Introduction to Financial Accounting

Prentice Hall Series in Accounting

Charles T. Horngren, Consulting Editor

Introduction to Financial Accounting

Sixth Edition

Charles T. Horngren
Stanford University

Gary L. Sundem
University of Washington—Seattle

John A. Elliott
Cornell University

 Prentice Hall Upper Saddle River, NJ 07458

Acquisition Editor: Annie Todd
Production Service: Editorial Services of New England
Managing Editor: Katherine Evancie
Interior Design: Jean Hammond
Cover Designer: Lorraine Castellano
Design Director: Patricia Wosczyk
Marketing Manager: Deborah H. Emry
Manufacturing Buyer: Paul Smolenski
Assistant Editor: Natacha St. Hill
Editorial Assistant: Christopher A. Ruel
Production Coordinator: Renée Pelletier
Cover Art: James Russell/IMA USA, Inc.

©1996, 1993, 1990, 1988, 1987, 1984, 1981 by Prentice-Hall, Inc.
A Simon & Schuster Company
Upper Saddle River, New Jersey 07458

Printed in the United States of America
10 9 8 7 6 5 4 3 2 1

ISBN 0-13-230145-8

Prentice-Hall International (UK) Limited, *London*
Prentice-Hall of Australia Pty. Limited, *Sydney*
Prentice-Hall Canada Inc., *Toronto*
Prentice-Hall Hispanoamericana, S.A., *Mexico*
Prentice-Hall of India Private Limited, *New Delhi*
Prentice-Hall of Japan, Inc., *Tokyo*
Simon & Schuster Asia Pte. Ltd., *Singapore*
Editora Prentice-Hall do Brasil, Ltda., *Rio de Janeiro*

To Joan, Scott, Mary, Susie,
Cathy, Liz, Garth, Jens,
Laura, and Dawn

■ **Charles T. Horngren** is the Edmund W. Littlefield Professor of Accounting at Stanford University. A graduate of Marquette University, he received his MBA from Harvard University and his Ph.D. from the University of Chicago. He is also the recipient of honorary doctorates from Marquette University and De Paul University.

A Certified Public Accountant, Horngren has served on the Accounting Principles Board, the Financial Accounting Standards Board Advisory Council, the Council of the American Institute of Certified Public Accountants, and as a trustee of the Financial Accounting Foundation.

A member of the American Accounting Association, Horngren has been its President and its Director of Research. He received the Outstanding Accounting Educator Award in 1973. The California Certified Public Accountants Foundation gave Horngren its Faculty Excellence Award in 1975 and its Distinguished Professor Award in 1983. In 1985 the American Institute of Certified Public Accountants presented its first Outstanding Educator Award to Horngren. In 1990 he was elected to the Accounting Hall of Fame.

Professor Horngren is also a member of the National Association of Accountants. He was a member of the Board of Regents, Institute of Certified Management Accountants, which administers the CMA examinations.

Horngren is the co-author of six other books published by Prentice Hall including: *Cost Accounting: A Managerial Emphasis*, Eighth Edition (with George Foster and Srikant M. Datar); *Introduction to Management Accounting*, Tenth Edition (with Gary L. Sundem and William O. Stratton); *Accounting*, Third Edition (with Walter T. Harrison, Jr., and Michael A. Robinson), and *Financial Accounting*, Second Edition (also with Harrison). In addition he is the Consulting Editor for the Prentice Hall Series in Accounting.

■ **Gary L. Sundem** is Professor of Accounting at the University of Washington, Seattle. He received his B.A. degree from Carleton College and his MBA and Ph.D. degrees from Stanford University.

Professor Sundem was the 1992–93 President of the American Accounting Association, served as Executive Director of the Accounting Education Change Commission, 1989–91, and as Editor of *The Accounting Review*, 1982–86.

A member of the National Association of Accountants, Sundem is past-president of the Seattle chapter. He has served on NAA's national Board of Directors, Committee on Academic Relations, and the Research Committee.

Professor Sundem has numerous publications in accounting and finance journals, including *Issues in Accounting Education, The Accounting Review, Journal of Accounting Research*, and *The Journal of Finance*. He received an award for the most notable contribution to accounting literature in 1978. He was selected as the Outstanding Accounting Educator by the Washington Society of CPAs in 1987. He has made more than 100 presentations at universities in the United States and abroad.

■ **John A. Elliott** is an Associate Professor of Accounting at the Johnson Graduate School of Management at Cornell University. He received his B.S. and MBA degrees from the University of Maryland and his Ph.D. degree from Cornell University. He is currently Director of the Ph.D. program at the Johnson School and has acted as associate dean for academic affairs.

A certified public accountant, Elliott worked for Arthur Anderson & Co. and for Westinghouse before returning for his advanced degrees. He currently teaches financial accounting and international accounting at the Johnson School. Prior teaching has included auditing and taxation as well as intermediate accounting and financial statement analysis. Over 25 years as an educator, Professor Elliott has taught at the University of Maryland, St. Lawrence University, Central Washington State College, and the University of Chicago. In addition to executive teaching for Cornell, he has conducted various corporate training programs in the United States and internationally.

As a member of the American Accounting Association, he was the founding president of the Financial Accounting and Reporting Section. As a member of the Financial Accounting Standards Committee he has frequently responded to FASB exposure drafts and worked to integrate academic study with practice. His research has been published in accounting and economics journals and deals primarily with the use of accounting information to assess the financial condition of an enterprise.

Professor Elliott served on the Hangar Theatre Board of Trustees for nine years, and was president for four of those years. He currently serves as Treasurer of the Board of the Cayuga Medical Center at Ithaca.

Brief Contents

Contents

4   **Accounting Adjustments and Financial Statement Preparation**   135

5   **Accounting Cycle: Recording and Formal Presentation**   179

Part Three ■ Additional Elements of Financial Statements

Preface

Introduction to Financial Accounting is the first member of a matched pair of books that provides full coverage of the essentials of financial and managerial accounting. The second book is *Introduction to Management Accounting*. In combination, the pair can be used throughout two semesters or three quarters of introductory accounting.

This book takes the view that business is an exciting process and that accounting is the perfect window through which to understand how economic events affect businesses. Since we believe accounting is an aid to understanding economic events, and that accounting builds on simple principles, this book introduces a number of concepts earlier than other textbooks do. However, the early introductions are at the simplest level and are illustrated with carefully chosen examples from real companies that emphasize the basics. Thus, in Chapter 2 we introduce the concept of earnings per share and how the share price of a company may change when an earnings announcement occurs. But it is not until Chapter 15 that details of calculation of earnings per share under complex conditions are addressed. In Chapter 2 we introduce the price-earnings ratio and dividend yield as ratios that are used by investors. Throughout the book we add ratios in each chapter that enhance students' understanding of the accounting topics addressed. Finally, in Chapter 15, the prior coverage is enriched and integrated to provide a complete coverage of financial statement analysis that includes management's discussion and segment reporting. In Chapter 2 we introduce the simplest possible statement of cash flow to emphasize the role of this statement in the family of accounting reports. The statement is revisited periodically throughout the remainder of the text. Chapter 11 provides an integrated exploration of the cash flow consequences of material covered to that point, and subsequent chapters explore new issues.

These examples illustrate our philosophy: Introduce the simple concepts early. Revisit the concepts at more complex levels as the reader gains sophistication and understanding. Provide real world examples at every stage that illustrate the topics consistent with the theoretical treatment in the chapter. Always view accounting as a tool that enhances our understanding of economic events. After this transaction, are we better off or worse off? One of our colleagues, Hal Bierman, often focuses on an economic event by asking, "are you happy or are you sad?" We believe that accounting provides a way to understand what is happening and to answer that question. You might think of the basic financial statements as scorecards in the most fundamental economic game of all. Each year the financial statements help you answer the most important questions:

Are you happy or are you sad? Did you make money or lose money? Are you prospering, or are you just surviving, or are you failing?

President Carter's financial statements, the Golden Gate Bridge District's loss of $26.20 of ferry tickets, and the 1985 financial implications of a baseball players strike are all classic examples that we decided to retain in the current problem material. While the baseball strike of 1985 is ancient history, the 1994–95 version has just ended and the next one is probabley right around the corner. We believe there is great value in extensive current examples, and we provide them. Accounting changes constantly, and we stay on top of those changes. But the reality is that "...the more things change the more they stay the same...." and our mix of constructed problems and old and new real world examples is intended to find the right balance.

Introduction to Financial Accounting is a textbook for introductory accounting courses that presupposes no prior knowledge of accounting. It deals with important topics that all students of management should study. Our goals have been to choose *relevant* subject matter, including many examples drawn from actual companies, and to present it *clearly* and *flexibly*. Although the focus is on U.S. accounting methods, numerous references to international practices and standards are found throughout the text. The book is oriented to the user of financial statements, but it gives ample attention to the needs of potential accounting practitioners.

Because financial accounting is so pervasive, an understanding of its uses and limitations is valuable whether the student eventually becomes a company president, a sales manager, a professional accountant, a hospital administrator, or a politician. In particular, knowledge of accounting for business is worthwhile because all of us relate to companies in one or more of the following ways: investors, managers, customers, creditors, government regulators, observers, or critics.

A philosopher once said, "You have to know what something *is* before you know what it *is used for*. When you know what it is used for, then you can decide what changes deserve serious thought." *Introduction to Financial Accounting* describes the most widely used accounting theory and practice. Emphasis is on *what accounting is* rather than *what it should be*. After all, beginning students must know what accounting today is really like before they can make judgments as to what changes in practice are desirable. Ample consideration is given to proposed changes in accounting throughout the book (especially in Chapter 16), but the thrust is toward understanding generally accepted theory and practice.

This text stresses underlying concepts, but it makes them concrete with profuse illustrations, many taken from corporate annual reports. Moreover, accounting procedures such as transaction analysis, journalizing, and posting are given abundant consideration. For example, see the sections on transaction analysis in Chapter 1. In this way, the reader obtains a thorough grasp of the fundamentals of accounting. The study of concepts develops understanding of procedures, and the study of procedures enriches understanding of concepts. A major objective is to equip students with enough fundamental concepts and terminology so that they can comprehend a typical corporate annual report.

Flexibility has been a driving force in writing this book. Are you among the many instructors who favor solidifying the fundamentals by using many journal entries, T-accounts, work sheets, and special journals? Then see Chapters 3, 4, and 5, including its appendixes, and the appendixes to Chapters 10 and 11. Are you among the other instructors who favor downplaying the details and emphasizing concepts? Then consider skipping some of the material just cited, in whole or in part (especially Chapter 5).

The flexibility of the book is illustrated by the use of chapter appendixes. They give the instructor latitude in picking and choosing among various topics. In short, greater depth and breadth are available, depending on the preferences of the teacher. Moreover, parts of the bodies of some chapters can be omitted if desired. Numerous candidates for exclusion can be found in Chapters 6–16. Examples include materials in Chapter 6 other than the valuation of accounts receivable, and the presentation of consolidated statements in Chapter 13.

A major feature is the use of the fundamental accounting equation as a central thread throughout the book for explaining new concepts and analyzing transactions. For example, consider the presentations in Chapter 10 on bonds, Chapter 11 on the statement of cash flows, Chapter 13 on intercompany investments, and Chapter 14 on interperiod income tax allocation. Such presentations give instructors immense latitude. They can use journal entries, or T-accounts, or the balance sheet equation format *exclusively,* if desired.

Additional features of this book include attempts to spark the reader's curiosity from the outset by:

1. Introducing financial statements of *actual companies* throughout the text beginning in Chapter 1.

2. Using published financial information as a basis for much of the assignment material in each chapter.

3. Showcasing interesting illustrations of chapter topics in boxed-off features in each chapter.

4. Including references to international accounting standards and practices throughout the text, rather than relegating them to the end.

5. Including a complete set of financial statements for Wal-Mart, the largest retailer in the United States, and having one problem in each chapter's assignment materials based on these statements. One problem in each chapter allows students to use the Compact D™/SEC Academic Edition from Disclosure® , a computerized database of financial statements. We have also added a new ethics problem in each chapter.

6. Integrating a few financial ratios in Chapter 2, a few more in Chapter 4, a few more in Chapter 6, and so on. The goal is to make financial statement analysis a natural element of the process. We do not relegate the interpretation of financial statements to the rear of the book.

7. Using a minimum of technical detail to introduce relatively complicated subjects, and examining the subjects in more depth in chapter appendixes. For example, we treat the details of the statement of cash flows in an appendix to Chapter 11, and pooling of interests is relegated to the appendix in Chapter 13.

8. Providing a solid conceptual foundation in the first two chapters before covering the mechanics of journals, ledgers, and related procedural matters in Chapter 3.
9. Introducing simple income tax aspects in Chapter 4 rather than later. Income taxes are not only important, they stimulate reader interest.
10. Listing learning objectives at the start of each chapter, and highlighting each objective again in the margin as it is discussed, which is a key student review tool.
11. Emphasizing key terms by offering marginal glossary definitions.

Alternative Ways of Using This Book

Texts are fundamentally teaching instruments. Teaching is highly personal and heavily influenced by the backgrounds and interests of assorted students and faculty in various settings. To satisfy this audience, a book must be a pliable tool, not a straitjacket.

In our opinion, the first twelve chapters provide the foundation for the field of financial accounting. These twelve chapters may be amplified by assigning other chapters in a variety of sequences that do not disrupt the readers' flow of thought. The most obvious candidates for alternate order and selective inclusion are:

Chapters 1, 2, 3, 4, 5, 6, 7, 8, 9, 10, 11 and any of 12–16.
　　　　　　　　　　　　↑　　　　　↑
　　　　　　　　　　　11　　　13
　　　　　　　　　　　16　　　16

Chapter 8 deals with internal controls. Often this topic is omitted in introductory financial accounting courses. It is placed in Chapter 8 because the authors believe the topic is extremely important. Further, it is less technical than other chapters, so it provides a change of pace for students in the midst of heavily technical material. However, it can be delayed until anytime later in the course without loss of continuity.

Chapter 11 on cash flows may be assigned after Chapter 7 (or even pages 487-504 after Chapter 5); it is placed as Chapter 11 because the statement of cash flows is an excellent vehicle for reviewing all the fundamentals of financial accounting.

Assignment Material

Careful choices among the wide variety of assignment material in each chapter will slant the course toward various combinations of breadth and depth, theory and procedures, simplicity and complexity. Many exercises and problems marked with an icon use information presented in actual corporate annual reports or news stories. In this way, some major points in the chapter can be underscored by "real world" illustrations. Most of the annual reports used are relatively recent but some classics are retained. One complete annual report, that of Wal-Mart Stores, Inc., is included as Appendix A at the end of the text. It is the basis for the next-to-last problem in each chapter. Using these problems will assure students that they can cope with real financial statements.

Special review assignment material is contained in Chapters 5 and 16. In addition, some assignments in Chapters 13-16 tend to crystallize previous work. The review assignment material for Chapter 16 is especially noteworthy. It uses corporate annual reports as a basis for review of all parts of the course. These cases or problems provide a splendid test of the student's overall comprehension. Their successful solution enhances a student's confidence enormously, especially because he or she is dealing with real companies' financial statements.

The front of the solutions manual contains several alternate detailed assignment schedules and ample additional suggestions to teachers regarding how best to use this book.

Features of This Edition

Users of the fifth edition gave the assignment material high marks regarding quality, quantity, and range. They especially liked the references in the text and the assignment materials to actual companies. The sixth edition enhances the latter feature because it spurs student interest and enthusiasm.

We have expanded and revised the "boxed" items that highlight real-world issues related to the chapter coverage. For example, in the inventory chapter, one box deals with why some firms do not use LIFO, and another box describes the classic salad oil fraud, in which management used complex deceptions to substantially overstate their inventory and earnings. In the first chapter a box discusses how *The New York Times* grades annual reports and the letter to shareholders, while nearby text relates earnings announcements to changes in share prices on an April day in 1995. A later box details how internal control failures permitted thieves to steal over $300,000 from an unsuspecting woman's bank account. Such real-world examples heighten student interest.

We have devoted enormous attention to the assignment material for each chapter. The beginning of the Chapter 1 Assignment Material explains the format and the various ways of using the material. If they desire, instructors may select materials exclusively from those "real-world" exercises and problems identified with the logo and cover all the essentials of financial accounting.

Of special note is Chapter 11, "Statement of Cash Flows." This chapter provides an especially easy-to-learn explanation of the statement. In particular, the readers need not contend with either a long series of "things to do" or awkward work sheets. Instead, the chapter employs the familiar balance sheet equation that threads throughout the entire book. Thus readers can quickly understand why as well as how the statement dovetails with balance sheets and income statements. A chapter appendix covers the T-account approach for those instructors who favor such a technique.

Another valuable feature of this edition is the series of Wal-Mart problems at the end of each chapter's assignment material. These problems directly link the chapter's subject matter to the actual financial statements of Wal-Mart, which are reproduced in Appendix A at the end of the book. As students progress through the course, they will grow increasingly comfortable with the real-world report of a publicly-held company.

All chapters were updated. Consider the following distinguishing features:

- Learning objectives and accounting vocabulary definitions placed in chapter margins for emphasis.
- New ethics problem in each chapter.
- Examples of the use of accounting information for decision making in Chapter 1.
- Brief introduction to Statement of Cash Flows and simple ratios in Chapter 2.
- Introduction to formats found on non-U.S. balance sheets in Chapter 4.
- Expanded discussion of auditing in Chapter 5.
- Emphasis on what expenditures should be capitalized in Chapter 9.
- Examples woven throughout Chapter 13 on intercorporate investments to illustrate the extent and nature of intercorporate relations and motivate the need for diverse accounting practice.
- Clarified and expanded discussion of permanent and timing differences between the reporting to tax authorities and the reporting to shareholders in Chapter 14.
- More integrated coverage of the use of historical results to predict future results in Chapter 15, together with brief coverage of foreign currency translation.
- Expanded section on non-U.S. financial statements in Chapter 16, focusing on Japan, Germany, and France.

Supplements for Instructors

Instructor's Manual—includes learning objectives, chapter overviews, chapter outlines, quizzes, transparency masters, and selected readings.

Solutions Manual—provides solutions for all end-of-chapter assignment material. All solutions were prepared by the authors.

Solutions Transparencies—provides selected solutions on acetates.

Test Item File—consists of approximately 15 true/false questions, 50 multiple-choice questions, and 10 exercises per chapter. The learning objective and level of difficulty are indicated for each question.

ABC News/Prentice Hall Video Library—offers high-quality feature and documentary-style videos with carefully researched selections from award-winning ABC news shows. The accompanying video guide provides a synopsis, learning objectives, and discussion questions for each video segment.

Prentice Hall Custom Test—offers a computerized testing package in both DOS and Windows formats.

Supplements for Students

Study Guide—includes a detailed review of key ideas for each chapter plus practice test questions and problems along with the worked-out solutions.

Working Papers—include tear-out forms, organized by chapter, for solving the problem assignments.

The New York Times Dodger—a complimentary "mini-newspaper" supplement for students that consists of recent articles pertaining to the field of accounting. This supplement is updated annually for timeliness.

Compact D™ from Disclosure® —software database that contains detailed profiles and financial data for 100 publicly traded companies. Each chapter of the text includes a generic financial statement problem that can be assigned in conjunction with this software package. Compact D/SEC™ Academic Edition 30 contains the profiles and financial data of 30 companies. Compact D/SEC™ Academic Edition 100 contains profiles and financial data of 100 companies.

Lotus (R) Templates—provides pre-prepared templates for selected problems from the text.

Practice Sets: *Runners Corporation* (Manual & Computerized)

Reading and Applications in Financial Accounting, Third Edition, by Rankine/Stice—available shrinkwrapped with the text.

Acknowledgments

Our appreciation extends to our present and former colleagues and students. This book and our enthusiasm for accounting grow out of their collective contributions to our knowledge and experience. We particularly appreciate the following individuals who supplied helpful comments and reviews of the previous edition or of drafts of this edition: Schlomi Benartzi, University of Southern California; James Bond, Winthrop College; Averil Brent, Columbia University; Alice Cooperstein, Central Connecticut State University; William Colye, Babson College; Patricia Dougherty, Boston University; Julia D'Souza, Cornell University; Pete Dukes, University of Washington; Anita Feller, University of Illinois; Richard Frankel, University of Michigan; Al Hartgraves, Emory University; Yuji Ijiri, Carnegie Mellon University; Dale Janouski, State University of New York at Buffalo; Donna Kilpatrick, University of Washington; Robert Libby, Cornell University; Barbara Lougee, Cornell University; Don Lucy; Joan Luft, Michigan State University; Carol Marquardt, Cornell University; Maureen McNichols, Stanford University; W. Timothy O'Keefe; Mohamed Onsi, Syracuse University; Joseph Paperman, University of Washington; Moses Pava, Yeshiva University; Laura Philips, White House Office of Science and Technology; Morton Pincus, University of Iowa; James Sander, Butler University; Rudolph Schattke, University of Colorado at Boulder; Bob Swieringa, Financial Accounting Standards Boards; and Christine Wiedman, College of William and Mary. Graeme W. Rankin and Earl K. Stice co-authored some of the boxes in the text. Donna Phoenix skillfully typed the solutions manual.

Finally, our thanks to the following people at Prentice Hall: Annie Todd, Rich Wohl, Debbie Emry, Diane deCastro, Natacha St. Hill, Christopher Ruel, Katherine Evancie, Paul Smolenski, Vincent Scelta, Patricia Wosczyk, Carol Burgett, Patti Dant, and Lisa DiMaulo.

Comments from users are welcome.

Charles T. Horngren
Gary L. Sundem
John A. Elliott

1

Entities and Balance Sheets

Learning Objectives

Learning objectives will be found at the beginning of each chapter. They specify some of the important knowledge and skills you should have after completing your study of the chapter and your solving of the assignment material.

1 Explain the nature of accounting and its role in decision making.

2 Define and describe a balance sheet and its major elements.

3 Explain the need for generally accepted accounting principles and the basic concepts of entity and reliability.

4 Record transactions and analyze their effect on the balance sheet equation.

5 Understand the advantages and disadvantages of the three types of business organizations and how to account for each.

6 Explain the notion of credibility and the function of auditing.

7 Describe public and private accounting and the role of ethics in the accounting profession.

This chapter provides a glimpse of the entire field of accounting. It describes the nature of accounting and its role in providing useful information for a wide variety of decisions. It introduces the financial statements that accountants prepare to provide this information. The chapter also looks at some of the generally accepted accounting principles used by accountants, and it examines types of business organizations. An introduction to the basic terms accountants use—the accounting vocabulary—is an overall theme of the chapter.

Although accounting is often called the language of business, its usefulness extends well beyond the business world. Anyone living in modern society without a basic knowledge of accounting is like someone living in a foreign country without knowing the language. A knowledge of accounting helps people of all ages in all countries to understand their economic environment and to manage their everyday affairs.

For example, a student with limited funds can use accounting procedures to design a budget and record actual expenses. A comparison of the budget with actual expenses can be likened to analysis of financial statements. The budget analysis allows the student to monitor progress in meeting financial goals and to make decisions on how remaining funds can be spent. Analysis of financial statements helps managers to manage the business, allows investors to select among investments, and provides our elected officials critical information to use in directing government. The study of accounting is important to everyone even if they do not plan to become accountants or enter the field of business.

■ THE NATURE OF ACCOUNTING

Objective 1

Explain the nature of accounting and its role in decision making.

Accounting is the major means of organizing and summarizing information about economic activities. This information is provided to decision makers in the form of financial statements. To prepare these statements, accountants analyze, record, quantify, accumulate, summarize, classify, report, and interpret economic events and their financial effects on the organization.

Accountants design their accounting systems after considering the types of information desired by managers and other decision makers. Bookkeepers and computers then perform the more routine tasks of following detailed procedures designed by accountants. While some accounting systems may be highly complex and require the skills and talents of many people, the real value of any accounting system lies in the information it provides.

Accounting as an Aid to Decision Making

Accounting information is useful to anyone who must make judgments and decisions that have economic consequences. Such decision makers include managers, owners, investors, and politicians. For example,

- The engineering department of Apple Computer has developed a new personal computer. An accountant is asked to develop a report on the potential profitability of the product, including the estimated sales receipts and the costs incurred to produce and sell the product. Management uses the accountant's report to help decide whether to produce and market the product.

- Meadowdale Nursery School has one empty classroom. The school's director asks the accountant to estimate the additional tuition that would be received and costs that would be incurred if an additional class were added. The accountant prepares a report based on information about costs incurred for other similar classes. The director uses the accountant's report to decide on the financial feasibility of adding the class.

- An investor is considering an investment in either General Motors or Volvo. She uses published financial statements to compare the most recent financial results of the companies to help her predict their future profitability and the riskiness of an investment in either company.

- A U.S. presidential candidate proposes a new medical-care system for the country. Of course, the proposal has a major effect on the country's budget. Accounting numbers are used to identify the added tax receipts and government expenditures required to implement the plan.

Accounting helps decision making by showing where and when money has been spent and commitments have been made, by evaluating performance, and by indicating the financial implications of choosing one plan rather than another. Accounting also helps predict the future effects of decisions, and it helps direct attention to current problems, imperfections, and inefficiencies, as well as opportunities.

Consider some fundamental relationships in the decision-making process:

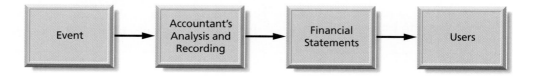

Here are some examples of decision makers and the decisions they must make:

Decision Makers	Decisions
Managers of organizations	Where to expand or reduce operations? How did subordinates perform? Whom to reward?
Lenders of money	Grant a loan? Which lending terms to specify?
Suppliers of goods and services	Extend credit? How much? How long?
Shareholders of organizations	Increase or reduce their investments?
Income tax authorities	Is taxable income measured properly?
U.S. Securities and Exchange Commission	Do the financial statements of a publicly held corporation conform to requirements of securities laws?

Evaluating the Annual Report

The *New York Times* recently assessed and graded the "Letters to Shareholders" that many companies use in their annual reports to reflect on the year's performance.

First Chicago, a major bank, was given a grade of D. They suffered a 14% decline in performance but did not explain the reasons clearly. The chairman reported the "trading results were significantly lower, due largely to very difficult market conditions." In other words, times were hard because times were hard.

This was also the year in which Intel, the computer chip producer, experienced grave difficulties. They discovered that their pentium computer chip made an infrequent, but predictable, mistake in certain calculations. At first they claimed that the mistake was very rare and should only worry rocket scientists. Their large user base responded angrily, and they gradually moved to a policy of complete replacement of the faulty chip. The financial consequences were significant, costing Intel about $475 million. And, as you will discover in this book, the financial statements will explain this process to educated readers. Intel evaluated its actions in the management letter in its annual report. Chairman Gordon Moore reported that "1994 was the best of times—and the worst of times. We received a crash course in consumer relations." Forthright confrontation of the problem and a direct explanation in their management letter earned Intel an "A" from *The New York Times*.

Sometimes the cover or format of the annual report says something about the company. In 1994 IBM issued its annual report on a CD and also made it available on the Internet. Could there be a more perfect marriage of communication, product emphasis, and corporate identity? A few companies are taking a minimalist approach. Can you imagine a corporation issuing an annual report without including the name of the corporation on the cover? Picture a black and white billboard. The background is white. A black silhouette of a beverage bottle appears above the caption, "Quick. Name a soft drink." If you thought Coca-Cola, you are right. If we reproduced the shape of the bottle for you, black against the white background, you too would probably know it was not Pepsi.

Ultimately, the annual report is both an informational document and a marketing document. In this accounting class we will prepare you to understand the information in the financial statements and in the management's analysis in the annual report. We will leave the decisions about the cover and about which photographs to use in the annual report to our colleagues who teach other courses. ■

Source: From Patrice Duggan Samuels, "Annual Reports: Upfront and Unstarched," The New York Times, April 9, 1995, page f5.

Accounting as a Measure of Financial Success

All organizations have financial goals. For example, business firms must make a profit to continue in business. Accountants measure the financial results of the activities of an organization and report those results in financial statements. This is the *scorekeeping role* of accounting. Decision makers use the financial statements to help assess how successfully an organization has met its financial goals.

Investors are particularly interested in the financial success of a firm as indicated in its financial statements. Investors provide resources to the firm, usually by investing cash. The firm then uses the invested cash to produce goods and services, which are sold to customers or clients. The goal is to sell the goods and services for more than it costs to provide them. The excess of receipts over disbursements is profit, which can be distributed to the investors.

Investors in business firms are major users of financial statements. They use these summaries of financial results to evaluate the performance of managers in generating profits and to predict a firm's ability to generate future profits. For example, investors in IBM saw profits fall from $5.8 billion in 1988 to a loss of

$2.8 billion in 1991 before reaching $3.0 billion in 1994. Meanwhile, investors in McDonald's Corporation saw a steady increase in profits from $0.6 billion in 1988 to $0.9 billion in 1991 to $1.2 billion in 1994. These profitability numbers and various other pieces of information in financial statements allow investors to make intelligent decisions about whether to invest more or less in a particular firm.

Managers are also concerned with financial statements. Managers are paid to generate profits for investors. Financial statements are their scorecard. Just as a baseball player is judged and rewarded on the basis of batting average, home runs, and other measures of performance, many managers of business firms are evaluated on the basis of financial statements. In fact, many companies pay bonuses to managers based directly on results reported in the firm's financial statements. Therefore, managers predict the effects of their decisions on the financial statements and try to take actions that enhance the values shown in the statements.

The primary questions regarding a firm's financial success that decision makers want answered are, What is the financial picture of the organization on a given day? and How well did it do during a given period? The accountant answers these questions with four major financial statements: *balance sheet, income statement, statement of cash flows,* and *statement of retained income.* The balance sheet, which is introduced later in this chapter, focuses on the financial picture as of a given day. The other financial statements, which are covered in Chapter 2, focus on the performance over time.

annual report A combination of financial statements, management discussion and analysis, and graphs and charts that is provided annually to investors.

Stockholders and potential investors use the information in financial statements to evaluate a firm's performance and to make investment decisions. The most common source of this information is the *annual report.* The **annual report** contains not only the financial statements but also management's discussion and analysis of a firm's performance in recent years. Firms distribute their annual report to stockholders. Interested investors may request the report by calling the investor relations department of the company. You may want to skim over the Wal-Mart annual report condensed in Appendix A on pages 775 to 792. The material in Appendix A does not give a complete picture of the elaborate, glossy, and expensive annual reports produced by many leading corporations. Photographs and charts are used extensively to communicate the firm's message. In this text we concentrate on the financial status of the entity as revealed in the four primary financial statements, but management's discussion and verbal assessment are also important, and Chapter 15 provides additional insight on these issues.

■ WATCHING THE EARNINGS ANNOUNCEMENTS

Suppose Uncle Harry opened the *Wall Street Journal* on Tuesday morning and noticed that Tantalizing Taco, his favorite fast food chain, announced earnings per share of $1.20 the previous day. Delighted with these results, since he expected earnings of only $.99 per share, Harry called his broker to buy another 200 shares. Mary Philips, his broker of twenty years, said "Sorry Harry, Tantalizing Taco shares rose 15% yesterday to $25.00 per share. The early birds caught all the worms."

Earnings information often affects the prices of securities. Consider various earnings announcements on April 24, 1995. The *Wall Street Journal* reported that Crane, a Stamford, Connecticut, maker of engineering products, reported earnings of $ .44 per share for the first quarter of its 1995 year, significantly higher than analysts' expected level of $ .31 per share. Investors concluded that Crane was doing very well and efforts to purchase shares drove prices up $2.00 per share, or more than 6%. As in our example of Uncle Harry, these price changes often occur very quickly. Within minutes of the announcement of the earnings news, informed investors begin to buy or sell securities based on their revised beliefs about the company.

Barron's, a weekly news magazine, helps its readers by publishing a schedule of anticipated earnings announcements. They present the actual quarterly earnings from the previous year and the earnings that analysts expect to be reported for this year. The following summary shows the *Barron's* predictions and the subsequent actual reported earnings for Monday, April 24, 1995. As the summary shows, the announcement often causes a change in share prices on the day of announcement.

Company	Prior Year	Forecast	Current Year	Change in Share Price	
				Amount	*Percentage*
Boeing	$.86	$.43	$.53	$1.125	2.02%
Hershey	.61	.70	.70	0.00	0.00
Union Carbide	.42	1.22	1.57	.50	1.67
United Technology	.73	.93	1.03	1.25	1.72
USX-Steel	−.56	.98	.89	−1.375	−4.55

In markets where a stock price might be expected to change by 12% per year, changes of over 1% in a single day are large. Because large changes are often associated with an earnings announcement, investors pay special attention to when earnings are announced and develop expectations about what the announcement will be.

Not all large changes are associated with releases of accounting information. That same April day, shares of Telefonos de Mexico, the Mexican telephone company whose shares trade on the New York Stock Exchange, rose in value by 6%. The *Wall Street Journal* attributed the increase to an announcement by the International Monetary Fund that the expected recession in Mexico was likely to be short-lived. An even larger 7.7% increase occurred that day for Texas Instruments shares. The *Wall Street Journal* concluded that investors believed the soaring value of the yen would make Japanese-manufactured D-Ram products much more expensive and allow Texas Instruments to capture a larger share of this very profitable market.

A Note on Nonprofit Organizations

The major focus of this book is on profit-seeking organizations, such as business firms. However, the fundamental accounting principles also apply to nonprofit (that is, not-for-profit) organizations. Managers and accountants in hospitals, universities, government agencies, and other nonprofit organizations use financial statements. Money must be raised and spent, budgets must be prepared, and financial performance must be judged. Nonprofit organizations need to use their limited resources wisely, and financial statements are essential for judging their use of resources. The mid-1990s are a time of increased public interest in the financial performance of government agencies and many other nonprofit organizations.

Good accounting records and reports are essential to good government. Politicians and administrators are much better equipped to understand the financial implications of their policies if they understand accounting. For example, the U.S. government has made loan guarantees to college students, small businesses (through the Small Business Administration), large companies such as Chrysler, and to banks and savings and loan institutions. The financial ramifications of these guarantees are being felt by all U.S. citizens. Guarantees to depositors in savings and loan companies alone may cost the government as much as $400 billion.

Local officials, including members of the city council, school board, park board, and other policy or advisory committees, will perform better if they understand accounting. And voters, who must judge the performance (including financial performance) of elected officials, will also make better decisions if they understand the financial statements of various government agencies.

Financial and Management Accounting

financial accounting The field of accounting that serves external decision makers, such as stockholders, suppliers, banks, and government agencies.

The financial statements discussed in this book are common to all areas of accounting. "Financial accounting" is often distinguished from "management accounting." The major distinction between them is their use by two different classes of decision makers. The field of **financial accounting** serves *external* decision makers, such as stockholders, suppliers, banks, and government agencies. **Management accounting** serves *internal* decision makers, such as top executives, department heads, college deans, hospital administrators, and people at other management levels *within* an organization.[1] The two fields of accounting share many of the same procedures for analyzing and recording the effect of individual transactions.

management accounting The field of accounting that serves internal decision makers, such as top executives, department heads, college deans, hospital administrators, and people at other management levels within an organization.

The more that managers know about accounting, the better they are able to plan and control their organization. In their dealings with both inside and outside parties, managers will be handicapped if their comprehension of accounting is sketchy or confused. So the learning of accounting is a wise investment, no matter what the manager's specialty. Moreover, managers' performance and rewards often hinge on how accounting measurements are made. Therefore managers have a natural self-interest in learning about accounting.

■ THE BALANCE SHEET

balance sheet (statement of financial position, statement of financial condition) A financial statement that shows the financial status of a business entity at a particular instant in time.

One of the major financial statements prepared by accountants is the **balance sheet**, which shows the financial status of a business entity at a particular instant in time. The balance sheet has two counterbalancing sections. The left side lists *assets*, which represent the resources of the firm. The right side lists *liabilities* and *owners' equity*, which represent claims against the resources.

---

[1] For a book-length presentation of the field, see Charles T. Horngren, Gary L. Sundem, and William O. Stratton, *Introduction to Management Accounting*, 10th ed. (Upper Saddle River, NJ: Prentice Hall, 1996), the companion volume to this textbook.

Objective 2

Define and describe a balance sheet and its major elements.

Although *balance sheet* is a widely used term, it is not as descriptive as its newer substitute terms: **statement of financial position** or **statement of financial condition**. But old terms die hard, so *balance sheet* will be used in this book.

For example, suppose George Smith, a salaried employee of a local bicycle company, decides to quit his job and open his own bicycle shop. Smith has heard about the troubles of new businesses that lack money, so he invests plenty: $400,000. Then Smith, acting for the business (which he has named Biwheels Company), borrows $100,000 from a local bank for business purposes. The opening balance sheet of this new business enterprise follows:

Biwheels Company
Balance Sheet
December 31, 19X1

Assets		Liabilities and Owner's Equity	
Cash	$500,000	Liabilities (note payable)	$100,000
		Smith, capital	400,000
Total assets	$500,000	Total liabilities and owner's equity	$500,000

balance sheet equation Assets = Liabilities + Owners' equity.

assets Economic resources that are expected to benefit future cash inflows or help reduce future cash outflows.

liabilities Economic obligations of the organization to outsiders or claims against its assets by outsiders.

notes payable Promissory notes that are evidence of a debt and state the terms of payment.

owners' equity The residual interest in, or remaining claim against, the organization's assets after deducting liabilities.

The entries in this balance sheet show the financial status of the Biwheels Company as of December 31, 19X1.[2] The company's assets at this point in time ($500,000) are listed on the left. They are balanced on the right by an equal amount of liability and owner's equity ($100,000 liability owed to the bank plus $400,000 paid in by Smith).

Because the balance sheet shows the financial status at a particular point in time, it is always dated. The left and right sides are always kept in balance.

The items in the balance sheet form the **balance sheet equation**:

$$\text{Assets} = \text{Liabilities} + \text{Owners' equity}$$

The terms in this equation are specifically defined as follows:

Assets are economic resources that are expected to benefit future cash inflows or help reduce future cash outflows. Examples are cash, inventories, and equipment.

Liabilities are economic obligations of the organization to outsiders, or claims against its assets by outsiders. An example is a debt to a bank. The usual evidence of this type of debt is a promissory note that states the terms of payment. Accountants use the term **notes payable** to describe the existence of promissory notes.

Owners' equity is the *residual interest* in, or remaining claims against, the organization's assets after deducting liabilities. At the inception of a business, the owners' equity is measured by the total amount invested by the owners. As illustrated by "Smith, capital" in the Biwheels Company example, the accountant often uses the term *capital* instead of owners' equity to designate an owner's investment in the business.

A mature business will have earned profits. As Chapter 2 will explain, the owners' equity will then consist of the total amounts invested by the owner (or owners) plus any cumulative profits retained in the business.

---

[2] Throughout this book, years will usually be designated 19X1, 19X2, 19X3, and so on.

The right side of the balance sheet equation represents outsider and owner "claims against" the total assets shown on the left side. Many accountants prefer to think of the right side as "interests in" or "sources of" the total assets. The residual, or "leftover," nature of owners' equity is often emphasized by reexpressing the balance sheet equation as follows:

$$\text{Owners' equity} = \text{Assets} - \text{Liabilities}$$

■ GENERALLY ACCEPTED ACCOUNTING PRINCIPLES AND BASIC CONCEPTS

Objective 3

Explain the need for generally accepted accounting principles and the basic concepts of entity and reliability.

Financial statements are the result of a measurement process that rests on a set of principles. If every accountant used a different set of measurement rules, decision makers would find it difficult to use and compare financial statements. For example, consider the recording of an asset such as a machine on the balance sheet. If one accountant listed the purchase cost, another the amount for which the used machine could be sold, and others listed various other amounts, the readers of financial statements would be confused. It would be as if each accountant were speaking a different language. Therefore, accountants have agreed to apply a common set of measurement principles—that is, a common language—to record information on financial statements. But, as we shall see throughout this text, even a common language leaves some ambiguities and room for interpretation.

generally accepted accounting principles (GAAP) A term that applies to the broad concepts or guidelines and detailed practices in accounting, including all the conventions, rules, and procedures that together make up accepted accounting practice at a given time.

Generally accepted accounting principles (GAAP) is the term that applies to the broad concepts or guidelines and detailed practices in accounting. It includes all the conventions, rules, and procedures that together make up accepted accounting practice at a given time. Around the world different choices have been made regarding how to determine GAAP. In this book we will concentrate on the GAAP that exists today in the United States. But we will frequently use practices from other countries and financial reports for non-U.S. firms to illustrate the extent of global diversity in practice. There is not one correct answer to providing economic information about an organization's performance, but each country has found it useful to narrow the range of possible practices to a few acceptable ones. In some countries the national government carefully specifies each rule. In others there is substantial variety in acceptable practices.

Accounting principles become "generally accepted" by agreement. Such agreement is not influenced solely by formal logical analysis. Experience, custom, usage, and practical necessity contribute to a set of principles. Accordingly, it might be preferable to call them conventions. Why? Because *principles* erroneously connotes that GAAP is the product of airtight logic. Nevertheless, accountants use the term *principles* rather than *conventions* to describe the entire framework that guides their work.

The Entity Concept

entity An organization or a section of an organization that stands apart from other organizations and individuals as a separate economic unit.

The first basic concept or principle in accounting is the entity concept. An accounting **entity** is an organization or a section of an organization that stands apart from other organizations and individuals as a separate economic unit. Accounting draws sharp boundaries around each entity to avoid confusing its affairs with those of other entities.

An example of an entity is General Motors Corporation, an enormous entity that encompasses many smaller entities such as the Chevrolet Division and the Buick Division. In turn, Chevrolet encompasses many smaller entities such as a Michigan assembly plant and an Ohio assembly plant. Managers want accounting reports that are confined to their particular entities.

The key point here is that the entity concept helps the accountant relate events to a clearly defined area of accountability. For example, *business* entities should not be confused with *personal* entities. A purchase of groceries for merchandise inventory is an accounting transaction of a grocery store (the business entity), but the store owner's purchase of a stereo set with a personal check is a transaction of the owner (the personal entity).

The Reliability Concept

The accounting process focuses on reliable recording of events that affect an organization. While many events may affect a company—including wars, elections, and general economic booms or depressions—the accountant recognizes only specified types of events as being worthy of formal recording as accounting transactions.

Consider an illustration. Suppose the president of Exxon is killed in an airplane crash, and the company carries no life insurance for him or her. The accountant would not record this event. Suppose further that Exxon discovers that an employee has embezzled $1,000 in cash, and the company carries no employee theft insurance. The accountant would record this event. The death of the president may have considerably more economic or financial significance for Exxon than the embezzlement. But the monetary effect is hard to measure in any objective way. Accountants measure the impact of events in a systematic, reliable manner.

Users of financial statements want assurance that the numbers are not fabricated by management. Consequently, accountants seek and prize reliability as one of their major strengths and regard it as an essential characteristic of measurement. **Reliability** is a quality of information that assures decision makers that the information captures the conditions or events it purports to represent. Reliable data are accurate. Moreover, reliable data are supported by convincing evidence that can be verified by independent accountants.

reliability The quality of information that assures decision makers that the information captures the conditions or events it purports to represent.

Without the reliability concept, accounting records might be based on whims and opinions open to dispute. So to ensure reliability, the accountant would record the $1,000 financial impact of the Exxon embezzlement but would not record the unreliable financial impact of the Exxon president's death, wars, or elections.

■ BALANCE SHEET TRANSACTIONS

transaction Any event that both affects the financial position of an entity and can be reliably recorded in money terms.

A **transaction** is any event that both affects the financial position of an entity and can be reliably recorded in terms of money. Each transaction requires two counterbalancing entries so that the total assets always equal the total liabilities and owners' equity. That is, the equality of the balance sheet equation cannot be destroyed by any transaction. An accountant who prepares a balance sheet that does not balance knows that a clerical error has been made. The balance sheet *must* balance.

The following examples use the Biwheels Company to illustrate typical transactions and their effects on the balance sheet.

Objective 4

Record transactions on the balance sheet and analyze their effect on the balance sheet equation.

Transaction 1, Initial Investment.   The first Biwheels transaction was the investment by the owner on December 31, 19X1. Smith deposited $400,000 in a business bank account entitled Biwheels Company. The accounting equation is affected as follows:

	Assets	=	Liabilities	+	Owner's Equity
	Cash				*Smith, Capital*
(1)	+ 400,000	=			+ 400,000
					(owner investment)

This transaction increases both the assets, specifically Cash, and the owner's equity of the business, specifically Smith, Capital. Liabilities are unaffected. Why? Because Smith's business has no obligation to an outside party arising from this transaction. A parenthetical note, "owner investment," is used to identify the reason for the transaction's effect on owner's equity. The total amounts on the left side of the equation are equal to the total amounts on the right side, as they should be.

Transaction 2, Loan from Bank.   On January 2, 19X2, Biwheels Company borrows from a bank, signing a promissory note for $100,000. The $100,000 is added to the business's cash. The effect of this loan transaction on the accounting equation is:

	Assets	=	Liabilities	+	Owner's Equity
			Note		
	Cash		*Payable*		*Smith, Capital*
(1)	+ 400,000	=			+ 400,000
(2)	+ 100,000	=	+100,000		
Bal.	500,000	=	100,000		400,000
	500,000			500,000	

The loan increases the asset, Cash, and increases the liability, Note Payable, by the same amount, $100,000. After the transaction is completed, Biwheels has assets of $500,000, liabilities of $100,000, and owner's equity of $400,000. The sums of the individual *balances* (abbreviated Bal.) on each side of the equation are equal. This equality must always exist.

Transaction 3, Acquire Inventory for Cash. On January 2, 19X2, Biwheels acquires bicycles from a manufacturer for $150,000 cash.

	Assets		=	Liabilities	+	Owner's Equity
	Cash	Merchandise Inventory		Note Payable		Smith, Capital
Bal.	500,000		=	100,000		400,000
(3)	− 150,000	+ 150,000	=			
Bal.	350,000	150,000	=	100,000		400,000
		500,000			500,000	

inventory Goods held by a company for the purpose of sale to customers.

This transaction, the cash purchase of inventory, increases one asset, Merchandise Inventory, and decreases another asset, Cash, by the same amount. **Inventory** refers to goods held by the company for the purpose of sale to customers. The form of the assets changed, but the total amount of assets is unchanged. Moreover, the right-side items are completely unchanged.

After any transaction has been completed, Biwheels can prepare a balance sheet.

**Biwheels Company
Balance Sheet
January 2, 19X2**

Assets		Liabilities and Owner's Equity	
Cash	$350,000	Liabilities (note payable)	$100,000
Merchandise inventory	150,000	Smith, capital	400,000
Total assets	$500,000	Total liabilities and owner's equity	$500,000

Transaction Analysis

account A summary record of the changes in a particular asset, liability, or owners' equity.

Accountants record transactions in an organization's *accounts*. An **account** is a summary record of the changes in a particular asset, liability, or owners' equity, and the *account balance* is the total of all entries to the account to date. The analysis of transactions is the nucleus of accounting. For each transaction, the accountant determines (1) which specific accounts are affected, (2) whether the account balances are increased or decreased, and (3) the amount of the change in each account balance.

Exhibit 1-1 shows how a series of transactions may be analyzed using the balance sheet equation. The transactions are numbered for easy reference. Please examine how the first three transactions that were discussed earlier are analyzed in Exhibit 1-1.

Consider how each of the following additional transactions is analyzed:

4. Jan. 3. Biwheels buys bicycles for $10,000 from a manufacturer. The manufacturer requires $4,000 by January 10 and the balance in thirty days.

5. Jan. 4. Biwheels acquires assorted store equipment for a total of $15,000. A cash down payment of $4,000 is made. The remaining balance must be paid in sixty days.

6. Jan. 5. Biwheels sells a store showcase to a business neighbor after Smith decides he dislikes it. Its selling price, $1,000, happens to be exactly equal to its cost. The neighbor agrees to pay within thirty days.

7. Jan. 6. Biwheels returns some inventory (which had been acquired on January 3 for $800) to the manufacturer for full credit (an $800 reduction of the amount that Biwheels owes the manufacturer).

8. Jan. 10. Biwheels pays $4,000 to the manufacturer described in transaction 4.
9. Jan. 12. Biwheels collects $700 of the $1,000 owed by the business neighbor for transaction 6.
–. Jan. 12. Smith remodels his home for $35,000, paying by check from his personal bank account.

To check your comprehension, use the format in Exhibit 1-1 to analyze each transaction. Try to do your own analysis of each transaction before looking at the entries shown for it in the exhibit. For example, you could cover the numerical entries with a sheet of paper or a ruler and then proceed through each transaction, one by one.

Exhibit 1-1

Biwheels Company
Analysis of Transactions for December 31, 19X1–
January 12, 19X2

Description of Transactions	Cash	+ Accounts Receivable +	Merchandise Inventory +	Store Equipment =	Note Payable +	Accounts Payable +	Smith, Capital
(1) Initial investment	+ 400,000			=			+ 400,000
(2) Loan from bank	+ 100,000			=	+ 100,000		
(3) Acquire inventory for cash	– 150,000		+ 150,000	=			
(4) Acquire inventory on credit			+ 10,000	=		+ 10,000	
(5) Acquire store equipment for cash plus credit	– 4,000			+ 15,000 =		+ 11,000	
(6) Sale of equipment		+1,000		– 1,000 =			
(7) Return of inventory acquired on January 3			– 800	=		– 800	
(8) Payments to creditors	– 4,000			=		– 4,000	
(9) Collections from debtors	+ 700	– 700					
Balance, January 12, 19X2	342,700	+ 300 +	159,200 +	14,000 =	100,000 +	16,200 +	400,000
			516,200			516,200	

Transaction 4, Purchase on Credit.   The vast bulk of purchases among manufacturers, wholesalers, and retailers throughout the world are conducted on a *credit* basis rather than on a *cash* basis. An authorized signature of the buyer is usually sufficient to assure payment; no formal promissory note is necessary. This practice is known as buying on **open account**; the debt is shown on the buyer's balance sheet as an **account payable**. Thus an account payable is a liability that results from a purchase of goods or services on open account. As Exhibit 1-1 shows for this merchandise purchase on account, the merchandise inventory (an asset account) of Biwheels is increased and an account payable (a liability account) is also increased in the amount of $10,000 to keep the equation in balance.

open account
Buying or selling on credit, usually by just an "authorized signature" of the buyer.

account payable
A liability that results from a purchase of goods or services on open account.

	Assets		=	Liabilities	+	Owner's Equity
	Cash	Merchandise Inventory		Note Payable	Accounts Payable	Smith, Capital
Bal.	350,000	150,000	= 100,000			400,000
(4)		+10,000	=		+ 10,000	
Bal.	350,000	160,000	= 100,000		10,000	400,000
	510,000				510,000	

Transaction 5, Purchase for Cash Plus Credit. This transaction illustrates a **compound entry** because it affects more than two balance sheet accounts (two asset accounts and one liability account in this case). Store equipment is increased by the full amount of its cost regardless of whether payment is made in full now, in full later, or partially now and partially later. Therefore Biwheels' Store Equipment (an asset account) is increased by $15,000, Cash (an asset account) is decreased by $4,000, and Accounts Payable (a liability account) is increased by the difference, $11,000.

compound entry
A transaction that affects more than two accounts.

	Assets			=	Liabilities		+	Owner's Equity
	Cash	Merchandise Inventory	Store Equipment		Note Payable	Accounts Payable		Smith, Capital
Bal.	350,000	160,000		= 100,000		10,000		400,000
(5)	– 4,000		+ 15,000	=		+ 11,000		
Bal.	346,000	160,000	15,000	= 100,000		21,000		400,000
	521,000					521,000		

Transaction 6, Sale on Credit. This transaction is similar to a purchase on credit except that Biwheels is now the seller. Accounts Receivable (an asset account) of $1,000 is created, and Store Equipment (an asset account) is decreased by $1,000. We are purposely avoiding transactions that result in profits or losses until the next chapter. Instead we are concentrating on elementary changes in the balance sheet equation. In this case, the transaction affects assets only; liabilities and owner's equity are unchanged.

	Assets				=	Liabilities		+	Owner's Equity
	Cash	Accounts Receivable	Merchandise Inventory	Store Equipment		Note Payable	Accounts Payable		Smith, Capital
Bal.	346,000		160,000	15,000	= 100,000		21,000		400,000
(6)		+ 1,000		– 1,000	=				
Bal.	346,000	1,000	160,000	14,000	= 100,000		21,000		400,000
	521,000						521,000		

Transaction 7, Return of Inventory to Supplier. When a company returns merchandise to its suppliers for credit, its merchandise inventory account is reduced and its liabilities are reduced. In this instance, the amount of the decrease on each side of the equation is $800.

	Assets				=	Liabilities		+	Owner's Equity
	Cash	Accounts Receivable	Merchandise Inventory	Store Equipment		Note Payable	Accounts Payable		Smith, Capital
Bal.	346,000	1,000	160,000	14,000	=	100,000	21,000		400,000
(7)			– 800		=		– 800		
Bal.	346,000	1,000	159,200	14,000	=	100,000	20,200		400,000
			520,200				520,200		

creditor One to whom money is owed.

Transaction 8, Payments to Creditors. A **creditor** is one to whom money is owed. The manufacturer is an example of a creditor. These payments decrease both assets (Cash) and liabilities (Accounts Payable) by $4,000.

	Assets				=	Liabilities		+	Owner's Equity
	Cash	Accounts Receivable	Merchandise Inventory	Store Equipment		Note Payable	Accounts Payable		Smith, Capital
Bal.	346,000	1,000	159,200	14,000	=	100,000	20,200		400,000
(8)	– 4,000				=		– 4,000		
Bal.	342,000	1,000	159,200	14,000	=	100,000	16,200		400,000
			516,200				516,200		

debtor One who owes money.

Transaction 9, Collections from Debtors. A **debtor** is one who owes money. Here the business neighbor is the debtor, and Biwheels is the creditor. These collections increase one of Biwheels' assets (Cash) and decrease another asset (Accounts Receivable) by $700.

	Assets				=	Liabilities		+	Owner's Equity
	Cash	Accounts Receivable	Merchandise Inventory	Store Equipment		Note Payable	Accounts Payable		Smith, Capital
Bal.	342,000	1,000	159,200	14,000	=	100,000	16,200		400,000
(9)	+ 700	– 700			=				
Bal.	342,700	300	159,200	14,000	=	100,000	16,200		400,000
			516,200				516,200		

Note that transactions 4 through 9 illustrate the entity concept in that they all relate to Smith's *business* entity, the Biwheels Company. When Smith remodels his home for $35,000, paying by check from his personal bank account, the transaction is a nonbusiness transaction of Smith's *personal* entity. It is not recorded by the business. Our focus is solely on the business entity.

Preparing the Balance Sheet

A cumulative total may be drawn at *any* date for each *account* in Exhibit 1-1. The following balance sheet uses the totals at the bottom of Exhibit 1-1. Observe once again that a balance sheet represents the financial impact of an accumulation of transactions at a specific point in time, here January 12, 19X2.

Biwheels Company
Balance Sheet
January 12, 19X2

Assets		Liabilities and Owners' Equity	
Cash	$342,700	Note payable	$100,000
Accounts receivable	300	Accounts payable	16,200
Merchandise		Total liabilities	$116,200
inventory	159,200		
Store equipment	14,000	Smith, capital	400,000
Total	$516,200	Total	$516,200

As noted earlier, Biwheels could prepare a new balance sheet after each transaction. Obviously, such a practice would be awkward and unnecessary. Therefore balance sheets are usually produced once a month.

Examples of Actual Corporate Balance Sheets

To become more familiar with the balance sheet and its equation, consider the following condensed excerpts from two actual recent financial reports. Some terms vary among organizations, but the essential balance sheet equation does not.

Delta Airlines, Inc.
(in millions)

Assets		Liabilities and Owners' Equity	
Cash	$ 1,710	Notes payable	$ 238
Accounts receivable	886	Accounts payable	1,552
Flight equipment	5,214	Other liabilities	8,639
Other equipment	1,148	Total liabilities	$10,429
Other assets	2,938	Owners' equity	1,467
		Total liabilities and	
Total assets	$11,896	owners' equity	$11,896

The Delta Airlines 1994 balance sheet illustrates the prominence of flight equipment as a major component of an airline's assets. Moreover, the total liabilities exceed the owners' equity, which is commonplace for airlines, but not for most large industrial and service organizations. The other liabilities consist largely of long-term debt that usually arises in conjunction with the acquisition of long-term assets such as airplanes.

Nike, Inc.
(in thousands)

Assets		Liabilities and Owners' Equity	
Cash	$ 518,816	Notes payable	$ 127,378
Accounts receivable	703,682	Accounts payable	210,578
Inventories	470,023	Other liabilities	294,910
Property, plant, and		Total liabilities	$ 632,866
equipment	405,845	Owners' equity	1,740,949
Other assets	275,449	Total liabilities and	
Total assets	$2,373,815	owners' equity	$2,373,815

As you might expect, Nike has a significant amount of inventories; Delta's inventories are confined to a relatively insignificant amount of supplies classified as other assets. Nike's total liabilities of $632,866 are easily exceeded by the owners' equity of $1,740,949. Some readers might expect the $405,845 of property, plant, and equipment to be much larger. However, Nike does not produce much of its own merchandise. Instead Nike contracts with various manufacturers to make goods in accordance with Nike's specifications.

Appendix A at the end of this book contains a complete set of the actual 1995 financial statements of Wal-Mart Stores, Inc. As you proceed from chapter to chapter, you should examine the pertinent parts of the Wal-Mart financial statements. In this way, you will become increasingly comfortable with actual financial reports. For example, the general format and major items in the Wal-Mart balance sheet (Appendix A) should be familiar by now. Details will gradually become understandable as each chapter explains the nature of the various major financial statements.

■ TYPES OF OWNERSHIP

Business entities can take one of three forms. Owners must decide whether to organize as sole proprietorships, partnerships, or corporations.

Sole Proprietorships

sole proprietorship A separate organization with a single owner.

A **sole proprietorship** is a separate organization with a single owner. Most often the owner is also the manager. Therefore sole proprietorships tend to be small retail establishments and individual professional businesses such as those of dentists, physicians, and attorneys. From an *accounting* viewpoint, each sole proprietorship is an individual entity that is separate and distinct from the proprietor.

Partnerships

partnership A special form of organization that joins two or more individuals together as co-owners.

A **partnership** is a special form of organization that joins two or more individuals together as co-owners. Many retail establishments, as well as dentists, physicians, attorneys, and accountants, conduct their activities as partnerships. Indeed, partnerships can sometimes be gigantic. For instance, the largest independent accounting firms have more than two thousand partners. Again, from an *accounting* viewpoint, each partnership is an individual entity that is separate from the personal activities of each partner.

Corporations

corporation An organization that is an "artificial being" created by individual state laws.

publicly owned A corporation in which shares in the ownership are sold to the public.

privately owned A corporation owned by a family, a small group of shareholders, or a single individual, in which shares of ownership are not publicly sold.

Corporations are organizations created under state law in the United States. Individuals form a corporation by applying to the state for approval of the company's *articles of incorporation*, which include information on shares of ownership. Most large corporations are **publicly owned** in that shares in the ownership are sold to the public. The owners of the corporation are then identified as *shareholders* (or *stockholders*). Large publicly owned corporations can have thousands of shareholders. Some corporations are **privately owned** by families, small groups of shareholders, or a single individual, and shares of ownership are not publicly sold. Many states allow having only one shareholder.

In the United States the laws governing the creation of a corporation vary from state to state. In spite of its small size, Delaware is the state in which many corporations are legally created because its rules are less restrictive than those of most other states. In addition, its fees are low and its legal system and the judges who hear business cases are experienced and efficient at resolving disputes and lawsuits. The exact rights and privileges of a corporation also vary from state to state and from country to country.

Internationally, distinct legal organizations are very common. In the United Kingdom they are frequently indicated by the word *limited* (Ltd) in the name. In many countries whose laws trace back to Spain, the initials *S.A.* refer to a "society anonymous" in which multiple owners stand behind the company. A necessary condition for modern market economies is a mechanism that permits investment capital to be accumulated in support of larger economic efforts. A corporate type of form has proven effective worldwide.

Once a corporation has been established, it is a *legal* entity apart from its owners. The management and business activities are conducted completely apart from the activities of the owners. The corporation is also, of course, an *accounting* entity.

Advantages and Disadvantages

limited liability
A feature of the corporate form of organization whereby corporate creditors ordinarily have claims against the corporate assets only. The owners' personal assets are not subject to the creditors' grasp.

The corporate form of organization has many advantages. Perhaps most notable is the **limited liability** of owners, which means that corporate creditors (such as banks or suppliers) ordinarily have claims against the corporate assets only. Therefore, if a corporation drifts into financial trouble, its creditors cannot look for repayment beyond the corporate entity; that is, generally the owners' personal assets are not subject to the creditors' grasp. In contrast, the owners of proprietorships and partnerships typically have *unlimited liability*, which means that business creditors can look to the owners' personal assets for repayment. For example, if Biwheels were a partnership, *each* partner would bear a personal liability for full payment of the $100,000 bank loan.

capital stock certificate (stock certificate) Formal evidence of ownership shares in a corporation.

Another advantage of the corporation is easy transfer of ownership. In selling shares in its ownership, the corporation usually issues **capital stock certificates** (often called simply **stock certificates**) as formal evidence of ownership. These shares may be sold and resold among present and potential owners. Stock exchanges make trading of shares easy. More than 250 million shares are bought and sold on an average day on the New York Stock Exchange (NYSE) alone. Further, trading is not limited to U.S. markets. Shares of many large U.S. firms are also traded on international exchanges such as those in Tokyo and London. And many Japanese and British firms have shares traded on the NYSE. The total market value of stocks traded in U.S. markets is over $4.5 trillion, compared with $4 trillion in Japan and $1 trillion in London.

Objective 5

Understand the advantages and disadvantages of the three types of business organizations and how to account for each.

In contrast to proprietorships and partnerships, corporations have the advantage of ease in raising ownership capital from hundreds or thousands of potential stockholders. Indeed, AT&T has nearly 2.5 million stockholders, owning a total of over 1 billion shares of stock.

The corporation also has the advantage of continuity of existence. Life is indefinite in the sense that it continues even if its ownership changes. In contrast, proprietorships and partnerships officially terminate upon the death or complete withdrawal of an owner.

The effects of the form of ownership on income taxes may vary significantly. For example, a corporation is taxed as a separate entity (as a corporation). But no income taxes are levied on a proprietorship (as a proprietorship) or on a partnership (as a partnership). Instead the income earned by proprietorships and partnerships is attributed to the owners as personal taxpayers. In short, the income tax laws regard corporations as being taxable entities, but proprietorships or partnerships as not being taxable entities. Whether the corporation provides tax advantages depends heavily on the personal tax situations of the owners.

Regardless of the economic and legal advantages or disadvantages of each type of organization, some small-business owners incorporate simply for prestige. That is, they feel more important if they can refer to "my corporation" and if they can refer to themselves as "chairman of the board" or "president" instead of "business owner" or "partner."

capital A term used to identify owners' equities for proprietorships and partnerships.

In terms of numbers of entities, there are fewer corporations in the United States than there are proprietorships or partnerships. However, the corporation has far more economic significance. Corporations conduct a sheer money volume of business that dwarfs the volume of other forms of organization. Moreover, almost every reader of this book interacts with, owes money to, or invests in corporations. For these reasons, this book emphasizes the corporate entity.

Accounting for Owners' Equity

stockholders' equity (shareholders' equity) Owners' equity of a corporation. The excess of assets over liabilities of a corporation.

The basic accounting concepts that underlie the owners' equity are unchanged regardless of whether the organization is a proprietorship, a partnership, or a corporation. However, owners' equities for proprietorships and partnerships are often identified by the word **capital**. In contrast, owners' equity for a corporation is usually called **stockholders' equity** or **shareholders' equity**. Examine the possibilities for the Biwheels Company that are shown in the accompanying table.

Owners' Equity for Different Organizations

Owner's Equity for a Proprietorship *(Assume George Smith is the sole owner)*	
George Smith, capital	$400,000

Owners' Equity for a Partnership *(Assume Smith has two partners)*	
George Smith, capital	$320,000
Alex Handl, capital	40,000
Susan Eastman, capital	40,000
Total partners' capital	$400,000

Owners' Equity for a Corporation	
Stockholders' equity:	
Paid-in capital:	
Capital stock, 10,000 shares issued at par value of $10 per share	$100,000
Paid-in capital in excess of par value of capital stock	300,000
Total paid-in capital	$400,000

paid-in capital The total capital investment in a corporation by its owners at the inception of business and subsequently.

The accounts for the proprietorship and the partnership show owners' equity as straightforward records of the *capital* invested by the owners. For a corporation, the total capital investment in a corporation by its owners at the inception of business and subsequently is called **paid-in capital**. It is recorded in two parts: capital stock at par value and paid-in capital in excess of par value.

The Meaning of Par Value

par value (stated value) The nominal dollar amount printed on stock certificates.

Stock certificates typically have some printed nominal dollar amount that is required by most states. This amount is determined by the board of directors and is usually called **par value** or **stated value**. Typically, the stock is sold at a price that is higher than its par value. The difference between the total amount received for the stock and the par value is called **paid-in capital in excess of par value**.

paid-in capital in excess of par value When issuing stock, the difference between the total amount received and the par value.

To alter our example to the corporate form, assume 10,000 shares of Biwheels stock have been sold for $40 per share. The par value is $10 per share, and therefore the paid-in capital in excess of par value is $30 per share. Thus, the total ownership claim of $400,000 arising from the investment is split between two equity claims, one for $100,000 "capital stock, at par" and one for $300,000 "paid-in capital in excess of par" or "additional paid-in capital."

The following formulas show these components of the total paid-in capital account:

$$\text{Total paid-in capital} = \text{Capital stock at par} + \text{Paid-in capital in excess of par}$$
$$\$400,000 = \$100,000 + \$300,000$$
$$\text{Capital stock at par} = \text{Number of shares issued} \times \text{Par value per share}$$
$$\$100,000 = 10,000 \times \$10$$
$$\text{Paid-in capital in excess of par} = \text{Total paid-in capital} - \text{Common stock at par}$$
$$\$300,000 = \$400,000 - \$100,000$$
$$\text{Total paid-in capital} = \text{Number of shares issued} \times \text{Average issue price per share}$$
$$\$400,000 = 10,000 \times \$40$$

Originally, par value was conceived as a measure of protection for creditors because it established the minimum legal liability of a stockholder. In this way, the creditors would be assured that the corporation would have at least a minimum amount of ownership capital ($10 for each share issued). Indeed, the stockholder had a commitment to invest at least $10 per share in the corporation.

Examples of Paid-in Capital in Actual Corporate Balance Sheets

common stock Stock representing the class of owners having a "residual" ownership of a corporation.

In most states, it is illegal to issue shares unless their par value is fully paid in. As a result, the par (or stated) values are usually set far below the full market price of the shares upon issuance, as illustrated by the following excerpts from recent actual corporate balance sheets. The excerpts use the term *common stock* to describe capital stock. Sometimes more than one type of capital stock is issued by a corporation (as explained in Chapter 12). But there is always **common stock**, which represents the "residual" ownership.

Sun Microsystems, Inc.

Common stock, $0.00067 par value, 300,000,000 shares authorized; issued106,394,200 shares	$ 72,000
Additional paid-in capital	1,066,571,000

The extremely small amount of par value in comparison with the additional paid-in capital is common and illustrates the insignificance of "par value" in today's business world. Also note the use of a frequently encountered term, "additional paid-in capital," as a short synonym for "paid-in capital in excess of par value of common stock." Finally, note that the number of "shares authorized" is the maximum number of shares that the company can issue as designated by the company's articles of incorporation.

Microsoft

Common stock and paid-in-capital— shares authorized 2,000,000,000 issued and outstanding 581,000,000	$1,086,000,000

Microsoft does not split the paid-in capital into two lines and does not even mention the par value, which is $.00001 per share. Inasmuch as par value is usually small and has little significance, this approach is praiseworthy.

In summary, both of these actual corporate presentations can be described accurately with a simple term, *total paid-in capital*, which will be distinguished from other ownership equity arising from profitable operations in later chapters.

■ CREDIBILITY AND THE ROLE OF AUDITING

Objective 6

Explain the notion of credibility and the function of auditing.

The credibility of financial statements is the ultimate responsibility of the managers who are entrusted with the resources under their command. In proprietorships, the owner is usually the top manager. In partnerships, top management may be shared by the owners. In corporations, the ultimate responsibility for management is delegated by stockholders to the *board of directors*, as indicated in the following diagram:

An advantage of the corporate form of organization is separation of ownership and management. Stockholders invest resources but do not need to devote time to managing, and managers can be selected for their managerial skills, not their ability to invest large sums in the firm. The board of directors is the link between stockholders and the actual managers. It is the board's duty to ensure that managers act in the interests of shareholders.

The board of directors is elected by the shareholders, but the slate of candidates is often selected by management. Sometimes, the chairman of the board is also the top manager and the major shareholder. For example, for over thirty years Henry Ford II was the major stockholder, the chairman of the board, and the chief executive officer (CEO) of the Ford Motor Company. Other top managers such as the president, financial vice president, and marketing vice president are routinely elected to the board of directors of the company they manage. Therefore, the interests of both stockholders and managers are usually represented on the board of directors.

Membership on a board of directors is often extended to CEOs and presidents of other corporations, to university presidents and professors, and to attorneys. For example, the sixteen-member board of General Mills includes five General Mills managers, eight present or former CEOs of other companies, two professors, and one attorney. In many cases, these members of the board are also stockholders of the corporation.

In fulfilling its management responsibilities, the board of directors relies on financial statements to assess the corporation's performance. Because financial statements are prepared by managers (or by accountants employed by the managers), there is a chance that the statements will portray an overly rosy picture of the firm—thereby enhancing the image of management. Long ago stockholders, as well as external parties such as banks who lend money to the firm, wanted some third-party assurance about the credibility of the financial statements. The profession of public accounting arose to serve this purpose—to provide a means for examining financial statements and the transactions underlying them and to provide an opinion on the statements' credibility.

The Certified Public Accountant

Public accountants' opinions on financial statements will add credibility only if such accountants have a reputation for expertise and integrity and provide assurance that their examination of the financial statements was thorough. To assure expertise and integrity, public accountants are certified.

certified public accountant (CPA)
In the United States, a person earns this designation by a combination of education, qualifying experience, and the passing of a two-day written national examination.

A **certified public accountant (CPA)** in the United States earns this designation by a combination of education, qualifying experience, and the passing of a two-day written national examination. The examination is administered and graded by a national organization, the American Institute of Certified Public Accountants (AICPA). The institute is the principal professional association in the private sector that regulates the quality of the public accounting profession. Other English-speaking nations have similar arrangements but use the term *chartered accountant* (CA) instead of certified public accountant.

The CPA examination covers four major topical areas: auditing, accounting theory, business law, and accounting practice. The last is a series of accounting problems covering a wide variety of topics, including income taxes, cost accounting, and accounting for nonprofit institutions.

Although the AICPA prepares and grades the CPA examination on a national basis, the individual states have their own regulations concerning the qualifications for taking and passing the examination and for earning the right to practice as a CPA. These regulations are determined and enforced by state boards of accountancy.[3]

The Auditor's Opinion

audit An examination of transactions and financial statements made in accordance with generally accepted auditing standards.

auditor's opinion (independent opinion) A report describing the auditor's examination of transactions and financial statements. It is included with the financial statements in an annual report issued by the corporation.

To assess management's financial disclosure, public accountants conduct an **audit**, which is an examination of transactions and financial statements made in accordance with generally accepted auditing standards developed primarily by the AICPA. This audit includes miscellaneous tests of the accounting records, internal control systems, and other auditing procedures as deemed necessary. The examination is described in the **auditor's opinion** (also called an **independent opinion**) that is included with the financial statements in an annual report issued by the corporation. Standard phrasing is used for auditors' opinions, as illustrated by the following opinion rendered by a large CPA firm, Deloitte & Touche, for Microsoft Corporation.

To the Board of Directors and Stockholders of Microsoft Corporation:

We have audited the accompanying balance sheets of Microsoft Corporation and subsidiaries as of June 30, 1993 and 1994, and the related statements of income, stockholders' equity, and cash flows for each of the three years in the period ended June 30, 1994. These financial statements are the responsibility of the Company's management. Our responsibility is to express an opinion on these financial statements based on our audits.

We conducted our audits in accordance with generally accepted auditing standards. Those standards require that we plan and perform the audit to obtain reasonable assurance about whether the financial statements are free of material misstatement. An audit includes examining, on a test basis, evidence supporting the amounts and disclosures in the financial statements. An audit also includes assessing the accounting principles used and significant estimates made by management, as well as evaluating the overall financial statement presentation. We believe that our audits provide a reasonable basis for our opinion.

In our opinion, such financial statements present fairly, in all material respects, the financial position of Microsoft Corporation and subsidiaries as of June 30, 1993 and 1994, and the results of their operations and their cash flows for each of the three years in the period ended June 30, 1994 in conformity with generally accepted accounting principles.

DELOITTE & TOUCHE

---

[3] The Certificate in Management Accounting (CMA) is the internal accountant's counterpart to the CPA. The major objective of the CMA is to establish management accounting as a distinct profession. Information can be obtained from the Institute of Management Accountants, 10 Paragon Dr., Montvale, NJ, 07645-1760.

This book will explore the meaning of such phrases as "present fairly" and "generally accepted accounting principles." For now, reflect on the fact that auditors do not prepare a company's financial statements. Rather, the auditor's opinion is the public accountant's stamp of approval on *management's* financial statements.

■ THE ACCOUNTING PROFESSION

public accounting
The field of accounting where services are offered to the general public on a fee basis.
private accounting
Accountants who work for businesses, government agencies, and other nonprofit organizations.

Objective 7

Describe public and private accounting and the role of ethics in the accounting profession.

The accounting profession can be classified in many ways. A major classification is **public accounting** and **private accounting**. "Public" accountants are those whose services are offered to the general public on a fee basis. Such services include auditing, income taxes, and management consulting. "Private" accountants are all the rest. They consist not only of those individuals who work for businesses but also of those who work for government agencies, including the Internal Revenue Service, and other nonprofit organizations.

Public Accounting Firms

Public accounting firms vary in size and in the type of accounting services performed. There are small proprietorships, where auditing may represent as little as 10% or less of annual billings. *Billings* are the total amounts charged to clients for services rendered to them. The bulk of the work of these firms is income taxes and "write-up" work (the actual bookkeeping services for clients who are not equipped to do their own accounting).

There are also a handful of gigantic firms that have over two thousand partners with offices located throughout the world. Such enormous firms are necessary because their clients are also enormous. For instance, a large CPA firm has reported that its annual audit of one client takes the equivalent of seventy-two accountants working a full year. Another client has three hundred separate corporate entities in forty countries that must ultimately be consolidated into one set of overall financial statements.

The six largest public international accounting firms are known collectively as the "Big-Six":

- Arthur Andersen & Co.
- Coopers & Lybrand
- Deloitte & Touche
- Ernst & Young
- KPMG Peat Marwick
- Price Waterhouse

Of the companies listed on the New York Stock Exchange, 97% are clients of these six firms. These accounting firms have annual billings in excess of a billion dollars each. A majority of the billings is attributable to auditing services. The top partners in big accounting firms are compensated on about the same scale as their corporate counterparts. Huge accounting firms tend to receive more publicity than other firms. However, please remember that there are thousands of other able accounting firms, varying in size from sole practitioners to giant international partnerships.

Other Opportunities for Accountants

In the accompanying diagram, the long arrows indicate how accountants often move from public accounting firms to positions in business or government. Obviously, these movements can occur at any level or in any direction.

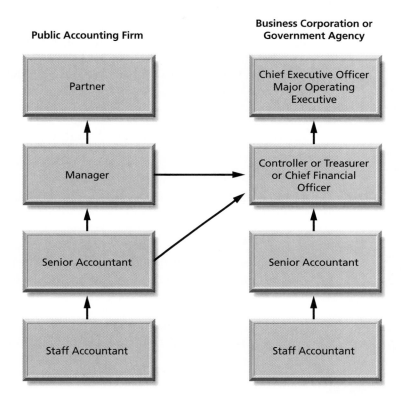

Accounting cuts across all management functions, including purchasing, manufacturing, wholesaling, retailing, and a variety of marketing and transportation activities. It provides an excellent opportunity for gaining broad knowledge. Senior accountants or controllers in a corporation are sometimes picked as production or marketing executives. Why? Because they may have impressed other executives as having acquired general management skills.

Accounting was recently ranked as the most important business school course for future managers. *Business Week* recently reported that "more CEOs [chief executive officers] started out in finance or accounting than in any other area."

Professional Ethics

Members of the American Institute of Certified Public Accountants must abide by a code of professional conduct. Surveys of public attitudes toward CPAs have consistently ranked the accounting profession as having high ethical standards.

The code of professional conduct is especially concerned with integrity and independence. For example, independent auditors are forbidden to own shares of their client corporations. Moreover, the auditors must satisfy themselves that their clients' financial statements are prepared in accordance with GAAP.

The emphasis on ethics extends beyond public accounting. For example, members of the Institute of Management Accountants are expected to abide by that organization's code of ethics for management accountants. Auditors and management accountants have professional responsibilities regarding competence, confidentiality, integrity, and objectivity. Professional accounting organizations and state regulatory bodies have procedures for reviewing behavior alleged to violate codes of professional conduct. Chapter 8 contains a more extensive discussion of professional ethics.

Summary Problems for Your Review

Problem One

Review Exhibit 1-1 (p. 13). Analyze the following additional transactions of Biwheels Company. Begin with the balances shown for January 12, 19X2, in Exhibit 1-1. Prepare an ending balance sheet for Biwheels Company (say, on January 16 after these additional transactions).

   i. Biwheels pays $10,000 on the bank loan (ignore interest).

  ii. Smith buys furniture for his home for $5,000, using his family charge account at Macy's.

 iii. Biwheels buys merchandise inventory for $50,000. Half the amount is paid in cash, and half is owed on open account.

 iv. Biwheels collects $200 more from its business debtor.

Exhibit 1-2

Biwheels Company
Analysis of Additional January Transactions

Description of Transaction	Cash	Accounts + Receivable +	Merchandise Inventory +	Store Equipment =	Note Payable	Accounts + Payable +	Smith, Capital
		Assets			**=**	**Liabilities + Owner's Equity**	
Balance, January 12, 19X2	342,700 +	300 +	159,200 +	14,000	= 100,000 +	16,200 +	400,000
(i) Payment on bank loan	– 10,000				=– 10,000		
(ii) Personal; no effect							
(iii) Acquire inventory, half for cash	– 25,000		+ 50,000		=	+ 25,000	
Collection of receivable	+ 200	– 200					
Balance, January 16	307,900 +	100 +	209,200 +	14,000	= 90,000 +	41,200 +	400,000
		531,200			=	531,200	

Exhibit 1-3	Assets		Liabilities and Owner's Equity	
Biwheels Company			Liabilities:	
Balance Sheet	Cash	$307,900	Note payable	$ 90,000
January 16, 19X2	Accounts receivable	100	Accounts payable	41,200
	Merchandise inventory	209,200	Total liabilities	$131,200
	Store equipment	14,000	Smith, capital	400,000
	Total	$531,200	Total	$531,200

Solution to Problem One

See Exhibits 1-2 and 1-3. Note that transaction ii is ignored because it is wholly personal. However, visualize how Smith's personal balance sheet would be affected. His assets, Home Furniture, would rise by $5,000 and his liabilities, Accounts Payable, would also rise by $5,000.

Problem Two

"If I purchase 100 shares of the outstanding stock of General Motors Corporation (or Biwheels Company), I invest my money directly in that corporation. General Motors must record that event." Do you agree? Explain.

Solution to Problem Two

Money is invested directly in a corporation when the entity originally issues the stock. For example, 100,000 shares of stock may be issued at $80 per share, bringing in $8 million to the corporation. This is a transaction between the corporation and the stockholders. It affects the corporate financial position:

Cash **$8,000,000**   Stockholders' equity **$8,000,000**

Subsequently, 100 shares of that stock may be sold by an original stockholder (Michael Jordan) to another individual (Meg Ryan) for $130 per share. This is a private transaction; no cash is received by the corporation. Of course, the corporation records the fact that 100 shares originally owned by Jordan are now owned by Ryan, but the corporate financial position is unchanged. Accounting focuses on the business entity; subsequently, private dealings of the owners have no effect on the financial position of the entity, although the corporation records the owners' identities.

Problem Three

"One individual can be an owner, an employee, and a creditor of a corporation." Do you agree? Explain.

Solution to Problem Three

Yes. The corporation enters contracts, hires employees, buys buildings, and conducts other business. The chairman of the board, the president, the other officers, and all the workers are employees of the corporation. Thus Katharine Graham could own some of the capital stock of the Washington Post and also be an employee (CEO). Since money owed to employees for salaries is a liability, she could be an owner, an employee, and a creditor. Similarly, an employee of a telephone company who is a stockholder of the company could also be receiving telephone services from the same company. She is an owner, employee, *customer*, and debtor of the company.

Highlights to Remember

Financial statements provide information for decision making to managers, creditors, and owners of all types of organizations. The balance sheet (or statement of financial position) provides a "snapshot" of the financial position of an organization at any instant. That is, it answers the basic question, Where are we? The balance sheet equation is Assets = Liabilities + Owners' Equity. This equation must always be in balance.

Using the entity concept, the accountant relates transactions to a sharply defined area of accountability. Entities may take different forms, including proprietorships, partnerships, or corporations. There are also entities within entities. For example, the University of California contains various schools and departments within schools. The department is an accounting entity nested within the school, which is a larger entity nested within the university.

Transaction analysis is the heart of accounting. Transactions are events that require recording in an organization's accounts. For each transaction, an accountant must determine what accounts are affected and by how much. The transactions of a personal entity should not be mingled with those of a business entity.

Corporations are especially important entities because so much business is conducted by corporations. The ownership equity of a corporation is usually called stockholders' equity. It initially takes the form of common stock at par, or stated, value plus additional paid-in capital.

Separation of ownership from management in corporations creates a demand for auditing, a third-party examination of financial statements. The public accounting profession gives credibility to audits by specifying qualifications for certified public accountants, including ethical standards, and by developing generally accepted auditing standards to ensure thoroughness of audits. Because accountants work with managers in all management functions, accounting positions are fertile training grounds for future top managers.

Accounting Vocabulary

An "Accounting Vocabulary" section will be found at the end of each chapter. Vocabulary is an extremely important and often troublesome phase of the learning process. A fuzzy understanding of terms will hamper the learning of concepts and the ability to solve accounting problems.

Before proceeding to the assignment material or to the next chapter, be sure you understand the following words or terms. Their meaning is explained in the chapter and also in the glossary at the end of this book:

account, *p. 12*

account payable, *p. 13*

annual report, *p. 5*

assets, *p. 8*

audit, *p. 23*

auditor's opinion, *p. 23*

balance sheet, *p. 7*

balance sheet equation, *p. 8*

capital, *p. 19*

capital stock certificate, *p. 18*

certified public accountant (CPA), *p. 22*

common stock, *p. 20*

compound entry, *p. 14*
corporation, *p. 17*
creditor, *p. 15*
debtor, *p. 15*
entity, *p. 9*
financial accounting, *p. 7*
GAAP, *p. 9*
generally accepted accounting
   principles, *p. 9*
independent opinion, *p. 23*
inventory, *p. 12*
liabilities, *p. 8*
limited liability, *p. 18*

management accounting, *p. 7*
notes payable, *p. 8*
open account, *p. 13*
owners' equity, *p. 8*
paid-in capital, *p. 20*
paid-in capital in excess of par
   value, *p. 20*
partnership, *p. 17*
par value, *p. 20*
private accounting, *p. 24*
privately owned, *p. 18*
public accounting, *p. 24*

publicly owned, *p. 17*
reliability, *p. 10*
shareholders' equity, *p. 19*
sole proprietorship, *p. 17*
stated value, *p. 20*
statement of financial condition,
   p. 7
statement of financial position,
   p. 7
stock certificate, *p. 18*
stockholders' equity, *p. 19*
transaction, *p. 10*

Formulate good habits now. Check your understanding of these words or terms as a routine part of your study. The habit of checking your accounting vocabulary, chapter by chapter, is a good investment of your time. To aid your understanding and review, key vocabulary items appear in the margins within the chapter.

Assignment Material

The assignment material for each chapter is divided into Questions, Exercises, and Problems. The assignment material contains problems based on fictitious companies and problems based on real-life situations. We hope our use of actual companies and news events enhances your interest in accounting.

Problems based on real companies are identified with a logo in the margin. These problems underscore a major objective of this book: to increase the reader's ability to read, understand, and use published financial reports and news articles. In later chapters, these problems provide the principal means of reviewing not only the immediate chapter but also the previous chapters. In particular, note the Wal-Mart and Compact D from Disclosure problems at the end of each chapter's assignment material.

Questions

1-1. Give three examples of decisions that are likely to be influenced by financial statements.

1-2. Give three examples of users of financial statements.

1-3. Briefly distinguish between *financial accounting* and *management accounting*.

1-4. Give four examples of accounting entities.

1-5. Give two synonyms for *balance sheet*.

1-6. Explain the difference between a *note payable* and an *account payable*.

1-7. Give two synonyms for *owners' equity*.

1-8. Explain the meaning of *limited liability*.

1-9. Why does this book emphasize the corporation rather than the proprietorship or the partnership?

1-10. "The idea of par value is insignificant." Explain.

1-11. What is a CPA and how does someone become one?

Exercises

 1-12   Describing Underlying Transactions
LTC Company, which was recently formed, is engaging in some preliminary transactions before beginning full-scale operations for retailing laptop computers. The balances of each item in the company's accounting equation are given at the top of page 30 for May 10 and for each of the next nine business days.

Required   State briefly what you think took place on each of these nine days, assuming that only one transaction occurred each day.

	Cash	Accounts Receivable	Computer Inventory	Store Fixtures	Accounts Payable	Owners' Equity
May 10	$ 6,000	$4,000	$18,000	$ 3,000	$ 4,000	$27,000
11	11,000	4,000	18,000	3,000	4,000	32,000
12	11,000	4,000	18,000	7,000	4,000	36,000
15	8,000	4,000	21,000	7,000	4,000	36,000
16	8,000	4,000	26,000	7,000	9,000	36,000
17	11,000	1,000	26,000	7,000	9,000	36,000
18	6,000	1,000	26,000	14,000	11,000	36,000
19	3,000	1,000	26,000	14,000	8,000	36,000
22	3,000	1,000	25,600	14,000	7,600	36,000
23	1,000	4,000	25,600	14,000	7,600	34,000

1-13 Describing Underlying Transactions

The balances of each item in Lansdown Company's accounting equation are given below for August 31 and for each of the next nine business days.

Required State briefly what you think took place on each of these nine days, assuming that only one transaction occurred each day.

	Cash	Accounts Receivable	Computer Inventory	Store Fixtures	Accounts Payable	Owners' Equity
Aug. 31	$2,000	$8,000	$ 9,000	$ 7,500	$ 5,500	$21,000
Sept.1	4,000	6,000	9,000	7,500	5,500	21,000
2	4,000	6,000	9,000	10,000	8,000	21,000
3	1,000	6,000	9,000	10,000`	8,000	18,000
4	2,000	9,000	5,000	10,000	8,000	18,000
5	2,000	9,000	10,000	10,000	8,000	23,000
8	1,500	9,000	10,000	10,000	7,500	23,000
9	1,000	9,000	10,000	13,000	10,000	23,000
10	1,000	9,000	10,000	12,700	9,700	23,000
11	4,000	6,000	10,000	12,700	9,700	23,000

1-14 Prepare Balance Sheet

Sacremento Corporation's balance sheet at March 30, 19X1, contained only the following items (arranged here in random order):

Cash	$10,000	Accounts payable	$ 7,000
Notes payable	10,000	Furniture and fixtures	3,000
Merchandise inventory	40,000	Long-term debt payable	12,000
Paid-in capital	81,000	Building	20,000
Land	6,000	Notes receivable	2,000
Accounts receivable	14,000	Machinery and equipment	15,000

On March 31, 19X1, these transactions and events took place:

1. Purchased merchandise on account, $2,500.
2. Sold at cost for $1,000 cash some furniture that was not needed.
3. Issued additional capital stock for machinery and equipment valued at $12,000.

4. Purchased land for $25,000, of which $5,000 was paid in cash, the remaining being represented by a five-year note (long-term debt).

5. The building was valued by professional appraisers at $50,000.

Required   Prepare in good form a balance sheet for March 31, 19X1, showing supporting computations for all new amounts.

1-15   Prepare Balance Sheet

Geary Corporation's balance sheet at November 29, 19X1 contained only the following items (arranged here in random order):

Paid-in capital	$195,000	Machinery and equipment	$ 20,000
Notes payable	20,000	Furniture and fixtures	8,000
Cash	21,000	Notes receivable	8,000
Accounts receivable	10,000	Accounts payable	15,000
Merchandise inventory	29,000	Building	230,000
Land	46,000	Long-term debt payable	142,000

On the following day, November 30, these transactions and events occurred:

1. Purchased machinery and equipment for $14,000, paying $3,000 in cash and signing a ninety-day note for the balance.

2. Paid $5,000 on accounts payable.

3. Sold on account some land that was not needed for $6,000, which was the Geary Corporation's acquisition cost of the land.

4. The remaining land was valued at $240,000 by professional appraisers.

5. Issued capital stock as payment for $23,000 of the long-term debt, that is, debt due beyond one year.

Required   Prepare in good form a balance sheet for November 30, 19X1, showing supporting computations for all new amounts.

Problems

1-16   Prepare Balance Sheet

Alexis Brentano is a realtor. She buys and sells properties on her own account, and she also earns commissions as a real estate agent for buyers and sellers. Her business was organized on November 24, 19X1, as a sole proprietorship. Brentano also owns her own personal residence. Consider the following on November 30, 19X1:

1. Brentano owes $90,000 on a mortgage on some undeveloped land, which was acquired by her business for a total price of $175,000.

2. Brentano had spent $15,000 cash for a Century 21 real estate franchise. Century 21 is a national affiliation of independent real estate brokers. This franchise is an asset.

3. Brentano owes $100,000 on a personal mortgage on her residence, which was acquired on November 20, 19X1, for a total price of $180,000.

4. Brentano owes $2,800 on a personal charge account with Nordstrom's Department Store.

5. On November 28, Brentano hired David Goldstein as her first employee. He was to begin work on December 1. Brentano was pleased because Goldstein was one of the best real estate salesmen in the area. On November 29, Goldstein was killed in an automobile accident.

6. Business furniture of $17,000 was acquired on November 25 for $6,000 on open account plus $11,000 of business cash. On November 26, Brentano sold a $1,000 business chair for $1,000 to her next-door business neighbor on open account.

7. Brentano's balance at November 30 in her business checking account after all transactions was $9,500.

Required   Prepare a balance sheet as of November 30, 19X1, for Alexis Brentano, realtor.

1-17 Analysis of Transactions

Use the format of Exhibit 1-1 (p. 13) to analyze the following transactions for April of Kijewski Cleaners. Then prepare a balance sheet as of April 30, 19X1. Kijewski was founded on April 1.

1. Issued 1,000 shares of $1 par common stock for cash, $60,000.
2. Issued 1,000 shares of $1 par common stock for equipment, $60,000.
3. Borrowed cash, signing a note payable for $30,000.
4. Purchased equipment for cash, $20,000.
5. Purchased office furniture on account, $10,000.
6. Disbursed cash on account (to reduce the account payable), $4,000.
7. Sold equipment on account at cost, $8,000.
8. Discovered that the most prominent competitor in the area was bankrupt and was closing its doors on April 30.
9. Collected cash on account, $3,000. See transaction 7.

1-18 Analysis of Transactions

Walgreen Company is a well-known drugstore chain. A condensed balance sheet for August 31, 1993 follows (in thousands):

Assets		Liabilities and Stockholders' Equity	
Cash	$ 91,597	Notes payable	$ 99,590
Accounts receivable	139,313	Accounts payable	427,185
Inventories	1,094,053	Other liabilities	629,665
Property and		Stockholders' equity	1,378,751
other assets	1,210,228		
Total	$2,535,191	Total	$2,535,191

Required   Use a format similar to Exhibit 1-1 (p. 13) to analyze the following transactions for the first two days of September. (Dollar amounts are in thousands.) Then prepare a balance sheet as of September 2.

1. Issued 1,000 shares of common stock to employees for cash, $22.
2. Issued 1,500 shares of common stock for the acquisition of special equipment from a supplier, $33.
3. Borrowed cash, signing a note payable for $120.
4. Purchased equipment for cash, $125.
5. Purchased inventories on account, $90.
6. Disbursed cash on account (to reduce the accounts payable), $354.
7. Sold display equipment to retailer on account at cost, $14.
8. Collected cash on account, $84.

1-19 Analysis of Transactions

Nike, Inc. had the following condensed balance sheet on May 31, 1994 (in thousands):

Assets		Liabilities and Owner's Equity	
Cash	$ 518,816	Notes payable	$ 127,378
Accounts receivable	703,682	Accounts payable	210,578
Inventories	470,023	Other liabilities	294,910
Equipment and		Total liabilities	$ 632,866
other assets	681,294	Owners' equity	1,740,949
		Total liabilities and	
Total assets	$2,373,815	owners' equity	$2,373,815

Consider the following transactions that occurred during the first three days of June (in thousands of dollars):

1. Inventories were acquired for cash, $150.
2. Inventories were acquired on open account, $200.
3. Unsatisfactory shoes acquired on open account in March were returned for full credit, $40.
4. Equipment of $120 was acquired for a cash down payment of $30 plus a six-month promissory note of $90.
5. To encourage wider displays, special store equipment was sold on account to New York area stores for $400. The equipment had cost $400 in the preceding month.
6. Jodie Foster produced, directed, and starred in a movie. As a favor to a Nike executive, she agreed to display Nike shoes in a basketball scene. No fee was paid by Nike.
7. Cash was disbursed on account (to reduce accounts payable), $170.
8. Collected cash on account, $180.
9. Borrowed cash from a bank, $500.
10. Sold additional common stock for cash to new investors, $900.
11. The president of the company sold 5,000 shares of his personal holdings of Nike stock through his stockbroker.

Required

1. Using a format similar to Exhibit 1-1(p. 13), prepare an analysis showing the effects of the June transactions on the financial position of Nike.
2. Prepare a balance sheet as of June 3.

1-20 Analysis of Transactions

Consider the following January transactions:

1. ABC Corporation is formed on January 1, 19X1, by three persons, Aldor, Binge, and Chin. ABC will be a wholesale distributor of electronic games. Each of the three investors is issued 20,000 shares of common stock ($2 par value) for $10 cash per share. Use two stockholders' equity accounts: Capital Stock (at par) and Additional Paid-in Capital.
2. Merchandise inventory of $200,000 is acquired for cash.
3. Merchandise inventory of $85,000 is acquired on open account.
4. Unsatisfactory merchandise that cost $11,000 in transaction 3 is returned for full credit.
5. Equipment of $40,000 is acquired for a cash down payment of $10,000 plus a three-month promissory note of $30,000.
6. As a favor, ABC sells equipment of $4,000 to a business neighbor on open account. The equipment had cost $4,000.
7. ABC pays $20,000 on the account described in transaction 3.
8. ABC collects $2,000 from the business neighbor. See transaction 6.

9. ABC buys merchandise inventory of $100,000. One-half of the amount is paid in cash, and one-half is owed on open account.
10. Chin sells half of his common stock to Loring for $13 per share.

Required   1. Using a format similar to Exhibit 1-1 (p. 13), prepare an analysis showing the effects of January transactions on the financial position of ABC Corporation.
2. Prepare a balance sheet as of January 31, 19X4.

1-21   Analysis of Transactions

You began a business as a wholesaler of gloves, scarves, and caps. The following events have occurred:

1. On March 1, 19X1, you invested $150,000 cash in your new sole proprietorship, which you call Alaska Products.
2. Acquired $20,000 inventory for cash.
3. Acquired $8,000 inventory on open account.
4. Acquired equipment for $15,000 in exchange for a $5,000 cash down payment and a $10,000 promissory note.
5. A large retail store, which you had hoped would be a big customer, discontinued operations.
6. You take gloves home for your family. The gloves were carried in Alaska's inventory at $600. (Regard this as a borrowing by you from Alaska Products.)
7. Gloves that cost $300 in transaction 2 were of the wrong style. You returned them and obtained a full cash refund.
8. Gloves that cost $800 in transaction 3 were of the wrong color. You returned them and obtained gloves of the correct color in exchange.
9. Caps that cost $500 in transaction 3 had an unacceptable quality. You returned them and obtained full credit on your account.
10. Paid $5,000 on promissory note.
11. You use your personal cash savings of $5,000 to acquire some equipment for Alaska. You consider this as an additional investment in your business.
12. Paid $3,000 on open account.
13. Two scarf manufacturers who are suppliers for Alaska announced a 7% rise in prices, effective in sixty days.
14. You use your personal cash savings of $1,000 to acquire a new TV set for your family.
15. You exchange equipment that cost $4,000 in transaction 4 with another wholesaler. However, the equipment received, which is almost new, is smaller and is worth only $1,500. Therefore the other wholesaler also agrees to pay you $500 in cash now and an additional $2,000 in cash in sixty days. (No gain or loss is recognized on this transaction.)

Required   1. Using Exhibit 1-1 (p. 13) as a guide, prepare an analysis of Alaska's transactions for March. Confine your analysis to the effects on the financial position of Alaska Products.
2. Prepare a balance sheet for Alaska Products as of March 31, 19X1.

1-22   Personal and Professional Entities

Kate Green, a recent graduate of a law school, was penniless on December 25, 19X1.

1. On December 26, Green inherited an enormous sum of money.
2. On December 27, she placed $80,000 in a business checking account for her unincorporated law practice.
3. On December 28, she purchased a home for a down payment of $100,000 plus a home mortgage payable of $250,000.

4. On December 28, Green agreed to rent a law office. She provided a $1,000 cash damage deposit (from her business cash), which will be fully refundable when she vacates the premises. This deposit is a business asset. Rental payments are to be made in advance on the first business day of each month. (The first payment of $700 is not to be made until January 2, 19X2.)

5. On December 28, Green purchased a computer for her law practice for $5,000 cash plus a $5,000 promissory note due in ninety days.

6. On December 28, she also purchased legal supplies for $1,000 on open account.

7. On December 28, Green purchased office furniture for her practice for $4,000 cash.

8. On December 29, Green hired a legal assistant receptionist for $380 per week. He was to report to work on January 2.

9. On December 30, Green's law practice lent $2,000 of cash in return for a one-year note from G. Keefe, a local candy store owner. Keefe had indicated that she would spread the news about the new lawyer.

Required

1. Use the format demonstrated in Exhibit 1-1 (p. 13) to analyze the transactions of Kate Green, lawyer. To avoid crowding, put your numbers in thousands of dollars. Do not restrict yourself to the account titles in Exhibit 1-1.

2. Prepare a balance sheet as of December 31, 19X1.

1-23 Bank Balance Sheet

Consider the following balance sheet accounts of Bank of America (in millions):

Assets		Liabilities and Stockholders' Equity	
Cash	$ 13,470	Deposits	$ 141,618
U.S. government and		Other liabilities	28,171
other securities	32,162	Total liabilities	$ 169,789
Loans receivable	122,871	Stockholders' equity	17,144
Premises and equipment	3,631		
Other assets	14,799	Total liabilities and	
Total assets	$186,933	stockholders' equity	$186,933

This balance sheet illustrates how banks gather and use money. Nearly 75% of the total assets are in the form of investments in loans, and over 80% of the total liabilities and stockholders' equity are in the form of deposits, the major liability. That is, these financial institutions are in the business of raising funds from depositors and, in turn, lending those funds to businesses, homeowners, and others. The stockholders' equity is usually tiny in comparison with the deposits (only about 6% in this case).

Required

1. What Bank of America accounts would be affected if you deposited $1,000?
2. Why are deposits listed as liabilities?
3. What accounts would be affected if the bank loaned Joan Kessler $50,000 for home renovations?
4. What accounts would be affected if Isabel Garcia withdrew $4,000 from her savings account?

1-24 Presenting Paid-in Capital

Consider excerpts from two balance sheets (amounts in thousands):

Occidental Petroleum Corporation

Common stock, $0.20 par value; authorized	
400 million shares; shares outstanding 305,603,000	$ 61,000
Additional paid-in capital	5,212,000

IBM

Common stock par value—$1.25 —outstanding 581,388,475	
shares (includes capital in excess of par value)	$6,980,000

1. How would the presentation of Occidental's stockholders' equity accounts be affected if one million more shares were issued for $50 cash per share?
2. How would the presentation of IBM's stockholders' equity accounts be affected if one million more shares were issued for $50 cash per share? Be specific.

1-25 Presenting Paid-in Capital
Honeywell, Inc., maker of thermostats and a variety of complex control systems, presented the following in its balance sheet of January 1, 1994:

Common stock—$1.50 par value, 188,328,570 shares issued	?
Additional paid-in capital	$431,500,000

What amount should be shown on the common stock line? What was the average price per share paid by the original investors for the Honeywell common stock? How do your answers compare with the $31 market price of the stock on January 2, 1995? Comment briefly.

1-26 Presenting Paid-in Capital
Mitsubishi Kasei Corporation is Japan's premier integrated chemical company. The following items were presented in its balance sheet of March 31, 1991:

Common stock— ¥50 par value, 1,408 million shares issued and outstanding	?
Additional paid–in capital (in millions of yen)	¥105,982

Note: ¥ is the symbol for Japanese yen.

1. What amount should be shown on the common stock line?
2. What was the average price per share paid by the original investors for the Mitsubishi Kasei common stock?
3. How do your answers compare with the ¥580 market price of the stock? Comment briefly.

1-27 Prepare Balance Sheet
Microsoft is the world's leading software company. Microsoft's 1994 annual report included the following balance sheet items (in millions of dollars):

Property, plant, and equipment	867
Accounts payable	239
Inventories	127
Capital stock	1,086
Cash	?
Total stockholders' equity	?
Long-term debt	0
Total assets	3,805
Accounts receivable	338
Other assets	310
Additional stockholders' equity	?
Other liabilities	324

Required   Prepare a condensed balance sheet, including amounts for

1. Cash.
2. Additional and total stockholders' equity.
3. Total liabilities.

1-28 Prepare Balance Sheet
Procter & Gamble Company has many popular products, including Tide, Jif, and Crest. Its balance sheet of June 30, 1994 contained the following items (in millions):

Long-term debt payable	$ 4,980
Cash	(1)
Total shareholders' equity	(2)
Total liabilities	(3)
Accounts receivable	3,115
Common stock	684
Inventories	2,877
Accounts payable	3,264
Property, plant, and equipment	10,024
Additional shareholders' equity	8,148
Other assets	7,146
Other liabilities	8,459
Total assets	25,535

Required Prepare a condensed balance sheet, including amounts for

1. Cash. What do you think of its relative size?
2. Total shareholders' equity.
3. Total liabilities.

1-29   Accounting and Ethics

A survey of high school seniors and college freshmen by the American Institute of Certified Public Accountants showed that accountants are given high marks for their ethics. Professional associations for both internal accountants and external auditors place much emphasis on their standards of ethical conduct. Discuss why maintaining a reputation for ethical conduct is important for (1) accountants within an organization,and (2) external auditors. What can accountants do to foster a reputation for high ethical standards and conduct.

1-30   Wal-Mart Annual Report

This and similar problems in succeeding chapters focus on the financial statements of an actual company. Wal-Mart Stores, Inc., is the largest retailer in the United States.

As each homework problem is solved, readers gradually strengthen their understanding of actual financial statements in their entirety.

Refer to the Wal-Mart balance sheet in Appendix A at the end of the book and answer the following questions:

1. How much cash did Wal-Mart have on January 31, 1995? (Include cash equivalent as part of cash.)
2. What were the total assets on January 31, 1995? January 31, 1994?
3. Write the company's accounting equation as of January 31,1995, by filling in the dollar amounts:

Assets = Liabilities + Stockholders' equity. Consider long-term obligations under capital leases and deferred income taxes to be liabilities.

1-31   Compact D from Disclosure

Each chapter will have one problem that requires use of Compact D (or a similar database of financial statements).

Select the financial statements of any company, and focus on the balance sheet.

Required
1. Identify the amount of cash (including cash equivalents, if any) shown on the most recent balance sheet.
2. What were the total assets shown on the most recent balance sheet? The total liabilities plus stockholders' equity? How do these two months compare?
3. Compute total liabilities and total stockholders' equity. (Assume that all items on the right side of the balance sheet that are not explicitly listed as stockholders' equity are liabilities.) Compare the size of the liabilities to stockholders' equity, and comment on the comparison. Write the company's accounting equation as of January 31, 1995, by filling in the dollar amounts.

2

Income Measurement: The Accrual Basis

Learning Objectives

After studying this chapter, you should be able to

1 Explain how revenues and expenses combine to measure income for an accounting time period.

2 Compare the accrual basis and cash basis accounting methods and use the concepts of recognition, matching, and cost recovery to record revenues and expenses.

3 Prepare an income statement and show how it is related to a balance sheet.

4 Prepare a statement of cash flows and show how it differs from an income statement.

5 Account for cash dividends and prepare a statement of retained income.

6 Identify the major organizations that influence generally accepted accounting principles.

7 Compute and explain earnings per share, price-earnings ratio, dividend-yield ratio, and dividend-payout ratio.

The measurement of income is one of the most important and controversial topics in accounting. This chapter presents the rudiments of measuring income, including a discussion of revenues and expenses. It also defines three basic financial statements prepared by accountants: *the income statement, statement of cash flows,* and *statement of retained income*. We enlarge our understanding of generally accepted accounting principles (GAAP) and how they are determined. Finally, four financial ratios that decision makers use to analyze the performance and prospects of a business entity are introduced.

Income is a measure of accomplishment—a means of evaluating an entity's performance over a period of time. Although income could be measured many ways, accountants have agreed to use the accrual basis in reporting an entity's net income, so that is the major focus of this chapter. An alternative, the cash basis, has supporters, and accountants prepare another statement, the statement of cash flows, to provide information about how the company obtains and uses cash.

Investors eagerly await reports about a company's annual income. Stock prices generally reflect investors' expectations about income, but often actual reported income differs from what was expected. When this happens, stock prices can have large swings. For example, both Fisher Price, the toy company, and Marvel Entertainment Group, creator and publisher of comic books, reported their 1991 income on the same day. Apparently Marvel Entertainment's income of $16.1 million was above expectations; its price per share increased from $55 to $66 in the week of the announcement. In contrast, Fisher Price's income of $4 million must have been below expectations because its price per share dropped from $39 to $34 that week.

■ INTRODUCTION TO INCOME MEASUREMENT

Almost all of us have a reason for learning about how accountants measure income. For example, we want to know how we are doing as individuals, as corporations, as hospitals, or as universities. Even nonprofit institutions use a concept of income as a way of determining how much they can afford to spend to accomplish their objectives. Investors use a concept of income to measure their successes and failures and to compare the performance of their existing and potential holdings. Indeed, *income* is the primary way of evaluating the economic performance of people, corporations, other entities, and economies as a whole.

The accountant's measurements of income are the major means of evaluating a business entity's performance. But measuring income is not straightforward. Most people agree that income should be a measure of the increase in the "wealth" of an entity over a period of time. However, disputes arise over how to define wealth and how to measure the increase in wealth for a specific entity for a specific time period. These disputes will never be fully resolved. Nevertheless, accountants have decided that a common set of rules for measuring income should be applied by all companies so that decision makers such as investors can more easily compare the performance of one company with that of another. These rules provide the basis for the following discussion of income measurement. We begin by discussing the time period over which income is measured and then proceed to measures of accomplishments (revenues) and efforts (expenses).

Operating Cycle

Most corporations and business entities follow a similar, somewhat rhyth-
mic, pattern of economic activity during which income is measured. An
operating cycle (also called a *cash cycle* or *earnings cycle*) is the time span
during which cash is used to acquire goods and services, which in turn are
sold to customers, who in turn pay for their purchases with cash. Consider
the following example. A retail business usually engages in some version of
the operating cycle in order to earn profits:

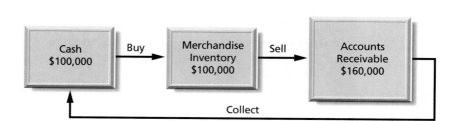

The box for Accounts Receivable (amounts owed to the entity by customers) is larger than the other two boxes because the objective is to sell goods
at a price higher than the acquisition cost. Retailers and nearly all other businesses buy goods and services and perform acts (such as placing them in a convenient location or changing their form) that merit selling prices that yield an
expected profit. The total amount of profit earned during a particular period
depends on the excess of selling prices over costs of the goods and additional
expenses and on the speed of the operating cycle.

The Accounting Time Period

The only way to be certain of how successfully a business has performed is to
close its doors, sell all its assets, pay all liabilities, and return any leftover cash
to the owner. Indeed in the 1400s, Venetian merchant traders did exactly that.
For each voyage, cash was invested, goods were acquired and exported to foreign markets, and sold for cash. The proceeds were distributed to the original
investors. However, today owners, managers, and others want periodic reports
on how well an entity has performed before the entity is terminated. The
accountant's measurements of income are a major means of evaluating
progress during the accounting time period.

The calendar year is the most popular time period for measuring income or
profits. However, about 40% of large companies use a **fiscal year**, which is the
year established for accounting purposes, that ends on some date other than
December 31. The fiscal year-end date is often the low point in annual business
activity. For example, many retailers such as Kmart and JC Penney use a fiscal
year ending on January 31. Why? Because Christmas sales and post-Christmas
sales are over, and inventories, which are at their lowest point of the year, can
be counted more easily and valued with greater accuracy.

Users of financial statements also want to know how well the business is
doing each month, each quarter, and each half-year. Therefore, companies

interim periods The time span established for accounting purposes that are less than a year.

prepare financial statements for **interim periods**, which are the time spans established for accounting purposes that are less than a year.

Revenues and Expenses

revenues Gross increases in owners' equity arising from increases in assets received in exchange for the delivery of goods or services to customers.

Revenues and expenses are the key components in measuring income. These terms apply to the inflows and outflows of assets that occur during a business entity's operating cycle. More specifically, **revenues** are gross increases in owners' equity arising from increases in assets received in exchange for the delivery of goods or services to customers. **Expenses** are decreases in owners' equity that arise because goods or services are delivered to customers. Together these items define the fundamental meaning of **income** (or **profit** or **earnings**), which can simply be defined as the excess of revenues over expenses. The additional owners' equity generated by income or profits is **retained income**.

expenses Decreases in owners' equity that arise because goods or services are delivered to customers.

Consider again the Biwheels Company presented in Chapter 1. Exhibit 2-1 is a direct reproduction of Exhibit 1-1, which summarized the nine transactions of George Smith's business. Assume now that Smith has incorporated his business so that the company is a corporation instead of a sole proprietorship. That is, the owner's equity account is no longer George Smith, Capital. In Exhibit 2-1, it is stockholders' equity.

income (profit, earnings) The excess of revenues over expenses.

Now consider some additional transactions. Suppose Biwheels' sales for the entire month of January amount to $160,000 on open account. The cost to Biwheels of the inventory sold is $100,000. Note that the January sales and other transactions illustrated here are recorded as *summarized* transactions. The company's sales do not all take place at once, nor do purchases of inventory, collections from customers, or disbursements to suppliers.

retained income Additional owners' equity generated by income or profits.

The accounting for the summarized sales transaction has two phases, a *revenue phase* (10a) and an *expense phase* (10b):

	Assets		=	Liabilities	+	Stockholders' Equity
	Accounts Receivable	Merchandise Inventory				Retained Income
(10a) Sales on open account	+160,000		=			+160,000 (sales revenues)
(10b) Cost of merchandise inventory sold		−100,000	=			−100,000 (cost of goods sold expenses)

This transaction records the $160,000 sale on open account of inventory that had cost $100,000. Two things happen simultaneously in the balance sheet equation: an inflow of assets in the form of accounts receivable (10a) in *exchange* for an outflow of assets in the form of merchandise inventory (10b). Liabilities are completely unaffected, so stockholders' equity rises by $160,000 (sales revenues) − $100,000 (cost of goods sold expense), or $60,000.

Exhibit 2-1

Biwheels Company
Analysis of Transactions for December 31, 19X1–
January 12, 19X2 (in dollars)

			Assets		=	Liabilities +	Stockholders' Equity	
Description of Transactions	**Cash +**	**Accounts Receivable +**	**Merchandise Inventory +**	**Store Equipment =**		**Note Payable +**	**Accounts Payable +**	**Stockholders' Equity**
(1) Initial investment	+400,000				=			+400,000
(2) Loan from bank	+100,000				=	+100,000		
(3) Acquire inventory for cash	−150,000		+150,000		=			
(4) Acquire inventory on credit			+ 10,000		=		+10,000	
(5) Acquire store equipment for cash plus credit	− 4,000			+15,000 =			+11,000	
(6) Sales of equipment		+1,000		− 1,000 =				
(7) Return of inventory acquired on January 3			− 800		=		− 800	
(8) Payments to creditors	− 4,000				=		− 4,000	
(9) Collections from debtors	+ 700	− 700						
Balance, January 12, 19X2	+342,700	300 +	1 59,200 +	14,000 =		100,000 +	16,200 +	400,000
			516,200				516,200	

As entries 10a and 10b show, revenue from sales is recorded as an increase in assets, namely, Accounts Receivable, and an increase in Retained Income, a stockholders' equity account. In contrast, the expense of the goods sold is recorded as a decrease in assets, namely, the Merchandise Inventory account, and a decrease in Retained Income. So expenses are negative entries to stockholders' equity accounts. These relationships can be illustrated as follows:

Assets = Liabilities + Stockholders' equity

Assets = Liabilities + Paid-in capital + Retained income

Accounts receivable + Inventory = Liabilities + Paid-in capital + Revenues − Expenses
160,000   (−100,000)   0   +   0   + (+160,000) − (+100,000)

Increase in assets   60,000 = Increase in retained income   60,000

Revenue is recorded when a sale on open account is made and an asset, accounts receivable, is recorded; recording is not delayed until cash is received. Likewise, expenses are recorded when goods or services are delivered or assets are used for operations, not when items are purchased or when payments are made. Therefore, accountants measure income by the increases and decreases in assets, not solely by cash receipts and cash disbursements.

accrual basis
Recognizes the impact of transactions on the financial statements in the time periods when revenues and expenses occur.

cash basis Accounting method that recognizes the impact of transactions on the financial statements only when cash is received or disbursed.

Objective 2

Compare the accrual basis and cash basis accounting methods and use the concepts of recognition, matching, and cost recovery to record revenues and expenses.

■ METHODS FOR MEASURING INCOME

Accrual Basis and Cash Basis

Income measurement is anchored to the **accrual basis** of accounting, as distinguished from the cash basis. The accrual basis recognizes the impact of transactions on the financial statements in the time periods when revenues and expenses occur. That is, revenue is recorded as it is earned, and expenses are recorded as they are incurred—not necessarily when cash changes hands.

In contrast, the **cash basis** recognizes the impact of transactions on the financial statements only when cash is received or disbursed.

For many years accountants debated the merits of accrual basis versus cash-basis accounting. Supporters of the accrual basis maintained that the cash basis provides an incomplete measure of performance—it ignores activities that increase or decrease assets other than cash. Supporters of the cash basis pointed out that companies with good records of income went bankrupt because they did not generate enough cash to meet their obligations. Both camps were right. Income under the accrual basis is the better measure for relating overall operating accomplishments to efforts. Why? Because it includes a more complete summary of the entity's value-producing activities. The cash basis focuses on the narrow but important issue of an entity's ability to generate cash from its current operations. The cash flow from operations is an important part of the cash flow statement to be introduced later in this chapter.

Accrual versus Cash Accounting for Governments

Most governments in the world use cash-basis, not accrual-basis, accounting. Many accountants and economists claim that the cash-basis system does not give a true picture of the financial health of a national economy.

Using cash-basis accounting, the economic performance of a country is measured by the difference between its cash receipts and cash disbursements. During the mid-1980s many countries had large annual deficits, meaning that disbursements greatly exceeded receipts. The difference had to be made up by heavy borrowing.

By the 1990s many European countries, such as Britain and Germany, had reduced their annual deficits so that their economic picture looked rosier, at least according to their cash-basis accounting records. But much of the deficit reduction came from delaying expenditures on assets such as roads, bridges, and education. At the same time, they were using up assets that had been purchased in the past. Their cash-basis accounting system did not measure this depletion in the countries' asset bases. If

companies ignored depletion of their assets, they would soon be out of business. Governments must also face this reality sooner or later.

Accrual accounting separates outlays for assets, which have value that carries over into future years, from outlays for resources that are consumed immediately. If these governments had used accrual accounting, they would have learned the extent of the negative impact of using up more assets than are being replaced. National wealth was decreasing even though cash disbursements did not greatly exceed cash receipts.

One government—New Zealand's—has recently changed to an accrual-accounting system. The government leaders believe the accrual balance sheet and income statement will provide a better measure of the financial performance and position of the country than did the cash-basis system. ■

Sources: "Budget by Balance Sheet," The Economist (January 25, 1992), p. 18; R. Khalaf, "Lies, Damned Lies, and the Budget Deficit," Forbes (December 9, 1991), p. 71.

Recognition of Revenues

recognition A test for determining whether revenues should be recorded in the financial statements of a given period. To be recognized, revenues must be earned and realized.

A major convention accountants use to measure income on an accrual basis is **recognition** of revenues, which is a test for determining whether revenues should be recorded in the financial statements of a given period. To be recognized, revenues must ordinarily meet *two* criteria:

1. Be *earned*. For revenues to be earned, the goods or services must be fully rendered. The usual evidence is delivery to customers.

2. Be *realized*. Revenues are realized when cash or claims to cash are received in exchange for goods or services. The usual evidence is a market transaction whereby the buyer pays or promises to pay cash and the seller delivers merchandise or services. If cash is not received directly, the eventual collectibility of cash must be reasonably assured.

Revenue recognition for most retail companies such as Wal-Mart, Safeway, and McDonald's is straightforward. Revenue is both earned and realized at the point of sale. For other companies, revenue may be earned and realized at different times. When this occurs, revenue recognition is delayed until the second event. Consider the following examples:

- *Newsweek* receives prepaid subscriptions. The revenue is realized when the subscription is received, but it is not earned until delivery of each issue.
- A real estate company "sells" land in the Arizona desert on an installment basis but without credit investigations. Often when collectibility is questionable, revenue recognition may be delayed until cash is received.

Matching and Cost Recovery

product costs Costs that are linked with revenues and are charged as expenses when the related revenue is recognized.

Expenses are recognized and recorded in the financial statements of the period in which their economic benefits are consumed or used up. Expenses of any period are of two types: (1) those linked with the revenues earned that period, and (2) those linked with the time period itself.

Some costs, such as cost of goods sold or sales commissions, are naturally linked with revenues. If there are no revenues, there is no cost of goods sold or sales commissions. Such costs are called **product costs** and are charged as expenses when revenue from the goods is recognized. The concept of *matching*, a favorite buzzword of accountants, describes the recognition of these product costs. **Matching** is the recording of expenses in the same time period as the related revenues are recognized.

matching The recording of expenses in the same time period as the related revenues are recognized.

period costs Items identified directly as expenses of the time period in which they are incured.

Other expenses, such as rent expense and many administrative expenses, occur regardless of the level of sales in a particular period. Their benefits are consumed by the passage of time rather than the level of sales. Such items are identified directly as expenses of the time period and are called **period costs**.

cost recovery The concept by which some purchases of goods or services are recorded as assets because their costs are expected to be recovered in the form of cash inflows (or reduced cash outflows) in future periods.

The heart of recognizing expense in the accounts is the *cost recovery* concept. Under **cost recovery**, some purchases of goods or services are recorded as assets because the costs are expected to be recovered in the form of cash inflows (or reduced cash outflows) in future periods. For example, the purchase price of goods or services that are acquired in the current period but will not be fully used until a future period should be initially recorded as an asset. When the good or service is used, the accountant reduces the asset account and records an expense. Rent paid in advance is such an asset. Suppose a firm pays an annual rental of $12,000 on January 1. An asset account, *prepaid rent*, is increased by $12,000 because the rental services have not yet been used. Each month the prepaid rent account is reduced by $1,000, and rent expense is increased by $1,000, recognizing the using up of the prepaid rent asset.

Notice that prepaid rent is an *intangible* asset. Assets are defined as economic resources. They are not confined to tangible items that you can see or touch, such as cash or inventory. Assets also include the intangible legal rights to future services, such as the use of facilities.

Applying Matching and Cost Recovery

To focus on the matching and cost recovery concepts, assume that the Biwheels Company has only two expenses other than the cost of goods sold: rent expense and depreciation expense. Transaction 11 (see Exhibit 2-2, which merely continues Exhibit 2-1) is the payment of store rent of $6,000 covering January, February, and March of 19X2. Rent is $2,000 per month, payable quarterly in advance. (Assume that this initial payment was made on January 16, although rent is commonly paid at the start of the rental period.)

The rent disbursement acquires the right to use store facilities for the next three months. The $6,000 measures the *future* benefit from these services, so the amount is recorded in an asset account, Prepaid Rent:

	Assets		= Liabilities +	Stockholders' Equity
	Cash	*Prepaid Rent*		*Retained Income*
(11) Pay rent in advance	−6,000	+6,000	=	
(12) Recognize rent expense		−2,000	=	−2,000 (increase rent expense)

Transaction 11, made at the time of disbursement, shows no effect on stockholders' equity in the balance sheet equation. One asset, cash, is simply exchanged for another, prepaid rent.

Transaction 12 is recorded at the end of January. It recognizes that one-third of the rental services has expired, so the asset is reduced, and stockholders' equity is also reduced by $2,000 as rent expense for January. This recognition of rent *expense* means that $2,000 of the asset, Prepaid Rent, has been "used up" in the conduct of operations during January.

Prepaid rent of $4,000 is carried forward as an asset as of January 31 because the accountant was virtually certain of cost recovery. Why? Because without the prepayment, cash outflows of $2,000 each would have to be made for February and March. So the cost of the prepayment will be recovered in the sense that future cash outflows will be reduced by $4,000. Furthermore, future revenues (sales) are expected to be high enough to ensure the recovery of the $4,000.

Exhibit 2-2

Biwheels Company Analysis of Transactions for January 19X2 (in dollars)

Desription of Transactions	Cash	+ Accounts Receivable	+ Merchandise Inventory	+ Prepaid Rent	+ Store Equipment	=	Note Payable	+ Accounts Payable	+ Paid-in Capital	+ Retained Income
(1)–(9) See Exhibit 2-1 Balance, January 12, 19X2	342,700	300	159,200		14,000	=	100,000	16,200	400,000	
(10a) Sales on open account (inflow of assets)		+160,000				=				+ 160,000 (sales revenue)
(10b) Cost of merchandise inventory sold (outflow of assets)			–100,000			=				– 100,000 (increase cost of goods sold expense)
(11) Pay rent in advance	– 6,000			+6,000						
(12) Recognize expiration of rental services				–2,000		=				– 2,000 (increase rent expense)
(13) Recognized expiration of equipment services (depreciation)					– 100	=				– 100 (increase depreciation expense)
Balance, January 31, 19X2	336,700	+ 160,300	+ 59,200	+ 4,000	+ 13,900	=	100,000	+ 16,200	+ 400,000	+ 57,900
	574,100					=	574,100			

depreciation The systematic allocation of the acquisition cost of long-lived or fixed assets to the expense accounts of particular periods that benefit from the use of the assets.

The same matching and cost recovery concepts that underlie the accounting for prepaid rent apply to **depreciation**, which is the systematic allocation of the acquisition cost of *long-lived* or *fixed assets* to the expense accounts of particular periods that benefit from the use of the assets. These assets are tangible physical assets such as buildings, equipment, furniture, and fixtures owned by the entity. Land is not subject to depreciation.

In both prepaid rent and depreciation, the business purchases an asset that gradually wears out or is used up. As the asset is being used, more and more of its original cost is transferred from an asset account to an expense account. The sole difference between depreciation and prepaid rent is the length of time taken before the asset loses its usefulness. Buildings, equipment, and furniture remain useful for many years; prepaid rent and other prepaid expenses usually expire within a year.

Transaction 13 in Exhibit 2-2 records the depreciation expense for the Biwheels equipment. A portion of the original cost of $14,000 becomes depreciation expense in each month of the equipment's useful life, say, 140 months. Under the matching concept, the depreciation expense for January is $14,000 / 140 months, or $100 per month:

	Assets	=	Liabilities	+	Stockholders' Equity	
	Store Equipment				Retained Income	
(13) Recognize depreciation expense	−100	=			−100 (increase depreciation expense)	

In this transaction, the asset account, Store Equipment, is decreased as is the stockholders' equity account, Retained Income. The general concept of expense should be clear by now. The purchases and uses of goods and services (for example, inventories, rent, equipment) ordinarily consist of two basic steps: (1) the *acquisition* of the assets (transactions 3, 4, and 5 in Exhibit 2-1 and transaction 11 in Exhibit 2-2), and (2) the *expiration* of the assets as *expenses* (transactions 10b, 12, and 13 in Exhibit 2-2). As these examples show, when prepaid expenses and fixed assets are used up, the total assets and owners' equity are decreased. When sales to customers bring new assets to the business, its total assets and owners' equity are increased. Expense accounts are basically deductions from stockholders' equity. Similarly, revenue accounts are basically additions to stockholders' equity.

Recognition of Expired Assets

Assets such as inventory, prepaid rent, and equipment may be thought of as stored costs that are carried forward to future periods rather than immediately charged against revenue:

Thus, assets are unexpired costs held back from the expense stream and carried in the balance sheet to await expiration in future periods. Assets have future potential to produce revenue.

The analysis of the inventory, rent, and depreciation transactions in Exhibit 2-2 distinguishes between acquisition and expiration. The unexpired costs of inventory, prepaid rent, and equipment are assets until they are used up and become expenses.

Services such as advertising are often acquired and used almost instantaneously. Conceptually, these costs should, at least momentarily, be viewed as assets upon acquisition before being written off as expenses. For example, suppose newspaper advertising was acquired for $1,000 cash. To abide by the acquisition-expiration sequence, the transaction could be analyzed in two phases; see alternative 1 below.

		Assets		=	Liabilities +	Stockholders' Equity	
Transaction	Cash +	Other Assets +	Prepaid Advertising =			Paid-in Capital +	Retained Income
ALTERNATIVE 1: TWO PHASES							
Phase (a) Prepay for advertising	−1,000		+1,000	=			
Phase (b) Use up advertising			− 1,000	=			−1,000 (advertising expense)
ALTERNATIVE 2: ONE PHASE							
Phases (a) and (b) together	−1,000			=			−1,000 (advertising expense)

In practice, however, many services are acquired and used up so quickly that accountants do not bother recording the asset, Prepaid Advertising. Instead the shortcut in alternative 2 is usually recorded. When financial statements are prepared, this presents the correct result, but the two-step alternative 1 underscores what the entity actually does. The entity acquires goods and services, not expenses per se. These goods and services become expenses as they are used to generate revenue.

Some of the most difficult issues in accounting center on *when* an unexpired cost expires and becomes an expense. For example, some accountants believe that research and development costs should be accounted for as unexpired costs, shown on balance sheets among the assets, and written off to expense in some systematic manner over a period of years. After all, companies engage in research and product development activities because they expect them to create future benefits. But regulators in the United States and most other countries have ruled that such costs have vague future benefits that are difficult to measure reliably and thus have required writing them off as expenses immediately. In such cases, research costs are not found on balance sheets. In contrast, Italy and Spain allow research and development costs to be recognized initially as an asset and to be shown on the balance sheet.

Analyzing the Balance Sheet Equation

Recall from page 43:

(1) Assets (A) = Liabilities (L) + Stockholders' equity (SE)

(2) Assets   = Liabilities + Paid-in capital + Retained income

(3) Assets   = Liabilities + Paid-in capital + Revenue − Expenses

Revenue and expense accounts are nothing more than subdivisions of stockholders' equity—temporary stockholders' equity accounts, as it were. Their purpose is to summarize the volume of sales and the various expenses so that income can be measured.

    The analysis of each transaction in Exhibits 2-1 and 2-2 illustrates the dual nature of the balance sheet equation, which is always kept in balance. If the items affected are confined to one side of the equation, the total amount added is equal to the total amount subtracted on that side. If the items affected are on both sides, then equal amounts are simultaneously added or simultaneously subtracted on each side.

    The striking feature of the balance sheet equation is its universal applicability. No transaction has ever been conceived, no matter how simple or complex, that cannot be analyzed via the equation. Business leaders and accountants employ the balance sheet equation constantly to be sure they understand the effects of business transactions they are planning.

■ THE INCOME STATEMENT

income statement
A report of all revenues and expenses pertaining to a specific time period.

net income The remainder after all expenses have been deducted from revenues.

Chapter 1 showed that a balance sheet is a summary of the net result of all of the transactions recorded in an entity's accounts. Another basic financial statement, the *income statement*, focuses on the revenue and expense transactions recorded in the retained income account. An **income statement** is a report of all revenues and expenses pertaining to a specific time period. **Net income** is the famous "bottom line" on an income statement—the remainder after *all* expenses (including income taxes, which are illustrated later) have been deducted from revenue.

Exhibit 2-3

**Biwheels Company
Income Statement
for the Month Ended
January 31, 19X2**

Sales (revenues)		$ 160,000
Deduct expenses:		
Cost of goods sold	$100,000	
Rent	2,000	
Depreciation	100	
Total expenses		102,100
Net income		$ 57,900

Look back at Exhibit 2-2 and notice that four transactions affect the Biwheels Company's retained income account: sales revenue, cost of goods sold expense, rent expense, and depreciation expense. Exhibit 2-3 shows how an income statement displays these transactions. The net income is $57,900.

Notice that the income statement measures performance for a *span of time*, whether it be a month, a quarter, or longer. Therefore the income statement must always indicate the exact period covered. In Exhibit 2-3, the Biwheels income statement clearly shows it is for the *month* ended January 31, 19X2. Recall that the balance sheet shows the financial position at an *instant of time*, and therefore the balance sheet must always indicate the exact date, not a period of time.

Public companies in the United States generally publish income statements quarterly. In some other countries, only semi-annual or annual statements are published. Nevertheless, most companies prepare such statements monthly or weekly for internal management purposes. Some top managers even insist on a daily income statement to keep up-to-date on the performance of their operations.

Objective 3

Prepare an income statement and show how it is related to a balance sheet.

Decision makers use the income statement to assess the performance of an entity or its management over a span of time. The income statement shows how the entity's operations for the period have increased net assets through revenues and decreased net assets by consuming resources (expenses). *Net income* measures the amount by which the increase in assets exceeds the decrease. (A *net loss* means that the value of the assets used exceeded the revenues.) In essence, net income is one measure of the wealth created by an entity during the accounting period. By tracking net income from period to period, comparing changes in net income to economy-wide and industry averages, and examining changes in the revenue and expense components of net income, investors and other decision makers can evaluate the success of the period's operations.

For example, the management of Nike explained its 18% decrease in net income in 1994 as follows:

> A decrease in revenues and increased selling and administrative expenses were the primary factors in reduced earnings for fiscal 1994, while increased revenues and improved gross margins, offset partially by increased selling and administrative expenses, were the highlight of earnings growth in fiscal 1993. Despite a sluggish economy in the United States and abroad, the Company has been able to sustain its worldwide market share. The company faces a mature market in the United States, where industry sources expect growth rates to range between 3% and 5%. The Company's international markets are less mature, however, and offer more potential for future growth. Accordingly, the Company has continued to invest in international infrastructure in order to prepare for that future growth, resulting in an increase in selling and administrative expenses as a percentage of revenues. Through its aggressive worldwide marketing efforts and international infrastructure spending, the Company hopes to exceed those underlying market growth rates and thereby continue to increase its worldwide market share. However, until economies in the United States and Europe show full recovery, the Company may not realize those growth rates.

The above passage stresses the critical role of international markets for Nike. Nike is a U.S. company whose income statement reflects U.S. GAAP.

However, income statements throughout the world have the same basic format, although international differences in terminology do arise. For example, the British use the term *turnover* instead of *revenues*. Thus, the first line of British Petroleum's income statement reads (where £ is the British monetary unit, the pound):

Turnover £ 34,950,000,000

Relationship Between Income Statement and Balance Sheet

The income statement is the major link between two balance sheets:

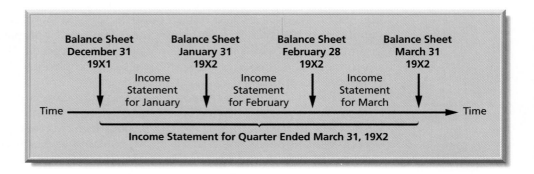

Remember that the balance sheet provides a snapshot of an entity's financial position at an *instant* of time; in contrast, the income statement provides a moving picture of events over a *span* of time.

For example, the Biwheels Company balance sheet for December 31, 19X1 was given in Chapter 1, page 8. At that date, the balance sheet showed assets of $500,000 and, to balance the equation, liabilities of $100,000 plus stockholders' equity of $400,000. There was no retained income. The January transactions analyzed in Exhibit 2-2 showed revenues of $160,000 and expenses of $102,100 recorded in the retained income account. The income statement in Exhibit 2-3 displays these revenues and expenses for the time span, the month of January. The next balance sheet, on January 31, 19X2, will include these changes in retained earnings (sales revenue of $160,000 and expenses of $102,100). The stockholders' equity account, Retained Income, will be $160,000 − $102,100 = $57,900 greater on January 31, 19X2 than it was on December 31, 19X1.

■ STATEMENT OF CASH FLOWS

Income versus Cash Flows

Recall what triggers the recognition of revenues when measuring income: the receipt of any asset, such as an account receivable, not just the receipt of cash. Revenues should eventually entail a cash receipt, but the important factor in assessing an entity's performance is the generation of a new asset, not the conversion of the asset into cash. Likewise, expenses are recorded when an entity gives up or uses up an asset, not when it acquires or pays for the asset. For example, when Wal-Mart purchases and pays for inventory, it is exchanging one asset, cash, for another, inventory. Value is neither created nor lost. But when a product is delivered to a customer, an asset is given up (in exchange for a promise to pay for it), and the expense should be matched with revenues to calculate the income that we use for evaluating performance.

You can think of income as a measure of the entity's performance in generating net assets (that is, assets less liabilities). Increases in retained income are accompanied by increases in assets or decreases in liabilities. However, income does not measure the entity's performance in generating cash.

Because a business enterprise is usually formed to return cash to the owners, and because creditors must be paid in cash, many decision makers want a financial statement focused on cash in addition to the income statement that focuses on changes in net assets. The *statement of cash flows* is prepared to fill this need. The **statement of cash flows** (or **cash flow statement**) reports the cash receipts and cash payments of an entity during a particular period. Like the income statement, it summarizes activities over a *span of time*, so it must be labeled with the exact period covered. Furthermore, like the income statement, which shows changes in retained income, the statement of cash flows details the changes in one balance sheet account, the cash account.

Introduction to Statement of Cash Flows

The fundamental approach to the statement of cash flows is simple: (1) list the activities that increased cash (that is, cash inflows) and those that decreased cash (cash outflows), and (2) place each cash inflow and outflow into one of three categories according to the type of activity that caused it: operating activities, investing activities, and financing activities.

Operating activities include the sale and the purchase or production of goods and services, including collections from customers, payments to suppliers or employees, and payments for items such as rent, taxes, and interest. *Investing activities* include acquiring and selling long-term assets and securities held for long-term investment purposes. *Financing activities* include obtaining resources from owners and creditors and repaying amounts borrowed.

Consider our Biwheels example from its inception in December 19X1 through the end of January 19X2. Part I of Exhibit 2-4 lists the transactions that affect cash, and Part II shows the statement of cash flows. Notice that at the bottom of the statement the changes in cash during the month are added to the beginning balance to give the January 31, 19X2, balance in the cash account.

PART I: TRANSACTIONS AFFECTING CASH

Transaction	Amount	Type of Activity
(1) Initial investment	$400,000	Financing
(2) Loan from bank	100,000	Financing
(3) Acquire inventory for cash	(150,000)	Operating
(5) Acquire store equipment for cash	(4,000)	Investing
(8) Payments to trade creditors	(4,000)	Operating
(9) Sale of store equipment	700	Investing
(11) Pay rent in cash	(6,000)	Operating

PART II: STATEMENT OF CASH FLOWS

CASH FLOWS FROM OPERATING ACTIVITIES	
Cash payments to suppliers	$ (154,000)
Cash payments for rent	(6,000)
Net cash used for operating activities	$(160,000)
CASH FLOWS FROM INVESTING ACTIVITIES	
Cash payments for purchases of equipment	$ (4,000)
Cash receipts from sales of equipment	700
Net cash used for investing activities	$ (3,300)
CASH FLOWS FROM FINANCING ACTIVITIES	
Proceeds from initial investment	$ 400,000
Proceeds from bank loan	100,000
Net cash provided by financing activities	$ 500,000
Net increase in cash	$ 336,700
Cash balance, December 1, 19X1	0
Cash balance, January 31, 19X2	$ 336,700

The statement of cash flows gives a direct picture of where cash came from and where it went. The dominant reason that cash increased by $336,700 is that $500,000 of new financing was obtained. A total of $160,000 was paid to support operating activities. It is not unusual to have large cash outflows for operating activities in the early periods of a business's life or when an entity is growing quickly. Cash payments for inventories and pre-payments for operating expenses often exceed receipts. In the Biwheels example, all sales were on open account and no cash was received before the end of January, so all operating cash flows were outflows. Despite income of $57,900 for January, Biwheels has not yet started to generate any cash from operating activities.

Summary Problem for Your Review

If you have never studied accounting before, or if you studied it long ago, do not proceed further until you have solved the following problem. There are no shortcuts. Pushing a pencil is an absolute necessity for becoming comfortable with accounting concepts. The cost-benefit test will easily be met: your gain in knowledge will exceed your investment of time. Please do the work on your own. In particular, do not ask for help from professional accountants or advanced accounting students. They might introduce new terms beyond those already covered that will only confuse, not clarify, at this stage. Instead, scrutinize Exhibits 2-1 through 2-4. Note how each transaction affects the balance sheet equation and how the financial statements are prepared. Then solve the problem that follows.

Problem One

Biwheels' transactions for January were analyzed in Exhibits 2-1 and 2-2, pages 43 and 47. The balance sheet, January 31, 19X2, is

Biwheels Company
Balance Sheet
January 31, 19X2

Assets		Liabilities and Stockholders' Equity		
Cash	$ 336,700	Liabilities:		
Accounts receivable	160,300	Note payable		$ 100,000
Merchandise		Accounts payable		16,200
inventory	59,200	Total liabilities		$ 116,200
Prepaid rent	4,000	Stockholder's equity:		
Store equipment	13,900	Paid-in capital	$400,000	
		Retained income	57,900	
		Total stockholders' equity		457,900
		Total liabilities and		
Total assets	$574,100	stockholders' equity		$574,100

The following series of transactions occurred during February:

(14) Collection of accounts receivable, $130,000.
(15) Payments of accounts payable, $15,000.
(16) Acquisitions of inventory on open account, $80,000, and for cash, $10,000.
(17) Merchandise carried in inventory at a cost of $110,000 was sold for $176,000, of which $125,000 was on open account and $51,000 was for cash.
(18) Recognition of rent expense for February.
(19) Recognition of depreciation expense for February.
(20) Borrowing of $10,000 from the bank was used to buy $10,000 of store equipment on February 28.

Required

1. Prepare an analysis of transactions, employing the equation approach demonstrated in Exhibit 2-2.
2. Prepare a balance sheet as of February 28, 19X2, and an income statement and statement of cash flows for the month of February.

Solution to Problem One

1. *Analysis of transactions.* The answer is in Exhibit 2-5. All transactions are straightforward extensions or repetitions of the January transactions.
2. *Preparation of financial statements.* Exhibit 2-6 contains the balance sheet, income statement, and statement of cash flows, which have been described earlier. Notice that the balance sheet lists the ending balances in all the accounts in Exhibit 2-5. The income statement summarizes the revenue and expense entries in retained income, and the statement of cash flows summarizes the entries to the cash account.

Exhibit 2-5 Biwheels Company Analysis of Transactions for February 19X2 (in dollars)

Description of Transactions	Assets						=	Liabilities			Owners' Equity	
											Stockholders' Equity	
	Cash	+	Accounts Receivable	+	Merchandise Inventory	+	Prepaid Rent	+	Store Equipment	=	Notes Payable	+	Accounts Payable	+	Paid-in Capital	+	Retained Income
Balance, January 31, 19X2	336,700	+	160,300	+	59,200	+	4,000	+	13,900	=	100,000	+	16,200	+	400,000	+	57,900
(14) Collection of accounts receivable	+130,000		−130,000														
(15) Payments of accounts payable	− 15,000									=			−15,000				
(16) Acquisitions of inventory on open account and for cash	− 10,000				+ 90,000					=			+80,000				
(17a) Sales on open account and for cash	+ 51,000		+125,000							=							+176,000 (increase sales revenue)
(17b) Cost of inventory sold					−110,000					=							−110,000 (increase cost of goods sold expense)
(18) Recognize expiration of rental services							−2,000			=							− 2,000 (increase rent expense)
(19) Recognize expiration of equipment services (depreciation)									− 100	=							− 100 (increase depreciation expense)
(20a) Borrow from bank	+ 10,000									=	+10,000						
(20b) Purchase store equipment	− 10,000								+10,000								
Balance, February 28, 19X2	492,700	+	155,300	+	39,200	+	2,000	+	23,800	=	110,000	+	81,200	+	400,000	+	121,800

713,000

713,000

713,000

Exhibit 2-6

Biwheels Company
Balance Sheet
February 28, 19X2

Assets		Liabilities and Stockholders' Equity		
Cash	$492,700	Liabilities:		
Accounts receivable	155,300	Notes payable	$110,000	
Merchandise inventory	39,200	Accounts payable	81,200	$191,200
Prepaid rent	2,000	Stockholders' equity:		
Store equipment	23,800	Paid-in capital	$400,000	
		Retained income	121,800	521,800
Total	$713,000	Total		$713,000

Biwheels Company
Income Statement
for the Month Ended
February 28, 19X2

Sales		$176,000
Deduct expenses:		
Cost of goods sold	$110,000	
Rent	2,000	
Depreciation	100	112,100
Net income		$ 63,900

Biwheels Company
Statement of Cash
Flows for the Month
Ended February 28,
19X2

CASH FLOWS FROM OPERATING ACTIVITIES	
Cash collections from customers	$181,000
Cash payments to suppliers	(25,000)
Net cash provided by operating activities	$156,000
CASH FLOWS FROM INVESTING ACTIVITIES	
Purchase of store equipment	$ (10,000)
Net cash used for investing activities	$ (10,000)
CASH FLOWS FROM FINANCING ACTIVITIES	
Loan from bank	$ 10,000
Net cash provided by financing activities	$ 10,000
Net increase in cash	$156,000
Cash balance, February 1, 19X2	336,700
Cash balance, February 28, 19X2	$492,700

■ ACCOUNTING FOR DIVIDENDS AND RETAINED INCOME

Objective 5

Account for dividends and prepare a statement of retained income.

A corporation's revenues and expenses for a particular time period are recorded in the stockholders' equity account, Retained Income. Because net income is the excess of revenues over expenses, retained income increases by the amount of net income reported during the period. (If expenses exceed revenues, retained income decreases by the amount of the period's net loss.)

Cash Dividends

cash dividends
Distributions of cash to stockholders that reduce retained income.

In addition to revenues and expenses, cash dividends are recorded in the Retained Income account. **Cash dividends** are distributions of cash to stockholders that reduce retained income. Corporations pay out cash dividends to stockholders to provide a return on the stockholders' investment in the corporation. The ability to pay dividends is fundamentally a result of profitable operations. Retained income increases as profits accumulate, and it decreases as dividends are paid out.

Although cash dividends decrease retained income, they are not expenses like rent and depreciation. They should not be deducted from revenues because dividends are not directly linked to the generation of revenue or the costs of operating activities. For example, assume that on February 28, cash dividends of $50,000 are declared by the Biwheels board of directors and are disbursed to stockholders. This transaction (21) is analyzed as follows:

	Assets	= Liabilities	+	Stockholders' Equity
	Cash			Retained Income
(21) Declaration and payment of cash dividends	−50,000 =			−50,000 (dividends)

Transaction 21 shows the decrease in Retained Income and the decrease in Cash.

Cash dividends distribute some of the company's assets (cash) to shareholders, thus reducing their residual interest in Biwheels. Sufficient cash must be available for dividends to be paid. Because of the need for cash, many companies try to avoid paying dividends that exceed the amount of cash provided by operating activities.

As a successful company grows, the Retained Income account can soar enormously if dividends are not paid. It can easily be the largest stockholders' equity account. Its balance is the cumulative, lifetime earnings of the company less its cumulative, lifetime losses and dividends. For example, Eastman Kodak's retained earnings are $4,469 million compared with paid-in capital of $1,161 million.

The amount of cash dividends declared by the board of directors of a company depends on many factors. For example, the amount of a dividend often is some fraction of net income, but dividends are not necessarily tied to current net income. Although profitable operations and the existence of a balance in Retained Income are generally essential, dividend policy is also influenced by the company's cash position and future needs for cash to pay debts or to purchase additional assets. Dividends are also influenced by whether the company is committed to a stable dividend policy or to a policy that normally ties dividends to fluctuations in net income. Under a stable policy, dividends may be paid consistently even if a company encounters a few years of little or no net income. Many companies maintain a stable dividend from year to year because it gives stockholders the ability to plan on a steady cash return from their investment. (More is said about dividends in Chapter 12.)

Dividends or withdrawals are often spoken of as "distributions of profits" or "distributions of retained income." Dividends are often erroneously described as being "paid out of retained income." In reality, cash dividends are distributions of assets that reduce a portion of the ownership claim. The distribution is made possible by both profitable operations and the existence of cash.

Dividend Transactions

Transaction 21 combined the declaration and payment of a dividend into a single transaction as if everything had occurred on the same day. However, corporations usually approach dividend matters in steps. The board of directors declares a dividend on one date (declaration date) payable to those stockholders on record as owning the stock on a second date (record date) and actually pays the dividend on a third date (payment date).

The *Wall Street Journal* lists dividend announcements as follows:

Company	Period	Amt.	Payable Date	Record Date
Ford Motor Company	Q*	$.26	3-1-95	1-30
Giant Food	Q*	.18	3-3-95	2-3

*Q indicates that the dividend is typically declared quarterly.

Such dividend actions entail two accounting transactions. First, the *declaration* affects the corporation's financial position because the shareholders also become creditors for the amount of the legally declared dividend. Second, the resulting liability is reduced only when the cash is disbursed. Consequently, transaction 21 must be divided into two phases:

	Assets	=	Liabilities	+	Stockholders' Equity
	Cash	=	Dividends Payable	+	Retained Income
(21a) Date of declaration		=	+50,000		−50,000 (dividends)
(21b) Date of payment	−50,000	=	−50,000		
The net effect is eventually the same as in 21 above	−50,000	=	0		−50,000

Although the ultimate effect is the same as that shown originally in transaction 21, a balance sheet prepared *between* the date of declaration and the date of payment must show dividends payable as a *liability*. Note too that although a corporation may be expected to pay dividends, no legal liability occurs until a board of directors formally declares a dividend.

Retained Income and Cash

The existence of retained income enables a board of directors to *declare* a dividend. The existence of cash enables the corporation to *pay* the dividend. Cash and Retained Income are two entirely separate accounts sharing no necessary relationship. Consider the following illustration:

Step 1. Assume an opening balance sheet of

Cash	$ 100	Paid-in capital	$100

Step 2. Purchase inventory for $50 cash. The balance sheet now reads

Cash	$ 50	Paid-in capital	$100
Inventory	50		
Total assets	$ 100		

Step 3. Now sell the inventory for $80 cash, which produces a retained income of $80 – $50 = $30:

Cash	$ 130	Paid-in capital	$100
		Retained income	30
		Total owners' equity	$130

At this stage, the retained income might be reflected by a $30 increase in cash. But the $30 in retained income connotes only a *general* claim against *total assets*. This can be clarified by the transaction that follows.

Step 4. Purchase inventory and equipment, in the amounts of $60 and $50, respectively. Now,

Cash	$ 20	Paid-in capital	$100
Inventory	60	Retained income	30
Equipment	50		
Total assets	$130	Total owners' equity	$130

Where is the $30 in retained income reflected? Is it reflected in Cash, in Inventory, or in Equipment? The answer is indeterminate. Since there is only $20 in Cash, and Retained Income is $30, the claim is not exclusively on Cash. Part of the results of profitable sales have been reinvested in inventory and equipment. This example helps to explain the nature of the Retained Income account. It is a *residual claim*, not a pot of gold. Retained income is increased by profitable operations, but the cash inflow from sales may be used to buy more inventory or equipment (Step 4). Retained income (and also paid-in capital) is a *general* claim against, or *undivided* interest in, *total* assets, *not* a specific claim against cash or against any other particular asset. Do not confuse the assets themselves with the claims against the assets.

statement of retained income A statement that lists the beginning balance in retained income, followed by a description of any changes that occurred during the period, and the ending balance.

Statement of Retained Income

Exhibit 2-7 shows another financial statement prepared by accountants. The **statement of retained income** lists the beginning balance (in this case, January 31) in Retained Income, followed by a description of any major changes (in this case, net income and dividends) that occurred during the period, and the ending balance (February 28) for the Biwheels Company.

Exhibit 2-7	Retained income, January 31, 19X2	$ 57,900
	Net income for February	63,900
Biwheels Company	Total	$121,800
Statement of	Dividends declared	50,000
Retained Income for	Retained income, February 28, 19X2	$ 71,800
the Month Ended		
February 28, 19X2		

Frequently, the statement of retained income is added to the bottom of the income statement. If that is done, the combined statements are called a **statement of income and retained income**. For example, the income statement in Exhibit 2-6 combined with Exhibit 2-7 and retitled appears as shown in Exhibit 2-8.

statement of income and retained income
A statement that includes a statement of retained income at the bottom of an income statement.

Note how Exhibit 2-8 is anchored to the balance sheet equation:

$$\text{Assets} = \text{Liabilities} + \text{Paid-in capital} + \text{Retained income}$$

$$\text{Ending balance} = \left[\text{Beginning balance} + \text{Revenues} - \text{Expenses} - \text{Dividends} \right]$$

$$\text{Bal. Feb. 28 after dividends} = \left[57,900 + 176,000 - 112,100 - \$50,000 \right] = 71,800$$

Exhibit 2-8	Sales	$176,000
	Deduct expenses:	
Biwheels Company	Cost of goods sold	$110,000
Statement of Income	Rent	2,000
and Retained Income	Depreciation	100 112,100
for the Month Ended	Net income	$ 63,900 *
February 28, 19X2	Retained income, January 31, 19X2	57,900
	Total	$121,800
	Dividends declared	50,000
	Retained income, February 28, 19X2	$ 71,800

* Note how the income statement ends here. The $63,900 simultaneously becomes the initial item on the statement of retained income portion of this combined statement.

Customs of Presentation

Exhibits 2-7 and 2-8 illustrate some customs that accountants follow when they prepare financial statements. To save space accountants often place a subtotal on the right side of the final number in a column, as is illustrated by the $112,100 in Exhibit 2-8. Under this arrangement, the expenses caption is used only once.

Dollar signs are customarily used at the beginning of each column of dollar amounts and for net income. Some statements also use dollar signs with the subtotals, the $63,900 and the $121,800 in Exhibit 2-8. Double-underscores (double rulings) are typically used to denote final numbers.

Summary Problem for Your Review

Problem Two

(The first problem appeared earlier in the chapter.)

The following interpretations and remarks are frequently encountered with regard to financial statements. Do you agree or disagree? Explain fully.

1. "Sales show the cash coming in from customers, and the various expenses show the cash going out for goods and services. The difference is net income."
2. Consider the following June 30, 1991 accounts of Delta, a leading U.S. airline:

Common stock, par value $3.00 per share,	
54,384,941 shares issued	$ 163,155,000
Additional paid-in capital	883,888,000
Retained earnings	1,761,103,000
Total stockholders' equity	$2,808,146,000

A shareholder commented, "Why can't that big airline pay higher wages and dividends too? It can use its hundreds of millions of dollars of retained earnings to do so."

3. "The total Delta stockholders' equity measures the amount that the shareholders would get today if the corporation were liquidated."

Solution to Problem Two

1. Cash receipts and disbursements are not the fundamental basis for the accounting recognition of revenues and expenses. Credit, not cash, lubricates the economy. Therefore, if services or goods have been delivered to a customer, a legal claim to future cash in the form of a receivable is deemed sufficient justification for recognizing revenue. Similarly, if services or goods have been used up, a legal obligation in the form of a payable is justification for recognizing expense.

   This approach to the measurement of net income is known as the accrual method. Revenue is recognized as it is (a) earned by goods or services rendered and (b) realized. Expenses are recorded when goods or services are used up in the obtaining of revenue (or when such goods or services cannot justifiably be carried forward as an asset because they have no potential future benefit). The expenses and losses are deducted from the revenue, and the result of this matching process is net income, the net increase in stockholders' equity from the conduct of operations. Cash flow from operations can be larger or smaller than net earnings.

2. As the chapter indicated, retained earnings is not cash. It is a stockholders' equity account that represents the accumulated increase in ownership claims due to profitable operations. This claim or interest may be partially liquidated by the payment of cash dividends, but a growing company will reinvest cash in receivables,

inventories, plant, equipment, and other assets so necessary for expansion. As a result, the ownership claims measured by retained earnings may become "permanent" in the sense that, as a practical matter, they will never be liquidated as long as the company remains a going concern.

The fallacy of linking retained earnings and cash is illustrated by the fact that Delta's cash was less than $764 million on the balance sheet date when its retained earnings exceeded $1.7 billion.

Not all retained earnings balances grow indefinitely. To demonstrate what can happen to retained earnings, consider what actually happened to Delta. The early 1990s were a period of extreme competition in the airline industry. Airlines were striving to cut wage costs, not to increase them. New non-union airlines were opening low-cost service on highly traveled and previously very profitable routes. By June 30, 1994, the $1.7 billion of retained earnings from 1991 had been wiped out. Delta lost $0.5 billion in 1992, $1 billion in 1993, and another $0.4 billion in 1994. This transformed the positive retained earnings balance to a negative one.

In spite of this operating performance during the three-year period, Delta had $1.7 billion in cash on June 30, 1994, as noted on p. 16 in Chapter 1. Why? In part because an airline records very large amounts of depreciation each year, reducing net income for significant non-cash expenses. Thus net income can be negative, while a firm is still generating positive cash flow from operations. Recall that Biwheels had net income in February 19X2 of $63,900, but cash flow from operations was substantially higher at $156,000 (see p. 57).

3. Stockholders' equity is a difference, the excess of assets over liabilities. If the assets were carried in the accounting records at their liquidating value today and the liabilities were carried at the exact amounts needed for their extinguishment, the remark would be true. But such valuations would be coincidental because assets are customarily carried at *historical cost* expressed in an unchanging monetary unit. Intervening changes in markets and general price levels in inflationary times may mean that the assets are woefully understated. Investors may make a critical error if they think that balance sheets indicate current values.

Furthermore, the "market values" for publicly owned shares are usually determined by daily trading conducted in the financial marketplaces such as the New York Stock Exchange. These values are affected by numerous factors, including the *expectations* of (a) price appreciation and (b) cash flows in the form of dividends. The focus is on the future; the present and the past are examined as clues to what may be forthcoming. Therefore the present stockholders' equity is usually of only incidental concern.

For example, Delta's 1991 stockholders' equity was $2,808,146,000 ÷ 54,384,941 shares, or almost $52 per share. During 1991 Delta's market price per common share fluctuated between $52 and $75. By 1994 Delta's stockholders' equity fell to $1,467,000,000 ÷ 54,469,491 shares, or about $27 per share. During 1994 Delta's market price per share fluctuated between $39 and $57.

■ THE LANGUAGE OF ACCOUNTING IN THE REAL WORLD

Unfortunately for the new student of accounting, organizations use different terms to describe the same concept or account, creating a multitude of synonyms. These terms are not introduced here to confuse you. Our objective is to acquaint you with the real world of accounting vocabulary so that you will not be surprised when a company's financial statement uses different terms than you learned initially.

retained earnings (reinvested earnings) A synonym for retained income.

statement of income (statement of operations, results of operations, statement of earnings, operating statement, statement of revenues and expenses, P&L statement) A synonym for income statement.

sales (sales revenues) A synonym for revenues.

cost of goods sold (cost of sales) The original acquisition cost of the inventory that was sold to customers during the reporting period.

The terms *income*, *earnings*, and *profits* are often used interchangeably. Indeed, many companies will use net *income* on their income statements but will refer to retained income as retained *earnings*. As Exhibit 2-9 shows, Anheuser-Busch, H. J. Heinz, and Colgate-Palmolive are examples. In short, retained income is frequently called **retained earnings** or **reinvested earnings**.

The term *earnings* is becoming increasingly popular because it has a preferable image. *Earnings* apparently implies compensation for honest toil, whereas *income* or *profit* evidently inspires cartoonists to portray managers as greedy, evil-looking individuals.

The income statement is frequently called the **statement of income, statement of operations, results of operations,** or **statement of earnings.** Other terms sometimes encountered are the **operating statement** and **statement of revenues and expenses.** For many years, the most popular name for this statement was statement of profit and loss, often termed the **P&L statement.** Such a label is justifiably fading into oblivion. After all, the ultimate result is either a profit *or* a loss.

The terms **sales** and **sales revenues** are synonyms for revenues.

The term **cost of sales** is a synonym for **cost of goods sold.** For example, Bethlehem Steel Corporation uses *cost of sales*, not *cost of goods sold*. Both terms mean the entity's original acquisition cost of the inventory that was sold to customers during the reporting period.

Fortunately, some accounting terms have no synonyms. Examples are *expenses* and *dividends*.

Exhibit 2-9

Some Synonyms in Accounting

Term Initially Used in This Book	Examples of Synonyms	Example of Companies
1. Net income		Anheuser-Busch, H. J.Heinz, Colgate-Palmolive
	Net earnings	General Mills, Chrysler, Johnson & Johnson
	Profit	Caterpillar
2. Retained income		General Motors
	Retained earnings	Anheuser-Busch, H. J. Heinz, Colgate-Palmolive
	Reinvested earnings	Scott Paper, Coca-Cola
	Earnings retained for use in the business	Ford Motor
	Profit employed in the business	Caterpillar

■ MORE ON NONPROFIT ORGANIZATIONS

The examples in this chapter have focused on profit-seeking organizations, but balance sheets and income statements are also used by nonprofit organizations. For example, hospitals and universities have income statements, although they are called statements of *revenue* and *expense*. The "bottom line" is frequently called "excess of revenue over expense" or "net financial result" rather than "net income."

The basic concepts of assets, liabilities, revenue, expense, and operating statements are applicable to all organizations, whether they be utilities, symphony orchestras, private, public, American, or Asian. However, some non-profit organizations have been slow to adopt some ideas that are widely used in progressive companies. For example, many government organizations use only the cash basis of accounting, not the accrual basis. This practice hampers the evaluation of the performance of such organizations. A recent annual report of the New York Metropolitan Museum of Art stated: "As the Museum's financial operations have begun to resemble in complexity those of a corporation, it has become necessary to make certain changes in our accounting.... Operating results are reported on an accrual rather than the previously followed cash basis. Thus, revenue and expenses are recorded in the proper time period."

An article in *Forbes* commented:

Shoddy, misleading accounting has not been the cause of our cities' problems but it has prevented us from finding solutions. Or even looking for solutions until it's too late. Chicago's schools, for example, suddenly found themselves unable to pay their teachers. Had the books been kept like any decent corporation's, that could never have happened. The most basic difference is in the common use of cash accounting rather than the accrual method that nearly all businesses use.

■ MORE ON GENERALLY ACCEPTED ACCOUNTING PRINCIPLES (GAAP)

This section continues our study of accounting principles. So far in this chapter, the accrual basis and the concepts of recognition, matching, and cost recovery have been discussed.

Stable Monetary Unit

The monetary unit (called the dollar in the United States, Canada, Australia, New Zealand, and elsewhere) is the principal means for measuring assets and equities. It is the common denominator for quantifying the effects of a wide variety of transactions. Accountants record, classify, summarize, and report in terms of the monetary unit.

Such measurement assumes that the monetary unit, the dollar, is an unchanging yardstick. Yet we all know that a 1995 dollar did not have the same purchasing power that a 1985 or a 1975 dollar had. Furthermore, the change in the purchasing power of the monetary unit varies among countries. During the 1980s, the U.S. dollar lost 5.0% of its purchasing power per year, while the Japanese yen lost only 2.2%, and the Italian lira lost 10.1%. Therefore, accounting statements that include assets measured in different years must be interpreted and compared with full consciousness of the limitations of the basic measurement unit. Chapter 16 discusses ways to account for changes in the monetary unit.

Accounting Standard-Setting Bodies

The existence of generally accepted accounting principles (GAAP) implies that someone must decide which principles are generally accepted and which are not. This decision falls to regulatory agencies or professional associations. In the

Financial Accounting Standards Board (FASB) A private-sector body that determines generally accepted accounting standards in the United States.

Accounting Principles Board (APB) The predecessor to the Financial Accounting Standards Board.

AICPA American Institute of Certified Public Accountants, the leading organization of the auditors of corporate financial reports.

FASB Statements The FASB's rulings on generally accepted accounting principles.

APB Opinions A series of thirty-one opinions of the Accounting Principles Board, many of which are still the "accounting law of the land."

Securities and Exchange Commission (SEC) The agency designated by the U.S. Congress to hold the ultimate responsibility for authorizing the generally accepted accounting principles for companies whose stock is held by the general investing public.

United States, GAAP is set primarily in the private sector (with government oversight), but in many countries, such as France, the government sets the standards.

In the United States, generally accepted accounting principles have been determined primarily by two private-sector bodies, the **Financial Accounting Standards Board (FASB)** and its predecessor, the **Accounting Principles Board (APB)**. The FASB consists of seven qualified individuals who work full-time. The board is supported by a large staff and an annual $16 million budget.

The FASB is an independent creature of the private sector and is financially supported by various professional accounting associations (such as the leading organization of auditors, the American Institute of Certified Public Accountants, also known as the **AICPA**). The FASB's rulings on GAAP are called **FASB Statements**.

The FASB was established in 1973 as the replacement for the APB. The APB consisted of a group of eighteen accountants (mostly partners in large accounting firms) who worked part-time. The APB issued a series of thirty-one **APB Opinions** during 1962 to 1973, many of which are still the "accounting law of the land." Many of these *APB Opinions* and *FASB Statements* will be referred to in succeeding chapters of this book.

The U.S. Congress has designated the **Securities and Exchange Commission (SEC)** as holding the ultimate responsibility for authorizing the generally accepted accounting principles for companies whose stock is held by the general investing public. However, the SEC has informally delegated much rule-making power to the FASB. This public sector–private sector authority relationship can be sketched as follows:

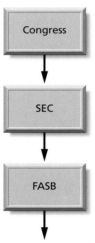

Issues pronouncements on various accounting issues. These pronouncements govern the preparation of typical financial statements.

Objective 6

Identify the major organizations that influence generally accepted accounting principles.

Reconsider the three-tiered structure above. Note that Congress can overrule both the SEC and the FASB, and the SEC can overrule the FASB. Such undermining of the FASB occurs rarely, but pressure is exerted on all three tiers by corporations if they think an impending pronouncement is "wrong." Hence the setting of accounting principles is a complex process involving heavy interactions among the affected parties: public regulators (Congress and the SEC), private regulators (FASB), companies, the public accounting profession, representatives of investors, and other interested groups.

Recent years have seen a growing interest in developing a common set of accounting principles throughout the world. Often called *harmonization of accounting standards*, the movement seeks to eliminate differences in accounting principles that are not caused by cultural or environmental differences between countries. Leading the way is the **International Accounting Standards Committee (IASC)**, which represents more than one hundred accountancy bodies from over seventy-five countries. Like the FASB, the IASC is a private-sector body that issues standards—so far over thirty of them. Although compliance with IASC standards is voluntary, a growing number of countries and multinational companies are adopting the methods advocated by the IASC.

Also affecting international accounting standards is the European (Economic) Community (EC). Via a series of *Directives*, which have the force of law, the EC is reducing the variations in financial statements of companies in its twelve member nations.

International Accounting Standards Committee (IASC) An organization representing over one hundred accountancy boards from over seventy-five countries that is developing a common set of accounting standards to be used throughout the world.

■ FOUR POPULAR FINANCIAL RATIOS

Objective 7

Compute and explain earnings per share, price-earnings ratio, dividend-yield ratio, and dividend-payout ratio.

To underscore how financial statements are used, this book will gradually introduce you to various financial ratios. Because stock market prices are quoted on a per-share basis, many ratios are expressed per share (and after income taxes).

A financial ratio is computed by dividing one number by another. For a set of complex financial statements, literally hundreds of ratios can be computed if desired. Every analyst has a set of favorite ratios, but one is so popular that it dwarfs all others: earnings per share of common stock (EPS).

In its *Statement on Objectives*, the Financial Accounting Standards Board, which is described in this chapter, stresses that the main focus of financial reporting is on earnings. The income statement and its accompanying earnings per share are paramount to many users of financial reports, so accounting authorities have specified how various items therein must be displayed.

The accounting regulators have promulgated the requirement that EPS data appear on the face of the income statement of publicly held corporations. This is the only instance where a financial ratio is required as a part of the body of financial statements.

Earnings per Share (EPS)

When the owners' equity is relatively simple, the computation of EPS is straightforward. For example, consider Pepsico Corporation, the well-known beverage and food company. The bottom of two of its income statements showed:

Pepsico

	1993	1990
Net income	$1,587,900,000	$1,076,900,000
Net income per share of common stock	$ 1.96	$ 1.35

The earnings per share (called *net income per share* by Pepsico) was calculated as follows:

$$\text{EPS} = \frac{\text{Net income}}{\text{Average number of shares outstanding}}$$

$$1993 \text{ EPS} = \frac{\$1,587,900,000}{810,153,061} = \$1.96 \quad 1990 \text{ EPS} = \frac{\$1,076,900,000}{798,700,000} = \$1.35$$

The Pepsico computation is relatively simple because the company has only one type of capital stock, little fluctuation of shares outstanding throughout the year, and no unusual items affecting the computation of net income. EPS calculations can become more difficult when such complications arise. See Chapter 15 for further discussion.

Price-Earnings (P-E) Ratio

Another popular ratio is the price-earnings (P-E) ratio:

$$\text{P-E Ratio} = \frac{\text{Market price per share of common stock}}{\text{Earnings per share of common stock}}$$

The numerator is typically today's market price; the denominator, the EPS for the most recent twelve months. Thus the P-E ratio varies throughout a given year, depending on the fluctuations in the stock price. For example, Pepsico's P-E ratio would be:

Pepsico

	Using Highest Market Price During Fourth Quarter	Using Lowest Market Price During Fourth Quarter
1990 P-E	$\dfrac{\$26}{\$1.35} = 19.3$	$\dfrac{\$22}{\$1.35} = 16.3$
1993 P-E	$\dfrac{\$42}{\$1.96} = 21.4$	$\dfrac{\$37}{\$1.96} = 18.9$

The *Wall Street Journal* publishes P-E ratios daily on its stock page. P-E ratios are rarely carried out to any decimal places when published in the business press. The P-E ratio is sometimes called the *earnings multiple*. It measures how much the investing public is willing to pay for the company's prospects for earnings. Note especially that the P-E ratio is a consensus of the marketplace. This earnings multiplier may differ considerably for two companies within the same industry. It may also change for the same company through the years. Glamour stocks often have astronomical ratios. In general, a high P-E ratio indicates that investors predict that the company's net income will grow at a fast rate. Consider Microsoft's 1995 ratio of 30 compared with the 8 of Bank of America.

Dividend-Yield Ratio

Individual investors are usually interested in the profitability of their personal investments in common stock. That profitability takes two forms: cash dividends and market-price appreciation of the stock. Two popular ratios are the *dividend-yield ratio* (the current dividend per share divided by the current market price of the stock) and the price-earnings ratio (just discussed). The *dividend-yield ratio* (or *dividend-yield percentage*), also simply called *dividend yield*, is computed as follows:

$$\text{Dividend yield} = \frac{\text{Common dividends per share}}{\text{Market price per share}}$$

Pepsico

	Using Highest Market Price During Fourth Quarter		Using Lowest Market Price During Fourth Quarter	
1990 Dividend yield =	$\dfrac{\$.48}{\$26}$	= 1.8%	$\dfrac{\$.48}{\$22}$	= 2.2%
1993 Dividend yield =	$\dfrac{\$.61}{\$42}$	= 1.5%	$\dfrac{\$.61}{\$37}$	= 1.7%

When published in the business press, dividend yields are ordinarily carried to one decimal place. Dividend ratios may be of particular importance to those investors in common stock who seek regular cash returns on their investments. For example, an investor who favored high current returns would not buy stock in growth companies. Growth companies have conservative dividend policies because they are using most of their profit-generated resources to help finance expansion of their operations.

Market prices at which stocks are traded in organized marketplaces, such as the New York Stock Exchange, are quoted in the daily newspapers. The dividend yields are also published, as measured by annual disbursements based on the last quarterly dividends.

Consider the following stock quotations for Pepsico regarding trading on a particular day in 1995:

52 Weeks										
High	Low	Stock	Div.	Sales 100s	Yld. %	P-E Ratio	High	Low	Close	Net Chg.
41⅛	29¼	Pepsico	.72	21,815	2.1	16	35½	34¾	34¾	-¾

Reading from left to right, the highest price at which Pepsico common stock was traded in the preceding fifty-two weeks was $41.125 per share; the lowest price, $29.25. The current dividend rate for twelve months is $.72 per share, producing a yield of 2.1% based on the day's closing price of the stock. The P-E ratio is 16, also based on the closing price. Total sales for the day were 2,181,500 shares. The highest price at which the stock was traded was $35.50 per share; the lowest $34.75. The closing price was that of the last trade for the day, $34.75, which was $.75 lower than the preceding day's last trade.

Keep in mind that transactions in publicly traded shares are between *individual investors* in the stock, not between the *corporation* and the individuals. Thus a "typical trade" results in the selling of, say, 100 shares of Pepsico stock held by Ms. Johnson in Minneapolis to Ms. Davis in Atlanta for $3,475 cash. These parties would ordinarily transact the trade through their respective stock-brokers, who represent individual shareholders. Pepsico Corporation would not be directly affected by the trade except that its records of shareholders would be changed to show the 100 shares were now held by Davis, not Johnson.

Dividend-Payout Ratio

Although not routinely published, the dividend-payout ratio also receives much attention from analysts. Consider McDonald's, the well-known fast-food chain. The formula for its payout computation is given below, followed by McDonald's ratio, using figures from a recent annual report:

$$\text{Dividend-payout ratio} = \frac{\text{Common dividends per share}}{\text{Earnings per share}}$$

$$\text{Dividend-payout ratio} = \frac{\$.42}{\$2.91} = 14\%$$

McDonald's fits into the category of a low-payout company. As long as McDonald's continues its worldwide expansion, a minimal payout can be anticipated. Some fast-growing companies such as Microsoft pay no dividends. In contrast, companies without exceptional growth tend to pay a higher percentage of their earnings as dividends. Public utilities will ordinarily have a payout ratio of 60% to 70%. For instance, Pacific Gas and Electric Company paid dividends amounting to 80% of 1993 earnings. Pepsico falls between the extremes, with a 1993 payout ratio of ($.61 ÷ 1.96) = 31%.

Financial ratios are also covered in Chapters 4, 6, 7, 10, 12, and especially 15.

Highlights to Remember

This chapter focused on how accountants measure income, the excess of revenues over expenses for a particular time period, on an accrual basis. In accrual accounting, revenue is seldom accompanied by an immediate cash receipt; therefore, *revenue* should not be confused with the term *cash receipt*. Similarly, an expense is seldom accompanied by an immediate cash disbursement; *expense* should not be confused with the term *cash disbursement*.

The concept of recognition means that revenues are assigned to the period in which they are earned and realized. Under the concepts of matching and cost recovery, expenses are assigned to a period in which the pertinent goods and services are either used or appear to have no future benefit. Revenues and expenses are components of stockholders' equity. Revenues increase stockholders' equity; expenses decrease stockholders' equity.

An income statement shows an entity's revenues and expenses for a particular span of time. The net income links to the balance sheet because it is an addition to retained income.

Income based on accrual accounting focuses on an entity's performance in generating net assets. In contrast, the statement of cash flows focuses on an entity's ability to generate and use cash. A focus on cash is too narrow to provide a measure of overall performance, but it provides valuable information on the important function of cash generation and use.

Cash dividends are not expenses. They are distributions of cash to stockholders that reduce retained income. Corporations are not obligated to pay dividends, but once dividends are declared by the board of directors they become a legal liability until paid in cash.

Generally accepted accounting principles (GAAP) are based on many concepts. Among those covered in this chapter are the accounting time period, recognition, matching, cost recovery, and stable monetary unit. GAAP in the United States is generally determined by the Financial Accounting Standards Board (FASB), with oversight by the Securities and Exchange Commission (SEC). Growing interest in a common international GAAP has moved the International Accounting Standards Committee (IASC) into the forefront of standard setting.

Accounting Vocabulary

Accounting Principles Board (APB), *p. 66*
accrual basis, *p. 44*
AICPA, *p. 66*
APB Opinions, *p. 66*
cash basis, *p. 44*
cash dividends, *p. 57*
cash flow statement, *p. 53*
cost of goods sold, *p. 64*
cost of sales, *p. 64*
cost recovery, *p. 45*
depreciation, *p. 48*
earnings, *p. 42*
expenses, *p. 42*
Financial Accounting Standards Board (FASB), *p. 66*
FASB Statements, *p. 66*
fiscal year, *p. 41*

income, *p. 42*
income statement, *p. 50*
interim periods, *p. 42*
International Accounting Standards Committee (IASC), *p. 67*
matching, *p. 45*
net income, *p. 50*
operating cycle, *p. 41*
operating statement, *p. 64*
period costs, *p. 45*
product costs, *p. 45*
profit, *p. 42*
P&L statement, *p. 64*
recognition, *p. 45*
reinvested earnings, *p. 64*
results of operations, *p. 64*
retained earnings, *p. 64*

retained income, *p. 42*
revenues, *p. 42*
sales, *p. 64*
sales revenues, *p. 64*
Securities and Exchange Commission (SEC), *p. 66*
statement of cash flows, *p. 53*
statement of earnings, *p. 64*
statement of income, *p. 64*
statement of income and retained income, *p. 61*
statement of operations, *p. 64*
statement of retained income, *p. 60*
statement of revenues and expenses, *p. 64*

Assignment Material

Questions

2-1. "Expenses are negative stockholders' equity accounts." Explain.

2-2. What are the two tests of recognition of revenue?

2-3. Give two examples where revenue is not recognized at the point of sale, one where recognition is delayed because the revenue is not yet earned, and one because it is not yet realized.

2-4. "Expenses are assets that have been used up." Explain.

2-5. "The manager acquires goods and services, not expenses per se." Explain.

2-6. "Cash dividends are not expenses." Explain.

2-7. Identify the three categories of cash flows found on the statement of cash flows and list two activities that might appear in each of the categories.

2-8. What are the major defects of the cash basis?

2-9. "Retained income is not a pot of gold." Explain.

2-10. What is the meaning of a *general claim*?

2-11. Give two synonyms for *income statement*.

2-12. Give two synonyms for *net income*.

2-13. Give two synonyms for *retained income*.

2-14. "The term *earnings* is becoming increasingly popular because it has a preferable image." Explain.

2-15. "Changes in the purchasing power of the dollar hurt the credibility of financial statements." Do you agree? Explain.

2-16. Distinguish between GAAP, FASB, SEC, and APB.

2-17. Countries have different ways of choosing accounting standards. Outline at least one alternative to the U.S. approach.

2-18. What function does the International Accounting Standards Committee (IASC) have in setting GAAP?

Exercises

2-19 Synonyms and Antonyms

Consider the following terms: (1) unexpired costs, (2) reinvested earnings, (3) expenses, (4) net earnings, (5) prepaid expenses, (6) undistributed earnings, (7) statement of earnings, (8) used-up costs, (9) net profits, (10) net income, (11) revenues, (12) retained income, (13) sales, (14) statement of financial condition, (15) statement of income, (16) statement of financial position, (17) retained earnings, (18) statement of operations, and (19) cost of goods sold.

Required Group the items into two major categories, the income statement and the balance sheet. Answer by indicating the numbered items that belong in each group. Specify items that are assets and items that are expenses.

2-20 Special Meanings of Terms

A news story described the disappointing sales of a new model car, the Nova. An auto dealer said: "Even if the Nova is a little slow to move out of dealerships, it is more of a plus than a minus.... We're now selling 14 more cars per month than before. That's revenue. That's the bottom line."

Required Is the dealer confused about accounting terms? Explain.

2-21 Nature of Retained Income

This is an exercise on the relationships between assets, liabilities, and ownership equities. The numbers are small, but the underlying concepts are large.

1. Assume an opening balance sheet of:

Cash	$1,500	Paid-in capital	$1,500

2. Purchase inventory for $600 cash. Prepare a balance sheet. A heading is unnecessary in this and subsequent requirements.

3. Sell the entire inventory for $850 cash. Prepare a balance sheet. Where is the retained income in terms of relationships within the balance sheet? That is, what is the meaning of the retained income? Explain in your own words.

4. Buy inventory for $400 cash and equipment for $700 cash. Prepare a balance sheet. Where is the retained income in terms of relationships within the balance sheet? That is, what is the meaning of the retained income? Explain in your own words.

5. Buy inventory for $500 on open account. Prepare a balance sheet. Where is the retained income and account payable in terms of the relationships within the balance sheet? That is, what is the meaning of the account payable and the retained income? Explain in your own words.

2-22 Asset Acquisition and Expiration

The Lougee Company had the following transactions:

a. Paid $18,000 cash for rent for the next six months.

b. Paid $2,000 for stationery and wrapping supplies.

c. Paid $3,000 cash for an advertisement in the New York Times.

d. Paid $9,000 cash for a training program for employees.

Required Show the effects on the balance sheet equation in two phases: at acquisition and upon expiration at the end of the month of acquisition. Show all amounts in thousands.

2-23 Find Unknowns
The following data pertain to the Mosimar Corporation. Total assets at January 1, 19X1 were $100,000; at December 31, 19X1 $124,000. During 19X1, sales were $304,000, cash dividends were $4,000, and operating expenses (exclusive of cost of goods sold) were $150,000. Total liabilities at December 31, 19X1, were $55,000; at January 1, 19X1, $40,000. There was no additional capital paid in during 19X1.

Required
1. Stockholders' equity, January 1, 19X1
2. Net income for 19X1
3. Cost of goods sold for 19X1

2-24 Income Statement
A statement of an automobile dealer follows:

Adams Toyota, Inc.
Statement of Profit and Loss
December 31, 19X3

Revenues:		
Sales	$1,000,000	
Increase in market value of land and building	200,000	$1,200,000
Deduct expenses:		
Advertising	$ 100,000	
Sales commissions	50,000	
Utilities	20,000	
Wages	150,000	
Dividends	100,000	
Cost of cars purchased	700,000	1,120,000
Net profit		$ 80,000

Required List and describe any shortcomings of this statement.

2-25 Balance Sheet Equation
(Alternates are 2-26 and 2-41.) For each of the following independent cases, compute the amounts (in thousands) for the items indicated by letters, and show your supporting computations:

	Case		
	1	2	3
Revenues	$140	$ K	$290
Expenses	120	200	250
Dividends declared	–0–	5	Q
Additional investment by stockholders	–0–	40	35
Net income	E	20	P
Retained income:			
Beginning of year	30	60	100
End of year	D	J	110
Paid-in capital:			
Beginning of year	15	10	N
End of year	C	H	85

continued

	Case		
	1	*2*	*3*
Total assets:			
Beginning of year	85	F	L
End of year	100	280	M
Total liabilities:			
Beginning of year	A	90	105
End of year	B	G	95

2-26 Balance Sheet Equation
(Alternates are 2-25 and 2-41.) Reebok International's actual terminology and actual data (in millions of dollars) follow for a recent fiscal year:

Cost and expenses	B
Net income	$ 177
Dividends	34
Additional investments by stockholders	4
Assets, beginning of period	1,166
Assets, end of period	E
Liabilities, beginning of period	A
Liabilities, end of period	1,403
Paid-in capital, beginning of period	276
Paid-in capital, end of period	D
Retained earnings, beginning of period	565
Retained earnings, end of period	C
Revenues	2,159

Required   Find the unknowns (in millions), showing computations to support your answers.

2-27 Nonprofit Operating Statement
Examine the accompanying statement of the Oxbridge University Faculty Club. Identify the Oxbridge classifications and terms that would not be used by a profit-seeking hotel and restaurant. Suggest terms that the profit-seeking entity would use instead. (£ is the British pound.)

Oxbridge Faculty
Club
Statement of Income
and Expenses for
Fiscal Year 1991–92

Food Service:			
Sales			£545,128
Expenses:			
Food	£287,088		
Labor	272,849		
Operating costs	30,535	590,472	
Deficit			£(45,344)

Bar:		
Sales		£ 90,549
Expenses:		
Cost of liquor	£ 29,302	
Labor	5,591	

continued

Oxbridge Faculty
Club
Statement of Income
and Expenses for
Fiscal Year 1991–92

Operating costs		6,125	41,018
Surplus			49,531
Hotel:			
Sales			£ 33,771
Expenses			23,803
Surplus			9,968
Surplus from operations			£ 14,155
General income (members' dues,			
room fees, etc.)			95,546
General administration and operating			
expenses			(134,347)
Deficit before university subsidy			£(24,646)
University subsidy			30,000
Net surplus after university subsidy			£ 5,354

2-28   Earnings and Dividend Ratios

Study pages 67 to 70. Procter & Gamble's brand names include Tide, Crest, Jif, and Prell. The company's 1994 annual report showed earnings of $2,211 million. Cash dividends per share were $1.24. Procter & Gamble had 683,100,000 average number of common shares outstanding. No other type of stock was outstanding. The market price of the stock at the end of the year was $62 per share.

Required   Compute (1) earnings per share, (2) price-earnings ratio, (3) dividend yield, and (4) dividend-payout ratio.

2-29   Earnings and Dividend Ratios

Chevron Corporation is one of the largest oil companies in the world. The company's revenue in 1994 was $37 billion. Net income was $1,285,000,000. EPS was $3.89. The company's common stock is the only type of shares outstanding.

Required
1. Compute the average number of common shares outstanding during the year.
2. The dividend-payout ratio was 90%. What was the amount of dividends per share?
3. The average market price of the stock for the year was $44 per share. Compute (a) dividend yield and (b) price-earnings ratio.

Problems

2-30   Fundamental Revenue and Expense

Inkwell Corporation was formed on June 1, 19X2, when some stockholders invested $100,000 in cash in the company. During the first week of June, $85,000 cash was spent for merchandise inventory (sportswear). During the remainder of the month, total sales reached $110,000, of which $70,000 was on open account. The cost of the inventory sold was $60,000. For simplicity, assume that no other transactions occurred except that on June 28 Inkwell Corporation acquired $25,000 additional inventory on open account.

Required
1. Using the balance sheet equation approach demonstrated in Exhibit 2-2 (p. 47), analyze all transactions for June. Show all amounts in thousands.
2. Prepare a balance sheet, June 30, 19X2.
3. Prepare two statements for June, side by side. The first should use the accrual basis of accounting to compute net income, and the second the cash basis to compute net cash provided by (or used by) operating activities. Which basis provides a more informative measure of economic performance? Why?

2-31   Accounting for Prepayments

(Alternates are 2-33, 2-35, 2-37, and 2-40.) The Lopez Company, a wholesale distributor of home appliances, began business on July 1, 19X2. The following summarized transactions occurred during July:

1. Lopez's stockholders contributed $220,000 in cash in exchange for their common stock.
2. On July 1, Lopez signed a one-year lease on a warehouse, paying $60,000 cash in advance for occupancy of twelve months.
3. On July 1, Lopez acquired warehouse equipment for $100,000. A cash down payment of $40,000 was made and a note payable was signed for the balance.
4. On July 1, Lopez paid $24,000 cash for a two-year insurance policy covering fire, casualty, and related risks.
5. Lopez acquired assorted merchandise for $35,000 cash.
6. Lopez acquired assorted merchandise for $190,000 on open account.
7. Total sales were $200,000, of which $30,000 were for cash.
8. Cost of inventory sold was $160,000.
9. Rent expense was recognized for the month of July.
10. Depreciation expense of $2,000 was recognized for the month.
11. Insurance expense was recognized for the month.
12. Collected $35,000 from credit customers.
13. Disbursed $80,000 to trade creditors.

For simplicity, ignore all other possible expenses.

Required

1. Using the balance sheet equation format demonstrated in Exhibit 2-2 (p. 47), prepare an analysis of each transaction. Show all amounts in thousands. What do transactions 8 to 11 illustrate about the theory of assets and expenses? (Use a Prepaid Insurance account, which is not illustrated in Exhibit 2-2.)
2. Prepare an income statement for July on the accrual basis.
3. Prepare a balance sheet, July 31, 19X2.

2-32   Net Income and Cash Flows from Operating Activities

(Alternates are 2-34, 2-36, and 2-38.) Refer to the preceding problem. Suppose Lopez measured performance on the cash basis instead of the accrual basis. Compute the net cash provided by (or used for) operating activities. Which measure, net income or net cash provided by (or used for) operating activities, provides a better measure of overall performance? Why?

2-33   Analysis of Transactions, Preparation of Statements

(Alternates are 2-31, 2-35, 2-37, and 2-40.) The Philips Company was incorporated on April 1, 19X2. Philips had ten holders of common stock. Rita Philips, who was the president and chief executive officer, held 51% of the shares. The company rented space in chain discount stores and specialized in selling ladies' shoes. Philips's first location was in a store that was part of Century Market Centers, Inc.

The following events occurred during April:

1. The company was incorporated. Common stockholders invested $140,000 cash.
2. Purchased merchandise inventory for cash, $45,000.
3. Purchased merchandise inventory on open account, $35,000.
4. Merchandise carried in inventory at a cost of $37,000 was sold for cash for $25,000 and on open account for $65,000, a grand total of $90,000. Philips (not Century) carries and collects these accounts receivable.
5. Collection of the above accounts receivable, $15,000.
6. Payments of accounts payable $28,000. See transaction 3.

7. Special display equipment and fixtures were acquired on April 1 for $36,000. Their expected useful life was thirty-six months. This equipment was removable. Philips paid $12,000 as a down payment and signed a promissory note for $24,000. Also see transaction 11.

8. On April 1, Philips signed a rental agreement with Century. The agreement called for a flat $2,000 per month, payable quarterly in advance. Therefore Philips paid $6,000 cash on April 1.

9. The rental agreement also called for a payment of 10% of all sales. This payment was in addition to the flat $2,000 per month. In this way, Century would share in any success of the venture and be compensated for general services such as cleaning and utilities. This payment was to be made in cash on the last day of each month as soon as the sales for the month had been tabulated. Therefore Philips made the payment on April 30.

10. Employee wages and sales commissions were all paid for in cash. The amount was $35,000.

11. Depreciation expense of $1,000 was recognized ($36,000 / 36 months). See transaction 7.

12. The expiration of an appropriate amount of prepaid rental services was recognized. See transaction 8.

Required

1. Prepare an analysis of Philips Company's transactions, employing the equation approach demonstrated in Exhibit 2-2 (p. 47). Show all amounts in thousands.
2. Prepare a balance sheet as of April 30, 19X2, and an income statement for the month of April. Ignore income taxes.
3. Given these sparse facts, analyze Philips's performance for April and its financial position as of April 30, 19X2.

2-34 Net Income and Cash Flows from Operating Activities
(Alternates are 2-32, 2-36, and 2-38.) Refer to the preceding problem. Suppose Philips measured performance on the cash basis instead of the accrual basis. Compute the net cash provided by (or used for) operating activities. Which measure, net income or net cash provided by (or used for) operating activities, provides a better measure of overall performance? Why?

2-35 Analysis of Transactions, Preparation of Statements
(Alternates are 2-31, 2-33, 2-37, and 2-40.) H. J. Heinz Company's actual condensed balance sheet data for May 1, 1994, follows (in millions):

Cash	$ 68	Accounts payable	$ 533
Accounts receivable	979	Other liabilities	3,967
Inventories	1,185	Paid-in capital	242
Other assets	2,427	Retained earnings	2,079
Property, plant, and equipment	2,162		
Total	$6,821	Total	$6,821

The following summarizes some transactions during May (in millions):

1. Ketchup carried in inventory at a cost of $3 was sold for cash of $2 and on open account of $8, a grand total of $10.
2. Acquired inventory on account, $5.
3. Collected receivables, $3.
4. On May 2, used $12 cash to prepay some rent and insurance for 12 months.
5. Payments on accounts payable (for inventories), $2.

6. Paid selling and administrative expenses in cash, $1.
7. Prepaid expenses of $1 for rent and insurance expired in May.
8. Depreciation expense of $1 was recognized for May.

Required   1. Prepare an analysis of Heinz's transactions, employing the equation approach demonstrated in Exhibit 2-2 (p. 47). Show all amounts in millions. (For simplicity, only a few transactions are illustrated here.)
2. Prepare a statement of earnings for the month ended May 31 and a balance sheet, May 31. Ignore income taxes.

2-36   Net Income and Cash Flows from Operating Activities
(Alternates are 2-32, 2-34, and 2-38.) Refer to the preceding problem. Suppose Heinz measured performance on the cash basis instead of the accrual basis. Compute the net cash provided by (or used for) operating activities. Which measure, net income or net cash provided by (or used for) operating activities, provides a better measure of overall performance? Why?

2-37   Analysis of Transactions, Preparation of Statements
(Alternates are 2-31, 2-33, 2-35, and 2-40.) Wm. Wrigley Jr. Company manufactures and sells chewing gum. The company's actual condensed balance sheet data for a recent December 31 follows (in millions):

Cash	$ 86	Accounts payable	$ 63
Receivables	118	Dividends payable	12
Inventories	177	Other liabilities	158
Other current assets	121	Paid-in capital	17
Property, plant, and equipment	240	Retained earnings	565
Other assets	73		
Total	$815	Total	$815

The following summarizes some major transactions during January (in millions):

1. Gum carried in inventory at a cost of $40 was sold for cash of $20 and on open account of $52, a grand total of $72.
2. Collection of receivables, $50.
3. Depreciation expense of $2 was recognized.
4. Selling and administrative expenses of $24 were paid in cash.
5. Prepaid expenses of $5 expired in January. These included fire insurance premiums paid in the previous year that applied to future months. The expiration increases selling and administrative expense and reduces other current assets.
6. The December 31 liability for dividends was paid in cash on January 25.
7. On January 30, the company declared a $2 dividend, which will be paid on February 25.

Required   1. Prepare an analysis of Wrigley's transactions, employing the equation approach demonstrated in Exhibit 2-2 (p. 47). Show all amounts in millions. (For simplicity, only a few major transactions are illustrated here.)
2. Prepare a statement of earnings and also a statement of retained earnings for the month ended January 31. Also prepare a balance sheet, January 31. Ignore income taxes.

2-38   Net Income and Cash Flows from Operating Activities
(Alternates are 2-32, 2-34, and 2-36.) Refer to the preceding problem. Suppose Wrigley measured performance on the cash basis instead of the accrual basis. Compute the net cash provided by (or used for) operating activities. Which measure, net income or net cash provided by (or used for) operating activities, provides a better measure of overall performance? Why?

2-39 Prepare Financial Statements

The Lazolli Corporation does not use the services of a professional accountant. However, at the end of its second year of operations, 19X2, the company's financial statements were prepared by its office manager. Listed below in random order are the items appearing in these statements:

Accounts receivable	$ 27,700	Office supplies inventory	$2,000
Paid-in capital	100,000	Notes payable	7,000
Trucks	33,700	Merchandise inventory	61,000
Cost of goods sold	156,000	Accounts payable	14,000
Salary expense	86,000	Notes receivable	2,500
Unexpired insurance	1,800	Utilities expenses	5,000
Rent expense	19,500	Net income	4,200
Sales	280,000	Retained income:	
Advertising expense	9,300	January 1, 19X2	18,000
Cash	14,500	December 31, 19X2	22,200

You are satisfied that the statements in which these items appear are correct except for several matters that the office manager overlooked. The following information should have been entered on the books and reflected in the financial statements:

a. The amount shown for rent expense includes $1,500 that is actually prepaid for the first month in 19X3.

b. Of the amount shown for unexpired insurance, only $800 is prepaid for periods after 19X2.

c. Depreciation of trucks for 19X2 is $5,000.

d. About $1,200 of the office supplies in the inventory shown above was actually issued and used during 19X2 operations.

e. Cash dividends of $3,000 were declared in December 19X2 by the board of directors. These dividends are to be distributed in February 19X3.

Required   Prepare in good form the following corrected financial statements, ignoring income taxes:

1. Income statement for 19X2
2. Statement of retained income for 19X2
3. Balance sheet at December 31, 19X2

It is not necessary to prepare a columnar analysis to show the transaction effects on each of the elements of the accounting equation.

2-40 Transaction Analysis and Financial Statements, Including Dividends

(Alternates are 2-31, 2-33, 2-35, and 2-37.) Consider the following balance sheet of a wholesaler of party supplies:

Valory Supplies Company
Balance Sheet
December 31, 19X1

Assets		Liabilities and Stockholders' Equity		
		Liabilities:		
Cash	$ 200,000	Accounts payable		$ 700,000
Accounts receivable	$ 400,000	Stockholders' equity:		
Merchandise inventory	860,000	Paid-in capital	$300,000	
Prepaid rent	40,000	Retained income	600,000	
Equipment	100,000	Total stockholders'		
		equity		900,000
Total	$1,600,000	Total		$1,600,000

The following is a summary of transactions that occurred during 19X2:

a. Acquisitions of inventory on open account, $1 million.

b. Sales on open account, $1.4 million; and for cash, $200,000. Therefore, total sales were $1.6 million.

c. Merchandise carried in inventory at a cost of $1.2 million was sold as described in b.

d. The warehouse twelve-month lease expired on September 1, 19X2. However, the lease was immediately renewed at a rate of $84,000 for the next twelve-month period. The entire rent was paid in cash in advance.

e. Depreciation expense for 19X2 for the warehouse equipment was $20,000.

f. Collections on accounts receivable, $1.25 million.

g. Wages for 19X2 were paid in full in cash, $200,000.

h. Miscellaneous expenses for 19X2 were paid in full in cash, $70,000.

i. Payments on accounts payable, $900,000.

j. Cash dividends for 19X2 were paid in full in December, $100,000.

Required

1. Prepare an analysis of transactions, employing the equation approach demonstrated in Exhibit 2-2 (p. 47). Show the amounts in thousands of dollars.

2. Prepare a balance sheet, statement of income, and statement of retained income. Also prepare a combined statement of income and retained income.

3. Reconsider transaction j. Suppose the dividends were declared on December 15, payable on January 31, 19X3, to shareholders of record on January 20. Indicate which accounts and financial statements in requirement 2 would be changed and by how much. Be complete and specific.

2-41   Balance Sheet Equation

(Alternates are 2-25 and 2-26.) Nordstrom, Inc., the fashion retailer, had the following actual data for its 1994 fiscal year (in millions):

Assets, beginning of period	$2,053
Assets, end of period	2,177
Liabilities, beginning of period	A
Liabilities, end of period	E
Paid-in capital, beginning of period	155
Paid-in capital, end of period	D
Retained earnings, beginning of period	897
Retained earnings, end of period	C
Sales and other revenues	3,590
Cost of sales, and all other expenses	3,450
Net earnings	B
Dividends	28
Additional investment by stockholders	2

Required

Find the unknowns (in thousands), showing computations to support your answers.

2-42   Statement of Cash Flows

Kang Company imports Asian goods and sells them in eight import stores on the West Coast. On August 1, 19X4, Kang's cash balance was $164,000. Summarized transactions during August were:

1. Sales on open account, $580,000.

2. Collections of accounts receivable, $450,000.

3. Purchases of inventory on open account, $305,000.
4. Payment of accounts payable, $280,000.
5. Cost of goods sold, $325,000.
6. Salaries and wages expense, $105,000, of which $90,000 was paid in cash and $15,000 remained payable on August 31.
7. Rent expense for August, $35,000, paid in advance in July.
8. Depreciation expense, $46,000.
9. Other operating expenses, $60,000, all paid in cash.
10. Borrowed from bank on August 31, $50,000, with repayment (including interest) due on December 31.
11. Purchased fixtures and equipment for San Diego store on August 31, $120,000; half paid in cash and half due in October.

Required

1. Prepare a statement of cash flows, including the cash balance on August 31.
2. Prepare an income statement.
3. Explain why net income differs from net cash provided by (or used for) operating activities.

2-43   Two Sides of a Transaction
For each of the following transactions, show the effects on the entities involved. As was illustrated in the chapter, use the A = L + OE equation to demonstrate the effects. Also name each amount affected, show the dollar amount, and indicate whether the effects are increases or decreases. The following transaction is completed as an illustration.

Illustration

The Massachusetts General Hospital collects $1,000 from the Blue Cross Health Care Plan.

		A		=	L	+ OE
Entity	*Cash*	*Receivables*	*Trucks*		*Payables*	
Hospital	+1,000	−1,000		=		
Blue Cross	−1,000			=	−1,000	

1. Borrowing of $100,000 on a home mortgage from Fidelity Savings by Evan Porteus.
2. Payment of $10,000 principal on the above mortgage. Ignore interest.
3. Purchase of a two-year subscription to *Time* magazine for $80 cash by Carla Bonini.
4. Purchase of trucks by the U.S. Postal Service for $10 million cash from the U.S. General Services Administration. The trucks were carried in the accounts at $10 million by the General Services Administration.
5. Purchase of U.S. government bonds for $100,000 cash by Lockheed Corporation.
6. Cash deposits of $10 on the returnable bottles sold by Safeway Stores to a retail customer, Philomena Simon.
7. Collections on open account of $100 by Sears store from a retail customer, Kenneth Arrow.
8. Purchase of traveler's checks of $1,000 from American Express Company by Michael Harrison.
9. Cash deposit of $500 in a checking account in Bank of America by David Kreps.
10. Purchase of a United Airlines "super-saver" airline ticket for $500 cash by Robert Wilson on June 15. The trip will be taken on September 10.

McDonald's Corporation

2-44 Net Income and Retained Income

McDonald's Corporation is a well-known fast-food restaurant company. The following data are from a recent annual report (in millions):

Retained earnings, beginning of year	$6,727.3	Dividends paid	$ 197.2
Revenues	7,408.1	General, administrative, and selling expenses	941.1
Interest and other non-operating expenses	308.3	Franchise expenses	318.4
Provisions for income taxes	593.2	Retained earnings, end of year	7,612.6
Food and packaging	1,735.1	Occupancy and other operating expenses	1,138.3
Wages and salaries	1,291.2		

Required

1. Prepare the following for the year:
   a. Income statement. The final three lines of the income statement were labeled as income before provision for income taxes, provision for income taxes, and net income.
   b. Statement of retained earnings.
2. Comment briefly on the relative size of the cash dividend.

2-45 Earnings Statement, Retained Earnings

The Procter & Gamble Company has many well-known products. Examples are Tide, Crest, Jif, and Prell. The following amounts were in the financial statements contained in its 1994 annual report (in millions):

Net sales and other income	$30,296	Retained earnings at beginning of year	6,248
Cash	2,373		
Interest expense and other	234	Cost of products sold	17,355
Income taxes	1,135	Dividends to shareholders	847
Accounts payable—Trade	2,604	Marketing, administrative,	
Cash provided by operations	3,649	and other expenses	9,361

Required

Choose the relevant data and prepare (1) the income statement for the year and (2) the statement of retained income for the year. The final three lines of the income statement were labeled as earnings before income taxes, income taxes, and net earnings.

2-46 Financial Ratios

Study pages 67 to 70. Following is a list of several well-known companies and selected financial data included in a letter sent by a stock brokerage firm to some of its clients:

	Per-share Data			Ratios and Percentages		
Company	Price	Earnings	Dividends	Price–Earnings	Dividend Yield	Dividend–Payout
Airborne Freight	$17	$1.76	$ —	$ —	—%	17%
B. F. Goodrich	37	—	2.12	—	—	42
Lockheed	—	5.30	1.80	6.4	—	—
Northern States Power	34	—	2.32	12.0	6.8	—
Texaco	60	5.18	—	—	5.3	—
USX Corp.	30	3.14	1.40	—	—	—
Wells Fargo	—	—	4.00	—	6.8	30

The missing figures for this schedule can be computed from the data given.

1. Compute the missing figures and identify the company with
   a. The highest dividend yield
   b. The highest dividend-payout percentage
   c. The lowest market price relative to earnings
2. Assume that you know nothing about any of these companies other than the data given and the computations you have made from the data. Which company would you choose as
   a. The most attractive investment? Why?
   b. The least attractive investment? Why?

2-47 Classic Case of the President's Wealth

This is a classic case in accounting. From the *Chicago Tribune*, August 20, 1964:

- Accountants acting on President Johnson's orders today reported his family wealth totaled $3,484,098.

- The statement of capital, arrived at through conservative procedures of evaluation, contrasted with a recent estimate published by *Life* magazine, which put the total at 14 million dollars.

- The family fortune, which is held in trust while the Johnsons are in the White House, was set forth in terms of book values. The figures represent original cost rather than current market values on what the holdings would be worth if sold now.

- Announced by the White House press office, but turned over to reporters by a national accounting firm at their Washington branch office, the financial statement apparently was intended to still a flow of quasi-official and unofficial estimates of the Johnson fortune....

Assets:		
Cash		$ 132,547
Bonds		398,540
Interest in Texas Broadcasting Corp		2,543,838
Ranch properties and other real estate		525,791
Other assets, including insurance policies		82,054
Total assets		$3,682,770
Liabilities:		
Note payable on real estate holding, 5 percent due 1971	$150,000	
Accounts payable, accrued interest, and income taxes	48,672	
Total liabilities		$198,672
Capital		$3,484,098

- The report apportions the capital among the family, with $37,081 credited to the President; $2,126,298 to his wife Claudia T., who uses the name Lady Bird; $490,141 to their daughter Lynda Bird; and $489,578 to their daughter Luci Baines.

- The statement said the family holdings—under the names of the President, his wife, and his two daughters, Lynda Bird and Luci Baines—had increased from $737,730 on January 1, 1954, a year after Johnson became Democratic leader of the Senate, to $3,484,098 on July 31 this year, a gain of $2,746,368....

- A covering letter addressed to Johnson said the statement was made "in conformity with generally accepted accounting principles applied on a consistent basis."

- By far the largest part of the fortune was listed as the Johnsons' interest in the Texas Broadcasting Corporation, carried on the books as worth $2,543,838.

- The accountants stated that this valuation was arrived at on the basis of the cost of the stock when the Johnsons bought control of the debt-ridden radio station between 1943 and 1947, plus accumulated earnings ploughed back as equity, less 25% capital gains tax.[1]

Editorial, Chicago Tribune, August 22, 1964:

- An accounting firm acting on Mr. Johnson's instructions and employing what it termed "generally accepted auditing standards" has released a statement putting the current worth of the Lyndon Johnson family at a little less than 3½ million dollars....
- Dean Burch, chairman of the Republican National Committee, has remarked that the method used to list the Johnson assets was comparable to placing the value of Manhattan Island at $24, the price at which it was purchased from the Indians. The Johnson accounting firm conceded that its report was "not intended to indicate the values that might be realized if the investment were sold."
- In fact, it would be interesting to observe the response of the Johnson family if a syndicate of investors were to offer to take Texas Broadcasting off the family's hands at double the publicly reported worth of the operation....

Required

1. Evaluate the criticisms, making special reference to fundamental accounting concepts or "principles."
2. The financial statements of President and Mrs. Carter are shown in Exhibit 2-10. Do you prefer the approach taken by the Carter statements as compared with the Johnson statements? Explain.
3. The Carter statements in Exhibit 2-10 indicate that the Carter residence cost $45,000. Its estimated current value is shown as $54,090. Which number do you believe is more accurate? More relevant? Which number, $45,000 or $54,090, would be used by a business in its statement of assets?
4. Have the Carters earned income of $54,090 – $45,000 on their residence?
5. Suppose you were asked tomorrow to prepare your family's (or your individual) statement of assets and liabilities. Could you do it? How would you measure your wealth?

2-48   Revenue Recognition and Ethics

Kendall Square Research Corporation (KSR), located in Waltham, Massachusetts, produced high-speed computers and competed against companies such as Cray Research and Sun Microsystems.

In August 1993 the common stock of KSR reached an all-time high of $25.75 a share; by mid-December it had plummeted to $5.25. Its financial policies were called into question in an article in *Financial Shenanigan Busters*, Winter 1994, p. 3. The main charge was that the company was recording revenues before it was appropriate.

---

[1] You need not be concerned about the details of this method of accounting until you study Chapter 13. In brief, when an investor holds a large enough stake in a corporation, such investment is accounted for at its acquisition cost plus the investor's pro rata share of the investee's net income (or net loss) minus the investor's share of dividends. For example, suppose the Texas Broadcasting Corporation earned $500,000 in a given year and that Johnson owned 20% of the corporation. In this situation, the Johnson financial statements would show an increase in Interest in Texas Broadcasting Corp. of $100,000 less the $25,000 income tax that would become payable upon disposition of the investment. (Today's accountants would prefer to increase the Investment account by the full $100,000 and the liabilities by $25,000. See the Carter financial statements.)

Exhibit 2-10

Perry, Chambliss,
Sheppard and
Thompson
Certified Public
Accountants
Americus, Georgia
James Earl Carter, Jr.
and Rosalynn Carter
Statement of Assets
and Liabilities
December 31, 1977
(unaudited)

Assets	Cost Basis	Estimated Current Value
Cash	$204,979.04	$ 204,979.04
Cash Value of Life Insurance	45,506.88	45,506.88
U.S. Savings Bonds, Series E	1425.00	1,550.94
Loan receivable	50,000.00	50,000.00
Overpayment of 1977 Income Taxes	51,121.27	51,121.27
Personal Assets Trust—Note 3	151,097.87	557,717.11
Residence, Plains, Georgia	45,000.00	54,090.00
Lot in Plains, Georgia	1,100.00	3,155.00
Automobile	4,550.75	2,737.50
Total assets	$554,780.81	$ 970,857.74

Liabilities and Capital		
Miscellaneous accounts payable, estimated	$ 1,500.00	$ 1,500.00
Provision for possible income taxes on unrealized asset appreciation—Note 4	–0–	174,000.00
Total liabilities	$ 1,500.00	$ 175,500.00
Excess of assets over liabilities (Capital)	$553,280.81	$ 795,357.75

NOTE 1: Estimated market values of real estate are 100% of the fair market values as determined by county tax assessors except as to certain assets held in the personal assets trust, which are stated at book value.

NOTE 2: This statement excludes campaign fund assets and liabilities.

NOTE 3: The interest in Carter's Warehouse partnership, the capital stock of Carter's Farms, Inc., the remainder interest in certain real estate and securities and a commercial lot in Plains, Georgia, were transferred to a personal assets trust in January, 1977. The primary purpose of the trust is to isolate the President from those of his assets which are most likely to be affected by actions of the federal government. The President was responsible as a general partner for obligations of the partnership before his partnership interest was transferred to the trust. The transfer to the trust did not affect such responsibility.

NOTE 4: If the market values of the assets were realized, income taxes would be payable at an uncertain rate. A provision for such income taxes has been made at rates in effect for 1977.

NOTE 5: The amounts in the accompanying statements are based principally upon the accrual basis method of accounting.

KSR sold expensive computers to universities and other research institutions. Often the customers took delivery before they knew how they might pay for the computers. Sometimes they anticipated receiving grants that would pay for the computers, but other times they had no prospective funding. KSR also recorded revenue when computers were shipped to distributors who did not yet have customers to buy them and when computers were sold contingent on future upgrades.

Required   Comment on the ethical implications of KSR's revenue recognition practices.

✓ **2-49   Wal-Mart Annual Report**
Refer to the financial statements of the actual company, Wal-Mart, in Appendix A at the end of the text and answer the following questions:

Required
1. What was the amount of total revenues for the 1995 fiscal year? The net income?
2. What was the total amount of cash dividends for the 1995 fiscal year?
3. What was the title of the financial statement that contained the dividend amount? Did it differ from the title you expected? Explain.

2-50 Compact D from Disclosure

Select the financial statements of any company from those available on Compact D.

1. What was the amount of sales or total revenues for the most recent year? The net income?

2. What was the total amount of cash dividends for the most recent year?

3. What was the amount of cash provided by (or used for) operating activities in the most recent year? Compare the amount to the net income.

4. What was the ending balance in retained income in the most recent year? What were the two most significant items during the year that affected the retained income balance?

3

The Recording Process: Journals and Ledgers

Learning Objectives

After studying this chapter, you should be able to

1 Explain the double-entry accounting system, the role of ledger accounts, and the meaning of debits and credits.

2 Describe the sequence of steps in recording transactions and explain how transactions are journalized and posted.

3 Analyze transactions for journalizing and posting and explain the relationship of revenues and expenses to stockholders' equity.

4 Prepare journal entries and post them to the ledger.

5 Prepare a trial balance and understand its role relative to the income statement and balance sheet.

6 Correct erroneous entries and describe how errors affect accounts.

7 Use T-accounts to aid the discovery of unknown amounts.

8 Understand the significance of computers in data processing.

9 Explain the meaning of the concepts of going concern, materiality, and cost-benefit.

To intelligently use the reports prepared by accountants, decision makers must understand the methods used to record and analyze accounting data. This chapter focuses on the double-entry accounting system that is universally used to record and process information about an entity's transactions. We concentrate primarily on specific procedures and techniques instead of new accounting concepts.

The chapter begins by describing the building blocks of a double-entry system—ledgers and journals. It then defines terms that accountants use daily, such as *debit* and *credit*, but that often seem strange to nonaccountants. Next, the chapter traces the process of recording transactions, from the original entry into the accounts to the completed financial statements. It includes treatment of errors in the records and methods for creating entries from incomplete files and data sources. Finally, the gradual introduction of basic concepts continues with coverage of the going concern convention, materiality, and the cost-benefit criterion.

Methods of processing accounting data have changed dramatically in the last decade or two, as computerized systems have replaced manual ones. However, the steps in recording, storing, and processing accounting data have not changed. Moving from pencil-and-paper accounting records to computerized ones is like starting to drive a car with an automatic transmission after driving one with a manual transmission. Less time must be spent on routine tasks, but a basic understanding of the system is still required. Whether data are entered into the system by pencil, keyboard, or optical scanner, the same basic data are required. Whether reports are automatically produced by a computer or painstakingly assembled by hand, understanding and interpreting the reports requires basic knowledge about how the underlying data were processed. Therefore, this chapter is important to anyone who *uses* accounting reports, as well as to someone who plans to *produce* such reports.

■ THE DOUBLE-ENTRY ACCOUNTING SYSTEM

double-entry system
The method usually followed for recording transactions, whereby at least two accounts are always affected by each transaction.

In a large business such as a Sears or Wal-Mart store, hundreds or thousands of transactions occur hourly. Accounting procedures must be used to keep track of these transactions in a systematic manner. The method usually followed for recording all of a business entity's transactions is the **double-entry system**, whereby at least two accounts are always affected by each transaction. Each transaction must be analyzed to determine which accounts are involved, whether the accounts are increased or decreased, and the amount of the change in each account balance.

Recall the first three transactions of the Biwheels Company introduced in Chapter 1:

Objective 1

Explain the double-entry accounting system, the role of ledger accounts, and the meaning of debits and credits.

	A		=	L	+	SE
	Cash	Merchandise Inventory		Note Payable		Paid-in Capital
(1) Initial investment by owner	+400,000		=			+400,000
(2) Loan from bank	+100,000		=	+100,000		
(3) Acquire inventory for cash	−150,000	+150,000	=			

This balance sheet equation illustrates the basic concepts of the double-entry system by showing two entries for each transaction. It also emphasizes that the equation Assets = Liabilities + Stockholders' Equity must always remain in balance.

The balance sheet equation approach is unwieldy as a means for recording each and every transaction that occurs. In practice, *ledgers* are used to record the individual transactions in the proper accounts.

Ledger Accounts

ledger A group of related accounts kept current in a systematic manner.

general ledger The collection of accounts that accumulates the amounts reported in the major financial statements.

T-account Simplified version of ledger accounts that takes the form of the capital letter T.

A **ledger** contains a group of related accounts kept current in a systematic manner. The ledger may be in the form of a bound record book, a loose-leaf set of pages, or some kind of electronic storage element such as magnetic tape or disk. You can think of a ledger as a book with one page for each account. When you hear reference to "keeping the books" or "auditing the books," the word *books* refers to the ledger. A firm's **general ledger** is the collection of accounts that accumulates the amounts reported in the firm's major financial statements.

The ledger accounts used here are simplified versions of those used in practice. They are called **T-accounts** because they take the form of the capital letter T. The vertical line in the T divides the account into left and right sides for recording increases and decreases in the account. The account title is on the horizontal line. For example, consider the format of the Cash account:

Cash	
Left side	Right side
Increases in cash	Decreases in cash

The T-accounts for the first three Biwheels Company transactions are as follows:

Assets   =   Liabilities + Stockholders' Equity

Cash			
Increases		Decreases	
(1)	400,000	(3)	150,000
(2)	100,000		

Note Payable			
Decreases		Increases	
		(2)	100,000

Merchandise Inventory			
Increases		Decreases	
(3)	150,000		

Paid-in Capital			
Decreases		Increases	
		(1)	400,000

These entries are in accordance with the rules of the double-entry system. Two accounts are affected by each transaction.

In practice, accounts are created as needed. The process of writing a new T-account in preparation for recording a transaction is called *opening the account*. For transaction 1, we opened Cash and Paid-in Capital. For transaction 2, we opened Note Payable, and for transaction 3 we opened Merchandise Inventory.

Each T-account summarizes the changes in a particular asset, liability, or stockholders' equity. Each transaction is keyed in some way, such as by the numbering used in this illustration or by the date or by both. This keying helps

balance The differ-
ence between the total
left-side and right-
side amounts in an
account at any partic-
ular time.

the rechecking (auditing) process by aiding the tracing of entries in the ledger account to the original transactions. A **balance** is the difference between the total left-side and right-side amounts in an account at any particular time.

Asset accounts have *left-side balances*. They are increased by entries on the left side and decreased by entries on the right side. Liabilities and owners' equity accounts have *right-side balances*. They are increased by entries on the right side and decreased by entries on the left side.

Consider the analysis and entries for each Biwheels transaction. Notice that each transaction has a left-side entry and a right-side entry of the same amount.

1. **Transaction:** Initial investment by owners, $400,000 cash.
   Analysis: The asset **Cash** is increased.
   The stockholders' equity **Paid-in Capital** is increased.
   Entry:

Cash		Paid-in Capital	
(1) 400,000			(1) 400,000

2. **Transaction:** Loan from bank, $100,000.
   Analysis: The asset **Cash** is increased.
   The liability **Note Payable** is increased.
   Entry:

Cash		Note Payable	
(1) 400,000			(2) 100,000
(2) 100,000			

3. **Transaction:** Acquired inventory for cash, $150,000.
   Analysis: The asset Cash is decreased.
   The asset Merchandise Inventory is increased.
   Entry:

Cash		
(1) 400,000	(3)	150,000
(2) 100,000		

Merchandise Inventory	
(3) 150,000	

Accounts such as these exist to keep an up-to-date record of the changes in specific assets and equities. Financial statements can be prepared at any instant if the account balances are up to date. The information accumulated in the accounts provides the necessary summary balances for the financial statements. For example, the balance sheet after the first three transactions contains the following account balances:

Assets		Liabilities + Owners' Equity	
Cash	$350,000	Liabilities:	
Merchandise		Note payable	$100,000
inventory	150,000	Stockholders' equity:	
		Paid-in capital	400,000
Total	$500,000	Total	$500,000

■ THE DEBIT-CREDIT LANGUAGE

debit An entry or balance on the left side of an account.

credit An entry or balance on the right side of an account.

charge A word often used instead of debit.

You have just seen that the double-entry system features entries on left sides and right sides of various accounts. Accountants use the term **debit** to denote the left-side entries and the term **credit** to denote right-side entries. For instance, suppose a CPA were asked how to analyze and record transaction 1. She would say, "That's easy. Debit Cash and credit Paid-in Capital." By so doing, she enters $400,000 on the *left* side of Cash and $400,000 on the *right* side of Paid-in Capital.

In short, *debit* means *left* and *credit* means *right*. The word **charge** is often used instead of *debit*, but no single word is used as a synonym for credit. Abbreviations may be used—*dr.* for debit and *cr.* for credit.

The words *debit* and *credit* have a Latin origin. They were used when double-entry bookkeeping was introduced in 1494 by Pacioli, an Italian monk. (Indeed, it has been said, probably by an accountant, that the most important event of the 1490s was the creation of double-entry bookkeeping, not Columbus's ocean crossing.) Even though *left* and *right* are more descriptive words, *debit* and *credit* are too deeply entrenched to avoid.

Debit and *credit* are used as verbs, adjectives, and nouns. "Debit $1,000 to cash, and credit $1,000 to accounts receivable" are examples of uses as verbs, meaning that $1,000 should be placed on the left side of the Cash account and on the right side of the Accounts Receivable account. Similarly, in phrases such as "a debit is made to cash" or "cash has a debit balance of $12,000," the word *debit* is a noun or an adjective that describes the status of a particular account. Thus *debit* and *credit* are short words packed with meaning.

In our everyday conversation, we sometimes use the words *debit* and *credit* in a general sense that may completely diverge from their technical accounting uses. For instance, we may give praise by saying, "She deserves plenty of credit for her good deed," or we may give criticism by saying, "That misplay is a debit on his ledger." When you study accounting, forget these general uses and misuses of the words. Merely think right or left—that is, right side or left side.

■ RECORDING TRANSACTIONS: JOURNALS AND LEDGERS

Although Biwheels transactions 1, 2, and 3 were entered directly in the ledger in the previous section, in actual practice the recording process does not start with the ledger. The sequence of steps in recording transactions is as follows:

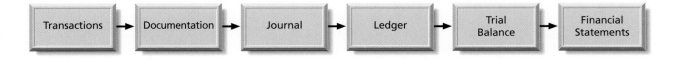

Transactions → Documentation → Journal → Ledger → Trial Balance → Financial Statements

source documents The supporting original records of any transaction; they are memorandums of what happened.

The recording steps begin when the transaction is substantiated by **source documents**. These are supporting original records of any transaction. Examples of source documents include sales slips or invoices, check stubs, purchase orders, receiving reports, cash receipt slips, and minutes of the board of directors. Source documents are kept on file so they can be used to verify the accuracy of recorded transactions if necessary.

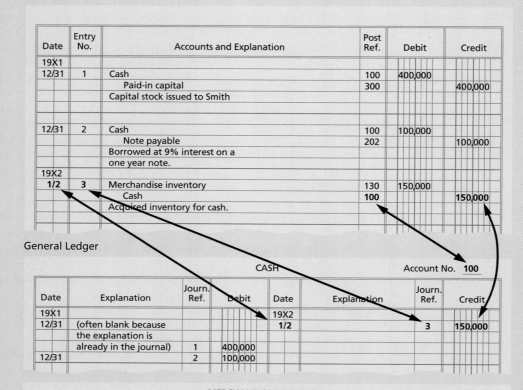

General Journal

Date	Entry No.	Accounts and Explanation	Post Ref.	Debit	Credit
19X1					
12/31	1	Cash	100	400,000	
		Paid-in capital	300		400,000
		Capital stock issued to Smith			
12/31	2	Cash	100	100,000	
		Note payable	202		100,000
		Borrowed at 9% interest on a			
		one year note.			
19X2					
1/2	3	Merchandise inventory	130	150,000	
		Cash	100		150,000
		Acquired inventory for cash.			

General Ledger

CASH   Account No. **100**

Date	Explanation	Journ. Ref.	Debit	Date	Explanation	Journ. Ref.	Credit
19X1				19X2			
12/31	(often blank because the explanation is already in the journal)			1/2		3	150,000
12/31		1	400,000				
		2	100,000				

MERCHANDISE INVENTORY   Account No. **130**

Date	Explanation	Journ. Ref.	Debit	Date	Explanation	Journ. Ref.	Credit
19X2							
1/2		3	150,000				

NOTE PAYABLE   Account No. 202

Date	Explanation	Journ. Ref.	Debit	Date	Explanation	Journ. Ref.	Credit
				19X1			
				12/31		2	100,000

PAID-IN CAPITAL   Account No. 300

Date	Explanation	Journ. Ref.	Debit	Date	Explanation	Journ. Ref.	Credit
				19X1			
				12/31		1	400,000

book of original entry A formal chronological record of how the entity's transactions affect the balances in pertinent accounts.

general journal The most common example of a book of original entry; a complete chronological record of transactions.

In the second step, an analysis of the transaction is placed in a **book of original entry**, which is a formal chronological record of how each transaction affects the balances in particular accounts. The most common example of a book of original entry is the **general journal**. An entire transaction is recorded in one place in the journal, in contrast to the ledger, where only part of a transaction is recorded in a particular ledger account. The general journal is thus a complete, chronological record that can be likened to a diary of all of the events in an entity's life.

The timing of the steps will differ. Transactions occur constantly and documentation is prepared continuously. Depending on the size and nature of the organization, the accounting operation may be very large and transaction analysis may also occur continuously or the operation may be small and the analysis of transactions and recording in the journal may be less frequent. As discussed previously, the ledger is the collection of information about specific accounts. Information in the ledger is updated periodically by recording each piece of each transaction in the ledger account where it belongs This process might occur weekly or even less frequently in very small organizations.

The fourth step, preparation of the trial balance, serves two purposes. It verifies clerical accuracy and assists in preparing financial statements. Thus it occurs as needed, perhaps each month or each quarter as the firm prepares its financial statements. The final step, the preparation of financial statements occurs at least once a quarter, every three months, for publicly traded companies in the United States. These statements, which include the balance sheet, the income statement, the statement of cash flows, and the statement of changes in retained earnings were described in Chapter 2.

Some companies prepare financial statements more frequently for management's benefit. Recently many companies are watching results at Springfield ReManufacturing Corp in the Ozark mountains of southern Missouri. Springfield is a leader in "open-book management." The phrase "open books" refers to the company's accounting results. Management and all employees meet monthly to examine the results in detail. Extensive training is provided to employees on how the accounting process works and what the numbers mean. This new management process increased efficiency and profitability at Springfield. In summary, the timing of the steps in the accounting cycle must conform to the needs of the users of the data.

Journalizing Transactions

journalizing The process of entering transactions into the journal.

journal entry An analysis of the effects of a transaction on the accounts, usually accompanied by an explanation.

The process of entering transactions into the journal is called **journalizing**. A **journal entry** is an analysis of the effects of a transaction on the accounts, usually accompanied by an explanation. The accounts to be debited and credited are identified. For example, the top of Exhibit 3-1 shows how the opening three transactions for Biwheels are journalized.

The conventional form of the general journal includes the following:

1. The date and identification number of the entry make up the first two columns.

2. The accounts affected are shown in the next column, Accounts and Explanation. The title of the account or accounts to be *debited* is placed flush left. The title of the account or accounts to be *credited* is indented in a consistent way. The journal entry is followed by the narrative explanation, which can be brief or extensive. The length of the explanation depends on the complexity of the transaction and whether management wants the journal itself to contain all relevant information. Most often, explanations are brief, and details are available in the file of supporting documents.

3. The Post Ref. (posting reference) column in Exhibit 3-1 contains the number that is assigned to each account and is used for cross-referencing to the ledger accounts.

4. The money columns are for recording the amounts in the debit (left) or credit (right) columns for each account. No dollar signs are used.

Objective 2

Describe the sequence of steps in recording transactions and explain how transactions are journalized and posted.

Chart of Accounts

chart of accounts
A numbered or coded list of all account titles.

Organizations have a **chart of accounts**, which is normally a numbered or coded list of all account titles. These numbers are used as references in the Post Ref. column of the journal, as Exhibit 3-1 demonstrates. The following is the chart of accounts for Biwheels:

Account Number	Account Title	Account Number	Account Title
100	Cash	202	Note payable
120	Accounts receivable	203	Accounts payable
		300	Paid-in capital
130	Merchandise inventory	400	Retained income
		500	Sales revenues
140	Prepaid rent	600	Cost of goods sold
170	Store equipment		
170A	Accumulated depreciation, store equipment (explained later)	601	Rent expense
		602	Depreciation expense

Although an outsider may not know what the code means, accounting employees become so familiar with the code that they think, talk, and write in terms of account numbers instead of account names. Thus an outside auditor may find entry 3, the acquisition of Merchandise Inventory (Account 130) for Cash (Account 100), journalized as follows:

MONEY COLUMNS

19X2			dr.	cr.
Jan. 2	130	. . . .	150,000	
	100	. . . .		150,000

This journal entry is the employee's shorthand. Its brevity and lack of explanation would hamper any outsider's understanding of the transaction, but the entry's meaning would be clear to anyone within the organization.

Posting Transactions to the Ledger

posting The transferring of amounts from the journal to the appropriate accounts in the ledger.

Posting is the transferring of amounts from the journal to the appropriate accounts in the ledger. It is a mechanical process that is ideally suited to computers. The accountant places the journal entry in the general journal, and the computer is programmed to transfer the relevant information to the ledger. To demonstrate, consider transaction 3 for Biwheels. Exhibit 3-1 shows with bold arrows how the credit to cash is posted.

The sample of the general ledger in Exhibit 3-1 is in the form of elaborate T-accounts; that is, debits are on the left side and credits on the right side. Note how cross-referencing occurs between the journal and the ledger. The date is recorded in the journal and the ledger, and the journal entry number is placed in the reference column of the ledger. The process of numbering or otherwise specifically identifying each journal entry and each posting is known as the **keying of entries**, or **cross-referencing**. It allows users to find the other parts of the transactions no matter where they start. It also helps auditors to find and correct errors and reduces the frequency of initial errors.

keying of entries (cross-referencing) The process of numbering or otherwise specifically identifying each journal entry and each posting.

Professional accountants and financial managers frequently think about complicated transactions in terms of how they would be analyzed in a journal or in T-accounts. These bookkeeping devices become models of the organization. Accountants or managers often ask, "How would you journalize that transaction?" or "How would the T-accounts be affected?" By answering these questions, they can see how a transaction will affect the financial statements. In short, accountants and managers have found that they can think straighter if they visualize the transaction in terms of the balance sheet equation and debits and credits.

Running Balance Column

Exhibit 3-2 shows a popular ledger account format that adds an additional column to provide a *running balance*. Notice the similarity of the running balance format for the cash account and your checkbook. The debit column records deposits, the credit column records checks written, and the balance column has an up-to-date cash balance. The running balance feature is easily achieved by computers.

Above all, note that the same postings to Cash (or any other pertinent accounts) are made regardless of the account format used: T-account (Exhibit 3-1) or running balance (Exhibit 3-2).

Exhibit 3-2

Ledger Account with Running Balance Column

CASH						Account No. 100
Date	Explanation	Journ. Ref.	Debit	Credit	Balance	
19X1						
12/31	(often blank because the explanation is already	1	400,000		400,000	
12/31	in the journal)	2	100,000		500,000	
19X2						
1/2		3		150,000	350,000	

■ ANALYZING TRANSACTIONS FOR THE JOURNAL AND LEDGER

Objective 3

Analyze transactions for journalizing and posting and explain the relationship of revenue and expenses to stockholders' equity.

As we have seen, transactions are analyzed mentally and then are journalized before being posted to the ledger. This process can now be extended to the Biwheels Company's transactions 4 through 13 as a continuation of the journal entries 1 through 3 in Exhibit 3-1.

4. Transaction: Acquired inventory on credit, $10,000.
    Analysis: The asset **Merchandise Inventory** is increased.
              The liability **Accounts Payable** is increased.
       Entry: In the journal (explanation omitted):

          Merchandise inventory   10,000
               Accounts payable   10,000

         Post to the ledger (postings are indicated by circled amounts):

Merchandise Inventory*				Accounts Payable	
(3)	150,000			(4)	(10,000)
(4)	(10,000)				

* If it is the only type of inventory account, it is often simply called Inventory.

simple entry An entry for a transaction that affects only two accounts.

Transaction 4, like transactions 1, 2, and 3, is a **simple entry** in that only the two accounts shown are affected by the transaction. Note that the balance sheet equation always remains in balance.

5. Transaction: Acquired store equipment for $4,000 cash plus $11,000 trade credit.
    Analysis: The asset **Cash** is decreased.
              The asset **Store Equipment** is increased.
              The liability **Accounts Payable** is increased.
       Entry: In the journal:

          Store equipment   15,000
             Cash   4,000
                 Accounts payable   11,000

         Post to the ledger:

Cash				Accounts Payable	
(1)	400,000	(3)	150,000	(4)	10,000
(2)	100,000	(5)	(4,000)	(5)	(11,000)

Store Equipment	
(5)	(15,000)

compound entry An entry for a transaction that affects more than two accounts.

Transaction 5 is a **compound entry**, which means that more than two accounts are affected by a single transaction. Whether transactions are simple or compound, the total of all left-side entries always equals the totals of all right-side entries. The net effect is *always* to keep the accounting equation in balance:

$$\text{Assets} = \text{Liabilities} + \text{Stockholders' equity}$$
$$15,000 - 4,000 = + 11,000$$

Helpful hint: When analyzing a transaction, initially pinpoint the effects (if any) on cash. Did cash increase or decrease? Then think of the effects on other accounts. In this way, you get off to the right start. Usually, it is much easier to identify the effects of a transaction on cash than to identify the effects on other accounts.

6. Transaction: Sold unneeded showcase to neighbor for $1,000 on open account.
   Analysis: The asset **Accounts Receivable** is increased.
   The asset **Store Equipment** is decreased.
   Entry: In the journal:

Accounts receivable	1,000	
Store equipment		1,000

Post to the ledger:

Accounts Receivable		
(6)	1,000	

Store Equipment				
(5)	15,000	(6)	1,000	

In transaction 6, one asset goes up, and another asset goes down. No liability or owners' equity account is affected.

7. Transaction: Returned inventory to supplier for full credit, $800.
   Analysis: The asset **Merchandise Inventory** is decreased.
   The liability **Accounts Payable** is decreased.
   Entry: In the journal:

Accounts payable	800	
Merchandise inventory		800

Post to the ledger:

Merchandise Inventory					Accounts Payable			
(3)	150,000	(7)	800	(7)	800	(4)	10,000	
(4)	10,000					(5)	11,000	

8. Transaction: Paid cash to creditors, $4,000.
   Analysis: The asset **Cash** is decreased.
   The liability **Accounts Payable** is decreased.
   Entry: In the journal:

Accounts payable	4,000	
Cash		4,000

Post to the ledger:

Cash					Accounts Payable			
(1)	400,000	(3)	150,000	(7)	800	(4)	10,000	
(2)	100,000	(5)	4,000	(8)	4,000	(5)	11,000	
		(8)	4,000					

9. **Transaction:** Collected cash from debtors, $700.
   Analysis: The asset **Cash** is increased.
                  The asset **Accounts Receivable** is decreased.
   Entry: In the journal:

   Cash   700
       Accounts receivable   700

   Post to the ledger:

Cash			
(1)	400,000	(3)	150,000
(2)	100,000	(5)	4,000
(9)	(700)	(8)	4,000

Accounts Receivable			
(6)	1,000	(9)	(700)

Transactions 7, 8, and 9 are all simple entries. In transactions 7 and 8 an asset and a liability both go down. In transaction 9 one asset goes up while another asset goes down.

Revenue and Expense Transactions

Revenue and expense transactions deserve special attention because their relation to the balance sheet equation is less obvious. Focus on the balance sheet equation:

$$\text{Assets} = \text{Liabilities} + \text{Stockholders' equity} \tag{1}$$
$$\text{Assets} = \text{Liabilities} + (\text{Paid-in capital} + \text{Retained income}) \tag{2}$$

Recall from Chapter 2 that if we ignore dividends, retained income is merely the accumulated revenue less expenses. Therefore the T-accounts can be grouped as follows:

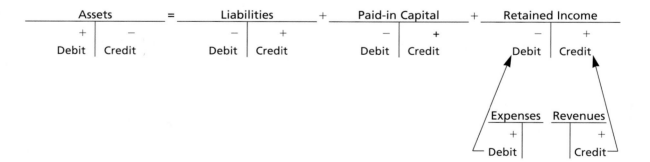

Assets have a left-hand balance; that is, debit entries increase the balance in an asset account. In contrast, liabilities, paid-in capital, and retained income have right-hand balances; credit entries increase their balances. Expense and Revenue accounts are part of Retained Income. You can think of them as separate compartments within the larger Retained Income account. The Revenue account collects items that increase retained income. Any credit to Revenue is essentially a credit to Retained Income; both revenue and retained income are increased by such a credit entry. The Expense account collects items that decrease retained income. A debit to Expense is essentially a debit to Retained Income. *While a debit entry increases expenses, it results in a decrease in retained income.*

Consider transactions 10a and 10b in detail:

10a. Transaction: Sales on credit, $160,000.
     Analysis: The asset **Accounts Receivable** is increased.
                 The stockholders' equity **Sales Revenues** is increased.
         Entry: In the journal:

Accounts receivable	160,000	
Sales revenues		160,000

Post to the ledger:

Accounts Receivable				Sales Revenues		
(6)	1,000	(9)	700		(10a)	160,000
(10a)	160,000					

The Sales Revenues account is increased by a credit, or right-side, entry in this transaction, essentially increasing the stockholders' equity account, Retained Income.

10b. Transaction: Cost of merchandise inventory sold, $100,000.
     Analysis: The asset Merchandise Inventory is decreased.
                 The stockholders' equity is decreased by creating an expense account,
                 Cost of Goods Sold, which is essentially a negative stockholders' equity
                 account.
         Entry: In the journal:

Cost of goods sold	100,000	
Merchandise inventory		100,000

Post to the ledger:

Merchandise Inventory				Cost of Goods Sold		
(3)	150,000	(7)	800	(10b)	100,000	
(4)	10,000	(10b)	100,000			

In this transaction, the expense account, Cost of Goods Sold, is increased by a debit, or left-side, entry. The effect is to decrease the stockholders' equity account, Retained Income.

Before proceeding, reflect on the logic illustrated by transactions 10a and 10b. Revenues increase stockholders' equity because the revenue accounts and the stockholders' equity accounts are right-side balance accounts. Expenses decrease stockholders' equity because expenses are left-side balance accounts. They are offsets to the normal right-side balances of stockholders' equity. Therefore *increases* in expenses are *decreases* in stockholders' equity. The following logic applies to the analysis of the $100,000 Cost of Goods Sold expense:

If only a lone stockholders' equity account is used:

Stockholders' Equity	
Decreases	Increases
(100,000)	

If two stockholders' equity accounts are used without a revenue or expense account:

Paid-in Capital		Retained Income	
Decreases	Increases	Decreases	Increases
		(100,000)	

If revenue and expense accounts are created that will eventually be summarized into a single net effect on retained income:

Expenses		Revenues	
Increases			Increases
(100,000)			

Revenue and expense accounts are really "little" stockholders' equity accounts. *That is, they are fundamentally a part of stockholders' equity.* The revenue and expense accounts are periodically summarized into one number, *net income*, which increases retained income (or *net loss*, which decreases retained income).

Exhibit 3-3 presents the rules of debit and credit and the normal balances of the accounts discussed in this section. It demonstrates the basic principles of the balance sheet equation and the double-entry accounting system:

$$\text{Left side} = \text{Right side}$$
$$\text{Debit} = \text{Credit}$$

Exhibit 3-3   Rules of Debit and Credit and Normal Balances of Accounts

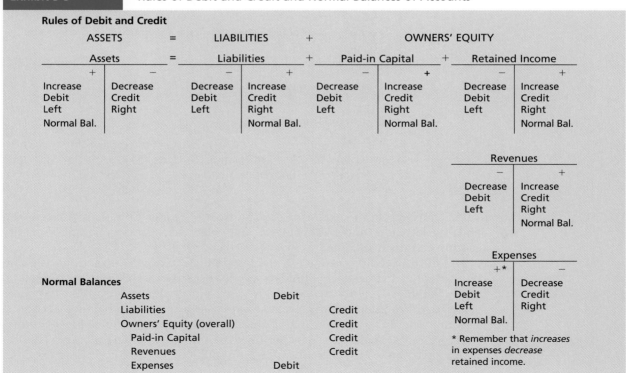

Rules of Debit and Credit

| | ASSETS | = | LIABILITIES | + | | OWNERS' EQUITY | | |

Assets		=	Liabilities		+	Paid-in Capital		+	Retained Income	
+	−		−	+		−	+		−	+
Increase	Decrease		Decrease	Increase		Decrease	Increase		Decrease	Increase
Debit	Credit		Debit	Credit		Debit	Credit		Debit	Credit
Left	Right		Left	Right		Left	Right		Left	Right
Normal Bal.				Normal Bal.			Normal Bal.			Normal Bal.

Revenues	
−	+
Decrease	Increase
Debit	Credit
Left	Right
	Normal Bal.

Expenses	
+*	−
Increase	Decrease
Debit	Credit
Left	Right
Normal Bal.	

Normal Balances

Assets	Debit	
Liabilities		Credit
Owners' Equity (overall)		Credit
Paid-in Capital		Credit
Revenues		Credit
Expenses	Debit	

* Remember that *increases* in expenses *decrease* retained income.

The exhibit also emphasizes that revenues increase stockholders' equity; hence they are recorded as credits. Because expenses decrease stockholders' equity, they are recorded as debits.

Note in Exhibit 3-3 that Retained Income is a balance sheet account. All *changes* in retained income between balance sheet dates could be recorded directly in the account. However, keeping revenues and expenses, which are changes in retained income resulting from operations, in separate accounts makes it easier to prepare an income statement. Revenues and expenses are summarized as net income (or net loss) on the income statement. In essence, the income statement provides the detailed explanation of how operations caused the retained income shown on the balance sheet to change during the period.

Prepaid Expenses and Depreciation Transactions

Recall from Chapter 2 that prepaid expenses, such as prepaid rent, and depreciation expenses relate to assets having a useful life that will expire some time in the future. Biwheels transactions 11, 12, and 13 demonstrate the analysis for journalizing and posting of prepaid rent expenses and depreciation of store equipment.

11. Transaction: Paid rent for three months in advance, $6,000.
    Analysis: The asset **Cash** is decreased.
                The asset **Prepaid Rent** is increased.
       Entry: In the journal:

Prepaid rent	6,000	
Cash		6,000

Post to the ledger:

Cash			
(1)	400,000	(3)	150,000
(2)	100,000	(5)	4,000
(9)	700	(8)	4,000
		(11)	(6,000)

Prepaid Rent		
(11)	(6,000)	

Transaction 11 represents the acquisition of the asset. It affects only asset accounts—Cash is decreased (credited) and Prepaid Rent is increased (debited). Transaction 12 represents the subsequent expiration of one-third of the asset as an expense.

12. Transaction: Recognized expiration of rental services, $2,000.
    Analysis: The asset **Prepaid Rent** is decreased.
                The negative stockholders' equity **Rent Expense** is increased.
       Entry: In the journal:

Rent expense	2,000	
Prepaid rent		2,000

Post to the ledger:

Prepaid Rent				Rent Expense	
(11)	6,000	(12)	(2,000)	(12)	(2,000)

Remember that in this transaction, the effect of the $2,000 increase in Rent Expense is a decrease in stockholders' equity on the balance sheet.

13. Transaction: Recognized depreciation, $100.
      Analysis: The asset-reduction account **Accumulated Depreciation, Store Equipment** is increased.
                      The negative stockholders' equity **Depreciation Expense** is increased.
         Entry: In the journal:

Depreciation expense	100	
Accumulated depreciation, store equipment		100

Post to the ledger:

Accumulated Depreciation, Store Equipment		Depreciation Expense	
	(13) (100)	(13) (100)	

In transaction 13, a new account, *Accumulated Depreciation*, is opened. While it is described as an *asset-reduction* account in our analysis and corresponding journal entry, a more popular term is *contra account*. A **contra account** is a separate but related account that offsets or is a deduction from a companion account. A contra account has two distinguishing features: (1) it always has a companion account, and (2) it has the opposite balance of the companion account. In our illustration, accumulated depreciation is a **contra asset** account because it is a contra account offsetting an asset. The asset and contra asset accounts on January 31, 19X2, are:

Asset:	Store equipment	$14,000
Contra asset:	Accumulated depreciation, equipment	100
Net asset:	Book value	$13,900

The **book value** or **net book value** or **carrying amount** or **carrying value** is defined as the balance of an account shown on the books, net of any contra accounts. In our example, the book value of Store Equipment is $13,900, the original acquisition cost less the contra account for accumulated depreciation.

A Note on Accumulated Depreciation

The balance sheet distinguishes between the store equipment's original cost and its accumulated depreciation. As the name implies, **accumulated depreciation** (sometimes called **allowance for depreciation**) is the cumulative sum of all depreciation recognized since the date of acquisition of the particular assets described. Published balance sheets routinely report both the original cost and accumulated depreciation.

Why is there an Accumulated Depreciation account? Why not reduce Store Equipment directly by $100? Conceptually, a direct reduction is indeed justified. However, accountants have traditionally preserved the original cost in the original asset account throughout the asset's useful life. Accountants can then readily refer to that account to learn the asset's initial cost. Such information may be sought for reports to management, government regulators, and tax authorities. Moreover the original $14,000 cost is the height of accuracy; it is a reliable, objective number. In contrast, the Accumulated Depreciation is an *estimate*, the result of a calculation whose accuracy depends heavily on the accountant's less reliable prediction of an asset's useful life.

In addition, users can estimate the average age of the assets by computing the percentage of the original cost that has been depreciated. For example, Microsoft has accumulated depreciation of $314 million on an original cost of

---

contra account A separate but related account that offsets or is a deduction from a companion account. An example is accumulated depreciation.

contra asset A contra account that offsets an asset.

book value (net book value, carrying amount, carrying value) The balance of an account shown on the books, net of any contra accounts. For example, the book value of equipment is its acquisition cost minus accumulated depreciation.

accumulated depreciation (allowance for depreciation) The cumulative sum of all depreciation recognized since the date of acquisition of the particular assets described.

plant and equipment of $1,037 million, making it 30% depreciated. Most of Microsoft's assets must be quite young, which is what would be expected for a fast-growing company. In contrast, the German diversified industrial company VIAG Aktiengesellschaft has accumulated depreciation of DM 17.1 billion on an original cost of DM 24.5 billion (DM stands for the German currency deutsche marks). Therefore, its assets are 17.1 ÷ 24.5 = 70% depreciated.

Objective 4

Prepare journal entries and post them to the ledger.

■ RECORDING TRANSACTIONS IN THE JOURNAL AND LEDGER

Exhibit 3-4 shows the formal journal entries for Biwheels' transactions 4 through 13 as analyzed in the previous section. The posting reference (Post

Exhibit 3-4

General Journal of Biwheels Company

Date	Entry No.	Accounts and Explanation	Post Ref.	Debit	Credit
19X2	4	Merchandise inventory	130	10,000	
		Accounts payable	203		10,000
		Acquired inventory on credit.			
	5	Store Equipment	170	15,000	
		Cash	100		4,000
		Accounts payable	203		11,000
		Acquired store equipment for cash plus credit.			
		(This is an example of a *compound journal entry*,			
		whereby more than two accounts are affected by			
		the same transaction.)			
	6	Accounts receivable	120	1,000	
		Store equipment	170		1,000
		Sold store equipment to business neighbor.			
	7	Accounts payable	203	800	
		Merchandise inventory	130		800
		Returned some inventory to supplier.			
	8	Accounts payable	203	4,000	
		Cash	100		4,000
		Payments to creditors.			
	9	Cash	100	700	
		Accounts receivable	120		700
		Collections from debtors.			
	10a	Accounts receivable	120	160,000	
		Sales	500		160,000
		Sales to customers on credit.			
	10b	Cost of goods sold	600	100,000	
		Merchandise inventory	130		100,000
		To record the cost of inventory sold.			
	11	Prepaid rent	140	6,000	
		Cash	100		6,000
		Payment of rent in advance.			
	12	Rent expense	601	2,000	
		Prepaid rent	140		2,000
		Recognize expiration of rental service.			
	13	Depreciation expense	602	100	
		Accumulated depreciation, store equipment	170A		100
		Recognize depreciation for January.			

Ref.) column uses the account numbers from the Biwheels chart of accounts given earlier in this chapter. These account numbers also appear on each account in the Biwheels general ledger.

Exhibit 3-5 shows the Biwheels general ledger in T-account form. Pause and trace each of the following journal entries to its posting in the general ledger:

1. Initial investment
2. Loan from bank
3. Acquire merchandise inventory for cash
4. Acquire merchandise inventory on credit
5. Acquire store equipment for cash plus credit
6. Sale of equipment on credit
7. Return of merchandise inventory for credit

8. Payments to creditors
9. Collections from debtors
10a. Sales on credit
10b. Cost of merchandise inventory sold
11. Pay rent in advance
12. Recognize expiration of rental services
13. Recognize depreciation

It is customary *not* to use dollar signs in either the journal or the ledger. Note too that negative numbers are never used in the journal or the ledger; the effect on the account is conveyed by the side on which the number appears.

In the ledger the account balance may be kept as a running balance, or it may be updated from time to time as desired. There are many acceptable techniques for updating. Accountants' preferences vary. The double horizontal lines in Exhibit 3-5 mean that all postings above the double lines are summarized as a single balance immediately below the double lines. Therefore all amounts above the double lines should be ignored for purposes of computing the next updated balance. (Many accountants prefer to use single horizontal lines instead of the double lines used in this book.)

The accounts without double lines in Exhibit 3-5 contain a lone number. This number automatically serves also as the ending balance. For example, the Note Payable entry of $100,000 also serves as the ending balance for the account.

trial balance A list of all accounts with their balances.

■ PREPARING THE TRIAL BALANCE

Once journal entries have been posted to the ledger, the next step in the process of recording transactions is the preparation of a **trial balance**. A trial balance is a list of all accounts with their balances. The word *trial* was well chosen; the list is prepared as a *test* or *check* before proceeding further. Thus the purpose of the trial balance is twofold: (1) to help check on accuracy of posting by proving whether the total debits equal the total credits, and (2) to establish a convenient summary of balances in all accounts for the preparation of formal financial statements. The trial balance is an internal report that helps accountants to prepare financial statements. The public sees only the published financial statements, not the trial balance.

Exhibit 3-5

General Ledger of
Biwheels Company

Assets	Liabilities and Stockholders' Equity
(Increases on left, decreases on right)	*(Decreases on left, increases on right)*

Cash — Account No. 100

(1)	400,000	(3)	150,000
(2)	100,000	(5)	4,000
(9)	700	(8)	4,000
		(11)	6,000
1/31 Bal. 336,700			

Accounts Receivable   120

(6)	1,000	(9)	700
(10a)	160,000		
1/31 Bal. 160,300			

Merchandise Inventory   130

(3)	150,000	(7)	800
(4)	10,000	(10b)	100,000
1/31 Bal. 59,200			

Prepaid Rent   140

(11)	6,000	(12)	2,000
1/31 Bal. 4,000			

Store Equipment   170

(5)	15,000	(6)	1,000
1/31 Bal. 14,000			

**Accumulated Depreciation,
Store Equipment   170A**

		(13)	100

Note Payable   202

		(2)	100,000

Accounts Payable   203

(7)	800	(4)	10,000
(8)	4,000	(5)	11,000
		1/31 Bal. 16,200	

Expense and Revenue Accounts

Cost of Goods Sold   600

(10b)	100,000

Rent Expense   601

(12)	2,000

Depreciation Expense   602

(13)	100

Paid-in Capital   300

		(1)	400,000

Retained Income   400

	1/31 Bal. 57,900*

Sales Revenues   500

		(10a)	160,000

* The details of the revenue and expense accounts appear in the income statement. Their net effect is then transferred to a single account, Retained Income, in the balance sheet. In this case, $160,000 − $100,000 − $2,000 − $100 = $57,900$. The procedures for accomplishing this transfer, called "closing the books," are explained in Chapter 5.

Note: An ending balance is shown on the side of the account with the larger total.

A trial balance may be taken at any time the accounts are up to date, for example, on January 2, 19X2, after the first three transactions of Biwheels:

Biwheels Company
Trial Balance
January 2, 19X2

Account Number	Account Title	Balance Debit	Credit
100	Cash	$350,000	
130	Merchandise inventory	150,000	
202	Note payable		$100,000
300	Paid-in capital		$400,000
	Total	$500,000	$500,000

Obviously, the trial balance becomes more detailed (and more essential) when there are many more accounts.

Exhibit 3-6 shows the trial balance of the general ledger in Exhibit 3-5. As shown, the trial balance is normally prepared with the balance sheet accounts listed first, in the order of assets, liabilities, and stockholders' equity. These are followed by the income statement accounts, Revenues and Expenses. Note that the last stockholders' equity account listed, Retained Income, has no balance here because it was zero at the start of the period in our example. The revenues and expenses for the current period that are on the list constitute the change in retained income for the current period. When the accountant prepares a formal balance sheet, the revenue and expense accounts will be deleted and their net effect will be added to the Retained Income account.

Exhibit 3-6

Biwheels Company
Trial Balance
January 31, 19X2

	Debits	Credits
Cash	$336,700	
Accounts receivable	160,300	
Merchandise inventory	59,200	
Prepaid rent	4,000	
Store equipment	14,000	
Accumulated depreciation, store equipment		$ 100
Note payable		100,000
Accounts payable		16,200
Paid-in capital		400,000
Retained income		0 *
Sales revenues		160,000
Cost of goods sold	100,000	
Rent expense	2,000	
Depreciation expense	100	
Total	$676,300	$676,300

* Of course, if a Retained Income balance existed at the start of the accounting period, it would appear here. However, in our example Retained Income was zero at the start of the period.

As can be seen, the trial balance assures the accountant that the debits and credits are equal. It is also the springboard for the preparation of the balance sheet and the income statement, as shown in Exhibit 3-7. The income statement accounts are summarized later as a single number, net income, which then becomes part of Retained Income in the formal balance sheet.

Exhibit 3-7

Trial Balance, Balance Sheet, and Income Statement

Biwheels Company
Trial Balance
January 31, 19X2

	Debits	Credits
Cash	$336,700	
Accounts receivable	160,300	
Merchandise inventory	59,200	
Prepaid rent	4,000	
Store equipment	14,000	
Accumulated depreciation, store equipment		$ 100
Note payable		100,000
Accounts payable		16,200
Paid-in capital		400,000
Retained income		0
Sales revenues		160,000
Cost of goods sold	100,000	
Rent expense	2,000	
Depreciation expense	100	
Total	$676,300	$676,300

Biwheels Company
Balance Sheet
January 31, 19X2

Assets			Liabilities and Stockholders' Equity		
Cash		$336,700	**Liabilities:**		
Accounts receivable		160,300	Note payable		$100,000
Merchandise inventory		59,200	Accounts payable		16,200
Prepaid rent		4,000	Total liabilities		$116,200
Store equipment	14,000		**Stockholders' equity:**		
Less accumulated depreciation	100	13,900	Paid-in capital	$400,000	
			Retained income	57,900	
			Total stockholders' equity		457,900
Total assets		$574,100	Total liabilities and stockholders' equity		$574,100

Biwheels Company
Income Statement
For the Month Ended January 31, 19X2

Sales revenues		$160,000
Deduct expenses:		
Cost of goods sold	$100,000	
Rent	2,000	
Depreciation	100	
Total expenses		102,100
Net income		$ 57,900

107

While the trial balance helps alert the accountant to possible errors, a trial balance may balance even when there are recording errors. For example, a $10,000 cash receipt on account may erroneously be recorded as $1,000. Then both Cash and Accounts Receivable would be in error by offsetting amounts of $9,000. Another example would be the recording of a $10,000 cash receipt on account as a credit to Sales Revenues rather than as a credit reducing Accounts Receivable. Sales Revenues and Accounts Receivable would both be overstated by $10,000. Nevertheless, the trial balance would still show total debits equal to total credits.

■ EFFECTS OF ERRORS

Objective 6

Correct erroneous entries and describe how errors affect accounts.

When a journal entry contains an error, the entry can be erased or crossed out and corrected—if the error is discovered immediately. However, if the error is detected later, typically after posting to ledger accounts, the accountant makes a *correcting entry*, as distinguished from a correct entry. Consider the following examples:

1. A repair expense was erroneously debited to Equipment on December 27. The error is discovered on December 31:

CORRECT ENTRY

12/27 Repair Expense	500	
Cash		500

ERRONEOUS ENTRY

12/27 Equipment	500	
Cash		500

CORRECTING ENTRY

12/31 Repair Expense	500	
Equipment		500

The correcting entry shows a credit to Equipment to cancel or offset the erroneous debit to Equipment. Moreover, the entry debits Repair Expense correctly. Notice that the credit to Cash was correct and therefore was not changed.

2. A collection on account was erroneously credited to Sales on November 2. The error is discovered on November 28:

CORRECT ENTRY

11/2 Cash	3,000	
Accounts Receivable		3,000

ERRONEOUS ENTRY

11/2 Cash	3,000	
Sales		3,000

CORRECTING ENTRY

11/28 Sales	3,000	
Accounts Receivable		3,000

The debit to Sales in the correcting entry offsets the incorrect credit to Sales in the erroneous entry. The credit to Accounts Receivable in the correcting entry places the collected amount where it belongs. The debit to Cash is unaffected by the correcting entry.

Some Errors Are Counterbalanced

Accountants' errors can affect a variety of items, including revenues and expenses for a given period. Some errors are counterbalanced by offsetting errors in the ordinary bookkeeping process in the next period. Such errors misstate net income in both periods, but they only affect the balance sheet of the first period, not the second.

Consider a payment of $1,000 in December 19X1 for rent. Suppose this was for January 19X2's rent. Instead of recording it as prepaid rent, the payment was listed as Rent Expense:

INCORRECT ENTRY

December 19X1 Rent expense	1,000	
Cash		1,000
One month's rent.		

CORRECT ENTRY

December 19X1 Prepaid rent	1,000	
Cash		1,000
Payment for January 19X2's rent.		
January 19X2 Rent Expense	1,000	
Prepaid rent		1,000
Expiration of January's rent.		

The effects of this counterbalancing error would (1) overstate rent expense for the first year (which understates pretax income) and understate year-end assets by $1,000 and (2) understate rent expense for the second year (which overstates income by $1,000). These errors have no effect on the second year's ending assets. The *total* of the incorrect pretax incomes for the two years would be identical with the *total* of the correct pretax incomes for the two years. The retained income balance at the end of the second year would be correct on a pretax basis.

Some Errors Are Not Counterbalanced

Accountants' errors that are undetected can affect a variety of accounts. As we have just seen, some errors may be counterbalanced in the ordinary course of the next period's transactions. However, other errors may not be counterbalanced in the ordinary bookkeeping process. Until specific correcting entries are made, all subsequent balance sheets will be in error.

For example, overlooking a depreciation expense of $2,000 in *one year only* (1) would overstate pretax income, assets, and retained income by $2,000 in that year, and (2) would continue to overstate assets and retained income on successive balance sheets for the life of the fixed asset. But observe that pretax income for each subsequent year would not be affected unless the same error is committed again.

■ INCOMPLETE RECORDS

Accountants must sometimes construct financial statements from incomplete data. For example, documents may be stolen, destroyed, or lost. T-accounts help organize an accountant's thinking and aid the discovery of unknown amounts. For example, suppose the proprietor of a local sports shop asks you to prepare an income statement for 19X5. She provides the following accurate but incomplete information:

List of customers who owe money:	
December 31, 19X4	$ 4,000
December 31, 19X5	6,000
Cash receipts from customers during 19X5	
appropriately credited to customer's accounts	280,000

You want to compute revenue (sales) on the accrual basis. Assume that all sales were made on account. Shortcuts may be available, but the following steps demonstrate a general approach to the reconstruction of incomplete accounts:

Step 1: Enter all known items into the key T-account. Knowledge of the usual components of such an account is essential. Let S equal sales on account. We know that credit sales are debited to Accounts Receivable:

Accounts Receivable			
Bal. 12/31/X4	4,000	Collections	280,000
Sales	S		
Total debits	(4,000+S)	Total credits	280,000
Bal. 12/31/X5	6,000		

Step 2: Find the unknown. Simple arithmetic will often suffice; however, the following solution illustrates the algebraic nature of the relationships in an asset T-account:

$$\text{Total debits} - \text{Total credits} = \text{Balance}$$
$$(4{,}000 + S) - \quad 280{,}000 = 6{,}000$$
$$S = 6{,}000 + 280{,}000 - 4{,}000$$
$$S = 282{,}000$$

Obviously, the analyses become more complicated if more entries have affected a particular account. Nevertheless, the key idea is to fill in the account with all known debits, credits, and balances. Then solve for the unknown.

■ DATA PROCESSING AND COMPUTERS

data processing
The totality of the procedures used to record, analyze, store, and report on chosen activities.

Data processing is a general term that usually means the totality of the procedures used to record, analyze, store, and report on chosen activities. An accounting system is a data-processing system. For instructional ease, most introductory accounting textbooks focus on the manual (pen-and-ink) methods that were once used in all businesses. Today almost all organizations use advanced technology, ranging from a simple cash register to bar-code scanners at grocery store checkouts to massive computer systems that automatically record and bill billions of telephone transactions per month.

Objective 8

Understand the significance of computers in data processing.

The physical forms of journals and ledgers are generally magnetic tape or disks or some other form of computer record, not paper. Nevertheless, whatever their form, journals and ledgers remain the backbone of accounting systems. Each transaction can be journalized by entering the appropriate account numbers and amounts into a computer. The computer then does the posting to the ledger. If managers desire, they can have a new balance sheet each day.

The microcomputer has enabled small organizations to process data more efficiently than ever. When you check out at a pharmacy or clothing store, the cash register often does more than just record a sale. It may also record a decrease in inventory. It may activate an order to a supplier if the inventory level is low. If a sale is on credit, the machine may check a customer's credit limit, update the accounts receivable, and eventually prepare monthly statements for mailing to the customer.

Automation has decreased data processing costs. Consider the oil companies. Amoco Oil Company once received 650,000 separate sales slips daily. But today most credit sales are recorded by computers reading the magnetic strips on credit cards. Many stations have the card-reading equipment built into the gasoline pumps, eliminating the need for sales clerks. Information about each credit sale is electronically submitted to a central computer, which prepares all billing documents and financial statements. Millions of transactions are recorded automatically into the general journal without any paperwork or keyboard entry. Imagine the increase in accuracy in addition to the savings in time and money.

Computers Have Changed Accounting

Midway through your first experience of posting a pageful of journal entries to the ledger, you probably thought, "Couldn't a computer do this?" Yes, computers can and do post journal entries. Data entry and sorting were among the first large-scale uses of computers. Herman Hollerith, founder of one of the companies that eventually combined to form IBM, used punch cards and a forerunner of the computer to tabulate data as early as the 1890 U.S. census.

During World War II intricate calculations such as those used to design the atomic bomb at Los Alamos spawned development of electronic computers. Early computers primarily solved complex scientific calculations, such as the differential equations needed to guide a missile toward a moving airplane.

At first, computers were too expensive for routine business data processing and accounting. However, since 1950, the cost of computing has been cut in half approximately every three years. By the late 1970s, even some small businesses used computers. Doctors used them for billing; bowling alleys used them for tabulating league standings; and many small businesses did payrolls and general accounting on computers. But these computers were primitive by today's standards. They offered only 16 kilobytes of internal memory but nevertheless cost from $15,000 to $30,000.

By the mid-1990s a small business could buy a computer with more than 100 megabytes of memory for less than $1,000. The computing power that once filled a room can now easily be carried in a briefcase. Combined with the appropriate software, such a computer is capable of managing the accounting functions of the business. Because computers can now do the routine bookkeeping functions, some students wonder why they should study debits, credits, journals, and ledgers. It is useful to remember what has been said about computers from the beginning: The power of a computer depends on the knowledge and abilities of the operator. ■

Sources: S. Engelbourg, International Business Machines: A Business History *(Arno Press, 1976); F. M. Fisher, J. W. McKie, and R. B. Mancke,* IBM and the U.S. Data Processing Industry: An Economic History *(Praeger, 1983); L. G. Tesler, "Networked Computing in the 1990s,"* Scientific American *(September, 1991), p. 86.*

■ MORE ON GENERALLY ACCEPTED ACCOUNTING PRINCIPLES

Objective 9

Explain the meaning of the concepts of going concern, materiality, and cost-benefit.

Basic concepts of accounting theory are too vast to consume in one gulp, so they are being introduced gradually as we proceed. Previous chapters discussed some basic concepts of accounting, such as entity, recognition, matching and cost recovery, and stable monetary unit. We now consider three other major ideas that are part of the body of generally accepted accounting principles: going concern, materiality, and cost-benefit.

Going Concern Convention

going concern convention (continuity convention) The assumption that in all ordinary situations an entity persists indefinitely.

The **going concern convention**, or **continuity convention**, is the assumption that in all ordinary situations an entity persists indefinitely. This notion implies that existing *resources*, such as plant assets, *will be used* to fulfill the general purposes of a continuing entity *rather than sold* in tomorrow's real estate or equipment markets. It also implies that existing liabilities will be paid at maturity in an orderly manner.

For example, suppose some old specialized equipment has a book value (that is, original cost less accumulated depreciation) of $10,000, a replacement cost of $12,000, and a realizable value of $7,000 on the used-equipment market. The going concern convention is often cited as the justification for adhering to the $10,000 book value (or acquisition cost less depreciation) as the primary basis for valuing such an asset. Some critics believe that replacement cost ($12,000) or realizable values upon liquidation ($7,000) would be more informative. Defenders of using $10,000 as an appropriate asset valuation argue that a going concern will generally use the asset as originally intended to produce revenue over its useful life. Allocating historical cost over time provides an objective matching of revenue and expense. Other values are not as germane because replacement or disposal will not occur en masse as of the balance sheet date. Moreover, replacement costs and realizable values are less objective, less easily determined, and likely to be estimated differently by different parties. They do not arise from a completed, arms-length transaction.

The opposite view of this going concern, or continuity, convention is an immediate-liquidation assumption whereby all items on a balance sheet are valued at the amounts appropriate if the entity were to be liquidated in piecemeal fashion within a few days or months. This liquidation approach to valuation is usually used only when the probability is high that the company will be liquidated.

Materiality Convention

materiality convention The concept that states that a financial statement item is material if its omission or misstatement would tend to mislead the reader of the financial statements under consideration.

Because accounting is a practical art, the practitioner often tempers accounting reports by applying judgments about *materiality*. The **materiality convention** asserts that a financial statement item is *material* if its omission or misstatement would tend to mislead the reader of the financial statements under consideration.

Many acquisitions that should theoretically be recorded as assets are immediately written off as expenses because of their insignificance. For example, many corporations require the immediate write-off to expense of all outlays under a specified minimum such as $100, regardless of the useful life of the asset acquired. For example, coat hangers may last indefinitely but never appear in the balance sheet as assets. The resulting $100 understatement of assets and stockholders' equity is considered too trivial to worry about. In general, GAAP need not be applied to immaterial items. The FASB regularly includes the following statement in its standards: "The provisions of this statement need not be applied to immaterial items."

When is an item material? There will probably never be a universal, clear-cut answer. What is trivial to General Motors may be material to Evelyn's Boutique. A working rule is that an item is material if its proper accounting would probably affect the decision of a knowledgeable party. In sum, materiality is an important convention. But it is difficult to use anything other than prudent judgment to tell whether an item is material.

Cost-Benefit Criterion

cost-benefit criterion As a system is changed, its expected additional benefits should exceed its expected additional costs.

Accounting systems vary in complexity, from the minimum crude records kept by a small business to satisfy government authorities to the sophisticated budgeting and feedback schemes that are at the heart of management planning and control in a huge, multinational corporation. The **cost-benefit criterion** means that as a system is changed, its expected additional benefits should exceed its expected additional costs. Often the benefits are difficult to measure, but this criterion at least implicitly underlies the decisions about the design and change of accounting systems. Reluctance to adopt suggestions for new ways of measuring financial position and performance is often due to the fact that the apparent benefits do not exceed the obvious costs of gathering and interpreting the information.

The FASB uses a cost-benefit criterion in judging new standards. It safeguards the cost-effectiveness of its standards by (1) assuring that a standard does not "impose costs on the many for the benefit of a few," and (2) seeking alternative ways of handling an issue that are "less costly and only slightly less efficient."

Room for Judgment

Accounting is commonly misunderstood to be a precise discipline that produces exact measurements of a company's financial position and performance. As a result, many individuals regard accountants as mechanical tabulators who grind out financial reports after processing an imposing amount of detail in accordance with stringent predetermined rules. Accountants do take methodical steps with masses of data, but their rules of measurement require judgment. As business practices evolve, new types of transactions and contracts must be incorporated into the accounts. Managers and accountants must make judgments, guided by the basic concepts, techniques, and conventions called generally accepted accounting principles. The basic concepts that guide these judgments will become clearer as these concepts are applied in future chapters.

Summary Problems for Your Review

Problem One

Do you agree with the following statements? Explain.

1. To charge an account means to credit it.
2. One person's debit is another person's credit.

3. A charge account may be credited.
4. My credit is my most valuable asset.
5. When I give credit, I debit my customer's account.

Solution to Problem One

Remember that in accounting, *debit* means left side and *credit* means right side.

1. No. *Charge* and *debit* and *left side* are synonyms.
2. Yes, in certain situations. The clearest example is probably the sale of merchandise on open account. The buyer's account payable would have a credit (right) balance, and the seller's account receivable would have a debit (left) balance.
3. Yes. When collections are received, Accounts Receivable is credited (right).
4. Note that "charge" as used in "charge account" is not a synonym for debit. As used in this statement, "my credit" refers to "my ability to borrow," not which side of a balance sheet is affected. "My ability to borrow" may indeed be a valuable right, but the accountant does not recognize that ability (as such) as an asset to be measured and reported in the balance sheet. When borrowing occurs, the borrower's assets are increased (debited, increased on the left side) and the liabilities are increased (credited, increased on the right side).
5. Yes. Accounts Receivable is debited (left). "Give credit" in this context means that the seller is allowing the customer to defer payment. The corresponding account payable on the customer's accounting records will be increased (credited, right).

Problem Two

The trial balance of Hassan Used Auto Co. on March 31, 19X1, follows:

Account Title	Balance	
	Debit	Credit
Cash	$ 10,000	
Accounts receivable	20,000	
Automobile inventory	100,000	
Accounts payable		$ 3,000
Notes payable		70,000
Hassan, owner's equity		57,000
Total	$130,000	$130,000

The Hassan business entity is not incorporated; it is a proprietorship. The equity account used here is Hassan, Owner's Equity; in practice, it is often called Hassan, Capital.

Hassan rented operating space and equipment on a month-to-month basis. During April, the business had the following summarized transactions:

a. Hassan invested an additional $20,000 cash in the business.
b. Collected $10,000 on accounts receivable.
c. Paid $2,000 on accounts payable.

d. Sold autos for $120,000 cash.
e. Cost of autos sold was $70,000.
f. Replenished inventory for $60,000 cash.
g. Paid rent expense in cash, $14,000.
h. Paid utilities in cash, $1,000.
i. Paid selling expense in cash, $30,000.
j. Paid interest expense in cash, $1,000.

Required

1. Open the following T-accounts in the general ledger: cash; accounts receivable; automobile inventory; accounts payable; notes payable; Hassan, owner's equity; sales; cost of goods sold; rent expense; utilities expense; selling expense; and interest expense. Enter the March 31 balances in the appropriate accounts.
2. Journalize transactions *a–j* and post the entries to the ledger. Key entries by transaction letter.
3. Prepare the trial balance at April 30, 19X1.
4. Prepare an income statement for April. Ignore income taxes.

Solution to Problem Two

The solutions to requirements 1 through 4 are in Exhibits 3-8 through 3-11. The opening balances are placed in the appropriate accounts in Exhibit 3-9; the journal entries are prepared in Exhibit 3-8 and posted to the ledger in Exhibit 3-9; a trial balance is prepared in Exhibit 3-10; and the income statement is shown in Exhibit 3-11.

Exhibit 3-8

Hassan Used
Auto Co.
General Journal

Entry	Accounts and Explanation	Post Ref.*	Debit	Credit
a.	Cash	✓	20,000	
	Hassan, owner's equity	✓		20,000
	Investment in business by Hassan.			
b.	Cash	✓	10,000	
	Accounts receivable	✓		10,000
	Collected cash on accounts.			
c.	Accounts payable	✓	2,000	
	Cash	✓		2,000
	Disbursed cash on accounts owed to others.			
d.	Cash	✓	120,000	
	Sales (or Sales Revenue)	✓		120,000
	Sales for cash.			
e.	Cost of goods sold	✓	70,000	
	Automobile inventory	✓		70,000
	Cost of inventory that was sold to customers.			
f.	Automobile inventory	✓	60,000	
	Cash	✓		60,000
	Replenished inventory.			
g.	Rent expense	✓	14,000	
	Cash	✓		14,000
	Paid April rent.			

continued

Entry	Accounts and Explanation	Post Ref.*	Debit	Credit
h.	Utilities expense	✓	1,000	
	Cash	✓		1,000
	Paid April utilities.			
i.	Selling expense	✓	30,000	
	Cash	✓		30,000
	Paid April selling expenses.			
j.	Interest expense	✓	1,000	
	Cash	✓		1,000
	Paid April interest expense.			

* Ordinarily, account numbers are used to denote specific posting references. Otherwise check marks are used to indicate that the entry has been posted to the general ledger.

Exhibit 3-9

Hassan Used
Auto Co.
General Ledger

Cash				Accounts Payable				Hassan, Owner's Equity		
Bal.*	10,000	(c)	2,000	(c)	2,000	Bal.*	3,000		Bal.*	57,000
(a)	20,000	(f)	60,000			Bal.	1,000		(a)	20,000
(b)	10,000	(g)	14,000						Bal.	77,000
(d)	120,000	(h)	1,000	**Notes Payable**						
	160,000	(i)	30,000			Bal.*	70,000		**Sales**	
		(j)	1,000						(d)	120,000
			108,000 †	**Cost of Goods Sold**						
Bal.	52,000			(e)	70,000				**Rent Expense**	
								(g)	14,000	
Accounts Receivable				**Selling Expense**						
Bal.*	20,000	(b)	10,000	(i)	30,000				**Interest Expense**	
Bal.	10,000							(j)	1,000	
				Utilities Expense						
Automobile Inventory				(h)	1,000					
Bal.*	100,000	(e)	70,000							
(f)	60,000									
Bal.	90,000									

* Balances denoted with an asterisk are as of March 31; balances without asterisks are as of April 30. A lone number in any account also serves as an ending balance.

† Subtotals are included in the Cash account. They are not an essential part of T-accounts. However, when an account contains many postings, subtotals ease the checking of arithmetic.

Exhibit 3-10

Hassan Used
Auto Co.
Trial Balance
April 30, 19X1

Account Title	Balance	
	Debit	Credit
Cash	$ 52,000	
Accounts receivable	10,000	
Automobile inventory	90,000	
Accounts payable		$ 1,000
Notes payable		70,000
Hassan, owner's equity		77,000
Sales		120,000
Cost of goods sold	70,000	
Rent expense	14,000	
Utilities expense	1,000	
Selling expense	30,000	
Interest expense	1,000	
Total	$268,000	$268,000

Exhibit 3-11

Hassan Used
Auto Co.
Income Statement
For the Month
Ended April 30, 19X1

Sales		$120,000
Deduct expenses:		
Cost of goods sold	$70,000	
Rent expense	14,000	
Utilities expense	1,000	
Selling expense	30,000	
Interest expense	1,000	116,000
Net Income		$ 4,000

Problem Three

A recent annual report of Kobe Steel, Ltd., one of the world's largest producers of iron and steel, showed (in billions of Japanese yen):

Property, plant, and equipment, at cost	¥2,062	
Accumulated depreciation	1,051	¥1,011

Required

1. Open T-accounts for (a) Property, Plant, and Equipment, (b) Accumulated Depreciation, and (c) Depreciation Expense. Enter the above amounts therein.
2. Assume that during the ensuing month no additional property, plant, and equipment were acquired, but depreciation expense of ¥ 80 billion was incurred. Prepare the journal entry, and post to the T-accounts.
3. Show how Kobe Steel would present its property, plant, and equipment accounts in its balance sheet after the journal entry in requirement 2.

Solution to Problem Three

1. Amounts are in billions of Japanese yen.

Property, Plant, and Equipment		Accumulated Depreciation, Property, Plant, and Equipment	
2,062			1,051
		(2)	80
		Bal.	1,131

Depreciation Expense	
(2)	80

2. Depreciation expense   80
    Accumulated depreciation, property, plant,
        and equipment   80

3. The plant and equipment section would appear as follows:
    Property, plant, and equipment, at cost   ¥2,062
    Accumulated depreciation   1,131   ¥931

Highlights to Remember

The accountant's recording process concentrates on the journal and the general ledger. The journal provides a chronological record of transactions, whereas the general ledger provides a dated summary of the effects of the transactions on all accounts, account by account. This book uses a simplified version of general ledger accounts called T-accounts. Accountants at all levels use T-accounts to help think through complex transactions.

Accountants use the terms *debit* and *credit* repeatedly. Remember that debit simply means "left side" and credit means "right side."

Journal entries are a convenient, simple way to analyze a transaction. Journal entries are always posted to the general ledger.

Revenues and expenses are essentially stockholders' equity accounts. Don't be confused by the fact that both assets and expenses normally have debit balances. Expenses have debit balances because they are reductions in stockholders' equity. In other words, expenses are a negative component of stockholders' equity.

Trial balances are internal reports that are used for detecting errors in the accounts and to aid in preparing financial statements. Trial balances that fail to balance are inevitably the result of careless or rushed journalizing or posting. The good news is that the out-of-balance condition lets you know that an error has been made.

Basic concepts in accounting are difficult to digest in one gulp. Therefore, they are introduced gradually in this book. Going concern, materiality, and cost-benefit are important concepts introduced in this chapter. All three concepts require accountants to exercise judgment.

Despite precautions, errors sometimes occur in accounting entries. Such errors should be corrected when discovered, adjusting account balances so that they equal the amounts that would have existed if the correct entry had been made.

T-accounts help organize thinking and aid in the discovery of unknown amounts. The key idea is to fill in the related accounts with all known debits, credits, and balances, and then solve for the unknown amounts.

Pause before proceeding. There is no shortcut to learning debits and credits. Learning occurs by solving homework problems. Whether such homework is satisfying depends largely on your approach. Before you prepare journal entries, think hard about the relationships among the accounts. The mechanics of the journal and the ledger then become much easier to understand.

Accounting Vocabulary

accumulated depreciation, *p. 102*
allowance for depreciation, *p. 102*
balance, *p. 90*
book of original entry, *p. 93*
book value, *p. 102*
carrying amount, *p. 102*
carrying value, *p. 102*
charge, *p. 91*
chart of accounts, *p. 94*
compound entry, *p. 97*
continuity convention, *p. 112*

contra account, *p. 102*
contra asset, *p. 102*
cost-benefit criterion, *p. 113*
credit, *p. 91*
cross-referencing, *p. 95*
data processing, *p. 110*
debit, *p. 91*
double-entry system, *p. 88*
general journal, *p. 93*
general ledger, *p. 89*
going concern convention, *p. 112*

journal entry, *p. 94*
journalizing, *p. 93*
keying of entries, *p. 95*
ledger, *p. 89*
materiality convention, *p. 112*
net book value, *p. 102*
posting, *p. 95*
simple entry, *p. 96*
source document, *p. 91*
T-account, *p. 89*
trial balance, *p. 104*

Assignment Material

Questions

3-1. "Double entry means that amounts are shown in the journal and ledger." Do you agree? Explain.

3-2. "Increases in cash and stockholders' equity are shown on the right side of their respective accounts." Do you agree? Explain.

3-3. "Debit and credit are used as verbs, adjectives, or nouns." Give examples of how debit may be used in these three meanings.

3-4. Name three source documents for transactions.

3-5. "The ledger is the major book of original entry because it is more essential than the journal." Do you agree? Explain.

3-6. "Revenue and expense accounts are really little stockholders' equity accounts." Explain.

3-7. "Accumulated depreciation is the total depreciation expense for the year." Do you agree? Explain.

3-8. Give two synonyms for book value.

3-9. "A trial balance assumes that the amounts in the financial statements are correct." Do you agree? Explain.

3-10. "If debits equal credits in a trial balance, you can be assured that no errors were made." Do you agree? Explain.

3-11. "In double-entry accounting, errors are not a problem because they are self-correcting." Do you agree? Explain.

3-12. Are all data processing systems computerized? Explain.

3-13. "This idea implies that existing equipment will be used rather than sold in tomorrow's equipment markets." What is the name of this idea?

3-14. "What is trivial to General Electric may be significant to Don's Hobby Shop." What idea is being described?

Exercises

3-15   Debits and Credits

For each of the following accounts, indicate whether it normally possesses a debit or a credit balance. Use *Dr.* or *Cr.*:

1. Sales
2. Accounts payable
3. Accounts receivable
4. Supplies expense
5. Supplies inventory

6. Retained income
7. Depreciation expense
8. Dividends payable
9. Paid-in capital
10. Subscription revenue

3-16   Debits and Credits

Indicate for each of the following transactions whether the account *named in parentheses* is to be debited or credited:

1. Bought merchandise on account (Merchandise Inventory), $4,000.
2. Paid Fassi Associates $3,000 owed them (Accounts Payable).
3. Received cash from customers on accounts due (Accounts Receivable), $1,000.
4. Bought merchandise on open account (Accounts Payable), $5,000.
5. Sold merchandise (Merchandise Inventory), $1,000.
6. Borrowed money from a bank (Notes Payable), $10,000.

3-17   Debits and Credits

For the following transactions, indicate whether the accounts *in parentheses* are to be debited or credited. Use *Dr. or Cr.*:

1. Merchandise was sold on credit (Accounts Receivable).
2. Dividends were declared and paid in cash (Retained Income).
3. A county government received property taxes (Tax Revenue).
4. Wages were paid to employees (Wages Expense).
5. A newsstand sold magazines (Sales Revenue).
6. A three-year fire insurance policy was acquired (Prepaid Expenses).

3-18   True or False

Use *T* or *F* to indicate whether each of the following statements is true or false:

1. Repayments of bank loans should be charged to Notes Payable and credited to Cash.
2. Asset debits should be on the left and liability debits should be on the right.
3. Inventory purchases on account should be credited to Accounts Payable and debited to an expense account.
4. In general, all credit entries are recorded on the right side of accounts and represent decreases in the account balances.
5. Cash collections of accounts receivable should be recorded as debits to Cash and credits to Accounts Receivable.
6. Credit purchases of equipment should be debited to Equipment and charged to Accounts Payable.
7. In general, entries on the right side of asset accounts represent decreases in the account balances.
8. Increases in liability and revenue accounts should be recorded on the left side of the accounts.
9. Decreases in retained income are recorded as debits.
10. Both increases in assets and decreases in liabilities are recorded on the debit sides of accounts.
11. In some cases, increases in account balances are recorded on the right sides of accounts.

✓ **3-19 Matching Transaction Accounts**

Listed here are a series of accounts that are numbered for identification. Accompanying this problem are columns in which you are to write the identification numbers of the accounts affected by the transactions described. The same account may be used in several answers. For each transaction, indicate which account(s) are to be debited and which are to be credited.

1. Cash
2. Accounts receivable
3. Inventory
4. Equipment
5. Accumulated depreciation, equipment
6. Prepaid insurance
7. Accounts payable

8. Notes payable
9. Paid-in capital
10. Retained earnings
11. Sales revenues
12. Costs of goods sold
13. Operating expense

	Debit	Credit
(a) Purchased new equipment for cash plus a short-term note.	4	1, 8
(b) Made sales on credit. Inventory is accounted for as each sale is made.		
(c) Paid cash for salaries and wages for work done during the current fiscal period.		
(d) Collected cash from customers on account.		
(e) Paid some old trade bills with cash.		
(f) Purchased three-year insurance policy on credit.		
(g) Sold for cash some old equipment at cost.		
(h) Paid off note owed to bank.		
(i) Bought regular merchandise on credit.		
(j) Paid cash for inventory that arrived today.		
(k) In order to secure additional funds, 400 new shares of common stock were sold for cash.		
(l) Some insurance premiums have expired.		
(m) Recorded the entry for depreciation on equipment for the current fiscal period.		
(n) Paid cash for ad in today's *Chicago Tribune*.		

3-20 Journalizing and Posting

(Alternate is 3-21.) Prepare journal entries and post to T-accounts the following transactions of Renaldo's Catering Company:

a. Cash sales, $11,000.
b. Collections on accounts, $7,000.
c. Paid cash for wages, $3,000.
d. Acquired inventory on open account, $5,000.
e. Paid cash for janitorial services, $400.

3-21 Journalizing and Posting

(Alternate is 3-20.) Prepare journal entries and post to T-accounts the following transactions of Rita Rosen, Realtor:

a. Acquired office supplies of $1,000 on open account. Use a Supplies Inventory account.
b. Sold a house and collected a $9,000 commission on the sale. Use a Commissions Revenue account.

c.   Paid cash of $700 to a local newspaper for current advertisements.
d.   Paid $800 for a previous credit purchase of a desk.
e.   Recorded office supplies used of $300.

✓ 3-22   Reconstruct Journal Entries

(Alternate is 3-23.) Reconstruct the journal entries (omit explanations) that resulted in the postings to the following T-accounts of a consulting firm:

Cash				Equipment		Revenue from Fees	
(a) 60,000	(b) 1,000		(c) 15,000			(d)	90,000
	(c) 5,000						

Accounts Receivable		Note Payable	
(d) 90,000		(c)	10,000

Supplies Inventory		Paid-in Capital		Supplies Expense	
(b) 1,000	(e) 300		(a) 60,000	(e) 300	

3-23   Reconstruct Journal Entries

(Alternate is 3-22.) Reconstruct the journal entries (omit explanations) that resulted in the postings to the following T-accounts of a small computer retailer:

Cash				Accounts Payable		Paid-in Capital	
(a) 40,000	(e) 30,000		(e) 30,000	(b) 90,000		(a)	40,000

Accounts Receivable	
(c) 100,000	

Inventory		Cost of Goods Sold		Sales	
(b) 90,000	(d) 57,000	(d) 57,000		(c)	100,000

3-24   Effects of Errors

The bookkeeper of Hyland Legal Services included the cost of a new computer, purchased on December 30 for $15,000 and to be paid in January, as an operating expense instead of as an addition to the proper asset account. What was the effect of this error ("no effect," "overstated," or "understated"?—use symbols n, o, or u, respectively) on:

1. Operating expenses for the year ended December 31   _____
2. Profit from operations for the year   _____
3. Retained earnings as of December 31 after the books are closed _____
4. Total assets as of December 31   _____
5. Total liabilities as of December 31   _____

3-25   Effects of Errors

Assume Matheson Company is a going concern and analyze the effect of the following errors on the net profit figures for 19X1 and 19X2. Choose one of three answers: understated (u), overstated (o), or no effect (n). Problem a has been answered as an illustration.

a. EXAMPLE: Failure to adjust at end of 19X1 for prepaid rent that had expired during December 19X1. The remaining prepaid rent was charged in 19X2. 19X1: *o*; 19X2: *u*. (*Explanation*: In 19X1, expenses would be understated and profits overstated. This error would carry forward so that expenses in 19X2 would be overstated and profits understated.)

b. Omission of Depreciation on Office Machines in 19X1 only. Correct depreciation was taken in 19X2.

c. During 19X2 $300 of office supplies were purchased and debited to Office Supplies, an asset account. At the end of 19X2 only $100 worth of office supplies were left. No entry had recognized the use of $200 of office supplies during 19X2.

d. Machinery, cost price $500, bought in 19X1, was not entered in the books until paid for in 19X2. Ignore depreciation; answer in terms of the specific error described.

e. Three months' rent, paid in advance in December 19X1, for the first quarter of 19X2 was debited directly to Rent Expense in 19X1. No prepaid rent was on the books at the end of 19X1.

Problems

3-26 Account Numbers, Journal, Ledger, Trial Balance

Journalize and post the entries required by the following transactions for Kowalski Construction Company. Prepare a trial balance, April 30, 19X6. Ignore interest. Use dates, posting references, and the following account numbers:

Cash	100	Note payable	130	
Accounts receivable	101	Paid-in capital	140	
Equipment	111	Retained income	150	
Accumulated depreciation,		Revenues	200	
equipment	111A	Expenses	300, 301, etc.	
Accounts payable	120			

- April 1, 19X6. The Kowalski Construction Company was formed with $95,000 cash upon the issuance of common stock.
- April 2. Equipment was acquired for $75,000. A cash down payment of $25,000 was made. In addition, a note for $50,000 was signed.
- April 3. Sales on credit to a local hotel, $2,200.
- April 3. Supplies acquired (and used) on open account, $200.
- April 3. Wages paid in cash, $600.
- April 30. Depreciation expense for April, $1,000.

3-27 Account Numbers, T-Accounts, and Transaction Analysis

Consider the following (in thousands):

Kwality Printing
Trial Balance
December 31, 19X4

Account Number	Account Titles	Balance Debit	Credit
10	Cash	$ 50	
20	Accounts receivable	115	
21	Note receivable	100	
30	Inventory	130	
40	Prepaid insurance	12	
70	Equipment	120	

continued

Account Number	Account Titles	Balance Debit	Balance Credit
70A	Accumulated depreciation, equipment		$ 30
80	Accounts payable		135
100	Paid-in capital		60
110	Retained income		182
130	Sales		950
150	Cost of goods sold	550	
160	Wages expense	200	
170	Miscellaneous expense	80	
		$1,357	$1,357

The following information had not been considered before preparing the trial balance:

1. The note receivable was signed by a major customer. It is a three-month note dated November 1, 19X4. Interest earned during November and December was collected at 4 p.m. on December 31. The interest rate is 12% per year.
2. The Prepaid Insurance account reflects a one-year fire insurance policy acquired for cash on August 1, 19X4.
3. Depreciation for 19X4 was $15,000.
4. Wages of $13,000 were paid in cash at 5 p.m. on December 31.

Required

1. Enter the December 31 balances in a general ledger. Number the accounts. Allow room for additional T-accounts.
2. Prepare the journal entries prompted by the additional information. Show amounts in thousands.
3. Post the journal entries to the ledger. Key your postings. Create logical new account numbers as necessary.
4. Prepare a new trial balance, December 31, 19X4.

3-28   Trial Balance Errors
Consider the following trial balance (in thousands of dollars):

Delgado Auto
Parts Store
Trial Balance for the
Year Ended
December 31, 19X7

	Debit	Credit
Cash	$ 15	
Equipment	33	
Accumulated depreciation, equipment	15	
Accounts payable	42	
Accounts receivable	15	
Prepaid insurance	1	
Prepaid rent		$ 4
Inventory	129	
Paid-in capital		12
Retained income		10
Cost of goods sold	500	
Wages expense	100	
Miscellaneous expenses	80	
Advertising expense		30
Sales		788
Note payable	40	
	$970	$844

Required List and describe all the errors in the above trial balance. Be specific. On the basis of the available data, prepare a corrected trial balance.

3-29 Journal, Ledger, and Trial Balance
(Alternates are 3-31 through 3-36.) Appleton Bazaar is a retailer. The entity's balance sheet accounts had the following balances on October 31, 19X5:

Cash	$ 39,000	
Accounts receivable	90,000	
Inventory	10,000	
Prepaid rent	2,000	
Accounts payable		$ 25,000
Paid-in capital		100,000
Retained income		16,000
	$141,000	$141,000

Following is a summary of the transactions that occurred during November:

a. Collections of accounts receivable, $85,000.
b. Payments of accounts payable, $19,000.
c. Acquisitions of inventory on open account, $80,000.
d. Merchandise carried in inventory at a cost of $70,000 was sold on open account for $86,000.
e. Recognition of rent expense for November, $1,000.
f. Wages paid in cash for November, $8,000.
g. Cash dividends declared and disbursed to stockholders on November 29, $15,000.

Required 1. Prepare journal entries (in thousands of dollars).
2. Enter beginning balances in T-accounts. Post the journal entries to T-accounts. Use the transaction letters to key your postings.
3. Prepare a trial balance, November 30, 19X5.
4. Explain why accounts payable increased by so much during November.

3-30 Financial Statements
Refer to problem 3-29. Prepare a balance sheet as of November 30, 19X5, and an income statement for the month of November. Prepare a statement of retained income. Prepare the income statement first.

3-31 Journal, Ledger, and Trial Balance
(Alternates are 3-29, and 3-32 through 3-36.) The trial balance of Kim Appliance Co. on December 31, 19X4, follows:

	Balance	
Account Title	*Debit*	*Credit*
Cash	$ 25,000	
Accounts receivable	30,000	
Merchandise inventory	120,000	
Accounts payable		$ 35,000
Notes payable		80,000
Paid-in capital		29,000
Retained income		31,000
Total	$175,000	$175,000

Operating space and equipment are rented on a month-to-month basis. A summary of January transactions follows:

a. Collected $26,000 on accounts receivable.
b. Sold appliances for $70,000 cash and $40,000 on open account.
c. Cost of appliances sold was $60,000.
d. Paid $18,000 on accounts payable.
e. Replenished inventory for $63,000 on open account.
f. Paid selling expense in cash, $33,000.
g. Paid rent expense in cash, $7,000.
h. Paid interest expense in cash, $1,000.

Required

1. Open the appropriate T-accounts in the general ledger. In addition to the seven accounts listed in the trial balance of December 31, open accounts for Sales, Cost of Goods Sold, Selling Expense, Rent Expense, and Interest Expense. Enter the December 31 balances in the accounts.
2. Journalize transactions *a–h*. Post the entries to the ledger, keying by transaction letter.
3. Prepare a trial balance, January 31, 19X5.

3-32   Journal, Ledger, and Trial Balance
(Alternates are 3-29, 3-31, 3-33, 3-34, 3-35, and 3-36.) Jessica Howard owned and managed a franchise of Taco Tents, Inc. The accompanying trial balance existed on September 1, 19X5, the beginning of a fiscal year.

Howard's Taco Tent
Trial Balance
September 1, 19X5

Cash	$ 2,300	
Accounts receivable	25,200	
Merchandise inventory	77,800	
Prepaid rent	4,000	
Store equipment	21,000	
Accumulated depreciation, store equipment		$ 5,750
Accounts payable		45,000
Paid-in capital		30,000
Retained income		49,550
	$130,300	$130,300

Summarized transactions for September were:

1. Acquisitions of merchandise inventory on account, $52,000.
2. Sales for cash, $39,300.
3. Payments to creditors, $29,000.
4. Sales on account, $38,000.
5. Advertising in newspapers, paid in cash, $3,000.
6. Cost of goods sold, $40,000.
7. Collections on account, $33,000.
8. Miscellaneous expenses paid in cash, $8,000.
9. Wages paid in cash, $9,000.
10. Entry for rent expense. (Rent was paid quarterly in advance, $6,000 per quarter. Payments were due on February 1, May 1, August 1, and November 1.)
11. Depreciation of store equipment, $250.

1. Enter the September 1 balances in a general ledger.
2. Prepare journal entries for each transaction.
3. Post the journal entries to the ledger. Key your postings.
4. Prepare an income statement for September and a balance sheet as of September 30, 19X5.

3-33   Journalizing, Posting, Trial Balance
(Alternates are 3-29, 3-31, 3-32, 3-34, 3-35, and 3-36.) Alou Gardens, a retailer of garden supplies and equipment, had the accompanying balance sheet accounts, December 31, 19X3:

Assets			Liabilities and Stockholders' Equity	
Cash		$ 20,000	Accounts payable*	$111,000
Accounts receivable		39,000	Paid-in capital	40,000
Inventory		131,000	Retained income	79,000
Prepaid rent		4,000		
Store equipment	$60,000			
Less: Accumulated depreciation	24,000	36,000		
Total		$230,000	Total	$230,000

* For merchandise only.

Following is a summary of transactions that occurred during 19X4:

a. Purchases of merchandise inventory on open account, $550,000.
b. Sales, all on credit, $810,000.
c. Cost of merchandise sold to customers, $450,000.
d. On June 1, 19X4, borrowed $80,000 from a supplier. The note is payable at the end of 19X8. Interest is payable yearly on December 31 at a rate of 15% per annum.
e. Disbursed $25,000 for the rent of the store. Add to Prepaid Rent.
f. Disbursed $165,000 for wages through November.
g. Disbursed $76,000 for miscellaneous expenses such as utilities, advertising, and legal help. (Combined here to save space. Debit Miscellaneous expenses.)
h. On July 1, 19X4, lent $20,000 to the office manager. He signed a note that will mature on July 1, 19X5, together with interest at 10% per annum. Interest for 19X4 is due on December 31, 19X4.
i. Collections on accounts receivable, $690,000.
j. Payments on accounts payable $470,000.

The following entries were made on December 31, 19X4:

k. Previous rent payments applicable to 19X5 amounted to $3,000.
l. Depreciation for 19X4 was $6,000.
m. Wages earned by employees during December were paid on December 31, $5,000.
n. Interest on the loan from the supplier was disbursed.
o. Interest on the loan made to the office manager was received.

1. Prepare journal entries in thousands of dollars.
2. Post the entries to the ledger, keying your postings by transaction letter.
3. Prepare a trial balance, December 31, 19X4.

3-34   Transaction Analysis, Trial Balance

(Alternates are 3-29, 3-31, 3-32, 3-33, 3-35 and 3-36.) Tulalip Appliance Repair Service, Incorporated, had the accompanying trial balance on January 1, 19X5.

**Tulalip Appliance
Repair Service, Inc.
Trial Balance
January 1, 19X5**

Cash	$ 5,000	
Accounts receivable	4,000	
Parts inventory	2,000	
Prepaid rent	2,000	
Trucks	36,000	
Equipment	8,000	
Accumulated depreciation, trucks		$15,000
Accumulated depreciation, equipment		5,000
Accounts payable		2,800
Paid-in capital		17,000
Retained income		17,200
Total	$57,000	$57,000

During January, the following summarized transactions occurred:

Jan 2 Collected accounts receivable, $3,000.

3 Rendered services to customers for cash, $2,200 ($700 collected for parts, $1,500 for labor). Use two accounts, Parts Revenue and Labor Revenue.

3 Cost of parts used for services rendered, $300.

7 Paid legal expenses, $400 cash.

9 Acquired parts on open account, $900.

11 Paid cash for wages, $1,100.

13 Paid cash for truck repairs, $500.

15 Paid cash for utilities, $400.

19 Billed customer for services, $4,000 ($1,200 for parts and $2,800 for labor).

19 Cost of parts used for services rendered, $500.

24 Paid cash for wages, $1,300.

27 Paid cash on accounts payable, $1,500.

31 Rent expense for January, $1,000 (reduce Prepaid Rent).

31 Depreciation for January: trucks, $600; equipment, $200.

31 Paid cash to local gas station for gasoline for trucks for January, $300.

31 Paid cash for wages, $900.

Required

1. Enter the January 1 balances in T-accounts. Leave room for additional accounts.
2. Record the transactions in the journal.
3. Post the journal entries to the T-accounts. Key your entries by date. (Note how keying by date is not as precise as by transaction number or letter. Why? Because there is usually more than one transaction on any given date.)
4. Prepare a trial balance, January 31, 19X5.

3-35   Transaction Analysis, Trial Balance

(Alternates are 3-29, 3-31 through 3-34, and 3-36.) McDonald's Corporation is a well-known fast-foods restaurant company. Examine the accompanying condensed trial balance, which is based on McDonald's annual report and actual terminology.

McDonald's Corporation
Trial Balance
January 1, 1994
(in millions)

Cash	$ 186	
Accounts and notes receivable	315	
Inventories	43	
Prepaid expenses	119	
Property and equipment, at cost	13,459	
Other assets	1,291	
Accumulated depreciation		$ 3,378
Notes and accounts payable		589
Other liabilities		5,172
Paid-in capital		1,026
Retained earnings		5,248
Total	$15,413	$15,413

Consider the following assumed partial summary of transactions for 1994 (in millions):

a. Revenues in cash, company-owned restaurants, $2,200.
b. Revenues, on open account from franchised restaurants, $500. Set up a separate revenue account for these sales.
c. Inventories acquired on open account, $827.
d. Cost of the inventories sold, $820.
e. Depreciation, $226. (Debit Depreciation Expense.)
f. Paid rents and insurance premiums in cash in advance, $42. (Debit Prepaid Expenses.)
g. Prepaid expenses expired, $37. (Debit Operating Expenses.)
h. Paid other liabilities, $148.
i. Cash collections on receivables, $590.
j. Cash disbursements on notes and accounts payable, $747.
k. Paid interest expense in cash, $100.
l. Paid other expenses in cash, mostly payroll and advertising, $1,510. (Debit Operating Expenses.)

Required

1. Record the transactions in the journal.
2. Enter beginning balances in T-accounts. Post the journal entries to the T-accounts. Key your entries with the transaction letters used here.
3. Prepare a trial balance, December 31, 1994.

3-36   Transaction Analysis, Trial Balance
(Alternates are 3-29, and 3-31 through 3-35.) Kellogg Company's major product line is ready-to-eat breakfast cereals. Examine the condensed trial balance at the top of page 130, which is based on Kellogg's annual report.

Consider the following assumed partial summary of transactions for 1994 (in millions):

a. Acquired inventories for $1,700 on open account.
b. Sold inventories that cost $1,600 for $2,500 on open account.
c. Collected $2,550 on open account.
d. Disbursed $1,650 on open accounts payable.

Kellogg Company
Trial Balance
January 1, 1994
(in millions)

Cash	$ 98.1	
Accounts receivable	536.8	
Inventories	403.1	
Prepaid expenses	121.6	
Property and equipment	4,272.5	
Other assets	309.1	
Accumulated depreciation		$1,504.1
Accounts payable		308.8
Other liabilities		2,214.9
Paid-in capital		149.6
Retained earnings		1,563.8
Total	$5,741.2	$5,741.2

e.   Paid cash of $300 for advertising expenses. (Use an Operating Expenses account.)

f.   Paid rent and insurance premiums in cash in advance, $20. (Use a Prepaid Expenses account.)

g.   Prepaid expenses expired, $18. (Use an Operating Expenses account.)

h.   Other liabilities paid in cash, $110.

i.   Interest expense of $13 was paid in cash. (Use an Interest Expense account.)

j.   Depreciation of $50 was recognized. (Use an Operating Expenses account.)

Required

1. Record the transactions in the journal.
2. Enter beginning balances in T-accounts. Post the journal entries to the T-accounts. Key your entries with the transaction letters used here.
3. Prepare a trial balance, December 31, 1994.
4. Explain why cash increased more than five-fold during 1994.

✓**3-37   Preparation of Financial Statements from Trial Balance**
Heart Technology, Inc., prepared a condensed trial balance in late June to be used in compiling financial statements for the six months ended June 30, 19X4. The company, located in the high-tech corridor east of Seattle, makes the Rotablator® system used in coronary care to clear clogged arteries. Production rates are about 60,000 systems per year. The trial balance follows (in thousands):

	Debits	Credits
Current assets	$56,964	
Property and equipment, net	14,760	
Intangible assets, net	2,416	
Other assets	51	
Current liabilities		$ 4,481
Long-term debt		0
Stockholders' equity*		69,195
Revenue		24,973
Cost of goods sold	11,364	
Research and development expenses	1,472	
Selling, general, and administrative expenses	10,047	
Interest income		925
Shareholder litigation settlement expense	2,500	
Total	$99,574	$99,574

*Includes *beginning* retained earnings.

Required

1. Prepare Heart Technology's income statement for the six months ended June 30, 1994.
2. Prepare Heart Technology's balance sheet as of June 30, 1994.

3-38   Reconstructing Journal Entries, Posting
NEC Corporation is a leading international supplier of electronic products, including computers. The NEC annual report at the end of the 1993 fiscal year included the following balance sheet items (in millions of Japanese yen):

Cash	¥397,715
Receivables	997,565
Prepaid expenses	49,256
Land	77,574
Accounts payable	738,329

Consider the following assumed transactions that occurred immediately subsequent to the balance sheet date (in millions of yen):

a. Collections from customers	¥940,000
b. Purchase of land for cash	20,000
c. Purchase of insurance policies on account	12,000
d. Disbursements to trade creditors	690,000

Required

1. Enter the five account balances in T-accounts.
2. Journalize each transaction.
3. Post the journal entries to T-accounts. Key each posting by transaction letter.

3-39   Reconstructing Journal Entries, Posting
(Alternate is 3-40.) Procter & Gamble has many popular products, including Tide, Crest, and Jif. A partial income statement from its annual report for the 1993 fiscal year showed the following actual numbers, nomenclature, and format (in millions):

Income:	
Net sales	$ 30,433
Interest and other income	445
	30,878
Costs and expenses:	
Cost of products sold	17,683
Marketing, administrative, and other expenses	9,589
Interest expense	552
Other expenses	2,705
	30,529
Earnings before income taxes	$ 349

Required

1. Prepare six summary journal entries for the given data. Label your entries *a* through *f*. Omit explanations. For simplicity, assume that all transactions (except for cost of products sold) were for cash.
2. Post to a ledger for all affected accounts. Key your postings by transaction letter.
3. The company uses *income* as a heading for the first part of its income statement. Suggest a more descriptive term. Why is your term more descriptive?

3-40   Reconstructing Journal Entries, Posting

(Alternate is 3-39.) General Mills, Inc., has many popular products, including Cheerios and Wheaties. A partial income statement from its annual report for the 1993 fiscal year showed the following actual numbers, nomenclature, and format (in millions):

Sales		$8,134.6
Cost and expenses:		
Cost of sales, exclusive of items below	$4,297.6	
Selling, general, and administrative expenses	2,645.2	
Depreciation expenses	274.2	
Interest expense	73.6	
Total costs and expenses		7,290.6
Earnings before income taxes		$ 844.0

Required

1. Prepare five summary journal entries for the given data. Label your entries *a* through *e*. Omit explanations. For simplicity, assume that all transactions (except for cost of sales and depreciation expense) were for cash.
2. Post to a ledger for all affected accounts. Key your postings by transaction letter.

3-41   Plant Assets and Accumulated Depreciation

Georgia-Pacific, the pulp, paper, and building products company, had the following in its 1993 annual report (in millions):

Total property, plant, and equipment, at cost	$10,986
Accumulated Depreciation	5,538
Property, Plant, and Equipment, Net	$ 5,448

Required

1. Open T-accounts for (a) Property, Plant, and Equipment; (b) Accumulated Depreciation, Property, Plant, and Equipment; and (c) Depreciation Expense. Enter the above amounts into the T-accounts.
2. Assume that in 1994 no assets were purchased or sold. Depreciation expense for 1994 was $600 million. Prepare the journal entry, and post to the T-accounts.
3. Prepare the property, plant, and equipment section of Georgia-Pacific's balance sheet at the end of 1994.
4. Land comprises $237 million of Georgia-Pacific's property, plant, and equipment, and land is not depreciated. Comment on the age of the company's depreciable assets (that is, all property, plant, and equipment except land) at the end of 1994.

3-42   Management Incentives, Financial Statements, and Ethics

Margarita Reynolds was controller of the St. Louis Electronic Components (SLEC) division of a major medical instruments company. On December 30, 1995, Reynolds prepared a preliminary income statement and compared it with the 1995 budget:

St. Louis Electronic Components Division Income Statement for the Year Ended December 31, 1995 (in thousands)

	Budget	Preliminary Actual
Sales revenues	$1,200	$1,600
Cost of goods sold	600	800
Gross margin	600	800
Other operating expenses	450	500
Operating income	$ 150	$ 300

The top managers of each division had a bonus plan that paid each a 10% bonus if operating income exceeded budgeted income by more than 20%. It was obvious to Reynolds that the SLEC division had easily exceeded the $180,000 of operating income needed for a bonus. In fact, she wondered if it wouldn't be desirable to reduce operating income this year—after all, the higher the income this year, the higher top management is likely to set the budget next year. Besides, if some of December's sales could just be held back and recorded in January, the division would have a running start on next year.

Reynolds had always been a team player, and she saw holding back sales as the best strategy for her team of managers. Therefore, she recorded only $1,500,000 of sales in 1995—the other $100,000 was recorded as January 1996 sales. Operating income for 1995 then became $250,000 and there was a head start of $50,000 on 1996's operating income.

Required Comment on the ethical implications of Reynolds's decision.

✓**3-43   Wal-Mart Annual Report**

This problem helps to develop skill in recording transactions by using an actual company's account titles. Refer to the financial statements of Wal-Mart in Appendix A at the end of the book. Note the following summarized items from the income statement for the 1995 fiscal year (in millions):

Revenues		$83,412
Cost of sales	$65,586	
Operating, selling, and general and administrative expenses	12,858	
Interest costs	706	79,150
Income before income taxes		$ 4,262

Required

1. Prepare four summary journal entries for the given data. Use the Wal-Mart account titles and label your entries *a* through *d*. Omit explanations. For simplicity, assume that all transactions (except for cost of sales) were for cash.
2. Post to a ledger for all affected accounts. Key your postings by transaction letter.

3-44   Compact D from Disclosure

Select the financial statements of any company available on Compact D.

Required

1. Prepare an income statement in the following format:

   Total sales (or revenues)
   Cost of goods sold
   Gross margin
   Other expenses
   Income before income taxes

   Be sure that all revenues are included in the first line and that all expenses (except income taxes) are included in either Cost of goods sold or Other expenses.
2. Prepare three summary journal entries for the income statement data you prepared. Use the given account titles and label your entries *a*, *b*, and *c*. Omit explanations. For simplicity, assume that all "Other expenses" were paid in cash.
3. Post to a ledger for all affected accounts. Key your postings by transaction letter.

4

Accounting Adjustments and Financial Statement Preparation

Learning Objectives

After studying this chapter, you should be able to

1 Explain the meaning of explicit and implicit transactions, and tell why adjustments to the accounts are important.

2 Understand and make adjustments for the expiration of unexpired costs.

3 Understand and make adjustments for the earning of unearned revenues.

4 Understand and make adjustments for the accrual of unrecorded expenses, including accrued wages, interest, and income taxes.

5 Understand and make adjustments for the accrual of unrecorded revenues.

6 Give the sequence of the final steps in the recording process and describe the relationship between cash flows and adjusting entries.

7 Prepare a classified balance sheet and use the current asset and current liability classifications to assess solvency.

8 Prepare single- and multiple-step income statements and use ratios based on income statement categories to assess profitability.

Before preparing financial statements, an accountant makes *adjusting entries* in the accounting records. This chapter describes these entries, why they are necessary, and how to make them. The chapter then discusses the preparation of balance sheets and income statements, with special attention to the format of each. Finally, it shows how to assess solvency using financial ratios based on balance sheet data and how to assess profitability using financial ratios based on income statement data.

Like Chapter 3, this chapter focuses on procedures and techniques rather than concepts. Remember, however, that the concept of double-entry, accrual accounting is the foundation of the procedures. You will understand better the procedures and techniques if you appreciate *why* they are being done.

Entities as large as IBM or Exxon and as small as Mama's Mexican Cafe use accrual accounting and must make adjusting entries before preparing financial statements. Accountants in nonprofit as well as for-profit organizations, and accountants in France, Kenya, China, and every other country in the world, must be able to apply the procedures and techniques of this chapter. In addition, decision makers throughout the world must be able to understand and interpret the financial statements that are prepared.

■ ADJUSTMENTS TO THE ACCOUNTS

explicit transactions
Events such as cash receipts and disbursements, credit purchases, and credit sales that trigger nearly all day-to-day routine entries.

implicit transactions
Events (such as the passage of time) that are temporarily ignored in day-to-day recording procedures and are recognized via end-of-period adjustments.

adjustments (adjusting entries)
The key final process (before the computation of ending account balances) of assigning the financial effects of transactions to the appropriate time periods.

The majority of events in the life of a business entity are recorded by accountants when they occur. In addition, at the end of an accounting period, the accountant makes *adjustments* to the accounts. The need for these adjusting entries stems from the fact that some transactions are *implicit* rather than *explicit*.

Explicit transactions are events such as cash receipts and disbursements, credit purchases, and credit sales that trigger nearly all day-to-day routine entries. Recording of *explicit transactions* is straightforward. Entries for such transactions are supported by explicit evidence, usually in the form of miscellaneous source documents (for example, sales slips, purchase invoices, and employee payroll checks). Note that some explicit transactions do not involve actual exchanges of goods and services between the entity and another party. For instance, the losses of assets from fire or theft are also explicit transactions even though no market exchange occurs.

On the other hand, the events that trigger *implicit transactions* are not so obvious. **Implicit transactions** are events (such as the passage of time) that are temporarily ignored in day-to-day recording procedures and are recognized only at the end of an accounting period. For example, entries for depreciation expense and expiration of prepaid rent are prepared at the end of an accounting period from special schedules or memorandums, not because an explicit event occurred.

The accountant uses *adjustments* to record implicit transactions at the end of each reporting period. **Adjustments** (also called **adjusting entries**, *adjusting the books*, and *adjusting the accounts*) can be defined as the key final process (before the computation of ending account balances) of assigning the financial effects of implicit transactions to the appropriate time periods. Thus adjustments are made at periodic intervals, usually when the financial statements are about to be prepared.

accrue Accumulation of a receivable or payable during a given period even though no explicit transaction occurs.

Adjusting entries are at the heart of accrual accounting. **Accrue** means the accumulation of a receivable or payable during a given period even though no explicit transaction occurs. Examples of accruals are the wages of employees for partial payroll periods and the interest on borrowed money before the interest payment date. The receivables or payables grow as the clock ticks; as some services are continously acquired and used, so they are said to accrue (accumulate).

Objective 1

Explain the meaning of explicit and implicit transactions, and tell why adjustments to the accounts are important.

Adjustments help provide a complete and accurate measure of efforts, accomplishments, and financial position. They are an essential part of accrual accounting because they improve the *matching* of revenues and expenses to a particular period. For example, consider the $5 million annual contract of a baseball star, such as Ken Griffey, Jr., or Barry Bonds, for the 1996 season. If all $5 million is paid in cash in 1996, it is an obvious explicit transaction. But suppose only $2 million is paid in cash and $3 million is deferred until 1997 or later. The $2 million cash payment is an explicit transaction and is recorded as an expense when the payment is made. Since no explicit transaction for the $3 million occurs during the period, it is not routinely entered into the accounting record. However, since the entire $5 million contract was incurred for the benefit of the 1996 season, the $3 million deferred payment is an expense for 1996 that arises because of an implicit transaction for the period. Thus, at the end of the period, when the 1996 financial statements are being prepared, an adjustment is necessary to record the deferred $3 million payment as an expense and to record a $3 million liability for its payment.

The principal adjustments can be classified into four types:

I. Expiration of unexpired costs
II. Realization (earning) of unearned revenues
III. Accrual of unrecorded expenses
IV. Accrual of unrecorded revenues

Each of the four will be explained in the following sections.

■ I. EXPIRATION OF UNEXPIRED COSTS

Objective 2

Understand and make adjustments for the expiration of unexpired costs.

Recall from previous chapters that some costs expire because of the passage of time. The adjustments to the accounts for the cost of these assets were illustrated in Chapter 2 by the recognition of monthly depreciation expense and rent expense. The examples in Chapter 3 described the analysis of these transactions for entry into the journal and ledger. Thus we will not dwell on expiration of unexpired costs here. Other examples of adjusting for asset expirations include the write-offs to expense of such assets as Office Supplies Inventory, Advertising Supplies Inventory, and Prepaid Fire Insurance. A characteristic of these items is that an explicit transaction in the past has created an asset and the implicit transaction adjusts the asset to its appropriate book value.

unearned revenue (deferred revenue, deferred credit) Revenue received and recorded before it is earned.

■ II. EARNING OF UNEARNED REVENUES

Just as some assets are acquired and then expire over time, some revenue is received and then earned over time. **Unearned revenue** (also called **deferred**

revenue or **deferred credit**) is revenue that is received and recorded before it is earned. That is, payment is received in exchange for a commitment to provide services (or goods) at a later date.

Objective 3

Understand and make adjustments for the earning of unearned revenues.

The analysis of adjusting entries for unearned revenue is easier to understand if we visualize the financial positions of both parties to a contract. For example, recall the Biwheels Company's January advance payment of $6,000 for three months' rent. Compare the financial impact on Biwheels Company with the impact on the owner of the property, who received the rental payment:

	Owner of Property (Landlord, Lessor)			Biwheels Company (Tenant, Lessee)		
	A =	*L*	+ *SE*	*A*	= *L* +	*SE*
		Unearned Rent	*Rent*		*Prepaid*	*Rent*
	Cash	*Revenue*	*Revenue*	*Cash*	*Rent*	*Expense*
(a) Explicit transaction (advance payment of three months' rent)	+6,000 =	+6,000		−6,000	+6,000 =	
(b) January adjustment (for one month's rent)	=	−2,000	+2,000		−2,000 =	−2,000
(c) February adjustment (for one month's rent)	=	−2,000	+2,000		−2,000 =	−2,000
(d) March adjustment (for one month's rent)	=	−2,000	+2,000		−2,000 =	−2,000

The journal entries for (a) and (b) follow:

OWNER (LANDLORD)

(a) Cash	6,000	
Unearned rent revenue		6,000
(b) Unearned rent revenue	2,000	
Rent revenue		2,000

BIWHEELS CO. (TENANT)

(a) Prepaid rent	6,000	
Cash		6,000
(b) Rent expense	2,000	
Pepaid rent.		2,000

(Entries for (c) and (d) are the same as for (b).)

We are already familiar with the analysis from Biwheels' point of view. The $2,000 monthly entries for Biwheels are examples of the first type of adjustments, the expiration of unexpired costs. From the viewpoint of the owner of the rental property, transaction *a* recognizes the receipt of unearned revenue. The balancing amount for the increase in cash is recorded as a *liability* because the lessor is obligated to deliver the rental services (or to refund the money if the services are not delivered). Sometimes this account is called Rent Collected in Advance, rather than Unearned Rent Revenue as in our example, but it is an unearned revenue type of liability account no matter what its label. That is, it is revenue collected in advance that has not yet been earned.

Franchises and Revenue Recognition

In a franchise arrangement, a central organization, such as McDonald's or the National Basketball Association, sells the right to use the company name and company products to a franchisee. The franchisee also receives the benefit of centralized advertising, management assistance, and product development. There are more than 500,000 franchise outlets of various types in the United States, with sales totaling more than $700 billion.

Franchising raises an interesting accounting problem. How does the central organization account for the franchise fees? At first glance, it might seem clear that such fees should be recorded as revenue. However, under accrual accounting, revenue should be recorded only after two conditions have been satisfied: (1) The "work" has been completed, and (2) Collectability of the fee is reasonably assured.

Jiffy Lube, a subsidiary of Pennzoil Company, is a franchisor of fast oil-change centers and provides an example of receipt of franchise fees before the related work is performed. Jiffy Lube sells its franchisees area development rights, which grant the franchisee the exclusive right to develop Jiffy Lube outlets in a certain area. In return for these rights, Jiffy Lube receives an upfront fee. Should Jiffy Lube record the fee as revenue? No, because Jiffy Lube's work is not done until the franchisee actually opens the outlets. In the interim, Jiffy Lube must report the fees as unearned revenue.

Porta-John, which acquires chemical toilets and sells the right to service the toilets to franchisees, illustrates the collectability condition. The franchisees agree to pay Porta-John an upfront fee. However, only 10% of the fee is collected in cash, and historically, franchisees have taken up to 10 years to pay the remainder of the fee. The fact is that many of the franchisees don't stick with the portable toilet business for very long, so the collectability of the total fee is quite uncertain. Accordingly, Porta-John is required to account for the fees using the cash basis, reporting revenue only as the franchise fees are actually received in cash. ■

Sources: Statistical Abstract of the United States: 1991, *U.S. Bureau of the Census, Table 1368; K. Weisman and R. Khalaf, "Number Pumpers," Forbes (November 11, 1991), p. 110; P. Wang, "Claiming Tomorrow's Profits Today," Forbes (October 17, 1988), p. 78; Pennzoil 1993 Annual Report.*

Notice that transaction *a* does not affect stockholders' equity. The revenue is recognized (earned) when the adjusting entries are made in transactions *b*, *c*, and *d*. That is, as the liability Unearned Rent Revenue is decreased (debited), the stockholders' equity account Rent Revenue is increased (credited). The net effect is an increase in stockholders' equity at the time the revenue is recognized.

Adjustments I and II (p. 137) are really mirror images of each other. If one party to a contract has a prepaid expense, the other has an unearned revenue. A similar analysis could be conducted for, say, a three-year fire insurance policy or a three-year magazine subscription. The buyer recognizes a prepaid expense (asset) and uses adjustments to spread the initial cost to an expense account over the useful life of the services. In turn, the seller, such as a magazine publisher, must initially record its liability, Unearned Subscription Revenue, on receipt of payment for the three-year subscription. For example, the publisher of *Time* magazine showed a liability of over $600 million as of January 1, 1995, calling it Unearned Portion of Paid Subscriptions. The unearned revenue is then systematically recognized as *earned* revenue when magazines are delivered throughout the life of the subscription. The following diagrams show that explicit cash transactions in such situations are initially recorded as balance sheet items and are later transformed into income statement items via periodic adjustments:

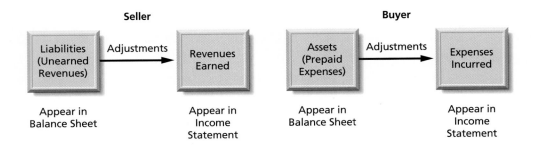

Unearned revenues are essentially advances from customers who have paid for goods or services to be delivered at a future date. For instance, airlines often require advance payments for special-fare tickets. American Airlines showed a recent balance of over $1.5 billion in an unearned revenue account labeled Air Traffic Liability. Other descriptions of unearned revenues used in recently published financial statements include:

Commerce Clearing House:	
Unearned revenue	$277,733,000
Dun & Bradstreet:	
Unearned subscription income	$263,700,000
Albertson's:	
Unearned income	$19,927,000
National Computer Systems:	
Deferred income	$18,956,000

Commerce Clearing House includes a typical footnote describing this account: "Unearned revenue on the balance sheet reflects the revenue to be recognized in the future (primarily within one year) on subscription and representation contracts."

Note that Albertson's uses *unearned income* and National Computer Systems uses *deferred income*, but revenue is a more accurate description than income. The latter is, strictly speaking, a difference, or "what's left over" after deducting appropriate expenses from revenue. When unearned revenue becomes earned, the expenses matched with the revenue are also recognized. Income is the amount by which the earned revenue exceeds the related cost of goods or services delivered to customers.

■ III. ACCRUAL OF UNRECORDED EXPENSES

It is awkward and unnecessary to make hourly, daily, or even weekly formal recordings in the accounts for many accrued expenses. The cost of such detailed recording would certainly exceed the benefits. Consequently, adjustments are made to bring each expense (and corresponding liability) account up to date just before the formal financial statements are prepared in order to match the expense to the period.

Accounting for Payment of Wages

Consider wages. Most companies pay their employees at predetermined times. Here is a sample calendar for January:

			January			
S	M	T	W	T	F	S
	1	2	3	4	5	6
7	8	9	10	11	12	13
14	15	16	17	18	19	20
21	22	23	24	25	26	27
28	29	30	31			

Objective 4

Understand and make adjustments for the accrual of unrecorded expenses, including accrued wages, interest, and income tax.

The Biwheels Company, for example, pays its employees each Friday for services rendered during that week. Thus, wages paid on January 26 are compensation for the week ended January 26. The cumulative total wages paid on the Fridays during January amount to $20,000, or $5,000 per five-day workweek, or $1,000 per day. Biwheels uses the popular method described in Chapter 3 to make routine entries for wage payments at the end of each week in January. At the end of January, the balance sheet shows the summarized amounts and their effect on the accounting equation:

	Assets A =	Liabilities L	+	Stockholders' Equity SE
	Cash			Wages Expense
(a) Routine entries for explicit transactions	−20,000 =			−20,000

Accounting for Accrual of Wages

Suppose the Biwheels accountant wishes to prepare financial statments at the end of January. In addition to the $20,000 actually paid to employees during the month, Biwheels owes $3,000 for employee services rendered during the last three days of the month. The employees will not be paid for these services until Friday, February 2. To ensure accurate financial statements for the month of January, adjustments must be made to account for the accrual of these unrecorded wages, which are owed but not paid in January. Transaction *a* shows the total of the routine entries in the journal for the explicit wage payments made to employees, and transaction *b* shows the entries for the accrued wages.

(a) Wages expense	20,000	
Cash		20,000
(b) Wages expense	3,000	
Accrued wages payable		3,000

The *total* effects of wages on the balance sheet equation for the month of January are as follows:

	A	=	L	+	SE
	Cash		Accrued Wages Payable		Wages Expense
(a) Routine entries for explicit transactions	−20,000 =				− 20,000
(b) Adjustment for implicit transaction, the accrual of unrecorded wages	=		+3,000		− 3,000
Total effects	−20,000 =		+3,000		− 23,000

Entry **b** is the first example in this book that shows an expense that is offset by an increase in a liability instead of a decrease in an asset. On February 2, the liability will be paid off, together with the wages expense for February 1 and 2:

Wages expense (February 1 and 2)	2,000	
Accrued wages payable.	3,000	
Cash		5,000
(To record wages expense for February 1 and 2 and to pay wages for the week ended February 2.)		

These entries clearly demonstrate the matching principle. The routine entries and the adjusting entries match the wage expenses to the periods in which they help generate revenues.

Accrual of Interest

Other examples of accrued expenses include sales commissions, property taxes, income taxes, and interest paid on borrowed money. *Interest* is "rent" paid for the use of money, just as rent is paid for the use of buildings. The interest accumulates (accrues) as time unfolds, regardless of when the actual cash for interest is paid.

Recall that Biwheels borrowed $100,000 on December 31, 19X1. Assume that the principal ($100,000) plus interest on the one-year loan is payable on December 31, 19X2. The interest rate is 9%. (Unless stated otherwise, quoted interest rates typically imply an interest rate *per year*.)

As of January 31, Biwheels has had the benefit of a $100,000 bank loan for one month. Biwheels owes the bank for these services (the use of money); the amount is $\frac{1}{12} \times 0.09 \times \$100,000 = \$750$. These money services costing $750 have been acquired *and* used up. Therefore, an adjusting entry is required for the month of January. Since the amount is not actually paid in January, it is a liability, Accrued Interest Payable. The adjustment is analyzed and recorded in a fashion similar to the adjustment for accrued wages:

	A =	L	+	SE
		Accrued Interest Payable		*Interest Expense*
Adjustment to accrue January interest not yet recorded	=	+750		−750

The adjusting journal entry is:

Interest expense.	750	
Accrued interest payable		750

If the adjusting entry is omitted, liabilities will be understated. At the end of January, Biwheels owes the bank $100,750, not $100,000. The adjusting entry matches the $750 interest expense with the period in which it occurred.

Accrual of Income Taxes

As income is generated, income tax expense should be accrued. Income taxes are worldwide, although rates and details differ from country to country and from state to state. Corporations in the United States are subject to federal and state corporate income taxes. Tax rates are progressive; that is, the current federal tax rate is 15% for the first $50,000 of taxable income, 25% for the next $25,000, and 34% for the next $25,000. Taxable income over $100,000 is taxed between 34% and 39%. The rates are changed almost yearly by either the U.S. Congress or the state legislatures or both. For many corporations, the federal-plus-state income tax rates hover around 40%.

Various labels are used for income taxes on the income statement: *income tax expense, provision for income taxes*, and just plain *income taxes* are found most frequently. For multinational firms income tax expense may include tax obligations in every country in which they operate. About 85% of publicly held U.S. companies show income taxes as a separate item just before net income. This arrangement is logical because income tax expense is based on income before taxes. In contrast, the other 15% list income taxes along with other operating expenses such as wages. A recent McDonald's annual report contains the format adopted by the vast majority of companies:

Income before provision for income taxes	$1,675,700,000
Provision for income taxes	593,200,000
Net income	$1,082,500,000

PolyGram, Europe's leading recorded music company, has slightly different terminology but the same information (in millions of Netherlands guilders):

Income before taxes	NLG 927
Income taxes	(264)
Income after taxes	NLG 663

pretax income
Income before income taxes.

Income tax expenses are accrued each month (not just once a year) as pretax income is generated. **Pretax income** is a popular synonym for income before income taxes. The amount of the accrual for income taxes obviously depends on the amount of pretax income.

■ IV. ACCRUAL OF UNRECORDED REVENUES

Objective 5

Understand and make adjustments for the accrual of unrecorded revenues.

The accrual of unrecorded revenues is the mirror image of the accrual of unrecorded expenses. The adjusting entries show the recognition of revenues that have been earned but not yet shown in the accounts. According to the revenue recognition principle, then, revenues affect stockholders' equity in the period they are earned, not received.

Suppose First National Bank had loaned the $100,000 to Biwheels. As of January 31, First National Bank has earned $750 on the loan. The following tabulations show the mirror-image effect:

	First National Bank, as a Lender			Biwheels, as a Borrower		
	A	= L +	SE	A=	L +	SE
	Accrued Interest Receivable		Interest Revenue		Accrued Interest Payable	Interest Expense
January interest	+750	=	+750	=	+750	−750

The adjusting journal entries are:

FIRST NATIONAL BANK (LENDER)

Accrued interest receivable	750	
Interest revenue		750

BIWHEELS (BORROWER)

Interest expense	750	
Accrued interest payable		750

Other examples of accrued revenues and receivables include "unbilled" fees. For example, attorneys, public accountants, physicians, and advertising agencies may earn hourly fees during a particular month but not send out bills to their clients until the completion of an entire contract or engagement. Under the accrual basis of accounting, such revenues should be recorded in the month in which they were earned rather than at a later time. Suppose an attorney renders $10,000 of services during January that will not be billed until March 31.

Before the attorney's financial statements can be prepared for January, an adjustment for unrecorded revenue for the month is necessary:

	A	= L	+	SE
	Accrued (Unbilled) Fees Receivable			**Fee Revenue**
Adjustment for fees earned	+10,000	=		+10,000

The adjusting journal entry is:

$$\text{Accrued (unbilled) fees receivable} \dots\dots\dots\dots \quad 10{,}000$$
$$\text{Fee revenue} \dots\dots\dots\dots\dots\dots\dots\dots \quad\quad 10{,}000$$

Utilities often recognize unbilled revenues for services provided but not yet billed. For example, American Water Works Company, a utility that provides water supply services to more than 1.6 million customers in 625 communities in 20 states, includes more unbilled revenues than accounts receivable among its current assets:

Customer accounts receivable	$46,795,000
Unbilled revenues	57,298,000

■ THE ADJUSTING PROCESS IN PERSPECTIVE

Chapter 3 demonstrated the various steps in recording transactions:

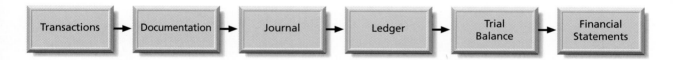

These steps have a final aim: financial statements prepared on the accrual basis. To accomplish this goal, adjusting entries are needed to record implicit transactions, and the final steps in the process are divided further as follows:

Each adjusting entry affects at least one income statement account—a revenue or an expense. The other side of the entry is a balance sheet account—an asset or a liability. No adjusting entry debits or credits cash. Why? Because cash transactions are explicit transactions that are routinely recorded as they happen. The end-of-period adjustment process is reserved for the implicit transactions that must be recognized by the accrual basis of accounting. Exhibit 4-1 summarizes the major adjusting entries.

Exhibit 4-1	Adjusting Entry	Type of Account Debited	Type of Account Credited
Summary of Adjusting Entries	I. Expiration of unexpired costs	Expense	Prepaid Expense, Accumulated Depreciation
	II. Realization (earning) of unearned revenues	Unearned Revenue	Revenue
	III. Accrual of unrecorded expenses	Expense	Payable
	IV. Accrual of unrecorded revenues	Receivable	Revenue

Objective 6

Give the sequence of the final steps in the recording process and describe the relationship between cash flows and adjusting entries.

Cash Flows and Adjusting Entries

Cash flows (that is, cash receipts and disbursements) may precede or follow the adjusting entry that recognizes the related revenue or expense. The accompanying diagrams underscore the basic differences between the cash flows and the accrual accounting entries.

Entries for adjustments I and II, expiration of unexpired costs and realization (earning) of unearned revenues, are usually made *subsequent* to the cash flows. For example, the cash received or disbursed for rent had an *initial* impact on the balance sheet. The adjustment process was used to show the *later* impact on the income statement.

I. Expiration of Unexpired Costs.

II. Realization (Earning) of Unearned Revenues.

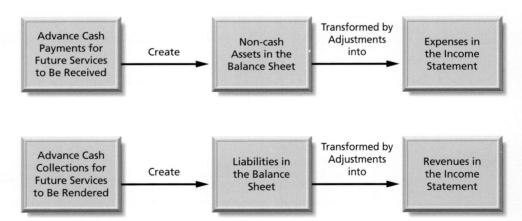

Entries for adjustments III and IV, accrual of unrecorded expenses and accrual of unrecorded revenues, are made *before* the related cash flows. The income statement is affected *before* the cash receipts and disbursements occur. The accounting entity must compute the amount of goods or services provided or received prior to any cash receipt or payment.

III. Accrual of Unrecorded Expenses.

IV. Accrual of Unrecorded Revenues.

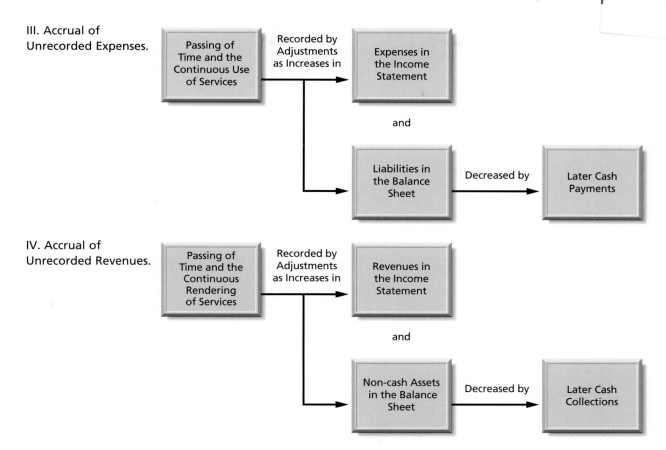

Summary Problem for Your Review

Problem One

Chan Audio Co. is a retailer of stereo equipment. Chan Audio has been in business one month. The company's *unadjusted* trial balance, January 31, 19X2, has the following accounts:

Cash	$ 71,700	
Accounts receivable	160,300	
Note receivable	40,000	
Merchandise inventory	250,200	
Prepaid rent	15,000	
Store equipment	114,900	
Note payable		$100,000
Accounts payable		117,100
Unearned rent revenue		3,000
Paid-in capital		400,000
Sales		160,000
Cost of goods sold	100,000	
Wages expense	28,000	
Total	$780,100	$780,100

Consider the following adjustments on January 31:

a. January depreciation, $1,000.

b. On January 2, rent of $15,000 was paid in advance for the first quarter of 19X2, as shown by the debit balance in the Prepaid Rent account. Adjust for January rent.

c. Wages earned by employees during January but not paid as of January 31 were $3,750.

d. Chan borrowed $100,000 from the bank on January 1. This explicit transaction was recorded when the business began, as shown by the credit balance in the Note Payable account. The principal and 9% interest are to be paid one year later (January 1, 19X3). However, an adjustment is necessary now for the interest expense of ½ × 0.09 × $100,000 = $750 for January.

e. On January 1, a cash loan of $40,000 was made to a local supplier, as shown by the debit balance in the Note Receivable account. The promissory note stated that the loan is to be repaid one year later (January 1, 19X3), together with interest at 12% per annum. On January 31, an adjustment is needed to recognize the interest earned on the note receivable.

f. On January 15, a nearby corporation paid $3,000 cash to Chan Audio Co. as an advance rental for Chan's storage space and equipment to be used temporarily from January 15 to April 15 (three months). This $3,000 is the credit balance in the Unearned Revenue account. On January 31, an adjustment is needed to recognize the rent revenue earned for one-half month.

g. Income tax expense was accrued on January income at a rate of 50% of income before taxes.

Required

1. Enter the trial-balance amounts in the general ledger. Set up the new asset account, Accrued Interest Receivable, and the new asset-reduction account, the contra account, Accumulated Depreciation, Store Equipment. Set up the following new liability accounts: Accrued Wages Payable, Accrued Interest Payable, and Accrued Income Taxes Payable. Set up the following new expense and revenue accounts: Depreciation Expense, Rent Expense, Interest Expense, Interest Revenue, Rent Revenue, and Income Tax Expense.

2. Journalize adjustments *a-g* and post the entries to the ledger. Key entries by transaction letter.

3. Prepare an adjusted trial balance as of January 31, 19X2.

Solution to Problem One

The solutions to requirements 1 through 3 are in Exhibits 4-2 (p. 149), 4-3 (p. 150), and 4-4 (p. 151). Accountants often refer to the final trial balance, Exhibit 4-4, as the adjusted trial balance. Why? Because all the necessary adjustments have been made, and the trial balance provides the data necessary for the formal financial statements.

Exhibit 4-2

Chan Audio Co.
Journal Entries

(a)	Depreciation expense	1,000	
	Accumulated depreciation, store equipment ..		1,000
	Depreciation for January.		
(b)	Rent expense	5,000	
	Prepaid rent		5,000
	Rent expense for January.		
(c)	Wages expense	3,750	
	Accrued wages payable		3,750
	Wages earned but not paid.		
(d)	Interest expense	750	
	Accrued interest payable		750
	Interest for January.		
(e)	Accrued interest receivable	400	
	Interest revenue		400
	Interest earned for January:		
	$\frac{1}{2} \times \$40,000 \times .12 = \$400$.		
(f)	Unearned rent revenue	500	
	Rent revenue		500
	Rent earned for January. Rent per month is		
	$\$3,000 \div 3 = \$1,000$; for one-half month, \$500.		
(g)	Income tax expense	11,200	
	Accrued income taxes payable		11,200
	Income tax on January income:		
	$.50 \times [160,000 + 400 + 500 - 100,000 - 31,750 - 1,000 - 5,000 - 750]$		

classified balance sheet A balance sheet that groups the accounts into subcategories to help readers quickly gain a perspective on the company's financial position.

current assets Cash plus assets that are expected to be converted to cash or sold or consumed during the next twelve months or within the normal operating cycle if longer than a year.

current liabilities Liabilities that fall due within the coming year or within the normal operating cycle if longer than a year.

■ CLASSIFIED BALANCE SHEET

Accounts are listed on the balance sheet according to the major categories of assets, liabilities, and stockholders' equity as we have seen throughout this book thus far. A **classified balance sheet** groups the accounts into subcategories to help readers quickly gain a perspective on the company's financial position. The classifications help to draw attention to certain amounts or groups of accounts.

Assets are frequently classified into two groupings: current assets and long-term assets. Liabilities are similarly classified: current liabilities and long-term liabilities. In this section we concentrate on current assets and liabilities; long-term assets and liabilities are covered in detail in Chapters 9 and 10.

Current Assets and Liabilities

Current assets are cash plus assets that are expected to be converted to cash or sold or consumed during the next twelve months or within the normal operating cycle if longer than a year. Similarly, **current liabilities** are those liabilities that fall due within the coming year or within the normal operating cycle if longer than a year. (Long-term assets and liabilities are expected to affect cash at some time beyond a year, or beyond the length of the normal operating cycle if it is longer than a year.) Companies that build ships or construct buildings are examples of companies that may take more than a year to complete an operating cycle.

Exhibit 4-3

Chan Audio Co.
General Ledger

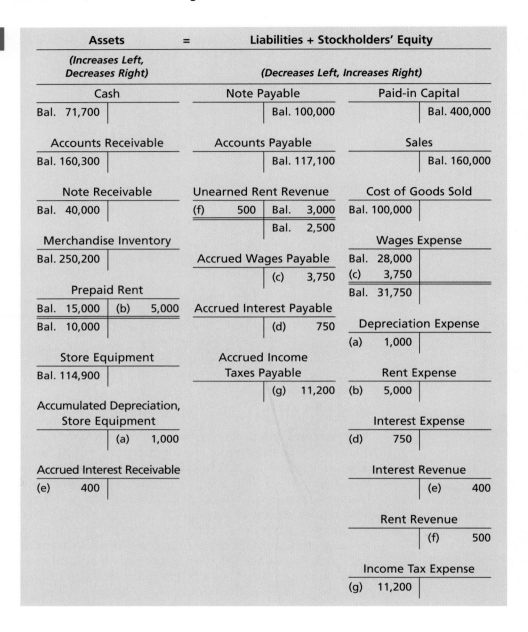

	Assets	=	Liabilities + Stockholders' Equity

(Increases Left, Decreases Right)   *(Decreases Left, Increases Right)*

Cash
Bal. 71,700

Note Payable
Bal. 100,000

Paid-in Capital
Bal. 400,000

Accounts Receivable
Bal. 160,300

Accounts Payable
Bal. 117,100

Sales
Bal. 160,000

Note Receivable
Bal. 40,000

Unearned Rent Revenue
(f)   500 | Bal.   3,000
Bal.   2,500

Cost of Goods Sold
Bal. 100,000

Merchandise Inventory
Bal. 250,200

Accrued Wages Payable
(c)   3,750

Wages Expense
Bal.   28,000
(c)   3,750
Bal.   31,750

Prepaid Rent
Bal. 15,000 | (b)   5,000
Bal. 10,000

Accrued Interest Payable
(d)   750

Depreciation Expense
(a)   1,000

Store Equipment
Bal. 114,900

Accrued Income Taxes Payable
(g)   11,200

Rent Expense
(b)   5,000

Accumulated Depreciation, Store Equipment
(a)   1,000

Interest Expense
(d)   750

Accrued Interest Receivable
(e)   400

Interest Revenue
(e)   400

Rent Revenue
(f)   500

Income Tax Expense
(g)   11,200

Objective 7

Prepare a classified balance sheet and use the current asset and current liability classifications to assess solvency.

Exhibit 4-5 shows the classified balance sheet for Chan Audio Company, which is prepared from the adjusted trial balance for the company (shown in Exhibit 4-4). On the balance sheet, the current asset accounts are generally listed in the order in which they will be converted to cash during the coming year. Thus, Cash is listed first (since it is already in the form of cash). Accounts Receivable are listed next since cash payments will be received within weeks or months. Note Receivable and Accrued Interest Receivable, which are listed as the third and fourth accounts, will be converted to cash by the end of the year. Nonmonetary assets, such as inventories and prepaid expenses (in this case, Merchandise Inventory and Prepaid Rent) are usually listed last in the current assets section of the balance sheet. As shown in Exhibit 4–5, current liability accounts are also listed in the order in which they will draw on, or decrease, cash during the coming year.

Exhibit 4-4

Chan Audio Co.
Adjusted Trial
Balance January 31,
19X2

Account Title	Balance		
	Debit	Credit	
Cash	$ 71,700		
Accounts receivable	160,300		
Note receivable	40,000		
Merchandise inventory	250,200		
Prepaid rent	10,000		
Store equipment	114,900		
Accumulated depreciation, store equipment		$ 1,000	Balance
Accrued interest receivable	400		Sheet
Note payable		100,000	Exhibit 4-5
Accounts payable		117,100	
Unearned rent revenue		2,500	
Accrued wages payable		3,750	
Accrued interest payable		750	
Accrued income taxes payable		11,200	
Paid-in capital		400,000	
Sales		160,000	
Cost of goods sold	100,000		
Wages expense	31,750		
Depreciation expense	1,000		Income
Rent expense	5,000		Statement,
Interest expense	750		Exhibit 4-8
Interest revenue		400	
Rent revenue		500	
Income tax expense	11,200		
Total	$797,200	$797,200	

working capital
The excess of current assets over current liabilities.

The excess of current assets over current liabilities is known as **working capital.** In the case of the Chan Audio Company, the working capital on January 31, 19X2, is $297,300 ($532,600 – $235,300).

Exhibit 4-5 shows only one long-term asset, Store Equipment (and its related accumulated depreciation) and no long-term liabilities. However, most balance sheets contain several long-term assets and at least one type of long-term debt.

The stockholders' equity is $400,000 of paid-in capital plus January net income of $11,200, or $411,200. Note that the $11,200 does not appear as a separate number in the adjusted trial balance (Exhibit 4-4). Instead the $11,200 is the net effect of all the balances in the revenue and expense accounts. The balance sheet condenses the $11,200 effect as retained income. (The next chapter will explain the journal entries necessary to achieve this effect.)

Current Ratio

solvency An entity's ability to meet its financial obligations as they become due.

current ratio (working capital ratio) Current assets divided by current liabilities.

The classifications of current assets and current liabilities can help readers of financial statements assess a business entity's **solvency**, which is its ability to meet its financial obligations as they become due. The **current ratio** (also called the **working capital ratio**), which is widely used to evaluate solvency, is found by dividing current assets by current liabilities. Chan Audio's current ratio, for example, is:

$$\text{Current ratio} = \frac{\text{Current assets}}{\text{Current liabilities}} = \frac{\$532,600}{\$235,300} = 2.3$$

Other things being equal, the higher the current ratio, the more assurance creditors have about being paid in full and on time. Conversely, a current ratio that is too high may indicate excessive holdings of cash, accounts receivable, or inventories. Analysts will compare a company's current ratio with those of past years and with those of similar companies to make judgments about the company's solvency.

An old rule of thumb was that the current ratio should be greater than 2.0. However, a better assessment can be made by comparing a company's current ratio with the average in its industry. For example, recently IBM's ratio was 1.2 compared with an industry average of 1.7. Microsoft's current ratio of 5.1 was more than four times as large as IBM's. Utilities often have low current ratios because of low inventories and stable cash flows. For example, NYNEX, the telephone company in New York and New England, has a current ratio of 0.6.

Although the current ratio is widely used as a measure of short-term debt-paying ability, a budget (prediction) of cash receipts and disbursements is more useful. Whether cash is too low or too high really depends on the predictions of operating requirements over the coming months. Intelligent management calls for trying to invest any temporary excess cash to generate additional income.

| Exhibit 4-5 | Chan Audio Co.   Balance Sheet, January 31, 19X2 |

Assets			Liabilities and Owners' Equity		
Current assets:			Current liabilities:		
Cash		$ 71,700	Note payable		$100,000
Accounts receivable		160,300	Accounts payable		117,100
Note receivable		40,000	Unearned rent revenue		2,500
Accrued interest receivable		400	Accrued wages payable		3,750
Merchandise inventory		250,200	Accrued interest payable		750
Prepaid rent		10,000	Accrued income taxes payable		11,200
Total current assets		$532,600	Total current liabilities		$235,300
Long-term asset:			Stockholders' equity:		
Store equipment	$114,900		Paid-in capital	$400,000	
Accumulated depreciation	1,000	113,900	Retained income	11,200	411,200
Total		$646,500	Total		$646,500

Managing Working Capital

The traditional view is that large amounts of working capital and high current ratios are good—they show that a company is likely to remain solvent. However, maintaining solvency is not as big a problem for most companies as generating profits. Large amounts of working capital may needlessly tie up funds that could profitably be used elsewhere in the company.

The main components of working capital for the typical company are accounts receivable plus inventories less accounts payable. In the 1990s building inventories and accounts receivable fell out of fashion. Each dollar not invested in working capital is a dollar of free cash available for investing in value-adding activities—activities that actually create and deliver products or services to customers. In addition, there is another downside to large accounts receivable or inventories. Receivables may grow because of increasing sales, but they can also zoom upward when collection of receivables slows down. Soaring inventories may mean increased ability to deliver orders on time; they may also mean that sales are not keeping up with production or that the company is incurring excessive storage and handling costs for inventory. Companies with large inventories may also lack the ability to adapt products quickly to customers' wishes.

You can see that there are mixed signals in measures such as working capital and current ratio. In the 1990s many companies have made a concerted effort to reduce working capital and hence lower their current ratios. For example, in the fiscal year ending May 1994, Campbell Soup reduced its working capital by $80 million. This meant that Campbell had an extra $80 million to invest in new products, corporate acquisitions, or whatever other opportunity presented itself. Another food company, Quaker Oats, reduced its working capital by $200 million, primarily by smoothing out its production runs. Instead of building inventories and then offering huge discounts to entice customers to take delivery, Quaker now produces its cereals and other products just in time to ship them. Each product is produced once a week instead of once every six weeks or so. Of course, this requires more time resetting machines to produce a different product. By streamlining its procedures, one Quaker Oats factory spent only $20,000 a year on the extra machine setups compared with the annual savings of $500,000 from lowering inventories.

A measure of working capital that is increasingly popular is working capital per dollar of sales. The Fortune 500 firms have an average ratio of $.20 for every dollar of sales. Recent figures for Quaker Oats and Campbell Soup are $.07 and $.14, respectively.

Reduction of working capital is not just a U.S. phenomenon. Consider Wabco UK, the British auto products manufacturer. In the last five years, its working capital has gone from $13 million to a negative $154,000. Currently, payables exceed receivables by $2.35 million and inventories are only $2.2 million. How did it accomplish this? Partly by cutting cycle time—the time from receipt of an order to delivery of the product. For example, a vacuum pump that took three weeks to build in 1989 can now be built in six minutes. Wabco is also collecting receivables more quickly—42 days compared with 54 days five years ago.

Many companies have set a target of zero working capital and therefore a current ratio of 1.0. As these efforts prove to be successful, the rule of thumb of a desirable current ratio of 2.0 is being revised. Companies with twice as many current assets as current liabilities may be solvent but may lose out in the long run. Why? Because they may not be using their capital as profitably as possible. ∎

Sources: Shawn Tully, "Raiding a Company's Hidden Cash," Fortune (August 22, 1994), p. 82-87; Campbell Soup, Annual Report, 1994; Quaker Oats, Annual Report, 1994.

Formats of Balance Sheets

The particular detail and format of balance sheets and other financial statements vary among companies. Yet, all balance sheets contain the same basic information, regardless of format. For example, consider the reproduction of the balance sheet of Walgreen Co., the drugstore chain, as shown in Exhibit 4-6. The format and classifications are those actually presented. Note the

report format A classified balance sheet with the assets at the top.

account format A classified balance sheet with the assets at the left.

captions used for noncurrent items. Captions such as *long-term assets* and *long-term liabilities* might be used instead of noncurrent assets and noncurrent liabilities, respectively. Some accountants prefer to omit a general caption for noncurrent items when there are only one or two items within a specific class.

Exhibit 4-6 presents a classified balance sheet in the **report format** (assets at top) in contrast to the **account format** (assets at left) that has previously been illustrated (Exhibit 4-5). Either format is acceptable. A recent survey of six hundred U.S. companies indicated that 70% use the report format and 30% use the account format.

Exhibit 4-6

Walgreen Co.
Balance Sheet
August 31, 1993
(in thousands)

Assets	
Current Assets:	
Cash	$ 91,597
Marketable securities	29,695
Accounts receivable	139,313
Inventories	1,094,035
Other current assets	108,493
Total current assets	1,463,133
Noncurrent Assets:	
Property and equipment, at cost, less accumulated depreciation and amortization	927,333
Other noncurrent assets	144,725
Total Assets	$2,535,191

Liabilities and Shareholders' Equity	
Current Liabilities:	
Trade accounts payable	$ 427,185
Accrued expenses and other liabilities	434,640
Income taxes	21,682
Total current liabilities	883,507
Noncurrent Liabilities:	
Deferred income taxes	173,343
Other noncurrent liabilities	99,590
Total noncurrent liabilities	272,933
Shareholders' Equity:	
Common stock, $.625 par value; authorized 400,000,000 shares; issued and outstanding 123,070,536 at stated value	76,919
Retained earnings	1,301,832
Total shareholders' equity	1,378,751
Total Liabilities and Shareholders' Equity	$2,535,191

Non-U.S. companies may use other formats. Exhibit 4-7 shows a condensed balance sheet for British Petroleum Company. Notice that fixed assets (that is, long-term assets) are listed before current assets. Current liabilities are deducted from current assets to give a direct measure of working capital (called *net current assets* by British Petroleum). Note that British Petroleum has negative working capital of £46 million. As suggested in the boxed example on p.153, Managing Working Capital, zero or negative working capital is becoming more common as companies reduce their inventories and accounts receivable. More is said about classifications and the analysis of the balance sheet in succeeding chapters, especially Chapter 15.

Exhibit 4-7		
British Petroleum Company Balance Sheet December 31, 1993 (in millions)		
Fixed assets		£22,706
Current assets	£8,311	
Current liabilities	8,357	
Net current assets		(46)
Total assets less current liabilities		£22,660
Long-term liabilities		12,912
Shareholders' interests		£ 9,748

■ INCOME STATEMENT

Most investors are vitally concerned about a company's ability to produce long-run earnings and dividends. In this regard, income statements are often considered much more important than balance sheets. Like the balance sheet, income statements may be prepared with subcategories that draw attention to certain accounts or groups of accounts.

Single- and Multiple-Step Income Statements

single-step income statement An income statement that groups all revenues together and then lists and deducts all expenses together without drawing any intermediate subtotals.

The adjusted trial balance for Chan Audio Company (Exhibit 4-4) provides the data for two formats of income statements shown in Exhibit 4-8. The statement in Part A of the exhibit is called a **single-step income statement** because it groups all revenues together (sales plus interest and rent revenues) and then lists and deducts all expenses together without drawing any intermediate subtotals.

multiple-step income statement An income statement that contains one or more subtotals that highlight significant relationships.

Another major form of income statement is the **multiple-step income statement**. It contains one or more subtotals that highlight significant relationships. For example, Exhibit 4-8, Part B, shows a *gross profit* figure. **Gross profit** is defined as the excess of sales revenue over the cost of the inventory that was sold. It is also called **gross margin**.

gross profit (gross margin) The excess of sales revenue over the cost of the inventory that was sold.

operating income (operating profit) Gross profit less all operating expenses.

The next section of the multiple-step statement usually contains a group of recurring expenses that are often labeled as operating expenses because they pertain to the firm's routine, ongoing operations. Examples are wages, rent, depreciation, and various other expenses such as telephone, heat, and advertising. These operating expenses are deducted from the gross profit to obtain **operating income**, which is also called **operating profit**. Cost of goods sold could

Objective 8

Prepare single- and multiple-step income statements and use ratios based on income statement categories to assess profitability.

also be viewed as an operating expense because it is also deducted from sales revenue to obtain "operating income." However, because of its size and importance, it is usually deducted separately from sales revenue, as shown here.

The next grouping is usually called *other revenue and expense* (or *other income* or *other expense* or *nonoperating items* or some similar catchall title). These are not directly related to the mainstream of a firm's operations. The revenues are usually minor in relation to the revenues shown at the top of the income statement. The expenses are also minor, with one likely exception, interest expense.

Exhibit 4-8, Part A

Single-Step Income Statement
Chan Audio Co.
Income Statement
for the Month Ended
January 31, 19X2

Sales		$160,000
Rent revenue		500
Interest revenue		400
Total sales and other revenues		$160,900
Expenses:		
Cost of goods sold	$100,000	
Wages	31,750	
Depreciation	1,000	
Rent	5,000	
Interest	750	
Income taxes	11,200	
Total expenses		149,700
Net income		$ 11,200

Exhibit 4-8, Part B

Multiple-Step
Income Statement
Chan Audio Co.
Income Statement
for the Month Ended
January 31, 19X2

Sales		$160,000
Cost of goods sold		100,000
Gross profit		$ 60,000
Operating expenses:		
Wages	$ 31,750	
Depreciation	1,000	
Rent	5,000	37,750
Operating income		$ 22,250
Other revenues and expenses:		
Rent revenue	$ 500	
Interest revenue	400	
Total other revenue	$ 900	
Deduct: Interest expense	750	150
Income before income taxes		$ 22,400
Income taxes (at 50%)		11,200
Net income		$ 11,200

Accountants have usually regarded interest revenue and interest expense as "other" items because they arise from lending and borrowing money—activities that are distinct from the ordinary selling of goods or services. Some companies make heavy use of debt, which causes high interest expenses, whereas other

Financial Statement Classification

The grouping of items in balance sheets and income statements is intended to emphasize the most important items and to highlight their relationships. For many firms, particularly retailers such as Wal-Mart and manufacturers such as Caterpillar, the relationship between sales and cost of goods sold is crucial and is thus highlighted as gross profit in a multiple-step income statement. However, gross profit is not the most significant relationship in all businesses. For example, how would a bank report cost of goods sold? Instead of gross profit, banks typically highlight the relationship between interest revenue (what the bank makes on its loans) and interest expense (what the bank pays to depositors). As the first two items in its 1993 income statement, Citicorp reported interest revenue of $23,811 million and interest expense of $16,121 million; the difference of $7,690 million was called *net interest revenue*.

Some firms find that the most useful format for the income statement is to group revenues and expenses by functional area. In its 1993 Income Statement, Walt Disney reported revenues and expenses for three areas: theme parks and resorts ($3,441 million revenue and $2,694 million expense), filmed entertainment ($3,673 million revenue and $3,051 million expense), and consumer products ($1,415 million revenue and $1,060 million expense).

The assets and liabilities in almost all balance sheets are separated into current and noncurrent categories. However, the arrangement of the categories can differ. Utilities typically list noncurrent assets before the current assets because the plant and equipment of a utility are far and away their most important assets. Portland General Corporation, the Oregon electric utility company, lists Net Utility Plant of $1,476 million before its Current Assets of $297 million and Other Assets of $338 million.

Most British firms show current liabilities as a subtraction from current assets. In its December 31, 1993 balance sheet, British Aerospace reported Net Current Assets of £2,323 million, consisting of current assets of £6,612 million minus current liabilities of £4,289 million. This arrangement highlights the fact that the acquisition of current assets is typically financed through current liabilities and that only the net amount, often called working capital, requires financing from long-term debt or equity sources. ■

Sources: 1993 Annual Reports of Citicorp, Walt Disney, Portland General Corporation, and British Aerospace.

companies incur little debt and have low interest expenses. Because interest revenue and expense appear in a separate category, comparisons of operating income between years and between companies can be made easily.

Examples of Actual Income Statements

Exhibits 4-9 and 4-10 demonstrate how two different companies use assorted terminology and formats for their individual statements of income. Note that extremely condensed income statement information is provided in published reports (as opposed to the detail that is shown for internal use).

The H. J. Heinz income statement in Exhibit 4-9 uses a *multiple-step* format, as do 65% of all corporate external reports in the United States. The multiple-step format has subtotals to highlight significant relationships. In addition to net income, the format also presents two key measures of performance, gross profit and operating income.

Accountants use the label *net* to denote that some amounts have been deducted in computing the final result. Thus *other expenses, net* in the Heinz statement, means that some revenue items and some expense items have been combined into one number. In a statement of income, the term *net* is not ordinarily used to describe any subtotals of income that precede the final net income number. For example, the Heinz statement shows *"income* before income taxes," not *"net income* before income taxes."

Wm. Wrigley Jr. Company, maker of chewing gum, uses a *single-step* format for its income statement in Exhibit 4-10, as do 35% of corporate external reports in the United States. Wrigley follows the single-step model and groups all revenues together and all expenses together without drawing subtotals within revenue and expense categories.

Exhibit 4-9		
H. J. Heinz Co. Statement of Income (in thousands) for the Year Ended April 27, 1994		

Sales		$7,046,738
Cost of products sold		4,381,745
Gross profit		2,664,993
Operating expenses		1,596,650
Operating income		1,068,343
Interest income	$ (36,771)	
Interest expense	149,243	
Other expenses, net	33,485	145,957
Income before income taxes		922,386
Provision for income taxes		319,442
Net Income		$ 602,944

Exhibit 4-10	
Wm. Wrigley Jr. Company Statement of Earnings (in thousands) for the Year Ended December 31, 1993	

Revenues:	
Net sales	$1,428,504
Investment income	11,938
Total revenues	1,440,442
Costs and expenses:	
Cost of sales	617,156
Selling, distribution, and general administrative expenses	542,944
Interest	1,507
Total costs and expenses	1,161,607
Earnings before income taxes	278,835
Income taxes	103,944
Net earnings	$ 174,891

However, note where income taxes appear. Most companies follow this practice of showing income taxes as a separate item immediately above net income (regardless of the grouping of other items on the income statement).

As Wrigley shows, the term *costs and expenses* is sometimes found instead of just *expenses*. Expenses would be an adequate description. Why? Because the "costs" listed on the income statement are expired costs, such as cost of sales, and thus are really expenses of the current period.

profitability evaluation The assessment of the likelihood that a company will provide investors with a particular rate of return on their investment.

■ PROFITABILITY EVALUATION RATIOS

Income statements provide information useful for evaluating a company's profitability. In its ultimate sense, **profitability evaluation** is the assessment of the likelihood that a company will provide investors with a particular rate of return on their investment. Profitability measures are also useful decision-making tools for company managers. Profitability comparisons through time and within and among industries are thus used as a basis for predictions and decisions by both external and internal users of financial statements. Consider three of the most popular ratios for measuring profitability:

gross profit percentage (gross margin percentage) Gross profit divided by sales.

1. A ratio based on gross profit (sales revenues minus cost of goods sold) is particularly useful to a retailer in choosing a pricing strategy and in judging its results. This measure, the **gross profit percentage**, or **gross margin percentage**, is defined as gross profit divided by sales. The Chan Audio gross profit percentage for January was

$$\text{Gross profit percentage} = \text{Gross profit} \div \text{Sales}$$
$$= \$60,000 \div \$160,000$$
$$= 37.5\%$$

These relationships can also be presented as follows:

	Amount	Percentage
Sales	$160,000	100.0%
Cost of goods sold	100,000	62.5
Gross profit	$ 60,000	37.5%

Gross profit percentages vary greatly by industry. Software companies have high gross profit percentages—Microsoft's is 83%. Why? Because most costs are in research and development and sales and marketing, not in cost of goods sold. In contrast, retail companies have lower gross margin percentages because product costs are their main expense. For example, the gross profit percentage for Safeway is 27%. Other gross margin percentages fall between the extremes, such as General Mills at 47% and Nike at 39%.

return on sales ratio Net income divided by sales.

2. A ratio based on a comparison of expenses and sales will be carefully followed by managers from month to month. The **return on sales ratio** shows the relationship of net income, the famous "bottom line," after all expenses have been deducted from all revenues, to sales revenue. Chan Audio's return on sales ratio is computed as follows:

$$\text{Return on sales} = \text{Net income} \div \text{Sales}$$
$$= \$11,200 \div \$160,000$$
$$= 7\%$$

return on stockholders' equity ratio Net income divided by invested capital (measured by average stockholders' equity).

3. The **return on stockholders' equity ratio** also uses net income but compares it with invested capital (as measured by average stockholders' equity) instead of sales. This ratio is widely regarded as the ultimate measure of overall accomplishment. The calculation for Chan Audio is:

$$\text{Return on stockholders' equity} = \text{Net income} \div \text{Average stockholders' equity}$$
$$= \$11,200 \div 1/2 \text{ (January 1 balance, } \$400,000 + \text{January 31}$$
$$\text{balance, } \$411,200)$$
$$= \$11,200 \div \$405,600$$
$$= 2.8\% \text{ (for one month)}$$

Some recent examples of actual annual return on sales and return on stockholders' equity ratios are:

	Return on Sales	Return on Stockholders' Equity
Microsoft	25%	35%
Nike	9%	22%
McDonald's	15%	17%
Bell Atlantic	11%	17%
Walgreens	3%	17%
British Petroleum (United Kingdom)	2%	6%
Nordstrom	4%	12%
Kobe Steel (Japan)	1%	3%

These three profitability ratios are being introduced at this early stage because they are so widely encountered. Chan Audio's 37.5% gross profit is relatively low compared with the usual 40% to 45% for the retail stereo industry. However, Chan Audio has maintained excellent expense control because its 7% return on sales and its 33.6% return on stockholders' equity (an annual rate of $2.8\% \times 12 = 33.6\%$) are higher than the 6% and 18% annual returns usually earned by the industry.

Statistical studies have shown that *profitability evaluation ratios* such as the three just discussed have higher power than *solvency determination ratios* (such as the current ratio) for predicting performance regarding *both* income and solvency. Later chapters study the uses and limitations of these and other ratios. For example, Chapter 7 explores the analytical role of gross profit percentages, and Chapter 15 reviews the most widely used ratios.

Summary Problem for Your Review

The first problem appeared earlier in the chapter, page 147.

Problem Two

Johnson & Johnson (maker of Tylenol, Band-Aids, and other products) uses a statement of earnings and retained earnings, as follows:

Johnson & Johnson
Statement of
Earnings and
Retained Earnings
(dollars in millions
except per share
figures)

Sales to customers	$14,138
Cost of products sold	4,791
Selling, distribution, and administrative expenses	5,771
Research expense	1,182
Interest income	(80)
Interest expense	126
Other expense	16
	11,806
Earnings before provision for taxes on income	2,332
Provision for taxes on income	545
Net earnings	1,787
Retained earnings at beginning of period	6,648
Cash dividends paid	(708)
Retained earnings at end of period	$ 7,727
Net earnings per share	$ 2.74

Required

1. Is this a single-step or a multiple-step statement of earnings? Explain your answer.
2. What term would Wm. Wrigley Jr. use as a label for the line having the $11,806 figure? (Refer to the Wrigley income statement on page 158.)
3. Suggest an alternative term for interest income.
4. Compute the gross profit.
5. What is the amount of the famous "bottom line" that is so often referred to by managers?
6. Net earnings per share is defined as net earnings divided by the average number of common shares outstanding. Compute the average number of common shares outstanding during the year.

Solution to Problem Two

1. As is often the case, Johnson & Johnson uses a hybrid of single-step and multiple-step income statements. However, it is closer to a single-step than a multiple-step statement. A purebred single-step statement would place interest income with sales to obtain total revenues.
2. Wrigley would use "total costs and expenses" to describe the $11,806 figure.
3. Interest *revenue* is preferable to interest *income*.
4.

Sales to customers	$14,138	100%
Cost of products sold	4,791	34
Gross profit	$ 9,347	66%

5. The bottom line in total is net earnings of $1,787 million. The bottom line per average common share outstanding is $2.74.
6. As Chapter 2 explains, net earnings per share is required to be shown on the face of the income statement.

$$\text{Earnings per share (EPS)} = \frac{\text{Net earnings}}{\text{Average number of common shares outstanding}}$$

$$\$2.74 = \frac{\$1,787,000,000}{\text{Average shares}}$$

$$\text{Average shares} = \$1,787,000,000 \div \$2.74$$

$$\text{Average shares} = 652,189,781$$

Highlights to Remember

At the end of each accounting period, adjustments must be made so that financial statements can be presented on a full-fledged accrual basis. The major adjustments are for (1) the expiration of unexpired costs, (2) the earning of unearned revenues, (3) the accrual of unrecorded expenses, and (4) the accrual of unrecorded revenues. Frequently, accounting adjustments are clarified when they are seen as mirror images by looking at both sides of the adjustment simultaneously. For example, (a) the expiration of unexpired costs (the tenant's rent expense) is accompanied by (b) the earning of unearned revenues (the landlord's rent revenue). Similarly, (a) the accrual of unrecorded expenses (a borrower's interest expense) is accompanied by (b) the accrual of unrecorded revenues (a lender's interest revenue).

The adjusting entries can either precede or follow the related cash flows. Entries for the expiration of unexpired costs and the recognition (earning) of unearned revenues follow the cash flows, while entries for the accrual of unrecorded expenses and the accrual of unrecorded revenues precede the cash flows.

Classified balance sheets divide various items into subcategories. For example, assets and liabilities are separated into current and long-term. These subcategories are used in analysis. For example, current assets minus current liabilities is called working capital. The current ratio, defined as current assets divided by current liabilities, is used to help assess solvency.

Income statements may appear in single-step or multiple-step form. Regardless of the format, published income statements are highly condensed and summarized compared with reports used within an organization.

Income statement ratios are used to assess profitability. Among the most useful are gross margin (or gross profit), return on sales, and return on stockholders' equity.

Accounting Vocabulary

account format, *p. 154*
accrue, *p. 137*
adjusting entries, *p. 136*
adjustments, *p. 136*
classified balance sheet, *p. 149*
current assets, *p. 149*
current liabilities, *p. 149*
current ratio, *p. 152*
deferred credit, *p. 137*
deferred revenue, *p. 137*
explicit transactions, *p. 136*

gross margin, *p. 155*
gross margin percentage, *p. 159*
gross profit, *p. 155*
gross profit percentage, *p. 159*
implicit transactions, *p. 136*
multiple-step income statement, *p. 155*
operating income, *p. 155*
operating profit, *p. 155*
pretax income, *p. 144*
profitability evaluation, *p. 158*

report format, *p. 154*
return on sales ratio, *p. 159*
return on stockholders' equity ratio, *p. 159*
single-step income statement, *p. 155*
solvency, *p. 152*
unearned revenue, *p. 137*
working capital, *p. 151*
working capital ratio, *p. 152*

Assignment Material

Questions

4-1. Give two examples of an explicit transaction.

4-2. Give two examples of an implicit transaction.

4-3. Give two synonyms for *deferred revenue*.

4-4. Explain the difference between *incur* and *accrue*.

4-5. "Accountants often use routine shortcuts when they record expenses." Explain, giving an illustration.

4-6. Distinguish between the return *on* investment and the return *of* investment.

4-7. Give a popular synonym for *income before income taxes*.

4-8. Give a synonym for *income tax expense*.

4-9. Explain why income tax expense is usually the final deduction on both single-step and multiple-step income statements.

4-10. "The accrual of previously unrecorded revenues is the mirror image of the accrual of previously unrecorded expenses." Explain, using an illustration.

4-11. What types of adjusting entries are made before the related cash flows? What types after the related cash flows?

4-12. Why are current assets and current liabilities grouped separately from long-term assets and long-term liabilities?

4-13. Explain the difference between a *single-step* and a *multiple-step* income statement.

4-14. Why does interest expense appear below operating income on a multiple-step income statement?

4-15. The term "costs and expenses" is sometimes found instead of just "expenses" on the income statement. Would "expenses" be an adequate description? Why?

4-16. Name three popular ratios for measuring profitability, and indicate how to compute each of the three.

Exercises

4-17   True or False

Use *T* or *F* to indicate whether each of the following statements is true or false:

1. Retained Earnings should be accounted for as a current asset item.
2. Cash should be classified as a stockholders' equity item.
3. Machinery used in the business should be recorded as a noncurrent asset item.
4. The cash balance is the best evidence of stockholders' equity.
5. From a single balance sheet you can find stockholders' equity for a period of time but not for a specific day.
6. It is not possible to determine changes in the condition of a business from a single balance sheet.

4-18   Tenant and Landlord

The Eugster Company, a retail hardware store, pays quarterly rent on its store at the beginning of each quarter. The rent per quarter is $15,000. The owner of the building in which the store is located is the Omen Corporation.

Required   Using the balance sheet equation format, analyze the effects of the following on the tenant's and the landlord's financial position:

1. Eugster pays $15,000 rent on July 1.
2. Adjustment for July.
3. Adjustment for August.
4. Adjustment for September. Also prepare the journal entries for Eugster and Omen for September.

4-19   Customer and Airline

The Scott Paper Company decided to hold a managers' meeting in Hawaii in February. To take advantage of special fares, Scott purchased airline tickets in advance from American Airlines at a total cost of $70,000. These were acquired on December 1 for cash.

Required   Using the balance sheet equation format, analyze the impact of the December payment and the February travel on the financial position of both Scott and American. Also prepare journal entries for February.

4-20   Accruals of Wages

Consider the following calendar:

September						
S	M	T	W	T	F	S
		1	2	3	4	5
6	7	8	9	10	11	12
13	14	15	16	17	18	19
20	21	22	23	24	25	26
27	28	29	30			

The Melrose Department Store commenced business on September 1. It is open every day except Sunday. Its total payroll for all employees is $6,000 per day. Payments are made each Tuesday for the preceding week's work through Saturday.

Required   Using the balance sheet equation format, analyze the financial impact on Melrose of the following:

1. Disbursements for wages on September 8, 15, 22, and 29.
2. Adjustments for wages on September 30. Also prepare the journal entry.

4-21   Accrued Vacation Pay

Delta Airlines had the following as a current liability on its balance sheet, June 30, 1993:

Accrued vacation pay	$194,174,000

Under the accrual basis of accounting, vacation pay is ordinarily accrued throughout the year as workers are regularly paid. For example, suppose a Delta baggage handler earns $650 per week for fifty weeks and also gets paid $1,300 for two weeks' vacation. Accrual accounting requires that the obligation for the $1,300 be recognized as it is earned rather than when the payment is disbursed. Thus, in each of the fifty weeks Delta would recognize a wage expense (or vacation pay expense) of $1,300 ÷ 50 = $26.

Required

1. Prepare the weekly Delta adjusting journal entry called for by the $26 example.
2. Prepare the entry for the $1,300 payment of vacation pay.

4-22   Placement of Interest in Income Statement

Two companies have the following balance sheets as of December 31, 19X2:

Jupiter Company

Cash	$ 50,000	Note payable*	$100,000
Other assets	150,000	Stockholders' equity	100,000
Total	$200,000	Total	$200,000

* 12% interest.

Saturn Company

Cash	$ 50,000	Stockholders' equity	$200,000
Other assets	150,000		
Total	$200,000		

In 19X6, each company had sales of $450,000 and expenses (excluding interest) of $400,000. Ignore income taxes.

Required Did the two companies earn the same net income? The same operating income? Explain, showing computations of operating income and net income.

4-23   Effects of Interest on Lenders and Borrowers

Prudential lent Harshman Paint Manufacturing Company $800,000 on March 1, 19X1. The loan plus interest of 12% is payable on March 1, 19X2.

Required

1. Using the balance sheet equation format, prepare an analysis of the impact of the transactions on both Prudential's and Harshman's financial position on March 1, 19X1. Show the summary adjustments on December 31, 19X1, for the period March 1–December 31.
2. Prepare adjusting journal entries for Prudential and Harshman on December 31,19X1.

4-24   Identification of Transactions

Sherwin Corporation's financial position is represented by the nine balances shown on the first line of the following schedule (in thousands of dollars). Assume that a single transaction took place for each of the following lines, and describe what you think happened, using one short sentence for each line.

	Cash	Accounts Receivable	Inventory	Equipment	Accounts Payable	Accrued Wages Payable	Unearned Rent Revenue	Paid-in Capital	Retained Income
Bal.	19	32	54	0	29	0	0	55	21
(1)	29	32	54	0	29	0	0	65	21
(2)	29	32	54	20	29	0	0	85	21
(3)	29	32	66	20	41	0	0	85	21
(4a)	29	47	66	20	41	0	0	85	36
(4b)	29	47	58	20	41	0	0	85	28
(5)	35	41	58	20	41	0	0	85	28
(6)	15	41	58	20	21	0	0	85	28
(7)	20	41	58	20	21	0	5	85	28
(8)	20	41	58	20	21	2	5	85	26
(9)	20	41	58	19	21	2	5	85	25
(10)	20	41	58	19	21	2	3	85	27

4-25 Effects on Balance Sheet Equation

Following is a list of effects of accounting transactions on the basic accounting equation: Assets equal Liabilities plus Stockholders' Equity.

a. Increase in assets, increase in liabilities
b. Increase in assets, decrease in liabilities
c. Increase in assets, increase in stockholders' equity
d. Increase in assets, decrease in assets
e. Decrease in assets, decrease in liabilities
f. Increase in liabilities, decrease in stockholders' equity
g. Decrease in assets, increase in liabilities
h. Decrease in liabilities, increase in stockholders' equity
i. Decrease in assets, decrease in stockholders' equity
j. None of these

Which of the foregoing relationships defines the accounting effect of each of the following?

1. The adjusting entry to recognize periodic depreciation.
2. The adjusting entry to record accrued salaries.
3. The adjusting entry to record accrued interest receivable.
4. The collection of interest previously accrued.
5. The settlement of an account payable by the issuance of a note payable.
6. The recognition of an expense that had been paid for previously. A "prepaid" account was increased upon payment.
7. The earning of income previously collected. Unearned Revenue was increased when collection was made in advance.

4-26 Effects of Errors in Adjustments

What will be the effect—understated (u), overstated (o), or no effect (n)—upon the income of the present and future periods if the following errors were made. In all cases assume that amounts carried over into 19X4 would affect 19X4 operations via the routine accounting entries of 19X4.

		Period	
		19X3	*19X4*
1.	Revenue has been collected in advance, but earned amounts have not been recognized at the end of 19X3. Instead, all revenue was recognized as earned in 19X4.	_____	_____
2.	Revenue for services rendered has been earned, but the unbilled amounts have not been recognized at the end of 19X3.	_____	_____
3.	Accrued wages payable have not been recognized at the end of 19X3.	_____	_____
4.	Prepaid items like rent have been paid (in late 19X3) through half of 19X4, but not adjusted at the end of 19X3. The payments have been debited to Prepaid Rent. They were written off in mid-19X4.	_____	_____

4-27   Effects of Adjustments and Corrections

Listed below are a series of accounts that are numbered for identification. All accounts needed to answer the parts of this question are included. Prepare an answer sheet with columns in which you are to write the identification numbers of the accounts affected by your answers. The same account may be used in several answers.

1.	Cash	15.	Notes payable
2.	Accounts receivable	16.	Accrued wages and salaries payable
3.	Notes receivable	17.	Accrued interest payable
4.	Inventory	18.	Unearned subscription revenue
5.	Accrued interest receivable	19.	Capital stock
6.	Accrued rent receivable	20.	Sales
7.	Fuel on hand	21.	Fuel expense
8.	Unexpired rent	22.	Sales and wages
9.	Unexpired insurance	23.	Insurance expense
10.	Unexpired repairs and maintenance	24.	Repairs and maintenance expense
		25.	Rent expense
11.	Land	26.	Rent revenue
12.	Buildings	27.	Subscription revenue
13.	Machinery and equipment	28.	Interest revenue
14.	Accounts payable	29.	Interest expense

Required   Prepare any necessary adjusting or correcting entries called for by the following situations, *which were discovered at the end of the calendar year*. With respect to each situation, assume that no entries have been made regarding the situation other than those specifically described (i.e., no monthly adjustments have been made during the year). *Consider each situation separately*. These transactions were not necessarily conducted by one business firm. Amounts are in thousands of dollars. *Illustration:* Purchased new equipment for $100 cash, plus a $300 short-term note. The bookkeeper failed to record the transaction. The answer would appear as follows:

	Account		Amount	
	Debit	Credit	Debit	Credit
Illustration	13	1 & 15	400	100 & 300
a.	—		—	
b.	—		—	
c.	—		—	
etc.	—		—	

a. A $300 purchase of equipment on December 5 was erroneously debited to Accounts Payable. The credit was correctly made to Cash.

b. A business made several purchases of fuel oil. Some purchases ($800) were debited to Fuel Expense, while others ($1,100) were charged to an assets account. An oil gauge revealed $400 of fuel on hand at the end of the year. There was no fuel on hand at the beginning of the year.

c. On April 1, a business took out a fire insurance policy. The policy was for two years, and the premium paid was $400. It was debited to Insurance Expense on April 1.

d. On December 1, $400 was paid in advance to the landlord for four months' rent. The tenant debited Unexpired Rent for $400 on December 1. What adjustment is necessary on December 31 on the tenant's books?

e. Machinery is repaired and maintained by an outside maintenance company on an annual fee basis, payable in advance. The $240 fee was paid in advance on September 1 and charged to Repairs and Maintenance Expense. What adjustment is necessary on December 31?

f. On November 16, $800 of machinery was purchased. $200 cash was paid down and a ninety-day, 5% note payable was signed for the balance. The November 16 transaction was properly recorded. Prepare the adjustment for the interest.

g. A publisher sells subscriptions to magazines. Customers pay in advance. Receipts are originally credited to Unearned Subscription Revenue. On August 1, many one-year subscriptions were collected and recorded, amounting to $12,000.

h. On December 30, certain merchandise was purchased for $1,000 on open account. The bookkeeper debited Machinery and Equipment and credited Accounts Payable for $1,000. Prepare a correcting entry.

i. A 120-day, 7%, $7,500 cash loan was made to a customer on November 1. The November 1 transaction was recorded correctly.

Problems

4-28   Adjusting Entries

(Alternates are 4-30, 4-31, and 4-32.) Jennifer Blair, certified public accountant, had the following transactions (among others) during 19X2:

a. For accurate measurement of performance and position, Blair uses the accrual basis of accounting. On August 1, she acquired office supplies for $2,000. Office Supplies Inventory was increased, and Cash was decreased by $2,000 on Blair's books. On December 31, her inventory was $800.

b. On September 1, a client gave Blair a retainer fee of $48,000 cash for monthly services to be rendered over the following twelve months. Blair increased Cash and Unearned Fee Revenue.

c. Blair accepted an $8,000 note receivable from a client on October 1 for tax services. The note plus interest of 12% per year were due in six months. Blair increased Note Receivable and Fee Revenue by $8,000.

d. As of December 31, Blair had not recorded $400 of unpaid wages earned by her secretary during late December.

Required   For the year ended December 31, 19X2, prepare all adjustments called for by the above transactions. Assume that appropriate entries were routinely made for the explicit transactions described above. However, no adjustments have been made before December 31. For each adjustment, prepare an analysis in the same format used when the adjustment process was explained in the chapter (i.e., the balance sheet equation format). Also prepare the adjusting journal entry.

4-29   Multiple-Step Income Statement

(Alternate is 4-33.) From the following data, prepare a multiple-step income statement for the Redmond Company for the fiscal year ended May 31, 19X6 (in thousands except for percentage). *Hint*: see page 156.

Sales	$890	Cost of goods sold	$440
Interest expense	72	Depreciation	30
Rent expense	52	Rent revenue	10
Interest revenue	14	Wages	200
Income tax rate	40%		

✓4-30   Four Major Adjustments

(Alternates are 4-28, 4-31, and 4-32.) Judith Noller, an attorney, had the following transactions (among others) during 19X2, her initial year in practicing law:

a. On August 1, Noller leased office space for one year. The landlord (lessor) insisted on full payment in advance. Prepaid Rent was increased and Cash was decreased by $24,000 on Noller's books. Similarly, the landlord increased Cash and increased Unearned Rent Revenue.

b. On October 1, Noller received a retainer fee of $18,000 cash for services to be rendered to her client, a local trucking company, over the succeeding twelve months. Noller increased Cash and Unearned Fee Revenue. The trucking company increased Prepaid Expenses and decreased Cash.

c. As of December 31, Noller had not recorded $400 of unpaid wages earned by her secretary during late December.

d. During November and December, Noller rendered services to another client, a utility company. She had intended to bill the company for $5,400 services through December 31, but she decided to delay formal billing until late January when the case would probably be settled.

Required   1. For the year ended December 31, 19X2, prepare all adjustments called for by the above transactions. Assume that appropriate entries were routinely made for the explicit transactions described above. However, no adjustments have been made before December 31. For each adjustment, prepare an analysis in the same format used when the adjustment process was explained in the chapter (i.e., the balance sheet equation format). Prepare two adjustments for each transaction, one for Noller and one for the other party to the transaction. In part **c**, assume that the secretary uses the accrual basis for his personal entity.

2. For each transaction, prepare the journal entries for Judith Noller *and* the other entities involved.

4-31   Four Major Adjustments

(Alternates are 4-28, 4-30, and 4-32.) The Goodyear Tire and Rubber Company included the following items in its January 1, 1994 balance sheet (in millions):

| Prepaid expenses (a current asset) | $371.1 |
| United States and foreign taxes (a current liability) | 373.1 |

Required

Analyze the impact of the following transactions on the financial position of Goodyear. Prepare your analysis in the same format used when the adjustment process was explained in the chapter. Also show adjusting journal entries.

1. On January 31, an adjustment of $3 million was made for the rentals of various retail outlets that had originally increased Prepaid Expenses but had expired.
2. During December 1993, Goodyear sold tires for $2 million cash to U-Haul, but delivery was not made until January 28. Unearned Revenue had been increased in December. No other adjustments had been made since. Prepare the adjustment on January 31.
3. Goodyear had lent cash to several of its independent retail dealers. As of January 31, the dealers owed $4 million of interest that had been unrecorded.
4. On January 31, Goodyear increased its accrual of federal income taxes by $21 million.

4-32   Four Major Adjustments
(Alternates are 4-28, 4-30, and 4-31.) Alaska Airlines had the following items in its balance sheet, December 30, 1995, the end of the fiscal year:

Inventories and supplies	$ 41,269,000
Prepaid expenses and other current assets	56,498,000
Air traffic liability	108,360,000
Accrued wages, vacation pay, and payroll taxes	40,192,000

A footnote stated: "Passenger ticket sales are recorded as revenue when the transportation is used. The value of unused tickets is included in current liabilities in the financial statements." The title of this current liability is Air Traffic Liability.

The income statement included:

| Passenger revenues | $1,001,975,000 |
| Wages and benefits expense | 368,152,000 |

Required

Analyze the impact of the following assumed transactions on the financial position of Alaska. Prepare your analysis in the same format used when the adjustment process was explained in the chapter. Also show adjusting journal entries.

1. Rented a sales office in a Transamerica office building for one year, beginning December 1, 1995, for $18,000 cash.
2. On December 30, 1995, an adjustment was made for the rent in requirement 1.
3. Sold two charter flights to Apple Computer for $100,000 each. Cash of $200,000 was received in advance on November 20, 1995. The flights were for transporting marketing personnel to two business conventions in New York.
4. As the financial statements were being prepared on December 30, accountants for both Alaska and Apple Computer independently noted that the first charter flight had occurred in late December. The second would occur in early February. An adjustment was made on December 30.
5. Alaska had lent $2 million to Boeing. Interest of $160,000 was accrued on December 30.
6. Additional wages of $140,000 were accrued on December 30.

4-33 Budweiser Financial Statements

(Alternate is 4-29.) Anheuser-Busch (maker of Budweiser beer) is the largest beer producer in the United States. Some actual financial data and nomenclature from its 1993 annual report were (in millions):

Anheuser-Busch,
Inc.

Interest expense, net	$ 166	Cash dividends declared	$?
Sales	11,505	Other income	4
Gross profit	4,085	Net income	594
Operating income	1,212	Retained earnings:	
Other operating expenses	565	Beginning of year	5,795
Marketing, administrative,		End of year	6,023
and research expenses	?	Provision for income taxes	
Cost of products sold	?	(income tax expense)	456

Required

1. Prepare a combined multiple-step statement of income and retained earnings for the year ended December 31, 1993. *Hint*: see page 156.
2. Compute the percentage of gross profit on sales and the percentage of net income on sales.
3. The average stockholders' equity for the year was $4,438 million. What was the percentage of net income on average stockholders' equity?

4-34 Accounting for Dues

(Alternate is 4-35.) The Pebble Island Golf Club provided the following data from its comparative balance sheets:

	December 31	
	19X3	*19X2*
Dues receivable	$90,000	$75,000
Unearned dues revenue	—	$30,000

The income statement for 19X3, which was prepared on the accrual basis, showed dues revenue earned of $720,000. No dues were collected in advance during 19X3.

Required Prepare journal entries and post to T-accounts for the following:

1. Earning of dues collected in advance.
2. Billing of dues revenue during 19X3.
3. Collection of dues receivable in 19X3.

4-35 Accounting for Subscriptions

(Alternate is 4-34.) A French magazine company collects subscriptions in advance of delivery of its magazines. However, many magazines are delivered to magazine distributors (for newsstand sales), and these distributors are billed and pay later. The subscription revenue earned for the month of March on the accrual basis was FF200,000 (FF refers to the French franc). Other pertinent data were:

	March	
	31	*1*
Unearned subscription revenue	FF190,000	FF140,000
Accounts receivable	7,000	9,000

Required Reconstruct the entries for March. Prepare journal entries and post to T-accounts for the following:

1. Collections of unearned subscription revenue of $140,000 prior to March 1.
2. Billing of accounts receivable (a) of $9,000 prior to March 1, and (b) of $80,000 during March. (Credit Revenue Earned)
3. Collections of cash during March and any other entries that are indicated by the given data.

4-36 Financial Statements and Adjustments

Marcella Wholesalers, Inc., has just completed its fourth year of business, 19X3. A set of financial statements was prepared by the principal stockholders' eldest child, a college student who is beginning the third week of an accounting course. Following is a list (in no systematic order) of the items appearing in the student's balance sheet, income statement, and statement of retained income:

Accounts receivable	$183,100	Advertising expense	$ 98,300
Note receivable	36,000	Merchandise inventory	201,900
Cash	99,300	Cost of goods sold	590,000
Paid-in capital	620,000	Unearned rent revenue	4,800
Building	300,000	Insurance expense	2,500
Accumulated depreciation,		Unexpired insurance	2,300
building	20,000	Accounts payable	52,500
Land	169,200	Interest expense	600
Sales	936,800	Telephone expense	2,900
Salary expense	124,300	Notes payable	20,000
Retained income:		Net income	110,500
December 31,19X2	164,000	Miscellaneous expense	3,400
December 31,19X3	274,500	Maintenance expense	4,300

Assume that the statements in which these items appear are current and complete except for the following matters not taken into consideration by the student:

a. Salaries of $5,200 have been earned by employees for the last half of December 19X3. Payment by the company will be made on the next payday, January 2, 19X4.

b. Interest at 10% per annum on the note receivable has accrued for two months and is expected to be collected by the company when the note is due on January 31, 19X4.

c. Part of the building owned by the company was rented to a tenant on November 1, 19X3, for six months, payable in advance. This rent was collected in cash and is represented by the item labeled Unearned Rent Revenue.

d. Depreciation on the building for 19X3 is $6,100.

e. Cash dividends of $60,000 were declared in December 19X3, payable in January 19X4.

f. Income tax at 40% applies to 19X3, all of which is to be paid in the early part of 19X4.

Required Prepare the following corrected financial statements:

1. Multiple-step income statement for 19X3.
2. Statement of retained income for 19X3.
3. Classified balance sheet at December 31, 19X3. (Show appropriate support for the dollar amounts you compute.)

4-37 Mirror Side of Adjustments

Problem 4-28 described some Blair adjustments. Repeat the requirement for each adjustment as it would be made by the client in transactions *b* and *c* and by the secretary in transaction *d*. For our purposes here, assume that the secretary keeps personal books on the accrual basis.

4-38   Mirror Side of Adjustments

Problem 4-31 described some Goodyear adjustments. Repeat the requirements for each adjustment as it would be made by (1) landlords, (2) U-Haul, (3) retail dealers, and (4) U.S. and foreign governments. Assume that all use accrual accounting.

4-39   Mirror Side of Adjustments

Problem 4-32 described some Alaska Airlines adjustments numbered 1 to 6. Repeat the requirements for each adjustment as it would be made by the other party in the transaction. Specifically, (1) and (2) Transamerica, (3) and (4) Apple Computer, (5) Boeing, and (6) employees. Assume that all use accrual accounting.

4-40   Journal Entries and Posting

Nike, Inc., has many well-known products, including footwear. The company's balance sheet included (in thousands):

	May 31	
	1993	*1992*
Prepaid expenses	$42,452	$32,977
Income taxes payable	17,150	42,422

Suppose that during the fiscal year ended May 31, 1993, $210,000,000 cash was disbursed and charged to Prepaid Expenses. Similarly, $254,772,000 was disbursed for income taxes and charged to Income Taxes Payable.

Required

1. Assume that the Prepaid Expenses account relates to outlays for miscellaneous operating expenses (for example, supplies, insurance, and short-term rentals). Prepare summary journal entries for (a) the disbursements and (b) the expenses for fiscal 1993. Post the entries to the T-accounts.
2. Assume that there were no other accounts related to income taxes. Prepare summary journal entries for (a) the disbursements and (b) the expenses for fiscal 1993. Post the entries to T-accounts.

4-41   Advance Service Contracts

Diebold, Incorporated, a manufacturer of automated teller machines (ATMs), showed the following balance sheet account:

	December 31	
	1993	*1992*
Deferred income	$45,001,000	$41,522,000

A footnote to the financial statements stated: "Deferred income is recognized for customer billings in advance of the period in which the service will be performed and is recognized in income on a straight-line basis over the contract period."

Required

1. Prepare summary journal entries for the creation in 1992 and subsequent earning in 1993 of the deferred income of $41,522,000. Use the following accounts: Accounts Receivable, Deferred Income, and Income from Advance Billings.
2. A one-year job contract was billed to Keystone Bank on January 1, 1993, for $36,000. Work began on January 1. The full amount was collected on February 15. Prepare all pertinent journal entries through February 28, 1993. ("Straight-line" means an equal amount per month.)

4-42   Journal Entries and Adjustments

Northern States Power Company is a public utility in Minnesota. An annual report included the following footnote:

Revenues—Because customer utility meters are read and billed on a cycle basis, unbilled revenues are estimated and recorded for services provided from the monthly meter-reading dates to month-end.

The income statements showed:

	1993	1992
Operating revenues	$2,403,992,000	$2,159,522,000
Operating income	303,886,000	256,016,000

The balance sheet showed as part of current assets:

	December 31	
	1993	1992
Accounts receivable	$266,531,000	$224,618,000
Unbilled utility revenues	111,296,000	100,172,000

Required   Prepare the adjusting journal entry for (a) the unbilled revenues at the end of 1993 and (b) the eventual billing and collection of the unbilled revenues. Ignore income taxes.

4-43   Postal Service Accounting

The U.S. Postal Service is a separate federal entity created by the Postal Reform Act. The Postal Service financial statements are audited by an independent accounting firm. Its current liabilities for a given year included:

Prepaid permit mail and box rentals	$329,355,000
Estimated prepaid postage-Note 1	770,000,000

Note 1 stated: "Estimated prepaid postage represents the estimated revenue collected prior to the end of the year for which services will be subsequently rendered."

The Postal Service's statement of operations showed "operating revenue" of $19,133,041,000.

The current assets included "Receivables, U.S. Government," of $126,890,000.

Required
1. Provide alternative descriptions for the two current-liability accounts.
2. A large retailer, Sears, has rented boxes in thousands of post offices to accelerate receipts from customers. Suppose $1 million of those rentals that were prepaid by Sears had expired as of September 30. Journalize a $1 million adjustment for expired rentals on the accounts of the Postal Service and Sears.
3. Many mail-order retailers prepay postage. In addition, millions of citizens buy rolls of postage stamps for later use. Note 1 describes how the Postal Service recognizes such prepayments. Suppose in a given year that Sears used $2 million of its prepaid postage that had not been adjusted for. Journalize a $2 million adjustment on the accounts of the Postal Service and Sears.
4. The Postal Service's statement of operations included the following as a separate addition to its operating revenue:

Operating appropriations (for revenue forgone for certain classes of mail)	$789,108,000

A footnote stated that the Postal Reform Act authorizes "to be appropriated each year a sum determined by the Postal Service to be equal to revenue forgone by it in providing certain mail services to the U.S. Government at free or reduced rates." Journalize the effects on the accounts of the Postal Service of an adjustment as of September 30 that increases appropriations by $20 million. Also journalize the effects on the accounts of the U.S. government. For simplicity, assume that no cash had changed hands as yet regarding these appropriations.

4-44   Classified Balance Sheet and Current Ratio

Fisher Imaging Corporation is a Denver-based high-technology company that produces x-ray imaging systems for the medical profession. Major products include minimally invasive systems for diagnosis and treatment of breast cancer, heart disease, and vascular disease. The company's balance sheet for December 31, 1993 contained the following items:

Property and equipment, net	4,526,575
Accrued salaries and wages	2,461,997
Cash	161,520
Other assets	8,046,411
Other noncurrent liabilities	1,535,779
Short-term bank loans	1,824,148
Inventories	19,131,834
Other current liabilities	6,344,662
Notes payable	8,169,702
Other current assets	3,084,997
Trade accounts payable	5,769,111
Trade accounts receivable	21,599,625
Long-term debt	?
Stockholders' equity	27,033,116

Required

1. Prepare a December 31, 1993 classified balance sheet for Fisher Imaging Corporation. Include the correct amount for long-term debt.
2. Compute the company's working capital and current ratio.
3. Comment on the company's current ratio. In 1991 the ratio was 1.5; in 1989 it was 1.6. The industry average is 2.0.
4. During 1993 Fisher Imaging increased its short-term borrowing from banks by $3.3 million. Suppose the company had not increased its short-term borrowing but had instead increased its long-term debt by $3.3 million. How would this have affected Fisher Imaging's current ratio? How would it have affected the company's solvency?

4-45   Multiple-Step Income Statement

Kimberly-Clark Corporation has many well-known products, including Kleenex and Huggies. Its 1993 annual report contained the following data and actual terms (in millions):

Cost of products sold	$4,581	Advertising, promotion, and selling expense	$1,068
Research expense	159	Provision for income taxes	
Interest expense	113	(income tax expense)	284
Interest and other income	32	General and other expense	371
Gross profit	2,392		

Required   Prepare a multiple-step statement of income.

4-46   Single-Step Income Statement

A. T. Cross Company's best-known products are writing instruments such as ballpoint pens. The Cross 1992 annual report contained the following items (in thousands):

Interest and other income	$ 3,206	Selling, general, and administrative expenses	$ 76,029
Cost of goods sold	111,600	Retained earnings at end	
Provision for income taxes		of year	125,187
(income tax expense)	5,191	Cash dividends	21,648
Sales	200,432		

Required

1. Prepare a combined single-step statement of income and retained earnings for the year.
2. Compute the percentage of gross profit on sales and the percentage of net income on sales.
3. The average stockholders' equity for the year was about $156 million. What was the percentage of net income on average stockholders' equity?
4. In 1990 the gross profit percentage was 46.6%, the percentage of net income to sales was 12.2%, and the return on average stockholders' equity was 6.9%. Comment on the changes between 1990 and 1992.

4-47   Retail Company Financial Statements

Kmart Corporation is one of the world's largest retailers. The 1993 annual report included the data shown below (in millions of dollars). Unless otherwise specified, the balance sheet amounts are the balances at the end of the 1993 fiscal year.

Sales	$38,124	Interest expense	$ 432
Cash dividends	455	Long-term debt	3,237
Merchandise inventories	8,752	Cash	611
Cost of merchandise sold	28,485	Selling & administrative expense	7,781
Paid-in capital	1,836	Accrued taxes payable	614
Accounts receivable	1,146	Accrued payroll and other current	
Retained earnings:		liabilities	1,332
Beginning of year	5,214	Provision for income taxes	485
End of year	5,700	Property & equipment, net	6,405
Notes payable	590	Other noncurrent assets	2,017
Accounts payable	2,959	Other noncurrent liabilities	2,663

Required

1. Prepare a combined multiple-step statement of income and retained earnings.
2. Prepare a classified balance sheet.
3. The average stockholders' equity for the year was about $7,213 million. What was the percentage of net income on average stockholders' equity?
4. Compute (a) gross profit percentage and (b) percentage of net income to sales.
5. Optional: Why might stockholders want to invest in a company with such a consistently low percentage of net income to sales?

✔ 4-48   Preparation of Financial Statements from Trial Balance

ConAgra, the Omaha company that produces consumer foods such as Armour and Swift meats, Banquet and Morton frozen foods, and Healthy Choice brands, prepared the following (slightly modified) trial balance as of May 29, 1994, the end of the company's fiscal year:

ConAgra, Inc.
Trial Balance
May 29, 1994
(in millions)

	Debits	Credits
Cash and cash equivalents	$ 166.4	
Receivables	1,589.6	
Inventories	2,884.4	
Prepaid expenses	216.9	
Other current assets	286.0	
Property, plant, and equipment, at cost	4,150.4	
Accumulated depreciation, property, plant, and equipment		$ 1,564.1
Brands, trademarks, and goodwill, net	2,626.4	
Other assets	365.8	

continued

Notes payable		419.0
Accounts payable		1,937.0
Accrued payroll		262.4
Advances on sales (deferred revenues)		914.9
Other current liabilities		1,219.5
Long-term debt		2,206.8
Other noncurrent liabilities		1,079.7
Preferred stock		455.6
Common stock, $5 par value		1,263.6
Retained earnings		1,167.0
Additional paid-in capital		304.9
Treasury and restricted stock*	764.3	
Net sales		23,512.2
Cost of goods sold	20,452.2	
Selling, administrative, and general expenses	2,091.0	
Interest expense	254.2	
Other income		5.2
Income taxes	282.9	
Cash dividends	181.4	
Total	$36,311.9	$36,311.9

*Part of stockholders' equity.

Required

1. Prepare ConAgra's income statement for the year ended May 29, 1994, using a multiple-step format.

2. Prepare ConAgra's income statement for the year ended May 29, 1994, using a single-step format. Which format for the income statement is more informative? Why?

3. Prepare ConAgra's classified balance sheet as of May 29, 1994.

4-49   Professional Football Income

Examine the accompanying condensed income statement of the Green Bay Packers, Inc. for a recent year.

Income:		
Regular season:		
Net receipts from home games	$ 3,223,803	
Out-of-town games	2,288,967	
Televison and radio programs	14,322,244	$19,835,014
Preseason:		
Net recepts from preseason games	1,356,751	
Television and radio programs	355,032	1,711,783
Miscellaneous:		
Club allocation of league receipts	784,988	
Other income	511,516	1,296,504
Total income		22,843,301
Expenses:		
Salaries and other season expenses	16,243,729	
Training expense	725,079	
Overhead expense	4,744,336	
Severance pay	656,250	22,369,394
Income from operations		473,907
Interest income		1,203,281
Income before taxes		1,677,188
Provision for income taxes		167,000
Net income		$ 1,510,188

Required
1. Do you agree with the choice of terms in this statement? If not, suggest where a preferable label should be used.
2. Is this a single-step income statement? If not, which items would you shift to prepare a single-step statement?
3. Identify the major factors that affect the Packers' net income.

4-50 Adjusting Entries and Ethics

By definition, adjusting entries are not triggered by an explicit event. Therefore, accountants must initiate adjusting entries. For each of the following adjusting entries, discuss a potential unethical behavior that an accountant or manager might undertake:

a. Recognition of expenses from the prepaid supplies account.

b. Recognition of revenue from the unearned revenue account.

c. Accrual of interest payable.

d. Accrual of fees receivable.

✓4-51 Wal-Mart Annual Report

This problem uses an actual company's accounts to develop skill in preparing adjusting journal entries. Refer to the financial statements of Wal-Mart (Appendix A at the end of the book). Note the following balance sheet items:

	January 31	
	1995	*1994*
Prepaid expenses	$ 329,000,000	$ 182,000,000
Accrued liabilities	1,819,000,000	1,473,000,000

Suppose that during the 1995 fiscal year, $2,400,000,000 cash was disbursed and charged to Prepaid Expenses and $8,200,000,000 of accrued liabilities were paid.

Required
1. Assume that the Prepaid Expenses account relates to outlays for miscellaneous Operating Expenses (for example, supplies, insurance, and short–term rentals). Prepare summary journal entries for (a) the disbursements and (b) the expenses (for our purposes, debit Operating, Selling, and General and Administrative Expenses) for fiscal 1995. Post the entries to the T-accounts.
2. Prepare summary journal entries for (a) the disbursements and (b) the expenses related to the accrued liabilities for fiscal 1995. (For our purposes, debit Operating, Selling, and General and Administrative Expenses.) Post the entries to the T-accounts.

4-52. Compact D from Disclosure

Select any two companies from those available on Compact D.

Required
1. For each company, determine the amount of working capital and the current ratio.
2. Compare the current ratios. Which company has the larger ratio, and what do the ratios tell you about the solvency of the companies?
3. Compute the gross margin percentage, the return on sales, and the return on stockholders' equity.
4. Compare the profitability of the two companies.

5

Accounting Cycle: Recording and Formal Presentation

Learning Objectives

After studying this chapter, you should be able to

1 Explain the accounting cycle and analyze transactions, including those that relate to the adjustments of the preceding period.

2 Analyze cash transactions used in the statement of cash flows.

3 Prepare closing entries for pertinent accounts.

4 Explain the role of auditors of financial statements.

5 Use a work sheet to prepare adjustments, financial statements, and closing entries (Appendix 5A).

6 Prepare adjustments when alternative recording methods are used for the related originating transactions (Appendix 5B).

7 Use special journals to process transactions (Appendix 5C).

This chapter describes the accounting cycle, which is the process of recording transactions from the beginning of a period to its end in order to produce the firm's financial statements. The chapter identifies the steps in the cycle and uses the transactions of an example company to review the techniques for recording data that will be used in the financial statements. The transactions necessary to close the books after the statements have been prepared are also demonstrated. Three chapter appendices provide more details on the processing of accounting data.

This chapter includes primarily a review of materials covered in Chapters 1 through 4 and the addition of some technical data-processing details. Therefore, some instructors may elect to omit it. Nevertheless, we recommend that any student who had difficulty with the processing of transactions in the earlier chapters pay particular attention to pages 186–194. In addition, students planning to become accountants and those who want a complete understanding of how financial statements are produced should learn the procedures for closing the books, as described on pages 196–200.

The major focus in this chapter is on how the recording process leads to the final output of the accounting cycle. The financial statements present a picture of the firm's financial standing. They show the efficiency of its operations and its ability to generate profits. The role of auditing, which is also discussed at the end of this chapter, is crucial in assuring readers that the financial statements fairly present the firm's results for the period.

Although accounting serves different purposes in different countries, the accounting cycle and double-entry bookkeeping are mainstays of accounting throughout the world. Socialist governments have tried to outlaw Western accounting methods (including double-entry systems) as capitalist. They have tried to develop "moneyless" bookkeeping systems. Nevertheless, accounting systems based on double-entry bookkeeping have always emerged as the preferred method for recording and reporting the economic events and transactions of an organization, regardless of the type of economic system employed. As many formerly socialist countries have moved to embrace capitalism, training in accounting and the development of reliable information for investors have emerged as high priorities.

■ THE ACCOUNTING CYCLE

accounting cycle
The multistage process by which accountants produce an entity's financial statements.

The **accounting cycle** is the multistage process by which accountants produce an entity's financial statements. Exhibit 5-1 shows the principal steps in the cycle.

As previous chapters have demonstrated, many transactions are journalized and posted to ledger accounts during the period of the cycle. At the end of the period, an *unadjusted* trial balance or a work sheet may be prepared to assist in the analysis of adjusting entries and corrections to the accounts. The adjusting entries are then journalized and posted, and an *adjusted* trial balance is prepared. Finally, the formal financial statements are prepared, and the books are closed for the period.

Objective 1

Explain the accounting cycle and analyze transactions, including those that relate to the adjustments of the preceding period.

A Practical Exercise in the Accounting Cycle

The financial statements of the Oxley Company, a retailer of nursery products for lawns and gardens, are used in this section and the following one to illustrate the principal steps in the accounting cycle. (Preparation of the optional work sheet is described in Appendix 5A.) Although many simplifying assumptions have been made, the Oxley Company illustration provides both a review of previous chapters and a sequential view of the accounting cycle in its entirety.

Exhibit 5-1

Steps in the Accounting Cycle

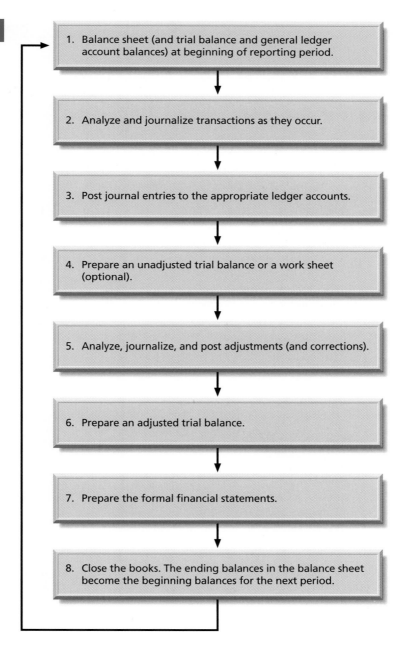

1. Balance sheet (and trial balance and general ledger account balances) at beginning of reporting period.

2. Analyze and journalize transactions as they occur.

3. Post journal entries to the appropriate ledger accounts.

4. Prepare an unadjusted trial balance or a work sheet (optional).

5. Analyze, journalize, and post adjustments (and corrections).

6. Prepare an adjusted trial balance.

7. Prepare the formal financial statements.

8. Close the books. The ending balances in the balance sheet become the beginning balances for the next period.

comparative financial statements Statements that present data for two or more reporting periods.

Exhibits 5-2, 5-3, and 5-4 display Oxley Company's balance sheet, income statement, and statement of retained income, respectively. Oxley's accounting cycle is for a year, but it could occur monthly, quarterly, or for any other period as desired. The exhibits contain **comparative financial statements**, which present data for two or more reporting periods. Note that the most

Exhibit 5-2				
Oxley Company **Balance Sheet** **(in thousands)**			December 31	
Assets		19X2		19X1
Current assets:				
Cash		$150		$ 57
Accounts receivable		95		70
Accrued interest receivable		15		15
Inventory of merchandise		20		60
Prepaid rent		10		—
Total current assets		$290		$202
Long-term assets*				
Long-term note receivable		288		288
Equipment, at original cost	$200		$200	
Deduct: Accumulated depreciation	120		80	
Equipment, net		80		120
Total assets		$658		$610
Liabilites and Stockholders' Equity				
Current liabilities:				
Accounts payable		$ 90		$ 65
Accrued wages payable		24		10
Accrued income taxes payable		16		12
Accrued interest payable		9		9
Unearned sales revenue		—		5
Note payable, current portion		80		—
Total current liabilities		$219		$101
Long-term note payable		40		120
Total liabilities		$259		$221
Stockholders' equity:				
Paid-in capital †		$102		$102
Retained income		297		287
Total stockholders' equity		$399		$389
Total liabilities and stockholders' equity		$658		$610

* This caption is frequently omitted. Instead the long-term note receivable, the equipment, and other categories are merely listed as separate items following the current assets.

† Details are often shown in a supplementary statement or in footnotes. In this case, there are 200,000 common shares outstanding: $.25 par per share, or 200,000 × $.25 = $50,000. Additional paid-in capital is $52,000, the total being the $102,000 shown here.

recent data are usually shown in the first column, as is the case with the Oxley Company data. In a series of years, the oldest data generally appear in the last column on the right. Publicly held corporations in the United States generally present comparative income statements for three periods and balance sheets for two periods.

Exhibit 5-3

Oxley Company
Statement of Income
(in thousands except
earnings per share)

		For the Year Ended December 31, 19X2		For the Year Ended December 31, 19X1
Sales			$999	$800
Cost of goods sold			399	336
Gross profit (or gross margin)			$600	$464
Operating expenses:				
Wages	$214			$150
Rent	120			120
Miscellaneous	100			50
Depreciation	40	474		40 360
Operating income (or operating profit)			$126	$104
Other revenue and expense:				
Interest revenue	$ 36			$ 36
Deduct: Interest expense	12	24		12 24
Income before taxes			$150	$128
Income tax expense			60	48
Net income			$ 90	$ 80
Earnings per common share*			$.45	$.40

* Dividends per share, $.40 and $.20, respectively. For publicly held companies, there is a requirement to show earnings per share on the face of the income statement, but it is not necessary to show dividends per share. Calculations of earnings per share: $90,000 ÷ 200,000 = $.45, and $80,000 ÷ 200,000 = $.40.

Consider the Oxley balance sheet for December 31, 19X1, as the start of our illustration of the accounting cycle. The following Oxley transactions, which are condensed here, occurred during 19X2 (amounts are in thousands):

a. Acquired merchandise inventory on account, $359.
b. Delivered merchandise to customers who had previously paid $5 in full in advance.
c. Sales of merchandise (all on account and excluding transaction *b*) during 19X2 were $994.
d. The cost of merchandise sold (including that in transaction *b*) during 19X2 was $399.
e. Cash collected on account was $969.
f. The note receivable was from a key industrial customer. The $288 principal is payable on August 1, 19X4. Interest of 12.5% per annum is collected each August 1 (to be computed).

Cash was disbursed as follows for

g. Accounts payable, $334.

Exhibit 5-4

Oxley Company
Statement of
Retained Income
(in thousands)

	For the Year Ended December 31	
	19X2	**19X1**
Retained income, beginning of year	$287	$247
Add: Net income	90	80
Total	$377	$327
Deduct: Dividends declared	80	40
Retained income, end of year	$297	$287

h. Wages, $200, including the $10 accrued on December 31, 19X1.

i. Income taxes, $56, including the $12 accrued on December 31, 19X1.

j. Interest on note payable, including the $9 accrued on December 31, 19X1. Interest of 10% per annum on the $120 principal is paid each March 31 (to be computed).

k. Rent, $130 for 13 months, which was debited to Prepaid Rent.

l. Miscellaneous expenses, $100.

m. Dividends, $80. A separate account called Dividends Declared was created. For simplicity, assume that declaration and payment occurred on the same day.

No interim statements were prepared, so no adjusting entries were made until December 31, 19X2, when the following were recognized:

n. Accrual of interest receivable (to be computed, see item f).

o. The disbursements for rent included $10 paid on December 31, 19X2, pertaining to the month of January 19X3 (see item k).

p. Accrual of wages payable, $24.

q. Accrual of interest payable (to be computed, see item j).

r. Depreciation for 19X2, $40.

s. Two-thirds of the principal of the note payable is transferred to Note Payable, Current Portion, because two-thirds is due March 31, 19X3. The other third is payable on March 31, 19X5 (see item j).

t. Accrual of income taxes payable. The total income tax expense for 19X2 is 40% of the income before income taxes (to be computed).

Required

1. Prepare a general ledger in T-account form, entering the account balances as of December 31, 19X1. Provide space for additional accounts.
2. Analyze and journalize all transactions for 19X2, including the year-end adjustments.
3. Post the entries in requirement 2 to the T-accounts.
4. Prepare an adjusted trial balance as of December 31, 19X2. If it fails to balance, check to see that all items were posted to the correct sides of the accounts.
5. Prepare a multiple-step income statement for 19X2.
6. Prepare a statement of retained income for 19X2.
7. Prepare a comparative classified balance sheet for December 31, 19X1 and 19X2.
8. Prepare a statement of cash flows for 19X2.
9. Journalize and post the entries necessary to "close the books" for 19X2.

You are *urged* to try to solve requirements 1-4 on your own before examining the solution. The general ledger (requirements 1 and 3), illustrated in Exhibit 5-6, incorporates all of the 19X2 transactions including yearly transactions and adjusting entries. The general journal (requirement 2) is illustrated in

Exhibit 5-5. Note how the accounts are numbered. Posting and journalizing are keyed to facilitate cross-checking. The adjusted trial balance (requirement 4) is illustrated in Exhibit 5-7.

Requirements 5 through 7 were illustrated in Exhibits 5-2, 5-3, and 5-4. Requirements 8 and 9 are described later in this chapter, requirement 8 in the section on "Statement of Cash Flows" and requirement 9 in the section entitled "Closing the Accounts."

Exhibit 5-5

Journal Entries

Date	Entry No.	Accounts and Explanation	Post Ref.	Debit	Credit
19X2				(in thousands of dollars)	
Dates					
are	a	Inventory of merchandise	130	359	
varied		Accounts payable	200		359
and		Acquired inventory on account			
are					
not	b	Unearned sales revenue	237	5	
entered		Sales	320		5
in this		Delivery of merchandise to customers who had paid			
illus-		in advance			
tration	c	Accounts receivable	110	994	
except		Sales	320		994
for		Sales on account			
Dec. 31					
	d	Cost of goods sold	340	399	
		Inventory of merchandise	130		399
		To record the cost of inventory sold			
	e	Cash	100	969	
		Accounts receivable	110		969
		Collections from customers			
	f	Cash	100	36	
		Accrued interest receivable	111		15
		Interest revenue	330		21
		Collection of interest (12.5% of $288 = $36)			
	g	Accounts payable	200	334	
		Cash	100		334
		Payments to creditors			
	h	Accrued wages payable	210	10	
		Wages expense	350	190	
		Cash	100		200
		Payments of wages			
	i	Accrued income taxes payable	220	12	
		Income tax expense	395	44	
		Cash	100		56
		Payments of income taxes			
	j	Accrued interest payable	230	9	
		Interest expense	380	3	
		Cash	100		12
		Payment of interest (10% of $120)			
	k	Prepaid rent	140	130	
		Cash	100		130
		Disbursements for rent			

Exhibit 5-5

Continued

Date	Entry No.	Accounts and Explanation	Post Ref.	Debit	Credit
				(in thousands of dollars)	
19X2					
	l	Miscellaneous expenses	364	100	
		Cash	100		100
		Disbursements for miscellaneous expense items such as utilities, repairs etc.			
	m	Dividends declared	310A	80	
		Cash	100		80
		Declaration and payment of dividends			
		Year-End Adjusting Entries			
Dec.31	n	Accrued interest receivable	111	15	
		Interest revenue	330		15
		Accrual of interest for five months at 12.5% on $288: (12.5%) ($288) (5/12) = $15			
Dec.31	o	Rent expense	360	120	
		Prepaid rent	140		120
		To record 19X2 rent expense at $10 per month. (Note that this leaves a $10 debit balance in Prepaid Rent for January, 19X3.)			
Dec.31	p	Wages expense	350	24	
		Accrued wages payable	210		24
		To recognize wages accrued but unpaid at December 31, 19X2			
Dec.31	q	Interest expense	380	9	
		Accrued interest payable	230		9
		Accrual of interest for nine months at 10% on $120: (10%) ($120) (9/12) = 9			
Dec.31	r	Depreciation expense	370	40	
		Accumulated depreciation, equipment	170A		40
		To record depreciation for 19X2.			
Dec.31	s	Long-term note payable	280	80	
		Note payable, current	240		80
		To reclassify $80 as a current liability			
Dec.31	t	Income tax expense	395	16	
		Accrued income tax payable	220		16
		To record the income tax expense, which is 40% of the income before income taxes, or .40 x $150 = $60. (Of this amount, $44 has already been paid and charged to expense in entry i, leaving $16 of expense accrued but not paid.)			

Detailed Analysis of Transactions

This section presents a step-by-step analysis of all 19X2 transactions for the Oxley Company shown in Exhibits 5-5 and 5-6. It is presented as a review for readers who need to strengthen their understanding. Some readers, however, may need to study only the analysis of transactions they did not analyze correctly in solving requirements 1-4 in the Oxley Company exercise.

Exhibit 5-6   General Ledger of Oxley Company

Assets	Liabilities + Stockholders' Equity
(Increases Left, Decreases Right)	*(Decreases Left, Increases Right)*

Cash   Account No.100

Bal.*	57	(g)	334
(e)	969	(h)	200
(f)	36	(i)	56
		(j)	12
		(k)	130
		(l)	100
		(m)	80
	1,062		912
†	150		

Accounts Payable 200

(g)	334	*	65
		(a)	359
		†	90

Accrued Wages Payable 210

(h)	10	*	10
		(p)	24
		†	24

Accrued Income Taxes Payable 220

(i)	12	*	12
		(t)	16
		†	16

Accounts Receivable 110

*	70	(e)	969
(c)	994		
†	95		

Accrued Interest Payable 230

(j)	9	*	9
		(q)	9
		†	9

Unearned Sales Revenue 237

(b)	5	*	5
		†	0

Note Payable, Current Portion 240

		(s)	80
		†	80

Accrued Interest Receivable 111

*	15	(f)	15
(n)	15		
†	15		

Long-term Note Payable 280

(s)	80	*	120
		†	40

Paid-In Capital 300

		*	102
		†	102

Dividends Declared 310A

(m)	80		

Retained Income 310

		*	287

Inventory of Merchandise 130

*	60	(d)	399
(a)	359		
†	20		

Cost of Goods Sold 340

(d)	399		

Wages Expense 350

(h)	190		
(p)	24		

Prepaid Rent 140

(k)	130	(o)	120
†	10		

Rent Expense 360

(o)	120		

Miscellaneous Expense 364

(l)	100		

Long-term Note Receivable 160

*	288		
†	288		

Depreciation Expense

(r)	40		

Interest Expense 380

(j)	3		
(q)	9		

Sales 320

		(b)	5
		(c)	994

Equipment 170

*	200		
†	200		

Accumulated Depreciation Equipment 170A

		*	80
		(r)	40
		†	120

Income Tax Expense 395

(i)	44		
(t)	16		

Interest Revenue 330

		(f)	21
		(n)	15

* All amounts denoted with an asterisk are balances, December 31, 19X1.
† All amounts denoted with a dagger are balances, December 31, 19X2.

Exhibit 5-7		
Oxley Company Adjusted Trial Balance December 31, 19X2 (in thousands)		
Cash	$ 150	
Accounts receivable	95	
Accrued interest receivable	15	
Inventory of merchandise	20	
Prepaid rent	10	
Long-term note receivable	288	
Equipment	200	
Accumulated depreciation, equipment		$ 120
Accounts payable		90
Accrued wages payable		24
Accrued income taxes payable		16
Accrued interest payable		9
Note payable, current portion		80
Long-term note payable		40
Paid-in capital		102
Retained income, December 31, 19X1		287
Dividends declared	80	
Sales		999
Interest revenue		36
Cost of goods sold	399	
Wages expense	214	
Rent expense	120	
Miscellaneous expense	100	
Depreciation expense	40	
Interest expense	12	
Income tax expense	60	
	$1,803	$1,803

Helpful hint: Entries for interest, wages, income taxes, and other accruals (for example, see *f, h, i,* and *j*) have a common theme: They relate to the adjustments of the preceding period. The explicit subsequent transaction involves a cash inflow or outflow. Part of each cash flow in this example relates to the accrual made at the end of 19X1. *Failure to remember the accruals may result in double-counting of expenses (or revenues).* A common error, for instance, would be to recognize the entire $12,000 disbursement for interest in entry *j* as an expense of 19X2, whereas $9,000 was already recognized as an expense in 19X1 and is properly charged in entry *j* to the liability account Accrued Interest Payable.

a. Transaction: Acquired merchandise inventory on account, $359.
    Analysis: The asset **Inventory of Merchandise** is increased.
              The liability **Accounts Payable** is increased.
        Entry: In the journal (explanation omitted):

Inventory of merchandise   359
    Accounts payable   359

Post to the ledger (postings are indicated by the circled amounts):

Inventory of Merchandise		Accounts Payable	
Bal.	60	Bal.	65
(a)	(359)	(a)	(359)

b. Transaction: Delivered merchandise to customers who had previously paid $5.
    Analysis: The liability **Unearned Sales Revenue** is decreased.
              The stockholders' equity **Sales** is increased.
        Entry: In the journal:

Unearned sales revenue   5
    Sales   5

Post to the ledger:

Unearned Sales Revenue			Sales	
(b)	(5)	Bal. 5	(b)	(5)

c. Transaction: Sales of merchandise on account, $994.
    Analysis: The asset **Accounts Receivable** is increased.
              The stockholders' equity **Sales** is increased.
        Entry: In the journal:

Accounts receivable   994
    Sales   994

Post to the ledger:

Accounts Receivable		Sales	
Bal.	70	(b)	5
(c)	(994)	(c)	(994)

d. Transaction: The cost of merchandise sold, $399.
    Analysis: The Asset **Inventory of Merchandise** is decreased.
              The negative stockholders' equity **Cost of Goods Sold** is increased.
              Recall that all expense accounts are reductions in stockholders' equi-
              ty; thus expense accounts can be regarded as negative stockholders'
              equity.
        Entry: In the journal:

Cost of goods sold   399
    Inventory of merchandise   399

Post to the ledger:

Inventory of Merchandise		Cost of Goods Sold	
Bal. 60	(d) (399)	(d) (399)	
(a) 359			

e. Transaction: Cash collected on account from customers, $969.

Analysis: The asset **Cash** is increased.
The asset **Accounts Receivable** is decreased.

Entry: In the journal:

Cash	969	
Accounts receivable		969

Post to the ledger:

Cash		Accounts Receivable	
Bal. 57		Bal. 70	(e) (969)
(e) (969)		(c) 994	

f. Transaction: Collection of interest on August 1, 12.5% of $288 = $36.

Analysis: The asset **Cash** is increased.
The asset **Accrued Interest Receivable** is decreased.
The stockholders' equity **Interest Revenue** is increased.
Interest revenue earned is $36 \div 12 = \$3$ per month. Seven months $\times$ $3 = \$21. The $15 decrease in Accrued Interest Receivable pertains to revenue earned during the preceding year.

Entry: In the journal:

Cash	36	
Accrued interest receivable		15
Interest revenue		21

Post to the ledger:

Cash		Accrued Interest Receivable	
Bal. 57		Bal. 15	(f) (15)
(e) 969			
(f) (36)			

		Interest Revenue	
		(f)	(21)

g. Transaction: Payments to trade creditors on account, $334.

Analysis: The asset **Cash** is decreased.
The liability **Accounts Payable** is decreased.

Entry: In the journal:

Accounts payable	334	
Cash		334

Post to the ledger:

Cash		Accounts Payable	
Bal. 57	(g) (334)	(g) (334)	Bal. 65
(e) 969			(a) 359
(f) 36			

h. Transaction: Payments of wages, $200.

   Analysis: The asset **Cash** is decreased.
   The liability **Accrued Wages Payable** is decreased. The negative stock-holders' equity **Wages Expense** is increased. The Accrued Wages Payable was $10, as shown in the balance sheet in Exhibit 5-2.

   Entry: In the journal:

Accrued wages payable	10	
Wages expense	190	
Cash		200

Post to the ledger:

Cash					Accrued Wages Payable		
Bal.	57	(g)	334	(h)	⑩	Bal.	10
(e)	969	(h)	⑳⓪				
(f)	36						

	Wages Expense	
(h)	⑲⓪	

i. Transaction: Payments of income taxes, $56.

   Analysis: The asset **Cash** is decreased.
   The liability **Accrued Income Taxes Payable** is decreased.
   The negative stockholders' equity **Income Tax Expense** is increased.
   The payable was $12, as shown in the balance sheet in Exhibit 5-2.

   Entry: In the journal:

Accrued income taxes payable	12	
Income tax expense	44	
Cash		56

Post to the ledger:

Cash					Accrued Income Taxes Payable		
Bal.	57	(g)	334	(i)	⑫	Bal.	12
(e)	969	(h)	200				
(f)	36	(i)	㊴				

	Income Tax Expense	
(i)	㊹	

j. Transaction: Payment of interest on March 31, 10% of $120 = $12.

   Analysis: The asset **Cash** is decreased.
   The liability **Accrued Interest Payable** is decreased. The negative stockholders' equity **Interest Expense** is increased. Interest expense is $12 ÷ 12 = $1 per month; three months × $1 = $3. The $9 decrease in Accrued Interest Payable pertains to interest expense during the preceding year.

   Entry: In the journal:

Accrued interest payable	9	
Interest expense	3	
Cash		12

Post to the ledger:

Cash

Bal.	57	(g)	334
(e)	969	(h)	200
(f)	36	(i)	56
		(j)	(12)

Accrued Interest Payable

(j)	(9)	Bal.	9

Interest Expense

(j)	(3)		

k. Transaction: Payment of rent, $130.
Analysis: The asset **Cash** is decreased.
The asset **Prepaid Rent** is increased.
Entry: In the journal:

Prepaid rent	130	
Cash		130

Post to the ledger:

Cash

Bal.	57	(g)	334
(e)	969	(h)	200
(f)	36	(i)	56
		(j)	12
		(k)	(130)

Prepaid Rent

(k)	(130)		

l. Transaction: Payment of miscellaneous expenses, $100.
Analysis: The asset **Cash** is decreased.
The negative stockholders' equity **Miscellaneous Expenses** is increased.
Entry: In the journal:

Miscellaneous expenses	100	
Cash		100

Post to the ledger:

Cash

Bal.	57	(g)	334
(e)	969	(h)	200
(f)	36	(i)	56
		(j)	12
		(k)	130
		(l)	(100)

Miscellaneous Expenses

(l)	(100)		

m. Transaction: Dividends declared and paid, $80.
Analysis: The asset **Cash** is decreased.
The negative stockholders' equity **Dividends Declared** (an offsetting account to Retained Income) is increased.
Entry: In the journal:

Dividends declared	80	
Cash		80

Post to the ledger:

Cash				Dividends Declared	
Bal.	57	(g)	334	(m)	(80)
(e)	969	(h)	200		
(f)	36	(i)	56		
		(j)	12		
		(k)	130		
		(l)	100		
		(m)	(80)		

n. Transaction: Accrual of interest receivable for 5 months × $3 = $15.
    Analysis: The asset **Accrued Interest Receivable** is increased.
               The stockholders' equity **Interest Revenue** is increased.
        Entry: In the journal:

Accrued interest receivable	15	
Interest revenue		15

               Post to the ledger:

Accrued Interest Receivable				Interest Revenue	
Bal.	15	(f)	15	(f)	21
(n)	(15)			(n)	(15)

o. Transaction: Recognition of rent expense.
    Analysis: All prepaid rent has expired except for $10 for the month of January 19X3.
               The asset **Prepaid Rent** is decreased.
               The negative stockholders' equity **Rent Expense** is increased.
        Entry: In the journal:

Rent expense	120	
Prepaid rent		120

               Post to the ledger:

Prepaid Rent				Rent Expense	
(k)	130	(o)	(120)	(o)	(120)

p. Transaction: Accrual of wages payable, $24.
    Analysis: The liability **Accrued Wages Payable** is increased.
               The negative stockholders' equity **Wages Expense** is increased.
        Entry: In the journal:

Wages expense	24	
Accrued wages payable		24

               Post to the ledger:

Accrued Wages Payable				Wages Expense	
(h)	190	Bal.	10	(h)	190
		(p)	(24)	(p)	(24)

q. Transaction: Accrual of interest payable for 9 months × $1 = $9. (See transaction j.)
    Analysis: The liability **Accrued Interest Payable** is increased.
               The negative stockholders' equity **Interest Expense** is increased.
        Entry: In the journal:

| Interest expense | 9 | |
| Accrued interest payable | | 9 |

Post to the ledger:

Accrued Interest Payable					Interest Expense		
(j)	9	Bal.	9	(j)	3		
		(q)	⑨	(q)	⑨		

r. Transaction: Depreciation, $40.

   Analysis: The asset reduction account **Accumulated Depreciation, Equipment** is increased.
   The negative stockholders' equity **Depreciation Expense** is increased.

   Entry: In the journal:

| Depreciation expense | 40 | |
| Accumulated depreciation, equipment | | 40 |

Post to the ledger:

Accumulated Depreciation, Equipment					Depreciation Expense		
		Bal.	80	(r)	④⓪		
		(r)	④⓪				

s. Transaction: Reclassification of note payable ⅔ × $120 = $80.

   Analysis: The liability **Long-term Note Payable** is decreased.
   The liability **Note Payable, Current** portion is increased.

   Entry: In the journal:

| Long-term note payable | 80 | |
| Note payable, current | | 80 |

Post to the ledger:

Long-term Note Payable					Note Payable, Current		
(s)	⑧⓪	Bal.	120			(s)	⑧⓪

t. Transaction: Income tax expense for the year. Income before taxes must be computed and then 40% thereof recognized as expense (.40 × $150 = $60). Moreover, the accrued liability must be accurate. Therefore, because $44 has already been paid for the current year and charged to expense (see transaction *i*), the amount remaining ($60 − $44 = $16) must be charged to expense.

   Analysis: The liability **Accrued Income Taxes Payable** is increased.
   The negative stockholders' equity **Income Tax Expense** is increased.

   Entry: In the journal:

| Income tax expense | 16 | |
| Accrued income taxes payable | | 16 |

Post to the ledger:

Accrued Income Taxes Payable					Income Tax Expense		
(i)	12	Bal.	12	(i)	44		
		(t)	⑯	(t)	⑯		

A Note on Dividends Declared

A corporation must declare a dividend before paying it. The board of directors alone has the authority to declare a dividend. The corporation has no obligation to pay a dividend unless the board declares one; however, when declared, the dividend becomes a legal liability of the corporation.

The overall approach to accounting for cash dividends was explained in Chapter 2. As shown there, some companies reduce Retained Income directly when their board of directors declares dividends. However, as shown in transaction *m* in Exhibits 5-5 and 5-6, other companies prefer to use a separate "temporary" stockholders' equity account (Dividends Declared or simply Dividends) to compile the cumulative amounts of the dividends for a given year. Publicly held U.S. companies generally declare dividends quarterly. Internationally, many companies pay dividends twice a year.

Oxley's transaction *m* summarized the overall effect of $80,000 dividend payments throughout the year. In the real world, $20,000 would have been declared and paid quarterly. The declaration is usually made on one date, and the payment follows declaration by a few weeks. Oxley would have made the following entries for the first quarter, specific dates assumed:

February 10	Dividends declared..............................	20	
	Dividends payable............................		20
	To record quarterly declaration of dividends.		
February 27	Dividends payable	20	
	Cash...		20
	To record payment of dividends.		

Dividends Payable is a current liability. If a balance sheet is prepared between the date of declaration and the date of payment, Dividends Payable will be listed with the other current liabilities. For example, J. M. Smucker, the jam company, declared $13,642 million in dividends in fiscal 1994, of which $3,639 million was listed among its payables at the end of 1994.

Consider another example. The journal entry for a quarterly dividend recently declared by the H. J. Heinz Company would be:

Dividends declared	83,366,580	
Dividends payable		83,366,580
To record declaration of $.33 per share		
dividend on 252,626,000 shares.		

The Dividends Declared account will have a normal left-side balance. It represents a reduction in Retained Income and Stockholders' Equity.

■ STATEMENT OF CASH FLOWS

Objective 2

Analyze cash transactions used in the statement of cash flows.

The emphasis so far in this chapter has been on the Oxley Company's balance sheet, income statement, and statement of retained income (Exhibits 5-2, 5-3, and 5-4) because they are prepared directly from the general ledger accounts. But we should not forget the other required financial statement, the *statement of cash flows*. It was described briefly in Chapter 2 and will be covered in more detail in Chapter 11.

The statement of cash flows provides details on the entries to the cash account. Oxley's transactions *e* through *m* affect cash, as shown in the Cash

T-account in Exhibit 5-6. Therefore, these items are included in the statement of cash flows in Exhibit 5-8. Recall that the statement of cash flows classifies activities affecting cash into three categories: operating activities, investing activities, and financing activities. Eight of the nine items, all except payment of cash dividends, are operating activities. Payment of dividends is a financing activity because it provides a return to stockholders who supplied capital to the company. Oxley had no investment activities during 19X2. The items in Exhibit 5-8 explain why Oxley's cash increased by $93,000, from $57,000 to $150,000, during 19X2.

Exhibit 5-8		
	CASH FLOWS FROM OPERATING ACTIVITIES	
Oxley Company	Cash collections from customers	$ 969
Statement of	Interest received	36
Cash Flows	Cash payments to suppliers	(334)
for the Year Ended	Cash payments to employees	(200)
December 31, 19X2	Cash payments for income taxes	(56)
(in thousands)	Cash payments for interest	(12)
	Cash payments for rent	(130)
	Cash payments for miscellaneous expenses	(100)
	Net cash provided by operating activities	$173
	CASH FLOWS FROM INVESTING ACTIVITIES	
	None	
	CASH FLOWS FROM FINANCING ACTIVITIES	
	Cash dividends	$ (80)
	Net cash used by financing activities	$ (80)
	Net increase in cash	$ 93
	Cash balance, December 31, 19X1	57
	Cash balance, December 31, 19X2	$150

■ CLOSING THE ACCOUNTS

closing the books The final step taken in the accounting cycle to update retained earnings and facilitate the recording of the next year's transactions.

After preparing financial statements, accountants must get ledger accounts ready to record the next period's transactions. This process is called *closing the books*.

Transferring and Summarizing

closing entries Entries that transfer the revenues, expenses, and dividends declared balances from their respective accounts to the retained income account.

Closing the books is the final step taken in the accounting cycle to update retained earnings and facilitate the recording of the *next* year's transactions. This step is called *closing*, but *transferring and summarizing* or *clearing* are better labels. All balances in the "temporary" stockholders' equity accounts (revenue, expense, and dividends declared accounts) are summarized and transferred to a "permanent" stockholders' equity account, Retained Income. **Closing entries** transfer the revenues, expenses, and dividends declared balances from their respective accounts to the retained income account.

When the closing entries are completed, the revenue, expense, and dividends declared accounts have zero balances. Closing is a clerical procedure.

It is devoid of any new accounting theory. Its main purpose is to set the revenue and expense meters back to zero so that those accounts can be used afresh in the new year. For instance, without the closing process the sales account of a business like Shell Oil would continue to cumulate revenue, so that the balance would be the sum of many years of sales rather than only one year of sales.

Objective 3

Prepare closing entries for pertinent accounts.

Exhibit 5-9 shows the closing (transferring) process for the Oxley Company. How does the debit-credit process accomplish this summarizing and transferring?

Step 1. An Income Summary account, which has a life of one day (or an instant), is typically created. As Exhibit 5-9 indicates, the Income Summary account is a convenience. It facilitates an orderly sequence of events and helps auditors trace transactions through to their impact on the financial statements. However, it is not absolutely necessary; many accountants prefer to accomplish the entire closing process by a single (massive) compound entry to Retained Income.

Exhibit 5-9   General Effects of Closing the Accounts   (Data are from Exhibit 5-6, p. 187)

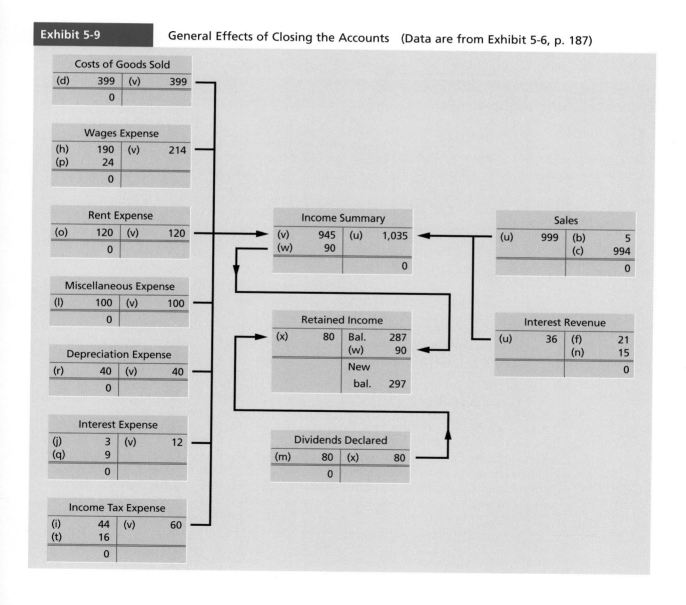

Step 2. The credit balances of the revenue accounts are debited to those accounts in entry *u* in Exhibit 5-9. The balances in Sales and Interest Revenues are now zero. They have been "closed." Their meters are back to zero, but their amounts have not vanished. Instead, the amounts now rest in aggregate form as a credit of $1,035 in Income Summary.

Step 3. The debit balances of the expense accounts are credited to each expense account, as shown in entry *v*. Their individual amounts also now reside in aggregate form as a debit of $945 in Income Summary.

Step 4. The net income is computed and transferred from Income Summary to its "permanent" home, Retained Income, as shown in entry *w*. Thereafter, the Income Summary account has a balance of zero.

Step 5. The Dividends Declared account is then closed directly to Retained Income, as shown in entry *x*. Note that the Income Summary account is not used for closing the Dividends account because dividends are *not* expenses and do *not* affect net income.

How Long Does It Take to Close the Books?

If closing the books at the end of the fiscal year were merely a mechanical process, computers would have the job completed by the time the Rose Bowl started on January 1. However, because of the large amount of accounting judgment required, the process takes longer. Company accountants must decide what adjusting entries are necessary and also what estimates (about bad debts and depreciation, for example) are appropriate. Then these judgments and estimates must be scrutinized by the independent auditors as part of their examination of the fairness of the financial statements.

After the year ends, the first piece of information provided to the public is typically a preliminary earnings announcement. Firms with shares listed on the New York Stock Exchange usually make a preliminary earnings announcement sometime in January or February. For middle- and large-sized firms, these announcements are published in the *Wall Street Journal*. A selection of announcement dates for IBM and Chrysler are listed below:

	1993	1990	1980	1970
IBM	1/26/94	1/18/91	1/19/81	1/18/71
Chrysler	1/19/94	2/8/91	3/2/81	2/10/71

For most companies, the date of the preliminary earnings announcement is fairly constant year after year. In fact, market participants have come to expect earnings announcements for cer-

tain firms on certain dates. Late announcements are generally interpreted as bad news. It is no coincidence that Chrysler announced its 1980 earnings almost a month later than usual. Chrysler lost $1.71 billion in 1980. Since 1990 Chrysler has speeded up its closing of the books and is now reporting its earnings nearly three weeks earlier than it did before 1990.

Some time after the preliminary earnings announcement is made, the auditors finish their work and sign their audit opinion. IBM's independent audit report for 1993 is dated February 16, 1994, twenty-one days after its earnings announcement appeared in the *Wall Street Journal*. The final annual report is then compiled, printed, and mailed out to stockholders, analysts, the stock exchange, and the SEC. By law, all companies with publicly traded stock must file an annual report (called a 10-K) with the SEC within 90 days of the end of the fiscal year. Just as many individuals delay filing their tax returns until April 15, a large number of firms wait to file their 10-Ks until March 31. ■

Sources: Wall Street Journal Index, *1994, 1991, 1981, and 1971; A. E. Chambers and S. H. Penman, "Timeliness of Reporting and the Stock Price Reaction to Earnings Announcements,"* Journal of Accounting Research *(Spring 1984), pp. 21–47.*

At the end of Step 5, the Retained Income account has been brought up to date. The books (the journal and ledger) are now ready for a new year. Exhibit 5-9 presents zero balances for all temporary accounts. In essence, all revenue and expense meters have been set back to zero.

Detailed Analysis of Closing Transactions

Because the discussion of Exhibit 5-9 did not show formal journal entries recorded in the general journal, the following analysis gives the journal entries for the closing transactions:

u. Transaction: Clerical procedure of transferring the ending balances of revenue accounts to the Income Summary account.

Analysis: The stockholders' equity accounts **Sales** and **Interest Revenue** are decreased.
The stockholders' equity account **Income Summary** is increased.

Entry: In the journal:

Sales	999	
Interest revenue	36	
Income summary		1,035

To close the revenue accounts by transferring their ending balances to Income Summary.

Post to the ledger:

Sales			
(u)	(999)	(b)	5
		(c)	994
			0

Income Summary		
	(u)	(1,035)

Interest Revenue			
(u)	(36)	(f)	21
		(n)	15
			0

v. Transaction: Clerical procedure of transferring the ending balances of expense accounts to the Income Summary account.

Analysis: The negative stockholders' equity accounts **Cost of Goods Sold, Wages Expense**, etc., are decreased. The stockholders' equity account **Income Summary** is decreased.

Entry: In the journal:

Income summary	945	
Cost of goods sold		399
Wages expense		214
Rent expense		120
Miscellaneous expense		100
Depreciation expense		40
Interest expense		12
Income tax expense		60

To close the expense accounts by transferring their ending balances to Income Summary.

Post to the ledger:

Cost of Goods Sold				Income Summary		
(d)	399	(v)	(399)	(v)	(945)	(u)	1,035
	0						

Rent Expense				Wages Expense		
(o)	120	(v)	(120)	(h)	190	(v)	(214)
				(p)	24		
	0				0		

Depreciation Expense				Miscellaneous Expense		
(r)	40	(v)	(40)	(l)	100	(v)	(100)
	0				0		

Interest Expense				Income Tax Expense		
(j)	3	(v)	(12)	(i)	44	(v)	(60)
(q)	9			(t)	16		

w. Transaction: Clerical procedure of transferring the ending balance of Income Summary account to the Retained Income account.

   Analysis: The stockholders' equity account **Income Summary** is decreased. The stockholders' equity account **Retained Income** is increased.

   Entry: In the journal:

Income summary	90
Retained income	90

To close Income Summary by transferring net income to Retained Income.

Post to the ledger:

Income Summary				Retained Income		
(v)	945	(u)	1,035			Bal.	287
(w)	(90)					(w)	(90)
			0				

x. Transaction: Clerical procedure of transferring the ending balance of Dividends Declared to the Retained Income account.

   Analysis: The negative stockholders' equity account **Dividends Declared** is decreased. The stockholders' equity account **Retained Income** is decreased.

   Entry: In the journal:

Retained Income	80
Dividends declared	80

To close Dividends Declared by transferring the ending balance to Retained Income.

Post to the ledger:

Dividends Declared				Retained Income		
(m)	80	(x)	(80)	(x)	(80)	Bal.	287
						(w)	90
	0					Bal.	297

Terminology of Types of Accounts

temporary accounts Accounts that are subjected to periodic closing, i.e., revenue, expense, and dividends declared accounts.

Accounts that are subjected to periodic closing are frequently called **temporary accounts**, as distinguished from *permanent accounts*. The temporary accounts are the revenues, expenses, and dividends declared. They are all really subparts of ownership equity. They are created to provide a detailed explanation for the changes in retained income from period to period. They are the ingredients of the income statement and the statement of retained income.

permanent accounts Balance sheet accounts.

In contrast, the **permanent accounts** are the balance sheet accounts. The word *permanent* may be misleading. After all, the balances of permanent accounts fluctuate. Moreover, some permanent accounts come and go. For example, unearned sales revenue appears on Oxley's balance sheet of December 31, 19X1, but not on December 31, 19X2.

Computers and the Accounting Cycle

Computer software can do all the steps in the accounting cycle except generate the numbers for initial journal entries and for many adjusting entries. Many computer systems produce paper output that looks much like the examples of journals and ledgers in this book. Computers eliminate the drudgery of posting, writing and rewriting, and adding and subtracting. Best of all, they make no mathematical errors and can be programmed to check for many other common errors.

Computer systems have made many time-honored manual accounting methods obsolete. For example, the entire "closing the books" process, including the use of Income Summary accounts, was designed in large part to control clerical errors. But computers do not make such errors. Furthermore, an ordinary journal is unnecessary if a computer can indefinitely store the effects of accounting transactions in its memory and print an analysis of any transaction upon command.

■ AUDITING THE FINANCIAL STATEMENTS

Objective 4

Explain the role of auditors of financial statements.

It is management's responsibility to carry out the steps in the accounting cycle (see Exhibit 5-1, page 181) and produce formal financial statements. If the company's stock is traded in the U.S. capital markets, statements must then be published as part of the company's annual report and submitted to the Securities and Exchange Commission. Because managers have a personal stake in the results reported in financial statements, stockholders, creditors, government officials, and other external users often want assurance that the financial statements fairly present the company's financial results. Indeed, managers also want to assure the public that the statements are not misleading. Why? So that investors and creditors are willing to buy stock or lend the company money when it needs additional capital. Therefore, it is in everyone's interest to hire an **auditor**, who provides an independent examination of financial statements.

auditor An accountant who provides an independent examination of the financial statements.

In the United States, auditors are not government officials but professionals who are licensed (or certified) to attest to the accuracy of financial statements. Most countries have an auditing profession and rules for evaluating financial disclosures by management. However, in the newly emerging countries of the former USSR the independent auditing profession is less established. Why? Because under the Communist system there was no external ownership that required assurance as to the reliability of financial reports.

What does the auditor do? Certainly an auditor cannot check every transaction recorded in the accounting system; the costs would surely exceed the benefits. But by systematically checking a sample of transactions and by studying the system that records and stores transaction data and prepares statements from the data, the auditor forms an opinion about whether the financial statements "present fairly" the financial position and results of the period. In the United Kingdom, the auditors use the words "give a true and fair view" instead of "present fairly," but the effect is the same. The opinion, an example of which is in Chapter 1, is published with the financial statements.

Because auditors examine only a sample of transactions, they cannot provide 100% assurance that financial statements are accurate. Furthermore, although auditors technically are hired by the board of directors, they work closely with management and might be unduly influenced by management's position. To guard against this, auditors must meet high technical and ethical standards. Auditors are valuable only if the public has a high regard for their competence and integrity, so they are careful to protect their reputations. To assure the public that an audit is thorough, auditors follow standard audit procedures developed by the American Institute of CPAs and others, and they make sure the statements conform to GAAP as determined by the FASB.

Auditing is a costly but valuable service. An audit might cost a small nonprofit organization only a few hundred dollars, but major corporations pay millions of dollars. For example, the annual audit fee for huge companies like Ford and General Motors can exceed $4 million. But without the assurance provided by auditors, widespread trading in the stock of companies would be severely curtailed.

Summary Problems for Your Review

Problem One

Review the transactions for the Oxley Company during 19X2. Suppose wages expense accrued but unpaid at the end of 19X2 were $34 instead of $24. What numbers would be changed on the income statement for 19X2 and on the balance sheet, December 31, 19X2? What would be the new numbers? The financial statements are on pages 182-184.

Solution to Problem One

Income Statement Items	For the Year Ended December 31, 19X2	
	As in Exhibit 5-3	Revised
Wages expense	$214	$224
Total operating expenses	474	484
Operating income	126	116
Income before income taxes	150	140
Income tax expense (at 40%)	60	56
Net income	90	84

Balance Sheet Accounts	December 31, 19X2	
	As in Exhibit 5-2	Revised
Accrued wages payable	$ 24	$ 34
Accrued income taxes payable	16	12
Retained income	297	291

Note the effects on the year-end balance sheet. Retained income would be decreased by $6, and total liabilities would be increased by a net of $6. Accrued wages payable increase by $10, but accrued income taxes payable decrease by $4 (40% of the $10 decrease in income before taxes).

Problem Two

The balance sheet of Coca-Cola Bottling Co. showed Accrued Interest of $11,042,000 under current liabilities at the beginning of a recent year. Interest payments of $31,928,000 were disbursed during the year. Prepare the journal entry that summarizes those disbursements.

Solution to Problem Two

Accrued interest	11,042,000	
Interest expense	20,886,000	
Cash		31,928,000

To record disbursements for interest; interest expense is $31,928,000 less $11,042,000, or $20,886,000.

The nomenclature used here illustrates why beginners in accounting should be alert to how the account description is used by a particular entity. That is, the term *Accrued Interest* is basically unclear. Does it mean *receivable* or *payable*? The answer is obvious in the annual report of Coca-Cola because the account is classified as a current liability. But some other company may use the same term, *Accrued Interest*, to describe a receivable. Hence, for clarity this textbook generally uses *accrued interest receivable* or *accrued interest payable* rather than *accrued interest* alone.

Highlights to Remember

The accounting cycle refers to the recording process that leads from the initial recording of transactions to the ending financial statements. In addition to recording explicit transactions as they occur, the accounting cycle includes making adjustments for implicit transactions. It is especially important to recognize how adjustments for implicit transactions in the preceding period affect the proper accounting in the current period for related explicit transactions. For example, if wages are accrued at the end of the prior period, the first payroll of the current period will eliminate that payable.

Moving to a new accounting period is aided by closing the books, which is a clerical procedure that transfers balances for revenues and expenses into retained income and gets the books ready for the start of a new accounting cycle.

Although closing the books and preparing financial statements complete the accounting cycle, auditors often examine the statements before they are released to the public. An audit adds credibility to the statements.

Appendix 5A: The Work Sheet

Purpose of Work Sheet

work sheet (working paper) A columnar approach to moving from a trial balance to the finished financial statements.

The body of this chapter described the rudiments of the accounting cycle. This appendix explores the cycle in more detail by explaining a favorite tool of the accountant. The **work sheet** (also called a **working paper**) is a columnar approach to moving from a trial balance to the finished financial statements. It provides an orderly means for (1) preparing adjusting entries, (2) computing net income, (3) preparing the formal financial statements, and (4) closing the books.

Although a work sheet is not essential to obtaining financial statements, it is a valuable informal device for bringing everything together in a single place, especially when there are numerous accounts and year-end adjustments. It helps assure the accountant that potential errors and overlooked adjustments will be discovered.

For learning purposes, the work sheet is usually prepared with a pencil. However, as already mentioned, accountants typically use electronic spreadsheets for work sheets, as discussed at the end of this appendix.

Steps in Preparation

Objective 5

Use a work sheet to prepare adjustments, financial statements, and closing entries.

Because the work sheet is an informal tool, there is no unique way of preparing it. However, a typical work sheet is illustrated in Exhibit 5-10. A step-by-step description of its preparation follows.

1. The accountant initially prepares an "unadjusted" trial balance as the first pair of columns in the work sheet. Then adjusting entries are listed in the second pair of columns. This provides a systematic and convenient way of reviewing the unadjusted trial balance together with the adjustments to make sure that nothing is overlooked.

The numbers in the first pair of columns come from the balances in the general ledger in Exhibit 5-6 *after* the last entry for the period's explicit transactions (entry *m*) but *before* the first entry for the end-of-period adjustments (entry *n*). This preparation of the unadjusted trial balance provides a check on the general accuracy of the ledger *before* adjustments are entered. Thus it provides an early chance to catch errors. As students and practicing accountants will testify, frequent use of self-checks as detailed work proceeds inevitably saves time. Few accounting tasks are more maddening than trying to trace an error discovered at a final stage back through a maze of interrelated journal entries and ledgers.

Concentrate on the first pair of columns, the Unadjusted Trial Balance. Many accounts are listed in their appropriate locations even though they have zero balances (for example, Accrued Wages Payable). Why? Because through experience the accountant knows that such accounts are almost always affected by the adjustment process. Listing all the accounts can help avoid overlooking required adjustments. However, inasmuch as the work sheet is an informal document, some accountants prefer first to list only the accounts with balances and later to list the additional accounts (below the $1,699 total in this illustration) when adjustments are made.

2. The second pair of columns is used for preparing the adjusting entries *n* through *t*. These columns are also totaled as a check on accuracy.

3. After the adjustments have been made, the third pair of columns represents the net effects of the first pair plus the second pair. That is, the unadjusted trial balance plus the adjustments equals the adjusted trial balance. Note how check after check is built into the work sheet.

4. The fourth pair of columns provides an income statement; the fifth pair, a statement of retained income; the sixth pair, a balance sheet. By tracing the numbers in those columns to the formal statements in Exhibits 5-2, 5-3, and 5-4 (pp. 182-184), you can readily see how a work sheet aids the preparation of the formal statements.

The Income Statement columns are sometimes used to compute income before taxes and the income tax expense for the year. That is why income tax expense appears below the subtotals. The net income amount is then transferred to the fifth pair of columns for the statement of retained income. Again, as in every pair, the columns are totaled to check accuracy.

The Income Statement and the Retained Income columns often guide the preparation of closing entries. Note how the Income Statement columns contain all the details necessary for the closing process; indeed, you can visualize the pair as a detailed Income Summary T-account used for closing. Similarly, the Retained Income columns can be visualized as the Retained Income T-account.

The final step is to move the ending balance of Retained Income from the fifth pair of columns to the sixth pair, the Balance Sheet columns.

The detailed sequence for the fourth, fifth, and sixth pairs of columns follows:

a. Add each of the two Income Statement columns and calculate the difference, as follows:

Credit column total (revenues)	$1,035
Debit column total (expenses)	885
Income before income taxes	$ 150

b. Compute the income tax expense, which is .40 × $150 = $60. Extend the $60 on the Income Tax Expense line as a debit in the Income Statement columns. Net income amounts to $150 − $60 = $90.

c. Add "net income" to the list of account titles. Place the $90 amount in the Income Statement debit column and in the Statement of Retained Income credit column. Note that this is akin to the closing journal entry that transfers net income from Income Summary to Retained Income.

d. Add each of the two Income Statement columns to see that the totals are equal.

e. Add the two Statement of Retained Income columns and calculate the difference, as follows:

Credit column total (beginning balance of retained income plus net income for the period)	$377
Debit column total (dividends declared)	80
Retained income balance, December 31, 19X2	$297

Exhibit 5-10 Oxley Company Work Sheet for the Year Ended December 31, 19X2

Accounts Titles (in thousands of dollars)	Unadjusted Trial Balance Debit	Credit	Adjustments Debit	Credit	Adjusted Trial Balance Debit	Credit	Income Statement Debit	Credit	Statement of Retained Income Debit	Credit	Balance Sheet Debit	Credit
Cash	150				150						150	
Accounts receivable	95				95						95	
Accrued interest receivable			(n) 15		15						15	
Inventory of merchandise	20				20						20	
Prepaid rent	130			(o) 120	10						10	
Long-term note receivable	288				288						288	
Equipment	200				200						200	
Accumulated depreciation, equipment		80		(r) 40		120						120
Accounts payable		90				90						90
Accrued wages payable				(p) 24		24						24
Accrued income taxes payable				(t) 16		16						16
Accrued interest payable				(q) 9		9						9
Note payable–current portion				(s) 80		80						80
Long-term note payable		120	(s) 80			40						40
Paid-in capital		102				102						102
Retained income, December 31, 19X1		287				287				287		
Dividends declared	80				80				80			
Sales		999				999		999				
Interest revenue		21		(n) 15		36		36				
Cost of goods sold	399				399		399					
Wages expense	190		(p) 24		214		214					
Rent expense			(o) 120		120		120					
Miscellaneous expense	100				100		100					
Depreciation expense			(r) 40		40		40					
Interest expense	3		(q) 9		12		12					
	1699	1699					885	1035				
Income tax expense	44		(t) 16		60		60					
			304	304	1803	1803						
Net income							90			90		
							1035	1035	80	377		
Retained income, December 31, 19X2									297			297
									377	377	778	778

(n) Accrual of interest receivable, $15   (o) Rent expense, $120   (p) Accrual of wages, $24   (q) Accrual of interest payable, $9   (r) Depreciation expense, $40
(s) Reclassification of note, $80   (t) Income tax expense, .40 × $150 income before income taxes = $60. Adjustment for accrued portion is $16.

f.   Add "retained income, December 31, 19X2," to the list of account titles. Place the $297 amount in the Statement of Retained Income debit column and in the Balance Sheet credit column.

g.   Add each of the two Statement of Retained Income columns to see that the totals are equal.

h.   Add each of the two Balance Sheet columns to see that the totals are equal. When they are equal, the accountant is ready to prepare the formal statements. When they are not equal, the accountant seldom smiles. He or she faces the labor of rechecking the preceding steps in reverse order to find the errors.

Flexibility of Uses

Ponder the work sheet in its entirety. It is a clever means of summarizing masses of interrelated data. Accountants often use the work sheet to prepare monthly and quarterly financial statements. Adjustments may be necessary for preparing these interim statements, but the accountant may not wish to enter adjustments formally in the journal and ledger each month. For example, suppose the work sheet in Exhibit 5-10 were for January 19X2. Adjustments entered on the work sheet as shown would not be made in the journals and ledgers. Formal interim financial statements can be prepared without the books being cluttered by the elaborate adjusting and closing entries each month.

Electronic Spreadsheet

Exhibit 5-11 shows the work sheet from Exhibit 5-10 as it would be prepared using an electronic spreadsheet. An Excel spreadsheet was used, but the format would be basically the same with Lotus 1-2-3, QuatroPro, or any other spreadsheet. Note that the spreadsheet contains columns that are labeled with letters and rows that are labeled with numbers. After the spreadsheet is set up, the accountant must simply enter in the cells the first four columns of numbers, and the computer will prepare the rest. The general procedure for using the spreadsheet follows:

1.   List the accounts.

2.   Enter the trial balance amount of each account as shown in the columns B and C of Exhibit 5-11.

3.   Enter the adjustment amounts in columns E and G; if desired, you can key the entries to the corresponding journal entries by entering the appropriate letter in column D or F, as was done in the example.

4.   Program the spreadsheet to calculate the adjusted trial balance amounts and place them in columns H and I. For example, the adjusted trial balance amount for prepaid rent is in cell $H9$ and is calculated as follows:

$$H9 = B9 + E9 - G9$$

For a credit-balance account, consider the long-term note payable, cell $I18$:

$$I18 = C18 - E18 + G18$$

5.   Program the spreadsheet to place the amount from the adjusted trial balance into the correct financial statement column. Rows 5 through 19 are placed in the appropriate (debit or credit) column of the balance sheet, rows 20 and 21 in the statement of retained income, and rows 22 through 29 and 31 in the income statement.

6. Program the spreadsheet to compute column totals. Be sure that the total debits equal the total credits in each pair of columns. (Note that subtotals are computed in columns *J*, *K*, *L*, and *M*. Such subtotals are handy but are not necessary.)

Major advantages of the electronic spreadsheet include the following:

1. The format is stored and can be used repeatedly. This avoids laborious writing of column heads and account titles.
2. Revisions of the basic format are easy.
3. Mathematical computations and placements of each account are achieved via computer. Speed and accuracy are maximized. Drudgery is minimized.
4. "What if" analysis is easily conducted. For example, suppose a manager wants to know the effects of various contemplated expense or revenue transactions on the income statement and balance sheet. Electronic spreadsheets can answer such questions instantly.

Appendix 5B: Variety in Data Processing and Journalizing

This appendix stresses that there are many appropriate data-processing paths to the same objectives. The focus should be on the final product, not on whether one path is theoretically better than other paths. For example, should we use manual or computer methods? Should we use one pattern of journal entries or another? The answers to the questions of data-processing alternatives are inherently tied to the *overall* costs and benefits of the possible competing systems in a *specific* organization. What is good for General Motors is probably not good for Sophia's Pizza House, and vice versa.

Objective 6

Prepare adjustments when alternative recording methods are used for the related originating transactions.

Variety in Recording Assets

Oxley Company's entries for rent (see entries **k** and **o** reproduced below from our chapter illustration) exemplify how accountants might adopt different patterns for journalizing:

Entry	As in Chapter: All Asset Now; Recognize Expense Later		Alternative: All Expense Now; Recognize Asset Later	

k. Cash payment	Prepaid rent
	  Cash
		130
		
			Rent expense
			  Cash
				130

		130		130

o. End-of-period adjustment	Rent expense
	  Prepaid rent
		120
		
			Prepaid rent
			  Rent expense
				10

		120		10

Is one choice better than another? Both produce the same final account balances. However, from a strict theory point of view, the method used in the chapter is superior because of its straightforward recognition that all acquisitions of goods and services are assets that expire and become expenses later. Under this method, entry **k** regards all acquisitions as assets, and entry **o** writes off the prepayments that have expired. Good theory often also makes good

Exhibit 5-11   Oxley Company   Work Sheet for the Year Ended December 31, 19X2

Account titles	Unadjusted Trial Balance Debit	Credit	Adjustments Debit	Credit	Adjusted Trial Balance Debit	Credit	Income Statement Debit	Credit	Statement of Retained Income Debit	Credit	Balance Sheet Debit	Credit
(in thousands of dollars)												
Cash	150				150						150	
Accounts receivable	95				95						95	
Accrued interest receivable			(n) 15		15						15	
Inventory of merchandise	20				20						20	
Prepaid rent	130			(o) 120	10						10	
Long-term note receivable	288				288						288	
Equipment	200				200						200	
Accumulated depreciation, equipment		80		(r) 40		120						120
Accounts payable		90				90						90
Accrued wages payable				(p) 24		24						24
Accrued income taxes payable				(t) 16		16						16
Accrued interest payable				(q) 9		9						9
Note payable—current portion				(s) 80		80						80
Long-term note payable		120	(s) 80			40						40
Paid-in capital		102				102						102
Retained income, December 31, 19X1		287				287				287		
Dividend declared	80				80				80			
Sales		999				999		999				
Interest revenue		21		(n) 15		36		36				
Cost of goods sold	399				399		399					
Wages expense	190		(p) 24		214		214					
Rent expense			(o) 120		120		120					
Miscellaneous expense	100				100		100					
Depreciation expense			(r) 40		40		40					
Interest expense	3		(q) 9		12		12					
							885	1035				
Income tax expense	44		(t) 16		60		60					
	1699	1699	304	304	1803	1803						
Net income							90			90		
							1035	1035				
Retained income, December 31, 19X2									297	377		297
									377	377	778	778

practice. For example, it is often easier to review asset accounts to determine what should be expensed than it is to review expense accounts to determine what should not have been expensed.

The altenative is to record as expenses such items as rent (or insurance premiums or office supplies) when cash is disbursed (or when a liability such as accounts payable is created) upon their acquisition, as entry *k* illustrates. Adjustments such as entry *o* are made at the end of the reporting period to reduce the expenses that would otherwise be overstated and to increase the assets for the unused part of the prepayments. This alternative is frequently encountered in practice.

Either alternative is acceptable. The accountant should choose the easiest one. By far the most important point is that any of the alternatives, properly applied, will lead to the same answers—the correct expense and the correct ending asset balance.

Variety in Recording Liabilities

As in the recording of assets, alternative recordings of liabilities are acceptable, provided that they ultimately result in the proper ending balances for the expense and liability accounts. Consider the entries for income taxes:

Entry	As in Chapter: Pay Old Liability and Recognize Expense; Recognize More Expense Later			Alternative: Recognize Expense Now; Adjust to Get Correct Balances Later		
i. Cash payment	Accrued income taxes payable	12		Income tax expense	56	
	Income tax expense	44		Cash		56
	Cash		56			
t. End-of-period adjustment	Income tax expense	16		Income tax expense	4	
	Accrued income taxes payable		16	Accrued income taxes payable		4

The chapter entries *i* and *t* followed the most theoretically defensible position. Entry *i* recognized that $12 of the $56 disbursement pertained to the liability carried over from the preceding period. Entry *t* recognized that the year-end liability arising from the current period was $16.

In the alternative, all disbursements are initially recorded as expenses. The U.S. government does not want to wait until after the end of the year to get its income taxes. Interim payments of estimated income taxes must be made and are frequently debited to income tax expense before the exact amount of the annual income tax expense is computed. At year-end (entry *t*), the income tax of $60 is computed, and the additional expense of $60 − $56 = $4 is charged. The accrued income taxes payable becomes the beginning balance of $12 plus the addition of $4, or $16 in total.

Temporarily Incorrect Balances

The major lesson of this appendix deserves emphasis. For sensible reasons governing day-to-day recording procedures, accountants may routinely debit expense for the *full amount* when cash changes hands. This may result in temporarily incorrect balances in a number of accounts throughout a reporting period. However, the accountant is aware that such a condition is commonplace. Adjustments become necessary to achieve the correct balances for the reporting period.

The justification for such "full amount" approaches centers on costs and benefits. On a day-to-day basis, an accountant or a clerk or a computer does not have to be concerned with remembering whether routine cash flows really affect past accruals. Instead, all receipts or disbursements are handled in *identical fashion* throughout the year. To the extent that such routines (used by, say, a computer or a lower-level clerk) cause temporary errors in accruals, the year-end adjustments (prepared by, say, a higher-level accountant) produce the necessary corrections.

Reversing Entries

reversing entries
Entries that switch back all debits and credits made in a related preceding adjusting entry.

Reversing entries are sometimes used to cope with the proper accounting for accruals. As the name implies, **reversing entries** switch back all debits and credits made in a related preceding adjusting entry. To illustrate their effect, compare the pattern of journal entries illustrated in the chapter with the pattern of reversing entries that would be employed, as shown in Exhibit 5-12. The adjustments (and the closing entries, not shown) would be identical whether reversing entries are used or not. The differences occur only for the routine journalizing during the following year, 19X3, as Exhibit 5-12 demonstrates.

Some accountants favor using reversing entries because they or their clerks or their computers do not have to be concerned with whether a later routine cash disbursement (or receipt) applies to any accrued liabilities (or assets) that were recognized at the end of the preceding period. So reversing entries are creatures of practical data processing, especially in manual systems. They have no theoretical merit, and, with the widespread use of computers, their use is diminishing.

Appendix 5C: Processing Data Using Special Journals

Objective 7

Use special journals to process transactions.

special journals
Journals used to record particular types of voluminous transactions; examples are the sales journal and the cash receipts journal.

Elsewhere in this textbook, the only book of original entry is a general journal. This appendix describes the use of special journals in addition to a general journal. This material is important to anyone who wants to know the details about how an accounting system processes data.

Chapters 4 and 5 use the general journal as the basic step in data processing. However, in all but the smallest accounting systems, *special journals* (or procedures akin to special journals) are used in addition to the general journal. **Special journals** are used to record particular types of recurring voluminous transactions. We will discuss two special journals, the sales journal and the cash receipts journal. These two special journals illustrate how special journals aid data processing. In practice you will find many other special journals including a purchases journal, cash disbursements journal, sales returns and allowances journal, and purchase returns and allowances journal.

Exhibit 5-12

	Without Reversing Entries: the Pattern Illustrated in Chapter	With Reversing Entries
Adjustment December 31, 19X2 Entry **p** from the chapter example.	Wages expense 24 Accrued wages payable 24	Wages expense 24 Accrued wages payable 24

Books closed for 19X2 (Entries would be identical and therefore are not shown here. The key point is that, under either approach, closing the books brings the balance in Wages Expense to zero at the start of 19X3.)

	Without Reversing Entries	With Reversing Entries
Reversal January 2, 19X3.	None	Accrued wages payable 24 Wages expense 24
Disbursements during 19X3 (assumed a total of 210).	Accrued wages payable 24 Wages expense 186 Cash 210	Wages expense 210 Cash 210

Postings during 19X3

Without Reversing Entries:

Accrued Wages Payable

24	Bal. 24

Wages Expense

24	
186	
186	

With Reversing Entries:

Accrued Wages Payable

24	Bal. 24

Wages Expense

| 210 | 24 |
| 210 | 24 |

Every accounting system has a general journal, whether kept in pen and ink or on computer tape or disk. But a general journal is not an efficient device for recording numerous repetitive transactions. How would you enjoy using a general journal to debit Accounts Receivable and credit Sales for each credit sale made in a Wal-Mart store on a busy Saturday? Moreover, how would you like to post each journal entry to the general ledger accounts for accounts receivable and sales? Not only would the work be long, tedious, and dull, but it would be outrageously expensive.

As we will see, all entries in each specialized journal have common features. Combining multiple similar transactions allows us to post only the totals and provides speed, efficiency, and economy of data processing.

Sales Journal

The sales journal in Exhibit 5-13 is probably better called a *credit sales journal* because it includes only credit sales, cash sales being recorded in the cash receipts journal. If a general journal were used for these five credit sales transactions, five separate entries debiting Accounts Receivable and crediting Sales would be required. In addition, five separate postings would be made to these accounts in the general ledger. Obviously, if five thousand sales occurred in June, journalizing and posting each individual transaction would become oppressive.

Consider the details in Exhibit 5-13. As each sale is entered, the accountant debits the *subsidiary* ledger account for the particular customer. The invoice reference provides a trail to any underlying details of the sale. A check mark is put in the Post column as each amount is posted to the individual subsidiary accounts.

The general ledger accounts, Accounts Receivable and Sales, are not written out as entries are being made in the sales journal. The dollar amount is entered once, not twice, for each sale. Column totals are posted to the general ledger periodically, usually at the end of the month. Posting the $6,400 total to the two accounts eliminates the need for a journal entry, but it has the same effect as if the following general journal entry were made:

	POST	AMOUNTS	
Accounts receivable........	4	6,400	
Sales..............	88		6,400

Of course, the direct posting from the sales journal eliminates having the above general journal entry.

The sum of the balances in the subsidiary ledger must agree with the Accounts Receivable account in the general ledger. When there is a subsidiary ledger, its corresponding summary account in the general ledger is often called a controlling account. The existence of a subsidiary ledger for a particular general ledger account is often denoted by adding the word *control* to the latter's title—for example, Accounts Receivable Control.

Cash Receipts Journal

Special journals may have a single money column, as in the sales journal just illustrated, or they may have several columns, as Exhibit 5-14 demonstrates. The number of columns depends on the frequency of transactions affecting

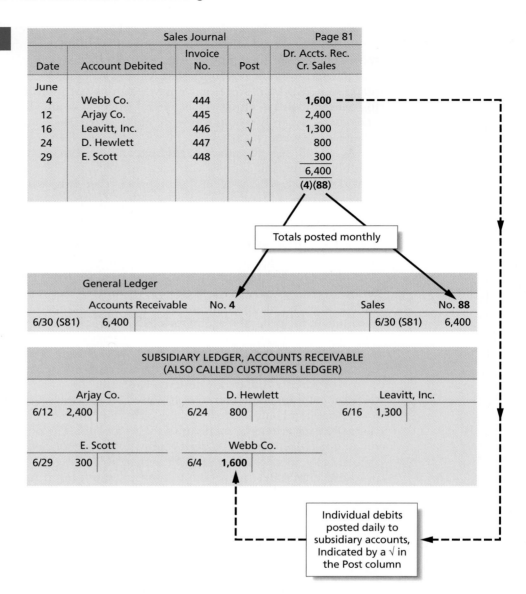

Exhibit 5-13

Sales Journal and Postings

particular accounts. Moreover, as the cash receipts journal in Exhibit 5-14 shows, the most frequently affected columns might be placed at the far right—regardless of whether the amounts therein are debits or credits. The important point about debits and credits is that they are ultimately entered on the correct sides of the *ledger* accounts, even though the format of some special *journals* places debit columns on the right-hand side of the page.

Cash sales and collections on accounts receivable are the two most common types of cash receipts, so special columns are formed for Cash, Sales, and Accounts Receivable. The amounts of the cash sales are entered in the Cash and Sales columns. The amounts of the collections on accounts are entered in the

Exhibit 5-14 Cash Receipts Journal and Postings

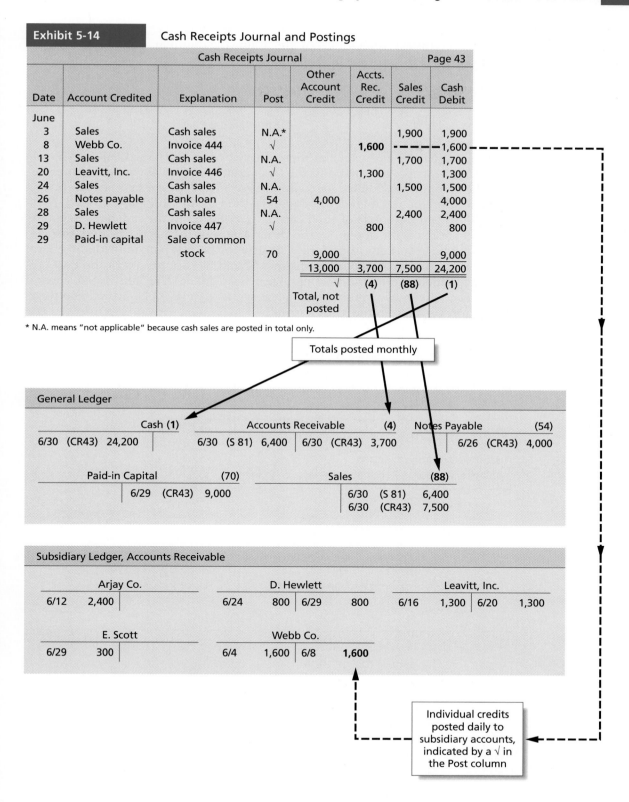

	Cash Receipts Journal						Page 43
Date	Account Credited	Explanation	Post	Other Account Credit	Accts. Rec. Credit	Sales Credit	Cash Debit
June							
3	Sales	Cash sales	N.A.*			1,900	1,900
8	Webb Co.	Invoice 444	√		1,600		1,600
13	Sales	Cash sales	N.A.			1,700	1,700
20	Leavitt, Inc.	Invoice 446	√		1,300		1,300
24	Sales	Cash sales	N.A.			1,500	1,500
26	Notes payable	Bank loan	54	4,000			4,000
28	Sales	Cash sales	N.A.			2,400	2,400
29	D. Hewlett	Invoice 447	√		800		800
29	Paid-in capital	Sale of common stock	70	9,000			9,000
				13,000	3,700	7,500	24,200
				√ Total, not posted	(4)	(88)	(1)

* N.A. means "not applicable" because cash sales are posted in total only.

Totals posted monthly

General Ledger

Cash (1)		Accounts Receivable (4)		Notes Payable (54)
6/30 (CR43) 24,200		6/30 (S 81) 6,400 | 6/30 (CR43) 3,700		6/26 (CR43) 4,000

Paid-in Capital (70)	Sales (88)
6/29 (CR43) 9,000	6/30 (S 81) 6,400
	6/30 (CR43) 7,500

Subsidiary Ledger, Accounts Receivable

Arjay Co.	D. Hewlett	Leavitt, Inc.
6/12 2,400	6/24 800 | 6/29 800	6/16 1,300 | 6/20 1,300

E. Scott	Webb Co.
6/29 300	6/4 1,600 | 6/8 1,600

Individual credits posted daily to subsidiary accounts, indicated by a √ in the Post column

Cash and Accounts Receivable columns. This specialized approach replaces the need for countless repetitions of the following familiar entries that would otherwise have to be made in the general journal:

Cash	xx	
Sales		xx
Cash	xx	
Accounts receivable		xx

Infrequent cash receipts, such as those illustrated for the bank loan and the sale of common stock, are entered in the Cash and the Other Accounts columns.

The columns are totaled (accountants say *footed*) at the end of each month to make sure that the total debits equal the total credits: 13,000 + 3,700 + 7,500 = 24,200. Then the totals of each column are posted to the indicated accounts in the general ledger. Of course, the Other Accounts total is not posted. Instead, the individual amounts therein are posted to the relevant individual general ledger accounts. The account numbers (54 and 70) are placed in the Post column as evidence that the postings have been made. The illustrated general ledger accounts now contain postings from the cash receipts journal and those made previously from the sales journal.

The only subsidiary ledger in this illustration is for Accounts Receivable. The postings from the cash receipts journal are made in the same manner as those from the sales journal. A principal internal control feature is illustrated by the monthly schedule of the individual customer balances. The sum should agree with the general ledger balance, June 30:

Arjay Co.	$2,400
E. Scott	300
Balance, subsidiary ledger	$2,700
Balance, Accounts Receivable in general ledger	$2,700

Accounting Vocabulary

accounting cycle, *p. 180*
auditor, *p. 201*
closing entries, *p. 196*
closing the books, *p. 196*

comparative financial statements, *p. 182*
permanent accounts, *p. 201*
reversing entries, *p. 211*

special journals, *p. 211*
temporary accounts, *p. 201*
working paper, *p. 204*
work sheet, *p. 204*

Assignment Material

Questions

5-1. How many years are usually covered by the comparative income statements and balance sheets of publicly held corporations?

5-2. "It's a several-stage process by which accountants produce an entity's financial statements

for a specific period of time." What is the term that describes the process?

5-3. What is the purpose of a Dividends Declared account?

5-4. "A corporation has no obligation to pay a dividend

on its common stock." Do you agree? Explain.

5-5. A company declared a dividend of $100,000. Using a Dividends Declared account, prepare a journal entry for the transaction.

5-6. "Cash dividends that are payable are a part of stockholders' equity." Do you agree? Explain.

5-7. "Dividends Declared has a normal left-side balance. It represents a reduction in Retained Income and Stockholders' Equity." Do you agree? Explain.

5-8. "Closing is a clerical procedure. It is devoid of any new accounting theory." Do you agree? Explain.

5-9. "Net assets are always equal to stockholders' equity." Do you agree? Explain.

5-10. "Closing the books might better be called clearing the revenue and expense accounts." Do you agree? Explain.

5-11. "The word *permanent* to describe balance sheet accounts is misleading." Explain.

5-12. "If it were up to management, there would be no auditors." Do you agree? Explain.

5-13. Why do auditors protect their reputations so carefully?

5-14. Appendix 5A. Why are work sheets used?

5-15. Appendix 5A. "Preparing a work sheet using an electronic spreadsheet is more trouble than it is worth." Do you agree? Explain.

5-16. Appendix 5B. "Variety in recording accounting transactions is unacceptable diversity." Do you agree? Explain.

5-17. Appendix 5B. "Liabilities can have temporary debit balances." Explain.

5-18. Appendix 5C. Name two common special journals, and briefly describe the types of entries to each.

Exercises

5-19 Journal Entry Explanations

Prepare possible explanations for the following journal entries:

a.	Accounts receivable	4,000	
	Sales		4,000
b.	Cash	3,000	
	Accounts receivable		3,000
c.	Accrued wages payable	2,500	
	Wages expense	400	
	Cash		2,900
d.	Long-term note payable	1,800	
	Notes payable, current		1,200
	Cash		600
e.	Unearned sales revenue	1,500	
	Sales		1,500
f.	Dividend payable	300	
	Cash		300

5-20 Effects of Adjustments of Preceding Period

The Big Pine Boat Company had the following balances as of December 31, 19X5:

Unearned sales revenue	$100,000
Accrued interest receivable	120,000
Accrued wages payable	190,000

During early 19X6, cash was collected for interest of $170,000. Cash was disbursed for wages of $900,000. Total sales of $700,000 included $100,000 of deliveries to all customers who had made advance payments during 19X5.

Required Set up T-accounts and prepare the journal entries for the 19X6 transactions described. Post to the T-accounts.

5-21   Closing the Accounts

The following accounts show their final balances before closing and their closing entries (in thousands). Prepare the closing journal entries that were evidently made. What is the balance in Retained Income after closing?

Cost of Goods Sold	
500	500

Dividends Declared	
70	70

Other Revenues	
40	40

Income Summary	
840	930
90	

Sales	
890	890

Retained Income	
70	500
	90

Other Expenses	
340	340

5-22   Dividends

On March 10, Liverpool Music Company declared dividends of £.25 per share for each of the 100,000 shares outstanding. Payment was made on March 31. (£ is the symbol for British pounds.)

Required   Prepare journal entries pertaining to dividends in March. Include appropriate dates and explanations.

5-23   Income Versus Cash Flow

Pedro's Equipment sells farm implements. January 19X6 was a slow month. The only sale was one tractor, sold for $30,000 with a $15,000 cash down payment and $15,000 due in six months. The tractor was purchased for inventory in 19X5 for $18,000 cash. January's operating expenses were $9,000; $7,000 was paid in cash and $2,000 was depreciation.

Required   1. Compute net income for January. Ignore taxes.
2. Compute net cash flows from operating activities for January.
3. Why do the amounts in requirements 1 and 2 differ?

Problems

5-24   Journalize, Post, and Prepare Trial Balance

Consider the trial balance for Limacher Software Consultants, Inc., shown at the top of the next page.

The following additional information pertains to June 29 and 30, which is the end of Limacher's fiscal year (amounts in thousands):

a. Wages incurred but unpaid, $12.
b. One-third of the prepaid insurance had expired. (Increase Miscellaneous Expenses.)
c. The note is payable on July 31. It is a 16%, seven-month note. Principal and interest are payable at maturity.
d. Depreciation expense for the fiscal year is $10.
e. Billed clients for $15.
f. Paid the liability for dividends.
g. Unbilled revenue as of June 30, based on time logged on various client projects, was $60. (Increase Unbilled Client Receivables.)
h. Half the prepaid trade association dues had expired. (Increase Miscellaneous Expenses.)
i. Received $14 cash advance from a client for services to be rendered after June 30.
j. Income tax rate was 35%.

Limacher Software
Consultants, Inc.
Trial Balance
June 28, 19X5
(in thousands)

	Debit	Credit
Cash	$ 38	
Accounts receivable	95	
Unbilled client receivables	—	
Prepaid trade association dues	6	
Prepaid insurance	3	
Equipment	59	
Accumulated depreciation, equipment		$ 8
Accounts payable		21
Note payable		75
Accrued interest payable (on note)		5
Dividends payable		10
Accrued wages payable		—
Accrued income taxes payable		—
Unearned fee revenue		—
Paid-in capital		50
Retained income		20
Dividends declared	10	
Fee revenue		840
Rent expense	21	
Wages expense	400	
Depreciation expense	—	
Miscellaneous expense	362	
Interest expense	5	
Income tax expense	30	
Total	$1,029	$1,029

Required

1. After posting the above balances to T-accounts, analyze and journalize all entries arising from the above information.
2. Post the journal entries to T-accounts. Use check marks as posting references in the journal.
3. Prepare an adjusted trial balance, June 30, 19X5.

5-25   Effects of Adjustments of Preceding Period

(Alternates are 5-26 and 5-27.) The New York Times Company showed the following actual balances and descriptions in its balance sheet, January 1, 1994:

Current liabilities:	
Payrolls	$ 71,256,000
Unexpired subscriptions	130,627,000

Suppose the company also showed Interest Receivable of $550,000.

During early 1994, assume the following: $852,000 was collected for interest; cash of $98,054,000 was disbursed for payrolls; and deliveries of $33,621,000 were made of the company's publications that had been subscribed to and fully collected before 1994.

Required Set up T-accounts and prepare the journal entries for the 1994 transactions. Post to the T-accounts.

5-26   Effects of Adjustments of Preceding Period
(Alternates are 5-25 and 5-27.) The Times Mirror Company engages principally in publishing, notably the *Los Angles Times, Newsday, Sporting News, Golf,* and *Popular Science.* Its annual report included the following balances, January 1, 1994.

Accounts receivable	$550,102,000
Employees' compensation payable	104,737,000
Unearned income	198,619,000

Assume that during early 1994, accounts receivable of $527,462,000 was collected in cash. Cash of $210,417,000 was disbursed for employees' compensation. Deliveries of $58,162,000 were made of magazines and newspapers that had been subscribed to and fully collected before 1994.

Required Set up T-accounts and prepare the journal entries for the 1994 transactions. Post to the T-accounts.

Class **5-27   Journal Entries**
(Alternates are 5-25 and 5-26.) Delta Air Lines, Inc., had the following three actual balance sheet items in its 1993 annual report (in thousands):

Maintenance and operating supplies	$ 90,593
Air traffic liability	1,189,883
Accrued rent	200,471

A footnote stated: "Passenger ticket sales are recorded as revenue when the transportation is provided. The value of unused tickets is included in current liabilities as air traffic liability." Therefore air traffic liability is an unearned revenue account.

Required Set up T-accounts and prepare journal entries and postings for the following transactions that occurred subsequent to the date of the balance sheet in the 1993 annual report. All numbers are in thousands.

1. Use of $70,000 of maintenance and operating supplies.
2. Sales of $900,000 of tickets in advance of air travel. (Increase Cash.)
3. Revenues of $4,440,000 including $1,200,000 of transportation provided for passengers who paid in advance.
4. Additional accruals of rent payable, $180,000.
5. Payments of rent, $187,041.

Indicate the balances in Maintenance and Operating Supplies, Air Traffic Liability, and Accrued Rent after posting for the five transactions.

5-28   Journal Entries
Cincinnati Bell, Inc., provides communications services, mainly telephone services, in parts of Ohio, Kentucky, and Indiana. Its total revenues for a recent year were $1,089,637,000. Its balance sheets showed:

	End of Year	Beginning of Year
Advance billing and customers' deposits	$31,553,000	$26,464,000

To save space, annual reports often combine accounts. In this instance, Advance Billing is really one account, an unearned revenue account. For example, customers typically are billed for their basic monthly phone charges in advance of the service rendered.

Customers' Deposits is another account. For example, a new customer may be required to make a security deposit of $300. When the customer terminates the service, the deposit is usually returned in cash.

Required   Post all entries to three T-accounts. (Use Cash, Advance Billing and Customers' Deposits, and Operating Revenues.)

1. Prepare a summary journal entry to show how the $26,464,000 was initially recorded.

2. (a) During the year, additional amounts of advance billings and deposits amounted to $17 million. (b) Moreover, $3 million of customers' deposits was returned in cash to customers. Prepare summary journal entries for these events.

3. At the end of the year, prepare the necessary adjusting journal entry to obtain the balance given for the year.

5-29   Closing Entries

(Alternates are 5-30 through 5-32.) Limacher Software Consultants, Inc., had the following accounts included in an adjusted trial balance, June 30, 19X5 (in thousands):

Retained income	$ 20	Rent expense	$ 21	Miscellaneous	
Dividends		Wages expense	412	expenses	$366
declared	10	Depreciation		Interest expense	6
Fee revenue	915	expense	10	Income tax	
				expense	35

Required   After posting the above balances to T-accounts, journalize and post the entries necessary to close the books. Number your entries as 1, 2, etc. What is the balance in Retained Income after closing?

5-30   Closing Entries

(Alternates are 5-29, 5-31, and 5-32.) Post the following balances to T-accounts. Then, journalize and post the entries required to close the books (in thousands):

Retained income		Wages expense	$300
(before closing entries)	$245	Miscellaneous	
Sales	890	expenses	40
Interest revenue	30	Income tax expense	15
Cost of goods sold	500	Dividends declared	30

What is the balance in Retained Income after closing entries?

5-31   Closing Entries
(Alternates are 5-29, 5-30, and 5-32.) Albertson's, Inc., is a prominent supermarket chain located in the southern and western United States. The actual balances and descriptions that follow pertain to the 1994 fiscal year and are in millions of dollars:

Sales	$11,284	Other expenses	$ 78
Cost of sales	8,492	Income taxes	212
Operating and		Cash dividends	91
administrative expenses	2,162	Retained earnings,	
		beginning of year	1,251

Required   After posting the balances to T-accounts, journalize and post the entries required to close the books. What is the balance in Retained Earnings after closing entries?

5-32   Closing Entries
(Alternates are 5-29 through 5-31.) In addition to ketchup, pickles, and other products with the Heinz brand name, H. J. Heinz Company produces foods with the brands Ore-Ida, StarKist, and Weight Watchers. The accompanying actual balances and descriptions pertain to a recent year and are in millions of dollars.

Retained earnings,		Selling, general, and	
beginning of year	$3,356	administrative expenses	$1,597
Sales	7,047	Interest and other expenses, net	146
Cost of products sold	4,382	Provision for income taxes	319
		Cash dividends	326

Required   After posting the balances to T-accounts, journalize and post the entries required to close the books. What is the balance in Retained Earnings after closing entries?

5-33   Adjustments and Closing
Consider the accompanying Soderstrom Company trial balance.

Soderstrom Company Unadjusted Trial Balance December 31, 19X2 (in thousands of dollars)

	Debit	Credit
Cash	$ 32	
Accounts receivable	89	
Notes receivable	50	
Merchandise inventory	120	
Prepaid rent	12	
Equipment	95	
Accumulated depreciation, equipment		$ 25
Accounts payable		132
Paid-in capital		100
Retained income		66
Sales		990
Cost of goods sold	570	
Wages expense	200	
Miscellaneous expense	120	
Income tax expense	25	
Total	$1,313	$1,313

The following additional information is not reflected in the trial balance (amounts are in thousands):

a. Interest accrued on notes receivable, $5.

b. Depreciation, $9.

c. Wages accrued but unpaid, $7.

d. Utilities accrued but unpaid, $4. (Increase Miscellaneous Expenses.)

e. Rent expired, $5.

f. Dividend declared but unpaid, $14. Use a Dividends Declared account, which is really just an offset to Retained Income.

g. A cash receipt of $2 from a credit customer was credited erroneously to Accounts Payable, so a correction must be made.

h. Additional income tax expense must be accrued. The income tax rate is 40% of pretax income. Compute the additional tax after computing the effects of the above adjustments to revenue and expense accounts.

Required

1. After posting the above balances to T-accounts, analyze and journalize all entries arising from the descriptions in *a* through *h* above. Use new accounts as necessary.

2. Post your journal entries to T-accounts. Use check marks as posting references in the journal.

3. Prepare an adjusted trial balance, December 31, 19X2. Allow space for four columns, placing your numbers for this requirement in the first pair of columns.

4. Prepare and post the closing journal entries to T-accounts. Key the entries as *i, j*, etc.

5. Prepare a postclosing trial balance by placing the appropriate numbers in the second pair of columns in your answer to requirement 3 above.

5-34 Prepare Financial Statements

Consider the accompanying Soccer Specialties, Inc. adjusted trial balance.

Soccer Specialties, Inc. Adjusted Trial Balance December 31, 19X5 (in thousands)

	Debit	Credit
Accounts payable		$ 85
Accounts receivable	$ 65	
Accrued income taxes payable		10
Accrued interest payable (due annually)		4
Accrued wages payable		20
Accumulated depreciation, building		70
Accumulated depreciation, equipment		47
Building	130	
Cash	68	
Cost of goods sold	488	
Dividends declared	11	
Equipment	70	
Income tax expense	20	
Interest expense	6	
Inventory	120	
Long-term note payable (due in 19X8)		50
Other operating expenses	110	
Paid-in capital		110
Prepaid insurance	2	
Retained income		34
Sales		960
Wages expense	300	
Total	$1,390	$1,390

1. Prepare a multiple-step income statement.
2. Prepare a statement of retained income.
3. Prepare a classified balance sheet.
4. Compute the working capital and the current ratio.

5-35   Income and Cash Flows

Following are the summarized transactions of Dr. Rose Francisco, a dentist, for 19X7, her first year in practice:

1. Acquired equipment and furniture for $60,000 cash. Depreciation expense for 19X7 is $10,000.
2. Fees collected, $85,000. These fees included $3,000 paid in advance by some patients on December 31, 19X7.
3. Rent is paid at the rate of $500 monthly, payable on the twenty-fifth of each month for the following month. Total disbursements during 19X7 for rent were $6,500.
4. Fees billed but uncollected, December 31, 19X7, $15,000.
5. Utilities expense paid in cash, $600. Additional utility bills unpaid at December 31, 19X7, $100.
6. Salaries expense of dental assistant and secretary, $15,000 paid in cash. In addition, $2,000 was earned but unpaid on December 31, 19X7.

Required   1. Prepare an income statement and a statement of cash provided by operating activities. Ignore taxes.
2. Compare operating income with net cash provided by operating activities. Which basis do you prefer as a measure of Dr. Francisco's performance? Why?

5-36   Prepare Income Statement and Balance Sheet

Nancy Yamaguchi runs a small consulting-engineering firm that specializes in designing and overseeing the installation of environmental-control systems. However, even though she is the president, she has had no formal training in management. She has been in business one year and has prepared the following income statement for her fiscal year ended June 30, 19X4:

Yamaguchi
Consulting
Engineers, Inc.
Income Statement
for the Year Ended
June 30, 19X4

Fees collected in cash		$455,000
Expenses paid in cash except for depreciation:		
Rent	$ 12,500	
Utilities	10,000	
Wages	150,000	
President's salary	46,000	
Office supplies	14,000	
Travel	40,000	
Miscellaneous	80,000	
Depreciation	10,000	$362,500
Operating income		$ 92,500

Yamaguchi realized that the entire $50,000 cost of equipment acquired on July 1, 19X3 should not be an expense of one year. She predicted a useful life of five years, a terminal value of zero, and deducted $10,000 as depreciation for the first year.

Yamaguchi is thinking about future needs for her expanding business. For example, although she now uses rented space in an office building, she is considering buying a small building. She showed her income statement to a local banker, who reacted: "Nancy, this statement may suffice for filing income tax forms, but the bank will not consider any long-term financing until it receives a balance sheet and income statement prepared on the accrual basis of accounting. Moreover, the statements must be subjected to an audit by an independent certified public accountant."

As a CPA, you are asked to audit her records and fulfill the bank's request.

The following data have been gathered:

1. On July 1, 19X3, Yamaguchi invested $25,000 cash, and two friends each invested $2,000 cash in the firm in return for capital stock.
2. Yamaguchi acquired $50,000 of equipment on July 1, 19X3. A down payment of $20,000 cash was made. A $30,000 two-year note bearing an annual interest rate of 15% was signed. Principal plus interest were both payable at maturity.
3. On June 30, 19X4, clients owed Yamaguchi $95,000 on open accounts.
4. Salaries are paid on the fifteenth of every month. As business expanded throughout the fiscal year, additional employees were hired. The total payroll paid on June 15, 19X4, including the president's monthly salary of $4,000, was $40,000.
5. Rent was paid in advance on the fifteenth of every month. An initial payment of $1,500 covered July 1, 19X3–August 15, 19X3. Payments of $1,000 monthly were paid beginning August 15, 19X3.
6. Office Supplies on hand on June 30, 19X4, were $5,000.
7. On April 1, 19X4, a local oil refinery gave Yamaguchi a retainer fee of $40,000 cash in exchange for twelve months of consulting services beginning at that date.

Required

1. Using the accrual basis of accounting, prepare an income statement for the fiscal year. Submit supporting computations properly labeled.
2. Prepare a balance sheet, dated June 30, 19X4. Assume that the cash balance is $111,500.

5-37   Prepare Statement of Cash Flows

Refer to the preceding problem. Prepare a statement of cash flows that proves that the ending cash balance is indeed $111,500. Label your analysis fully. Note that interest payments are operating cash flows. Explain why net income differs from net cash provided by operating activities.

5-38   Financial Statements

Mitsubishi Kasei Corporation, Japan's premier diversified chemical company, has annual sales of more than $12 billion. The company's 1993 annual report included the items listed below (in billions of yen). The balance sheet items included here are the amounts at March 31, 1993, unless otherwise indicated.

Property, plant, and equipment, original cost	¥1,327
Accumulated depreciation	848
Net sales	1,181
Interest expense	36
Interest income	11
Bank loans payable	288
Retained earnings, March 31, 1992	82
Common stock	108
Cost of sales	930
Provision for income taxes	9
Marketable securities	99
Accrued income taxes	5
Long-term debt	404
Additional paid-in capital	106

continued

Selling, general, and administrative expenses	217
Dividends declared	12
Inventories	160
Prepaid expenses	23
Other income	6
Accounts payable	247
Accounts receivable	360
Other current liabilities	49
Accrued expenses	47
Other liabilities (noncurrent)	85
Cash and time deposits	101
Other assets (noncurrent)	193

Required

1. Prepare a combined multi-step statement of income and retained earnings.
2. Prepare the classified balance sheet as of the end of the year.
3. Compute the working capital and the current ratio.

✓ **5-39   Preparation of Financial Statements from Trial Balance**
Apple Computer, Inc., prepared the following (slightly modified) trial balance as of September 30, 1994, the end of the company's fiscal year:

Apple Computer, Inc.
Trial Balance
September 30, 1994
(in millions)

	Debits	Credits
Cash and cash equivalents	$ 1,204	
Short-term investments	54	
Accounts receivable	1,581	
Inventories	1,088	
Prepaid income taxes	293	
Other current assets	256	
Property, plant, and equipment, at cost	1,452	
Accumulated depreciation and amortization		$ 785
Other assets	159	
Notes payable		292
Accounts payable		882
Accrued compensation and employee benefits		137
Accrued marketing and distribution expenses		178
Other current liabilities		455
Long-term debt		304
Deferred income taxes		671
Common stock, no par value		298
Retained earnings		1,831
Net sales		9,189
Cost of sales	6,845	
Research and development expenses	565	
Selling, general, and administrative expenses	1,384	
Other operating expenses (revenues)		127
Interest and other expenses, net	22	
Provision for income taxes	190	
Cash dividends	56	
Total	$15,149	$15,149

Required
1. Prepare Apple Computer's income statement for the year ended September 30, 1994.
2. Prepare Apple Computer's balance sheet as of September 30, 1994.

5-40   Summarized Corporate Annual Report

Inspect an annual report of a publicly held corporation. (Your instructor will give more specific instructions regarding how to obtain access to such reports at your school.) Read the report. The report will contain many details not covered in your study to date. Nevertheless, you will see the general picture portrayed by the balance sheet, income statement, and other statements. Complete the following. If the item is not reported by the corporation, write "not available."

1. Name of company.
2. Location of corporate headquarters.
3. Principal products or services.
4. Main geographic area of activity.
5. Name and title of chief executive officer (CEO).
6. Ending date of latest operating year reported.
7. Indicate the terms (if any) used instead of (a) balance sheet, (b) income statement, (c) retained income, (d) stockholders' equity, (e) revenues, (f) expenses.
8. Total assets.
9. Total liabilities.
10. Total stockholders' equity.
11. Total revenues (you may need to compute this).
12. Total expenses (you may need to compute this).
13. Net income (see above and subtract item 12 from item 11, then check the result with reported net income).
14. Total cash dividends declared.
15. Earnings per share of common stock (EPS).
16. Annual dividends per share of common stock.
17. Market in which stock is traded (see *Wall Street Journal* or local newspapers).
18. Latest market price of common stock (see *Wall Street Journal* or local newspapers).
19. Price-earnings ratio (compute or see *Wall Street Journal* or local newspapers).
20. Dividend yield (compute or see *Wall Street Journal* or local newspapers).
21. Dividend-payout ratio (you may need to compute this).
22. Name of independent public accountants.
23. Did they certify that all amounts were correct? If not, what did they say? (Do not simply copy the actual wording; be brief.)
24. Total number of shareholders.
25. Total number of employees.
26. Total number of shares of common stock outstanding.
27. Common stockholders' equity per share (book value per share).
28. Comparative statistics (financial and operating data) were reported for how many years?
29. Give very briefly your general impression of this report (for example, quality, scope, usefulness, format, readability, interest to you, etc.).

5-41   External Auditors and Ethics

Managers (with the help of staff accountants) prepare the financial statements, which are then examined by external auditors. Compare and contrast the types of ethical responsibilities of external auditors with those of managers and staff accountants.

5-42   Comprehensive Review

This is a comprehensive review of Chapters 1 through 5. Mallard Clothing, a retail corporation, had the following postclosing trial balance, December 31, 19X4 (in thousands of dollars):

Account Number	Name of Account	Dr.	Cr.
10	Cash	30	
20	Accounts receivable	91	
34	Notes receivable, current	100	
35	Accrued interest receivable	16	
40	Merchandise inventory	160	
52	Prepaid fire insurance	3	
62	Notes receivable, long-term	100	
74	Equipment	120	
74A	Accumulated depreciation, equipment		76
100	Accounts payable		90
111	Accrued wages payable		8
123	Accrued income taxes payable		4
137	Unearned sales revenue		10
200	Paid-in capital		110
230	Retained income		322
		620	620

The following summarized transactions (in thousands of dollars) occurred during 19X5:

a.   Merchandise inventory purchased on open account was $480.

b.   Total sales were $890, of which 80% were on credit.

c.   The sales in *b* were exclusive of the deliveries of goods to customers who had paid in advance as of December 31, 19X4. All of those goods ordered in advance were indeed delivered during 19X5.

d.   The cost of goods sold for 19X5, including those in *c*, was $440.

e.   Collections from credit customers were $682.

f.   The notes receivable are from a major supplier of belts. Interest for twelve months on all notes was collected on May 1. The rate is 12% per annum. The accounting system provides for cash collections of interest to be credited first to existing accrued interest receivable carried over from the preceding period.

g.   The principal of the current notes receivable was collected on May 1, 19X5. The principal of the remaining notes is payable on May 1, 19X6 (see entry *r*).

h.   As of December 31, 19X5, customers had made a total of $7 in advance cash payments for "layaway" plans and for merchandise not yet in stock. These payments were exclusive of any other transactions described above.

Cash disbursements were:

i.   To trade creditors, $470.

j.   To employees for wages, $193. The accounting system for wages is to debit any existing accrued payables first and debit any remainder of a disbursement to expense.

k.   For miscellaneous expenses such as store rents, advertising, utilities, and supplies, which were all paid in cash, $189. (These items are combined here to reduce the detailed recording of items that are basically accounted for alike.)

l. For new equipment acquired on July 1, 19X5, $74.

m. To the insurance company for a new three-year fire insurance policy effective September 1, 19X5, $36 (rates had increased). Prepayments of expenses are routinely debited to asset accounts.

n. To the federal and state governments for income taxes, $19. Income tax expense was debited for $15 of the $19. (For your general information, most businesses must pay income taxes regularly throughout the year.)

o. The board of directors declared cash dividends of $26 on December 15 to stockholders of record, January 5, and to be paid on January 21, 19X6. (Note that this is not a cash disbursement until payment has been made.) Debit Dividends Declared, which is really just an offset to Retained Income.

The following adjustments were made on December 31, 19X5:

p. For the interest on notes receivable.

q. For insurance. The prepaid insurance of December 31, 19X4, had expired too.

r. For reclassification of the notes receivable.

s. For depreciation. Depreciation expense for 19X5 was $30.

t. Wages earned but unpaid, December 31, 19X5, $15.

u. Total income tax expense for 19X5 is $20, computed as 40% of pretax income of $50. (Note that part of the 19X5 tax expense has already been recorded and paid, as indicated in transaction *n*.)

Required

1. After posting the opening balances to T-accounts, analyze and journalize all transactions, including adjustments, for 19X5.
2. Post all journal entries to T-accounts. Be painstaking as you post. Use the given account numbers as posting references. For accounts not in the trial balance of December 31, 19X4, use check marks as posting references instead.
3. Prepare a trial balance, December 31, 19X5.
4. Prepare a multiple-step income statement for 19X5.
5. Prepare a statement of retained income for 19X5.
6. Prepare classified comparative balance sheets for December 31, 19X4 and 19X5. Classify the prepaid insurance, December 31, 19X4, as a current asset even though a portion thereof might justifiably be classified as a long-term asset.
7. Journalize and post the entries necessary to "close the books" for 19X5.

5-43 Work Sheet

Study Appendix 5A. Refer to the preceding problem. Examine the accompanying unadjusted trial balance that includes the results of transactions *a* through *o* (in thousands).

Required

1. Prepare a twelve-column work sheet, using the unadjusted trial balance as the first pair of columns. Add pairs of columns for adjustments, adjusted trial balance, income statement, statement of retained income, and balance sheet. When entering the unadjusted trial balance on the work sheet, allow space for new accounts as follows: two spaces after Accounts Receivable, two spaces after Accounts Payable, and three spaces between Miscellaneous Expense and Income Tax Expense.
2. Enter the adjustments for transactions *p* through *u*.
3. Complete the work sheet. Check the accuracy of your work by comparing the work sheet results with the formal financial statements prepared in the solution to Problem 5-42.

Mallard Clothing
Unadjusted Trial Balance

Account Title	Debit	Credit
Cash	$ 40	
Accounts receivable	121	
Merchandise inventory	200	
Prepaid fire insurance	39	
Notes receivable, long-term portion	100	
Equipment	194	
Accumulated depreciation, equipment		$ 76
Accounts payable		100
Dividends payable		26
Unearned sales revenue		7
Paid-in capital		110
Retained income		322
Dividends declared	26	
Sales		900
Interest revenue		8
Cost of goods sold	440	
Wages expense	185	
Miscellaneous expense	189	
Income tax expense	15	
Total	$1,549	$1,549

5-44 Work Sheet

Study Appendix 5A. An unadjusted trial balance for Gonzales Sporting Goods is on the accompanying work sheet on page 231. The following additional information is available.

a. Wages earned but unpaid, $2,050.

b. Adjustment for prepaid rent. Rent was paid quarterly in advance, $9,000 per quarter. Payments were due on January 1, April 1, July 1, and October 1.

c. The store equipment originally cost $16,800 on February 1, 19X1. It is being depreciated on a straight-line basis over seven years with zero expected terminal value.

d. The note payable is based on a one-year loan of $20,000. The note is dated November 1, 19X1. Principal plus 12% interest is payable at maturity.

e. Income taxes are to be accrued. The applicable income tax rate is 30%.

Required   Enter the adjustments and complete the work sheet.

5-45 Work Sheet

Study Appendix 5A. Refer to problem 5-24. Prepare a complete work sheet, including pairs of columns for unadjusted trial balance, adjustments and other entries, adjusted trial balance, income statement, and statement of retained income, and balance sheet for Limacher Software Consultants, Inc.

5-46 Work Sheet

Study Appendix 5A. Refer to problem 5-33. Prepare a complete work sheet, including pairs of columns for unadjusted trial balance, adjustments and other entries, adjusted trial balance, income statement, and statement of retained income, and balance sheet for Soderstrom Company. If you did not solve Problem 5-33, prepare closing journal entries now.

5-47 Alternative Analyses of Transactions

(Alternate is 5-48.) Study Appendix 5B. Consider the following balances, December 31, 19X1:

Gonzales Sporting Goods   Work Sheet for the Month Ended February 28, 19X2

Account Title	Unadjusted Trial Balance		Adjustments		Adjusted Trial Balance		Income Statement		Statement of Retained Income		Balance Sheet	
	Debit	Credit	Debit	Credit	Debit	Credit	Debit	Credit	Debit	Credit	Debit	Credit
Cash	24800											
Accounts receivable	36000											
Merchandise inventory	112000											
Prepaid rent	6000											
Store equipment	16800											
Accumulated depreciation, equip.		2400										
Accounts payable		62000										
Note payable		20000										
Accrued interest payable		750										
Paid-in capital		50000										
Retained income		45250										
Sales		90200										
Cost of goods sold	50000											
Advertising expense	4000											
Wages expense	11000											
Miscellaneous expenses	10000											
	270600	270600										

Accrued interest receivable	$ 8,000
Prepaid rent	12,000
Accrued wages payable	16,000

During 19X2, $24,000 cash was received for interest for one year on a long-term note of $200,000. Interest was due yearly on September 1. In addition, half the principal of the note was paid on September 1, 19X2.

During 19X2, cash disbursements of $78,000 were made for rent. The rent was payable, $18,000 quarterly in advance on March 1, June 1, September 1, and December 1. The rent was raised to $24,000 quarterly beginning December 1, 19X2.

During 19X2, $800,000 was disbursed for wages. The ending balance of accrued wages payable, December 31, 19X2, was $26,000.

In responding to the requirement for journal entries, use the following format:

	Requirement 1		Requirement 2	
Explanation of Entry	*(in thousands of dollars)*			
Summary cash receipts or disbursements	Journal entry		Journal entry	
End-of-period adjustments	Journal entry		Journal entry	
Example: Paid insurance of $40,000	Prepaid insurance Cash	40 40	Insurance expense Cash	40 40
Adjustment so that ending balance of prepaid insurance is $30,000	Insurance expense Prepaid insurance	10 10	Prepaid insurance Insurance expense	30 30

Required

1. Assume that the accounting system provides for the appropriate portions of the above cash collections and cash disbursements to be applied to any balances of accruals and prepayments carried over from the preceding period. Given the above data, prepare summary journal entries, including the adjusting entries, for 19X2. Post the entries to T-accounts. Do not prepare the entry for the repayment of the principal on the note.

2. Assume that the accounting system regards all the above cash collections and cash disbursements as revenues or expenses. Adjustments are then made at the end of each year to recognize the appropriate accruals and prepayments. Given the above data, prepare summary journal entries, including the adjusting entries for 19X2. Post the entries to T-accounts.

3. Which set of data-processing procedures do you prefer, those in requirement 1 or those in requirement 2? Explain.

5-48 Alternate Analyses of Transactions
(Alternate is 5-47.) Study Appendix 5B. Consider the following balances, December 31, 19X4 (in thousands of dollars):

Accrued interest receivable	$16
Prepaid fire insurance	3
Accrued wages payable	8

The accounting system provides for cash collections of interest to be credited first to any existing accrued interest receivable carried over from the preceding period. Cash collections for interest during 19X5 were $26. Label this as entry *f*.

The accounting system for wages is to debit any existing accrued payables first and debit any remainder of the disbursement to expense. Cash disbursements for wages during 19X5 were $193. Label this as entry *i*.

Prepayments of expenses are routinely debited to asset accounts. A cash disbursement for a three-year insurance policy, effective September 1, 19X5, was $36. Label this as entry *l*.

Required

1. Prepare T-accounts for Accrued Interest Receivable, Interest Revenue, Prepaid Fire Insurance, Insurance Expense, Accrued Wages Payable, and Wages Expense. Post the opening balances therein, December 31, 19X4. Journalize and post the above entries *f*, *i*, and *l* to the appropriate accounts. (At the same time, you may wish to use a Cash T-account to complete the postings. However, the Cash T-account is not required for purposes of this problem.)

2. The following correct balances were applicable at the end of 19X5:

Accrued interest receivable	$10
Prepaid fire insurance	?
Accrued wages payable	15

Journalize and post the adjusting entries, December 31, 19X5. Label them as *o*, *p*, and *s*. Assume that the prepaid insurance of December 31, 19X4, expired during 19X5.

3. Assume the same data as in requirements 1 and 2. However, suppose the following summarized journal entries had been made during 19X5:

			Debit	Credit
Entry	**Accounts and Explanation**	**Post Ref.**	**(in thousands of dollars)**	
f	Cash	✓	26	
	Interest revenue	✓		26
	Collection of interest.			
i	Wages expense	✓	193	
	Cash	✓		193
	Payments of wages.			
l	Insurance expense	✓	36	
	Cash	✓		36
	Payment of insurance.			

Given these revised entries *f*, *i*, and *l*, prepare alternate adjusting journal entries *o*, *p*, and *s*, December 31, 19X5. Post the entries to a new set of T-accounts having the same opening balances given in the first paragraph of this problem. How do the ending balances in the accounts affected by the adjustments compare with the ending balances in the same accounts in requirement 2?

4. Which set of data-processing procedures do you prefer for interest, wages, and insurance, those in requirements 1 and 2 or those in requirement 3? Explain.

5-49 Special Journals

(Alternate is 5-50.) Study Appendix 5C. The Cambridge Trading Company uses a sales journal, a cash receipts journal, and a general journal. It has a general ledger and sub-sidiary ledgers for accounts receivable. For simplicity, only a few transactions of each kind are illustrated in the accompanying list of transactions. Moreover, the beginning balances of the pertinent accounts are not given, nor are they necessary for the purposes of this problem. The currency is British pounds, £.

The numbers of some pertinent accounts are:

Cash	No. 10
Accounts receivable	30
Allowance for bad debts	32
Notes payable	75
Paid-in capital	80
Sales	90
Bad debts expense	99

Consider the following list of transactions.

July	Description	Invoice Date	Invoice No.	Terms	Check No.	Amount
2	Cash sales	—	—	—	—	£ 2,000
3	Credit sales to Major	—	319	n30	—	1,200
8	Collection of Invoice 319	—	—	—	—	1,200
10	Credit sale to Ramakrishnan	—	320	n30	—	2,800
13	Cash sales	—	—	—	—	1,900
16	Credit sale to Haynes	—	321	n30	—	1,800
20	Collection of Invoice 321	—	—	—	—	1,800
23	Credit sale to Cyert	—	322	n30	—	900
24	Cash sales	—	—	—	—	2,000
26	Borrowed from bank, 60-day loan	—	—	—	—	5,000
28	Cash sales	—	—	—	—	2,500
29	Credit sale to Holford	—	323	n30	—	600
31	Sale of additional common stock for cash	—	—	—	—	10,000
31	Addition to allowance for uncollectible accounts	—	—	—	—	100

Required

1. Journalize the transactions for July, using the appropriate journals.
2. Post the effects of the transactions to the general and subsidiary ledgers. Show posting details such as dates and account numbers.
3. Prepare a listing of the accounts receivable subsidiary ledger balances. Make sure that the total agrees with the related general ledger account.

5-50 Special Journals
(Alternate is 5-49.) Study Appendix 5C. Huang Company, a wholesaler of luggage, uses a general journal and two special journals with amount columns as shown:

- General journal: two columns, debit and credit
- Sales journal: single amount column
- Cash receipts journal: debit columns for Cash and for Sales Discounts; credit columns for Sales, Accounts Receivable, and Other Accounts

The general-ledger accounts needed for this problem are included in the table following with their account numbers and June 1, 19X1, balances, if any:

Cash (10)	$ 5,000	
Accounts receivable (25)	18,000	
Office supplies (40)	2,000	
Office equipment (44)	21,000	
Accounts payable (84)		$12,000
Notes payable (88)		
Sales (142)		
Sales returns and allowances (143)		
Sales discounts (144)		
Purchases (162)		
Purchase returns and allowances (163)		
Purchase discounts (164)		
All other accounts (300)	46,000	80,000
Total	$92,000	$92,000

The subsidiary ledger accounts needed and their June 1 balances, if any, are:

Accounts Receivable
Stratton Co.
Davey & Ramos
Maxson's, Inc.
Joy Bros., $18,000 debit balance

Required

1. Set up journals and ledgers, entering beginning account balances, if any.
2. Enter the transactions described below in the appropriate journals.
3. Post amounts from all journals to T-accounts, showing details: dates, account numbers, and posting references.
4. Take a trial balance of the general ledger at June 30.
5. Prepare a schedule for the accounts receivable subsidiary ledger to prove its agreement with the controlling account at June 30.

Transactions

June 4	Cash sales of merchandise, $1,800.
6	Sold merchandise to Stratton Co., $9,000; terms 2/10, n/30; invoice number 1063.
10	Sold merchandise to Davey & Ramos, $12,000; terms 2/10, n/30; invoice number 1064.
*12	Purchased office equipment from Langley Co., $5,400; terms n/30.
14	Received cash to settle Stratton Co. invoice 1063, less 2% cash discount. (Use only one line for this entry in the cash receipts journal.)
15	Sold merchandise to Maxson's, Inc., $15,000; terms 2/10, n/30; invoice number 1065.
21	Borrowed $18,000 for ninety days from First National Bank at 15% interest to be paid at due date of note.
*24	Issued credit memo number 88 for $600 to Davey & Ramos for unsatisfactory merchandise sold June 10.

* These transactions are to be entered in the general journal. Be sure to post the debit and credit amounts for receivables to the subsidiary ledger accounts as well as to the related controlling accounts.

5-51 Wal-Mart Annual Report

Refer to the financial statements of Wal-Mart in Appendix A. This problem will familiarize you with some of the accounts of this actual company.

Required

1. Which balance sheet format does Wal-Mart use, the account format or the report format?
2. Name the company's largest current asset and current liability.
3. How much were total current assets and total current liabilities at January 31, 1995? What is the current ratio at January 31, 1995?
4. What was the original cost of the Property, plant, and equipment assets on January 31, 1995? What was the book value of the Property, plant, and equipment assets at January 31, 1995?

5-52 Compact D for Disclosure

Select any company whose financial statements are available on Compact D. Examine the most recent financial statements, focusing on the balance sheet.

Required

1. Identify the company's auditor. What is the auditor's role in relation to the financial statements?
2. Name the company's largest current asset and the largest current liability.
3. How much were total current assets and total current liabilities at the most recent balance sheet date? What was the current ratio at that date?
4. What was the original cost of the Property, plant, and equipment assets at the most recent balance sheet date? What was the book value of the Property, plant, and equipment assets at that date?

6

Sales Revenue, Cash, and Accounts Receivable

Learning Objectives

After studying this chapter, you should be able to

1 Determine the proper time to record a particular revenue item on the income statement.

2 Explain how to account for sales returns and allowances, sales discounts, and bank credit card sales.

3 Explain why cash is important and how it is managed.

4 Explain how uncollectible accounts affect the valuation of accounts receivable.

5 Estimate bad debts expense under the allowance method using (a) percentage of sales, (b) percentage of ending accounts receivable, and (c) aging of accounts.

6 Understand techniques for assessing the level of accounts receivable.

In this chapter we consider sales revenue and related current assets. Combining these topics in one chapter stresses their interrelated character. When sales are recognized in the income statement, a corresponding change occurs in the firm's asset composition. The firm receives either cash or the promise of cash. Income statement and balance sheet effects are intertwined.

The creation and delivery of a product or service occur in very different ways in different industries. When a barber cuts hair and receives payment there is little uncertainty about when the service is complete and when the revenue is earned. Other transactions are not so well defined, and the accountant's task is to determine when transactions are sufficiently complete to warrant the recording of sales revenue.

A related question is, How much revenue should be recognized? Or stated another way, How valuable is the customer's promise to pay? Suppose you sold a $5,000 oriental rug to a local realtor who promised to pay you in five monthly payments of $1,000. Two months later, after receiving the second check, you read in the paper that the realtor had declared personal bankruptcy and was not expected to be able to repay his debts. How can we report this transaction to capture the economic reality of what happened? Such issues occupy our attention in this chapter.

■ RECOGNITION OF SALES REVENUE

Objective 1

Determine the proper time to record a particular revenue item on the income statement.

Why is the timing of revenue recognition important? Because it is critical to the measurement of net income. Under the *matching principle*, described in Chapter 2, the cost of the items sold is reported in the same period in which revenue is recognized. Net income is the excess of revenues over the cost of goods sold and related expenses.

Managers often receive higher salaries or greater bonuses for increasing sales and net income. Therefore, they prefer to recognize sales revenue as soon as possible. Owners and potential investors, on the other hand, want to be sure the economic benefits of the sale are guaranteed before recognizing revenue. Because of these different perspectives, accountants must carefully assess when revenue should be recognized.

Chapter 2 described the principles that accountants use to determine when revenue is recognized in the financial statements. Under *cash-basis accounting*, accountants recognize revenue when cash is collected for sales of goods and services. Under *accrual-basis accounting*, however, recognition of revenue requires a two-pronged test: (1) goods or services must be delivered to the customers (that is, the revenue is *earned*); and (2) cash or an asset virtually assured of being converted into cash must be received (that is, the revenue is *realized*).

Most revenue is recognized at the point of sale. Suppose you buy a compact disc at a local music store. Both revenue recognition tests are generally met at the time of purchase. You receive the merchandise, and the store receives cash, a check, or a credit card slip. Because both checks and credit card slips are readily converted to cash, the store can recognize revenue at the point of sale regardless of which of these three methods of payment you use.

Sometimes the two revenue recognition tests are not met at the same time. In such cases, revenue is generally recognized only when both tests are met.

Consider magazine subscriptions. The *realization* test is met when the publisher receives cash. However, revenues are not *earned* until magazines are delivered. Therefore revenue recognition is delayed until the time of delivery.

Sometimes accountants must exercise judgment in deciding when the recognition criteria are met. For example, accounting for long-term contracts might require such judgment. Suppose Lockheed signs a $40 million contract with the U.S. government to produce a part for the space shuttle. The contract is signed, and work begins on January 2, 19X1. The completion date is December 31, 19X4. Payment will be made upon delivery of the part. Lockheed expects to complete one-fourth of the project each year. When should the $40 million of revenue be recorded on the income statement?

The most common answer is that one-fourth of the revenue is *earned* each year, so $10 million of the revenue should be recognized annually. Generally, payments on contracts with the government or with major corporations are reasonably certain. Therefore, revenues on such contracts are recognized as the work is performed. Because collection from the government is virtually certain, realization can be said to occur because the work has been performed and the government has an obligation. For other customers, where payment on the contract is uncertain, the *realization* test may not be met until the product is delivered and a bill is sent. In such a case, all revenues might be recognized at completion of the project.

As another example, consider a land developer with a three-hundred-acre tract of bare desert land that is being subdivided and sold in one-acre vacation lots. The sales office has a scale model showing each lot as being "available" or "sold." It also shows the (future) municipal park, (future) paved roads and sidewalks, (future) community building, (future) swimming pool, and so on. A customer who likes the model, the $5,000 price for a lot, and the payments of $20 per month (for a very long time) signs a contract, making the minimum down payment of $50.

Is this transaction a sale? The developer might think so. He or she cashes the $50 deposit and records "sold" on the scale model. The developer believes that other customers, impressed by the rapid sale, might be more inclined to buy.

What can go wrong in this type of situation? Financially distressed customers can walk away from their deposits and payment contracts. The developer can fail to complete the promised amenities, and existing lot owners can sue for refunds or completion. Given these conditions and others that can prevent fulfillment of the contract by either the customer or the seller, recognition of the sale based on a small deposit is not sound practice. Creditors, potential investors in the development company, or buyers of lots can be misled by financial statements that treat sales contracts with minimal down payments as completed sales.

■ MEASUREMENT OF SALES REVENUE

Cash and Credit Sales

After deciding when revenue is to be recognized, the accountant must determine *how much* revenue to record. In other words, how should accountants measure revenue? Ordinarily, accountants approximate the *net realizable value*

Objective 2

Explain how to account for sales returns and allowances, sales discounts, and bank credit card sales.

of the asset inflow from the customer. That is, the revenue is measured in terms of the present cash equivalent value of the asset received.

Revenue is recorded equal to the asset received:

```
Cash . . . . . . . . . . . . . . . . . . . . . . . . . . . . .    xxx
          Sales revenue  . . . . . . . . . . . . . . . .           xxx
OR
Accounts receivable   . . . . . . . . . . . . . . .    xxx
          Sales revenue  . . . . . . . . . . . . . . . .           xxx
```

Notice that a cash sale increases Sales Revenue, an income statement account, and increases Cash, a balance sheet account. A credit sale on open account is recorded much like a cash sale except that the balance sheet account Accounts Receivable is increased instead of Cash.

In fact, the realizable value of a credit sale is often less than that of a cash sale. Why? Because some accounts receivable may never be collected. Adjustments for uncollectible accounts are discussed later in this chapter in the "Credit Sales and Accounts Receivable" section beginning on page 246.

Merchandise Returns and Allowances

Suppose revenue is recognized at the point of sale, but later the customer decides to return the merchandise. He or she may be unhappy with the product for many reasons, including color, size, style, quality, or simply changing of the mind. The supplier (vendor) calls these **sales returns**; the customer calls them **purchase returns**. Such merchandise returns are minor for manufacturers and wholesalers but are major for retail department stores. For instance, returns of 12% of gross sales are not abnormal for stores such as Marshall Field's or Macy's.

Or suppose that instead of returning the merchandise, the customer demands a reduction of the selling price (the original price previously agreed upon). For example, a customer may complain about finding scratches on a household appliance or about buying a toaster for $40 on Wednesday and seeing the same item for sale in the same store or elsewhere for $35 on Thursday. Such complaints are often settled by the seller's granting a **sales allowance**, which is essentially a reduction of the selling price. The buyer calls such a price reduction a **purchase allowance**.

Gross sales revenue equal to the sales price must be decreased by the amount of the returns and allowances to give the **net sales**. But instead of directly reducing the revenue (or sales) account, managers of retail stores typically use a contra account, Sales Returns and Allowances, which combines both returns and allowances in a single account. Managers use a contra account so they can watch changes in the level of returns and allowances. For instance, a change in the percentage of returns in fashion merchandise may give early signals about changes in customer tastes. Similarly, a buyer of fashion or fad merchandise may want to keep track of purchase returns to help assess the quality of products and services of various suppliers.

Consider an example of how to account for sales and sales returns and allowances. Suppose a JC Penney Department Store has $900,000 gross sales on credit and $80,000 sales returns and allowances. The analysis of transactions would show:

sales returns (purchase returns) Products returned by the customer.

sales allowance (purchase allowance) Reduction of the selling price (the original price previously agreed upon).

gross sales Total sales revenue before deducting sales returns and allowances.

net sales Total sales revenue reduced by sales returns and allowances.

	A	=	L +	SE
Credit sales on open account	+900,000 Increase Accounts Receivable	=		+900,000 Increase Sales
Returns and allowances	-80,000 Decrease Accounts Recievable	=		-80,000 Increase Sales Returns and Allowances

The journal entries (without explanations) are:

Accounts receivable	900,000	
Sales		900,000
Sales returns and allowances	80,000	
Accounts receivable		80,000

The income statement would begin:

Gross sales	$900,000
Deduct: Sales returns and allowances	80,000
Net sales	$820,000
or	
Sales, net of $80,000 returns and allowances	$820,000

trade discounts
Reductions to the gross selling price for a particular class of customers to arrive at the actual selling price (invoice price).

Discounts from Selling Prices

There are two major types of sales discounts: *trade* and *cash*. **Trade discounts** apply one or more reductions to the gross selling price for a particular class of customers in accordance with a company's management policies. These discounts are price concessions or ways of quoting the actual prices that are charged to various customers. An example is a discount for large-volume purchases. The seller might offer no discount on the first $10,000 of merchandise per year but a 2% discount on the next $10,000 and 3% on all sales to a customer in excess of $20,000.

Companies set trade discount terms for various reasons. If common in the industry, the seller may offer trade discounts to be competitive. Discounts may also be used to encourage certain customer behavior. For example, manufacturers with seasonal products (gardening supplies, snow shovels, fans, Christmas gifts, and so on) might offer price discounts on early orders and deliveries to smooth out production throughout the year and minimize the cost of storing the inventory. The gross sales revenue recognized from a trade discount sale is the price received after deducting the discount.

cash discounts
Reductions of invoice prices awarded for prompt payment.

In contrast to trade discounts, **cash discounts** are rewards for prompt payment. The terms of the discount may be quoted in various ways on the invoice:

Credit Terms	Meaning
n/30	The full billed price (net price) is due on the thirtieth day after the invoice date.
1/5, n/30	A 1% discount can be taken for payment within five days of the invoice date; otherwise the full billed price is due in thirty days.
15 E.O.M.	The full price is due within fifteen days after the end-of-the-month of sale. An invoice dated December 20 is due January 15.

Consider an example. A manufacturer sells $30,000 of toys to Kmart, a retailer, on terms 2/10, n/60. Therefore, Kmart may remit $30,000 less a cash discount of 0.02 × $30,000, or $30,000 − $600 = $29,400, if payment is made within ten days after the invoice date. Otherwise the full $30,000 is due in sixty days.

Cash discounts entice prompt payment and reduce the manufacturer's need for cash. Early collection also reduces the risk of bad debts. Favorable credit terms with attractive cash discounts are also a way to compete with other sellers. That is, if one seller grants such terms, competitors tend to do likewise.

Should cash discounts be taken by purchasers? The answer is usually yes, but the decision depends on the relative costs of interest. Suppose Kmart decides not to pay the $30,000 invoice for sixty days. It has the use of $29,400 for an extra fifty days (60 − 10) for an "interest" payment of $600. Based on a 365-day year, that is an effective interest rate of approximately:

$$\frac{\$600}{\$29,400} = \begin{array}{l}\text{2.04\% for 50 days, or 14.9\% for 365 days (14.9\% is 2.04\%}\\\text{multiplied by 365 ÷ 50, or 7.3 periods of 50 days each)}\end{array}$$

Most well-managed companies, such as Kmart, can usually obtain funds for less than 14.9% interest per annum, so their accounting systems are designed to take advantage of all cash discounts automatically. However, some retailers pass up the discounts. Why? Because they have trouble getting loans or other financing at interest rates lower than the annual rates implied by the cash discount terms offered by their suppliers. Usage of cash discounts varies through time and from one industry to another. You may be familiar with some gas stations that offer a lower price for cash payment, while other stations do not.

Accounting for Net Sales Revenue

Cash discounts and sales returns and allowances are recorded as deductions from Gross Sales. Consequently, a detailed income statement will often contain:

Gross sales		xxx
Deduct:		
Sales returns and allowances	x	
Cash discounts on sales	x	xxx
Net sales		xxx

Reports to shareholders often omit details and show only net revenues. For example, when Nike shows "Revenues... $3,789,668,000" on its income statement, the number refers to its *net* revenues. Note also that in many countries outside the United States, the word **turnover** is used as a synonym for *sales* or *revenues*. British Petroleum began its income statement with "Turnover... £ 34,950,000,000."

Turnover A synonym for sales or revenues in many countries outside the United States.

An important feature of the income statement is the fact that returns, allowances, and discounts are offsets to gross sales. Management may design an accounting system to use one account, Sales, or several accounts, as shown above. If only one account is used, all returns, allowances, and cash discounts are direct decreases to the sales account. If a separate account is used for cash discounts on sales, the following analysis is made, using the numbers in our Kmart example:

	A	= L +	SE
1. Sell at terms of 2/10,n/60	+30,000 Increase Accounts Receivable	=	+30,000 Increase Sales

Followed by either 2 or 3

	A	= L +	SE
2. Either collect $29,400 ($30,000 less 2%)	+29,400 Increase Cash −30,000 Decrease Accounts Receivable	=	−600 Increase Cash Discounts on Sales
or			
3. collect $30,000	+30,000 Increase Cash −30,000 Decrease Accounts Receivable	=	(no effect)

The journal entries follow:

```
1. Accounts receivable . . . . . . . . . . . . . .  30,000
       Sales  . . . . . . . . . . . . . . . . . . . . . .            30,000
2. Cash  . . . . . . . . . . . . . . . . . . . . . . . .  29,400
   Cash discounts on sales  . . . . . . . . . . .     600
       Accounts receivable . . . . . . . . . . . .            30,000
   OR
3. Cash  . . . . . . . . . . . . . . . . . . . . . . . .  30,000
       Accounts receivable . . . . . . . . . . . .            30,000
```

Recording Bank Card Charges

Cash discounts also occur when retailers accept bank cards such as Visa or MasterCard or similar cards, such as American Express, Carte Blanche, or

Diner's Club. Retailers do so for three major reasons: (1) to attract credit customers who would otherwise shop elsewhere, (2) to get cash immediately rather than wait for customers to pay in due course, and (3) to avoid the cost of keeping track of many customers' accounts.

Retailers can deposit VISA slips in their bank accounts daily (just like cash). But this service costs money, and this cost must be included in the calculations to determine net sales revenue. Service charges for bank cards are usually from 1% to 3% of gross sales, although large-volume retailers bear less cost as a percentage of sales. For example, JC Penney had an arrangement where it paid 4.3 cents per transaction plus 1.08% of the gross sales using bank cards.

With the 3% rate, credit sales of $10,000 will result in cash of only $10,000 − 0.03 ($10,000), or $10,000 − $300, or $9,700. The $300 amount may be separately tabulated for management control purposes:

	A	= L	+	SE
				+10,000 [Increase Sales]
Sales using Visa	+9,700 [Increase Cash]	=		
				−300 [Increase Cash Discounts for Bank Cards]

Cash	9,700	
Cash discounts for bank cards	300	
Sales		10,000

■ CASH

Revenue is generally accompanied by an increase in either cash or accounts receivable. This section discusses cash, and the next discusses accounts receivable.

Cash has the same meaning to organizations that it does to individuals. Cash encompasses all the items that are accepted for deposit by a bank, notably paper money and coins, money orders, and checks. Banks do not accept postage stamps (which are really prepaid expenses), notes receivable, or post-dated checks as cash. Indeed, although deposits are often credited to the accounts of bank customers on the date received, the bank may not provide cash for a check until it "clears" through the banking system. If the check fails to clear because its writer has insufficient funds, its amount is deducted from the depositor's account.

Many companies combine cash and *cash equivalents* on their balance sheets. **Cash equivalents** are highly liquid short-term investments that can easily be converted into cash with little delay. For example, the 1994 balance sheet of Chrysler begins with "Cash and equivalents. . . $5,145 million." Chrysler describes its cash equivalents as "highly liquid investments with a maturity of three months or less at the date of purchase." Examples of cash equivalents include money market funds and treasury bills.

Cash equivalents
Highly liquid short-term investments that can easily be converted into cash.

Compensating Balances

compensating balances Required minimum cash balances on deposit when money is borrowed from banks.

Sometimes the entire cash balance in a bank account is not available for unrestricted use. Banks frequently require companies to maintain **compensating balances**, which are required minimum balances on deposit to compensate the bank for providing loans. The size of the minimum balance often depends on either the amount borrowed or the amount of credit available, or both.

Compensating balances increase the effective interest rate paid by the borrower. When borrowing $100,000 at 10% per year, annual interest will be $10,000. With a 10% compensating balance, the borrower can use only $90,000 of the loan, raising the effective interest rate on the usable funds to 11.1% ($10,000 ÷ $90,000).

To prevent any misleading information regarding cash, annual reports must disclose the state of any compensating balances. For example, a footnote in the annual report of North Carolina Natural Gas Corporation disclosed a requirement for a compensating balance "of 10% of the annual average loan outstanding."

Management of Cash

Cash is usually a small portion of the total assets of a company. Yet, managers spend much time managing cash. Why? For many reasons. First, although the cash balance may be small at any one time, the flow of cash can be enormous. Weekly receipts and disbursements of cash may be many times as large as the cash balance. Second, because cash is the most liquid asset, it is enticing to thieves and embezzlers. Safeguards are necessary. Third, adequate cash is essential to the smooth functioning of operations. Managers must carefully plan for the acquisition and use of cash. Finally, cash itself does not earn income, so it is important not to hold excess cash.

reconcile a bank statement To verify that the bank balance for cash is consistent with the accounting records.

Most organizations have detailed, well-specified procedures for receiving, recording, and disbursing cash. Cash is usually placed in a bank account, and the company's books are periodically reconciled with the bank's records. To **reconcile a bank statement** means to verify that the bank balance and the accounting records are consistent. The two balances are rarely identical. A company accountant records a deposit when made and a payment when the check is written. The bank, however, may receive or record the deposit several days after the accountant recorded it because of postal delay, deposit on a bank holiday or weekend, and so on. The bank may also process a check days, weeks, or even months after it was issued.

In addition to reconciling the bank balance, other internal control procedures (discussed in Chapter 8) are set up to safeguard cash. Briefly, the major procedures include the following:

1. The individuals who receive cash do not also disburse cash.
2. The individuals who handle cash cannot access accounting records.
3. Cash receipts are immediately recorded and deposited and are not used directly to make payments.
4. Disbursements are made by serially numbered checks, only upon proper authorization by someone other than the person writing the check.
5. Bank accounts are reconciled monthly.

Why are such controls necessary? Consider a person who handles cash and makes entries into the accounting records. That person could take cash and cover it up by making the following entry in the books:

Operating expenses	xxx	
Cash		xxx

Besides guarding against dishonest actions, the procedures help ensure accurate accounting records. Suppose a check is written but not recorded in the books. Without serially numbered checks, there would be no way of discovering the error before receiving a bank statement showing that the check was paid. But if checks are numbered, an unrecorded check can be identified, and such errors can be discovered early.

■ CREDIT SALES AND ACCOUNTS RECEIVABLE

accounts receivable (trade receivables, receivables) Amounts owed to a company by customers as a result of delivering goods or services and extending credit in the ordinary course of business.

Credit sales on open account increase **accounts receivable**, which are amounts owed to the company by its customers as a result of delivering goods or services and extending credit for these goods or services. Accounts receivable, sometimes called **trade receivables** or simply **receivables**, should be distinguished from deposits, accruals, notes, and other assets not arising out of everyday sales.

Uncollectible Accounts

uncollectible accounts (bad debts) Receivables determined to be uncollectible because debtors are unable or unwilling to pay their debts.

Granting credit entails cost and benefits. One *cost* is **uncollectible accounts** or **bad debts**, receivables that some credit customers are either unable or unwilling to pay. Accountants often label this major cost as **bad debts expense**. Another cost is administration and collection. The *benefit* is the boost in sales and profit that would otherwise be lost if credit were not extended. That is, many potential customers would not buy if credit were unavailable.

bad debts expense The cost of granting credit that arises from uncollectible accounts.

The extent of nonpayment of debts varies. It often depends on the credit risks that managers are willing to accept. For instance, many small retail establishments will accept a higher level of risk than larger stores such as Sears. The extent of a nonpayment can also depend on the industry. The problem of uncollectible accounts is especially difficult in the health-care field. For example, the Bayfront Medical Center of St. Petersburg, Florida, suffered bad debts equal to 21% of gross revenue. Some hospitals and physicians hire a collection agency for a fee that is based on collections attained, while others attempt to collect their own delinquent accounts rather than pay the collection agency fee.

Objective 4

Explain how uncollectible accounts affect the valuation of accounts receivable.

Deciding When and How to Grant Credit

Competition and industry practice affect whether and how companies offer credit. Offering credit involves costs such as credit administration and uncollectible accounts. Companies offer credit only when the additional earnings on credit sales exceed these costs. Suppose bad debts are 5% of credit sales, administrative costs of a credit department are $5,000 per year, and $20,000 of credit sales (with earnings of $8,000 before credit costs) are achieved. Assume that none of the credit sales would have been made without granting credit. The earnings of $8,000 exceeds the credit costs of $6,000 (5% × $20,000 + $5,000), so offering credit is worthwhile.

Latin American Debt Crisis

In the banking business, 1987 was a tough year, particularly in the United States. On February 20, 1987, Brazil suspended interest and principal payments on $67 billion of medium- and long-term loans. Many U.S. banks with substantial loans to less-developed countries (LDCs), including Brazil, Argentina, and Mexico, were affected by the Brazilian decision.

Three months later, on May 19, 1987, after the close of business on the New York Stock Exchange, Citicorp, the largest U.S. bank, announced an increase in its loan loss reserves for LDC debt of $3 billion. This raised Citicorp's loan loss reserves to 25% of total LDC debt outstanding. To give you an idea of just how large that is, Citicorp's loan loss reserves for U.S. consumer debt were below 1%. The table below indicates that the $4.6 billion allowance for possible credit losses in 1987 was about three times higher than in the two previous years. On the 19th, Citicorp's stock price fell by 3.1% in anticipation of a major announcement, but it rose by 10.1% in the next two days. The popular press attributed this rise in stock price to a perception that Citicorp had a strategy to deal with its LDC debt problem.

By July 24, 1987, forty-five other major U.S. banks announced significant increases in their loan loss reserves. The forty-five major banks also experienced a substantial increase in stock prices on average over the three days surrounding their announcements. The positive impact of the loan loss reserve announcements is consistent with the banks' having the financial strength and the willingness to deal with their LDC problems.

Some seven months later, on December 14, 1987, the Bank of Boston announced that it would increase loan loss reserves by an additional $200 million, write off $200 million of LDC debt, and reclassify $470 million of LDC debt as non-revenue-producing. After such an announcement by one company, investors may reassess the status of other similar companies. Over the three-day period beginning the day before the Bank of Boston announcement, twelve large banks suffered an average 5% loss of share value. These banks had the greatest exposure to LDC debt, and their weak financial condition limited their ability to withstand large loan losses.

Because receivables from outstanding loans are such a large part of a bank's total assets, small changes in the probability of collectibility can lead to large bad debt expenses. Without the "unusual" $3 billion bad debt expense in 1987, Citicorp would have had a very respectable income before taxes of $2.7 billion.

There are several lessons in this tale. (1) Accounting estimates are not rapidly, easily, or perfectly made. Ten months elapsed from February 20 to December 14 while many banks assessed their loss exposure, provided for estimated losses and revised their provisions. (2) Markets interpret announcements in complex ways. Citicorp shares rose in value at the original $3 billion provision. Investors expected something to happen; they assessed Citicorp's provision compared to what they expected. (3) One bank's action has implications for other banks; the Bank of Boston's December announcement led to market losses for other banks.

The final lesson is that problems recur. At the end of 1994 Mexico faced a financial crisis again, the peso fell sharply and security values on the Mexican Bolsa (stock exchange) dropped. Investors became concerned about collectibility and valuation of Mexican debt. Citicorp announced its 1994 financial results very early in 1995 to reassure investors that its potential losses on Mexican obligations were modest as compared to 1987.

Source: Citicorp, 1986-1994 Annual Reports; John A. Elliott, Doug A. Hanna, and Wayne H. Shaw, "The Evaluation by the Financial Markets of Changes in Bank Loan Loss Reserve Levels," The Accounting Review, 66(1991), pp. 847-861.

Information from Citicorp's Financial Statements (in millions of U.S. dollars)

	1994	1988	1987	1986
Provision for Possible Credit Losses (Bad Debt Expense)	1,881	1,330	4,410*	1,825
Income before Taxes	4,611	2,707	(288)	1,645
Year-end Balance in the Allowance for Possible Credit Losses	5,155	4,205	4,618	1,698
Year-end Balance of Stockholders' Equity	17,769	9,864	8,810	9,060
Year-end Balance of Total Assets	250,489	211,647	203,607	196,124

* Due to $3.0 billion provision relating to LDC loans.

■ MEASUREMENT OF UNCOLLECTIBLE ACCOUNTS

Suppose Compuport has credit sales of $100,000 (two hundred customers averaging $500 each) during 19X1. Collections during 19X1 were $60,000. The December 31, 19X1, accounts receivable of $40,000 includes the accounts of eighty different customers who have not yet paid for their 19X1 purchases:

Customer	Amount Owed
1. Jones	$ 1,400
2. Slade	125
⎰	⎰
42. Monterro	600
⎰	⎰
79. Weinberg	700
80. Porras	11
Total receivables	$40,000

How should Compuport account for this situation? There are two basic ways: the specific write-off method and the allowance method.

Specific Write-off Method

specific write-off method This method of accounting for bad debt losses assumes all sales are fully collectible until proved otherwise.

A company that rarely experiences a bad debt might use the **specific write-off method**, which assumes that all sales are fully collectible until proved otherwise. When a specific customer account is identified as uncollectible, the account receivable is reduced. Because no specific customer's account is deemed to be uncollectible at the end of 19X1, the December 31, 19X1, Compuport balance sheet would show an Account Receivable of $40,000.

Now assume that during the second year, 19X2, the retailer identifies Jones and Monterro as customers who are not expected to pay. When the chances of collection from specific customers become dim, the amounts in the *particular* accounts are written down and the *bad debts expense* is recognized:

Bad debts expense	2,000	
Accounts receivable, Jones		1,400
Accounts receivable, Monterro		600

Effects of the specific write-off method on the balance sheet equation in 19X1 and 19X2 are (ignoring the collections of accounts receivable):

Specific Write-off Method	A	= L +	SE
19X1 Sales	+100,000 ⎡ Increase Accounts Receivable ⎤	=	+100,000 ⎡ Increase Sales ⎤

continued

Specific Write-off Method	A	= L +	SE
19X2 Write-off	−2,000 ⎡ Decrease Accounts Receivable ⎤	=	−2,000 ⎡ Increase Bad Debts Expense ⎤

The specific write-off method has been criticized justifiably because it fails to apply the matching principle of accrual accounting. The $2,000 bad debts expense in 19X2 is related to (or caused by) the $100,000 of 19X1 sales. Matching requires recognition of the bad debts expense at the same time as the related revenue, that is, in 19X1, not 19X2. The specific write-off method produces two errors. First, 19X1 income is overstated by $2,000 because no bad debts expense is charged. Second, 19X2 income is understated by $2,000. Why? Because 19X1's bad debts expense of $2,000 is charged in 19X2. Compare the specific write-off method with a correct matching of revenue and expense:

	Specific Write-off Method: Matching Violated		Matching Applied Correctly	
	19X1	19X2	19X1	19X2
Sales revenue	100,000	0	100,000	0
Bad debts expense	0	2,000	2,000	0

allowance method
Method of accounting for bad debt losses using estimates of the amount of sales that will ultimately be uncollectible and a contra asset account, allowance for doubtful accounts.

The principal arguments in favor of the specific write-off method are based on cost-benefit and materiality. The method is simple. Moreover, no great error in measurement of income occurs if amounts of bad debts are small and similar from one year to the next.

Allowance Method

allowance for uncollectible accounts (allowance for doubtful accounts, allowance for bad debts, reserve for doubtful accounts)
A contra asset account that offsets total receivables by an estimated amount that will probably not be collected.

Most accountants oppose the specific write-off method because it violates the matching principle. An alternate method makes use of an estimate of uncollectible accounts that can be better matched to the related revenue. Suppose that Compuport knows from experience that 2% of sales is never collected. Therefore 2% × $100,000 = $2,000 of the 19X1 sales can be estimated to be uncollectible. However, the exact customer accounts that will not be collected are unknown at December 31, 19X1. (Of course, all $2,000 must be among the $40,000 of accounts receivable because the other $60,000 has already been collected.) Bad debts expense can be recognized in 19X1, before the specific uncollectible accounts are identified, by using the **allowance method**, which has two basic elements: (1) an *estimate* of the amount of sales that will ultimately be uncollectible and (2) a *contra account*, which records the estimate and is deducted from the accounts receivable. The contra account is usually called **allowance for uncollectible accounts** (or **allowance for doubtful accounts, allowance for bad debts,** or **reserve for doubtful accounts**). It measures the amount of receivables estimated to be uncollectible from as yet unidentified customers. The effects of the allowance method on the balance sheet equation follow:

	A	= L +	SE
Allowance Method:			
19X1 Sales	+100,000 Increase Accounts Receivable	=	+100,000 Increase Sales
19X1 Allowance	−2,000 Increase Allowance for Uncollectible Accounts	=	−2,000 Increase Bad Debts Expense
19X2 Write-off	+2,000 Decrease Allowance for Uncollectible Accounts		
	−2,000 Decrease Accounts Receivable	=	(No effect)

The associated journal entries are:

19X1 Sales	Accounts receivable	....	100,000	
	Sales	....		100,000
19X1 Allowances	Bad debts expense	....	2,000	
	Allowance for uncollectible accounts	...		2,000
19X2 Write-offs	Allowance for uncollectible accounts	....	2,000	
	Accounts receivable, Jones	....		1,400
	Accounts receivable, Monterro	....		600

Objective 5

Estimate bad debts expense under the allowance method using (a) percentage of sales, (b) percentage of ending accounts receivable, and (c) aging of accounts.

The principal argument in favor of the allowance method is its superiority in measuring accrual accounting income in any given year. That is, the $2,000 of 19X1 sales that is estimated never to be collected should be recorded in 19X1, the period in which the $100,000 sales revenue is recognized.

The allowance method results in the following presentation in the Compuport balance sheet, December 31, 19X1:

Accounts receivable	$40,000
Less: Allowance for uncollectible accounts	2,000
Net accounts receivable	$38,000

Other formats for presenting the allowance method on recent balance sheets of actual companies include:

	1994
Pepsico. Inc. (in millions):	
Accounts and notes receivable,	
less allowance: $150.6	$ 2,050.9
Chrysler (in millions):	
Accounts receivable–trade and other,	
less allowance for doubtful accounts: $58	$ 1,695

Allowance methods are based on historical experience and assume the current year is similar to prior years in terms of economic circumstances (growth versus recession, interest rate levels, and so on) and in terms of customer composition. Estimates are revised when conditions change. For example, if a local employer closed or drastically reduced employment, Compuport might increase expected bad debts.

Applying the Allowance Method Using a Percentage of Sales

percentage of sales method An approach to estimating bad debts expense and uncollectible accounts based on the historical relations between credit sales and uncollectibles.

A contra asset account is created under the allowance method because of the inability to write down a specific customer's account at the time bad debts expense is recognized. A **percentage of sales method** based on historical relations between credit sales and uncollectibles is one method used to estimate the amount recorded in this contra account. In our example, at the end of 19X1 the retailer has $40,000 in Accounts Receivable. On the basis of experience, a bad debts expense is recognized at a rate of 2% of total credit sales, or 0.02 × $100,000, or $2,000.

Visualize the relationship between the general ledger item Accounts Receivable and its supporting detail (which is a form of supporting ledger, called a *subsidiary ledger*) on December 31, 19X1. The sum of the balances of all the customer accounts in the subsidiary ledger must equal the accounts receivable balance in the general ledger.

Compuport General Ledger, December 31, 19X1

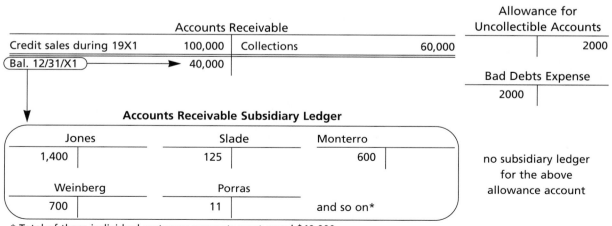

* Total of these individual customer accounts must equal $40,000.

In 19X2, after exhausting all practical means of collection, the retailer judges the Jones and Monterro accounts to be uncollectible. Recording the $2,000 write-off for Jones and Monterro in 19X2 has the following effect:

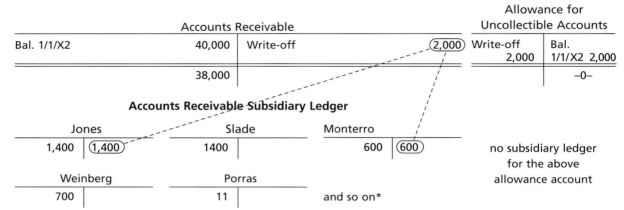

Compuport General Ledger, December 31, 19X1

* Total of these individual customer accounts must equal $38,000.

Convince yourself that the ultimate write-off has no effect on total assets:

	Before Write-off	After Write-off
Accounts receivable	$40,000	$38,000
Allowance for uncollectible accounts	2,000	—
Book value (net realizable value)	$38,000	$38,000

Applying the Allowance Method Using a Percentage of Accounts Receivable

percentage of accounts receivable method An approach to estimating bad debts expense and uncollectible accounts at year end using the historical relations of uncollectibles to accounts receivable.

Like the percentage of sales method, the **percentage of accounts receivable method** uses historical experience, but the estimate of uncollectible accounts is based on the historical relations of uncollectibles to year-end gross accounts receivable, not sales.

The additions to the Allowance for Bad Debts are calculated to achieve a desired balance in the Allowance account. This addition to the allowance equals the Bad Debts Expense, as shown below. Consider the historical experience in the following table:

	Accounts Receivable at End of Year	Bad Debts Deemed Uncollectible and Written Off
19X1	$100,000	$ 3,500
19X2	80,000	2,450
19X3	90,000	2,550
19X4	110,000	4,100
19X5	120,000	5,600
19X6	112,000	2,200
Six-year total	$612,000	$20,400
Average (divide by 6)	$102,000	$3,400

Average percentage not collected $= 3,400 \div 102,000 = 3.33\%$

At the end of 19X7, assume the accounts receivable balance is $115,000. The 19X7 addition to the Allowance for Bad Debts is computed as follows:

1. Divide average bad debt losses of $3,400 by average ending accounts receivable of $102,000 to calculate average percentage not collected of 3.33%.
2. Apply the percentage not collected to the ending Accounts Receivable balance for 19X7 to determine the balance that should be in the Allowance account at the end of the year: 3.33% × $115,000 receivables at the end of 19X6 is $3,833.
3. Prepare an adjusting entry to bring the Allowance to the appropriate amount. Suppose the books show a $700 credit balance in the Allowance account at the end of 19X7. Then the adjusting entry for 19X7 is $3,833 – $700, or $3,133 to record the Bad Debts expense. The journal entry is:

Bad debts expense	3,133	
Allowance for bad debts		3,133
To bring the Allowance to the level		
justified by bad debt experience during		
the past six years.		

The percentage of accounts receivable method differs from the percentage of sales method in two ways: (1) the percentage is based on the ending accounts receivable balance rather than on sales, and (2) the dollar amount calculated using the percentage is the appropriate *ending balance* in the allowance account, not the amount added to the account for the year.

Applying the Allowance Method
Using the Aging of Accounts Receivable

aging of accounts receivable An analysis of the elements of individual accounts receivable according to the time elapsed after the dates of billing.

A refinement on the percentage of accounts receivable approach is the **aging of accounts receivable** method, which considers the composition of the end-of-year accounts receivable. As time elapses after the sale, ultimate collection becomes less likely. The seller may send the buyer a late notice thirty days after the sale, a second reminder after sixty days, make a phone call after ninety days, and place the account with a collection agency after 120 days. Companies that analyze the age of their accounts receivable for credit management purposes naturally incorporate this evidence into estimates of the allowance for uncollectibles. For example, the $115,000 balance in Accounts Receivable on December 31, 19X7, might be aged as follows:

Name	Total	1–30 Days	31–60 Days	61–90 Days	Over 90 Days
Oxwall Tools	$ 20,000	$20,000			
Chicago Castings	10,000	10,000			
Estee	20,000	15,000	$ 5,000		
Sarasota Pipe	22,000		12,000	$10,000	
Ceilcote	4,000			3,000	$1,000
Other accounts (each detailed)	39,000	27,000	8,000	2,000	2,000
Total	$115,000	$72,000	$25,000	$15,000	$3,000
Historical bad debt percentages		0.1%	1%	5%	90%
Bad debt allowance to be provided	$ 3,772 =	$ 72 +	$ 250 +	$ 750 +	$2,700

This aging schedule produces a different target balance for the Allowance account than the percentage of accounts receivable method did: $3,772 versus $3,833. Similarly, the journal entry is slightly different. Given the same $700 credit balance in the Allowance account, the journal entry to record the Bad Debts Expense is $3,772 – $700, or $3,072:

Bad debts expense	$3,072	
Allowance for uncollectible accounts . . .		$3,072
To bring the Allowance to the level justified by		
prior experience using the aging method.		

Whether the percentage of sales, percentage of accounts receivable, or aging method is used to estimate bad debts expense and the Allowance for Uncollectible Accounts, the subsequent accounting for write-offs is the same—a decrease in Accounts Receivable and a decrease in the allowance for Uncollectible Accounts.

Bad Debt Recoveries

bad debt recoveries Accounts receivable that were written off as uncollectible but then collected at a later date.

A few accounts will be written off as uncollectible, but then collection occurs at a later date. When such **bad debt recoveries** occur, the write-off should be reversed, and the collection handled as a normal receipt on account. In this way, a company will be better able to keep track of the customer's true payment history. Return to the Compuport example and assume that Monterro's account for $600 is written off in February 19X2 and collected in October 19X2. The following journal entries produce a complete record of the transactions in Monterro's individual accounts receivable account.

Feb. 19X2	Allowance for uncollectible accounts	600	
	Accounts receivable		600
	To write off uncollectible account of		
	Monterro, a specific customer.		
Oct. 19X2	Accounts receivable	600	
	Allowance for uncollectible accounts		600
	To reverse February 19X2 write-off of		
	account of Monterro.		
	Cash	600	
	Accounts receivable		600
	To record the collection on account.		

Note that these 19X2 entries have no effect on the level of bad debt expense in 19X1. At the end of 19X1, journal entries created bad debt expense based on the expected level of uncollectibles. Briefly, in 19X2 Compuport thought that Monterro would be a nonpaying customer. This was not ultimately the case, and the records now reflect Monterro's payment.

■ ASSESSING THE LEVEL OF ACCOUNTS RECEIVABLE

accounts receivable turnover Credit sales divided by average accounts receivable.

Management and financial analysts assess the firm's ability to *control* accounts receivable. Can the firm generate sales without excessive growth in receivables? One measure of this ability is the **accounts receivable turnover**, which is calculated by dividing the credit sales by the average accounts receivable for the period during which the sales were made:

$$\text{Accounts receivable turnover} = \frac{\text{Credit sales}}{\text{Average accounts receivable}}$$

Objective 6

Understand techniques for assessing the level of accounts receivable.

Suppose credit sales (or sales on account) in 19X2 were $1 million and beginning and ending accounts receivable were $115,000 and $112,000 respectively.

$$\text{Accounts receivable turnover} = \frac{1,000,000}{0.5\,(115,000+112,000)} = 8.81$$

Credit managers, bank loan officers, and auditors evaluate trends in this ratio. They may compare it with ratios of similar-sized companies in the industry. Reductions in the accounts receivable turnover are generally unwelcome.

Alternatively, receivables can be assessed in terms of how long it takes to collect them. Here, the **days to collect accounts receivable,** or **average collection period,** is calculated by dividing 365 by the accounts receivable turnover. For our example:

days to collect accounts receivable (average collection period) 365 divided by accounts receivable turnover.

$$\begin{aligned}\text{Days to collect} \atop \text{accounts receivable} &= \frac{365\text{ days}}{\text{Accounts receivable turnover}} \\ &= \frac{365\text{ days}}{8.81} \\ &= 41.4\text{ days}\end{aligned}$$

The following illustrates the variability in accounts receivable turnover levels among industries.

	Median Levels	
Industry	**Accounts Receivable Turnover**	**Days to Collect Accounts Receivable**
Automobile Retailer	57.7	6.3
Department Stores	33.1	11.0
Furniture Retailer	17.2	21.2
Jewelry Retailer	6.9	52.9
Management Consulting Firms	5.4	67.6

Source: Robert Morris Associates, *Annual Statement Studies for 1994.*

The high accounts receivable turnovers for automobile retailers and department stores correspond to the way customers finance purchases. For automobiles, customers generally finance through banks or through the credit arms of the automobile manufacturer. For department stores, credit is increasingly obtained via national credit cards such as Visa and MasterCard. In both industries the seller receives cash quickly. The other three industries more frequently involve direct granting of credit by the selling firm.

Summary Problems for Your Review

Problem One

Hector Lopez, marketing manager for Fireplace Distributors, sold twelve woodstoves to Woodside Condominiums, Inc. The sales contract was signed on April 27, 19X1. The list price of each wood stove was $1,200, but a 5% quantity discount was allowed. The wood-stoves were to be delivered on May 10, and a cash discount of 2% of the amount owed was offered if payment was made by June 10. Fireplace distributors delivered the woodstoves as promised and received the proper payment on June 9.

Required

1. How much revenue should be recognized in April? in May? in June? Explain.
2. Suppose Fireplace Distributors has a separate account titled "Cash Discounts on Sales." What journal entries would be made on June 9 when the cash payment is received?
3. Suppose Fireplace Distributors has another account titled "Sales Returns and Allowances." Suppose further that one of the woodstoves had a scratch, and Fireplace Distributors allowed Woodside to deduct $100 from the total amount due. What journal entries would be made on June 9 when the cash payment is received?

Solution to Problem One

1. Revenue of $13,680 (12 × $1,200 less a 5% quantity discount of $720) would be recognized in May and none in April or June. The key is whether the revenue is earned and the asset received from the buyer is realized. The revenue is not earned until the merchandise is delivered; therefore revenue cannot be recognized in April. Provided that Woodside Condominiums has a good credit rating, the receipt of cash is reasonably ensured before the cash is actually received. Therefore recognition of revenue need not be delayed until June. On May 10 both revenue recognition tests were met, and the revenue would be recorded on May's income statement.

2. The original revenue recorded was $13,680. The 2% cash discount is 2% × $13,680 = $273.60. Therefore the cash payment is $13,680 − $273.60 = $13,406.40:

Cash	13,406.40	
Cash discounts on sales	273.60	
Accounts receivable		13,680.00

3. The only difference from requirement 2 is a $100 smaller cash payment and a $100 debit to sales returns and allowances:

Cash	13,306.40	
Cash discounts on sales	273.60	
Sales returns and allowances	100.00	
Accounts receivable		13,680.00

Problem Two

H. J. Heinz Company sells many popular food products, including its best-selling Heinz ketchup. Its balance sheet showed the following (in thousands):

	April 27,1994	April 28,1993
Receivables	$827,908	$995,234
Less allowance for doubtful accounts	15,407	16,299
	$812,501	$978,935

Required

Suppose a large grocery chain that owed Heinz $2 million announced bankruptcy on April 28, 1994. Heinz decided that chances for collection were virtually zero. The account was immediately written off. Show the balances as of April 28, 1994, after the write-off. Explain the effect of the write-off on income for the year beginning April 28, 1994.

Solution to Problem Two

Receivables ($827,908 – $2,000)	$825,908
Less allowance for doubtful accounts ($15,407 – $2,000)	13,407
	$812,501

Because Heinz has an account labeled allowance for doubtful accounts, it must use the allowance method. The write-off will not affect the *net* carrying amount of the receivables, which is still $812,501,000. Moreover, the income will be unaffected. Why? Because the estimated expense has already been recognized in prior periods. Under the allowance method, net assets and income are affected when the estimation process occurs, not when the write-off happens.

HIGHLIGHTS TO REMEMBER

Revenue is generally recognized when two tests are met: (1) the revenue is earned, and (2) the asset received in return is realized. Most often, revenue is recognized at the point of sale, when the product is delivered to the customer. In offering products for sale many special practices produce differences between the list price at which a product is offered and the final price which a customer is charged. The term *net sales* represents the final proceeds to the seller—gross sales less offsetting amounts for returns, allowances, and cash discounts.

Sales made for cash are the most easily recorded and valued. However, cash creates a number of procedural problems for the firm. Protecting cash from theft or loss, adequately planning for the availability of cash as needed, and reconciling the firm's accounting records with the bank's records were introduced in this chapter, and they will receive greater attention in Chapter 8.

Potential uncollectible accounts reduce the amount of accounts receivable reported on the balance sheet. Reporting the uncollectible portion of credit sales requires estimates that may be based on a percentage of sales, a percentage of accounts receivable, or an aging of accounts receivable. These estimates permit the financial statements to (1) properly reflect asset levels on the balance sheet, and (2) properly match bad debts expense with revenue on the income statement.

Companies and analysts use ratios to assess the level of accounts receivable. The accounts receivable turnover ratio and the days to collect accounts receivable both relate the average dollar value of accounts receivable to the level of sales activity during the year. Comparisons with other companies in the same industry or examination of a particular company over time draw attention to unusual circumstances and possible problems.

Accounting Vocabulary

accounts receivable, *p. 246*
accounts receivable turnover, *p. 254*
aging of accounts receivable, *p. 253*
allowance for bad debts, *p. 249*
allowance for doubtful accounts, *p. 249*
allowance for uncollectible accounts, *p. 249*

allowance method, *p. 249*
average collection period, *p. 255*
bad debt recoveries, *p. 254*
bad debts, *p. 246*
bad debts expense, *p. 246*
cash discounts, *p. 241*
cash equivalents, *p. 244*
compensating balances, *p. 245*

days to collect accounts receivable, *p. 255*
gross sales, *p. 240*
net sales, *p. 240*
percentage of accounts receivable method, *p. 252*
percentage of sales method, *p. 251*

Assignment Material

Questions

6-1. Describe the two alternatives for the timing of revenue recognition on a $50 million long-term government contract with work spread evenly over five years. Which method do you prefer? Explain.

6-2. Why is the realizable value of a credit sale often less than that of a cash sale?

6-3. Distinguish between a *sales allowance* and a *purchase allowance*.

6-4. Distinguish between a *cash discount* and a *trade discount*.

6-5. "Trade discounts should not be recorded by the accountant." Do you agree? Explain.

6-6. "Retailers who accept Visa or MasterCard are foolish because they do not receive the full price for merchandise they sell." Comment.

6-7. Describe and give two examples of *cash equivalents*.

6-8. "A compensating balance essentially increases the interest rate on money borrowed." Explain.

6-9. "Cash is only 3% of our total assets. Therefore we should not waste time designing systems to manage cash. We should use our time on matters that have a better chance of affecting our profits." Do you agree? Explain.

6-10. The El Camino Hospital uses the allowance method in accounting for bad debts. A journal entry was made for writing off the accounts of Jane Jensen, Eunice Belmont, and Samuel Maze: Do you agree with this entry? If not, show the correct entry and the correcting entry.

Bad debts expense	14,321	
Accounts receivable . .		14,321

6-11. Distinguish between the allowance method and the specific write-off method for bad debts.

6-12. "The Allowance for Uncollectible Accounts account has no subsidiary ledger, but the Accounts Receivable account does." Explain.

6-13. Z Company received a $100 cash payment from a customer and immediately deposited the cash in a bank account. Z Company *debited* its Cash account, but the bank statement showed the deposit as a *credit*. Explain.

6-14. "The cash balance on a company's books should always equal the cash balance shown by its bank." Do you agree? Explain.

6-15. How can a credit balance arise in an Accounts Receivable subsidiary ledger? How should it be accounted for?

6-16. "Under the allowance method, there are three popular ways to estimate the bad debts expense for a particular year." Name the three.

6-17. What is meant by "aging of accounts"?

6-18. Describe why a write-off of a bad debt should be reversed if collection occurs at a later date.

6-19. What is the relationship between the average collection period and the accounts receivable turnover?

6-20. Distinguish between the percentage of sales approach to applying the allowance method and the aging of accounts receivable approach.

6-21. How can a debit balance arise in the allowance for bad debts account?

6-22. What is the cost-benefit relationship in deciding whether or not to offer credit to customers? Whether or not to accept bank credit cards?

6-23. You are opening a new department store and setting policy on merchandise returns. Would you grant cash refunds or store credit only? Would you require receipts? Would you base the refund on the price at which the transaction occurred or on the selling price when the return occurred?

6-24. What are the advantages to accepting bank credit cards rather than having your own, store-specific credit card?

6-25. If a company accepts bank credit cards, why might they accept specific cards rather than all of them? For example, some retailers accept Visa and MasterCard, but not American Express or Diner's Club, while the exact opposite is true for some restaurants.

6-26. It is common in sub shops and pizza parlors around the Cornell University campus to find signs that say "Your purchase is free if the clerk does not give you a receipt" or "Two free lunches if your receipt has a red star." What is management trying to accomplish with these free offers?

Exercises

6-27   Revenue Recognition, Cash Discounts, and Returns

Campus Bookstore ordered 1,000 copies of an introductory economics textbook from Prentice Hall on July 17, 19X0. The books were delivered on August 12, at which time a bill was sent requesting payment of $40 per book. However, a 2% discount was allowed if Prentice Hall received payment by September 12. Campus Bookstore sent the proper payment, which was received by Prentice Hall on September 10. On December 18 Campus Bookstore returned 60 books to Prentice Hall for a full cash refund.

Required
1. Prepare the journal entries (if any) for Prentice Hall on (a) July 17, (b) August 12, (c) September 10, and (d) December 18. Include appropriate explanations.
2. Suppose this was the only sales transaction in 19X0. Prepare the revenue section of Prentice Hall's income statement.

6-28   Revenue Recognition

Godoy Logging Company hired Atencio Construction Co. to build a new bridge across the Gray River. The bridge would extend a logging road into a new stand of timber. The contract called for a payment of $10 million upon completion of the bridge. Work was begun in 19X0 and completed in 19X2. Total costs were:

19X0	$2 million
19X1	2 million
19X2	3 million
Total	$7 million

Required
1. Suppose the accountant for Atencio Construction Co. judged that Godoy Logging might not be able to pay the $10 million. Still, the chance of a $3 million profit makes the contract attractive enough to sign. How much revenue would you recognize each year?
2. Suppose Godoy Logging is a subsidiary of a major wood-products company. Therefore receipt of payment on the contract is reasonably certain. How much revenue would you recognize each year?

6-29   Compensating Balances

Pegasus Company borrowed $100,000 from First Bank at 9% interest. The loan agreement stated that a compensating balance of $10,000 must be kept in the Pegasus checking account at First Bank. The total Pegasus cash balance rose to $45,000 as a result.

Required
1. How much usable cash did Pegasus Company receive for its $100,000 loan?
2. What was the real interest rate paid by Pegasus?
3. Prepare a footnote for the annual report of Pegasus Company explaining the compensating balance.

6-30   Sales Returns and Discounts

Phoenix Electronics Wholesalers had gross sales of $700,000 during the month of March. Sales returns and allowances were $50,000. Cash discounts granted were $22,000.

Required Prepare an analysis of the impact of these transactions on the balance sheet equation. Also show the journal entries. Prepare a detailed presentation of the revenue section of the income statement.

6-31 Gross and Net Sales

Sausilito, Inc., reported the following in 19X0 (in thousands):

Net sales	$520
Cash discounts on sales	20
Sales returns and allowances	35

Required
1. Prepare the revenue section of the 19X0 income statement.
2. Prepare journal entries for (a) initial revenue recognition for 19X0 sales, (b) sales returns and allowances, and (c) collection of accounts receivable. Assume that all sales were on credit and all accounts receivable for 19X0 sales were collected in 19X0. Omit explanations.

6-32 Cash Discounts Transactions

AV Wholesalers sells on terms of 2/10, n/30. It sold equipment to Beaulieu Retailers for $200,000 on open account on January 10. Payment (net of cash discount) was received on January 19. Using the equation framework, analyze the two transactions for AV. Also prepare journal entries.

6-33 Entries for Cash Discounts and Returns on Sales

The Napa Wine Company is a wholesaler of California wine that sells on credit terms of 2/10, n/30. Consider the following transactions:

June 9 Sales on credit to Riordan Wines, $20,000.
June 11 Sales on credit to Marty's Liquors, $12,000.
June 18 Collected from Riordan Wines.
June 26 Accepted the return of six cases from Marty's, $1,000.
July 10 Collected from Marty's.
July 12 Riordan returned some defective wine that she had acquired on June 9 for $100. Napa issued a cash refund immediately.

Required Prepare journal entries for these transactions. Omit explanations. Assume that the full appropriate amounts were exchanged.

6-34 Credit Terms, Discounts, and Annual Interest Rates

As the struggling owner of a new Thai restaurant, you suffer from a habitual shortage of cash. Yesterday the following invoices arrived:

Vendor	Face Amount	Terms
Val Produce	$ 600	n/30
Rose Exterminators	90	EOM
Top Meat Supply	500	15,EOM
John's Fisheries	1,000	1/10, n/30
Garcia Equipment	2,000	2/10, n/30

Required 1. Write out the exact meaning of each of the terms.

2. You can borrow cash from the local bank on a ten-, twenty-, or thirty-day note bearing an annual interest rate of 16%. Should you borrow to take advantage of the cash discounts offered by the last two vendors? Why? Show computations. For interest rate computations, assume a 360-day year.

6-35   Accounting for Credit Cards

The Byard Clothing Store has extended credit to customers on open account. Its average experience for each of the past three years has been:

	Cash	Credit	Total
Sales	$500,000	$300,000	$800,000
Bad debts expense	—	6,000	6,000
Administrative expense	—	10,000	10,000

Cynthia Byard is considering whether to accept bank cards (e.g., Visa, MasterCard). She has resisted because she does not want to bear the cost of the service, which would be 5% of gross sales.

The representative of Visa claims that the availability of bank cards would have increased overall sales by at least 10%. However, regardless of the level of sales, the new mix of the sales would be 50% bank card and 50% cash.

Required

1. How would a bank card sale of $200 affect the accounting equation? Where would the discount appear on the income statement?
2. Should Byard adopt the bank card if sales do not increase? Base your answer solely on the sparse facts given here.
3. Repeat requirement 2, but assume that total sales would increase 10%.

6-36   Trade-Ins Versus Discounts

Many states base their sales tax on gross sales less any discount. Trade-in allowances are not discounts, so they are not deducted from the sales price for sales tax purposes. Suppose Sven Gustafson had decided to trade in his old car for a new one with a list price of $20,000. He will pay cash of $12,000 plus sales tax. If he had not traded in a car, the dealer would have offered a discount of 15% of the list price. The sales tax is 8%.

Required

How much of the $8,000 price reduction should be called a discount? How much a trade-in? Mr. Gustafson wants to pay as little sales tax as legally possible.

6-37   Uncollectible Accounts

During 19X2, the Seattle Paint Store had credit sales of $800,000. The store manager expects that 2% of the credit sales will never be collected, although no accounts are written off until ten assorted steps have been taken to attain collection. The ten steps require a minimum of fourteen months.

Assume that during 19X3, specific customers are identified who are never expected to pay $14,000 that they owe from the sales of 19X2. All ten collection steps have been completed.

Required

1. Show the impact on the balance sheet equation of the above transactions in 19X2 and 19X3 under (a) the specific write-off method and (b) the allowance method. Which method do you prefer? Why?
2. Prepare journal entries for both methods. Omit explanations.

6-38   Bad Debts

Prepare all journal entries regarding the following data. Consider the following balances of a hospital, December 31, 19X1: Receivables from patients, $200,000; and Allowance for Doubtful Receivables, $50,000. During 19X2, total billings to individual patients, excluding the billings to third-party payers such as Blue Cross and Medicare, were $3 million. Past experience indicated that 20% of such individual billings would ultimately be uncollectible. Write-offs of receivables during 19X2 were $590,000.

6-39   Bad Debt Allowance

Holtz Appliance had sales of $1,000,000 during 19X2, including $600,000 of sales on credit. Balances on December 31, 19X1, were Accounts Receivable, $45,000; and Allowance for Bad Debts, $4,000. Data for 19X2: Collections on accounts receivable were $530,000. Bad debts expense was estimated at 2% of credit sales, as in previous years. Write-offs of bad debts during 19X2 were $11,000.

Required
1. Prepare journal entries regarding the above information for 19X2.
2. Show the ending balances of the balance sheet accounts, December 31, 19X2.
3. Based on the given data, what questions seem worth raising with Ingrid Holtz, the president of the store?

6-40   Bad Debt Recoveries

Cayuga Department Store has many accounts receivable. The Cayuga balance sheet, December 31, 19X1, showed Accounts Receivable, $950,000 and Allowance for Uncollectible Accounts, $40,000. In early 19X2, write-offs of customer accounts of $30,000 were made. In late 19X2, a customer, whose $3,000 debt had been written off earlier, won a $1 million sweepstakes cash prize. She immediately remitted $3,000 to Cayuga. The store welcomed her money and her return to a high credit standing. Prepare the journal entries for the $30,000 write-off in early 19X2 and the $3,000 receipt in late 19X2.

6-41   Subsidiary Ledger

An appliance store makes credit sales of $800,000 in 19X4 to a thousand customers: Schumacher, $4,000; Cerruti, $7,000; others, $789,000. Total collections during 19X4 were $700,000 including $4,000 from Cerruti, but nothing was collected from Schumacher. At the end of 19X4 an allowance for uncollectible accounts was provided of 3% of credit sales.

Required
1. Set up appropriate general ledger accounts plus a subsidiary ledger for Accounts Receivable. The subsidiary ledger should consist of two individual accounts plus a third account called Others. Post the entries for 19X4. Prepare a statement of the ending balances of the individual accounts receivable to show that they reconcile with the general ledger account.
2. On March 24, 19X5, the Schumacher account was written off. Post the entries.

Problems

6-42   Allowance for Credit Losses

BankAmerica Corp. included the following in the footnotes to its 1993 annual report: The following is a summary of changes in the allowance for credit losses (in millions):

	1993
Balance, beginning of year	$3,921
Credit losses	(1,599)
Credit loss recoveries	484
Provision for credit losses	803
Other additions (deductions)	(111)
Balance, end of year	$3,498

Required
1. Terminology in bank financial statements sometimes differs slightly from that in statements of industrial companies. Explain what is meant by "allowance for credit losses," "provisions for credit losses," and "credit losses" in the footnote.

2. Prepare the 1993 journal entries to record the writing off of specific credit losses, the recovery of previously written off credit losses, and the charge for credit losses against 1993 income. Omit explanations.

3. Suppose BankAmerica analyzed its loans at the end of 1993 and decided that an allowance for credit losses equal to the 1992 amount ($3,921 million) was required. Compute the provision for credit losses that would be charged in 1993. In other words, instead of a provision for credit losses of $803 million, what provision would have been charged?

4. BankAmerica had net income of $1,954 million in 1993. Compute the net profit (loss) if the allowance for credit losses at the end of 1993 had been the same as at the end of 1992. Ignore income tax effects.

6-43 Aging of Accounts

Consider the following analysis of Accounts Receivable, February 28, 19X1:

Name of Customer	Total	Remarks
White Nurseries	$ 20,000	50% over 90 days, 50% 61-90 days
Michael's Landscaping	8,000	75% 31-60 days, 25% under 30 days
Shoven Garden Supply	10,000	60% 61-90 days, 40% 31-60 days
Bonner Perennial Farm	16,000	all under 30 days
Hjortshoj Florists	4,000	25% 61-90 days, 75% 1-30 days
Other accounts (each detailed)	80,000	50% 1-30 days, 30% 31-60 days, 15% 61-90 days, 5% over 90 days
Total	$138,000	

Required

Prepare an aging schedule, classifying ages into four categories: 1-30 days, 31-60 days, 61-90 days, and over 90 days. Assume that the prospective bad debt percentages for each category are 0.2%, 0.8%, 10%, and 80%, respectively. What is the ending balance in the Allowance for Uncollectible Accounts?

6-44 Percentage of Ending Accounts Receivable

Consider the following data.

	Accounts Receivable at End of Year	Accounts Receivable Deemed Uncollectible and Written Off During Subsequent Years
19X1	$210,000	$ 8,000
19X2	170,000	6,000
19X3	180,000	6,400
19X4	230,000	9,000
19X5	250,000	12,000
19X6	220,000	9,000

Required   The unadjusted credit balance in Allowance for Uncollectible Accounts at December 31, 19X7, is $500. Using the percentage of ending accounts receivable method, prepare an adjusting entry to bring the Allowance to the appropriate amount at December 31, 19X7 when the Accounts Receivable balance is $230,000.

Class

6-45   Estimates of Uncollectible Accounts

Yakamora Company has made an analysis of its sales and accounts receivable for the past five years. Assume that all accounts written off in a year relate to sales of the preceding year and were part of the accounts receivable at the end of that year. That is, no account is written off before the end of the year of the sale, and all accounts remaining unpaid are written off before the end of the year following the sale. The analysis showed:

	Sales	Ending Accounts Receivable	Bad Debts Written Off During the Year
19X1	$680,000	$ 90,000	$12,000
19X2	750,000	97,000	12,500
19X3	750,000	103,000	14,000
19X4	850,000	114,000	16,500
19X5	850,000	110,000	17,600

The balance in Allowance for Uncollectible Accounts on December 31, 19X4, was $16,000.

Required
1. Determine the bad debts expense for 19X5 and the balance of the Allowance for Uncollectible Accounts for December 31, 19X5, using the percentage of sales method.
2. Repeat requirement 1 using the percentage of ending accounts receivable method.

6-46   Percentage of Sales and Percentage of Ending Accounts Receivable

The Daniel's Playgrounds had credit sales of $4 million during 19X7. Most customers paid promptly (within 30 days), but a few took longer; an average of 1.5% of credit sales were never paid. On December 31, 19X7, accounts receivable were $300,000. The Allowance for Bad Debts account, before any recognition of 19X7 bad debts, had an $800 debit balance.

Daniel's produces and sells playground equipment and other outdoor children's toys. Most of the sales (about 80%) come in the period of March through August; the other 20% is spread almost evenly over the other six months. Over the last six years, an average of 18% of the December 31 accounts receivable has not been collected.

Required
1. Suppose Daniel's Playgrounds uses the percentage of sales method to calculate an allowance for bad debts. Present the accounts receivable and allowance accounts as they should appear on the December 31, 19X7, balance sheet. Give the journal entry required to recognize the bad debts expense for 19X7.
2. Repeat requirement 1 except assume that Daniel's Playgrounds uses the percentage of ending accounts receivable method.
3. Which method do you prefer? Why?

6-47   Average Collection Period

Consider the following:

	19X3	19X2	19X1
Sales	$4,000,000	$5,000,000	$4,800,000

	December 31		
	19X3	19X2	19X1
Accounts receivable	$ 390,000	$ 380,000	$ 370,000

Eighty percent of the sales are on account.

Required   Compute the average collection period for the years 19X2 and 19X3. Comment on the results.

— **6-48   Bank Cards**

Visa and MasterCard are used to pay for a large percentage of retail purchases. The financial arrangements are similar for both bank cards. A news story said:

> If a cardholder charges a pair of $60 shoes, for instance, the merchant deposits the sales draft with his bank, which immediately credits $60 less a small transaction fee (usually 2% of the sale) to the merchant's account. The bank that issued the customer his card then pays the shoe merchant's bank $60 less a 1.5% transaction fee, allowing the merchant's bank a 0.5% profit on the transaction.

Required   1. Prepare the journal entry for the sale by the merchant.
2. Prepare the journal entries for the merchant's bank regarding (a) the merchant's deposit and (b) the collection from the customer's bank that issued the card.
3. Prepare the journal entry for the customer's bank that issued the card.
4. The national losses from bad debts for bank cards are about 1.8% of the total billings to cardholders. If so, how can the banks justify providing this service if their revenue from processing is typically 1.5% to 2.0%?

6-49   Student Loans

A recent annual report of the University of Washington includes information about its receivables from student loans in a footnote to the financial statements (in thousands):

	Year 1		Year 2	
Student Loans:				
Federal programs	$30,905		$33,109	
Less—allowances	2,793	$28,112	2,378	$30,731
University funds	$ 4,748		$ 4,999	
Less—allowances	337	4,411	271	4,728
Total, net		$32,523		$35,459

Required   1. Compare the quality of the loans under federal programs with the quality of those using university funds. Compare the quality of the loans outstanding at the end of Year 2 with the quality of those outstanding at the end of Year 1.
2. Using the allowance method, which accounts would be affected by an allowance for bad debts of an appropriate percentage of $200,000 of new loans in Year 2 from university funds? Choose a percentage.

6-50   Hospital Bad Debts

Hospital Corporation of America is a health-care company that operates over 350 hospitals and other medical facilities. A note to the 1990 earnings statement reported the following about net revenue (in thousands):

Operating revenues	$6,642,837
Less provision for contractual adjustments and policy discounts	2,011,767
Net revenues	$4,631,070

Required

1. Prepare a reasonable footnote to accompany the above presentation. What do you think is the purpose of contractual adjustments?
2. Prepare the summary journal entries for the $6,642,837 and the $2,011,767.

6-51   Discounts and Doubtful Items

Scott Paper Company includes the following in the notes to the financial statements (in millions):

	December 25 1993
Customer receivables	$516.6
Allowance for discounts and doubtful items	(25.3)
	$491.3

Required

1. Compute the ratio of the allowance for discounts and doubtful items to gross accounts receivable for December 25, 1993. In 1988 and 1987 this ratio was 5.2% and 5.1% respectively. In 1990, it was 4.8%. What are some possible reasons for the change in this ratio?
2. Assume that all discounts are cash discounts, not trade discounts. Why does the allowance for cash discounts exist?
3. Independent of Scott Paper's actual balances, prepare a journal entry to write off an uncollectible account of $100,000 on December 26, 1993.

6-52   Uncollectible Accounts

Nike, Inc., is a worldwide supplier of athletic products. Its balance sheet on May 31, 1994 included the following data (in thousands):

Accounts receivable, less allowance for doubtful accounts of $28,291	$518,816

Required

1. The company uses the allowance method for accounting for bad debts. Suppose the company added $20 million to the allowance during the year ending May 31, 1994. Write-offs of uncollectible accounts were $19 million. Show (a) the impact on the balance sheet equation of these transactions and (b) the journal entries.
2. Suppose Nike had used the specific write-off method for accounting for bad debts. Using the same information as in requirement 1, show (a) the impact on the balance sheet equation and (b) the journal entry.
3. How would the Nike balance sheet amounts above have been affected if the specific write-off method had been used up to that date? Be specific.

6-53   Uncollectible Accounts

Exxon Corporation is the world's largest producer of oil and gas. Its balance sheet included the following actual presentation:

	December 31	
	1993	1992
	(millions of dollars)	
Notes and accounts receivable less estimated doubtful accounts	$6,860	$8,079

Required

1. Footnote 5 to Exxon's financial statements revealed that estimated doubtful notes and accounts receivable were $118 million at the end of 1993 and $145 million at the end of 1992. Suppose that during 1993 Exxon had added $300 million to its allowance for estimated doubtful accounts. (a) Calculate the write-offs of uncollectible accounts and show (b) the impact on the balance sheet equation of these transactions and (c) the journal entries.
2. Assume that Exxon had used the specific write-off method for accounting for bad debts. Using the same information as in requirement 1, show (a) the impact on the balance sheet equation and (b) the journal entry.
3. How would the Exxon balance sheet amounts have been affected if the specific write-off method had been used? Be specific.

➤ 6-54   Allowance for Doubtful Accounts and 10-K Disclosures

The following is schedule VIII, taken from the 10-K filing of Sears Roebuck Corporation for the year ending December 31, 1993. The 10-K is a required filing that companies must make with the Securities and Exchange Commission each year in order for their common stock to be traded publicly in the United States. It includes more detail than is often found in the annual report that is sent to all shareholders. This schedule describes exactly what occurred in the allowance for doubtful accounts. Use the information in schedule VIII to reproduce the journal entries affecting the allowance for doubtful accounts during the year ending December 31, 1993.

Sears Roebuck Corporation
Schedule VIII—Valuation and Qualifying Accounts
(in millions)

	Column A	Column B	Column C	Column D	Column E
		Additions			
		(1)	(2)		
Description	Balance at Beginning of Period	Charged to Cost and Expenses	Charged to Other Accounts	Deductions From Reserves	Balance at End of Period
Accounts receivable—allowance for doubtful accounts:					
Year Ended December 31, 1993	$ 891.7	$632.6	$181.8	$718.2	$987.9
Year Ended December 31, 1992	$ 642.3	$765.6	$ 95.7	$611.9	$891.7

NOTES: (A) Column C: Recoveries of accounts previously written off.
    (B) Column D: Write-off of accounts receivable.

6-55   Sales, Accounts Receivable and Ethics

Writing in *Corporate Cashflow* in September 1993, Howard Schillit described how the market value of Comptronix fell from $238 million to $67 million in a few hours when it was revealed that management had "cooked the books." Comptronix provides contract manufacturing services to makers of electronic equipment. Its 1991 financial results looked strong:

	1991	1990	Change
Sales	$102.0 million	$70.2 million	+45%
Accounts receivable	12.6 million	12.0 million	+5%
Accounts receivable turnover	8.1	5.9	

However, the relationship between sales and accounts receivable sent signals to knowledgeable analysts.

Required

1. Discuss the relationship that you would expect between sales and accounts receivable in a normal situation.
2. What unethical actions might cause sales to grow so much faster than accounts receivable? What unethical actions might cause the opposite, that is, for accounts receivable to grow faster than sales?
3. What is the most likely type of "cooking the books" that occurred at Comptronix?

6-56   Wal-Mart Annual Report

Refer to the Wal-Mart financial statements (Appendix A).

Required

1. Wal-Mart combines cash and cash equivalents on the balance sheet. Define cash equivalents and give an example.
2. Calculate the average collection period for 1995 assuming all sales were on account.
3. Independent of requirement 2, assume that Wal-Mart's average collection period was 45 days. What percentage of sales would this imply were on credit?
4. In fact, Wal-Mart makes no reference to a bad debts expense or an allowance for bad debts. Why might Wal-Mart simultaneously have $700 million in accounts receivable and no significant allowance for bad debts?

6-57   Compact D From Disclosure

Select an industry and choose two companies within that industry.

Required

Calculate the accounts receivable turnover and days to collect accounts receivable for the two companies for two years and comment on the results.

7

Valuing Inventories, Cost of Goods Sold, and Gross Profit

Learning Objectives

After studying this chapter, you should be able to

1. Explain the importance of inventory in measuring profitability.

2. Explain and illustrate the differences between perpetual and periodic inventory systems.

3. Identify the items included in the cost of merchandise acquired.

4. Explain the four principal inventory valuation methods and their effect on measurement of assets and net income.

5. Understand the reasons for choosing and using the inventory methods.

6. Explain the meaning and impact of LIFO liquidation and LIFO reserves.

7. Explain why the lower-of-cost-or-market method is used to value inventories.

8. Show the effects of inventory errors on financial statements.

9. Explain the uses of the gross profit percentage and inventory turnover measures.

This chapter introduces the details involved in assigning value to inventories and calculating the cost of goods sold. These important measures are used to determine a firm's gross profits. Since a firm's goal is profitable sales, we need effective accounting techniques to measure profitability. This chapter covers the methods and procedures for valuing inventory on the balance sheet and for recording costs of goods sold on the income statement. As in prior chapters, the chapter also presents ratios to assess the profitability of the firm and the effective management of inventory levels.

This chapter continues to link the preparation of the income statement and the balance sheet. When inventory is acquired it initially appears on the balance sheet as an asset. Under the matching principle, when revenue is recognized, the cost of the sale is also recognized. Thus, when a sale occurs the costs of the inventory become an expense, cost of goods sold, in the income statement. The chapter also explains how different inventory valuation techniques affect financial statements.

The accounting procedures discussed in this chapter are responses to a reporting need encountered in every nation of the world. While the dominant practices differ slightly from country to country, the issues remain. Even within a country, many different procedures are encountered. Thus, the reader of financial statements must understand alternative practices in order to intelligently compare the economic performance of different firms.

■ GROSS PROFIT AND COST OF GOODS SOLD

Objective 1

Explain the importance of inventory in measuring profitability.

For firms that purchase and resell merchandise, a beginning guide to assessing profitability is *gross profit* (also called *profit margin* or *gross margin*), which is defined as the difference between sales revenues and the costs of the goods sold. These calculations rely on the value of the firms' inventories, which are goods that are being held for resale.

Sales revenue must cover the cost of goods sold and provide a gross profit sufficient to cover all other costs, including research and development, selling and marketing, administration, and so on. As illustrated in Exhibit 7-1, prior to sale, items held for sale are reported as inventory, a current asset in the balance sheet. When the goods are sold, the costs of the inventory become an expense, Cost of Goods Sold, in the income statement. This expense is deducted from Net Sales to determine Gross Profit, and additional expenses are deducted from Gross Profit to determine Net Income.

The Basic Concept of Inventory Accounting

The key to calculating the cost of goods sold is accounting for inventory. Conceptually, the process is very simple. Suppose Christina sells T-shirts. Periodically, she orders many shirts of various sizes and colors. They sell, she orders more, and her business operating cycle continues. After a year, to evaluate her success, Christina prepares financial statements. To calculate the value of inventory on hand, she obtains a *physical count* of inventory items remaining at year end. She then develops a **cost valuation**, which assigns a specific value from the historical cost records to each item in ending inventory. With 100 shirts remaining at a cost of $5.00 each, Christina's total ending inventory is $500. Suppose she had no shirts at the beginning of the year, and total

cost valuation
Process of assigning specific historical costs to items counted in the physical inventory.

purchases for the year were $26,000. Her cost of goods sold is $25,500 ($26,000 of available shirts minus $500 of unsold shirts).

In practice, the process is not this simple. Complexity arises from many sources. The following sections describe alternate techniques for measuring inventories and how they differ.

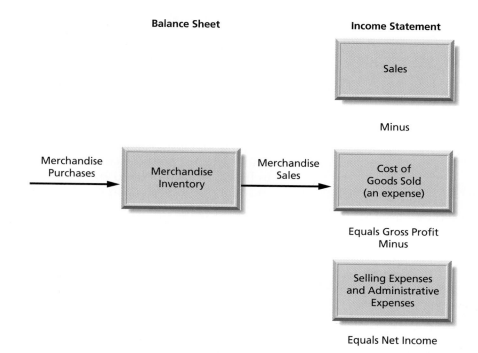

PERPETUAL AND PERIODIC INVENTORY SYSTEMS

perpetual inventory system A system that keeps a running, continuous record that tracks inventories and the cost of goods sold on a day-to-day basis.

There are two fundamental ways of keeping inventory records for merchandise: perpetual and periodic. The **perpetual inventory system** (which has been assumed in previous chapters) keeps a running, continuous record that tracks inventories and the cost of goods sold on a day-to-day basis. Such a record helps managers control inventory levels and prepare interim financial statements. Nonetheless, physical inventory counts should be taken at least once a year to check on the accuracy of the clerical records.

Previous chapters have described the inventory cycle as follows:

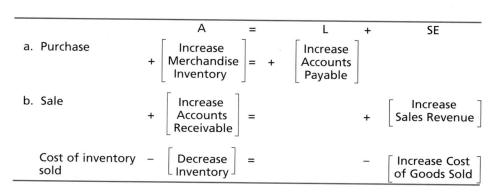

In the perpetual inventory system, the journal entries are:

a. When inventory is purchased:
    Merchandise inventory xxx
        Accounts payable   xxx
b. When inventory is sold:
    Accounts receivable (or cash) xxx
        Sales revenue   xxx
    Cost of goods sold xxx
        Inventory   xxx

Thus, in the perpetual inventory system, the sale and the inventory reduction are recorded simultaneously.

periodic inventory system The system in which the cost of goods sold is computed periodically by relying solely on physical counts without keeping day-to-day records of units sold or on hand.

The **periodic inventory system,** conversely, does *not* involve a day-to-day record of inventories or of the cost of goods sold. Instead the cost of goods sold and an updated inventory balance are computed only at the end of an accounting period, when a physical count of inventory is taken. The cost of the goods purchased is accumulated by recording the individual purchase transactions throughout any given reporting period, such as a year. The accountant computes the cost of goods sold by subtracting the ending inventories (determined by physical count) from the sum of the opening inventory and purchases. Christina applied the periodic inventory method to her T-shirt business.

While the cost of goods sold under the perpetual system is computed instantaneously as goods are sold, under the periodic system, the computation is delayed:

$$\underbrace{\begin{array}{c}\text{Beginning}\\\text{inventory}\end{array} + \text{Purchases} -}_{\text{Goods available for sale}} \quad \underbrace{\begin{array}{c}\text{Ending}\\\text{inventory}\end{array}}_{-\text{ Inventory left over }} = \quad \underbrace{\begin{array}{c}\text{Cost of}\\\text{goods sold}\end{array}}_{= \text{ Cost of goods sold}}$$

cost of goods available for sale Sum of beginning inventory plus current year purchases.

The periodic system computes cost of goods sold as a *residual amount*. First, the beginning inventory is added to the purchases to obtain the total **cost of goods available for sale.** Then the ending inventory is counted, and its cost is deducted from the cost of goods available for sale to obtain the cost of goods sold.

	Periodic System		Perpetual System
Exhibit 7-2	**Periodic System**		**Perpetual System**
Inventory Systems	Beginning inventories (by physical count)	xxx	Cost of goods sold (kept on a day-to-day basis rather than being determined periodically)*
	Add: Purchases	xxx	
	xxx		
	Cost of goods available for sale	xxx	
	Less: Ending inventories (by physical count)	xxx	
	Cost of goods sold	xxx	

* Such a condensed figure does not preclude the presentation of a supplementary schedule similar to that on the left.

Comparison of Systems

Explain and illustrate the differences between perpetual and periodic inventory systems.

Exhibit 7-2 compares the perpetual and periodic inventory systems. For annual financial statements, the two methods give equivalent results. Historically, the perpetual system has been used for low-volume, high-value items. The periodic system has been preferred for high-volume, low-value, and mixed-value inventory operations. The more expensive and cumbersome perpetual system was typically implemented when it gave significant managerial information to aid in pricing or ordering. Sometimes it improved control over loss and theft of inventory. Computerized inventory systems and optical scanning equipment at checkout counters have made implementation of perpetual inventory systems less costly.

The perpetual system does not eliminate the need for a physical count and valuation of the inventory. While the perpetual system captures information about goods purchased and sold, the physical inventory allows management to delete from inventory goods that are damaged or obsolete. It also reveals disagreements between perpetual records and the physical count that may arise from **inventory shrinkage.** Inventory shrinkage refers to theft, breakage, and loss, which are substantial factors in some businesses.

inventory shrinkage
Difference between (a) the value of inventory that would occur if there were no theft, breakage, or losses of inventory and (b) the value of inventory when it is physically counted.

If the physical count differs from the perpetual inventory amount, the following result might be obtained:

| Perpetual inventory record: | Part 1F68X | 142 units @ $20 | $2,840 |
| Physical count: | Part 1F68X | 125 units @ $20 | $2,500 |

Seventeen units (142 units – 125 units) have disappeared without being charged as cost of goods sold. The journal entry to adjust inventory from $2,840 to $2,500 is:

Inventory shrinkage	340	
Merchandise inventory		340
To adjust the ending inventory to its balance per physical count.		

In summary, the perpetual system is more accurate in providing timely information, but it is more costly. The periodic system is less accurate, especially for monthly or quarterly statements. It is less costly because there is no day-to-day processing regarding cost of goods sold. However, if theft or the accumulation of obsolete merchandise is likely, periodic systems often prove to be more expensive in the long run.

Physical Inventory

physical count The process of counting all the items in inventory at a moment in time.

Good inventory control procedures require a **physical count** of each item being held in inventory at least annually in both periodic and perpetual inventory systems. The physical count is an imposing, time-consuming, and expensive process. You may have seen "closed for inventory" signs. To simplify counting and valuation, firms often choose fiscal accounting periods so that the year ends when inventories are low. For example, Kmart and JC Penney have late January year ends, which follow the holiday season.

The physical inventory is so important to income determination that external auditors usually observe the client's physical count and confirm the accuracy of the subsequent valuation. Some audit firms hire outside experts to assist them. For example, assessing a jeweler's inventory might require an expert to test the color, size, clarity, and imperfections in the diamonds on hand. Similarly, the client and auditor might rely on an engineer to measure the physical dimensions of an electric utility's coal pile so the volume and weight could be estimated without actually weighing the coal itself.

The Classic Salad Oil Swindle

On Thursday, November 21, 1963, reports linked the suspension of two Wall Street brokerage firms to uncollectible loans made to an obscure company named Allied Crude Vegetable Oil and Refining. Collateral for the loans had been $175 million worth of vegetable oil supposedly stored in forty converted gasoline storage tanks in Bayonne, New Jersey. Investigation revealed that, instead of being filled with vegetable oil, the tanks contained sea water, soap stock, and "sludge." In response to these reports, the Dow Jones Industrial Average experienced its largest decline in more than a year. However, news of the unfolding "Great Salad Oil Swindle" was rapidly overshadowed when, on the following day, President John F. Kennedy was assassinated in Dallas.

The case of Allied's missing salad oil offers an interesting illustration of the problems associated with verifying the reported level of inventory. Since the late 1930s, auditors have been required to physically observe the counting of inventory in order to issue an opinion on the fairness of financial statements. Allied used some ingenious techniques to hide their shortfall from the watchful auditors. Because the forty storage tanks were connected by pipes, the vegetable oil was pumped from tank to tank during the week required to complete the inventory count—that is, the same vegetable oil was counted over and over. Moreover, no one tank was ever completely filled with the oil. Allied welded shut all but one opening to the tank. Beneath this working opening the company then welded a pipe, which was filled with a few hundred pounds of real oil. When the auditors took samples, they were actually testing what was in this pipe, not what was in the tank. The tank itself was filled with sea water. After the fraud was uncovered, a faucet on one tank was opened, and water poured out for twelve days. Through these manipulations, Allied created 1.9 billion pounds of fictitious vegetable oil. At one point, the amount of soybean and cottonseed oil supposedly stored in the tank farm in Bayonne was almost twice as much as the Census Bureau counted in the entire United States. ■

Source: Norman C. Miller, The Great Salad Oil Swindle *(New York: Coward McCann, 1965).*

■ COST OF MERCHANDISE ACQUIRED

Measuring Cost of Merchandise Acquired

Objective 3

Identify the items included in the cost of merchandise acquired.

Some of the complexity in inventory accounting stems from the question of what constitutes the cost of the merchandise. To be more specific, does cost include all or part of the following: invoice price, transportation charges, trade and cash discounts, cost of handling and placing in stock, storage, purchasing department, receiving department, and other indirect charges? In practice, accountants usually consider the cost of merchandise to include only the invoice price plus the directly identifiable transportation charges less any offsetting discounts. The costs of the purchasing and receiving departments are treated as period costs and appear on the income statement as they are incurred.

The accounting for *purchase* returns, *purchase* allowances, and cash discounts on *purchases* is just the opposite of their sales counterparts. Using the periodic inventory system, suppose gross purchases are $960,000 and purchase returns and allowances are $75,000. The summary journal entries are:

Purchases	960,000	
Accounts payable		960,000
Accounts payable	75,000	
Purchase returns and allowances		75,000

Suppose also that cash discounts of $5,000 are taken upon payment of the remaining $960,000 − $75,000 = $885,000 of payables. The summary journal entry is:

Accounts payable	885,000	
Cash discounts on purchases		5,000
Cash		880,000

The accounts Cash Discounts on Purchases and Purchase Returns and Allowances are deducted from Purchases in calculating cost of goods sold.

Car dealers sometimes sell cars "below cost" or "$100 below invoice." Do dealers lose money on such sales? Probably not, because gross invoice cost to the dealer and final cost of goods sold may differ. Dealers receive incentives from the manufacturers such as volume discounts or special discounts to push particular models. The dealer's invoice shows the list price before discounts and allowances, not the final net dealer cost.

Inward Transportation

F.O.B. destination Seller pays freight costs from the shipping point of the seller to the receiving point of the buyer.

The major cost of transporting merchandise is typically the freight charges from the shipping point of the seller to the receiving point of the buyer. When the seller bears this cost, the terms are stated on the sales invoice as **F.O.B.** (free on board) **destination**. When the buyer bears this cost, the terms are stated as **F.O.B. shipping point.**

F.O.B. shipping point Buyer pays freight costs from the shipping point of the seller to the receiving point of the buyer.

In theory, any transportation costs borne by the buyer should be added to the cost of the inventory acquired. In practice, several different items are typically ordered and shipped simultaneously. Therefore it is often difficult to allocate freight costs among the items. In addition, management may want to compile freight costs separately to see how they compare with regard to periods and modes of transportation. Consequently, accountants frequently use a separate transportation cost account, labeled as Freight In, Transportation In, Inbound Transportation, or Inward Transportation.

freight in (inward transportation) An additional cost of the goods acquired during the period, which is often shown in the purchases section of an income statement.

Freight in (or **inward transportation**) appears in the purchases section of an income statement as an additional cost of the goods acquired during the period. On the other hand, **freight out** represents the costs borne by the *seller* and is shown as a "shipping expense," which is a form of selling expense. Thus Freight In affects the gross profit section of an income statement for the buyer, but Freight Out does not and therefore appears below the gross profit line on the seller's income statement. A detailed gross profit section is often arranged as follows (figures in thousands are assumed):

freight out The transportation costs borne by the seller of merchandise and often shown as a "shipping expense."

Gross sales			$1,740
Deduct: Sales returns and allowances		$ 70	
Cash discounts on sales		100	170
Net sales			$1,570
Deduct: Cost of goods sold:			
Merchandise inventory, December 31, 19X1		$ 100	
Purchases (gross)	$960		
Deduct: Purchase returns and allowances	$75		
Cash discounts on purchases	5	80	
Net purchases		$880	
Add: Freight in		30	
Total cost of merchandise acquired		910	
Cost of goods available for sale		$1,010	
Deduct: Merchandise inventory,			
December 31, 19X2		140	
Cost of goods sold			870
Gross profit			$ 700

While management may find such detail valuable, summary information is much more common in the annual report to shareholders:

Net Sales	$1,570
Cost of Goods Sold	870
Gross Profit	$ 700

■ COMPARING ACCOUNTING PROCEDURES FOR PERIODIC AND PERPETUAL INVENTORY SYSTEMS

A Detailed Example

GoodEarth Products, Inc., has a balance of $100,000 in merchandise inventory at the beginning of 19X2 (December 31, 19X1). A summary of transactions for 19X2 follows:

a. Purchases	$990,000
b. Purchase returns and allowances	80,000

Net purchases were therefore $990,000 less $80,000, or $910,000. The physical count of the ending inventory for 19X2 led to a cost valuation of $140,000. Note how these figures can be used to compute the $870,000 cost of goods sold:

$$\underset{\text{inventory}}{\text{Beginning}} + \text{Net purchases} - \underset{\text{inventory}}{\text{Ending}} = \underset{\text{goods sold}}{\text{Cost of}}$$

$$\$100,000 + \$910,000 - \$140,000 = \$870,000$$

$$\underset{\substack{\text{Cost of goods} \\ \text{available for sale}}}{} - \underset{\substack{\text{Cost of goods} \\ \text{left over}}}{} = \underset{\substack{\text{Cost of} \\ \text{goods sold}}}{}$$

$$\$1,010,000 - \$140,000 = \$870,000$$

The periodic and perpetual procedures would record these transactions differently. As Exhibit 7-3 shows, the perpetual system entails directly increasing the Inventory account by the $990,000 purchases (entry *a*) and decreasing it by the $80,000 in returns and allowances (entry *b*) and the $870,000 cost of goods sold (entry *C*). The Cost of Goods Sold account would be increased daily as sales are made. In a nutshell, these entries should be familiar. The only new aspect here is the purchase returns and allowances, which directly reduce the Inventory account. Although no purchase (cash) discounts are illustrated, their treatment would parallel purchase returns and allowances.

Before proceeding, reflect on how the perpetual system in Exhibit 7-3 creates the ending inventory of $140,000.

GoodEarth Products, Inc. General Ledger at December 31, 19X2 (amounts in thousands) Perpetual Inventory

	Inventory				Cost of Goods Sold		
Balance 12/31/X1	100	(b)	80	(c)	870	(d3)	870
(a)	990	(c)	870				
Balance 12/31/X2	140						

The periodic system is called "periodic" because neither the Cost of Goods Sold account nor the Inventory account is computed on a daily basis. Moreover, Purchases and Purchase Returns and Allowances are accounted for in a separate account, as entries *a* and *b* indicate. Entries *d1* and *d2* at the bottom of Exhibit 7-3 show the eventual periodic calculation of cost of goods sold in the Cost of Goods Sold Account.

Exhibit 7-3 Comparison of Perpetual and Periodic Inventory Entries (amounts in thousands)

	Perpetual Records				Periodic Records		
a. Gross purchases:	Inventory	990			Purchases	990	
	Accounts payable		990		Accounts payable		990
b. Returns and allowances:	Accounts payable	80			Accounts payable	80	
	Inventory		80		Purchase returns and allowances		80
c. As goods are sold:	Cost of goods sold	870			No entry		
	Inventory		870				
d. At the end of the accounting period:	d1. ⎫ d2. ⎬ No entry				d1. Cost of goods sold	1,010	
					Purchase returns and allowances	80	
					Purchases		990
					Inventory		100
					d2. Inventory	140	
					Cost of goods sold		140
	d3. Income summary	870			d3. Income summary	870	
	Cost of goods sold		870		Cost of goods sold		870

Entry *d1* transfers the beginning inventory balance, purchases, and purchase returns and allowances, totaling $1,010,000, to cost of goods sold. This provides the cost of goods available for sale, the first step in calculating cost of goods sold.

Next, the ending inventory is physically counted and its cost is computed. Entry *d2* recognizes the $140,000 ending inventory and reduces the $1,010,000 cost of goods available for sale by $140,000 to obtain a final cost of goods sold of $870,000. All of these details can be shown in the cost of goods sold section of the income statement. However, published income statements usually include only a single cost of goods sold number.

The periodic system may seem awkward when compared with the perpetual system. The beginning inventory and cost of goods sold accounts are untouched until the end of the period. However, the periodic system avoids the costly process of calculating the cost of goods sold for each sale.

GoodEarth
Products, Inc.
General Ledger at
December 31, 19X2
(amounts in
thousands)
Periodic Inventory

	Inventory					Cost of Goods Sold		
Balance,					(d1)	1,010	(d2)	140
12/31/X1	100	(d1)	100				(d3)	870
(d2)	140							
Balance,								
12/31/X2	140							

As shown in entry *d3*, the cost of goods sold is closed to Income Summary under either method (see Chapter 5, p. 196):

Note that the periodic method produces the same final balances in Inventory and Income Summary as the perpetual method. However, as entries *d1* and *d2* demonstrate, the cost of goods sold is computed at the end of the year; consequently, the related journal entries and postings are made then.

Note that in the perpetual system, the Inventory and Cost of Goods Sold account balances are always up to date, without special action by the accountant. In contrast, under the periodic system, more accounts are in use and information is simply being accumulated. No balance appears in the Cost of Goods Sold account until the company prepares financial statements and uses an adjusting journal entry to properly state inventory balances and cost of goods sold.

■ PRINCIPAL INVENTORY VALUATION METHODS

Objective 4

Explain the four principal inventory valuation methods and their effect on measurement of assets and net income.

Each period, accountants must divide the cost of beginning inventory and merchandise acquired between cost of goods sold and cost of items remaining in ending inventory. Under a perpetual system, a cost must be assigned to each item sold. Under a periodic system, the costs of the items remaining in ending inventory must be measured. Regardless of the inventory system, costs of individual items must be determined by some inventory valuation method. Four principal inventory valuation methods have been generally accepted in the United States: specific identification, FIFO, LIFO, and weighted-average. Each will be explained and compared in this section.

If unit prices and costs did not fluctuate, all inventory methods would show identical results. But prices change, and these changes raise central issues regarding cost of goods sold (income measurement) and inventories (asset measurement). As a simple example of the valuation method choices facing management, consider Emilio, a new vendor of a cola drink at the fairgrounds, who begins the week with no inventory. He buys one can on Monday for 30 cents; a second can on Tuesday for 40 cents; and a third can on Wednesday for 56 cents. He then sells one can on Thursday for 90 cents. What is his gross profit? His ending inventory? Answer these questions in your own mind before reading on.

Four Major Methods

Panel I of Exhibit 7-4 provides a first glimpse of the nature of the four generally accepted methods for inventory valuation. As the exhibit shows, Emilio's choice of an inventory method can significantly affect the amount reported as cost of goods sold (and hence gross profit and net income) and ending inventory. Note, for example, that three different gross profit margins may occur under the specific identification method. FIFO yields a 60 cent profit, while LIFO yields only a 34 cent profit.

specific identification method This inventory method concentrates on the physical tracing of the particular items sold.

1. Specific identification method. This method concentrates on the *physical* linking of the *particular* items sold. Suppose Emilio could tell which can of cola was purchased on each day. If he reached for the Monday can instead of the Wednesday can, the *specific identification* method would show different results. Thus Panel I of Exhibit 7-4 indicates that gross profit for operations of Monday through Thursday could be 60 cents, 50 cents, or 34 cents, depending on the particular can handed to the customer. Emilio could choose which can to sell and affect reported results by doing so.

first-in, first-out (FIFO) This method of accounting for inventory assumes that the units acquired earliest are used or sold first.

2. First-in, first-out (FIFO). This method assumes that the stock acquired earliest is sold (used up) first. It does not track the physical flow of individual items except by coincidence. Thus the Monday can of cola is deemed to have been sold regardless of the actual can delivered. In times of rising prices, FIFO usually shows the *largest* gross profit (60 cents in Panel I of Exhibit 7-4).

last-in, first-out (LIFO) This inventory method assumes that the units acquired most recently are used or sold first.

3. Last-in, first-out (LIFO). This method assumes that the stock acquired most recently is sold (used up) first. Thus the Wednesday can of cola is deemed to have been sold regardless of the actual can delivered. In times of rising prices, LIFO generally shows the lowest gross profit (34 cents in Panel I of Exhibit 7-4).

weighted-average cost This inventory method computes a unit cost by dividing the total acquisition cost of all items available for sale by the number of units available for sale.

4. Weighted-average cost. This method computes a unit cost by dividing the total acquisition cost of all items available for sale by the number of units available for sale. Exhibit 7-4 shows the calculations Emilio would make. The weighted-average method usually produces a gross profit somewhere between that obtained under FIFO and that under LIFO (48 cents as compared with 60 cents and 34 cents in Panel I of Exhibit 7-4).

Exhibit 7-4	Emilio's Cola Sales Comparison of Inventory Methods (all monetary amounts are in cents)					
	(1) Specific Identification			(2) FIFO	(3) LIFO	(4) Weighted Average
	(1A)	(1B)	(1C)			
Panel I						
Income Statement for the Period Monday through Thursday						
Sales	90	90	90	90	90	90
Deduct cost of goods sold:						
1 30¢ (Monday) unit	30			30		
1 40¢ (Tuesday) unit		40				
1 56¢ (Wednesday) unit			56		56	
1 weighted-average unit [(30 + 40 + 56) ÷ 3 = 42]						42
Gross profit for Monday through Thursday	60	50	34	60	34	48
Thursday's ending inventory, 2 units:						
Monday unit @ 30¢		30	30		30	
Tuesday unit @ 40¢	40		40	40	40	
Wednesday unit @ 56¢	56	56		56		
Weighted-average units @ 42¢						84
Total ending inventory on Thursday	96	86	70	96	70	84
Panel II						
Income Statement for Friday						
Sales, 2 units @ 90¢	180	180	180	180	180	180
Cost of goods sold (Thursday ending inventory from above)	96	86	70	96	70	84
Gross profit, Friday only	84	94	110	84	110	96
Panel III						
Gross profit for full week						
Monday through Thursday (Panel 1)	60	50	34	60	34	48
Friday (Panel II)	84	94	110	84	110	96
Total gross profit	144	144	144	144	144	144

Inventory Methods and the Matching Principle

Under the matching principle, we must link the cost of goods sold with the sales revenue generated when the product is delivered to a customer. What is challenging is to *measure* cost of goods sold. Panel I of Exhibit 7-4 identifies four measurement methods—specific identification, FIFO, LIFO, and weighted-average cost—each with both strengths and weaknesses.

Think of these methods as expressions of how Emilio might physically store and sell his cola. He could mark each can with its cost and record that cost as cost of goods sold when the can was handed to a customer. Specific identification captures this procedure. He could put each new can, as it is acquired, into the top of a cooler. At each customer purchase, the top can is the one sold. LIFO reflects this procedure. In contrast, each new can could be placed at the back of the cooler to chill and the oldest, coldest can sold first. FIFO captures this physical flow. If the cans are mixed together, the weighted-average method is a rough approximation of what Emilio knows about the cost of each can sold.

Because the physical flow of products has little importance to the financial success of most businesses, the accounting profession has concluded that companies may choose any of the four methods to record cost of goods sold. Since the method is not linked to the physical flow of merchandise, inventory methods are often referred to as *cost flow assumptions*. For example, when we decide that the cost of the first inventory item purchased will be matched with the sales revenue from the first item sold to calculate the gross profit from the sale, we are adopting the FIFO cost flow assumption.

Suppose Emilio sells his remaining inventory on Friday and enters a more attractive business. Panel II of Exhibit 7-4 shows Friday's gross profit. Panel III of Exhibit 7-4 shows that the *cumulative* gross profit over the life of Emilio's business would be the same $1.44 under any of the inventory methods. What makes the choice of method important is our having to match particular costs to particular periods *during* the life of the business in order to prepare financial statements and evaluate performance.

The Consistency Convention

consistency
Conformity from period to period with unchanging policies and procedures.

While companies have broad latitude in choosing their inventory cost flow assumption, they are expected to use the chosen method consistently over time. The FASB has referred to **consistency** as "conformity from period to period with unchanging policies and procedures." Interpreting financial performance over time involves comparing the results of different periods. If accounting methods for inventory were changed often, meaningful comparisons over time would be impossible. Exhibit 7-4 illustrates the extreme difference that the choice of inventory method produces for Emilio's reported gross profits in different periods.

Occasionally a change in market conditions or other circumstances may justify a change in inventory method. With its auditor's approval, a firm may change method. But the firm is required to note the change in its financial statements, and the auditor will also refer to the change in the audit opinion so that financial statement readers are alerted to the possible effects of the change on their analysis.

■ CHOOSING AND USING INVENTORY METHODS

Objective 5

Understand the reasons for choosing and using the inventory methods.

The four inventory methods have different benefits and drawbacks. Among the issues facing management when choosing a method are such questions as: Which method provides the highest reported net income? Which method provides management the most flexibility to affect reported earnings? How do the methods affect income tax obligations? Which methods are inexpensive to apply? Which method provides an inventory valuation that approximates the actual value of the inventory?

Consider the link between cost of goods sold and the valuation of ending inventory. Emilio's three cola cans had a total cost of goods available for sale of $1.26. At the end of the period, this $1.26 must be allocated either to cans sold or to cans in ending inventory. The higher the cost of goods sold, the lower the ending inventory. Exhibit 7-5 illustrates that interdependence. At one extreme, FIFO treats the 30 cent cost of the first can acquired as cost of goods sold and 96 cents as ending inventory. At the other extreme, LIFO treats the 56 cent cost of the last can acquired as cost of goods sold and 70 cents as ending inventory.

Before considering each method in detail, one other general relation is worth studying. Note from columns 2 and 3 of Exhibit 7-4 that during this period of rising prices, FIFO yields higher inventory *and* higher gross profit than LIFO. This result is consistent with the accounting equation that requires that A = L + SE. If inventory is higher under FIFO (higher assets) and the equation is to balance, either liabilities or stockholders' equity must also be higher. Higher gross profit under FIFO implies higher net income and higher stockholder's equity (SE in the equation). Note that nothing in our choice of methods would affect accounts payable. We record each new inventory purchase at its cost and recognize a liability in that amount in the same way under all of these methods.

Exhibit 7-5			

Emilio's Cola Sales Diagram of Inventory Methods (data are from Panel I, Exhibit 7-4; monetary amounts are in cents)

Beginning inventory	+	Merchandise purchases	=	Cost of goods available for sale
0	+	126	=	126
Cost of goods available for sale	−	Cost of goods sold	=	Ending inventory

$$
\begin{array}{c}
1 @ 30 \\
1 @ 40 \\
1 @ 56
\end{array}
\left\{
\begin{array}{ccccc}
126 & - & \left\{\begin{array}{c}30 \\ \text{or} \\ 40 \\ \text{or} \\ 56\end{array}\right\} & = & \left\{\begin{array}{c}96 \\ \text{or} \\ 86 \\ \text{or} \\ 70\end{array}\right\} \quad \text{Specific identification} \\
126 & - & 30 & = & 96 \quad \text{FIFO} \\
126 & - & 56 & = & 70 \quad \text{LIFO} \\
126 & - & 42 & = & 84 \quad \text{Weighted average}
\end{array}
\right.
$$

Specific Identification

The specific identification method, which uses physical observation or the labeling of items in stock with individual numbers or codes, is easy and economically justifiable for relatively expensive low-volume merchandise like custom artwork, diamond jewelry, and automobiles. However, most organizations have vast segments of inventories that are too numerous and insufficiently valuable per unit to warrant such individualized attention. Since the cost of goods sold is determined by the specific item handed to the customer, this method permits managers to manipulate income and inventory values by filling a sales order from a number of physically equivalent items with different historical costs.

FIFO

FIFO is sometimes referred to as LISH (Last In, Still Here). When the first costs represent goods sold, the last costs represent goods still on hand. By using the latest costs to measure the ending inventory, FIFO tends to provide inventory valuations that closely approximate the actual market value of the inventory at the balance sheet date. In addition, in periods of rising prices, FIFO leads to higher net income. Higher reported incomes may favorably affect investor attitudes toward the company. Similarly, higher reported incomes may lead to higher salaries, higher bonuses, or higher status for the management of the company. Unlike specific identification, FIFO specifies the order in which acquisition costs will become cost of goods sold, so management cannot affect income by choosing to sell one identical item rather than another.

LIFO

While FIFO associates the most recent costs with inventories, LIFO treats the most recent costs as costs of goods sold. LIFO provides an income statement perspective in the sense that net income measured using LIFO combines current sales prices and current acquisition costs. *In a period of rising prices and constant or growing inventories, LIFO yields lower net income.* Why is lower net income such an important feature of LIFO? Because in the United States LIFO is an acceptable inventory accounting method for income tax purposes. When lower income is reported to the tax authorities, lower taxes are paid, so it is not surprising that almost two-thirds of U.S. corporations use LIFO for at least some of their inventories. The Internal Revenue Code requires that if LIFO is used for tax purposes, it must also be used for financial reporting purposes.

During a recent period of higher inflation, the *Wall Street Journal* reported that many small firms changed from FIFO to LIFO. As an example, Chicago Heights Steel Co. "boosted cash by 5% to 10% by lowering income taxes when it switched to LIFO." When Becton, Dickinson and Company changed to LIFO, its annual report stated that its "change to the LIFO method... for both financial reporting and income tax purposes resulted in improved cash flow due to lower income taxes paid." Indeed, some observers maintain that executives are guilty of serious mismanagement by not adopting LIFO when FIFO produces significantly higher taxable income.

LIFO does permit management to influence reported income by the *timing of purchases* of inventory items. Consider Emilio's case. Suppose that acquisition prices increase from 56 cents on Wednesday to 68 cents on Thursday, the day of the sale of the one unit. How is net income affected if one more unit is acquired on Thursday? Under LIFO, cost of goods sold would change to 68 cents, and profit would fall by 12 cents. In contrast, FIFO cost of goods sold and gross profit would be unchanged.

	LIFO		FIFO	
	As in Exhibit 7-4	If One More Unit Acquired	As in Exhibit 7-4	If One More Unit Acquired
Sales	90¢	90¢	90¢	90¢
Cost of goods sold	56¢	68¢	30¢	30¢
Gross profit	34¢	22¢	60¢	60¢
Ending inventory:				
First layer, Monday	30¢	30¢		
Second layer, Tuesday	40¢	40¢	40¢	40¢
Third layer, Wednesday		56¢	56¢	56¢
Fourth layer, Thursday				68¢
	70¢	126¢	96¢	164¢

Paying FIFO Taxes: Your Favorite Charity

In times of inflation, using LIFO results in higher reported cost of goods sold than using FIFO. Higher cost of goods sold means lower gross profit and lower net income. On the one hand, you might expect that firms would be reluctant to use LIFO in times of inflation because they wouldn't want to report lower net income to their stockholders and creditors. On the other hand, you might expect firms to use LIFO in times of inflation to lower their income taxes. With these conflicting incentives, which inventory method do firms choose in times of inflation?

In 1974, the inflation rate in the United States, as measured by change in the Consumer Price Index, reached double digits for the first time. In response, more than forty U.S. corporations switched from FIFO to LIFO, apparently deciding the benefit of lower income taxes exceeded the cost of reporting lower profits. These tax savings were not trivial. For example, by switching from FIFO to LIFO, DuPont saved more than $200 million in taxes in 1974 and could anticipate greater savings in the future. The savings are real, but they are not permanent. In effect, adopting LIFO allowed DuPont to postpone some of its tax obligations for what might be a very long time.

Which firms did *not* switch to LIFO? Professor Gary Biddle, writing on the editorial page of the *Wall Street Journal*, identified several firms that paid tens of millions of dollars in extra taxes because they did not change from FIFO to LIFO. Why? One possibility suggested tongue in cheek by Biddle is that these firms were very civic-minded and continued using FIFO in order to voluntarily pay extra taxes. Other possible reasons include the high bookkeeping costs of implementing the switch, reluctance by management to make an accounting switch reducing reported income and possibly reducing management bonuses, fear that banks would view the reduction in income unfavorably in loan negotiations, and belief that lower reported income would result in a lower stock price. We cannot know what was in each manager's mind. But we can be sure that some firms were well advised not to switch to LIFO. Even when prices were rising in general, some industries, such as the computer business, faced lower prices. For them, FIFO minimized their tax obligations.

Sources: Gary C. Biddle, "Paying FIFO Taxes: Your Favorite Charity?" Wall Street Journal (January 19, 1981), p. 18; Thomas J. Bray, "More Companies Alter Accounting Methods to Neutralize Inflation," Wall Street Journal (October 7, 1974), p. 1.

Weighted Average

Exhibit 7-4 illustrates that the weighted average costing method produces less extreme results than either LIFO or FIFO relative to both the income statement and the balance sheet. The weighted average is also subject to minimal manipulation by management action. The term *weighted* average can be better understood by assuming Emilio bought two cans rather than one on Monday at 30 cents each. To get the weighted average, we must consider not only the price paid, but also the number purchased as follows:

$$\text{Weighted average} = \text{Cost of goods available for sale} \div \text{Units available for sale}$$
$$\text{Weighted average} = [(2 \times 30¢) + (1 \times 40¢) + (1 \times 56¢)] \div 4$$
$$= 156¢ \div 4$$
$$= 39¢$$

Summarizing the Four Methods

LIFO is the most popular inventory method for large U.S. companies. As we said, about two-thirds of the companies use LIFO for at least *some* of their inventories. Over 60% use FIFO, and 40% use weighted average for a *portion* of their inventories. Less than 10% use any other method, including specific identification. Over half the companies use more than one inventory method.

In a study by the American Institute of Certified Public Accountants, fewer than 25% of the respondents in the following industries used LIFO: electronics, business equipment, ship building, and railway equipment. If tax benefits are so important, why doesn't everyone use LIFO? Recall that LIFO yields lower net income and lower taxes *in a period of rising prices and constant or growing inventories.* One answer is that some industries don't face rising prices. For such industries, FIFO yields lower net income and lower taxes. In electronics, for example, technology has consistently driven prices down. Think back to two decades of constant reductions in prices for radios, stereo systems, clocks, and watches. The situation is similar for business equipment such as word processors and computers. With ship building and railway equipment, specific identification is an appropriate method since each unit is large and expensive.

■ CHARACTERISTICS AND CONSEQUENCES OF LIFO

Objective 6

Explain the meaning and impact of LIFO liquidation and LIFO reserves.

Given the dominant role that LIFO has in inventory accounting in the United States, this section addresses some of the peculiarities of the LIFO inventory method. But remember that LIFO's dominant role is more a result of an inflationary world and tax benefits than any theoretical dominance over other methods. Internationally, LIFO is not common. In many countries—for example, in Brazil and Australia—it is not permitted at all. In Canada it is disallowed for tax purposes. LIFO is a minority practice in many countries. The predominant choice worldwide is an average cost method, and the next most common choice is FIFO.

Holding Gains and Inventory Profits

replacement cost
The cost at which an inventory item could be acquired today.

holding gain (inventory profit)
Increase in the replacement cost or other measure of current value of the inventory held during the current period.

LIFO's income statement orientation provides a reasonable economic interpretation of operating performance in inflationary periods. Consider Emilio. For him to be as well off after selling the can of cola as he was before, he must be able to replace it with the proceeds from his sale. If he must spend 56 cents to replace the can that was sold, we might call 56 cents the **replacement cost** of the inventory. The 26 cent difference between the historical cost of, say, 30 cents (the Monday can) and 56 cents (the Wednesday replacement cost) is called a **holding gain**. This holding gain is sometimes called an **inventory profit**. Because LIFO matches recent acquisition costs with sales revenue, LIFO cost of goods sold typically offers a close approximation to replacement cost, and reported net income rarely contains significant holding gains. The LIFO profit is 90 − 56 = 34 cents. In contrast, recall that using FIFO Emilio reports a profit of 60 cents (90 cents − 30 cents). This profit contains two parts, the economic profit of 34 cents calculated as sales price less replacement costs, plus the inventory profit or holding gain of 26 cents that arose because the value of the inventory item rose with the passage of time.

In commenting on inventory profits, a *Newsweek* article said:

> In an inflationary world, parts acquired for inventory tend to appreciate in value by the time they are used in the manufacturing process. The company then reflects the difference in its selling price—and takes an "inventory profit." It must restock at the new, higher cost, of course, but as long as the inflation continues, so does the inventory-profit process.

LIFO Layers

LIFO layer (LIFO increment) A separately identifiable additional segment of LIFO inventory.

The ending inventory under LIFO may contain prices from many different periods. With Emilio, the ending inventory contained two cans, one acquired on Monday at 30 cents and one acquired on Tuesday for 40 cents. Each distinct element of inventory might be called a **LIFO layer** (also called **LIFO increment**), an identifiable addition to inventory. As a company grows, the LIFO layers tend to pile on top of one another over the years. Suppose Emilio's business grew for years, ending each year with two more cans in inventory than the year before. Each year would have an identifiable LIFO layer, much like the rings that grow on a tree each year. After five years of inventory growth and rising prices, his ending inventory might be structured as follows:

Year 1	layer 1——1 can @.30	
	layer 2——1 can @.40	.70
Year 2	layer 3——2 cans @.45	.90
Year 3	layer 4——2 cans @.50	1.00
Year 4	layer 5——2 cans @.55	1.10
Total inventory		$3.70

Many LIFO companies show inventories that have ancient layers going back as far as 1940, when LIFO was first used. Reported LIFO inventory values may therefore be far below what the true market value or current replacement value of the inventory might be.

LIFO Inventory Liquidations

The existence of old LIFO layers can cause problems if inventory decreases. Examine Exhibit 7-6. Suppose Harbor Electronics bought an inventory of 100 units at $10 per unit on December 31, 19X0. The company bought and sold 100 units each year, 19X1 through 19X4, at the purchase and selling prices shown. The example assumes replacement costs and sales prices rise in tandem with a difference per unit of $3. In 19X5 100 units were sold but none were purchased.

Compare the gross profit each year under LIFO with that under FIFO in Exhibit 7-6. LIFO gross profit is generally less than FIFO gross profit because prices were rising. But what happened in 19X5? The old 19X0 inventory became the cost of goods sold under LIFO because inventory was depleted. Consequently, gross profit under LIFO soared to $1,300, well above the FIFO gross profit, which was stable at $500. In general, when the physical amount of inventory decreases, LIFO charges the cost of old LIFO layers as cost of goods sold, beginning with the most recent layers. This treatment can create a very low cost of goods sold and high gross profit. In a sense a LIFO liquidation means that the cumulative inventory profit from years of increasing prices is reflected in the income statement in one year.

In general, prices have been rising throughout the world for many years. Companies that have been on LIFO for a number of years typically have many LIFO layers, some at unit prices that are relatively old and low. Occasionally, circumstances (such as a prolonged strike or the discontinuance of a segment of the business) call for the liquidation of some or all of the LIFO layers. This decrease in the physical levels of inventories would cause unusually low cost of goods sold, high income, and high income tax expense in comparison with FIFO. For example, LIFO inventory liquidations by Amoco, an international oil company, increased its 1993 net income by $50 million, about 3% of its $1.8 billion income before tax.

| Exhibit 7-6 | Harbor Electronics | | | | | | | | | |

Effect of Inventory Liquidations under LIFO (Purchases and sales of 100 units in 19X1-19X4. Purchases but no sales in 19X0; sales but no purchases in 19X5.)

| Year | Purchase Price Per Unit | Selling Price Per Unit | Revenue | FIFO | | | LIFO | | |
				Cost of Goods Sold	Gross Profit	Ending Inventory	Cost of Goods Sold	Gross Profit	Ending Inventory
19X0	$10	—	—	—	—	$1,000	—	—	$1,000
19X1	12	$15	$ 1,500	$ 1,000	$ 500	1,200	$1,200	$ 300	1,000
19X2	14	17	1,700	1,200	500	1,400	1,400	300	1,000
19X3	16	19	1,900	1,400	500	1,600	1,600	300	1,000
19X4	18	21	2,100	1,600	500	1,800	1,800	300	1,000
19X5		23	2,300	1,800	500	0	1,000	1,300	0
Total			$ 9,500	$7,000	$2,500		$7,000	$2,500	

LIFO reserve The difference between a company's inventory valued at LIFO and what it would be under FIFO.

A company's **LIFO reserve,** which is generally defined as the difference between inventories valued at LIFO and what they would be under FIFO, measures the potential effects of inventory liquidations. Refer to Exhibit 7-6. What is Harbor Electronics' LIFO reserve at the end of 19X1? It is $1,200 – $1,000 = $200, the difference in the LIFO and FIFO ending inventories. Note that it is the same as the difference in gross profit of $200. What about year 19X2? The LIFO reserve is $400 (FIFO ending inventory of $1,400 less LIFO ending inventory of $1,000). This difference represents the cumulative effect on earnings (or gross profit) over the first two years the company was in business. The specific effect on earnings *during* 19X2 is the *change* in the LIFO reserve, or $200. Exhibit 7-7 summarizes these effects.

From Exhibit 7-7 note that the *annual* difference between gross profit using FIFO and that using LIFO is the yearly *change* in the LIFO reserve. Finally, when all of the inventory is sold in 19X5, the liquidation of the LIFO inventory leads to recognition of higher earnings than under FIFO by the amount of the LIFO reserve. LIFO recognizes inventory profits when inventory levels are reduced. The LIFO reserve indicates the *cumulative* gross profit effect over all prior years due to LIFO.

How significant are the effects of LIFO? Ford Motor Company reported 1994 inventory of $6.5 billion. LIFO was used for the U.S. inventories. If FIFO had been used for all inventories, the total inventory would have been $1.4 billion higher (over a 20% difference). This means that over time, Ford has reported lower income on its tax returns and paid lower taxes of approximately $560 million ($1.4 billion times approximately a 40% tax rate) as a result of its decision to use LIFO rather than FIFO.

	Ending Inventory				Gross Profit Effect	
Year	FIFO	LIFO	LIFO Reserve	Change in Reserve	Current	Cumulative
X0	$ 1,000	$ 1,000	$ 0	$ 0	$ 0	$ 0
X1	1,200	1,000	200	200	200	200
X2	1,400	1,000	400	200	200	400
X3	1,600	1,000	600	200	200	600
X4	1,800	1,000	800	200	200	800
X5	0	0	0	(800)	(800)	0

■ LOWER-OF-COST-OR-MARKET METHOD

lower-of-cost-or-market method (LCM) The superimposition of a market-price test on an inventory cost method.

Under the **lower-of-cost-or-market method (LCM)**, a market-price test is run on an inventory costing method. The *current market price* is compared with *historical cost* derived under one of the four primary methods: specific identification, FIFO, LIFO, or average. The lower of the two—current market value or historical cost—is conservatively selected as the basis for the valuation of goods at a specific inventory date. When market value is lower and is used for valuing the ending inventory, the effect is to increase the amount reported as cost of goods sold.

conservatism Selecting the methods of measurement that yield lower net income, lower assets, and lower stockholders' equity in the early years.

LCM is an example of conservatism. **Conservatism** means selecting methods of measurement that yield lower net income, lower assets, and lower stockholders' equity in the early years. Conservatism was illustrated in accounts receivable with the use of an allowance for bad debts. We estimated and recorded losses on uncollectible accounts before they were certain. With inventories, conservatism dictates the use of the LCM method.

Conservatism has been criticized as being inherently inconsistent. If replacement market prices are sufficiently objective and verifiable to substitute for cost when market prices are declining, why are they not sufficient to use when market values are rising? Accountants reply by saying that erring in the direction of conservatism usually has less severe economic consequences than erring in the direction of overstating assets and net income. The accountant's conservatism balances management's optimism. Management prepares the financial statements. The conservatism principle moderates management's human tendency to hope for, and expect, the best.

Objective 7

Explain why the lower-of-cost-or-market method is used to value inventories.

Role of Replacement Cost

Under GAAP, the definition of *market* is complex. For our purposes we will think of it as the *replacement cost* of the inventory item—that is, the cost that would be incurred to buy the inventory item today. Implicit in the method is the assumption that when replacement costs decline in the wholesale market, so do the retail selling prices. Consider the following example. The Ripley Company has 100 units in its ending FIFO inventory on December 31, 19X1. Its gross profit for 19X1 has been tentatively computed as follows:

Sales	$2,180
Cost of goods available for sale	$1,980
Ending inventory of 100 units, at cost	$ 790
Cost of goods sold	$1,190
Gross profit	$ 990

Assume a sudden decline in market prices during the final week of December from $7.90 per unit to $4 per unit. If the lower market price is indicative of lower ultimate sales prices, an inventory **write-down** of ($7.90 – $4.00) ×100 units, or $390, is in order. A write-down is a reduction in carrying value to below cost in response to a decline in value. The required journal entry is:

write-down A reduction in carrying value to below cost in response to a decline in value.

Loss on write-down of inventory (or cost of goods sold)	390	
Inventory		390
To write down inventory from $790 cost to $400 market value.		

The write-down of inventories increases cost of goods sold by $390. Therefore reported income for 19X1 would be lowered by $390:

	Before $390 Write-Down	After $390 Write-Down	Difference
Sales	$2,180	$2,180	
Cost of goods available	$1,980	$1,980	
Ending inventory	790	400	– $390
Cost of goods sold	$1,190	$1,580	+ $390
Gross profit	$ 990	$ 600	– $390

The theory states that of the $790 historical cost, $390 is considered to have expired during 19X1 because the cost cannot be justifiably carried forward to the future as an asset. Furthermore, the decision to purchase was made during 19X1, and the fluctuation in the replacement market price occurred during the same period. This decline in price caused the inventory to lose some value, some revenue-producing power, because the decline in replacement cost generally corresponds to a decline in selling price.

If *selling prices* are not likely to fall, the revenue-producing power of the inventory will be maintained and no write-down would be justified. In sum, if predicted selling prices will be *unaffected* by the fact that current replacement costs are below the carrying cost of the inventory, do nothing. If predicted selling prices will be lower, use replacement cost.

If a write-down occurs, the new $4 per unit replacement cost valuation becomes, for accounting purposes, the unexpired cost of the inventory. Thus, if replacement prices subsequently rise to $8 per unit in January 19X2, no restoration of the December write-down will be permitted. In short, the lower-of-cost-or-market method would regard the December 31 $4 cost as the "new historical cost" of the inventory. Historical cost is the ceiling for valuation under generally accepted accounting principles.

Conservatism in Action

Compared with a pure cost method, the lower-of-cost-or-market method reports less net income in the period of decline in market value of the inventory and more net income in the period of sale. More generally, cumulative net income (the sum of all net income amounts from the inception of the firm to the present date) is never lower and is usually higher under the strict cost method. The lower-of-cost-or-market method affects how much income is reported in each year but not the total income over the company's life. Exhibit 7-8 underscores this point. Suppose the Ripley Company goes out of business in early 19X2. That is, no more units are acquired. There are no sales in 19X2 except for the disposal of the inventory in question at $8 per unit (100 × $8 = $800). Neither combined gross profit nor combined net income for the two periods will be affected by the LCM method, as the bottom of Exhibit 7-8 reveals.

Exhibit 7-8		Cost Method		Lower-of-Cost-or-Market Method	
The Ripley Company Effects of Lower-of-Cost-or-Market		**19X1**	**19X2**	**19X1**	**19X2**
	Sales	$2,180	$800	$2,180	$800
	Cost of goods available	$1,980	$790	$1,980	$400
	Ending inventory	790	—	400*	—
	Cost of goods sold	$1,190	$790	$1,580	$400
	Gross profit	$ 990	$ 10	$ 600	$400

Combined gross profit for two years:
   Cost method: $990 + $10 = $1,000
   Lower-of-cost-or-market method: $600 + $400 = $1,000

* The inventory is shown here after being written down by $390, from $790 to $400. For internal purposes, many accountants prefer to show the write-down separately, presenting a gross profit before write-down of inventory, the write-down, and a gross profit after write-down.

This example shows that conservatism can be a double-edged sword in the sense that net income in a current year will be hurt by a write-down of inventory (or any asset), and net income in a future year will be helped by the amount of the write-down. As Exhibit 7-8 illustrates, 19X2 income is $390 higher because of the $390 write-down of 19X1.

A full-blown lower-of-cost-or-market method is rarely encountered in practice. Why? Because it is expensive to get the correct replacement costs of hundreds or thousands of different products in inventory. Still, auditors definitely feel that the costs of inventories should be fully recoverable from future revenues. Therefore auditors inevitably make market-price tests of a representative sample of the ending inventories. In particular, auditors want to write down the subclasses of inventory that are obsolete, shopworn, or otherwise of only nominal value.

■ EFFECTS OF INVENTORY ERRORS

Inventory errors can arise from many sources. Examples are wrong physical counts (possibly because goods that are in receiving or shipping areas instead of the inventory stockroom were omitted when physical counts were made) and clerical errors.

An undiscovered inventory error usually affects two reporting periods. It is counterbalanced by the ordinary accounting process in the next period. That is, the error affects income by identical offsetting amounts. An undiscovered inventory error affects the balance sheet at the end of the first period but not at the end of the second. For example, suppose ending inventory in 19X7 is understated by $10,000 because of errors in the physical count. The year's cost of goods sold would be overstated, pretax income understated, assets understated, and retained income understated.

These effects are easier to understand when a complete illustration is studied. Consider the following income statements (all numbers are in thousands), which assume ending 19X7 inventory is reported to be $10 too low.

19X7	Correct Reporting		Incorrect Reporting*		Effects of Errors
Sales		$ 980		$ 980	
Deduct: Cost of goods sold:					
Beginning inventory	$ 100		$ 100		
Purchases	500		500		
Cost of goods available for sale	$ 600		$ 600		
Deduct: Ending inventory	70		60		Understated by $10
Cost of goods sold		530		540	Overstated by $10
Gross profit		$ 450		$ 440	Understated by $10
Other expenses		250		250	
Income before income taxes		$ 200		$ 190	Understated by $10
Income tax expense at 40%		80		76	Understated by $4
Net income		$ 120		$ 114	Understated by $6
Ending balance sheet items:					
Inventory		$ 70		$ 60	Understated by $10
Retained income includes current net income of		120		114	Understated by $6
Income tax liability†		80		76	Understated by $4

* Because of error in ending inventory.
† For simplicity, assume that the entire income tax expense for the year will not be paid until the succeeding year. Therefore the ending liability will equal the income tax expense.

Think about the effects of the uncorrected error on the following year, 19X8. The beginning inventory will be $60,000 rather than the correct $70,000. Therefore *all* the errors in 19X7 will be offset by counterbalancing errors in 19X8. Thus the retained income at the end of 19X8 would show a cumulative effect of zero. This is because the net income in 19X7 would be understated by $6,000, but the net income in 19X8 would be overstated by $6,000.

The point to stress is that the ending inventory of one period is also the beginning inventory of the succeeding period. Assume that the operations during 19X8 are a duplication of those of 19X7 except that the ending inventory is correctly counted as $40,000. Note the role of the error in the beginning inventory.

19X8	Correct Reporting	Incorrect Reporting*	Effects of Errors
Sales	$ 980	$980	
Deduct: Cost of goods sold:			
Beginning inventory	$ 70	$ 60	Understated by $10
Purchases	500	500	
Cost of goods available for sale	$ 570	$ 560	Understated by $10
Deduct: Ending inventory	40	40	
Cost of goods sold	530	520	Understated by $10
Gross profit	$ 450	$ 460	Overstated by $10
Other expenses	250	250	
Income before income taxes	$ 200	$ 210	Overstated by $10
Income tax expense at 40%	80	84	Overstated by $4
Net income	$120	$126	Overstated by $6
Ending balance sheet items:			
Inventory	$ 40	$ 40	Correct
Retained income includes:			
Net income of previous year	120	114	Counterbalanced and
Net income of current year	120	126	thus now correct in total
Two-year total	240	240	
Income tax liability:			
End of previous year	80	76	Counterbalanced and
End of current year	80	84	thus now correct in total[†]
Two-year total	160	160	

* Because of error in beginning inventory.
† The $84 really consists of the $4 that pertains to income of the previous year plus $80 that pertains to income of the current year.

The complete illustration shows the full detail of the inventory error, but we can use the accounting equation to develop our intuition. A useful generalization is: If ending inventory is understated, retained income is understated. If ending inventory is overstated, retained income is overstated. These relations are clear from the accounting equation. The presence of taxes means only that the effects need to be considered in two parts. Understated inventory implies overstated cost of goods sold and therefore lower current-year income and lower taxes. The shortcut analysis follows:

	A	=	L	+	SE
	Inventory		Income Tax Liability		Retained Income
Effects of error	$10,000 understated	=	$4,000 understated	+	$6,000 understated*

* Cost of goods overstated $10,000
Pretax income understated $10,000
Income taxes understated   4,000
Net income, which is included in ending retained income, understated $ 6,000

■ THE IMPORTANCE OF GROSS PROFITS

As we have seen, gross profits are the result of sales revenue less the cost of goods sold as determined by one of the accounting methods for inventory valuation. Management and investors are intensely interested in gross profit and its changes. Will gross profits be large enough to cover operating expenses and produce a net income?

Gross Profit Percentage

Objective 9

Explain the uses of the gross profit percentage and inventory turnover measures.

Gross profit is often expressed as a percentage of sales. Consider the following information on a past year for a typical Safeway grocery store:

	Amount	Percentage
Sales	$10,000,000	100%
Net cost of goods sold	7,500,000	75%
Gross profit	$ 2,500,000	25%

The *gross profit percentage*—gross profit divided by sales—here is 25%. The following illustrates the extent to which gross profit percentages vary among industries.

Industry	Gross Profit (%)
Auto retailers	12.3
Auto manufacturers	17.6
Jewelry retailers	47.6
Grocery retailers	22.6
Grocery wholesalers	16.1
Drug manufacturers	40.8

Source: Robert Morris Associates, *Financial Statement Studies for 1994*.

wholesaler An intermediary that sells inventory items to retailers.

retailer A company that sells items directly to the final users, individuals.

The gross profit percentages range from a low of 12.3% to a high of 47.6%. Several patterns are evident. **Wholesalers** sell in larger quantity and incur fewer selling costs because they sell to other companies rather than individuals. As a result of competition and high volumes, they have smaller gross profit percentages than **retailers**. Retailers sell directly to individuals. Among retailers, jewelers have twice the gross profits of grocers because of expensive inventory and extensive personal selling. High gross profit percentages for drug manufacturers derive from patent protection and the need for substantial research and development outlays (up to 15% of sales). In contrast, auto manufacturers face more direct competition and earn lower gross profit percentages.

Estimating Intraperiod Gross Profit and Inventory

Exact ending inventory balances are not usually available for monthly or quarterly reports. The physical count required for an exact inventory count and accurate cost of goods sold calculation is too costly to obtain other than for year-end annual statements and reports. Interim reports thus use estimates derived from percentage or ratio methods. When the actual ending inventory is unavailable for monthly and quarterly financial statements, the gross profit percentage is often used to estimate the amount.

For example, assume that past sales of Tip Top Variety Store have usually resulted in a gross profit percentage of 25%. (Unless otherwise stated, any gross profit percentage given is based on net sales, not cost.) The accountant would estimate gross profit to be 25% of sales. If the monthly sales are $800,000, the cost of goods sold can be estimated as follows:

$$\text{Sales} - \text{Cost of goods sold} = \text{Gross profit}$$
$$S - CGS = GP$$
$$\$800,000 - CGS = 0.25 \times \$800,000 = \$200,000$$
$$CGS = \$600,000$$

If we know Tip Top's beginning inventory is $30,000 and purchases are $605,000, we can estimate ending inventory to be $35,000 as follows:

$$\text{Beginning inventory} + \text{Purchases} - \text{Ending inventory} = CGS$$
$$BI + P - EI = CGS$$
$$\$30,000 + \$605,000 - EI = \$600,000$$
$$EI = \$35,000$$

In retailing, profit margins may be expressed as "markups" on cost. When an item costing $60 is sold for $80 it is a 25% profit margin as defined in this accounting text, but marketing professionals might call it a 33⅓% markup on cost ($20 markup ÷ $60 cost).

Gross Profit Percentage and Turnover

inventory turnover
The cost of goods sold divided by the average inventory held during the period.

Retailers often attempt to increase total profits by increasing sales levels. They lower prices and hope to increase their gross profits by selling their inventories more quickly, replenishing, selling again, and so forth. Managers speak of improving their **inventory turnover**, which is defined as cost of goods sold divided by the average inventory held during a given period. Average inventory is usually the sum of beginning inventory and ending inventory divided by 2. For the Tip Top Variety Store, the average inventory is ($30,000 + $35,000) ÷ 2 = $32,500. The inventory turnover is computed as follows:

$$\text{Turnover} = \text{Cost of goods sold} \div \text{Average inventory}$$
$$= \$600,000 \div \$32,500 = 18.5$$

Suppose the inventory sells twice as quickly if prices are lowered. With a 5% reduction in sales price, sales revenue on the current level of business drops from $800,000 to (0.95 × $800,000), or $760,000. But twice as many units are sold, so total revenue becomes 2 × $760,000, or $1,520,000. How profitable is Tip Top? Cost of goods sold doubles from $600,000 to $1,200,000. Total gross profit is $320,000. The inventory turnover doubles: $1,200,000 divided by $32,500 (the unchanged average inventory) is 36.9. However, the gross profit percentage falls from 25% to 21% ($320,000 divided by $1,520,000).

Is the company better off? Maybe. Certainly, in the current month gross profit has risen. However, strategic questions remain. *Is this new sales level maintainable?* For some products, when prices fall, consumers sharply increase purchases and stockpile the extras for later consumption. There is little increase in underlying demand, just a shift of future purchases to the present.

Another strategic question is, *What will the competition do?* If Tip Top's increased sales came at a competitor's expense, the competitor's response may be a similar decrease in prices. The competition might recover most of its old customers, with each buying a little more at the new price than at the old. But the whole market would see, not a doubling of sales, but perhaps a 20% sales growth. Tip Top would be worse off in the aggregate; the 20% growth would not cover the 5% price reduction.

Exhibit 7-9 illustrates two principles. Panel A shows that if a firm can increase inventory turnover while maintaining a constant gross profit percentage, it should do so. However, as shown in panel B, if the increased inventory turnover results from a decrease in sales price, the gross margin percentage may fall. The desirability of the change depends on whether the sales gain could offset the decreased margin. In the Tip Top Variety Store example, when a 5% price reduction produces a 20% increase in units sold, the new gross margin of $192,000 is still less than the initial $200,000. Dropping the price is not justified even though the inventory turnover rises to 22.2 from 18.5. However, at a 50% increase in sales volume, the new gross margin of $240,000 exceeds the original $200,000.

Exhibit 7-9

Tip Top Variety Store
Effects of Increased Inventory Turnover (in thousands)

		Unit Sales Increase		
Panel A	Original	20%	50%	100%
No change in sales price				
Sales	$ 800	$ 960	$1,200	$ 1,600
Cost of goods sold (75%)	600	720	900	1,200
Gross margin (25%)	$ 200	$ 240	$ 300	$ 400
Inventory turnover	18.5	22.2	27.7	36.9
Panel B				
5% reduction in sales price				
Sales (95% of above)	$ 760	$ 912	$1,140	$ 1,520
Cost of goods sold (as above)	600	720	900	1,200
Gross margin (21% of sales)	$ 160	$ 192	$ 240	$ 320
Inventory turnover (as above)	18.5	22.2	27.7	36.9

The industry variability in gross margin percentages referred to earlier is also reflected in inventory turnover percentages.

Industry	Gross Profit (%)	Inventory Turnover
Grocery wholesalers	16.1	14.7
Grocery retailers	22.6	16.9
Drug manufacturers	40.8	3.3
Jewelry retailers	47.6	1.4

Source: Robert Morris Associates, *Financial Statement Studies for 1994.*

The data are ordered from lowest gross profit percentage to highest for the industries displayed. There is a tendency for the inventory turnovers to move in the opposite direction.

When ratios are being calculated it is important to keep the accounting methods in mind. Consider the following data for Ford Motor Company:

Ford Motor
Company
($ in millions)

| | 1994 Inventory | | | Cost of |
	Beginning	Ending	Average	Goods Sold
LIFO	$5,538	$6,487	$6,012.5	$96,180
LIFO Reserve	1,342	1,383	1,362.5	
FIFO	$6,880	$7,870	$7,375.0	$96,139

Using reported LIFO results for Ford Motor Company, we can calculate the inventory turnover and gross profit percentages (sales of $107,137 million) to be:

LIFO

Gross profit percentage: (107,137 − 96,180) ÷ 107,137 = 10.23%

Inventory turnover: 96,180 ÷ 6,012.5 = 16.00

FIFO

Gross profit percentage: (107,137 − 96,139) ÷ 107,137 = 10.27%

Inventory turnover: 96,139 ÷ 7,375.0 = 13.04

LIFO tends to *decrease* the gross profit percentage and to *increase* the inventory turnover relative to FIFO. Why? Because, under LIFO, cost of goods sold is usually greater and inventory values are lower.

Adjusting from LIFO to FIFO

Ford Motor Company uses LIFO and therefore reports higher cost of goods sold and lower inventory levels than it would if FIFO were used. Ford reports the *LIFO reserve* to aid analysts in understanding this difference. The LIFO reserve concept was illustrated on page 288 for Harbor Electronics. Here we use the Ford data to extend our understanding. Note that Ford's LIFO reserve increased from $1,342 million to $1,383 million during the year. This increase of $41 million in the LIFO reserve is exactly the amount by which the cost of goods sold for the year under LIFO exceeds the cost of goods sold under FIFO ($96,180 million − $96,139 million = $41 million, see above).

Why is the LIFO cost of goods sold higher? Because costs are rising and under LIFO the new higher costs flow directly to the cost of goods sold reported in the earnings statement. In contrast, under FIFO the new higher costs flow into ending inventory, while older lower costs are used to calculate cost of goods sold. Cumulatively, this process has happened year after year for Ford. We can use the LIFO reserve to answer two questions. The *change* in the LIFO reserve from one year to the next answers the question "How much did this year's LIFO cost of goods sold differ from what the cost of goods sold would have been if FIFO were used?" In contrast, the end of year *level* of the LIFO reserve is the answer to the question "During the years that Ford has used LIFO, what has the total, cumulative effect been on cost of goods sold over all those years?" To see this, do the mental experiment of having Ford sell all of its 1994 year-end inventory for $10,000 million. This complete *liquidation* would produce *higher* profits under LIFO. These higher profits in the final liquidation year are equal to the cumulative amount by which gross profits were lower under LIFO in past years. The hypothetical liquidation of Ford inventories would show:

	LIFO	FIFO	Difference
Sales	$10,000	$10,000	—
Cost of goods sold	6,487	7,870	(1,383)
Gross profit	$ 3,513	$ 2,130	1,383

Gross Profit Tests

Auditors, including those from the Internal Revenue Service (IRS), use the gross profit percentage to help satisfy themselves about the accuracy of records. For example, the IRS compiles gross profit percentages by types of retail establishment. If a company shows an unusually low percentage compared with similar companies, IRS auditors may suspect that the taxpayer has failed to record all cash sales. Similarly, managers watch changes in gross profit percentages to judge operating profitability and to monitor how well employee theft and shoplifting are being controlled.

Suppose an internal revenue agent, a manager, or an outside auditor had gathered the following data for a particular jewelry company for the past three years (in millions):

	19X3	19X2	19X1
Net sales	$350	$300	$300
Cost of goods sold	210	150	150
Gross profit	$140	$150	$150
Gross profit percentage	40%	50%	50%

gross profit test
The comparing of gross profit percentages to detect any phenomenon worth investigating.

These data illustrate a **gross profit test** whereby the gross profit percentages are compared to detect any phenomenon worth investigating. Obviously, the decline in the percentage might be attributable to many factors. Possible explanations include the following:

1. Competition has intensified, resulting in intensive price wars that reduced selling prices.
2. The mix of goods sold has shifted so that, for instance, the $350 million of sales in 19X3 is composed of relatively more products bearing lower gross margins (e.g., more costume jewelry bearing low margins and less diamond jewelry bearing high margins).
3. Shoplifting or embezzling has soared out of control. For example, a manager may be pocketing and not recording cash sales of $70 million. After all, sales in 19X3 would have been $210 × 2 = $420 million if the past 50% margin had been maintained.

Reports to Shareholders

The importance of gross profits to investors is demonstrated in the following example based on a quarterly report to shareholders of Superscope, Inc., a real-life manufacturer and distributor of stereophonic equipment that encountered rocky times. The following condensed income statement was presented for a three-month period (in thousands):

	Current Year	Previous Year
Net sales	$ 40,000	$40,200
Cost and expenses:		
Cost of sales	33,100	28,200
Selling, general, and administrative	11,200	9,900
Interest	2,000	1,200
Total costs and expenses	46,300	39,300
Income (loss) before income tax provision (benefit)	(6,300)	900
Income tax provision (benefit)	(3,000)	200
Net income (loss)	$ (3,300)	$ 700

Although the statement does not show the amount of gross profit, the gross profit percentages can readily be computed as ($40,000 − $33,100) ÷ $40,000 = 17% and ($40,200 − $28,200) ÷ $40,200 = 30%. To show how seriously these percentages are considered, the chairman's letter to shareholders began as follows:

> I shall attempt herein to provide you with a candid analysis of the Company's present condition, the steps we have instituted to overcome current adversities, and the potential which we believe can, in due course, be realized by the Company's realistic positive determination to regain profitability.
> In the second quarter the Company's gross profit margins decreased to 17% compared to 30% in the corresponding quarter of a year ago. For the first six months gross profit margins were 22%, down from 31% for the corresponding period of a year ago.
> Essentially, the gross profits and consequential operating losses in the second quarter, as reflected in the condensed financial statements appearing in this report, resulted from lower than anticipated sales volume and from the following second quarter factors: liquidation of our entire citizens band inventory; increases in dealer cash discounts and sales incentive expenses; gross margin reductions resulting from sales of slow moving models at less than normal prices; and markdown of slow moving inventory on hand to a realistic net realizable market value.

Summary Problems for Your Review

Problem One

Examine Exhibit 7-10. The company uses the periodic inventory system. Using these facts, prepare a columnar comparison of income statements for the year ended December 31, 19X2. Compare the FIFO, LIFO, and weighted-average inventory methods. Assume that other expenses are $1,000. The income tax rate is 40%.

Exhibit 7-10

Facts for Summary
Problem One

	Purchases	Sales	Inventory
December 31, 19X1			200 @ $5 = $1,000
January 25	170@ $6 = $1,020		
January 29		150*	
May 28	190@ $7 = $1,330		
June 7		230*	
November 20	150@ $8 = $1,200		
December 15		100*	
Total	510	$3,550	480*
December 31, 19X2			230 @ ?

* Selling prices were $9, $11, and $13,
respectively, providing total sales of:

			Summary of costs:	
	150 @ $ 9 = $1,350	Beginning inventory	$ 1,000
	230 @ $11 = $2,530	Purchases	$ 3,550
	100 @ $13 = $1,300	Cost of goods available	
Total sales	480 $5,180	for sale	$4,550

Exhibit 7-11   Comparison of Inventory Methods for the Year Ended December 31, 19X2

	FIFO		LIFO		Weighted Average
Sales, 480 units		$5,180		$5,180	$5,180
Deduct cost of goods sold:					
Beginning inventory, 200 @ $5		$ 1,000		$ 1,000	$ 1,000
Purchases, 510 units (from Exhibit 7-10)*		3,550		3,550	3,550
Available for sale, 710 units †		$4,550		$4,550	$4,550
Ending inventory, 230 units ‡					
150 @ $8	$1,200				
80 @ $7	560	1,760			
or					
200 @ $5			$1,000		
30 @ $6			180	1,180	
or					
230 @ $6.408					1,474
Cost of goods sold, 480 units		2,790		3,370	3,076
Gross profit		$ 2,390		$1,810	$2,104
Other expenses		1,000		1,000	1,000
Income before income taxes		$ 1,390		$ 810	$1,104
Income taxes at 40%		556		324	442
Net income		$ 834		$ 486	$ 662

*Always equal across all three methods.
†These amounts will not be equal in general across the three methods because beginning inventories will generally be different. They are equal here only because beginning inventories were assumed to be equal.
‡Under FIFO, the ending inventory is composed of the last purchases plus the second-last purchases, and so forth, until the costs of 230 units are compiled. Under LIFO, the ending inventory is composed of the beginning inventory plus the earliest purchases of the current year until the costs of 230 units are compiled. Under weighted average, the ending inventory and cost of goods sold are accumulations based on a unit cost. The latter is the cost of goods available for sale divided by the number of units available for sale: $4,550 ÷ 710 = $6.408.

Solution to Problem One

See Exhibit 7-11.

Problem Two

"When prices are rising, FIFO results in fool's profits because more resources are needed to maintain operations than previously." Do you agree? Explain.

Solution to Problem Two

The merit of this position depends on the concept of income favored. LIFO gives a better measure of "distributable" income than FIFO. Recall the Emilio's Cola Sales example in the chapter (Exhibit 7-4, p. 280). The gross profit under FIFO was 60 cents, and under LIFO it was 34 cents. The 60¢ – 34¢ = 26¢ difference is a fool's profit because it must be reinvested to maintain the same inventory level as previously. It arises from a profit on holding inventory as prices change rather than from buying at wholesale and selling at retail. Therefore the 26 cents cannot be distributed as a cash dividend without reducing the current level of operations.

Problem Three

Fay's Incorporated operates about 260 super drugstores in the Northeast and 321 stores in total, including a chain of discount auto supply stores and 29 Paper Cutter stores. Some results for fiscal 1994 were (in thousands):

Sales	$919,719
Cost of merchandise sold	649,078
Net earnings	5,223
Beginning merchandise inventory	137,896
Ending merchandise inventory	153,627

Required

1. Calculate the 1994 gross profit and gross profit percentage for Fay's Incorporated.
2. Calculate the inventory turnover ratio.
3. What gross profit would have been reported if inventory turnover in 1994 had been 7, the gross profit percentage calculated in requirement 1 had been achieved, and the level of inventory was unchanged?

Solution to Problem Three

1. Gross profit = Sales – Cost of merchandise sold

= $919,719 – $649,078

= $270,641

Gross profit percentage = Gross profit ÷ Sales

= $270,641 ÷ $919,719

= 29.4%

2. Inventory turnover = Cost of merchandise sold ÷ Average merchandise inventory

$$= \$649,078 \div [(\$137,896 + \$153,627) \div 2]$$

$$= \$649,078 \div \$145,762$$

$$= 4.45$$

3. Cost of merchandise sold = Inventory turnover × Average merchandise inventory

$$= 7 \times \$145,762$$

$$= \$1,020,334$$

Gross profit percentage = (Sales − Cost of merchandise sold) ÷ Sales

$$29.4\% = (S − \$1,020,334) \div S$$

$$0.294 \times S = S − \$1,020,334$$

$$S − (0.294 \times S) = \$1,020,334$$

$$S \times (1 − 0.294) = \$1,020,334$$

$$S = \$1,020,334 \div (1 − 0.294)$$

$$S = \$1,445,232$$

Gross profit = Sales − Cost of merchandise sold

$$= \$1,445,232 − \$1,020,334$$

$$= \$424,898$$

The increase in inventory turnover from 4.45 to 7.0 would raise gross profit from $270,641 to $424,898.

Problem 4

At the end of 19X1, a $1,000 error was made in the physical inventory so the inventory value was understated. The error went undetected. The subsequent inventory at the end of 19X2 was done correctly. Assess the effect of this error on income before tax, taxes, net income, and retained earnings for 19X1 and 19X2, assuming a 40% tax rate.

Solution to Problem 4

First calculate the effect on Cost of Goods Sold.

	19X1	19X2
Beginning Inventory	ok	too low
Purchases	ok	ok
Goods available for sale	ok	too low
Ending Inventory	too low	ok
Cost of goods sold	too high	too low

Note that 19X1 Ending Inventory becomes 19X2 Beginning Inventory, reversing the effects on Cost of Goods Sold.

The 19X1 Cost of Goods Sold being too high causes 19X1 income before tax to be too low by $1,000. Therefore taxes will be too low by .40 × $1,000 = $400 and net income will be too low by $600, causing retained income to be too low by $600 also.

In 19X2 the effects reverse and by year's end retained income is correctly stated.

Highlights to Remember

Inventory accounting involves allocating the cost of goods available for sale between cost of goods sold and ending inventory as of the balance sheet date. Under the *perpetual* system, this allocation occurs continually; cost of goods sold is recorded for each sale. Under the *periodic* system, the allocation occurs via an adjusting entry at year end. A physical inventory is conducted under either system. The goods on hand are counted, and a cost is calculated for each item from purchase records. The cost of an item of inventory includes not only the purchase price but also inward transportation costs.

Under the *periodic* system the physical inventory is the basis for the year-end adjusting entry to recognize cost of goods sold. Under the perpetual system the physical inventory is used to confirm the accounting records. Differences, if any, lead to adjustments to cost of goods sold and ending inventory. Adjustments reflect inventory shrinkage due to theft, spoilage, damage, and so on, or to accounting errors in the perpetual records.

Valuation of inventories involves the assignment of specific historical costs of acquisition either to units sold or to units on hand. Four major inventory valuation methods are in use: specific identification, weighted average, FIFO, and LIFO. When prices are rising and inventories are constant or growing, less income is shown by LIFO than by FIFO. LIFO liquidation refers to the relatively higher profits generated under LIFO when reductions in inventory levels cause older, lower inventory costs to be used in calculating cost of goods sold. Notice that even with declining inventories, with rising costs the *cumulative* taxable income is always less under LIFO than FIFO because the inventory valuation is less and the cumulative cost of goods sold is higher.

LIFO is popular in the United States among companies who face rising prices, for whom lower profits under LIFO mean lower taxes. The U.S. tax law contains a conformity requirement that allows LIFO for tax purposes only if it is used also for financial reporting purposes.

Conservatism leads to the lower-of-cost-or-market method, which treats cost as the maximum value of inventory. Inventory is reduced to replacement cost (with a corresponding increase in cost of goods sold) when acquisition prices fall below historical cost levels.

The nature of accrual accounting for inventories creates a self-correcting quality about errors in counting or valuing the ending inventory. This occurs because the ending inventory in one period becomes the beginning inventory of the subsequent period.

Financial analysts and managers use gross profit percentages as a measure of profitability and inventory turnover as a measure of efficient asset use. These measures are compared with prior levels to examine trends and with current levels of other industry members to assess relative performance.

Appendix 7: Inventory in a Manufacturing Environment

In the chapter, inventory accounting is covered from the viewpoint of a wholesaler or retailer, companies that acquire their inventory by purchase from another company. When a company *manufactures* products, the cost of inventory is a combination of the acquisition cost of raw material, the wages paid to workers who combine the raw materials into finished products, and an allocation of the costs of space, energy, and equipment used by the workers as they transform the various elements into a finished product.

Consider how costs are accumulated in a manufacturing environment for Packit, a company that makes backpacks. The raw materials are heavy fabric, glue, and thread. The transformation occurs when workers use cutters to make the panels that other workers sew and glue together. The costs of manufacture include depreciation on the manufacturing building, depreciation on the sewing machines and cutters, and utilities to support the effort in the form of heat, power, and light. The finished goods are backpacks.

The accounting process is easiest to understand when calculating the cost of a complete year of production. In the example below, 100,000 backpacks are produced during Packit's first year at a total cost of $800,000, providing a cost per backpack of $8.00 each ($800,000 ÷ 100,000 units). At year end, if all have been sold, the financial statements would include $800,000 in cost of goods sold.

Calculation of cost of manufacturing for a year's production of 100,000 backpacks:

Beginning inventory	—
Fabric purchased and used	$200,000
Wages paid to workers	300,000
Thread and glue used	50,000
Depreciation on building and equipment	220,000
Utilities	30,000
Total Costs to Manufacture	$800,000
Cost per backpack ($800,000 ÷ 100,000)	$8.00

In the above example, all of the materials acquired during the year are transformed into finished products before year end and sold. In fact, if we take a snapshot of the typical backpack manufacturer at year end we would observe bolts of fabric, spools of thread and gallons of glue waiting to be put into production. We call these items held for use in the manufacturing of a product **raw material inventory.** In addition we would also observe fabric already cut but not assembled and some partially completed backpacks.

raw material inventory Includes the cost of materials held for use in the manufacturing of a product.

We refer to the material, labor and other costs accumulated for partially completed items as **work in process inventory**. When manufacture is complete and the goods are ready to deliver to customers, the inventory is called **finished goods inventory**. The accounting system for managing these costs is illustrated in Exhibit 7-12 for the second year of production of our backpack manufacturer. During this second year 120,000 backpacks are completed and 110,000 are sold. Some remain in the assembly process at year end, and unused fabric thread and glue are held in preparation for future production.

work in process inventory Includes the cost incurred for partially completed items, including raw materials, labor, and other costs.

The schematic in Exhibit 7-12 captures the production process. You might think of each of the accounts as corresponding to a physical reality. The raw material is stored in a locked room, ready for use. The work-in-process is located in the production room and as it is finished it is physically transfered to a storage site. When goods are sold they are removed from that storage site and are given to the customer in exchange for cash or an account receivable. Raw materials, work-in-process, and finished goods are all forms of inventory and appear on the balance sheet as current assets. They are simply in different stages of completion. The act of sale converts the asset into an expense to be reported on the income statement. At year end, Packit will show total inventory on its year 2 balance sheet of $126,000, as follows:

finished goods inventory The accumlulated costs of manufacture for goods that are complete and ready for sale.

Raw Materials Inventory	$25,000
Work in Process Inventory	22,000
Finished Goods Inventory	79,000
Total Inventory	$126,000

Exhibit 7-12

Packit Company
Accounting for
Manufacturing
Costs

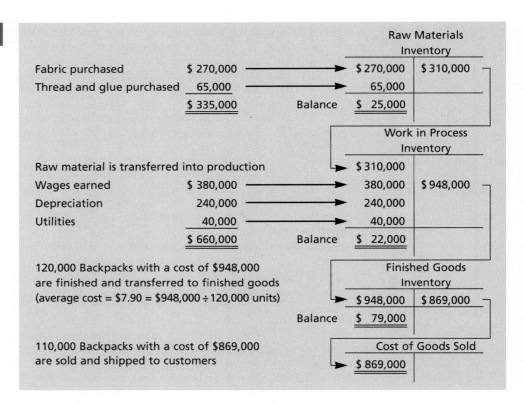

The summary journal entries to record these events for year 2 would be:

```
Purchase of raw material:
    Raw material inventory  . . . . . . . . . . . . .   335,000
        Accounts payable  . . . . . . . . . . . . .              335,000
Production activity:
    Work in process inventory  . . . . . . . . . . .   310,000
        Raw materials inventory  . . . . . . . . .              310,000
    Work in process inventory  . . . . . . . . . . .   660,000
        Wages payable  . . . . . . . . . . . . . . .              380,000
        Accumulated depreciation  . . . . . . .              240,000
        Utilities payable  . . . . . . . . . . . . . .               40,000
Completion of production:
    Finished goods inventory  . . . . . . . . . . . .   869,000
        Work in process inventory . . . . . . . .              869,000
```

Accounting Vocabulary

conservatism, *p. 288*
consistency, *p. 281*

cost of goods available for sale,
     p. 292

cost valuation, *p. 270*
finished goods inventory, *p. 303*

Assignment Material

Questions

7-1. "There are two major steps in accounting for inventories at year end." What are they?

7-2. Distinguish between *F.O.B. destination* and *F.O.B. shipping point*.

7-3. "Freight out should be classified as a direct offset to sales, not as an expense." Do you agree? Explain.

7-4. What are the two phases of accounting for a sales transaction?

7-5. Distinguish between the *perpetual* and *periodic* inventory systems.

7-6. "An advantage of the perpetual inventory system is that a physical count of inventory is unnecessary. The periodic method requires a physical count to compute cost of goods sold." Do you agree? Explain.

7-7. Name the four inventory cost flow assumptions or valuation methods that are generally accepted in the United States. Give a brief phrase describing each.

7-8. What is *consistency*, and why is it an important accounting principle?

7-9. "An inventory profit is a fictitious profit." Do you agree? Explain.

7-10. LIFO produces absurd inventory valuations. Why?

7-11. "Purchases of inventory at the end of a fiscal period can have a direct effect on income under LIFO." Do you agree? Explain.

7-12. "There is a single dominant reason why more and more U.S. companies have adopted LIFO." What is the reason?

7-13. "Conservatism always results in lower reported profits." Do you agree? Explain.

7-14. "Accountants have traditionally favored taking some losses but no gains before an asset is exchanged." What is this tradition or convention called?

7-15. What does *market* mean in inventory accounting?

7-16. "The lower-of-cost-or-market method is inherently inconsistent." Do you agree? Explain.

7-17. Express the cost of goods sold section of the income statement as an equation.

7-18. "Gross profit percentages help in the preparation of interim financial statements." Explain.

7-19. "Inventory errors are counterbalancing." Explain.

7-20. If a company uses a FIFO cost flow assumption, will it report the same cost of goods sold using the periodic inventory method that it reports using the perpetual method? Why or why not?

7-21. Assume that the physical level of inventory is constant at the beginning and end of year and that the cost of inventory items is rising. Which will produce a higher ending inventory value, LIFO or FIFO?

7-22. Will LIFO or FIFO produce higher cost of goods sold during a period of *falling* prices? Explain.

7-23. Which of the following items would a company be likely to account for using a perpetual inventory system and the specific identification inventory method?

a. Corporate jet aircraft   **e.** Timex watches

b. Large sailboats   **f.** Automobiles

c. Pencils   **g.** Books

d. Diamond rings   **h.** Compact discs

Exercises

7-24   Gross Profit Section

Given the following, prepare a detailed gross profit section for Ramon's Jewelry Wholesalers for the year ended December 31, 19X1 (in thousands):

Cash discounts on purchases	$ 6	Cash discounts on sales	$ 5
Sales returns and allowances	40	Purchase returns and	
Gross purchases	650	allowances	27
Merchandise inventory,		Merchandise inventory,	
December 31, 19X0	103	December 31, 19X1	180
Gross profit	360	Freight in	50

7-25   Gross Margin Computations and Inventory Costs

On January 15, 19X4, Ruth Burton valued her inventory at cost, $40,000. Her statements are based on the calendar year, so you find it necessary to establish an inventory figure as of January 1, 19X4. You find that from January 2 to January 15, sales were $71,000; sales returns, $2,100; goods purchased and placed in stock, $54,000; goods removed from stock and returned to suppliers, $2,000; freight in, $500. Calculate the inventory cost as of January 1, assuming that goods are priced to provide a 23% gross profit.

7-26   Journal Entries

Castellon Inc., had sales of $24 million during the year. The goods cost Castellon $16 million. Give the journal entry or entries at the time of sale under the perpetual and the periodic inventory systems.

7-27   Valuing Inventory and Cost of Goods Sold

Hurman Ltd., had the following inventory transactions during the month of January.

1/1 beginning inventory,	4,000 units @ $2.00	$ 8,000
week 1, purchases	2,000 units @ $2.10	4,200
week 2, purchases	3,000 units @ $2.20	6,600
week 3, purchases	1,000 units @ $2.30	2,300
week 4, purchases	1,000 units @ $2.40	2,400

On January 31, a count of the ending inventory was completed, and 5,500 units were on hand. Using the periodic inventory system, calculate the cost of goods sold and ending inventory using LIFO, FIFO, and weighted-average inventory methods.

7-28   Entries for Purchase Transactions

The Vanhonacker Company is a Swiss wholesaler of small giftware. Its unit of currency is the Swiss franc (Sfr.). Vanhonacker uses a periodic inventory system. Prepare journal entries for the following summarized transactions (omit explanations):

Aug.   2 Purchased merchandise, Sfr. 300,000, terms 2/10, n/45.

Aug.   3 Paid cash for freight in, Sfr. 10,000.

Aug.   7 Vanhonacker complained about some defects in the merchandise acquired on August 2. The supplier hand-delivered a credit memo granting an allowance of Sfr. 20,000.

Aug. 11 Cash disbursement to settle purchase of August 2.

7-29   Cost of Inventory Acquired

On July 5, Solanski Company purchased on account a shipment of sheet steel from Oregon Steel Co. The invoice price was $ 160,000, F.O.B. shipping point. Shipping cost from the steel mill to Solanski's plant was $12,000. When inspecting the shipment, Neisha, the Solanski receiving clerk, found several flaws in the steel. Neisha informed Oregon's sales representative of the flaws, and after some negotiation, Oregon granted an allowance of $16,000.

To encourage prompt payment, Oregon grants a 2% cash discount to customers who pay their accounts within thirty days of billing. Solanski paid the proper amount on August 1.

Required

1. Compute the total cost of the sheet steel acquired.
2. Prepare the journal entries for the transaction. Omit explanations.

7-30   Entries for Periodic and Perpetual Systems

Viteri Co. had an inventory of $250,000, December 31, 19X1. Data for 19X2 follow:

Gross purchases	$960,000
Cost of goods sold	920,000
Inventory, December 31, 19X2	200,000
Purchase returns and allowances	90,000

Required

Using the data, prepare comparative journal entries, including closing entries, for a perpetual and a periodic inventory system.

7-31   Entries for Purchase Transactions

Winbush Landscape Wholesalers uses a periodic inventory system. Prepare journal entries for the following summarized transactions for 19X2 (omit explanations). For simplicity, assume that the beginning and ending balances in accounts payable were zero.

1. Purchases (all using trade credit), $900,000.
2. Purchase returns and allowances, $60,000.
3. Freight in, $72,000 paid in cash.
4. Cash discounts on purchases, $10,000.

7-32   Closing Entries, Periodic Inventory System

Refer to the data in the preceding problem. Inventories were: December 31, 19X1, $81,000; December 31, 19X2, $130,000. Sales were $1,300,000. Prepare the closing journal entries, December 31, 19X2. Omit explanations.

7-33   Closing Entries, Periodic Inventory System

Consider the following data taken from the adjusted trial balance of the Silva Company, December 31, 19X3 (in millions):

Purchases	$125	Sales	$244
Sales returns and allowances	5	Purchase returns and	
Freight in	14	allowances	6
Cash discounts on purchases	1	Cash discounts on sales	8
Inventory (beginning of year)	25	Other expenses	80

Required

Prepare the closing journal entries. The ending inventory was $30 million.

7-34 Reconstruction of Transaction

Apple Computer, Inc., produces the well-known Macintosh computer. Consider the following account balances (in thousands):

	September 30	
	1994	**1993**
Inventories	$355,473	$475,377

Required

The purchases of inventories during the 1994 fiscal year were $2,486,319,000. The income statement had an item "cost of sales." Compute its amount.

7-35 Reconstruction of Records

An earthquake caused heavy damage to the Bebop Record Store on May 3, 19X1. All the merchandise was destroyed. Some accounting data are missing. In conjunction with an insurance investigation, you have been asked to estimate the cost of the inventory destroyed. The following data for 19X1 are available:

Cash discounts on purchases	$ 1,000	Inventory, December 31, 19X0	$ 19,000
Gross sales	140,000	Purchase returns and allowances	4,000
Sales returns and allowances	12,000	Inward transportation	3,000
Gross purchases	80,000	Gross profit percentage on net sales	45%

7-36 Cost of Inventory Destroyed by Fire

E. Ravelo requires an estimate of the cost of merchandise lost by fire on March 9. Merchandise inventory on January 1 was $70,000. Purchases since January 1 were $190,000; freight in, $28,000; purchase returns and allowances, $10,000. Sales are made at a gross margin of 20% of *sales* and totaled $200,000 up to March 9. What was the cost of the merchandise destroyed?

7-37 Inventory Shortage

An accounting clerk of the Bettis Company absconded with cash and a truck full of the entire electronic merchandise on May 14, 19X2. The following data have been compiled:

Beginning inventory, January 1	$ 80,000
Sales to May 14, 19X2	280,000
Average gross profit rate	25%
Purchases to May 14, 19X2	180,000

Required

Compute the estimated cost of the missing merchandise.

7-38 Inventory Errors

At the end of his first business year, Irving counted and priced the inventory. A few very high-value items were hidden in a dark corner of the storage shelves and Irving understated his 1995 inventory by $10,000. His business financial statements and his tax return were affected. Assume a 40% tax rate.

Required

1. Calculate the effect on taxable income, taxes, net income, and retained earnings for 1995.

2. Repeat requirement 1 for 1996, assuming the 1996 ending inventory is correctly calculated.

7-39 Decision about Pricing

Rivera Jewelers, Inc., a retail jewelry store, had gross profits of $880,000 on sales of $1,600,000 in 19X3. Average inventory was $720,000.

Required

1. Compute inventory turnover.
2. Jaime Rivera is considering whether to become a "discount" jeweler. For example, Jaime believes that a cut of 20% in average selling prices would have increased turnover to 1.5 times per year. Beginning and ending inventory would be unchanged. Suppose Jaime's beliefs are valid. Would the gross profit in 19X3 have improved? Show computations.

7-40 LIFO and FIFO

The inventory of the Childers Chat Company on June 30 shows 1,000 tons at $9 per ton. A physical inventory on July 31 shows a total of 1,200 tons on hand. Revenue from sales of gravel for July totals $98,000. The following purchases were made during July:

July 8	5,000 tons @ $10 per ton
July 13	1,000 tons @ $11 per ton
July 22	1,100 tons @ $12 per ton

Required

1. Compute the inventory cost as of July 31, using (a) LIFO and (b) FIFO.
2. Compute the gross profit, using each method.

7-41 Lower-of-Cost-or-Market

(A lternate is 7-67.) Saeki Company uses the inventory method "cost or market, whichever is lower." There were no sales or purchases during the periods indicated, although selling prices generally fluctuated in the same directions as replacement costs. At what amount would you value merchandise on the dates listed below?

	Invoice Cost	Replacement Cost
December 31, 19X1	$200,000	$180,000
April 30, 19X2	200,000	190,000
August 31, 19X2	200,000	220,000
December 31, 19X2	200,000	165,000

7-42 Reconstruction of Transactions

Consider the following account balances of Nike, maker of athletic wear (in thousands):

	May 31,	
	1994	1993
Inventories	$470,023	$592,986

Required

The income statement for the fiscal year included the item "cost of sales" of $2,301,423. Compute the net cost of the acquisition of inventory for the 1994 fiscal year.

7-43   Profitability and Turnover

Dano's Garden Supply began 19X1 with inventory of $170,000. Dano's 19X1 sales were $800,000, purchases of inventory totaled $680,000, and ending inventory was $230,000.

Required

1. Prepare a statement of gross profit for 19X1.
2. What was Dano's inventory turnover?

Problems   7-44   **Detailed Income Statement**

(Alternate is 7-47.) Following are accounts taken from the adjusted trial balance of the Myrick Building Supply Company, December 31, 19X5. The company uses the periodic inventory system. Prepare a detailed income statement for 19X5. All amounts are in thousands:

Sales salaries and commissions	$160	Freight in	$ 50
Inventory, December 31, 19X4	200	Miscellaneous expenses	13
Allowance for bad debts	14	Sales	1,080
Rent expense, office space	10	Bad debts expense	8
Gross purchases	600	Cash discounts on purchases	15
Depreciation expense, office equipment	3	Inventory, December 31, 19X5	325
Cash discounts on sales	10	Office salaries	60
Advertising expense	40	Rent expense, selling space	90
Purchase returns and allowances	40	Income tax expense	44
Delivery expense	20	Sales returns and allowances	50
		Office supplies used	6
		Depreciation expenses, trucks, and store fixtures	29

7-45   Perpetual Inventory Calculations

Park Electric is a wholesaler for commercial builders. The company uses a perpetual inventory system and a FIFO cost-flow assumption. The data concerning QuiteQuiet Switches for the year 19X2 follows:

	Purchased		Sold	Balance
December 31, 19X1				110 @ $5 = $550
February 10, 19X2	80 @ $6 =	$ 480		
April 14			60	
May 9	110 @ $7 =	$ 770		
July 14			120	
October 21	100 @ $8 =	$ 800		
November 12			80	
Total	290	$2,050	260	

Required   Calculate the ending balance in units and dollars.

7-46   Gross Profit and Turnover

Retailers closely watch a number of financial ratios, including the gross profit (gross margin) percentage and inventory turnover. Suppose the results for the furniture department in a large store in a given year were:

Sales	$3,000,000
Cost of goods sold	1,800,000
Gross profit	$1,200,000
Beginning inventory	$ 650,000
Ending inventory	550,000

Required

1. Compute the gross profit percentage and the inventory turnover.
2. Suppose the retailer is able to maintain a reduced inventory of $450,000 throughout the succeeding year. What inventory turnover would have to be obtained to achieve the same $1,200,000 gross profit? Assume that the gross profit percentage is unchanged.
3. Suppose the retailer maintains inventory at the $450,000 level throughout the succeeding year but cannot increase the inventory turnover from the level in requirement 1. What gross profit percentage would have to be obtained to achieve the same total gross profit?
4. Suppose the average inventory of $600,000 is maintained. Compute the total gross profit in the succeeding year if there is

   a. A 10% increase of the gross profit *percentage* (that is, 10% of the percentage, not an additional ten percentage points) and a 10% decrease of the inventory turnover; or

   b. A 10% decrease of the gross profit percentage and a 10% increase of the inventory turnover.

5. Why do retailers find the above types of ratios helpful?

7-47   Detailed Income Statement
(Alternate is 7-44.) Hartmarx Corporation is a clothing company with many retail outlets, including Country Miss and Kuppenheimer. The company's annual report contained the following actual data for the year ended November 30, 19X1 (in thousands):

Net sales	$1,310,126
Cost of goods sold	806,237
Selling, administrative, and occupancy expenses	492,147
Other expenses (net)	106,552
Profit (or loss) before tax	$ (94,810)

The balance sheets included the following actual data (in thousands of dollars):

	November 30	
	19X1	19X0
Allowance for doubtful accounts	$ 13,980	$ 12,755
Inventories	409,599	473,999

Consider the following additional assumed data (in thousands of dollars):

Bad debts expense	$ 5,400	Freight in	$ 32,000
Gross purchases	737,837	Advertising expense	29,000
Cash discounts on sales	10,000	Sales returns and allowances	35,000
Sales salaries and compensation	279,747	Depreciation expense	26,000
Purchase returns and		Cash discounts on purchases	4,000
allowances	24,000	Rent expense	100,000
Freight out	52,000	Miscellaneous other	
		expenses (net)	106,552

Required

Prepare a detailed multistep income statement that ends with profit (or loss) before tax. You need not subclassify the selling, administrative, and occupancy expenses into three separate categories.

7-48 Comparison of Inventory Methods

(Alternates are 7-60 and 7-62.) The Caen Co. is a wholesaler for commercial builders. The company uses a periodic inventory system. The data concerning Airvent Grill RD8 for the year 19X2 follow:

	Purchases	Sold	Balance
December 31, 19X1			110 @ $5 = $550
February 10, 19X2	80 @ $6 = $480		
April 14		60	
May 9	120 @ $7 = $840		
July 14		120	
October 21	100 @ $8 = $800		
November 12		80	
Total	300 $2,120	260	
December 31, 19X2			150 @ ?

The sales during 19X2 were made at the following selling prices:

60 @ $ 8=	$ 480
120 @ 10 =	1,200
80 @ 11 =	880
260	$2,560

Required

1. Prepare a comparative statement of gross profit for the year ended December 31, 19X2, using FIFO, LIFO, and weighted-average inventory methods.
2. By how much would income taxes differ if Caen used LIFO instead of FIFO for Airvent Grill RD8? Assume a 40% income tax rate.

7-49 Effects of Late Purchases

(Alternates are 7-61 and 7-63.) Refer to the preceding problem. Suppose 100 extra units had been acquired on December 30 for $8 each, a total of $800. How would net income and income taxes have been affected under FIFO? under LIFO? Show a tabulated comparison.

7-50   LIFO, FIFO, and Lower-of-Cost-or-Market

DRP Company began business on March 15, 19X0. The following are DRP's purchases of inventory.

March 17	100 units @ $10	$1,000
April 19	50 units @ $12	600
May 14	100 units @ $13	1,300
Total		$2,900

On May 25, 140 units were sold, leaving inventory of 110 units. DRP Company's accountant was preparing a balance sheet for June 1, at which time the replacement cost of the inventory was $12 per unit.

Required

1. Suppose DRP Company uses LIFO, without applying lower-of-cost-or-market. Compute the June 1 inventory amount.
2. Suppose DRP Company uses lower-of-LIFO-cost-or-market. Compute the June 1 inventory amount.
3. Suppose DRP Company uses FIFO, without applying lower-of-cost-or-market. Compute the June 1 inventory amount.
4. Suppose DRP Company uses lower-of-FIFO-cost-or-market. Compute the June 1 inventory amount.

7-51   Inventory Errors

(Alternate is 7-58.) The following data are from the 19X1 income statement of the Woolen Carpet Stores (in thousands):

Sales		$1,600
Deduct Cost of goods sold:		
Beginning inventory	$ 390	
Purchases	720	
Cost of goods available for sale	$1,110	
Deduct: Ending inventory	370	
Cost of goods sold		740
Gross profit		$ 860
Other expenses		610
Income before income taxes		$ 250
Income tax expense at 40%		100
Net income		$ 150

The ending inventory was overstated by $30,000 because of errors in the physical count. The income tax rate was 40% in 19X1 and 19X2.

Required

1. Which items in the income statement are incorrect? By how much? Use *O* for overstated, *U* for understated, and *N* for not affected. Complete the following tabulation:

	19X1	19X2
Beginning inventory	N	0 $30
Ending inventory	?	?
Cost of goods sold	?	?
Gross margin	?	?
Income before income taxes	?	?
Income tax expense	?	?
Net income	?	?

2. What is the dollar effect of the inventory error on retained income at the end of 19X1? at the end of 19X2?

7-52 LIFO, FIFO, Prices Rising and Falling

The Romero Company has a periodic inventory system. Inventory on December 31, 19X1, consisted of 10,000 units @ $10 = $100,000. Purchases during 19X2 were 13,000 units. Sales were 12,000 units for sales revenue of $20 per unit.

Required Prepare a four-column comparative statement of gross margin for 19X2:

1. Assume purchases were at $12 per unit. Assume FIFO and then LIFO.
2. Assume purchases were at $8 per unit. Assume FIFO and then LIFO.
3. Assume an income tax rate of 40%. Suppose all transactions were for cash. Which inventory method in requirement 1 would result in more cash for Romero Company? by how much?
4. Repeat requirement 3. Which inventory method in requirement 2 would result in more cash for Romero Company? by how much?

7-53 LIFO, FIFO, Cash Effects

In 19X2, Inverness Company had sales revenue of £ 370,000 for a line of woolen scarves. The company uses a periodic inventory system. Pertinent data for 19X2 included:

Inventory, December 31, 19X1	14,000 units @ £ 6	£ 84,000
January purchases	20,000 units @ £ 7	140,000
July purchases	32,000 units @ £ 8	256,000
Sales for the year	30,000 units	

Required

1. Prepare a statement of gross margin for 19X2. Use two columns, one assuming LIFO and one assuming FIFO.
2. Assume a 40% income tax rate. Suppose all transactions were for cash. Which inventory method would result in more cash for Inverness Company? by how much?

7-54 FIFO and LIFO

Two companies, the LIFO Company and the FIFO Company, are in the scrap metal warehousing business as arch competitors. They are about the same size and in 19X1 coincidentally encountered seemingly identical operating situations. Only their inventory accounting systems differed.

Their beginning inventory was 10,000 tons; it cost $50 per ton. During the year, each company purchased 50,000 tons at the following prices:

- 20,000 @ $60 on March 17
- 30,000 @ $70 on October 5

Each company sold 45,000 tons at average prices of $100 per ton. Other expenses in addition to cost of goods sold but excluding income taxes were $650,000. The income tax rate is 40%.

Required

1. Compute net income for the year for both companies. Show your calculations.
2. As a manager, which method would you prefer? Why? Explain fully. Include your estimate of the overall effect of these events on the cash balances of each company, assuming that all transactions during 19X1 were direct receipts or disbursements of cash.

7-55   Effects of LIFO and FIFO

The GHS Company is starting in business on December 31, 19X0. In each *half year*, from 19X1 through 19X4, it expects to purchase 1,000 units and sell 500 units for the amounts listed below. In 19X5, it expects to purchase no units and sell 4,000 units for the amount indicated in the following table:

	19X1	19X2	19X3	19X4	19X5
Purchases:					
First 6 months	$ 2,000	$ 4,000	$ 6,000	$ 6,000	0
Second 6 months	4,000	9,000	6,000	8,000	0
Total	$ 6,000	$13,000	$12,000	$14,000	0
Sales (at selling price)	$10,000	$10,000	$10,000	$10,000	$40,000

Assume that there are no costs or expenses other than those shown above. The tax rate is 40%, and taxes for each year are payable on December 31 of each year. GHS Company is trying to decide whether to use periodic FIFO or LIFO throughout the five-year period.

Required

1. What was net income under FIFO for each of the five years? under LIFO? Show calculations.
2. Explain briefly which method, LIFO or FIFO, seems more advantageous, and why.

➤ 7-56   Effects of LIFO on Purchase Decisions

The Bihan Corporation is nearing the end of its first year in business. The following purchases of its single product have been made:

	Units	Unit Price	Total Cost
January	1,000	$10	$ 10,000
March	1,000	10	10,000
May	1,000	11	11,000
July	1,000	13	13,000
September	1,000	14	14,000
December	4,000	15	60,000
	9,000		$118,000

Sales for the year will be 5,000 units for $120,000. Expenses other than cost of goods sold will be $20,000.

The president is undecided about whether to adopt FIFO or LIFO for income tax purposes. The company has ample storage space for up to 7,000 units of inventory. Inventory prices are expected to stay at $15 per unit for the next few months.

Required

1. What would be the net income before taxes, the income taxes, and the net income after taxes for the year under (a) FIFO and (b) LIFO? Income tax rates are 30% on the first $25,000 of net taxable income and 50% on the excess.

2. If the company sells its year-end inventory in Year 2 @ $24 per unit and goes out of business, what would be the net income before taxes, the income taxes, and the net income after taxes under (a) FIFO and (b) LIFO? Assume that other expenses in Year 2 are $20,000.
3. Repeat requirements 1 and 2, assuming that the 4,000 units @ $15 purchased in December were not purchased until January of the second year. Generalize on the effect on net income of the timing of purchases under FIFO and LIFO.

7-57   Changing Quantities and LIFO Reserve
Consider the following data for the year 19X2:

	Units	Unit Cost
Beginning inventory	2	*
Purchases:	3	24
	3	28
Ending inventory	2	†

* FIFO, $20; LIFO, $16.
† To be computed.

Required

1. Prepare a comparative table computing the cost of goods sold, using columns for FIFO and LIFO. In a final column, show (a) the difference between FIFO and LIFO inventories (the LIFO reserve) at the beginning of the year and at the end of the year, and (b) how the *change* in this amount explains the difference in cost of goods sold.
2. Repeat requirement 1, except assume that the ending inventory consisted of (a) three units, (b) zero units.
3. In your own words, explain why, for a given year, the increase in the LIFO reserve measures the amount by which cost of goods sold is higher under LIFO than FIFO.

7-58   Inventory Errors, Three Years
(Alternate is 7-51.) The Rohm Company had the accompanying data for three successive years (in millions):

	19X3	19X2	19X1
Sales	$200	$160	$175
Deduct Cost of goods sold:			
Beginning inventory	15	25	40
Purchases	135	100	90
Cost of goods available for sale	150	125	130
Ending inventory	30	15	25
Cost of goods sold	120	110	105
Gross profit	80	50	70
Other expenses	70	30	30
Income before income taxes	10	20	40
Income tax expense at 40%	4	8	16
Net income	$ 6	$ 12	$ 24

In early 19X4, a team of internal auditors discovered that the ending inventory for 19X1 had been overstated by $20 million. Furthermore, the ending inventory for 19X3 had been understated by $10 million. The ending inventory for December 31, 19X2, was correct.

Required

1. Which items in the income statement are incorrect? by how much? Prepare a tabulation covering each of the three years.

2. Is the amount of retained income correct at the end of 19X1, 19X2, and 19X3? If it is erroneous, indicate the amount and whether it is overstated (*O*) or understated (*U*).

7-59   Review of Chapters 1-7. Adjusting and Correcting Entries
Examine the accompanying Unadjusted Trial Balance as of December 31, 19X2.

Mantle Cloak
Company
Unadjusted Trial
Balance
December 31, 19X2

Account	Debit	Credit
1. Cash	$ 5,000	
2. Note receivable	1,000	
3. Accounts receivable	10,300	
4. Allowance for bad debts		$ 300
5. Inventory balance, as of January 1, 19X2	20,000	
6. Unexpired insurance	600	
7. Office supplies on hand	400	
8. Unexpired rent		
9. Equipment	4,000	
10. Accumulated depreciation, equipment		500
11. Accounts payable		10,000
12. Long-term 8% mortgage payable		3,000
13. Accrued interest payable		
14. Accrued wages payable		
15. Mantle capital		18,500
16. Sales		130,000
17. Sales returns	1,000	
18. Cash discounts on sales	1,000	
19. Purchases	81,000	
20. Purchase returns		1,000
21. Wages	22,000	
22. Rent and heat	10,000	
23. Bad debts expense		
24. Other operating expenses	7,000	
25. Supplies expense		
26. Insurance expense		
27. Depreciation		
28. Interest expense		
	$163,300	$163,300

For each of the following items 1 through 12 prepare the necessary entries. Select only from the accounts listed in the Trial Balance. The same account may be used in several answers. Answer by using account *numbers* and indicating the dollar amounts of debits and credits. For example, item 1 would call for a debit to Cash (1) for $200, a debit to Equipment (9) for $300, and a credit to Mantle Capital (15) for $500. (*Note:* The accounts that carry no balances are listed in the table for your convenience in making adjustments. All accounts needed to answer the questions are included.)

Required

1. On December 30, the owner invested $200 in cash plus equipment valued at $300. The bookkeeper has not recorded the transaction.

2. It is estimated that the Allowance for Bad Debts should be *increased* by an amount equal to 0.5% of 19X2 gross sales.

3. A correct entry was made, early in December, for $500 worth of goods sold to a customer on open account. The customer returned these goods on December 29. The bookkeeper has made no entry for the latter transaction, although a credit memo was issued, December 31.

4. Unexpired insurance was $450 on December 31, 19X2.

5. The interest on the mortgage is payable yearly on January 2. (Adjust for a *full year's* interest. Do not refine the arithmetic for one or two days' interest.)

6. There was a $1,000 payroll robbery on December 15. Wages had been debited for $1,000 and Cash credited for $1,000 for the original payroll. A substitute payroll was made up on December 16, Wages again debited for $1,000, and Cash again credited for $1,000. However, the loss was covered by insurance. On December 20, the insurance company remitted $1,000, and the Mantle bookkeeper debited Cash and credited Sales.

7. The equipment cost is being allocated to operations on the basis of an estimated useful life of ten years and no residual value.

8. Mantle withdrew $500 in cash on December 31. The bookkeeper has not recorded the transaction.

9. A $400 rental charge for January 19X3 was paid in cash to the DiMaggio Realty Company on December 31. The Mantle Company bookkeeper did not record the transaction.

10. Wages of salesclerks earned, but not paid, amount to $100.

11. A physical count of the office supplies revealed that there is a balance of $250 on hand as of December 31, 19X2.

12. On December 20, a customer paid the Mantle Company $980 for a $1,000 invoice, deducting a 2% discount. The bookkeeper made the appropriate entries. On December 30, Mr. Mantle discovered that the customer should have paid the full $1,000 because the discount period had expired on December 17. He sent the customer another invoice for the extra $20. The bookkeeper has not recorded the last transaction.

7-60 Comparison of Inventory Methods
(Alternates are 7-48 and 7-62.) Unisys Corporation is a producer of computer-based information systems. The following actual data and descriptions are from the company's fiscal 1993 annual report (in millions):

	December 31	
	1993	1992
Inventories	$753.9	$873.8

A footnote states: "Inventories are valued at the lower of cost or market. Cost is determined principally on the first-in, first-out method."
The income statement for the fiscal year ended December 31, 1993, included (in millions):

Net revenue from sales, service, and maintenance	$7,742.5
Cost of products sold, service, and maintenance	4,844.3

Assume that Unisys used the periodic inventory system. Suppose a division of Unisys had the accompanying data regarding the use of its computer parts that it acquires and resells to customers for maintaining equipment (dollars are *not* in millions):

	Units	Total
Inventory (December 31, 1993)	100	$400
Purchase (February 20, 1994)	200	1,000
Sales, March 17, 1994 (at $9 per unit)	150	
Purchase (June 25, 1994)	160	960
Sales, November 7, 1994 (at $10 per unit)	160	

Required

1. For these computer parts only, prepare a tabulation of the cost of goods sold section of the income statement for the year ended December 31, 1994. Support your computations. Round totals to the nearest dollar. Show your tabulation for four different inventory methods: (a) FIFO, (b) LIFO, (c) weighted-average, and (d) specific identification.

   For requirement *d*, assume that the purchase of February 20 was identified with the sale of March 17. Also assume that the purchase of June 25 was identified with the sale of November 7; the additional units sold were identified with the beginning inventory.

2. By how much would income taxes differ if Unisys used (a) LIFO instead of FIFO for this inventory item? (b) LIFO instead of weighted-average? Assume a 40% tax rate.

7-61   Effects of Late Purchases

(Alternates are 7-49 and 7-63.) Refer to the preceding problem. Suppose Unisys acquired 60 extra units @ $7 each on December 29, 1994, a total of $420. How would gross profit and income taxes be affected under FIFO? That is, compare FIFO results before and after the purchase of 60 extra units. Under LIFO? That is, compare LIFO results before and after the purchase of 60 extra units. Show computations and explain.

7-62   Comparison of Inventory Methods

(Alternates are 7-48 and 7-60.) Texas Instruments is a major producer of semiconductors and other electrical and electronic products. Semiconductors are especially vulnerable to price fluctuations. The following actual data and descriptions are from the company's annual report (in millions):

	December 31	
	1994	1993
Inventories	$882	$822

Texas Instruments uses a variety of inventory methods, but for this problem assume that only FIFO is used.

Net revenues for the fiscal year ended December 31, 1994, were $10,315 million. Cost of revenues was $7,471 million.

Assume that Texas Instruments had the accompanying data regarding one of its semiconductors. Assume a periodic inventory system.

	In	Out	Balance
December 31, 1993			80 @ $5 = 400
February 25, 1994	50 @ $6 = $ 300		
March 29		60* @ ?	
May 28	80 @ $7 = $ 560		
June 7		90* @ ?	
November 20	90 @ $8 = $ 720		
December 15		50* @ ?	
Total	220 $1,580	200	
December 31, 1994			100 @ ?

* Selling prices were $9, $11, and $13, respectively:

	60 @ $ 9 = $ 540	
	90 @ 11 = 990	
	50 @ 13 = 650	
Total sales	200 $2,180	

Summary of costs to account for:

Beginning inventory	$ 400
Purchases	1,580
Cost of goods available for sale	$1,980
Other expenses for this product	$ 500
Income tax rate, 40%	

Required

1. Prepare a comparative income statement for the 1994 fiscal year for the product in question. Use the FIFO, LIFO, and weighted-average inventory methods.
2. By how much would income taxes have differed if Texas Instruments had used LIFO instead of FIFO for this product?
3. Suppose Texas Instruments had used the specific identification method. Compute the gross margin (or gross profit) if the ending inventory had consisted of (a) 90 units @ $8, and 10 units @ $7; and (b) 60 units @ $5, and 40 units @ $8.

7-63   Effects of Late Purchases
(Alternates are 7-49 and 7-61.) Refer to the preceding problem. Suppose Texas Instruments had acquired 50 extra units @ $8 each on December 30, 1994, a total of $400. How would income before income taxes have been affected under FIFO? That is, compare FIFO results before and after the purchase of 50 extra units. Under LIFO? That is, compare LIFO results before and after the purchase of 50 extra units. Show computations and explain.

7-64   Classic Switch From LIFO to FIFO
Effective January 1, 1970, Chrysler Corporation adopted the FIFO method for inventories previously valued by the LIFO method. The 1970 annual report stated: "This... makes the financial statements with respect to inventory valuation comparable with those of the other United States automobile manufacturers."

The *Wall Street Journal* reported:

The change improved Chrysler's 1970 financial results several ways. Besides narrowing the 1970 loss by $20 million it improved Chrysler's working capital. The change also made the comparison with 1969 earnings look somewhat more favorable because, upon restatement, Chrysler's 1969 profit was raised by only $10.2 million from the original figures.

Finally, the change helped Chrysler's balance sheet by boosting inventories, and thus current assets, by $150 million at the end of 1970 over what they would have been under LIFO. As Chrysler's profit has collapsed over the last two years and its financial position tightened, auto analysts have eyed warily Chrysler's shrinking ratio of current assets to current liabilities.

To get the improvements in its balance sheet and results, however, Chrysler paid a price. Roger Helder, vice president and comptroller, said Chrysler owed the government $53 million in tax savings it accumulated by using the LIFO method since it switched from FIFO in 1957. The major advantage of LIFO is that it holds down profit and thus tax liabilities. The other three major auto makers stayed on the FIFO method. Mr. Helder said Chrysler now has to pay back that $53 million to the government over 20 years, which will boost Chrysler's tax bills about $3 million a year.

Required Given the content of this text chapter, do you think the Chrysler decision to switch from LIFO to FIFO was beneficial to its stockholders? Explain, being as specific as you can.

7-65 LIFO, FIFO, Purchase Decisions, and Earnings Per Share
Pete's Pots, a company with one million shares of common stock outstanding, had the following transactions during 19X1, its first year in business:

Sales:	1,000,000 units @ $5
Purchases:	800,000 units @ $2
	300,000 units @ $3

The current income tax rate is a flat 50%; the rate next year is expected to be 40%.

It is December 20 and Pete, the president, is trying to decide whether to buy the 600,000 units he needs for inventory now or early next year. The current price is $4 per unit. Prices on inventory are expected to remain stable; in any event, no decline in prices is anticipated.

Pete has not chosen an inventory method as yet, but will pick either LIFO or FIFO. Other expenses for the year will be $1.4 million.

Required
1. Using LIFO, prepare a comparative income statement assuming the 600,000 units (a) are not purchased, (b) are purchased. The statement should end with reported earnings per share.
2. Repeat requirement 1, using FIFO.
3. Comment on the above results. Which method should Pete choose? Why? Be specific.
4. Suppose that in Year 2 the tax rate drops to 40%, prices remain stable, 1 million units are sold @ $5, enough units are purchased at $4 so that the ending inventory will be 700,000 units, and other expenses are reduced to $800,000.

   a. Prepare a comparative income statement for the second year showing the impact of each of the four alternatives on net income and earnings per share for the second year.

   b. Explain any differences in net income that you encounter among the four alternatives.

   c. Why is there a difference in ending inventory values under LIFO even though the same amount of physical inventory is in stock?

   d. What is the total cash outflow for income taxes for the two years together under the four alternatives?

   e. Would you change your answer in requirement 3 now that you have completed requirement 4? Why?

7-66 Eroding the LIFO Base

Many companies on LIFO are occasionally faced with strikes or material shortages that necessitate a reduction in their normal inventory levels in order to satisfy current sales demands. A few years ago several large steel companies requested special legislative relief from the additional taxes that ensued from such events.

A news story stated:

> As steelworkers slowly streamed back to the mills this week, most steel companies began adding up the tremendous losses imposed by the longest strike in history. At a significant number of plants across the country, however, the worry wasn't losses but profits—"windfall" bookkeeping profits that for some companies may mean painful increases in corporate income taxes.
>
> These outfits have been caught in the backfire of a special mechanism for figuring up inventory costs on tax returns. It's known to accountants as LIFO, or last in, first out. Ironically, it's designed to slice the corporate tax bill in a time of rising prices.
>
> *Biggest Bite*—Most of the big steel companies—16 out of the top 20—as well as 40 percent of all steel warehousers, use LIFO accounting in figuring their taxes. But the tax squeeze from paper LIFO profits won't affect them all equally. It will put the biggest bite on warehousers that kept going during the strike—and as a result, the American Steel Warehouse Assn. may ask Congress for a special tax exemption on these paper profits....
>
> Companies such as Ryerson and Castle have been caught because they have had to strip their shelves bare in order to satisfy customer demands during the strike. And they probably won't be able to rebuild their stocks by the time they close their books for tax purposes.

To see how this situation can happen, consider the following example. Suppose a company adopted LIFO in 1976. At December 31, 1996, its LIFO inventory consisted of three "layers":

From 1976:	100,000 units @ $1.00	$100,000
From 1977:	50,000 units @ 1.10	55,000
From 1978:	30,000 units @ 1.20	36,000
		$191,000

In 1997, prices rose enormously. Data follow:

Sales	500,000 units @ $3.00 = $1,500,000
Purchases	340,000 units @ $2.00 = $ 680,000
Operating expenses	500,000

A prolonged strike near the end of the year resulted in a severe depletion of the normal inventory stock of 180,000 units. The strike was settled on December 28, 1997. The company intended to replenish the inventory as soon as possible.

The applicable income tax rate is 60%.

Required

1. Compute the income taxes for 1997.
2. Suppose the company had been able to meet the 500,000-unit demand out of current purchases. Compute the income taxes for 1997 under those circumstances.

7-67   Lower-of-Cost-or-Market

(Alternate is 7-41.) Polaroid Corporation's annual report stated: "Inventories are valued on a first-in, first-out basis at the lower of cost or market value." Assume that severe price competition in 1995 necessitated a write-down on December 31 for a class of camera inventories with a cost of $11 million. The appropriate valuation at market was deemed to be $8 million.

Suppose the product line was terminated in early 1996 and the remaining inventory was sold for $8 million.

Required

1. Assume that sales of this line of camera for 1995 were $19 million and cost of goods sold was $14 million. Prepare a statement of gross margin for 1995 and 1996. Show the results under a strict FIFO cost method in the first two columns and under a lower-of-FIFO-cost-or-market method in the next two columns.
2. Assume that Polaroid did not discontinue the product line. Instead a new marketing campaign spurred market demand. Replacement cost of the cameras in the December 31 inventory was $9 million on January 31, 1996. What inventory valuation would be appropriate if the inventory of December 31, 1995, was still held on January 31, 1996?

7-68   LIFO Liquidation

Maytag Corporation reported 1993 pretax income of $89,870,000. Footnotes to Maytag's financial statements read: "Inventories are stated at the lower of cost or market. Cost is determined by the last-in, first-out (LIFO) method for 79% of the company's inventory.... If the first-in, first-out (FIFO) method of inventory accounting, which approximates current cost, had been used, inventories would have been $76.3 million and $78.1 million higher than reported at December 31, 1993 and 1992, respectively."

Required

1. Calculate the pretax income that Maytag would have reported if the FIFO inventory method had been used.
2. Suppose Maytag's income tax rate is 34%. What were Maytag's income taxes using LIFO? What would they have been if Maytag had used FIFO?
3. How could Maytag have avoided the extra taxes?

7-69   LIFO Reserve

Brunswick Corporation reported inventories of $321.4 million on its 1993 balance sheet. A footnote to the financial statements indicated that if "the FIFO method of inventory accounting had been used by the Company for inventories valued at LIFO, inventories would have been $73.9 million higher than reported."

Required

1. Has the cost of Brunswick's inventory generally been increasing or decreasing? Explain.
2. Suppose Brunswick sold its entire inventory for $500 million in 1994 and did not replace it. Compute the gross profit from the sale of this inventory (a) as Brunswick would report it using LIFO and (b) as it would have been reported if Brunswick had always used FIFO instead of LIFO. Which inventory method creates higher 1994 gross profit? Explain.

7-70   Inventory Errors

IBM had inventories of $8.3 billion at December 31, 1993, and $9.2 billion one year earlier.

Required

1. Suppose the beginning inventory for fiscal 1993 had been overstated by $50 million because of errors in physical counts. Which items in the financial statements would be incorrect? By how much? Use O for overstated, U for understated, and N for not affected. Assume a 40% tax rate.

| | Effect on Fiscal Year | |
	1993	1992
Beginning inventory	O by $50	N
Ending inventory	?	?
Cost of sales	?	?
Gross profit	?	?
Income before taxes on income	?	?
Taxes on income	?	?
Net income	?	?

2. What is the dollar effect of the inventory error on retained earnings at the end of fiscal 1992? 1993?

7-71   LIFO Liquidation

(Bob Libby, adapted) The inventory footnote taken from the 1990 annual report of PACCAR is printed below. PACCAR reported Income Before Income Taxes of $46,105,000 in 1990.

| | Inventories | |
(in thousands)	1990	1989
Inventories at FIFO cost:		
Finished products	$ 199,341	$ 227,095
Work in process and raw materials	115,715	127,356
	315,056	354,451
Less excess of FIFO over LIFO	(123,481)	(128,945)
	$191,575	$225,506

Inventories valued using the LIFO method comprised 87% and 75% of consolidated inventories at FIFO cost at December 31, 1990 and 1989, respectively. In 1990 and 1989, inventory quantities were reduced, resulting in liquidations of LIFO inventory quantities carried at the lower costs prevailing in prior years. The effects of these liquidations increased net income approximately $9,900 in 1990, $13,900,000 in 1989, and $3,000,000 in 1988.

Required

1. What would PACCAR have reported as Income Before Income Taxes for 1990 had they used FIFO to account for all their inventories?
2. How does the change in the LIFO reserve relate to the effect of the LIFO liquidation?

7-72   Year-End Purchases and LIFO

A company engaged in the manufacture and sale of jewelry maintained an inventory of gold for use in its business. The company used LIFO for the gold content of its products.

On the final day of its fiscal year, the company bought 10,000 ounces of gold at $400 per ounce. Had the purchase not been made, the company would have penetrated its LIFO layers for 8,000 ounces of gold acquired at $260 per ounce.

The applicable income tax rate is 40%.

Required

1. Compute the effect of the year-end purchase on the income taxes of the fiscal year.
2. On the second day of the next fiscal year, the company resold the 10,000 ounces of gold to its suppliers. What do you think the Internal Revenue Service should do if it discovers this resale? Explain.

7-73   Comparison of Gross Profit Percentages and Inventory Turnover

JC Penney and Kmart are competitors in the retail business, although they target slightly different markets. The gross margin for each company and average inventory appear below for the indicated years (both have January year ends; 1994 refers to the year ending in January of 1994).

JC Penney

	1994	1992	1990
	(in millions)		
Retail sales	18,983	16,201	16,103
Cost of goods sold*	12,997	11,099	10,492
Gross profit	5,986	5,102	5,611
Average inventory	3,402	2,777	2,407

KMart

	1994	1992	1990
	(in millions)		
Retail sales	34,156	29,042	29,533
Cost of goods sold*	25,646	21,243	21,745
Gross profit	8,510	7,799	7,788
Average inventory	8,002	6,912	6,302

*Both companies classify costs of occupancy, buying, and warehousing with cost of goods sold.

Required   Calculate gross profit percentages and inventory turnovers for 1990, 1992, and 1994 for each company and compare them. What trends do you observe? Which company appears to perform better? To what extent do their different performances seem to relate to their relative positions in the retail market?

7-74   LIFO and Ethical Issues

McMullen Instrument Distributors is a wholesaler of electronic instruments. McMullen has used the LIFO inventory method since 1971. Near the end of 1995 the company's inventory of a particular instrument listed three LIFO layers, two of which were from earlier years and one from 1995 purchases:

	No. of Units	Unit Cost
Layer One	4,000	$40
Layer Two	2,500	50
1995 Purchases	30,000	60
Total available	36,500	

In 1995, McMullen sold 32,500 units, leaving 4,000 units in inventory.

On December 27, 1995, McMullen had a chance to buy a minimum of 15,000 units of the instrument at a unit cost of $70. The offer was good for ten days, and delivery would be immediate upon placing the order.

Roberta Donellen, chief purchasing manager of McMullen, was trying to decide whether to make the purchase, and, if it is made, whether to make it in 1995 or 1996. The controller had told her that she should buy immediately, because the company would save $70,000 in taxes. The tax rate is 40%.

Required

1. Explain why $70,000 of taxes would be saved.
2. Are there any ethical considerations that would influence this decision? Explain.

7-75   Manufacturing Costs

Study Appendix 7. Erik made custom T-shirts for himself and his friends for years before trying to treat it seriously as a business. January 1, 19X1, he decided to become more serious. He bought some screening equipment for $5,000 that he figured was good for 10,000 screenings. He decided to use units of production depreciation. He acquired 2,000 shirts for $4,000 and rented a studio for $500 per month. During the month he paid an assistant $1,600 and together they created three designs, screened 1,500 shirts, and sold 1,200 at $8 each. At month end, there were 500 shirts unused, 300 finished shirts ready for sale, and Erik was trying to figure out how he was doing.

Required

1. Calculate the cost of goods sold and the value of ending inventory (including raw material and finished goods).
2. Prepare an income statement for Erik's first month of operations. Assume a 30% tax rate.

7-76   Wal-Mart Annual Report

Refer to the Wal-Mart financial statements in Appendix A.

Required

1. Assume that Wal-Mart uses the periodic inventory procedure. Compute the amount of merchandise inventory purchased during fiscal 1995. (Hint: Use the inventory T-account.)
2. Assume that Wal-Mart has always used "replacement cost" (which is close to FIFO cost) rather than LIFO. Calculate cost of goods sold under "replacement cost" for 1995.
3. In fact, Wal-Mart has always used LIFO. How has this choice affected the retained earnings balance as of January 31, 1995?
4. Compute the 1995 inventory turnover for Wal-Mart.
5. Worldwide, Wal-Mart had 2,176 Wal-Mart Stores and 453 Sam's Clubs as of January 31, 1995. About one hundred new Wal-Mart Stores are opened per year. Does the opening of new stores tend to increase or decrease the inventory turnover?
6. Calculate the gross margin percentage during 1993, 1994, and 1995. Comment on any changes.

7-77   Compact D from Disclosure

Select an industry and identify two firms within that industry.

Required

1. Identify the inventory accounting method used by each.
2. Calculate gross profit percentages and inventory turnovers. Comment on the comparison and any trends.

8

Internal Control and Ethics

Learning Objectives

After studying this chapter, you should be able to

1   Describe the elements of internal control.

2   Explain the role of the audit committee.

3   Judge an internal control system using the checklist of internal control.

4   Describe how computers have changed the internal control environment.

5   Explain the basics of controlling cash and inventories.

6   Incorporate ethical judgments into decision making.

This chapter focuses on the internal accounting controls that detect and prevent errors and generally safeguard the firm's assets. The chapter describes the elements of internal control and the roles of management and the audit committee. An internal control checklist is provided, and its applicability to computer systems is considered along with the special types of controls required for large computer systems. The chapter contains a special section on ethical standards that are essential to good internal control, and two appendices extend our discussion of cash and inventories.

CFO magazine reports that American businesses lose some $50 billion a year to internal thievery. At its simplest, this refers to employees walking out the door with their employers' assets, although the process is often more complicated. For example, an accounts payable clerk at a pharmaceuticals company embezzled $25,000 by writing checks to companies that he created. Following a standard practice, his employer had an executive authorize payments by initialing invoices. The resulting checks, for small amounts, were created by the clerk, mechanically signed and mailed. The extra payments to the clerk's companies were detected one day when the clerk called in sick and his coworker noted checks written to an unfamiliar vendor. In another case, a bookkeeper wrote fraudulent paychecks to seasonal employees and cashed them himself. The theft was revealed when a seasonal employee objected that the W-2 form, sent to the government at year end to report his annual earnings for income tax purposes, reported too much income. Good systems of internal control would reduce such losses.

Internal controls extend beyond theft prevention. The chapter examines federal laws that require management to maintain accounting controls to assure management policies and procedures are followed. The law arose when Congress became concerned that secret payments and bribes were occuring internationally, apparently without the knowledge of top management. The law merely emphasizes the fundamental responsibility of corporate leadership. The board of directors sets broad policy on how the company will function. These policies determine what management may do and should do in pursuit of the shareholders' interests. In turn, management must establish boundaries around allowable actions to assure that employees execute their responsibilites without taking unacceptable risks. When employees exceed their authority, signficant losses may result for the company even when the employee receives no direct personal gain. For example, an employee of Spectra-Physics lost millions for the company by circumventing management restrictions on foreign currency trading. To make up for losses in one quarter, in the next quarter the employee engaged in transactions well beyond the authorized limits. When exchange rates moved in the "wrong" way, the extra trading compounded the loss. General Electric also suffered hundreds of millions in losses when a trader in its Kidder Peabody subsidiary apparently violated corporate trading limits.

The need for internal control also extends to nonprofit organizations, which often suffer from defective systems. An auditor's report on the U.S. Department of Energy commented that the department "does not have an effective system of recording, managing, and disposing of government property." A Febuary 11, 1995, *San Francisco Chronicle* article entitled "Park Service Trips Over Sloppy Books" noted that the National Park Service had not produced reliable financial statements for three years and could not vouch for the accuracy of its reported $68 million in long-term debt. Further, "inadequate recordkeeping also means that the Park Service cannot always bill for the money that it is owed, even though the agency carries a balance of $73 million in its receivable account."

■ OVERVIEW OF INTERNAL CONTROL

The essence of internal control is the creation of a system of checks and balances that assures that all actions occurring within the company are in accord with organizational objectives and have the general approval of top management. At one level this means that a highly placed manager should not expose the company to unauthorized, speculative losses from, for example, trading exotic derivatives securities. Here internal control seeks to tie daily decisions to corporate strategy. At another level it means that a salesperson at the clothing-store giant, The GAP, should not be able to walk out of the store with holiday gifts for the family without paying for them. Here internal control refers to protection of firm assets from theft and loss. Therefore, an electronic tag on a leather coat is an internal control device and so is the requirement that checks over $200 have the approval of two people.

In its broadest sense, **internal control** refers to both *administrative* control and *accounting* control:

> **internal control**
> Refers to both internal administrative control and internal accounting control.

1. *Administrative controls* include the plan of organization (for example, the formal organizational chart concerning who reports to whom) and all methods and procedures that facilitate management planning and control of operations. Examples are departmental budgeting procedures, reports on performance, and procedures for granting credit to customers.
2. *Accounting controls* include the methods and procedures for authorizing transactions, safeguarding assets, and ensuring the accuracy of the financial records. Good accounting controls help *maximize* efficiency; and they help *minimize* waste, unintentional errors, and fraud.

Our focus is on internal accounting controls, which should provide reasonable assurance concerning

1. *Authorization.* Transactions are executed in accordance with management's general or specific intentions.
2. *Recording.* All authorized transactions are recorded in the correct amounts, periods, and accounts. No fictitious transactions are recorded.
3. *Safeguarding.* Precautions and procedures appropriately restrict access to assets.
4. *Reconciliation.* Records are compared with other independently kept records and physical counts. Such comparisons help ensure that other control objectives are attained.
5. *Valuation.* Recorded amounts are periodically reviewed for impairment of values and necessary write-downs.

> **Objective 1**
>
> Describe the elements of internal control.

The first three general objectives—authorization, recording, and safeguarding—relate to establishing the system of accountability and are aimed at *prevention* of errors and irregularities. The final two objectives—reconciliation and valuation—are aimed at *detection* of errors and irregularities.

A sixth objective of an internal control system should be added: *promoting operating efficiency.* Management should recognize that an internal control system's purpose is as much a positive one (promoting efficiency) as a negative one (preventing errors and fraud).

The Accounting System

> **accounting system** A set of records, procedures, and equipment that routinely deals with the events affecting the financial performance and position of the entity.

An entity's **accounting system** is a set of records, procedures, and equipment that *routinely* deals with the events affecting the entity's financial performance and position. The system maintains accountability for the firm's assets and liabilities.

The $346,770 Overdraft

Karen Smith was amazed when her credit union notified her that her account was overdrawn by $346,770. How could that kind of money turn up missing? Did she mistakenly add three extra zeros to a check? No, but she did leave her bank card in her wallet, locked inside her van during a high school football game on a Friday night. Two thieves broke into the van, stole the bank card, and visited local cash machines.

Think about how bank internal control procedures should stop theives. Automated teller machines (ATM) require the use of a customer's specific personal identification number (the "pin" number). As a secondary precaution, ATM machines normally restrict withdrawals to a maximum amount, perhaps $200 per day, per account. Thieves cannot randomly guess pin numbers. The computer tracks "unauthorized" accesses. After several incorrect pin numbers the ATM keeps the card and notifies the user to reclaim it at the bank.

Nonetheless, these thieves hit the jackpot. Karen stored her pin number on her social security card, in the stolen wallet. Luckier yet, the Oregon TelCo Credit Union was updating some computer programs and their $200 limit per account per day was inoperative. To access all the funds in Karen's account, the thieves put the card in and withdrew $200, time after time. Eventually the ATM ran out of bills, but the thieves visited many more on a circuitous, five county, 500 mile route.

A third internal control should have limited the thieves to the balance in Karen's account. Something else went wrong. Most financial institutions only permit immediate withdrawal of certified checks or checks drawn on accounts at the institution. Deposits may be unavailable for days while the institution verifies that the check is written on a good bank against a bonafide account with sufficient funds. Checks on in-state institutions may take two days to "clear" while out-of-state checks take three or four days. Deposits into an ATM machine are generally unavailable until the next banking day so the bank can verify the deposit, subject to the rules just described.

Unfortunately,the TelCo system was giving immediate credit for deposits made into automated tellers. The thieves "deposited" $820,500, by inserting empty deposit envelopes and recording large deposits on the ATM keypad. They exhausted the cash in the ATM machines in their five county area by 2:30 am on Monday and headed to Reno to buy a new truck and enjoy their wealth.

One piece of TelCo's internal control worked. Hidden cameras photographed the thieves. The perpetrators, David Gallagher and his wife Terry were easily identified. David has been in prison five times and has 21 felony convictions. Federal sentencing guidelines could bring up to 63 years in prison. ∎

Source: The New York Times, *(February 12, 1995),* *p. 36.*

Regardless of the entity's size or type, and regardless of whether it is held privately or publicly, managers and accountants should be alert to the importance of accounting systems and controls. Accounting records are kept for a variety of purposes. A major purpose is to help managers operate their entities more efficiently and effectively. Any business must keep records of receivables from customers and payables to creditors, and it must record and manage cash disbursements and receipts. The cost-benefit test is easily met. Unless orderly compilation of records occurs, intolerable chaos results. In short, an accounting system is a wise business investment.

Chapters 3 and 4 provided an overview of the heart of the accounting system: source documents, journal entries, postings to ledgers, trial balances, adjustments, and financial reports. The focus of the system is on repetitive, voluminous transactions, which almost always fall into four categories:

1. Cash disbursements.
2. Cash receipts.
3. Purchase of goods and services, including employee payroll.
4. Sales or other rendering of goods and services.

The magnitude of the physical handling of records is often staggering. For example, consider telephone companies or credit card companies. They must process *millions* of transactions daily. Without computers and data-processing systems, most modern organizations would be forced to halt operations.

Too often, systems are regarded as a necessary evil. But systems deserve a loftier status. Well-designed and well-run accounting systems are positive contributions to organizations and the economy. For example, Federal Express created a dominant position in the overnight delivery market by developing an efficient system for continuous tracking of an item from pickup to delivery. And Wal-Mart's extraordinary success as a low-price retailer is partly due to their development of an integrated inventory control and ordering system that allows its computer to interact automatically with suppliers such as Procter & Gamble to generate orders and reduce delivery times.

Advances in computer technology continue to be awesome. The description of a specific accounting system is likely to be ancient history before it comes off the presses. Consequently, this chapter emphasizes the *general* features of accounting systems that persist regardless of specific computer programs and hardware. The purpose is not to develop skills as a systems designer, but to understand the scope and nature of accounting systems and controls. Any manager or would-be manager must understand the primary attributes of a suitable internal control system.

Management's Responsibility

Chapters 1 and 5 explained that outside auditors attest to the financial reports of an entity. However, management bears the *primary responsibility* for a company's financial statements. Most annual reports of publicly held companies in the United States contain an explicit statement of management responsibility for its financial statements.

management reports
Explicit statements in annual reports of publicly held companies that management is responsible for all audited and unaudited information in the annual report.

These **management reports** state that management is responsible for all audited and unaudited information in the annual report, and they include a statement on the adequacy of internal control. They also include a description of the composition and duties of the audit committee as well as the duties of the independent auditor. These features are highlighted in Exhibit 8-1, the statement of McDonald's Corporation, franchiser of more than 10,000 restaurants in over fifty countries.

Foreign Corrupt Practices Act and Internal Control

Foreign Corrupt Practices Act A U.S. law that makes it an explicit responsibility of management to report on the adequacy of internal control.

In the United States, public reporting on the adequacy of internal control is an explicit responsibility of management under the **Foreign Corrupt Practices Act**. The name derives from the act's origins; Congress passed it after major public disclosures about bribes and other corrupt actions by U.S. corporations in international settings. Worse yet, managers testified before Congress that they were unaware of these actions by their employees.

Nonetheless, the act's provisions pertain to the internal control systems of all publicly held companies, *even if they do no business outside the United States*. The act contains not only specific prohibitions against bribery and other corrupt practices, but also requirements (1) for maintaining accounting records in reasonable detail and accuracy and (2) for maintaining an appropriate system of internal accounting controls.

Exhibit 8-1

McDonald's
Corporation

Management's Report

Management is responsible for the preparation, integrity, and fair presentation of the consolidated financial statements and financial comments appearing in this annual report. The financial statements were prepared in accordance with generally accepted accounting principles and include certain amounts based on management's judgment and best estimates. Other financial information presented in the annual report is consistent with the financial statements.

The Company maintains a system of internal control over financial reporting including safeguarding of assets against unauthorized acquisition, use, or disposition, which is designed to provide reasonable assurance to the Company's management and Board of Directors regarding the preparation of reliable published financial statements and such asset safeguarding. The system includes a documented organizational structure and appropriate division of responsibilities; established policies and procedures which are communicated throughout the Company; careful selection, training, and development of our people; and utilization of an internal audit program. Policies and procedures prescribe that the Company and all employees are to maintain the highest ethical standards and that business practices throughout the world are to be conducted in a manner which is above reproach.

There are inherent limitations in the effectiveness of any system of internal control, including the possibility of human error and the circumvention or overriding of controls. Accordingly, even an effective internal control system can provide only reasonable assurance with respect to financial statement preparation and safeguarding of assets. Furthermore, the effectiveness of an internal control system can change with circumstances. The Company believes that at December 31, 1994, it maintained an effective system of internal control over financial reporting and safeguarding of assets against unauthorized acquisition, use, or disposition.

The consolidated financial statements have been audited by independent auditors, Ernst & Young LLP, who were given unrestricted access to all financial records and related data. The audit report of Ernst & Young LLP is presented herein.

The Board of Directors, operating through its audit committee composed entirely of outside Directors, provides oversight to the financial reporting process. Ernst & Young LLP has independent access to the Audit Committee and periodically meets with the Committee to discuss accounting, auditing, and financial reporting matters.

McDonalds's Corporation
Oak Brook, Illinois
January 26, 1995

Under the act, managers must focus on systems of internal control. Boards of directors assure themselves of compliance with the act and with SEC requirements by obtaining documentation of the internal control system, and compiling written evidence of management's evaluation and ongoing review of the system. The biggest impact of the act has been the mandatory documentation of an evaluation of internal control *by management* rather than only by auditors.

The Foreign Corrupt Practices Act is only one item in the recent focus on internal control. The Committee of Sponsoring Organizations of the Treadway Commission (COSO) published "Internal Control–Integrated Framework" to define internal control and provide guidance on implementation. The American Institute of Certified Public Accountants asks management to issue separately audited reports on internal controls. The Federal Deposit Insurance Corporation Act requires some insured banks to report annually on internal controls. Internal controls are a key management tool in reaching corporate objectives.

Internal control requirements were extended to managers in the public sector by the Federal Managers' Financial Integrity Act. Briefly, the act requires each executive agency to establish a system of internal accounting and administrative control that meets prescribed standards. They must also report annually, based on an evaluation conducted in accordance with established guidelines, to the president, Congress, and the public on the extent to which the agency's systems comply with the standards.

The documentation of internal control should systematically refer to (1) management's cost-benefit choices regarding the system and (2) management's evaluation of how well the internal control system is working. Documentation includes memos, minutes of meetings discussing internal control concepts with all affected individuals, written statements of compliance, flowcharts, procedures manuals, and the like. Moreover, there should be a written program for ongoing review and evaluation of the system. Finally, there should be letters from independent auditors stating that they found no material weaknesses in internal control during their audit, or that necessary improvements have been made.

■ THE AUDIT COMMITTEE

Objective 2

Explain the role of the audit committee.

audit committee
A committee of the board of directors that oversees the internal accounting controls, financial statements, and financial affairs of the corporation.

The first objective of internal accounting control is authorization; transactions should be executed in accordance with management's intentions. Moreover, management bears primary responsibility for the entity's financial statements. This authority and responsibility extends upward to the board of directors. Most boards have an **audit committee,** which oversees the internal accounting controls, financial statements, and financial affairs of the corporation. Indeed, such committees are required of companies whose shares are listed on the New York Stock Exchange.

Audit committees typically have three or more "outside" board members. Not everyday employees of the company, they are considered to be more independent than the "inside" directors—employees who serve as part of the corporation's management.[1] The committee provides contact and communication among the board, the external auditors, the internal auditors, the financial executives, and the operating executives. These relationships are depicted in Exhibit 8-2.

Exhibit 8-2 shows only one of many possible arrangements. Above all, note how the audit committee serves as the main pipeline to the board of directors, especially for individuals responsible for the accounting function. In Exhibit 8-2, the internal audit manager is directly responsible (solid line) through the controller on up to the board. The dashed lines indicate that the audit committee should communicate with and gather information directly from the internal auditors as well as the external auditors.

These relationships are evolving. For example, the internal auditing department sometimes is directly responsible to the executive vice-president. But increasingly the internal audit department is directly responsible to the audit committee itself and is totally independent of the financial officers.

The audit committee meets at least twice annually. The first meeting is typically to review the annual external audit plan; the second, to review the audited financial statements before their publication. Additional meetings may be held (1) to consider the retention or replacement of the independent external auditors; (2) to review the company's accounting system, particularly the internal controls; and (3) to review any special matters raised by internal audits. At least

[1] Mobil Corporation, the oil company, has a typical board composition. Of sixteen directors, six are also members of management and ten are "outside" directors. Five of the outside directors form the audit committee.

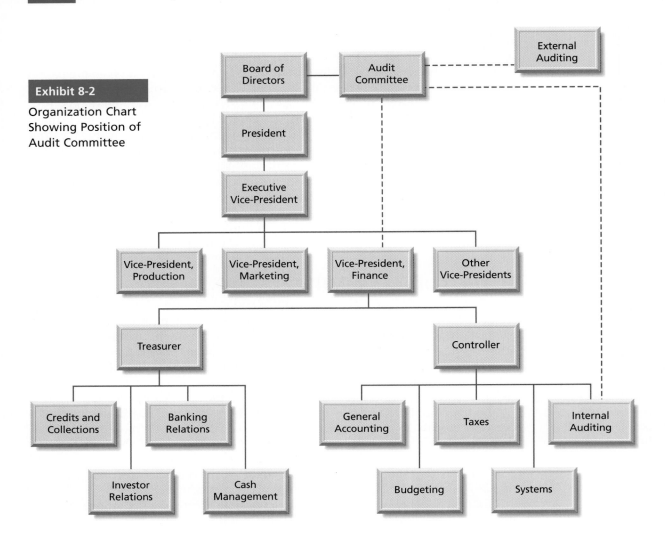

Exhibit 8-2

Organization Chart Showing Position of Audit Committee

once a year, the committee should discuss with the independent auditors their evaluation of corporate management (without the presence of the latter). Similarly, the committee should obtain management's evaluation of the independent auditors.

Many companies include an audit committee report in their annual report. Merck & Co., the pharmaceutical firm, included the report shown in Exhibit 8-3.

Objective 3

Judge an internal control system using the checklist of internal control.

■ CHECKLIST OF INTERNAL CONTROL

All good systems of internal control have certain features in common. These features can be summarized in a *checklist of internal control*, which may be used to appraise any specific procedures for cash, purchases, sales, payroll, and the like. This checklist is sometimes called *principles* or *rules* or *concepts*

Exhibit 8-3	The Audit Committee of the Board of Directors is comprised of five outside directors. The members of the Committee are Charles E. Exley, Jr., Chairman; Carolyn K. Davis, Ph.D., Vice Chair; Sir Derek Birkin; William N. Kelley, M.D.; and Dennis Weatherstone. The committee held three meetings during 1993.
Merck & Co. Audit Committee's Report	The Audit Committee meets with the independent public accountants, management, and internal auditors to assure that all are carrying out their respective responsibilities. The Audit Committee reviews the performance and fees of the independent public accountants prior to recommending their appointment and meets with them, without management present, to discuss the scope and results of their audit work, including the adequacy of internal controls and the quality of financial reporting. Both the independent public accountants and the internal auditors have full access to the Audit Committee.

or *characteristics* or *features* or *elements*. The following checklist summarizes the guidance that is found in much of the systems and auditing literature.[2]

1. Reliable Personnel with Clear Responsibilities

The most important element of successful control is personnel. Incompetent or dishonest individuals can undermine a system, no matter how well it meets the other items on the checklist. Procedures to hire, train, motivate, and supervise employees are essential. Individuals must be given authority, responsibility, and duties commensurate with their abilities, interests, experience, and reliability. Yet many employers use low-cost talent that may prove exceedingly expensive in the long run, not only because of fraud but because of poor productivity.

Assessing responsibility means tracking actions as far down in the organization as is feasible, so that results can be related to individuals. It means having salesclerks sign sales slips, inspectors initial packing slips, and workers sign time cards and requisitions. Grocery stores often assign each cashier a separate money tray; therefore shortages can easily be traced to the person responsible. The psychological impact of fixing responsibility tends to promote care and efficiency. Employees often perform better when they must explain deviations from required procedures.

The possibility of employee theft is distasteful to most managers, but it must be taken seriously. The National Mass Retailing Institute estimates that retailers lose about 2% of sales to theft and mistakes. Shoplifting accounts for part of this, but employee theft causes much larger losses than shoplifting. The institute estimates that an average retail store loses $10 per shift per clerk. Convenience stores and fast-food restaurants are especially vulnerable to employee theft. Such businesses need to be especially concerned with internal control systems.

2. Separation of Duties

The separation of duties not only helps ensure accurate compilation of data but also limits the chances for fraud that would require the collusion of two or more persons. This extremely important and often neglected element can be subdivided into four parts:

---

[2] For an expanded discussion, see A. Arens and J. Loebbecke, *Auditing*, 5th ed. (Upper Saddle River, NJ: Prentice Hall, 1991), Chap. 9.

1. *Separation of operational responsibility from recordkeeping responsibility.* The entire accounting function should be divorced from operating departments. For example, product inspectors, not machine operators, should count units produced; inventory records clerks or computers, not material handlers, should keep perpetual inventory records. Why? Because those keeping the records should have nothing to gain by falsifying the records. A material handler should not be able to steal materials and cover up the theft by recording the issue of the materials to production.

2. *Separation of the custody of assets from accounting.* This practice reduces temptation and fraud. For example, the bookkeeper should not handle cash, and the cashier should not have access to ledger accounts such as the individual records of customers. A person with both accounting and cash-handling duties could pocket cash that is received and make a false entry in the accounting records.

   In a computer system, a person with custody of assets should not have access to programming or any input of records. In a classic example, a programmer in a bank rounded transactions to the next lower cent rather than the nearest cent and had the computer put the fraction of a cent into his account. For example, a customer amount of $10.057 became $10.05, and the programmer's account received $.007. With millions of transactions, the programmer's account became very large.

3. *Separation of the authorization of transactions from the custody of related assets.* To the extent feasible, persons who authorize transactions should not have control over the related asset. For instance, the same individual should not authorize the payment of a supplier's invoice and also sign the check in payment of the bill. Nor should an individual who handles cash receipts have the authority to indicate which accounts receivable should be written off as uncollectible.

   The latter separation of powers prevents such embezzlement as the following: A bookkeeper opens the mail, removes a $1,000 check from a customer, and somehow cashes it. To hide the theft, the bookkeeper prepares the following journal entry:

Allowance for bad debts	1,000	
Accounts receivable		1,000
To write off an amount owed by a customer.		

4. *Separation of duties within the accounting function.* An employee should not be able to record a transaction from its origin to its ultimate posting in a ledger. Independent performance of various phases will help ensure control over errors. Even a small company should have some separation of duties. For example, if there is only one bookkeeper who writes checks and keeps the accounting records, the owner can at least sign the checks and reconcile the monthly bank statement.

A main goal of the separation of duties is to make sure that one person, acting alone, cannot defraud the company. It is more difficult, although not impossible, for two or more employees to collude in a fraud. This is why movie theaters have a cashier selling tickets and an usher taking them. The cashier takes in cash, the usher keeps the ticket stubs, and in an audit step performed by a third person, the cash is compared with the number of stubs. But suppose they do collude. The ticket seller pockets the cash and issues a fake ticket. The usher accepts the fake ticket and allows entry. Separation of duties alone will not prevent collusive theft.

3. Proper Authorization

The Foreign Corrupt Practices Act stresses proper authorization. Authorization can be either *general* or *specific*. General authorization is usually found in

writing. It often sets definite limits on what price to pay (whether to fly econc ,
or first class), on what price to receive (whether to offer a sales discount), on
what credit limits to grant to customers, and so forth. There may also be complete prohibitions (against paying extra fees or bribes or overtime premiums).

Specific authorization usually means that a superior manager must permit
(typically in writing) any particular deviations from the limits set by general
authorization. For example, the plant manager, rather than the lathe supervisor, may have to approve any overtime. Another example is the need for
approval from the board of directors regarding expenditures for capital assets
in excess of a specific limit.

4. Adequate Documents

Documents and records vary considerably, from source documents such as
sales invoices and purchase orders to journals and ledgers. Immediate, complete, and tamper-proof recording is the aim. It is encouraged by optical scanning of bar-coded data, by having all source documents prenumbered and
accounted for, by using devices such as cash registers, and by designing forms
for ease of recording.

Immediate recording is especially important for handling cash sales.
Devices used to ensure immediate recording include "rewards" to customers if
they are not offered a receipt at the time of sale and forcing clerks to make
change by pricing items at $1.99, $2.99, and $3.99 rather than at $2, $3, and $4.
(Historically, such pricing was originally adopted to force clerks to make
change as well as for its psychological impact on potential customers.) The
need to access the change drawer forces the clerk to ring up the sale so the
drawer will open.

5. Proper Procedures

Most organizations have *procedures manuals*, which specify the flow of documents
and provide information and instructions to facilitate adequate recordkeeping.

Routine and automatic checks are major ways of attaining proper procedures. In a phrase, this means doing things "by the numbers." Repetitive procedures may be prescribed for order taking, order filling, collating, and
inspecting. The use of general routines permits specialization of effort, division
of duties, and automatic checks on previous steps in the routine.

6. Physical Safeguards

Obviously, losses of cash, inventories, and records are minimized by safes,
locks, guards, and limited access. For example, many companies (such as
Boeing and Hewlett-Packard) require all *visitors* to sign a register and wear a
name tag. Often *employees* will also wear name tags that are coded to show the
facilities to which they have access. Doors to research areas or computer rooms
often may be opened only with special keys or by use of a specific code.

Sometimes small businesses are especially vulnerable to theft of physical
assets. For example, retail stores use alarm systems, guard dogs, security
guards, special lighting, and many other safeguards to protect their property.

7. Bonding, Vacations, and Rotation of Duties

Key people may be subject to excessive temptation. Thus, top executives, branch managers, and individuals who handle cash or inventories should have understudies, be required to take vacations, and be bonded.

Rotating employees and requiring them to take vacations ensures that at least two employees know how to do each job so that an absence due to illness or a sudden resignation does not create major problems. Further, the practice of having another employee periodically perform their duties discourages employees from engaging in fraudulent activities that might be discovered when someone else has access to their records.

Rotation of duties is illustrated by the common practice of having employees such as receivables and payables clerks periodically exchange duties. Or a receivables clerk may handle accounts from *A* to *C* for three months and then be rotated to accounts *M* to *P* for three months, and so forth.

Incidentally, the act of *bonding*—that is, buying insurance against embezzlement—is not a substitute for vacations, rotation of duties, and similar precautions. Insurance companies will pay only when a loss is proved; establishing proof is often difficult and costly in itself.

8. Independent Check

All phases of the system should be subjected to periodic review by outsiders (for example, by independent public accountants) and by internal auditors. Auditors have a degree of objectivity that allows them to spot weaknesses overlooked by managers immersed in day-to-day operations. It is too costly for external auditors to examine all transactions, so they inspect a sample of the transactions. By first evaluating the system of internal control and testing the extent to which it is being followed, the auditor decides on the likelihood of undetected errors. If internal controls are weak, there is a greater probability of significant errors in the accounting records. Then the auditor must examine many transactions to provide reasonable assurance that existing errors will be found. If internal controls are strong, the auditor can use a smaller sample to develop confidence in the accuracy of the accounting records.

Internal auditors are company employees who help design control systems and assess the degree of compliance with the existing systems. Their main goal is to enhance efficiency of operations by promoting adherence to both administrative and accounting controls and to continuously improve the system.

The idea of an independent check extends beyond the work performed by professional auditors. For example, bank statements should be reconciled with book balances. The bank provides an independent record of cash. Furthermore, the monthly bank reconciliations should be conducted by some clerk other than the cash, receivables, or payables clerks. Other examples of independent checks include monthly statements sent to credit customers and physical counts of inventory to check against perpetual records.

9. Cost-Benefit Analysis

Highly complex systems tend to strangle people in red tape, impeding rather than promoting efficiency. Besides, the "cost of keeping the costs" sometimes gets out of hand. Investments in more costly systems must be compared with the

Reengineering the Accounting Function

The last decade has witnessed the emergence of "reengineering," a process in which existing approaches to work are fundamentally reexamined. The process is often characterized as redesigning a task starting with a clean sheet of paper. In manufacturing, the goal may be to reduce the number of separate parts in a product by 50% or to cut the inventory levels needed to support production by 90%.

This process is equally applicable to systems for accounting and maintaining data. Historically, most large accounting systems were maintained on single large mainframe computers. The systems were managed by large computing staffs, and data were processed in large batches, once a day or once a week or once a month. When the computer was busy on a big job, nothing else could be done.

Many companies are reengineering these systems and switching to client/server systems. In such systems, the data are maintained on a smaller, fast machine (the server) that interacts with many clients, which are personal computers like those in university computer labs or many homes and offices. The worker downloads data from the server and processes them as required, returning the result to the server.

Motorola, a $13.5 billion electronics firm, has had great success with its transformation to client/server systems. From 1989 to 1993, its financial and manufacturing systems, both domestically and internationally, have been transformed. Tony Knapp, the vice president and controller, reported "Our systems are driving our cost-saving initiatives, our cycle-time reduction initiatives, and our quality initiatives. We're not just replacing the old system, we're also reengineering activities to be more productive and efficient."

One example is the accounts payable function. In the old system, the process looked like a production line. One employeee opened the envelope, one entered data in the computer, another checked vendor numbers—paper traveled from person to person, and when a supplier called with a question, often no one knew where the relevant papers were. In the reengineering process, the team thought of their supplier as their customer for service and information. The new system makes each clerk responsible for a series of suppliers. As each invoice arrives, the responsible clerk enters it into the system. It is automatically linked to other data such as the record of receipt of the goods and the purchase order. Documents handled per person are up 85%, the number of employees has remained steady while volume has risen 25%, and suppliers are happier because their needs for accurate information and timely payments are better met. Checks are written several times a day, not several times a week.

Other Motorola activities are copying this success story. One group reported saving $800,000 per year by trashing their mainframe in favor of a client/server accounting system. ■

Source: L Calabro, "All Eyes on Internal Contol," and S. Barr, "When System Change Means Process Change," CFO, (August 1993), pp 51–53 and 37–45.

---

expected benefits. Unfortunately it is easier to relate new lathes or production methods to cost savings in manufacturing than to link a new computer to cost savings in inventory control. Yet efforts must be made. For example, the accounting firm of KPMG Peat Marwick completed a study of office automation for a client. After examining the jobs of 2,600 white-collar workers, KPMG Peat Marwick quantified a cost-benefit relationship: "A single investment of $10 million would result in a productivity savings equal to $8.4 million every year."

Although many companies implement more complex procedures to improve internal control, a few have taken a reverse course. They have decided that the increased costs of additional scrutiny are not worth the expected savings from catching mistakes or crooks. For example, an aerospace manufacturer routinely pays the invoice amounts without checking supporting documentation except on a random-sampling basis. An aluminum company sends out a blank check with its purchase orders, and then the supplier fills out the check and deposits it.

No framework for internal control is perfect in the sense that it can prevent some shrewd individual from "beating the system" either by outright embezzlement or by producing inaccurate records. The task is not total prevention of fraud, nor is it implementation of operating perfection; rather, the task is the designing of a *cost-effective* tool that will help achieve efficient operations and reduce temptation.

■ EFFECTS OF COMPUTERS ON INTERNAL CONTROL

Objective 4

Describe how computers have changed the internal control environment.

The nine items in the preceding checklist on pages 334 to 339 apply to both computer and manual accounting systems. However, computers change the focus of internal control in two ways:

1. The computer can accomplish traditional internal control functions more efficiently.
2. But, additional controls must be put in place to ensure the accuracy and reliability of computer-processed data.

Computers Change the Control Environment

The computer has allowed relatively inexpensive processing of huge volumes of accounting data. However, internal control over computerized operations is essential. Consider an error that a human might make once a month. Such an error would be repeated thousands of times a day in a computer program for processing vast quantities of data. Further, errors that would be obvious by scanning journal entries could go undetected because data are "invisible," stored on tape or disks. Input and output data transmitted over phone lines may be vulnerable to unauthorized access. Thus the installation of internal control systems must accompany computerization.

Computers are amazingly accurate. The focus of internal control is not *computer* errors. Invariably, the computer has done exactly what it was told (or programmed) to do. Errors usually result because someone entered the wrong data, programmed the computer incorrectly, ran the wrong program, or asked for the wrong output.

Types of Control for Computer Systems

The greatest source of errors in computerized systems is the data input. Both the original recording (for example, a sales slip) and the transcription of the data to computer-readable form (for example, key-punching cards or direct entry from a remote terminal) are frequent sources of error. Other possible sources of errors are managed by processing, output, and general controls.

input controls
Internal accounting controls that help guard against the entry of false or erroneous data.

Input controls can help guard against the entry of false or erroneous data, especially those due to multiple steps in handling the data when human processing is involved. Such controls include using standardized forms and verifying data input. Accountants also program the computer to verify that all required data are included on each input document, identify key numbers outside a range of reasonableness, and conduct other such checks. Use of optical scanning equipment can also limit data-recording errors.

processing controls
Internal accounting controls relating to the design, programming, and operation of the system.

Processing controls start with the design and programming of the system, including complete documentation. They also include control of operations, including normal separation and rotation of duties. For example, programmers should not be allowed to operate the computers. A computer consultant commented that he had immense stealing opportunities when he ran computer operations for a large bank: "I alone designed the dividend-payment operation, wrote the program for it, and ran the job on the machine. The operation was so big that it had a mistake tolerance of nearly $100,000. I could have paid at least half that much to myself, in small checks, and the money wouldn't even have been missed."

output controls
Internal accounting controls that check output against input and ensure that only authorized persons receive reports.

Output controls check output against input, possibly by random manual processing of data. Output controls should also ensure that only authorized persons receive the reports. Computers often generate literally tons of printed output. A paper shredder can be an important control tool to safeguard privileged information.

General controls focus on the organization and operation of the data-processing activity. Good internal control requires well-defined procedures for developing, testing, and approving new systems and programs or changing old ones. Access to equipment and files should be restricted. But most important, as in any system, manual or computerized, are personnel controls. Hiring reliable personnel and keeping temptation from their doorsteps through common-sense controls are important goals of any internal control system.

general controls
Internal accounting controls that focus on the organization and operation of the data-processing activity.

■ EXAMPLES OF INTERNAL CONTROL

This section discusses specific internal control considerations for cash and inventories. Additional details are provided in Appendix 8A and Appendix 8B.

Internal Control of Cash

Objective 5

Explain the basics of controlling cash and inventories.

Cash is almost always the most enticing asset for potential thieves and embezzlers. Therefore, internal controls are far more elaborate for cash than for, say, the paper clips and desks on the premises. The following points are especially noteworthy:

1. As previously mentioned, the function of receiving cash should be separated from the function of disbursing cash. Moreover, individuals who handle cash or checks should not have access to the accounting records.

2. All receipts should be deposited intact daily. That is, none of the currency and checks received each day should be used directly for any other purposes. For example, sales in retail establishments are recorded in a cash register. A supervisor compares the locked cash register tape with the actual cash in the register drawer. Then the cash receipts are deposited, and the tape is forwarded to the accounting department as a basis for accounting entries. If cash from the till is sometimes used to pay suppliers, there is a serious internal control weakness.

3. All major disbursements should be made by serially numbered checks. Gaps should be investigated. The *Wall Street Journal* cited an example of good controls used poorly: "A bookkeeping assistant [was] under strict orders to note every missing number.... But no one checked to see how many were missing or why."

4. Bank accounts should be reconciled monthly. (This recommendation also applies to personal banking accounts.) A **bank reconciliation** is an analysis that explains any difference between the cash balance shown by the depositor and that shown by the bank. It is surprising how many businesses (some of substantial size) do not reconcile their bank accounts regularly.

bank reconciliation
An analysis that explains any difference between the cash balance shown by the depositor and that shown by the bank.

Control of cash requires procedures for handling both checks and currency. To control checks, many organizations use check protectors that perforate or otherwise establish an unalterable amount on the face of each check. Dual signatures are frequently required on large checks.

Currency is probably the most alluring form of cash. Businesses that handle much currency, such as gambling establishments, restaurants, and bars, are particularly subject to theft and false reporting. For example, many owners of small retail outlets do not record all of their cash receipts, a procedure known as *skimming*. Why? To save income taxes.

A recent news story reported: "Federal undercover agents in New York City opened an attack on the underground economy, which spawns billions of dollars yearly in untaxed income through off-the-books transactions." According to the affidavits, the establishments searched by the agents grossed more than $5 million while reporting on their tax returns only $3.6 million.

Recall from Chapter 7 that tax authorities often use known gross profit margins for an industry to assess the reasonableness of the profits based on reported revenues and costs of goods sold for a particular company. Measures such as industry average sales per square foot of store space allow assessment of the adequacy of reported revenue.

Comparing reported results with averages is not foolproof. An exclusive clothing store in San Francisco paid a percentage of sales for rent. Reported sales for a recent year were $11.2 million; an independent audit later disclosed actual sales of $20.5 million. The lessor always compared sales per square foot of floor space with those of similar stores. No clue to any impropriety arose. In fact, the lessor termed the reported sales per square foot "extraordinary" and the actual results as "unheard of."

Internal Control of Inventories

In many organizations, inventories are more easily accessible than cash. Therefore they become a favorite target for thieves.

Retail merchants must contend with inventory shrinkage, a polite term for shoplifting by customers and embezzling by employees. As defined in Chapter 7, *inventory shrinkage* is the difference between (1) the value of inventory that would occur if there were no pilferage, misclassifications, breakage, or clerical errors and (2) the value of inventory when it is physically counted. Consider the following footnote from a recent annual report of Associated Dry Goods, one of the largest operators of department and discount stores in the country: "Physical inventories are taken twice each year. Department store inventory shrinkage at retail, as a percent of retail sales, was 2.4% this year compared with 2.1% last year. Discount store inventory shrinkage as a percent of retail sales was 0.4% and 0.3%, respectively." Some department stores have suffered shrinkage losses of 4% to 5% of their sales volume. Compare this with the typical net profit margin of 5% to 6%.

A management consulting firm has demonstrated how widespread shoplifting has become. The firm concentrated on a midtown New York City department store. Five hundred shoppers, picked at random, were followed from the moment they entered the store to the time they departed. Forty-two shoppers, or one out of every twelve, took something. They stole $300 worth of merchandise, an average of $7.15 each. Similar experiments were conducted in Boston (1 of 20 shoplifted), Philadelphia (1 of 10), and again in New York (1 of 12).

Experts on controlling inventory shrinkage generally agree that the best deterrent is an alert employee at the point of sale. Retail stores use sensitized tags on merchandise; if not detached or neutralized by a salesclerk, these miniature transmitters trip an alarm as the culprit begins to leave the store.

Many libraries use a similar system to safeguard their books. Macy's in New York has continuous surveillance with over fifty television cameras.

Retailers must also scrutinize their own personnel, because they account for at least 30% to 40% of inventory shortages. Some stores have actors pose as shoplifters, who are then subjected to fake arrests. If potential thieves see the arrests, they may be deterred. Such ploys have helped reduce thefts by employees at major retail chains.

The problem of stealing is not confined to profit-seeking entities. According to the student newspaper at Northwestern University, $14,000 worth of silverware, glasses, and china was stolen from the university dining halls annually. That amounts to $4.71 for every regular customer. Signs posted at the end of each school term requesting the return of "borrowed" goods have had little success. The food service director commented: "Two years ago, we put up really nice signs and set out boxes for returns. Kids saw the boxes and stole them for packing."

The imposing magnitude of retail inventory shrinkage demonstrates how management objectives may differ among industries. For example, consider the grocery business, where net income is about 1% of sales. You can readily see why a prime responsibility of the store manager is to control inventory shrinkage rather than boost gross sales volume. The trade-off is clear: If the operating profit is 2% of sales, to offset a $1,000 increase in shrinkage requires a $50,000 boost in gross sales.

Shrinkage in Perpetual and Periodic Inventory Systems

Measuring inventory shrinkage is straightforward for companies that use a perpetual inventory system. Shrinkage is simply the difference between the cost of inventory identified by a physical count and the clerical inventory balance. Consider the following example:

Sales	$100,000
Cost of goods sold (perpetual inventory system)	$ 80,000
Beginning inventory	$ 15,000
Purchases	$ 85,000
Ending inventory, per clerical records	$ 20,000
Ending inventory, per physical count	$ 18,000

Shrinkage is $20,000 – $18,000 = $2,000. The journal entries under a perpetual inventory system would be:

Inventory shrinkage	2,000	
Inventory		2,000
To adjust ending inventory to its balance per physical count.		
Cost of goods sold	2,000	
Inventory shrinkage		2,000
To close inventory shrinkage to cost of goods sold.		

The total cost of goods sold would be $80,000 + $2,000 = $82,000.

By definition, a periodic inventory system has no clerical balance of the inventory account. Inventory shrinkage is automatically included in cost of goods sold.

Why? Because beginning inventory plus purchases less ending inventory measures all inventory that has flowed out, whether it went to customers, shoplifters, or embezzlers, or was simply lost or broken. Our example would show:

Beginning inventory	$ 15,000
Plus: Purchases	85,000
Goods available for sale	$100,000
Less: Ending inventory, per physical count	18,000
Cost of goods sold	$ 82,000

To assess shrinkage, we need some way to *estimate* what the ending inventory *should be*. The difference between this *estimate* and the physical count is inventory shrinkage. Appendix 8B describes how these estimates are made. No journal entries are necessary.

■ ETHICS AND INTERNAL CONTROL

Objective 6

Incorporate ethical judgments into decision making.

Employees' ethical standards play a large part in internal control. Ethical failures that went undetected by internal control systems have led to widely publicized cases—from security traders benefitting from the use of inside information, to savings and loan executives diverting company funds for their own personal use, to managers lying about their company's financial prospects as they approach bankruptcy. Although such ethical failures are rare, there is a public perception that they are widespread. Most businesses realize that, as Roger Smith, former Chairman and CEO of General Motors said, "Ethical practice is, quite simply, good business."

Corporate Codes of Ethics

To help employees make ethical decisions, a majority of large companies have a "corporate code of ethics." For example, General Motors has a booklet, "Guidelines for Employee Conduct," which includes the following:

> It would be comforting to have a booklet which sets forth clear-cut rules that would apply in all our business dealings. This would help us balance the seemingly contradictory obligations we owe to our fellow stockholders, customers, dealers, suppliers, communities—and to ourselves and families. But the world is not neat and orderly, and arriving at an ethical decision can be difficult. It has been wisely observed that: "It is easy to do what is right; it is hard to know what is right."... In the final analysis, each of us must exercise individual judgment and answer to our own conscience. As General Motors employees, we should never do anything we would be ashamed to explain to our family or afraid to see on the front page of the local newspaper.[3]

Some companies have a more detailed code, and some have less detail. Supporters of general guidelines maintain that a detailed list of "do's" and

---

[3] R. B. Smith, "Ethics in Business: An Essential Element of Success," *Management Accounting* (June 1990), p. 50.

"don'ts" leads to a legalistic view of ethics—any action not prohibited by the code is seen as acceptable. Supporters of more detail say that general guidelines are unenforceable platitudes that are easily ignored. There is no easy answer.

Regardless of the exact form of the code, top management support is essential for its success in influencing employee behavior. The code should be approved at the Board of Directors or CEO level, and the need to adhere to the code must be continually communicated throughout the organization. A common practice is to have employees sign a statement of compliance each year.

Professional Codes of Ethics

Accountants have an additional motivation to behave ethically. As professionals, they are expected to maintain higher standards of ethical conduct than other members of society. Professionals have an expertise that is hard for nonprofessionals to judge. Just as a patient lacks the knowledge to judge a physician, users of accounting information generally lack the expertise to evaluate the accountant who prepares or audits the information. Therefore, it is important that the public have confidence in accountants, that they be able to rely on accountants' honesty, integrity, and competence. To ensure this confidence, professional accounting organizations have developed codes of ethics for their members. They also have procedures for reviewing alleged behavior that is not consistent with the standards and enforcing penalties for violators of the standards.

CPAs adhere to the *AICPA Code of Professional Conduct*. The code includes both broad basic philosophical principles and explicit rules of conduct. The *principles* set a target, an ideal standard to aim for. The *rules* set a minimum standard; conduct below the minimum standard is unsatisfactory and results in penalties. Topics for which rules of conduct exist include independence, integrity and objectivity, competence, confidential client information, contingent fees, and advertising. The Institute of Management Accountants, which focuses on accountants in industry and government, has developed *Standards of Ethical Conduct for Management Accountants*.

Ethical Dilemmas

Despite corporate and professional codes of ethical conduct, making ethical choices is not always easy. Managers and accountants should have no difficulty choosing between clearly ethical and unethical alternatives. Unfortunately, most ethical dilemmas are not that clear-cut. The most difficult situations arise when there is strong pressure to take an action that is "borderline" ethical, or when two ethical standards conflict.

Sometimes two ethical objectives cannot both be achieved. For example, maintaining client confidentiality can conflict with a CPA's goals of objective reporting and professional integrity. Suppose you are a CPA who audits a local bank and also a manufacturing firm that is one of the bank's customers. The manufacturing firm has a $5 million loan from the bank. From your audit of the manufacturer, you know that the company is in deep financial trouble and may default on the loan. The bank does not yet realize this and still has the loan receivable listed as a $5 million asset. Should you tell the bank about the possible default so that it can reduce its asset and plan for a possible default? Or should you respect the confidentiality of the manufacturer? Both decisions have ethical pros and cons.

Borderline ethical actions also create problems. Rationalizations such as "it's legal, so it must be acceptable" or "everyone does it" are often heard in such situations. Suppose you are an accountant in a division of a large company. A major sale is completed just after the close of the fiscal year. The division manager has asked you to record the sale in the current year instead of next year. The manager is your boss, and you believe she will give you a much better evaluation if you go along with her request. In fact, she could make your life difficult if you don't go along. It is unlikely that anyone will find out—and besides, it's simply a matter of timing, not one of recording fictitious sales. It might be clear that recording the sale in the next period is the ethical thing to do, but the pressure to record it in the current period is great. You might see many personal benefits and few costs to recording it in the current period. Ethics might not be the dominant factor in the decision.

In summary, ethical dilemmas are just that—dilemmas. There are no easy answers. The important thing is to recognize the ethical dimensions of a decision and weigh them when forming your judgment.

Framework for Ethical Judgments: An Example

To carefully weigh ethical considerations in making decisions, it helps to have a framework. Consider the following six steps:

1. Determine the facts.
2. Identify the ethical issues.
3. Identify major principles, rules, and values.
4. Specify the alternatives.
5. Assess the possible consequences.
6. Make the decision.

We will now apply these steps to the following situation.[4]

Sylvia Feldberg was a new staff assistant in the internal audit department of Melman Metals, Inc. In undertaking her part of an audit, Sylvia discovered an error in the previous year's audit. The error was not insignificant, but it was not large enough to cause major problems. The person in charge of that part of the audit last year, David Williams, is currently in charge of the overall audit. David had advanced rapidly with the firm and had an excellent reputation with his superiors. He was known to be rather hard on his staff assistants, particularly if they failed to meet their time budget.

Sylvia is trying to decide what to do. She knows that David will be preparing a form rating her performance on the audit. She also knows that she overran the budgeted time for her work because of the need to investigate the error. What are the ethical issues? What should Sylvia do? Let us apply the six-step framework.

1. *Determine the facts.* These should be clear from the description of the case.
2. *Identify the ethical issues.* The ethical issues revolve around the effects on the people involved. Individuals who might be affected include Sylvia, David, other internal auditors reporting to David, and various other employees of Melman Metals. Sylvia

---

[4]Adapted from the case "Let Bygones Be Bygones" in W. W. May, ed., *Ethics in the Accounting Curriculum: Cases and Readings* (American Accounting Association, 1990).

might examine her integrity versus her job protection and David's reputation. She might judge the importance of David's reputation versus other junior accountants' interests and the interests of the internal audit department and Melman Metals.

3. *Identify major principles, rules, and values.* Among the items to be considered are integrity, job security, reputation (David's and Sylvia's), obligations to a colleague, obligation to disclose important information, concern for the welfare of others, the firm's right to know, morale among staff members, and loyalty (to self, to colleagues, to the firm).

4. *Specify the alternatives.* There are at least three alternatives: (a) report the error to David, (b) report the error to a manager one step above David, and (c) correct the error, put a note in the files, but say nothing.

5. *Assess the possible consequences.* (a) Reporting the error to David may lead him to penalize Sylvia, or it might lead him to reward her for careful work and for exhibiting integrity in reporting the error. It will also preserve Sylvia's integrity and probably cause the error to be corrected, possibly without any notice to the firm's management. (b) Reporting to a manager above David's level will result in the error being corrected but at the expense of David's reputation. David may penalize Sylvia, and surely their working relationship will be damaged. Sylvia will maintain her integrity, and other young accountants may be treated more fairly. (c) Correcting the error but saying nothing avoids a confrontation with David, possibly creating in Sylvia a mixed feeling of relief and uneasiness with ducking the issue. Management may or may not discover the error and its correction. If they discover it, they may do nothing, praise Sylvia for careful work in correcting it, or reprimand her for not reporting it. If they discover it, they may also confront David, who might criticize Sylvia for not reporting the error to him.

6. *Make the decision.* As in most ethical dilemmas, there is no obviously correct decision. Sylvia must weigh the probabilities of the various consequences and the relative importance of the principles, rules, and values involved. Even though the framework does not lead to an easy decision, it makes sure the relevant factors are considered in the decision. The authors favor reporting the error to David. Internal auditors must protect their integrity, and Sylvia has a responsibility to keep the firm from being unpleasantly surprised.

Manipulation of Reported Income

We often think of ethical violations where managers scheme to line their own pockets at the expense of the company, other employees, or shareholders. However, many recent ethical problems have arisen not for direct personal gain but to meet top management expectations for growth and profits.

Although many managers may not be directly lured by cash or inventories, they may nevertheless attempt to manipulate financial results. Why? Because bonuses, salary raises, and promotions are frequently affected by reported sales or income. For example, the achieving of a budgeted net income for a specific quarter or year may mean a tidy bonus.

Examples of manipulation of profits appear periodically. For instance, a few years ago several executives of H. J. Heinz Company felt that they were under pressure to produce smooth earnings growth from quarter to quarter. These executives would prepay for advertising services near the end of a highly profitable quarter, charging the outlay to expense. They would then obtain the actual advertising services in the next quarter. In effect, such manipulation hurts the current quarter's profits by overstating its expenses and helps the subsequent quarter's profits by understating its expenses.

In a highly publicized case, E. F. Hutton, a securities brokerage firm, pleaded guilty to two thousand counts of fraud for writing checks for more than it had in its checking accounts. *Business Week* indicated that "Hutton's top management put in place incentives to encourage mid-level employees to boost cash-management income but neglected to set up systems to monitor the overdrafting of checking accounts."

A little later, the manipulation of earnings at Boston Company was disclosed. This banking subsidiary of Shearson Lehman Hutton, Inc., is a leader in administering pension funds, mutual funds, and trusts. Earnings were inflated by $30 million, primarily by the improper deferral of expenses. The disclosure was followed by the firing of Boston Company's president and the resignation of its chief financial officer and senior vice-president. *Business Week* reported that "some clients and Shearson insiders believe Boston Co. felt impelled by Shearson to produce extraordinary results at a time when most other units of Shearson were struggling."

Undue pressures for profits also induce the recording of phony sales and tempt marketing executives to sell to marginal customers who never pay. The best protection against such manipulations is paying attention to these points in the checklist of internal control: (1) reliable personnel, (2) separation of duties, (3) proper authorization, and (4) independent check.

Above all, to ensure adequate control, a "control consciousness" must become embedded in the managers throughout the organization. Such consciousness must come from the top down. Unless top managers provide clear messages and examples of proper behavior, subordinates will be unlikely to take their responsibilities for control seriously. A *Business Week* editorial commented: "Middle management in a lot of companies is under excruciating pressure to meet profit goals that are too tough. There may be more indictments unless top management takes a more realistic view of its business."

Control consciousness begins with an unequivocal communication of a positive tone from the very top. Various incentives may drive managers to struggle for profits, to increase revenues, and to control costs. But such pressures must be counterbalanced by a clear, consistent message: "Thou shalt not cook the books. If you do, you're history. This firm stands for quality and honesty."

Summary Problems for Your Review

Problem One

Identify the internal control weaknesses in each of the following situations:

a. Mike Reynolds performs all purchasing functions for Bayside Marine. He orders merchandise, oversees its delivery, and approves invoices for payment.

b. The Winthrop Mudhens, a minor league baseball team, is struggling financially. To save costs, and because all seating is general admission, the team has eliminated ticket takers. The ticket seller simply lets fans go through the gate when they pay the admission fee.

c. Cash and checks received by mail from customers who purchased items on open account are opened by an accounts receivable clerk, who deposits the cash and checks in the bank and prepares the appropriate accounting journal entry.

d. Ruth Ann Kilstrom is a trusted and dedicated employee. In fact, she is so dedicated that she has not taken a vacation in five years. Her boss appreciates her dedication because no one could do her job if she were gone.

e. Employees in Wing Point Grocery do a variety of jobs. When business is slack, they stock shelves and perform other necessary tasks. When the checkout stands are busy, everyone is expected to help with checkouts by operating whatever cash register is available. Each employee works at an average of four different checkout stands in an average shift, and every checkout stand is manned by an average of six different persons each day.

Solution to Problem One

a. A single person should not perform all these functions. Reynolds could order fictitious merchandise, record its delivery, and authorize payment to his own (or a confederate's) account.

b. There is no control against the ticket seller's letting friends in free or pocketing cash without issuing a ticket, by simply letting the fans go through the gate.

c. The accounts receivable clerk performs too many functions. The clerk could keep cash (or forge an endorsement of a check) and make a false entry in the accounts, such as writing off the account as a bad debt.

d. There are at least two problems with Kilstrom's dedication. First, because no one else could do her job, the company would be in dire straits if something happened to her or if she resigned suddenly. Second, she has too great an opportunity to perpetrate a fraud without anyone discovering it. If someone replaced her periodically, he or she might be in a position to discover any fraud.

e. Responsibility is not well defined. If a shortage of cash occurs at any checkout stand, it will be impossible to identify the employee responsible.

Problem Two

A news story reported:

> A federal grand jury indicted seven former Cenco, Inc., officials, accusing them of an inventory overstatement scheme that led the concern to report about $25 million in false profits. The indictment charged that the overstatement was accomplished by increasing the number of products shown on inventory tabulating cards and making up new cards. The inflation of inventory lessened the reported cost of sales and thereby resulted in a greater reported profit figure.

Given this description, were any assets stolen? What is the major feature in the chapter checklist of internal control that is aimed at preventing such dishonesty? Indicate how such dishonest acts could be accomplished and how the dishonest officials might have expected to benefit from those acts.

Solution to Problem Two

Assets in the form of inventories were probably not stolen. Recall the section "Effects of Inventory Errors" in Chapter 7, page 291; overstatement of ending inventory also causes overstatement of net income in the current period. Major motives were job security (by means of a display of higher net income) and greed (by means of management bonuses and raises in future salaries). Indeed, the manager who began the scheme was hired on a four-year contract with Cenco, giving him a modest annual base salary of $40,000 plus a bonus that added 1% to his salary for every 1% increase in the Cenco Medical Health (CMH) Group's net income. Net profits soared during the life of the manager's contract. The manager reaped total compensation far in excess of his base salary.

Two subordinate managers had no incentive bonus plans, but they played along with the inventory scheme to please their boss. A variety of ways were used to overstate inventories. For example, three boxes of gauze pads would become twenty-three. The auditors were fooled with the help of fake invoices and lies. The scheme was uncovered when a subordinate informed the company treasurer. Three executives were given prison terms ranging from one to three years.

The major feature that should prevent such dishonesty is *separation of duties*. Collusion makes dishonest acts harder to accomplish. Nevertheless, as the Cenco case illustrates, separation of duties is not enough to detect fictitious inventories when there is collusion.

Reliable personnel with clear responsibilities is an additional feature on the checklist that is illustrated by this case. Personnel must be not only competent and honest but also adequately instructed and supervised. Immediate supervisors should know enough about underlying operations so that they can sense any significant unauthorized conduct. *Independent check* is another feature that helps. That is why outside auditors conduct their own counts and observe management's counts.

Highlights to Remember

It is tempting to delegate internal control decisions to accountants. However, managers at all levels have a major responsibility for the success of internal controls. In fact, in the United States there is a federal law that explicitly places the ultimate responsibility for the adequacy of internal controls of publicly held companies on top management. To help monitor internal control, boards of directors appoint audit committees, which oversee accounting controls, the financial statements, and general financial affairs of the company.

The following general characteristics form a checklist that can be used as a starting point for judging the effectiveness of internal control:

1. Reliable personnel with clear responsibilities
2. Separation of duties
3. Proper authorization
4. Adequate documents
5. Proper procedures
6. Physical safeguards
7. Bonding, vacations, and rotation of duties
7. Independent check
9. Cost-benefit analysis

Managers and accountants should recognize that the role of an internal control system is as much a positive one (enhancing efficiency) as a negative one (reducing errors and fraud).

The checklist of internal controls applies to both computerized and manual systems. However, computerized systems change the emphasis of internal controls. Although computers process data exactly as instructed, controls over programming and data input are especially important.

Control systems for cash and inventories are usually well developed because these assets are often the targets of theft or embezzlement.

Internal control is enhanced by high ethical standards among employees. Companies and professional organizations develop codes of ethical conduct to provide guidelines. Nevertheless, ethical dilemmas exist—situations where the ethical choice is not clear. It is important to recognize the ethical dimensions of a decision, even if ethical values and norms do not always lead to a clear-cut choice.

Appendix 8A: Internal Control of Cash

This appendix describes how organizations control cash. Most cash is kept in bank accounts. Therefore the focus is on understanding bank statements and transactions.

The Bank Statement

Exhibit 8-4 displays a bank statement for account number 96848602, one of thousands of the bank's deposits. Together, these accounts form the subsidiary ledger that supports the bank's general ledger account *Deposits*, a liability.

The supporting documents for the detailed checks on the statement are canceled checks; for additional deposits, deposit slips. Notice that the minimum balance, $ – 33.39, is negative. This indicates an *overdraft*, which is a negative account balance arising from the bank's paying a check even though the depositor had insufficient funds available at the instant the check was presented.

Overdrafts are permitted as an occasional courtesy by the bank. However, the depositor is rarely given more than a day or two to eliminate the overdraft by making a deposit. Moreover, the bank may levy a fee (e.g. $10 or $30) for each overdraft.

Banks often provide (for a fee plus interest) "automatic" loan privileges, short-term loans (from ten to thirty days or more) to cover overdrafts. That is, when a depositor has insufficient funds, the bank increases the depositor's account with an "automatic" loan. The depositor avoids any embarrassment or risks of a bank's delaying payment of a check to await an additional deposit.

Bank Reconciliations

Exhibit 8-5 demonstrates how an independent check of cash balances works for any bank depositor (individual or business entity). First, note how parallel records are kept. The balance on December 31 is an asset (Cash) on the depositor's books and a liability (Deposits) on the bank's books. The terms *debit* and *credit* as used by banks may seem strange. Banks *credit* the depositor's account for additional deposits because the bank has a liability to the depositor. Banks *debit* the account for checks cleared and canceled (paid) by the bank. When the $2,000 check drawn by the depositor on January 5 is paid by the bank on January 8, the bank's journal entry would be:

```
Jan. 8 Deposits . . . . . . . . . . . . . . . . . . . . . . . . .   $2,000
          Cash . . . . . . . . . . . . . . . . . . . . . . . . .              $2,000
          To decrease the depositor's account.
```

SEAFIRST BANK

University Branch
4701 University Way NE
Seattle WA 98145

Richard B. Sandstrom   777
2420 Highline Rd.
Redmond WA 98110

Account Number
96848602
Statement Period
11-21-95 to 12-20-95

SUMMARY OF YOUR ACCOUNTS	
CHECKING	
First Choice Minimum Balance	96848602
Beginning Balance	368.56
Deposits	5,074.00
Withdrawals	3,232.92
Service Charges/Fees	16.00
Ending Balance	2,193.64
Minimum Balance on 12-9-95	-33.39

CHECKING ACTIVITY

Deposits

Posted	Amount	Description
11-21	700.00	Deposit
11-25	1,810.00	Payroll Deposit
12-10	1,810.00	Payroll Deposit
12-16	754.00	Deposit

Withdrawals

Ck No	Paid	Amount
1606	12-02	1134.00
1607	11-28	561.00
1609*	12-09	12.00
1617*	12-05	7.00
1629*	11-26	10.00
1630	11-25	16.95
1639*	12-02	96.00
1641*	12-09	1025.00
1642	12-05	50.00
1643	12-15	236.25
1644	12-17	84.72

* = Gap in check sequence
Total number of checks = 10

A credit balance on the bank's books means that the bank owes money to the depositor.

A monthly *bank reconciliation* (see p.341) is conducted by the depositor to make sure that all cash receipts and disbursements are accounted for. Bank reconciliations take many forms, but the objective is unchanged: to explain all differences in the cash balances shown on the bank statement and in the depositor's general ledger at a given date. Using the data in Exhibit 8-5:

Bank Reconciliation January 31, 19X2	Balance per books (also called *balance per check register, register balance*)	$ 8,000
	Deduct: Bank service charges for January not recorded on the books (also include any other charges by the bank not yet deducted)*	20
	Adjusted (corrected) balance per books	$ 7,980
	Balance per bank (also called *bank statement balance, statement balance*)	$10,980
	Add: Deposits not recorded by bank (also called *unrecorded deposits, deposits in transit*), deposit of 1/31	7,000
	Total	$17,980
	Deduct: Outstanding checks, check of 1/29	10,000
	Adjusted (corrected) balance per bank	$ 7,980

* Note that new entries on the depositor's books are required for all previously unrecorded additions and deductions made to achieve the adjusted balance per books.

As the bank reconciliation indicates, an adjustment is necessary on the books of the depositor:

Jan. 31 Bank service charge expense   20
                 Cash   20
          To record bank charges for printing checks.

This popular format has two major sections. The first section begins with the balance per books (that is, the balance in the Cash T-account). Adjustments are made for items not entered on the books but already entered by the *bank*, such as deduction of the $20 service charge. No additions are shown in the illustrated section, but an illustrative addition would be the bank's collection of a customer receivable on behalf of the company. The second section begins with the balance per bank. Adjustments are made for items not entered by the *bank* but already entered in the books. After adjustments, each section should end with identical adjusted cash balances. This is the amount that should appear as cash in bank on the depositor's balance sheet.

Paperless Bank Transactions

Each passing year brings us closer to so-called paperless banking. For example, many employees never see their payroll checks. Instead the employer deposits the "checks" in the employees' bank accounts. This is an example of an "automatic" deposit. If the employee forgets to add the amount to his or her check register, the bank's books would show a higher balance than the depositor's books. Similarly, some 75% of transactions in "branch banking" offices occur at automatic teller machines (ATM). Many depositors may forget to record these, but will find them when they reconcile their bank statement with their books (check register).

Petty Cash

imprest basis A method of accounting for petty cash.

Every organization desires to minimize red tape—for example, avoiding unjustifiably complicated procedures for minor disbursements. Consequently, petty cash funds are usually created and accounted for on an **imprest basis**. An imprest petty cash fund is initiated with a fixed amount of currency and coins. As the currency

Exhibit 8-5

Comparative
Cash Balances,
January 19X2

Depositor's Records			
Cash in Bank			
(receivable from bank)			
1/1/X2 Bal.	11,000	1/5	2,000
		1/15	3,000
1/10	4,000		
		1/19	5,000
1/24	6,000		
1/31	7,000	1/29	10,000
	28,000		20,000
1/31/X2 Bal.	8,000		

Bank's Records			
Deposits (payable)			
1/8	2,000	1/1/X2 Bal.	11,000
1/20	3,000		
		1/11	4,000
1/28	5,000	1/26	6,000
1/31	20*		
	10,020		21,000
		1/31/X2 Bal.	10,980

* Service charge for printing checks.

Date	Depositor's General Journal	Debit	Credit
1/5	Accounts payable	2,000	
	Cash		2,000
	Check No. 1.		
1/10	Cash	4,000	
	Accounts receivable		4,000
	Deposit slip No. 1.		
1/15	Income taxes payable	3,000	
	Cash		3,000
	Check No. 2.		
1/19	Accounts payable	5,000	
	Cash		5,000
	Check No. 3.		
1/24	Cash	6,000	
	Accounts receivable		6,000
	Deposit No. 2.		
1/29	Accounts payable	10,000	
	Cash		10,000
	Check No. 4.		
1/31	Cash	7,000	
	Accounts receivable		7,000
	Deposit No. 3.		

is used, petty cash receipts or vouchers are prepared to show the purposes of the disbursements. When the balance of currency gets low, the fund is restored to its original level by drawing and cashing a single check for the exact amount of the needed cash replenishment. The following are typical journal entries:

Petty cash	100	
Cash in bank		100
To set up a fund for miscellaneous minor office disbursements. (A check is drawn, cashed, and proceeds placed with some responsible person.)		
Postage	10	
Freight in	40	
Miscellaneous office expenses	35	
Cash in bank		85
To replenish the petty cash fund and record expenses paid therefrom.		

Examples of petty cash outlays include special post-office charges for certifying or insuring mail, collections by delivery personnel, and dinner money given to an employee when working overtime.

Note that after inception, the Petty Cash account itself is never directly charged or credited unless the $100 initial amount of the fund is increased or decreased. Further, the cash on hand plus the receipts (or vouchers) should always equal the $100 amount of the petty cash fund.

Appendix 8B: Inventory Control via Retail Method, Cost Ratios, and Cutoffs

Retail Method of Inventory Control

retail inventory method (retail method) A popular inventory costing method based on sales prices, often used as a control device and for obtaining an inventory valuation for financial statement purposes.

A popular inventory costing method, known as the **retail inventory method**, or simply **retail method**, is often used as a control device. Its role in obtaining an inventory valuation (at cost) for financial statement purposes will be discussed in the next section; for now, concentrate on its internal control characteristics. Consider how a food store might use the retail method to control grocery inventories. Merchandise is accounted for at *retail prices* as follows:

		Retail Prices
	Inventory, January 5 (by surprise count by branch auditors)	$ 15,000
	Purchases (shipments to store from branch warehouse)	101,000
	Additional retail price changes:	
	Markups (from initial retail prices)	2,000
	Markdowns (from initial retail prices)	(5,000)
(1)	Total merchandise to account for	$113,000
	Sales (per cash-register records)	$100,000
	Allowable shrinkage (shoplifting, breakage, etc., usually a predetermined percentage of sales)	1,000

continued

		Retail Prices
(2)	Total deductions	$101,000
(1) – (2)	Inventory, February 11 (should be)	$ 12,000
	Inventory, February 11 (by physical count)	11,100
	Excess shrinkage	$ 900

The total retail value of merchandise to account for is $113,000. What happens to it? Most is sold, some disappears as shrinkage, and some remains in ending inventory. Cash-register tabulations indicate sales of $100,000. If there were absolutely no shrinkage, the ending inventory at retail should be $113,000 – $100,000 = $13,000. But suppose "normal" shrinkage is 1% of sales, or $1,000. Therefore the expected inventory is $13,000 – $1,000 = $12,000. The actual physical count provides a retail valuation of $11,100. Thus the total shrinkage is $1,900, including $900 of excess shrinkage ($12,000 – $11,100 = $900). If the inventory shrinkage is not within predetermined limits, the manager usually bears prime responsibility.

Computerized checkout systems help to control inventory shrinkage. Such systems record each individual item that is sold, allowing a store to keep an item-by-item perpetual inventory. Pinpointing the items that are disappearing allows additional control measures to be applied to these items.

Role of Cost Ratios and Gross Profit Percentages

While retail inventory values provide a satisfactory basis for internal control, inventories in financial statements are reported at cost. Therefore the retail values of inventories must be converted to costs. This is accomplished using the ratio of cost to retail value. Consider the data in our prior illustration with a "cost" column added.

		Retail Prices	Cost
	Inventory, January 5 (by surprise count by branch auditors)	$ 15,000	$12,300
	Purchases (shipments to store from branch warehouse)	101,000	78,100
	Additional retail price changes:		
	Markups (from initial retail prices)	2,000	
	Markdowns (from initial retail prices)	(5,000)	
(1)	Total merchandise to account for	$113,000	$90,400
	Ratio of cost to retail value		80%
	Sales (per cash-register records)	$100,000	$80,000
	Allowable shrinkage (shoplifting, breakage, etc., usually a predetermined percentage of sales)	1,000	800
(2)	Total deductions	$101,000	$80,800
(1) – (2)	Inventory, February 11 (should be)	$ 12,000	$ 9,600
	Inventory, February 11 (by physical count)	11,100	8,880
	Excess shrinkage	$ 900	$ 720

The line denoted as (1) provides the basis for a ratio of cost to retail value:

$$\$90,400 \div \$113,000 = .80$$

This critical ratio[5] is then used to develop the key subsequent amounts at cost:

	Retail Prices		Average Ratio of Cost To Retail Value		Cost
Allowable shrinkage	$ 1,000	×	.80	=	$ 800
Inventory per physical count	11,100	×	.80	=	8,880
Excess shrinkage	900	×	.80	=	720

These amounts can be used in an income statement for a company with a periodic inventory system:

Sales		$100,000
Cost of sales:		
Beginning inventory per physical count	$12,300	
Purchases	78,100	
Available for sale	$90,400	
Ending inventory per physical count	8,880	
Cost of sales (including $800 allowable shrinkage and $720 excess shrinkage)		81,520
Gross margin (after inventory shrinkage)		$ 18,480

This approach is used over and over again as periods unfold. The ending inventory of $8,880 becomes the beginning inventory of the next reporting period. Purchases are then added at cost, a new ratio of cost to retail value is developed, and shrinkage and ending inventory values are approximated:

1. Compute the goods available for sale at retail value and cost.
2. Compute the ratio of cost to retail value.
3. Count the ending inventory and value it at retail value.
4. Convert the retail value of the ending inventory to cost by using the ratio of cost to retail value.

The *cost* of shrinkage, which can be divided into normal and excess components, is approximated by using the ratio of cost to retail value.

Note that the ratio of cost to retail value is the complement of the gross profit ratio. In this illustration, the gross profit percentage is 100% − 80% = 20%. Thus the gross profit percentage or its related ratio of cost to retail value is a key element of internal control.

---

[5] Both markdowns and markups are included in this illustrative computation. Many retailers prefer to exclude markdowns because a lower cost ratio is developed:

$$\$90,400 \div (\$113,000 + \$5,000 \text{ Markdowns}) = .7661$$

This ratio would provide a "more conservative" ending inventory. Advocates of this approach say that it yields a better approximation of the lower-of-cost-or-market method.

Cutoff Errors, Consignments, and Inventory Valuation

cutoff error Failure to record transactions in the correct time period.

The accrual basis of accounting should include the physical counting and careful valuation of inventory at least once yearly. Auditors routinely search for **cutoff errors**, which are failures to record transactions in the correct time period. For example, assume a periodic inventory system. Suppose a physical inventory is conducted on December 31. Inventory purchases of $100,000 arrive in the receiving room during the afternoon of December 31. The acquisition is included in Purchases and Accounts Payable but excluded from the ending inventory valuation. Such an error would understate ending inventory, thereby overstating cost of goods sold and understating gross profit. On the other hand, if the acquisition were not recorded until January 2, the error would understate both the ending inventory and Accounts Payable as of December 31. However, cost of goods sold and gross profit would be correct because Purchases and the ending inventory would be understated by the same amount.

The general approach to recording purchases and sales is keyed to the legal transfer of ownership. Some major points follow:

1. Ownership typically changes hands when the goods are delivered by the seller to the purchaser. These terms are usually F.O.B. destination. If the terms are F.O.B. shipping point, ownership passes to the purchaser when the goods are delivered to the transportation company.

consignment Goods shipped for future sales, title remaining with the shipper (consignor), for which the receiver (consignee), upon his or her acceptance, is accountable. The goods are part of the consignor's inventory until sold.

2. Sometimes goods are shipped on **consignment**. These are goods shipped for future sale, title remaining with the shipper (consignor), for which the receiver (consignee), upon his or her acceptance, is accountable. Even though such goods are physically elsewhere, they are part of the consignor's inventory until sold. For example, a manufacturer of bicycles might ship 20 units on consignment to a new retailer. Under such terms, the bicycles are included in the manufacturer's inventory and excluded from the retailer's inventory.

Auditors are especially careful about cutoff tests because the pressure for profits sometimes causes managers to postpone the recording of bona fide purchases of goods and services. Similarly, the same managers may deliberately include sales *orders* near year end (rather than bona fide completed sales) in revenues. For example, consider the case of Datapoint, a maker of small computers and telecommunications equipment. A news story reported: "Datapoint's hard-pressed sales force was still logging orders that might not hold up after shipment." In the wake of an accounting scandal, Datapoint's president declared a three-week "amnesty period" during which scheduled shipments could be taken off the books, no questions asked.

A similar news story referred to difficulties at McCormick & Co., a firm known for its spices: "The investigation also found that improprieties included the company's accounting for sales. In a longstanding practice, the company recorded as sales, goods that had been selected and prepared for shipment rather than waiting until after they had been shipped as is the customary accounting practice."

Accounting Vocabulary

Assignment Material

Questions

8-1. "The words *internal control* are commonly misunderstood to refer only to those facets of the accounting system that are supposed to help prevent embezzling." Comment.

8-2. Distinguish between *internal accounting control* and *internal administrative control*.

8-3. Into what four categories of transactions can the most repetitive, voluminous transactions in most organizations be divided?

8-4. "Business operations would be a hopeless tangle without the paperwork that is often regarded with disdain." Explain.

8-5. "The primary responsibility for internal controls rests with the outside auditors." Do you agree? Explain.

8-6. "The Foreign Corrupt Practices Act governs the acts of multinational companies." Do you agree? Explain.

8-7. What are the major ways the board of directors ensures compliance with the Foreign Corrupt Practices Act regarding internal control systems?

8-8. Give three examples of documentation of an internal accounting control system.

8-9. Name five objectives of the Foreign Corrupt Practices Act with respect to internal accounting controls.

8-10. What is the primary responsibility of the audit committee?

8-11. "Internal control systems have both negative and positive objectives." Do you agree? Explain.

8-12. Prepare a checklist of important factors to consider in judging an internal control system.

8-13. "The most important element of successful control is personnel." Explain.

8-14. What is the essential idea of separation of duties?

8-15. Authorization can be general or specific. Give an example of each.

8-16. Internal control of a computerized system consists of applications controls and general controls. What are the three types of applications controls?

8-17. Briefly describe how a bottler of soda water might compile data regarding control of breakage of bottles at the plant, where normal breakage can be expected.

8-18. The branch manager of a national retail grocery chain has stated: "My managers are judged more heavily on the basis of their merchandise-shrinkage control than on their overall sales volume." Why? Explain.

8-19. What is a corporate code of ethics? Why do organizations adopt such a code?

8-20. Why do accountants generally adhere to a higher ethical standard than other members of society?

8-21. "It is easy to be ethical. Just identify the ethical choice and then do it." Do you agree? Explain.

8-22. "Our managers know they are expected to meet budgeted profit targets. We do not take excuses. Good managers find a way to make budget." Discuss the possible consequences of this policy.

8-23. Pressure for profits extends beyond managers in profit-seeking companies. A news story reported: "The profit motive, even in nonprofit hospitals, is steadily eroding the traditional concern to provide care to the medically indigent." Why does the profit motive affect even nonprofit organizations?

Exercises

8-24   Management's Responsibility for Internal Controls

The Lorentzen Company has always tried to prepare informative annual reports. A few years ago, Maureen Lorentzen, president, heard about the Foreign Corrupt Practices Act, but she assumed that it did not affect her company. After all, not only did Lorentzen Company refrain from corrupt foreign practices, but the company had no foreign operations or export sales.

Required   Explain how the Foreign Corrupt Practices Act affects a company such as Lorentzen. How does it affect Lorentzen's annual report?

8-25   Internal Control Weaknesses

Identify the internal control weaknesses in each of the following situations and indicate what change or changes you would recommend to eliminate the weaknesses.

a. The internal audit staff of MacDougall Aerospace, Inc., reports to the controller. However, internal audits are undertaken only when a department manager requests one, and audit reports are confidential documents prepared exclusively for the manager. Internal auditors are not allowed to talk to the external auditors.

b. Alice Walker, president of Northwestern State Bank, a small-town midwestern bank, wants to expand the size of her bank. She hired Fred Howell to begin a foreign-loan department. Howell had previously worked in the international department of a London bank. The president told him to consult with her on any large loans, but she never specified exactly what was meant by "large." At the end of Howell's first year, the president was surprised and pleased by his results. Although he had made several loans larger than any made by other sections of the bank and had not consulted with her on any of them, the president hesitated to say anything because the financial results were so good. Walker certainly did not want to upset the person most responsible for the bank's excellent growth in earnings.

c. Michael Grant is in charge of purchasing and receiving watches for Blumberg, Inc., a chain of jewelry stores. Grant places orders, fills out receiving documents when the watches are delivered, and authorizes payment to suppliers. According to Blumberg's procedures manual, Grant's activities should be reviewed by a purchasing supervisor. But to save money, the supervisor was not replaced when she resigned three years ago. No one seems to miss the supervisor.

8-26   Multiple Choice
Choose the best answer for each of the four questions that follow:

1. Which of the following internal control procedures would be *most* likely to prevent the concealment of a cash shortage resulting from the improper write-off of a trade account receivable?
    a. Write-offs must be authorized by company field sales employees who are in a position to determine the financial standing of the customers.
    b. Write-offs must be approved by a responsible officer after review of credit department recommendations and supporting evidence.
    c. Write-offs must be supported by an aging schedule showing that only receivables overdue several months have been written off.
    d. Write-offs must be approved by the cashier who is in a position to know if the receivables have, in fact, been collected.

2. Which of the following is an effective internal accounting control over accounts receivable?
    a. The billing function should be assigned to persons other than those responsible for maintaining accounts receivable subsidiary records.
    b. Only persons who handle cash receipts should be responsible for the preparation of documents that reduce accounts receivable balances.
    c. Responsibility for approval of the write-off of uncollectible accounts receivable should be assigned to the cashier.
    d. Balances in the subsidiary accounts receivable ledger should be reconciled to the general ledger control account once a year, preferably at year end.

3. Internal control over cash receipts is weakened when an employee who receives customer mail receipts also
    a. Prepares bank deposit slips for all mail receipts.
    b. Maintains a petty cash fund.
    c. Prepares initial cash receipts records.
    d. Records credits to individual accounts receivable.

4. Which of the following activities would be *least* likely to strengthen a company's internal control?

a. Carefully selecting and training employees.

b. Separating accounting from other financial operations.

c. Maintaining insurance for fire and theft.

d. Fixing responsibility for the performance of employee duties.

8-27 Assignment of Duties

The Drafting Supply Corporation is a distributor of several popular lines of drawing and measuring instruments. It purchases merchandise from several suppliers and sells to hundreds of retail stores. Here is a *partial list* of the company's necessary office routines:

1. Verifying and comparing related purchase documents: purchase orders, purchase invoices, receiving reports, etc.

2. Preparing vouchers for cash disbursements and attaching supporting purchase documents.

3. Signing above vouchers to authorize payment (after examining vouchers with attached documents).

4. Preparing checks for above.

5. Signing checks (after examining voucher authorization and supporting documents).

6. Mailing checks.

7. Daily sorting of incoming mail into items that contain money and items that do not.

8. Distributing the above mail: money to cashier, reports of money received to accounting department, and remainder to various appropriate offices.

9. Making daily bank deposits.

10. Reconciling monthly bank statements.

The company's chief financial officer has decided that no more than five people will handle all of these routines, including himself as necessary.

Required Prepare a chart to show how these operations should be assigned to the five employees, including the chief financial officer. Use a row for each of the numbered routines and a column for each employee: Financial Officer, A, B, C, D. Place a check mark for each row in one or more of the columns. Observe the rules of the textbook checklist for internal control, especially separation of duties.

8-28 Multiple Choice; Discovering Irregularities

In questions 1 through 3, you are given a well-recognized procedure of internal control. You are to identify the irregularity *that will be discovered or prevented by each procedure*. Write the numbers 1 through 3 on your answer sheet. Then place the letter of your chosen answer next to your numbers.

1. The general-ledger control account and the subsidiary ledger of Accounts Receivable are reconciled monthly. The two bookkeepers are independent.

   a. When friends purchase merchandise, the salesclerk allows them an employee discount by using an employee name on the sales slip and deducting the discount on the slip. This is against company policy.

   b. The Accounts Receivable subsidiary-ledger bookkeeper charges a sale to Mr. Smith instead of Mr. Smithe (that is, the wrong customer). The error is due to misreading the sales slip.

   c. The Accounts Receivable subsidiary-ledger bookkeeper charges a customer with $72 instead of $74, the correct amount. The error is due to misreading the sales slip. The credit-sales summary for the day has the correct amount of $74.

   d. The employee opening mail takes funds without making a record of their receipt. Customer accounts are not credited with their payments.

e. The general-ledger bookkeeper takes funds and covers the loss by charging "Miscellaneous General Expenses."

2. Both cash and credit customers are educated to expect a sales receipt. Receipts are serially numbered. All numbers are accounted for daily.

   a. Customers complain that goods ordered are not received.

   b. Customers complain that their monthly bills contain items that have already been paid.

   c. Some customers have the correct change for the merchandise purchased. They pay and do not wait for a sales receipt.

   d. Customers complain that they are billed for goods they did not purchase.

   e. Salesclerks destroy duplicate sales receipts for the amount of cash stolen.

3. At a movie theater box office, all tickets are prenumbered. At the end of each day, the beginning ticket number is subtracted from the ending number to give the number of tickets sold. Cash is counted and compared with the number of tickets sold.

   a. Tickets from a previous day are discovered in the ticket taker's stub box despite the fact that tickets are stamped "Good on Date of Purchase Only."

   b. The ticket taker admits his or her friends without a ticket.

   c. The manager gives theater passes for personal expenses. This is against company policy.

   d. The box office gives too much change.

   e. A test check of customers entering the theater does not reconcile with ticket sales.

8-29   Simple Bank Reconciliation

Study Appendix 8A. The Good Samaritan Hospital has a bank account. Consider the following information:

   a. Balances as of July 31: per books, $48,000; per bank statement, $28,880.

   b. Cash receipts of July 31 amounting to $10,000 were recorded and then deposited in the bank's night depository. The bank did not include this deposit on its July statement.

   c. The bank statement included service charges of $120.

   d. Patients had given the hospital some bad checks amounting to $13,000. The bank marked them NSF and returned them with the bank statement after charging the hospital for the $13,000. The hospital had made no entry for the return of these checks.

   e. The hospital's outstanding checks amounted to $4,000.

Required

1. Prepare a bank reconciliation as of July 31.
2. Prepare the hospital journal entries required by the given information.

8-30.   Petty Cash Fund

(Alternate is 8-31.) Study Appendix 8A. On July 1, 19X2, the treasurer of Holtzer Company established an imprest petty cash fund of $200 by writing a check on the company's regular bank account payable to "Cash." This check was cashed by the office receptionist, who became responsible for the fund. On July 30, there was cash of $93 in the fund along with petty cash "vouchers" (signed receipts for disbursements) as follows: airport limousine fares, $22; postage, $13; office supplies, $35; delivery charges for incoming merchandise, $17; and "supper money" for two secretaries who worked late, $20.

Required

1. Prepare journal entries for (a) creation of the petty cash fund and (b) reimbursement of the fund on July 31 for the payments made from it.
2. Assume that the petty cash fund had been replenished on July 31. Where would its balance appear in the financial statements?
3. Suppose the cash balance in the fund had been only $88 instead of $93 just before its replenishment. Comment briefly.
4. Suppose that sometime in December 19X2 the treasurer decided to decrease the

fund to $175. Prepare the journal entry for the transaction.

8-31   Imprest Petty Cash
(Alternate is 8-30.) Study Appendix 8A. The Stanford Business School created an imprest petty cash fund of $130 on January 2.

During January the following outlays were made from petty cash:

Auto mileage at 25¢ per mile for secretary to deliver documents to alumni office in San Francisco, round trip 80 miles	$20.00
Dinner allowance for mail clerk working overtime	9.00
Postal charges for insuring mail	4.50
Payments to delivery personnel	22.40
Purchase of special posters	12.75
Total	$68.65

Required   Prepare journal entries for

1. Creation of the fund on January 2.
2. Replenishment of the fund on January 31.
3. Reduction of the fund from $130 to $90 on February 15.

8-32   Retail Method and Inventory Shrinkage

Study Appendix 8B. The following figures pertain to the Nadir Gift Store for the two-month period June and July, 19X2:

Sales	$170,000	Purchases (at sales price)	$ 80,000
Additional markups	10,000	Inventory at June 1, 19X2:	
Markdowns	25,000	At cost price	90,000
Purchases (at cost price)	45,000	At selling price	160,000

Required

1. What should the inventory amount to at July 31, 19X2, at retail price using the conventional retail inventory method?
2. Suppose the allowable shrinkage is 2% of sales. The physical inventory at retail prices at July 31 amounts to $50,000. What is the excess inventory shrinkage?
3. Compute the ratio of cost to retail value and the cost of ending inventory.

Problems

8-33   Audit Committee Role
In a recent court decision, a U.S. corporation was required to delegate certain responsibilities to its audit committee. Management was required to

1. Consult with its independent auditors before deciding any significant or material accounting question or policy.
2. Retain independent auditors to perform quarterly reviews of all financial statements prior to public issuance.
3. Conduct internal audits, with personnel reporting directly to the audit committee (internal auditors must report quarterly to the audit committee).
4. Retain or dismiss independent and internal auditors.
5. Consult with the independent auditors on their quarterly reviews of financial statements.

6. Review all monthly corporate and division financial statements and the auditor's management letter.

7. Receive quarterly reports from independent auditors on internal control deficiencies.

8. Review and approve all reports to shareholders and the SEC before dissemination. The court also ruled that the audit committee must be composed of at least three outside directors who have no business dealings with the firm other than directors' fees and expense reimbursements.

Required

a. Prepare a partial corporation organization chart to depict these requirements. Use boxes only for Audit Committee, Independent Auditors, Internal Auditing, Finance Vice-President, and Board of Directors. Connect the appropriate boxes with lines: solid lines for direct responsibility, dashed lines for information and communications. Place numbers on these lines to correspond to the eight items specified by the court decision.

b. Identify the main elements of the chapter checklist of internal control that seem most relevant to this system design.

8-34 Use of Credit Cards

A faculty member used an American Express card for a variety of purchases. When checking her monthly bill, she compared her original copy with a duplicate copy for a gasoline purchase made at a local convenience store. The original copy showed a purchase of $14.25; the duplicate had been raised to $19.25.

Required

Who obtained the extra $5? How can the system be improved to prevent such thievery?

8-35 Embezzlement of Cash Receipts

Leboe Company is a small wholesaler of exercise equipment. It has only a few employees.

The owner of Leboe Company, who is also its president and general manager, makes daily deposits of customers' checks in the company bank account and writes all checks issued by the company. The president also reconciles the monthly bank statement with the books when the bank statement is received in the mail.

The assistant to Leboe Company's president renders secretarial services, which include taking dictation, typing letters, and processing all mail, both incoming and outgoing. Each day the assistant opens the incoming mail and gives the president the checks received from customers. The vouchers attached to the checks are separated by the assistant and sent to the bookkeeper, along with any other remittance advices that have been enclosed with the checks.

The bookkeeper makes prompt entries to credit customers' accounts for their remittances. From these accounts, the bookkeeper prepares monthly statements for mailing to customers.

Other employees include marketing and warehouse personnel.

Required

For the thefts described below, explain briefly how each could have been concealed and what precautions you would recommend for forestalling the theft and its concealment:

1. The president's assistant takes some customers' checks, forges the company's endorsements, deposits the checks in a personal bank account, and destroys the check vouchers and any other remittance advices that have accompanied these checks.

2. The same action is taken as above, except that the vouchers and other remittance advices are sent intact to the bookkeeper.

8-36 Appraisal of Payroll System

(CPA, adapted) Maryland Savings and Loan Company has one hundred branch loan offices. Each office has a manager and four or five subordinates who are employed by the manager. Branch managers prepare the weekly payroll, including their own salaries, and pay their employees from cash on hand. The employee signs the payroll sheet, signifying receipt of his or her salary. Hours worked by hourly personnel are inserted in the payroll sheet from time cards prepared by the employees and approved by the manager.

The weekly payroll sheets are sent to the home office along with other accounting statements and reports. The home office compiles employee earnings records and prepares all federal and state salary reports from the weekly payroll sheets.

Salaries are established by home-office job-evaluation schedules. Salary adjustments, promotions, and transfers of full-time employees are approved by a home-office salary committee, on the basis of the recommendations of branch managers and area supervisors. Branch managers advise the salary committee of new full-time employees and of terminations. Part-time and temporary employees are hired without referral to the salary committee.

Required Based on your review of the payroll system, how might payroll funds be embezzled?

8-37   Film Processing

(W. Crum) Write not more than one page about the possible areas where internal controls should be instituted in the business described briefly below. Keep in mind the size of the business and do not suggest controls of a type impossible to set up in a firm of this sort. Make any reasonable assumptions about management duties and policies not expressly set forth below.

You have a film-developing service in Glendale, with ten employees driving their own cars six days a week to contact about forty places each, where film is left to be picked up and developed. Routes cover all parts of Los Angeles. Drivers bring film in one day and return the processed film the second or third day later. Stores pay the driver for his charges made on film picked up at their store, less a percentage for their work as an agency. The driver then turns this cash in to the Glendale office, where all film is developed and books are kept. Six to ten employees work at the office in Glendale, depending on the volume of work. You run the office and have one full-time accounting-clerical employee. Route drivers are paid monthly by miles of route covered.

8-38 State and County Fairs

Nonprofit entities take various forms. For example, state and county fairs are usually important sources of revenue because the state gets a percentage of the bets made on horse races. In past years, the carnivals would bid for the rights to appear at the fair. The winner would be willing to pay the fair a higher percentage of some measure of its revenue generated from rides, games, and food booths.

Required What types of major internal control problems arise from such percentage revenue agreements? Which item or items in the chapter checklist of internal control seem most critical in these cases?

8-39   Appraisal of Internal Control System

From the *San Francisco Chronicle*:

> The flap over missing ferry fares was peacefully—and openly—resolved at a meeting of the Golden Gate Bridge District finance committee yesterday.
>
> Only a week ago, the subject was a matter of furious dispute in which bridge manager Dale W. Luehring was twice called a liar and there were prospects of a closed meeting on personnel matters.
>
> But yesterday, after a week of investigation, the meeting turned out to be public after all, and attorney Thomas M. Jenkins revealed the full total of stolen ferry tickets equaled $26.20.
>
> The controversy began when auditor Gordon Dahlgren complained that there was an auditing "problem" and that he had not been informed when four children swiped $13.75 worth of tickets February 28. Committee chairman Ben K. Lerer, of San Francisco, ordered a full investigation.
>
> Jenkins said the situation was complicated because children under 5 have been allowed to ride the ferry without a ticket, but after May 1 everyone will have to have a ticket, allowing for a closer audit.

Secondly, Jenkins explained, the "vault" in which tickets are deposited was proved insecure (resulting in two thefts totaling $26.20 worth of tickets) but has been replaced.

In the future, it was decided, all thefts of cash or tickets must be reported immediately to the California Highway Patrol or the local police, the bridge lieutenant on duty, the general manager, the security officer, the auditor-controller, and the transit manager.

In addition, employees must make a full written report within 24 hours to the president of the district board, the chairman of the finance-auditing committee, the auditor-controller, the attorney, the bus transit manager, the water transit manager, the toll captain, and the chief of administration and security.

Required   What is your reaction to the new system? Explain, giving particular attention to applicable criteria for appraising an internal control system.

8-40   Casino Skimming

An article in the *Wall Street Journal* reported that about $7 million in quarters disappeared from the slot machines of four casinos of Argent Corporation in an 18-month period. The coins weighed nearly 150 tons, and the odds against such a payout to players of the slot machines is one in 3,875,000,000,000,000,000,000,000,000,000,000,000,000,000,000,000—an extremely unlikely event, to say the least. The disappearance was part of the biggest known skim operation ever. *Skimming* is taking a portion of gambling revenues before they can be counted for tax purposes.

Internal control is especially important in casinos. Meters in the slot machines record the winnings paid to customers. Coins are taken immediately to the slot counting room when machines are emptied. In the counting rooms coins are weighed, and a portion is returned to the change booths.

Required   What items in the chapter checklist of internal control seem especially important regarding slot machine operations? How could the money from slot machine operations have been stolen in such large amounts?

8-41   Employee Dishonesty

Consider the following true newspaper reports of dishonesty:

a. At a small manufacturer, supervisors had access to time cards and gave out W-2 forms each year. The supervisors pocketed $80,000 a year in the paychecks for phantom workers.

b. A manager at a busy branch office of a copying service had a receipt book of his own. Jobs of $200 and $300 were common. The manager stole cash by simply giving customers a receipt from his book instead of one of the company's numbered forms.

c. A purchasing agent received tiny kickbacks on buttons, zippers, and other trims used at a successful dress company. The agent got rich, and the company was overcharged $10 million.

Required   Specify what control or controls would have helped avoid each of the listed situations.

8-42   Internal Control Weaknesses

Identify the internal control weaknesses in each of the following situations:

a. Rodney Williams, a football star at the local university, was hired by D.A. Mount to work in the accounting department of Mount Electronics during summer vacation. Providing summer jobs is one way that Mount supports the team. After a week of training, Williams opened the mail containing checks from customers, recorded the payment in the books, and prepared the bank deposit slip.

b. Jim Sanchez manages a local franchise of a major twenty-four-hour convenience store. Sanchez brags that he keeps labor costs well below the average for such stores by operating with only one clerk. He has not granted a pay increase in four years.

He loses a lot of clerks, but he can always find replacements.

c. Martha McGuire operates an Exxon service station. Because it takes much extra time for attendants to walk from the gas pumps to the inside cash register, McGuire placed a locked cash box next to the pumps and gave each attendant a key. Cash and credit card slips are placed in the cash box. Each day the amounts are counted and entered in total into the cash register.

d. Lazlo Perconte trusts his employees. The former manager purchased fidelity bonds on employees who handle cash. Perconte decided that such bonds showed a lack of trust, so he ceased purchasing them. Besides, the money saved helped Perconte meet his budget for the year.

8-43   Overstatements of Results

Saxon Industries, Inc., sold office copiers before undergoing bankruptcy proceedings.

Forbes reported that Saxon's inventory had been overstated by at least $100 million out of a reported total inventory of $120 million. A news study reported that possible motives included "inflating earnings or increasing the company's borrowing capacity."

Regarding the manipulations, *Forbes* referred to the Saxon inventory methods as "not LIFO or FIFO but Presto!"

Required

1. How does overstating inventory enhance reported results? Be specific.
2. How are such overstatements accomplished? prevented? Be specific.

8-44   Inventory Shrinkage

Jose Chavez, owner of Handy Hardware Company, was concerned about his control of inventory. In December 19X2, he installed a computerized perpetual inventory system. In April, his accountant brought him the following information for the first three months of 19X3:

Sales	$350,000
Cost of goods sold	295,000
Beginning inventory (per physical count)	65,000
Merchandise purchases	315,000

Chavez had asked his public accounting firm to conduct a physical count of inventory on April 1. The CPAs reported inventory of $70,000.

Required

1. Compute the ending inventory shown in the books by the new perpetual inventory system.
2. Provide the journal entry to reconcile the book inventory with the physical count. What is the corrected cost of goods sold for the first three months of 19X3?
3. Do your calculations point out areas about which Chavez should be concerned? Why?

8-45   Cheating on Inventories

The *Wall Street Journal* reported: "Cheating on inventories is a common way for small businesses to chisel on their income taxes.... A New York garment maker, for example, evades a sizable amount of income tax by undervaluing his firm's inventory by 20 percent on his tax return. He hides about $500,000 out of a $2.5 million inventory."

The news story concluded: "When it's time to borrow, business owners generally want profits and assets to look fat." The garment maker uses a different fiscal period for financial statements to his bank: "After writing down the inventory as of Dec. 31, he writes it up six months later when the fiscal year ends. In this way, he underpays the IRS and impresses his banker. Some describe that kind of inventory accounting as WIFL— Whatever I Feel Like."

1. At a 40% income tax rate, what amount of federal income taxes would the owner evade according to the news story?
2. Consider the next year. By how much would the ending inventory have to be understated to evade the same amount of income taxes?

Use the following table and fill in the blanks:

| | (in dollars) | | | |
| | Honest Reporting | | Dishonest Reporting | |
	First Year	Second Year	First Year	Second Year
Beginning inventory	$ 3,000,000	$?	$ 3,000,000	$?
Purchases	10,000,000	10,000,000	10,000,000	10,000,000
Available for sale	13,000,000	?	13,000,000	?
Ending inventory	2,500,000	2,500,000	2,000,000	?
Cost of goods sold	$10,500,000	$?	$11,000,000	$?
Income tax savings @ 40%*	$ 3,150,000	$?	$?	$?
Income tax savings for two years together		$?		$?

* This is the income tax effect of only the cost of goods sold. To shorten and simplify the analysis, sales and operating expenses are assumed to be the same each year.

8-46   Ethics and Sensitive Data

(Adapted from a case prepared by T. H. Rowley and published in *Ethics in the Accounting Curriculum*, edited by W. W. May and published by the American Accounting Association.) Greg Schwartz, an internal auditor for Ajax Products Company, is pursuing a graduate degree on a part-time basis. Greg and another graduate student, Linda Stephens, have an assignment to produce an accounting information database. Greg's company has a site license for a relational database management system on a local area network (LAN). Linda is a full-time student with no access to the needed database management system.

Greg invites Linda to work at his office after hours to complete the project. He greets her at the security desk, cosigns her identification card, and leads her to his office. Greg describes to Linda how to access the database management system. He first enters his user-ID and password to gain access to the LAN, and then lets Linda enter the commands to start the database management system. Linda misunderstands Greg's instructions and mistakenly types a transposed set of characters. The computer responds with the message, "Access Code? _____." Greg comments that he's never had to do that before and leans over and types his password. The computer screen flickers, then a colorful display of the company's logo appears above the words "Welcome to Ajax Company's Executive Information System." Instinctively, Linda presses the enter key and the computer screen presents a menu listing of ten files and programs available, including such entries as "Budgets," "Plans," and "Benefits."

Greg comments that he's unfamiliar with that menu and asks Linda if she remembers what she typed when she signed on. "Whatever you told me to type," she replies. Curious, Greg selects "Benefits" and, after a moment, a list of the top company officers appears on the screen along with a summary of their salary and benefits package plus an entry for the projected bonus for the current year. Greg is somewhat shocked to see substantial bonuses, and by quickly paging down, recognizes that the total in the bonus category for twelve executives is in the high six figures. Since Ajax is a privately held company, none of the data would be released to the public. What is shocking and disturbing to Greg is that the company recently announced a work-force reduction plan, which was going to result in a work-force reduction of 6% in the coming weeks. Greg says to Linda, "And this is the company that parades its Code of Ethics in public, with the CEO constantly talking of honesty, integrity, and fairness." Greg recovers his poise in a moment and remarks, "I don't think that this is the system that we want." He types "BYE" and exits the executive information system. At the LAN system prompt, he accesses the database management system. They work for several hours developing the database and then sign off and go home after saving the file.

At home that night, Greg muses about what he had seen and the fact that Linda, an outsider to the firm, saw everything. If he reports the breach in the computer security system, it will be suspected that he has seen confidential information. If he doesn't report the breach, someone else may access the sensitive data and exploit it. The LAN operating system audit log will show that he gained access to the executive information system. Greg is responsible for reviewing the log and reporting unauthorized access or access attempts. Is his access to the executive information system actually a security breach? Internal audit routinely has access to all applications and data due to their job function. Does he have a moral obligation to two long-term friends whose jobs will be terminated due to the work-force reduction?

The Institute of Internal Auditors' Code of Ethics suggests that internal auditors should be loyal to their employer. However, internal auditors should avoid actions that violate the law. Additionally, he knows that internal auditors should refrain from disclosing information for personal benefit or in a way that will damage the employer.

Required   What are the ethical issues? What should Greg do?

8-47.   Ethics and International Operations

(Adapted from a case in *Ethics in the Accounting Curriculum*, edited by W. W. May and published by the American Accounting Association.) Marjorie Singer is a senior partner in a major CPA firm that has foreign affiliates in a number of countries. Clients of the foreign affiliates include firms based in other countries as well as operations owned by or controlled by American multinational corporations. Marjorie is working in her office one day when she receives a call from Peter Slater, a partner in a foreign affiliate.

Peter:	Marjorie, I thought that I'd better clear an issue with the U.S. National Office involving one of your multinational corporations.
Marjorie:	OK, tell me what's going on.
Peter:	Well, you know that business over here isn't quite the same as in the U.S. Our situation here is that if wheels aren't 'greased' occasionally, nothing happens. As you can guess from that preamble, we have a transaction which we've identified as a $300,000 cash payment to a political figure. The management of our client insists that it qualifies as a 'grease payment' under the Foreign Corrupt Practices Act (FCPA) rather than as an 'illegal payment.'
Marjorie:	What is your judgment?
Peter:	I believe that it could be construed as a bribe, but it seems debatable and, as is typical in these settings, there is little hard evidence. As a matter of fact, one of the client managers 'slipped' and explained the nature of the payment, much to the apparent chagrin of his peers. If we pushed hard on this with the client, it is possible that they would reverse the representation. We wouldn't be very popular with senior management, though.
Marjorie:	Are alternative procedures available to gain sufficient evidence so that we could clarify the nature of the payment?
Peter:	Not really; we have to respect the client's confidentiality. Moreover, I doubt that the apparent recipient would acknowledge the payment in any case. Keep in mind that this is a multimillion dollar operation. Hence the $300,000 payment is literally a drop in the bucket.

Marjorie:	I hear you, but as you well know, materiality takes on another dimension when we're dealing with the FCPA. That's especially the case due to the implications of illegality from a monetary, punitive, and reputation perspective.
Peter:	A real problem may arise if we push this, because the sole basis of support is one manager's statement that may well be disclaimed by his peers. They can argue that he was not involved and that he really didn't know what he was talking about.
Marjorie:	What does your 'gut' say?
Peter:	If 'nervousness' is a criterion, my view is that we're standing on the edge.
Marjorie:	Let's take the worst case scenario. Assume the client states it is merely a loss of $300,000 and the nature of the loss is unknown. Further assume it is uncovered down the line, where does that leave us?
Peter:	Well, our workpapers document the manager's explanation about the real purpose of the payment. While we would document the reversal by the client, there's definitely a 'black hole' that's apparent. The question would remain as to who should be informed of this missing $300,000 and/or speculations as to its nature.
Marjorie:	I understand why you called; this is a 'can of worms.'

Required   What are the ethical issues? What should Marjorie do?

8-48   Pressure for Profits

The *Wall Street Journal* stated that "Datapoint Corp. reported its first quarterly loss in nearly a decade, partly reflecting the reversal of about $15 million in revenue generated in previous quarters by questionable sales practices." Datapoint makes small computer systems and telecommunications equipment.

The news report stated that excessive product returns in recent months led Datapoint to investigate the sales practices of its domestic marketing division. Certain marketing officials, determined to continue a string of thirty-nine quarters of record profits, resorted to questionable practices of recording revenue. Their methods eventually backfired.

The practices included shipping computer equipment to customers who failed to meet Datapoint's credit requirements, executives using their own money to pay warehousing fees so that distributors would accept shipments they did not have room for, and, in one instance, shipping to an imaginary customer "just to get a shipment out the door and revenue logged."

Required   On what specific items on the checklist of internal control should Datapoint concentrate to prevent a recurrence of these questionable marketing practices?

8-49   Manipulation of Profits

Throughout the decade, H. J. Heinz Company had a publicly stated objective: to seek an increase in earnings at a steady and consistent rate. For example, a Heinz annual report said: "... the annual compound growth rate has been 11.7% for the past 10 years and 14.0% for the past five years, which is consistent with the company's financial objectives for a compound growth rate in earnings per share of 10% to 12% per year."

Shortly after issuing that annual report, Heinz disclosed that several managers had engaged in "profit-switching" practices for the past seven years. These practices resulted in the improper transfer of $16.4 million in pretax income to the most recent fiscal year. A news story reported that "the intent of the practices was to smooth out earnings increases to create the appearance of consistent, orderly growth."

For your information, "profit-switching" and "improper transfer" refer to keeping records so that profits that appropriately belong in one reporting period are actually reported in a different reporting period.

Required   Given this description, were any assets stolen by management? Identify at least one way to falsely defer profit to a future period. What features in the chapter checklist of internal control are aimed at preventing the practice you describe?

8-50   Cooking the Books

In *The Accounting Wars* (Macmillan, 1985), author Mark Stevens presents a chapter on "Book Cooking, Number Juggling, and Other Tricks of the Trade." He quotes Glen Perry, a former chief accountant of the SEC's Enforcement Division: "Companies play games with their financial reports for any number of reasons, the most common being the intense pressure on corporate management to produce an unbroken stream of increasing earnings reports." Stevens then lists Perry's "terrible ten of accounting frauds—ploys used to misrepresent corporate financial statements":

1. Recognition of revenues before they are realized.
2. Recognition of rentals to customers as sales.
3. Inclusion of fictitious amounts in inventories.
4. Improper cutoffs at year end.
5. Improper application of LIFO.
6. Creation of fraudulent year-end transactions to boost earnings.
7. Failure to recognize losses through write-offs and allowances.
8. Inconsistent accounting practices without disclosures.
9. Capitalization or improper deferral of expenses.
10. Inclusion of unusual gains in operating income.

Required Suppose you were a division manager in a major corporation. Give a brief specific example of each of the ten methods.

8-51   Straightforward Bank Reconciliation

Study Appendix 8A. The Village of Pennington has a checking account with the Kitsap National Bank. The Village cash balance on February 28, 19X1, was $30,000. The deposit balance on the bank's books on February 28, 19X1, was also $30,000. The following transactions occurred during March:

Date	Check Number	Amount	Explanation
3/1	492	$11,000	Payment of previously billed consulting fee
3/6	493	8,000	Payment of accounts payable
3/10		12,000	Collection of taxes receivable
3/14	494	14,000	Acquisition of equipment for cash
3/17		16,000	Collection of license fees receivable
3/28	495	9,000	Payment of accounts payable
3/30	496	21,000	Payment of interest on municipal bonds
3/31		25,000	Collection of taxes receivable

All cash receipts are deposited via a night depository system after the close of the municipal business day. Therefore the receipts are not recorded by the bank until the succeeding day.

On March 31, the bank charged the Village of Pennington $95 for miscellaneous bank services.

Required
1. Prepare the journal entries on the bank's books for check 493 and the deposit of March 10.
2. Prepare the journal entries for all March transactions on the books of the Village of Pennington.
3. Post all transactions for March to T-accounts for the Village's Cash in Bank account and the bank's Deposit account. Assume that only checks 492-494 have been presented to the bank in March, each taking four days to clear the bank's records.

4. Prepare a bank reconciliation for the Village of Pennington, March 31, 19X1. The final three Village of Pennington transactions of March had not affected the bank's records as of March 31. What adjusting entry in the books of the Village of Pennington is required on March 31?
5. What would be the cash balance shown on the balance sheet of the Village of Pennington on March 31, 19X1?

8-52   Semicomplex Bank Reconciliation

Study Appendix 8A. An employee, Anne Burns, has a personal bank account. Her employer deposits her weekly paycheck automatically each Friday. The employee's check register (checkbook) for October is summarized as follows:

Reconciled cash balance, September 30, 19X1			$ 100
Additions:			
Weekly payroll deposits:	October		
	3		800
	10		800
	17		800
	24		800
Deposit of check received for gambling debt	25		500
Deposit of check received as winner of cereal contest	31		400
Subtotal			$4,200
Deductions:			
Checks written #325-#339	1-23	$3,300	
Check #340	26	70	
Check #341	30	90	
Check #342	31	340	3,800
Cash in bank, October 31, 19X1			$ 400

The bank statement is summarized in Exhibit 8-8. Note that NSF means "not sufficient funds." The check deposited on October 25 bounced; by prearrangement with Burns, the bank automatically lends sufficient amounts (in multiples of $100) to ensure that her balance is never less than $100.

Exhibit 8-8

Bank Statement of Anne Burns

SUMMARY OF YOUR CHECKING ACCOUNTS	
Beginning Balance	100.00
Deposits	4,600.00
Withdrawals	3,870.00
Service Charges/Fees	25.00*
Ending Balance	805.00
Minimum Balance on 10-28	**-80.00**

*$10.00 for returned check;
  $15.00 monthly service charge

continued

Exhibit 8-8
Bank Statement of Anne Burns
(Continued)

CHECKING ACTIVITY

Deposits

Posted	Amount	Description
10-13	800.00	Payroll Deposit
10-10	800.00	Payroll Deposit
10-17	800.00	Payroll Deposit
10-24	800.00	Payroll Deposit
10-25	500.00	Deposit
10-28	100.00	Automatic Loan
10-31	800.00	Payroll Deposit

Withdrawals

Ck No		Paid	Amount
325-339 Various dates in October. These would be shown by specific amounts, but are shown here as a total.			3,300.00
340		10-27	70.00
NSF		10-28	500.00

Total Number of checks = 16

Required

1. Prepare Burns's bank reconciliation, October 31, 19X1.
2. Assume that Burns keeps a personal set of books on the accrual basis. Prepare the compound journal entry called for by the bank reconciliation.

8-53   Bank Versus Book Records

Study Appendix 8A. The Mead Corporation, primarily a forest products company, lists the following among its current assets and current liabilities (in millions):

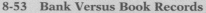

	December 31,	
	1993	**1992**
As part of current assets:		
Cash and cash equivalents	$ 9.3	$ 18.4
As part of current liabilities:		
Accounts payable:		
Trade	238.6	256.5
Affiliated companies	34.7	27.0
Outstanding checks	77.0	81.2

It is unusual to find a liability account labeled "Outstanding Checks."

Required

1. Most companies have checks outstanding at any balance sheet date. Why is it unusual to have a liability for outstanding checks?
2. Suppose you examined the "Cash and Cash Equivalents" account in Mead's general ledger. What balance would you find for December 31, 1993? for December 31, 1992?
3. Why do you suppose Mead reported outstanding checks as a liability?

8-54   Retail Method and Inventory Shrinkage

Study Appendix 8B. The following data are for a lawn and garden department in a large Kmart store at retail selling prices:

Net sales	$1,900,000	Transfers in from other branches	$26,000
Discounts granted to		Transfers out to other branches	8,000
employees, churches, etc.	19,500	Additional markups	10,000
Beginning inventory	900,000	Markdowns	79,000
Net purchases	2,068,000		

Required

1. What should be the ending inventory at retail prices using the conventional retail inventory method and assuming no allowances for losses (shrinkage)?
2. Suppose the estimated shrinkage is 1% of sales. What should be the ending inventory at retail prices? Suppose the cost ratio is 62%—that is, the *cost* of the ending inventory is approximated at 62% of retail price. What should be the ending inventory at cost? Again, assume 1% shrinkage.
3. The actual ending physical inventory at retail is $950,000. What is the total shrinkage at retail? at cost? Prepare a section of the income statement through gross profit on sales. Assume that beginning inventory at cost was $580,000 and that applicable net purchases (including transfer effects) at cost were $1,280,000.

8-55   Control of Retail Shoe Inventory

Study Appendix 8B. Athletic Shoes, Inc., reported an ending inventory of shoes that seemed significantly smaller than usual despite no apparent deviations from the usual amounts of beginning inventory, purchases, and sales. Employee theft was suspected. Reported data included:

Beginning inventory:		Purchases:	
At cost prices	$ 60,000	At cost prices	$110,000
At retail prices	120,000	At retail prices	210,000
Sales	200,000	Markdowns	25,000
Additional markups	5,000	Ending physical inventory, retail	108,600

The company's auditing department discovered that the supplementary merchandise records showed an arithmetically incorrect total for purchases at retail prices. The correct total is $220,000.

Required

1. Use the uncorrected data and assume that the allowable inventory shrinkage is 0.6% of sales. Compute the apparent inventory shortage.
2. Compute the apparent inventory shortage by using the corrected figure for purchases at retail prices.
3. Assume that the arithmetical error in determining the total purchases at retail prices had been deliberately committed to conceal a merchandise theft of an equal amount. Using a ratio of cost to retail value of 55%, compute the estimated cost of the inventory that may have been stolen.
4. See the chapter checklist of internal control. Briefly explain what precautions should be used to forestall such a theft and its concealment by employees.

8-56   Retail Method and Inventory Shrinkage

Study Appendix 8B. Safeway Stores is a large food chain. Its 1995 sales exceeded $15 billion. Safeway uses the retail method of inventory control for many parts of its operations. Suppose the following data pertain to the grocery department of one of its stores for a given period (at retail prices in thousands):

Beginning inventory	$200,000	Sales	$1,040,000
Markups	30,000	Purchases	1,020,000
Markdowns	50,000		

Required

1. Using the retail inventory method, compute the retail value of the ending inventory (in accordance with the given data).
2. Suppose the allowable shrinkage is 1% of sales. The physical inventory at retail prices at December 31 amounts to $142,000. Compute the excess shrinkage.
3. Consider the following additional data (at cost): beginning inventory, $150,000; purchases, $690,000. Compute the ratio of cost to retail value. Compute the cost value of the ending inventory for inclusion in the financial statements.

8-57   Ethics and Bank Reconciliations

The Springfield Chamber of Commerce recently hired you as an accounting assistant. Upon assuming your position on September 15, one of your first tasks was to reconcile the August bank statement. Your immediate supervisor, Ms. Ratelli, had been in charge of nearly all accounting tasks, including paying bills, preparing the payroll, and recording all transactions in the books. She has been very helpful to you, providing assistance on all the tasks she has asked you to do. The reconciliation was no different. Without assistance, you were able to locate the following information from the bank statement and the Chamber's books:

Balance per books	$16,710
Balance per bank statement	16,500
Bank service charges	30
NSF check returned	3,000
Deposit in transit	4,600
Outstanding checks	9,750

You also found a deposit on the bank statement of $3,300 that was incorrectly recorded as $3,030 on the Chamber's books.

When you could not reconcile the book and bank balances, you asked Ms. Ratelli for help. She responded that an additional $2,600 deposit was in transit. By coincidence, you noticed a $2,600 check, signed by Ms. Ratelli, to an individual whose name you did not recognize.

Required

1. Assume that all the information given is accurate and complete. Prepare the August bank reconciliation with the original information, showing that the book and bank balances do not reconcile.
2. Prepare a reconciliation using the new number, $7,200, for deposits in transit.
3. Why might Ms. Ratelli have instructed you to add $2,600 to the deposits in transit? What might she be trying to hide? If there were deceit, when might it be discovered?
4. What actions would you take if you were the accounting assistant?

8-58 Wal-Mart Annual report

Study Appendix 8B for requirement 2. Examine the 1995 amounts for cost of sales from the income statement and inventories from the balance sheet of Wal-Mart (Appendix A at the end of the book.)

Required

1. Suppose Wal-Mart uses a perpetual inventory system, and the balance in inventories (at LIFO) at the end of fiscal 1995 was $14,345,280,000 before taking a physical count. Compute the amount of inventory shrinkage, and prepare the journal entries to recognize the shrinkage and close it to cost of sales.
2. Suppose Wal-Mart uses a periodic inventory system and the retail method of inventory control. Purchases of merchandise during fiscal 1995 totaled $68,636,000,000. The ratio of cost to retail value was .78, and normal shrinkage is 1% of sales. Compute (a) the cost of sales before shrinkage, (b) the allowable shrinkage, (c) the excess shrinkage, and (d) the total cost of sales including all shrinkage.

8-59   Compact D from Disclosure
Study Appendix 8B for requirement 2. Select a retail company or a consumer products company from the list of companies available on Compact D. Note the amount of the cost of goods (or cost of sales) and the beginning and ending inventory levels.

Required

1. Assume your company uses a perpetual inventory system. Suppose that 1% of the cost of goods sold (or cost of sales) is a charge for inventory shrinkage. Prepare the summary journal entry that recorded the cost of the items actually sold and the journal entry that recognized inventory shrinkage.
2. Assume your company uses a periodic inventory system. Suppose the ending inventory value shown on the balance sheet is based on a physical count. An estimate of what the inventory level should be is 2% higher than the amount shown on the balance sheet. Normal shrinkage is 1.5% of the ending inventory based on the physical count. Compute the amount of normal shrinkage and excess shrinkage, and prepare a journal entry to recognize cost of goods sold and the charge for shrinkage.

9

Long-Lived Assets and Depreciation

Learning Objectives

After studying this chapter, you should be able to

1   Distinguish between tangible and intangible assets, and explain how the costs of each are charged.

2   Measure the acquisition cost of tangible assets such as land, buildings, and equipment.

3   Compute depreciation for buildings and equipment using various depreciation methods.

4   Differentiate financial statement depreciation from income tax depreciation.

5   Explain how depreciation affects cash flow.

6   Discuss changes in estimates and timing of acquisition.

7   Distinguish expenses from expenditures that should be capitalized.

8   Compute gains and losses on disposal of fixed assets.

9   Explain how to account for depletion of natural resources.

10   Describe how to account for various intangible assets.

This chapter shows how to account for long-lived assets. It discusses the differences in accounting for various kinds of assets—land, buildings and equipment, natural resources, and intangible assets. The main issue is when to charge the cost of a long-lived asset as an expense on the income statement. For example, if an asset lasts ten years, how much of its cost should be assigned to each of the ten years it is used?

Long-lived assets are especially significant for companies with large capital investments. Consider the plant and equipment in the balance sheets of the following companies (in millions):

Company	Total Assets	Plant and Equipment	
		Total	*Percentage*
NYNEX	$ 29,458	$20,250	69%
Kmart	17,029	6,280	37
CITICORP	250,489	4,062	2

Objective 1

Distinguish between tangible and intangible assets, and explain how the costs of each are charged.

NYNEX, the telephone company for the northeastern United States, invests heavily in plant and equipment. Kmart, like many retailers, has more investment in inventories than in long-lived assets. Finally, banks such as CITICORP have primarily financial assets and relatively minor plant and equipment.

Much of this chapter focuses on depreciation—both understanding the nature of depreciation and learning about the various depreciation methods. Companies in the United States freely choose depreciation methods. In contrast, in countries such as Japan, Germany, and France, depreciation methods are specified by government (tax) authorities.

■ OVERVIEW OF LONG-LIVED ASSETS

long-lived assets
Resources that are held for an extended time, such as land, buildings, equipment, natural resources, and patents.

Most business entities hold such major assets as land, buildings, equipment, natural resources, and patents. These resources are described as **long-lived assets** because they provide benefits for an extended time. These assets facilitate the production and sale of goods or services to customers. They are not available for sale in the ordinary course of business. Thus a delivery truck is a long-lived asset for nearly all companies. However, a truck dealer would regard trucks as merchandise inventory.

tangible assets (fixed assets, plant assets)
Physical items that can be seen and touched, such as land, natural resources, buildings, and equipment.

Tangible and Intangible Assets

Long-lived assets are often divided into tangible and intangible categories. **Tangible assets** (also called **fixed assets** or **plant assets**) are physical items that can be seen and touched. Examples are land, natural resources, buildings, and equipment. In contrast, **intangible assets** are rights or economic benefits, such as franchises, patents, trademarks, copyrights, and goodwill that are not physical in nature.

intangible assets
Rights or economic benefits, such as franchises, patents, trademarks, copyrights, and goodwill, that are not physical in nature.

Land is unique in that it does not wear out or become obsolete. Therefore it is reported in the financial records at its historical cost. Other long-lived assets may be used up, worn out, or become obsolete, so accountants charge their historical cost to expense over the period of time during which the firm

Exhibit 9-1

Summary of
Accounting for Long-
Lived Assets

Balance Sheet	Income Statement
Land ———————————————→	—
Buildings and equipment ————————→	Depreciation
Natural resources ————————————→	Depletion
Intangible assets (for example, franchises or patents) ——→	Amortization

amortization The systematic reduction of a lump-sum amount. When referring to long-lived assets, it usually means the allocation of the costs of intangible assets to the periods that benefit from these assets.

depletion The process of allocating the cost of natural resources to the period in which the resources are used.

benefits from their use. The word **amortization** is the general term that means the systematic reduction of a lump-sum amount and it might be used to describe any allocation of the acquisition cost of long-lived assets to the time periods of their use. In practice different words are used to describe the allocation of costs over time. For tangible assets such as buildings, machinery, and equipment, the allocation is called depreciation. For natural resources the allocation is called **depletion**. By convention, *amortization* is typically used to refer to the allocation of the costs of intangible assets to the periods that benefit from these assets. These terms are summarized in Exhibit 9-1.

Companies maintain careful detailed records of their long-lived assets and of the accumulated depreciation, depletion and amortization of those assets over time. However, when the financial results are reported to shareholders, only summary totals are shown for large classes of assets and all of the accumulated depreciation, depletion, and amortization is typically shown in one total as evidenced by the following excerpt from AT&T's annual report:

**AT&T Company
Property, Plant,
and Equipment
(in millions)**

	At January 1,	
	1994	**1993**
Land and improvements	$ 761	$ 757
Buildings and improvements	9,240	8,608
Machinery, electronic, and other equipment	$35,981	$33,930
Total property, plant, and equipment	45,982	43,295
Less: Accumulated depreciation	$23,947	$22,280
Property, plant, and equipment—net	$22,035	$21,015

■ ACQUISITION COST OF TANGIBLE ASSETS

The acquisition cost of all long-lived assets is their cash-equivalent purchase price, including incidental costs required to obtain title, to transport the asset, and to prepare it for use.

Land

Objective 2

Measure the acquisition cost of tangible assets such as land, buildings, and equipment.

The acquisition cost of land includes charges to the purchaser for the cost of land surveys, legal fees, title fees, realtors' commissions, transfer taxes, and even the demolition costs of old structures that might be torn down to get the land ready for its intended use. Under historical-cost accounting, land is carried indefinitely at its original cost. After many years of persistent inflation, its carrying amount is likely to be far below its current market value.

Should land acquired and held since 1936 be placed on a 1996 balance sheet at cost expressed in 1936 dollars? Accountants do exactly that. For example, Weyerhaeuser lists 5.9 million acres of land at $125 million (only $21 per acre). Critics of the basic historical-cost framework of accounting claim that some type of accounting for inflation should be mandatory. Inflation adjustment is common in many countries where double-digit inflation rates are the norm. This worrisome problem of inflation is discussed in Chapter 16.

Buildings and Equipment

Unlike land, buildings and equipment wear out or become obsolete. In other words, the services provided by buildings and equipment are consumed. Depreciation recognizes the consumption of these services. The cost of buildings, plant, and equipment should include all costs of acquisition and preparation for use. Consider the following example for some used packaging equipment:

Invoice price, gross	$100,000
Deduct 2% cash discount for payment within 30 days	2,000
Invoice price, net	$ 98,000
State sales tax at 8% of $98,000	7,840
Transportation costs	3,000
Installation costs	8,000
Repair costs prior to use	7,000
Total acquisition cost	$123,840

capitalized A cost that is added to an asset account, as distinguished from being expensed immediately.

The $123,840 would be the total *capitalized cost* added to the Equipment account. A cost is described as being **capitalized** when it is added to an asset account, as distinguished from being "expensed" immediately. Note that ordinary repair costs incurred *after* equipment is being used are expensed.

Under GAAP, interest cost is usually an expense. However, interest on expenditures during an extended construction period should be added to the acquisition cost of the fixed asset under construction. Suppose a $2 million plant was constructed over two years. If no construction payments were made before the plant was completed, no interest would be capitalized. However, suppose $1 million was paid at the end of the first year, and $1 million at completion. Assume the interest rate on recent borrowing was 12%. Interest of $1,000,000 × 0.12 = $120,000 would be part of the capitalized cost of the plant.

basket purchase The acquisition of two or more types of assets for a lump-sum cost.

Frequently, companies acquire more than one type of long-lived asset for a single overall outlay. For instance, suppose a company acquires land and a building for $1 million. The acquisition of two or more types of assets for a lump-sum cost is sometimes called a **basket purchase**. How much of the $1 million should the company allocate to land and how much to the building? Invariably, the cost is allocated in proportion to some estimate of relative sales value for the land and the building as separate items. For example, if an appraiser indicates that the market value of the land is $480,000 and of the building, $720,000, the cost would be allocated as follows:

	(1)	(2)	(3)	(2) × (3)
	Appraised Value	Weighting	Total Cost To Allocate	Allocated Costs
Land	$ 480,000	480/1,200 (or 40%)	$1,000,000	$ 400,000
Building	720,000	720/1,200 (or 60%)	1,000,000	600,000
Total	$1,200,000			$1,000,000

Objective 3

Compute deprecia-
tion for buildings
and equipment
using various depre-
ciation methods.

Allocating a basket purchase cost to the individual assets can significantly affect future reported income if the useful lives of various assets differ. In our example, if less cost is allocated to the land, more cost is allocated to the building, which is depreciable. In turn, depreciation expenses are higher, operating income is lower, and fewer income taxes are paid. Within the bounds of the law, tax-conscious managers load as much cost as possible on depreciable assets rather than on land.[1]

■ DEPRECIATION METHODS

Depreciation is a key factor distinguishing accrual accounting from cash-basis accounting. Suppose a long-lived asset is purchased for cash. Cash-basis accounting would recognize the entire cost of the asset when it is purchased. In contrast, accrual accounting allocates the cost in the form of depreciation over the periods the asset is used.

depreciable value
The amount of the
acquisition cost to be
allocated as deprecia-
tion over the total use-
ful life of an asset. It is
the difference between
the total acquisition
cost and the predicted
residual value.

Equipment and similar long-lived assets are initially recorded at *cost*. The major accounting difficulties center on the choice of a pattern of depreciation—that is, the allocation of the original cost to the particular periods that benefit from the use of assets. Depreciation is frequently misunderstood. It is *not* a process of *valuation*. In everyday use, we might say that an auto depreciates in value, meaning a decrease in its current market value. But to an accountant, depreciation is *not* a technique for approximating current values such as replacement costs or resale values. It is simply *cost allocation*.

residual value
(terminal value, dis-
posal value, salvage
value, scrap value)
The amount received
from disposal of a
long-lived asset at the
end of its useful life.

The amount of the acquisition cost to be allocated over the total useful life of the asset as depreciation is the **depreciable value**. It is the difference between the total acquisition cost and the predicted *residual value*. The **residual value** is the amount received from disposal of a long-lived asset at the end of its useful life. Synonyms for residual value are **terminal value**, **disposal value**, **salvage value**, and **scrap value**.

useful life (economic
life) The time period
over which an asset is
depreciated.

Depreciation allocates the depreciable value to the income statement during the **useful life** (or **economic life**) of the asset. The useful life, the time period over which an asset is depreciated, is determined as the shorter of the physical

---

[1] The allocation of a lump-sum cost of a sports team, which includes player contracts, has been the subject of litigation between taxpayers and the Internal Revenue Service. Buyers want to allocate as much of the cost to player contracts as possible. Such contracts may be depreciated (amortized) for income tax purposes, but the sports franchise itself may not. (See Problem 9-70 for an example.)

life of the asset before it wears out or the economic life of the asset before it is obsolete. Given the rapidly increasing speed and decreasing cost of computers in recent time, most companies replace them long before they wear out. That is, their economic life is shorter than their physical life. Sometimes an asset's life is measured directly in terms of the benefit it provides rather than the time period over which it is used. For example, the useful life of a truck might be measured as the total miles to be driven. This might be 100,000 or 200,000 miles. If a truck were purchased for $500,000, the depreciation would be $.50 per mile if it was expected to last 100,000 miles with no salvage value.

depreciation schedule The listing of depreciation amounts for each year of an asset's useful life.

A list of depreciation amounts for each year of an asset's useful life is called a **depreciation schedule**. We will use the following symbols and amounts to compare various depreciation schedules:

Symbols	Amounts for Illustration
Let	
C = total acquisition cost on December 31, 19X2	$41,000
R = residual value	$ 1,000
n = useful life (in years or miles)	4 years; 200,000 miles
D = amount of depreciation (or amortization)	Various

Straight-Line Depreciation

straight-line depreciation A method that spreads the depreciable value evenly over the useful life of an asset.

Straight-line depreciation spreads the depreciable value evenly over the useful life of an asset. It is by far the most popular method for corporate reporting to shareholders. It is used by almost 95% of major companies for at least part of their fixed assets, and 70% use it exclusively.

Exhibit 9-2 shows how the asset would be displayed in the balance sheet if a straight-line method of depreciation were used. The annual depreciation expense that would appear on the income statement is:

$$\text{Depreciation expense} = \frac{\text{Acquisition cost} - \text{Residual value}}{\text{Years of useful life}}$$

$$= \frac{C - R}{n}$$

$$= \frac{\$41,000 - \$1,000}{4} = \$10,000 \text{ per year}$$

Depreciation Based on Units

unit depreciation A method based on units of service when physical wear and tear is the dominating influence on the useful life of the asset.

When physical wear and tear is the dominating influence on the useful life of the asset, accountants often base depreciation on *units of service* or *units of production* rather than on the units of time (years) so commonly used. Depreciation based on units of service is called **unit depreciation**. Suppose the asset in our example were a large truck with a useful life of 200,000 miles.

Depreciation computed on a mileage basis is:

$$D = \frac{C - R}{n}$$

$$= \frac{\$41,000 - \$1,000}{200,000 \text{ miles}}$$

$$= \$.20 \text{ per mile}$$

For some assets, such as transportation equipment, this depreciation pattern may have more logical appeal than the straight-line method. However, the unit depreciation method is not widely used, probably for two major reasons:

1. Straight-line depreciation frequently produces approximately the same yearly depreciation amounts.

2. Straight-line depreciation is easier because the entire depreciation schedule can be set at the time of acquisition, and detailed records of units of service are not necessary.

Exhibit 39-2

Straight-Line Depreciation Schedule

	Balances at End of Year			
	1	2	3	4
Plant and equipment (at original acquisition cost)	$41,000	$41,000	$41,000	$41,000
Less: Accumulated depreciation (the portion of original cost that has already been charged to operations as expense)	10,000	20,000	30,000	40,000
Net book value (the portion of original cost that will be charged to future operations as expense)	$31,000	$21,000	$11,000	$ 1,000

accelerated depreciation Any depreciation method that writes off depreciable costs more quickly than the ordinary straight-line method based on expected useful life.

A commonly encountered example of unit depreciation relates to the use of mining equipment. Instead of writing such costs off on a time basis, most mining companies depreciate the equipment costs at a rate per ton of minerals extracted.

Double-Declining-Balance Depreciation

double-declining-balance depreciation (DDB) The most popular form of accelerated depreciation. It is computed by doubling the straight-line rate and multiplying the resulting DDB rate by the beginning book value.

Any pattern of depreciation that writes off depreciable costs more quickly than the ordinary straight-line method based on expected useful life is called **accelerated depreciation**.[2] Although an infinite number of accelerated depreciation methods are possible, the most popular form of accelerated depreciation is the **double-declining-balance (DDB)** method. DDB is computed as follows:

1. Compute a rate by dividing 100% by the years of useful life. This result is the straight-line rate. Then double the rate.[3] In our example, the straight-line rate is 100% ÷ 4 years = 25%. The DDB rate would be 2 × 25%, or 50%.

2. To compute the depreciation for any year, ignore the residual value and multiply the beginning book value for the year by the DDB rate.

---

[2] About 20% of major U.S. companies use accelerated depreciation for part of their fixed assets in reporting to shareholders.

[3] *Double*-declining-balance requires doubling the rate. Other declining-balance methods use other multiples. For instance, 150% declining-balance requires the straight-line rate to be multiplied by 1.5.

The DDB method can be illustrated as follows:

$$\text{DDB rate} = 2 \times (100\% \div n)$$
$$\text{DDB rate, 4-year life} = 2 \times (100\% \div 4) = 50\%$$
$$\text{DDB depreciation} = \text{DDB rate} \times \text{Beginning book value}$$

For year 1: D = .50 ($41,000)
         = $20,500

For year 2: D = .50 ($41,000 – $20,500)
         = $10,250

For year 3: D = .50 [$41,000 – ($20,500 + $10,250)]
         = $5,125

For year 4: D = .50 [$41,000 – ($35,875)]
         = $2,563

Cumulative 3-year total = $35,875

In this example, by coincidence, the depreciation amount for each year happens to be half the preceding year's depreciation. However, this is a special case; it happens only with a four-year life. As the equations show, the basic approach is to apply the depreciation rate to the beginning book value.

Comparing Depreciation Methods

Exhibit 9-3 compares the results of straight-line and DDB depreciation. Note that the DDB method will not write off the full depreciable cost of $40,000. Thus, some companies that use DDB change to the straight-line method part way through the asset's depreciable life. Straight-line depreciation over the remaining useful life is applied to the remaining depreciable value, thereby fully writing off the depreciable value. The change comes when the next year's straight-line depreciation first exceeds the amount in the original DDB schedule.

Consider the DDB section of Exhibit 9-3, for example. The company could switch to the straight-line method at the beginning of the fourth year. The total accumulated depreciation for the first three years is $35,875. Because the maximum depreciation allowed for this asset over its four-year life is $40,000, the company would charge depreciation expense of $40,000 – $35,875, or $4,125, in the fourth year (rather than the $2,563 shown in Exhibit 9-3).

In this way, the company writes off the complete depreciable amount, as shown below:

Year	Unmodified DDB Schedule	Straight-Line Depreciation on the Remaining Depreciable Amount	Modified DDB Schedule: Switch to Straight-Line in Year 4
1	$20,500	$40,000 ÷ 4 = $10,000	$20,500
2	10,250	($40,000 – $20,500) ÷ 3 = $6,500	10,250
3	5,125	($40,000 – $30,750) ÷ 2 = $4,625	5,125
4	2,563	($40,000 – $35,875) ÷ 1 = $4,125	4,125
	$38,438		$40,000

Exhibit 9-3	Depreciation: Two Popular Methods (assume equipment costs $41,000, four-year life, predicted residual value of $1,000)

	Straight-Line*		Declining Balance at Twice the Straight-Line Rate (DDB)†	
	Annual Depreciation	Book Value	Annual Depreciation	Book Value
At acquisition		$41,000		$41,000
Year				
1	$10,000	31,000	$20,500	20,500
2	10,000	21,000	10,250	10,250
3	10,000	11,000	5,125	5,125
4	10,000	1,000	2,563	2,562
Total	$40,000		$38,438	

* Depreciation is the same each year, 25% of ($41,000 − $1,000).

†100% / 4 = 25%. The double rate is 50%. Then 50% of $41,000; 50% of ($41,000 − $20,500); 50% of [$41,000 − ($20,500 + $10,250)]; etc. Unmodified, this method will never fully depreciate the existing book value. Therefore, in the later years of an asset's life, companies typically switch to a straight-line method. See the text for a fuller explanation.

The switch would come in Year 4; the company would charge depreciation of $4,125 instead of $2,563 in the fourth year.

Companies do not necessarily use the same depreciation methods for all types of depreciable assets. For example, consider the annual report of Kobe Steel, Ltd., a major Japanese company: "Buildings and structures in all locations and machinery and equipment located in the Kakogawa Works, the Kobe Works, the Takasago Works, the Mooka Plant, and the Chofu Plant are depreciated using the straight-line method, and all other machinery and equipment are depreciated using the declining balance method over estimated useful lives."

Objective 4

Differentiate financial statement depreciation from income tax depreciation.

■ INCOME TAX REPORTING AND SHAREHOLDER REPORTING

In accounting for long-lived assets, reporting to stockholders and reporting to the income tax authorities may differ. Reports to stockholders must abide by GAAP. In contrast, reports to income tax authorities must abide by the income tax rules and regulations. These rules are often consistent with GAAP but they sometimes diverge. Therefore there is nothing immoral or unethical about keeping two sets of records. In fact, it is necessary.

Depreciation on Tax Reports

Congress changes the U.S. tax rules in some way almost every year. However, since 1986 the tax authorities have required the *Modified Accelerated Cost Recovery System (MACRS)* for computing accelerated depreciation, although taxpayers may use straight-line depreciation. MACRS approximates *(a) double-declining-balance*[4] depreciation *(b)* applied over *shorter lives* than previously allowed. In combination, *a* and *b* provide greater acceleration of depreciation than was allowed before 1986. Congress hoped to spur investment in long-lived assets. Most companies use straight-line depreciation over an asset's useful life for shareholder reporting, even though they use MACRS for tax purposes.

The key factor in tax depreciation for most companies is *accelerated* depreciation. The earlier the depreciation expense is recognized, the earlier the company gets a reduction in income taxes. MACRS gives higher depreciation in the early years of an asset's service life than with the straight-line method. Shorter MACRS lives also accelerate depreciation. Carried to its extreme, an accelerated depreciation method would call for immediate total write-off in the year of acquisition. For example, tax authorities in some countries permit taxpayers to write off the full cost of new equipment as an expense in the year acquired. Tax reporting of depreciation is treated in detail in Chapter 14.

Shareholder Reporting

While tax authorities may use special rates, very short lives, or immediate write-off to increase the tax benefits of investing in long-lived assets, shareholder reporting is driven by efforts to use depreciation to match the costs of ownership to the income statements during the years of benefit from that ownership.

Most companies use straight-line depreciation for reporting to shareholders. Practical reasons for adopting straight-line depreciation are simplicity, convenience, and the reporting of higher earnings in early years than would be reported under accelerated depreciation. Managers tend not to choose accounting methods that hurt reported earnings in the early years of long-lived assets.

An additional reason given in support of straight-line depreciation is the assumption that depreciation is a function of time rather than of use. Therefore the "service potential" of the asset is assumed to decline by an equal amount each period; the total cost of the services consumed in any period is the same regardless of actual use. Further, suppose the benefit from using an asset is the same each period. The matching principle would require that the cost be spread equally to all periods.

For income-tax-reporting purposes, most corporations use *accelerated depreciation* to postpone payments of income taxes. A few companies also use some form of accelerated depreciation for reporting to shareholders. For example, Ford Motor Company states that assets placed in service before January 1, 1993, are depreciated using an accelerated method. Assets placed in service after December 31, 1992, are depreciated using the straight-line method.

Proponents of accelerated depreciation for shareholder reporting maintain that it is the more conservative option. They also point out that the full cost of using an asset includes depreciation *plus* repairs and maintenance. They claim that accelerated methods record high depreciation charges initially when repair and mainte-

---

[4] Some categories of assets use a 150% declining-balance method, and residential rental property and nonresidential real estate are depreciated using the straight-line method.

nance costs are low. Then depreciation charges fall as repair and maintenance costs rise, keeping the full cost of using the asset relatively stable over its life.

■ DEPRECIATION AND CASH FLOW

Objective 5

Explain how depreciation affects cash flow.

Too often, the relationships between depreciation expense, income tax expense, cash, and accumulated depreciation are confused. For example, the business press frequently contains misleading quotations such as "... we're looking for financing $3.75 billion. Of that, about 60% will be recovered in depreciation and amortization." As another example, consider a *Business Week* news report concerning an airline company: "And with a hefty boost from depreciation and the sale of $6 million worth of property, its cash balance rose by $10 million in the year's first quarter."

These statements imply that depreciation somehow generates cash. It does not. Depreciation simply allocates the original cost of an asset to the periods in which the asset is used, nothing more and nothing less. Accumulated depreciation is a summation of the amounts of the original cost already written off to expense in prior periods. Thus accumulated depreciation is *not* a pile of cash waiting to be used.

Effects of Depreciation on Cash

To illustrate that depreciation does not generate cash, consider Acme Service Company, which began business with cash and common stock equity of $100,000. On the same day, equipment was acquired for $40,000 cash. The equipment had an expected four-year life and zero predicted residual value. The first year's operations generated cash sales of $103,000 and cash operating expenses of $53,000. These facts are depicted visually below, and in Exhibit 9-4. Straight-line depreciation in Panel I is ¼ × $40,000 = $10,000. Accelerated depreciation (double-declining-balance) in Panel II for the first year is 2 × 25% × $40,000 = $20,000.

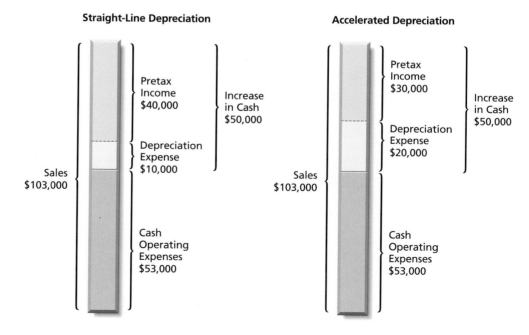

Exhibit 9-4   Acme Service Company   Analysis of Transactions (in thousands of dollars)

		A			L		SE	
	Cash	+ Equipment	− Accumulated Depreciation	=	Liabilities	+	Paid-in Capital	+ Retained Income
Panel I.	**STRAIGHT-LINE DEPRECIATION**							
Initial investment	+ 100			=			+ 100	
Acquisition	− 40	+ 40		=				
Cash sales	+ 103			=				+103 Sales
Cash operating expenses	− 53			=				− 53 Expense
Depreciation, Year 1			−10	=				− 10 Expense
Ia. Bal. Dec. 31 before taxes	+ 110	+ 40	−10	=			+ 100	+ 40
Income taxes (40% of 40)	− 16			=				− 16 Expense
Ib. Bal. Dec. 31 after taxes	+ 94	+ 40	−10	=			+ 100	+ 24
Panel II.	**ACCELERATED DEPRECIATION**							
Initial investment	+ 100			=			+ 100	
Acquisition	− 40	+ 40		=				
Cash sales	+ 103			=				+103 Sales
Cash operating expenses	− 53			=				− 53 Expense
Depreciation, Year 1			−20	=				− 20 Expense
IIa. Bal. Dec. 31 before taxes	+ 110	+ 40	−20	=			+ 100	+ 30
Income taxes (40% of 30)	− 12			=				− 12 Expense
IIb. Bal. Dec. 31 after taxes	+ 98	+ 40	−20	=			+ 100	+ 18
Panel III.	**SUMMARY**							
BEFORE TAX BALANCES, DEC 31								
Line Ia. Straight Line	+ 110	+ 40	−10				+ 100	+ 40
Line IIa. Accelerated	+ 110	+ 40	−20				+ 100	+ 30
Change	0	0	−10				0	− 10
AFTER TAX BALANCES, DEC 31								
Line Ib. Straight Line	+ 94	+ 40	−10				+ 100	+ 24
Line IIb. Accelerated	+ 98	+ 40	−20				+ 100	+ 18
Change	+ 4	0	−10				0	− 6

Focus first on the December 31 balances before taxes in Exhibit 9-4, denoted Ia. and IIa. Comparing the before-tax amounts stresses the role of depreciation expense most vividly. At year end, the cash balance *before taxes* is $110,000, regardless of the depreciation method used. Before taxes, changes in the depreciation method affect only the accumulated depreciation and retained earnings accounts. The before-tax ending cash balances are completely unaffected. Panel III shows the before-tax equality of cash in summary form.

Consider next the effect of depreciation on the before-tax income statement. The relevant amounts are in the last column of Exhibit 9-4, but the first two columns of Exhibit 9-5 present the same numbers in a more useful format. The cash provided by operations before income taxes is $50,000, regardless of the depreciation method used. Pretax income under straight-line differs from that under accelerated depreciation only because of differences in the noncash depreciation expense.

Suppose depreciation were $40,000. Before reading on, compute the pretax income and increase in cash. You should have obtained pretax income of only $10,000. However, the increase in cash remains at $50,000. Why? Because cash received from sales is $103,000 and cash expenses are $53,000, leaving $50,000 cash provided by operations, so long as we ignore taxes.

	Exhibit 9-5	Income Statement and Statement of Cash Flows for the Year Ended December 31, 19X1		
		Acme Service Company (in thousands)		

	Before Taxes		**After Taxes**	
	Straight-Line Depreciation	*Accelerated Depreciation*	*Straight-Line Depreciation*	*Accelerated Depreciation*
Panel I. INCOME STATEMENT				
Sales	$103	$103	$103	$103
Operating expenses	53	53	53	53
Depreciation expense	10	20	10	20
Pretax income	40	30	40	30
Income tax expense (40%)	—	—	16	12
Net income	$ 40	$ 30	$ 24	$ 18
Panel II. STATEMENT OF CASH FLOWS				
Cash collections	$103	$103	$103	$103
Cash operating expenses	53	53	53	53
Cash tax payments	—	—	16	12
Cash provided by operations*	$ 50	$ 50	$ 34	$ 38

* Sometimes called cash flow from operations or just cash flow. But it is usually simply called cash provided by operations, which is typically defined as cash collected on sales (a) less all operating expenses requiring cash and (b) less income taxes.

Effects of Depreciation on Income Taxes

Now consider the after-tax portions of Exhibits 9-4 and 9-5. Depreciation is a deductible noncash expense for income tax purposes. Hence, the higher the depreciation allowed to be deducted in any given year, the lower the taxable income, and therefore the lower the cash disbursement for income taxes. In short, if depreciation expense is higher, more cash is conserved and kept for use in the business. To emphasize the point, we assume the depreciation method used for financial reporting is the same as for tax purposes. This does not have to be true, but aids our comparsion. From the first column of Exhibit 9-4 or the last two columns of Exhibit 9-5, you can see that Acme would pay $16,000 of income taxes using straight-line depreciation but only $12,000 using acceler-ated depreciation. Therefore, compared with the straight-line depreciation method, the accelerated method results in a higher cash balance *after* income tax ($98,000 instead of $94,000). At a 40% income tax rate, a $10,000 higher depreciation expense postpones $4,000 of income taxes.

Some strange results occur here. The reported net income is *lower* under accelerated than under straight-line depreciation, but the cash balance is *higher*. Thus, suppose managers were forced to choose one depreciation method for all purposes. Managers who are concerned about reported net income to shareholders would prefer straight-line to accelerated depreciation. Those trying to minimize taxes would prefer accelerated depreciation. This dilemma is not faced by managers in the United States, because straight-line depreciation can be used for shareholder purposes while accelerated deprecia-tion is used for income tax purposes. You may recall from Chapter 7 that companies using the LIFO-inventory method for tax purposes are required to use LIFO for reporting to shareholders. Such is *not* the case with depreciation, where methods for tax and shareholder reporting are allowed to differ. See Chapter 14 for additional explanation.

Governments throughout the world have increasingly tolerated a wide vari-ety of depreciation methods "to provide more cash for industrial expansion." Cash benefits occur only if higher depreciation reduces taxes paid.

There is one primary source of cash from operations: the cash provided through *sales to customers*. As the Acme Service Company example shows, the effect of more depreciation on cash is *indirect*; it reduces income taxes by 40% of the extra depreciation of $10,000, or $4,000. Therefore, accelerated depreci-ation keeps more cash in the business for a longer span of time only because of the postponement of cash disbursements for income taxes.

■ OTHER FACTORS AFFECTING DEPRECIATION

Changes in Depreciation Estimates

Objective 6

Discuss changes in estimates and tim-ing of acquisition.

Actual useful lives and residual values are seldom exactly equal to their pre-dicted amounts. If the differences are material, how should we adjust the affected accounts? Consider the example of the $41,000 asset with a $1,000 residual value. Use the straight-line method. Suppose it is the beginning of Year 3. The firm's economists and engineers have altered their expectations; the asset's new expected useful life is five instead of four years. Moreover, the new expected residual value is $3,000 instead of $1,000. There are two ways to incor-porate this new information into the depreciation schedules, the *prospective* and *retroactive* methods, which are explained on the next page.

Depreciation Calculation	Original	Retroactive (Adjust Past)	Prospective (Change Future)
Cost	$41,000	$41,000	$41,000
Useful life	4 years	5 years	5 years
Residual value	$ 1,000	$ 3,000	$ 3,000
Straight-line depreciation per year:			
Old, $40,000 ÷ 4	$10,000		
New, retroactively*		$ 7,600	
New, prospectively			
First 2 years			$10,000
Last 3 years			$ 6,000

*($41,000 − $3,000) ÷ 5 = $7,600

These modifications to predictions are "changes in accounting estimates." GAAP requires that they be accounted for "prospectively" rather than "retroactively," in the sense that the records through Year 2 would not be adjusted. Instead, the *remaining* depreciable amount would be written off over the new *remaining* useful life:

Book value at end of Year 2 (beginning of Year 3): Cost less accumulated depreciation	$41,000 − 2 ($10,000) = $21,000
Revised residual value	3,000
Revised depreciable amount	$18,000
Divide by remaining useful life in years, ÷ 3	
New straight-line depreciation per year	$ 6,000

Critics of the foregoing "prospective" method assert that it misstates the yearly depreciation throughout the entire life of the asset. That is, depreciation in early years is overstated and in later years is understated. This can be illustrated by comparing the prospective method in our example with the retroactive method (which uses perfect hindsight):

Year	Original	Prospective Method	Retroactive Method
1	$10,000	$10,000	$ 7,600
2	10,000	10,000	7,600
3	10,000	6,000	7,600
4	10,000	6,000	7,600
5	—	6,000	7,600
	$40,000	$38,000	$38,000

Although the retroactive method correctly matches expenses and revenues, it requires restating the accounts of prior periods, a procedure that many accountants oppose. The critics argue that the past accounting was as accurate as possible given the knowledge then existing. They fear that users of financial reports would be confused by frequent restatement and would lose confidence in financial statements that were often "corrected" after being issued. Therefore, GAAP requires that "a change in estimate should not be accounted for by restating amounts reported in financial statements of prior periods."

Depreciation for Parts of a Year

Assets are rarely acquired exactly at the start of a year or a month. To simplify recordkeeping, various assumptions are made about depreciation within the year. Each assumption must be reasonable and be consistently applied. For example, one of two methods might be used to determine when certain specified assets are placed in service:

1. *Half-year convention.* Treat all assets placed in service during the year as if they had been placed in service at the year's midpoint.
2. *Modified half-year convention.* Treat each asset placed in service during the first half of a year as if it had been placed in service on the first day of that year. Treat each asset placed in service during the last half of the year as if it had been placed in service on the first day of the *following* year.

Suppose our $41,000 asset had been acquired on October 1, 19X1, and DDB depreciation was used. As shown on page 384, the depreciation for the first year of use would be $20,500 and for the second year would be $10,250. Assume that the company's fiscal year and calendar year are the same and that depreciation is to be included for the full month of October. The depreciation schedule could appear as follows (in thousands of dollars):

Asset Year	Modified DDB Depreciation from Page 384	19X1	Allocation to Each Calendar Year 19X2	19X3	19X4	19X5
1	20,500	5,125*	15,375†			
2	10,250		2,563	7,687		
3	5,125			1,281	3,844	
4	4,125				1,031	3,094
	40,000	5,125	17,938	8,968	4,875	3,094

* 3/12 of Year 1's depreciation affects 19X1
† 9/12 of Year 1's depreciation affects 19X2

For interim reporting, yearly depreciation is usually spread uniformly *within* a given fiscal year (an equal amount for each month), regardless of whether straight-line or accelerated depreciation is used to compute the total amount for the year. The monthly statements in October, November, and December, 19X1, would each have depreciation expense of $5,125 ÷ 3 = $1,708. In turn, the monthly statements of 19X2 would each have depreciation expense of $17,938 ÷ 12 = $1,495.

■ EXPENSES VERSUS EXPENDITURES

expenditures The purchases of goods or services, whether for cash or on credit.

Expenditures are defined by accountants as the purchases of goods or services, whether for cash or on credit. Asset-related expenditures that are expected to benefit more than the current accounting year are *capitalized* (that is, added to an asset account) and are sometimes called *capital expenditures*. Such capital expenditures generally add new fixed assets or increase the capacity, efficiency,

Objective 7

Distinguish expenses from expenditures that should be capitalized.

or useful life of an existing fixed asset. Expenditures deemed to have a life of one year or less are charged as *expenses* in the current year.

All expenditures eventually become expenses. Expenditures benefiting the current period are matched with current revenues and therefore become expenses in the current period. Expenditures that are capitalized benefit *future* revenues, and they are charged as expenses over future periods.

The Decision to Capitalize

The decision whether to capitalize an expenditure is often subjective. Auditors from both the public accounting firms and the income tax authorities regularly investigate whether a given outlay should be capitalized or expensed. For example, is an engine repair properly classified as an asset or an expense? The public accountant (who tends to prefer conservatism) is usually on the alert for any tendencies to understate current expenses through the unjustified charging of a repair to an asset account. In contrast, the income tax auditor is looking for the unjustified charging to an expense account (which provides an immediate income tax deduction).

Wherever doubt exists, there is a general tendency in practice to charge an expense rather than an asset account for repairs, parts, and similar items. First, many of these expenditures are minor, so the cost-benefit test of recordkeeping (the concept of materiality) justifies such action. Setting up an asset account and a depreciation schedule is not worth the cost. For instance, many companies have a policy of charging to expense all expenditures that are less than a specified minimum such as $100, $500, or $1,000. Second, there is the temptation of an immediate deduction for income tax purposes (if, indeed, the deductions are allowable as reasonable expenses).

To Capitalize or Not to Capitalize

Late in the afternoon on St. Patrick's Day, 1992, Chambers Development Company, a rapidly growing waste-management firm, announced that it was changing the way it accounted for certain costs associated with landfill development. Instead of capitalizing indirect costs associated with landfill projects and listing them with the assets on the balance sheet, Chambers announced that it would follow industry practice and report those expenditures as expenses of the period in which they are incurred. The change had the effect of reducing reported income for 1991 from $49.9 million to $1.5 million.

To some observers, an accounting decision such as what to capitalize and what to charge immediately to expense is not very interesting. However, stockholders of Chambers Development soon became extremely interested. Chambers Development's stock price dropped from $30.50 to $11.50 the day after the announcement, a fall of 62%.

Chambers Development's management defended the change, maintaining that the capitalization in previous years had been warranted because Chambers had been a company in development. Now as an operating company, expensing seemed appropriate. At issue were costs such as the salaries of executives for that portion of their time spent on developing new landfills. Also in question were the company's costs related to the public relations and legal aspects of the landfills. The firm's auditor approved both the previous method and the change. In fact, speculation arose that the auditor *forced* the change because the amount of capitalized development costs had become so large that the amounts did not realistically represent costs that would be recovered in the future. Therefore the costs did not qualify as assets.

There is no easy answer as to what should be capitalized. Chambers spent millions to gain landfill permits, and there certainly is value to such permits. However, many accountants favor a conservative approach that recognizes all questionable items as expenses as soon as possible. The one thing that is clear is that decisions to capitalize expenditures can greatly affect stockholders. ■

Source: G. Stern and L. P. Cohen, "Chambers Development Switches Accounting Plan," Wall Street Journal (March 19, 1992), p. B4.

Repairs and Maintenance Versus Capital Improvements

Repairs and maintenance costs are necessary to maintain a fixed asset in operating condition. The costs of repairs and maintenance are usually compiled in a single account and are regarded as expenses of the current period. *Repairs* are sometimes distinguished from *maintenance* as follows. *Repairs* include the occasional costs of restoring a fixed asset to its ordinary operating condition after breakdowns, accidents, or damage. *Maintenance* includes the routine recurring costs of oiling, polishing, painting, and adjusting. However, accountants spend little effort distinguishing between repairs and maintenance expenditures since both are period costs.

improvement (betterment, capital improvement) An expenditure that is intended to add to the future benefits from an existing fixed asset.

On the other hand, an **improvement** (sometimes called a **betterment** or a **capital improvement**) is an expenditure that is intended to add to the future benefits from an existing fixed asset by decreasing its operating cost, increasing its rate of output, or prolonging its useful life. An improvement differs from repairs and maintenance because the latter helps ensure a level of current benefits but does not enlarge the expected future benefits. Improvements are generally *capitalized*. Examples of capital improvements or betterments include the rehabilitation of an apartment house that will allow increased rents and the rebuilding of a packaging machine that increases its speed or extends its useful life.

In Exhibit 9-2 (p. 383), suppose that at the start of Year 3 a major overhaul costing $7,000 occurred. If this is judged to extend the useful life from four to five years, the required accounting would be:

1. Increase the book value of the asset (now $41,000 − $20,000 = $21,000) by $7,000. This is usually done by adding the $7,000 to Equipment.[5]
2. Assume straight-line depreciation. Revise the depreciation schedule so that the new unexpired cost is spread over the remaining three years, as follows:

	Original Depreciation Schedule		Revised Depreciation Schedule	
	Year	Amount	Year	Amount
	1	$10,000	1	$10,000
	2	10,000	2	10,000
	3	10,000	3	9,000*
	4	10,000	4	9,000
			5	9,000
Accumulated depreciation		$40,000		$47,000†

* New depreciable amount is [($41,000 − $20,000 + $7,000) − $1,000 residual value] = $27,000. New depreciation expense is $27,000 divided by remaining useful life of 3 years, or $9,000 per year.

† Recapitulation: Original cost $41,000
                    Major overhaul   7,000
                                               48,000
                    Less residual   1,000
                    Depreciable cost $47,000

---

[5] A few accountants prefer to debit Accumulated Depreciation instead of Equipment. They argue that a portion of past depreciation is being "reversed" or "made good" by the improvement or betterment. Both accounting approaches increase the net book value of the equipment and increase subsequent depreciation in identical amounts.

■ GAINS AND LOSSES ON SALES OF FIXED ASSETS

Objective 8

Compute gains and losses on disposal of fixed assets.

Gains or losses on the disposal of property, plant, and equipment are inevitable. They are usually measured in a cash sale by the difference between the cash received and the net book value (net carrying amount) of the asset given up.[6]

Recording Gains and Losses

Suppose the equipment in Exhibit 9-2 (p. 383) were sold at the end of Year 2 for $27,000. The sale would have the following effects:

A				= L	+ SE
+$27,000 −	$41,000 +	$20,000	=		+ $6,000
Increase Cash	Decrease Equipment	Decrease Accumulated Depreciation			Increase Gain on Sale of Equipment

Note that the disposal of the equipment requires the removal of its carrying amount or book value, which appears in *two* accounts, not one. Therefore *both* the Accumulated Depreciation account and the Equipment account are affected when dispositions occur.

If the selling price were $17,000 rather than $27,000:

+$17,000 −	$41,000 +	$20,000	=	−$4,000
Increase Cash	Decrease Equipment	Decrease Accumulated Depreciation		Increase Loss on Sale of Equipment

The T-account presentations and journal entries are in Exhibit 9-6. Note especially that the disposal of the equipment necessitates the removal of the original cost of the equipment *and* the accompanying accumulated depreciation. Of course, the net effect is to eliminate the $21,000 carrying amount of the equipment (cost of $41,000 less accumulated depreciation of $20,000).

---

[6] When an old asset is traded for a silimar new asset, the new asset is valued at its cash-equivalent value for purposes of computing gain or loss. For example, consider the trade-in of a five-year-old truck for a new truck. The cash-equivalent value of the old truck is the difference between the cash cost of the new truck without the trade-in and the cash paid with the trade-in. The trading of assets can become complex and is expalined in advanced accounting texts.

| Exhibit 9-6 | Journal and Ledger Entries Gain or Loss on Sale of Equipment (in thousands of dollars) |

Sale at $27,000:

Cash	27	
Accumulated depreciation	20	
Equipment		41
Gain on sale of equipment		6

Cash		Equipment		Gain on Sale of Equipment
27		* 41	41	6

Accumulated
Depreciation,
Equipment

20	* 20

Sale at $17,000:

Cash	17	
Accumulated depreciation	20	
Loss on sale of equipment	4	
Equipment		41

Cash		Equipment		Loss on Sale of Equipment
17		* 41	41	4

Accumulated
Depreciation,
Equipment

20	* 20

*Beginning balance

Income Statement Presentation

In most instances, gains or losses on disposition of plant assets are not significant, so they are buried as a part of "other income" on the income statement and are not separately identified. For example, W. R. Grace & Co. includes an item on its income statement immediately after sales labeled "Dividends, interest, and other income." AT&T shows "Other income, net (Note D)" on a separate line after operating income in a recent annual report. Note D lists Gains (loss) on sale of fixed assets, $9.0 million, out of a total of $251.8 million of net other income.

When Gain on Sale of Equipment is shown as a separate item on an income statement, it is usually shown as a part of "other income" or some similar category. In single-step income statements, the gain is shown at the top along with other revenue items. For example:

Revenue:	
Sales of products	$xxx
Interest income (or interest revenue)	x
Other income: Gain on sale of equipment	x
Total sales and other income	$xxx

When a multiple-step income statement is used, the gain (or loss) is usually excluded from the computation of major profit categories such as gross profit or operating profit. Therefore the gain or loss appears in some type of "other income" or nonoperating income section in the lower part of the income statement. For example, Coca-Cola Enterprises Inc. showed a $59.3 million "Gain on sale of operations" as one of four items in the category labeled "Nonoperating income (deductions)."

■ DEPLETION OF NATURAL RESOURCES

Objective 9

Explain how to account for depletion of natural resources.

Natural resources such as minerals, oil, and timber are sometimes called *wasting assets. Depletion* is the accounting measure of the gradual exhaustion of the original resources acquired. Depletion differs from depreciation because depletion narrowly focuses on a physical phenomenon while depreciation focuses more broadly on any reduction of the economic value of a fixed asset, including physical deterioration and obsolescence.

The costs of natural resources are usually classified as fixed assets. However, the investment in natural resources can be likened to a lump-sum acquisition of massive quantities of inventories under the ground (iron ore) or above the ground (timber). Depletion expense is the measure of that portion of this "long-term inventory" that is used up in a particular period. For example, a coal mine may cost $20 million and originally contain an estimated one million tons. The depletion rate would be $20 million ÷ 1 million tons = $20 per ton. If 100,000 tons were mined during the first year, the depletion would be 100,000 × $20, or $2 million for that year; if 150,000 tons were mined the second year, depletion would be 150,000 × $20, or $3 million; and so forth.

As the above example shows, depletion is measured on a units-of-production basis. The annual depletion may be accounted for as a direct reduction of the mining asset, or it may be accumulated in a separate contra account similar to accumulated depreciation.

Another example is timber. Boise Cascade Corporation, a large producer of forest products, describes its approach to depletion as follows:

> Timber and timberlands are shown at cost, less the cost of company timber harvested. Costs of company timber harvested and amortization of logging roads are determined on the basis of timber removals at rates based on the estimated volume of recoverable timber and are credited to the respective asset accounts.

The "cost of company timber harvested" is Boise Cascade's synonym for "depletion" of timber.

■ AMORTIZATION OF INTANGIBLE ASSETS

Objective 10

Describe how to account for various intangible assets.

Intangible assets are a class of long-lived assets that are not physical in nature. They are rights to expected benefits deriving from their acquisition and continued possession. Examples of intangible assets are *patents, copyrights, franchises,* and *goodwill.*

Intangible assets are accounted for like plant and equipment. That is, the acquisition costs are capitalized as assets and are then amortized over estimated useful lives. Because of obsolescence, the *economic lives* of intangible assets tend to be shorter than their *legal lives.*

An intangible asset is shown on a company's balance sheet only if the rights to some benefit are *purchased.* Equally valuable assets may be created by internal expenditures, but they are not recognized as assets. For example, suppose Pfizer spent $5 million to internally develop and patent a new drug. Pfizer would charge $5 million to expense; no asset would be recognized. In contrast, if Pfizer paid $5 million to another company for their patent on an identical drug, Pfizer would record the $5 million as an intangible asset. The difference in treatment acknowledges that it is difficult for management to honestly and objectively value the results of its internal research and development efforts, while an independent transaction between separate companies realistically measures the value.

Examples of Intangible Assets

patents Grants by the federal government to an inventor, bestowing (in the United States) the exclusive right for 17 years to produce and sell the invention.

Patents are grants by the federal government to an inventor, bestowing (in the United States) the exclusive right for 17 years to produce and sell the invention. Suppose a company acquires such a patent from the inventor for $170,000. Suppose further that because of fast-changing technology, the *economic life* (the expected useful life) of the patent is only five years. The amortization would be $170,000 ÷ 5 = $34,000 per year, rather than $170,000 ÷ 17 = $10,000 per year.

The write-offs of intangible assets are usually made via direct reductions of the accounts in question. Thus accounts such as Accumulated Amortization of Patents are rarely found. Furthermore, the residual values of intangible assets are nearly always zero.

Balance sheets seldom contain a separate line for patents or for any other single intangible asset. Patents are usually lumped with other items in a category labeled "intangible assets" or simply "other assets." A footnote often provides details. For example, a footnote in United States Surgical Corporation's 1994 annual report describes the amortization policy for its $124 million in other assets.

Other Assets. The Company capitalizes and includes in Other Assets the costs of acquiring patents on its products, the costs of computer software developed and used in its information-processing systems, goodwill arising from the excess of cost over the fair value of net assets of purchased businesses, and deferred start-up costs incurred prior to 1991 relating to the Company's entrance in 1991 into the suture portion of the wound management market. These costs are amortized on the straight-line basis over the following estimated useful lives:

	Years
Patents	10
Computer software costs	3 to 4
Deferred start-up costs	5
Goodwill	10 to 40

copyrights Exclusive rights to reproduce and sell a book, musical composition, film, and similar items.

Copyrights are exclusive rights to reproduce and sell a book, musical composition, film, and similar items. These rights are issued (in the United States) by the federal government and provide protection to a company for 75 years. The original costs of obtaining copyrights from the government are nominal, but a company may pay a large sum to purchase an existing asset from the owner. For example, a publisher of paperback books will pay the author of a popular novel in excess of a million dollars for his or her copyright. The economic lives of such assets may be no longer than two or three years, so amortization occurs accordingly.

trademarks Distinctive identifications of a manufactured product or of a service taking the form of a name, a sign, a slogan, a logo, or an emblem.

Trademarks are distinctive identifications of a manufactured product or of a service taking the form of a name, a sign, a slogan, a logo, or an emblem. An example is an emblem for Coca-Cola. Trademarks, trade names, trade brands, secret formulas, and similar items are property rights with economic lives depending on their length of use. For stockholder-reporting purposes, their costs are amortized over their useful lives, but no longer than 40 years.

Remember that trademarks are recorded as intangible assets only if they are purchased. Companies like Coca-Cola, who have spent millions of advertising dollars creating public awareness of their brands, show no intangible asset, even though their trademark may be extremely valuable.

If a company has trademarks or other intangible assets that cease to have value, they should be immediately written off as an expense. For example, Brown-Forman Corporation had $60 million of intangible assets associated with the brand California Cooler when it decided the assets no longer provided future benefits. The $60 million expense reduced the company's income before taxes from $218 million to $158 million.

franchises (licenses) Privileges granted by a government, manufacturer, or distributor to sell a product or service in accordance with specified conditions.

Franchises and **licenses** are privileges granted by a government, manufacturer, or distributor to sell a product or service in accordance with specified conditions. An example is the franchise of a baseball team or the franchise of a local owner of a Holiday Inn. The lengths of the franchises vary from one year to perpetuity. Again, the acquisition costs of franchises and licenses are amortized over their economic lives rather than their legal lives.

goodwill The excess of the cost of an acquired company over the sum of the fair market value of its identifiable individual assets less the liabilities.

Goodwill, which is discussed in more detail in Chapter 13, is defined as the excess of the cost of an acquired company over the sum of the fair market values of its identifiable individual assets less the liabilities. For example, General Motors (GM) acquired Hughes Aircraft for $5 billion but could assign only $1 billion to various identifiable assets such as receivables, plant, and patents less liabilities assumed by GM; the remainder, $4 billion, is goodwill. Identifiable intangible assets, such as franchises and patents, may be acquired singly, but goodwill cannot be acquired separately from a related business. This excess of the purchase price over the fair market value is called "goodwill" or "purchased goodwill" or, more accurately, "excess of cost over fair value of net identifiable assets of businesses acquired."

The accounting for goodwill illustrates how an *exchange* transaction is a basic concept of accounting. After all, there are many owners who could obtain a premium price for their companies. But such goodwill is *never* recorded. Only the goodwill arising from an *actual acquisition* with arm's-length bargaining is shown as an asset on the purchaser's records.

For shareholder-reporting purposes, goodwill must be amortized, generally in a straight-line manner, over the periods benefited. The maximum amortization period is forty years. The minimum amortization period is not specified by U.S. GAAP, but a lump-sum write-off on acquisition is forbidden.

Special Case of Research and Development

Before 1975, many companies regarded *research and development (R&D) costs* as intangible assets. R&D costs were capitalized and amortized over the years of expected benefit, usually three to six years. Such costs result from planned research or critical investigation aimed at obtaining new products or processes or significant improvements in existing products or processes. Since 1975, Financial Accounting Standards Board Statement Number 2 has required that all such costs be charged to expense when incurred. The FASB recognized that research and development generates many long-term benefits, but the uncertainty about the life and value of future benefits led to conservative accounting in the form of immediate write-off.

Practice varies internationally. For example, in Korea and India R&D expenditures are capitalized and later amortized. Even in the United States there is an exception to the immediate expensing of all research and development costs. The costs of developing computer software to be sold or leased should be expensed only until the *technological feasibility* of the product is established. Thereafter, software production costs should be capitalized and amortized over the estimated economic life of the product.

Software development costs can be significant. Consider BMC Software, a Texas-based maker of software to support IBM mainframe systems. It began capitalizing software development costs in fiscal 1987, and in 1991 such costs were 36% of the company's noncurrent assets. During fiscal 1991, costs of $5,043,000 were capitalized, compared with only $1,388,000 of amortization. If all these costs had been expensed, income before taxes would have been $5,043,000 – $1,388,000 = $3,655,000 lower:

BMC Software	With Capitalization of Software Development Costs	Without Capitalization of Software Development Costs
Income before software development costs	$19,045,000	$19,045,000
Amortization of software development costs	1,388,000	
Software development cost expense		5,043,000
Income before taxes	$17,657,000	$14,002,000
	Difference = $3,655,000	

This phenomenon continues as long as the rate of new software development continues to grow. By 1994, BMC's rate of new development leveled off. In that year, $4,771,000 amortization of previously capitalized software exactly equaled the 1994 software development cost. The consolidated balance sheet reported software costs as follows:

BMC Software
Balance Sheet
(in thousands)

	1994	1993
Software development costs, net of accumulated amortization of $14,519 and $9,748.	$14,750	$14,750

Amortization of Leaseholds and Leasehold Improvements

Leaseholds and *leasehold improvements* are frequently classified with plant assets although they are technically intangible assets. The lessee owns the right to use the leased items, not the items themselves.

leasehold The right to use a fixed asset for a specified period of time, typically beyond one year.

A **leasehold** is the right to use a fixed asset (such as a building or some portion thereof) for a specified period of time beyond one year. A **leasehold improvement** incurred by a lessee (tenant) can take various forms. Examples are the installation of new fixtures, panels, walls, and air-conditioning equipment that are not permitted to be removed from the premises when a lease expires.

leasehold improvement
Investments by a lessee in items that are not permitted to be removed from the premises when a lease expires, such as installation of new fixtures, panels, walls, and air-conditioning equipment.

deferred charges
Similar to prepaid expenses, but they have longer-term benefits.

The costs of leases and leasehold improvements are amortized over the life of the lease, even if the physical life of the leasehold improvement is longer. The straight-line method is used almost exclusively, probably because accelerated methods have not been permitted for income tax purposes. For more on leases, see Appendix 10B, page 462.

Amortization of Deferred Charges

Sometimes prepaid expenses are lumped with *deferred charges* as a single amount, *prepaid expenses and deferred charges*, that appears on the balance sheet at the bottom of the current asset classification or at the bottom of all the assets as an "other asset." **Deferred charges** are like prepaid expenses, but they have longer-term benefits. For example, the costs of relocating a mass of employees to a different geographical area, or the costs of rearranging an assembly line or developing new markets, may be carried forward as deferred charges and written off as expense over a three- to five-year period. This procedure is often described as the amortization of deferred charges.

Another example of deferred charges is *organization costs*, which include certain types of expenditures made in forming a corporation: fees for legal and accounting services, promotional costs for the sale of corporate securities, and the printing costs of stock certificates. These costs theoretically benefit the corporation indefinitely, but they are usually amortized for both shareholder and tax purposes over five years (which happens to be the minimum span allowed by the Internal Revenue Service).

Conservatism and Inconsistencies

The attitude of the regulatory bodies toward accounting for intangible assets has become increasingly conservative. Before 1970, the amortization of goodwill, trademarks, and franchises with indefinite useful lives was not mandatory. But the Accounting Principles Board ruled in 1970 that the values of all intangible assets eventually disappear, and therefore such assets must be amortized. However, the new requirement for amortization was not imposed retroactively. Consequently, many companies *are* currently amortizing intangible assets acquired after 1970 but *are not* amortizing intangible assets acquired before that date. For example, American Brands, maker of Titleist golf balls, Master locks, and many other consumer products, states in its annual report: "Intangibles resulting from business acquisitions, comprising brands and trademarks and cost in excess of net assets of businesses acquired, are considered to have a continuing value over an indefinite period and are not being amortized, except for intangibles acquired after 1970, which are being amortized on a straight-line basis over 40 years."

Conservatism produces inconsistencies between the accounting for tangible and intangible long-lived assets. Provocative and knotty theoretical issues arise because accountants sometimes overlook the underlying reality of future economic benefits. Their preoccupation with physical evidence often results in the expensing of outlays that should be treated as assets. Thus expenditures for research, advertising, employee training, and the like are generally expensed, although it seems clear that in an economic sense such expenditures represent expected future benefits.

The difficulty of measuring future benefits is the reason usually advanced for expensing these items. GAAP requires that *internal* research, advertising, and other such costs be written off to expense as incurred. In contrast, purchases of patents, trademarks, and similar intangibles that were incurred outside the firm are recorded as assets.

In summary, accounting practice for intangible assets is not consistent. An annual report of Omark Industries exemplifies this inconsistency: "Costs of internally developed patents, trademarks, and formulas are charged to current operations. Costs of purchased patents, trademarks, and formulas are amortized over their legal or economic lives."

Conflicts with Income Tax Purposes

As mentioned earlier in this chapter, accounting for shareholder purposes is usually similar to accounting for income tax purposes. Tax and shareholder accounting for leaseholds, leasehold improvements, patents, and copyrights have generally coincided. However, historically the acquisition costs of perpetual franchises, trademarks, and goodwill have been amortized for shareholder reporting but must *not* be amortized for income tax purposes. After years of conflict, Congress recently authorized amortization over 15 years for tax purposes, under certain circumstances.

Summary Problems for Your Review

Problem One

"The net book value of plant assets is the amount that would be spent today for their replacement." Do you agree? Explain.

Solution to Problem One

Net book value of the plant assets is the result of deducting accumulated depreciation from original cost. It is a result of cost allocation, not valuation. This process does not attempt to reflect all the technological and economic events that may affect replacement value. Consequently, there is little assurance that net book value will approximate replacement cost.

Problem Two

"Accumulated depreciation provides cash for the replacement of fixed assets." Do you agree with this quotation from a business magazine? Explain.

Solution to Problem Two

Accumulated depreciation is a contra asset. It is the amount of the asset already used up and in no way represents a direct stockpile of cash for replacement.

Problem Three

Refer to Exhibit 9-3 (p. 385). Suppose the predicted residual value had been $5,000 instead of $1,000.

1. Compute depreciation for each of the first two years using straight-line and double-declining-balance methods.
2. Assume that DDB depreciation is used and that the equipment is sold for $20,000 cash at the end of the second year. Compute the gain or loss on the sale. Show the effects of the sale in T-accounts for the equipment and accumulated depreciation. Where and how would the sale appear in the income statement?
3. Assume that straight-line depreciation is used and that the equipment is sold for $20,000 cash at the end of the second year. Compute the gain or loss on the sale. Compare this amount to the gain or loss computed in the previous question.

Solution to Problem Three

1.

	Straight-Line Depreciation $= \dfrac{C - R}{n}$	DDB Depreciation $= $ Rate* $\times$ (Beginning Book Value)
Year 1	$36,000/4 = $9,000	.50 ($41,000) = $20,500
Year 2	$36,000/4 = $9,000	.50 ($41,000 − $20,500) = $10,250

* Rate = 2(100% ÷ n) = 2(100% ÷ 4) = 50%

2.

Revenue	$20,000
Expense: Net book value of equipment sold is $41,000 − ($20,500 + $10,250), or $41,000 − $30,750 =	10,250
Gain on sale of equipment	$ 9,750

The effect of removing the book value is a $10,250 decrease in assets. Note that the effect of a *decrease* in Accumulated Depreciation (by itself) is an *increase* in assets:

Equipment

Acquisition cost	41,000	Cost of equipment sold	41,000

Accumulated Depreciation, Equipment

Accumulated depreciation on equipment sold	30,750	Depreciation for:	
		Year 1	20,500
		Year 2	10,250
			30,750

The $9,750 gain is usually shown as a separate item on the income statement as Gain on Sale of Equipment or Gain on Disposal of Equipment.

3.

Revenue	$20,000
Expense:	
$41,000 − ($9,000 + $9,000)	23,000
Loss on sale of equipment	$ 3,000

There is a loss of $3,000 instead of a gain of $9,750 because the book value is $12,750 higher. The amount of gains or losses on disposed-of equipment depends on the depreciation method used.

Problem Four

Review the important chapter illustration in the section "Depreciation and Cash Flow," page 387. Suppose the equipment had been acquired for $80,000 instead of $40,000. The predicted residual value remains zero and the useful life remains four years.

Required
1. Prepare a revised Exhibit 9-5, which is on page 389. Assume an income tax rate of 40%; round all income tax computations to the nearest thousand.
2. Indicate all items affected by these changes. Also tabulate all differences between the final two columns in your revised exhibit as compared with Exhibit 9-5.

Solution to Problem Four

1. The revised income statements are in Exhibit 9-7.

Exhibit 9-7

Income Statement and Statement of Cash Flows for the Year Ended December 31, 19X1

Acme Service Company   (in thousands)

	Before Taxes		After Taxes	
	Straight-Line Depreciation	Accelerated Depreciation	Straight-Line Depreciation	Accelerated Depreciation
Panel I. INCOME STATEMENT				
Sales	$103	$103	$103	$103
Operating expenses	53	53	53	53
Depreciation expense	20	40	20	40
Pretax income	30	10	30	10
Income tax expense (40%)	—	—	12	4
Net income	$ 30	$ 10	$ 18	$ 6
Panel II. STATEMENT OF CASH FLOWS				
Cash collections	$103	$103	$103	$103
Cash operating expenses	53	53	53	53
Cash tax payments	—	—	12	4
	$ 50	$ 50	$ 38	$ 46

2. The following comparisons of Exhibits 9-7 and 9-5 are noteworthy. *Sales, operating expenses, and cash provided by operations before income taxes are unaffected by the change in depreciation.* Because of higher depreciation, net income would be lower in all four columns of Exhibit 9-7 than in Exhibit 9-5. Comparison of the final two columns of the exhibits follows:

| | As Shown in | | |
	Exhibit 9-7	Exhibit 9-5	Difference
Straight-line depreciation	20	10	10 higher
Accelerated depreciation	40	20	20 higher
Income tax expense based on:			
Straight-line depreciation	12	16	4 lower
Accelerated depreciation	4	12	8 lower
Net income based on:			
Straight-line depreciation	18	24	6 lower
Accelerated depreciation	6	18	12 lower
Cash provided by operations based on:			
Straight-line depreciation	38	34	4 higher
Accelerated depreciation	46	38	8 higher

Especially noteworthy is the phenomenon that higher depreciation *decreases* net income but also decreases cash outflows for income taxes. As a result, cash provided by operations *increases*.

Highlights to Remember

Long-lived assets are either tangible—physical in nature—or intangible—rights or benefits that are not physical. Depreciation, depletion, and amortization are similar concepts, providing for systematic write-offs of the acquisition costs of long-lived assets over their useful lives. Depletion usually refers to natural resources, depreciation to other tangible assets, and amortization to intangible assets. The acquisition cost includes both the purchase price and all incidental costs necessary to get the asset ready for use.

Land is not depreciated; it remains on the books at acquisition cost. Buildings and equipment can be depreciated using the straight-line method, units of production method, or an accelerated method, such as double-declining balance.

Financial reports to shareholders often differ from the reports to tax authorities. Keeping two sets of records to satisfy these two purposes is necessary, not illegal or immoral.

By itself, depreciation does not provide cash. Customers provide cash. However, depreciation is deductible for income tax purposes. Therefore the larger the depreciation reported on the tax return in any given year, the greater the amount of cash from customers that may be kept by the business instead of being disbursed to the income tax authorities.

Expenditures can be capitalized or expensed. Expenditures with benefits extending beyond the current year should be capitalized—other expenditures should be expensed.

When fixed assets are sold, the difference between the amount received from the sale and the book value of the asset is a gain or loss, which is generally included with "other income" on the income statement.

Intangible assets, such as patents, trademarks, or goodwill, are shown on the balance sheet if they were purchased. However, equally valuable items that were generated by internal expenditures are not recorded as assets.

Accounting Vocabulary

accelerated depreciation, *p. 383*
amortization, *p. 379*
basket purchase, *p. 380*
betterment, *p. 394*
capital improvement, *p. 394*
capitalized, *p. 380*
copyrights, *p. 398*
deferred charges, *p. 401*
depletion, *p. 379*
depreciable value, *p. 381*
depreciation schedule, *p. 382*
disposal value, *p. 381*

double-declining-balance
   depreciation (DDB), *p. 383*
economic life, *p. 381*
expenditures, *p. 392*
fixed assets, *p. 378*
franchises, *p. 399*
goodwill, *p. 399*
improvement, *p. 394*
intangible assets, *p. 378*
leasehold, *p. 400*
leasehold improvement, *p. 401*
licenses, *p. 399*

long-lived assets, *p. 378*
patents, *p. 398*
plant assets, *p. 378*
residual value, *p. 381*
salvage value, *p. 381*
scrap value, *p. 381*
straight-line depreciation, *p. 382*
tangible assets, *p. 378*
terminal value, *p. 381*
trademarks, *p. 398*
unit depreciation, *p. 382*
useful life, *p. 381*

Assignment Material

Questions

9-1. Distinguish between *tangible* and *intangible* assets.

9-2. Distinguish between *amortization, depreciation,* and *depletion*.

9-3. "The cash discount on the purchase of equipment is income to the buyer during the year of acquisition." Do you agree? Explain.

9-4. "When an expenditure is capitalized, stockholders' equity is credited." Do you agree? Explain.

9-5. "Accumulated depreciation is a sum of cash being accumulated for the replacement of fixed assets." Do you agree? Explain.

9-6. "The accounting process of depreciation is allocation, not valuation." Explain.

9-7. "Keeping two sets of books is immoral." Do you agree? Explain.

9-8. Compare the choice between straight-line and accelerated depreciation with the choice between FIFO and LIFO. Give at least one similarity and one difference.

9-9. "Most of the money we'll spend this year for replacing our equipment will be generated by depreciation." Do you agree? Explain.

9-10. Criticize: "Depreciation is the loss in value of a fixed asset over a given span of time."

9-11. "Accelerated depreciation saves cash but shows lower net income." Explain.

9-12. "Changes in accounting estimates should be reported prospectively rather than retroactively." Explain.

9-13. The manager of a division reported to the president of the company: "Now that our major capital improvements are finished, the division's expenses will be much lower." Is this really what he means to say? Explain.

9-14. "The gain on sale of equipment should be reported fully on the income statement." Explain what the complete reporting would include.

9-15. Name and describe four kinds of intangible assets.

9-16. Explain how goodwill is computed.

9-17. "Internally acquired patents are accounted for differently than externally acquired patents." Explain the difference.

9-18. "Goodwill may have nothing to do with the personality of the manager or employees." Do you agree? Explain.

9-19. "Accountants sometimes are too concerned with physical objects." Explain.

9-20. "Accounting for research and development is more conservative than it was before 1975." Explain.

Exercises

9-21   Computing Acquisition Costs

From the following data, calculate the cost to be added to the Land account and the Building account of St. Mary's Hospital.

On January 1, 19X9, the hospital acquired a twenty-acre parcel of land immediately adjacent to its existing facilities. The land included a warehouse, parking lots, and driveways. The hospital paid $500,000 cash and also gave a note for $2 million, payable at $200,000 per year plus interest of 10% on the outstanding balance.

The warehouse was demolished at a cash cost of $250,000 so that it could be replaced by a new hospital building. The construction of the building required a cash down payment of $3 million plus a mortgage note of $7 million. The mortgage was payable at $400,000 per year plus interest of 10% on the outstanding balance.

Required   Prepare journal entries (without explanations) to record the above transactions.

9-22   Government Equipment

A tax agency of the state of Texas acquired some used computer equipment. Installation costs were $7,000. Repair costs prior to use were $10,000. The purchasing manager's salary is $47,000 per annum and he spent one month evaluating equipment and completing the transaction. The invoice price was $400,000. The seller paid its salesman a commission of 4% and offered the buyer a cash discount of 2% if the invoice was paid within sixty days. Freight costs were $4,400, paid by the agency. Repairs during the first year of use were $9,000.

Required   Compute the total capitalized cost to be added to the Equipment account. The seller was paid within sixty days.

9-23   Basket Purchase

On February 21, 19X2, FastLube, an auto service chain, acquired an existing building and land for $720,000 from a local gas station that had failed. The tax assessor had placed an assessed valuation on January 1, 19X2, as follows:

Land	$220,000
Building	380,000
Total	$600,000

Required   How much of the $720,000 purchase price should be attributed to the building? Why?

9-24   Basket Purchase of Sports Franchise

William Rooney wants to acquire the assets of the 1995 world champion San Francisco football team, including the player contracts. The total cost is $120 million. The largest assets are the franchise and the contracts. Assume that for reporting to the IRS, the franchise has an indefinite useful life while the contracts have a five-year useful life. Other assets are relatively minor. The seller shows the following book values of the assets (in millions):

Player contracts	$3
Franchise	5
Total book value	$8

Required As Rooney, if you have complete discretion for tax purposes, how much of the $120 million price would you allocate to the contracts? Explain.

9-25   Journal Entries for Depreciation
(Alternates are 9-26 and 9-27.) On January 1, 19X1, the Marcos Company acquired 10 assembly robots for $660,000 cash. The robots had an expected useful life of ten years and an expected terminal scrap value of $60,000. Straight-line depreciation was used.

Required
1. Set up T-accounts and prepare the journal entries for the acquisition and for the first annual depreciation charge. Post to T-accounts.
2. One of the robots with an original cost of $66,000 on January 1, 19X1, and an expected terminal scrap value of $6,000 was sold for $40,000 cash on December 31, 19X3. Prepare the journal entry for the sale.
3. Refer to requirement 2. Suppose the robot had been sold for $55,000 cash instead of $40,000. Prepare the journal entry for the sale.

9-26   Journal Entries for Depreciation
(Alternates are 9-25 and 9-27.) The American Air Lines balance sheet, December 31, 1994, included the following (in millions):

Flight equipment at cost	$13,323
Less: Accumulated depreciation	3,435
	$ 9,888
Purchase deposits	116
	$10,004
Other equipment	$ 4,046
Less accumulated depreciation	2,030
	$ 2,016

Assume that on January 1, 1995, some new maintenance equipment was acquired for $850,000 cash. The equipment had an expected useful life of five years and an expected terminal scrap value of $50,000. Straight-line depreciation was used.

Required
1. Prepare the journal entry that would be made annually for depreciation on the new equipment.
2. Suppose some of the equipment with an original cost of $214,000 on January 1, 1995, and an expected terminal scrap value of $14,000 was sold for $150,000 cash two years later. Prepare the journal entry for the sale.
3. Refer to requirement 2. Suppose the equipment had been sold for $120,000 cash instead of $150,000. Prepare the journal entry for the sale.

9-27   Journal Entries for Depreciation
(Alternates are 9-25 and 9-26.) The Coca-Cola Company balance sheet, December 31, 1994, included the following:

Property, plant, and equipment	$3,221,000,000
Less allowances for depreciation	1,352,000,000
	$1,869,000,000

Note that the company uses "allowances for" rather than "accumulated" depreciation. Assume that on January 1, 1995, some new bottling equipment was acquired for $870,000 cash. The equipment had an expected useful life of five years and an expected terminal scrap value of $70,000. Straight-line depreciation was used.

Required   1. Prepare the journal entry that would be made annually for depreciation.
2. Suppose some of the equipment with an original cost of $55,000 on January 1, 1995, and an expected terminal scrap value of $5,000 was sold for $30,000 cash two years later. Prepare the journal entry for the sale.
3. Refer to requirement 2. Suppose the equipment had been sold for $45,000 cash instead of $30,000. Prepare the journal entry for the sale.

9-28   Simple Depreciation Computations

A company acquired the following assets:

    a. Conveyor, five-year useful life, $38,000 cost, straight-line method, $3,000 residual value.

    b. Truck, three-year useful life, $18,000 cost, DDB method, $1,500 residual value.

Required   Compute the first three years of depreciation.

9-29   Depreciation on a Group of Assets

Horwath Company has just purchased the assets of a division of Sportsgear, Inc. for $4.3 million. Of the purchase price, $1.8 million was allocated to assets that will be depreciated on a straight-line basis over a useful life of six years (assume no residual value). Another $800,000 was for special production machinery that will be depreciated on a DDB basis over a useful life of five years. A total of $300,000 was for land. The remainder was goodwill, which Horwath will amortize by the straight-line method over forty years.

Required   Compute the total depreciation and amortization expense generated by the acquired assets for each of the first two years.

9-30   Units-of-Production Method

The Rockland Transport Company has many trucks that are kept for a useful life of 300,000 miles. Depreciation is computed on a mileage basis. Suppose a new truck is purchased for $97,000 cash. Its expected residual value is $7,000. Its mileage during Year 1 is 60,000 and during Year 2 is 90,000.

Required   1. What is the depreciation expense for each of the two years?
2. Compute the gain or loss if the truck is sold for $55,000 at the end of Year 2.

9-31   Fundamental Depreciation Approaches

(Alternates are 9-33 and 9-34.) Consolidated Freight acquired some new trucks for $1 million. Their predicted useful life is five years, and predicted residual value is $100,000.

Required   Prepare a depreciation schedule similar to Exhibit 9-3, page 385, comparing straight-line and double-declining-balance.

9-32   Units-of-Production, Straight-Line, and DDB

Montana Mining Company buys special drills for $440,000 each. Each drill can extract about 100,000 tons of ore, after which it has a $40,000 residual value. One such drill was bought in early January, 19X1. Projected tonnage figures for the drill are 40,000 tons in 19X1, 40,000 tons in 19X2, and 20,000 tons in 19X3. Montana is considering units-of-production, straight-line, or double-declining-balance depreciation for the drill.

Required   Compute depreciation for each year under each of the three methods.

9-33   Comparison of Popular Depreciation Methods

(Alternates are 9-31 and 9-34.) Elm Lumber Company acquired a machine for $32,000 with an expected useful life of five years and a $2,000 expected residual value. Prepare a tabular comparison (similar to Exhibit 9-3, p. 385) of the annual depreciation and book value for each year under straight-line and double-declining-balance depreciation. (Note that this is a comparison of methods used for reporting to shareholders. Such methods may differ from those used for reporting to the income tax authorities.)

9-34 Fundamental Depreciation Policies

(Alternates are 9-31 and 9-33.) The Mailing Services department of Bank of America acquired some new package-handling equipment for $380,000. The equipment's predicted useful life is eight years and predicted residual value is $28,000.

Required Prepare a depreciation schedule similar to Exhibit 9-3 (p. 385), comparing straight-line and double-declining-balance. Show all amounts in thousands of dollars (rounded to the nearest thousand). Limit the schedule to each of the first three years of useful life. Show the depreciation for each year and the book value at the end of each year. (Note that this is a comparison of methods used for reporting to shareholders. Such methods may differ from those used for reporting to the income tax authorities.)

9-35 Depreciation, Income Taxes, and Cash Flow

Fleck Company began business with cash and common stock equity of $150,000. The same day, December 31, 19X1, equipment was acquired for $50,000 cash. The equipment had an expected useful life of five years and a predicted residual value of $5,000. The first year's operations generated cash sales of $160,000 and cash operating expenses of $85,000.

Required
1. Prepare an analysis of transactions for December 31, 19X1, plus the year 19X2, using the balance sheet equation format as illustrated in Exhibit 9-4. Assume (a) straight-line depreciation and (b) DDB depreciation. Assume zero income taxes. Exhibit 9-4 is on page 388.
2. Repeat requirement 1, but assume an income tax rate of 40%. Income taxes are paid in cash. The company uses the same depreciation method for reporting to shareholders and to income tax authorities.
3. Prepare columnar (a) income statements for 19X2 and (b) balance sheets as of December 31, 19X2, that compare the effects of the four alternatives covered in requirements 1 and 2. (*Hint*: See the illustration in the chapter, pp. 387-390.)
4. Compare your answers to requirements 1 and 2. Does depreciation provide cash? Explain as precisely as possible.
5. Refer to requirement 1. Suppose depreciation were tripled under straight-line and DDB methods. How would cash be affected? Be specific.

9-36 MACRS Versus Straight-Line

San Pedro Machinery bought special tooling equipment for $3 million. The useful life is five years, with no residual value. For tax purposes, assume MACRS specifies a three-year, DDB depreciation schedule. San Pedro uses the straight-line depreciation method for reporting to shareholders.

Required
1. Explain the two factors that account for acceleration of depreciation for tax purposes.
2. Compute the first year's depreciation (a) for shareholder reporting and (b) for tax purposes. (Ignore complications in the tax law that are not introduced in this chapter.)

9-37 Leasehold Improvements

A Taco Bell has a ten-year lease on space in a suburban shopping center. Near the end of the sixth year of the lease, Taco Bell exercised its rights under the lease, removing walls and replacing floor coverings and lighting fixtures. The cost was $200,000. The useful life of the redesigned facilities was predicted to be twelve years.

Required What accounts would be affected by the $200,000 expenditure? What would be the annual amortization?

9-38 Classic Case from the Business Press

A news story regarding Chrysler Corporation stated:

> Yet the $7.5 billion that John J. Riccardo, its money man, estimates the company
> will need to finance a recovery over the next five years is huge by any standard. But,

says Riccardo, "half is charged to the P&L [profit and loss] as incurred, so we're looking for $3.75 billion. Of that, about 60% will be recovered in depreciation and amortization. That leaves a balance of $1.5 billion over the five years, to be financed through earnings, borrowings, and divestitures. Over the period, that overall number is manageable."

Required

Explain or comment on the following:
1. "Half is charged to the P&L as incurred, so we're looking for $3.75 billion."
2. "Of that, about 60% will be recovered in depreciation and amortization."

9-39   Changes in Depreciation Estimates

Cascade Company acquired equipment for $50,000 with an expected useful life of five years and a $5,000 expected residual value. Straight-line depreciation was adopted. Suppose it is the end of Year 3. The company's engineers have altered their expectations; the equipment's new expected useful life is six instead of five years. Furthermore, the expected residual value is $2,000 instead of $5,000.

Required

1. Using the "prospective" method, compute the new annual straight-line depreciation.
2. Critics of the "prospective" method favor using the "retroactive" method instead. Prepare a table comparing annual depreciation throughout the eight-year life using the prospective method and the retroactive method. Which method do you favor? Why?

9-40   Capital Expenditures

Consider the following transactions:

a.   Paid principal on building mortgage.
b.   Paid cash dividends.
c.   Paid plumbers for repair of leaky faucets.
d.   Acquired new air-conditioning system for the building.
e.   Replaced smashed front door (not covered by insurance).
f.   Paid travel expenses of sales personnel.
g.   Acquired building for a down payment plus a mortgage payable.
h.   Paid interest on building mortgage.
i.   Paid janitorial wages.
j.   Paid security guard wages.

Required

Answer by letter:
1. Indicate which transactions are capital expenditures.
2. Indicate which transactions are expenses in the current year.

9-41   Capital Expenditures

Consider each of the following transactions. For each one, indicate whether it is a capital expenditure (C) or an expense in the current year (E).

a.   Paid for a tune-up on one of the autos in the company's fleet.
b.   Paid a consultant to advise on marketing strategy.
c.   Installed new lighting fixtures in a leased building.
d.   Paid for routine maintenance on equipment.
e.   Acquired a patent for $50,000.
f.   Paid for overhaul of machinery that extends its useful life.
g.   Developed a patentable product by paying for research and development.
h.   Paid organization costs to incorporate a new company.

9-42   Depreciation for Parts of Year

Rubanko Company acquired material-handling equipment on April 2, 19X1, for $280,000 cash. Its expected useful life was five years, and its expected residual value was $40,000. The double-declining balance method of depreciation was adopted. Prepare a schedule of depreciation for the first three calendar years of use. Show the total amount of depreciation for each calendar year affected.

9-43   Repairs and Improvements

Harui Grain Company acquired harvesting equipment for $88,000 with an expected useful life of five years and an $8,000 expected residual value. Straight-line depreciation was used. During its fourth year of service, expenditures related to the equipment were as follows:

1. Oiling and greasing, $200.
2. Replacing belts and hoses, $450.
3. Major overhaul during the final week of the year, including the replacement of an engine. The useful life of the equipment was extended from five to seven years. The cost was $20,000. The residual value is now expected to be $11,000 instead of $8,000.

Required   Indicate in words how each of the three items would affect the income statement and the balance sheet. Prepare a tabulation that compares the original depreciation schedule with the revised depreciation schedule.

9-44   Disposal of Equipment

Tompkins Community Hospital's Convenient Care Center acquired x-ray equipment for $35,000 with an expected useful life of five years and a $5,000 expected residual value. Straight-line depreciation was used. The equipment was sold at the end of the fourth year for $16,000 cash.

Required
1. Compute the gain or loss on the sale. Show the effects of the sale on the balance sheet equation, identifying all specific accounts by name. Where and how would the sale appear on the income statement?
2. (a) Show the journal entries for the transaction in requirement 1. (b) Repeat 2a, assuming that the cash sales price was $7,000 instead of $16,000.

9-45   Gain or Loss on Sales of Fixed Assets

Ontime Delivery Company purchased a van in early 19X1 for $30,000. It was being depreciated on a straight-line basis over its useful life of five years. Estimated residual value was $5,000. The van was sold in early 19X3 after two years of depreciation had been recognized.

Required
1. Suppose Ontime received $22,000 for the van. Compute the gain or loss on the sale. Prepare the journal entries for the sale of the van.
2. Suppose Ontime received $15,000 for the van. Compute the gain or loss on the sale. Prepare the journal entries for the sale of the van.

9-46   Depletion

A zinc mine contains an estimated 900,000 tons of zinc ore. The mine cost $13.5 million. The tonnage mined during 19X4, the first year of operations, was 120,000 tons.

Required
1. What was the depletion for 19X4?
2. Suppose that in January 19X5 it was discovered that the mine originally contained 1 million tons. What was the estimated depletion for 19X5, assuming that 100,000 tons were mined?

9-47   Balance Sheet Presentation

Consider the presentation of the Procter & Gamble Company, whose brands include *Tide, Jif, Charmin, Folger's,* and *Crest* (in millions of dollars) for 1994 and 1990:

	June 30	
	1994	1990
PROPERTY, PLANT, AND EQUIPMENT		
Buildings	$ 3,027	$ 1,862
Machinery and equipment	12,249	9,506
Land	550	230
Timberlands, less depletion	70	191
	15,896	11,789
Less accumulated depreciation	5,872	4,353
	$10,024	$ 7,436

Required   Do any features of this presentation seem unusual? Explain.

9-48   Various Intangible Assets
Consider the following:

1. On December 29, 19X1, a publisher acquires the copyright for a book by Robert Ludlum for $2 million. Most sales of this book are expected to take place uniformly during 19X2 and 19X3. What will be the amortization for 19X2?

2. On January 4, 19X1, Company X acquires Company Y for $45 million and can assign only $35 million to identifiable individual assets. What is the minimum amount of amortization of the goodwill for 19X1? Could the entire amount be written off in 19X1? Why?

3. In 19X1, Company C spent $10 million in its research department, which resulted in new valuable patents. In December 19X1, Company D paid $10 million to an outside inventor for some valuable new patents. How would the income statements for 19X1 for each company be affected? How would the balance sheets as of December 31, 19X1, be affected?

4. On December 28, 19X8, Scholes Company purchased a patent for a calculator for $360,000. The patent has ten years of its legal life remaining. Technology changes fast, so Scholes expects the patent to be worthless in five years. What will be the amortization for 19X9?

9-49   Various Intangible Assets
1. On December 29, 1995, CBS Corporation purchased a patent on some broadcasting equipment for $600,000. The patent has sixteen years of its legal life remaining. Because technology moves rapidly, CBS expects the patent to be worthless at the end of five years. What is the amortization for 1996?

2. An annual report of Associated Hosts, owner and operator of many restaurants and hotels, including the Beverly Hillcrest Hotel, stated: "It is the company's policy to defer preopening costs during periods of construction of new units or remodeling of existing units and to amortize such costs over a period of 12 to 24 months commencing on the opening date."

    During the year, preopening costs of $582,000 were capitalized. The beginning-of-the-year asset balance for preopening costs was $779,000, and the end-of-the-year balance was $617,000. Compute the amortization for the year.

3. Philip Morris purchased General Foods for $5.6 billion. Philip Morris could assign only $1.7 billion to identifiable individual assets. What is the amount of goodwill created by the acquisition? What is the minimum amount of amortization in the first year?

4. (a) In 1994, DuPont spent over $1 billion in its research departments, and this resulted in valuable new patents. (b) Suppose that in December 1994, DuPont had paid $1 billion to various outside companies for the same new patents. How would the income statement for 1994 have been affected under a and b? How would the balance sheet on December 31, 1994, be affected?

9-50   Various Intangible Assets
Consider the following:

1. (a) Dow Chemical Company's annual report indicated that research and development expenditures for the year were $1,136 million. How did this amount affect operating income, which was $2,818 million? (b) Suppose the entire $1,136 million arose from outlays for patents acquired from various outside parties on December 30. What would be the operating income for the year? (c) How would Dow's December 31 balance sheet be affected by b?

2. On January 1, American Telephone and Telegraph Company (AT&T) acquired new patents on some communications equipment for $10 million. Technology changes quickly. The equipment's useful life is expected to be five years rather than the seventeen-year life of the patent. What will be the amortization for the first year?

3. Hilton Hotels has an account classified under assets in its balance sheet called preopening costs. A footnote said that these costs "are charged to income over a three-year period after the opening date." Suppose expenditures for preopening costs in 1995 were $2,000,000 and the preopening costs account balance on December 31, 1995, was $1,840,000 and on December 31, 1994, was $2,390,000. What amount was amortized for 1995?

4. The Gannett Co., Inc., publisher of many newspapers, including *USA Today*, purchased radio stations KKBQ-AM and FM in Houston and WDAE-AM in Tampa for a total of $41 million. A footnote in the annual report stated that goodwill is "amortized over a period of 40 years." Assume that both purchases were made on January 2 and that Gannett could assign only $33 million to identifiable individual assets. What is the minimum amount of amortization of goodwill for the first year? Could the entire amount be written off immediately? Explain.

Problems

9-51   Basket Purchase and Intangibles
A tax newsletter stated: "When a business is sold, part of the sales price may be allocated to a 'covenant not to compete' and another part to 'goodwill.' How this allocation is made can have important tax consequences to both the buyer and seller."

A large law firm, organized as a professional services corporation, purchased a successful local firm for $145,000. Only $45,000 was assigned to individual assets. The other $100,000 was for both a covenant not to compete for five years and goodwill. Suppose the buyer has legally supportable latitude concerning how to allocate this amount, as follows:

	Allocation One	Allocation Two
Covenant	$ 65,000	$ 50,000
Goodwill	35,000	50,000
Total for two assets	$100,000	$100,000

Required

1. For income tax purposes, which allocation would the buyer favor? Why?
2. For shareholder reporting purposes, which allocation would the buyer favor? Why?

9-52   Popular Depreciation Methods

The annual report of Alaska Airlines contained the following footnote:

PROPERTY, EQUIPMENT, AND DEPRECIATION—Property and equipment are recorded at cost and depreciated using the straight-line method over the estimated useful lives, which are as follows:

Buildings	10–30 years
Flight equipment	10–18 years
Other equipment	3–15 years

Required   Consider a Boeing 727-100 airplane, which was acquired for $26 million. Its useful life is ten years, and its expected residual value is $4 million. Prepare a tabular comparison of the annual depreciation and book value for each of the first three years of service life under straight-line and double-declining-balance depreciation. Show all amounts in thousands of dollars (rounded to the nearest thousand). (Note that this is a comparison of methods used for reporting to shareholders. Such methods may differ from those used for reporting to the income tax authorities.) *Hint*: See Exhibit 9-3, page 385.

9-53   Depreciation Practices

The 1994 annual report of General Mills, maker of *Wheaties*, *Cheerios*, and *Betty Crocker* baking products, contained the following (in millions):

	1994	1993
Total land, buildings, and equipment	$4,689.8	$4,239.5
Less accumulated depreciation	(1,597.2)	(1,379.9)
Net land, buildings, and equipment	$3,092.6	$2,859.6

During 1994, depreciation expense was $303.8 million, and General Mills acquired land, buildings, and equipment worth $559.5 million. Assume that no gain or loss arose from the disposition of land, buildings, and equipment and that cash of $22.7 million was received from such disposals.

Required   Compute (1) the gross amount of assets written off (sold or retired), (2) the amount of accumulated depreciation written off, and (3) the book value of the assets written off. *Hint:* The use of T-accounts may help your analysis.

9-54   Reconstruction of Plant Asset Transactions

(J. Patell, adapted.) The Ford Motor Company's balance sheets included (in millions of dollars):

Ford Motor Company

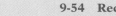

	December 31	
	1994	1993
Property:		
Land, plant, and equipment	$42,534	$37,489
Less accumulated depreciation	(22,738)	(20,691)
Net land, plant, and equipment	19,796	16,798
Unamortized special tools	7,252	6,261
Net property	$27,048	$23,059

The following additional information was available from the notes to the income statement for 1994 (in millions):

Depreciation	$2,297
Amortization	2,129

The account Unamortized Special Tools is increased by new investments in tools, dies, jigs, and fixtures necessary for new models and production processes. These investments are then amortized over various periods. Hence the account is called "unamortized" because its amount will become amortized during future periods.

Hint: Analyze with the help of T-accounts.

Required

1. There were no disposals of special tools during 1994. Compute the cost of new acquisitions of special tools.
2. Suppose the proceeds from the sales of land, plant, and equipment during 1994 were $92 million, and the loss on sale of land, plant, and equipment was $25 million. Compute the original cost *and* the accumulated depreciation of the land, plant, and equipment that was sold.
3. Compute the cost of the new acquisitions of land, plant, and equipment.

9-55   Average Age of Assets
NYNEX, owner of New England Telephone and New York Telephone, had the following on its January 1, 1994, balance sheet (in millions):

Total depreciable property, plant, and equipment	$34,447.1
Less: Accumulated depreciation	14,843.7
	$19,603.4

A footnote states that "all [depreciation] rates are calculated on a straight-line basis." Annual depreciation expense is approximately $2,600 million.

Required

1. Estimate the average useful life of NYNEX's depreciable assets.
2. Estimate the average age of NYNEX's depreciable assets on January 1, 1994.

9-56   Depreciation, Income Tax, and Cash Flow
(Alternates are 9-57, 9-58, and 9-74.) Morales Metal Products Co. had the following balances, among others, at the end of December 19X1: Cash, $300,000; Equipment, $400,000; Accumulated Depreciation, $100,000. Total revenues (all in cash) were $900,000. Cash operating expenses were $600,000. Straight-line depreciation expense was $50,000. If accelerated depreciation had been used, depreciation expense would have been $80,000.

Required

1. Assume zero income taxes. Fill in the blanks in the accompanying table. Show the amounts in thousands.
2. Repeat requirement 1, but assume an income tax rate of 40%. Assume also that Morales uses the same depreciation method for reporting to shareholders and to income tax authorities.
3. Compare your answers to requirements 1 and 2. Does depreciation provide cash? Explain as precisely as possible.
4. Assume that Morales had used straight-line depreciation for reporting to shareholders and to income tax authorities. Indicate the change (increase or decrease and amount) in the following balances if Morales had used accelerated depreciation

instead of straight-line: Cash, Accumulated Depreciation, Operating Income, Income Tax Expense, and Retained Income.

5. Refer to requirement 1. Suppose depreciation were tripled under both straight-line and accelerated methods. How would cash be affected? Be specific.

Table for Problem 9-56
(amounts in thousands)

| | 1. Zero Income Taxes | | 2. 40% Income Taxes | |
	Straight-Line Depreciation	Accelerated Depreciation	Straight-Line Depreciation	Accelerated Depreciation
Revenues	$	$	$	$
Cash operating expenses				
Cash provided by operations before income taxes				
Depreciation expense				
Operating income				
Income tax expense				
Net income	$	$	$	$
Supplementary analysis:				
Cash provided by operations before income taxes	$	$	$	$
Income tax payments				
Net cash provided by operations	$	$	$	$

9-57 Depreciation, Income Taxes, and Cash Flow
(Alternates are 9-56, 9-58, and 9-74.) The annual report of Kmart, a major retailing company, listed the following property and equipment (in millions):

Property and equipment, at cost	$8,339
Less: Accumulated depreciation	3,978
Property and equipment, net	$4,361

The cash balance was $278,000,000.

Depreciation expense during the year was $497,000,000. The condensed income statement follows (in millions):

Revenues	$32,462
Expenses	31,316
Operating income	$ 1,146

For purposes of this problem, assume that all revenues and expenses, excluding depreciation, are for cash. Thus, cash operating expenses were $31,316,000,000 − $497,000,000 = $30,819,000,000.

Required

1. Kmart uses straight-line depreciation. Suppose accelerated depreciation had been $597,000,000 instead of $497,000,000. Assume zero income taxes. Fill in the blanks in the accompanying table (in millions of dollars).

2. Repeat requirement 1, but assume an income tax rate of 40%. Assume also that Kmart uses the same depreciation method for reporting to shareholders and to income tax authorities.
3. Compare your answers to requirements 1 and 2. Does depreciation provide cash? Explain as precisely as possible.
4. Assume that Kmart had used straight-line depreciation for reporting to shareholders and to income tax authorities. Indicate the change (increase or decrease and amount) in the following balances if Kmart had used accelerated depreciation instead of straight-line during that year: Cash, Accumulated Depreciation, Operating Income, Income Tax Expense, and Retained Income. What would be the new balances in Cash and Accumulated Depreciation?
5. Refer to requirement 1. Suppose depreciation were increased by an extra $300,000,000 under both straight-line and accelerated methods. How would cash be affected? Be specific.

Table for Problem 9-57
(amounts in millions)

	1. Zero Income Taxes		2. 40% Income Taxes	
	Straight-Line Depreciation	Accelerated Depreciation	Straight-Line Depreciation	Accelerated Depreciation
Revenues	$	$	$	$
Cash operating expenses				
Cash provided by operations before income taxes				
Depreciation expense				
Operating income				
Income tax expense				
Net income	$	$	$	$
Supplementary analysis:				
Cash provided by operations before income taxes	$	$	$	$
Income tax payments				
Net cash provided by operations	$	$	$	$

9-58   Depreciation, Income Taxes, and Cash Flow

(Alternates are 9-56, 9-57, and 9-74.) Mitsubishi Kasei Corp. is Japan's premier integrated chemical company. The company's annual report showed the following balances (translated into thousands of U.S. dollars):

Revenues	$8,964,335
Operating expenses	8,529,216
Operating income	$ 435,119

Mitsubishi Kasei had depreciation expense of $441,614,000 (included in operating expenses). The company's ending cash balance was $1,013,257.

Mitsubishi Kasei reported its property and equipment in the following way (in thousands of U.S. dollars):

Property, plant, and equipment, at cost	
Land	$ 756,044
Buildings	1,903,990
Machinery and equipment	5,715,985
Construction in process	217,234
	8,593,253
Less: Accumulated depreciation	5,348,046
Net property and equipment	$3,245,207

For purposes of this problem, assume that all revenues and expenses, excluding depreciation, are for cash.

Required

1. Mitsubishi Kasei used declining-balance depreciation. Suppose straight-line depreciation had been $341,614,000 instead of $441,614,000. Assume zero income taxes. Fill in the blanks in the accompanying table (in thousands of dollars).
2. Repeat requirement 1, but assume an income tax rate of 60%. Assume also that Mitsubishi Kasei uses the same depreciation method for reporting to shareholders and to income tax authorities.
3. Compare your answers to requirements 1 and 2. Does depreciation provide cash? Explain as precisely as possible.
4. Mitsubishi Kasei used declining-balance depreciation for reporting to shareholders and to income tax authorities. Indicate the change (increase or decrease and amount) in the following balances if Mitsubishi Kasei had used straight-line depreciation rather than declining-balance: Cash, Accumulated Depreciation, Operating Income, Income Tax Expense, and Retained Income. What would be the new balances in Cash and Accumulated Depreciation?
5. Refer to requirement 1. Suppose depreciation were doubled under both straight-line and declining-balance methods. How would cash be affected? Be specific.

Table for Problem 9-58
(amounts in thousands)

	1. Zero Income Taxes		2. 60% Income Taxes	
	Straight-Line Depreciation	Declining-Balance Depreciation	Straight-Line Depreciation	Declining-Balance Depreciation
Revenues	$	$	$	$
Cash operating expenses				
Cash provided by operations before income taxes				
Depreciation expense				
Operating income				
Income tax expense				
Net income	$	$	$	$
Supplementary analysis:				
Cash provided by operations before income taxes	$	$	$	$
Income tax expense				
Net cash provided by operations	$	$	$	$

9-59   Depreciation, Income Taxes, and Cash Flow

Mr. Kuhlmann, president of the Bremen Shipping Company, had read a newspaper story that stated: "The Frankfurt Steel Company had a cash flow last year of 1,500,000 DM, consisting of 1,000,000 DM of net income plus 500,000 DM of depreciation. New plant facilities helped the cash flow, because depreciation was 25 percent higher than in the preceding year." "Cash flow" is frequently used as a synonym for "cash provided by operations," which, in turn, is cash revenue less cash operating expenses and income taxes. (DM stands for Deutschmark, the German unit of currency.)

Kuhlmann was encouraged by the quotation because Bremen Shipping Company had just acquired a vast amount of new transportation equipment. These acquisitions had placed a severe financial strain on the company. Kuhlmann was heartened because he thought that the added cash flow from the depreciation of the new equipment should ease the financial pressures on the company.

The income before income taxes of the Bremen Shipping Company last year (19X2) was 200,000 DM. Depreciation was 200,000 DM; it will also be 200,000 DM on the old equipment in 19X3.

Revenue in 19X2 was 2.1 million DM (all in cash), and operating expenses other than depreciation were 1.7 million DM (all in cash).

In 19X3, the new equipment is expected to help increase revenue by 1 million DM. However, operating expenses other than depreciation will increase by 800,000 DM.

Required

1. Suppose depreciation on the new equipment for financial reporting purposes is 100,000 DM. What would be the "cash flow" from operations (cash provided by operations) for 19X3? Show computations. Ignore income taxes.
2. Repeat requirement 1, assuming that the depreciation on the new equipment is 50,000 DM. Ignore income taxes.
3. Assume an income tax rate of 40%. (a) Repeat requirement 1; (b) repeat requirement 2. Assume that the same amount of depreciation is shown for tax purposes and for financial reporting purposes.
4. In your own words, state as accurately as possible the effects on "cash flow" of depreciation. Comment on requirements 1, 2, and 3 above in order to bring out your points. This is a more important requirement than requirements 1, 2, and 3.

9-60   Rental Cars

An annual report of the Hertz rental car company contained the following footnote:

> Depreciable assets—the provisions for depreciation and amortization are computed on a straight-line basis over the estimated useful lives of the respective assets.... Hertz follows the practice of charging maintenance and repairs, including the costs of minor replacements, to maintenance expense accounts. Costs of major replacement of units of property are charged to property and equipment accounts and depreciated.... Upon disposal of revenue earning equipment, depreciation expense is adjusted for the difference between the net proceeds from sale and the remaining book value.

Required

1. Assume that some new cars are acquired on October 1, 1995, for $120 million. The useful life is one year. Expected residual values are $84 million. Prepare a summary journal entry for depreciation for 1995. The fiscal year ends on December 31.
2. Prepare a summary journal entry for depreciation for the first six months of 1996.
3. Assume that the automobiles are sold for $96 million cash on October 1, 1996. Prepare the journal entry for the sale. Automobiles are considered "revenue earning equipment."
4. What is the total depreciation expense for 1996? If the $96 million proceeds could have been predicted exactly when the cars were originally acquired, what would depreciation expense have been in 1995? In 1996? Explain.

9-61   Nature of Research Costs

Maria Gersteli, a distinguished scientist of international repute, had developed many successful drugs for a well-established pharmaceutical company. Having an entrepreneurial spirit, she persuaded the board of directors that she should resign her position as vice-president of research and launch a subsidiary company to produce and market some powerful new drugs for treating arthritis. However, she did not predict overnight success. Instead, she expected to gather a first-rate research team that might take three to five years to generate any marketable products. Furthermore, she admitted that the risks were so high that conceivably no commercial success might result. Nevertheless, she had little trouble obtaining an initial investment of $5 million. The Gersteli Pharmaceuticals Company was 80% owned by the parent and 20% by Maria.

Maria acquired a team of researchers and began operations. By the end of the first year of the life of the new subsidiary, $2 million had been expended on research activities, mostly for researchers' salaries, but also for related research costs.

No marketable products had been developed, but Maria and other top executives were extremely pleased about overall progress and were very optimistic about getting such products within the next three or four years.

Required

How would you account for the $2 million? Would you write it off as an expense in Year 1? Carry it indefinitely? Write it off systematically over three years or some longer span? Why? Explain, giving particular attention to the idea of an asset as an unexpired cost.

9-62   Meaning of Book Value

Sanchez Company purchased an office building twenty years ago for $1.2 million, $400,000 of which was attributable to land. The mortgage has been fully paid. The current balance sheet follows:

Cash		$300,000	Stockholders'	
Land		400,000	equity	$850,000
Building at cost	$800,000			
Accumulated depreciation	650,000			
Net book value		150,000		
Total assets		$850,000		

The company is about to borrow $1.8 million on a first mortgage to modernize and expand the building. This amounts to 60% of the combined appraised value of the land and building before the modernization and expansion.

Required

Prepare a balance sheet after the loan is made and the building is expanded and modernized. Comment on its significance.

9-63   Capital Expenditures

Disputes sometimes arise between the taxpayer and the Internal Revenue Service regarding whether legal costs should be deductible as expenses in the year incurred (revenue expenditures) or be considered as capital expenditures because they relate to defining or perfecting title to business property.

Consider three examples from court cases:

Example 1

Several years after Rock set up his stone-quarrying business, Smalltown passed an ordinance banning it. Rock spent $1,000 to invalidate the ordinance.

Example 2

Now suppose Rock decided to expand his business. He applied to Smalltown for a permit to build an additional crusher. It was denied because an ordinance prohibited the expansion of nonconforming uses, including quarrying. Rock sued to invalidate the ordinance and won after spending $2,000. He then built the crusher.

Example 3

Smalltown's zoning board established a restrictive building (setback) line across Rock's business property. The line lowered the property's value. Rock spent $3,000 trying unsuccessfully to challenge it.

Required Indicate whether each example should be deemed (a) an expense or (b) a capital expenditure. Briefly explain your answer.

9-64   Change in Service Life

An annual report of TWA contained the following footnote:

> Note 2. *Change in accounting estimate.* TWA extended the estimated useful lives of Boeing 727-100 aircraft from principally sixteen years to principally twenty years. As a result, depreciation and amortization expense was decreased by $9,000,000.

The TWA annual report also contained the following data: depreciation, $235,518,000; net income, $42,233,000.

The cost of the 727-100 aircraft subject to depreciation was $800 million. Residual values were predicted to be 10% of acquisition cost.

Required Assume a combined federal and state income tax rate of 46% throughout all parts of these requirements.

1. Was the effect of the change in estimated useful life a material difference? Explain, including computations.
2. The same year's annual report of Delta Air Lines contained the following footnote:

   > Depreciation—Substantially all of the flight equipment is being depreciated on a straight-line basis to residual values (10% of cost) over a 10-year period from dates placed in service.

   The Delta annual report also contained the following data: depreciation, $220,979,000; net income, $146,474,000. Suppose Delta had used a twenty-year life instead of a ten-year life. Assume a 46% applicable income tax rate. Compute the new depreciation and net income.
3. Suppose TWA had used a ten-year life instead of a twenty-year life on its 727-100 equipment. Compute the new depreciation and net income. For purposes of this requirement, assume that the equipment cost $800 million and has been in service one year and that reported net income based on a twenty-year life was $42,233,000.

9-65   Disposal of Equipment

(Alternate is 9-66.) Alaska Airlines acquired a new Boeing 727-100 airplane for $26 million. Its expected residual value was $6 million. The company's annual report indicated that straight-line depreciation was used based on an estimated service life of ten years. In addition, the company stated: "The cost and related accumulated depreciation of assets sold or retired are removed from the appropriate accounts, and gain or loss, if any, is recognized in Other Income (Expense)."

Required Show all amounts in millions of dollars.

1. Assume that the equipment is sold at the end of the sixth year for $15 million cash. Compute the gain or loss on the sale. Show the effects of the sale on the balance sheet equation, identifying all specific accounts by name. Where and how would the sale appear on the income statement?
2. (a) Show the journal entries for the transaction in requirement 1. (b) Repeat 2a, assuming that the cash sales price was $9 million instead of $15 million.

9-66   Disposal of Property and Equipment

(Alternate is 9-65.) Rockwell International is an advanced technology company operating primarily in aerospace and electronics. The company's annual report indicted that both accelerated and straight-line depreciation were used for its property and equipment. In addition, the annual report said: "Gains or losses on property transactions are recorded in income in the period of sale or retirement."

Rockwell received $27.9 million for property that it sold.

Required

1. Assume that the total property in question was originally acquired for $150 million and the $27.9 million was received in cash. There was a gain of $8.5 million on the sale. Compute the accumulated depreciation on the property and equipment sold. Show the effects of the sale on the balance sheet equation, identifying all specific accounts by name.
2. For this requirement, round your entries to the nearest tenth of a million dollars. (a) Show the journal entries and postings to T-accounts for the transaction in requirement 1. (b) Repeat 2a, assuming that the cash sales price was $17.9 million cash instead of $27.9 million.

9-67   Gain on Airplane Crash

In August 1988, a Delta Air Lines 727 crashed in Dallas. The crash resulted in a gain of $.11 per share for Delta. How could this happen? Consider the accounting for airplanes. Airlines insure their craft at market value, $6.5 million for Delta's 727. However, the planes' book values are often much less because of large accumulated depreciation amounts. The book value of Delta's 727 was only $962,000.

Required

1. Suppose Delta received the insurance payment and immediately purchased another 727 for $6.5 million. Compute the effect of the crash on pretax income. Also compute the effect on Delta's total assets.
2. Do you think a casualty should generate a reported gain? Why?

9-68   Disposal of Equipment

Airline Executive reported on an airline as follows:

> Lufthansa's highly successful policy of rolling over entire fleets in roughly ten years—before the aircrafts have outlived their usefulness—got started in a "spectacular" way when seven first-generation 747s were sold.
>
> The 747s were bought six to nine years earlier for $22-28 million each and sold for about the same price.

Required

1. Assume an average original cost of $25 million each, an average original expected useful life of ten years, a $2.5 million expected residual value, and an average actual life of eight years before disposal. Use straight-line depreciation. Compute the total gain or loss on the sale of the seven planes.
2. Prepare a summary journal entry for the sale.

9-69   Depreciation of Professional Sports Contracts

"Accounting Professor Says the Owners Lost $27 Million" read the headline on July 10, 1985. Major league baseball players and owners were engaged in contract negotiations. The owners claimed to have lost $43 million in 1984, and the Players Association maintained that the owners had made a profit of as much as $10 million. George Sorter, Professor of Accounting at New York University, fixed the loss at $27 million, primarily because he added back "initial roster depreciation" to adjust the owners' figure. "That depreciation, an amount that arises when a team is purchased and a portion of the purchase price that makes up player contracts is paid off [amortized] over several years, should not be treated as an operating expense," Sorter said. When a team is sold, an amount representing the value of current player contracts is put into an intangible asset account and amortized (or depreciated) over several years.

Required Explain why such an intangible asset account is created. Should this asset be amortized (or depreciated), thereby reducing income? Why would Professor Sorter eliminate this expense when assessing the financial operating performance of the major league teams?

9-70   Valuation of Intagible Assets of Football Team

New owners acquired the Los Angeles Rams football team for $7.2 million. They valued the contracts of their forty players at a total of $3.5 million, the franchise at $3.6 million, and other assets at $100,000. For income tax purposes, the Rams amortized the $3.5 million over five years; therefore they took a tax deduction of $700,000 annually.

The Internal Revenue Service challenged the deductions. It maintained that only $300,000 of the $7.2 million purchase price was attributable to the player contracts, and that the $3.2 million of the $3.5 million in dispute should be attributed to the league franchise rights. Such franchise rights are regarded by the Internal Revenue Service as a valuable asset with an indefinite future life; therefore no amortization is permitted for tax-reporting purposes.

Suppose the operating income for each of the five years (before any amortization) was $1 million.

Required 1. Consider the reporting to the Internal Revenue Service. Tabulate a comparison of annual operating income (after amortization) according to two approaches, (a) the Rams' and (b) the IRS's. What is the difference in annual operating income?
2. Consider the reporting to shareholders. Reports to shareholders by American companies amortize franchise fees. The Rams had been using a five-year life for player contracts and a forty-year life for the league franchise rights. Tabulate a comparison of operating income (after amortization) using (a) this initial approach and (b) the approach whereby only $300,000 would have been attributed to player contracts. What is the difference in annual operating income?
3. Comment on the results in requirements 1 and 2. Which alternative do you think provides the more informative report of operating results? Why?

9-71   Deferred Charges

Simmons Airlines, Inc., was a Chicago-based regional carrier in the Midwest that was owned by American Airlines. Consider the following item under "Other assets" in its annual report:

	19X7	19X6
Deferred development costs, net of amortization (19X7, $329,000; 19X6, $285,000)	$385,000	$514,000

A footnote to the annual report stated: "Deferred development and preoperating costs: Costs related to the introduction of new types of aircraft are deferred and amortized over five years."

Required 1. Suppose no new deferred development or preoperating costs were recorded during 19X7. Calculate the amount of deferred development costs amortized during 19X7.
2. Suppose Simmons took delivery of new Boeing 737s halfway through 19X8 and incurred $42,000 of training costs associated with the introduction of the new aircraft. Show the journal entries for recording these costs (assume that payment was in cash) and for recognizing amortization at the end of the year.

9-72   Acquisition of Intagible Assets

Forbes reported that CGA Computer Associates, a computer software marketer, had acquired another software company, Allen Services Corporation, for $19 million. CGA got only $1.2 million in net tangible assets.

The CGA president insisted that "the premium was justified because Allen had built up a huge inventory of software that was not reflected in the books. The reason: Spending on developing new software systems is treated as research and development and therefore written off immediately. In this case, CGA had to book $11.7 million of the $17.8 million discrepancy as software and the rest as goodwill."

The software would be amortized over its useful life, five years, because of the pace of developments in computers. Goodwill would be amortized over forty years.

Required

1. Compute the expenses for (a) amortization of software and (b) amortization of goodwill for the first complete year after the acquisition.
2. How would operating income (before taxes) for the first complete year after the acquisition have been affected if the excess of $19 million over $1.2 million had all been recorded as goodwill?

9-73   Software Development Costs

Microsoft, Incorporated, is one of the largest producers of software for personal computers. One of its divisions began working on some special business applications software for Apple MacIntosh computers. Suppose $400,000 had been spent on the project by the end of 19X1, but it was not yet clear whether the software was technologically feasible.

On about July 1, 19X2, after spending another $200,000, management decided that the software was technologically feasible. During the second half of 19X2, the division spent another $500,000 on this project. In December 19X2 the product was announced, with deliveries to begin in March 19X3. No research and development costs for the software were incurred after December 19X2. Projected sales were: 19X3, $400,000; 19X4, $700,000; 19X5, $600,000; 19X6, $200,000; and 19X7, $100,000.

Required

1. Prepare journal entries to account for the research and development expenses for the software for 19X1 and 19X2. Assume that all expenditures were paid in cash.
2. Would any research and development expenses affect income in 19X3? If so, prepare the appropriate journal entry. Actual 19X3 sales were $400,000.

9-74   Depreciation Policies and Ethics

Some companies have depreciation policies that differ substantially from the norm of their industry. For example, Cineplex Odeon depreciates its theater seats, carpets, and related equipment over 27 years, much longer than most of its competitors. Another example is Blockbuster Entertainment, which depreciates the videotapes it rents over 36 months. Others depreciate them over a period as short as nine months.

Growing companies can increase their current income by depreciating fixed assets over a longer period of time. Sometimes companies lengthen the depreciable lives of their fixed assets when a boost in income is desired. Comment on the ethical implications of choosing an economic life for depreciation purposes, with special reference to the policies of Cineplex Odeon and Blockbuster.

9-75   Wal-Mart Annual Report

Refer to the financial statements of Wal-Mart in Appendix A. Wal-Mart uses straight-line depreciation for all assets, as explained in Note 1, page 783. Depreciation and amortization expense was $1,070,000,000 in fiscal 1995. For purposes of this problem, assume that all revenues and expenses, except depreciation and amortization, are for cash. Therefore cash expenses for fiscal 1995 were $79,150,000,000 – 1,070,000,000 = 78,080,000,000.

Required

1. Suppose Wal-Mart had used DDB instead of straight-line depreciation, and therefore depreciation and amortization expense was $1,570,000,000 instead of $1,070,000,000. Assume zero income taxes. Fill in the blanks in the table on the next page (in thousands of dollars).
2. Repeat requirement 1, but assume an income tax rate of 40.0%. Assume also that Wal-Mart uses the same depreciation method for reporting to shareholders and to the IRS.

3. Compare your answers to requirements 1 and 2. Does depreciation provide cash? Explain as precisely as possible.

9-76   Compact D from Disclosure
Select two distinct industries and identify two companies in each industry.

Required

1. Identify the depreciation methods used by each company.
2. Calculate gross and net plant, property, and equipment as a percentage of total assets for each company. What differences do you observe between industries? Within industries?
3. Do the notes disclose any unusual practices with regard to long-lived assets? For example, Wal-Mart reports substantial amounts of capitalized interest during construction and an unusual practice called "pre-opening" costs. Watch for similar practices in your four companies and comment.

Wal-Mart
(amounts in thousands)

	1. Zero Income Taxes		2. 40% Income Taxes	
	Straight-Line Depreciation	*DDB Depreciation*	*Straight-Line Depreciation*	*DDB Depreciation*
Revenues	$	$	$	$
Cash expenses				
Cash provided before income taxes				
Depreciation expense				
Income before income taxes				
Income taxes				
Net income	$	$	$	$
Supplementary analysis:				
Cash provided before income taxes	$	$	$	$
Income taxes				
Net cash provided	$	$	$	$

10 Liabilities and Interest

Learning Objectives

After studying this chapter, you should be able to

1 Provide a perspective on why information about liabilities is so important to readers of financial statements.

2 Explain the accounting for current liabilities.

3 Describe the contractual nature of various long-term liabilities.

4 Use present value techniques in valuing long-term liabilities.

5 Value and account for bond issues over their entire life.

6 Explain the nature of pensions and other postretirement benefits.

7 Define contingent liabilities and explain why they are often disclosed by footnote rather than in the statements themselves.

8 Apply ratio analysis to assessing the debt levels of an entity.

9 Compute and interpret present and future values (Appendix 10A).

10 Describe, value, and account for long-term lease transactions (Appendix 10B).

This chapter considers the very broad categories of economic obligations that accountants classify as liabilities. It describes many kinds of liabilities and how they are reported. The accounting for common liabilities—such as the responsibility to repay a loan or to compensate an employee—is presented in more detail here than in earlier chapters. In addition, the fundamentals of compound interest are used as the basis for measuring and reporting long-term liabilities. These compound interest principles are applied to various types of bond issues, to the accounting for leases, and to obligations for pensions and other employee benefits. The chapter also describes the disclosure of potential liabilities, such as the obligations that *may* arise if a lawsuit against an entity is concluded in favor of the plaintiff.

The chapter closes with a consideration of the common ratios analysts use to evaluate the level of a firm's indebtedness. When individuals seek to buy a car or a house, lenders assess the buyer's financial position carefully and pay special attention to the size of the down payment the buyer will make. The larger the down payment, the more "equity" the borrower has in the purchase, and the more comfortable the lender is in making the loan. Similarly, potential investors in the common stock or bonds of a company carefully evaluate the amount of debt the company has relative to the amount of stockholders' equity to assess the potential risk of their investment. Thus a major element of generally accepted accounting principles in the United States is the careful definition of what constitutes a liability and how best to disclose the liability to readers of financial statements.

Dow Corning was sued for several millions of dollars by customers claiming injury from the silicon gel implants the company manufactured. Is there a liability involved? When should it be recognized? Accountants have decided the answer depends on details about the case, the level of insurance coverage, and other factors. We consider this case in more detail in a boxed discussion.

■ LIABILITIES IN PERSPECTIVE

Objective 1

Provide a perspective on why information about liabilities is so important to readers of financial statements.

Liabilities, as defined in previous chapters, are one entity's obligations to pay cash or to provide goods and services to other entities. Liabilities include wages due to employees, payables to suppliers, taxes to the government, interest and principal due to lenders, and so on. Ordinarily, these obligations arise from some transaction with an outside party such as a supplier, a lending institution, or an employee. However, obligations also arise from the imposition of taxes or the loss of a lawsuit.

Investors, financial analysts, management, and creditors consider existing liabilities of the firm when valuing the firm's common stock, when evaluating a new loan to the company, and in numerous other decisions. When companies show signs of excessive debt or of an inability to meet existing obligations, problems emerge. Suppliers who normally sell on credit may refuse to ship new items or may ship only C.O.D. (collect on delivery). Lenders may refuse to provide new loans. Customers worried about the reliability of warranties and product service may prefer to buy elsewhere. Valued employees concerned about promotion prospects may seek greener pastures. As problems multiply, conditions can worsen quickly.

When the debt burden is so heavy that the company cannot pay, the creditors can pursue legal channels to collect the debt. Depending on the type of obligation, creditors may be able to force sale of specific assets, take over the board of directors, or force the company out of business. Readers of financial statements are very concerned about debt levels, and the preparers of financial statements are careful to disclose fully the company's liabilities.

long-term liabilities
Obligations that fall due beyond one year from the balance sheet date.

The actual example of a balance sheet presentation of liabilities, shown in Exhibit 10-1, is from the annual report of The Timberland Company. Timberland manufactures and markets footwear, apparel, and accessories.

Consistent with common practice, Timberland classifies liabilities as either current or long-term, which helps financial statement readers interpret the immediacy of the company's obligations. **Long-term liabilities** are obligations that fall due more than one year beyond the balance sheet date. *Current liabilities* are obligations that fall due within the coming year or within the normal operating cycle if longer than a year. Some long-term obligations are paid gradually, in yearly or monthly installments. As the Timberland example illustrates, the current portion of the company's long-term obligations is included as a part of its current liabilities.

Accounts payable are amounts owed to suppliers who extended credit for purchases on open account. These open account purchases from trade creditors are ordinarily supported by signatures on purchase orders or similar business documents. *Notes payable* are short-term loans backed by formal promissory notes held by a bank or by business creditors.

Exhibit 10-1		December 31	
The Timberland Company Liabilities Section of Balance Sheet (in thousands)		**1994**	**1993**
	Current liabilities		
	Notes payable	$ 22,513	$ 10,061
	Current maturities of long-term obligations	8,048	682
	Accounts payable	37,035	32,526
	Accrued expenses		
	Payroll and related	6,038	8,873
	Interest and other	24,459	9,609
	Taxes	9,029	3,672
	Total current liabilities	107,122	65,423
	Long-term obligations, less current maturities	206,767	90,809
	Total liabilities	$313,889	$156,232

As explained in earlier chapters, the accrual basis of accounting recognizes expenses as they pertain to the operations of a given time period regardless of when they are paid in cash. In the general ledger, separate accounts are maintained for liabilities such as wages, salaries, commissions, interest, and similar items. A report to shareholders may combine these liabilities and show them as a single current liability labeled *accrued liabilities* or *accrued expenses payable*. Sometimes the adjective *accrued* is deleted so that these liabilities are labeled simply taxes payable, wages payable, and so on. Similarly, the term *accrued* may be used, and *payable* may be deleted.

Conceptually, a liability is best measured as the amount of cash required to discharge the obligation. For current liabilities, the accounting process is straightforward, and the measurement is relatively easy. Accounting for these current obligations is considered before turning to the more difficult task of measuring and reporting long-term obligations.

■ ACCOUNTING FOR CURRENT LIABILITIES

Objective 2

Explain the accounting for current liabilities.

Some current liabilities are recorded automatically as a result of a transaction with an outside entity, such as a lender or supplier. Other liabilities are recorded with an adjusting journal entry to acknowledge an obligation arising over time, such as interest or wages. In this section, accounting for various current liabilities is discussed in detail.

Accounts Payable

As defined in Chapter 1, *accounts payable* (or *trade accounts payable*) are obligations resulting from purchasing goods and services on credit. They are amounts owed to suppliers. Disbursements for accounts payable tend to be voluminous and repetitive. Therefore special data-processing and internal control systems are usually designed for these transactions, similar to the systems described in Chapter 8 for cash receipts. Over 90% of major U.S. companies show accounts payable as a separate line under current liabilities on their balance sheet. However, a few combine accounts payable with accrued liabilities.

Notes Payable

promissory note
A written promise to repay principal plus interest at specific future dates.

Obligations represented by a promissory note given by the borrower to the creditor are called *notes payable*. A **promissory note** is a written promise to repay principal plus interest at specific future dates. Most notes are payable to banks.

Only notes that are payable within the next year are shown as current liabilities; others are long-term liabilities. Some companies combine notes payable with other short-term obligations in a single account. For example, Chevron includes the current portion of long-term debt with notes payable in an account called *short-term debt*. Pfizer, a pharmaceutical company, calls a similar account *short-term borrowings*.

line of credit An agreement with a bank to provide automatically short-term loans up to some preestablished maximum.

Notes payable often result from **lines of credit**, which are agreements with a bank to provide automatically short-term loans up to some preestablished maximum. In the notes to the 1990 financial statements, Timberland disclosed various lines of credit totaling $55 million. At December 31, 1990, $12 million had actually been borrowed. Between 1990 and 1994 Timberland grew to rely more heavily on long-term debt, and on December 15, 1994, Timberland terminated its credit lines.

Accrued Employee Compensation

The accrual process is described in Chapter 4. Expenses that have been incurred and recognized on the income statement but not yet paid are *accrued liabilities*.

Employee-related liabilities account for a large part of most companies' accrued liabilities. In fact, a majority of companies have a separate current-liability account for such items, with a label such as *salaries, wages, and commissions payable*. Timberland follows this practice by separately stating "Payroll and Related" accrued liabilities.

Estimating Litigation Liabilities

Late in the 1980s a company was confronting substantial accusations from patients who were dissatisfied with silicone implants made by the company and surgically installed for reconstructive or cosmetic purposes. The accusations became lawsuits over time, and the company was confronted with a significant product liability. What should be disclosed? How much was the liability? How many cases would there be? How much would be involved in financial settlements? What portion of these costs would be covered by insurance companies?

In 1995, the answers to these questions remain uncertain. Notice that the questions posed are financial accounting questions. There are significant philosophical issues about responsibility for the safety of products. There are equally important questions about how to determine scientifically what is safe. While these are important social questions, our immediate concern is about what constitutes a liability. How should companies measure their obligations, disclose the nature of the obligations, and record these amounts in financial statements.

The company, Dow Corning, Inc., has worked on this problem for almost a decade. In the late 1980s the issue was disclosure. There were not yet many cases in the courts, and there was little experience in how they would be resolved. Significant product liability insurance policies with multiple carriers would mitigate the direct cost to the company. So for several years the financial statements disclosed the litigation in some detail, but the balance sheet and income statement did not show specific numbers.

It is instructive to examine the last five years. In 1991, the company recorded $25 million of pretax costs and in 1992 another $69 million. Remember that each of these was intended to be a best estimate of future costs to be incurred. The product was produced and delivered years before. Production ceased in 1992. The United States Food and Drug Administration (FDA) asked producers to suspend the sale and use of the product pending further investigation. Dow Corning did so, and shortly thereafter announced it would not resume production.

But the amounts provided through 1992 were woefully inadequate. In 1993, Dow Corning recorded another pretax charge of $640 million. Combined with expected insurance coverage exceeding $600 million, the total exceeded $1.2 billion. Dow Corning and other manufacturers joined together to structure a settlement that would assure plaintiffs of reasonable compensation, minimize legal costs, and allow the companies to survive. The deal required an agreement between the plaintiffs, the companies, and the insurance carriers. In late 1994 agreement seemed close. Dow Corning provided another pretax charge of $241 million. Combined with additional expected insurance costs the amounts set aside for injured parties approached $2 billion from Dow Corning and another similar amount from other manufacturers. There were over 19,000 pending lawsuits on this product.

In May of 1995, Dow Corning declared bankruptcy. They indicated that too many plaintiffs were unwilling to agree to the settlement. This changes the whole situation and leaves the final outcome very much in doubt. As this book is printed and used, the final outcome of the case will develop. However, the facts to date demonstrate the difficulty of predicting the cost of litigation. An initial extimate of $25 million was too low, by a big margin. ∎

Source: Corning 1994 Annual Report.

Chapter 4 described compensation to employees in an elementary way. We assumed that an employee earned, say, $100 per week and, in turn, received $100 in cash on payday. In actuality, however, the complexities of payroll accounting can be awesome. First, employers must *withhold* some employee earnings and pay them instead to the government, insurance companies, labor unions, charitable organizations, and so forth.

For example, consider the withholding of income taxes and social security taxes (also called FICA taxes, for Federal Insurance Compensation Act). Assume a $100,000 monthly payroll and, for simplicity, assume that the only amounts withheld are $15,000 for income taxes and $7,000 for social security taxes. The withholdings are not additional employer costs. They are part of the employee wages and salaries that are payable to third parties. The journal entry for this $100,000 payroll is:

Compensation expense 100,000	
Salaries and wages payable	78,000
Income tax withholding payable . .	15,000
Social security withholding payable	7,000

A second complication is the existence of payroll taxes and fringe benefits. These are employee-related costs *in addition* to salaries and wages. *Payroll taxes* are amounts paid to the government for items such as the employer's portion of social security, federal and state unemployment taxes, and workers' compensation taxes. *Fringe benefits* include employee pensions, life and health insurance, and vacation pay. Liabilities are accrued for each of these costs. If they have not yet been paid at the balance sheet date, they are included among the current liabilities.

For example, employers typically pay an additional FICA tax equal to the amount withheld from the employee and might also pay 10% of gross wages into a retirement account. This would generate the following journal entry.

Employee Benefit Expense 17,000	
Employer Social Security Payable . . .	7,000
Pension Liability Payable	10,000

Income Taxes Payable

A corporation must pay income taxes as a percentage of its earnings. (To review the basic accounting for income taxes, see Chapter 5.) Corporations make periodic installment payments based on their estimated tax for the year. Therefore the accrued liability for income taxes at year-end is generally much smaller than the annual income tax expense.

To illustrate, suppose a corporation has an estimated taxable income of $100 million for the calendar year 19X0. At a 40% tax rate, the company's estimated taxes for the year are $40 million. Payments must be made as follows:

	April 15	June 15	September 15	December 15
Estimated taxes (in millions)	$10	$10	$10	$10

The final income tax return must be filed, and payment must be made by March 15, 19X1. Suppose the actual taxable income is $110 million instead of the estimated $100 million. On March 15, the corporation must pay the $4 million additional tax on the additional $10 million of taxable income. The accrued liability on December 31, 19X0, would be:

Income taxes payable	$4,000,000

For simplicity, the illustration assumed equal quarterly payments. However, the estimated taxable income for a calendar year may change as the year unfolds. The corporation must change its quarterly payments accordingly. There will nearly always be a tax payment or refund due on March 15.

Current Portion of Long-Term Debt

A company's long-term debt often includes some payments due within a year that should be reclassified as current liabilities. The journal entry for recognizing the current portion of long-term debt reclassifies a noncurrent liability as a current liability. Using the Timberland illustration in Exhibit 10-1, the reclassification journal entry for 1994 would be:

Long-term obligations	8,048	
Current portion of long-term obligations ...		8,048

Sales Tax

When retailers collect sales taxes, they are agents of the state or local government. For example, suppose a 7% sales tax is levied on sales of $10,000. The total collected from the customer must be $10,000 + $700, or $10,700. The impact on the entity is:

A	=	L	+	SE
+ 10,700 Increase Cash or Accounts Receivable	=	+ 700 Increase Sales Tax Payable		+ 10,000 Increase Sales

The sales tax payable appears on the balance sheet as a liability until the taxes are paid to the government. The sales shown on the income statement would be $10,000, not $10,700. The sales tax never affects the income statement. The $700 received for taxes affects the current liability account Sales Tax Payable and is shown on the balance sheet until it is paid to the government. The journal entries (without explanations) are:

Cash or accounts receivable	10,700	
Sales		10,000
Sales tax payable		700
Sales tax payable	700	
Cash		700

Product Warranties

Some current liabilities are not measured with the same degree of certainty as the previous examples. A noteworthy example is the liability arising from product guarantees and warranties. If warranty obligations are material, they must be accrued when products are sold because the obligation arises then, not when the actual services are performed. Ford describes its accounting as follows: "Anticipated costs related to product warranty are accrued at the time of sale."

The *estimated* warranty expenses are typically based on past experience for replacing or remedying defective products. Although the estimates should be close, they are rarely precisely correct. Therefore any differences between the estimated and actual results are usually added to or subtracted from the current warranty expense account as additional information unfolds. The accounting entry at the time of sale is:

Warranty expense	600,000	
Liability for warranties (or some similar title) . . .		600,000

To record the estimated liability for warranties arising from current sales. The provision is 3% of current sales of $20 million, or $600,000.

When a warranty claim arises, an entry such as the following is made:

Liability for warranties	1,000	
Cash, accounts payable, accrued wages payable,		
and similar accounts		1,000

To record the acquisition of supplies, outside services, and employee services to satisfy claims for repairs.

If the estimate for warranty expense is accurate, the entries for all claims will total about $600,000.

Returnable Deposits

Customers occasionally make money deposits that are to be returned in full, sometimes with interest and sometimes not. Well-known examples of returnable deposits are those with banks and similar financial institutions. Savings deposits are *interest-bearing deposits*, on which an explicit rate of interest is paid. In contrast, many checking deposits do not bear interest and are thus interest-free or *non-interest-bearing deposits*.

Other examples of deposits include those for returnable containers such as soft-drink bottles, oil drums, or beer kegs. Moreover, many lessors (landlords) require damage deposits that are to be returned in full if specified conditions are met by their lessees (tenants).

Companies that receive deposits view them as a form of payable, although the word *payable* may not be a part of their specific labeling. The accounting entries by the *recipients* of deposits have the following basic pattern (numbers assumed in thousands of dollars):

	Interest-Bearing		Non-Interest-Bearing	
1. Deposit	Cash	100	Cash	100
	Deposits (payable)	100	Deposits (payable)	100
2. Interest	Interest expense	9	No entry	
recognized	Deposits	9		
3. Deposit	Deposits	109	Deposits	100
returned	Cash	109	Cash	100

The account Deposits is a current liability of the company receiving the deposit. Ordinarily the recipient of the cash deposit may use the cash for investment purposes from the date of deposit to the date of its return to the depositor. For example, banks lend the cash deposited by some customers to other customers in order to earn interest revenue.

Unearned Revenue

Chapter 4 explained that revenue collected in advance is usually a current liability. The seller either must deliver the product or service or is obligated to make a full refund. Examples include lease rentals, magazine subscriptions, insurance premiums, advance airline or theater ticket sales, and advance repair service contracts.

The accounting entries follow (in dollars):

Cash	100,000	
Unearned sales revenue		100,000
To record advance collections from customers.		
Unearned sales revenue	100,000	
Sales		100,000
To record sales revenue when products are delivered to customers who paid in advance.		

Unearned revenues are also called *revenues collected in advance*. A more specific title may also be used. For example, Dow Jones & Company lists "Unexpired subscriptions," and Wang Laboratories shows "Unearned service revenue." These advance collections are frequently referred to as *deferred credits*. Why? Because, as the second entry shows, the ultimate accounting entry is a "credit" to revenue, but such an entry has been deferred to a later accounting period.

■ LONG-TERM LIABILITIES

How do accountants measure the value of obligations that are not due for at least a year? Such measurement must recognize the "time value of money." A dollar to be paid (or received) in the future is not worth as much as a dollar today. For example, suppose a company owes $105, due in one year. It can put $100 in a savings account that pays 5% interest. In one year, the original $100 plus the $5 interest earned can be used to pay the $105 obligation. Satisfying the $105 obligation took only 100 of today's dollars. Therefore a current balance sheet should include an obligation of $100, not $105.

To understand the accounting for long-term liabilities, you need to understand the principles of *compound interest* and related terms such as *future value* and *present value*. If you do not already have a thorough understanding of these items, carefully study Appendix 10A before reading further. You can test your understanding by solving Summary Problems Three and Four on pages 456 to 457.

Nature of Long-Term Liabilities

Objective 3

Describe the contractual nature of various long-term liabilities.

Long-term liabilities are generally recorded at the present value of all future payments, discounted at the market interest rate in effect when the liability was incurred. Consider a loan for a new car. Michelle Young graduated from college and wishes to buy a $14,000 car on January 1, 19X0. She has only $4,000 cash. She borrows $10,000 at 10% interest, agreeing to pay $3,154.71

each December 31 from 19X0 through 19X3. (Normally payments would be each December 31 from 19X0 through 19X3. (Normally payments would be made monthly, but for simplicity we assume annual payments.) The loan is illustrated in Exhibit 10-2.

Michelle's total payments are $4 \times \$3,154.71 = \$12,618.84$. However, the *present value* of the payments at 10% is only $3.1699 \times \$3,154.71 = \$10,000$. (The 3.1699 factor is from the four-year row and 10% column of Table 3, page 466). What is the proper measure of her liability at January 1, 19X0? It is $10,000, the *present value* of the future payments, not the total of those payments. Most contracts would allow her to repay the amount borrowed without penalty at any time, so in a literal sense she could give the lender $10,000 on January 1, 19X0 and discharge her liability.

Exhibit 10-2   Analysis of Car Loan

Year	(1) Beginning Liability	(2) Interest @ 10% (1) × 0.10	(3) End-of-Year Cash Payment	(4) Reduction of Principal (3) – (2)	(5) Ending Liability (1) – (4)
19X0	$10,000.00	$1,000.00	$3,154.71	$2,154.71	$7,845.29
19X1	7,845.29	784.53	3,154.71	2,370.18	5,475.11
19X2	5,475.11	547.51	3,154.71	2,607.20	2,867.91
19X3	2,867.91	286.79	3,154.71	2,867.92	– 0.01*

* Rounding error; should be 0.

private placement A process whereby notes are issued by corporations when money is borrowed from a few sources, not from the general public.

Several types of obligations are classified as long-term liabilities. Notes and bonds are most common. Corporations issue notes when money is borrowed from a few sources. These issues are known as **private placements** because they are not held or traded among the general public. Instead the creditors are financial institutions such as insurance companies or pension funds. Private placements provide over half the capital borrowed by corporations in the United States.

bonds Formal certificates of indebtedness that are typically accompanied by (1) a promise to pay interest in cash at a specified annual rate plus (2) a promise to pay the principal at a specific maturity date.

Corporations have heavy demands for borrowed capital, so they often borrow from the general public by issuing bonds. **Bonds** are formal certificates of indebtedness that typically represent (1) a promise to pay interest in cash at a specified annual rate (often called the **nominal interest rate, contractual rate, coupon rate,** or **stated rate**) plus (2) a promise to pay the principal (often called the **face amount** or **par value**) at a specific maturity date. The interest is usually paid every six months. Fundamentally, bonds are individual promissory notes issued to many lenders.

nominal interest rate (contractual rate, coupon rate, stated rate) A contractual rate of interest paid on bonds.

Pension and lease obligations are also long-term liabilities that are recorded at the present value of future payments. The FASB has decided that both are appropriately listed as liabilities and has provided specific rules for their measurement.

Almost every company has a liability for deferred income taxes. This important liability is described in Chapter 13. It is the prime example of a long-term liability that is *not* discounted. Accountants measure the total tax payments that have been deferred, not their present values.

Mortgage Bonds and Debentures

face amount (par value) The principal as indicated on the certificates of bonds or other debt instructions.

Different lenders have different priority claims in collecting their money. As described below, mortgage bondholders have high priority claims on specific firm assets, while subordinated claims have very low priority claims on assets. A **mortgage bond** is a form of long-term debt that is secured by the pledge of specific property. In case of default, these bondholders can sell the pledged property to satisfy their claims. Moreover, the holders of mortgage bonds have a further unsecured claim on the corporation if the proceeds from the pledged property are insufficient.

mortgage bond A form of long-term debt that is secured by the pledge of specific property.

In contrast, a **debenture** is a debt security with a general claim against the *total* assets, rather than a particular asset. Suppose a company defaults and is liquidated to repay the creditors. *Liquidation* means converting assets to cash and terminating outside claims. A debenture bondholder shares the available assets with other general creditors such as trade creditors and employees who seek to recover their accounts payable or wages payable claims. **Subordinated debentures** are debt securities whose holders have claims against only the assets that remain after the claims of general creditors are satisfied. To clarify these ideas, suppose a liquidated company had a single asset, a building, that was sold for $110,000 cash. The balance sheet immediately after liquidation is:

debenture A debt security with a general claim against all assets rather than a specific claim against particular assets.

subordinated debentures Debt securities whose holders have claims against only the assets that remain after the claims of general creditors are satisfied.

Assets		Equities	
Cash	$110,000	Accounts payable	$ 50,000
		First-mortgage bonds payable	80,000
		Subordinated debentures payable	40,000
		Total liabilities	170,000
		Stockholders' equity (negative)	(60,000)
Total assets	$110,000	Total equities	$110,000

The mortgage bondholders, having a direct claim on the building, will be paid in full ($80,000). The trade creditors will be paid the remaining $30,000 for their $50,000 claim ($0.60 on the dollar). The other claimants will get nothing. If the debentures were **unsubordinated**, the bondholders would have a general claim on assets with a priority like an account payable. The $30,000 of cash remaining after paying $80,000 to the mortgage holders would be used to settle the $90,000 claims of the unsecured creditors proportionally as follows:

unsubordinated debenture A bond that is unsecured by specific pledged assets, giving its owner a general claim with a priority like an account payable.

To trade creditors	$5/9 \times $30,000 = $16,667
To debenture holders	$4/9 \times $30,000 = 13,333
Total cash distributed	$30,000

A *mortgage bond*, which has a specific lien on particular assets, is an inherently safer investment than the company's *debentures*, which have no specific lien on any asset. However, the relative attractiveness of specific bonds depends *primarily* on the credit-worthiness of the issuer. Thus IBM can issue billions of dollars of debentures at relatively low interest rates when compared with the mortgage bonds that might be issued by real estate companies.

Bond Provisions

Bonds typically have a par value of $1,000, but they are quoted in terms of *percentages of par*. Some bonds are traded on the New York Stock Exchange. A daily quotation for IBM follows:

Description	Current Yield	Volume	Close*	Net Change
IBM 9S98	8.5	39	105-3/4	– 1/8

* The price of one $1,000 bond is 105-3/4% of $1,000 = $1,057.50.

current yield Annual interest payments divided by the current price of a bond.

IBM's bonds carrying a 9% coupon rate and maturing in 1998 closed at a price of $1,057.50 (105-3/4% of $1,000) at the end of the day. The **current yield** is calculated as the annual interest divided by the current price, or 8.5%. Thirty-nine bonds were traded, each having a face, or par, value of $1,000. The closing price was down one-eighth from that of the previous day.

trust indenture A contract whereby the issuing corporation of a bond promises a trustee that it will abide by stated provisions.

An issue of bonds is usually accompanied by a **trust indenture** whereby the issuing corporation promises a *trustee* (usually a bank or trust company) that it will abide by stated provisions, often called **protective covenants** or simply **covenants**. The indenture is designed primarily to protect the safety of the bond-holders. The provisions pertain to payments of principal and interest, sales of pledged property, restrictions on dividends, and like matters. The trustee's major function is to represent the collective claims and concerns of the bondholders.

protective covenant (covenant) A provision stated in a bond, usually to protect the bondholders' interests.

For example, MacMillan Bloedel, the large forest products company, indicated in a recent annual report that "*trust indentures* securing the company's debentures contain provisions limiting the amount of indebtedness the company can incur." Gordon Jewelry Corporation, a major jewelry company listed on the New York Stock Exchange, mentioned many constraints in a recent annual report: "The note agreement contains restrictive *covenants* regarding the nature of the business, liabilities, financial ratios, indebtedness, liens, investments, leases, company stock, mergers, and dispositions."

registered instrument Bonds that require the interest and maturity payments to be made to specific owners.

Bonds issued by U.S. industrial corporations are normally **registered instruments**, which means that the interest and maturity payments are made to a specific owner. In contrast, bonds issued before 1983 by U.S. government bodies such as municipalities are normally **unregistered,** or **bearer, instruments,** which means that the interest is paid to the individual who presents the interest *coupons* attached to the bond. Similarly, the principal is paid to the individual who presents the bond at the maturity date. Bearer instruments are like cash; they are more vulnerable to theft than are registered bonds. In the United States, companies file statements (Form 1099) with the Internal Revenue Service reporting interest paid to each registered bondholder. Some investors prefer bearer bonds because the owner can evade (illegally) the income tax on the interest by not reporting it.

unregistered instrument (bearer instrument) Bonds requiring interest to be paid to the individual who presents the interest coupons attached to the bond.

Callable, Sinking Fund, and Convertible Bonds

callable bonds Bonds subject to redemption before maturity at the option of the issuer.

Some bonds are **callable**, which means that they are subject to redemption before maturity at the option of the issuer. Typically the call is at a redemption price in excess of par. The excess over par is referred to as a **call premium**. A

call premium The amount by which the redemption price exceeds par.

sinking fund bonds Bonds with indentures that require the issuer to make annual payments to a sinking fund.

sinking fund Cash or securities segregated for meeting obligations on bonded debt.

convertible bonds Bonds that may, at the holder's option, be exchanged for other securities.

Objective 4

Use present value techniques in valuing long-term liabilities.

underwriters A group of investment bankers that buys an entire bond or stock issue from a corporation and then sells the bonds to the general investing public.

premium on bonds The excess of the proceeds over the face amount of a bond.

discount on bonds The excess of face amount over the proceeds upon issuance of a bond.

yield to maturity (market rate, effective interest rate) The interest rate that equates market price at issue to the present value of principal and interest.

bond issued in 1995 with a 2015 maturity date might be callable any time after 2010. Then it may be subject to call for an initial price in 2010 of 105 (105% of par), in 2011 of 104, in 2012 of 103, and so on. The call premium declines from $50 per $1,000 bond to $40 in 2011 and so on.

Sinking fund bonds require the issuer to make annual payments into a sinking fund. A **sinking fund** is cash or securities segregated for meeting obligations on bonded debt. It is an asset that is usually classified as part of an asset category called "investments" or "other assets." The sinking fund helps assure the bondholders that sufficient cash will be accumulated to repay the principal at maturity.

Convertible bonds are those bonds that may, at the holder's option, be exchanged for other securities. The conversion is usually for a predetermined number of common shares of the issuing company. Because of the conversion feature, convertible bondholders are willing to accept a lower interest rate than on a similar bond without the conversion privilege.

Most companies have an assortment of long-term debt, including a variety of bonds payable. There are too many types of bonds to discuss exhaustively here. Textbooks on corporate finance contain detailed descriptions. The body of the balance sheet usually summarizes such debt on one line. In contrast, the details in the footnotes can occupy an entire page.

◼ ACCOUNTING FOR BOND TRANSACTIONS

Market Valuation of Bonds

Bonds are typically sold through a syndicate (special group) of investment bankers called **underwriters.** That is, the syndicate buys the entire issue from the corporation, thus guaranteeing that the company will obtain all of its desired funds. In turn, the syndicate sells the bonds to the general investing public.

A company's board of directors sets the stated or nominal interest rate. The investment banker who manages the underwriting syndicate provides advice. The nominal rate is usually set as close to the current market rate as possible. Many factors affect this rate, notably general economic conditions, industry conditions, risks of the use of the proceeds, and specific features of the bonds (examples include callability, sinking fund, convertibility). On the day of issuance, the proceeds to the issuer may be above par or below par, depending on market conditions. If the proceeds are above par, the bonds have been sold at a **premium;** if the proceeds are below par, the bonds are sold at a **discount.** Therefore the **yield to maturity (market rate, effective interest rate)**—the rate of interest demanded by investors in a bond—frequently differs from the *nominal interest rate.* The interest paid in cash, usually semiannually, is determined by the nominal rate, not the effective rate. The yield to maturity is the interest rate at which all contractual cash flows for interest and principal have a present value equal to the proceeds at issue.

Note that issuing bonds at a discount does not mean that the creditworthiness of the issuer is especially bad, nor does issuing bonds at a premium mean that credit-worthiness is especially good. Discounts and premiums are determined by market forces that fluctuate from day to day and by the choice of the nominal rate of interest, relative to the then-current market rate of interest for bonds of similar risk.

Chrysler Bonds: 1982-1993

Some people may think of bonds as boring investments that provide semiannual interest payments until the eventual repayment of the original principal. What these people fail to realize is that the resale value of a bond may rise and fall substantially over its life as market conditions change. Large changes in value may accompany general changes in interest rates or changes in the specific circumstances of the issuing firm.

During October 1973, Chrysler issued 8% bonds with principal value of $1,000 maturing in 1998. The bonds were sold at $1,000 because the market rate of interest on equivalent risk bonds was also 8% per year.

What was the market price of Chrysler's bonds ten years after issuance, in October 1982? October 1983-93? Implicitly, investors calculate the price they are willing to pay for Chrysler's bonds using the market interest rate for bonds of equivalent risk at that time and the number of periods until maturity. At October 1982, Chrysler's bonds matured in sixteen years, or in thirty-two periods of half a year, and the market interest rate for bonds of equivalent risk was 17.6%, or 8.8% per half-year. The market value of the bonds can be calculated as the present value of the $40 interest payments made every half-year ($1,000 × 8% × 1/2 = $40) and the present value of the $1,000 principal payment at maturity:

Interest:	PV of $40 per period for 32 periods at 8.8% per period	= $423.96
Principal:	PV of $1,000 at maturity in 32 periods at 8.8% per period	= 67.28
Market Value:		= $491.24

The historical market value of Chrysler's bonds can be found in past issues of *Moody's Bond Record*. Moody's provides bond ratings that measure the likelihood that the issuer will be able to pay back the debt. They range from Aaa (highest) to Baa (middle) to C (lowest). When the Chrysler bonds were issued in 1973, Moody's assigned them an A rating. The table below shows the market value and bond rating in October for 1973 and 1982-93. Notice that in 1982 the price of the bonds fell to $491.24. Why? One reason is that Chrysler bonds became riskier, as indicated by the fall in Moody's rating from A to Caa. During the next year Chrysler's condition improved significantly, its bond rating rose, and owners of these bonds earned a return of 50% including interest and appreciation. ■

Market Value of Chrysler 8% Bonds Due 1998

Date	Market Value	Moody's Rating
Oct. 1973	$1,000.00	A
∫	∫	∫
Oct. 1982	491.24	Caa
Oct. 1983	665.00	B2
Oct. 1984	621.25	Ba2
Oct. 1985	753.75	Baa3
Oct. 1986	922.50	Baa3
Oct. 1987	840.00	Baa1
Oct. 1988	912.50	Baa1
Oct. 1990	750.00	Baa3
Oct. 1991	680.00	Ba3
Oct. 1992	968.75	B1
Oct. 1993	1,021.25	Baa3

Source: Moody's Bond Record, 1982-1993.

A typical bond consists of a promise to pay interest evey six months until maturity and a promise to pay a lump sum at maturity. Suppose a two-year $1,000 bond is issued that bears a nominal interest rate of 10%. Consider how the investor would value the bond, using the tables on pages 465-66.

Exhibit 10-3 shows how the bond would be valued, using three different interest rates. Note that:

1. Although the quoted bond rates imply a rate per annum, the bond markets do not mean that rate literally. Thus a 10% bond really pays 5% interest each semiannual period. A two-year bond has four periods, a ten-year bond has twenty periods, and so on.
2. The *higher* the effective (or market) rate of interest, the *lower* the present value.
3. When the market interest rate equals the coupon rate of 10%, the bond is worth $1,000. We say such a bond is issued at *par*.
4. When the market interest rate of 12% exceeds the 10% coupon rate, the bond sells at a discount (i.e., for less than par).
5. When the market interest rate of 8% is less than the coupon rate, the bond sells at a premium (i.e., for more than par).

| Exhibit 10-3 | | Computation of Market Value of Bonds (in dollars) | | | | | | |

	Present Value Factor	Total Present Value	Sketch of Cash Flows by Period				
			0	1	2	3	4
Valuation at 10% per year, or 5% per half-year:							
Principal, 4-period line, Table 2 .8227 × $1,000 = $822.70	.8227	822.70					1,000
Interest, 4-period line, Table 3 3.5460 × $50 = $177.30	3.5460	177.30		50	50	50	50
Total		1,000.00					
Valuation at 12% per year, or 6% per half-year:							
Principal	.7921	792.10					1,000
Interest	3.4651	173.25		50	50	50	50
Total		965.35					
Valuation at 8% per year, or 4% per half-year:							
Principal	.8548	854.80					1,000
Interest	3.6299	181.50		50	50	50	50
Total		1,036.30					

Bonds Issued at Par

Objective 5

Value and account for bond issues over their entire life.

Suppose that on December 31, 1996, a company issued 10,000 two-year, 10% debentures, at par. Therefore, the proceeds of the sale were equal to the face amount of 10,000 × $1,000 = $10 million. Exhibit 10-4 shows how the issuer would account for the bonds throughout their life, assuming that they are held to maturity. Because the bonds were issued at par, the interest expense equals the amount of the interest payments, 5% × $10 million = $500,000 each six months. The interest expense and the cash payments for interest each totals $2,000,000 over the four semiannual periods. The journal entries for the issue follow:

1. Cash	10,000,000		
Bonds payable		10,000,000	

    To record proceeds upon issuance of 10%
    bonds maturing on December 31, 1998.

2. Interest expense	500,000	
Cash		500,000

    To record payment of interest each six-
    month period.

3. Bonds payable	10,000,000	
Cash		10,000,000

    To record payment of maturity value of
    bonds and their retirement.

The issuer's balance sheet at December 31, 1996, and December 31, 1997 (at the end of the first year, after paying semi-annual interest) shows:

Bonds payable, 10% due December 31, 1998	$10,000,000

Exhibit 10-4

Analysis of Bond Transactions: Issued at Par (in thousands of dollars)

	A	=	L	+	SE
	Cash		**Bonds Payable**		**Retained Income**
Issuer's records					
1. Issuance	+10,000	=	+10,000		
2. Semiannual interest (repeated twice a year for two years)	−500	=			−500 ⎡Increase Interest Expense⎤
3. Maturity value (final payment)	−10,000	=	−10,000		
Bond-related totals (total of 4 semi-annual payments)	− 2,000		0		−2,000

Bonds Issued at a Discount

Suppose the 10,000 bonds described in the preceding section are issued at a discount when annual market interest rates are 12%. Proceeds of the sale are 10,000 × $965.35 = $9,653,500, which reflects an effective interest rate of 6% per semiannual period, as shown in Exhibit 10-3. Therefore a discount of $10,000,000 − $9,653,500 = $346,500 is recognized at issuance. The discount is the excess of the face amount over the proceeds. The company has use of only $9,653,500, not $10,000,000. The journal entry at issue is:

Cash	9,653,500	
Discount on bonds payable	346,500	
Bonds payable		10,000,000

The discount on bonds payable is a *contra account*. It is deducted from bonds payable. The bonds payable account usually shows the face amount, and the difference between bonds payable and discount on bonds payable is the net *carrying amount* or net liability:

Issuer's Balance Sheet	December 31, 1996
Bonds payable, 10% due December 31, 1998	$10,000,000
Deduct: Discount on bonds payable	346,500
Net liability	$ 9,653,500

For bonds issued at a discount, interest takes two forms, semiannual cash outlays of 5% × $10 million = $500,000 plus an extra lump-sum cash payment of $346,500 at maturity (total payment of $10,000,000 at maturity when only $9,653,500 was actually borrowed). The extra $346,500 is another cost of using the proceeds over the four semiannual periods. It should be spread over all four periods, not simply charged at maturity. The spreading of the discount over the life of the bonds is called **discount amortization.**

discount amortization The spreading of bond discount over the life of the bonds as expense.

How much of the $346,500 should be amortized each semiannual period? A simple alternative is *straight-line amortization*:

Cash interest payment, 0.05 × $10,000,000	$500,000
Amortization of discount, $346,500 ÷ 4 periods	86,625
Total semiannual interest expense	$586,625

The discount is used as an adjustment of nominal interest to obtain the real interest. Notice that the amortization of bond discount increases the interest expense of the issuer. The straight-line amortization is simple, but it is conceptually flawed because it implies a different effective interest rate each period.

During the first six months, the implied interest rate would be 6.08% ($586,625 interest expense divided by proceeds or carrying value of $9,653,500). The $86,625 of amortized discount would increase the carrying value or book value of the debt to $9,740,125 in the second six months yielding an implied interest rate of 6.02% ($586,625 ÷ $9,740,125).

effective-interest amortization (compound interest method) An amortization method that uses a constant interest rate.

A preferred amortization method that uses a constant interest rate is **effective-interest amortization,** also called the **compound interest method.** The FASB requires its use for bond discounts and premiums. The key to effective-interest amortization is that each period bears an interest expense equal to the carrying value of the debt, (the net liability or the face amount less unamortized discount) multiplied by the market interest rate in effect when the bond was issued. The product is the *effective-interest amount*. The difference between the effective-interest amount and the cash interest payment is the amount of discount amortized for the period.

Consider our example with a market rate of 12% (or 6% each semiannual period) when the bond was issued. The effective-interest amortization schedule is shown in Exhibit 10-5. Notice that the discount amortized is not the same amount each period.

The balance sheet disclosure of the bond payable is the ending net liability calculated as the difference between the face or par value and the unamortized discount. Thus at June 30, 1997, the balance sheet would reflect a liability of $9,732,707. The calculation might be shown on the balance sheet or in the footnotes as:

Issuer's Balance Sheets	12/31/96	6/30/97	12/31/97	6/30/98	12/31/98*
Bonds payable, 10% due 12/31/98	$10,000,000	$10,000,000	$10,000,000	$10,000,000	$10,000,000
Deduct: Unamortized discount	346,500	267,293	183,334	94,337	—
Net liability	$9,653,500	$9,732,707	$9,816,666	$9,905,663	$10,000,000

*Before payment at maturity.

Exhibit 10-5 shows the complete worksheet and journal entries for the effective-interest method of amortizing the bond discount. Be sure you understand this important exhibit before proceeding further. Note that the interest expense each period is the market rate of interest at issue times the carrying value or book value of the bond. (See column (2) of Exhibit 10-5.) This value changes each semiannual period. The cash payment is a constant $500,000 calculated as one-half the coupon rate (10% ÷ 2) times the par value ($10,000,000).

Exhibit 10-5		Effective-Interest Amortization of Bond Discount					
	(1)	(2)	(3)	(4)	Ending Liability		
For Six Months Ended	Beginning Net Liability	Effective Interest* @ 6%**	Nominal Interest† @ 5%	Discount Amortized (2) – (3)	Face Amount	Unamortized Discount	Ending Net Liability
12/31/96	—	—	—	—	$10,000,000	$346,500	$ 9,653,500
6/30/97	$9,653,500	$579,207	$500,000	$79,207	10,000,000	267,293++	9,732,707
12/31/97	9,732,707	583,959	500,000	83,959	10,000,000	183,334	9,816,666
6/30/98	9,816,666	588,997	500,000	88,997	10,000,000	94,337	9,905,663
12/31/98	9,905,663	594,337	500,000	94,337	10,000,000	0	10,000,000

* Market interest rate when issued times beginning net liability, column (1).
** To avoid rounding errors, an unrounded actual effective rate slightly under 6% was used. The table used to calculate the proceeds of the issue has too few significant digits to calculate the exact present value of a number as large as $10 million. The more exact issue price would be $9,653,489.
† Nominal (coupon interest) rate times par value (face value), for six months.
++ $346,500 – $79,207 = $267,293; $267,293 – $83,959 = $183,334; etc.

Journal entries:
Discount
Amortization (without explanations)

12/31/96	1.	Cash		9,653,500	
		Discount on bonds payable		346,500	
		Bonds payable			10,000,000
6/30/97	2.	Interest expense		579,207	
		Discount on bonds payable			79,207
		Cash			500,000
12/31/97		Interest expense		583,959	
		Discount on bonds payable			83,959
		Cash			500,000
6/30/98		Interest expense		588,997	
		Discount on bonds payable			88,997
		Cash			500,000
12/31/98		Interest expense		594,337	
		Discount on bonds payable			94,337
		Cash			500,000
12/31/98	3.	Bonds payable		10,000,000	
		Cash			10,000,000

Exhibit 10-6		A	=	L		+	SE

Exhibit 10-6

Effective-Interest Amortization of Bond Discount (rounded to thousands of dollars)

	Cash	Bonds Payable	Discount on Bonds Payable		Retained Income	
Issuer's records:						
1. Issuance	+9,654	+10,000	−346	[Increase Discount]		
2. Semiannual interest Six months ended:						
6/30/97	−500		+79		−579	
12/31/97	−500		+84	[Decrease	−584	[Increase
6/30/98	−500		+89	Discount]	−589	Interest
12/31/98	−500		+94		−594	Expense]
3. Maturity value (final payment)	−10,000	−10,000	0			
Bond-related totals	− 2,346	0	0		−2,346	

Bonds Issued at a Premium

Accounting for bonds issued at a premium is not difficult after you have mastered bond discounts. The differences are reversed from discount bonds:

1. The cash proceeds *exceed* the face amount.
2. The amount of the contra account Premium on Bonds Payable is *added* to the face amount to determine the net liability reported in the balance sheet.
3. The amortization of bond premium *decreases* the interest expense.

To illustrate, suppose the 10,000 bonds described earlier were issued when annual market interest rates were 8% (and semiannual rates 4%). Proceeds would be 10,000 × $1,036.30 = $10,363,000 as shown in Exhibit 10-3. Exhibits 10-7 and 10-8 show how the effective-interest method is applied to the bond premium. The key concept remains the same as for amortization of bond discount: The interest expense equals the net liability multiplied by the market interest rate in effect when the bond was issued. Balance sheets show the net liability calculated as the face amount plus unamortized premium. The premium reduces to zero over the life of the bond:

Issuer's Balance Sheets	12/31/96	6/30/97	12/31/97	6/30/98	12/31/98[*]
Bonds payable, 10% due 12/31/98	$10,000,000	$10,000,000	$10,000,000	$10,000,000	$10,000,000
Add: Premium on bonds payable	363,000	277,517	188,615	96,157	0
Net liability	$10,363,000	$10,277,517	$10,188,615	$10,096,157	$10,000,000

*Before payment at maturity.

Journal entries:
Premium
Amortization
(without
explanations)

12/31/96	1.	Cash	10,363,000	
		Premium on bonds payable ...		363,000
		Bonds payable		$10,000,000
6/30/97	2.	Interest expense	414,517	
		Premium on bonds payable	85,483	
		Cash		500,000
12/31/97		Interest expense	411,098	
		Premium on bonds payable	88,902	
		Cash		500,000
6/30/98		Interest expense	407,542	
		Premium on bonds payable	92,458	
		Cash		500,000
12/31/98		Interest expense	403,843	
		Premium on bonds payable	96,157	
		Cash		500,000
12/31/98	3.	Bonds payable	10,000,000	
		Cash		10,000,000

Exhibit 10-7	Effective-Interest Amortization of Bond Premium

	(1)	(2)	(3)	(4)	Ending Liability		
For Six Months Ended	Beginning Net Liability	Effective Interest* @ 4%**	Nominal Interest† @ 5%	Premium Amortized (3) – (2)	Face Amount	Unamortized Premium	Ending Net Liability
12/31/96	—	—	—	—	$10,000,000	$363,000	$10,363,000
6/30/97	$10,363,000	$414,517	$500,000	$85,483	10,000,000	277,517‡	10,277,517
12/31/97	10,277,517	411,098	500,000	88,902	10,000,000	188,615	10,188,615
6/30/98	10,188,615	407,542	500,000	92,458	10,000,000	96,157	10,096,157
12/31/98	10,096,157	403,843	500,000	96,157	10,000,000	0	10,000,000

* Market interest rate when issued times beginning net liability, column (1).
** To avoid rounding errors, an unrounded actual effective rate slightly under 4% was used.
† Nominal (coupon interest) rate times par value (face values), for six months.
‡ $363,000 – $85,483 = $277,517; $277,517 – $88,902 = $188,615; etc.

Early Extinguishment

Investors often dispose of bonds before maturity by selling them to other investors. Such a sale does not affect the issuer's books. However, the issuer may redeem its *own* bonds by purchases on the open market or by exercising its call option. Gains or losses on these early extinguishments of debt are computed in the usual manner. That is, the difference between the cash paid and the net carrying amount of the bonds (face, less unamortized discount or plus unamortized premium) is the gain or loss.

Consider the bonds issued at a discount and described in Exhibit 10-5. Suppose the issuer purchases all of its bonds on the open market for 96 on December 31, 1997 (after all interest payments and amortization were recorded for 1997):

Carrying amount:

Face or par value	$10,000,000	
Deduct: Unamortized discount on bonds*	183,334	$ 9,816,666
Cash required, 96% of $10,000,000		9,600,000
Difference, gain on early extinguishment of debt		$ 216,666

* See Exhibit 10-5, page 444. Of the original $346,500 discount, $79,207 + $83,959 = $163,166 has been amortized, leaving $183,334 of the discount unamortized.

Exhibit 10-8

Effective-Interest Amortization of Bond Premium (rounded to thousands of dollars)

	A	=	L		+	SE	
	Cash	Bonds Payable	Premium on Bonds Payable			Retained Income	
Issuer's records:							
1. Issuance	+10,363	+10,000	363	[Increase Premium]			
2. Semiannual interest Six months ended:							
6/30/97	−500		−85			−415	[Increase
12/31/97	−500		−89	[Decrease		−411	Interest
6/30/98	−500		−92	Premium]		−408	Expense]
12/31/98	−500		−96			−404	
3. Maturity value (final payment)	−10,000	−10,000					
Bond-related totals	− 1,637	0	1*			−1,638*	

* Rounding error; should equal 0 and 1637.

Exhibit 10-9 presents an analysis of the transaction (rounded to thousands of dollars). The $216,666 gain on extinguishment of debt would be shown on an income statement below operating income as a separate classification called an extraordinary item. The journal entry on December 31, 1997, is:

Bond payable	10,000,000	
Discount on bonds payable		183,334
Gain on early extinguishment of debt		216,666
Cash		9,600,000
To record open-market acquisition of entire issue of 10% bonds at 96.		

Exhibit 10-9

Analysis of Early Extinguishment of Debt on Issuer's Records (in thousands of dollars)

	A	=	L		+	SE	
	Cash		Bonds Payable	Discount on Bonds Payable		Retained Income	
Redemption, December 31, 1997	−9,600	= −10,000	+183	[Decrease Discount]	+217	[Gain on Early Extinguishment]	

Bonds Sold between Interest Dates

Bond interest payments are typically made semiannually. Suppose the company in our example had its $10 million, 10% bonds printed and ready for issuance on December 31, 1996, but then market conditions delayed issuance of the bonds. On

January 31, 1997, one month after the originally planned issuance date, the bonds were issued at par. The indenture requires the payment of $500,000 interest every six months, beginning June 30, 1997.

Bonds sold between interest dates command the market price *plus accrued interest*. Thus the market quotations you see for bonds *always* mean that the investor must pay an extra amount for any *unearned* interest to be received at the next interest payment date. In our example, the price to be paid is:

Market price of bonds at 100 on 1/31/97	$10,000,000
Accrued interest, 0.10 × $10,000,000 × ½	83,333
Market price plus accrued interest	$10,083,333

Note that the $500,000 interest payment due on June 30, 1997 is spread over the first six months of 1997 by the straight-line method, that is, with an equal amount to each month.

Exhibit 10-10 presents an analysis of these transactions (rounded to thousands of dollars). Note that the interest expense for the first half of 1997 is properly measured as $500,000 − $83,333 = $416,667, pertaining to only five months that the money was actually in use. The journal entries follow:

1/31/97	Cash	$10,083,333	
	Bonds payable		$10,000,000
	Accrued interest payable		83,333
6/30/97	Accrued interest payable	83,333	
	Interest expense	416,667	
	Cash		500,000

	A	=	L	+	SE
			Bonds	**Accrued**	
	Cash		**Payable**	**Interest Payable**	**Retained Income**
Issuance, 1/31/97	+10,083 =		+10,000	+83	
Interest payment, 6/30/97	−500 =			−83	−417 ⎡Increase Interest Expense⎤

Obviously, the analysis of transactions can be made more complicated by combining the acquisitions of bonds between interest dates with discounts and premiums. However, these are mechanical details that do not involve any new accounting concepts.

Non-Interest-Bearing Notes and Bonds

Some notes and bonds do not bear explicit interest. Instead they contain a promise to pay a lump sum at a specified date. An example is *zero coupon bonds*. To call such notes *non-interest-bearing* is misleading. These instruments cannot be marketed at face value. The investor demands interest revenue. Therefore the investor pays less than the face value. The investor discounts the maturity value, using the market rate of interest for notes having similar terms and risks. The discount is amortized, or systematically reduced, as interest over the life of the note.

Banks often discount both long-term and short-term notes when making loans. Consider a two-year, non-interest-bearing, $10,000 face-value note issued on December 31, 1995, when semiannual market interest rates were 5%. In exchange for a promise to pay $10,000 on December 31, 1997, the bank provides the borrower with cash equal to the present value (PV) of the $10,000 payment:

PV of $1.00 from Table 2, page 465, 5% column, 4-period row = 0.8227

PV of $10,000 note = $10,000 × 0.8227 = $8,227

implicit interest (imputed interest) An interest expense that is not explicitly recognized in a loan agreement.

The note has no specific interest payments. However, there is **implicit interest** (or **imputed interest**), which is an interest expense that is not explicitly recognized in a loan agreement. The imputed interest amount is based on an **imputed interest rate,** which is the market rate that equates the proceeds with the present value of the loan payments.

In this example, the $10,000 payment on December 31, 1997 will consist of $8,227 repayment of principal and $1,773 ($10,000 – $8,227) of imputed interest. At issue, the note is shown on the borrower's balance sheet as follows:

imputed interest rate The market interest rate that equates the proceeds from a loan with the present value of the loan payments.

Note payable, due December 31, 1997	$10,000
Deduct: Discount on note payable	1,773
Net liability	$ 8,227

Exhibit 10-11 shows how interest expense is recognized for each semiannual period. Each amortization of discount decreases the discount account and increases the net carrying amount.

The appropriate journal entries follow:

12/31/95	Cash	8,227	
	Discount on note payable	1,773	
	Note payable		$10,000
6/30/96	Interest expense	411	
	Discount on note payable		411
12/31/96	Interest expense	432	
	Discount on note payable		432
6/30/97	Interest expense	454	
	Discount on note payable		454
12/31/97	Interest expense	476	
	Discount on note payable		476
	Note payable	10,000	
	Cash		10,000

Exhibit 10-11

Analysis of Transactions of Borrower, Discounted Notes

	A =	L		+	SE
	Cash	Notes Payable	Discount on Notes Payable		Retained Income
Proceeds of loan	+ 8,227	+10,000	−1,773 [Increase Discount]		
Semiannual amortization					
Six months ended:					
6/30/1996			+411		−411
12/31/1996			+432 [Decrease Discount]		−432 [Increase Interest Expense]
6/30/1997			+454		−454
12/31/1997			+476		−476
Payment of note	−10,000	−10,000			
Bond-Related Totals	− 1,773	0	0		−1773

■ PENSIONS AND OTHER POSTRETIREMENT BENEFITS

pensions Payments to former employees after they retire.

other postretirement benefits Benefits provided to retired workers in addition to a pension, such as life and health insurance.

Objective 6

Explain the nature of pensions and other postretirement benefits.

Most U.S. companies continue to pay retired employees reduced wages after they stop working. Such payments are commonly called **pensions**. In addition, retirees often continue to receive health insurance, life insurance, or other employee benefits, which are commonly called **other postretirement benefits.** The details of how these are accounted for are complex and are therefore covered in more advanced courses. However, the concepts are important and are dealt with briefly here.

Accrual accounting matches expenses with the associated revenue. Since the worker "earns" the right to postretirement payments during the working years, accrual accounting requires recognition of the growing liability for future payments as the years pass. Imagine a firm with a forty-five-year-old employee. The employee has worked for twenty years earning $50,000 per year. She will receive a pension of $25,000 per year after retirement at age 65. The firm has a liability, and using present value concepts, we can calculate it. Assume an interest rate of 10% and a life expectancy of 20 years after retirement. The employee will collect a twenty-year annuity, which will have a present value of $212,840 (8.5136 from Table 3, p. 466, times $25,000) at retirement. Today, twenty years before retirement, the present value is $31,628 (0.1486 from Table 2 times $212,840). Firms must disclose a number of this type in the notes to their financial statements.

Estimating this number requires estimates of life expectancy, future work lives, ages at retirement, and levels of future pension payments to retirees. The formal calculations are normally done by actuaries, specialists at making such predictions. In addition the firm must choose an interest rate for calculating the present value. The liabilities can be very large.

The U.S. tax law provides incentives for companies to make payments into a pension fund that is independent of the company and controlled by a trustee. These payments during the employees' working years assure that assets will be available to meet the pension obligation at retirement.

Suppose a company's current pension expense is $100,000, $90,000 of which is paid in cash to a pension fund. The accounting for pensions has the following fundamental framework:

	A	=	L	+	SE	
	Cash		Accrued Pensions Payable		Retained Income	
Current pension expense	−90,000	=	+10,000		−100,000	[Increase Pension Expense]

The journal entry would be:

Pension expense	100,000	
Cash		90,000
Accrued pensions payable		10,000
To record pension expense for the year.		

The expense of life insurance, health insurance, and similar benefits paid for retirees is conceptually similar to pensions. Therefore, a liability equal to the present value of expected payments should be recorded. Increases in the liability will be recognized as a current expense.

Suppose the present value of obligations for other postretirement benefits is $100,000 at the beginning of 19X1 and $120,000 at the end of the year. The summary journal entry for 19X1 is:

Other postretirement benefits expense	$20,000	
Accrued postretirement benefits payable		$20,000

The balance sheets thus include the following:

	December 31,	
	19X1	**19X0**
Long-Term Liabilities:		
Other postretirement benefits	$120,000	$100,000

In the international context, practice varies widely regarding pensions and other postretirement benefits. Variations arise in part from differences in business practices. For example, many countries provide the majority of retirement income through individual savings or through tax-supported government transfers akin to the U.S. social security system. When company-sponsored pensions are modest or nonexistent, there is no material information to be reported. In approximately half of the forty-four countries examined in a recent survey, it was common practice for pensions to be managed by an independent outside trustee with *funding* from the sponsoring company through periodic payments to the trustee, in accord with U.S. practice. This separate fund complicates accounting disclosure somewhat but provides substantial security to employees that their future pensions claims will be honored. In the United States, prior to the 1970s it was very common for companies to go out of business and for their current and future retirees to be left without pensions. Today outside trustees maintain financial assets on behalf of current workers, and the Pension Benefit Guarantee Corporation provides some "pension insurance" for workers.

■ CONTINGENT LIABILITIES

contingent liability
A potential liability that depends on a future event arising out of a past transaction.

A **contingent liability** is a *potential* (possible) liability that depends on a *future* event arising out of a *past* transaction. Sometimes it has a definite amount. For instance, a company may guarantee the payment on a related company's note payable. This means that the guarantor will pay if, and only if, the primary borrower fails to pay. Such a note is the liability of the primary borrower and the contingent liability of the guarantor.

More often, a contingent liability has an indefinite amount. A common example is a lawsuit. Many companies have lawsuits pending against them. These are possible obligations of indefinite amounts.

Some companies show contingent liabilities on the balance sheet. Most often they are listed after long-term liabilities but before stockholders' equity. United Technologies has sales of over $21 billion in providing "high-technology products and support services to customers in the aerospace, building, and automotive industries worldwide." Its 1994 balance sheet has a line labeled "Commitments and contingent liabilities (Notes 4 and 14)" at the end of the liabilities. As is usually the case, no amount is shown in the body of the balance sheet; the item is listed solely to direct readers to the details in the footnotes. The United Technologies footnotes are lengthy. Note 4 describes the commitments that the company often makes to customers to provide relatively long-term financing for future purchases. Note 14 describes potential liability for environmental contamination at some 100 waste-disposal sites.

Footnote disclosure of lawsuits is very common. The result of such *litigation* is extremely hard to estimate. Some years ago IBM lost a multimillion-dollar lawsuit for patent violation. On appeal, the verdict was reversed, and IBM ended up collecting damages from the plaintiff. Another example of uncertainty is the case of Eagle Picher, a company subject to extensive product liability claims over asbestos. The company initially estimated its costs to settle existing and future claims at $270 million and recorded them in the financial statements as an expense, with a related liability. Later it became apparent that the earlier estimate was substantially in error, and the asbestos liability was increased by $544 million.

To recapitulate, there are definite liabilities either of definite amounts (accounts payable) or of estimated amounts (product warranties). There are also contingent liabilities either of definite amounts (guaranteeing a note) or of estimated amounts (income tax dispute with IRS).

■ DEBT RATIOS AND INTEREST-COVERAGE RATIOS

Commonly encountered ratios for assessing a firm's debt load include:

$$\text{Debt-to-equity ratio} = \frac{\text{Total liabilities}}{\text{Total shareholders' equity}}$$

$$\text{Long-term-debt-to-total-capital ratio} = \frac{\text{Total long-term debt}}{\text{Total shareholders' equity} + \text{long-term debt}}$$

$$\text{Debt-to-total-assets ratio} = \frac{\text{Total liabilities}}{\text{Total assets}}$$

$$\text{Interest-coverage ratio} = \frac{\text{Pretax income} + \text{interest expense}}{\text{Interest expense}}$$

Note that the first three ratios are alternate ways of expressing the same thing: What part of the firm's resources is obtained by borrowing and what part is invested by the owners. Many other definitions of debt ratios exist. The interest coverage ratio measures the firm's ability to meet its interest obligation.

The debt burden varies greatly from firm to firm and industry to industry. For example, retailing companies, utilities, and transportation companies tend to have debt of more than 60% of their assets. Computer companies and textile firms have debt levels of about 45% of assets.

Debt-to-equity ratios that were thought to be too high a few years ago are becoming commonplace today. The average debt-to-total-assets ratio for major U.S. industrial companies grew from about 35% in 1960 to nearly 60% in the 1990s.

Many high debt-to-equity ratios result from leveraged buyouts (LBOs). In an LBO, a buyer takes over a company using the company's assets as collateral to borrow the money necessary for the buyout. For example, management might borrow against the firm's assets and use the proceeds to buy back all the outstanding stock.

The purchase of RJR Nabisco by Kohlberg Kravis Roberts was a $25 billion LBO. The resulting company had debt of $23 billion and equity of $7 billion for a debt-to-equity ratio of 23 to 7, or about 3.3 to 1. The debt-to-total-assets percentage was 23 ÷ 30 = 77%. Henry Kravis was quoted in *Fortune* that this debt-to-equity ratio was low compared with other LBOs: "We've rarely bought a company with a ratio that low.... It's usually 10 or 12 to 1. Others have gone as high as 25 to 1."

The following ratios demonstrate the variation among industries and among countries:

Company	Industry	Country	Debt-Total Capital	Interest-Coverage
RJR Nabisco	Tobacco	USA	76%	1
IBM	Computers	USA	24%	7
Eli Lilly	Drugs	USA	5%	33
Glaxo Holdings	Drugs	UK	1%	30
Exxon	Oil	USA	19%	8
Royal Dutch	Oil	Holland	9%	10
Repsol	Oil	Spain	6%	5
Ford	Autos	USA	66%	1
Volvo	Autos	Sweden	17%	1
Toyota	Autos	Japan	22%	8

Standard & Poor's Corporation (S&P) rates bonds issued by corporations according to their credit worthiness. High proportions of debt and low interest-coverage ratios usually lead to lower bond ratings. Why? Because they imply less ability to meet bond obligations and hence more risk for bondholders.

Investors use bond ratings to evaluate the bond's price. Lower ratings lead to lower prices and therefore higher yields on the bond. As of 1991 and 1995, the average yields for industrial bonds rated by S&P were as follows, by rating category:

Rating	AAA	AA	A	BBB	BB	B
Yield 1991	8.67	9.22	9.67	10.03	11.78	14.17
Yield 1995	7.82	7.85	8.44	8.78	9.69	11.38

Note that in each year the yields rise uniformly as the ratings decrease. Interest rates have fallen significantly during the early 1990s. To assign the ratings, S&P often interviews management in addition to analyzing financial data. AAA bonds have the lowest debt ratios and the highest interest-coverage ratios, as you would expect. Investors will pay more (accept a lower yield) for debt issued by the least risky companies.

In assessing the riskiness of a company's securities, U.S. analysts rely heavily on the debt level. In the United States debt obligations are legally enforceable, and many examples exist where creditors have forced a company to liquidate in order to pay interest or to repay principal. But financial analysis must be adapted to the realities facing the specific companies. In Japan, for example, debt ratios tend to be much higher than in the United States. This difference partly reflects banking practices. Japanese banks lend very large sums to the biggest and most creditworthy corporations. While the transaction has the form of debt, it tends to be part of a very long-term relationship between bank and customer. The banks end up with long-term rights that look somewhat like the rights of a U.S. shareholder.

Summary Problems for Your Review

Problem One

Suppose that on December 31, 1996, Exxon issued $12 million of ten-year, 10% debentures. Assume that the annual market interest rate at issuance was 10%.

Required

1. Compute the proceeds from issuing the debentures.
2. Prepare an analysis of the following items: (a) issuance of the debentures; (b) the first two semiannual interest payments; and (c) the payment of the maturity value. Use the balance sheet equation (similar to Exhibit 10-4, p. 442). Round to the nearest thousand dollars.
3. Prepare journal entries for the items in requirement 2.

Solution to Problem One

1. Because the market interest rate and the nominal rate are both 10%, the proceeds equal the face amount of $12 million. This can also be computed as the present value (PV) of the twenty $600,000 interest payments and the $12 million maturity value at 5% per semiannual period:

PV of interest payments: 12.4622 × $600,000	$ 7,477,320
PV of maturity value: .3769 × $12,000,000	4,522,800
Total proceeds (exceeds $12 million due to rounding error)	$12,000,120

2. See Exhibit 10-12.

3.

12/31/96: Cash	12,000,000	
Bonds payable		12,000,000
6/30/97: Interest expense	600,000	
Cash		600,000
12/31/97: Interest expense	600,000	
Cash		600,000
12/31/96: Bonds payable	12,000,000	
Cash		12,000,000

Exhibit 10-12

Analysis of Exxon's Bond Transactions: Problem One (rounded to thousands of dollars)

	A	=	L	+	SE
	Cash		Bonds Payable		Retained Income
Exxon's records:					
1. Issuance	12,000		12,000		
2. Semiannual interest Six months ended:					
6/30/97	−600				−600
12/31/97	−600				−600
3. Maturity value (final payment)	12,000		−12,000		
Bond-related totals*	−12,000		0		−12,000

For rows 6/30/97 and 12/31/97, Retained Income column: [Increase Interest Expense]

* Totals after all 20 interest payments and payment at maturity (20 × 600).

Problem Two

Suppose that on December 31, 1996, Exxon issued $12 million of ten-year, 10% debentures. Assume that the annual market interest rate at issuance was 14%.

Required

1. Compute the proceeds from issuing the debentures.
2. Prepare an analysis of the following items: (a) issuance of the debentures; (b) the first two semiannual interest payments; and (c) the payment of the maturity value. Use the balance sheet equation (similar to Exhibit 10-6, p. 445). Round to the nearest thousand dollars. Use a bond discount account.
3. Prepare journal entries for the items in requirement 2. Use a bond discount account.

Solution to Problem Two

1. Because the market interest rate exceeds the nominal rate, the proceeds will be less than the face amount. This can be computed as the present value (PV) of the twenty $600,000 interest payments and the $12 million maturity value at 7% per semiannual period:

PV of interest payments: 10.5940 × $600,000	$6,356,400
PV of maturity value: 0.2584 × $12,000,000	3,100,800
Total proceeds	$9,457,200

2. See Exhibit 10-13.

3.

12/31/96:	Cash	9,457,200	
	Discount on bonds payable	2,542,800	
	Bonds payable		12,000,000
6/30/97:	Interest expense	662,004	
	Discount on bonds payable		62,004
	Cash		600,000
12/31/97:	Interest expense	666,344	
	Discount on bonds payable		66,344
	Cash		600,000
12/31/96:	Bonds payable	12,000,000	
	Cash		12,000,000

Exhibit 10-13

Analysis of Exxon's
Bond Transactions:
Problem Two
(rounded to thou-
sands of dollars)

	A	=		L	+	SE
	Cash	Bonds Payable		Discount on Bonds Payable		Retained Income
Exxon's records:						
1. Issuance	+9,457	+12,000		−2,543 [Increase Discount]		
2. Semiannual interest Six months ended:						
6/30/97	−600			+62 [Decrease		−662* [Increase
12/31/97	−600			+66 Discount]		−666* Interest Expense]
3. Maturity value (final payment)	−12,000	−12,000				
Bond-related totals†	−14,543	0		0		−14,543

* 7% × 9,457 = 662; 7% × (9,457 + 66) = 666.
† Totals after payment at maturity and all 20 entries for discount amortization and interest payments are made.

Problem Three

Xerox Corporation plans to enter some new communications business. The company
expects to accumulate sufficient cash from its new operations to pay a lump sum of $200
million to Prudential Insurance Company at the end of five years. Prudential will lend
money on a promissory note now, will take no payments until the end of five years, and
desires 12% interest compounded annually.

Required

1. How much money will Prudential lend Xerox?
2. Prepare journal entries for Xerox at the inception of the loan and at the end of each
   of the first two years.

Solution to Problem Three

The initial step in solving present value problems focuses on a basic question, Which
table should I use? No computations should be made until you are convinced that you
are using the correct table.

1. Use Table 2. The $200 million is a future amount. Its present value is

$$PV = \$200{,}000{,}000 \times \frac{1}{(1 + 0.12)^5}$$

The conversion factor, $1/(1 + 0.12)^5$, is in row 5 and the 12% column. It is 0.5674.

$$PV = \$200{,}000{,}000 \times 0.5674 = \$113{,}480{,}000$$

2.

Cash	113,480,000	
Long-term note payable (or long-term debt) ...		113,480,000
To record borrowing that is payable in a lump sum at the end of five years at 12% interest compounded annually.		
Interest expense	13,617,600	
Long-term note payable		13,617,600
To record interest expense and corresponding accumulation of principal at the end of the first year: 0.12 × $113,480,000 = $13,617,600.		

Interest expense 15,251,712
    Long-term note payable 15,251,712
To record interest expense and corresponding
accumulation of principal at the end of the
second year: $0.12 \times (\$113,480,000 + \$13,617,600)$.

Reflect on the entries for interest. Note how the interest expense becomes larger if no interest payments are made from year to year. This mounting interest expense occurs because the unpaid interest is being added to the principal to form a new higher principal each year.

Problem Four

Refer to the preceding problem. Suppose Xerox and Prudential agree on a 12% interest rate compounded annually. However, Xerox will pay a *total* of $200 million in the form of $40 million annual payments at the end of *each* of the next five years. How much money will Prudential lend Xerox?

Solution to Problem Four

Use Table 3. The $40 million is a uniform periodic payment at the end of a series of years. Therefore it is an annuity. Its present value is:

$$PV_A = \text{Annual payment} \times \text{Present value factor}$$
$$= \$40 \text{ million} \times \text{Present value factor for 5 years at 12\%}$$
$$= \$40 \text{ million} \times 3.6048$$
$$= \$144,192,000$$

In particular, note that Prudential is willing to lend more than in Problem Four even though the interest rate is the same. Why? Because Prudential will get its money back more quickly.

Highlights to Remember

Liabilities are recognized obligations to pay money or to provide goods or services. An entity's liability level is important to analysts because unpaid liabilities may produce difficulties ranging from an inability to raise additional capital to forced liquidation. To help assess debt levels, financial statements typically separate liabilities requiring payment within one year as *current liabilities*. Accounting for current liabilities is a straightforward extension of procedures covered in earlier chapters. Transactions are recorded as they occur, and accruals at the end of a period capture incomplete transactions such as accruing interest, wages, utilities, or taxes.

Long-term liabilities are more complex contracts that convey many rights and responsibilities over long periods of time. When contracts require multiple cash payments over time, present value techniques are used to determine the value of these future payments as of the current time period.

Bonds, a common long-term liability, are originally recorded at the amount received from investors at issue. This equals the present value of all of their future payments as of the issue date, calculated at the market rate of interest.

During the life of the bond, interest expense is recognized each period equal to the market rate at issue times the carrying value.

Pensions and other postretirement benefits involve long-term obligations to make future payments in retirement to current employees. Under the matching principle companies report the expense of these benefits during the employees' active working years.

Contingent liabilities are uncertain in amount and timing of payment. Examples include lawsuits, contract disputes, possible losses on multiyear contracts, and environmental liabilities. Footnote disclosure is used to alert interested parties to the uncertain, unmeasurable future possibilities.

Debt ratios and interest-coverage ratios are two measures used to evaluate the level of a company's indebtedness. The more debt a company has, the more problems it will face if cash flow is inadequate to meet liabilities as they fall due.

Appendix 10A: Compound Interest, Future Value, and Present Value

Objective 9

Compute and interpret present and future values.

For the borrower, interest is the cost of using money. It is the rental charge for cash, just as rental charges are often made for the use of automobiles or boats. For the investor, *interest* is the return on investment or the fee for lending money. Contracts that bear interest have many forms, from simple short-term promissory notes to multimillion-dollar issues of long-term notes often called bonds. Commonly encountered terms include

- **Principal:** the amount invested, borrowed, or used on which interest accrues
- **Interest:** the rental charge for the use of principal

interest rate The percentage applied to a principal amount to calculate the interest charged.

interest period The time period over which the interest rate applies.

simple interest For any period, interest rate multiplied by an unchanging principal amount.

compound interest For any period, interest rate multiplied by a changing principal amount. The unpaid interest is added to the principal to become the principal for the new period.

Calculation of the amount of interest depends on the **interest rate**—a specified percentage of the principal—and the **interest period**—the time period over which this interest rate is applied.

Simple interest is calculated by multiplying an interest rate by an unchanging principal amount. Simple interest is rarely encountered in U.S. financial practice. In contrast, **compound interest** is calculated by multiplying an interest rate by a principal amount that is changed each interest period by the previously accumulated (unpaid) interest. The accumulated interest is added to the principal to become the principal for the new period.

Future Value

Consider an example. Suppose Christina's T-shirt business has $10,000 in cash that is not needed at this moment. Rather than hold the $10,000 in her business checking account, which does not pay interest, she can deposit $10,000 in a financial institution that pays 10% interest per annum, compounded annually. She plans to let the amount accumulate for three years before withdrawing the full balance of the deposit. The amount accumulated in the account, including principal and interest, is called the **future value.**

Compound interest provides interest on interest. That is, the principal changes from period to period. Interest in year 1 is paid on $10,000: 10% × $10,000 = $1,000. If the interest is not withdrawn, the principal for year 2 includes the intial

future value The amount accumulated, including principal and interest.

$10,000 deposit plus the $1,000 of interest earned in the first year, $11,000. Interest in year 2 is paid on the $11,000: 10% × $11,000 = $1,100. The future value of the deposit at the end of three years with compound interest would be $13,310:

	Principal	Compound Interest	Balance End of Year
Year 1	$10,000	$10,000 × 10 = $1,000	$11,000
Year 2	11,000	11,000 × 10 = 1,100	12,100
Year 3	12,100	12,100 × 10 = 1,210	13,310

More generally, suppose you invest S dollars for two periods and earn interest at an interest rate i. After one period, the investment would be increased by the interest earned, Si. You would have $S + Si = S(1 + i)$. In the second period you would again earn interest ($i[S(1 + i)]$). After two periods you would have :

$$[S(1 + i)] + (i[S(1 + i)]) = S(1 + i)(1 + i) = S(1 + i)^2$$

The general formula for computing the future value (FV) of S dollars n years hence at interest rate i is

$$FV = S(1 + i)^n$$

In general, n refers to the number of periods the funds are invested. Periods can be years, months, days, or any other time period. However, the interest rate must be consistent with the time period. That is, if n refers to days, i must be expressed as X% per day.

The "force" of compound interest can be staggering. For example:

Compound Interest		Future Values at End of		
		10 Years	20 Years	40 Years
$10,000 × (1.10)^{10}$ = $10,000 × 2.5937 =		$25,937		
$10,000 × (1.10)^{20}$ = $10,000 × 6.7275 =			$67,275	
$10,000 × (1.10)^{40}$ = $10,000 × 45.2593 =				$452,593

Hand calculations of compound interest can quickly become burdensome. Therefore compound interest tables have been constructed to ease computations. Table 1, page 464, shows the future values of $1 for various periods and interest rates. In the table each number is the solution to the expression $(1 + i)^n$. The value of i is given in the column heading. The value of n is given in the row label for number of periods. Notice that the three-year, 10% future value factor is 1.3310 (the third row, seventh column). This number is calculated as $(1 + 0.10)^3$.

Suppose you want to know how much $800 will grow to if left in the bank for nine years at 8% interest. Multiply $800 by $(1 + 0.08)^9$. The value for $(1 + .08)^9$ is found in the nine-year row and 8% column of Table 1.

$$\$800 × 1.9990 = \$1,599.20$$

The factors in the tables in this appendix are rounded to four decimal places. The examples in this text use these rounded factors. If you use tables with different rounding, or if you use a hand calculator or personal computer, your answers may differ from those given because of a small rounding error.

Present Value

present value The value today of a future cash inflow or outflow.

Accountants generally use *present values* rather than future values to record long-term liabilities. The **present value** is the value today of a future cash inflow or outflow.

Suppose you invest $1.00 today. As shown in the discussion of future values, the $1.00 will grow to $1.06 in one year at 6% interest; that is, $1 \times 1.06 = $1.06. At the end of the second year its value is ($1 \times 1.06) \times 1.06 = $1 \times (1.06)^2 = $1.124. In general, $1.00 grows to $(1 + i)^n$ in n years at i% interest.

We know how to calculate the future value (FV) of S dollars invested at a known interest rate i for n periods. We can reverse the process to calculate the present value when we know the future value. If

$$FV = S (1 + i)^n$$

then the present value (PV) is S, or

$$S = \frac{FV}{(1 + i)^n}$$

If $1.00 is to be received in one year, it is worth $1 \div 1.06 = $0.9434 today. Suppose you invest $0.9434 today. In one year you will have $0.9434 \times 1.06 = $1.00. Thus $0.9434 is the *present value* of $1.00 a year hence at 6%. If the dollar will be received in two years, its present value is $1.00 \div (1.06)^2 = $0.8900. If $0.89 is invested today, it will grow to $1.00 at the end of two years. The general formula for the present value (PV) of a future value (FV) to be received or paid in n periods at an interest rate of i% per period is

$$PV = \frac{FV}{(1 + i)^n} = FV \times \frac{1}{(1 + i)^n}$$

discount rates The interest rates used in determining present values.

Table 2 gives factors for $1/(1 + i)^n$ (which is the present value of $1.00) at various interest rates (often called **discount rates**) over several different periods. Present values are also called *discounted* values, and the process of finding the present value is *discounting*. You can think of this as discounting (decreasing) the value of a future cash inflow or outflow. Why is the value discounted? Because the cash is to be received or paid in the future, not today.

Assume that a prominent city is issuing a three-year non-interest-bearing note payable that promises to pay a lump sum of $1,000 exactly three years from now. You desire a rate of return of exactly 6%, compounded annually. How much would you be willing to pay now for the three-year note? The situation is sketched as follows:

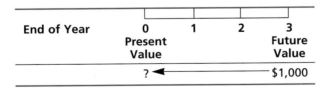

The factor in the Period 3 row and 6% column of Table 2 is 0.8396. The present value of the $1,000 payment is $1,000 × 0.8396 = $839.60. You would be willing to pay $839.60 for the $1,000 to be received in three years.

Suppose interest is compounded semiannually rather than annually. How much would you be willing to pay? The three years become six interest payment periods. The rate per period is half the annual rate, or 6% ÷ 2 = 3%. The factor in the Period 6 row and 3% column of Table 2 is 0.8375. You would be willing to pay $1,000 × 0.8375, or only $837.50 rather than $839.60.

As a further check on your understanding, review the earlier example of compound interest. Suppose the financial institution promised to pay $13,310 at the end of three years. How much would you be willing to deposit at time zero if you desired a 10% rate of return compounded annually? Using Table 2, the Period 3 row and the 10% column show a factor of 0.7513. Multiply this factor by the future amount and round to the nearest dollar:

$$PV = 0.7513 \times \$13,310 = \$10,000$$

Pause for a moment. Use Table 2 to obtain the present values of

1. $1,600, @ 20%, to be received at the end of 20 years.
2. $8,300, @ 10%, to be received at the end of 12 years.
3. $8,000, @ 4%, to be received at the end of 4 years.

Answers

1. $1,600 (0.0261) = $41.76.
2. $8,300 (0.3186) = $2,644.38.
3. $8,000 (0.8548) = $6,838.40.

Present Value of an Ordinary Annuity

annuity Equal cash flows to take place during successive periods of equal length.

An ordinary **annuity** is a series of equal cash flows to take place at the end of successive periods of equal length. Its present value is denoted PV_A. Assume that you buy a non-interest-bearing *serial note* from a municipality that promises to pay $1,000 at the end of *each* of three years. How much should you be willing to pay if you desire a rate of return of 6%, compounded annually?

You could solve this problem using Table 2. First, find the present value of each payment, and then add the present values as in Exhibit 10-14. You would be willing to pay $943.40 for the first payment, $890.00 for the second, and $839.60 for the third, a total of $2,673.00.

Exhibit 10-14

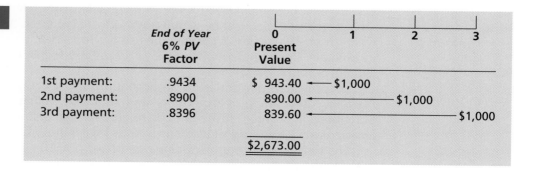

	End of Year 6% PV Factor	Present Value			
		0	1	2	3
1st payment:	.9434	$ 943.40 ←—$1,000			
2nd payment:	.8900	890.00 ←————————$1,000			
3rd payment:	.8396	839.60 ←————————————$1,000			
		$2,673.00			

Since each cash payment is $1,000 with equal one-year periods between them, Table 3 provides a shortcut method. The present value in Exhibit 10-14 can be expressed as

$$PV_A = (\$1,000 \times .9434) + (\$1,000 \times .8900) + (\$1,000 \times .8396)$$
$$= \$1,000\,(.9434 + .8900 + .8396)$$
$$= \$1,000\,(2.6730)$$
$$= \$2,673.00$$

The three terms in brackets are the first three numbers from the 6% column of Table 2, and their sum is in the third row of the 6% column of Table 3: 0.9434 + 0.8900 + 0.8396 = 2.6730.

This shortcut is especially valuable if the cash payments or receipts extend over many periods. Consider an annual cash payment of $1,000 for 20 years at 6%. The present value, calculated from Table 3, is $1,000 × 11.4699 = $11,469.90. To use Table 2 for this calculation, you would perform twenty multiplications and then add the twenty products.

The factors in Table 3 can be calculated using the following general formula:

$$PV_A = \frac{1}{i}\left[1 - \frac{1}{(1+i)^n}\right]$$

Applied to our illustration:

$$PV_A = \frac{1}{0.06}\,(1 - 0.83962) = \frac{0.16038}{0.06} = 2.6730$$

Use Table 3 to obtain the present values of the following ordinary annuities:

1. $1,600 to be received at the end of each year for 20 years, assuming interest at 20%.
2. $8,300 to be received at the end of each year for 12 years, assuming interest at 10%.
3. $8,000 to be received at the end of each year for 4 years, assuming interest at 4%.

Answers

1. $1,600 (4.8696) = $7,791.36.
2. $8,300 (6.8137) = $56,553.71.
3. $8,000 (3.6299) = $29,039.20.

In particular, note that the higher the interest rate, the lower the present value. Why? Because, at a higher interest rate, you would need to invest less now to obtain the same future value.

APPENDIX 10B: ACCOUNTING FOR LEASES

lease A contract whereby an owner (lessor) grants the use of property to a second party (lessee) for rental payments.

Leasing is a big business. Any asset imaginable, from television sets to jumbo aircraft to buildings, can be acquired via a *lease* contract. A **lease** is a contract whereby an owner (lessor) grants the use of property to a second party (lessee) in exchange for rental payments. This discussion focuses on leasing from the lessee's point of view.

Leasing is important from an accounting perspective because lease contracts create both property rights and financial obligations for the lessee. Sometimes it becomes difficult to distinguish the economic characteristics of a lease contract from the rights conveyed by ownership of the property.

The Financial Accounting Standards Board (FASB) asserted that many noncancelable leases are substantially equivalent to purchases. The lessee has full use

<table>
<tr><td>

Objective 10

Describe, value, and account for long-term lease transactions.

</td><td>

of the asset and a legal obligation to make payments, the same as if money were borrowed and the asset purchased. Moreover, the lessee often commits to use the asset for its full economic life, to incur all repair and maintenance costs, to insure it against all risks of loss and damage, and so on. In Statement No. 13, the FASB concluded that such leases should be recorded by the lessee as a leasehold *asset* and leasehold *liability* even though no legal title has passed. That is, legal passage of title (the form) is secondary; accountants should record the assumption of the risks and rewards of ownership by the lessee (economic substance).

</td></tr>
</table>

Kmart's 1995 annual report reveals that "The company conducts operations primarily in leased facilities. Kmart store leases are generally for terms of 25 years with multiple five-year renewal options, which allow the company... to extend the life of the lease up to 50 years beyond the initial noncancellable term." Many of these leases also require Kmart to pay taxes, maintenance, and insurance. GAAP in the United States, as more fully described later in this chapter, accounts for such lease or rental contracts "as if" Kmart borrowed money and purchased the leased stores. Kmart records both an asset (called "leased property under capital leases") and a liability called a "capital lease obligation" and shows them on the balance sheet. But treatment varies across the globe. If Kmart were incorporated and issuing financial reports in seventeen of the forty-four countries whose accounting practices were recently surveyed by the Center for International Financial Analysis & Research, no disclosure of these long-term lease commitments would be required. These countries include Austria, Brazil, Sri Lanka, and Taiwan. Most other countries follow lease disclosure practices similar to the United States.

Operating and Capital Leases

Leases are divided into two major kinds: capital leases and operating leases. **Capital leases** (or **financing leases**) transfer substantially all the risks and benefits of ownership to the lessee. They are equivalent to installment sale and purchase transactions. The asset must be recorded essentially as having been sold by the lessor and having been purchased by the lessee.

All other leases are **operating leases**. Examples are telephones rented by the month and rooms rented by the day, week, or month. Operating leases are accounted for as ordinary rent expenses; no balance sheet accounts are affected by operating leases.

Consider a simple example to see how the accounting differs for operating and capital leases. Suppose the Bestick Company can acquire a truck that has a useful life of four years and no residual value under either of the following conditions:

capital lease (financing lease) A lease that transfers substantially all the risks and benefits of ownership to the lessee.

operating lease A lease that should be accounted for by the lessee as ordinary rent expenses.

Buy Outright	or	Capital Lease
Cash outlays, $50,000 Borrow $50,000 cash to be repaid in four equal installments at 12% interest compounded annually		Rental of $16,462 per year, payable at the end of each of four years

There is no basic difference between an outright purchase or an irrevocable capital lease for four years. The Bestick Company uses the asset for its entire useful life and must pay for repairs, property taxes, and other operating costs under either plan.

Table 1

Future Value of $1

$$FV = 1(1 + i)^n$$

Periods	3%	4%	5%	6%	7%	8%	10%	12%	14%	16%	18%	20%	22%	24%	25%
1	1.0300	1.0400	1.0500	1.0600	1.0700	1.0800	1.1000	1.1200	1.1400	1.1600	1.1800	1.2000	1.2200	1.2400	1.2500
2	1.0609	1.0816	1.1025	1.1236	1.1449	1.1664	1.2100	1.2544	1.2996	1.3456	1.3924	1.4400	1.4884	1.5376	1.5625
3	1.0927	1.1249	1.1576	1.1910	1.2250	1.2597	1.3310	1.4049	1.4815	1.5609	1.6430	1.7280	1.8158	1.9066	1.9531
4	1.1255	1.1699	1.2155	1.2625	1.3108	1.3605	1.4641	1.5735	1.6890	1.8106	1.9388	2.0736	2.2153	2.3642	2.4414
5	1.1593	1.2167	1.2763	1.3382	1.4026	1.4693	1.6105	1.7623	1.9254	2.1003	2.2878	2.4883	2.7027	2.9316	3.0518
6	1.1941	1.2653	1.3401	1.4185	1.5007	1.5869	1.7716	1.9738	2.1950	2.4364	2.6996	2.9860	3.2973	3.6352	3.8147
7	1.2299	1.3159	1.4071	1.5036	1.6058	1.7138	1.9487	2.2107	2.5023	2.8262	3.1855	3.5832	4.0227	4.5077	4.7684
8	1.2668	1.3686	1.4775	1.5938	1.7182	1.8509	2.1436	2.4760	2.8526	3.2784	3.7589	4.2998	4.9077	5.5895	5.9605
9	1.3048	1.4233	1.5513	1.6895	1.8385	1.9990	2.3579	2.7731	3.2519	3.8030	4.4355	5.1598	5.9874	6.9310	7.4506
10	1.3439	1.4802	1.6289	1.7908	1.9672	2.1589	2.5937	3.1058	3.7072	4.4114	5.2338	6.1917	7.3046	8.5944	9.3132
11	1.3842	1.5395	1.7103	1.8983	2.1049	2.3316	2.8531	3.4785	4.2262	5.1173	6.1759	7.4301	8.9117	10.6571	11.6415
12	1.4258	1.6010	1.7959	2.0122	2.2522	2.5182	3.1384	3.8960	4.8179	5.9360	7.2876	8.9161	10.8722	13.2148	14.5519
13	1.4685	1.6651	1.8856	2.1329	2.4098	2.7196	3.4523	4.3635	5.4924	6.8858	8.5994	10.6993	13.2641	16.3863	18.1899
14	1.5126	1.7317	1.9799	2.2609	2.5785	2.9372	3.7975	4.8871	6.2613	7.9875	10.1472	12.8392	16.1822	20.3191	22.7374
15	1.5580	1.8009	2.0789	2.3966	2.7590	3.1772	4.1772	5.4736	7.1379	9.2655	11.9737	15.4070	19.7423	25.1956	28.4217
16	1.6047	1.8730	2.1829	2.5404	2.9522	3.4259	4.5950	6.1304	8.1372	10.7480	14.1290	18.4884	24.0856	31.2426	35.5271
17	1.6528	1.9479	2.2920	2.6928	3.1588	3.7000	5.0545	6.8660	9.2765	12.4677	16.6722	22.1861	29.3844	38.7408	44.4089
18	1.7024	2.0258	2.4066	2.8543	3.3799	3.9960	5.5599	7.6900	10.5752	14.4625	19.6733	26.6233	35.8490	48.0386	55.5112
19	1.7535	2.1068	2.5270	3.0256	3.6165	4.3157	6.1159	8.6128	12.0557	16.7765	23.2144	31.9480	43.7358	59.5679	69.3889
20	1.8061	2.1911	2.6533	3.2071	3.8697	4.6610	6.7275	9.6463	13.7435	19.4608	27.3930	38.3376	53.3576	73.8641	86.7362
21	1.8603	2.2788	2.7860	3.3996	4.1406	5.0338	7.4002	10.8038	15.6676	22.5745	32.3238	46.0051	65.0963	91.5915	108.4202
22	1.9161	2.3699	2.9253	3.6035	4.4304	5.4365	8.1403	12.1003	17.8610	26.1864	38.1421	55.2061	79.4175	113.5735	135.5253
23	1.9736	2.4647	3.0715	3.8197	4.7405	5.8715	8.9543	13.5523	20.3616	30.3762	45.0076	66.2474	96.8894	140.8312	169.4066
24	2.0328	2.5633	3.2251	4.0489	5.0724	6.3412	9.8497	15.1786	23.2122	35.2364	53.1090	79.4968	118.2050	174.6306	211.7582
25	2.0938	2.6658	3.3864	4.2919	5.4274	6.8485	10.8347	17.0001	26.4619	40.8742	62.6686	95.3962	144.2101	216.5420	264.6978
26	2.1566	2.7725	3.5557	4.5494	5.8074	7.3964	11.9182	19.0401	30.1666	47.4141	73.9490	114.4755	175.9364	268.5121	330.8722
27	2.2213	2.8834	3.7335	4.8223	6.2139	7.9881	13.1100	21.3249	34.3899	55.0004	87.2598	137.3706	214.6424	332.9550	413.5903
28	2.2879	2.9987	3.9201	5.1117	6.6488	8.6271	14.4210	23.8839	39.2045	63.8004	102.9666	164.8447	261.8637	412.8642	516.9879
29	2.3566	3.1187	4.1161	5.4184	7.1143	9.3173	15.8631	26.7499	44.6931	74.0085	121.5005	197.8136	319.4737	511.9516	646.2349
30	2.4273	3.2434	4.3219	5.7435	7.6123	10.0627	17.4494	29.9599	50.9502	85.8499	143.3706	237.3763	389.7579	634.8199	807.7936

Table 2
Present Value of $1

$$PV = \frac{1}{(1 + i)^n}$$

Periods	3%	4%	5%	6%	7%	8%	10%	12%	14%	16%	18%	20%	22%	24%	25%
1	.9709	.9615	.9524	.9434	.9346	.9259	.9091	.8929	.8772	.8621	.8475	.8333	.8197	.8065	.8000
2	.9426	.9246	.9070	.8900	.8734	.8573	.8264	.7972	.7695	.7432	.7182	.6944	.6719	.6504	.6400
3	.9151	.8890	.8638	.8396	.8163	.7938	.7513	.7118	.6750	.6407	.6086	.5787	.5507	.5245	.5120
4	.8885	.8548	.8227	.7921	.7629	.7350	.6830	.6355	.5921	.5523	.5158	.4823	.4514	.4230	.4096
5	.8626	.8219	.7835	.7473	.7130	.6806	.6209	.5674	.5194	.4761	.4371	.4019	.3700	.3411	.3277
6	.8375	.7903	.7462	.7050	.6663	.6302	.5645	.5066	.4556	.4104	.3704	.3349	.3033	.2751	.2621
7	.8131	.7599	.7107	.6651	.6227	.5835	.5132	.4523	.3996	.3538	.3139	.2791	.2486	.2218	.2097
8	.7894	.7307	.6768	.6274	.5820	.5403	.4665	.4039	.3506	.3050	.2660	.2326	.2038	.1789	.1678
9	.7664	.7026	.6446	.5919	.5439	.5002	.4241	.3606	.3075	.2630	.2255	.1938	.1670	.1443	.1342
10	.7441	.6756	.6139	.5584	.5083	.4632	.3855	.3220	.2697	.2267	.1911	.1615	.1369	.1164	.1074
11	.7224	.6496	.5847	.5268	.4751	.4289	.3505	.2875	.2366	.1954	.1619	.1346	.1122	.0938	.0859
12	.7014	.6246	.5568	.4970	.4440	.3971	.3186	.2567	.2076	.1685	.1372	.1122	.0920	.0757	.0687
13	.6810	.6006	.5303	.4688	.4150	.3677	.2897	.2292	.1821	.1452	.1163	.0935	.0754	.0610	.0550
14	.6611	.5775	.5051	.4423	.3878	.3405	.2633	.2046	.1597	.1252	.0985	.0779	.0618	.0492	.0440
15	.6419	.5553	.4810	.4173	.3624	.3152	.2394	.1827	.1401	.1079	.0835	.0649	.0507	.0397	.0352
16	.6232	.5339	.4581	.3936	.3387	.2919	.2176	.1631	.1229	.0930	.0708	.0541	.0415	.0320	.0281
17	.6050	.5134	.4363	.3714	.3166	.2703	.1978	.1456	.1078	.0802	.0600	.0451	.0340	.0258	.0225
18	.5874	.4936	.4155	.3503	.2959	.2502	.1799	.1300	.0946	.0691	.0508	.0376	.0279	.0208	.0180
19	.5703	.4746	.3957	.3305	.2765	.2317	.1635	.1161	.0829	.0596	.0431	.0313	.0229	.0168	.0144
20	.5537	.4564	.3769	.3118	.2584	.2145	.1486	.1037	.0728	.0514	.0365	.0261	.0187	.0135	.0115
21	.5375	.4388	.3589	.2942	.2415	.1987	.1351	.0926	.0638	.0443	.0309	.0217	.0154	.0109	.0092
22	.5219	.4220	.3418	.2775	.2257	.1839	.1228	.0826	.0560	.0382	.0262	.0181	.0126	.0088	.0074
23	.5067	.4057	.3256	.2618	.2109	.1703	.1117	.0738	.0491	.0329	.0222	.0151	.0103	.0071	.0059
24	.4919	.3901	.3101	.2470	.1971	.1577	.1015	.0659	.0431	.0284	.0188	.0126	.0085	.0057	.0047
25	.4776	.3751	.2953	.2330	.1842	.1460	.0923	.0588	.0378	.0245	.0160	.0105	.0069	.0046	.0038
26	.4637	.3607	.2812	.2198	.1722	.1352	.0839	.0525	.0331	.0211	.0135	.0087	.0057	.0037	.0030
27	.4502	.3468	.2678	.2074	.1609	.1252	.0763	.0469	.0291	.0182	.0115	.0073	.0047	.0030	.0024
28	.4371	.3335	.2551	.1956	.1504	.1159	.0693	.0419	.0255	.0157	.0097	.0061	.0038	.0024	.0019
29	.4243	.3207	.2429	.1846	.1406	.1073	.0630	.0374	.0224	.0135	.0082	.0051	.0031	.0020	.0015
30	.4120	.3083	.2314	.1741	.1314	.0994	.0573	.0334	.0196	.0116	.0070	.0042	.0026	.0016	.0012
40	.3066	.2083	.1420	.0972	.0668	.0460	.0221	.0107	.0053	.0026	.0013	.0007	.0004	.0002	.0001

Table 3

Present Value of Ordinary Annuity of $1

$$PV_A = \frac{1}{i}\left[1 - \frac{1}{(1+i)^n}\right]$$

Periods	3%	4%	5%	6%	7%	8%	10%	12%	14%	16%	18%	20%	22%	24%	25%
1	.9709	.9615	.9524	.9434	.9346	.9259	.9091	.8929	.8772	.8621	.8475	.8333	.8197	.8065	.8000
2	1.9135	1.8861	1.8594	1.8334	1.8080	1.7833	1.7355	1.6901	1.6467	1.6052	1.5656	1.5278	1.4915	1.4568	1.4400
3	2.8286	2.7751	2.7232	2.6730	2.6243	2.5771	2.4869	2.4018	2.3216	2.2459	2.1743	2.1065	2.0422	1.9813	1.9520
4	3.7171	3.6299	3.5460	3.4651	3.3872	3.3121	3.1699	3.0373	2.9137	2.7982	2.6901	2.5887	2.4936	2.4043	2.3616
5	4.5797	4.4518	4.3295	4.2124	4.1002	3.9927	3.7908	3.6048	3.4331	3.2743	3.1272	2.9906	2.8636	2.7454	2.6893
6	5.4172	5.2421	5.0757	4.9173	4.7665	4.6229	4.3553	4.1114	3.8887	3.6847	3.4976	3.3255	3.1669	3.0205	2.9514
7	6.2303	6.0021	5.7864	5.5824	5.3893	5.2064	4.8684	4.5638	4.2883	4.0386	3.8115	3.6046	3.4155	3.2423	3.1611
8	7.0197	6.7327	6.4632	6.2098	5.9713	5.7466	5.3349	4.9676	4.6389	4.3436	4.0776	3.8372	3.6193	3.4212	3.3289
9	7.7861	7.4353	7.1078	6.8017	6.5152	6.2469	5.7590	5.3282	4.9464	4.6065	4.3030	4.0310	3.7863	3.5655	3.4631
10	8.5302	8.1109	7.7217	7.3601	7.0236	6.7101	6.1446	5.6502	5.2161	4.8332	4.4941	4.1925	3.9232	3.6819	3.5705
11	9.2526	8.7605	8.3064	7.8869	7.4987	7.1390	6.4951	5.9377	5.4527	5.0286	4.6560	4.3271	4.0354	3.7757	3.6564
12	9.9540	9.3851	8.8633	8.3838	7.9427	7.5361	6.8137	6.1944	5.6603	5.1971	4.7932	4.4392	4.1274	3.8514	3.7251
13	10.6350	9.9856	9.3936	8.8527	8.3577	7.9038	7.1034	6.4235	5.8424	5.3423	4.9095	4.5327	4.2028	3.9124	3.7801
14	11.2961	10.5631	9.8986	9.2950	8.7455	8.2442	7.3667	6.6282	6.0021	5.4675	5.0081	4.6106	4.2646	3.9616	3.8241
15	11.9379	11.1184	10.3797	9.7122	9.1079	8.5595	7.6061	6.8109	6.1422	5.5755	5.0916	4.6755	4.3152	4.0013	3.8593
16	12.5611	11.6523	10.8378	10.1059	9.4466	8.8514	7.8237	6.9740	6.2651	5.6685	5.1624	4.7296	4.3567	4.0333	3.8874
17	13.1661	12.1657	11.2741	10.4773	9.7632	9.1216	8.0216	7.1196	6.3729	5.7487	5.2223	4.7746	4.3908	4.0591	3.9099
18	13.7535	12.6593	11.6896	10.8276	10.0591	9.3719	8.2014	7.2497	6.4674	5.8178	5.2732	4.8122	4.4187	4.0799	3.9279
19	14.3238	13.1339	12.0853	11.1581	10.3356	9.6036	8.3649	7.3658	6.5504	5.8775	5.3162	4.8435	4.4415	4.0967	3.9424
20	14.8775	13.5903	12.4622	11.4699	10.5940	9.8181	8.5136	7.4694	6.6231	5.9288	5.3527	4.8696	4.4603	4.1103	3.9539
21	15.4150	14.0292	12.8212	11.7641	10.8355	10.0168	8.6487	7.5620	6.6870	5.9731	5.3837	4.8913	4.4756	4.1212	3.9631
22	15.9369	14.4511	13.1630	12.0416	11.0612	10.2007	8.7715	7.6446	6.7429	6.0113	5.4099	4.9094	4.4882	4.1300	3.9705
23	16.4436	14.8568	13.4886	12.3034	11.2722	10.3711	8.8832	7.7184	6.7921	6.0442	5.4321	4.9245	4.4985	4.1371	3.9764
24	16.9355	15.2470	13.7986	12.5504	11.4693	10.5288	8.9847	7.7843	6.8351	6.0726	5.4509	4.9371	4.5070	4.1428	3.9811
25	17.4131	15.6221	14.0939	12.7834	11.6526	10.6748	9.0770	7.8431	6.8729	6.0971	5.4669	4.9476	4.5139	4.1474	3.9849
26	17.8768	15.9828	14.3752	13.0032	11.8258	10.8100	9.1609	7.8957	6.9061	6.1182	5.4804	4.9563	4.5196	4.1511	3.9879
27	18.3270	16.3296	14.6430	13.2105	11.9867	10.9352	9.2372	7.9426	6.9352	6.1364	5.4919	4.9636	4.5243	4.1542	3.9903
28	18.7641	16.6631	14.8981	13.4062	12.1371	11.0511	9.3066	7.9844	6.9607	6.1520	5.5016	4.9697	4.5281	4.1566	3.9923
29	19.1885	16.9837	15.1411	13.5907	12.2777	11.1584	9.3696	8.0218	6.9830	6.1656	5.5098	4.9747	4.5312	4.1585	3.9938
30	19.6004	17.2920	15.3725	13.7648	12.4090	11.2578	9.4269	8.0552	7.0027	6.1772	5.5168	4.9789	4.5338	4.1601	3.9950
40	23.1148	19.7928	17.1591	15.0463	13.3317	11.9246	9.7791	8.2438	7.1050	6.2335	5.5482	4.9966	4.5439	4.1659	3.9995

Most lease rentals are paid at the *start* of each payment period, but to ease our computations we assume that each payment of $16,462 will occur at the end of the year. To make the comparison between leasing and purchasing, payments on the $50,000 loan in the purchase option must be calculated:

Let X = loan payment
$50,000 = PV of annuity of X per year for 4 years at 12%
$50,000 = 3.0373X$
X = $50,000 ÷ 3.0373
X = $16,462 per year

Note that this loan payment is exactly equal to the lease payment. Of course, we constructed the example this way deliberately because we want to stress the fundamental economic similarity between ownership and certain kinds of leases. Thus, from Bestick's perspective as lessee, both buying outright and leasing create an obligation for four $16,462 payments that have a present value of $50,000.

Suppose the lease contract were treated as an operating lease. Each year the journal entry would be:

Rent expense   16,462
    Cash   16,462
To record lease payment.

The total expense over the four years of the lease would be $65,848, the sum of four years of cash payments of $16,462 per year.

No leasehold asset or lease liability would appear on the balance sheet. However, under today's accounting rules, such a lease must be accounted for as a *capital lease*. This means that both a leasehold asset and a lease liability must be placed on the balance sheet at the present value of future lease payments, $50,000 in this illustration. The signing of the capital lease requires the following journal entry:

Truck leasehold   50,000
    Capital lease liability   50,000
To record lease payment.

At the end of each of the four years, the asset must be amortized. *Straight-line amortization*, which is used almost without exception, is $50,000 ÷ 4 = $12,500 annually.

The yearly journal entries for the leasehold expense are:

Leasehold amortization expense   12,500
    Truck leasehold   12,500

In addition, the annual lease payment must be recorded. Each lease payment consists of interest expense plus an amount that reduces the outstanding liability. The *effective-interest method* is used, as Exhibit 10-15 demonstrates. Study the exhibit before proceeding.

The yearly journal entries for lease payments are:

	YEAR 1		YEAR 2		YEAR 3		YEAR 4	
Interest expense	6,000		4,745		3,339		1,764	
Lease liability	10,462		11,717		13,123		14,698	
Cash		16,462		16,462		16,462		16,462

Leasehold assets and lease liabilities are illustrated by the following items from the annual report of Kmart for the year ending January 30, 1995:

KMart Company
Footnotes
(Selected Items)
(in millions)

	End of January	
	1995	**1994**
Assets:		
Leased property under capital leases, less accumulated amortization	$3,055 1,508 $1,547	$2,949 1,468 $1,481
Liabilities:		
Obligations under capital leases	$1,777	$1,720

Exhibit 10-15

Analytical Schedule
of Capital Lease
Payments

End of Year	*(1)* Capital Lease Liability at Beginning of Year	*(2)* Interest Expense at 12% Per Year	*(3)* Cash for Capital Lease Payment	*(4)* (3) – (2) Reduction in Lease Liability	*(5)* (1) – (4) Capital Lease Liability at End of Year
1	$50,000	$6,000	$16,462	10,462	$39,538
2	39,538	4,745	16,462	11,717	27,821
3	27,821	3,339	16,462	13,123	14,698
4	14,698	1,764	16,462	14,698	0

Differences in Income Statements

Exhibit 10-16 shows the major differences between the accounting for operating leases and the accounting for capital leases. The cumulative expenses are the same, $65,848, but the timing differs. In comparison with the operating-lease approach, the capital-lease approach tends to bunch heavier charges in the early years. The longer the lease, the more pronounced the differences will be in the early years. Therefore, immediate reported income is hurt more under the capital-lease approach.

Exhibit 10-16   Comparison of Annual Expenses: Operating versus Capital Leases

	Operating-Lease Method	Capital-Lease Method			Differences	
Year	*(a)* Lease Payment*	*(b)* Amortization of Asset†	*(c)* Interest Expense‡	*(d)* (b) + (c) Total Expense	*(e)* (a) – (d) Difference in Pretax Income	*(f)* Cumulative Difference in Pretax Income
1	$16,462	$12,500	$ 6,000	$18,500	$(2,038)	$(2,038)
2	16,462	12,500	4,745	17,245	(783)	(2,821)
3	16,462	12,500	3,339	15,839	623	(2,198)
4	16,462	12,500	1,764	14,264	2,198	0
Cumulative expenses	$65,848	$50,000	$15,848	$65,848	$ 0	

* Rent expense for the year under the operating-lease method.
† $50,000 ÷ 4 = $12,500.
‡ From Exhibit 10-15.

An operating lease affects the income statement as rent expense, which is the amount of the lease payment. A capital lease affects the income statement as amortization (of the asset) plus interest expense (on the liability).

Accounting for capital leases is similar to U.S. GAAP in most developed countries around the world. However, Australia, Germany, and the United Kingdom have been using this practice only since 1982. In France and Brazil most leases continue to be recorded as operating leases. However, in France extensive lease disclosures are required, and, at this writing, Brazil is contemplating adoption of a capitalization requirement.

Tests for Capital Leases

The capital lease approach was adopted in the United States in 1976 after many years of controversy within the accounting profession regarding which leases deserve capitalization as balance sheet items. Until then, almost no leases were capitalized. Many companies were criticized for "invisible debt" or "off-balance sheet financing" in the sense that noncancelable leases existed but were not included as liabilities on the balance sheet.

A *capital lease* exists if *one* or more of the following conditions are met:

1. Title is transferred to the lessee by the end of the lease term.
2. An inexpensive purchase option is available to the lessee at the end of the lease.
3. The lease term equals or exceeds 75% of the estimated economic life of the property.
4. At the start of the lease term, the present value of minimum lease payments is at least 90% of the property's fair value.

The lease structure determines whether a lease is operating or capital. Managers cannot choose how to treat an existing lease. However, some managers seek to structure leases so that they do not meet any of the criteria of a capital lease and therefore are not shown on the balance sheet.

As you can readily visualize, accounting for leases can become enormously complicated. For further discussion, see a textbook on intermediate or advanced accounting.

Accounting Vocabulary

annuity, *p. 461*

bearer instrument, *p. 438*

bonds, *p. 436*

callable bonds, *p. 438*

call premium, *p. 439*

capital lease, *p. 463*

compound interest, *p. 458*

compound interest method, *p. 443*

contingent liability, *p. 451*

contractual rate, *p. 436*

convertible bonds, *p. 439*

coupon rate, *p. 436*

covenant, *p. 438*

current yield, *p. 438*

debenture, *p. 437*

debt-to-equity ratio, *p. 452*

debt-to-total-assets ratio, *p. 452*

discount amortization, *p. 443*

discount on bonds, *p. 439*

discount rates, *p. 460*

effective-interest amortization, *p. 443*

effective interest rate, *p. 439*

face amount, *p. 437*

financing lease, *p. 463*

future value, *p. 459*

implicit interest, *p. 449*

imputed interest, *p. 449*

imputed interest rate, *p. 449*

interest, *p. 458*

interest-coverage ratio, *p. 452*

interest period, *p. 458*

interest rate, *p. 458*

lease, *p. 462*

line of credit, *p. 430*

long-term-debt-to-total-capital ratio, *p. 452*

long-term liabilities, *p. 429*

market rate, *p. 439*

mortgage bond, *p. 437*

Assignment Material

Questions

10-1. Distinguish between *current liabilities* and *long-term liabilities*.

10-2. Name and briefly describe five items that are often classified as current liabilities.

10-3. "Withholding taxes really add to employer payroll costs." Do you agree? Explain.

10-4. Distinguish between *employee* payroll taxes and *employer* payroll taxes.

10-5. "Product warranties expense should not be recognized until the actual services are performed. Until then you don't know which products might require warranty repairs." Do you agree? Explain.

10-6. Distinguish between a *mortgage bond* and a *debenture*. Which is safer?

10-7. Distinguish between *subordinated* and *unsubordinated* debentures.

10-8. "The face amount of a bond is what you can sell it for." Do you agree? Explain.

10-9. "Protective covenants protect the shareholders' interests in cases of liquidation of assets." Do you agree? Explain.

10-10. Bond covenants usually restrict the borrower's rights in various ways. An example might be a restriction that no additional long-term debt could be issued unless the debt-to-total assets ratio was below 0.5. Who benefits from such a covenant? How?

10-11. Many callable bonds have a call premium for "early" calls. Who does the call premium benefit, the issuer or the purchaser of the bond? How?

10-12. "The quoted bond interest rates imply a rate per annum, but the bond markets do not mean that rate literally." Explain.

10-13. Contrast *nominal* and *effective* interest rates for bonds.

10-14. "Discount *accumulation* is a better descriptive term than discount *amortization*." What would be the justification for making this assertion?

10-15. Distinguish between *straight-line* amortization and *effective-interest* amortization.

10-16. A company issued bonds with a nominal rate of 10%. At what market rates will the bonds be issued at a discount? At what market rates will they be issued at a premium?

10-17. What are the three main differences between accounting for a bond discount and accounting for a bond premium?

10-18. "A company that issues zero coupon bonds recognizes no interest expense until the bond matures." Do you agree? Explain.

10-19. "A contingent liability is a liability having an estimated amount." Do you agree? Explain.

10-20. "At the balance sheet date, a private high school has lost a court case for an uninsured football injury. The amount of damages has not been set. A reasonable estimate is between $800,000 and $2 million." How should this information be presented in the financial statements?

10-21. Suppose IBM won a lawsuit for $1 million against Innovative Software, a young company with assets of $20 million. Innovative has appealed the suit. How would each company disclose this event in financial statements prepared while the appeal was under way.

10-22. We observe higher debt levels in the automobile industry than in the pharmaceutical industry. Why?

10-23. Appendix 10A. "Future value and present value are two sides of the same coin." Explain.

10-24. Appendix 10B. Why might a company prefer to lease rather than to buy?

10-25. Certain leases are essentially equivalent to purchases. A company must account for such leases as if the asset had been purchased. Explain.

10-26. We observe extensive use of capital leases by airlines as a method for financing planes. Why might this be true? Does it make the airline seem to have lower debt ratios?

10-27. Discuss which characteristics of a lease are evaluated in deciding whether it is a capital lease.

10-28. Suppose New York State Electrical and Gas signed a contract to deliver a specific quantity of natural gas each year for the next 20 years. How would this be disclosed in its financial statements?

10-29. "Because a company never knows how much it will have to pay for pensions, no pension liability is recognized. Pension obligations are simply explained in a footnote to the financial statements." Do you agree? Explain.

10-30. Variation in international practice in the accounting for pensions can be explained in part by different financial practices in different countries. Discuss.

Exercises for Appendix A in Chapter 10

10–31 through 10–41 are arranged to correspond with Appendix 10A to provide practice for students newly familiar with present value concepts.

10-31   Exercises in Compound Interest

1. You deposit $5,000. How much will you have in four years at 8%, compounded annually? At 12%?
2. A savings and loan association offers depositors a lump-sum payment of $5,000 four years hence. If you desire an interest rate of 8% compounded annually, how much will you be willing to deposit? at an interest rate of 12%?
3. Repeat requirement 2, but assume that the interest rates are compounded semiannually.

10-32   Exercises in Compound Interest

A reliable friend has asked you for a loan. You are pondering various proposals for repayment.

1. Repayment of a lump sum of $40,000 four years hence. How much will you lend if your desired rate of return is (a) 10% compounded annually, (b) 20% compounded annually?
2. Repeat requirement 1, but assume that the interest rates are compounded semiannually.
3. Suppose the loan is to be paid in full by equal payments of $10,000 at the end of each of the next four years. How much will you lend if your desired rate of return is (a) 10% compounded annually, (b) 20% compounded annually?

10-33   Compound Interest and Journal Entries

Bruckner Company acquired equipment for a $250,000 promissory note, payable five years hence, non-interest-bearing, but having an implicit interest rate of 14% compounded annually. Prepare the journal entry for (1) the acquisition of the equipment and (2) interest expense for the first year.

10-34   Compound Interest and Journal Entries

A German company has bought some equipment on a contract entailing a DM 100,000 cash down payment and a DM 400,000 lump sum to be paid at the end of four years. The same equipment can be bought for DM 336,840 cash. DM refers to the German mark, a unit of currency.

Required

1. Prepare the journal entry for the acquisition of the equipment.
2. Prepare journal entries at the end of each of the first two years. Ignore entries for depreciation.

10-35.   Compound Interest and Journal Entries

A dry-cleaning company bought new presses for an $80,000 down payment and $100,000 to be paid at the end of each of four years. The applicable imputed interest rate is 10% on the unpaid balance. Prepare journal entries (1) for the acquisition and (2) at the end of the first year.

10-36 Exercises in Compound Interest

a. It is your sixtieth birthday. You plan to work five more years before retiring. Then you want to spend $10,000 for a Mediterranean cruise. What lump sum do you have to invest now in order to accumulate the $10,000? Assume that your minimum desired rate of return is

    (1) 6%, compounded annually.

    (2) 10%, compounded annually.

    (3) 20%, compounded annually.

b. You want to spend $3,000 on a vacation at the end of each of the next five years. What lump sum do you have to invest now in order to take the five vacations? Assume that your minimum desired rate of return is

    (1) 6%, compounded annually.

    (2) 10%, compounded annually.

    (3) 20%, compounded annually.

10-37 Exercises in Compound Interest

a. At age sixty, you find that your employer is moving to another location. You receive termination pay of $50,000. You have some savings and wonder whether to retire now.

    (1) If you invest the $50,000 now at 6%, compounded annually, how much money can you withdraw from your account each year so that at the end of five years there will be a zero balance?

    (2) If you invest it at 10%?

b. At 16%, compounded annually, which of the following plans is more desirable in terms of present value? Show computations to support your answer.

	Annual Cash Inflows	
Year	*Mining*	*Farming*
1	$100,000	$ 20,000
2	80,000	40,000
3	60,000	60,000
4	40,000	80,000
5	20,000	100,000
	$300,000	$300,000

10-38 Basic Relationships in Interest Tables

1. Suppose you borrow $15,000 now at 16% interest compounded annually. The borrowed amount plus interest will be repaid in a lump sum at the end of six years. How much must be repaid? Use Table 1 and basic equation: FV = Present amount × Future value factor.

2. Repeat requirement 1 using Table 2 and the basic equation: PV = Future amount × Present value factor.

3. Assume the same facts as in requirement 1 except that the loan will be repaid in equal installments at the end of each of six years. How much must be repaid each year? Use Table 3 and the basic equation: PV_A = Future annual amounts × Conversion factor.

10-39 Deferred Annuity Exercise

It is your thirty-fifth birthday. On your fortieth birthday, and on three successive birthdays thereafter, you intend to spend exactly $1,000 for a birthday celebration. What lump sum do you have to invest now in order to have the four celebrations? Assume that the money will earn interest, compounded annually, of 8%.

✓10-40 Discounted Present Value and Bonds

On December 31, 19X1, a company issued a three-year $1,000 bond that bears a nominal interest rate of 12%, payable 6% semiannually. Compute the discounted present value of the principal and the interest as of December 31, 19X1, if the market rate of interest for such securities is 12%, 14%, and 10%, respectively. Show your computations, including a sketch of cash flows. Round to the nearest dollar.

10-41 Discounted Present Value and Leases

Suppose Winn-Dixie Stores, Inc., signed a ten-year lease for a new store location. The lease calls for an immediate payment of $20,000 and annual payments of $15,000 at the end of each of the next nine years. Winn-Dixie expects to earn 16% interest, compounded annually, on its investments. What is the present value of the lease payments?

Exercises

10-42 Sales Taxes

(Alternate is 10-43.) The Riordan Store is in a midwestern state where the sales tax is 7%. Total sales for the month of April were $300,000, of which $250,000 was subject to sales tax.

Required
1. Prepare a journal entry that summarizes sales (all in cash) for the month.
2. Prepare a journal entry regarding the disbursement for the sales tax.

10-43 Sales Taxes

(Alternate is 10-42.) Most of the food sold in retail stores in California is not subject to sales taxes (for example, candy), but some items are (for example, soft drinks). Apparently, the candy lobbyists were more effective than soft drinks lobbyists when dealing with the state legislature. Most cash registers are designed to record taxable sales and nontaxable sales and automatically add the appropriate sales tax.

The sales for the past week in the local Safeway store were $130,000, $20,000 of which was taxable at a rate of 7%. Using the $A = L + SE$ equation, show the impact on the entity, both now and when the sales taxes are paid at a later date. Also prepare corresponding journal entries.

✓10-44 Product Warranties

During 19X9, the Shavez Company had sales of $1 million. The company estimates that the cost of servicing products under warranty will average 2% of sales.

Required
1. Prepare journal entries for sales revenue and the related warranty expense for 19X9. Assume all sales are for cash.
2. The liability for warranties was $11,100 at the beginning of 19X9. Expenditures (all in cash) to satisfy warranty claims during 19X9 were $17,400, of which $4,500 was for products sold in 19X9. Prepare the journal entry for the warranty expenditures.
3. Compute the end-of-19X9 balance in the Liability for Warranties account.

10-45 Priorities of Claims

Lustre Corporation is being liquidated. It has one major asset, an office building, which was converted into $18 million cash. The stockholders' equity has been wiped out by past losses. The following claims exist: accounts payable, $3 million; debentures payable, $5 million; first mortgage payable, $12 million.

Required
1. Assume the debentures are unsubordinated. How much will each class of claimants receive?

2. If the debentures are subordinated, how much will each class of claimants receive? How much will each class receive if the cash proceeds from the sale of the building amount to only $13.5 million?

10-46 Bond Quotations

Following is a bond quotation for American Telephone and Telegraph Company from 1995:

Description	Current Yield	Close	Net Change
AT&T 6S00	6.1	98	$-3/8$

Required

1. How was the current yield of 6.1% calculated?

2. What price (in total dollars) would you have paid for one bond?

3. What was the closing price (in total dollars) for the bond on the preceding day?

10-47 Accounting for Pensions

A company's current pension expense is $800,000, $200,000 of which is paid in cash to a trustee. Using the balance sheet equation format, show which accounts are affected by these data. Prepare the corresponding journal entry.

√10-48 Various Liabilities

(Alternate is 10-49.)

1. Lynn made a $24,000 savings deposit on August 1. On September 30, the bank recognized two months' interest thereon at an annual rate of 10%. On October 1, Lynn closed her account with the bank. Interest is payable from the date of deposit through the date before withdrawal. Prepare the bank's journal entries.

2. On August 31 the City Ballet sold season tickets for $4.8 million cash in advance of the ballet season, which begins on September 10. These tickets are for eight performance dates.

  a. What is the effect on the balance sheet, August 31? Prepare the appropriate journal entry for the sale of the tickets.

  b. Assume that seven dates remain after September 30. What is the effect on the balance sheet, September 30? Prepare the related summary journal entry for September.

3. Smith Corporation sells communications equipment. Experience has shown that warranty costs average 4% of sales. Sales for June were $10 million. Cash disbursements for rendering warranty service during June were $360,000. Prepare the journal entries for these transactions.

4. A wholesale distributor gets cash deposits for its returnable bottles. In July, the distributor received $160,000 cash and disbursed $120,000 for bottles returned. Prepare the journal entries for these transactions.

5. The city hospital has lost a lawsuit. Damages were set at $1 million. The hospital plans to appeal the decision to a higher court. The hospital's attorneys are 80% confident of a reversal of the lower court's decision. What liability, if any, should appear on the hospital's balance sheet?

10-49 Various Liabilities

(Alternate is 10-48.)

1. Maytag Corporation sells electric appliances, including automatic washing machines. Experience in recent years has indicated that warranty costs average 3.0% of sales. Sales of washing machines for April were $3 million. Cash disbursements and obligations for warranty service on washing machines during April totaled $80,000. Prepare the journal entries prompted by these facts.

2. Pepsi-Cola Company of New York gets cash deposits for its returnable bottles. In June it received $100,000 cash and disbursed $91,000 for bottles returned. Prepare the journal entries regarding the receipts and returns of deposits.

3. Bank of America received a $2,000 savings deposit on April 1. On June 30, it recognized interest thereon at an annual rate of 5%. On July 1, the depositor closed her account with the bank. Prepare the bank's necessary journal entries.

4. The Schubert Theater sold for $100,000 cash a "season's series" of tickets in advance of December 31 for four plays, each to be held in successive months beginning in January.

   a. What is the effect on the balance sheet, December 31? What is the appropriate journal entry for the sale of the tickets?

   b. What is the effect on the balance sheet, January 31? What is the related journal entry for January?

5. Suppose your local hospital has lost a lawsuit. Damages were set at $500,000. The hospital plans to appeal the decision to a higher court. The hospital's attorneys are 90% confident of a reversal of the lower court's decision. What liability, if any, should be shown on the hospital's balance sheet?

Problems

10-50 Accounting for Payroll
For the week ended January 27, the Ehlo River Manufacturing Company had a total payroll of $176,000. Three items were withheld from employees' paychecks: (1) social security (FICA) tax of 7.1% of the payroll; (2) income taxes, which average 21% of the payroll; and (3) employees' savings that are deposited in their Credit Union, which are $9,800. All three items were paid on January 30.

Required

1. Use the balance sheet equation to analyze the transactions on January 27 and January 30.
2. Prepare journal entries for the recording of the items in requirement 1.
3. In addition to the payroll, Ehlo River pays (1) payroll taxes of 9% of the payroll, (2) health insurance premiums of $13,000, and (3) contributions to the employees' pension fund of $16,000. Prepare journal entries for the recognition of these additional expenses.

10-51 Analysis of Payroll and Interest
Consider a bank loan of $800,000 to a church on August 31, 19X1. The loan bears interest at 9%. Principal and interest are due in one year. The church reports on a calendar-year basis.

Required

1. Prepare an analysis of transactions, using the balance sheet equation. Indicate the entries for the church for August 31, 19X1, December 31, 19X1, and August 31, 19X2. Allocate interest within the year on a straight-line basis. Show all amounts in thousands of dollars.
2. Prepare all the corresponding journal entries keyed as above.

✓ ### 10-52 Present Value and Sports Salaries
The *New York Times* reported that Jack Morris, a pitcher, signed a $4 million contract with the Detroit Tigers. His 1988 salary was $1,988,000, and his 1989 salary was $1,989,000. However, $1 million of his 1989 salary was paid in 1988. The *Times* reported that the advance payment increased the contract's value by about $50,000, pushing it over $4 million.

Assume that the contract was signed on December 1, 1987, that the 1988 and 1989 payments were both made on December 1 of the respective years, and that the appropriate discount rate was 10%.

Required
1. What was the present value of the contract on the day it was signed?
2. What would have been the present value of the contract if the $1 million advance payment had been paid in 1989 instead of 1988?
3. How much present value (as of December 1, 1987) did Morris gain by receiving the $1 million payment in 1988 rather than in 1989?
4. Do you agree that the contract was worth more than $4 million? Explain.

10-53 Bond Discount Transactions and Straight-Line Amortization
On December 31, 1995, ATP Technology issued $20 million of ten-year, 12% debentures. Proceeds were $19.5 million.

Required
Show all amounts in thousands of dollars.
1. Using the balance sheet equation format, prepare an analysis of bond transactions. Assume straight-line amortization. Show entries for the issuer regarding (a) issuance, (b) one semiannual interest payment, and (c) payment of maturity value.
2. Show all the corresponding journal entries keyed as above.
3. Show how the bond-related accounts would appear on the balance sheets as of December 31, 1995 and 2004.

10-54 Bonds Issued at Par
On December 31, 1995, Boz Computers issued $20 million of ten-year, 12% debentures at par.

Required
1. Compute the proceeds from issuing the debentures.
2. Using the balance sheet equation format, prepare an analysis of this bond transaction. Show entries for the issuer regarding (a) issuance, (b) the first semiannual interest payment, and (c) payment of maturity value.
3. Show all the corresponding journal entries keyed as in requirement 2.
4. Show how the bond-related accounts would appear on the balance sheet as of December 31, 1995, and June 30, 1996. Assume that the semiannual interest payment and amortization due on the balance sheet date have been recorded.

10-55 Bonds Issued at Par
On January 1, 1996, Capital Electronics issued $1 million of five-year, 11% debentures at par.

Required
1. Compute the proceeds from issuing the debentures.
2. Using the balance sheet equation format, prepare an analysis of this bond transaction. Show entries for the issuer regarding (a) issuance, (b) the first semiannual interest payment, and (c) payment of maturity value.
3. Show all the corresponding journal entries keyed as in requirement 2.
4. Show how the bond-related accounts would appear on the balance sheets as of January 1, 1996, and July 1, 1996. Assume that the semiannual interest payment and amortization due on the balance sheet dates have been recorded.

10-56 Bonds Issued at a Discount
On December 31, 1995, White Landscaping issued $20 million of ten-year, 12% debentures. The market interest rate at issuance was 14%.

Required
1. Compute the proceeds from issuing the debentures.
2. Using the balance sheet equation format, prepare an analysis of this bond transaction. Show entries for the issuer regarding (a) issuance, (b) the first semiannual interest payment and discount amortization, and (c) payment of maturity value. Round all amounts to the nearest thousand.
3. Show all the corresponding journal entries keyed as in requirement 2.
4. Show how the bond-related accounts would appear on the balance sheets as of December 31, 1995, and June 30, 1996. Assume that the semiannual interest payment and amortization due on the balance sheet dates have been recorded.

10-57 Bond Discount Transactions

(Alternates are 10-58 and 10-59.) On February 1, 1995, a local gas utility issued $200 million of twenty-year, 9% debentures. Proceeds were $182,382 million, implying a market interest rate of 10%.

Required Show all amounts in thousands of dollars.

1. Using the balance sheet equation format, prepare an analysis of bond transactions. Assume effective-interest amortization. Show entries for the issuer regarding (a) issuance, (b) the first semiannual interest payment, and (c) payment of maturity value.
2. Show all the corresponding journal entries for (a), (b), and (c) in requirement 1.
3. Show how the bond-related accounts would appear on the balance sheets as of February 1, 1995 and 1996. Assume the February 1 interest payment and amortization of bond discount have been made.

10-58 Bonds Issued at a Discount

(Alternates are 10-57 and 10-59.) On January 1, 1996, Private Electronics issued $1 million of five-year, 11% debentures. The market interest rate at issuance was 12%.

Required

1. Compute the proceeds from issuing the debentures.
2. Using the balance sheet equation format, prepare an analysis of this bond transaction. Show entries for the issuer regarding (a) issuance, (b) the first semiannual interest payment, and (c) payment of maturity value. Round to the nearest thousand.
3. Show all the corresponding journal entries keyed as in requirement 2.
4. Show how the bond-related accounts would appear on the balance sheets as of January 1, 1996, and July 1, 1996. Assume that the semiannual interest payment and amortization due on the balance sheet dates have been recorded.

10-59 Bond Discount Transactions

(Alternates are 10-57 and 10-58.) Assume that on December 31, 1995, Newcar Corporation issued $10 million of ten-year, 10% debentures. Proceeds were $7,881,000; therefore the market rate of interest was 14%.

Required

1. Using the balance sheet equation format, prepare an analysis of transactions for Newcar. Key your transactions as follows: (a) issuance, (b) first semiannual interest using effective-interest amortization of bond discount, and (c) payment of maturity value. Round all amounts to the nearest thousand.
2. Prepare corresponding journal entries keyed (a), (b), and (c) as in requirement 1.
3. Show how the bond-related accounts would appear on Newcar's balance sheets as of December 31, 1995, and June 30, 1996. Assume that the semiannual interest payments and amortization have been recorded.

10-60 Bonds Issued at a Premium

(Alternates are 10-61 and 10-62.) On December 31, 1996, Gray Chevrolet issued $20 million of ten-year, 12% debentures. The market interest rate at issuance was 10%.

Required

1. Compute the proceeds from issuing the debentures.
2. Using the balance sheet equation format, prepare an analysis of this bond transaction. Show entries for the issuer regarding (a) issuance, (b) the first semiannual interest payment and premium amortization, and (c) payment of maturity value. Round all amounts to the nearest thousand.
3. Show all the corresponding journal entries keyed as in requirement 2.
4. Show how the bond-related accounts would appear on the balance sheets as of December 31, 1996, and June 30, 1997. Assume that the semiannual interest payment and amortization due on the balance sheet dates have been recorded.

10-61 Bonds Issued at a Premium

(Alternates are 10-60 and 10-62) On January 1, 1996, General Sales issued $1 million of five-year, 10% debentures. The market interest rate at issuance was 8%.

Required

1. Compute the proceeds from issuing the debentures.
2. Using the balance sheet equation format, prepare an analysis of this bond transaction. Show entries for the issuer regarding (a) issuance, (b) the first semiannual interest payment, and (c) payment of maturity value. Round to the nearest thousand.
3. Show all the corresponding journal entries keyed as in requirement 2.
4. Show how the bond-related accounts would appear on the balance sheets as of January 1, 1996, and July 1, 1996. Assume that the semiannual interest payments and amortization due on the balance sheet date have been recorded.

10-62 Bond Premium Transactions

(Alternates are 10-60 and 10-61) Assume that on December 31, 1995, CBA issued $10 million of ten-year, 10% debentures. Proceeds were $11,359,000; therefore the market rate of interest was 8%.

Required

1. Using the balance sheet equation format, prepare an analysis of transactions for CBA. Key your transactions as follows: (a) issuance, (b) first semiannual interest using effective-interest amortization of bond discount, and (c) payment of maturity value. Round all amounts to the nearest thousand.
2. Prepare corresponding journal entries keyed (a), (b), and (c) as in requirement 1.
3. Show how the bond-related accounts would appear on CBA's balance sheets as of December 31, 1995, and June 30, 1996. Assume that the semiannual interest payments and amortization have been recorded.

10-63 Early Extinguishment of Debt

On December 31, 1994, Lansing Landscaping issued $20 million of ten-year, 12% debentures. The market interest rate at issuance was 14%. On December 31, 1995 (after all interest payments and amortization had been recorded for 1995), the company purchased all the debentures for $18.5 million. Throughout their life, the debentures had been held by a large insurance company.

Required

Show all amounts in thousands of dollars. Round to the nearest thousand.

1. Compute the gain or loss on early extinguishment.
2. Using the balance sheet equation, present an analysis of the transaction on the issuer's books.
3. Show the appropriate journal entry.
4. At what price on December 31, 1995 could Lansing Landscaping redeem the bonds and realize a $500,000 gain?

√10-64 Early Extinguishment of Debt

(Alternate is 10-63.) On December 31, 1995, a local ski slope issued $10 million of ten-year, 12% debentures. The market interest rate at issuance was 12%. Suppose that on December 31, 1996 (after all interest payments and amortization had been recorded for 1996), the company purchased all the debentures for $9.8 million. The debentures had been held by a large insurance company throughout their life.

Required

Show all amounts in thousands of dollars.

1. Compute the gain or loss on early extinguishment.
2. Using the balance sheet equation, present an analysis of the transaction on the issuer's books.
3. Show the appropriate journal entry.

10-65 Retirement of Bonds

(J. Patell, adapted) This is a more difficult problem than others in this group.

On January 2, 1986, the Liverpool Financial Corporation sold a large issue of Series A $1,000 denomination bonds. The bonds had a stated coupon rate of 6% (annual), had a term to maturity of twenty years, and made semiannual coupon payments. Market conditions at the time were such that the bonds sold at their face value.

During the ensuing ten years, market interest rates fluctuated widely, and by January 2, 1996, the Liverpool bonds were trading at a price that provided an annual yield of 10%. Liverpool's management was considering purchasing the Series A bonds in the open market and retiring them; the necessary capital was to be raised by a new bond issue—the Series B bonds. Series B bonds were to be $1,000 denomination coupon (semiannual) bonds with a stated annual rate of 8% and a twenty-year term. Management felt that these bonds could be sold at a price yielding no more than 10%, especially if the Series A bonds were retired.

Required
1. On January 2, 1996, at what price could Liverpool Financial purchase the Series A bonds? *Hint*: The applicable factors are 5% and 20 periods.
2. Show the journal entries necessary to record the following transactions:
   a. Issue of one Series B bond on January 2, 1996.
   b. Purchase and retirement of one Series A bond on January 2, 1996.
   c. The first coupon payment on a Series B bond on July 2, 1996. Liverpool uses the effective-interest method of accounting for bond premium and discount.
   d. The second coupon payment on a Series B bond on January 2, 1997.

10-66 Non-Interest Bearing Notes
(Alternate is 10-67.) A local theater borrowed from a bank on a one-year note due on July 31, 19X0. The face value of the note was $200,000. However, the bank deducted its interest "in advance" at 18% of the face value.

Required
Show the effects on the borrower's records at inception and at the end of the month:
1. Using the balance sheet equation, prepare an analysis of transactions.
2. Prepare journal entries.
3. What was the real rate of interest?

10-67 Non-Interest Bearing Notes
(Alternate is 10-66.) On July 31, 1995, a local vineyard borrowed money from a bank on a two-year note due on July 31, 1997. The face value of the note was $25,000. However, the bank deducted interest of $5,070 "in advance."

Required
Show the effects on the borrower's records. Show the effects at July 31, 1995 and 1996.
1. Using the balance sheet equation, prepare an analysis of transactions.
2. Prepare journal entries.
3. Calculate the effective annual rate of interest.

✓ 10-68 Zero Coupon Bonds
Since 1985, the U.S. Treasury has required issuers of "deep-discount" or "zero coupon" debt securities to use an effective-interest approach to amortization of discount rather than straight-line amortization. The Treasury claimed that the old tax law, which permitted straight-line amortization, resulted in overstatements of deductions in early years.

Required
1. Assume that J.C. Penney issues a ten-year zero coupon bond having a face amount of $20,000,000 to yield 10%. For simplicity, assume that the 10% yield is compounded annually. Prepare the journal entry for the issuer.
2. Prepare the journal entry for interest expense for the first full year and the second full year using (a) straight-line and (b) effective-interest amortization.
3. Assume an income tax rate of 40%. How much more income tax for the first year would the issuer have to pay because of applying effective-interest instead of straight-line amortization?

10-69 Zero Coupon Bonds
American Medical Holdings, Inc., operates 37 acute care facilities with over 9,000 beds. The company included the following information on its balance sheet:

	August 31	
	1994	**1993**
Zero Coupon Guaranteed Bonds due 1997, and 2002, $179.3 million face value, net of $83.6 million unamortized discount at August 31, 1994	$95,714,000	$84,577,000

Assume that none of the bonds were issued or retired in fiscal 1994.

1. Assume that the bonds were issued on August 31, 1993. Prepare the journal entry at issuance. Do not use a discount account.
2. Prepare the journal entry for recording interest expense on the bonds for fiscal 1994. Assume annual compounding of interest.
3. The bonds maturing in August of 1997 have a face value of $103 million and an effective annual interest rate of 14% compounded semi-annually. Calculate their value at August 31, 1994.
4. Given your answer to number 3 above, estimate the effective interest rate on the bonds maturing in 2002. Assume semi-annual compounding. (*Hint*: These values do not correspond exactly to tabulated values; an approximation is close enough.)

10-70 Bonds Sold Between Interest Dates

On December 31, 1994, a company had some bonds printed and ready for issuance. But market conditions soured. The bonds were not issued until February 28, 1995, at par. The indenture requires payment of semiannual interest on December 31 and June 30. The face value of the bonds is $10 million. The interest rate is 12%.

1. Compute the total proceeds of the issue on February 28.
2. Prepare an analysis of transactions, using the balance sheet equation. Show amounts in thousands of dollars. Show the effects on the issuer's records on February 28 and June 30, 1995.
3. Prepare corresponding journal entries.

10-71 Convertible Bonds

In recent years Kmart had 6% convertible bonds that could each be exchanged for 28.169 shares of common stock. The price of the common stock was $48 per share, and quarterly dividends were $.37 per share.

1. What was the total market price of the common stock that a holder of one bond could obtain by converting the bond to common stock?
2. What amount of semiannual dividends would be received on the stock obtained in requirement 1?
3. What amount of semiannual interest does the holder of the bond receive on the bond?
4. Will the holder of a convertible bond always exchange it for common stock when the market value of the stock exceeds that of the bond? Explain.
5. Under the terms of the agreement, Kmart decided to redeem the bonds for $1,024 per share plus accrued interest of $26.83. Bondholders could either convert or accept the cash payment. What would you expect to happen?

10-72 Debt to Equity Ratios

The total debt and stockholders' equity for four companies follows (in thousands):
The companies are described as follows:

- AT&T provides long-distance phone service and is a large, well-established company.
- NYNEX is a regional phone company that is diversifying into a variety of telecommunications and information systems areas.

- Micron Technology is a fast-growing producer of memory products for electronic systems.
- Amgen is a biotechnology company pioneering the development of products based on advances in recombinant DNA.

(in millions)	Total Debt		Stockholders' Equity	
	1994	**1987**	**1994**	**1987**
AT&T	$61,341	$24,936	$17,921	$14,455
NYNEX	21,043	13,809	8,416	9,197
Micron Technology	480	57	1,049	73
Amgen	595	13	1,172	84

Required

1. Compute debt-to-equity ratios for each company for 1987 and 1994.
2. Discuss the differences in the ratios across firms.
3. Discuss the changes in individual company ratios from 1987 to 1994.

10-73 Review of Chapters 9 and 10

Interpoint
Corporation

Interpoint Corporation, based in Redmond, Washington, produces hybrid microcircuit products for the electronics industry. Assets in 1994 were over $39 million. The company's 1994 annual report contained the following (in thousasnds):

	October 31	
	1994	**1993**
Property, plant, and equipment, at cost	$21,188	$19,697
Less accumulated depreciation	11,950	10,293
Net property, plant, and equipment	$ 9,238	$ 9,404
Long-term debt due within one year	$ 1,505	$ 1,607
Long-term debt	4,029	5,935

Purchases of buildings, machinery, and equipment during 1994 were $1,693,000. Depreciation expense for 1994 was $1,778,000.

Proceeds from issuance of *long-term debt* were $273,000 during 1994.

Required (The use of T-accounts should help your analysis.)

1. Compute the dollar amounts of
    a. Accumulated depreciation relating to properties and plants disposed of during 1994.
    b. Original acquisition cost of properties and plants disposed of during 1994.
2. Compute the dollar amounts of
    a. Long-term debt reductions
    b. The *net increase or decrease* in long-term debt.

10-74 Review of Chapters 9 and 10

(J. Patell, adapted) Here are excerpts from an annual report of Crane Company, a manufacturer of plumbing fixtures and related items.

From income statement (in thousands):

Depreciation	$23,178
Amortization of debt discount	779
Loss on disposal of property, plant, and equipment	84

Crane Company
From Balance Sheets
(in thousands of dollars)

	December 31	
	19X4	19X3
Investments and Other Assets:		
Unamortized debt discount	$ 1,938	$ 2,717
Property, Plant, and Equipment, at Cost:		
Land	$ 10,644	$ 10,751
Buildings and improvements	83,320	90,605
Machinery and equipment	303,063	314,732
	397,027	416,088
Less accumulated depreciation	269,078	269,896
	$127,949	$146,192
Long-Term Debt	$138,524	$202,232

Additional information (in thousands):

Additions to property, plant, and equipment during 19X4 amounted to $14,465. Reductions in long-term debt during 19X4 were $64,497.

Required (The use of T-accounts should help your analysis.) During 19X4, Crane's property, plant, and equipment accounts were affected by both purchases of new assets and disposals (sales) of old assets.

1. Determine the total original cost of the property, plant, and equipment sold by Crane during 19X4.
2. Determine the total dollar amount Crane received for the property, plant, and equipment that was sold during 19X4.
3. In 19X4, as well as in the several previous years, Crane issued long-term bonds at a discount. Rather than showing the bond discount as a contra account to long-term debt, Crane has shown it on the asset side of the balance sheet under the heading "Investments and Other Assets." All reductions in debt occurred through the normal maturity of outstanding bonds. There were no early retirements. Determine the face (or par) amount of the long-term debt issued during 19X4.
4. Determine the actual cash received by Crane for the bonds issued during 19X4.

10-75 Capital Lease
(Study Appendix 10B.) The Philbrick Packing Company acquired packaging equipment on a capital lease. There were annual lease payments of $40 million at the end of each of three years. The implicit interest rate was 18% compounded annually.

Required
1. Compute the present value of the capital lease.
2. Prepare journal entries at the inception of the lease and for each of the three years. Distinguish between the short-term and long-term classifications of the lease.

10-76 Comparison of Operating and Capital Lease
(Study Appendix 10B.) Refer to the preceding problem. Suppose the capital lease were regarded as an operating lease. Ignore income taxes. Fill in the blanks (prepare supporting computations):

	Operating Lease	Capital Lease	Difference
Total expenses:			
Year 1	?	?	?
Year 2	?	?	?
Two years together	?	?	?
End of year 1:			
Total assets	?	?	?
Total liabilities	?	?	?
Retained income	?	?	?
End of year 2:			
Total assets	?	?	?
Total liabilities	?	?	?
Retained income	?	?	?

10-77 Capital or Operating Lease

(Study Appendix 10B.) On December 31, 19X1, Emilio's Construction Company has been offered an electronically controlled automatic lathe (a) outright for $100,000 cash or (b) on a noncancelable lease whereby rental payments would be made at the end of each year for three years. The lathe will become obsolete and worthless at the end of three years. The company can borrow $100,000 cash on a three-year loan payable at maturity at 16% compounded annually.

Required

1. Compute the annual rental payment, assuming that the lessor desires a 16% rate of return per year.
2. If the lease were accounted for as an operating lease, what annual journal entry would be made?
3. The lease is a capital lease. Prepare an analytical schedule of each lease payment. Show the lease liability at the beginning of the year, interest expense, lease payment, and lease liability at end of year.
4. Prepare an analysis of transactions, using the balance sheet equation format.
5. Prepare yearly journal entries.

10-78 Leases

(Study Appendix 10B.) The following information appeared in a footnote to the 1994 annual report of Delta Air Lines, Incorporated, a June 30 fiscal-year-end company:

At June 30, 1994, the company's minimum rental commitments under capital leases and noncancelable operating leases with initial or remaining terms of more than one year were (in millions):

Years Ending June 30	Capital Leases	Operating Leases
1995	$ 18	$ 952
1996	18	965
1997	18	961
1998	15	940
1999	14	953
After 1999	44	12,605
Total minimum lease payment	$127	$17,376
Less: Amounts representing interest	$ 30	
Present value of future minimum capital lease payments	$ 97	

1. Suppose the minimum capital lease payments are made in equal amounts on September 30, December 31, March 31, and June 30 of each year. Compute the interest and principal to be paid on capital leases during the first half of fiscal 1995. Do calculations in millions with two decimal places. Assume an interest rate of 8% per annum, compounded quarterly.
2. Prepare the journal entries for the lease payments in requirement 1 on September 30 and December 31, 1995.
3. Suppose the operating leases were capital leases, the payments after 1999 were spread evenly over 12 years, and the payments were made annually at year-end. If operating leases were capitalized at 8% also, how much would long-term debt increase? Do calculations to closest million.

10-79   Leases
(Study Appendix 10B.) Consider footnote 10 from the 1994 annual report of American Telephone and Telegraph Company (AT&T):

Footnote 10:
   AT&T leases land, buildings, and equipment through contracts that expire in various years through 2025. Future minimum lease payments under noncancelable capital and operating leases at December 31, 1994 are as follows:

(Dollars in Millions)	Capital Leases	Operating Leases
Minimum lease payments for year ending December 31,		
1995	$ 52	$ 579
1996	30	445
1997	21	370
1998	10	301
1999	5	250
Later years	3	1,023
Total minimum lease payments	121	$2,968
Less: Estimated executory cost	1	
Imputed interest	15	
Present value of net minimum lease payments	$105	

1. Footnote 10 contains the minimum future lease payments due under AT&T's capital and operating leases. Compute the net present value of the *operating* lease payments as of December 31, 1994. Use a 10% implicit interest rate. For ease of computation, assume that each payment is made on December 31 of the designated year (i.e., the first $579 million payment is made on December 31, 1995) and that the final payment, labeled "Later," is made on December 31, 1999.
2. Suppose AT&T were to capitalize the operating leases examined in requirement 1. Show the journal entries necessary to
   a. Capitalize the leases on January 1, 1995. Ignore any prior period adjustments and do not break the lease obligation into current and long-term portions.
   b. Record the first payment on December 31, 1995.

10-80   Effect of Capital Leases
(Study Appendix 10B.) Deb Shops, Inc., a chain of specialty women's apparel stores, reported the following information about leases in its annual report (in thousands):

	January 31	
	1994	1993
Capital lease asset, gross	$1,982	$1,982
Less: Accumulated depreciation	$1,090	$ 991
Capital lease asset, net	$ 892	$ 991

The only asset under a capital lease is a warehouse and office building. The building has an economic life of twenty years and is being depreciated on a straight-line basis. Deb Shops had income before tax of $7,396,496 in fiscal 1994.

Required

1. Calculate the depreciation on the warehouse and office building for the fiscal year ending January 31, 1994.
2. On what date was the building placed into service? (*Hint*: How long would it take to build up the accumulated depreciation shown?)
3. The interest on the lease obligation was $464,000 in fiscal 1994. The total lease payment was $550,000. Reconstruct the 1994 journal entry.
4. Suppose this building had met the requirements for an operating lease rather than a capital lease. Calculate the operating income for Deb Shops in fiscal 1994.

10-81 Liabilities for Frequent Flier Miles and Ethics

Most airlines in the United States have frequent flier programs that grant free flights if a customer accumulates enough flight miles on the airline. For example, United Airlines offers a free domestic flight for every 25,000 miles flown on United. Delta Air Lines describes its program as follows in a footnote to the financial statements:

> The Company sponsors a travel incentive program whereby frequent travelers accumulate mileage credits that entitle them to certain awards including free travel. The company accrues the estimated incremental cost of providing free travel awards under its frequent flyer program when free travel award levels are achieved. The accrued incremental cost is recorded in current liabilities.

In a recent annual report, American Airlines reported a liability of $270 million for free flights, representing approximately 4 billion flight miles owed to customers. Assuming the average free flight is 2,000 miles, there is a $270 million liability for 2 million flights, an average of $135 per flight. However, some airlines maintain that the true liability is closer to $10 per flight including the cost of food, insurance, and other miscellaneous expenses. They argue that all other costs would be incurred even in the absence of the person traveling free.

Suppose airlines use one estimate of the cost of these "free" flights for their internal decision making and another for computing the liability for their publicly reported balance sheet. Comment on the ethical issues.

10-82 Wal-Mart Annual report

Refer to the Wal-Mart financial statements in Appendix A.

Required

1. Footnote 2 provides short-term debt information. Calculate and compare the interest expense on short-term debt during 1993, 1994, and 1995. Did short-term borrowing increase or decrease from 1993 to 1995?
2. Assume that all payments of principal on long-term debt occur as planned during 1996. Prepare the journal entry to record 1996 principal payments. Also prepare the journal entry to reclassify the current portion of long-term debt as of January 31, 1996.

3. Compute the following three ratios at January 31, 1994 and 1995.

    (a) Debt-to-equity ratio

    (b) Debt-to-total-assets ratio

    (c) Interest-coverage ratio

10-82 Compact D from Disclosure

Identify an industry and select two companies within the industry.

Required Calculate and compare the following ratios between the companies and through time.

    1. Debt-to-equity ratio

    2. Debt-to-total-assets ratio

    3. Interest-coverage ratio

11 Statement of Cash Flows

Learning Objectives

After studying this chapter, you should be able to

1 Explain the concept of the statement of cash flows.

2 Classify activities affecting cash as operating, investing, or financing activities.

3 Prepare a statement of cash flows using the direct method.

4 Calculate cash flows from operations using the indirect method.

5 Explain how depreciation affects cash flows provided by operating activities.

6 Describe several reconciling items between net income and cash provided by operating activities.

7 Explain treatment of gains and losses from fixed asset sales and debt extinguishments in the statement of cash flows (Appendix 11A).

8 Use the T-account approach to prepare the cash flow statement (Appendix 11B).

This chapter provides a detailed look at the statement of cash flows and the information it provides to readers of financial statements. We discuss how and why cash flows are classified into three categories: operating, financing, and investing. The cash flow statement may be *structured* in either the direct or indirect method, both of which are presented in the chapter. Some companies use the balance sheet approach, as presented in the chapter, to *prepare* the statement of cash flows. Others use the T-account approach, which is presented in Appendix 11B.

The accrual basis of accounting is the primary means of presenting financial position (balance sheet) and operating performance (income statement). But investors and managers are also concerned about an entity's ability to generate cash and to meet forthcoming obligations. Several large businesses have failed in the recent past because they did not produce enough cash to meet their obligations. Examples include Ames Department Stores, Eastern Airlines, and Penn Square Bank. The statement of cash flows is intended to enable investors to identify such risks in advance and to aid managers in avoiding the disastrous outcomes often associated with insufficient cash.

Until 1971, only the income statement and statement of financial position were required in the United States. In 1971, a third statement, which presented year-to-year changes in financial position, became required, and in 1987 the specific cash flow requirements discussed in this text took effect with FASB *Statement No. 95*. In many other countries a statement like the statement of cash flows is required, but the definitions and the structure of the statement differ widely. Moreover, in some countries, including Austria, India, and Uruguay, no such statement is common.

■ OVERVIEW OF STATEMENT OF CASH FLOWS

Purposes of Statement

Objective 1

Explain the concept of the statement of cash flows.

Rampant inflation in the late 1970s and early 1980s engendered many criticisms of the traditional accrual measures of income and financial position. One response has been a more intense focus on the effects of activities on cash. The FASB reacted to this change in focus by requiring the statement of cash flows as a basic financial statement.

A *statement of cash flows* reports the cash receipts and cash payments of an entity during a period. It explains the causes for the changes in cash by providing information about operating, financing, and investing activities. The statement of cash flows is a basic financial statement in corporate annual reports.

Why does the FASB require a statement of cash flows? Because:

1. It shows the relationship of net income to changes in cash balances. Cash balances can decline despite positive net income and vice versa.
2. It reports past cash flows as an aid to

   a. Predicting future cash flows.
   b. Evaluating management's generation and use of cash.
   c. Determining a company's ability to pay interest and dividends and to pay debts when they are due.

3. It identifies changes in the mix of productive assets.

The Cash Crunch

Can a profitable company go bankrupt? Can a corporate strategy fail for lack of cash? The answer is yes. National Convenience Stores (NCS), Inc., is a recent case. NCS operates 988 *Stop N Go* stores in seven markets in three Sunbelt states (California, Georgia, and Texas). The stores sell fresh foods, traditional fast foods, alcoholic and nonalcoholic beverages, tobacco products, groceries, and health and beauty aids. Approximately 80% of the stores are equipped with self-service gasoline dispensing facilities.

After battling fierce competition from gas stations expanding into the convenience store business, NCS began to implement a new merchandising strategy. The Neighborstore® concept linked each store's product mix directly to its local demographics and customer purchasing patterns. During 1991, the company expanded the strategy by joining forces with branded partners such as Pizza Hut® to offer fast-food, take-out items freshly prepared in store "eateries." The company also launched its "NCS Signature" fresh-food line.

Despite Chief Executive Officer (CEO) V. H. "Pete" VanHorn's efforts to improve the company's operating performance, NCS ran into financial difficulties. NCS posted a loss of $3.1 million for the quarter ending September 30, 1991, compared with a $1 million profit in that quarter a year earlier. Sales for the first quarter dropped 8.5% to $267 million from $292 million a year earlier. Cash was disappearing. In November 1991, the company deferred payment on $3.9 million in bank loans and stopped payment of preferred stock dividends. During the week ending December 6, 1991, NCS reported that it could not pay $1.3 million in mortgage debt coming due December 1, 1991. On December 9, 1991, NCS sought Chapter 11 bankruptcy protection after experiencing difficulties in obtaining credit from its major suppliers. Under Chapter 11, a company operates under court

protection from demands by its creditors for immediate payment while it designs a plan to repay its debts. NCS's bankruptcy filing listed the firm as having $277.5 million in assets and $192.6 million in liabilities.

For the five years prior to its bankruptcy filing, NCS reported the data in the following table. As the table shows, NCS's net income fluctuated wildly during the last five years, while its cash flow from operations generally declined. Cash flow problems were exacerbated by expenditures on new stores and store remodeling required to implement the company's new strategy. In the midst of it all, the economy moved into a serious recession, and Houston suffered a crime wave that hit NCS's stores. It was cash flow problems that finally forced bankruptcy.

In February 1993, the bankruptcy court confirmed the plan of reorganization as approved by the court and by votes of creditors and equity holders. Old securities were repaid or exchanged for new securities. In the process, the pre-reorganization shareholders had their interest in the firm reduced by half. But the company generated profits of $6.8 million in 1994 and had positive cash flow of $25 million from operations.

In response to the crime wave, NCS launched its Operation Safeguard program involving patrols by off-duty police and saftey-related technology, including video cameras, panic alarms, and signal-monitoring systems. NCS is also committed to point-of-sale technology, using scanners in 25% of its stores compared to 4% of other convenience stores nationally. Only time will determine whether the reorganization is a complete success. ∎

Sources: National Convenience Stores, Inc., Annual Reports, *10Ks, 1986-1994; Greg Hassell, "Stop N Go Plans No Layoffs,"* Houston Chronicle *(December 11, 1991), p. B1; Kevin Helliker, "National Convenience Stores Petition Bankruptcy Court for Chapter 11 Status,"* Wall Street Journal *(December 12, 1991), p. A10.*

	Year Ended June 30 (in thousands)				
	1991	**1990**	**1989**	**1988**	**1987**
Sales	$1,073,958	$1,062,183	$1,077,150	$917,533	$831,112
Gross Profit	270,578	293,056	277,211	253,302	223,442
Net Income (Loss)	(10,465)	4,963	(8,858)	6,754	(5,445)
Operating Cash Flow	15,090	6,704	23,585	36,122	31,599
Increase (Decrease) in Cash	11,448	1,112	(5,190)	3,762	5,580

Balance sheets show the status of an entity at a day in time. In contrast, statements of cash flows, income statements, and statements of retained income cover periods of time; they provide the explanations of why the balance sheet items have changed. This linkage is depicted in the accompanying diagram:

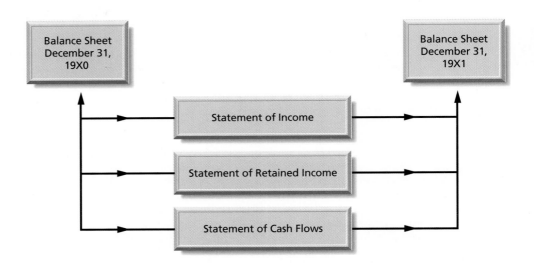

The statement of cash flows explains where cash came from during a period and where it was spent. The statement of cash flows usually explains changes in cash and cash equivalents. As explained in Chapter 6, *cash equivalents* are highly liquid short-term investments that can easily be converted into cash with little delay. Examples include money market funds and treasury bills. They are usually temporary investments of excess cash, and they can readily be converted into cash as obligations become due. Hereafter, when we refer to cash, we mean both cash and cash equivalents.

Readers of financial statements want information on a firm's activities in two primary areas: its operating management and its financial management. **Operating management** is largely concerned with the major day-to-day activities that generate revenues and expenses. The income statement, prepared on an accrual basis, is the primary statement used in assessing operating management.

operating management Is mainly concerned with the major day-to-day activities that generate revenues and expenses.

financial management Is mainly concerned with where to get cash and how to use cash for the benefit of the entity.

Financial management is largely concerned with where to get cash (*financing activities*) and how to use cash (*investing activities*). For example, financial managers decide about the issuance or retirement of long-term debt or additional capital stock and about how to invest the capital raised. The statement of cash flows reports the results of both financial management and operating management. It includes three categories of activities: operating activities, investing activities, and financing activities.

Typical Activities Affecting Cash

The following are typical activities in statements of cash flows:

Objective 2

Classify activities affecting cash as operating, investing, or financing activities.

OPERATING ACTIVITIES

Cash Inflows	*Cash Outflows*
Collections from customers	Cash payments to suppliers
Interest and dividends collected	Cash payments to employees
Other operating receipts	Interest and taxes paid
	Other operating cash payments

INVESTING ACTIVITIES

Cash Inflows	*Cash Outflows*
Sale of property, plant, and equipment	Purchase of property, plant, and equipment
Sale of securities that are not cash equivalents	Purchase of securities that are not cash equivalents
Receipt of loan repayments	Making loans

FINANCING ACTIVITIES

Cash Inflows	*Cash Outflows*
Borrowing cash from creditors	Repayment of amounts borrowed
Issuing equity securities	Repurchase of equity shares (including the purchase of treasury stock)
Issuing debt securities	Payment of dividends

operating activities
Transactions that affect the income statement.

investing activities
Activities that involve (1) providing and collecting cash as a lender or as an owner of securities and (2) acquiring and disposing of plant, property, equipment, and other long-term productive assets.

financing activities
In the statement of cash flows, obtaining resources as a borrower or issuer of securities and repaying creditors and owners.

As the lists of activities indicate, **operating activities** are generally transactions that affect the income statement. For example, sales are linked to collections from customers, and wage expenses are closely tied to cash payments to employees. **Investing activities** involve (1) providing and collecting cash as a lender or as an owner of securities and (2) acquiring and disposing of plant, property, equipment, and other long-term productive assets. **Financing activities** involve obtaining resources as a borrower or issuer of securities and repaying creditors and owners. Note that the two parties to a transaction treat it differently in the statement of cash flows. When stock is issued for cash to an investor, the issuer treats it as a financing activity and the investor treats it as an investing activity.

As a concrete example, consider the operating and financial management activities of the APT Company. The APT Company provides daily cleaning services for homes. Exhibit 11-1 displays its financial statements. APT pays all wages in cash daily, and all revenues are collected in cash daily. If these were the only transactions affecting income, net income would equal cash provided by operations. But APT owns a computer, and depreciation on the computer is allocated to the income statement over the computer's anticipated three-year life. Since depreciation does not involve a cash flow, it appears on the income statement as an expense but does not affect cash provided by operations.

Cleaning supplies are purchased for cash periodically, but the supplies are not necessarily paid for upon delivery. Moreover, supplies are kept in inventory to be used as needed, so all the supplies acquired are not immediately used. The income statement reports the $3,000 of supplies *used* during the period, while the cash flow statement reports the $3,200 of supplies *paid for* during the period.

In comparing the income statement and cash flows from operations, you can see that the only differences are for supplies and depreciation. The APT Company has only one investing activity, the purchase of a computer, and one financing activity, the payment of cash dividends.

| Exhibit 11-1 | | | | | | |

Balance Sheets for the Years Ended December 31

Assets	19X1	19X0	Liabilities and Stockholders' Equity	19X1	19X0
Cash	$1,200	$ 4,000	Accounts payable	$ 200	$ 200
Supplies	600	400	Stockholders'		
Computer	2,000	0	equity	3,600	4,200
Total assets	$3,800	$4,400	Total Liab. and SE	$3,800	$4,400

Income Statement for the Year Ended December 31, 19X1

Sales		$35,000
Wages	$20,000	
Depreciation	1,000	
Supplies	3,000	24,000
Net income		$11,000

Statement of Cash Flows for the Year Ended December 31, 19X1

CASH FLOWS FROM OPERATING ACTIVITIES:	
Collections from customers	$ 35,000
Payments to employees	(20,000)
Payments to suppliers	(3,200)
Net cash provided by operating activities	11,800
CASH FLOWS FROM INVESTING ACTIVITIES:	
Cash investment in computer	(3,000)
Net cash used for investing activities	(3,000)
CASH FLOWS FROM FINANCING ACTIVITIES:	
Cash dividend payments	(11,600)
Net cash used for financing activities	(11,600)
Decrease in cash	$ (2,800)
Cash balance December 31, 19X0	4,000
Cash balance December 31, 19X1	$ 1,200

cash flows from operating activities The first major section of the statement of cash flows. It shows the cash effects of transactions that affect the income statement.

direct method In a statement of cash flows, the method that calculates net cash provided by operating activities as collections minus operating disbursements.

indirect method In a statement of cash flows, the method that adjusts the accrual net income to reflect only cash receipts and outlays.

Approaches to Calculating the Cash Flow from Operating Activities

Two approaches can be used to compute **cash flow from operating activities** (or operations), the first major section of the statement of cash flows, which shows the cash effects of transactions affecting the income statement. Computing it as collections less operating disbursements is called the **direct method**. This is the method illustrated for APT. Adjusting the accrual net income to reflect only cash receipts and outlays is called the **indirect method**.

Under the direct method, we identify only the cash part of each item in the income statement. Since depreciation does not use cash, it is not part of the calculation. For APT we had only to do a calculation for supplies. By examining the balance sheet, we see that supplies inventory rose from $400 to $600. This suggests we bought more than we used, so cost of supplies in the income statement was smaller than purchases. But did we pay for what we bought? Yes, we paid for exactly the quantity purchased during the year because the Accounts Payable balance remained unchanged. Whatever the increases to the account were for new purchases, the decreases for payments were identical. So if we paid for all we bought, and we bought $200 more than we sold, we must have paid for $3,200. Therefore, net cash provided by operating activities must be cash sales of $35,000 less $20,000 in cash wages and $3,200 cash paid for supplies for a net of $11,800, as shown in Exhibit 11-1.

Alternatively, cash flow from operations can be calculated by the *indirect* method. The income statement provides an accrual-based net income of $11,000, and we can simply adjust it for the accrual elements that are different from the cash outlays. We deducted $1,000 of depreciation to calculate net income, but depreciation involved no cash, so let's add it back to get $12,000 ($11,000 plus $1,000). In addition we know we spent $200 more on supplies than we used, so let's subtract that $200 as an operating use of cash that does not appear in net income. By adjusting net income, we again calculate $11,800 ($11,000 + $1,000 – $200).

The FASB prefers the direct method because it shows operating cash receipts and payments in a way that is easier for investors to understand. However, the indirect method is more common. The two approaches are shown below:

**APT Company
Cash Flow from
Operating Activities**

	Direct Method		Indirect Method	
Collections from customers		$35,000	Net earnings	$11,000
Payments to employees	$20,000		Add depreciation*	1,000
Payments to suppliers	3,200	23,200	Deduct supplies†	(200)
Net cash provided by operating activities		$11,800		$11,800

*Depreciation was deducted to compute net earnings but did not involve a cash flow.
†Payments for supplies exceeded the amount charged as expense.

■ TRANSACTIONS AFFECTING CASH FLOWS FROM ALL SOURCES

The APT Company was an intentionally simplified illustration that gave us a first look at the principles behind the statement of cash flows. Now we will enlarge our scope.

Activities Affecting Cash

Exhibit 11-2 summarizes the effects of most major transactions on cash. The zeros in the "change in cash" column indicate that the transaction has no effect on cash. Examples are sales and purchases on account and even the accrual recording of cost of goods sold. Cash flow emphasizes the flow of cash to and from customers and suppliers; accrual accounting emphasizes the flow of goods and services.

Perhaps the most troublesome aspect of our summary is the classification of interest payments and dividend payments. Both of these represent cash flows to suppliers of capital to the firm. It would seem they might be treated the same, because both are disbursements related to financing activities. However, after much debate, the FASB followed tradition and decided to classify interest payments as cash flows associated with operations and dividend payments as financing cash flows. This classification maintains the long-standing distinction that dividend transactions with the owners (dividends) cannot be treated as expenses, while interest payments to creditors are expenses.

	Type of Transaction	Change in Cash
Exhibit 11-2	**OPERATING ACTIVITIES:**	
	Sales of goods and services for cash	+
Analysis of Effects of	Sales of goods and services on credit	0
Transactions on Cash	Receive dividends or interest	+
	Collection of accounts receivable	+
	Recognize cost of goods sold	0
	Purchase inventory for cash	–
	Purchase inventory on credit	0
	Pay trade accounts payable	–
	Accrue operating expenses	0
	Pay operating expenses	–
	Accrue taxes	0
	Pay taxes	–
	Accrue interest	0
	Pay interest	–
	Prepay expenses for cash	–
	Write off prepaid expenses	0
	Charge depreciation or amortization	0
	INVESTING ACTIVITIES:	
	Purchase fixed assets for cash	–
	Purchase fixed assets by issuing debt	0
	Sell fixed assets	+
	Purchase securities that are not cash equivalents	–
	Sell securities that are not cash equivalents	+
	Make a loan	–
	FINANCING ACTIVITIES:	
	Increase long-term or short-term debt	+
	Reduce long-term or short-term debt	–
	Sell common or preferred shares	+
	Repurchase and retire common or preferred shares	–
	Purchase treasury stock	–
	Pay dividends	–
	Convert debt to common stock	0
	Reclassify long-term debt to short-term debt	0

Cash Flow and Earnings

cash flow Usually refers to net cash provided by operating activities.

A focal point of the statement of cash flows is the net cash flow from operating activities. Frequently, this is called simply **cash flow**. The importance of cash flow has been stressed by Harold Williams, the former chairman of the Securities and Exchange Commission, quoted in *Forbes*: "If I had to make a forced choice between having earnings information and having cash flow information, today I would take cash flow information." Fortunately, we do not have to make a choice. Cash flow and income both convey useful information about an entity.

In prior years, some companies stressed a cash-flow-per-share-from-operations figure and provided it in addition to the required earnings-per-share figure. But net cash flow from operating activities gives an incomplete picture of management performance. Why? Because it ignores noncash expenses that are just as important as cash expenses for judging overall company performance. Moreover, a reported cash-flow-per-share says nothing about the cash needed for replacement and expansion of facilities. Thus, the entire per-share cash flow from operations may not be available for cash dividends. Because it gives an incomplete picture, a cash-flow-per-share figure can be quite misleading. Accordingly, the FASB has specifically prohibited the reporting of cash-flow-per-share amounts.

Both cash flow and accrual earnings data are useful. As Professor Loyd Heath said, "Asking which one is better, cash flow or earnings, is like asking which shoe is more useful, your right or your left?"

■ THE ECO-BAG COMPANY—A MORE-DETAILED EXAMPLE

Consider the Eco-Bag Company, whose financial statements are shown in Exhibit 11-3. The cash flow statement is prepared using the direct method.

Because the statement of cash flows explains the *causes* for the change in cash, the first step is always to compute the amount of the change (which represents the net *effect*):

Cash, December 31, 19X1	$ 25,000
Cash, December 31, 19X2	16,000
Net decrease in cash	$ 9,000

Eco-Bag Company's statement illustrates how this information is often shown at the bottom of a statement of cash flows. The beginning cash balance is added to the net change to compute the ending cash balance. Another common practice is to place the beginning cash balance at the top of the statement and the ending cash balance at the bottom. However, there is no requirement that beginning and ending cash balances be shown explicitly in the statement of cash flows. Showing only the net change is sufficient.

When business expansion occurs, as in this case, and where there is a strong cash position at the outset, cash often declines. Why? Because cash is usually needed for investment in various business assets required for expansion, including investment in accounts receivable and inventories.

Eco-Bag Company's statement gives a direct picture of where cash came from and where it went. In this instance, the excess of cash outflows over cash inflows reduced cash by $9,000. Without the statement of cash flows, the readers of the annual report would have to conduct their own analyses of the beginning and ending balance sheets, the income statement, and the statement of retained income to grasp the impact of financial management decisions.

Most important, this illustration demonstrates how a firm may simultaneously (1) have a significant amount of net income, as computed by accountants on the accrual basis, and yet (2) have a decline in cash that could become severe. Indeed, many growing businesses are desperate for cash even though reported net income zooms upward.

Exhibit 11-3

Eco-Bag Company
Balance Sheet as of
December 31
(in thousands)

Assets			Liabilities and Stockholders' Equity		
	19X2	19X1		19X2	19X1
Current assets:			Current liabilities:		
			Accounts payable	$ 74	$ 6
Cash	$ 16	$ 25	Wages and		
Accounts receivable	45	25	salaries payable	25	4
Inventory	100	60			
Total current assets	161	110	Total current liabilities	99	10
Fixed assets, gross	581	330	Long-term debt	125	5
Accum. depreciation	(101)	(110)	Stockholders' equity	417	315
Net	480	220			
			Total liabilities and		
Total assets	$641	$330	stockholders' equity	$641	$330

Eco-Bag Company
Statement of Income
for the Year Ended
December 31, 19X2
(in thousands)

Sales		$200
Cost and expenses:		
Cost of goods sold	$100	
Wages and salaries	36	
Depreciation	17	
Interest	4	
Total costs and expenses		$157
Income before income taxes		43
Income taxes		20
Net income		$ 23

Eco-Bag Company
Statement of Cash
Flows
for the Year Ended
December 31, 19X2
(in thousands)

CASH FLOWS FROM OPERATING ACTIVITIES:		
Cash collections from customers		$180
Cash payments:		
To suppliers	$ 72	
To employees	15	
For interest	4	
For taxes	20	
Total cash payments		(111)
Net cash provided by operating activities		$ 69
CASH FLOWS FROM INVESTING ACTIVITIES:		
Purchases of fixed assets	$(287)	
Proceeds from sale of fixed assets	10	
Net cash used by investing activities		(277)
CASH FLOWS FROM FINANCING ACTIVITIES:		
Proceeds from issue of long-term debt	$ 120	
Proceeds from issue of common stock	98	
Dividends paid	(19)	
Net cash provided by financing activities		199
Net decrease in cash		$ (9)
Cash, December 31, 19X1		25
Cash, December 31, 19X2		$ 16

■ PREPARING A STATEMENT OF CASH FLOWS— THE DIRECT METHOD

Changes in the Balance Sheet Equation

Objective 3

Prepare a statement of cash flows using the direct method.

Accountants use various techniques for preparing a statement of cash flows. The balance sheet approach is frequently used, but accountants may also use work sheets or T-accounts (described in Appendix 11B). The balance sheet provides the conceptual framework underlying all financial statements, including the statement of cash flows. The equation can be rearranged as follows:

$$\text{Assets} = \text{Liabilities} + \text{Stockholders' equity}$$

$$\text{Cash} + \text{Noncash assets} = \text{Liabilities} + \text{Stockholders' equity}$$

$$\text{Cash} = \text{Liabilities} + \text{Stockholders' equity} - \text{Noncash Assets}$$

$$\text{Cash} = \text{L} + \text{SE} - \text{NCA}$$

Any change (Δ) in cash must be accompanied by a change in one or more items on the right side to keep the equation in balance:

$$\Delta \text{ Cash} = \Delta \text{ L} + \Delta \text{ SE} - \Delta \text{ NCA}$$

Therefore:

$$\text{Change in cash} = \text{Change in all noncash accounts}$$

or

$$\text{What happened to cash} = \text{Why it happened}$$

The statement of cash flows focuses on the changes in the noncash accounts as a way of explaining how and why the level of cash has gone up or down during a given period. Thus, the major changes in the accounts on the right side of the equation appear in the statement of cash flows as *causes* of the change in cash. The left side of the equation measures the net *effect* of the change in cash.

Consider the following summary of 19X2 transactions for the Eco-Bag Company. In practice, this summary might be produced by a careful review of the general ledger accounts to combine similar transactions that occurred during the year. Those involving cash have an asterisk (*):

1. Sales on credit, $200,000.
*2. Collections of accounts receivable, $180,000.
3. Recognition of cost of goods sold, $100,000.
4. Purchases of inventory on account, $140,000.
*5. Payments of trade accounts payable, $72,000.
6. Recognition of wages expense, $36,000.
*7. Payments of wages, $15,000.
*8. Recognition of interest accrued and paid, $4,000.
*9. Recognition and payment of income taxes, $20,000.
10. Recognition of depreciation expense, $17,000.
*11. Acquisition of fixed assets for cash, $287,000.
*12. Sale of fixed assets at book value, $10,000.
*13. Issuance of long-term debt, $120,000.
*14. Issuance of common stock, $98,000.
*15. Declaration and payment of dividends, $19,000.

Exhibit 11-4 applies the balance sheet equation to the Eco-Bag Company data. We can see, step by step, how the statement of cash flows in Exhibit 11-3 is based on the same theoretical foundation that underlies the other financial statements.

When statements become complicated, accountants prefer to use work sheets or T-accounts to help their analysis. In any event, the totals in the tabulation of Exhibit 11-4 show that all transactions affecting cash have been accounted for. The $9,000 decrease in cash is explained by the changes in the liability, stockholders' equity, and noncash asset accounts. Each noncash account can be analyzed in detail if desired.

Exhibit 11-4		Δ Cash	=	Δ L	+ Δ SE	− Δ NCA
Conceptual Foundation: The Balance Sheet Equation (in thousands of dollars)	Operating activities:					
	1. Sales on credit		=		+200	− (+200)
	*2. Cash collections from customers	+180	=			− (− 180)
	3. Cost of goods sold		=		−100	− (− 100)
	4. Inventory purchases on account		=	+140		− (+140)
	*5. Payments to suppliers	− 72	=	− 72		
	6. Wages and salaries expense		=	+ 36	− 36	
	*7. Payments to employees	− 15	=	− 15		
	*8. Interest expense paid	− 4	=		− 4	
	*9. Income taxes paid	− 20	=		− 20	
	Net cash provided by operating activities, a subtotal	69				
	Expenses not requiring cash:					
	10. Depreciation		=		− 17	− (− 17)
	Net income, a subtotal				+ 23	
	Investing activities:					
	*11. Acquire fixed assets	−287	=			− (+287)
	*12. Dispose of fixed assets	+ 10	=			− (− 10)
	Financing activities:					
	*13. Issue long-term debt	+120	=	+120		
	*14. Issue common stock	+ 98	=		+ 98	
	*15. Pay dividends	− 19	=		− 19	
	Net changes	− 9	=	+209	+102	− (+320)

Computing Cash Flows from Operating Activities

The first major section in Eco-Bag Company's statement of cash flows (Exhibit 11-3, p. 496) is *cash flows from operating activities*. The section might also be called *cash flow from operations, cash provided by operations*, or, if operating activities decrease cash, *cash used for operations*.

Collections from sales to customers are almost always the major operating activity that increases cash. Correspondingly, disbursements for purchases of goods to be sold and operating expenses are almost always the major operating cash outflows. The excess of collections over disbursements is the net cash provided by operating activities. In Exhibit 11-3, collections of $180,000 minus the $111,000 of operating disbursements equals net cash provided by operating activities, $69,000.

Working from Income Statement Amounts to Cash Amounts

Many accountants build the statement of cash flows from the *changes* in balance sheet items, a few additional facts, and a familiarity with the typical causes of changes in cash. For instance, for convenience the $180,000 amount of cash collections from Eco-Bag Company customers for 19X2 was given in our example. However, most accounting systems do not provide such a balance. Therefore, accountants often compute the collections by beginning with the sales revenue shown on the income statement (an amount calculated using the accrual basis) and adding a decrease (or deducting an increase) in the accounts receivable balance. A detailed analysis of collections and other operating items follows.

a. Eco-Bag Company recognized $200,000 of revenue in 19X2, but because accounts receivable increased by $20,000, only $180,000 was collected from customers:

Sales	$200,000
+ Beginning accounts receivable	25,000
Potential collections	$225,000
− Ending accounts receivable	45,000
Cash collections from customers	$180,000

or

Sales	$200,000
Decrease (increase) in accounts receivable	(20,000)
Cash collections from customers	$180,000

Note that a decrease in accounts receivable means that collections exceeded sales. Conversely, an increase in accounts receivable means sales exceeded collections.

b. The difference between the $100,000 cost of goods sold and the $72,000 cash payment to suppliers is accounted for by changes in inventory *and* accounts payable. The $40,000 increase in inventory indicates that purchases exceeded the cost of goods sold by $40,000:

Ending inventory	$100,000
+ Cost of goods sold	100,000
Inventory to account for	$200,000
− Beginning inventory	(60,000)
Purchases of inventory	$140,000

Although purchases were $140,000, payments to suppliers were only $72,000. Why? Because trade accounts payable increased by $68,000, from $6,000 to $74,000:

Beginning trade accounts payable	$ 6,000
+ Purchases	140,000
Total amount to be paid	$ 146,000
− Ending trade accounts payable	(74,000)
Accounts paid in cash	$ 72,000

The effects of inventory and trade accounts payable can be combined as follows:

Cost of goods sold	$100,000
Increase (decrease) in inventory	40,000
Decrease (increase) in trade accounts payable	(68,000)
Payments to suppliers	$ 72,000

c. Cash payments to employees were only $15,000 because the wages and salaries expense of $36,000 was offset by a $21,000 increase in wages and salaries payable:

Beginning wages and salaries payable	$ 4,000
+ Wages and salaries expense	36,000
Total to be paid	$ 40,000
− Ending wages and salaries payable	(25,000)
Cash payments to employees	$ 15,000

or

Wages and salaries expense	$ 36,000
Decrease (increase) in wages and salaries payable	(21,000)
Cash payments to employees	$15,000

d. Notice that both interest payable and income taxes payable were zero at the beginning and at the end of 19X2. Therefore the entire $4,000 interest expense and the $20,000 income tax expense were paid in cash in 19X2.

Comparsion of Income Statement and Cash Flow Statement

Accrual-based measures of revenue and expense are reported in the income statement. Most of these are naturally linked to related asset or liability accounts and the cash effects of the revenue and expense transactions are moderated by changes in their related asset or liability accounts. The indirect method adjusts accrual-based values for changes in account balances. The following illustration emphasizes the process.

Exhibit 11-5

Comparison of Net Income and Net Cash Provided by Operating Activities

Panel I.   THE GENERAL CASE: Common Adjustments to Convert Income Statement Amounts to Cash Flow Amounts

Income Statement Amount	Related Noncash Asset	Related Liability
Sales revenue	Accounts receivable	Unearned revenue
Cost of goods sold	Merchandise inventory	Accounts payable
Wage expense	Prepaid wages	Wages payable
Rent expense	Prepaid rent	Rent Payable
Insurance expense	Prepaid insurance	Insurance payable
Depreciation expense	Plant, property, or equipment	
Amortization expense	Intangible asset	

Panel II.   THE ECO–BAG COMPANY EXAMPLE

Income Statement		Asset Change	Liability Change		Cash Flow Statement
		− Increases +Decreases	+ Increases −Decreases		
Sales revenue	$200,000	$ (20,000)		=	$180,000
Cost of goods sold	(100,000)	(40,000)	$68,000	=	(72,000)
Wage and salary expense	(36,000)		21,000	=	(15,000)
Interest expense	(4,000)			=	(4,000)
Income taxes	(20,000)			=	(20,000)
Depreciation	(17,000)	17,000			
Net income	$ 23,000	$ (43,000)	$89,000		$ 69,000

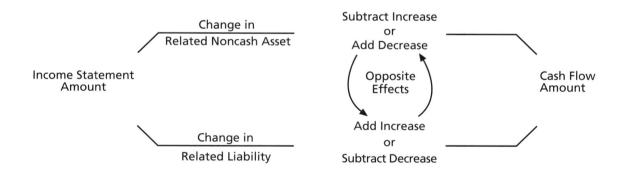

Income Statement Amount — Change in Related Noncash Asset → Subtract Increase or Add Decrease — Opposite Effects — Add Increase or Subtract Decrease ← Change in Related Liability → Cash Flow Amount

Note that liability changes have opposite effects from asset changes. Each revenue or expense account has a related asset and/or liability account, some examples of which are shown in Panel I of Exhibit 11-5.

Panel II of Exhibit 11-5 summarizes the application of this concept to the details of the Eco-Bag Company. For example, the $20,000 increase in accounts receivable indicates that not all of the sales were collected, so sales revenue is reduced from $200,000 to $180,000, the actual cash collected. Similarly, the $40,000 increase in inventory indicates that we might have paid for more goods than we sold, an additional use of cash. This effect is offset by the increase in accounts payable of $68,000. We delayed the use of cash by increasing our trade credit.

Computing Cash Flows from Investing and Financing Activities

cash flows from investing activities
The second major section of the statement of cash flows describing purchase or sale of plant, property, equipment, and other long-lived assets.

cash flows from financing activities
The third major section of the statement of cash flows describing flows to and from providers of capital.

The second and third major sections of the statement of cash flow are **cash flows from investing activities** and **cash flows from financing activities.** The former lists cash flows from the purchase or sale of plant, property, equipment, and other long-lived assets. The latter shows cash flows to and from providers of capital. If the necessary information regarding these cash flows is not directly available, accountants analyze *changes* in all balance sheet items *except* cash. The following rules pertain:

- *Increases in cash (cash inflows)*
    Increases in liabilities or stockholders' equity
    Decreases in noncash assets
- *Decreases in cash (cash outflows)*
    Decreases in liabilities or stockholders' equity
    Increases in noncash assets

Consider Eco-Bag Company's balance sheet (Exhibit 11-3, p. 496). All noncash *current* assets and *current* liabilities of the company were affected only by operating activities. Three *noncurrent* accounts—(a) fixed assets, (b) long-term debt, and (c) stockholders' equity—affect the cash flows from investing activities ($277,000 outflow) and financing activities ($199,000 inflow), respectively.

a. Net fixed assets increased by $260,000 in 19X2, as you can see by examining the balance sheet in Exhibit 11-3. Three items usually explain changes in net fixed assets: (1) assets acquired, (2) asset dispositions, and (3) depreciation expense for the period. Therefore:

Increase in net plant assets = Acquisitions – Disposals – Depreciation expense

Preparing the cash flow from investing activities requires some knowledge of the year's activity. But sometimes incomplete information can be used to figure out the unknown part. For example, you might know the increase in net plant assets, acquisitions of new fixed assets, and depreciation expense without knowing about Eco-Bag Company's asset disposals. The book value of disposals could be computed from the above equation:

$$\$260,000 = \$287,000 - \text{Disposals} - \$17,000$$
$$\text{Disposals} = \$287,000 - \$17,000 - \$260,000$$
$$\text{Disposals} = \$10,000$$

Eco-Bag Company received exactly the book value for the assets sold. (Appendix 11A discusses disposals for more or less than book value.) If the amount of disposals was known, but either acquisitions or depreciation expense was unknown, the missing item could be determined by applying this same equation. Both asset acquisitions and asset disposals are *investing activities* that affect cash.

b. Long-term debt increased by $125,000 – $5,000 = $120,000. Long-term debt was issued, a *financing activity* that increased cash.

c. The $102,000 increase in stockholders' equity can be explained by three factors: (1) issuance of capital stock, (2) net income (or loss), and (3) dividends. Therefore:

Increase in stockholders' equity = New issuance + Net income – Dividends

Cash Flows, Or Does It?

Although investors make important economic decisions on the basis of the so-called bottom line, one *Forbes* writer claims that earnings numbers reported by companies have become "virtually worthless" as a measure of what is really happening inside a company. In support of this claim the writer cited the case of Prime Motor Inns, the world's second-largest hotel operator, which reported earnings of $77 million on revenues of $410 million for 1989. That is a return on sales (net income ÷ revenues) of nearly 19%. Moreover, revenues increased by nearly 11% from the preceding year. Despite its impressive earnings performance, Prime lacked the cash to meet its obligations. Prime filed for Chapter 11 bankruptcy in September 1990. Under bankruptcy protection, a firm's obligations to its creditors are frozen as management figures out how to pay its creditors. How can a firm with $77 million in earnings file for bankruptcy about a year later?

Much of Prime's reported earnings in 1989 arose from *selling* hotels. When outside financing for the hotel sales became harder to obtain, Prime financed the sales itself by accepting notes and mortgages receivable from the buyer. Hotel sales cannot continue forever, and when the seller finances the transaction, the reported gain may exceed the cash received. In the same year that Prime reported a net income of $77 million, an astute analyst would have noted that Prime had a net cash *outflow* from operations of $15 million, compared with the net cash inflow of $58 million in the previous year.

On July 31, 1992, the plan of reorganization became effective. Prime entered bankruptcy with 141 hotels and emerged half as large, with 75 hotels and a new name, Prime Hospitality Corporation. The new company kept its great stock symbol, "PDQ," and investors who bought the new shares for about $1.50 when the reorganization occurred have done well. In May of 1995, the price was $9.63. On the other hand, the shareholders who bought the old company for $35 per share in 1989 watched their investment fall to under $1 in one year.

An analysis of the cash flow statement *in conjunction* with the earnings statement provides a complete perspective on the company's operating results. Surprisingly, given its usefulness, the cash flow statement is a latecomer to GAAP in the United States. The current form is specified in SFAS 95, which became effective in 1988. The value of this statement to investors is becoming more widely understood. For example, in the United Kingdom, British companies have been required to provide a cash flow statement since 1992. ∎

Sources: "Cash Flow Statements Should Be of Help in Diagnosing the Health of a Company," Financial Times *(February 21, 1992); Dana Wechsler Linden, "Lies of the Bottom Line,"* Forbes *(November 12, 1990), p. 106; John R. Dorfman, "Stock Analysts Increase Focus on Cash Flow,"* Wall Street Journal *(February 14, 1987), p. 35;* Prime Motor Inns, Inc., *1989 Annual Report;* Prime Hospitality Corporation, *1993 annual report,* NYSE Stock Reports, *February 1991 and 1995.*

Suppose data about the issuance of new capital stock had not been provided:

$$\$102,000 = \text{New issuance} + \$23,000 - \$19,000$$
$$\text{New issuance} = \$102,000 - \$23,000 + \$19,000$$
$$\text{New issuance} = \$98,000, \text{ an inflow of cash}$$

Both the issuance of new shares and the payment of cash dividends are *financing activities* that affect cash.

Reexamine the statement of cash flows in Exhibit 11-3. The asset acquisitions and disposals from paragraph **a** are listed with cash flows from investing activities, and the effects of debt and equity issues and dividend payments from paragraphs **b** and **c** are shown with cash flows from financing activities.

Noncash Investing and Financing Activities

Major investment and financing activities that do not affect cash must be reported in a schedule that accompanies the statement of cash flows. In our example, Eco-Bag Company did not have any noncash investing or financing activities. But suppose Eco-Bag Company had the following such activities:

1. Acquired a $14,000 fixed asset by issuing common stock.
2. Acquired a small building by signing a mortgage payable for $97,000.
3. Long-term debt of $35,000 was converted to common stock.

These items affect the balance sheet equation as follows:

	Δ Cash = Δ L	+ Δ SE	−	Δ NCA
1.	0 =	+$14,000 [Increase Common Stock]	− (+$14,000)	[Increase Fixed Asset]
2.	0 = +$97,000 [Increase Mortgage payable]		− (+$97,000)	[Increase Building]
3.	0 = −$35,000 [Decrease Long-term Debt]	+$35,000 [Increase Common Stock]		

None of these transactions affect cash, and therefore they do not belong in a statement of cash flows. On the other hand, each transaction is almost identical to one involving cash flows. For example, a company might accomplish the first by issuing common stock for $14,000 cash and immediately using the cash to purchase the fixed asset. Because of the similarities between these noncash transactions and ones involving cash, readers of statements of cash flows should be informed of such noncash activities. Therefore such items must be included in a separate schedule accompanying the statement of cash flows. Eco-Bag Company's schedule for these additional transactions would be:

Schedule of noncash investing and financing activities:	
Common stock issued to acquire fixed asset	$14,000
Mortgage payable for acquisition of building	$97,000
Common stock issued on conversion of long-term debt	$35,000

■ PREPARING A STATEMENT OF CASH FLOWS— THE INDIRECT METHOD

The Eco-Bag Company statement of cash flows in Exhibit 11-3 used the direct method to compute net cash provided by operating activities. The alternative, and often more convenient, *indirect method* of computing cash flows from operating activities reconciles net income to the net cash provided by operating activities. It also shows the link between the income statement and the statement of cash flows.

Using the direct method, the cash flow effect of each operating activity is calculated by adjusting the income statement amounts for changes in related asset and liability accounts. Simply stated, the indirect method considers the same changes in related asset and liability accounts but shows their effects directly on the net income number, rather than on the individual revenue and expense items that comprise net income.

Reconciliation of Net Income to Net Cash Provided by Operations

In the indirect method, the statement begins with net income. Then additions or deductions are made for changes in related asset or liability accounts, that is, for items that affect net income and net cash flow differently. Using the numbers in our Eco-Bag Company example, Exhibit 11-6 shows the reconciliation. As we saw in Exhibit 11-5, net cash provided by operating activities exceeds net income by $46,000. If a company uses the direct method, the FASB requires a reconciliation such as Exhibit 11-6 as a *supporting schedule* to the statement of cash flows.

Consider the logic applied in the reconciliation in Exhibit 11-6:

1. Depreciation is added back to net income because it was deducted in the computation of net income. To calculate cash provided by operations, the depreciation of $17,000 would not have been subtracted. Why? Because it used no cash. Since it *was* subtracted in computing net income, it must now be added back to income to get cash from operations. The addback simply cancels the earlier deduction.

2. Increases in noncash current assets such as receivables and inventory result in less cash flow from operations. For instance, suppose the $20,000 increase in receivables was a result of credit sales made near the end of the year. The $20,000 sales figure would be included in the computation of net income, but the $20,000 would not have increased cash flow from operations. Therefore the reconciliation deducts the $20,000 from the net income to help pinpoint the effects on cash.

Exhibit 11-6			
Eco-Bag Company Reconciliation of Net Income to Net Cash Provided by Operating Activities (in thousands)	Net income		$23
	Adjustments to reconcile net income to net cash provided by operating activities:		
	Depreciation	$ 17	
	Net increase in accounts receivable	(20)	
	Net increase in inventory	(40)	
	Net increase in accounts payable	68	
	Net increase in wages and salaries payable	21	
	Total additions and deductions		46
	Net cash provided by operating activities		$69

3. Increases in current liabilities such as accounts payable and wages payable result in more cash flow from operations. For instance, suppose the $21,000 increase in wages payable was attributable to wages earned near the end of the year, but not yet paid in cash. The $21,000 wages expense would be deducted in computing net income, but the $21,000 would not yet have decreased cash flow from operations. Therefore the reconciliation adds the $21,000 to net income to offset the deduction and thereby show the effect on cash.

The general rules for additions and deductions to adjust net income using the indirect method are identical to those for adjusting the line items of the income statement under the direct method. We focus on current assets and liabilities because they are most often tied to operations.

Changes in Noncash Current Assets	**Changes in Noncash Current Liabilities**
deduct increases	add increases
add decreases	deduct decreases
Examples: Accounts Receivable	Examples: Accounts Payable
Inventory	Wages Payable

A final step is to reconcile for gains and loses that are included in net income but arise from investing or financing activities (in contrast to operating activities). Examples, which are explained in Appendix 11A, are:

- Add loss (or deduct gain) from sale of fixed assets
- Add loss (or deduct gain) on extinguishment of debt

Role of Depreciation

The most crucial aspect of a statement of cash flows prepared by the indirect method is how depreciation and other expenses that do not require cash relate to the flow of cash. The way depreciation affects the indirect calculation of cash flow has led to widespread misunderstanding of the role of depreciation in financial reporting, so let us examine this point in detail.

Depreciation is an allocation of historical cost to expense and does not entail a current outflow of cash. Consider again the calculation of Eco-Bag Company's cash flows in Exhibit 11-5. Why is the $17,000 of depreciation added to net income to compute cash flow? Simply to cancel its deduction in calculating net income. Unfortunately, use of the indirect method may at first glance create an erroneous impression that depreciation is added because it, by itself, is a source of cash. If that were really true, a corporation could merely double or triple its bookkeeping entry for depreciation expense when cash was badly needed! What would happen? Cash provided by operations would be unaffected. Suppose depreciation for Eco-Bag Company is doubled:

	With Depreciation of $17,000	**With Depreciation of $34,000**
Sales	$200,000	$ 200,000
All expenses except depreciation (including income taxes)*	(160,000)	(160,000)
Depreciation	(17,000)	(34,000)
Net income	$ 23,000	$ 6,000
Nondepreciation adjustments †	29,000	29,000
Add depreciation	17,000	34,000
Net cash provided by operating activities	$ 69,000	$ 69,000

* $100,000 + $36,000 + $4,000 + $20,000 = $160,000
† From Exhibit 11-6, $(20,000) + $(40,000) + $68,000 + $21,000 = $29,000

The doubling affects depreciation and net income, but it has no direct influence on cash provided by operations, which, of course, still amounts to $69,000. (For additional discussion, see Chapter 9, page 387, the section called "Depreciation and Cash Flows." The effects of depreciation on income tax outflows are explained there.)

Reconciliation Items

We have seen that net income rarely coincides with net cash provided by operating activities. Consequently, many necessary additions or deductions are commonly shown to reconcile net income to net cash provided by operating activities, as explained earlier for depreciation and changes in noncash current assets and current liabilities.

Some other additions and deductions are listed below. Chapter references are shown in parentheses for readers who want to study the nature of the items in more depth:

ADD CHARGES AGAINST INCOME (EXPENSES) NOT REQUIRING CASH	DEDUCT CREDITS TO INCOME (REVENUES) NOT PROVIDING CASH
Depreciation (Chapter 9)	Amortization of premium on bonds payable (Chapter 10)
Depletion (Chapter 9)	Extraordinary and nonoperating gains (Chapter 15)
Amortization of long-lived assets such as patents, copyrights, and goodwill (Chapter 9)	Equity in earnings of affiliated companies (Chapter 13)
Amortization of discount on bonds payable (Chapter 10)	
Extraordinary and nonoperating losses (Chapter 15)	
Income tax expense arising from deferred income taxes (Chapter 14)	

Nike's Cash Flow Statement

Exhibit 11-7 contains a statement of cash flows for Nike, Inc., maker of running shoes and other athletic clothing and equipment. Other publicly held corporations may include more details, but the general format of the statement of cash flows is similar to that shown. Note that Nike uses the indirect method in the body of the statement of cash flows to report the cash flows from operating activities. Most companies use this format.

Most of the items in Exhibit 11-7 have been discussed earlier in the chapter, but one deserves mention here. Proceeds from exercise of options is *cash received* from issuance of shares to executives as part of a stock option compensation plan.

Summary Problems for Your Review

Problem One

The Buretta Company has prepared the data in Exhibit 11-8.

In December 19X2, Buretta paid $54 million cash for a new building acquired to accommodate an expansion of operations. This was financed partly by a new issue of long-term debt for $40 million cash. During 19X2, the company also sold fixed assets for $5 million cash, which was equal to their book value. All sales and purchases of merchandise were on credit.

Because the net income of $4 million was the highest in the company's history, Alice Buretta, the Chairman of the Board, was perplexed by the company's extremely low cash balance.

Exhibit 11-7

Nike, Inc.
Consolidated
Statement of
Cash Flows for the
Year Ended
May 31, 1994
(in thousands)

Cash provided (used) by operations:	
Net income	$298,794
Income charges (credits) not affecting cash:	
Depreciation	64,531
Deferred income taxes and purchased tax benefits	(23,876)
Other non-current liabilities	(3,588)
Other, including amortization	8,067
Changes in certain working capital components:	
Decrease (increase) in inventory	160,823
Decrease (increase) in accounts receivable	23,979
Decrease (increase) in other current assets	6,888
Increase (decrease) in accounts payable, accrued	
liabilities and income taxes payable	40,845
Cash provided by operations	576,463
Cash provided (used) by investing activities:	
Additions to property, plant, and equipment	(95,266)
Disposals of property, plant, and equipment	12,650
Acquisition of subsidiaries:	
Goodwill	(2,185)
Net assets acquired	(1,367)
Additions to other non-current assets	(5,450)
Cash used by investing activities	(91,618)
Cash provided (used) by financing activities:	
Additions to long-term debt	6,044
Reductions in long-term debt including current portion	(56,986)
Decrease in notes payable	(2,939)
Proceeds from exercise of options	4,288
Repurchase of stock	(140,104)
Dividends—common and preferred	(60,282)
Cash used by financing activities	(249,979)
Effect of exchange rate changes on cash	(7,334)
Net increase in cash and equivalents	227,532
Cash and equivalents, beginning of year	291,284
Cash and equivalents, end of year	$518,816

Required

1. Prepare a statement of cash flows from the Buretta data in Exhibit 11-8 on the next page. Ignore income taxes. You may wish to use Exhibit 11-3 (p. 496) as a guide. Use the direct method for reporting cash flows from operating activities.
2. Prepare a supporting schedule that reconciles net income to net cash provided by operating activities.
3. What is revealed by the statement of cash flows? Does it help you reduce Alice Buretta's puzzlement? Why?

Exhibit 11-8			
Buretta Co. **Income Statement** **and Statement of** **Retained Earnings** **for the Year Ended** **December 31, 19X2** **(in millions)**			

Sales			$ 100
Less cost of goods sold:			
Inventory, December 31, 19X1		$ 15	
Purchases		105	
Cost of goods available for sale		$ 120	
Inventory, December 31, 19X2		47	73
Gross profit			$ 27
Less other expenses:			
General expenses		$ 8	
Depreciation		8	
Property taxes		4	
Interest expense		3	23
Net income			$ 4
Retained earnings, December 31, 19X1			7
Total			$ 11
Dividends			1
Retained earnings, December 31, 19X2			$ 10

Trial Balances

	December 31 (in millions)		Increase (Decrease)
	19X2	**19X1**	
Debits			
Cash	$ 1	$ 20	$ (19)
Accounts receivable	20	5	15
Inventory	47	15	32
Prepaid general expenses	3	2	1
Fixed assets, net	91	50	41
	$ 162	$ 92	$ 70
Credits			
Accounts payable for merchandise	$ 39	$ 14	$ 25
Accrued property tax payable	3	1	2
Long-term debt	40	—	40
Capital stock	70	70	—
Retained earnings	10	7	3
	$ 162	$ 92	$ 70

Solution to Problem One

1. See Exhibit 11-9. Cash flows from operating activities were computed as follows (in millions):

Sales	$ 100
Less increase in accounts receivable	(15)
Cash collections from customers	$ 85
Cost of goods sold	$ 73
Plus increase in inventory	32
Purchases	$105
Less increase in accounts payable	(25)
Cash paid to suppliers	$ 80
General expenses	$ 8
Plus increase in prepaid general expenses	1
Cash payment for general expenses	$ 9
Cash paid for interest	$ 3
Property taxes	$ 4
Less increase in accrued property tax payable	(2)
Cash paid for property taxes	$ 2

Exhibit 11-9	**CASH FLOWS FROM OPERATING ACTIVITIES:**	
Buretta Company Statement of Cash Flows for the Year Ended December 31, 19X2 (in millions)	Cash collections from customers	$ 85
	Cash payments:	
	Cash paid to suppliers	$ (80)
	General expenses	(9)
	Interest paid	(3)
	Property taxes	(2) (94)
	Net cash used by operating activities	$ (9)
	CASH FLOWS FROM INVESTING ACTIVITIES:	
	Purchase of fixed assets (building)	$ (54)
	Proceeds from sale of fixed assets	5
	Net cash used by investing activities	(49)
	CASH FLOWS FROM FINANCING ACTIVITIES:	
	Long-term debt issued	$ 40
	Dividends paid	(1)
	Net cash provided by financing activities	39
	Net decrease in cash	$ (19)
	Cash balance, December 31, 19X1	20
	Cash balance, December 31, 19X2	$ 1

Exhibit 11-10	Net income (from income statement)	$ 4
Supporting Schedule to Statement of Cash Flows. Reconciliation of Net Income to Net Cash Provided by Operating Activities for the Year Ended December 31, 19X2 (in millions)	Adjustments to reconcile net income to net cash provided by operating activities:	
	Add: Depreciation, which was deducted in the computation of net income but does not decrease cash	8
	Deduct: Increase in accounts receivable	(15)
	Deduct: Increase in inventory	(32)
	Deduct: Increase in prepaid general expenses	(1)
	Add: Increase in accounts payable	25
	Add: Increase in accrued property tax payable	2
	Net cash used by operating activities	$ (9)

2. Exhibit 11-10 reconciles net income to net cash provided by operating activities.
3. The statement of cash flows shows where cash has come from and where it has gone. Operations used $9 million of cash. Why? The statement in Exhibit 11-9, which uses the direct method, shows the result clearly: $94 million in cash paid for operating activities exceeded $85 million in cash received from customers. The indirect method, in Exhibit 11-10, shows why, in a profitable year, operating cash flow could be negative. The three largest items differentiating net income from cash flow are changes in inventory, accounts receivable, and accounts payable. Sales during the period were not collected in full. Indeed, accounts receivable rose sharply, by $15 million, a 300% increase. Similarly, cash was committed to inventory growth, although much of that growth was financed by increased accounts payable. In summary, large increases in accounts receivable ($15 million) and inventory ($32 million), plus a $1 million increase in prepaid expenses, used $48 million of cash. In contrast, only $39 million (that is, $4 + $8 + $25 + $2 million) was generated.

Investing activities also consumed cash because $54 million was invested in a building, and only $5 million was received from sales of fixed assets. Financing activities generated $39 million cash, which was $19 million less than the $58 million used by operating and investing activities.

Alice Buretta should no longer be puzzled. The statement of cash flows shows clearly that cash payments exceeded receipts by $19 million. However, she may still be concerned about the depletion of cash. Either operations must be changed so that they do not require so much cash, or investment must be curtailed, or more long-term debt or ownership equity must be raised. Otherwise Buretta Company would soon run out of cash.

Problem Two

To understand how cash flow and net income vary during the life cycle of a business, consider the following example that portrays the four-year life of a short-lived merchandising company, Trend-2000. The first year the entrepreneurs bought twice as much as they sold because they were building their base inventory levels. Trend-2000 suppliers offered payment terms that resulted in 80% of each year's purchases being paid during that year and 20% in the next year. Sales were for cash with a 100% markup on cost. Selling activities were constant over the life of the business and were paid in cash. At the end of the fourth year the suppliers were paid in full and all of the inventory was sold. Use the following summary results to prepare four income statements and statements of cash flow from operations for Trend-2000, one for each year of its life.

	Year 1	Year 2	Year 3	Year 4
Purchases	2,000 units	1,500 units	1,500 units	1,000 units
$1 each	$2,000	$1,500	$1,500	$1,000
Sales	1,000 units	1,500 units	2,000 units	1,500 units
$2 each	$2,000	$3,000	$4,000	$3,000
Cost of sales	$1,000	$1,500	$2,000	$1,500
Selling expense	$1,000	$1,000	$1,000	$1,000
Merchandise payments*	$1,600	$1,600	$1,500	$1,300

*.8×2,000 = 1,600; (.2×2,000) + (.8×1,500) = 1,600; (.2×1,500) + (.8×1,500) = 1,500; (.2×1,500) + (1.0×1,000) = 1,300

Solution to Problem Two

	Year 1	Year 2	Year 3	Year 4	Total
Income statement					
Sales	$2,000	$3,000	$4,000	$3,000	$12,000
Cost of sales	1,000	1,500	2,000	1,500	6,000
Selling expenses	1,000	1,000	1,000	1,000	4,000
Net income	$ 0	$ 500	$1,000	$ 500	$ 2,000
Cash flows from Operations: Direct method					
Collections	$2,000	$3,000	$4,000	$3,000	$12,000
Payments on account	1,600	1,600	1,500	1,300	6,000
Payments for selling efforts	1,000	1,000	1,000	1,000	4,000
Cash flow from operations	$ (600)	$ 400	$1,500	$ 700	$ 2,000
Cash flows from Operations: Indirect method					
Net income	$ 0	$ 500	$1,000	$ 500	$ 2,000
– Increase in inventory	(1,000)				(1,000)
+Decrease in inventory			500	500	1,000
+Increase in accounts payable	400				400
– Decrease in accounts payable		(100)		(300)	(400)
	$ (600)	$ 400	$1,500	$ 700	$ 2,000

Balance Sheet Accounts at the end of:	Year 1	Year 2	Year 3	Year 4
Merchandise inventory	$1,000	$1,000	$ 500	$ 0
Accounts payable	$ 400	$ 300	$ 300	$ 0

This problem illustrates the difference between accrual-based earnings and cash flows. Observe that significant cash outflows occur for operations during the first year as payments to acquire inventory far exceed collections from customers. In fact, it is not until the third year that cash flow from operations exceeds net earnings for the year.

Highlights to Remember

The statement of cash flows focuses on the changes in cash and the activities that cause those changes. Accrual-based net income is a useful number, but we also ask, How did our cash position change? How much of the change in cash was caused by operating activities? By investing activities such as buying another company or new plant and equipment? By financing activities such as borrowing from a bank, issuing bonds, or paying dividends to shareholders?

The direct method of calculating net cash provided by operations requires that we restate each income element. We convert revenue to cash collected from customers, cost of goods sold to cash paid to suppliers, and so on. These cash items are then combined directly to yield cash from operations. The more common method in practice is the indirect method, which starts with net income and adjusts it for the differences, typically account by account, between accrual income and operating cash flow. Both methods yield the same result.

Under the indirect method, depreciation is added to net income because it is an expense not requiring the use of cash. In addition to depreciation, other items affect the reconciliation of net income to cash from operations. Examples covered in the text through Chapter 11 include depletion, amortization of bond premium and discount, and amortization of goodwill.

Appendix 11A: More on the Statement of Cash Flows

Objective 7

Explain treatment of gains and losses from fixed asset sales and debt extinguishments in the statement of cash flows.

This appendix describes two common items that affect the statement of cash flows. One need not be familiar with these items to have a basic understanding of the statement. However, the items occur frequently in the statements of cash flows of major corporations. Some instructors may wish to assign one but not both of the following sections. Each section independently introduces an item for Eco-Bag Company that was not considered in the chapter. An additional item is introduced in Chapter 13 regarding equity method investments and the statement of cash flows.

For purposes of this appendix, we will assume that Eco-Bag Company is concerned with preparing a supporting schedule that reconciles net income to net cash provided by operating activities. For simplicity, we will also assume that none of the changes introduced in this appendix affect income taxes.

Gain or Loss on Disposal of Fixed Assets

In the chapter, the Eco-Bag Company sold fixed assets for their book value of $10,000. More often a fixed asset is sold for an amount that differs from its book value. Suppose the fixed assets sold by Eco-Bag Company for $10,000 had a book value of $6,000 (original cost = $36,000; accumulated depreciation = $30,000). Therefore net income would be $27,000, comprising the $23,000 shown in Exhibit 11-3 (p. 496) plus a $4,000 gain on disposal of fixed assets. (Recall that we are assuming no tax effect.)

Consider first the disposal's effects on cash and income using the balance sheet equation:

$$\Delta \text{ Cash} = \Delta \text{ L} + \Delta \text{ SE} - \Delta \text{ NCA}$$
$$\text{Proceeds} = \quad \text{Gain} - (-\text{Book value})$$
$$\$10,000 = \quad \$4,000 - (-\$6,000)$$

The book value does not affect cash. The statement of cash flows again contains the following item under investing activities:

Proceeds from sale of fixed assets $10,000

The body of the statement of cash flows under the direct method, in the section "Cash flows from operating activities," would not include any gains (or losses) from the disposal of fixed assets. However, consider Exhibit 11-6, p. 505, which reconciles net income to net cash provided by operating activities. The new net income of $27,000, which is the starting point of the reconciliation, already includes the $4,000 gain. To avoid double counting (that is, showing inflows of $4,000 in operating activities and $10,000 in investing activities), Eco-Bag Company must deduct from net income the $4,000 gain on disposal:

Net income	$27,000
Plus adjustments in Exhibit 11-6	46,000
Less gain on disposal of fixed assets	(4,000)
Net cash provided by operating activities	$69,000

Losses on the disposal of assets would be treated similarly except that they would be added back to net income. Suppose the book value of the fixed assets sold by Eco-Bag Company was $17,000, creating a $7,000 loss on disposal and net income of $16,000. The reconciliation would show:

Net income	$16,000
Plus adjustments in Exhibit 11-6	46,000
Plus loss on disposal of assets	7,000
Net cash provided by operating activities	$69,000

Losses and gains on disposal are essentially nonoperating items that are included in net income. As such, their effect must be removed from net income when it is reconciled to net cash flow provided by operating activities.

Gain or Loss on Extinguishment of Debt

Issuing and retiring debt are financing activities. Any gain or loss on extinguishment of debt must be removed from net income in a reconciliation schedule. Suppose Eco-Bag Company paid $37,000 to retire long-term debt with a book value of $34,000, generating a $3,000 loss on extinguishment of debt. Net income would be $23,000 − $3,000 = $20,000. The balance sheet equation would show:

$$\Delta \text{ Cash} = \quad \Delta \text{ L} \quad + \quad \Delta \text{ SE} - \Delta \text{ NCA}$$
$$-\text{Payment} = -\text{Book value} \quad -\text{Loss}$$
$$-\$37,000 = -\$34,000 \quad -\$3,000$$

The $3,000 loss would be added back to net income to determine net cash provided by operating activities:

Net income	$20,000
Plus adjustments in Exhibit 11-6	46,000
Plus loss on retirement of debt	3,000
Net cash provided by operating activities	$69,000

The entire *payment* for debt retirement would be listed among the financing activities:

Proceeds from issue of long-term debt	$120,000
Payment to retire long-term debt	(37,000)
Proceeds from issue of common stock	98,000
Dividends paid	(19,000)
Net cash provided by financing activities	$162,000

Appendix 11B: T-Account Approach to Statement of Cash Flows

Many statements of cash flow can be prepared by using the steps described in the body of the chapter. However, as the facts become complicated, a T-account approach deserves serious consideration. When constructing any cash flow statement, we know that the increases and decreases of cash must total to the change in cash during the year. The T-account approach is simply a methodical procedure for being sure all items are identified.

To illustrate this approach, we will again use the Eco-Bag Company data from Exhibit 11-3. We will also use three facts disclosed earlier: Eco-Bag Company sold assets for their $10,000 book value, paid dividends of $19,000, and issued $98,000 in new stock. Exhibit 11-11 shows the T-accounts that represent the final result that will be obtained when we are finished.

T-Accounts and the Direct Method

This appendix shows how the direct method can be used with T-accounts. The T-accounts are reproduced in Exhibit 11-11. For the direct method, reasonably complete recreations of the summary journal entries for the year are required. The journal entries are shown below, keyed to the entries in Exhibit 11-11. Those involving cash have an asterisk (*).

The T-account approach displayed in Exhibit 11-11 is merely another way of applying the balance sheet equation described in the body of the chapter:

$$\Delta \text{ Cash} = \begin{array}{c}\Delta \text{ Current}\\\text{liabilities}\end{array} + \begin{array}{c}\Delta \text{ Long-term}\\\text{liabilities}\end{array} + \begin{array}{c}\Delta \text{ Stockholders'}\\\text{equity}\end{array} - \begin{array}{c}\Delta \text{ Noncash current}\\\text{assets}\end{array} - \begin{array}{c}\Delta \text{ Fixed assets,}\\\text{net}\end{array}$$

Δ Cash =	Δ Accounts and wages payable	+	Δ Long-term debt	+	Δ Stockholders' equity	−	Δ Accounts receivable and inventory	−	Δ Fixed assets, net
9	68		120		102		20		260
	21						40		
	89						60		

−9 = 89 + 120 + 102 − 60 − 260

1.	Sales on credit:			
	Accounts receivable		200	
	Sales			200
*2	Collection of accounts receivable:			
	Cash		180	
	Accounts receivable			180
3.	Recognition of cost of goods sold:			
	Cost of goods sold		100	
	Inventory			100
4.	Purchases of inventory on credit:			
	Inventory		140	
	Trade accounts payable			140

*5.	Payment of trade accounts payable:		
	Trade accounts payable	72	
	Cash		72
6.	Recognition of wages and salaries expense:		
	Wages and salaries expense	36	
	Wages and salaries payable		36
*7.	Payment of wages and salaries:		
	Wages and salaries payable	15	
	Cash		15
*8.	Recognition of interest accrued and paid:		
	Interest expense	4	
	Cash		4
*9.	Recognition and payment of income taxes:		
	Income tax expense	20	
	Cash		20
10.	Recognition of depreciation expense:		
	Depreciation expense	17	
	Fixed assets, net		17
*11.	Acquisition of fixed assets for cash:		
	Fixed assets, net	287	
	Cash		287
*12.	Sale of fixed assets at book value:		
	Cash	10	
	Fixed assets, net		10
*13.	Issuance of long-term debt:		
	Cash	120	
	Long-term debt		120
*14.	Issuance of common stock:		
	Cash	98	
	Stockholders' equity		98
*15.	Declaration and payment of dividends:		
	Dividends declared and paid	19	
	Cash		19

Again, we focus on the *changes* in the noncash accounts to explain why cash *changed*.

The summarized transactions for 19X2 entered in the Cash account are the basis for the preparation of the formal statement of cash flows, as can be seen by comparing the cash account from Exhibit 11-11 with the statement of cash flows in Exhibit 11-3 (p. 496).

Accounting Vocabulary

11-39, 40, 42, 43

Exhibit 11-11

Eco-Bag Company
T-Account Approach
Using Direct Method
Statement of Cash
Flows
for the Year Ended
December 31, 19X2
(in thousands)

Cash

Bal. 12/31/X1	25		

Operating Activities

2. Collection of accounts receivable	180	5. Pay accounts payable	72
		7. Pay wages and salaries	15
		8. Pay interest	4
		9. Pay taxes	20

Investing Activities

12. Disposal of fixed assets	10	11. Acquisition of fixed assets	287

Financing Activities

13. Issue long-term debt	120	15. Pay dividends	19
14. Issue common stock	98		
Total debits	408	Total credits	417
		Net decrease	9
Bal. 12/31/X2	16		

Accounts Receivable

Bal. 12/31/X1	25		
1. Sales	200	2. Collections	180
Net increase	20		
Bal. 12/31/X2	45		

Accounts Payable

		Bal. 12/31/X1	6
5. Payments	72	4. Purchases	140
		Net increase	68
		Bal. 12/31/X2	74

Inventory

Bal. 12/31/X1	60		
4. Purchases	140	2. Cost of goods sold	100
Net increase	40		
Bal. 12/31/X2	100		

Wages and Salaries Payable

		Bal. 12/31/X1	4
7. Payments	15	6. Accruals	36
		Net increase	21
		Bal. 12/31/X2	25

Fixed Assets, Net

Bal. 12/31/X1	220		
11. Acquisition	287	10. Depreciation	17
		12. Disposals	10
Net increase	260		
Bal. 12/31/X2	480		

Long-Term Debt

		Bal. 12/31/X1	5
		13. New issue	120
		Bal. 12/31/X2	125

Stockholders' Equity

		Bal. 12/31/X1	315
3. Cost of goods sold	100	1. Sales	200
		14. New issue	98
6. Wages	36		
8. Interest	4		
9. Income taxes	20		
10. Depreciation	17		
15. Dividends	19		
Total debits	196	Total credits	298
		Net increase	102
		Bal. 12/31/X2	417

Assignment Material

Special note: The following exercises and problems can be solved without reading beyond page 504, the end of "Preparing a Statement of Cash Flows: The Direct Method": 11-28 through 11-31, 11-34, 11-37, 11-41, 11-42, 11-44, 11-47, 11-49, 11-57, and 11-61.

Questions

11-1. "The statement of cash flows is an optional statement included by most companies in their annual reports." Do you agree? Explain.

11-2. What are the purposes of a statement of cash flows?

11-3. Distinguish between *operating management* and *financial management*.

11-4. Define *cash equivalents*.

11-5. What three types of activities are summarized in the statement of cash flows?

11-6. Name four major operating activities included in a statement of cash flows.

11-7. Name three major investing activities included in a statement of cash flows.

11-8. Name three major financing activities included in a statement of cash flows.

11-9. Where does interest received or paid appear on the statement of cash flows?

11-10. Why is there usually a difference between the cash collections from customers and sales revenue in a period's financial statements?

11-11. What are the two major ways of computing net cash provided by operating activities?

11-12. Demonstrate how the fundamental balance sheet equation can be recast to focus on cash.

11-13. The indirect method for reporting cash flows from operating activities can create an erroneous impression about noncash expenses (such as depreciation). What is the impression, and why is it erroneous?

11-14. An investor's newsletter had the following item: "The company expects increased cash flow in 1996 because depreciation charges will be substantially greater than they were in 1995." Comment.

11-15. "Net losses mean drains on cash." Do you agree? Explain.

11-16. "Depreciation is an integral part of a statement of cash flows." Do you agree? Explain.

11-17. "Cash flow per share can be downright misleading." Why?

11-18. XYZ Company's only transaction in 19X1 was the sale of a fixed asset for cash of $20,000. The income statement included only "Gain on sale of fixed asset, $5,000." Correct the following statement of cash flows:

Cash flows from operating activities:	
Gain on sale of fixed asset	$ 5,000
Cash flows from investing activities:	
Proceeds from sale of fixed asset	20,000
Total increase in cash	$25,000

11-19. Why are noncash investing and financing activities listed on a separate schedule accompanying the statement of cash flows?

11-20. The Lawrence Company sold fixed assets with a book value of $5,000 and recorded a $4,000 gain. How should this be reported on a statement of cash flows?(Appendix 11a).

11-21. A company acquired a fixed asset in exchange for common stock. Explain how this transaction should be shown, if at all, in the statement of cash flows. Why is your suggested treatment appropriate?

11-22. A company operated at a profit for the year, but cash flow from operations was negative. Why might this occur? What industry or industries might find this a common occurrence?

11-23. Suppose a company paid off a $1 million short-term loan to one bank with the proceeds from an identical loan from another bank. The change in the short-term debt account would be zero. Should anything appear in the statement of cash flows? Explain.

11-24. Suppose the loan in the preceding question was renewed at the same bank. Does this change the answer? Explain.

11-25. Do all changes in current assets and liabilities affect cash flows from operations? If not, give an example of an account that does not.

11-26. Suppose an auto company introduced a five-year, 50,000-mile warranty plan to replace the old two-year, 20,000-mile plan. Would this be likely to require an adjustment to cash flow from operations under the indirect method?

11-27. A company operated at a loss for the year, but cash flow from operations was positive. Why might this occur? What industry or industries might find this a common occurrence?

Exercises

11-28   Cash Received from Customers
Good Foods, Inc., had sales of $730,000 during 19X1, 80% of them on credit and 20% for cash. During the year, accounts receivable increased from $65,000 to $75,000, an increase of $10,000. What amount of cash was received from customers during 19X1?

11-29   Cash Paid to Suppliers
Cost of goods sold for Good Foods, Inc., during 19X1 was $480,000. Beginning inventory was $105,000, and ending inventory was $125,000. Beginning trade accounts payable were $24,000, and ending trade accounts payable were $44,000. What amount of cash was paid to suppliers?

11-30   Cash Paid to Employees
Good Foods, Inc., reported wage and salary expenses of $250,000 on its 19X1 income statement. It reported cash paid to employees of $215,000 on its statement of cash flows. The beginning balance of accrued wages and salaries payable was $20,000. What was the ending balance in accrued wages and salaries payable? Ignore payroll taxes.

11-31   Simple Cash Flows from Operating Activities
Beatty and Associates provides accounting and consulting services. In 19X2, net income was $185,000 on revenues of $470,000 and expenses of $285,000. The only noncash expense was depreciation of $30,000. The company has no inventory. Accounts receivable increased by $5,000 during 19X2, and accounts payable and salaries payable were unchanged.

Required   Prepare a statement of cash flows from operating activities. Use the direct method. Omit supporting schedules.

11-32   Net Income and Cash Flow
Refer to Problem 11-31. Prepare a schedule that reconciles net income to net cash flow from operating activities.

11-33   Book Value of Asset Disposals
The UPtown Broadcasting Company reported net fixed assets of $47 million at December 31, 19X5, and $53 million at December 31, 19X6. During 19X6, the company purchased fixed assets for $10 million and had $3 million of depreciation. Compute the book value of the fixed asset disposals during 19X6.

11-34   Financing Activities
During 19X3, the Bremen Shipping Company refinanced its long-term debt. It spent DM 175,000 to retire long-term debt due in 2 years and issued DM 200,000 of 15-year bonds at par. DM signifies deutsche mark, the German monetary unit. It then bought and retired common shares for cash of DM 35,000. Interest expense for 19X3 was DM 22,000, of which DM 20,000 was paid in cash; the other DM 2,000 was still payable at the end of the year. Dividends declared and paid during the year were DM 10,000.

Required   Prepare a statement of cash flows from financing activities.

11-35   Depreciation and Cash Flows
(Alternate is 11-46.) Aballo Company had sales of $970,000, all received in cash. Total operating expenses were $650,000. All except depreciation were paid in cash. Depreciation of $90,000 was included in the $650,000 of operating expenses. Ignore income taxes.

Required

1. Compute net income and net cash provided by operating activities.
2. Assume that depreciation is tripled. Compute net income and net cash provided by operating activities.

11-36 Loss on Disposal of Equipment

Study Appendix 11A. The Lynnwood Insurance Company sold a computer. It had purchased the computer five years ago for $100,000, and accumulated depreciation at the time of sale was $70,000.

Required

1. Suppose Lynnwood received $30,000 cash for the computer. How would the sale be shown on the statement of cash flows?
2. Suppose Lynnwood received $20,000 for the computer. How would the sale be shown on the statement of cash flows (including the schedule reconciling net income and net cash provided by operating activities)?
3. Redo requirement 2 assuming cash received was $50,000.

11-37 Identify Operating, Investing, and Financing Activities

The items listed below were found on the 1994 statement of cash flows of the American Telephone and Telegraph Company (AT&T). For each item, indicate which section of the statement should contain the item—the operating, investing, or financing section. Also indicate whether AT&T uses the direct or indirect method for reporting cash flows from operating activities.

a. Proceeds from long-term debt issuance
b. Net income (loss)
c. Dividends paid
d. Capital expenditures net of proceeds from sale or disposal of property, plant, and equipment
e. Issuance of common shares
f. Retirements of long-term debt
g. Increase in inventories
h. Increase in short-term borrowing—net
i. Depreciation

Problems 11-38 Cash Provided by Operations

Kellogg Company is the world's leading producer of ready-to-eat cereal products and manufactures numerous other food products. In 1994, net sales of $6.5 billion represented a 4% increase over 1993 and produced a 3.6% earnings increase to $705.4 million. To calculate net earnings, Kellogg recorded $256.1 million in depreciation and other items of revenue and expense not requiring cash reduced cash flow from operations by $51.5 million. Dividends of $313.6 million were paid during 1994. Among the changes in balance sheet accounts during 1994 were (in millions):

Accounts receivable	$ 27.7	increase
Inventories	6.8	decrease
Accrued liabilities	57.4	increase
Other current assets	5.4	increase
Accounts payable	25.7	increase

Required   Compute the net cash provided by operating activities using the indirect method.

— 11-39   Cash Flows from Operating Activities, Indirect Method

Deere & Company's 1994 annual report indicates that it "manufactures, distributes, and finances a full range of agricultural equipment; a broad range of industrial equipment for construction, forestry, and public works; and a variety of lawn and grounds care equipment." During 1994, Deere & Company earned $603.6 million on revenues of approximately $7.6 billion. The following summarized information relates to Deere's statement of cash flows:

	(millions of dollars)
Provision for depreciation	$292.8
Principal payments on long-term borrowing	590.7
Proceeds from long-term borrowing	188.5
Other noncash operating expenses	13.6
Decrease in accounts receivable	147.8
Decrease in inventories	164.5
Other increases in cash from operations due to changes in current assets and liabilities	121.1
Purchases of property and equipment	228.1
Dividends paid	171.8

Required   Compute the net cash provided by operating activities. All of the information necessary for that task is provided, together with some information related to other elements of the cash flow statement. Note that the format does not include parentheses to differentiate elements that increase cash from those that (decrease) cash, but the distinction should be clear from the captions.

— 11-40   Cash Flows from Financing Activities

Eli Lilly and Company is a global, research-based corporation that develops, manufactures, and markets pharmaceuticals, medical instruments, diagnostic products, and agricultural products. Its 1994 sales exceeded $6 billion. Lilly's 1994 statement of cash flows included the following items, among others:

Dividends paid	$ (708.4)
Repurchase of common stock	(25.8)
Additions to property and equipment	(633.5)
Depreciation and amortization	398.3
Stock issuances	19.8
Decrease in short-term borrowings	(152.7)
Additions to investments	(1,001.7)
Net income	(480.2)
Additions to long-term debt	383.8
Reductions of long-term debt	(39.8)

Required   Prepare the section "Cash flows from financing activities" from Eli Lilly's 1994 annual report. All items necessary for that section appear above. Some items from other sections have been omitted.

11-41   Statement of Cash Flows, Direct Method

MCI Communications Corporation had cash and cash equivalents of $262 million at the beginning of the year. The following items are on the company's statement of cash flows (in millions) for the year:

Cash received from customers	$7,551
Retirement of debt	(236)
Interest paid, net	(131)
Cash outflow to purchase communications system	(1,274)
Purchase of treasury stock	(24)
Sales of marketable securities	27
Increase in long-term debt	1,077
Cash paid to suppliers and employees	(5,593)
Issuance of common stock for employee stock plans	71
Dividend payments	(54)
Acquisition of Telecom, USA	(1,243)
Other investing activity	28
Taxes paid	(278)

Required   Prepare a statement of cash flows for MCI using the direct method. Include the balance of cash and cash equivalents at year end. Omit the schedule reconciling net income to net cash provided by operating activities and the schedule of noncash investing and financing activities.

11-42   Prepare a Statement of Cash Flows, Direct Method

(Alternate is 11-47.) Fix-it, Inc., is a chain of retail hardware stores. Its cash balance on December 31, 19X6, was $55 thousand, and net income for 19X7 was $414 thousand. Its 19X7 transactions affecting income or cash were (in thousands):

a. Sales of $1,600, all on credit. Cash collections from customers, $1,500.

b. The cost of items sold, $800. Purchases of inventory totaled $850; inventory and accounts payable were affected accordingly.

c. Cash payments on trade accounts payable, $825.

d. Salaries and wages: accrued, $190; paid in cash, $200.

e. Depreciation, $45.

f. Interest expense, all paid in cash, $11.

g. Other expenses, all paid in cash, $100.

h. Income taxes accrued, $40; income taxes paid in cash, $35.

i. Bought plant and facilities for $435 cash.

j. Issued long-term debt for $110 cash.

k. Paid cash dividends of $39.

Required   Prepare a statement of cash flows using the direct method for reporting cash flows from operating activities. Omit supporting schedules.

11-43   Reconcile Net Income and Net Cash Provided by Operating Activities

(Alternate is 11-48.) Refer to Problem 11-42. Prepare a supporting schedule that reconciles net income to net cash provided by operating activities.

11-44   Cash Flows from Investing Activities

Kmart is one of the world's largest retailers offering both discount store and specialty store retailing. For the year ended January 30, 1995, Kmart reported sales of $34,313 million with net earnings of $296 million. The Statement of Cash Flows for the fiscal year ended January 30, 1995, included the following elements:

	(millions)
Divestiture of subsidiary (net)	$ 590
Sale of interest in subsidiary	896
Net income	296
Acquisitions of other companies	(12)
Proceeds from issuance of long-term debt	66
Proceeds from sale of assets	945
Depreciation and amortization	724
(Increase) decrease in inventories	(716)
Reduction in long-term debt	(717)
Reduction in capital lease obligations	(124)
Other investing uses of cash—net	(12)
Capital expenditures—owned property	(1,247)

Required   Prepare the section "Cash flows from investing activities" for Kmart for the year ended January 30, 1995. All items necessary are among those listed in this problem.

11-45   Reconcile Net Income and Net Cash Provided by Operating Activities

Refer to Problem 11-44. Identify the elements in the list that would be part of a schedule reconciling net income to cash provided by operating activities. List at least two items that are missing from the list.

11-46   Depreciation and Cash Flows

(Alternate is 11-35.) The following condensed income statement and reconciliation schedule are from the annual report of Vinales Company (in millions):

Sales	$484
Expenses	460
Net income	$ 24

Reconciliation Schedule of Net Income to Net Cash Provided by Operating Activities

Net income	$ 24
Add noncash expenses:	
Depreciation	25
Deduct net increase in noncash	
operating working capital	(17)
Net cash provided by operating activities	$ 32

A shareholder has suggested that the company switch from straight-line to accelerated depreciation on its annual report to shareholders. He maintains that this will increase the cash flow provided by operating activities. According to his calculations, using accelerated methods would increase depreciation to $45 million, an increase of $20 million; net cash flow from operating activities would then be $52 million.

1. Suppose Vinales Company adopts the accelerated depreciation method proposed. Compute net income and net cash flow from operating activities. Ignore income taxes.

2. Use your answer to requirement 1 to prepare a response to the shareholder.

11-47 Prepare a Statement of Cash Flows

(Alternate is 11-42.) Nakata Importers is a wholesaler of Asian goods. By the end of 19X0, the company's cash balance had dropped to $20 thousand, despite net income of $254 thousand in 19X0. Its transactions affecting income or cash in 19X0 were (in thousands):

a. Sales were $2,510, all on credit. Cash collections from customers were $2,413.

b. The cost of items sold was $1,599.

c. Inventory increased by $56.

d. Cash payments on trade accounts payable were $1,653.

e. Payments to employees were $305; accrued wages payable decreased by $24.

f. Other operating expenses, all paid in cash, were $94.

g. Interest expense, all paid in cash, was $26.

h. Income tax expense was $105; cash payments for income taxes were $108.

i. Depreciation was $151.

j. A warehouse was acquired for $540 cash.

k. Sold equipment for $37; original cost was $196, accumulated depreciation was $159.

l. Received $28 for issue of common stock.

m. Retired long-term debt for $25 cash.

n. Paid cash dividends of $88.

Prepare a statement of cash flows using the direct method for reporting cash flows from operating activities. Omit supporting schedules.

11-48 Reconcile Net Income and Net Cash Provided by Operating Activities
(Alternate is 11-43.) Refer to Problem 11-47. Prepare a supporting schedule to the statement of cash flows that reconciles net income to net cash provided by operating activities.

11-49 Prepare Statement of Cash Flows from Income Statement and Balance Sheet
(Alternate is 11-61.) During 19X4, the Riley Software company declared and paid cash dividends of $10 thousand. Late in the year, the company bought new personal computers for its staff for a cash cost of $125 thousand, financed partly by its first issue of long-term debt. Interest on the debt is payable annually. Several old computers were sold for cash equal to their aggregate book value of $5 thousand. Taxes are paid in cash as incurred. The following data are in thousands:

Income Statement
for the Year Ended
December 31, 19X4

Sales		$316
Cost of sales		154
Gross margin		162
Salaries	$ 82	
Depreciation	40	
Cash operating expenses	15	
Interest	2	139
Income before taxes		23
Income taxes		8
Net income		$ 15

Balance Sheets

	December 31		Increase (Decrease)
	19X4	19X3	
Assets			
Cash and cash equivalents	$ 97	$ 5	$ 92
Accounts receivable	40	95	(55)
Inventories	57	62	(5)
Total current assets	194	162	32
Fixed assets, net	190	110	80
Total assets	$384	$272	$112
Liabilities and Stockholders' Equity			
Accounts payable	$ 21	$ 16	$ 5
Interest payable	2	—	2
Long-term debt	100	—	100
Paid-in capital	220	220	—
Retained income	41	36	5
Total liabilities and stockholders' equity	$384	$272	$112

Required   Prepare a statement of cash flows. Use the direct method for reporting cash flows from operating activities. Omit supporting schedules.

11-50   Indirect Method: Reconciliation Schedule in Body of Statement
Refer to Problem 11-49. Prepare a statement of cash flows that includes a reconciliation of net income to net cash provided by operating activities in the body of the statement.

11-51   Cash Flows, Indirect Method
The Edgardo Company has the following balance sheet data (in millions):

	December 31				December 31		
	19X7	19X6	Change		19X7	19X6	Change
Current assets:				Current liabilities (detailed)	$105	$ 30	$ 75
Cash	$ 13	$ 25	$(12)				
Receivables, net	50	15	35	Long-term debt	150	—	150
Inventories	100	50	50	Stockholders' equity	208	160	48
Total current assets	$163	$ 90	$ 73				
Plant assets (net of accumulated depreciation)	300	100	200				
Total assets	$463	$190	$273	Total liabilities and stockholders' equity	$463	$190	$273

Net income for 19X7 was $60 million. Net cash inflow from operating activities was $80 million. Cash dividends paid were $12 million. Depreciation was $30 million. Fixed assets were purchased for $230 million, $150 million of which was financed via the issuance of long-term debt outright for cash.

Edgardo Freytes, the President and majority stockholder of Edgardo, was a superb operating executive. He was imaginative and aggressive in marketing and ingenious and creative in production. But he had little patience with financial matters. After examining the most recent balance sheet and income statement, he muttered, "We've enjoyed ten years of steady growth; 19X7 was our most profitable ever. Despite such profitability, we're in the worst cash position in our history. Just look at those current liabilities in relation to our available cash! This whole picture of the more you make, the poorer you get, just does not make sense. These statements must be cockeyed."

Required

1. Prepare a statement of cash flows using the indirect method. Include a schedule reconciling net income to net cash provided by operating activities in the body of the statement.
2. Using the statement of cash flows and other information, write a short memorandum to Freytes, explaining why there is such a squeeze on cash.

11-52   Prepare Statement of Cash Flows
The Friedlander Company has assembled the accompanying (a) balance sheets and (b) income statement and reconciliation of retained earnings for 19X9.

Friedlander Co.
Balance Sheets as of December 31 (in millions)

	19X9	19X8	Change
Assets:			
Cash	$ 10	$ 25	$ (15)
Accounts receivable	40	28	12
Inventory	70	50	20
Prepaid general expenses	4	3	1
Plant assets, net	202	150	52
	$326	$256	$ 70
Liabilities and Shareholders' Equity:			
Accounts payable for merchandise	$ 74	$ 60	$ 14
Accrued tax payable	3	2	1
Long-term debt	50	—	50
Capital stock	100	100	—
Retained earnings	99	94	5
	$326	$256	$ 70

Friedlander Co.
Income Statement and Reconciliation of Retained Earnings for the Year Ended December 31, 19X9 (in millions)

Sales		$250
Less cost of goods sold:		
Inventory, Dec. 31, 19X8	$ 50	
Purchases	160	
Cost of goods available for sale	$210	
Inventory, Dec. 31, 19X9	70	140
Gross profit		$110
Less other expenses:		
General expense	$ 51	
Depreciation	40	
Taxes	10	101
Net income		$ 9
Dividends		4
Net income of the period retained		$ 5
Retained earnings, Dec. 31, 19X8		94
Retained earnings, Dec. 31, 19X9		$ 99

On December 30, 19X9, Friedlander paid $98 million in cash to acquire a new plant to expand operations. This was partly financed by an issue of long-term debt for $50 million in cash. Plant assets were sold for their book value of $6 million during 19X9. Because net income was $9 million, the highest in the company's history, Sidney Friedlander, the Chief Executive Officer, was distressed by the company's extremely low cash balance.

Required

1. Prepare a statement of cash flows using the direct method for reporting cash flows from operating activities. You may wish to use Exhibit 11-3, page 496, as a guide.
2. Prepare a schedule that reconciles net income to net cash provided by operating activities.
3. What is revealed by the statement of cash flows? Does it help you reduce Mr. Friedlander's distress? Why? Briefly explain to Mr. Friedlander why cash has decreased even though net income was $9 million.

11-53   Balance Sheet Equation

Refer to Problem 11-52, requirement 1. Support your financial statement by using a form of the balance sheet equation. Step by step, show in equation form how each item in the statement of cash flows affects cash.

11-54   Noncash Investing and Financing Activities

The Aaron Amusement Company operates a chain of video-game arcades. Among Aaron's activities in 19X7 were:

1. Traded four old video games to another amusement company for one new "Flightime" game. The old games could have been sold for a total of $9,000 cash.
2. Paid off $50,000 of long-term debt by paying $30,000 cash and signing a $20,000 six-month note payable.
3. Issued debt for $75,000 cash, all of which was used to purchase new games for its Northwest Arcade.
4. Purchased the building in which one of its arcades was located by assuming the $120,000 mortgage on the building and paying $15,000 cash.
5. Debtholders converted $66,000 of debt to common stock.
6. Refinanced debt by paying cash to buy back an old issue at its call price of $21,000 and issued new debt at a lower interest rate for $21,000.

Required

Prepare a schedule of noncash investing and financing activities to accompany a statement of cash flows.

11-55   Comprehensive Statement of Cash Flows

During the past 30 years, Cascade Toys, Inc., has grown from a single-location specialty toy store into a chain of stores selling a wide range of children's products. Its activities in 19X7 included the following:

a. Purchased 40% of the stock of Kansas Toy Company for $3,846,000 cash.
b. Issued $1,906,000 in long-term debt; $850,000 of the proceeds was used to retire debt that became due in 19X7 and was listed on the books at $900,000.
c. Property, plant, and equipment were purchased for $1,986,000 cash, and property with a book value of $576,000 was sold for $500,000 cash.
d. A note payable was signed for the purchase of new equipment; the obligation was listed at $516,000.
e. Executives exercised stock options for 8,000 shares of common stock, paying cash of $166,000.

f. On December 30, 19X7, bought Sanchez Musical Instruments Company by issuing common stock with a market value of $297,000.

g. Issued common stock for $3,000,000 cash.

h. Withdrew $800,000 cash from a money market fund that was considered a cash equivalent.

i. Bought $249,000 of treasury stock to hold for future exercise of stock options.

j. Long-term debt of $960,000 was converted to common stock.

k. Selected results for the year:

Net income	$ 679,000
Depreciation and amortization	615,000
Increase in inventory	72,000
Decrease in accounts receivable	13,000
Increase in accounts and wages payable	7,000
Increase in taxes payable	25,000
Interest expense	144,000
Increase in accrued interest payable	15,000
Sales	9,739,000
Cash dividends received from investments	159,000
Cash paid to suppliers and employees	8,074,000
Cash dividends paid	240,000
Cash paid for taxes	400,000

Required Prepare a statement of cash flows for 19X7 using the direct method. Include a schedule that reconciles net income to net cash provided by operating activities. Also include a schedule of noncash investing and financing activities.

11-56 Statement of Cash Flows, Direct and Indirect Methods
Nordstrom, Inc., the Seattle-based fashion retailer, had the following income statement for the year ended January 31 (in thousands):

Net sales		$2,893,904
Costs and expenses:		
Cost of sales	$2,000,250	
Selling, general, and administrative	747,770	
Interest	52,228	
Less: Other income	(84,660)	
Total costs and expenses		2,715,588
Earnings before income taxes		$ 178,316
Income taxes		62,500
Net earnings		$ 115,816

The company's net cash provided by operating activities, prepared using the indirect method, was:

Net earnings	$115,816
Adjustments to reconcile net earnings to net cash provided by operating activities:	
Depreciation and amortization	85,615
Changes in:	
Accounts receivable	(39,234)
Merchandise inventories	(28,368)
Prepaid expenses	(20,018)
Accounts payable	8,928
Accrued salaries and wages	24,982
Accrued interest	(963)
Other accrued expenses	6,551
Income taxes payable	(5,182)
Net cash provided by operating activities	$148,127

Required   Prepare a statement showing the net cash provided by operating activities using the direct method. Assume that all "other income" was received in cash and that prepaid expenses and accrued salaries and wages and other accrued expenses relate to selling, general, and administrative expenses.

11-57   Statement of Cash Flows, Direct Method, for a Utility
The Columbia Gas System had operating revenues of $2.4 billion from providing gas services ranging from exploration and production to pipeline transmission to final distribution to users. The company's statement of cash flows contained the following items (some have been slightly summarized):

	(in millions)
Issuance of common stock	$ 225.3
Retirement of long-term debt	(71.7)
Dividends paid	(103.9)
Cash received from customers	2,829.8
Other operating cash receipts	161.2
Capital expenditures	(600.1)
Issuance of long-term debt	204.5
Other financing activities—net	86.0
Cash paid to suppliers	(1,319.2)
Interest paid	(172.5)
Taxes paid	(256.3)
Other investments—net	(166.3)
Cash paid to employees and for their benefit	(445.2)
Other operating cash payments	(377.7)

Required   1. Prepare the statement of cash flows for Columbia Gas using the direct method. Omit the schedule reconciling net income to net cash provided by operating activities.
2. Discuss the relation between operating cash flow and investing and financing needs.

11-58 **Interpreting the Statement of Cash Flows**

The Kellogg Company statement of cash flows appears in Exhibit 11-12.

Required

Use that statement to answer two questions. Does Kellogg generate sufficient cash flow from operations to cover ongoing investing activities and pay dividends to its shareholders? How has Kellogg changed its debt-equity ratio during the period 1992 to 1994?

Exhibit 11-12

Kellogg Company
and Subsidiaries
Consolidated
Statement of Cash
Flows
Years ended
December 31

(millions)	1994	1993	1992
Operating activities			
Net earnings	$705.4	$680.7	$431.2
Items in net earnings not requiring (providing) cash:			
Cumulative effect of accounting change			251.6
Depreciation	256.1	265.2	231.5
Pre-tax gain on sale of subsidiaries	(26.7)	(65.9)	(58.5)
Deferred income taxes	24.5	(22.3)	.1
Other	(49.3)	11.9	34.7
Change in operating assets and liabilities:			
Accounts receivable	(27.7)	(17.7)	(99.1)
Inventories	6.8	13.3	(15.3)
Other current assets	(5.4)	(32.3)	(.9)
Accounts payable	25.7	(5.0)	24.0
Accrued liabilities	57.4	(27.7)	(57.4)
Net cash provided from operating activities	966.8	800.2	741.9
Investing activities			
Additions to properties	(354.3)	(449.7)	(473.6)
Proceeds from sale of subsidiaries	95.5	95.6	115.0
Property disposals	15.6	19.0	18.8
Other	7.8	(25.1)	(10.6)
Net cash used in investing activities	(235.4)	(360.2)	(350.4)
Financing activities			
Net borrowings of notes payable	(111.9)	176.7	21.6
Issuance of long-term debt	200.0	208.3	311.7
Reduction of long-term debt	(2.9)	(1.7)	(270.2)
Issuance of common stock	2.3	2.9	13.4
Common stock repurchases	(327.3)	(548.1)	(224.1)
Cash dividends	(313.6)	(305.2)	(286.4)
Other	(6.1)	2.9	11.4
Net cash used in financing activities	(559.5)	(464.2)	(422.6)
Effect of exchange rate changes on cash	(3.7)	(4.0)	(20.6)
Increase (decrease) in cash and temporary investments	168.2	(28.2)	(51.7)
Cash and temporary investments at beginning of year	98.1	126.3	178.0
Cash and temporary investments at end of year	$266.3	$ 98.1	$126.3

11-59 **Cash Flows from Operating Activities**

Boise Cascade Corporation, the forest products company with headquarters in Boise, Idaho, reported net income of over $75 million. The following data are condensed from the company's income statement and balance sheet (in thousands):

Revenues:	
Sales	$ 4,184,560
Costs and expenses:	
Nondepreciation expenses (summarized)	(3,737,780)
Depreciation	(212,890)
Income from operations	233,890
Interest expense	(116,620)
Interest income	4,130
Income before income taxes	121,400
Income tax provision	46,130
Net income	$ 75,270

		Increase (Decrease)
Current assets:		
Cash	$ 19,781	$ 66
Short-term investments	6,165	639
Receivables	412,558	(9,010)
Inventories	484,972	60,533
Other	74,107	13,038
Total current assets	$997,583	$ 65,266
Current liabilities:		
Current portion of long-term debt	$136,731	$ 106,341
Income taxes payable	140	(4,133)
Notes payable	40,000	40,000
Accounts payable	344,384	(47,158)
Accrued liabilities:		
Compensation and benefits	99,530	(14,552)
Interest payable	38,460	(1,611)
Other	99,127	1,261
Total current liabilities	$758,372	$ 80,148

You have determined that other current assets are all operating items, as are other accrued liabilities. Short-term investments are cash equivalents. Depreciation is the only noncash expense. Interest income is all in cash.

Required

1. Prepare a statement of cash flows from operating activities. Use the direct method that begins with cash collections from customers.
2. Reconcile net income to net cash provided by operating activities. (*Hint*: The cash outflow for nondepreciation expense is an aggregation of more specific outflows. There is no way to break the total amount into its component parts.)

11-60   Prepare Statement of Cash Flows, Indirect Method
The income statement and balance sheets in Exhibit 11-14 (pp. 535) are from a recent annual report of Data I/O, a world leader in developing and marketing computer-aided engineering tools. (The statements are slightly modified to avoid items beyond the scope of this text.) Assume the following information about activities in 19X8:

a.   Depreciation on fixed assets was $3,427,000, which is included in operating expenses.

b. Fixed assets were sold for their book value of $2,186,000; fixed assets were acquired at a cost of $2,351,000.

c. Common stock was purchased for $16,064,000 and retired. Additional common stock was issued for stock options.

d. No notes payable were retired.

Required   Prepare a 19X8 statement of cash flows for Data I/O. Use the indirect method in the body of the statement for reporting cash flows from operating activities.

11-61. Prepare Statement of Cash Flows from Income Statement and Balance Sheet (Alternate is 11-49.) Crevice Company had the following income statement and balance sheet items (in thousands):

Income Statement for the Year Ended December 31, 19X8

Sales	$ 870
Cost of goods sold	(510)
Gross margin	$ 360
Operating expenses	(210)
Depreciation	(60)
Interest	(10)
Income before taxes	$ 80
Income taxes	(25)
Net income	$ 55
Cash dividends paid	(35)
Total increase in retained earnings	$ 20

Balance Sheets

	December 31		Increase (Decrease)
	19X8	**19X7**	
Assets			
Cash	$ 20	$ 60	$ (40)
Accounts receivable	240	150	90
Inventories	450	350	100
Total current assets	$ 710	$560	$ 150
Fixed assets, gross	$ 890	$715	$175
Accumulated depreciation	(570)	(550)	(20)
Fixed assets, net	$ 320	$165	$ 155
Total assets	$1,030	$725	$305
Liabilities and Stockholders' Equity			
Trade accounts payable	$ 520	$300	$220
Long-term debt	245	180	65
Stockholders' equity	265	245	20
Total liabilities and stockholders' equity	$1,030	$725	$305

During 19X8, Crevice purchased fixed assets for $415,000 cash and sold fixed assets for their book value of $200,000. Operating expenses, interest, and taxes were paid in cash. No long-term debt was retired.

Required   Prepare a statement of cash flows. Use the direct method for reporting cash flows from operating activities. Omit supporting schedules.

11-62   Miscellaneous Cash Flow Questions

McDonald's Corporation is a well-known provider of food services around the world. McDonald's statement of cash flows for 1994 is reproduced with a few slight modifications and omissions as Exhibit 11-13. Use that statement and the additional information provided to answer the following questions:

1. In the Financing activities section, all parentheses for 1994 have been removed. Which numbers should be put in parentheses?

Exhibit 11-13   McDonald's Corporation   Consolidated Statement of Cash Flows

(In millions of dollars)	Years ended December 31, 1994	1993
Operating activities		
Net income	$ 1,224.4	$1,082.5
Adjustments to reconcile to cash provided by operations		
Depreciation and amortization	628.6	568.4
Deferred income taxes	(5.6)	52.4
Changes in operating working capital items		
Accounts receivable increase	(51.6)	(48.3)
Inventories, prepaid expenses and other current assets (increase) decrease	(15.0)	(9.6)
Accounts payable increase	105.4	45.4
Accrued interest payable decrease	(25.5)	(5.1)
Taxes and other liabilities increase (decrease)	95.2	26.5
Other–net	(29.7)	(32.4)
Cash provided by operations	1,926.2	1,679.8
Investing activities		
Property and equipment expenditures	1,538.6	(1,316.9)
Sales of restaurant businesses	151.5	114.2
Purchases of restaurant businesses	133.8	(64.2)
Notes receivable additions	15.1	(33.1)
Property sales	66.0	61.6
Notes receivable reductions	56.7	75.7
Other	92.6	(55.3)
Cash used for investing activities	1,505.9	(1,218.0)
Financing activities		
Net short-term borrowings	521.7	(8.9)
Long-term financing issuances	260.9	1,241.0
Long-term financing repayments	536.9	(1,185.9)
Treasury stock purchases	495.6	(620.1)
Common and preferred stock dividends	215.7	(201.2)
Other	39.4	62.6
Cash used for financing activities	426.2	(712.5)
Cash and equivalents increase (decrease)	a	(250.7)
Cash and equivalents at beginning of year	b	436.5
Cash and equivalents at end of year	$ c	$ 185.8

2. In the Investing activities section, all parentheses for 1994 have been removed. Which numbers should be put in parentheses?

3. Estimate the interest expense that was originally deducted in the income statement if interest paid was $323.9 million.

4. The 1994 values for the change in cash and cash equivalents and for beginning and end-of-year balances have been omitted and replaced with the letters *a*, *b*, and *c*. Provide the proper values for these three missing numbers.

5. Retained earnings at December 31, 1993, was $7,612.6 million. Calculate the retained earnings balance at December 31, 1994.

6. Comment on the relation between cash flow from operations and cash used for investing activities.

7. What do you conclude about changes in McDonald's debt-to-equity ratio during this period?

11-63   Statement of Cash Flows, Direct Method, for a Bank

Ithaca Bancorp, Inc., was a savings bank located in Ithaca, New York, with total assets of $541 million. Shortly before it was acquired by M & T Bank, its statement of cash flows contained the following items (some have been slightly summarized):

	(in thousands)
Interest received	$ 52,169
Net (decrease) increase in deposits	(1,360)
Proceeds from sales of real estate acquired through foreclosure	2,507
Fees and commissions received	4,500
Proceeds from security sales and maturities	9,535
Origination of loans held for sale	(34,566)
Proceeds from sales of loans	34,431
Repayments of FHLB borrowings	(59,000)
Principal collection on mortgage-backed securities	3,314
Acquisition of loans and securities	(11,273)
Interest paid	(37,806)
Cash paid to suppliers and employees	(15,989)
Other operating uses of cash	(1,783)
Other investing uses of cash	(1,346)
Proceeds from FHLB borrowings	56,000

Note: Because banks are noticeably different from manufacturing and service companies, their classifications of what constitutes operating, investing, and financing activities also differ. For example, banks treat as financing activities their transactions with the FHLB (Federal Home Loan Bank), which is a source of borrowing and lending. Similarly, the basic deposits that individuals make in the savings bank are treated as financing activities.

Required   Prepare Ithaca Bancorp's statement of cash flows in proper format, using the direct method. Omit the schedule reconciling net income to net cash provided by operating activities.

11-64   T-Account Approach

Study Appendix 11B. Refer to the facts concerning the Buretta Company's "Summary Problem for Your Review" in the chapter (p. 507). Prepare a set of T-accounts that supports the statement of cash flows shown in Exhibit 11-9 (p. 510). Use Exhibit 11-11 (p. 517) as a guide. Key your postings by number.

11-65 T-Account Approach

Study Appendix 11B. Refer to the facts concerning the Friedlander Company in Problem 11-52. Prepare a set of T-accounts that supports the statement of cash flows. Use Exhibit 11-11 (p. 517) as a guide. Key your postings by number.

11-66 T-Account Approach

Study Appendix 11B. Refer to the facts concerning Data I/O, Problem 11-60. Prepare a set of T-accounts that supports the statement of cash flows. Use the direct method for computing net cash flow from operating activities. (This differs from the requirements of 11-60, which asked you to use the indirect method.) Key your postings by number. Use Exhibit 11-11 (p. 517) as a guide. Assume that all sales are on open credit.

Exhibit 11-14

Data I/O

Income Statement at December 31, 19X8 (in thousands)

Net sales	$ 65,117
Cost of goods sold	(26,825)
	38,292
Operating expenses	(31,714)
Earnings before taxes on income	6,578
Taxes on income	(1,973)
Net earnings	$ 4,605

Balance Sheets at December 31 (in thousands)

Assets	19X8	19X7	Increase (Decrease)
Current Assets:			
Cash and cash equivalents	$20,344	$27,014	$ (6,670)
Trade accounts receivable, less allowance for doubtful accounts	14,811	13,796	1,015
Inventories	6,433	6,664	(231)
Prepaid operating expenses	1,317	4,602	(3,285)
Total current assets	42,905	52,076	(9,171)
Fixed assets, gross	34,608	38,091	(3,483)
Accumulated depreciation	(15,344)	(15,565)	221
Net fixed assets	19,264	22,526	(3,262)
Total assets	$62,169	$74,602	$(12,433)

Liabilities and Stockholders' Equity	19X8	19X7	Increase (Decrease)
Current Liabilities:			
Trade accounts payable	$ 2,185	$ 3,173	$ (988)
Accrued operating expenses	9,084	10,004	(920)
Income taxes payable	1,600	1,160	440
Notes payable	1,052	974	78
Total current liabilities	13,921	15,311	(1,390)
Stockholders' equity:			
Common stock, authorized, 30,000,000 shares; issued and outstanding, 6,530,496 and 8,649,672 shares	17,647	33,295	(15,648)
Retained earnings	30,601	25,996	4,605
Total shareholders' equity	48,248	59,291	(11,043)
Total liabilities and stockholders' equity	$62,169	$74,602	$(12,433)

11-67   Interpretation of the Statement of Cash Flows and Ethics
Megasoft was a successful developer of personal computer software in the early 1990s.
The company's peak year was 1992. Since then, both sales and profits have fallen. The
following information is from the company's 1994 annual report (in thousands):

	1994	1993	1992
Net income	$1,500	$4,500	$7,500
Accounts receivable (end of year)	900	1,800	6,000
Inventory (end of year)	1,050	2,100	2,850
Net cash provided by operations	675	1,050	2,250
Capital expenditures	900	1,050	1,350
Proceeds from sales of fixed assets	2,700	1,500	2,250
Net gain on sales of fixed assets plus net extraordinary gains	2,250	1,800	2,400

During 1995, $9 million of short-term loans became due. Megasoft paid off only
$2.25 million and was able to extend the terms on the other $6.75 million. Accounts
payable continued at a very low level in 1995, and the company maintained a large
investment in corporate equity securities, enough to generate $450,000 of dividends
received in 1995. Megasoft neither paid dividends nor issued stock or bonds in 1995. Its
1995 Statement of Cash Flows was as follows:

Megasoft Company Statement of Cash Flows for the Year Ended December 31, 1995 (in thousands)

Cash flows from operating activities:		
Net income	$ 1,050	
Adjustments to reconcile net income to net cash provided by operating activities:		
Depreciation and amortization	600	
Net decrease in accounts receivable	150	
Net decrease in inventory	225	
Investment revenue from equity investments, less $900 of dividends received	(600)	
Gains on sales of fixed assets	(2,100)	
Extraordinary loss on building fire	1,200	
Net cash provided by operating activities		$ 525
Cash flows from investing activities:		
Purchase of fixed assets	$ (600)	
Insurance proceeds on building fire	3,000	
Sale of plant assets	3,750	
Purchase of corporate equity securities	(2,250)	
Net cash provided by investing activities		3,900
Cash flows from financing activities:		
Principal payments on short-term debt to banks	$(2,250)	
Purchase of treasury stock	(900)	
Net cash used for financing activities		(3,150)
Net increase in cash		1,275
Cash, December 31, 1994		1,800
Cash, December 31, 1995		$ 3,075

Required

1. Interpret the Statement of Cash Flows for Megasoft.
2. Describe any ethical issues relating to the strategy and financial disclosures of Megasoft.

11-68 British Versus U.S. Cash Flow Statements

The "Group Cash Flow Statement" for British Petroleum is presented below.

Required

Discuss the differences between this British statement and the common U.S. equivalent.

British Petroleum Group Cash Flow Statement

	£ million	
For the year ended 31 December	1994	1993
Net cash inflow from operating activities	4,406	4,397
Servicing of finance and returns on investments		
Interest received	83	112
Interest paid	(617)	(723)
Dividends received	124	71
Dividends paid	(424)	(439)
Net cash outflow from servicing of finance and returns on investments	(834)	(979)
Taxation		
UK corporation tax	(157)	(149)
Overseas tax	(581)	(532)
Tax paid	(738)	(681)
Investing activities		
Capital expenditures	(2,405)	(2,800)
Acquisitions	–	(38)
Disposal proceeds	786	2,052
Net cash outflow from investing activities	(1,619)	(786)
Net cash inflow before financing	1,215	1,951
Financing		
Issue of ordinary share capital	(47)	(28)
Long-term borrowing	(228)	(290)
Repayments of long-term borrowing	1,323	1,341
Short-term borrowing	(849)	(544)
Repayments of short-term borrowing	818	1,399
Net cash outflow from financing	1,017	1,878
Increase in cash and cash equivalents	198	73
	1,215	1,951

Statement of total recognised gains and losses

Profit for the year	1,577	615
Currency translation differences	145	(200)
Total recognised gains and losses relating to the year	1,722	415
Prior year adjustment–change in accounting policy	–	(276)
Total recognised gains and losses since last annual report	1,722	139

11-69 Wal-Mart Annual Report

Refer to the financial statements contained in Appendix A at the end of the book.

1. Generally, companies have operating cash flow in excess of net earnings because of non-cash expenses such as depreciation. In 1993 and 1994, Wal-Mart's cash flow from operations was well below net income. What was the primary cause of this relation?
2. Why did the pattern from requirement 1 not continue in 1995?
3. Wal-Mart uses the indirect format for its statement of cash flows. Calculate the amount it would show as cash collections from customers using the direct method.

11-70   Compact D from Disclosure
Identify an industry and select two companies within that industry.

1. Determine whether cash flow from operations is stable through time.
2. Relate cash flow from operations to investing and dividend payment needs.
3. Compare cash flow from operations to net income. Explain why they differ.

12 Stockholders' Equity

Learning Objectives

After studying this chapter, you should be able to

1 Describe the rights of shareholders.

2 Differentiate among authorized, issued, and outstanding shares.

3 Explain the characteristics of preferred stock.

4 Discuss similarities and differences between bonds and preferred stock.

5 Identify the economic characteristics of stock splits and dividends.

6 Explain the accounting for stock splits.

7 Differentiate between the accounting for large-percentage and small-percentage stock dividends.

8 Account for treasury stock transactions.

9 Explain and record conversions of preferred stock into common stock.

10 Describe the motivation for and importance of restrictions on retained earnings.

11 Define and use the rate of return on common equity and book value per share.

Business entities obtain economic resources from two sources: debt and equity. The stockholders' equity section of the balance sheet and its related footnotes provide substantial information about the investments made by the owners of the firm. In this chapter we consider two types of equity securities—preferred and common stock—and discuss how to classify and report transactions involving them. Such transactions include issuance, redemption, and reissuance of securities and various types of distributions to the owners of the shares. These distributions may involve cash or other assets, and sometimes, as with stock splits, these distributions may alter the characteristics of the securities. Many of these transactions lead to changes in the retained earnings account.

Sole proprietorships and partnerships are more common business entities than are corporations, but the majority of business activity in terms of volume is conducted by corporations. Therefore we concentrate on the accounting for ownership in the corporate form. A number of the accounting practices for shareholders' equity are based on legal characteristics of corporations, so the chapter includes frequent reference to the rights and privileges of shareholders and the consequences of various financing decisions on the firm and its owners.

Internationally there is substantial variation in the structure of corporate activity and in accounting procedures used to disclose results. At the most basic level we are observing the conversion of many planned economies from state-owned-and-operated business entities into private ones. In regions of the former USSR, decisions are now being made about the geographic boundaries, the form of government, and the structure of private businesses *and* how to own and account for those businesses. Even in the West we increasingly observe that government is selling "public companies" to the private sector. Examples range from the United Kingdom's privatization of British Petroleum in the mid-1980s to New York City's 1994 sale of its public television station. From an accounting perspective, the key point is that many diverse legal structures worldwide lead to plentiful variation in accounting for stockholders' equity internationally.

■ STOCKHOLDERS' EQUITY IN PERSPECTIVE

The owners of a business have a *residual interest* in the assets of the firm after both current and long-term liabilities have been deducted. In prior chapters this residual interest has been separated into *paid-in* (or *contributed*) *capital* and *retained income*, which is the result of profitable operations in prior years. The following balance sheet presentation is condensed from the 1994 annual report of CSX Corporation, a family of international transportation companies offering a variety of rail-freight, container-shipping, and other transportation, warehousing, and distribution services.

CSX Corporation
Shareholders' Equity
(in millions of dollars)

	December 31	
	1994	**1993**
Common stock, $1 par value	$ 105	$ 104
Other capital	1,368	1,307
Retained earnings	2,258	1,769
Total shareholders' equity	$3,731	$3,180

In the footnotes to the financial statements, CSX provides additional disclosures, including the fact that almost 1 million new shares were issued during the year for approximately $57 million. The summary journal entry to record these new shares would be (in millions):

Cash	57	
Common stock		1
Other capital		56

As the journal entry shows, the issue price is far in excess of the par value. CSX labels that excess simply "Other Capital," but the amounts in excess of par value appear under many different names in various corporate balance sheets. Examples are:

- Paid-in capital (Kelly Services, Inc.)
- Additional paid-in capital (Sara Lee Corporation)
- Capital in excess of par value of stock (Ford Motor Company)
- Capital surplus (Coca-Cola Company)

Recall that some states require by law a minimum level of investment by the owners of a company, and this is the amount called par value. Some states use a conceptually equivalent term called the *stated value*, and other states permit issuance of common stock without either a par or a stated value. Thus for antiquated legal reasons the corporation may have two accounts for its common stock, one for par or stated value and one for additional paid-in capital. However, the economic substance of the stock issuance by CSX could be portrayed with one account, as indicated by the following journal entry (in thousands):

Cash	57	
Paid-in capital, common stock		57

Indeed, as you pursue your study of this chapter, keep in mind that distinguishing between the par or stated value, the additional paid-in capital, and retained income has little practical importance for ongoing corporations. To keep perspective, whenever feasible think of stockholders' equity as a single amount.

The highlights of the corporate form of ownership were covered in Chapter 1. In addition, Chapter 1 compared the sole proprietorship, partnership, and corporation on pages 17–19. Please review this material before proceeding.

Corporations are creatures of the state. They are artificial persons created by law. They exist separately from their owners. As persons, corporations may enter into contracts, may sue, and may even marry (by affiliating with another corporation) and produce offspring (corporation subsidiaries). Corporations are also subject to taxation as separate entities.

Shareholders' Rights

Objective 1

Describe the rights of shareholders.

Stockholders (or shareholders) are entitled to (1) vote, (2) share in corporate profits, (3) share residually in corporate assets upon liquidation, and (4) acquire more shares of subsequent issues of stock. The extent of the stockholders' powers is determined by the number and type of shares held.

corporate proxy
A written authority granted by individual shareholders to others to cast the shareholders' votes.

Corporations hold annual meetings of shareholders, when votes are taken on important matters. For example, the shareholders elect the board of directors. They may also vote on changing employee bonus plans, choosing outside auditors, and similar matters. Large corporations make heavy use of the proxy system. A **corporate proxy** is a written authority granted by a shareholder to others (usually members of corporate management) to cast the shareholders' votes. By using a proxy, shareholders may express (vote) their preference without traveling to the site of the annual meeting.

The ultimate power to manage a corporation almost always resides with the common shareholders. But shareholders of publicly owned corporations usually delegate that power to the top managers. As described in Chapter 1, the modern large corporation frequently has a team of professional managers, from the chairman of the board downward. The top managers may have only a token number of shares. The chief executive officer (CEO) is frequently the chairman of the board rather than the president.

preemptive rights
The rights to acquire a pro-rata amount of any new issues of capital stock.

professional corporation A form of corporation providing professional people some corporate benefits without limited liability.

Stockholders also generally have **preemptive rights,** which are the rights to acquire a pro-rata amount of any new issues of capital stock. The preemptive privilege allows present shareholders to purchase additional shares directly from the corporation before the shares can be sold to the general public. In this way, the shareholders are able to maintain their percentage of ownership.

unlimited liability
Legal responsibility not limited by law or contract; personal assets can be seized to satisfy corporate debts.

Perhaps the most important right of common shareholders is *limited liability*, which means that creditors of the corporation have claims only on the assets owned by the corporation, not on the assets of the owners of the corporation. In contrast, the creditors of a partnership have potential rights against the savings, homes, and automobiles of the individual partners. Only in the special case of **professional corporations** do shareholders have **unlimited liability.** Generally, society believes that professionals such as accountants, lawyers, and doctors must be personally responsible for their errors. To assure this responsibility, the states had prohibited them from practicing in the corporate form. In recent years, most states have introduced professional corporations, which provide many advantages of the corporate form (such as certain pension and tax benefits) but deny limited liability to the professionals who own the business.

authorized shares
The total number of shares that may legally be issued under the articles of incorporation.

issued shares The aggregate number of shares potentially in the hands of shareholders.

Authorized, Issued, and Outstanding Stock

outstanding shares
Shares in the hands of shareholders equal to issued shares less treasury shares.

treasury stock A corporation's issued stock that has subsequently been repurchased by the company and not retired.

The state approves the articles of incorporation, which includes authorization of the number and types of capital stock that can be issued. The total number of shares that may be issued is known as the **authorized shares**. When the company receives cash in exchange for stock certificates, the shares become **issued shares**. Shares that are issued and held by the stockholders are called **outstanding shares.** Sometimes a company reacquires shares by purchasing shares from its own shareholders. These shares are called **treasury stock.** They are *issued* but are no longer *outstanding*. As of December 31, 1994, Federal Paper Board Company had authorized 240 million shares of common stock. Of these, 42,573,000 shares had been issued. Since 46,000 shares had been reacquired as treasury shares, the remaining 42,527,000 shares were outstanding. A tabulation shows the relation among authorized, issued, and outstanding shares.

	Number of Shares (in thousands)
Federal Paper Board Company As of December 31, 1994	
Authorized	240,000
Unissued	197,427
Issued	42,573
Deduct: Shares held in treasury	46
Total shares outstanding	42,527

Objective 2

Differentiate among authorized, issued, and outstanding shares.

preferred stock Stock that has some priority over other shares regarding dividends or the distribution of assets upon liquidation.

Objective 3

Explain the characteristics of preferred stock.

■ PREFERRED STOCK

All corporations have common stock, and the shareholders who own it have the rights we have discussed, including the right to elect the board of directors and to vote on matters of policy. Some 25% of U.S. corporations also have *preferred stock* outstanding. As the name implies, some rights of the owners of **preferred stock** take precedence over the rights of common shareholders. These special rights generally pertain to receipt of dividends and receipt of assets if the company is liquidated, as we will discuss.

The preferred stock usually appears in the top part of the stockholders' equity section of the balance sheet, as illustrated in the ALLTEL 1994 annual report. ALLTEL provides telephone service to 1.2 million customers in twenty-five states and also provides cellular telephone services and related communications equipment and services.

ALLTEL
(dollars in thousands)

	December 31	
	1994	1993
Shareholders' equity:		
Preferred stock	$ 9,320	$ 9,405
Common stock	187,981	187,458
Additional capital	339,436	333,698
Unrealized holding gain on investments	84,275	121,507
Retained earnings	1,004,357	902,640
Total shareholders' equity	1,625,369	1,554,708
Total liabilities and capital	$4,713,878	$4,270,458

Preferred stock generally has a specified dividend rate, which does not change over time. For example, ALLTEL has *5% cumulative $25 par value* preferred stock outstanding. The 5% expresses the preferred dividend as a percentage of par, which means that the 5% preferred stock pays 0.05 × $25 = $1.25 per year as a dividend. In ALLTEL's case this occurs in four quarterly payments of $0.3125 per share. In contrast, common stock has no predetermined rate of dividends; the board of directors sets it each year. In fact the board may decide not to pay a dividend on preferred stock. If no dividend is paid on preferred, no dividend may be paid on the common stock. The *unrealized holding gain* is a new concept to be covered in Chapter 13.

cumulative A characteristic of preferred stock that requires that undeclared dividends accumulate and must be paid in the future before common dividends.

Cumulative Dividends

ALLTEL's **cumulative** preferred means that if the company fails to pay a preferred dividend, its obligation accumulates and all omitted dividends must be paid in the

dividend arrearages
Accumulated unpaid
dividends on preferred
stock.

future before any common dividends are paid. For example, if ALLTEL skips its $1.25 preferred dividend one year, it must pay $2.50 for each preferred share the next year before common dividends can be paid. The holders of cumulative preferred stock would receive all accumulated unpaid dividends (called **dividend arrearages**) before the holders of common shares receive anything. Moreover, in the event of liquidation, cumulative unpaid dividends must be paid before common stockholders receive any cash. However, the amount of dividends in arrears is *not* a liability, because no dividends are owed until declared. But dividends in arrears must be disclosed in a footnote to the balance sheet.

To illustrate these distinctions, consider the stockholders' equity of Acumulado Corporation on December 31, 19X0, and the consequences of subsequent years of net income and dividends:

Preferred stock, no par, cumulative, $5 annual dividend per share:	
Issued and outstanding, 1,000,000 shares	$ 50,000,000
Common stock, no par, 5,000,000 shares	100,000,000
Retained income	400,000,000
Total stockholders' equity	$550,000,000

In our example, Acumulado's board of directors elects not to declare and pay preferred dividends in 19X1 and 19X2. Is this realistic, given that Acumulado Corporation began 19X1 with $400,000,000 in the retained income account? It is very realistic. Recall that dividends are paid with cash or other assets. The large retained income balance results from many years of profitable operations, but in those prior years the company has reinvested the cash generated by operations into productive business assets. When a firm encounters losses such as Acumulado experienced in 19X1 and 19X2 cash flow may be reduced, and conserving cash may be prudent.

		Preferred Dividends		Common Dividends	Ending Balance, Retained
	Net Income	*Declared*	*In Arrears*	Declared	Income
19X0					$400,000,000
19X1	$(4,000,000)	—	$ 5,000,000	—	396,000,000
19X2	(4,000,000)	—	10,000,000	—	392,000,000
19X3	21,000,000	$ 3,000,000	12,000,000	—	410,000,000
19X4	49,000,000	17,000,000	—	$ 2,000,000	440,000,000
19X5	32,000,000	5,000,000	—	17,000,000	450,000,000

During 19X1 and 19X2 the omitted $5,000,000 cumulative dividends accumulate and total $10,000,000 by the end of 19X2. Operating results improve in 19X3, and the board declares and pays a partial dividend of $3,000,000. But the dividends in arrears grow by the undeclared unpaid $2,000,000 to a total of $12,000,000. In 19X4 Acumulado improves profitability and cash flow. Dividends to preferred shareholders of $17,000,000 cover the dividends in arrears and the 19X4 dividend. With preferred dividends now completely paid, the firm may pay a dividend to the common shareholders. Note that the ending balance in retained income in each year is equal to the beginning balance, plus net income (or minus a net loss) minus dividends declared.

Would you rather own cumulative or noncumulative preferred stock? In the above tabulation, a holder of noncumulative preferred stock would not be entitled to receive more than $5 million in any single year. Thus, despite three years of omitted or partial dividends, the preferred dividend payment in 19X4 would have been only $5 million. Consequently, most buyers of preferred shares insist on cumulative status, and in actual practice such shares far outnumber the noncumulative type.

Preference in Liquidation

liquidating value A measure of the preference to receive assets in the event of corporate liquidation.

In addition to the cumulative dividend feature, preferred stock usually has a **liquidating value,** which is a preference to receive assets in the event of corporate liquidation. The exact liquidating value is stated on the stock certificate; it is often the same as par value. Any dividends in arrears would also have preference ahead of common shareholders.

Consider an illustration of the liquidation of assets when short- and long-term debt, preferred stock, and common stock are all present. Exhibit 12-1 shows the distribution of cash to different claimants. The priority of the claims decreases as you move down the chart, except that unsubordinated debentures and accounts payable have equal priority, as explained in Chapter 10. The first column presents the book values. The next seven columns show the distributions to each class of claimant under different circumstances. The second column shows what the distribution would be if the company had $1,500,000 left in cash. The third column shows what the distribution would be if the company had $1,000,000 left in cash, and so on. The preferred stock has a liquidating value of $120 per share, which must be paid before common shareholders receive anything.

When cash available exceeds the claims of creditors and preferred shareholders, the excess goes to the common shareholders as residual claimholders. However, when cash is insufficient to pay the other claims, the common shareholders receive nothing, as demonstrated in the five rightmost columns of Exhibit 12-1. Note that the limited liability of common stockholders also extends to preferred shareholders and protects their personal assets from corporate claimants.

Other Features of Preferred Stock

In addition to claims to dividend payments and to cash at liquidation, preferred stock may have other features. Each characteristic affects the attractiveness of the security to potential investors. The issuing company chooses the mix of features that best meets its needs given the market conditions at the time the preferred stock is being offered.

participating A characteristic of preferred stock that provides increasing dividends when common dividends increase.

A **participating** preferred ordinarily receives a minimum dividend but also receives higher dividends when the company has a very good year and pays substantial dividends on common shares. *Participating* means that holders of these shares participate in the growth of the company because they share in the growing amount of dividends. This might be an especially attractive feature that a company with strong growth opportunities might use to make its preferred stock more attractive and thereby increase its price.

Exhibit 12-1	Liquidation of Claims under Various Alternatives (in thousands)

	Account Balances	\$1,500	\$1,000	\$500	\$450	\$350	\$200	\$100
		Assumed Total Cash Proceeds to Be Distributed						
Accounts payable	\$ 100	\$ 100	\$ 100	\$100	\$100	\$100	\$100	\$ 50*
Unsubordinated debentures	100	100	100	100	100	100	100	50*
Subordinated debentures	200	200	200	200	200	150		
Preferred stock (\$100 par value and \$120 liquidating value per share)	100	120	120	100	50			
Common stock and retained income	500	980	480					
Total liabilities and shareholders' equity	\$1,000							
Total cash proceeds distributed		\$1,500	\$1,000	\$500	\$450	\$350	\$200	\$100

* Ratio of 50:50 because each has a \$100,000 claim.

A **callable** preferred gives the issuing company the right to purchase the stock back from the owner upon payment of the call price, or **redemption price.** Investors may worry that the company will call the stock at a bad time— from their perspective—so redemption prices are typically set 5% to 10% above the par value or issuance price of the stock.

A **convertible** preferred gives the owner the option to exchange the preferred for common. Since the investor can convert when it benefits her to do so, a conversion feature is valuable. As a result, convertible securities typically carry a lower dividend rate. For example, a regular preferred offering an 8% dividend might sell for the same price as a 7% convertible preferred.

Comparing Bonds and Preferred Stock

Preferred stock and bonds are similar securities in the sense that each pays a specific return to the investor. The specific return to bondholders is called interest and appears on the earnings statement as an expense. In contrast, the specific return to preferred shareholders is a dividend and represents a distribution of profits, which reduces the retained income account directly. Both common and preferred dividends become liabilities only when the board declares them. In this sense preferred stock is like common stock, and the accounting for preferred dividends is exactly like the accounting for common dividends.

Preferred stock and bonds also differ in that bonds have specific maturity dates, at which time they must be repaid, but preferred stock typically has an unlimited life. From the investor's perspective, preferred stock is riskier than bonds because it never matures and the company does not have to declare dividends.

Just as some companies have many different bonds and other long-term loans outstanding at any particular time, some companies issue a variety of preferred stock. Often each issue is called a **series** and has distinct characteristics from other preferred stock issued by the company. For example the 5% $25 par value preferred of ALLTEL referred to earlier is only one series of stock. ALLTEL's preferred stock issues include other *series* of $25 par value shares issued at 5½% and 6%. All of the $25 par value series are callable by ALLTEL at par. In addition ALLTEL has a no-par issue that pays a $2.06 preferred dividend each year, and each share is convertible into 5.963 shares of common.

Like a bond, preferred stock is a contract between an investor and an issuer that spells out each party's rights and responsibilities. It is not possible to describe every type and kind of preferred stock because each investor and issuer has the opportunity to develop a unique security that exactly meets their needs, and they can adapt that security to the particular market conditions they face at the time.

■ CASH DIVIDENDS

Dividends are proportional distributions of assets to shareholders to satisfy their claims arising from the generation of net income. It is infrequent for assets other than cash to be distributed. In the United States the tendency is for dividends to be paid in equal amounts each quarter, although the board may declare, change, or eliminate a dividend at any time. Some firms do tend to pay a special, larger dividend once a year.

declaration date
The date the board of directors declares a dividend.

The date on which the board formally announces that it will pay a dividend is called the **declaration date**. The board specifies a **date of record,** a future date that determines which stockholders will receive the dividend. A person who holds the stock on the declaration date but sells before the date of record will not receive the dividend. The person who owns it on the date of record will receive it. The actual **payment date** is the day the checks are mailed and follows the date of record by a few days or weeks. ALLTEL has 61,141 shareholders who must be identified and to whom dividends must be paid. AT&T pays dividends to 2.3 million shareholders.

date of record The date when ownership is fixed for determining the right to receive a dividend.

The declaration will specify the amount of the dividend, and it becomes a liability on that date. No journal entry is required on the date of record, although the company's stock transfer agent must identify all parties to whom dividends will be paid as of that date. If a balance sheet is prepared between declaration and payment, a liability for the dividend payable will appear. The journal entries to record a $20,000 dividend declaration and its subsequent payment appear below:

payment date The date dividends are paid.

Date of Declaration	Sept. 26	Retained income	20,000	
		Dividends payable		20,000
		To record the declaration of dividends to be paid on November 15 to shareholders of record as of October 25.		

Date of Payment	Nov. 15	Dividends payable	20,000	
		Cash		20,000
		To pay dividends declared on September 26 to shareholders of record as of October 25.		

The amount of cash dividends declared by a board of directors depends on many factors. The least important factor is the amount of retained income, except in cases where the company is on the brink of bankruptcy or where the company has just been incorporated. In these two cases, the wisdom of declaring dividends is highly questionable.

The more important factors that affect dividends include the stock market's expectations that have crystallized over a series of years, the current and predicted earnings, and the corporation's current cash position and financial plans regarding spending on plant assets and repayments of debts. Remember that payment of cash dividends requires *cash*. Large amounts of net income or retained income do not mean that the necessary cash is available.

Some corporations try to increase the attractiveness of their shares by maintaining a stable quarterly dividend payment on common shares (say, $1 per share each quarter). Others pay a predictable fraction of current earnings per share (say, 60% of whatever is earned in the current year). Some corporations also try to show steady growth in dividends by increasing the dividend per share each year. Sometimes an "extra" payment occurs at the end of an especially profitable year. General Motors has followed the latter practice.

If a company has maintained a series of uninterrupted dividends over a span of years, it will make an effort to continue such payments even in the face of net losses. Indeed, companies occasionally borrow money for the sole purpose of maintaining dividend payments.

■ DISTRIBUTIONS OF ADDITIONAL STOCK

Objective 5

Identify the economic characteristics of stock splits and dividends.

Companies occasionally issue additional shares to current shareholders. A common approach is to issue one additional share for every share currently owned. Suppose the Allstar Equipment Company has 100,000 shares outstanding with a market value of $150 per share. The total market value of the stock is thus $15,000,000. If Allstar Equipment gives each shareholder an additional share for each share owned, the total number of shares would increase to 200,000.

If nothing else changes, the shareholder is no better or worse off. Allstar Equipment is unchanged because the shareholders did not provide any new resources. Since Allstar has the same assets, liabilities, and equity, the total value of the firm should still be $15,000,000. With 200,000 shares outstanding, the market value per share should drop to $75.

In practice distributions of new shares take a variety of forms that may involve changing the par value of the shares and may involve smaller increases in the shares. Such minor differences in the distribution lead to the use of a different term for the transaction and to somewhat different accounting.

Stock Splits and Stock Dividends

stock split Issuance of additional shares to existing stockholders for no payments by the stockholders.

A **stock split** refers to the issuance of additional shares to existing shareholders without any additional cash payment to the firm. Issuance of one additional share for each share currently owned is called a "two-for-one" split. Typically there is a corresponding adjustment to the par value. The following expands the Allstar Equipment example to show the whole stockholders' equity section. Suppose that 100,000 $10 par value shares of common are returned to Allstar in exchange for 200,000 $5 par value shares of common. Nothing changes in the stockholders' equity section of Allstar's balance sheet except the description of shares authorized, issued, and outstanding. As shown below, the aggregate par value is unchanged, no cash has changed hands, each owner has the same proportionate interest as before, and each has the same relative voting power:

	Before 2-for-1 Split	Changes	After 2-for-1 Split
Common stock, 100,000 shares @ $10 par	$ 1,000,000	−100,000 shares @ $10 par + 200,000 shares @ $5 par	$ 1,000,000
Additional paid-in capital	4,000,000		4,000,000
Total paid-in capital	$ 5,000,000		$ 5,000,000
Retained income	6,000,000		6,000,000
Stockholders' equity	$11,000,000		$11,000,000
Overall market value of stock @ assumed $150 per share	$15,000,000	@ assumed $75 per share	$15,000,000

stock dividends
Distribution to stock-holders of additional shares of any class of the distributing com-pany's stock, without any payment to the company by the stock-holders.

   Stock dividends are also issuances of additional shares to existing share-holders without additional cash payment, but the number of new shares issued is usually smaller than in a split, and the original par value is typically retained. For example, a 10% stock dividend involves issuance of one new share for every ten currently owned.

Why Use Stock Splits and Dividends?

Experts debate the importance of splits and stock dividends even as companies continue to use them. One observation is that most U.S. common stock sells at under $100 per share. In 1994, Wal-Mart stock sold for approximately $25 per share. During the prior thirteen years the stock split two-for-one on six occa-sions. An investor who purchased one share in 1981 would have sixty-four shares in 1994. Without any splits, one original Wal-Mart share would have been worth $1,600 in 1994. After these splits, a "round-lot" of 100 shares costs 100 × $25 = $2,500, a reasonable investment size. Without the splits, a round-lot would cost $1,600 × 100 = $160,000. Thus splits allow the company to maintain the stock price in a trading range accessible to small investors and company employ-ees. If one share cost $1,600, Wal-Mart might not have as many shareholders.
   Professor Willard Graham explained a stock split as being akin to taking a gallon of whiskey and pouring it into five individual bottles. The resulting pack-aging *might* attract a price for each fifth that would produce a higher total value than if the gallon had not been split. There is little evidence to suggest that Graham's speculation is true. But as he noted, there is some spillage when pouring the gallon into five bottles—that's the legal, printing, and clerical costs of physically issuing the new stock.
   Often a stock split or stock dividend accompanies other announcements, such as new corporate investment strategies or changes in cash dividend levels. Suppose a company issues a 10% stock dividend, issuing one new share for each ten shares held. The company may not change the normal cash dividend per share, which means total cash dividends to each shareholder will increase

Objective 6

Explain the accounting for stock splits.

by 10%. Why? Because dividends are received on eleven shares instead of ten. Or perhaps the firm has traditionally paid a special cash dividend at year-end but plans to substantially expand production, which will absorb available cash. The firm might combine the announcement of the planned expansion with an announcement of a small stock dividend. The small-percentage stock dividend will not draw on cash immediately but will provide stockholders with an increase in future cash dividends in proportion to the percentage of new shares issued.

Accounting for Stock Splits

In the Allstar Equipment Company's stock split, no entry occurs because the number of shares doubles and the par value is cut in half. Thus the total par value in the common stock account is unchanged.

However, Allstar Equipment might have chosen a different procedure to implement their plan to increase the number of shares outstanding. If Allstar did not want to bother physically exchanging the old $10 par value stock certificates for new $5 par value certificates, it could simply issue more of the $10 par value shares. Previously no accounting entry was required because total par value was unchanged. Issuing more $10 par value shares requires that the common stock account be increased by a credit to common stock. Since the investors did not contribute more capital to the company, this accounting procedure is just a rearrangement of owners' equity. Normally, the increase to the common stock account is transferred from the Additional Paid-in Capital. The company may choose instead to increase the common stock account by making a transfer from Retained Earnings. In this case different language is used to describe the two-for-one stock split. We say it is "accounted for as a stock dividend." The three alternative implementations are summarized below:

Option 1.	Exchange 200,000 new $5.00 par value shares for the old ones	No Entry		
Option 2.	Issue 100,000 new $10.00 par value shares	Additional Paid-in Capital Common Stock	100,000	100,000
Option 3.	Issue 100,000 new $10.00 par value shares and "account for it as a stock dividend"	Retained Earnings Common Stock	100,000	100,000

Large-Percentage Stock Dividends

Objective 7

Differentiate between the accounting for large-percentage and small-percentage stock dividends.

The U.S. accounting authorities differentiate between the sizes of stock dividends. Large-percentage stock dividends (typically those 20% or higher) are accounted for at par or stated value. As in the case of stock splits, the market value of the outstanding shares tends to adjust completely when additional shares are issued. When firms issue large-percentage stock dividends or splits, they usually lower the per-share dividend proportionately. Consider the Allstar Equipment Company and the effect of possible stock dividends on share price. Recall that the market value of the firm will be unchanged by simply changing the number of shares.

If the Allstar Equipment Company chose to double the outstanding number of shares by issuing a 100% stock dividend, the total amount of stockholders' equity would still be unaffected. However, its composition would change.

Possible Allstar
Stock Dividends;
Total Market Value
$15,000,000

Stock Dividend	Shares			Price per Share
	Original	New	Total	
None	100,000		100,000	$150.00
20%	100,000	20,000	120,000	125.00
40%	100,000	40,000	140,000	107.14
60%	100,000	60,000	160,000	93.75
80%	100,000	80,000	180,000	83.33
100%	100,000	100,000	200,000	75.00

	Before 100% Stock Dividend	Changes	After 100% Stock Dividend
Common stock, 100,000 shares @ $10 par	$ 1,000,000	+ (100,000 shares @ $10 par = $1,000,000)	$ 2,000,000
Additional paid-in capital	4,000,000		4,000,000
Total paid-in capital	$ 5,000,000		$ 6,000,000
Retained income	6,000,000	−$1,000,000 par value of "dividend"	5,000,000
Stockholders' equity	$11,000,000		$11,000,000

In substance, there is absolutely no difference between the 100% stock dividend and the two-for-one stock split. *In form*, the shareholder receiving a dividend has $10 par shares rather than $5 par shares. The stock dividend is accounted for as in Option 3 above for stock splits. Note, retained income is transferred to the par value account. Infrequently a company will transfer amounts from additional paid-in capital, as in Option 2. Regulations are not ironclad on this issue.

Small-Percentage Stock Dividends

When a stock dividend of less than 20% is issued, accountants require that the dividend be accounted for at market value, *not* at par value. This rule is not easy to defend. It is partly the result of tradition and partly because small-percentage stock dividends often accompany increases in the total dividend payments or other changes in the company's financial policies. It is argued that the decision to increase total dividends communicates management's conviction that future cash flows will rise to support these increased distributions, and this is a positive statement about the firm's prospects.

Reconsider our example of Allstar Equipment Company (before the split). Suppose the market value of common shares is $150 at the time of issuance of a 2% stock dividend. The effect on the stockholders' equity section is shown in the table on page 552.

As before the individual shareholder receives no assets from the corporation. Moreover, the shareholders' fractional interest is unchanged; if the shareholders sell the dividend shares, their proportionate ownership interest in the company will decrease. The major possible economic effect of a stock dividend is to signal increased cash dividends. Suppose the company in our example consistently paid cash dividends of $1 per share. Often this cash dividend level per share is maintained after a stock dividend. The recipient of the stock dividend can now expect a future annual cash dividend of $1 × 1,020 = $1,020 rather than $1 × 1,000 = $1,000. In this case, when the dividend rate per share is maintained, announcing a stock dividend of 2% has the same effect as announcing an increase of 2% in the cash dividend.

	Before 2% Stock Dividend	Changes	After 2% Stock Dividend
Common stock, 100,000 shares @ $10 par	$ 1,000,000	+ (2,000 shares @ $10 par) = + 20,000	$ 1,020,000
Additional paid-in capital	4,000,000	+ [2,000 shares @ ($150 – $10)] = + 280,000	4,280,000
Retained income	6,000,000	– (2,000 @ $150)	5,700,000
Stockholders' equity	$11,000,000	= – 300,000	$11,000,000
Overall market value of stock @ assumed $150 per share	$15,000,000	@ assumed $147.06 per share*	$15,000,000
Total shares outstanding	100,000		102,000
Individual shareholder:			
Assumed ownership of shares	1,000		1,020
Percentage ownership interest	1%		Still 1%

* Many simultaneous events affect the level of stock prices, including expectations regarding the general economy, the industry, and the specific company. Thus the market price of the stock may move in either direction when the stock dividend is declared. Theory and complicated case studies indicate that a small-percentage stock dividend should have zero effect on the total market value of the firm. Accordingly, the new market price per share should be $15,000,000 ÷ 102,000 shares = $147.06.

For small-percentage (under 20%) stock dividends the company records the transaction by transferring the *market value* of the additional shares from retained income to common stock and additional paid-in capital. The entry is often referred to as being a "capitalization of retained income." It is basically a signal to the shareholders that $300,000 of retained income is being invested for the long term in productive assets. In our example, the required journal entry would be:

Retained income	300,000	
Common stock		20,000
Additional paid-in capital		280,000

To record a 2% common stock dividend, resulting in the issuance of 2,000 shares. Retained income is reduced at the rate of the market value of $150 per share at date of issuance.

U.S. practice regarding the use of market values in accounting for small-percentage stock dividends is arbitrary and is not consistently adopted worldwide. For example, in Japan these journal entries are recorded at par value. The Japanese practice is one most accountants would support. The U.S. practice compounds the false notion that the recipients are getting a dividend akin to a cash dividend.

Relation of Dividends and Splits

Companies typically use large-percentage stock dividends to accomplish exactly the same purpose as a stock split. That is, the companies want a material reduction in the market price of their shares or they want to signal an increase in total dividend payments to shareholders. Stock splits frequently occur in the form of a stock "dividend" to save clerical costs. After all, swapping old $10-par certificates for new $5-par certificates is more expensive than merely printing and mailing additional $10-par certificates.

Review the typical accounting for stock splits and stock dividends:

- Stock splits—
  1. Change par value—no accounting entry.
  2. Retain par value—rearranging owners' equity by transferring paid-in capital or retained income to common stock.
- Stock dividends—shift from retained income to paid-in capital:
  1. Small-percentage dividends—reduce retained income by *market value* of the additional shares issued.
  2. Large-percentage dividends—reduce retained income or additional paid-in capital by only the *par value* of the additional shares issued.

Wal-Mart described its 1993 split in the following footnote to the 1994 annual report:

> On February 25, 1993, the company distributed a two-for-one stock split in the form of a 100% stock dividend. Consequently, stock option data and per share data reflect the stock split.

Fractional Shares

Corporations ordinarily issue shares in whole units. However, some shareholders are entitled to stock dividends in amounts equal to fractional units. Consequently, corporations issue additional shares for whole units plus cash equal to the market value of the fractional amount.

For example, suppose a corporation issues a 3% stock dividend. A shareholder has 160 shares. The market value per share on the date of issuance is $40. Par value is $2. The shareholder would be entitled to 0.03 × 160 = 4.8 shares. The company would issue 4 shares plus 0.8($40) = $32 cash. The journal entry is:

Retained income (4.8 × $40)	192	
Common stock, at par (4 × $2)		8
Additional paid-in capital (4 × $38) .		152
Cash (0.8 × $40)		32
To issue a stock dividend of 3% to a holder of 160 shares.		

The Investor's Accounting for Dividends and Splits

So far, we have focused on the corporation. What about the stockholder? Consider the *investor's* entries for the transactions described so far. Suppose Investor J is passive and takes no active voice in management. She bought 1,000 shares of the original issue of Allstar Equipment Company stock for $50 per share:

Investment in Allstar common stock	50,000	
Cash		50,000
To record investment in 1,000 shares of an original issue of Allstar Equipment Company common stock at $50 per share. The par value is $10 per share.		

Investor J holds the shares indefinitely. However, if Investor J sold the shares to Investor K at a subsequent price other than $50, a gain or loss would be recorded by J, and K would carry the shares at the amount paid to J. Meanwhile the stockholders' equity of Allstar Equipment Company would be completely unaffected by this sale by one investor to another. The company's underlying shareholder records would simply be changed to delete J and add K as a shareholder.

The following examples show how Investor J would record the stock split, cash dividends, and stock dividends, where each is treated as an independent event, not as sequential events. Note that several events that produced journal entries for Allstar, do not provide entries for Investor J:

a. Stock split at 2 for 1:

No journal entry, but a memorandum would be made in the investment account to show that 2,000 shares are now held at a cost of $25 each instead of 1,000 shares at a cost of $50 each.

b. Cash dividends of $2 per share:

Cash	2,000	
Dividend income		2,000
To record cash dividends on Allstar Equipment Company stock.		

or:

Alternatively, the following two entries might be used:

Date of declaration:

Dividends receivable	2,000	
Dividend income		2,000
To record dividends declared by Allstar Equipment Company.		

Date of receipt:

Cash	2,000	
Dividends receivable		2,000
To record the receipt of cash dividends.		

c. Stock dividends of 2%:

No journal entry, but a memorandum would be made in the investment account to show that (assuming the stock split in **a** had not occurred) 1,020 shares are now owned at an average cost of $50,000 ÷ 1,020, or $49.02 per share.

d. Stock split in form of a 100% dividend:

No journal entry, but a memorandum would be made in the investment account to show that (assuming the stock splits and stock dividends in **a** and **c** had not occurred) 2,000 shares are now owned at an average cost of $25 instead of 1,000 shares @ $50. Note that this memorandum has the same effect as the memorandum in **a** above.

■ REPURCHASE OF SHARES

Companies repurchase their own shares for two main purposes: (1) to permanently reduce shareholder claims, called *retiring stock*, and (2) to temporarily hold shares for later use, most often to be granted as part of employee bonus or stock purchase plans. Temporarily held shares are called *treasury stock* or *treasury shares*. By repurchasing shares, for whatever reason, a company liquidates some shareholders' claims, and the following journal entry results:

```
Stockholders' equity ................   xxx
        Cash ......................            xxx
Repurchase of outstanding shares.
```

The purpose of the repurchase determines *which stockholders' equity accounts* are affected. Consider an illustration of the Brecht Company, whose stock has a market value of $15 per share:

Common stock, 1,000,000 shares at $1 par	$ 1,000,000
Additional paid-in capital	4,000,000
Total paid-in capital	$ 5,000,000
Retained income	6,000,000
Stockholders' equity	$11,000,000
Overall market value of stock @ assumed $15 per share	$15,000,000
Book value per share = $11,000,000 ÷ 1,000,000 = $11.	

Book value per share refers to the historical investment by the shareholders in the company. The total stockholders' equity of $11,000,000 combines the original purchase price of shares in the past (par value plus paid-in capital) with the periodic earnings of the firm that have remained in the business (retained income). Dividing it by the number of shares gives the average per share, in this case $11,000,000 ÷ 1,000,000 = $11.

Retirement of Shares

Suppose the board of directors has decided that the $15 market value of its shares is "too low." Even though the market value exceeds the book value by $4 per share ($15 - $11), the board may think the market is too pessimistic regarding the company's shares. Because of inflation and other factors, it is not unusual to have the market value vastly exceed the book value.

The board might believe that the best use of corporate cash would be to purchase and retire a portion of the outstanding shares. In this way, the remaining shareholders would have the sole benefit of the predicted eventual increase in market value per share. Other motives include the desire to change the proportion of debt and equity in use to finance the firm. The company may wish to return cash to shareholders without creating expectations of permanent increases in dividends. It is not unusual for a firm to buy back its own stock.

Albertson's, Inc., operates 676 retail grocery stores in seventeen western and southern states. Their 1994 footnotes reveal a stock repurchase program:

> Since 1987, the Board of Directors has continuously adopted or renewed plans under which the Company is authorized, but not required, to purchase shares of its common stock on the open market. The current plan was adopted by the Board on March 7, 1994, and authorizes the Company to purchase up to 2.5 million shares through March 31, 1995. The Company has purchased and retired an equivalent of 12.4 million shares under these plans.

Suppose the Board of Brecht Company purchases and retires 5% of its outstanding shares @ $15 for a total of 50,000 × $15, or $750,000 cash. The total stockholders' equity is reduced or contracted. The stock certificates are canceled, and the shares are no longer issued and outstanding:

	Before Repurchase of 5% of Outstanding Shares	Changes Because of Retirement	After Repurchase of 5% of Outstanding Shares
Common stock, 1,000,000 shares @ $1 par	$ 1,000,000	– (50,000 shares @ $1 par) = –$50,000	$ 950,000
Additional paid-in capital	4,000,000	– (50,000 shares @ $4) = –$200,000	3,800,000
Total paid-in capital	$ 5,000,000		$ 4,750,000
Retained income	6,000,000	– (50,000 @ $10*) = –$500,000	5,500,000
Stockholders' equity	$11,000,000		$10,250,000
Book value per common share:			
$11,000,000 ÷ 1,000,000	$ 11.00		
$10,250,000 ÷ 950,000			$ 10.79

* $15 – the $5 (or $1 + $4) originally paid in.

The journal entry reverses the original average paid-in capital per share and charges the additional amount to retained income:

Common stock	50,000	
Additional paid-in capital	200,000	
Retained income	500,000	
Cash		750,000

To record retirement of 50,000 shares of stock for $15 cash per share. The original paid-in capital was $5 per share, so the additional $10 per share is debited to Retained Income.

dilution Reduction in stockholders' equity per share or earnings per share that arises from some changes among shareholders' proportionate interests.

The additional $10 is sometimes described as being tantamount to a special cash dividend paid to the owners of the 50,000 retired shares. Note how the book value per share of the outstanding shares has declined from $11.00 to $10.79. The phenomenon is called *dilution* of the common shareholders' equity. **Dilution** is usually defined as a reduction in shareholders' equity per share or earnings per share that arises from some changes among shareholders' proportionate interests. As a rule, boards of directors avoid dilution. However, boards sometimes favor deliberate dilution if expected future profits will more than compensate for a temporary undesirable reduction in book value per share.

Objective 8

Account for treasury stock transactions.

Treasury Stock

Suppose the Brecht Company's Board of Directors decides that the 50,000 repurchased shares will be held only temporarily and then resold. Perhaps the shares are needed for an employee stock purchase plan or for executive stock options. Such temporarily held shares are called *treasury stock*. As in the retirement of shares, the repurchase is a *decrease* in stockholders' equity. Treasury stock is NOT an asset. It indicates a liquidation of the ownership claim of one or more stockholders. Cash dividends are not paid on shares held in the treasury; cash dividends are distributed only to the shares outstanding (in the hands of stockholders), and treasury stock is not outstanding:

Shares issued	1,000,000
Less: Treasury stock	50,000
Total shares outstanding	950,000

Brecht's stockholders' equity section would be affected as follows:

	Before Repurchase of 5% of Outstanding Shares	Changes Because of Treasury Stock	After Repurchase of 5% of Outstanding Shares
Common stock, 1,000,000 shares @ $1 par	$ 1,000,000		$ 1,000,000
Additional paid-in capital	4,000,000		4,000,000
Total paid-in capital	$ 5,000,000		$ 5,000,000
Retained income	6,000,000		6,000,000
Total	$11,000,000		$11,000,000
Deduct:			
Cost of treasury stock	—	−$750,000	750,000
Stockholders' equity	$11,000,000		$10,250,000

The journal entry is:

```
Treasury stock ............................    750,000
      Cash ..................................              750,000
   To record acquisition of 50,000 shares of common
   stock @ $15 (to be held as treasury stock).
```

The Treasury Stock account is a contra account to Owners' Equity just as Accumulated Depreciation is a contra account to related asset accounts. Like the retirement of shares, the purchase of treasury stock decreases stockholders' equity by $750,000. Unlike retirements, common stock at par value, additional paid-in capital, and retained income remain untouched by treasury stock purchases. A separate treasury stock account is a deduction from total stockholders' equity on the balance sheet.

Remember that treasury stock is not an asset. A company's holding of shares in *another company* is an asset; its holding of its *own shares* is a negative element of stockholders' equity.

Why Buy Back Your Own Shares?

During the three-year period 1988 through 1990, total net income for The Coca-Cola Company was $4.2 billion, an average of $1.4 billion per year. What did Coca-Cola do with this $4.2 billion in assets generated? It isn't surprising that some of it was distributed to shareholders in the form of cash dividends. Total cash dividends for the three-year period were $1.5 billion, resulting in a dividend payout ratio (cash dividends/net income) of 35.7%. What may be a bit surprising is that during this same period, Coca-Cola used $2.2 billion to buy back some of its own shares of stock. We often think that cash dividends are the primary method corporations employ to distribute cash to shareholders, but frequently, as in the case of Coca-Cola, cash used in stock purchases exceeds the amount paid in cash dividends.

One reason firms give is that idle resources within the company could be more efficiently used by individual shareholders. In announcing a $10 billion stock buyback plan in 1989 following an impressive series of acquisitions during the 1980s, General Electric stated that it saw no further acquisitions that looked attractive and, thus, would return excess funds to the shareholders. Such a strategy decreases the likelihood that a firm will be an object of a takeover bid since takeover artists frequently target firms holding large amounts of inefficiently used assets.

Firms also use stock purchases to demonstrate confidence in their own prospects. The thinking is that investors are more likely to believe company claims of rosy prospects if the investors see the company putting its money where its mouth is by buying its own shares. This tactic was employed extensively in the wake of the market crash of October 1987. At the time, in a bid to prop up falling share prices, over 600 firms announced plans to repurchase their own shares.

Both Coca-Cola and General Electric remain committed to share repurchase programs. In August of 1994 Coca-Cola began a repurchase program of up to 10 million shares. In December of 1994 GE's board of directors authorized the repurchase of up to $5 billion in common shares.

To put these numbers in perspective, GE has issued 1.8 billion shares historically and raised $594 million in equity investments in the process. As a result of continual repurchase activity, 8% of those shares are now in the treasury at a cost of $5.3 billion. Almost ten times as much has been used to reacquire shares as was originally raised. ∎

Sources: 1990 and 1994 Annual Reports of The Coca Cola Company; Amal Kumar Naj, "General Electric Buy-Back Plan Signals New Tack, Reflects Earnings Optimism," Wall Street Journal (November 20, 1989), p. A3; 1994 Annual Report of General Electric.

Disposition of Treasury Stock

Treasury shares are often resold at a later date, perhaps in conjunction with an employee stock purchase plan. The sales price usually differs from the acquisition cost. Suppose the sales price is $18. The journal entry is:

Cash	900,000	
Treasury stock		750,000
Additional paid-in capital		150,000
To record sale of treasury stock, 50,000 shares @ $18. Cost was $15 per share.		

Suppose the price is $13:

Cash	650,000	
Additional paid-in capital	100,000	
Treasury stock		750,000
To record sale of treasury stock, 50,000 shares @ $13. Cost was $15 per share.		

If the treasury shares are resold below their cost, accountants tend to debit (decrease) Additional Paid-in Capital for the difference, $2 per share in this case. Additional Paid-in Capital is sometimes divided into several separate accounts that identify different sources of capital. For example:

- Additional paid-in capital—preferred stock
- Additional paid-in capital—common stock
- Additional paid-in capital—treasury stock transactions

If such accounts are used, a consistent accounting treatment would call for debiting only Additional Paid-in Capital—Treasury Stock Transactions (and no other paid-in capital account) for the excess of the cost over the resale price of treasury shares. If there is no balance in such a paid-in capital account, the debit should be made to Retained Income.

Suppose 25,000 of the treasury shares bought by Brecht are later sold for $17 and still later the other 25,000 shares are sold for $12. The company had no previous sales of treasury stock. The journal entries are:

Cash	425,000	
Treasury stock		375,000
Additional paid-in capital—treasury		
stock transactions		50,000
To record sale of treasury stock, 25,000 shares @ $17.		
Cost was $15 per share.		
Cash	300,000	
Additional paid-in capital—treasury		
stock transactions	50,000	
Retained income	25,000	
Treasury stock		375,000
To record sale of treasury stock, 25,000 shares @ $12.		
Cost was $15 per share.		

Although the specific accounting for transactions in the company's own stock may vary from company to company, one rule is paramount. Any differences between the acquisition costs and the resale proceeds of treasury stock must never be reported as losses, expenses, revenues, or gains in the income statement. Why? A corporation's own capital stock is part of its capital structure. It is *not* an asset of the corporation. Nor is stock intended to be treated like merchandise for sale to customers at a profit. Therefore changes in a corporation's capitalization should produce no gain or loss but should merely require direct adjustments to the owners' equity.

There is essentially no difference between unissued shares and treasury shares. In our example, Brecht Company could accomplish the same objective by (1) acquiring 50,000 shares, retiring them, and issuing 50,000 new shares, or (2) acquiring 50,000 shares and reselling them.

Effects of Repurchases on Earnings per Share

When shares are repurchased and retired or put in treasury, the number of shares outstanding is reduced. This will tend to increase earnings per share. To see this, suppose that Brecht was generating net income of $950,000 each year. Assume further that the use of $750,000 to repurchase shares does not reduce future net income. Under these circumstances earnings per share will rise as a result of repurchasing shares:

EPS = net income ÷ average number of shares outstanding
Before repurchase $950,000 ÷ 1,000,000 shares = $.95
After repurchase $950,000 ÷ 950,000 shares = $1.00

Note that the only time a repurchase lowers earnings per share is when using cash to repurchase shares leads to lower earnings.

■ OTHER ISSUANCES OF COMMON STOCK

Not all common stock is issued in exchange for cash. In some cases other assets are given to the company in exchange for its stock. In other cases another corporate security—a bond or preferred stock—is *converted* into common stock.

Noncash Exchanges

Often a company issues its stock to acquire land, a building, or even the common stock of another company. Such exchanges raise the question of the proper dollar value of the transaction to be recorded in both the buyer's and the seller's books. The proper amount is the "fair value" of either the securities or the exchanged assets, whichever is more objectively determinable. That amount should be used by both companies.

For example, suppose Company A acquires some equipment from Company B in exchange for 10,000 newly issued shares of A's common stock. The equipment was carried on B's books at the $200,000 original cost less accumulated depreciation of $50,000. Company A's stock is listed on the New York Stock Exchange; its current market price is $18 per share. Its par value is $1 per share. In this case, the market price of A's common stock would be regarded as a more objectively determinable fair value than the book value or the undepreciated cost of B's equipment. The accounts are affected as follows:

	Assets			=	Liabilities	+	Stockholders' Equity	
		Equipment					*Common Stock*	*Additional Paid-in Capital*
Issuance of stock by A		+ 180,000		=			+10,000	+170,000
	Investment in A Common Stock	*Equipment*	*Accumulated Depreciation*				*Retained Income*	
Disposal of equipment by B	+ 180,000	−200,000	+50,000	=			+30,000	[gain on disposal of equipment]

The journal entries (without explanations) are:

On issuer's books (A):	Equipment	180,000	
	Common stock		10,000
	Additional paid-in capital		170,000

On investor's books (B):	Investment in A common stock	180,000	
	Accumulated depreciation, equipment	50,000	
	Equipment		200,000
	Gain on disposal of equipment		30,000

Conversion of Securities

Objective 9

Explain and record conversions of preferred stock into common stock.

When companies issue *convertible* bonds or preferred stock, the conversion feature makes the securities more attractive to investors and increases the price the issuer receives (or, equivalently, reduces the interest or dividend it must pay). Ultimately, the buyer or some subsequent owner may exercise the conversion privilege. Since the conversion is a transaction of form rather than substance, the accounts are simply adjusted as if the common stock had been issued initially.

For example, suppose Company B had paid $160,000 for an investment in 5,000 shares of the $1 par value convertible preferred stock of Company A in 19X1. The preferred stock was converted into 10,000 shares of Company A common stock ($1 par value) in 19X8. The accounts of Company A (the issuer) would be affected as shown in Exhibit 12-2.

Exhibit 12-2   Analysis of Convertible Preferred Stock

	Assets	=	Liabilities	+	Stockholders' Equity			
						Additional Paid-in Capital,		Additional Paid-in Capital,
	Cash				Preferred Stock	Preferred	Common Stock	Common
Issuance of preferred (19X1)	+ 160,000	=			+5,000	+155,000		
Conversion of preferred (19X8)		=			−5,000	−155,000	+10,000	+150,000

The journal entries would be as follows:

On issuer's books (A):	19X1	Cash	160,000	
		Preferred stock, convertible		5,000
		Additional paid-in capital, preferred		155,000
		To record issuance of 5,000 shares of $1 par preferred stock convertible into two common shares for one preferred share.		
	19X8	Preferred stock, convertible	5,000	
		Additional paid-in capital, preferred	155,000	
		Common stock		10,000
		Additional paid-in capital, common		150,000
		To record the conversion of 5,000 preferred shares to 10,000 common shares.		

Company B (the investor) has experienced a change in form of the investment, with no change in historical cost. The carrying value, or book value, of the investment remains $160,000. To show that the form of the investment is now common stock rather than preferred stock, Company B might use a journal entry to transfer the $160,000 from one investment account to another. Alternatively, it might change subsidiary records that document the composition of a single general ledger account called Investments.

Federal Paper Board had $1.20 cumulative convertible preferred shares that were callable at a *redemption price* of $20 per share in 1991 and thereafter. Each share was convertible into five shares of common. Since Federal Paper Board common stock traded for about $25 per share during most of 1989 and 1990, you can see that the preferred stock was worth about $125 (five shares times $25) upon conversion. It is not surprising that some 32,000 shares of preferred were converted into over 150,000 shares of common during the three-year period 1988–90 and the process continues. As of December 31, 1994, only 52,000 shares of the $1.20 convertible preferred remained outstanding. The footnotes disclosed that 260,000 shares of the authorized but unissued common stock were reserved for the possible conversion of the preferred.

Accounting for these conversions merely rearranges Federal Paper Board's owners' equity. Conversions of the company's stock do not create accounting gains or losses. To record the conversion, Federal Paper Board would eliminate the par value of the $1.20 preferred and create the par value of the newly issued common. If the two par values are not equal in total, the difference either increases or decreases additional capital. Some companies maintain distinct accounts for the additional paid-in capital from each class of stock; others do not. Total stockholders' equity does not change. The entry to record conversion of 7,000 Federal Paper Board $1.20 preferred shares with a $1 par value into 35,000 common shares with a $5 par value would be (without explanation):

Preferred stock	7,000	
Other capital	168,000	
Common stock		175,000

While preferred stock is common in some countries, it does not exist in others. Japan, for example, does not have this form of security. Other countries that have classes of preferred stock may not follow U.S. practice with respect to priority in liquidation or special features such as cumulative dividends, convertibility, or callability.

■ RETAINED INCOME RESTRICTIONS

Objective 10

Describe the motivation for and importance of restrictions on retained earnings.

Directors can make decisions that benefit shareholders but hurt creditors. For example, directors might pay such large dividends that payments of creditors' claims would be threatened. To protect creditors, dividend-declaring power is restricted by either state laws or contractual obligations or both. Moreover, boards of directors can voluntarily restrict their declarations of dividends.

States typically do not permit dividends if stockholders' equity is less than total paid-in capital. Therefore retained income must exceed the cost of treasury stock. If there is no treasury stock, retained income must be positive. This restriction limits dividend payments and protects the position of the creditors. For example, consider the following (in millions):

	Before Dividends	After Dividend Payments of $10	$4
Paid-in capital	$25	$25	$25
Retained income	10	—	6
Total	$35	$25	$31
Deduct:			
Cost of treasury stock	6	6	6
Stockholders' equity	$29	$19	$25

Without restricting dividends to the amount of retained income in excess of the cost of the treasury stock, the corporation could pay a dividend of $10 million. This would reduce the stockholders' equity below the paid-in capital of $25 million. With the restriction, unrestricted retained income (and maximum legal payment of dividends) would be $10 million – $6 million, or $4 million. In this case treasury stock creates a restriction on the company's ability to declare dividends. The **restricted retained income** cannot be reduced by dividend declarations.

Most of the time, restrictions of retained income are disclosed by footnotes. Occasionally, restrictions appear as a line item on the balance sheet called *restricted retained income*. Restrictions of retained income are also sometimes called **appropriated retained income** or *reserves*. The term *reserve* can be misleading. Accountants *never* use the word reserve to indicate cash set aside for a particular purpose; instead they call such assets a *fund*. The word **reserve** has one of three broad meanings in accounting: (1) restrictions of dividend declarations, (2) offset to an asset, or (3) estimate of a definite liability of indefinite or uncertain amount. An example of a restriction on dividend payments is contained in the following footnote from the 1994 annual report of Echlin, Inc.:

> In July 1994, the company renegotiated its RCA which was due to expire on September 1, 1994. Under the terms of the new agreement with twelve banking institutions, the company has the availability through September 1, 1999, of maximum borrowings of $375 million. The company's RCA and senior note agreements contain restrictive covenants regarding the payment of cash dividends, the maintenance of working capital and shareholders' equity, and the issuance of new debt. Under the most restrictive covenant, cash dividends paid since September 1, 1993, shall not exceed the sum of $60 million plus 60% of cumulative net income, as defined, plus 50% of the net proceeds from the sale of common stock of the company since September 1, 1993. The company is in compliance with all covenants of these agreements. (Note: an RCA is a revolving credit agreement.)

The U.S. practice toward retained earnings reserves is restrictive. Some other countries, among them France, Germany, the Netherlands, and Japan,

restricted retained income (appropriated retained income) Any part of retained income that may not be reduced by dividend declarations.

reserve Has one of three meanings: (1) a restriction of dividend-declaring power as denoted by a specific subdivision of retained income, (2) an offset to an asset, or (3) an estimate of a definite liability of indefinite or uncertain amount.

allow purely discretionary reserves to be reported. The idea is to disclose specific intentions of management. An international company might use a "reserve for plant expansion" to communicate an intention to reinvest future earnings in new technology rather than to increase dividends.

■ STOCK OPTIONS

stock options
Special rights usually granted to executives to purchase a corporation's capital stock.

Stock options are rights often granted to executives to purchase a corporation's capital stock. Various conditions are specified for the options including the time period during which the stock may be purchased, the number of shares, and the price per share. Although options have assorted conditions, a typical option grants the holder the right to purchase shares (exercise the option) during some specified time in the *future* at *today's* market price (the exercise price, which is set at the date of grant).

Options are frequently given to corporate officers as a form of incentive compensation. For example, suppose Company A granted its top executives options to purchase 60,000 shares of $1 par value common stock at $15 per share, the market price today (date of grant). The options can be exercised over a five-year span, beginning three years hence. Such options clearly are valuable rights. The executives can gain the benefits of price increases without bearing the risks of price declines. However, measurement of the value of options at the time of grant is difficult because executive options may not be sold to others. Therefore currently accepted accounting attributes zero value to most of them as long as the exercise price is the same as the market price at the date of the grant. Thus the accounting approach is to make no entry at the time of grant. Subsequent financial statements must reveal (usually by a footnote) the number and type of options outstanding.

Suppose all options are exercised three years hence. The journal entry is:

```
Cash . . . . . . . . . . . . . . . . . . . . . . . . . . . . . . . . . . . .    900,000
        Common stock . . . . . . . . . . . . . . . . . . . . . .                       60,000
        Additional paid-in capital . . . . . . . . . . . . .                          840,000
    To record issue of 60,000 shares upon exercise
    of options to acquire them @ $15 per share.
```

Executives sometimes let their options lapse. For example, here the options will become worthless if the price of the common stock is no higher than $15 per share during the time they may be exercised. In such a case, no journal entry is made.

The FASB has considered this reporting issue and has chosen to require extensive disclosures of options, but not to require expense recognition.

■ FINANCIAL RATIOS RELATED TO STOCKHOLDERS' EQUITY

rate of return on common equity (ROE) Net income less preferred dividends divided by average common equity.

Many ratios aid in evaluating the performance of a company. One important question is how effectively the company uses resources provided by the shareholders. To assess this, analysts relate the net income generated by the firm to the historic investment by its shareholders. The **rate of return on common equity** (often abbreviated **ROE**) is defined as:

$$\text{Rate of return on common equity} = \frac{\text{Net income} - \text{Preferred dividends}}{\text{Average common equity}}$$

Objective 11

Define and use the rate of return on common equity and book value per share.

Consider the following data for Company Y:

	December 31	
	19X2	**19X1**
Stockholders' equity:		
$10 preferred stock, 100,000 shares, $100 par	$ 10,000,000	$ 10,000,000
Common stock, 5,000,000 shares, $1 par	5,000,000	5,000,000
Additional paid-in capital	35,000,000	35,000,000
Retained income	87,400,000	83,000,000
Total stockholders' equity	$137,400,000	$133,000,000
Net income for the year ended Dec. 31,19X2	$11,000,000	
Preferred dividends @ $10 per share	1,000,000	
Net income available for common stock	$10,000,000	

The common stockholders received dividends of $1.12 per share during 19X2, or 5 million × $1.12 = $5,600,000.

The rate of return on common equity is naturally of great interest to common stockholders. The rate focuses on the ultimate profitability based on the book value of the common equity. To determine the numerator of the ratio, preferred dividends are subtracted from net income to obtain net income available for common stock. The denominator is the average of the beginning and ending *common* equity balances. Note that the *common* equity balance is the total stockholders' equity less the preferred stock at book value. If the liquidating value of a company's preferred stock exceeds the book value, the liquidating value is deducted from the total stockholders' equity to determine the common equity balance:

$$\text{Rate of return on common equity} = \frac{\text{Net income} - \text{Preferred dividends}}{\text{Average common equity}}$$

$$= \frac{\$11,000,000 - \$1,000,000}{\tfrac{1}{2}[(\$133,000,000 - \$10,000,000) + (\$137,400,000 - \$10,000,000)]}$$

$$= \frac{\$10,000,000}{\tfrac{1}{2}(\$123,000,000 + \$127,400,000)}$$

$$= \frac{\$10,000,000}{\$125,200,000} = 8.0\%$$

book value per share of common stock Stockholders' equity attributable to common stock divided by the number of shares outstanding.

Return on stockholders' equity varies considerably among companies and industries. For example, Wal-Mart's return on equity in 1995 was almost 25%, while AT&T reported over 29%, but Federal Paper Board's return on equity was only 8%.

The *book value* of a company is the stockholders' equity, often expressed on a per share basis. When preferred stock is present the calculation of the **book value per share of common stock** adjusts for the preferred as follows:

$$\text{Book value per share of common stock} = \frac{\text{Total stockholders' equity} - \text{Book value of preferred stock}}{\text{Number of common shares outstanding}}$$

$$= \frac{\$137,400,000 - \$10,000,000}{5,000,000} = \$25.48$$

Suppose the market value is $35. Note the low book value as compared with market value. The shareholders are paying for future earning power rather than for the historical cost of assets. The usefulness of book value per share is highly questionable for most companies because book values are based on balance sheet values, which show the historical cost of assets. The current value of those assets may differ greatly from their historical cost. Consequently, some companies consistently have market prices in excess of book values, or vice versa.

Comparing book values with market values is useful primarily because it suggests questions. A market value well above the book value may be appropriate if the company has many unrecorded assets or appreciated assets. For example, Eli Lilly had a 1995 book value of about $18 and a market value per share over three times as large ($62). Why? Lilly has valuable patents on various drugs and additional research under way that are not reflected in the book values. Wal-Mart's mid-1995 market value of about $25 substantially exceeds its book value of about $5.50. Why? Presumably, this difference reflects beliefs of investors that Wal-Mart will be able to continue its ten-year-old pattern of sales growth of over 26% per year and return on equity in excess of 20%. In contrast, in mid-1992 Ford Motor Company had a $20 market value, well below its $22 book value (as adjusted for stock splits). During a series of bad years for auto sales, Ford suffered losses and cut its dividend payment sharply. The market price per share indicated a belief that Ford's production plants and other assets could not be liquidated for their book value. By 1994 Ford had recovered well. During 1994 its book value was around $30, and its share price ranged from $25 to $35.

Summary Problems for Your Review

Problem One

From the following data, prepare a detailed statement of stockholders' equity for the Sample Corporation, December 31, 19X1:

Additional paid-in capital, preferred stock	$ 50,000
Additional paid-in capital, common stock	1,000,000
9% preferred stock, $50 par value, callable at $55, authorized 20,000 shares, issued and outstanding 12,000 shares	
Common stock, no par, stated value $2 per share, authorized 500,000 shares, issued 400,000 shares of which 25,000 shares are held in the treasury	
Dividends payable	90,000
Retained income	2,000,000

The 25,000 shares of treasury stock cost $250,000.

Solution to Problem One

Dividends payable is a *liability*. It must therefore be excluded from a statement of stockholders' equity:

Sample Corporation
Statement of
Stockholders' Equity
December 31, 19X1

9% preferred stock, $50 par value, callable at $55, authorized 20,000 shares, issued and outstanding 12,000 shares		$ 600,000
Common stock, no par, stated value $2 per share, authorized 500,000 shares, issued 400,000 shares of which 25,000 shares are held in the treasury		800,000
Additional paid-in capital:		
Preferred	$ 50,000	
Common	1,000,000	1,050,000*
Retained income		2,000,000
Subtotal		$4,450,000
Less: Cost of 25,000 shares of common stock reacquired and held in treasury		250,000
Total stockholders' equity		$4,200,000

* Many presentations would not show the detailed breakdown of additional paid-in capital into preferred and common portions.

Problem Two

B Company splits its $10 par common stock 5 for 1. How will its balance sheet be affected? Its earnings per share? Assume 2,000 shares are originally outstanding.

Solution to Problem Two

The total amount of stockholders' equity would be unaffected, but there would be 10,000 outstanding shares (instead of 2,000) at $2 par rather than $10 par. Earnings per share would be one-fifth of that previously reported, assuming no change in total net income applicable to the common stock.

Suppose the question were framed as, the company recently issued a 5-for-1 stock split "accounted for" as a stock dividend. Then the par value per share would be retained, and a journal entry would increase the par value account for common stock by $80,000 (8,000 additional shares times $10 par value per share):

Retained earnings	80,000	
Common stock at par		80,000

Problem Three

C Company distributes a 2% stock dividend on its 1 million outstanding $5 par common shares. Its stockholders' equity section before the dividend was:

Common stock, 1,000,000 shares @ $5 par	$ 5,000,000
Paid-in capital in excess of par	20,000,000
Retained income	75,000,000
Total stockholders' equity	$100,000,000

The common was selling on the open market for $150 per share when the dividend was distributed.

How will the stockholders' equity section be affected? If net income were $10.2 million next year, what would be the earnings per share before considering the effects of the stock dividend? After considering the effects of the stock dividend?

Solution to Problem Three

Stockholders' equity:

	Before 2% Stock Dividend	Changes	After 2% Stock Dividend
Common stock, 1,000,000 shares @ $5 par	$ 5,000,000	+ (20,000 @ $5)	$ 5,100,000
Paid-in capital	20,000,000	+ [20,000 @ ($150 − $5)]	22,900,000
Retained income	75,000,000	− (20,000 @ $150)	72,000,000
Total	$100,000,000		$100,000,000

Earnings per share before considering the effects of the stock dividend would be $10,200,000 ÷ 1,000,000, or $10.20. After the dividend: $10,200,000 ÷ 1,020,000, or $10.

Note that the dividend has no effect on net income, the numerator of the earnings-per-share computation. But it does affect the denominator and causes a mild dilution which, in theory, should be reflected by a slight decline in the market price of the stock.

Problem Four

Metro-Goldwyn-Mayer Film Co. declared and distributed a 3% stock dividend. The applicable market value per share was $7.75. The par value of the 966,000 additional shares issued was $1.00 each. The total cash paid to shareholders in lieu of issuing fractional shares was $70,000. Prepare the appropriate journal entry.

Solution to Problem Four

Retained income	7,556,500	
Common stock, $1.00 par value		966,000
Capital in excess of par value		6,520,500
Cash		70,000

To record 3% stock dividend. Total shares issued were 966,000 at $7.75, a total market value of $7,486,500. In addition, cash of $70,000 was paid in lieu of issuing fractional shares. Total charge to retained earnings was $70,000 + (966,000 × $7.75) = $7,556,500. The account Capital in Excess of Par Value was the description actually used by MGM.

Highlights to Remember

On the balance sheet, stockholders' equity is reported as the book values of the residual interests of a corporation's owners. By incorporating, the company provides limited liability for its owners and provides them with various rights, including the right to vote. Among equity holders, preferred shareholders have more senior claims to dividends and may have other special rights, including cumulative dividends, participating dividends, conversion privileges, and preference in liquidation. While bonds pay legally enforceable interest and principle payments at maturity, preferred stock has an infinite life, and dividend payments to shareholders become legal obligations only if the board declares the dividend.

Stock splits and stock dividends alter the number of shares held by the owners. Accounting for them involves rearranging the owners' equity account balances. Par value accounts, paid-in capital accounts, and retained earnings may be rearranged without changing the total owners' equity. The exact procedure depends on whether the par value of the new shares changes and on the number of additional shares. Similarly, a rearrangement of owners' equity arises when convertible preferred shares are exchanged for common shares.

Companies sometimes acquire treasury stock, which are shares of their own stock purchased in the open market. These shares may later be retired, resold, or used to meet obligations under option agreements. Transactions in the company's own stock never give rise to gains and losses and do not affect the income statement. Such transactions with the shareholders give rise only to changes in the equity accounts.

Cash dividends to preferred and common shareholders will be declared only when cash is available for payment. But in most states, dividends may be paid legally only to the extent that retained earnings exceed the cost of treasury stock. Additional restrictions on the right to pay cash dividends are often built into debt contracts.

Security analysts use the return on common stockholders' equity as a primary ratio to assess the effectiveness of management and the profitability of the firm. Analysts often compare the market value per share with the book value per share. A higher market value should be associated with growth prospects and possibly unrecorded assets, such as internally developed patents.

Accounting Vocabulary

appropriated retained income, *p. 563*

authorized shares, *p. 542*

book value per share of common stock, *p. 565*

callable, *p. 546*

convertible, *p. 546*

corporate proxy, *p. 542*

cumulative, *p. 543*

date of record, *p. 547*

declaration date, *p. 547*

dilution, *p. 556*

dividend arrearages, *p. 544*

issued shares, *p. 542*

liquidating value, *p. 545*

outstanding shares, *p. 542*

participating, *p. 545*

payment date, *p. 547*

preemptive rights, *p. 542*

preferred stock, *p. 543*

professional corporation, *p. 542*

rate of return on common equity, *p. 564*

ROE, *p. 564*

redemption price, *p. 546*

reserve, *p. 563*

restricted retained income, *p. 563*

series, *p. 546*

stock dividends, *p. 549*

stock options, *p. 564*

stock split, *p. 548*

treasury stock, *p. 542*

unlimited liability, *p. 542*

Assignment Material

Questions

12-1. In what ways are corporations "artificial persons"?

12-2. What is the purpose of preemptive rights?

12-3. Can a share of common stock be outstanding but not authorized or issued? Why?

12-4. In what way is preferred stock similar to debt? To common stock?

12-5. "Treasury stock is unissued stock." Do you agree? Explain.

12-6. "Cumulative dividends are liabilities that must be paid to preferred shareholders before any dividends are paid to common shareholders." Do you agree? Explain.

12-7. "The liquidating value of preferred stock is the amount of cash for which it can currently be exchanged." Do you agree? Explain.

12-8. "Common shareholders have limited liability." Explain.

12-9. List the characteristics that distinguish debt and equity.

12-10. What is the proper measure for an asset newly acquired through an exchange (e.g., an exchange of land for securities)? Explain.

12-11. What are convertible securities?

12-12. "The only real dividends are cash dividends." Do you agree? Explain.

12-13. "The term *stock dividends* is a misnomer." Why?

12-14. "A stock split can be achieved by means of a stock dividend." Do you agree? Explain.

12-15. "A 2% stock dividend increases every shareholder's fractional portion of the company by 2%." Do you agree? Explain.

12-16. "When a company retires shares, it must pay the stockholders an amount equal to the original par value and additional capital contributed for those shares plus the stockholders' fractional portion of retained earnings." Do you agree? Explain.

12-17. "Treasury stock is not an asset." Explain.

12-18. "Gains and losses are not possible from a corporation's acquiring or selling its own stock." Do you agree? Explain.

12-19. Restrictions on dividend-declaring power may be voluntary or involuntary. Give an example of each.

12-20. Why might a board of directors voluntarily restrict its dividend-declaring power?

12-21. How may the distinction between contributed and accumulated capital be blurred by traditional accounting?

12-22. Many corporations choose Delaware as the state in which to incorporate. Why might this be true?

12-23. Which are riskier, bonds or preferred stock? Why? Whose perspective are you taking, the issuer's or the investor's?

12-24. Suppose a preferred stock issue had to be redeemed by the issuer on January 1, 2000. Would it still be correct to report this in the stockholders' equity section of the balance sheet?

12-25. "A common stock selling on the market far below its book value is an attractive buy." Do you agree? Explain.

12-26. If you were about to loan a company a substantial amount of money, what kinds of restrictions might you want to place on the company's use of that money? What other conditions might you include in the loan to increase the probability that you would be repaid?

12-27. Why do you suppose companies offer their employees stock options rather than simply paying higher salaries?

Exercises

12-28 Distinctions Between Terms

On January 1, 1995, McDonald's Corporation had 1.25 billion shares of common stock authorized. There were 830.3 million shares issued, and 136.6 million shares held as treasury stock. How many shares were issued and outstanding? How many shares were unissued? Label your computations.

12-29 Distinctions Between Terms

Clean-up Services, Inc., a waste-management company, had 4 million shares of common stock authorized on August 31, 19X8. Shares issued were 2,073,178. There were 20,000 shares held in the treasury. How many shares were issued and outstanding? How many shares were unissued? Label your computations.

12-30   Preferences as to Assets

The following are account balances of Shopper's Mart, Inc. (in thousands): common stock and retained income, $300; accounts payable, $300; preferred stock (5,000 shares; $20 par and $24 liquidating value per share), $100; subordinated debentures, $300; and unsubordinated debentures, $100. Prepare a table showing the distribution of the cash proceeds upon liquidation and dissolution of the corporation. Assume cash proceeds of (in thousands): $1,400; $1,000; $790; $500; $400; and $200, respectively.

12-31   Cumulative Dividends

The Blackfoot Corporation was founded on January 1, 19X1:

Preferred stock, no par, cumulative, $6 annual dividend per share:	
Issued and outstanding, 1,000,000 shares	$ 40,000,000
Capital stock, no par, 6,000,000 shares	90,000,000
Total stockholders' equity	$130,000,000

The corporation's subsequent net incomes (losses) were:

19X1	$(5,000,000)
19X2	(4,000,000)
19X3	14,000,000
19X4	30,000,000
19X5	12,000,000

Required   Assume that the board of directors declared dividends to the maximum extent permissible by law. The state prohibits dividend declarations that cause negative retained earnings.

1. Tabulate the annual dividend declarations on preferred and common shares. There is no treasury stock.
2. How would the total distribution to common shareholders change if the preferred were not cumulative?

12-32   Stock Split

The annual report of Dean Foods Company included the following in the statement of consolidated retained earnings:

Charge for stock split	$4,401,000

The balance sheets before and after the split showed:

	After	Before
Common stock $1 par value	$13,203,000	$8,802,000

Required   Define *stock split*. What did Dean Foods do to achieve its stock split? Does this conflict with your definition? Explain fully.

12-33   Cumulative Dividends

In recent years, the Manzanita Company had severe cash flow problems. In 19X4, the company suspended payment of common stock dividends. In 19X5, it ceased payment on its $4 million of outstanding 7% cumulative preferred stock. No common or preferred dividends were paid in 19X5 or 19X6. In 19X7, Manzanita's board of directors decided that $980,000 was available for cash dividends. Compute the preferred stock dividend and the common stock dividend for 19X7.

12-34   Reverse Stock Split

According to a news story, "The shareholders of QED approved a one-for-ten reverse split of QED's common stock." Accounting for a reverse stock split applies the same principles as accounting for a regular stock split. QED Exploration, Inc., is an oil-development company operating in Texas and Louisiana. QED's stockholders' equity section before the reverse split included:

Common stock, authorized 30,000,000 shares, issued 23,530,000 shares	$ 287,637
Additional paid-in capital	3,437,547
Retained income	2,220,895
Less treasury stock, at cost, 1,017,550 shares	(305,250)
Total stockholders' equity	$5,640,829

Required

1. Prepare QED's stockholders' equity section after the reverse stock split.
2. Comment on possible reasons for a reverse split.

12-35   Book Value and Return on Equity

Reach Company had net income of $10 million in 19X8. The stockholders' equity section of its 19X8 annual report follows:

	19X8	19X7
Stockholders' equity:		
9% Preferred stock, $50 par value, 400,000 shares authorized, 300,000 shares issued	$ 15,000,000	$ 15,000,000
Common stock, $1 par, 5,000,000 authorized, 2,000,000 and 1,800,000 issued	2,000,000	1,800,000
Additional paid-in capital	32,000,000	30,000,000
Retained earnings	69,000,000	65,000,000
Total stockholders' equity	$118,000,000	$111,800,000

Required

1. Compute the book value per share of common stock at the end of 19X8.
2. Compute the rate of return on common equity for 19X8.
3. Compute the amount of cash dividends on common stock declared during 19X8. (*Hint*: Examine the retained earnings T-account.)

12-36   Financial Ratios and Stockholders' Equity

Consider the following data for Crunch Company:

	December 31	
	19X2	19X1
Stockholders' equity:		
Preferred stock, 100,000 shares, $40 par, liquidation value $44	$ 4,000,000	$ 4,000,000
Common stock, 2,000,000 shares, $4 par	8,000,000	8,000,000
Additional paid-in capital	5,000,000	5,000,000
Retained income	3,000,000	1,400,000
Total stockholders' equity	$20,000,000	$18,400,000

Net income was $3 million for 19X2. The preferred stock is 10%, cumulative. The regular annual dividend was declared on the preferred stock, and the common shareholders received dividends of $.50 per share. The market price of the common stock on December 31, 19X2, was $10.50 per share.

Required   Compute the following statistics for 19X2: rate of return on common equity, earnings per share of common stock, price-earnings ratio, dividend-payout ratio, dividend-yield ratio, and book value per share of common stock. (You may want to review pages 564-66.)

12-37   Stock Options

Company Q granted its top executives options to purchase 5,000 shares of common stock (par $2) at $20 per share, the market price today. The options may be exercised over a four-year span, starting three years hence. Suppose all options are exercised three years hence, when the market value of the stock is $30 per share. Prepare the appropriate journal entry on the books of Company Q.

12-38   Stockholders' Equity Section

The following are data for the Bianchi Corporation. Prepare a detailed stockholders' equity section as it would appear in the balance sheet at December 31, 19X3:

6% cumulative preferred stock, $40 par value, callable at $42, authorized 100,000 shares, issued and outstanding 80,000 shares	$ 3,200,000
Treasury stock, common (at cost)	5,000,000
Additional paid-in capital, common stock	9,000,000
Dividends payable	100,000
Retained income	15,000,000
Additional paid-in capital, preferred stock	1,000,000
Common stock, $5 par value per share, authorized 900,000 shares, issued 600,000 shares of which 30,000 are held in the treasury	3,000,000

12-39   Shareholders' Equity Section

Consider the following data (in millions), which are from the 1991 and 1994 balance sheets of DuPont, a 200-year-old, international chemical company.

	1994	1991
Reinvested earnings	$7,406	$11,681
Preferred stock	237	237
Additional paid-in capital	4,771	4,418
Common shares: $.60 par value, 900,000,000 authorized, 680,000,000 shares issued and outstanding in 1994	408	403

Required   1. DuPont classified the above amounts as shareholders' equity. Prepare that section of the balance sheet for 1994.
2. Give the journal entry to record DuPont's $1.82 per share dividend on common for 1994.
3. Compare total shareholders' equity for 1991 and 1994. Comment on the change.

12-40   Effects on Stockholders' Equity

Indicate the effect (+ , – , or 0) on *total* stockholders' equity of General Electric for each of the following:

1. Operating loss for the period of $900,000.
2. Sale of 100 shares of General Electric by Jay Smith to Tom Jones.
3. Declaration of a stock dividend on common stock.

4. Issuance of a stock dividend on common stock.

5. Failing to declare a regular dividend on cumulative preferred stock.

6. Declaration of a cash dividend of $50,000 in total.

7. Payment of item 6.

8. Purchase of ten shares of treasury stock for $1,000 cash.

9. Sale of treasury stock, purchased in item 8, for $1,200.

10. Sale of treasury stock, purchased in item 8, for $900.

Problems

12-41   Dividends and Cumulative Preferred Stock

Commercial Decal, Inc., maker of ceramic decals and plastic foils, started 19X8 with retained income of $2,463,951. Commercial Decal's balance sheet showed:

6% Cumulative Convertible Preferred Stock, par value $10 a share, authorized 200,000 shares; issued 52,136 shares	$ 521,360
Common stock, par value $.20 a share, authorized 2,000,000 shares, issued 1,322,850 shares	264,570
Additional paid-in capital	2,063,351
Retained income	2,463,951
Less: Treasury stock, at cost:	
Preferred stock, 11,528 shares	(80,249)
Common stock, 93,091 shares	(167,549)
Total stockholders' equity	$5,065,434

Required

1. Suppose Commercial Decal had paid no dividends, preferred or common, in the prior year, 19X7. All preferred dividends had been paid through 19X6. Management decided at the end of 19X8 to pay $.05 per share common dividends. Calculate the preferred dividends that would be paid during 19X8. Prepare journal entries for recording both preferred and common dividends. Assume that no preferred or common shares were issued or purchased during 19X8.

2. Suppose 19X8 net income was $200,000. Compute the ending balance in the Retained Income account.

12-42   Dividend Reinvestment Plans

Many corporations have automatic dividend reinvestment plans. The shareholder may elect not to receive his or her cash dividends. Instead an equivalent amount of cash is invested in additional stock (at the current market value) that is issued to the shareholder.

Holiday Inns, Inc., had the following data during a recent year:

Holiday Inns, Inc.

Common stock: authorized 120,000,000 shares; $1.50 par value; issued 34,786,931 shares	$ 52,180,396
Capital surplus	271,004,000
Retained earnings	710,909,000

Required

1. Suppose Holiday Inns declared a cash dividend of $.14 per share. Holders of 10% of the company's shares decided to reinvest in the company under an automatic dividend reinvestment plan rather than accepting the cash. The market price of the shares upon issuance was $30 per share. Prepare the journal entry (or entries) for these transactions. There was no treasury stock.

2. A letter to the editor of *Business Week* commented:

Stockholders participating in dividend reinvestment programs pay taxes on dividends not really received.

If a company would refrain from paying dividends only to take them back as reinvestments, it would save paperwork, and the stockholder would save income tax.

Do you agree with the writer's remarks? Explain in detail.

12-43 Meaning of Stock Splits
A letter of January 31 to shareholders of United Financial, a California savings and loan company, said:

Once again, I want to take the opportunity of sending you some good news about recent developments at United Financial. Last week the board raised United's quarterly cash dividend 12½ percent and then declared a 5-for-4 stock split in the form of a 25 percent stock dividend. The additional shares will be distributed on March 15 to shareholders of record February 15.

On March 16, the board approved a merger between National Steel Corporation and United Financial. The agreement called for a cash payment of $33.60 on each outstanding United Financial share. The original National Steel offer (in early February) was $42 per share for the 5.8 million shares outstanding.

Required
1. As a recipient of the letter of January 31, you were annoyed by the five-for-four stock split. Prepare a letter to the chairman indicating the reasons for your displeasure.
2. Prepare a response to the unhappy shareholder in part 1.
3. A shareholder of United Financial wrote to the chairman in early March: "I'm confused about the change in the agreed upon price per share. I owned 100 shares and thought I'd receive $4,200. Now the price has dropped from $42.00 to $33.60." Prepare a response to the shareholder.

12-44 Stock Dividend and Fractional Shares
The Siegl Company decared and distributed a 2% stock dividend. The stockholders' equity before the dividend was:

Common stock, 5,000,000 shares, $2 par	$ 10,000,000
Additional paid-in capital	40,000,000
Retained earnings	50,000,000
Total stockholders' equity	$100,000,000

The market price of Siegl's shares was $20 when the stock dividend was distributed. Siegl paid cash of $30,000 in lieu of issuing fractional shares.

Required
1. Prepare the journal entry for the declaration and distribution of the stock dividend.
2. Show the stockholders' equity section after the stock dividend.
3. How did the stock dividend affect total stockholders' equity? How did it affect the proportion of the company owned by each shareholder?

12-45 Issuance and Retirement of Shares, Cash Dividends
On January 2, 19X1, Cherokee Investment Company began business by issuing 5,000 $2 par value shares for $100,000 cash. The cash was invested, and on December 26, 19X1, all investments were sold for $114,000 cash. Operating expenses for 19X1 were $5,000, all paid in cash. Therefore net income for 19X1 was $9,000. On December 27, the board of directors declared a $.70 per share cash dividend, payable on January 15, 19X2, to owners of record on December 31, 19X1. On January 30, 19X2, the company bought and retired 1,000 of its own shares on the open market for $19 each.

1. Prepare journal entries for issuance of shares, declaration and payment of cash dividends, and retirement of shares.
2. Prepare a balance sheet as of December 31, 19X1.

12-46 Issuance, Splits, Dividends
(Alternate is 12-49.)

1. Pemez Company issued 100,000 shares of common stock, $6 par, for $35 cash per share on December 31, 19X1. Prepare the journal entry.

2. Pemez Company had accumulated earnings of $5 million by December 31, 19X5. The board of directors declared a three-for-one stock split and immediately exchanged three $2 par shares for each share outstanding. Prepare the journal entry, if any. Present the stockholders' equity section of the balance sheet before and after the split.

3. Repeat requirement 2, but assume that instead of exchanging three $2 par shares for each share outstanding, two *additional* $6 par shares were issued for each share outstanding. Pemez said they issued a three-for-one stock split "accounted for as a stock dividend."

4. What journal entries would be made by the investor who bought 1,000 shares of Pemez Company common stock and held this investment throughout the time covered in requirements 1, 2, and 3?

12-47 Dividends
(Alternate is 12-48.)

1. The Provo Company issued 400,000 shares of common stock, $4 par, for $30 cash per share on March 31, 19X1. Prepare the journal entry.

2. Provo Company declared and paid a cash dividend of $2 per share on March 31, 19X2. Prepare the journal entry.

3. Provo Company had accumulated earnings of $9 million by March 31, 19X5. The market value of the common shares was $60 each. A common stock dividend of 5% was declared; the shares were issued on March 31, 19X5. Prepare the journal entry. Also present a tabulation that compares the stockholders' equity section before and after the declaration and issuance of the stock dividend. Also include at the bottom of the tabulation the effects on the overall market value of the stock, the total shares outstanding, and the number of shares and percentage ownership of an individual owner who originally bought 6,000 shares.

4. What journal entries would be made by the investor who bought 6,000 shares of the Provo common stock and held this investment throughout the time covered in requirements 1, 2, and 3?

5. Refer to requirement 4. Suppose the investor sold 200 shares for $58 each the day after receiving the stock dividend. Prepare the investor's journal entry for the sale of the shares.

12-48 Dividends
(Alternate is 12-47.)

1. Gomez Company issued 300,000 shares of common stock, $1 par, for $20 cash per share on December 31, 19X1. Prepare the journal entry.

2. Gomez Company declared and paid a cash dividend of $1 per share on December 31, 19X2. Prepare the journal entry. Assume that only the 300,000 shares from part 1 are outstanding.

3. Gomez Company had accumulated earnings of $7 million by December 31, 19X5. The market value of the common shares was $60 each. A common stock dividend of

3% was declared; the shares were issued on December 31, 19X5. Prepare the journal entry. Also present a tabulation that compares the stockholders' equity section before and after the declaration and issuance of the stock dividend. Also include at the bottom of the tabulation the effects on the overall market value of the stock, the total shares outstanding, and the number of shares and percentage ownership of an individual owner who originally bought 6,000 shares.

4. What journal entries would be made by the investor who bought 5,000 shares of Gomez Company common stock and held this investment throughout the time covered in requirements 1, 2, and 3?

5. Refer to requirement 4. Suppose the investor sold 100 shares for $58 each the day after receiving the stock dividend. Prepare the investor's journal entry for the sale of the shares.

12-49   Issuance, Splits, Dividends

(Alternate is 12-46.) AT&T's 1994 annual report contained the following:

Common stock, par value $1.00 per share	$1,569,000,000

 Required

1. Suppose AT&T had originally issued 200,000 shares of common stock, $2 par, for $15 cash per share many years ago, say, on December 31, 19X1. Prepare the journal entry.
2. AT&T had accumulated earnings of $5 billion by December 31, 19X5. The board of directors declared a two-for-one stock split and immediately exchanged two $1 par shares for each share outstanding. Prepare the journal entry, if any. Present the stockholders' equity section of the balance sheet before and after the split.
3. Repeat requirement 2, but assume that one additional $2 par share was issued by AT&T for each share outstanding (instead of exchanging shares).
4. What journal entries would be made by the investor who bought 2,000 shares of AT&T common stock and held this investment throughout the time covered in requirements 1, 2, and 3?

12-50   Stock Split and 100% Stock Dividend

The Hamada Company wishes to double its number of shares outstanding. The company president asks the controller how a two-for-one stock split differs from a 100% stock dividend. Hamada has 100,000 shares ($2 par) outstanding at a market price of $60 per share.

The current stockholders' equity section is:

Common shares, 100,000 issued and outstanding	$ 200,000
Additional paid-in capital	2,300,000
Retained income	4,500,000

Required

1. Prepare the journal entry for a two-for-one stock split.
2. Prepare the journal entry for a 100% stock dividend.
3. Explain the difference between a two-for-one stock split and a 100% stock dividend.

12-51   Treasury Stock

(Alternate is 12-56.) Minnesota Mining and Manufacturing Company (3M) presented the following data in its 1991 annual report:

	December 31	
	1991	1990
	(in millions)	
Stockholders' Equity:		
Common stock, without par value, 500,000,000 shares authorized, with 236,008,264 shares issued in 1991 and 1990	$ 296	$ 296
Reinvested earnings	6,996	6,751
Total	7,292	7,047
Less: Treasury stock, 16,867,905 shares at December 31, 1991, and 16,174,861 shares at December 31, 1990	(999)	(937)
Stockholders' Equity, Net	$6,293	$6,110

Required

1. During 1991, 3M reacquired 2,733,416 treasury shares for $240 million. Give the journal entry to record this transaction.
2. Given the information provided, calculate how many treasury shares were issued in 1991 pursuant to stock option plans.
3. Suppose that on January 2, 1992, 3M used cash to reacquire 175,000 shares for $100 each and held them in the treasury. Prepare the stockholders' equity section after the acquisition of treasury stock. Also prepare the journal entry.
4. Suppose the 175,000 shares of treasury stock are sold for $120 per share. Prepare the journal entry.
5. Suppose the 175,000 shares of treasury stock are sold for $80 per share. Prepare the journal entry.

12-52   Repurchase of Shares and Book Value per Share

Mobil repurchased 3.2 million of its own common shares during 1994. Mobil shares averaged $80 per share during the year. The condensed 1994 shareholders' equity section of the balance sheet showed (dollars and shares in millions):

Common stock, no par, 442 shares issued, 396 shares outstanding	$ 885
Retained earnings and other	18,334
Treasury stock (46 shares)	(2,073)
Total stockholders' equity	$17,146

Required

1. Prepare the journal entry to record the 1994 purchase of treasury shares.
2. Compute the book value per share at December 31, 1994.
3. Compute the book value per share as if the 1994 treasury stock purchase did not occur.

12-53   Retirement of Shares

Security Systems, Inc., has the following:

Common stock, 10,000,000 shares @ $1 par	$ 10,000,000
Paid-in capital in excess of par	40,000,000
Total paid-in capital	$ 50,000,000
Retained income	10,000,000
Stockholders' equity	$ 60,000,000
Overall market value of stock @ assumed $20	$200,000,000
Book value per share = $60,000,000 ÷ 10,000,000 = $6	

Required   The company used cash to reacquire and retire 200,000 shares for $20 each. Prepare the stockholders' equity section before and after this retirement of shares. Also prepare the journal entry.

12-54   Disposition of Treasury Stock

Visque Company bought 10,000 of its own shares for $12 per share. The shares were held as treasury stock. This was the only time Visque had ever purchased treasury stock.

Required
1. Visque sold 5,000 of the shares for $14 per share. Prepare the journal entry.
2. Visque sold the remaining 5,000 shares later for $11 per share. Prepare the journal entry.
3. Repeat requirement 2 assuming the shares were sold for $9 instead of $11 per share.
4. Did you record gains or losses in requirements 1, 2, and 3? Explain.

12-55   Effects of Treasury Stock on Retained Income

Assume that Kim Company has retained income of $20 million, paid-in capital of $50 million, and cost of treasury stock of $14 million.

Required
1. Tabulate the effects of dividend payments of (a) $9 million and (b) $4 million on retained income and total stockholders' equity.
2. Why do states forbid the payment of dividends if retained income does not exceed the cost of any treasury stock on hand? Explain, using the numbers from your answer to requirement 1.

12-56   Treasury Stock

(Alternate is 12-51.) Perry Company has the following:

Common stock, 2,000,000 shares @ $3 par	$ 6,000,000
Paid-in capital in excess of par	34,000,000
Total paid-in capital	$40,000,000
Retained income	18,000,000
Stockholders' equity	$58,000,000
Overall market value of stock @ assumed $35	$70,000,000
Book value per share = $58,000,000 ÷ 2,000,000 = $29.	

Required
1. The company used cash to reacquire 100,000 shares for $40 each and held them in the treasury. Prepare the stockholders' equity section after the acquisition of treasury stock. Also prepare the journal entry.
2. Suppose that all the treasury stock is sold for $50 per share. Prepare the journal entry.
3. Suppose that all the treasury stock is sold for $30 per share. Prepare the journal entry.
4. Recalculate book value after each transaction above.

12-57   Convertible Securities

Suppose Company G had paid $300,000 to Company H for an investment in 10,000 shares of the $5 par value preferred stock of Company H. The preferred stock was later converted into 10,000 shares of Company H common stock ($1 par value).

Required
1. Using the balance sheet equation, prepare an analysis of transactions of Company G and Company H.

2. Prepare the journal entries to accompany your analysis in requirement 1.

12-58 Issue of Common Shares

Intermec Corporation, a leader in the field of bar code data collection, issued the following common shares during a recent year:

a. 780,000 shares through a public offering for net cash of $10,765,977, an average price of $13.80 per share.

b. 16,900 shares as part of an employee stock purchase plan; $218,093, or $12.90 per share, was received.

c. 88,283 shares for the exercise of stock options; $355,275, or $4.02 per share, was received.

The stockholders' equity section of Intermec's balance sheet at the beginning of the year was the following:

Common stock: authorized 10,000,000 shares with $.60 par value, issued and outstanding 4,510,908 shares	$ 2,706,545
Additional paid-in capital	4,603,092
Retained earnings	8,128,230
Total stockholders' equity	$15,437,867

Net income for the year was $4,008,991. No dividends were paid.

Required
1. Prepare journal entries for the common stock issues in *a*, *b*, and *c*. Omit explanations.
2. Present the stockholders' equity section of the balance sheet at the end of the year.

12-59 Repurchases

During 1994 AT&T's outstanding $1 par common shares increased from 1,546,518,000 shares to 1,569,006,000. The change included issuance of 22,490,000 new shares for $976,000,000. Dividends of $1,940,000,000 were declared during the year. Retained income rose from a deficit of ($2.11 billion) to $687 million.

Required
1. Give the journal entry to record the newly issued stock.
2. Calculate how many shares AT&T repurchased during the year.
3. With the exception of dividends and net income, other items affecting retained income caused an increase of $29 million. Calculate net income. Comment on the relation between net income and dividends.

12-60 Non-Cash Exchanges

Suppose Jacquier Company acquires some equipment from Pawnee Company in exchange for issuance of 10,000 shares of Jacquier's common stock. The equipment was carried on Pawnee's books at the $520,000 original cost less accumulated depreciation of $140,000. Jacquier's stock is listed on the New York Stock Exchange; its current market value is $50 per share. Its par value is $1 per share.

Required
1. Using the balance sheet equation, show the effects of the transaction on the accounts of Jacquier Company and Pawnee Company.
2. Show the journal entries on the books of Jacquier Company and Pawnee Company.

12-61 Covenants and Leases

The notes to the financial statements of Mitchell Energy and Development, Inc., reveal the existence of certain debt agreement restrictions on the level of consolidated stockholders' equity as well as on various asset-to-debt ratios:

The debt agreements contain certain restrictions which, among other things, require consolidated stockholders' equity to be equal to at least $400,000,000 and require the maintenance of specified financial and oil and gas reserve and/or asset value to debt ratios.

Required

1. Given the existence of the asset-to-debt covenants, is Mitchell more likely to be able to enter into operating leases or capital leases without violating the covenants?
2. If Mitchell Energy and Development, Inc., had refused to agree to these conditions at the time of the debt issues, how would it have affected the market price of the debt they issued?

12-62   Stock Options

AIM Telephones, Inc., is one of the top five independent telecommunications equipment suppliers in the United States. Net income for a recent year was $1,018,000, and AIM paid no cash dividends. During the year, AIM issued 538,522 new shares at an average price of $7.853 per share. In addition, executives exercised stock options for 99,813 shares at an average price of $2.304 per share. The stockholders' equity at the beginning of the year was:

Common stock, par value $.01 per share	$ 39,000
Capital in excess of par value	4,962,000
Retained earnings	1,182,000
Total stockholders' equity	$6,183,000

Required

1. Prepare journal entries for (a) the newly issued shares and (b) the stock options that were exercised. Omit explanations. Round calculations to the nearest thousand dollars.
2. Prepare a statement of stockholders' equity at the end of the year.
3. Suppose all the stock options were exercised when the stock price for AIM was $7.50 per share. How much did the executives gain from exercising the stock options?
4. How much compensation expense did AIM record when the options were granted? When they were exercised?

12-63   Treasury Stock

The following information was provided in footnote 4 of the 1994 H. J. Heinz annual report.

4. Shareholders' Equity

Information related to stock issued and in treasury, and to additional capital follows:

(in thousands)	Cumulative Preferred Stock $1.70 First Series $10 Par Amount	Common Stock Issued Amount	Common Stock Issued Shares	Common Stock In Treasury Amount	Common Stock In Treasury Shares	Additional Capital Amount
Balance April 28, 1993	$438	$71,850	287,401	$1,046,905	33,036	$170,308
Reacquired	—	—	—	222,582	6,475	—
Conversion of preferred into common stock	(40)	—	—	(985)	(36)	(945)
Stock options exercised	—	—	—	(27,605)	(1,054)	267
Other, net	—	—	—	(1,720)	(61)	549
Balance April 27,1994	$398	$71,850	287,401	$1,239,177	38,360	$170,179
Authorized Shares— April 27, 1994	40		600,000			

Capital Stock: The preferred stock outstanding is convertible at a rate of one share of preferred stock into 9.0 shares of common stock. The company can redeem the stock at $28.50 per share.

Provide summary journal entries to account for the treasury stock transactions during the period April 28, 1993, to April 27, 1994. Omit the journal entry for "Other, net."

12-64   International Perspective
Shares in Honda Motor Company are traded in the United States, and therefore Honda provides some financial information in an English-language annual report. The following information appeared there:

	Common Stock	Capital Surplus	Legal Reserve	Retained Earnings	Adjustment from Foreign Currency Translation	Total Stockholders' Equity
	U.S. dollars (thousands)					
Balance at March 31, 1993	$831,013	$1,667,009	$228,182	$10,957,111	$(3,689,452)	$9,993,863
Net income for the year				229,753		229,753
Cash dividends $0.14 per share (note 10)				(132,147)		(132,147)
Transfer to legal reserve (note 10)			6,166	(6,166)		—
Common stock issued and capital surplus arising from conversion of debentures (note 9)	378	(39)				339
Adjustment from foreign currency translation					(713,766)	(713,766)
Balance at March 31, 1994	$831,391	$1,666,970	$234,348	$11,048,551	$(4,403,218)	$9,378,042

See accompanying notes to consolidated financial statements.

(9) Common Stock

During the years ended March 31, 1992, 1993, and 1994, the Company issued approximately 159 thousand, 812 thousand, and 89 thousand shares, respectively, of common stock in connection with the conversion of convertible debt. Conversions of convertible debt issued subsequent to October 1, 1982, into common stock and exercise of warrants were accounted for in accordance with the provisions of the Japanese Commercial Code by crediting one-half of the aggregate conversion price equally to the common stock account and the capital surplus account.

(10) Dividends and Legal Reserve

The Japanese Commercial Code provides that earnings in an amount equal to at least 10% of all appropriations of retained earnings that are paid in cash, such as cash dividends and bonuses to directors, shall be appropriated as a legal reserve until such reserve equals 25% of stated capital. This reserve is not available for dividends but may be used to reduce a deficit or may be transferred to stated capital. Certain foreign subsidiaries are also required to appropriate their earnings to legal reserves under laws of the respective countries of domicile.

Cash dividends and appropriations to the legal reserve charged to retained earnings during the years ended March 31, 1992, 1993, and 1994, represent dividends paid out during those years and the related appropriations to the legal reserve. The accompanying consolidated financial statements do not include any provision for the dividend of ¥7 ($0.07) per share aggregating ¥6,816 million ($66,079 thousand) to be proposed in June 1994 or for the related appropriation to legal reserve.

Required

1. Give journal entries to record the items shown for 1994 except the foreign currency translation.
2. Give the journal entry that Honda will make for the proposed dividend and transfer to the reserve in June 1994. Assume the transfer is 10% of the dividends.
3. If stated capital is defined as the common stock account, how much more must Honda pay in dividends and add to the legal reserve before the 25% limit is met?

12-65   Stock Options and Ethics

Bristol-Myers Squibb is the third largest pharmaceutical company in the world. In 1993 the company granted executives options to purchase 5,464,022 shares of common stock. Suppose that all shares were granted with an exercise price of $60 per share, which was the market price of the stock on the date the options were granted, and that all options could be exercised anytime between 3 and 5 years from the grant date, provided that the executive still works for Bristol-Myers Squibb.

Assume that, at the same time the stock options were issued, Bristol-Myers Squibb also issued warrants with the same $60 exercise price that are exercisable any time in the next five years. The company received $7 for each such warrant.

Required

1. How much expense was recorded at the issue of each stock option?
2. How much value was there to the executive for each stock option issued?
3. How much did it cost the firm for each stock option that was issued?
4. Might the fact that an executive holds stock options affect his or her decisions about declaring dividends? Comment on the ethics of this influence.

12-66   Wal-Mart Annual Report

Use the Wal-Mart financial statements and notes contained in Appendix A to answer the following questions.

Required

1. Give the journal entry to record dividends declared in fiscal 1995.
2. Give the journal entry Wal-Mart used to record the two-for-one stock split in fiscal 1993.
3. What else might Wal-Mart have done to record a transaction that doubled the number of outstanding shares? How would this differ from the transaction in (2)?
4. What was the average price of shares issued for stock options during fiscal 1995?

12-67   Compact D from Disclosure

Select a company and use the Compact D software to answer the following questions.

Required

1. Identify each transaction that affected Stockholders' Equity during the most recent two years. Indicate which accounts were affected and by how much. List any transactions that appear unusual. For example, many companies, including Wal-Mart, have a change in shareholders' equity that arises from tax benefits related to stock options. This and a few other common transactions are beyond our scope in this introductory course.

13

Intercorporate Investments, Including Consolidations

Learning Objectives

After studying this chapter, you should be able to

1 Describe the accounting for short-term investments in debt securities and equity securities.

2 Explain the accounting for long-term investments in bonds.

3 Contrast the equity and cost methods of accounting for investments.

4 Explain how equity-method investments affect the statement of cash flows.

5 Explain the preparation of consolidated financial statements.

6 Describe the use of minority interests in consolidated financial statements.

7 Explain how goodwill arises and how to account for it.

8 Contrast the purchase method and the pooling-of-interests method of accounting for business combinations (Appendix 13).

This chapter discusses investments made by corporations. It begins with short- and long-term investments in debt securities. The chapter also covers the complexities involved when one company makes long-term investments in the equity securities of another company. The accounting for consolidated financial statements and the accounting for purchased goodwill complete the chapter topics.

When you think of the Ford Motor Company, you probably know that it makes many models of cars and trucks under various Ford nameplates around the world. You may not know that Ford owns Jaguar, the prestigious British luxury car manufacturer. You also may not realize that Ford owns 25% of Mazda, the rapidly growing Japanese auto manufacturer. Indeed, Mazda assembles the Ford Probe at its Michigan plant. A primary objective of this chapter is to help you understand how the diverse elements of Ford's international activities are combined into one set of consolidated financial statements.

Examples throughout the chapter stress the fact that investments in securities arise from many different motives. The accounting for such investments differs depending on the purpose of the investment, on whether it is an equity or debt security, and on the degree of control the investor has over the issuer of the security. Our treatment concentrates on underlying concepts rather than tedious details. The topics—short-term investments, long-term investments in bonds, equity method for intercorporate investments, consolidated financial statements, and accounting for goodwill—can be studied separately or together.

■ AN OVERVIEW OF CORPORATE INVESTMENTS

As noted in previous chapters, when a firm has an excess of cash, sound management dictates that the cash be invested rather than remain idle in the company's checking account. Corporations frequently make both short- and long-term investments in securities issued by other corporations.

In many instances, companies invest in debt securities issued by governments, banks, or other corporations. Both short-term and long-term debt investments in securities are common. For example, Ford owned $6 billion in debt securities as part of its Financial Services subsidiary at December 31, 1994. Nike reported $518 million of cash and equivalents, including short-term debt securities with less than three months to maturity. It is a common practice to obtain interest income on temporarily idle cash. Note that the short-term nature of the debt allows Nike to have the cash as needed.

In addition to debt securities, companies also invest in other corporations' equity securities. These investments are typically long-term investments, and when they are large enough, they allow the investing company varying degrees of control over the company issuing the securities. The links among corporations created by such investments are common and arise from various motivations. Ford bought Jaguar in 1989 for approximately $2.5 billion after a fierce competition with General Motors (GM). GM already owned Lotus, and Chrysler acquired Lamborghini. These major U.S. auto companies were all committed to a strategy that required a full range of automobile offerings, including a luxury nameplate. Ford's motives in acquiring 25% of Mazda were different. Ford does not control Mazda; rather the two companies function as partners who share various production efficiencies and technical know-how.

Corporate Marriage and Divorce

Some marriages succeed, others fail. Some business combinations work and some do not. What if the combination does not work? At the worst, the assets are sold off, the proceeds are distributed to creditors, and the company disappears. But less extreme possibilities exist.

One interesting alternative is called a *spin-off*. Part of the company, a distinct business unit, is distributed to the shareholders. The spun-off subsidiary becomes a completely separate entity with its own board of directors, management, assets, liabilities, and owners.

Business combinations occur to create efficiency, to share management expertise, to increase access to capital, to integrate related operations, and so on. Spin-offs tend to separate dissimilar business segments to create opportunities for more creative and innovative growth or to offer management of those segments a chance to invest directly in the subsidiary, smaller company that they now control.

As of February 1992, *Forbes* magazine identified ten pending spin-offs. For example Burlington Resources was about to spin off its subsidiary, El Paso Natural Gas. General Dynamics was about to spin off its business aircraft subsidiary, Cessna. In January 1994 Eli Lilly, a giant in pharmaceuticals, announced its intent to create a medical-devices holding company to be spun off or sold. Historically, spin-offs have been profitable investments. A recent study of 146 spin-offs over thirty years concluded they outperform the stock market by an average of 35% in their first three years as separate companies.

Spin-offs are not the only option. Often the parent simply sells the subsidiary. Eli Lilly sold its cosmetic subsidiary, Elizabeth Arden, which proved to be too different from a pharmaceutical company to be easily integrated into existing operations.

The business combination is often only the beginning of the story. Sometimes the buyer plans a divestiture as part of the initial strategy. When Black & Decker purchased Emhart in 1989, the plan was to quickly sell Emhart's information services division. This activity was not central to the core strategy: manufacture and sale of tools, hardware, and small electronics. Cash from the sale would pay down the significant debt incurred in the purchase. However, no buyers appeared, and, as of 1995, the information division represented 17% of the company. There were still rumors of a possible sale.

While Black & Decker's planned sale did not occur, there are often unplanned dispositions in response to altered circumstances. The challenge is to combine and retain the right combination of people and products to succeed over the long haul. ■

Sources: Eric S. Hardy, "Healthy Babies," Forbes (February 3, 1992), p. 112; 1994 Annual Reports of Eli Lilly and Black and Decker, Inc.

After companies create intercorporate linkages, the accountant must develop ways to report on the financial results of these complicated entities. In 1994 Ford increased its ownership in Hertz from 49% to 100%. As you will see later in this chapter, accountants conclude that Jaguar and Hertz, which are 100% owned and controlled by Ford, should be merged into Ford's financial statements in a different way than Mazda, a 25%-owned company, which Ford can influence but cannot control.

All investments made by companies are classified on a balance sheet according to *purpose* or *intention*. An investment should be carried as a current asset if it is a short-term investment. Other investments are classified as non-current assets and usually appear as either (1) a separate *investments* category between current assets and property, plant, and equipment, or (2) a part of *other* assets below the plant assets category.

short-term investment A temporary investment in marketable securities of otherwise idle cash.

marketable securities Any notes, bonds, or stocks that can readily be sold via public markets. The term is often used as a synonym for short-term investments.

■ SHORT-TERM INVESTMENTS

As its name implies, **a short-term investment** is a temporary investment in marketable securities of otherwise idle cash. **Marketable securities** are notes, bonds, or stocks that can be readily sold. The short-term *investment portfolio*

Objective 1

Describe the accounting for short-term investments in debt securities and equity securities.

(total of securities owned) usually consists of *short-term debt securities* and *short-term equity securities*. The investments are highly liquid (easily convertible into cash) and have stable prices.

Ordinarily, short-term investments are expected to be completely converted into cash within a year after the balance sheet date. But some companies hold part of their portfolio of investments beyond a twelve-month period. Nevertheless, these investments are still classified as current assets if management intends to convert them into cash *when needed*. The key point is that conversion to cash is immediately available at the option of management.

Some companies use the term *marketable securities* to describe their short-term investments. Cash equivalents, discussed in Chapter 11, are usually marketable securities that mature quickly and are repaid by the issuer. Strictly speaking, marketable securities may be held as *either* short-term investments or long-term investments. Thus 100 shares of General Electric (GE) common stock may be held as a short-term investment by one company and another 100 shares of GE may be held as a long-term investment by a second company. Consequently, this book will not use the term *marketable securities* as a synonym for the more descriptive term *short-term investments*, a term which includes the intention of the owner.

Short-Term Securities

short-term debt securities Largely notes and bonds with maturities of one year or less.

Short-term debt securities consist largely of notes and bonds with maturities of one year or less. They represent interest-bearing debt of businesses and governments. Investors purchase debt securities to gain the interest income.

Typically, debt security investments include short-term obligations of banks, called **certificates of deposit,** and **commercial paper**, which consists of short-term notes payable issued by large corporations with top credit ratings. **U.S. Treasury obligations** refer to interest-bearing notes, bonds, and bills issued by the federal government. These debt securities may be held until maturity or may be resold in securities markets.

certificates of deposit Short-term obligations of banks.

commercial paper Short-term notes payable issued by large corporations with top credit ratings.

The investor's balance sheet shows short-term investments immediately after cash. These securities are initially recorded at cost. Because their market values are reliable and readily observable, when those market values differ from cost there is a requirement to write them either up or down to their market value. Interest income from short-term debt securities is recognized as it accrues.

U.S. Treasury obligations Interest-bearing notes, bonds, and bills issued by the U.S. government.

Some companies follow the reporting practice of Ford Motor Company, which combines marketable debt securities *and* accrued interest (in millions):

Marketable securities, at cost and accrued interest (approximates market)	$1,478.7

Some companies combine cash and short-term investments, as exemplified by the current asset section of Kmart (in millions):

Cash (includes temporary investments of $26)	$278

short-term equity securities Capital stock in other corporations held with the intention to liquidate within one year as needed.

Short-term equity securities consist of capital stock (shares of ownership) in other corporations. Equity securities are regularly bought and sold on the

New York Stock Exchange or other stock exchanges. If the investing firm intends to sell the equity securities it holds within one year or within its normal operating cycle, then the securities are considered a short-term investment.

FASB Statement 115 adds another set of important categories to the notion of short-term investments. The following from Ford Motor Company's 1994 annual report illustrates the existence of three important categories. Note the bold captions: trading securities, available-for-sale securities, and held to maturity securities.

NOTE 2. MARKETABLE AND OTHER SECURITIES

Automotive

Investments in securities by the automotive division at December 31, 1994, were as follows (in millions):

Ford Motor Company Footnote to financial statements

	Amortized Cost	Gross Unrealized Gains	Gross Unrealized Losses	Fair Value
Trading securities	$7,382	$3	$56	$7,329
Available-for-sale securities				
Debt securities issued by foreign government	23	0	0	23
Corporate securities	231	0	1	230
Total available-for-sale securities	254	0	1	253
Held-to-maturity securities				
Corporate securities	20	0	0	20
Total investments in securities	$7,656	$3	$57	$7,602

trading securities
Current investments in equity or debt securities held for short-term profit.

held-to-maturity securities Debt securities that the investor expects to hold until maturity.

available-for-sale securities
Investments in equity or debt securities that are not held for active trading but may be sold before maturity.

Trading securities are current investments, including both debt and equity securities, that the company acquires with a short-term profit motive. These securities are accounted for at market value. As the market value changes over time, gains and losses are recorded and recognized in the income statement. The market value (fair value) is the basis for valuation on the balance sheet.

Held-to-maturity securities are debt securities that the owner does not intend to sell. They are accounted for at amortized cost. In chapter 10 we examined the amortization of premium and discount on bonds payable by the issuer of the debt. Corporations that invest in bonds use the same approach, as illustrated below. Market value is not the basis of accounting for held-to-maturity investments. While trading securities are always short-term, held-to-maturity securities are classified according to the time remaining until they mature and are repaid. If the time to maturity is less that one year, they are current investments; otherwise they are long-term. The notes accompanying the Ford disclosure above state, "All debt securities classified as...held-to-maturity have contractual maturities of one year or less."

Available-for-sale securities include all securities that fall between trading and held-to-maturity in terms of intent. Ford provides a separate line under this category for debt securities issued by foreign governments and for corporate securities. The corporate securities may include both debt and equity issues. The accounting is based on market value, and market values are reported on the balance sheet. However, the gains or losses that arise as market values rise and fall are *not* recorded in the income statement. Instead, these unrealized gains and losses are carried in a separate account in the stockholders' equity section.

Ford combines these three categories of securities into one total that appears on the balance sheet as total marketable securities for the automotive division. For 1994, the total is $7.6 billion. Also, Ford has an additional $6.3 billion of marketable securities that are held by the financial services arm of the company.

Adjusting Security Values to Market

When marketable securities are held in a trading category or as available-for-sale, they are carried in the financial statements using the market method. Under the market method, the reported asset values in the balance sheet are the market values of the publicly traded securities. Although the two categories have identical asset values, they differ in how changes in values are reported. For trading securities, the changes in value appear as unrecognized gains or losses in the income statement. For available-for-sale securities, the changes in value do not affect the income statement. Instead, the difference between historical cost and current market value is reported as a valuation allowance in the owners' equity section of the balance sheet.

Suppose a portfolio cost $50 million and had the following market values at the end of four subsequent periods (in millions):

	End of Period			
	1	2	3	4
Assumed market value	50	45	47	54
Balance Sheet Presentation				
Short-term investment at cost	50	50	50	50
Valuation adjustment to market	0	(5)	(3)	4
Carrying value	50	45	47	54
For Trading securities:				
Income Statement Presentation				
Unrealized gain(loss) on changes in market	0	(5)	2	7
For Available-for-Sale-Securities:				
Additional Balance Sheet Presentation				
Valuation Allowance in Stockholders' Equity	0	(5)	(3)	4

The tabulation shows the results for four periods. Most companies will present the market value directly as a single line on the balance sheet. The valuation adjustment is shown to provide a linkage to cost and to emphasize that the valuation allowance in stockholders' equity for available-for-sale securities will have a balance equal to the difference between historical cost and market. Recall that the unrealized gain (loss) is periodically closed to retained income. Over the four periods, the loss of 5 and gains of 2 and 7 provide a net increase in retained income of 4.

The journal entries for the two classes of securities for periods 2, 3, and 4 would appear as follows, without explanations:

Period	Trading Securitites			Available-for-Sale Securities		
2	Unrealized loss.	5		Valuation Allowance.	5	
	Marketable Securities		5	Marketable Securities.		5
3	Marketable Securities.	2		Marketable Securities	2	
	Unrealized gain.		2	Valuation Allowance		2
4	Marketable Securities.	7		Marketable Securities	7	
	Unrealized gain.		7	Valuation Allowance		7

■ LONG-TERM INVESTMENTS IN BONDS

Chapter 10 explained the fundamental approach to accounting for bonds payable by the issuing firm. Recall that the issuer amortizes bond discounts and premiums as periodic adjustments of interest expense. Investors analyze bonds held-to-maturity in a parallel fashion. However, while the issuer typically keeps a separate account for unamortized discounts and premiums, investors do not (although they could if desired).

Objective 2

Explain the accounting for long-term investments in bonds.

Bonds-Held-to-Maturity

Exhibit 10-5 is reproduced here as Exhibit 13-1, except the phrase *book value* is substituted for *net liability* to emphasize our change in perspective to the view of the investor in the bond. Recall that *book value* refers to the amount reported under generally accepted accounting principles.

This table shows the values for 10,000 two-year bonds paying interest semiannually with a face value of $1,000 each and a 10% coupon rate (5% interest every six months). The bonds were issued to yield 12% per annum with semiannual compounding. Despite the face value of $10,000,000, an investor acquiring the whole issue would initially pay only $9,653,500 to acquire the bond issue. Interest (rental payment for the $9,653,500) will take two forms, four semiannual cash receipts of 5% × $10,000,000 = $500,000 plus an extra lump-sum receipt of $346,500 ($10 million face value less amount paid at issue) at maturity.

The extra $346,500 to be paid at maturity relates to the use of the proceeds over the two years. Therefore, like the issuer, the investor amortizes the discount:

	6/30/96	12/31/96	6/30/97	12/31/97
Semiannual interest revenue:				
Cash interest payments, .05 × $10 million	$500,000	$500,000	$500,000	$500,000
Amortization of $346,500 discount*	79,207	83,959	88,997	94,337
Semi-annual revenue	$579,207	$583,959	$588,997	$594,337

* For the amortization schedule, see column 4 of Exhibit 13-1. Note that $79,207 + $83,959 + $88,997 + $94,337 = $346,500.

As this tabulation shows, the discount is used to adjust nominal interest to obtain the real interest. Amortization of a discount *increases* the interest revenue of investors. (Investor accounting for bonds issued at a premium is similar except that amortization of premium *decreases* the interest revenue of investors.)

Exhibit 13-2 shows how the investor and the issuer account for the bonds throughout their life. Note that interest revenue and interest expense are identical in each period.

Exhibit 13-1	Effective-Interest Amortization of Bond Discount

For Six Months Ended	(1) Beginning Book Value	(2) Effective Interest @ 6%*	(3) Nominal Interest @ 5%	(4) Discount Amortized (2) – (3)	Ending Book Value		
					Face Amount	Unamortized Discount	Ending Book Value
12/31/95	—	—	—	—	$10,000,000	$346,500	$ 9,653,500
6/30/96	$9,653,500	$579,207	$500,000	$79,207	10,000,000	267,293†	9,732,707
12/31/96	9,732,707	583,959	500,000	83,959	10,000,000	183,334†	9,816,666
6/30/97	9,816,666	588,997	500,000	88,997	10,000,000	94,337	9,905,663
12/31/97	9,905,663	594,337	500,000	94,337	10,000,000	0	10,000,000

* To avoid rounding errors, an unrounded actual effective rate slightly under 6% was actually used.
† $346,500 – $79,207 = $267,293; $267,293 – $83,959 = $183,334; etc.

Exhibit 13-2	Accounting for Bonds

Investor's Records   **Issuer's Records**

12/31/95	1. Investment in bonds	9,653,500			1.	Cash	9,653,500	
	Cash		9,653,500			Discount on bonds payable	346,500	
						Bonds payable		10,000,000
6/30/96	2. Cash	500,000			2.	Interest expense	579,207	
	Investment in bonds	79,207				Discount on bonds payable		79,207
	Interest revenue		579,207			Cash		500,000
12/31/96	Cash	500,000				Interest expense	583,959	
	Investment in bonds	83,959				Discount on bonds payable		83,959
	Interest revenue		583,959			Cash		500,000
6/30/97	Cash	500,000				Interest expense	588,997	
	Investment in bonds	88,997				Discount on bonds payable		88,997
	Interest revenue		588,997			Cash		500,000
12/31/97	Cash	500,000				Interest expense	594,337	
	Investment in bonds	94,337				Discount on bonds payable		94,337
	Interest revenue		594,337			Cash		500,000
12/31/97	3. Cash	10,000,000			3.	Bonds payable	10,000,000	
	Investment in bonds		10,000,000			Cash		10,000,000

Early Extinguishment of Investment

Consider another illustration of parallel recording for the investor and the issuer. Suppose in our example that the issuer buys back all of its bonds on the open market for $9.6 million on December 31, 1996 (after all interest payments and amortization were recorded for 1996). The investor is affected as follows:

Carrying amount:		
Face or par value	$10,000,000	
Deduct: Unamortized discount on bonds*	183,334	$9,816,666
Cash received		9,600,000
Difference, loss on sale		$ 216,666

* The remaining discount is $88,997 + $94,337 = $183,334, or $346,500 − $79,207 − $83,959 = $183,334.

The appropriate journal entries for investor and issuer on December 31, 1996, are:

Investor's Records

Cash	9,600,000	
Loss on disposal of bonds	216,666	
Investment in bonds		9,816,666
To record the sale of bonds on the open market.		

Issuer's Records

Bonds payable	10,000,000	
Discount on bonds payable ..		183,334
Gain on early		
extinguishment		216,666
Cash		9,600,000

Recall that this same extinguishment of debt was initially analyzed from the issuer's viewpoint in Chapter 10, page 446.

■ THE MARKET AND EQUITY METHODS FOR INTERCORPORATE INVESTMENTS

Objective 3

Contrast the equity and cost methods of accounting for investments.

affiliated company
A company that has 20% to 50% of its voting shares owned by another company.

equity method
Accounting for an investment at acquisition cost adjusted for the investor's share of dividends and earnings or losses of the investee subsequent to the date of investment.

Long-term investments in the equity securities of one company are frequently made by another company. The accounting for equity securities from the issuer's point of view was discussed in Chapter 12. The investor's accounting depends on the relationship between the "investor" and the "investee." The question is, How much can the investor influence the operations of the investee? For example, the holder of a small number of shares in a company's stock is a passive investor and follows the *market method,* whereby the investment is carried at market and dividends are recorded as income when received. This type of investor cannot affect how the company invests its money, conducts its business, or declares and pays its dividends.

As an investor acquires more substantial holdings of a company's stock, the ability to influence the company changes. A stockholder with 2% or 3% ownership will have little difficulty making appointments to speak with management. At 5% ownership, U.S. law requires the investor to report the ownership publicly. As ownership interest rises to 20% and beyond, the investor begins to be able to affect decisions, to appoint directors, and so on.

Once the investor has "significant influence," a term that GAAP rather arbitrarily defines as about 20% to 25% ownership, the market method no longer adequately reflects the economic relationship between the potentially *active investor* and the investee (or **affiliated company**). In the United States, such an investor must use the **equity method,** which accounts for the investment at acquisition cost adjusted for the investor's share of dividends and earnings or losses of the investee subsequent to the date of investment. Accordingly, the carrying amount of the investment is increased by the investor's share of the investee's earnings. The carrying amount is reduced by dividends received from the investee and by the investor's share of investee's losses. The equity method is generally used for a 20% through 50% interest, because such a level of ownership is regarded as a presumption that the investor has the ability to exert significant influence, whereas the market method is generally used to account for interests of less than 20%. The treatment of an interest in excess of 50% is based on the belief that the investor has control. See the section entitled "Consolidated Financial Statements" on page 595.

Suppose Buyit invests $80 million in each of two companies, Passiveco and Influential. Influential has a total market value of $200 million, earnings of $30 million, and pays dividends of $10 million. Passiveco has a total market value of $800 million, earnings of $120 million, and pays dividends of $40 million. Buyit owns 40% of Influential and accounts for that investment using the equity method. Buyit owns only 10% of Passiveco and uses the market method in its accounting.

To compare the methods, consider how Buyit's balance sheet equation is affected differently by investee earnings and dividends, as follows:

| | Market Method–Passiveco | | | | Equity Method–Influential | | | |
| | A | | = | L + SE | A | | = | L + SE |
	Cash	Investments		Liab. SE	Cash	Investments		Liab. SE
1. Acquisition	−80	+80	=		−80	+80	=	
2. a. Net income of Passiveco	No entry and no effect							
b. Net income of Influential						+12	=	+12
3. a. Dividends from Passiveco	+ 4		=	+4			=	____
b. Dividends from Influential					+ 4	− 4		
Effects for year	−76	+80	=	+4	−76	+88	=	+12

Passiveco: Under the market method, the investment account is unaffected. The dividend increases the cash amount by $4 million. Dividend revenue increases stockholders' equity by $4 million.

Influential: Under the equity method, the investment account has a net increase of $8 million for the year. The dividend increases the cash account by $4 million. Investment revenue increases stockholders' equity by $12 million.

The following journal entries accompany the above table:

Cost Method-Passiveco			Equity Method-Influential		
1. Investment in Passiveco	80		1. Investment in Influential	80	
Cash		80	Cash		80
2. No entry			2. Investment in Influential	12	
			Investment revenue*		12
3. Cash	4		3. Cash	4	
Dividend revenue†		4	Investment in Influential		4

* Frequently called "equity in earnings of affiliated companies."
† Frequently called "dividend income."

Under the equity method, income is recognized by Buyit as it is earned by Influential rather than when dividends are received. Cash dividends from Influential do not affect net income; they increase Cash and decrease the Investment balance. In a sense, Buyit's claim on Influential grows by its share of Influential's net income. The dividend is a partial liquidation of Buyit's "claim." The receipt of a dividend is similar to the collection of an account receivable. The revenue from a sale of merchandise on account is recognized when the receivable is created; to include the collection also as revenue would be double-counting. Similarly, it would be double-counting to include the $4 million of dividends as income after the $12 million of income is already recognized as it is earned.

The major justification for using the equity method instead of the market method is that it more appropriately recognizes increases or decreases in the economic resources that the investor can influence. The reported net income of an equity investor is affected by its share of net income or net loss recognized by the investor. Unlike the market method, the reported net income of the "equity" investor is not affected by the dividend policies of the investee, over which the investor might have significant influence.

Sears, the world's largest retailer of general merchandise, holds ownership in several companies. For years Sears held a 23% interest in Roper Corporation, a manufacturer of household appliances. Sears used the equity method in accounting for the investment because an ownership interest in excess of 20% is presumed to be evidence of ability to exert significant influence.

Equity Affiliates and the Statement of Cash Flows

Objective 4

Explain how equity-method investments affect the statement of cash flows.

A company with equity affiliates may use the direct method or the indirect method to prepare its cash flow statement. If the *direct method* is used, no special problem arises because only the cash received from the affiliate as a dividend appears. However, if the *indirect method* is used, net earnings is increased by the investor's share of its affiliates' earnings or is decreased by its share of the affiliates' loss. We must adjust reported income to reflect cash flow from operations. Suppose the investor had net income of $7.6 million, including equity in earnings of an affiliate of $2.5 million, and received $1.3 in dividends from the affiliate. Cash flow is $1.3 million. Since net earnings includes $2.5 million, the indirect method must adjust net earnings by $2.5 − $1.3 = $1.2, the amount of the equity in earnings that was not received in cash. The first part of the Operating Activities section of Dow Chemical's Consolidated Statement of Cash Flows for 1992 and 1993 is reproduced below. Dow's share of the earnings of affiliated companies exceeded the dividends received by $27 million in 1992. In 1993, equity affiliates had losses of $111 million, although Dow Chemical received $36 million in dividends.

The Dow Chemical Company and Subsidiaries Consolidated Statement of Cash Flows

In Millions		1993	1992
Operating Activities	Net income	$ 644	$ 276
	Adjustments to reconcile net income to net cash provided by operating activities:		
	Depreciation and amortization	1,552	1,487
	Undistributed (earnings) losses of related companies	147	(27)

parent company A company owning more than 50% of the voting shares of another company, called the subsidiary company.

subsidiary A corporation owned or controlled by a parent company through the ownership of more than 50% of the voting stock.

consolidated statements Combinations of the financial positions and earnings reports of the parent company with those of various subsidiaries into an overall report as a single entity.

Objective 5

Explain the preparation of consolidated financial statements.

■ CONSOLIDATED FINANCIAL STATEMENTS

United States companies with substantial ownership of other companies constitute a single overall economic unit that is composed of two or more separate legal entities. This is almost always a parent-subsidiary relationship where one corporation (the **parent company**) owns more than 50% of the outstanding voting shares of another corporation (the **subsidiary**). Ford Motor Company, for example, has sixty separate legal entities just in the United States and owns many distinct non-U.S. entities as well.

Why have subsidiaries? Why not have the corporation take the form of a single legal entity? The reasons include limiting the liabilities in a risky venture, saving income taxes, conforming with government regulations with respect to a part of the business, doing business in a foreign country, and expanding in an orderly way. For example, there are often tax advantages in acquiring the capital stock of a going concern rather than its individual assets.

Consolidated statements combine the financial positions and earnings reports of the parent company with those of various subsidiaries into an overall report as if they were a single entity. The aim is to give the readers a better perspective than they could obtain by examining separate reports of individual companies.

Consolidated statements have been common in the United States since the turn of the century, when interconnected corporate entities first began to appear in the form of "holding companies," a parent with many subsidiaries. J. P. Morgan's U.S. Steel, formed in 1901, is a classic example. As this economic form spread to Great Britain and the Netherlands, so also did consolidated accounting begin to spread. However, all countries did not embrace it. As recently as 1977, consolidated accounts were rare in Japan. In 1977, the law was changed, and now both "parent-only" and consolidated statements are publicly available although the consolidated statements are generally released later. Some countries in Europe, for example Switzerland, have been slow to adopt consolidation, but in the 1992 culmination of the EEC, the Seventh Company Law Directive required full implementation of consolidation by EEC members of the European Community. Similarly, the International Accounting Standards Committee has encouraged this trend since 1976.

The Acquisition

To illustrate the concept of consolidated financial statements, consider two companies: the parent (P) and a subsidiary (S). Initially, they are separate companies with assets of $650 million and $400 million, respectively. P acquires all of the stock of S by purchasing the shares from their current owners for $213 million paid in cash. Exhibit 13-3 shows the two companies before and after this transaction. Figures in this and subsequent tables are in millions.

This purchase transaction is a simple exchange of one asset for another from P's perspective. In terms of the balance sheet equation, cash declines by $213 million and the asset account, Investment in S, increases by the same amount. *The subsidiary S is entirely unaffected from an accounting standpoint*, although it now has one centralized owner with unquestionable control over all economic decisions S may make in the future. In this example, the purchase price and the

"Investment in S" equal the stockholders' equity of the acquired company. The preparation of consolidated statements in situations where these two amounts differ is discussed later, in the section entitled "Accounting for Goodwill."

Note that the $213 million is paid to the *former owners* of S as private investors. The $213 million is *not* an addition to the existing assets and stockholders' equity of S. *That is, the books of S are unaffected by P's investment and P's subsequent accounting thereof.* S is not dissolved; it lives on as a separate legal entity but with a new owner, P.

To Consolidate or Not To Consolidate

Under a controversial rule issued by the Financial Accounting Standards Board (FASB), companies issuing financial statements with fiscal years ending after December 15, 1988, are required to consolidate all majority-owned subsidiaries. Previously, consolidation of dissimilar businesses was not required. For example, a manufacturing firm would not consolidate a financing subsidiary. Proponents of the new rule claimed that prior to this Statement 94, companies could arbitrarily keep significant debt off their balance sheets, reducing debt-equity ratios and making it difficult to compare the debt levels of companies in the same industry.

Some companies opposed the new rule. JC Penney claimed that combining its insurance company with its retailing operations would "junk up" their financial statements. General Motors Corporation claimed that the rule would cost up to $100,000 in new computer programming to produce its financial statements and that the rule's benefits did not exceed its costs. The FASB doesn't believe the new standard will make companies with different operations any more confusing than before. Supporting that view, an official from Standard & Poor's Corporation, a company that rates corporate debt, claimed that they saw no change in General Motors from a ratings standpoint.

Nevertheless, some companies with debt covenants that restrict the amount of debt they can maintain changed their corporate structure to avoid the higher debt ratios resulting from the FASB rule. A *Wall Street Journal* writer claimed that Tenneco, Inc., a Houston-based company, created a holding company that kept the debt of its pipeline company separate from the debt of its other businesses.

How much were corporate debt-equity ratios affected? One study of fifty-four companies with finance-related subsidiaries that were unconsolidated before 1988 (Textron, Ford Motor Credit Corporation, General Motors Acceptance Corporation, among others) showed that consolidation would significantly affect debt-equity ratios. For example, Textron's debt-equity ratio rose from 1.65 to 5.33 after its subsidiaries were consolidated.

What consolidation rules apply in other countries? The International Accounting Standards Committee requires majority-owned subsidiaries to be consolidated. But actual consolidation practices vary considerably among countries. Many analysts claim that it is less important to know how things are consolidated than it is to know detailed information about the pieces that constitute the whole.

In Japan, both "parent-only" statements and consolidated statements are prepared; however, "parent-only" statements receive the most attention. The difference between U.S. and Japanese accounting practice is driven in part by a very different pattern of intercorporate relations. In Japan, many companies own significant portions of other companies. Collectively they form closely linked groups called "Keiretsu", with extensive interlocking or cross-ownership such that it is hard to sort out controlling relationships. In the U.S., parent-subsidiary relations are more common, cross-ownership is infrequent and consolidated financial statements are more meaningful. ∎

Sources: Lee Berton, "FASB Issues Rule Making Firms Combine Data of All Their Majority-Owned Units," Wall Street Journal *(November 2, 1987), p. 39; Penelope Wang, "What's Off, What's On,"* Forbes *(February 20, 1989), p. 110; David F. Hawkins, "Dealing with International Accounting Diversity: International Accounting Standards,"* Accounting Bulletin No. 1 *(Merrill Lynch, May 1990); Joseph C. Rue and David E. Tosh, "Should We Consolidate Finance Subsidiaries,"* Management Accounting *(April 1987), pp. 45-50; Survey of the Use and Application of International Accounting Standards,* International Accounting Standards Committee, *1988.*

	Before Purchase		After Purchase	
	S	**P**	**S**	**P**
Cash	$100	$300	$100	$ 87
Net Plant	300	350	300	350
Investment in S				213
Total Assets	$400	$650	$400	$650
Accounts Payable	$187	$100	$187	$100
Bonds Payable	—	100	—	100
Stockholders' Equity	213	450	213	450
Total Liabilities and SE	$400	$650	$400	$650

The following journal entry occurs:

P Books

Investment in S	213	
Cash		213

S Books

No entry

Each legal entity has its individual set of books; the consolidated entity does not keep a separate set of books. Instead, working papers are used to prepare the consolidated statements.

Consider a consolidated balance sheet prepared immediately after the acquisition. The consolidated statement shows the details of all assets and liabilities of both the parent and the subsidiary. The Investment in S account on P's books is the evidence of an ownership interest, which is held by P but is really composed of all the assets and liabilities of S. The consolidated statements cannot show both the evidence of interest *plus* the detailed underlying assets and liabilities. So this double-counting is avoided by eliminating the reciprocal evidence of ownership present in two places: (a) the Investment in S on P's books and (b) the Stockholders' Equity on S's books:

Entity	**Types of Records**
P	Parent books
+ S	Subsidiary books
= Preliminary consolidated report	No separate books, but periodically P and S assets and liabilities are added together via work sheets
− E	"Eliminating entries" remove double-counting and appear on a consolidating worksheet, not on the books of P or S
= Consolidated report to investors	

On the work sheet for consolidating the balance sheet, the entry to eliminate the double-counting of ownership interest in journal format is:

Stockholders' equity (on S books)   213
    Investment in S (on P books)   213

Separately, after the purchase, P has assets of $650 and S has assets of $400 but when we consolidate and eliminate the double-counting the consolidated assets are $213 less, $837. The consolidated result, expressed in terms of the accounting equation, is:

	Assets			=	Liabilities	+	Stockholders' Equity
	Investment in S	+	*Cash and Other Assets*	=	*Accounts Payable, etc.*	+	*Stockholders' Equity*
P's accounts, Jan. 1:							
Before acquisition			650	=	200	+	450
Acquisition of S	+213		−213	=			
S's accounts, Jan. 1			400	=	187	+	213
Intercompany eliminations	−213			=			−213
Consolidated, Jan. 1	0	+	837	=	387	+	450

100% Purchase of S

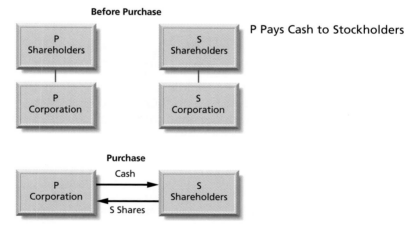

Before Purchase

P Pays Cash to Stockholders

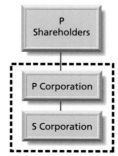

After Acquisition

After the initial acquisition, P accounts for its long-term investment in S by the same equity method used to account for an unconsolidated ownership interest of 20% through 50%. Suppose S has a net income of $50 million for the subsequent year (Year 1). If the parent company P were reporting alone using the equity method, it would account for the net income of its subsidiary by increasing its Investment in S account and its Stockholders' Equity account (in the form of Retained Income) by 100% of $50 million.

The income statements for the year are (numbers in millions assumed):

	P	S	Consolidated
Sales	$900	$300	$1,200
Expenses	800	250	1,050
Operating income	$100	$ 50	$ 150
Investment revenue*	50	—	
Net income	$150	$ 50	

*Pro-rata share (100%) of subsidiary net income.

P's parent-company-only income statement would show its own sales and expenses plus its pro-rata share of S's net income (as the equity method requires). The journal entry on P's books is:

```
Investment in S . . . . . . . . . . . . . . . . . . . . . . .   50
        Investment revenue* . . . . . . . . . . . .            50
```
* Or "equity in net income of subsidiary."

After this year's result is recorded by P, the entry to eliminate the Investment in S on the work sheet used for consolidating the balance sheets is $213 + $50 = $263.

Reflect on the changes in P's accounts, S's accounts, and the consolidated accounts (in millions of dollars):

	Assets			=	Liabilities	+	Stockholders' Equity
	Investment in S	+	Cash and Other Assets	=	Accounts Payable, etc.	+	Stockholders' Equity
P's accounts:							
Beginning of year	+213	+	437	=	200	+	450
Operating income			+100	=			+100*
Share of S income	+50			=			+50*
End of year	263	+	537	=	200	+	600
S's accounts:							
Beginning of year			400	=	187	+	+213
Net income			+50	=			+50*
End of year			450	=	187	+	263
Intercompany eliminations	−263			=			−263
Consolidated, end of year	0	+	987	=	387	+	600

* Changes in the retained income portion of stockholders' equity.

Review at this point to see that consolidated statements are the summation of the individual accounts of two or more separate legal entities. They are prepared periodically via work sheets. *The consolidated entity does not have a separate continuous set of books like the legal entities.* Moreover, a consolidated income statement is merely the summation of the revenue and expenses of the separate legal entities being consolidated after eliminating double-counting. The income statement for P shows the same $150 million net income as the consolidated income statement. The difference is that P's "parent-only" income statement shows its 100% share of S as a single $50 million item, whereas the consolidated income statement combines the detailed revenue and expense items for P and S.

Intercompany Eliminations

When two companies are consolidated, the accountant carefully avoids double-counting. In many cases the parent and subsidiary do business together. Suppose S charges P $12 for products that cost S $10, and the sale is made on credit. The following journal entries are made:

P's Records			S's Records		
Merchandise Inventory	12		Accounts Receivable	12	
Accounts Payable		12	Sales Revenue		12
			Cost of Goods Sold	10	
			Merchandise Inventory		10

But has anything happened economically? Not really. As far as the consolidated entity is concerned the product is just moved from one location to another. If P paid cash to S, the cash just shifts from "one pocket to another." So this transaction is not an important one from the perspective of the consolidated company, and it should be eliminated. It is important that each separate legal entity keep track of its transactions, but the accountant can undo these intercompany transactions when the consolidation is done. The accountant needs to eliminate the intercompany receivable and payable, eliminate the costs and revenues, and be sure the inventory is carried at its cost to the consolidated company, $10. The following consolidation journal entries are used in the work sheet consolidation process to accomplish that.

Accounts Payable (P)	12	
Accounts Receivable (S)		12
Sales Revenue (S)	12	
Cost of Goods Sold (S)		10
Merchandise Inventory (P)		2

The parenthetical letters show whose records contain the account balances. But remember, these entries *are not* recorded on the individual records of either company, only in the consolidation work sheet.

Objective 6

Describe the use of minority interests in consolidated financial statements.

Minority Interests

Our example of the consolidation of P and S assumes that P purchased 100% of S. This is often not true. One company can control another with just 51% of

minority interests
The outside shareholders' interests, as opposed to the parent's interests, in a subsidiary corporation.

the shares. For example, Corning owns 51% of Corning Asahi Video Products Company, and the remainder is owned by Asahi Glass America, Inc. Corning consolidates Asahi Video into its consolidated financial statements. But Asahi Glass has a claim on some of the consolidated assets and has a claim on some of Asahi Video's earnings. These claims are called *minority interests*. **Minority interests** represent the rights of nonmajority shareholders in the assets and earnings of a company that is consolidated into the accounts of its major shareholder. On the consolidated 1994 earnings statement, Corning shows a reduction of net income of $50.7 million due to "Minority interest in earnings of subsidiaries." On the consolidated balance sheet, Corning shows a $247 million "Minority Interest in Subsidiary Companies."

To make this idea more concrete, assume that our parent company (**P**) bought 90% of **S**. The next table, using the basic figures of the previous example, shows the overall approach to a consolidated balance sheet immediately after the acquisition. P's 90% of S cost 0.90 × $213, or $192 million. The minority interest is 10%, or $21 million. (All dollar amounts are rounded to the nearest million.)

90% Purchase of S:
P Pays Cash to Some
S Shareholders;
Some S Shareholders
Retain Minority Interest

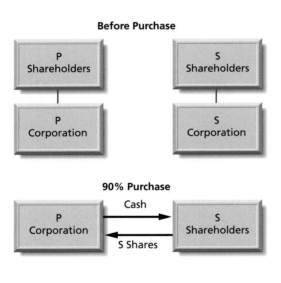

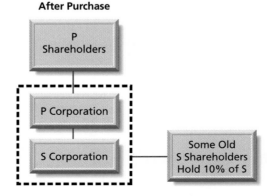

	Assets		=	Liabilities +		Stockholders' Equity		
	Investment in S	+	*Cash and Other Assets* =	*Accounts Payable, etc.*	+	*Minority Interest*	+	*Stockholders' Equity*
P's accounts, Jan. 1:								
Before acquisition			650 =	200			+	450
Acquisition of 90% of S	+192		−192 =					
S's accounts, Jan. 1:			400 =	187			+	213
Intercompany eliminations	−192		=			+21		−213
Consolidated, Jan. 1	0	+	858 =	387	+	21	+	450

Again, suppose S has a net income of $50 million for the year. The same basic procedures are followed by P and by S regardless of whether S is 100% owned or 90% owned. However, the presence of a minority interest changes the *consolidated* income statement slightly, as follows:

	P	S	Consolidated
Sales	$900	$300	$1,200
Expenses	800	250	1,050
Operating income	$100	$ 50	$ 150
Investment Revenue*	45	—	
Net income	$145	$ 50	
Minority interest (10%) in subsidiary's net income			5
Net income to consolidated entity			$ 145

*Pro-rata share (90%) of subsidiary net income.

Consolidated balance sheets at the end of the year would also be affected, as follows:

	Assets		=	Liabilities +		Stockholders' Equity		
	Investment in S	+	*Cash and Other Assets* =	*Accounts Payable, etc.*	+	*Minority Interest*	+	*Stockholders' Equity*
P's accounts:								
Beginning of year, before acquisition			650 =	200			+	450
Acquisition	192		−192 =					
Operating income			+100 =					+100
Share of S income	+45		=					+45
End of year	237	+	558 =	200			+	595
S's accounts:								
Beginning of year			400 =	187			+	213
Net income			+50 =					+50
End of year		+	450 =	187			+	263
Intercompany eliminations	−237		=			+26*		−263
Consolidated, end of year	0	+	1,008 =	387	+	26*	+	595

* Beginning minority interest plus minority interest in net income: 21 + .10(50) = 21 + 5 = 26.

Who Controls Whom?

Intercorporate investments occur worldwide, and different countries have made different choices ■ about how to define control and about when to consolidate the financial results of two related companies. Consolidation is appropriate when one entity can direct the use of the assets of another entity. In Australia, the definition of control and the decision to consolidate two firms is complex and relies on a combination of factors, including not only whether one firm owns 50% of another, but also whether it can control the membership of the board of directors and whether other investors own significant concentrated blocks of stock. Thus an Australian company might own only 40% of another company but might control it, because of board membership and because no other shareholder owned enough shares to care much about what happened.

In the United States, GAAP specifies three methods for accounting for intercorporate investments, and in 1995 "bright line" tests are used to choose among them. For ownership of less than 20% the market method is used, above 50% consolidation generally is required, and between the two the equity method is used. As this is being written, the FASB is debating whether to modify U.S. GAAP. If they do, it will no doubt move toward the more common and flexible definitions of control currently in use internationally.

In the Australian setting, Adelaide Steamship Group is a famous example of interlocking ownership. Adelaide Steamship was the top firm in such a system. Under U.S. rules none of the companies would have been consolidated, since none owned 50% of another. Three related companies each owned one third of a fourth company. Together they could direct the fourth company's every move, but none of the first three was consolidated with the fourth. Australia's new rules take these interconnections into account. It is not clear that consolidation and better disclosure would have saved the investors from the near total loss they suffered when the four companies collapsed a few years ago, but it would certainly have helped the investors understand the interconnected risks they faced with an investment in any of the three apparently "independent" companies.

Consider what control and influence might mean. USAir is a major airline in the U.S. that has one of the highest cost structures in the business. While United converted to employee ownership and American reached agreement on employee participation in profits during the early 1990s, USAir has struggled to engage its employees in similar agreements. The various unions have demanded representation on the board of directors as part of an arrangement to reduce wages and increase scheduling flexibility. USAir Chairman, Seth Schofield, may have favored such a plan, but could not accept it because British Airways PLC, owner of 24% of USAir, has adamantly opposed any voting role for the unions. Twenty-four percent of the shares provides British Airways with significant authority.

Also in the news at this writing is the termination of Joseph Antonini, former chairman of Kmart, a direct competitor of Wal-Mart. Ten years ago Kmart was the bigger company, and many predicted that Wal-Mart would never exceed Kmart on any financial measure. But Sam Walton, Wal-Mart's founder, generated spectacular growth while Kmart languished. Years after Wal-Mart passed Kmart, the board still supported Antonini. What finally lead to his dismissal? CALPERS, the California pension system, and other institutional holders of Kmart stock decided enough was enough. While none of them owned enough shares to individually have significant influence over the Kmart board, their collective voice was loud and clear. The Kmart board finally agreed.

These three examples show how different owners without 50% direct ownership of the firm can significantly direct managerial decisions. The accounting rules are intended to track the degree of influence, but the bright line tests described in this chapter may well change as the FASB considers more complex ways to assess control. Keep your eyes out for changes in the accounting rules and for the ways in which different forces guide the critical decisions that affect a firm's future and that may determine the risks and rewards faced by investors. ■

Source: K. Duncan, "Attributes of Dominant Control," Working Paper, Bond University, Australia, 1994.

As indicated in the table, the eliminating entry on the work sheet used for consolidating the balance sheet is:

Stockholders' equity (on S books)	263	
Investment in S (on P books)		237
Minority interest (on consolidated statements)		26

Thus the minority interest can be regarded as identifying the interests of those shareholders who own the 10% of the *subsidiary* stockholders' equity that is not eliminated by consolidation.

■ PURCHASED GOODWILL

The example in the previous section on consolidated financial statements assumed that the acquisition cost of Company S by Company P was equal to the *book value* of Company S. However, the total purchase price paid by P often exceeds the book values of the assets acquired. In fact, the purchase price also often exceeds the sum of the fair market values (current values) of the identifiable individual assets less the liabilities. Such excess of purchase price over fair market value is called *goodwill* or *purchased goodwill* or, more accurately, *excess of cost over fair value of net identifiable assets of businesses acquired*. Recall that Chapter 9 discusses goodwill on page 399. For example, Philip Morris paid $13 billion for Kraft, but only $2 billion was assigned to identifiable individual assets. The remaining $11 billion was goodwill. Similarly, Ford paid $2.5 billion for Jaguar, $2.0 billion of which was recorded as goodwill.

Why would Philip Morris rather buy Kraft as a going concern than pay less to buy trucks, buildings, copying machines, accounting systems, and so on that would produce the products that Kraft produces? When customers consider a purchase, they know that Kraft offers reliable quality. Customers pay more for that reputation than they would for an unbranded cheese. When grocery stores lay out their shelf space, they offer Kraft more space in better locations than they allow for unbranded, unknown products. Customers are more prone to buy well-displayed products in prime locations. These established patterns and reputations are why Kraft's *goodwill* is valuable.

Why would Ford rather buy Jaguar than start its own luxury car line? Why pay $2 billion more for Jaguar than its physical assets are worth? The answer to this question is not as obvious as the Kraft example. Recently, several Japanese manufacturers have proven it is possible to create new prestige labels: the Lexus and the Infiniti. But these may be a notch below Jaguar in price and status. And new labels lack the generations of image building that lead people to conceive of success as being *able* to own a Jaguar. Ford made a strategic choice about the future extra income that the Jaguar name will provide. Only time will tell if the $2 billion investment in goodwill was worth it, not to mention the additional investment to transform Jaguar production processes made by Ford in the early 1990s.

Accounting for Goodwill

Objective 7

Explain how goodwill arises and how to account for it.

To see the impact of goodwill on the consolidated statements, refer to our initial example on consolidations, where there was an acquisition of a 100% interest in S by P for $213 million. Suppose the price were $40 million higher, or a total of $253 million cash. For simplicity, assume that the fair values of the individual assets of S are equal to their book values. The balance sheets immediately after the acquisition are:

	Assets		=	Liabilities	+	Stockholders' Equity
	Investment in S	+	*Cash and Other Assets* =	*Accounts Payable, etc.*	+	*Stockholders' Equity*
P's accounts:						
Before acquisition			650 =	200	+	450
Acquisition	+253		−253 =			
S's accounts			400 =	187	+	213
Intercompany eliminations	−213		=			−213
Consolidated	40*	+	797 =	387	+	450

* The $40 million "goodwill" would appear in the consolidated balance sheet as a separate intangible asset account. It is often shown as the final item in a listing of assets. It is usually amortized in a straight-line manner as an expense in the consolidated income statement over a span of no greater than forty years.

As suggested in the table, the eliminating entry on the work sheet for consolidating the balance sheet is:

```
Stockholders' equity (on S books)  . . . . . . . . . . .   213
Goodwill (on consolidated balance sheet)  . . . . .    40
     Investment in S (on P books)  . . . . . . . . . .          253
```

Fair Values of Individual Assets

If the book values of the individual assets of S are *not* equal to their fair values, the usual procedures are:

1. S continues as a going concern and keeps its accounts on the same basis as before.
2. P records its investment at its acquisition cost (the agreed purchase price).
3. For consolidated reporting purposes, the excess of the acquisition cost over the book values of S is identified with the individual assets, item by item. (In effect, they are revalued at the current market prices prevailing when P acquired S.) Any *remaining* excess that cannot be identified is labeled as purchased goodwill.

Suppose the fair value of the other assets of S (e.g., machinery and equipment) exceeded their book value by $30 million in our example. The balance sheets immediately after acquisition would be the same as above. In consolidation, the $40 million goodwill would now be only $10 million. The remaining $30 million would appear in the consolidated balance sheet as an integral part of the other assets. That is, the S equipment would be shown at $30 million higher in the consolidated balance sheet than the carrying amount on S's books. Similarly, the depreciation expense on the consolidated income statement would be higher. For instance, if the equipment had five years of useful life remaining, the straight-line depreciation would be $30 million ÷ 5, or $6 million higher per year.

As in the preceding tabulation, the $10 million goodwill would appear in the consolidated balance sheet as a separate intangible asset account. The eliminating entry on the working papers for consolidating the balance sheet is:

```
Stockholders' equity (on S books)  . . . . . . . . . . .   213
Equipment (on consolidated balance sheet)  . . .    30
Goodwill (on consolidated balance sheet)  . . . . .    10
     Investment in S (on P books)  . . . . . . . . . .          253
```

Goodwill and Abnormal Earnings

Goodwill is frequently misunderstood. The layperson often thinks of goodwill as being the friendly attitude of the neighborhood store manager. But goodwill can have many aspects. A purchaser may be willing to pay more than the current values of the individual assets received because the acquired company is able to generate abnormally high earnings. The causes of this excess earning power may be traceable to personalities or skills of employees, to store locations, to operating methods, and so forth. For example, a purchaser may be willing to pay extra because excess earnings can be forthcoming from:

1. Saving in time and costs by purchasing a corporation having a share of the market in a type of business or in a geographical area where the acquiring corporation planned expansion
2. Excellent general management skills or a unique product line
3. Potential efficiency by combination, rearrangement, or elimination of duplicate facilities and administration

Of course, if goodwill exists to be purchased it is because the target company originally generated it internally. For example, a happy combination of advertising, research, management talent, and timing may give a particular company a dominant market position for which another company is willing to pay dearly. This ability to command a premium price for the total business is goodwill. However, such goodwill is not recorded by the original company because it is not possible to objectively value it. Therefore the *only* goodwill generally recognized as an asset is that identified when one company is purchased by another. The arms-length market transaction allows the purchasing company to reliably value the goodwill.

As you might suspect, the final price paid by the purchaser of an ongoing business is the culmination of a bargaining process. Therefore the exact amount paid for goodwill is subject to the negotiations regarding the total purchase price. A popular logic for determining the maximum price follows.

Goodwill is fundamentally the price paid for "excess" or "abnormal" earning power. The following steps might be taken regarding the possible acquisition of Company M or Company N:

	Ordinary Company M	Extraordinary Company N
1. Fair market value of identifiable assets, less liabilities	$800,000	$800,000
2. Normal annual earnings on net assets at 10%	80,000	80,000
3. Actual average annual earnings for past five years (including for Co. N an excess or abnormal return of $20,000)	80,000	100,000
4. Maximum price paid for normal annual earnings is ten times line 2	800,000	800,000
5. Maximum price paid for abnormal annual earnings (which are riskier and thus less valuable per dollar of expected earnings) is six times $20,000	—	120,000*
6. Maximum price a purchaser is willing to pay for the company (line 1 plus line 5)	800,000	920,000

* This is the most the purchaser is willing to pay for goodwill.

The preceding table uses a "capitalization rate" of 10% (earnings divided by 0.10 or earnings multiplied by 10) to arrive at a purchase price for a normal company. This normal rate varies by risk and by industry. For example, the normal rate for an oil exploration company will be higher (and the earnings multiplier lower) than for a retail food chain. Goodwill is attributed to the exceptional company, and the earnings multiplier paid for extra earnings (the abnormal layer) is less than the multiplier used for the basic earnings (the normal layer). The capitalization rate for the abnormal layer is 16⅔% (earnings divided by 0.1667 or earnings multiplied by 6):

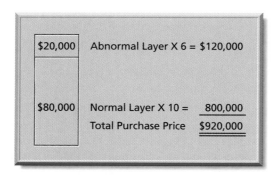

Amortization of Goodwill

Most long-lived assets other than land are depreciated or amortized over the period during which they benefit the firm. What about goodwill? Over what period does it benefit the firm? Does it have perpetual life? On the one hand, we might claim that reputations persist a long while. But they do so because the company continues to advertise, to produce a quality product, and to satisfy its customers. Coke and Pepsi are internationally known, distributed, and consumed, and they command a premium price over their generic competitors. Yet if one gave up the cola wars, the other would quickly gain market share. So goodwill can be maintained by continuous effort, but it does not have perpetual life.

How do accountants reflect this limited life in financial statements? Historically, international practice has ranged from recent British practice, which permitted immediate write-off of goodwill against stockholders' equity, to U.S. practice prior to 1970, which treated goodwill as infinitely lived. Notice that in both cases net income was unaffected by the presence of goodwill. Current U.S. GAAP requires that goodwill purchased after 1970 be amortized as an expense against net income over the period benefited, not to exceed forty years. The forty-year maximum is arbitrary and reflects the negotiated nature of many accounting principles. People could live with that flexibility. Amortization periods vary around the world. Germany and Japan require amortization over no more than five years, Australia limits the amortization period to twenty years, while Canada and the United Kingdom allow periods as long as forty years. Footnote disclosures of amortization practices for Ford, British Petroleum, and AT&T are reproduced below:

Ford:

> **Goodwill**. Goodwill represents the excess of the purchase price over the fair value of the net assets of acquired companies and is being amortized using the straight-line method principally over 40 years.

British Petroleum:

> **Goodwill**. Goodwill is the excess of purchase consideration over the fair value of net assets acquired. It is capitalized and amortized over its estimated useful economic life, limited to a maximum period of twenty years.

AT&T:

> **Goodwill**. Goodwill represents the excess of the purchase price over the fair value of net assets acquired in acquisitions accounted for using the purchase method. These amounts are amortized on a straight-line basis over the periods benefited, principally in the range of 10 to 15 years.

While the goodwill amounts are large and the annual amortization amounts are large in absolute terms, it is useful to keep them in perspective. For example, Ford's amortization is about $80 million per year, which was only 1% of 1994 pretax income. Of course, some companies have no goodwill since they have never purchased a subsidiary, while other companies have levels of goodwill larger than those considered here.

Managers, investors, and accountants tend to be uncomfortable about the presence of goodwill on the balance sheet. Somehow it is regarded as an inferior asset even though management decided that it was valuable enough to warrant a total outlay in excess of the total current value of the individual assets. As a practical matter, many accountants feel that the income-producing factors of goodwill are unlikely to have a value in perpetuity even though expenditures may be aimed at maintaining their value. Nevertheless, the generally accepted accounting principles do not permit the lump-sum write-off of goodwill upon acquisition.

■ PERSPECTIVE ON CONSOLIDATED STATEMENTS

Exhibit 13-4 provides summarized financial statements for Ford Motor Company for 1994. The circled items ①, ②, and ③ in the exhibits deserve special mention:

① The headings indicate that these are *consolidated* financial statements.

② Minority interests typically appear on the balance sheet, just above stockholders' equity. For Ford the minority interest is rather small. Footnote 7 to Ford's annual report indicates that the $24,920 million of other liabilities includes "Minority interest in net assets of subsidiaries" of $118 million. In the income statement the "Minority interests in net income of subsidiaries" appears as $152 million and is deducted to arrive at final net income of $5,308 million.

③ "Affiliated companies" are discussed in Ford's footnotes as follows: "Affiliates that are 20-50% owned, principally Mazda Motor Corporation, Autolatina, and Auto Alliance International, Inc., and subsidiaries where control is expected to be temporary, principally investments in certain dealerships, are generally accounted for on an equity basis." In the balance sheet, the "Equity in net assets of affiliated companies" appears with automotive assets in the amount of $3,554 million. On the income statement, the caption "Equity in net income of affiliated companies" describes the income associated with these affiliates in the amount of $271 million. Recall that the equity method attributes a share of the affiliates' *earnings or losses* to the investor. In 1990 these affiliates contributed a net loss of $96.6 million to Ford's consolidated income statement.

Exhibit 13-4

Ford Motor Company and Subsidiaries ① Consolidated Statement of Income for the Year Ended December 31, 1994 (in millions)

AUTOMOTIVE	
Sales	**$107,137**
Total costs and expenses	101,311
Operating Income	5,826
Net interest expense	(56)
③ Equity in net income of affiliated companies	271
Net (expense)/revenue from transactions with Financial Services	(44)
Income before income taxes—Automotive	**$ 5,997**
FINANCIAL SERVICES	
Revenues	**$ 21,302**
Total costs and expenses	18,554
Net revenue/(expense) from transactions with Automotive	44
Income before income taxes—Financial Services	**$ 2,792**
TOTAL COMPANY	
Income before income taxes	**$ 8,789**
Provision for income taxes	3,329
Income before minority interests	5,460
② Minority interests in net income of subsidiaries	152
Net Income	**$ 5,308**

Ford Motor Company and Subsidiaries ① Consolidated Balance Sheet December 31, 1994 (in millions)

ASSETS	
Automotive	
Total current assets	$ 26,863
③ Equity in net assets of affiliated companies	3,554
Property, net	27,048
Other assets	10,906
Total Automotive assets	68,371
Financial services	
Total Financial Services assets	150,983
Total Assets	**$219,354**
LIABILITIES AND STOCKHOLDERS' EQUITY	
Automotive	
Total current liabilities	$ 25,471
Long-term debt	7,103
② Other liabilities	24,920
Deferred income taxes	948
Total Automotive liabilities	58,442
Financial Services	
Total Financial Services liabilities	137,378
Preferred stockholders' equity in subsidiary company	1,875
Stockholders' equity	
Total stockholders' equity	21,659
Total Liabilities and Stockholders' Equity	**$219,354**

To help understand, consider the following simplified version of Ford Motor Company:

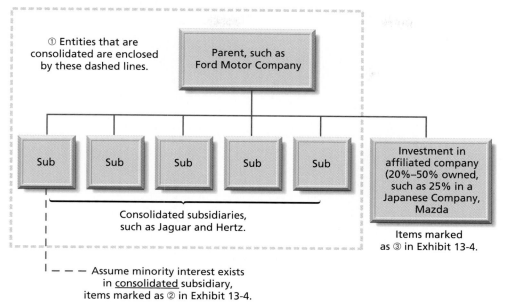

① Entities that are consolidated are enclosed by these dashed lines.

Parent, such as Ford Motor Company

Sub   Sub   Sub   Sub   Sub

Investment in affiliated company (20%–50% owned, such as 25% in a Japanese Company, Mazda

Consolidated subsidiaries, such as Jaguar and Hertz.

Items marked as ③ in Exhibit 13-4.

– – – Assume minority interest exists in <u>consolidated</u> subsidiary, items marked as ② in Exhibit 13-4.

The FASB requires that all subsidiaries be consolidated. That is, *all* subsidiaries, regardless of whether they are finance companies, brokerage companies, insurance companies, or other types, are an integral part of the complete consolidated entity. The FASB believes that excluding some subsidiaries from consolidation would result in the omission of significant amounts of assets, liabilities, revenues, and expenses.

There are exceptions to the general rule, but they are rare. A subsidiary shall not be consolidated if control is likely to be temporary or it does not rest with the majority owner.

Our discussion of item ③ for Ford Motor Company indicates that Ford sometimes owns dealerships that it will quickly resell to a new dealer and does not consolidate them. Ford's statements do reflect the consolidation of a manufacturing company with a financing company. Ford has chosen to structure the statements to clearly separate these two parts of its economic activity. The assets and liabilities of the Financial Services activity are listed separately as are the revenue and expense components. The footnotes provide additional detail on both segments of the business. Financial analysts pay particular attention to understanding the distinct parts of a business as they make predictions about the future. These issues are discussed in greater depth in Chapter 15, Analysis of Financial Statements.

■ RECAPITULATION OF INVESTMENTS IN EQUITY SECURITIES

Exhibit 13-5 summarizes all the relationships in intercorporate investments. Take a few moments to review the Ford financial statements in Exhibit 13-4 in conjunction with Exhibit 13-5. In particular, note that minority interests arise only in conjunction with *consolidated* subsidiaries. Why? Because consolidated balance sheets and income statements aggregate 100% of the detailed assets, liabilities, sales, and expenses of the subsidiary companies. Thus, if a minority interest were

Exhibit 13-5 Summary of Accounting for Equity Securities

Item in Exhibit 13-4	Percentage of Ownership	Type of Accounting	Balance Sheet Effects	Income Statement Effects	Major Journal Entries
①	100%	Consolidation	Individual assets, individual liabilities added together. For subsidiaries purchased for more than the fair value of identifiable assets, goodwill is shown.	Individual revenues, individual expenses added together. If goodwill exists, it must be amortized against net income.	None, except in work sheets for preparing consolidated statements; to eliminate reciprocal accounts, to avoid double-counting, and to recognize any goodwill.
②	Greater than 50% and less than 100%	Consolidation	Same as 1, but recognition given to minority interest in liability section.	Same as 1, but recognition given to minority interest near bottom of statement when consolidated net income is computed.	Same as 1, but recognition of minority interests is included in work sheet entries.

③	20% to and including 50%	Equity method	Investment carried at cost plus pro-rata share of subsidiary earnings less dividends received.	Equity in earnings (losses) of *affiliated or associated* companies shown on one line as addition to (deduction from) income.	Investment xx
					   Equity in earnings xx
					To record earnings.
					Cash xx
					   Investment xx
					To record dividends received.

not recognized, the stockholders' equity and net income of the consolidated enterprise would overstate the claims of the parent company shareholders.

In contrast, minority interests do not arise in connection with the accounting for investments in affiliated companies. Why? Because no detailed assets, liabilities, revenues, and expenses of the affiliated companies are included in the consolidated statements. The investor's interests in these companies have been recognized on a pro-rata basis only.

As we have seen, the accounting for investments *in voting stock* depends on the nature of the investment:

1. Investments that represent more than a 50% ownership interest are usually consolidated. A *subsidiary* is a corporation controlled by another corporation. The usual condition for control is ownership of a majority (more than 50%) of the outstanding voting stock.

2. **(a.)** The equity method is generally used for a 20% through 50% interest because such a level of ownership is regarded as a presumption that the owner has the ability to exert significant influence. Under the equity method, the cost at date of acquisition is adjusted for the investor's share of the earnings or losses of the investee subsequent to the date of investment. Dividends received from the investee reduce the carrying amount of the investment.

   (b.) Investments in corporate joint ventures should also be accounted for under the equity method. "Corporate joint ventures" are corporations owned and operated by a small group of businesses (the "joint venturers") as a separate business or project for the mutual benefit of the members of the group. Joint ventures are common in the petroleum and construction industries.

3. Marketable *equity* securities held as short-term investments are generally carried at market value. These investments are typically passive in the sense that the investor exerts no significant influence on the investee.

Summary Problems for Your Review

Problem One

Dow Chemical's annual report used the following asset nomenclature and classifications as of December 31, 1994 (in millions):

	$:
Marketable securities and interest-bearing deposits	565
	:
Total Current Assets	8,693
Investments:	
Capital stock at cost plus equity in accumulated earnings of 20%–50% owned companies	931
Other investments	1,529
Noncurrent receivables	330
Total Investments	2,790
Plant Properties	23,210
Less: Accumulated depreciation	14,484
Net Plant Properties	8,726
Goodwill	4,365
Deferred Charges and Other Assets	1,971
TOTAL	$26,545

Note that the statements are somewhat compressed and no detail for current assets is shown. Current assets may include some smaller holdings of equity securities that are valued at market.

Dow also shows "Minority Interests in Subsidiary Companies" of $2,506 million among its liabilities.

Required

1. Suppose "Marketable Securities" included a $24 million portfolio of equity securities. Their market values on the following March 31, June 30, and September 30 were $20, $23, and $28 million, respectively. Compute the following:
   a. Carrying amount of the portfolio on each of the three dates
   b. Gain (loss) on the portfolio for each of the three quarters
2. Suppose the $1,529 million of "Other Investments" included a $9 million investment in the debentures of an affiliate that was being held to maturity. The debentures had a par value of $10 million and a 10% nominal rate of interest, payable June 30 and December 31. Their market rate of interest when the investment was made was 12%. Prepare the Dow journal entry for the semiannual receipt of interest.
3. Suppose Dow's 20%-50% owned companies had net income of $200 million. Dow received cash dividends of $70 million from these companies. No other transactions occurred. Prepare the pertinent journal entries. Assume that on average Dow owns 40% of the companies.

Solution to Problem One

1. Amounts are in millions.
   a. Market: $20, $23, and $28.
   b. $20 – $24 = $4 loss; $23 – $20 = $3 gain; $28 – $23 = $5 gain. Gain or loss would be reported in the income statement for trading securities or in the stockholders' equity section for securities available-for-sale.

2.	Cash	500,000	
	Other investments (in bonds).	40,000	
	Interest revenue		540,000
	Six months' interest earned is .5 ×.12 ×		
	$9,000,000 = $540,000.		
	Amortization is $540,000 – cash received of		
	.5 × .10 × $10,000,000 = $540,000 – $500,000.		
3.	Investments in 20%-50% owned companies	80,000,000	
	Investment revenue		80,000,000
	To record 40% share of $200 million income.		
	Cash	70,000,000	
	Investments in 20%-50% owned companies ...		70,000,000
	To record dividends received from 20%–50% owned companies.		

Problem Two

1. Review the section on minority interests, pages 600-604. Suppose P buys 60% of the stock of S for a cost of 0.60 × $213, or $128 million. The total assets of P consist of this $128 million plus $522 million of other assets, a total of $650 million. The S assets and equities are unchanged from the amount given in the example on page 602. Prepare an analysis showing what amounts would appear in a consolidated balance sheet immediately after the acquisition.
2. Suppose S has a net income of $50 million for the year, and P has an operating income of $100 million. Other details are as described in the example on page 602. Prepare an analysis showing what amounts would appear in a consolidated income statement and year-end balance sheet.

Solution to Problem Two

1.

	Assets		=	Liabilities +		Stockholders' Equity		
	Investment in S	+	*Cash and Other Assets* =	*Accounts Payable, etc.*	+	*Minority Interest*	+	*Stockholders' Equity*
P's accounts, Jan. 1:								
Before acquisition		650 =	200				+	450
Acquisition of 60% of S	+128	−128 =						
S's accounts, Jan. 1		400 =	187				+	213
Intercompany eliminations	−128	=				+85		−213
Consolidated, Jan. 1	0	+ 922 =	387	+	85	+	450

2.

	P	S	Consolidated
Sales	$900	$300	$1,200
Expenses	800	250	1,050
Operating income	$100	$ 50	$ 150
Pro-rata share (60%) of unconsolidated subsidiary net income	30	—	
Net income	$130	$ 50	
Outside interest (40%) in consolidated subsidiary net income (minority interest in income)			20
Net income to consolidated entity			$ 130

	Assets		=	Liabilities +		Stockholders' Equity		
	Investment in S	+	*Cash and Other Assets* =	*Accounts Payable, etc.*	+	*Minority Interest*	+	*Stockholders' Equity*
P's accounts:								
Beginning of year	128	+	522* =	200			+	450
Operating income		+100 =					+	+100
Share of S income	+ 30							+ 30
End of year	158	+	622 =	200			+	580
S's accounts:								
Beginning of year		400 =	187				+	213
Net income		+ 50 =						+ 50
End of year		450 =	187				+	263
Intercompany eliminations	−158	=				+105†		− 263
Consolidated, end of year	0	+	1,072 =	387	+	105	+	580

* 650 beginning of year − 128 for acquisition = 522.
† 85 beginning of year + .40 × (50) = 85 + 20 = 105.

Highlights to Remember

The accounting for intercorporate investments depends on the purpose of the investment, on whether it is an equity or debt security, and on the level of control the investor has over the issuer of the security. For short-term *debt* securities and short-term *equity* securities, accounting is at market. Trading securities are held to be resold, and the gains and losses from changes in market value go directly to the income statement. Marketable securities that are available-for-sale are reported at market in the balance sheet, but gains and losses are carried in a separate account in stockholders' equity until the securities are sold.

When the investor's intention is to hold assets, the investor's accounting for *debt* securities uses the effective interest rate method in the same manner that the issuer does. That is, discount and premium are amortized to affect interest revenue. These securities are held-to-maturity. For *equity* securities held for the long-term, the accounting is linked to the investor's level of control of the issuer of the equity security. For ownership interests of less than 20%, accounting for equity securities requires classification as either available-for-sale or trading. The accounting is based on fair value.

As the ownership interest ranges from 20% to 50%, the increasing control the investor can exert over the issuer leads to earnings recognition in the income statement, proportional to the percentage ownership. The investment account is increased by this share of the issuer's earnings (or decreased by a proportionate share of losses). When dividends are received, the investment account is decreased with no effect on earnings. This is called the equity method.

As the ownership interest exceeds 50%, the investor controls the subsidiary. Consolidation is appropriate, which involves combining all of the assets and liabilities of the related corporate entities. For 100%-owned subsidiaries, the main concern is the elimination of intercompany transactions: sales, receivables, and payables. For less than 100%-owned subsidiaries, the rights of the minority shareholders must be recognized as a reduction of consolidated earnings on the income statement and as a liability on the balance sheet. Both amounts are calculated in proportion to the minority investors' share of the subsidiary.

The chapter's final consideration is valuation. When one company buys another, the purchase method recognizes the event as an opportunity to revalue the assets of the subsidiary. Identifiable assets may be recorded in consolidation at above their book value to the subsidiary, and goodwill may be recognized in the consolidated statements.

Appendix 13:   Pooling of Interests

Nature of Pooling

purchase method A way of accounting for the acquisition of one company by another; based on the market prices paid for the acquired company's assets.

The business combinations described in the body of the chapter were accounted for by using the *purchase method*, as contrasted with the *pooling-of-interests method*. The **purchase method** accounts for a business combination on the basis of the *market prices* actually paid for the acquired company's assets. Under the purchase method, one company is obviously acquiring another and typically paying cash to do so. The shareholders of the acquired company sell their stock and go away. The owners of the purchaser now own a different, bigger company.

Contrast the purchase method and the pooling-of-interests method of accounting for business combinations.

pooling-of-interests method A way of accounting for the combination of two corporations based on the book values of the acquired company's net assets, as distinguished from the purchase method.

Sometimes two companies approach each other and agree that they would be better off combining and further agree to combine by exchanging shares of stock in their original company for shares in a new combined company. In these instances it is less clear who is purchasing whom; it is more an integration of equals.

Suppose the two companies were privately held. No market existed for the stock. After the combination, all of the previous owners remained owners. It would be hard to attach values to the shares of stock or to the assets owned by the resulting company. Such transactions are called *poolings of interests*. The **pooling-of-interests method** is based on the *book values* of the acquired company's assets, not the market values.

Both the purchase and the pooling methods are acceptable under the appropriate circumstances, *but not as alternatives for the same business combination*. Pooling is a uniting of ownership interests of two or more companies by the exchange of common stock. The recorded assets and liabilities of the fused companies are carried forward at their book values by the combined corporation. To use pooling-of-interests accounting, the combination must completely adhere to a long list of restrictive conditions, including most importantly:

1. The acquirer must issue voting common shares (not cash) in exchange for substantially all (at least 90%) of the voting common shares of the acquired company.
2. The acquisition must occur in a single transaction.

Consider the way actual business combinations commonly occur:

1. The management of P and the management of S discuss the feasibility of P's acquiring S.
2. The *market value* of S as a going concern is established in a variety of ways, including the market values of securities, the appraisal values of individual assets, and negotiations between P and S. A final price is agreed upon.
3. P acquires S. The cash or stock issued by P is ultimately distributed to the individual shareholders of S, not to S itself. Thus, after the acquisition has been completed, S's assets, liabilities, and stockholders' equity are unchanged.
   a. P may issue shares for cash and then use the cash to buy S. The acquisition would be accounted for as a *purchase*.
   b. P may issue the *same number* of shares directly to shareholders of S. If various conditions are met, the acquisition would be accounted for as a *pooling*.
   c. Note especially that the owners of S would expect the *same total market value* for their shares sold to P, regardless of whether the transaction is accounted for as a purchase or a pooling. Also note that not all acquisitions by P's issuance of stock would necessarily be accounted for as a pooling. For example, P may fail to acquire at least 90% of the common shares of S. Or P may pay for S with half cash and half P shares. In either case, the transaction should be accounted for as a purchase.

Illustration of Pooling

Accounting for the basic data in the section "Accounting for Goodwill," page 604, provides the basis for the top of Exhibit 13-6. However, to provide a consistent transaction for comparison to the pooling method, we have added an extra step. P issues stock for $253 million cash at the beginning of the year and then uses the cash to acquire all the shares of S. This combination should be accounted for by using the purchase method, as illustrated.

| Exhibit 13-6 | Comparison of Purchase and Pooling for Business Combinations (in millions of dollars) |

	Assets			= Liabilities +		Stockholders' Equity
	Investment in S	+	Cash and Other Assets	=	Accounts Payable, etc.	+	Stockholders' Equity
PURCHASE METHOD						
P's accounts:						
Before issuance of stock			397	=	200	+	197
Issuance of stock			+253	=			+253
Acquisition of S	+253		−253	=			
S's accounts			400	=	187	+	213
Intercompany eliminations	−213						−213
Consolidated	40*	+	797	=	387	+	450
POOLING METHOD						
P's accounts:						
Before issuance of stock			397	=	200		197
Issuance of stock in acquisition of S	+213			=			+213
S's accounts			400	=	187	+	213
Intercompany eliminations	−213						−213
Consolidated	0	+	797	=	387	+	410

* Goodwill, as explained in the body of the chapter. See the section "Purchased Goodwill," page 604.

Instead of issuing its shares for $253 million cash, suppose P exchanges *the same number* of its shares for the shares of S. If all the conditions of pooling are met, the accounting would appear as shown in the bottom half of Exhibit 13-6.

The current value of Company S exceeds the recorded values by $40 million. Purchase accounting recognizes the fair values (current values) of the assets acquired, but pooling does not. Moreover, the future consolidated net income will be higher under pooling. Why? Because pooling has no $40 million goodwill to amortize as expense. Furthermore, net income is hurt doubly by the amortization of goodwill. Why? Because goodwill is generally not deductible for tax purposes. Assume a 40% income tax rate. Normally, a $10 expense would decrease net income by only $6 because the $10 reduction in pretax income will lower taxes by 40% × $10 = $4. In contrast, amortizing $10 of goodwill decreases net income by the full $10 because taxes are unaffected.

The magnitude of the difference between purchasing and pooling would become even more pronounced if S had several individual assets whose fair market values far exceeded book values. Examples are companies with large holdings of internally developed patents, copyrights, and trademarks. Under pooling, the combined company does not account for these market values. The asset values would not appear on its consolidated balance sheet nor would these assets be amortized as part of its expenses on future consolidated income statements.

Criticisms of Pooling

Many critics maintain that pooling-of-interests accounting should be completely banned. Pooling is defective because it ignores the asset values on which the parties have traded and substitutes a wholly irrelevant figure—the amount on the seller's books. Such accounting also permits the reporting of erroneous profits upon subsequent disposition of such assets. If the assets had been acquired for cash, the buyer's cost would be the amount of the cash. Acquisition for stock should make no difference.

The accounting essence is the amount of consideration, not its nature. Payment in cash or stock can be a matter of form, not substance. Suppose the seller wants cash. The buyer can first sell stock and turn over the proceeds to the seller, or the seller can take stock and promptly sell the stock for cash.

Some say that the elimination of pooling would impede mergers and thus is not in the national interest. Others say that accounting does not exist to aid or discourage mergers, but to account for them fairly. Elimination of pooling would remove the confusion that comes from the coexistence of pooling and purchase accounting. Above all, the elimination of pooling would remove an aberration in historical-cost accounting that permits an acquisition to be accounted for on the basis of the seller's historical cost rather than the more recently measured buyer's cost obtained in a bargained exchange of shares of stock.

Regardless of the strength of these arguments against the pooling-of-interests method, some business combinations are carefully structured so as to permit the purchaser to use pooling. A recent and visible example of this was the AT&T acquisition of NCR. AT&T gave NCR shareholders 2.839 shares of AT&T for every share of NCR in a deal valued at approximately $7.5 billion. As one of the final conditions of the deal, AT&T required NCR to stop paying certain special dividends that would have made it impossible to use pooling-of-interests accounting. AT&T sought approval of pooling accounting from its auditors and from the SEC before completing the deal. AT&T's preference for pooling-of-interest accounting was again affirmed in its 1994 acquisition of McCaw Cellular in a share-for-share exchange accounted for as a pooling.

Consolidating Owners' Equity in a Pooling

Exhibit 13-6 does not provide a detailed illustration of the consolidation process for pooling. A detailed approach follows:

1. Sum the individual assets and liabilities of P and S, line by line.
2. Sum the individual retained incomes. By definition of pooling, the retained incomes are combined in this way.
3. Adjust common stock at par and additional paid-in capital accounts. This adjustment is usually small; it involves increasing one of the two accounts and decreasing the other by a like amount.

To illustrate, reconsider Exhibit 13-6. Suppose the following detailed stockholders' equity accounts had existed before the pooling of interests (in millions of dollars):

	P	S
Common stock at par	8,000,000 shares @ $5 = 40	5,000,000 shares @ $4 = 20
Additional paid-in capital	87	140
Retained income	70	53
Total stockholders' equity	197	213

Assume that P pays $253 million to the owners of S, consisting of 4.6 million additional shares of P with a market value of $55 each (that is, 4.6 million × $55 = $253 million). In accounting for a pooling, the *number* of shares is pertinent, but their *value* is ignored.

In concept, a straightforward pooling would call for the following simple addition of all accounts (in millions of dollars):

	P	+	S	=	Consolidated
Cash and other assets	397	+	400	=	797
Accounts payable	200	+	187	=	387
Common stock at par	40	+	20	=	60*
Additional paid-in capital	87	+	140	=	227*
Retained income	70	+	53	=	123
	397		400		797

* Total paid-in capital = 60 + 227 = 287.

Indeed, in practice *the above addition does occur, including the noteworthy summing of retained incomes.* However, a modest change in the Common Stock at Par and Additional Paid-in Capital accounts is necessary to show the appropriate par value for all the P shares:

	Consolidated	
Common stock at par	Old P, 8,000,000 shares @ $5	= 40
	New P, 4,600,000 shares @ $5	= 23
	New total	63*
Additional paid-in capital	Old P	87
	Old S	140
	Adjustment	(3)
	New total	224*

* Total paid-in capital = 63 + 224 = 287.

Compare the $63 million with the $60 million in the preceding tabulation; also compare the $224 million with the $227 million. The numbers differ only because the $23 million par value of the new P shares differs from the $20 million par value of the S shares. To bring the par value account up to the required $63 million, $3 million must be transferred from additional paid-in capital to common stock at par.

Contrasting Pooling and Purchase

The following table summarizes the balance sheet effects of the pooling and purchase methods of accounting:

	Pooling	Purchase Compared with Pooling
1. Assets	No goodwill No fair value of other assets	Higher because of goodwill and fair values of other assets such as property, plant, and equipment
2. Retained income	P and S added together	Lower because S retained income not added; the consolidated retained income equals P retained income
3. Common stock at par	Sum of all P shares	Same as pooling
4. Additional paid-in capital	Adjusted to accommodate changes in par values	Higher because new shares affect equity at market values at time of acquisition of S

How do income statements differ between purchasing and pooling? Consider the year of the acquisition. Pooling merely sums revenues and expenses as though both P and S were together throughout the year:

	Pooling	Purchase Compared with Pooling
Revenue and expenses	Added together for entire year regardless of when acquisition occurred during the year	Added together only for time span subsequent to date of acquisition
Goodwill amortization	No goodwill	Amortized for time span subsequent to acquisition
Depreciation expense	Based on old book values	Based on fair values at date of acquisition

A widespread criticism of pooling has been that a P company can "artificially" boost its net income by acquiring an S company late in a year. Under pooling, regardless of the purchase date, P can include the S income for the entire year in consolidated results. Under purchasing, P can include only the S income earned subsequent to the acquisition.

Accounting Vocabulary

affiliated companies, *p. 593*

available-for-sale securities, *p. 589*

certificates of deposit, *p. 588*

commercial paper, *p. 588*

consolidated statements, *p. 596*

equity method, *p. 593*

held-to-maturity securities, *p. 589*

marketable securities, *p. 587*

minority interests, *p. 602*

parent company, *p. 596*

pooling-of-interests method, *p. 617*

purchase method, *p. 616*

short-term debt securities, *p. 588*

short-term equity securities, *p. 588*

short-term investment, *p. 587*

subsidiary, *p. 596*

trading securities, *p. 589*

U.S. Treasury obligations, *p 588*

Assignment Material

Questions

13-1. Why is *marketable securities* an ill-chosen term to describe short-term investments?

13-2. "The cost rule is applied to investments in short-term securities." Do you agree? Explain.

13-3. Suppose an investor buys a $1,000 face value bond for $950, a discount of $50. Will amortization of the discount increase or decrease the investor's interest income? Explain.

13-4. What is the equity method?

13-5. "The equity method is usually used for long-term investments." Do you think this is appropriate? Explain.

13-6. Contrast the *market* method with the *equity* method.

13-7. What criterion is used to determine whether a parent-subsidiary relationship exists?

13-8. Why have subsidiaries? Why not have the corporation take the form of a single legal entity?

13-9. Why does a consolidated balance sheet require "eliminating entries"?

13-10. What is a minority interest?

13-11. When is there justification for not consolidating majority-owned subsidiaries?

13-12. Distinguish between *control of* a company and *significant influence over* a company.

13-13. What are joint ventures, and how do companies account for them?

13-14. "Goodwill is the excess of purchase price over the book values of the individual assets acquired." Do you agree? Explain.

13-15. Suppose P company received $20,000 in cash dividends from Y company, a 40%-owned affiliated company. Y company's net income was $80,000. How will P's statement of cash flows show these items using the direct method?

13-16. Why does GAAP require amortization of goodwill against net income? What other options might exist?

13-17. Why might a company prefer to own 19.9% interest in an affiliate rather than a 20.1% interest?

13-18. Some years ago, finance subsidiaries and insurance subsidiaries owned by industrial companies were typically accounted for under the equity method rather than by consolidation. What was the argument for this procedure?

13-19. Suppose P company owns 90% of S company and S company earns $100,000. What is the amount of the minority interest shown in P company's consolidated income statement? What is the amount of the minority interest shown in S company's individual income statement?

13-20. Suppose P company owns 40% of S company. S company earns $200,000 and pays total dividends of $60,000 to its shareholders. What appears in the consolidated income statement of P company as a result of S company's activity? What would be the change in the account titled Investment in equity affiliates on P company's balance sheet?

13-21. "If a company is acquired by an exchange of stock, pooling-of-interests accounting must be used." Do you agree? Explain.

13-22. "Pooling is an inferior accounting method." What major reason is usually offered for making such a comment?

13-23. "Pooling should be allowed because its elimination would impede business combinations and thus would not be in the national interest." What is the counter argument to this assertion?

13-24. Would you expect the consolidated income statement to report higher net income if a business combination is accounted for as a pooling or as a purchase? Explain.

Exercises

13-25   Trading Securities

The Martinez Company has a portfolio of trading securities consisting of common and preferred stocks. The portfolio cost $160 million on January 1. The market values of the portfolio were (in millions): March 31, $150; June 30, $138; September 30, $152; and December 31, $168.

Required

1. Prepare a tabulation showing the balance sheet presentations and income statement presentations for interim reporting purposes.

2. Show the journal entries for quarters 1, 2, 3, and 4.

13-26   Bond Discount Transactions

On December 31, 1996, a company purchased $1 million of ten-year, 10% debentures for $885,295. The market interest rate was 12%.

Required

1. Using the balance sheet equation format, prepare an analysis of bond transactions. Assume effective-interest amortization. Show entries for the investor regarding (a) purchase, (b) the first semiannual interest payment, and (c) payment of maturity value.
2. Show the corresponding journal entries for (a), (b), and (c) above.
3. Show how the bond investment would appear on the balance sheets as of December 31, 1996, and June 30, 1997.

13-27 Bond Premium Transactions

On December 31, 1995, the Guzman company purchased $1 million of ten-year, 10% debentures for $1,135,915. The market interest rate was 8%.

Required

1. Using the balance sheet equation format, prepare an analysis of transactions for the investor's records. Key your transactions as follows: (a) purchase, (b) the first semiannual interest payment using effective-interest amortization of bond premium, and (c) payment of maturity value.
2. Prepare sample journal entries keyed as above.
3. Show how the bond-related accounts would appear on the balance sheets as of December 31, 1995, and June 30, 1996.

13-28 Market Method or Equity Method

Fred's Outdoors acquired 25% of the voting stock of Steve's Snowshoes for $40 million cash. In Year 1, Steve's had a net income of $32 million and paid a cash dividend of $20 million.

Required

1. Using the equity and the market methods, show the effects of the three transactions on the accounts of Fred's Outdoors. Use the balance sheet equation format. Also show the accompanying journal entries. Assume constant market value for Steve's.
2. Which method, equity or market, would Fred's use to account for its investment in Steve's? Explain.

13-29 Equity Method

Company X acquired 30% of the voting stock of company Y for $90 million cash. In Year 1, Y had a net income of $50 million and paid cash dividends of $20 million.

Required

Prepare a tabulation that uses the equity method of accounting for X's investment in Y. Show the effects on the balance sheet equation. What is the year-end balance in the Investment in Y account under the equity method?

13-30 Early Extinguishment of an Investment

On December 31, 1995, an insurance company purchased $10 million of ten-year, 10% debentures for $8,852,950. On December 31, 1996 (after all interest payments and amortization had been recorded for 1996), the insurance company sold all the debentures for $9.3 million. The market interest rate at issuance was 12%.

Required

1. Compute the gain or loss on the sale for the insurance company (i.e., the investor).
2. Prepare the appropriate journal entries for the insurance company (i.e., the investor).

13-31 Consolidations in Japan

A few years ago, Japan's finance ministry issued a directive requiring the six hundred largest Japanese companies to produce consolidated financial statements. The previous practice had been to use parent-company-only statements. A story in *Business Week* said: "Financial observers hope that the move will help end the tradition-honored Japanese practice of 'window dressing' the parent company financial results by shoving losses onto hapless subsidiaries, whose red ink was seldom revealed.... When companies needed to show a bigger profit, they would sell their product to subsidiaries at an inflated price.... Or the parent company charged a higher rent to a subsidiary company using its building."

Required

Could a parent company follow the quoted practices and achieve window dressing in its parent-only financial statements if it used the equity method of accounting for its intercorporate investments? Explain.

Problems

13-32   Effect of Transactions under the Equity Method
AT&T's footnotes revealed (in millions):

	December 31	
	1993	*1992*
Investments at equity	$698	$627

AT&T did not disclose the equity in earnings of these affiliates nor the dividends received, probably because the amounts were immaterial. They did disclose a gain of about $220 million on the sale of UNIX Systems Laboratories and Compagnie Industriali. Assume the carrying value of these two equity investments prior to sale was $100 million. Assume equity income from all investees totalled $25 million and dividends were $15 million.

Required
1. Estimate the additional investment that AT&T made in its equity affiliates during 1993. *Hint:* use a T-account to aid your analysis.
2. Describe how these items would affect the cash flow statement.

13-33   Trading Securities
On a recent December 31, Pennzoil Company held a portfolio of trading equity securities that cost $183,863,000 and had a market value of $159,127,000. Assume that the same portfolio was held until the end of the first quarter of the subsequent year. The market value of the portfolio was $174,531,000 at January 31, $169,680,000 at February 29, and $188,432,000 at March 31.

Required
1. Prepare a tabulation showing the balance sheet presentation and income statement presentation for monthly reporting purposes.
2. Show the journal entries for January, February, and March.
3. How would your answer to (1) change if the securities were classified as available-for-sale?

13-34   Equity Method and Cash Flows
The Sisly Company owns a 30% interest in the Rousseau Company. Sisly uses the equity method to account for the investment. During 19X6 Rousseau had net income of $100,000 and paid cash dividends of $70,000. Sisly's net income, including the effect of its investment in Rousseau, was $486,000.

Required
1. In reconciling Sisly's net income with its net cash provided by operating activities, the net income must be adjusted for Sisly's pro-rata share of the net income of Rousseau. Compute the amount of the adjustment. Will it be added to or deducted from net income?
2. Under the direct method, the dividends paid by Rousseau will affect the amounts Sisly lists under operating, investing, or financing activities. Which type(s) of activity will be affected? By how much? Will the amount(s) be cash inflows or cash outflows?

13-35   Consolidated Statements
Consider the following for Hane Company (the parent) as of December 31, 19X4:

	Hane	Subsidiary*
Assets	$800,000	$200,000
Liabilities to creditors	$300,000	$ 80,000
Stockholders' equity	500,000	120,000
Total equities	$800,000	$200,000

* 70 percent owned by Hane.

The $800,000 of assets of Hane include an $84,000 investment in the subsidiary. The $84,000 includes Hane's pro-rata share of the subsidiary's net income for 19X4. Hane's sales were

$990,000 and operating expenses were $922,000. These figures exclude any pro-rata share of the subsidiary's net income. The subsidiary's sales were $700,000 and operating expenses were $660,000. Prepare a consolidated income statement and a consolidated balance sheet.

13-36 Consolidated Financial Statements
The Parent Company owns 90% of the common stock of Company S-1 and 60% of the common stock of Company S-2. The balances as of December 31, 19X4, in the condensed accounts follow:

	(in thousands of dollars)		
	Parent	S-1	S-2
Sales	300,000	80,000	100,000
Investment in subsidiaries*	72,000	—	—
Other assets	128,000	90,000	20,000
Liabilities to creditors	100,000	20,000	5,000
Expenses	280,000	90,000	95,000
Stockholders' equity, including current net income	100,000	70,000	15,000

* Carried at equity in subsidiaries.

Required   Prepare a consolidated balance sheet as of December 31, 19X4, and a consolidated income statement for 19X4 (in millions of dollars).

13-37 Consolidated Financial Statements
Company P acquired a 100% voting interest in Company S for $110 million cash at the start of the year. Immediately before the business combination, each company had the following condensed balance sheet accounts (in millions):

	P	S
Cash and other assets	$500	$140
Accounts payable, etc.	$200	$ 30
Stockholders' equity	300	110
Total liab. & stk. eq.	$500	$140

Required   1. Prepare a tabulation of the consolidated balance sheet accounts immediately after acquisition. Use the balance sheet equation format.
2. Suppose P and S have the following results for the year:

	P	S
Sales	$600	$180
Expenses	450	160

Prepare income statements for the year for P, S, and the consolidated entity. Assume that neither P nor S sold items to the other.
3. Present the effects of the operations for the year on P's accounts and on S's accounts, using the balance sheet equation. Also tabulate the consolidated balance sheet accounts at the end of the year. Assume that liabilities are unchanged.
4. Suppose S paid a cash dividend of $10 million. What accounts in requirement 3 would be affected and by how much?

13-38   Minority Interests

This alters the preceding problem. However, this problem is self-contained because all the facts are reproduced below. Company P acquired an 80% voting interest in Company S for $88 million cash at the start of the year. Immediately before the business combination, each company had the following condensed balance sheet accounts (in millions):

	P	S
Cash and other assets	$500	$140
Accounts payable, etc.	$200	$ 30
Stockholders' equity	300	110
Total liab. & stk. eq.	$500	$140

Required

1. Prepare a tabulation of the consolidated balance sheet accounts immediately after acquisition. Use the balance sheet equation format.
2. Suppose P and S have the following results for the year:

	P	S
Sales	$600	$180
Expenses	450	160

Prepare income statements for the year for P, S, and the consolidated entity. Assume that neither P nor S sold items to the other.

3. Using the balance sheet equation format, present the effects of the operations for the year on P's accounts and on S's accounts. Also tabulate consolidated balance sheet accounts at the end of the year. Assume that liabilities are unchanged.
4. Suppose S paid a cash dividend of $10 million. What accounts in requirement 3 would be affected and by how much?

13-39   Goodwill and Consolidations

This alters Problem 13-37. However, this problem is self-contained because all the facts are reproduced below. Company P acquired a 100% voting interest in Company S for $150 million cash at the start of the year. Immediately before the business combination, each company had the following condensed balance sheet accounts (in millions):

	P	S
Cash and other assets	$500	$140
Accounts payable, etc.	$200	$ 30
Stockholders' equity	300	110
Total liab. & stk. equity	$500	$140

Assume that the fair values of the individual assets of S were equal to their book values.

Required

1. Prepare a tabulation of the consolidated balance sheet accounts immediately after the acquisition. Use the balance sheet equation format.
2. If goodwill is going to be amortized over forty years, how much was amortized for the first year? If over five years, how much was amortized for the first year?
3. Suppose the book values of the S individual assets are equal to their fair market values except for equipment. The net book value of equipment is $30 million and its fair market value is $50 million. The equipment has a remaining useful life of four years. Straight-line depreciation is used.

   a. Describe how the consolidated balance sheet accounts immediately after the acquisition would differ from those in requirement 1. Be specific as to accounts and amounts.

b. By how much will consolidated income differ in comparison with the consolidated income that would be reported in requirement 2? Assume amortization of goodwill over a forty-year period.

13-40   Purchased Goodwill

Consider the following balance sheets (in millions of dollars):

	Company A	Company B
Cash	150	20
Inventories	60	30
Plant assets, net	60	30
Total assets	270	80
Common stock and paid-in surplus	70	30
Retained income	200	50
Total liab. & stk. equity	270	80

A paid $110 million to B stockholders for all their stock. The "fair value" of the plant assets of B is $60 million. The fair value of cash and inventories is equal to their carrying amounts. A and B continued to keep separate books.

Required

1. Prepare a tabulation showing the balance sheets of A, of B, Intercompany Eliminations, and the consolidated balance sheet immediately after the acquisition.
2. Suppose that only $50 million rather than $60 million of the total purchase price of $110 million could logically be assigned to the plant assets. How would the consolidated accounts be affected?
3. Refer to the facts in requirement 1. Suppose A had paid $120 million rather than $110 million. State how your tabulation in requirement 1 would change.

13-41   Amortization and Depreciation

Refer to the preceding problem, requirement 3. Suppose a year passes, and A and B generate individual net incomes of $20 million and $13 million, respectively. The latter is after a deduction by B of $6 million of straight-line depreciation. Compute the consolidated net income if goodwill is amortized (a) over forty years and (b) over ten years. Ignore income taxes.

13-42   Allocationg Total Purchase Price to Assets

Two entities had the following balance sheet accounts as of December 31, 19X1 (in millions):

	Rosemont	Paradelt		Rosemont	Paradelt
Cash and receivables	$ 30	$ 22	Current liabilities	$ 50	$ 20
Inventories	120	3	Common stock	100	10
Plant assets, net	150	95	Retained income	150	90
Total assets	$300	$120	Total liab. and stk. eq.	$300	$120
Net income for 19X1	$ 19	$ 4			

On January 4, 19X2, these entities combined. Rosemont issued $180 million of its shares (at market value) in exchange for all the shares of Paradelt, a motion picture division of a large company. The inventory of films acquired through the combination had been fully amortized on Paradelt's books.

During 19X2, Paradelt received revenue of $21 million from the rental of films from its inventory. Rosemont earned $20 million on its other operations (that is, excluding Paradelt) during 19X2. Paradelt broke even on its other operations (that is, excluding the film rental contracts) during 19X2.

Required

1. Prepare a consolidated balance sheet for the combined company immediately after the combination on a purchase basis. Assume that $80 million of the purchase price was assigned to the inventory of films.
2. Prepare a comparison of Rosemont's net income between 19X1 and 19X2 where the cost of the film inventories would be amortized on a straight-line basis over four years. What would be the net income for 19X2 if the $80 million were assigned to goodwill rather than to the inventory of films and goodwill were amortized over forty years?

13-43   Pooling-of-Interest Accounting
Study Appendix 13. Refer to the previous problem.

Required

Calculate the following values assuming pooling-of-interests accounting is used.

1. Consolidated total assets, 1/4/X2.
2. Retained income, 1/4/X2.
3. 19X2 consolidated net income.

13-44   Prepare Consolidated Financial Statements

From the following data, prepare a consolidated balance sheet and an income statement of the Montufar Corporation. All data are in millions and pertain to operations for 19X2 or to December 31, 19X2:

Short-term investments at cost, which approximates current market	$ 40
Income tax expense	90
Accounts receivable, net	100
Minority interest in subsidiaries	90
Inventories at average cost	400
Dividends declared and paid on preferred stock	10
Equity in earnings of affiliated companies	20
Paid-in capital in excess of par	82
Interest expense	25
Retained income	218
Investments in affiliated companies	100
Common stock, 10 million shares, $1 par	10
Depreciation and amortization	20
Accounts payable	200
Cash	50
First-mortgage bonds, 10% interest, due December 31, 19X8	80
Property, plant, and equipment, net	120
Preferred stock, 2 million shares, $50 par, dividend rate is $5 per share, each share is convertible into one share of common stock	100
Accrued income taxes payable	30
Cost of goods sold and operating expenses, exclusive of depreciation and amortization	700
Subordinated debentures, 11% interest, due December 31, 19X9	100
Minority interest in subsidiaries' net income	20
Goodwill	100
Net sales and other operating revenue	950

13-45   Intercorporate Investments and Statements of Cash Flow
The 19X6 balance sheet of Fernandez Company contained the following three assets:

	19X6	19X5
Long-term debt investments held-to-maturity	$ 166,000	$ 166,000
Investment in Hull Company, 43% owned	$ 981,000	$ 861,000
Investment in Gavilan Company, 25% owned	$1,145,000	$1,054,000

The long-term-debt investments were shown at cost, which equaled maturity value. Interest income was $14,000 for these debt investments, which had been owned for several years. The equity method was used to account for both Hull Company and Gavilan Company. Results for 19X6 included:

	Hull Company	Gavilan Company
Fernandez Co. pro-rata share of net income	$120,000	$91,000
Cash dividends received by Fernandez Co.	$ 50,000	$ 0

Assume that Fernandez reported net income of $687,000 and depreciation of $129,000 in 19X6.

Required   A schedule that reconciles net income to net cash provided by operating activities contained the following:

Net income	$687,000
Depreciation	129,000
Increase in noncash working capital	(16,000)

Note: The increase in non-cash working capital is the net change in current assets and liabilities other than cash. Given the available data, complete the reconciliation.

13-46   Minority Interest
The consolidated financial statements of Caesars World, Inc., include the accounts of Caesars New Jersey, Inc., an 86.6%-owned subsidiary. Assume that Caesars New Jersey is Caesars World's only consolidated subsidiary. Caesars World's 1990 income statement contained the following (in thousands):

Income before minority interest and taxes	$65,778
Taxes	24,985
Minority interest in earnings of consolidated subsidiary	3,990
Net income	$36,803

Caesars World's account "Minority Interest in Consolidated Subsidiary" listed $25,112,000 at the beginning of 1990. Caesars New Jersey paid no dividends in 1990. Assume that Caesars World did not buy or sell any of its interest in Caesars New Jersey during 1990.

Required   1. Compute the 1990 net income of Caesars New Jersey.
2. What proportion of Caesars World's $36,803,000 net income was contributed by Caesars New Jersey?
3. Compute Caesars World's balance in "Minority Interest in Consolidated Subsidiary" at the end of 1990.

4. Comment on the reason for including a line for minority interest in the income statement and balance sheet of Caesars World.

13-47 Acquisition of RCA

The stockholders of RCA approved the sale of 100% of RCA's common stock to General Electric for $66.50 per share. Of the votes cast, over 90% were in favor of the $6.28 billion cash sale, the largest non-oil acquisition at the time. Assume that the $6.28 billion price was twice RCA's book value.

Required

1. Suppose the fair market values of RCA's net assets totaled $6.28 billion. Prepare the journal entry or entries to record the acquisition on General Electric's books.
2. Suppose the fair market values of RCA's tangible assets were equal to their book values. Fair market value of identifiable intangible assets was $800 million; their useful life was eight years. None of the intangible assets appeared on RCA's balance sheet. Prepare the journal entry or entries to record the acquisition on General Electric's books.
3. Refer to requirement 2. Assume that the acquisition took place on January 2. Prepare the December 31 journal entry or entries to recognize the first year's amortization of goodwill and other intangible assets. Assume that goodwill is amortized as slowly as possible.
4. Assume that the acquisition occurred on July 1 and that RCA's net income for the year was $500 million. RCA's net income was earned at a constant rate per unit of time during the year. How much of that net income would appear in General Electric's consolidated net income for the year ended December 31?

13-48 Purchase or Pooling

Study Appendix 13. Two companies had the following condensed balance sheet accounts at December 31, 19X6.

	P	S
Cash and other assets	$800	$220
Accounts payable, etc.	$300	$100
Stockholders' equity	500	120
Total liab. & stk. eq.	$800	$220

The fair value of the individual S assets is the same as their book values.

Required

1. Company P issued stock for $180 million cash at the beginning of 19X7 and then immediately used the cash to acquire all the shares of Company S. Prepare a consolidated balance sheet after the acquisition of S by P.
2. Instead of issuing its shares for $180 million cash, suppose P exchanges the same number of its shares for the shares of S. Assume that all conditions of pooling are met. Prepare a consolidated balance sheet.
3. Which set of future consolidated income statements will show higher income, the ones resulting from purchasing or from pooling? Explain.

13-49 Purchase and Pooling

Study Appendix 13. The B Company and the C Company have the following accounts at December 31, 19X1:

	B	C
Net assets	$99,000,000	$40,000,000
Stockholders' equity	$99,000,000	$40,000,000
Net income for 19X1	$10,000,000	$10,000,000

On December 31, 19X1, B combined with C by issuing stock with a market value of $50 million in exchange for the shares of C. Assume that the book value and the current value of the individual assets of C were equal.

Required

1. Show the balance sheet accounts and net income for 19X1 for the combined companies as they would appear if the combination were accounted for as (a) a $50 million purchase with recognition of purchased goodwill and (b) a pooling.
2. Assume that the same net incomes of $10 million each are generated by the subparts of the combined entity in 19X2 (before considering amortization of goodwill). Show the net income for 19X2 for the combined companies if the business combination had been accounted for as (a) a purchase and (b) a pooling. Any goodwill amortized is to be written off on a straight-line basis over five years. Comment on the results.
3. Redo part 2 assuming goodwill amortization over forty years.

13-50   More on Pooling of Interests
Study Appendix 13. Two companies had the following condensed balance sheet accounts at December 31, 19X1 (in millions):

	P	S
Cash and other assets	$700	$220
Accounts payable, etc.	$300	$100
Stockholders' equity:		
Common stock:		
4 million shares @ $4 par	16	
12 million shares @ $1 par		12
Additional paid-in capital	84	40
Retained income	300	68
Total stockholders' equity	$400	$120
Total liab. and stk. eq.	$700	$220

The fair values of the individual assets are the same as their book values.

Required

1. Company P issued 5 million shares of stock @ $40 for $200 million cash at the beginning of 19X2 and then immediately used the cash to acquire all the shares of Company S. Prepare a consolidated balance sheet after the acquisition of S by P.
2. Instead of issuing its shares for $200 million cash, suppose P exchanges the same number of its shares for the shares of S. Assume that all conditions of pooling are met. Prepare a consolidated balance sheet.
3. List the major differences between the two consolidated balance sheets immediately after the acquisition.
4. Suppose the acquisition occurred on December 1, 19X2. All other information is unchanged. How will the purchase and the pooling income statements differ for 19X2? Respond by listing the major differences. No numerical differences are required.

13-51   Equity Method, Consolidation, and Minority Interest
On January 2, 19X6, Magic Oil Company purchased 30% of Great Slave Lake Mining Company (GSLM) for $1.5 million cash. Before the acquisition, Magic had assets of $10 million and stockholders' equity of $8 million. GSLM had stockholders' equity of $5 million and liabilities of $1 million, and the fair values of its assets were equal to their book values.

GSLM reported 19X6 net income of $400,000 and declared and paid dividends of $200,000. Assume that Magic and GSLM had no sales to one another. Separate income statements for Magic and GSLM were as follows:

	Magic	GSLM
Sales	$12,500,000	$4,400,000
Expenses	11,100,000	4,000,000
Operating income	$ 1,400,000	$ 400,000

Required

1. Prepare the journal entries for Magic Oil (a) to record the acquisition of GSLM and (b) to record its share of GSLM net income and dividends for 19X6.
2. Prepare Magic Oil's income statement for 19X6 and calculate the balance in its investment in GSLM as of December 31, 19X6.
3. Suppose Magic had purchased 80% of GSLM for $4 million. Using the balance sheet equation format, prepare a tabulation of the consolidated balance sheet immediately after acquisition. Prepare the journal entries for both Magic and GSLM to record the acquisition. Omit explanations.
4. Prepare a consolidated income statement for 19X6, using the facts of requirement 3.

13-52   Equity Investments
Corning Inc.'s 1994 Consolidated Statements of Income reported equity in earnings of associated companies of $48.7 million. Its Consolidated Balance Sheets included investments in associated companies of $660.4 million in 1994 and $586.5 million in 1993. The Consolidated Statements of Cash Flow indicated that the equity in earnings of associated companies exceeded dividends received from these companies in 1994 by $.5 million.

Required

1. Compute the amount of additional investments in associated companies, if any, during 1994.
2. Suppose these associated companies were 40% owned and that Corning had acquired another 40% of these companies on the last day of 1994. Describe how the financial statements for 1994 would change as a result. Your answer should identify the accounts that would probably change and the direction of the probable change.

13-53   Intercorporate Investments and Ethics
Grover Jefferson and Alan Swenson were best friends at a small undergraduate college, and they fought side-by-side in the jungles of Vietnam. Upon returning to the United States, they went their separate ways to pursue MBA degrees, Grover to a prestigious East Coast Business school and Alan to an equally prestigious West Coast school. But 20 years later, their paths crossed again.

By 1992 Alan had become president and CEO of Butler Electronics after 18 years with the firm. Grover had started working for United Airlines, but had left after 9 years to start his own firm, Jefferson Transport. In April of 1992 Jefferson Transport was near bankruptcy when Grover approached his old friend for help. Alan Swenson answered his friend's call, and Butler Electronics bought 19% of Jefferson Transport.

In 1992, Jefferson paid no dividends, but in 1993 and 1994 it paid a total each year of $1,000,000 allowing Butler to record investment income of $190,000 each year. By 1995 Jefferson was financially stable and Butler was struggling. In fact, Alan Swenson thought his job as CEO might be in jeopardy if Butler did not report income up to expectations. Late in 1995 Alan approached Grover with a request — quadruple Jefferson's dividends so that Butler could recognize $760,000 of investment income. Although Jefferson had never paid dividends of more than 25% of net income and it had plenty of uses for excess cash, Grover felt a deep obligation to Alan. Thus he agreed to a $4,000,000 dividend on net income of $4,170,000.

Required

1. Why does the dividend policy of Jefferson Transport affect the income of Butler Electronics? Is this consistent with the intent of the accounting principles relating to the cost and equity methods for intercorporate investments? Explain.
2. Comment on the ethical issues in the arrangements between Grover Jefferson and Alan Swenson.

13-54   Wal-Mart Annual Report

Consult the Wal-Mart financial statements and footnotes in Appendix A in responding to the following. Also consult Note 7 from the 1992 annual report which is reproduced below. In 1992 reported sales were $43,886,902,000. From note 7 it is apparent that Wal-Mart owned McLane Company for the full year ended January 31, 1992. In contrast, Phillips Companies was acquired on November 26, 1991, and Western Merchandisers was acquired on May 6, 1991.

> Note 7
> Acquisitions
> On December 10,1990 the Company acquired all of the outstanding common stock of McLane Company, Inc. For its most recent fiscal year ended January 31, 1992, McLane Company, Inc., had sales of approximately $3,718,205,000, which included $1,203,205,000 in sales to the Company.
>
> On February 2, 1991, the Company acquired all of the outstanding common stock of The Wholesale Club, Inc. For the fiscal year ended February 2, 1991, The Wholesale Club, Inc., had sales of $725,944,000.
>
> On May 6, 1991, the Company acquired all of the outstanding common stock of Western Merchandisers, Inc., a wholesale distributor of books and prerecorded music. From the acquisition date through fiscal year ended January 31, 1992, Western Merchandisers, Inc., had sales of $181,448,000, which included $123,671,000 in sales to the Company
>
> On November 26, 1991, the Company acquired all of the outstanding common stock of Phillips Companies, Inc., which operates 20 food stores in Arkansas. For its most recent fiscal year ended January 31, 1992, Phillips Companies, Inc., had sales of $291,294,000, including $49,197,000 since the acquisition date.
>
> All four acquisitions were accounted for as purchases and the results of their operations since the dates of their acquisition have been included in the results of operation of the Company. Pro forma results of operation are not presented due to insignificant differences from the historical results presented.

Required

1. Estimate the total sales to be reported in the 1992 consolidated Wal-Mart Statements of Income if McLane had never been purchased.
2. Estimate the total sales to be reported in the 1992 consolidated Wal-Mart Statements of Income if Phillips Companies had never been purchased.
3. Estimate the total sales to be reported in the 1992 consolidated Wal-Mart Statements of Income if only 60% of Western Merchandisers had been acquired during 1991.
4. Estimate the total sales to be reported in the 1992 consolidated Wal-Mart Statements of Income if only 40% of Western Merchandisers had been acquired during 1991.
5. During 1994 Wal-Mart acquired selected assets of PACE Membership Warehouses Inc. Goodwill was recorded in the transaction. Estimate 1995 net income that would have been reported if the maximum life had been chosen for goodwill.

13-55   Compact D from Disclosure

Use the Compact D software to respond to the following. Select five companies in any industry.

Required

Review the financial statements to determine whether an acquisition occurred during the most recent year. For each acquisition identify as much as possible regarding each of the following:

1. Did the company use cash or stock?
2. What percentage of the target was purchased?
3. Can you determine whether the acquired company was previously either a customer or a supplier of the acquiring company? If so, which one?

14 Income Taxes, Including Interperiod Allocation

Learning Objectives

After studying this chapter, you should be able to

1 Distinguish temporary and permanent differences between tax rules and GAAP.

2 Explain how timing differences create deferred taxes.

3 Contrast tax (MACRS) and straight-line depreciation.

4 Explain why interperiod tax allocation is generally accepted.

5 Distinguish between tax credits and tax deductions.

6 Illustrate the importance of net operating losses (NOLs).

7 Differentiate the flow-through and deferral accounting methods for tax credits (Appendix 14).

Governments control a substantial part of a country's resources in order to provide education, roads, police and fire protection, defense, and, in some countries, health care. Often governments raise the money for providing these services through taxation. Taxes are varied and collected in many ways, including real estate taxes based on the value of real estate, sales taxes based on the value of items purchased, employment taxes based on wages earned, production taxes based on the value of items produced, inheritance taxes based on wealth at death, and income taxes based on income earned. In the United States all of these taxes are used except production taxes, which are generally called *value added taxes*. Often the different forms of taxes are used at different levels of government (federal, state, and local).

In this chapter we concentrate on income taxes: taxes that are based on the income earned by an individual or business during a specific period of time. These taxes are used at the federal level and by most states as a primary source of government revenue. This chapter provides an overview of the structure of income taxes and then focuses on how income taxes affect the financial statements of businesses. A primary difficulty for business in incorporating income taxes into the financial statements is that the definition of income used by the tax authorities to determine tax liabilities is not identical to the definition of income used for financial reporting purposes. These differences are examined in detail in the pages that follow.

GE *reported* income tax expense of $2.7 billion in its 1994 financial statements. GE *paid* $1.8 billion in income taxes during 1994. These figures stress two important characteristics of accounting for taxes: (1) That the amounts of money are immense is evident when one corporation owes $1.8 billion in taxes in one year and (2) that the accounting issues are complex is evident when the expense reported in the financial statement is 50% higher than the income tax actually paid or payable that year.

■ AN OVERVIEW OF INCOME TAXES

The income tax is a pervasive element of economic life around the world. Income tax laws are fiscal policies of governments. The primary objective of taxation is to provide revenue to finance government activities. In 1994 the majority of U.S. federal revenues came from individual and corporate income taxes. A related objective is to accomplish certain social goals by the way the tax rules are applied to taxpayers. For example, the individual income tax is *progressive*, which means that the tax rate increases as incomes increase. In 1994 an unmarried taxpayer faced a tax rate of 15% on the first $22,750 of taxable income, rising to 39.6% on income over $250,000. This accomplishes the social objective of shifting more of the tax burden to the higher-earning taxpayers.

The U.S. Congress passes the laws that govern income taxes. We are currently operating under the Internal Revenue Code (IRC) of 1986 as amended in subsequent years. Congress delegates many responsibilities for specifying tax procedures and collecting taxes to either the Treasury Department or the Internal Revenue Service (IRS). For corporations, the income tax is levied on *taxable income*, which is defined as taxable revenue items reduced by permitted **tax deductions**. In general, all revenue is taxable and all *ordinary and necessary* expenses of doing business are deductible. But there are notable, large exceptions to this generalization, which leads to potentially substantial differences

tax deduction An item that may be deducted on the tax return to calculate taxable income.

between taxable income on the tax return and the pretax income reported to shareholders and others.

Such differences do not exist in many countries. For example, in France, Germany, and Japan, the rules for financial reporting are largely the same as those for tax purposes. In the United States, however, differences between U.S. income tax rules and GAAP create special problems in financial accounting. The differences arise because GAAP is designed to provide useful information to investors, while the tax code is written to generate revenue for the government in a manner consistent with certain social and economic goals.

Good managers struggle to pay the least amount of income tax at the latest possible moment permitted within the law. This creates incentives to delay the reporting of taxable revenue as long as possible while deducting tax-deductible expense items as quickly as possible. Once these revenue and expense items are combined to calculate taxable income, the tax is determined by multiplying taxable income by the tax rate. U.S. corporations face *graduated* tax rates ranging from 15% on incomes under $50,000 to 35% on incomes over $335,000. Many states also levy an income tax, with tax rates varying from state to state. To simplify our illustrations, we will generally assume a flat (nongraduated) tax rate of 40%. This is a reasonable approximation of the combination of the federal 35% statutory (legally set) rate plus a state tax rate.

■ DIFFERENCES BETWEEN TAX AND SHAREHOLDER REPORTING

permanent differences
Differences between pretax income as reported to shareholders and taxable income as reported to the government because a revenue or expense item is recognized for one purpose but not the other.

municipal bond interest Interest paid by states and local governments that is not treated as taxable income by the United States government.

The government generally prohibits a company (or individual) from recognizing expenses on tax returns until cash is paid. This policy minimizes the extent of inflated expense reporting by taxpayers and reduces arguments between taxpayers and the Internal Revenue Service (IRS) over whether the taxpayer's expense estimates are excessive. Notice that this tax bias toward delayed expense recognition is exactly the opposite of the conservative bias built into GAAP. Under GAAP expenses are recognized as soon as they are both likely and capable of estimation.

The firm's income taxes are affected by revenue recognition rules, expense recognition rules, tax rates, and a unique feature of the tax system called tax credits. Revenue recognition and expense recognition rules for tax purposes can differ from GAAP rules on two dimensions: (1) *whether* an item is recognized (*permanent differences*) and (2) *when* it is recognized (*temporary differences*).

Permanent Differences

Permanent differences involve revenue and expense items that are recognized for tax purposes but not recognized under GAAP or not recognized for tax purposes but recognized under GAAP. For example, suppose a company owns a bond issued by the city of Seattle and periodically receives interest income. Under GAAP, this interest income is reported on the income statement. Under federal law, **interest on municipal bonds**—bonds issued by cities, states, and towns to fund community needs—is not taxed. This is an example of a nontaxable revenue item, a permanent difference between the tax law and GAAP. An example of an expense that is not deductible for tax purposes would be a fine levied on a trucking company for driving an overweight vehicle. Tax deduction for such an expense would be inconsistent with public policy.

Consider a company with taxable income of $120,000 and no permanent differences between GAAP requirements and the tax law. At a 40% tax rate, the tax due the government would be $48,000. This is Case A in the table below.

	Reporting	
	To Shareholders	On Income Tax Return
A. No permanent difference		
Pretax income	$120,000	$120,000
Income taxes @40%	$ 48,000	$ 48,000
B. Permanent expense difference		
Income before nondeductible expense	$120,000	$120,000
Permanent difference is nondeductible expense of $30,000	30,000	—
Pretax income	$ 90,000	$120,000
Income taxes	$ 48,000	$ 48,000
C. Permanent revenue difference		
Income before nontaxable interest	$120,000	$120,000
Permanent difference is interest revenue on municipal obligations	30,000	—
Pretax income	$150,000	$120,000
Income taxes	$ 48,000	$ 48,000

In Case B, a nondeductible expense reduces pretax income in the financial records without reducing taxable income.

In contrast, suppose the above company has a large portfolio of investments in tax-exempt municipal bonds, the permanent difference illustrated in Case C. The pretax income reported to shareholders *exceeds* the taxable income reported to the tax authorities.

Now consider how the financial statements appear. When there are no permanent differences, pretax income reported to shareholders is $120,000, tax expense is $48,000, and the earnings statement appears as in the first column (a) of the table on the next page. If $30,000 of expense is recorded on the books but is not deductible for tax purposes, as in column b, pretax income falls to $90,000, and the apparent tax rate rises to $48,000 ÷ $90,000 = 53.3%. An example might be a nondeductible fine for violating air pollution standards. Now suppose that, instead of a nondeductible expense, $30,000 of nontaxable revenue is added, as in the third column (c); pretax income rises to $150,000. Tax remains at $48,000. If you estimated the tax rate by dividing income taxes by pretax book income, the tax rate appears to be 32%.

	(a) No Permanent Differences	(b) Nondeductible Expense	(c) Nontaxable Revenue
Income before permanent differences	$120,000	$120,000	$120,000
Nontaxable revenue	—	—	30,000
Nondeductible expense	—	(30,000)	—
Pretax income	$120,000	$ 90,000	$150,000
Income tax	48,000	48,000	48,000
Net income	$ 72,000	$ 42,000	$102,000
Apparent tax rate Income tax ÷ pretax income in shareholder report	40%	53.3%	32%

Temporary Differences

Even items recognized for both tax purposes and GAAP may not be recognized at the same time. For example, GAAP requires that expected costs of providing warranty services be recognized at the time of sale. Thus Ford Motor Company uses estimates to record the expected lifetime warranty costs on each car when it is sold. The actual warranty services may be provided over many years. In contrast, the tax law allows Ford to deduct warranty expenses only as repairs are actually performed. This is a **timing difference**, or **temporary difference**, in that the same lifetime expense is recorded, but items are recognized in one period for tax purposes and in another period for shareholder reporting. There are four major categories of such temporary differences:

timing difference (temporary difference) A situation that arises whenever revenue or expense items are recognized in one period for tax purposes and in another period for shareholder reporting.

1. *Expenses* are deducted in determining taxable income *earlier* than they are deducted in determining pretax income for shareholder-reporting purposes. The major example is depreciation. Accelerated depreciation is often used for tax reporting by firms that use straight-line for shareholder reporting.

2. *Revenues* are included in taxable income *later* than they are included in pretax income for shareholder reporting. For instance, some firms use the percentage-of-completion method on long-term contracts for shareholder reporting and use the completed contract method on some contracts for income tax returns. Revenues and profits are generally recognized earlier under the percentage-of-completion method. Recent tax law changes have greatly limited this opportunity.

3. *Expenses* are deducted for income tax purposes *later* than they are deducted for shareholder reporting purposes. For instance, the estimated costs of product warranty contracts are not permitted to be deducted for tax purposes until the period paid or the period in which the warranty service is provided. For shareholder reporting, companies recognize estimated costs of product warranties as expenses when the related products are sold. Consider a simple example. Assume that a company stops offering warranty service on new sales at the start of Year 2 and that the first-year warranties are not paid in cash until the second year. The effects are:

	Shareholder Reporting		Income Tax Return	
	Year 1	Year 2	Year 1	Year 2
Income before warranty expenses	$600,000	$600,000	$600,000	$600,000
Warranty expenses	100,000	—	—	100,000
Pretax income	$500,000	$600,000	$600,000	$500,000

Note that the total pretax income for the two years is identical at $1,100,000 for both financial reporting and tax purposes. *Only the timing differs.*

4. *Revenues* are included in income for tax purposes *earlier* than they are included in pretax income for shareholder purposes. For instance, some fees, dues, and service contracts are taxed when collected but are usually deferred as unearned revenue for financial reporting purposes.

Tax Expense and Timing Differences

Objective 2

Explain how timing differences create deferred taxes.

A timing difference arises if a company is allowed to deduct the full cost of a long-lived asset on its tax return in the year of acquisition while depreciating it over its useful life for financial reporting purposes. Until recently, immediate write-off was permitted in the United Kingdom for certain assets. Indeed, it is currently permitted in the United States for the first $10,000 of asset acquisitions each year.

Suppose a small company earns $40,000 per year before deducting depreciation and taxes and pays taxes at a rate of 40% of taxable income. The company acquires a $10,000 asset with a two-year useful life. It will deduct the $10,000 immediately for tax purposes and will depreciate it at $5,000 per year for book purposes.

	Financial Reporting		Income Tax Return	
	Year 1	Year 2	Year 1	Year 2
Income before depreciation and taxes	$40,000	$40,000	$40,000	$40,000
Depreciation	5,000	5,000	10,000	0
Pretax income	$35,000	$35,000	$30,000	$40,000
Taxes payable at 40%			$12,000	$16,000

The total tax paid to the government over the two years will be $12,000 + $16,000 = $28,000, which is 40% of the two years of combined taxable income $30,000 + $40,000 = $70,000. How should this fact be shown for financial reporting purposes? One approach is to report the amount actually paid to the government each year, but the FASB does not permit this alternative. When timing differences arise, GAAP requires a hypothetical tax expense number. It is the tax that would have been paid if the pretax income used for shareholder reporting had also been reported to the tax authorities. Both approaches are illustrated in the table at the top of page 641.

In our example the company has a stable economic earnings pattern. When the tax expense is based on the financial reporting numbers, that stable pattern is evident in a constant $21,000 net income over the two years. However,

Alternate
Calculations of
Tax Expense for
Financial Reporting

	Tax Expense Based on Financial Reporting (Required)		Tax Expense Based on Tax Return (Not Allowed)	
	Year 1	Year 2	Year 1	Year 2
Pretax Income	$35,000	$35,000	$35,000	$35,000
Tax Expense	14,000*	14,000*	12,000†	16,000†
Net Income	$21,000	$21,000	$23,000	$19,000

* $14,000 is 40% of $35,000.
† From the tax return columns in the prior example: 40% x $30,000 = $12,000; 40% x $40,000 = $16,000.

when the actual tax paid is used to measure tax expense, the apparent pattern of net income is a declining one, from $23,000 to $19,000. Because the use of the actual tax amount paid to the government tends to distort the level and pattern of reported earnings, the FASB requires companies to calculate tax expense based on the accounting methods used for financial reporting purposes. This requirement correctly matches the income tax expense with the income to which it relates.

How is this hypothetical income tax expense number to be recorded? The payable to the government in Year 1 is $12,000, but an expense of $14,000 is being recorded. Think of it as a current payable for the $12,000 currently owed to the government and a $2,000 liability that arises because of predictable future taxes. This $2,000 liability is called a **deferred tax liability**, because it will be paid only when a future tax return is filed.

deferred tax liability
A tax liability that is predictable now because of timing differences but will only be payable when a future tax return is filed.

On the income statement, companies typically report one number for income tax expense. For example, in 1994 Kimberly-Clark reported $276 million of income taxes on pretax income of $741 million. In the footnotes, the income tax expense was reported to be made up of $245 million currently payable and $31 million of deferred tax. Over time these annual tax deferrals tend to build. The balance sheet showed total Deferred Income Taxes of $613 million. This is more than 9% of Kimberly-Clark's total liabilities and shareholders' equity of $6,716 million. The Deferred Tax Liability account will appear in the liability section, often just above Shareholders' Equity, as illustrated below.

Kimberly-Clark
(dollars in millions)

	For the Year Ended December 31	
	1994	1993
Current Liabilities (summarized)	$2,059	$1,909
Long-term Debt	930	933
Noncurrent Employee Benefit Obligations	439	430
Deferred Income Taxes	613	585
Minority Owners' Interests	80	67
Stockholders' Equity	2,595	2,457
Total Liabilities and Stockholders' Equity	$6,716	$6,381

■ TAX DEPRECIATION PROCEDURES

The majority of the $31 million of current-year deferred tax for Kimberly-Clark is related to timing differences in accounting for depreciation for financial reporting versus income tax purposes. Companies prefer to pay less tax, so they certainly prefer higher tax deductions for depreciation. Thus, for tax purposes, firms choose the shortest possible lives for their depreciable assets and employ the most accelerated method possible for allocating depreciation expense over the asset's life. In contrast, for financial reporting purposes, firms typically choose longer asset lives and employ straight-line depreciation.

Conflicts between the IRS and Taxpayers

The IRS audits the accuracy of tax reporting. When judgment enters into the reporting process the IRS and taxpayers often disagree. For example, a taxpayer might claim that a truck will last for only two years, while the IRS might believe that five years is a more appropriate life. The two alternatives give different depreciation amounts. For years the IRS was constantly taking taxpayers to the Tax Court and arguing that their depreciation claims were excessive.

Partly to eliminate this expensive, recurring conflict, Congress passed laws that state exactly how depreciation will be calculated for tax purposes for various classes of assets. Because depreciation timing differences are among the most common sources of deferred taxes, we will consider the tax depreciation procedures in some detail.

Modified Accelerated Cost Recovery System (MACRS)

Modified Accelerated Cost Recovery System (MACRS) The basis for computing depreciation for tax purposes in the United States. It is based on arbitrary "recovery" periods instead of useful lives.

Depreciation for tax purposes is generally based on the **Modified Accelerated Cost Recovery System (MACRS)** contained in the tax code. Depreciation deductions depend on arbitrary "recovery" periods instead of useful lives. As Exhibit 14-1 shows, property is classified by the number of years over which the acquisition cost is to be recovered through deductions.

For each class of property, schedules are provided that specify the percentage of cost that may be deducted during each year of the asset's use. An example of the three-, five-, and seven-year schedules is provided in Exhibit 14-2. These are the most accelerated depreciation deductions allowed under the tax law. Taxpayers may always choose to use the slower, straight-line depreciation method for any asset. For the 27.5-year and 31.5-year classes, the straight-line method is required for tax purposes.

Objective 3

Contrast tax (MACRS) and straight-line depreciation.

It may appear strange that the percentage in the first year is smaller than that in the second year for all three classes of property in Exhibit 14-2. This occurs because a *half-year convention* is built into the calculations. The half-year convention means that all assets are treated the same in their first year of use whether they are placed in service in January or December. On average, assets are used one-half year in their first year. For the 3-year property, the table is constructed using the double-declining balance method, which would normally charge two-thirds of the assets cost to the first year ($2 \times \frac{1}{3}$). The half-year convention leads to one-half of two-thirds being recorded in the first year. There is also a half year of depreciation in the year an asset is sold or retired from service.

Exhibit 14-1	Class	Examples of Types of Assets
Examples of Classifications in Modified Accelerated Cost Recovery System (MACRS)	3-year	Special tools for several specific industries; tractor units for over-the-road.
	5-year	Automobiles; trucks; research equipment; computers; airplanes; machinery and equipment in selected industries.
	7-year	Office furniture; railroad track; machinery and equipment in a majority of industries.
	10-year	Water transportation equipment (vessels, tugs, barges); machinery and equipment in selected industries.
	15-year	Most land improvements; machinery and equipment in selected industries.
	20-year	Farm buildings; electricity distribution (poles, cables, etc.); most electricity generation equipment.
	27.5-year	Residential rental property.
	31.5-year	Most nonresidential real property.

Exhibit 14-2

Examples of MACRS Depreciation Schedule of Yearly Percentages*

Year	3-Year Property	5-Year Property	7-Year Property
1	33%	20%	14%
2	45	32	24
3	15	19	18
4	7	12	13
5		12	9
6		5	9
7			9
8			4

* Rounded. For simplicity, these rounded percentages will be used in the examples in this chapter.

The table percentages are applied directly to the cost of the asset without regard to salvage value. For example, if a $1,000-asset in the five-year property class is acquired any time in 1998, the 1998 depreciation deduction would be $200 (or 20% × $1,000). In 1999 the deduction would be 32% × $1,000, or $320.

The MACRS method provides *accelerated* depreciation by (1) using depreciation periods shorter than useful lives and (2) assigning higher depreciation percentages in the earlier years than would be assigned under straight-line depreciation. Compare MACRS with the straight-line and double-declining balance (DDB) schedules applied based on a five-year economic life. Suppose General Motors bought special tooling for the manufacture of Buicks. The acquisition cost was $100 million, the useful life was five years, and there was no residual value. This is a three-year asset for MACRS purposes. Depreciation under the three methods is the following (in millions):

Year	Straight-Line	Double-Declining Balance	MACRS**
1	$ 20	$ 40.0	$ 33
2	20	24.0	45
3	20	14.4	15
4	20	10.8*	7
5	20	10.8	0
Total	$100	$100	$100

* Conversion to straight-line in Year 4, when straight-line rate on remaining balance exceeds DDB.

** Uses the rounded percentages as listed in Exhibit 14-2: 33% x 100 = $33; 45% x 100 = $45, etc.

Note that the total depreciation under all three methods is $100 million. The only difference is the *timing* of the depreciation. For many assets, MACRS accelerates depreciation even faster than the DDB method. Why? Because the recovery periods are shorter than useful lives. Because of the MACRS half-year convention, DDB exceeds MACRS for Year 1, but by the end of Year 2, MACRS cumulative deductions (78%) exceed DDB (64%).

■ DEFERRED FEDERAL INCOME TAXES

Corporations trying to minimize immediate income tax disbursements use MACRS depreciation methods for reporting to the income tax authorities even though straight-line depreciation may be used for financial reporting. This section explores the meaning of the deferred income taxes that result from timing differences between the tax return and financial reports.

A Matter of Timing

Consider the $100 million asset from the preceding section. Assume that it is depreciated using MACRS for tax purposes and straight-line for shareholder reporting (in millions):

	Shareholder Reporting			Tax Reporting		
	Beginning Book Value	*Depreciation Expense*	*Ending Book Value*	*Beginning Book Value*	*Depreciation Expense*	*Ending Book Value*
Year 1	$100	$20	$80	$100	$33	$67
Year 2	80	20	60	67	45	22
Year 3	60	20	40	22	15	7
Year 4	40	20	20	7	7	0
Year 5	20	20	0	0	0	0

Examine the situation at the end of Year 2. Under shareholder reporting, the book value is $60 million, meaning that $40 million of depreciation expense has been charged and $60 million remains to be charged. For tax reporting, the book value is $22 million; $78 million of depreciation expense has been charged and $22 million remains. The difference in book values is a result of the

What Is Income Tax Expense?

From 1973 through 1984, General Dynamics Corporation, a large defense contractor, reported total pretax income of $2.7 billion and total federal income tax expense of $1 billion. How much income tax did General Dynamics pay during this period? Zero! This is an extreme illustration of a very important point: For most companies in most years, the income reported to the shareholders is not the same as the income reported to the IRS, and the reported income tax expense is different from the cash paid for taxes.

The cause of the $1 billion difference between the income tax expense General Dynamics reported to its shareholders and the tax paid to the IRS is the accounting for long-term contracts. For financial accounting purposes, General Dynamics uses the percentage of completion method. A portion of the revenue and expense associated with a long-term contract (such as a contract to produce nineteen Ohio-class Trident submarines over multiple years) is reported each year according to the fraction of the total contract completed that year. For tax purposes, General Dynamics uses the completed contract method, in which no profit is reported until work under the contract is complete. Until a tax law change in 1982, General Dynamics was able to claim that contracts were not completed until the whole order was filled. This meant that General Dynamics could delay reporting profit from a contract

to produce and deliver, say, one hundred planes to the U.S. government until the hundredth plane was produced and delivered. The elapsed time sometimes exceeded ten years. In the early 1990s the IRS reexamined General Dynamics' tax returns for the years 1977 through 1986 to see whether the completed contract method was abused. Because General Dynamics and the IRS could not agree on what method was appropriate, the case has gone to the U.S. Tax Court. The resolution may take several years.

Remember that deviations between shareholder income and IRS income result in *deferral* of taxes, not cancellation of taxes. In the years 1987 through 1992, General Dynamics paid income taxes totaling $1.6 billion. As the timing differences reversed, income taxes paid to the government exceeded income tax expense reported to shareholders. In 1993 and 1994 tax expense and tax payments were approximately equal.

But the shareholders were happy. The decade of *delayed* taxes are equivalent to an interest-free loan from the government. ∎

Sources: 1991 *and* 1994 Annual Reports of General Dynamics Corporation; *James E. Wheeler and Edmund Outslay, "The Phantom Federal Income Taxes of General Dynamics Corporation,"* The Accounting Review, 61 *(October, 1986), p. 760.*

different timing of depreciation expense. It is a *temporary* difference because higher depreciation in the early years for tax purposes will be offset by higher depreciation in later years for shareholder reporting. At the end of Year 5, both methods have charged $100 million of depreciation and have a zero book value.

Note that the difference in book values of the asset reflects the differences in accumulated depreciation. Using straight-line depreciation, accumulated depreciation is 20 + 20 = 40 after two years, while under MACRS the accumulated depreciation is 33 + 45 = 78. The difference in accumulated depreciation of $38 equals the difference in ending book values after two years of $60 − $22 = $38.

Reporting Temporary Differences

How should these temporary differences affect *financial* or shareholder reporting? Suppose Cava Company is the owner of the $100 million asset described above. The company began on January 1, 19X1, with initial paid-in capital of $200 million cash. On January 2, 19X1, the company purchased the three-year MACRS asset for $100 million cash. For shareholder reporting, the estimated useful life is five years, the estimated residual value is zero, and the straight-line method is used. Prospective annual income before depreciation and income taxes is $45 million.

The income tax rate is 40% and is not expected to change over the life of the asset. Assume that all taxes are paid early in the next year after the income is earned.

Compare the MACRS depreciation used for tax purposes with the straight-line depreciation used for shareholder reporting (in millions):

	19X1	19X2	19X3	19X4	19X5	Total
MACRS depreciation*	$33	$45	$15	$ 7	$ 0	$100
Straight-line depreciation	20	20	20	20	20	100
Difference	$13	$25	$(5)	$(13)	$(20)	$ 0

* See Exhibit 14-2, page 643: 33% × $100 million = $33 million; 45% × $100 million = $45 million; etc.

Both methods charge $100 million of depreciation, but the *timing* of the charges differs.

Consider 19X1. The income tax return would show:

Income before depreciation	$45,000,000
MACRS depreciation, 33% × $100,000,000	33,000,000
Taxable income	$12,000,000
Income tax to be paid: .40 x $12,000,000, or	$ 4,800,000

Now examine Exhibit 14-3, which shows the Cava Company's transactions as they would be prepared for shareholder reporting. Stop for a moment after transaction *d*. If straight-line depreciation is used for shareholder reporting purposes, should *income tax expense* be based on MACRS cost recovery or straight-line depreciation?

Exhibit 14-3	Analysis of Transactions for Reporting to Cava Company Shareholders (in millions of dollars)

	A		=	L	+	SE	
	Cash	Equipment		Income Tax Payable	Deferred Tax Liability	Paid-in Capital	Retained Income
a. Formation	+200		=			+200	
b. Acquisition of equipment	−100	+100	=				
c. Income before depreciation and taxes	+ 45		=				+45
d. Straight-line depreciation		− 20	=				−20
e. Income tax expense—deferral			=	+4.8	+5.2		−10
Bal. Dec. 31, 19X1	+145	+ 80	=	+4.8	+5.2	+200	+15

Notes:
e. The 4.8 represents income taxes payable as calculated when using MACRS on the income tax return: .40 × 12 taxable income = 4.8. The 10 represents the income tax that would be payable if straight-line depreciation had been used on the income tax return. Taxable income would be 45 − 20 = 25; income tax expense would be .40 × 25 = 10. The deferred income tax is 10 − 4.8 = 5.2.

GAAP requires that income tax expense be based on the depreciation expense reported to shareholders, not on the typically higher depreciation deducted on the tax return. Thus, tax expense (in millions) is calculated as $0.4 \times (45 - 20) = 10$. Actual tax is calculated as $0.4 \times (45 - 33) = 4.8$. Entry e in Exhibit 14-3 shows the effect on the accounting equation. The 10 of depreciation expense reduces shareholders' equity, the 4.8 is shown as a liability to the government, and the difference of 5.2 appears as a *deferred tax liability*. Note that the 5.2 is exactly equal to the tax rate times the difference between MACRS and straight-line depreciation ($0.40 \times [33 - 20] = 5.2$). This represents additional taxes that will be paid in the future as the straight-line depreciation exceeds MACRS depreciation in the final years of the asset's life. In fact, recall that under MACRS there is no depreciation in Year 5 at all. The full life cycle is illustrated in the next section.

Interperiod Tax Allocation

Objective 4

Explain why interperiod tax allocation is generally accepted.

Before considering the relative merits of deferral and no deferral, study all parts of Exhibit 14-4. This exhibit provides a comparison for five years. The first part is a tabulation of the reports made to the IRS on income tax returns. The rightmost column is headed "net income." Technically, no number labeled net income is calculated on a tax return. In Exhibit 14-4 and elsewhere in the chapter, a column labeled net income is provided to allow comparison to total net income prepared for reporting to shareholders. This emphasizes the fact that depreciation timing differences merely reallocate deductions, taxes, and income through time without affecting totals. The second part of Exhibit 14-4 shows reports made to shareholders.

Note how the cumulative income tax paid is $50 million and the cumulative net income is $75 million in both cases. Furthermore, the comparison of tabulations *1* and *2* clearly demonstrates how the favorable effect of lower taxes and higher net income in earlier years is offset by higher taxes and lower net income in later years. *Temporary* or *timing* differences originate in one period and reverse, or "turn around," in one or more subsequent periods, as Exhibit 14-4 demonstrates.

tax deferral (interperiod tax allocation, tax allocation) A method that measures reported income as if it were subject to the full current tax rate even though a more advantageous accounting method was used for tax purposes.

Tabulation *2* in Exhibit 14-4 shows the **tax deferral**, which is also called **interperiod tax allocation,** or simply **tax allocation.** Tax allocation produces a deferred tax liability account that fluctuates as the cumulative difference between tax depreciation and financial reporting depreciation fluctuates. As Exhibit 14-4 shows, this results in a *smoothing effect* on income. Actual tax paid ranges from zero to $18 while tax expense is a constant $10 for financial reporting.

In Years 1 and 2, the deferred tax liability builds. Income taxes paid are less than the income tax expense. In essence, the company delays paying part of its income tax expense but recognizes an obligation to pay the remainder in later years. In Years 3, 4, and 5, the company pays more income taxes than it charges as income tax expense. It is paying the taxes deferred from Years 1 and 2 in addition to the income tax expense incurred in Years 3, 4, and 5. This can be summarized as follows (in millions):

	Income Tax Expense on Shareholder Reports (1)	Income Tax Payment (2)	Income Tax Deferred (1) – (2) (3)	Balance Sheet Cumulative Deferral (4)
19X1	$10	$ 4.8	$ 5.2	$ 5.2
19X2	10	0.0	10.0	15.2
19X3	10	12.0	(2.0)	13.2
19X4	10	15.2	(5.2)	8.0
19X5	10	18.0	(8.0)	0

Comparison of Alternative Reporting Practices for Depreciation and Income Taxes
Facts: Purchase asset for $100 million; five-year life; 40% tax rate. Company uses MACRS for tax purposes but straight-line depreciation for financial reporting purposes.

Exhibit 14-4

1. Reporting on Income Tax Returns

Year	Income Before Depreciation and Taxes	MACRS Cost Recovery	Taxable Income	Income Tax Paid @40%	Net Income
1	$ 45	.33 × $100 = $ 33	$ 12	$ 4.8	$ 7.2
2	45	.45 × $100 = 45	0	0.0	0.0
3	45	.15 × $100 = 15	30	12.0	18.0
4	45	.07 × $100 = 7	38	15.2	22.8
5	45		45	18.0	27.0
Cumulative	$225	$100	$125	$50.0	$75.0

2. Reporting to Shareholders
Straight-Line Depreciation and Tax Deferral (Required)

Year	Income Before Depreciation and Taxes	Straight-Line Depreciation	Pretax Income	Income Tax Expense — Tax Paid	Income Tax Expense — Tax Deferred	Income Tax Expense — Total Tax Expense	Net Income	Balance Sheet Effect: Deferred Tax Liability
1	$ 45	$ 20	$ 25	$ 4.8	$ 5.2	$10	$15	$ 5.2
2	45	20	25	0.0	10.0	10	15	15.2
3	45	20	25	12.0	–2.0	10	15	13.2
4	45	20	25	15.2	–5.2	10	15	8.0
5	45	20	25	18.0	–8.0	10	15	0
Cumulative	$225	$100	$125	$50.0	$ 0	$50	$75	—

In Years 1 and 2, the total income tax expense on reports to shareholders is $20 million, but only $4.8 million is paid to the government. The other $15.2 million will be paid in Years 3, 4, and 5; therefore there is a liability of $15.2 million at the end of Year 2. The total income tax expense on shareholder reports in Years 3, 4, and 5 is $30 million, but $45.2 million ($12.0 million + $15.2 million +

$18.0 million) is paid to the government. The extra $15.2 million is payment for the $15.2 million deferred in Years 1 and 2.

Another approach to computing the deferred tax liability is to focus directly on the difference between book value of the assets for tax and shareholder reporting. Exhibit 14-5 shows that the book values of the assets differ under straight-line and MACRS depreciation by $13 in Year 1, $38 in Year 2 and so on. These differences are the predictable timing differences that will reverse in the future. The *balance* in the deferred tax liability account must be the tax rate of 40% times the difference in book values; $5.2 in Year 1, $15.2 in Year 2, and so on. The final column shows the changes in these predicted balances each year; $5.2 in Year 1, $10.0 in Year 2, and so on. Note that these annual changes are exactly the annual "tax deferred" amounts calculated in panel 2 of Exhibit 14-4. As long as tax rates remain constant this will be true.

Exhibit 14-5	Deferred Taxes Based Directly on Book Value Differences (in millions)						
	Straight-Line		MACRS			Deferred	
	Depreciation Expense	Book Value*	Annual Depreciation Expense	Book Value*	Difference in Book Value	Tax Liability** @ 40%	Annual Change
Year 1	$20	$80	$33	$67	$13	$5.2	$ 5.2
Year 2	20	60	45	22	38	15.2	10.0
Year 3	20	40	15	7	33	13.2	(2.0)
Year 4	20	20	7	0	20	8.0	(5.2)
Year 5	20	0	0	0	0	0	(8.0)

* Book value at year end, $100 million cost less accumulated depreciation.
** 40% times difference in book value.

The balance sheet equation for the income tax items in our example are shown in Exhibit 14-6. The journal entries are as follows (without explanations):

```
19X1   Income tax expense ...................   10,000,000
           Deferred tax liability .............              5,200,000
           Cash (or income taxes payable) .....              4,800,000

19X2   Income tax expense ..................   10,000,000
           Deferred tax liability .............             10,000,000

19X3   Income tax expense .................   10,000,000
       Deferred tax liability ................    2,000,000
           Cash (or income taxes payable) .....             12,000,000

19X4   Income tax expense ..................   10,000,000
       Deferred tax liability ................    5,200,000
           Cash (or income taxes payable) .....             15,200,000

19X5   Income tax expense .................   10,000,000
       Deferred tax liability ................    8,000,000
           Cash (or income taxes payable) .....             18,000,000
```

Exhibit 14-6

Entries for Deferred
Taxes

Balance Sheet Equation:

	A	=		L		+		SE	
	Cash	=		Deferred Tax Liability		+		Retained Income	
19X1	−4.8	=	5.2	⎡Increase	⎤			−10	
19X2	0	=	10.0	⎣Deferred Tax Liability⎦				−10	⎡Income ⎤
19X3	−12.0	=	−2.0	⎡Decrease	⎤			−10	Tax
19X4	−15.2	=	−5.2	Deferred				−10	⎣Expense⎦
19X5	−18.0	=	−8.0	⎣Tax Liability	⎦			−10	

The Liability View of Deferred Taxes

The deferred tax liability arises because of timing differences– expenses are recognized at one time for financial reporting and at another time for tax purposes. In all of the examples given, the tax rate is held constant at 40% throughout the life of the asset. In addition, all examples illustrate early deduction for tax purposes and later deduction for financial reporting. Unlike depreciation timing differences, expenses for post-retirement items such as life and health insurance for retirees are often deducted earlier for financial reporting purposes than for tax purposes. When this occurs a deferred tax *asset* is recorded to acknowledge that the taxes being paid now are higher than the tax expense provided, based on pre-tax income reported for financial purposes. The FASB has dealt with this and other complex issues such as how to account for known future changes in tax rates and how to net deferred tax assets and liabilities together. The discussion of FASB Statement 109 that covers these details is deferred to more advanced courses.

Growth of Deferred Taxes

For growing companies, deferred tax liability accounts are likely to accumulate to enormous amounts that will never diminish as long as the company is growing and continues the replacement of old facilities used in its operations. For example, in Exhibit 14-4, if the company spent $100 million each year for more plant assets, the additional deferrals in each of these years would more than offset the decline in deferrals in Years 3, 4, and 5 associated with the original $100 million outlay. Exhibit 14-7 summarizes this point.

Critics of the deferral method point out that tax-allocation procedures should not apply if there is a relatively stable or growing investment in depreciable assets. Note from Year 4 in Exhibit 14-7 that the deferred tax liability will never decline if the company maintains its $100 million annual expenditure. In Year 5 MACRS cost recovery is $100 million and straight-line depreciation is also $100 million. This will remain true into the future, and the deferred tax liability will remain $41.6 million.

The proponents of deferral reject the growing-firm argument as incomplete. The ever-increasing deferred tax liability is a typical characteristic of growing companies that is also reflected in many other accounts. For example, accounts payable and liabilities for product warranties may also grow, but that is not justification for assuming that liabilities for these obligations are unnecessary.

Analysis of Growing Firm and Deferred Income Taxes

Facts: Same as in Exhibit 14-4 except that $100 million is spent each year for additional assets and income increases $45 million each year until leveling off in Year 6. In Year 6, the $100 million represents a replacement of the asset originally purchased in Year 1. All amounts are in millions.

Exhibit 14-7

1. Reporting for Tax Purposes

| Year | Income Before Depreciation and Taxes | MACRS Cost Recovery on Asset Purchased in Year | | | | | | Total | Taxable Income | Income Tax Paid | Net Income |
		1	2	3	4	5	6				
1	$ 45	$33						= $ 33	$ 12	$ 4.8	$ 7.2
2	90	45 + 33						= 78	12	4.8	7.2
3	135	15 + 45 + 33						= 93	42	16.8	25.2
4	180	7 + 15 + 45 + 33						= 100	80	32.0	48.0
5	225	7 + 15 + 45 + 33						= 100	125	50.0	75.0
6	225	7 + 15 + 45 + 33						= 100	125	50.0	75.0

2. Reporting to Shareholders
Straight-Line Depreciation and Tax Allocation

| Year | Income Before Depreciation and Taxes | Straight-Line Depreciation | Pretax Income | Income Tax Expense | | | Net Income | Balance Sheet Effect: Deferred Tax Liability |
				Tax Paid	Tax Deferred	Total Tax Expense		
1	$ 45	$ 20	$ 25	$ 4.8	$ 5.2	$10	$15	$ 5.2
2	90	40	50	4.8	15.2	20	30	20.4
3	135	60	75	16.8	13.2	30	45	33.6
4	180	80	100	32.0	8.0	40	60	41.6
5	225	100	125	50.0	—	50	75	41.6
6	225	100	125	50.0	—	50	75	41.6

Whatever your reactions to these conflicting arguments, the FASB's accounting *requirements* are clear. Income tax expense on the income statement for shareholders is based on the revenue and expenses on that statement, not those on the tax statement. Therefore income tax expense seldom equals the taxes payable to the government for any given period. Deferred tax liabilities are found on the balance sheets of nearly every company.

The following schedule illustrates the magnitude of the deferred tax liability as reported by various companies in 1994. The deferred tax liability is reported along with the total stockholders' equity and total assets to provide perspective (in millions):

Company	Deferred Tax	Stockholders' Equity	Total Assets
CSX Corporation	$ 2,570	$ 3,731	$13,724
DuPont	1,494	12,822	36,892
Exxon	11,435	37,415	87,862
McDonald's	841	6,885	13,591

Taxes Internationally

The tax arena illustrates how alternative approaches are used by different countries to solve a common problem. All governments raise revenue via taxation to pay for society's needs. Beyond that simple statement, we encounter huge international variation regarding how much tax revenue is raised, what kind of taxes are used to raise the revenue, and which social needs the government decides to support.

Our focus is financial reporting, so consider a very small, subordinate question. Is deferred income tax accounting such a good idea that all countries should (and do) adopt it as a generally accepted accounting principle? If not, why not and what are the other options? If the answer were a simple yes, this box would end here, but it doesn't.

The chapter has explained that the deferred tax payable account represents a liability to the government for future taxes that we can predict today based on events that have already happened. So long as we assume that the company remains profitable into the future and subject to income taxes, we can predict that these taxes will be paid. U.S. standard setters choose to report current income tax expense *as if* we report to the government much as we report to our shareholders. Income tax expenses include our current liability to the government for the current tax year plus (or minus) adjustments for future tax issues.

The whole issue becomes complicated because GAAP financial reporting and tax reporting originate from different perspectives. U.S. GAAP is designed to capture economic events in a manner useful to investors. The tax authorities seek to raise tax revenue in an efficient and equitable manner. These differences in intent produce many timing differences between GAAP and tax accounting for both revenue recognition and expense recognition. The United States resolves this conflict by requiring an artificial tax expense number that includes predictable future tax consequences. But this U.S. focus on future tax effects is not universal. In some countries, these issues disappear because the tax reporting and the financial reporting are identical. If there are no differences in revenue or expense, there is no timing pattern to worry about, and tax expense on the books equals the tax obligation on the tax return. This has been true historically in Italy, Norway, and Chile. In other regimes, the revenue and expense recognition differ between the tax returns and the financial reports, but the standard setters choose to rely on the current tax obligation as the most useful number. They mandate that it be reported as the income tax expense provision on the the income statement. If future tax policies and rates are highly uncertain, this choice is appropriate. Standard setters in France and Japan have made this choice. Canada and South Africa have rules similar to the United States.∎

The deferred tax liability, expressed as a percentage of total assets, varies for these four firms from 19% for CSX Corporation to 6% for McDonald's. For most companies the primary source of deferred taxes is timing differences related to depreciation.

In a recent survey of international practice, 60% of the countries surveyed required the use of deferred taxes when financial reporting of expenses differed from the timing of reporting of corresponding tax deductions.

■ ADDITIONAL FEATURES OF THE U.S. TAX LAW

The government often maximizes the effect of a particular tax law feature—aimed at achieving a certain social or economic goal—by offering *tax credits*.

tax credits Direct reductions in a company's income tax obligations.

Tax credits are direct reductions of the income tax itself, in contrast to *tax deductions*, which merely reduce the level of taxable income.

This section also considers the problem created by a one-year period for tax reporting. When companies have losses in one year and profits in another, a special feature called *net operating loss carryovers* allows companies to blend gains and losses from different periods to moderate the tax liability.

Tax Credits

Tax credits amount to the government saying to the taxpayer, "If you will do what I want, I will charge you less tax." For example, if the government wants to encourage investment in machinery, a tax credit could be given to taxpayers equal to 10% of their current-year new investment in machinery. The taxpayer who buys a $5,000 machine can directly reduce taxes by 0.10 x $5,000 = $500. This is like the government agreeing to pay for 10% of every piece of machinery acquired.

This example exactly parallels the *investment tax credit (ITC)*, which the government has used periodically to encourage investment. Various versions of an ITC were enacted, repealed, re-enacted, changed, and so on during the years from 1962 through 1986. As this text is being written, no ITC is in effect, but it remains a classic tool of government policy that may re-emerge if a decision is made to spur investment.

Congress enacted the investment tax credit to encourage businesses to invest in property such as machinery and equipment. To encourage research and development, Congress created a *credit for increased research expenditures*. It provided a tax credit equal to 20% of the amount by which qualified research expenditures exceed the average research expenses for a base period. For example, AT&T spent an average of $3 billion for research in 1992-1994. Assume AT&T spent an average of $3 billion on "qualified" research during the base period. If 1995 expenses totaled $3.2 billion, AT&T would have a tax credit of 20% × ($3.2 billion – $3 billion) = $40 million, which would directly reduce its income tax expense by $40 million.

Other recent tax credits have encouraged low-income housing, jobs for individuals in certain target groups (such as the handicapped), and use of alcohol fuels. Each credit is directed toward a specific social goal. The credit is kept only long enough to accomplish the goal.

"Flow-through" Accounting for Tax Credits

flow-through A method of accounting for tax credits whereby the entire tax savings reduces tax expense in the year the credit is earned.

The vast majority of U.S. companies use **flow-through** accounting for tax credits. Under this method of accounting, the tax credit reduces both the tax payment to the government and the tax expense for financial reporting in the year when the tax credit is earned. For example, suppose a company with a tax credit of $150,000 had taxable income of $3 million and pretax income for reporting to shareholders of $3.5 million:

	Reporting to Tax Authorities	Reporting to Shareholders
Pretax income	$3,000,000	$3,500,000
Income tax @ 40%	1,200,000	1,400,000
Less: tax credits	(150,000)	(150,000)
Total income taxes	1,050,000	1,250,000
Net income	$1,950,000	$2,250,000

The initial tax payment to the government of 40% of $3 million = $1,200,000 would be immediately reduced by the $150,000 tax credit to $1,050,000. For financial reporting purposes, the initial income tax expense of 40% of $3.5 million = $1,400,000 would be reduced by the $150,000 tax credit to $1,250,000.

Appendix 14 considers accounting for tax credits in more detail.

Net Operating Losses

Objective 6

Illustrate the importance of net operating losses (NOLs).

To illustrate the potential problem of one-year tax reporting, consider a company that earns $100,000 in even-numbered years and loses $50,000 in odd-numbered years. For simplicity, assume there are no permanent or timing differences between financial reporting and reporting to the tax authorities. Without a special provision the company would pay $40,000 in tax in each profitable year and none in unprofitable years. Over ten years, the company would earn $250,000 (5 × $100,000 – [5 × $50,000]) and pay tax of $200,000 (5 × $40,000).

In contrast, a company that earned $25,000 every year would pay only $100,000 in taxes (10 × $25,000 × 0.4). To avoid this inequity, the tax code provides for a **net operating loss (NOL)** to be offset against taxable income in other years. An *NOL* arises when permissible tax deductions in a given year exceed revenues. The current rules permit an NOL to be carried back for three years or forward for up to fifteen years. The details of exactly how this would affect a company's financial reporting are covered in intermediate accounting texts.

net operating loss (NOL) An operating loss for tax purposes that can be carried back three years or forward fifteen years to offset taxable income in other years.

Summary Problems for Your Review

Problem One

Kitsap Company bought a special-purpose tool for $200,000. The tool has a five-year economic life, is a three-year MACRS asset, and has no residual value. Kitsap uses straight-line depreciation in reports to shareholders and MACRS for tax purposes. The tax rate is 34%. For Years 1 through 5, compute the depreciation for tax purposes, the depreciation for shareholder reporting, and the deferred tax liability at the end of each year.

Solution to Problem One

In the following table, depreciation for shareholder reporting is in column (1), tax depreciation is in column (2), and the deferred tax liability is in column (5):

	(1) Straight-Line Depreciation	(2) MACRS Depreciation	(3) Difference in Depreciation Expense	(4) Tax Effect @ 34%	(5) Deferred Tax Liability
Year 1	$40,000	$66,000	$26,000	$ 8,840	$ 8,840
Year 2	$40,000	90,000	50,000	17,000	25,840
Year 3	$40,000	30,000	(10,000)	(3,400)	22,440
Year 4	$40,000	14,000	(26,000)	(8,840)	13,600
Year 5	$40,000	0	(40,000)	(13,600)	0

Problem Two

Examine Exhibit 14-7 on page 649. Suppose that rather than the $100 million spent in Years 1 through 6, $200 million was spent in Year 7 on additional three-year MACRS class assets with five-year useful lives. Income before depreciation and taxes reached $270 million. For Year 7, fill in all the columns in Exhibit 14-7 using a 40% tax rate.

Solution to Problem Two

For income tax authorities (in millions):

Year	Income Before Depreciation and Taxes	MACRS Cost Recovery	Taxable Income	Income Tax Paid	Net Income
7	$270	$7 + 15 + 45 + 66* = $133	$137	$54.8	$82.2

* .33 x $200 million = $66 million.

For shareholders (in millions):

Year	Income Before Depreciation and Taxes	Straight-Line Depreciation	Pretax Income	Income Tax Expense Paid	Income Tax Expense Deferred	Income Tax Expense Total	Net Income	Balance Sheet Effect: Deferred Tax Liability
7	$270	$120	$150	$54.8	$5.2	$60	$90	$46.8

Computations: 6 machines @ $20 of depreciation each = $120; .40 × 150 = 60; 60–54.8 = 5.2; 41.6 + 5.2 = 46.8.

Problem Three

The Solar Kitchen Corporation manufactures and sells energy-efficient additions to provide solar-heated eating areas next to existing kitchens. Because of good styling and marketing to an energy-conscious public, sales have grown briskly. Solar Kitchen has no pre-existing deferred tax liability. During 19X0 the following transactions occurred.

1. On January 1, 10,000 new shares of common were sold at $100 per share.
2. Half of the proceeds from the stock sale were immediately invested in tax-free bonds yielding 6% per annum. The bonds were held throughout the year, resulting in interest revenue of $500,000 ×.06 = $30,000.
3. Sales for the year were $4,500,000 with expenses of $3,800,000 reported under GAAP (exclusive of income tax expense).
4. MACRS depreciation exceeded depreciation included in item 3 above by $300,000.

5. For financial reporting purposes warranty costs are calculated at 1% of sales, and the resulting $45,000 is included in the $3,800,000 of expenses. Actual expenditures under warranty were $22,000. The difference is $23,000.

6. Tax credits received under various programs were $12,000.

Required

1. Calculate earnings before tax for shareholder reporting.
2. Calculate income tax payable to the tax authorities and income tax expense for shareholder reporting using a 40% tax rate.
3. Make the appropriate journal entry. Assume the 40% tax rate is expected to be maintained.

Solution to Problem Three

1. Earnings before taxes for shareholder reporting are:

Sales revenue	$4,500,000
Interest revenue	30,000
Less operating expenses	(3,800,000)
Pretax income	$ 730,000

2. Calculate income tax payable and income tax expense.

	Reporting to Tax Authorities	Reporting to Shareholders
Earnings before tax	$730,000	$730,000
Permanent differences:		
Nontaxable interest	(30,000)	(30,000)
Subtotal	700,000	700,000
Timing differences:		
Depreciation	(300,000)	—
Warranty expenses	23,000	—
Earnings on which tax is based:	423,000	700,000
Tax rate	.40	.40
Income tax before credits	169,200	280,000
Tax credit	12,000	12,000
Income tax payable	$157,200	
Income tax expense reported to shareholders		$268,000

a. The only permanent difference is the municipal interest revenue. It will never be taxed, so it is excluded from the income on which the tax is based for both tax and shareholder reporting.

b. The timing differences total $277,000. They include the MACRS difference of $300,000, which reduces taxable income because MACRS tax deductions exceed the straight-line deductions reported to shareholders. They also include $23,000 of warranty expenses under GAAP that are not deductible for tax purposes (.01 × $4,500,000 = $45,000 deducted under GAAP, less the $22,000 that is deductible for tax purposes).

3.

Income tax expense	268,000	
Income tax payable		157,200
Deferred tax liability		110,800

Note that the credit to the deferred tax account is the tax rate times the net temporary (or timing) differences: .40 × $277,000 = $110,800.

Highlights to Remember

Income tax rules differ from GAAP in terms of both whether and when certain revenue and expense items are recognized and reported. Permanent differences between GAAP and the tax laws are illustrated by such items as goodwill, which is never deductible for tax purposes, and municipal bond interest, which is not subject to federal income tax although it is clearly revenue under GAAP. Timing differences between GAAP and the tax laws are illustrated by such items as warranty expenses and depreciation where the tax laws specify different patterns of when the deductions will be recorded.

When tax and GAAP deductions occur at different times, taxable income does not equal book income before tax. Similarly, taxes currently payable do not equal tax expense calculated under GAAP. The deferred tax account is used to balance the two, generally as a deferred tax liability account that is conceptually similar to a long-term liability.

Straight-line depreciation amortizes the initial cost of an asset evenly over the expected economic life of the asset. MACRS is an accelerated method specified in the tax code that was adopted to encourage capital investment and to eliminate disputes between the IRS and taxpayers. Interperiod tax allocation is the name for the method that uses deferred taxes to capture such timing differences between GAAP and the tax law. It is required under GAAP because it better matches tax expense with the before-tax income being reported under GAAP.

Tax credits are immediate reductions of the amount of tax. Credits are created by Congress to encourage particular acts, such as investment in productive assets, increased research and development expenditures, job training, energy conservation, and the like. In contrast to tax credits, deductions reduce the amount subject to tax, not the tax itself.

The annual accounting period creates problems when profits and losses occur in a cycle over time. The government taxes profits, but does not generally share in business losses. The rules for net operating losses permit companies to offset losses in one year against profits in prior or subsequent years and, in a sense, to average out profits over time.

Appendix 14: Accounting for Investment Tax Credits

Objective 7

Differentiate the flow-through and deferral accounting methods for tax credits.

For many years, the largest tax credit available to corporations was the investment tax credit (ITC). Although Congress eliminated the ITC for investments made after 1985, the ITC will probably be reenacted when Congress again wants to stimulate business investment. Furthermore, many companies that used the deferral method (to be explained shortly) still show deferred investment tax credit liabilities on their balance sheets. Why? Because the tax credit was spread over the lives of the related assets, and many of the assets have not yet reached the end of their lives. For example, consider NYSEG, the company that provides utility services to much of upstate New York. On January 1, 1994, the unamortized investment tax credits were over $91 million. Amortization of these credits has averaged about $15 million each year.

Illustration of Financial Reporting Methods

The cost of equipment that generated an ITC must be spread over future years as depreciation expense. The tax saving from the associated ITC is received in the year the investment is made. Should the financial statements for investors recognize the entire tax savings from such a tax credit as an increase in net income for the year of purchase (the flow-through method)? Or should the tax savings be spread over the useful life of the asset (**deferral method**)? Both methods have been permitted. In many industries (such as airlines and others that have heavy capital expenditures), the method chosen for the investment tax credit has had a material effect on reported net income. Keep in mind that the controversy concerns reports to shareholders, not reports to the income tax authorities.

deferral method A method of accounting for tax credits associated with business investments whereby the tax savings reduce tax expense in each year of an asset's useful life.

To see the essence of the controversy regarding tax credits associated with investments in business property, consider the following problem:

A company begins business on January 1, 19X1, with $500,000 cash raised by an issue of common stock. All of its transactions throughout 19X1 were for cash. On December 31, it had pretax income of $50,000. The income tax rate is 40%. No income taxes will be due before early 19X2. An investment in equipment of $150,000 cash was made on December 31, 19X1. The equipment has a five-year life and an expected residual value of zero.

Exhibit 14-8 contains the complete analysis of transactions using the A = L + SE format. It shows the (a) effects of formation of the company, (b) effects of operating income on cash and retained income, (c) effects of acquisition of equipment, and (d) computation and effects of income taxes. Concentrate on items *a* through *d*. The reporting to shareholders would show an income tax liability of $20,000 and an income tax expense of $20,000. If there is no tax credit available, the matter ends here. That is, there is basically nothing new in the analysis of transactions *a* through *d*.

Exhibit 14-8	Analysis of Transactions (in thousands of dollars)						
		A	**=**	**L**		**+**	**SE**
	Cash	Equipment		Income Tax Payable	Deferred ITC Liability	Paid-in Capital	Retained Income
a. Formation	+500		=			+500	
b. Operations	+ 50		=				+50
c. Acquisition of equipment	−150	+150	=				
d. Income taxes			=	+20			−20
Bal. Dec. 31, 19X1	+400	+150	=	+20		+500	+30
e1. Flow-through			=	−15			+15
Bal. Dec. 31, 19X1, after e1	+400	+150	=	+5		+500	+45
e2. Deferral							
Bal. Dec. 31, 19X1, after e2 rather than e1	+400	+150	=	−15 +5	+15 +15	+500	+30

Suppose the company is eligible for a $15,000 tax credit. Items *e1* and *e2* illustrate two alternate ways of accounting for the investment tax credit. These are discussed below.

Flow-through

The flow-through method is shown as *e1* in Exhibit 14-8. The tax-related journal entries would be:

```
d.  Income tax expense  . . . . . . . . . . . . . . . .   20,000
         Income tax payable . . . . . . . . . . . . . .           20,000
e1. Income tax payable  . . . . . . . . . . . . . . . .   15,000
         Income tax expense  . . . . . . . . . . . . .            15,000
```

The proponents of the flow-through method claim that the entire amount of the tax credit is a selective reduction of income tax expense in the year in which taxes otherwise payable are reduced by the credit. It is not a determinant of cost of acquisition or use of the related assets. The majority of companies use this method. Entry *e1* reduces the $20,000 income tax expense and income tax payable shown in entry *d* by $15,000, making the actual expense and payable only $5,000.

Deferral

The deferral method is shown as *e2* in Exhibit 14-8. The tax-related journal-entries would be:

```
d.  Income tax expense  . . . . . . . . . . . . . . . .   20,000
         Income tax payable . . . . . . . . . . . . . .           20,000
e2. Income tax payable  . . . . . . . . . . . . . . . .   15,000
         Deferred ITC liability . . . . . . . . . . . .           15,000
```

Supporters of the deferral method are particularly critical of the idea that the amount spent for depreciable assets in a given year can directly affect net income; within constraints, the more the company *buys*, the more it earns. Such an implication conflicts with the generally accepted concept that net income is earned only by *using* assets to produce revenue from customers. The deferral method prevents current net income from being so significantly affected by unrelated management actions in buying depreciable assets.

Suppose 19X2 pretax income was again $50,000. However, no additional equipment is acquired. The journal entries for the deferral method would be:

```
d.  Income tax expense  . . . . . . . . . . . . . . . .   20,000
         Income tax payable . . . . . . . . . . . . . .           20,000
    To recognize income tax owed to
    government.
e2. Deferred ITC liability  . . . . . . . . . . . . . . .    3,000
         Income tax expense  . . . . . . . . . . . . .             3,000
    Amortization for 19X2 of ITC liability;
    $15,000 ÷ 5 years.
```

The amortization of the deferral spreads the $15,000 tax credit over the five years of useful life of the related equipment, 19X2 through 19X6. (Remember that the equipment was acquired at the *end* of 19X1.) The effect will be to reduce income tax expense (by crediting the Income Tax Expense account) and hence increase reported net income by $3,000 for each of five years. Note that flow-through companies report considerably higher net income than deferral companies in the year a tax credit is granted. In contrast, deferral companies report slightly higher net income each year of the deferral period. Exhibit 14-9 summarizes flow-through and deferral methods for the five-year life of the equipment, assuming pretax income is $50,000 each year.

The advocates of deferral maintain that the amount of the tax credit is associated primarily with the use of the property qualifying for the credit. Deferral of the credit and its subsequent amortization associates the credit with the useful life of the related property. This matching is consistent with the objectives of income measurement on the accrual basis because it spreads a purchase discount over the useful life of the asset purchased.

Exhibit 14-9	**19X1**	**19X2**	**19X3**	**19X4**	**19X5**	**19X6**
Investment Tax Credit—Flow-through and Deferral (in thousands of dollars)						
ON STATEMENT TO TAX AUTHORITIES:						
Taxable income	$50	$50	$50	$50	$50	$50
Income taxes @ 40%	20	20	20	20	20	20
Deduct: Tax credit	15					
Income tax paid (or payable)	$ 5	$20	$20	$20	$20	$20
ON STATEMENT TO SHAREHOLDERS:						
Flow-through method:						
Pretax income	$50	$50	$50	$50	$50	$50
Deduct: Income tax expense	5	20	20	20	20	20
Net income	$45	$30	$30	$30	$30	$30
Deferral method:						
Pretax income	$50	$50	$50	$50	$50	$50
Deduct: Income tax expense	20	17	17	17	17	17
Net income	$30	$33	$33	$33	$33	$33

Accounting Vocabulary

deferred tax liability, *p. 641*

deferral method, *p. 658*

flow-through, *p. 653*

interperiod tax allocation, *p. 647*

Modified Accelerated Cost Recovery System (MACRS), *p. 642*

municipal bond interest, *p. 637*

net operating loss (NOL), *p. 654*

permanent differences, *p. 637*

tax allocation, *p. 647*

tax credits, *p. 653*

tax deduction, *p. 636*

tax deferral, *p. 647*

temporary difference, *p. 639*

timing difference, *p. 639*

Assignment Material

Questions

14-1. "Taxes are a fact of life, and they have little effect on business decisions." Do you agree? Explain.

14-2. Why would the government pass a tax depreciation rule (MACRS) that provided depreciation deductions more rapidly than the straight-line method when this rule reduces the tax the government collects in the short run?

14-3. If the federal corporate tax rate is 35%, why are the illustrations in this book constructed at 40%?

14-4. Give two examples of permanent differences.

14-5. "Permanent differences are differences that persist beyond five years." Do you agree? Explain.

14-6. Give an example of a temporary difference where revenues are included in taxable income later than they are included in pretax income for stockholder reporting.

14-7. Give an example of a temporary difference where expenses are deducted from taxable income later than they are deducted for financial reporting purposes.

14-8. Give an example of a temporary difference where revenues are included in income tax for tax purposes earlier than they are for stockholder reporting purposes.

14-9. "A five-year MACRS asset provides depreciation deductions over six years." Explain.

14-10. "MACRS results in an acceleration of income tax disbursements." Do you agree? Explain.

14-11. "Tax laws allow more depreciation than is allowed for reporting to shareholders." Do you agree? Explain.

14-12. Why do deferred federal income taxes arise?

14-13. In brief, why did the Financial Accounting Standards Board favor deferral of income taxes?

14-14. An employee of a company used the phone extensively for personal phone calls but excused his behavior by thinking, "It doesn't cost the company anything because it is tax deductible." Comment.

14-15. Some people claim that deferred taxes are not a liability because in a growing company they will never be paid. Explain.

14-16. Why might some countries not have deferred tax accounting for financial reporting?

14-17. Congress considered enacting an investment tax credit to encourage economic growth during the recession period in 1991-92. Why would an investment tax credit have this effect?

14-18. In the United Kingdom, companies used to be able to write off goodwill directly against retained earnings when another company was acquired. If goodwill was never deductible for tax purposes, would goodwill be a temporary difference, a permanent difference, or neither in the United Kingdom under the old rules? Explain.

14-19. Are warranty expenses an example of temporary or permanent differences? Explain.

14-20. Suppose a company's income tax rate is 40%. The company has a $100,000 expenditure that can either be a deductible item or the company can receive a 25% tax credit. Which does the company prefer? Why?

14-21. "Tax credits are deductible as expenses for income tax purposes." Do you agree? Explain.

14-22. "Tax credits are better than deductible items because they directly reduce taxes." Critically discuss this statement.

14-23. "Operating losses are beneficial." Explain.

14-24. What are the two most widely used methods of accounting for the investment tax credit?

14-25. Which of the two methods of accounting for the investment tax credit will benefit reported current income the most?

14-26. Companies that use deferral of tax credits rather than flow-through show lower retained income. Why?

Exercises

14-27 MACRS Recovery Periods

Consider the following business assets: (1) heavy-duty truck, (2) underground power transmission lines, (3) commercial building, and (4) electron microscope used in industrial research. What is the recovery period for each of these assets under the prescribed MACRS method?

14-28 MACRS Depreciation

In 1996, the Castillo Manufacturing Company acquired the following assets and immediately placed them into service:

1. Equipment with a seven-year MACRS life, a useful life of seventeen years, and a cost of $30 million.
2. A desktop computer that cost $8,000.
3. An office desk that cost $2,000 but was sold sixteen months later.

Required Compute the depreciation for tax purposes, under the prescribed MACRS method, in 1996 and 1997. Assume that all assets were acquired on March 1, 1996.

14-29 Difference in Depreciation for Tax and Shareholder Reporting

International Paper Company is the world's largest producer of papers for food packaging and magazine printing. The company's 1994 depreciation on reports to shareholders was $885 million. A footnote stated that the use of MACRS depreciation for federal tax purposes and straight-line depreciation for shareholder reporting resulted in a decrease of $10 million in the deferred tax liability in 1994. The federal income tax rate was 35% and was expected to remain 35%. The income statement reported (in millions):

Earnings before income taxes	$664
Provision for income taxes	232
Net earnings	$432

Required
1. Compute the amount of depreciation reported on International Paper's tax return prepared for the Internal Revenue Service.
2. Collectively, all differences between shareholder and tax reporting caused a $42 million increase in the Deferred Tax Liability account. Prepare International Paper's summary journal entry to recognize income tax expense in 1994.
3. Explain why the increase in deferred taxes might be only $42 million when depreciation alone produced a $10 million decrease.

14-30 Incomplete Information

Consider the following facts about the Working Backwards Company in 19X0. The company had financial statement pretax income of $120,000 and was subject to tax at 40%. Income tax expense was $42,000, while the payable to the government for the year was only $18,000. The company had both permanent and timing differences during the year. Calculate the amount for each of these differences, and indicate whether each had the effect of increasing or decreasing taxable income relative to pretax financial statement income.

14-31 Incomplete Information

The Deductive Company had financial statement pretax income of $300,000 and was subject to a 40% tax rate. The journal entry for 19X0 to record income tax expense was:

Income tax expense	140,000	
Tax payable		100,000
Deferred taxes		40,000

Required Calculate both the permanent and timing differences.

14-32 Reconstruct Income Tax Transactions

Lincoln Logs, Ltd., sells easily assembled log home packages. Annual sales are slightly over $8 million. Its fiscal 1995 income statement included a provision for income taxes of $1,700. In the 1991 fiscal year, sales were $12 million and the tax provision was $117,000. Footnotes disclosed the following:

A summary of components of income taxes for the years ended January 31, 1991 and 1995 is as follows:

	1995	1991
Current expense:		
Federal	$ —	$ 91,700
State	1,700	4,000
	1,700	95,700
Deferred	—	21,300
	$1,700	$117,000

The Lincoln Logs 1991 balance sheet included:

	January 31	
	1991	1990
Long-term liabilities:		
Deferred tax liability	$49,800	$28,500

Required

1. Prepare summary journal entries for income tax expense for 1991.
2. Present possible reasons for the increase in the 1991 Deferred Tax Liability account.
3. Speculate on the absence of current and deferred federal amounts in 1995.

14-33 Tax versus Shareholder Reporting of Depreciation

On January 2, 19X1, a wholesale company bought several forklifts for use in its warehouse. The total amount paid was $80,000. The forklifts have an eight-year useful life with a zero residual value. The forklifts qualify as five-year assets for MACRS purposes. The company uses straight-line depreciation for shareholder reporting and has a combined federal and state income tax rate of 40%.

Required

For years 19X1 through 19X8, compute (1) depreciation for shareholder reporting, (2) depreciation for tax purposes, and (3) the deferred tax liability at the end of each year.

14-34 Deferred Tax Asset

Matlock Toy Company introduced an electronic car in the middle of 19X0. Sales were $110,000 in 19X0, and the car was discontinued after the Christmas season. There were no sales in 19X1. The cars were sold with a one-year warranty, and Matlock estimated that warranty expenses would be $8,000. All warranty claims were made in 19X1, and they totaled exactly $8,000. Assume that both 19X0 and 19X1 pretax income before deducting warranty expenses was $100,000 for both tax and shareholder reporting, and the combined state and federal income tax rate is 40%.

Required

1. Prepare journal entries for shareholder reporting to recognize both the warranty expense and income tax expense for 19X0.
2. Prepare journal entries relating to warranties and income tax expense for 19X1.

14-35 Tax Credits

The following cases are independent of each other.

Required

1. Felix Company has sales of $900,000, tax-deductible expenses of $790,000, and an income tax rate of 40%. The company is also entitled to a tax credit of $9,000. Compute the company's taxable income and income tax to be paid.
2. Niles Company receives a tax credit for hiring handicapped workers. The credit is equal to 20% of the wage paid to the qualifying workers. In addition, the wages are deductible when computing taxable income. In 19X0, wages paid to qualifying handicapped workers were $150,000. Total tax-deductible expenses, including the $150,000 of wages,

were $870,000. Sales revenues in 19X0 were $1.2 million. The income tax rate is 40%. Compute Niles Company's taxable income and the income tax to be paid for 19X0.

14-36 Research Tax Credit

An income tax credit is allowed for a company's research expenditures that exceed a base amount. The base amount is generally the average research expenditures for the past three years. Suppose the current rate for the credit is 25% of expenditures exceeding the base amount, and the income tax rate is 40% on taxable income of $100,000.

The Kwon Company incurred research expenses of $42,000 in 19X0, and research expenses for each of the past three years was $24,000. Assume that all expenses were paid in cash. The research tax credit was Kwon's only tax credit in 19X0.

Required
1. How much benefit did the Kwon Company receive from the 19X0 tax credit?
2. Suppose annual research expenses continue at $42,000 for 19X1, 19X2, and 19X3. Compute the research tax credit for each of the three years.

14-37 Net Operating Losses

Bagley Company's tax deductions exceeded its taxable revenues by $450,000 in 19X5. Taxes paid each of the last five years were:

19X0	$40,000
19X1	10,000
19X2	20,000
19X3	50,000
19X4	10,000

The income tax rate is 40%.

Required
1. Prepare the journal entry for 19X5 income taxes.
2. Prepare the bottom part of Bagley's 19X5 income statement, beginning with "Pretax loss... $(450,000)."

14-38 Net Income, Flow-through, and Deferral of ITC

Study Appendix 14. Suppose Congress reenacted the investment tax credit, allowing a credit equal to 5% of the cost of certain machinery. Lutz Manufacturing bought an assembly robot for $450,000 on the first day of 19X1. Assume that both tax and shareholder reporting use straight-line depreciation over ten years. Income before depreciation on the new robot and before taxes was $140,000. The tax rate is 40%. Assume that the new robot qualifies for the investment tax credit.

Required
1. Compute the taxes paid (or payable) to the government for 19X1.
2. Compute 19X1 net income reported to shareholders if the flow-through method is used for the investment tax credit.
3. Compute 19X1 net income reported to shareholders if the deferral method is used for the investment tax credit.

Problems

14-39 Fundamentals of Income Tax Allocation

Suppose the railroad division of Union Pacific Corporation purchases a group of highly specialized freight cars for $50 million. The cars have a ten-year life and no residual value. The company uses MACRS depreciation for tax purposes and straight-line depreciation for financial reporting purposes. The freight cars are seven-year MACRS property.

The income of this division before depreciation and taxes is $12 million each year. The applicable income tax rate is 30%.

Required

Show all amounts in thousands of dollars.

1. For the ten years, tabulate the details of how these facts would influence the Union Pacific reporting for tax purposes and for reporting to stockholders. *Hint*: See Exhibit 14-4 (p. 646).
2. How will the Deferred Tax Liability account be affected if capital expenditures are the same each year? If they grow each year?

14-40 MACRS and Deferred Taxes

Emery Air Freight Corporation provides overnight delivery of packages throughout the United States. The company acquired new equipment to expand its "Dayton Superhub" as part of its goal to reach $1 billion of sales. Suppose the equipment was acquired for $10 million cash and installed on January 2, 1995. For shareholder reporting purposes, the equipment's useful life is ten years. There is zero expected residual value. However, for income tax purposes, assume that MACRS prescribed a five-year recovery period.

Required

Show all dollar amounts in millions.

1. For simplicity, assume that this equipment is the only fixed asset subject to depreciation. Prepare a tabulation (similar to Exhibit 14-4, page 648) summarizing reporting to the Internal Revenue Service for the first six years. Assume that income before depreciation is $20 million each year and that the combined state and federal income tax rate is 40%.
2. Prepare a similar table summarizing reporting to shareholders. However, prepare a table for seven years. In the final column, show the balance sheet account Deferred Tax Liability at the end of each year. Assume straight-line depreciation.
3. Prepare the journal entry for Years 1 and 7 for income tax expense.

14-41 Deferred Income Taxes

(Alternates are 14-44 and 14-46.) Ruiz Company began business on January 1, 19X7, with initial paid-in capital of $60 million cash. On January 2, 19X7, the company purchases an asset for $30 million cash with an estimated useful life of five years and an estimated scrap value of zero. MACRS depreciation is used for tax purposes. The asset has a MACRS recovery period of three years. However, *the straight-line method is used for shareholder reporting purposes*. Prospective annual income before depreciation and income taxes is $14.9 million. The income tax rate is 40%. Assume that all taxes are paid early in the next year after the income is earned.

Required

1. Prepare an analysis of transactions for external reporting, using the balance sheet format. Show the effects of (a) formation, (b) acquisition, (c) income before depreciation and taxes, and (d) straight-line depreciation. Show the effects of (e1) no deferral and (e2) deferral of income taxes for 19X7.
2. Prepare a three-column comparison of reporting of income for 19X7 (a) to income tax authorities, (b) to shareholders if no deferral is used (i.e., tax expense based on tax return), and (c) to shareholders if deferral is used.

14-42 Tabulation of Effects of Deferral

(Alternates are 14-45 and 14-47.) Refer to the data in the preceding problem. Prepare a five-year schedule like Exhibit 14-4 (p. 648) for each of the three reporting methods of the problem requirement 2. Show all amounts in millions of dollars.

14-43 Growth of Deferred Taxes

The facts are the same as in Problem 14-41. However, $30 million is spent *each year* for additional assets, and income increases $14.9 million each year until leveling off in Year 6. The $30 million spent in Year 6 represents a replacement of the asset originally acquired in Year 1.

Required

Prepare two tabulations in millions of dollars. The first tabulation should display the effects of reporting for income tax purposes, assuming MACRS depreciation, including pretax income, income tax paid, and net income. The second tabulation should display the effects of reporting to stockholders, assuming straight-line depreciation and deferred income taxes. The second tabulation should include columns for pretax income, tax paid, tax deferred, total tax expense, net income, and the ending balance sheet effect on the Deferred Tax Liability.

14-44 Deferred Income Taxes
(Alternates are 14-41 and 14-46.) Monsanto Company produces chemicals and pharmaceuticals. The company's capital expenditures exceed $700 million annually. Suppose that on January 4, 1993, Monsanto purchased some special tools for the production of plastics. The acquisition cost was $30 million. The equipment's expected useful life is five years; expected residual value is zero. The MACRS class is three-year.

Assume that the combined state and federal income tax rate is 40%. No income tax payments will be due before early 1994. Assume that in 1993 Monsanto had pretax income of $700 million before considering depreciation related to this acquisition. For simplicity, assume also that this $700 million was the same for reporting to income tax authorities and to stockholders.

Regarding the $30 million acquisition, Monsanto uses straight-line depreciation for reporting to stockholders. However, the company uses the prescribed MACRS schedule for income tax purposes.

Required

1. Fill in the blanks in millions (based solely on the given data):

	1993 Reporting	
	To Income Tax Authorities	To Stockholders
Pretax income as given	$700	$700
Depreciation:		
MACRS (3-year recovery basis)	?	?
Straight-line (5-year useful life)	?	?
Pretax income	?	?
Income tax expense:		
To be paid in early 1994	?	?
Deferred	?	?
Total income tax expense	?	?
Net income	$?	$?

2. Prepare the summary journal entry, December 31, 1993, for Monsanto's 1993 income taxes.

14-45 Long-run Effects of Deferral
(Alternates are 14-42 and 14-47.)

1. Refer to the data in the preceding problem. Prepare a five-year schedule like Exhibit 14-4 (p. 648) for the two reporting methods of requirement 1. For each year, assume that income before the depreciation in question is $700 million and the income tax rate is 40%. Show all amounts in millions of dollars.
2. Prepare the journal entry for income tax expense for Year 5.

14-46 Deferred Income Taxes

(Alternates are 14-41 and 14-44.) Suppose that on January 5, 1993, USAir purchased some DC-10 aircraft for $400 million. The aircraft's expected useful life is ten years; expected residual value, zero.

Assume that the income tax rate is 40%. No income tax payments will be due before early 1994. Assume that in 1993 USAir had pretax income of $260 million before considering depreciation related to this acquisition. For simplicity, assume also that this $260 million was the same for reporting to income tax authorities and to stockholders.

Regarding the $400 million acquisition, USAir uses straight-line depreciation for reporting to stockholders. However, USAir uses the prescribed MACRS schedule for income tax purposes. Aircraft have a five-year recovery period.

Required

1. Fill in the blanks in millions (based solely on the given data):

	1993 Reporting	
	To Income Tax Authorities	To Stockholders
Pretax income as given	$260	$260
Depreciation:		
MACRS (5-year recovery basis)	?	?
Straight-line (10-year useful life)	?	?
Pretax income	?	?
Income tax expense:		
To be paid in early 1994	?	?
Deferred	?	?
Total income tax expense	?	?
Net income	$?	$?

2. Prepare the summary journal entry, December 31, 1993, for USAir's 1993 income taxes.

14-47 Long-run Effects of Deferral

(Alternates are 14-42 and 14-45.)

1. Refer to the data in the preceding problem. Prepare a seven-year schedule like Exhibit 14-4 (p. 648) for the two reporting methods in requirement 1. For each year, assume that the income before the depreciation in question is $260 million and the income tax rate is 40%. Show all amounts in millions of dollars. Do not continue the schedule beyond the seventh year; instead explain how the final three years would appear in a ten-year schedule.

2. Prepare the journal entry for income tax expense for Year 7.

14-48 Timing Differences

Effective January 1, 1992, Chrysler adopted SFAS No. 109, "Accounting for Income Taxes," which resulted in a favorable cumulative effect of the change in accounting principle of $218 million, or $0.74 per common share.

Earnings before income taxes and the cumulative effect of changes in accounting principles were attributable to the following sources:

In millions of dollars	1994	1993	1992
United States	$5,239	$3,191	$618
Foreign	591	647	316
Total	$5,830	$3,838	$934

The provision for income taxes on earnings before income taxes and the cumulative effect of changes in accounting principles included the following:

In millions of dollars	1994	1993	1992
Currently payable:			
United States	$ 876	$ 523	$ 66
Foreign	60	69	123
State and local	116	28	11
	$1,052	$ 620	$200
Deferred:			
United States	$ 820	$ 528	$220
Foreign	73	131	(27)
State and local	172	144	36
	1,065	803	229
Total	$2,117	$1,423	$429

The tax-effected temporary differences and carryforwards which comprised deferred tax assets and liabilities were as follows:

In millions of dollars	DECEMBER 31, 1994		DECEMBER 31, 1993	
	Deferred Tax Assets	Deferred Tax Liabilities	Deferred Tax Assets	Deferred Tax Liabilities
Nonpension postretirement benefits	$2,960	$ —	$2,783	$ —
Pensions	11	1,726	3	488
Accrued expenses	2,471	—	2,415	—
Lease transactions	—	1,713	—	1,673
Depreciation	—	1,678	—	1,665
Tax credit carryforwards	51	—	342	—
Alternative minimum tax credit carryforwards	751	—	825	—
State and local taxes	215	105	421	91
NOL carryforwards	109	—	136	—
Other	193	670	75	641
	6,761	5,892	7,000	4,558
Value allowance	(77)	—	(146)	—
Total	$6,684	$5,892	$6,854	$4,558

Required

1. Give the 1994 journal entry to record the provision for income tax expense.
2. Use the statutory federal tax rate of 35% to estimate the cumulative timing differences between depreciation taken for financial reporting and depreciation recorded for tax purposes.
3. Timing differences have arisen due to both pension and nonpension retirement benefits. In which case are expenses deducted more rapidly for tax purposes than for financial reporting purposes?

14-49 The Income Tax Footnote

Ryan's Family Steak Houses, Inc., develops, operates, and franchises family-style restaurants. The company reported total revenues of $273 million and generated net income of $24 million after recording income tax expense of $14 million. Depreciation and amortization of $10,520,000 appear in the income statement. The notes to the financial statements provided the following additional information:

Note 2. Income Taxes The components of income taxes are summarized as follows:

	1990
Current:	
Federal	$11,218,000
State	2,162,000
	13,380,000
Deferred:	
Federal	718,000
State	135,000
	853,000
Income taxes	$14,233,000

Deferred income taxes principally represent the income tax effects of the differences between depreciation and amortization methods for tax and financial reporting purposes.

Required

1. Recreate the journal entry Ryan's used to record income tax expense.
2. The federal tax rate was 34% in the year of this statement. Estimate the depreciation and amortization reported on the tax return.

14-50 The Income Tax Footnote

Norfolk Southern Corporation is a railway and motor carrier with 1994 operating revenues of approximately $4,581 million and net income of $682 million. Footnote 4 to the financial statements provided the following table:

The provision for income taxes consists of the following:

	1994	1993
	(In millions of dollars)	
Current:		
Federal	$236.0	$279.6
State	35.0	40.3
Total current	271.0	319.9
Deferred:		
Federal	95.2	78.0
State	19.0	14.9
Total deferred	114.2	92.9
Total	$ 385.2	$412.8

Other information explaining the sources of deferred income taxes indicated in 1994 that deferred tax assets included $27.8 million related to employee benefit timing differences and deferred tax liabilities included $2,679.8 million related to depreciation timing difference.

Required   1. Provide the journal entries to record income tax expense for 1994.
2. Were the employee benefit tax deductions larger or smaller than the expense recorded under GAAP?

14-51 Tax Credits and Tax-Exempt Income

International Container Systems, Inc., makes cases for the transporting of bottles and cans of various products, such as soft drinks. Recently the company's pretax income was $2,196,000. A footnote reported that normal state and federal income taxes would be 36.4% of taxable income. However, two items caused the actual rate on pretax income to differ from 36.4%: (1) tax-exempt income (possibly interest revenue from municipal bonds) totaled $25,000, and (2) the company received a research and development tax credit of $21,000.

Required   1. Compute the taxes paid or payable for the year. Round to the nearest thousand.
2. Compute the actual income tax percentage on pretax income.

14-52 Investment Credit and Deferred Taxes

Study Appendix 14. Finger Lakes Electronics had used accelerated depreciation for financial reporting and MACRS for tax purposes. It had also used the deferral method for the investment tax credit for financial reporting purposes. After enjoying steady growth in earnings for several years, the company encountered severe competition from foreign sources. This had a leveling effect on reported earnings per share.

In 19X8, the company invested over $70 million to update the equipment in one of its plants. The investment generated an investment tax credit of $3 million for 19X8. Management is seriously considering changing its method of reporting from that in requirement 2*a* to that in 2*d* below. Other data:

Useful life of the equipment, 15 years with no scrap value.

Net income before depreciation on new assets, income taxes, and investment tax credit effects, $20 million.

If the investment credit is deferred, a full year of amortization is taken in 19X8.

Depreciation on new assets for 19X8:

Straight-line	$ 4,666,667
Accelerated	8,750,000
MACRS	10,500,000

Required

Show all total amounts in thousands of dollars.
1. Compute taxable income and the total income taxes for 19X8. The tax rate is 40%.
2. Suppose Finger Lakes Electronics has a simple capital structure with 10 million common shares outstanding and no preferred shares outstanding. For financial reporting purposes, compute net income and earnings per share where
   a. The company uses accelerated depreciation and defers the investment credit.
   b. The company uses accelerated depreciation and "flows through" the investment credit.
   c. The company uses straight-line depreciation and defers the investment credit.
   d. The company uses straight-line depreciation and "flows through" the investment credit.

14-53 Amortization of Investment Tax Credit

Study Appendix 14A. On December 31, 1990, General Telephone and Electronics (GTE) had deferred investment tax credits of $631 million and retained earnings of $5,830 million. No new investment tax credits were available to GTE in 1986 or later years. GTE had net income of $1.5 billion in 1990. Assume that GTE's income after tax but before considering amortization of the investment tax credit is $1.6 billion for each of 1991, 1992, and 1993. Also assume that $100 million of deferred investment tax credits will be amortized in each of the next three years and that no dividends will be paid.

Required

1. Fill in the blanks in the following table (in millions, round to the nearest million):

	Year Ended December 31		
	1991	**1992**	**1993**
Income statement items:			
Income after tax but before amortization of ITC	$1,600	$1,600	$1,600
Amortization of ITC	?	?	?
Net income	?	?	?
Balance sheet items:			
Deferred investment tax credit	?	?	?
Retained earnings	?	?	?

2. Repeat requirement 1 except assume that GTE uses and has always used the flow-through method for the investment tax credit. (*Hint:* First compute the December 31, 1990, *retained earnings* balance *as if* GTE had been using the flow-through method.)
3. Assume that the entire $631 million of deferred investment tax credits is amortized in 1991, 1992, and 1993. Compute GTE's December 31, 1993, retained income under the conditions of requirement 1.
4. Assume that Congress does not reenact the investment tax credit. How long will GTE's financial statements be influenced by its accounting for the investment tax credit?

14-54 Tax Avoidance and Ethics

Meditron Company had pretax income in 1995 of $2,250,000. Of this income, $800,000 was from tax-free bonds. In addition, tax credits totaling $1,450,000 were obtained from increasing research activities and providing jobs to targeted groups. Therefore, Meditron paid no income taxes.

A local civic activist group received a copy of Meditron's tax statement from an anonymous source. The leader of the group called the local newspaper, and the headline the next day read, "Local Company Makes Millions, Pays No Taxes." The article went on to say how the shareholders of Meditron were making an excellent return on their investment at the expense of the taxpayers.

Required

1. Comment on the ethical issues involved in minimizing taxes. Did Meditron violate any ethical standards? Explain.

14-55 Wal-Mart Annual Report

Refer to the financial statements and footnotes for Wal-Mart contained in Appendix A. Use the information to respond to the following questions.

Required

1. Prepare a summary journal entry to recognize income tax expense in 1995.
2. Prepare summary journal entries to record cash disbursements for income taxes in 1995. (*Hint*: Use the change in the balance sheet accrual for the short-term liability to help you calculate the cash payment.)
3. Identify the main sources of timing differences between financial reporting to shareholders and tax reporting for Wal-Mart in 1995. Are the directional effects what you would expect for a rapidly growing retailer?

14-56 Compact D from Disclosure

Use the Compact D software to complete the following task. Identify one company in each of two industries and consult the notes to their financial statements.

Required

1. Prepare summary journal entries to recognize income tax expense for each company.
2. Identify the main sources of timing differences for each company. Compare and contrast the dominant sources in the two industries.
3. Calculate the provision for income taxes (income tax expense) as a percentage of earnings before taxes. Compare this percentage across the two industries. How does the percentage differ from the 40% we have typically used as an approximation? Explain whatever you can about the source(s) of the differences.

15 Analysis of Financial Statements

Learning Objectives

After studying this chapter, you should be able to

1 Describe many sources of financial and operating information about company performance.

2 Explain the different objectives of debt and equity investors in analyzing information.

3 Describe trend analysis and approaches to analyzing the components of a business.

4 Review the basic financial ratios.

5 Explain the relationship between ROA and ROE in evaluating corporate performance.

6 Calculate EPS when preferred stock exists, shares outstanding change during the year, and dilution is a possibility.

7 Characterize special items, extraordinary items, and discontinued operations.

8 Explain the importance of efficient markets to accounting disclosures.

9 Explain some effects on financial statements from translating foreign currencies.

financial statement analysis Using financial statements to assess a company's performance.

This chapter focuses on **financial statement analysis,** which means using financial statement data to assess a company's performance. Sources of information about companies, the objectives of financial statement analysis, and methods for evaluating financial statements are covered. The majority of the chapter deals with ratios and how to understand the financial statements as prepared under GAAP. A few additional steps in producing the financial statements are presented, including calculating earnings per share and preparing segmental disclosures of the parts of the business.

Disclosure practices in the United States have evolved with the specific purpose of providing information to investors, creditors, managers, suppliers, customers—anyone who wants to know about a company's financial position or prospects. The preceding chapters concentrated on how information is collected, aggregated, and disclosed. We have frequently provided examples of ratios and other tools of analysis and have demonstrated how the information might aid in making decisions. In this chapter we integrate prior material and discuss additional tools for analyzing and evaluating the company's financial position.

Internationally, financial statement analysis is significantly complicated by a variety of factors. Throughout the text we have considered differences in accounting methods used. In addition we should stress the obvious but easily forgotten differences in the language of reporting and the currency of measurement. For example, most U.S. analysts cannot read financial statements in Japanese and do not readily "have a feel for" the value of yen versus dollars. Last, but not least, is the fact that different structures for security markets, different tax laws, and different preferences among citizens of different countries all affect the relative value of financial assets.

■ SOURCES OF INFORMATION ABOUT COMPANIES

Objective 1

Describe many sources of financial and operating information about company performance.

Financial statement analysis focuses on techniques used by analysts external to the organization being analyzed, although managers use many of the same methods. These analysts rely on publicly available information.

Publicly available information refers primarily to published information and analysis that is broadly available to analysts and investors. Companies provide periodic press releases, which provide the financial community with news about company developments, including the following:

1. Changes in personnel.
2. Changes in dividends.
3. Issuance or retirement of debt.
4. Acquisition or sale of assets or business units.
5. New products.
6. New orders.
7. Changes in production plans.
8. Financial results.

Members of the financial press decide which information in press releases will be interesting and important. When a small company announces that thirty people will be laid off, the *Wall Street Journal* may ignore the event, while it will be front page news in the company's home town where many citizens are affected. Similarly, in certain regions, an industry focus determines what news is carried. The *Tulsa World* is a newspaper in Oklahoma that publishes significant details about oil exploration and production; for example, oil rigs in use, newly discovered oil or gas deposits, and changes in management of petroleum companies. The *Washington Post* in Washington, D.C., would not cover these issues but does provide up-to-date news on some thirty prominent firms that have a substantial employment or sales base in the nation's capital. The national business daily, the *Wall Street Journal*, does not publish as much detail in these specific areas as either the *Tulsa World* or the *Washington Post*.

A major source of information about an individual firm is the company's annual report. In addition to the financial statements (income statement, balance sheet, statement of cash flows, and statement of stockholders' equity), annual reports usually contain:

1. Footnotes to the financial statements.
2. A summary of the accounting principles used.
3. Management's discussion and analysis of the financial results.
4. The auditor's report.
5. Comparative financial data for a series of years.
6. Narrative information about the company.

To be useful, the financial statements and their accompanying footnotes and other disclosures must provide all significant or *material* information. Although analysts can learn much from the various parts of an annual report, we will focus most of our attention on the financial statements themselves.

Companies also prepare reports for the Securities and Exchange Commission (SEC). Form 10-K presents financial statement data in a standard format and is generally more comprehensive than the financial statements published in annual reports. Form 10-Q includes quarterly financial statements, so it provides more timely information than the annual reports, although the reports are less complete. Other SEC reports are required for certain specified events and for issuance of common shares or debt.

Both annual reports and SEC reports are issued well after the events being reported have occurred. More timely information is often available from company press releases and articles in the business press. The *Wall Street Journal*, *Business Week, Forbes, Fortune,* and *Barron's* are among the more popular publications. Services such as *Value Line*, Moody's Investors Services, and Standard and Poor's Industrial Surveys also provide useful information. In addition, stockbrokers prepare company analyses for their clients, and private investment services and newsletters supply information to their subscribers.

Heavy financial commitments, whether by investors purchasing many shares of the common stock of a company or by banks making large loans to a new customer, are preceded by thorough investigations. These investigations use information from many sources. When the amounts being invested are significant, investors and creditors often ask for a set of projected financial statements. Such a **pro forma statement** is a carefully formulated expression of predicted results. Major creditors expect the projections to include a schedule of the amounts and timings of cash repayments.

pro forma statement
A carefully formulated expression of predicted results.

Most investors and creditors are not able to request specific information from companies. For example, the typical trade creditor cannot afford the time or resources for an exhaustive investigation of every customer. Instead, such creditors rely on published information and reports from credit agencies such as Dun & Bradstreet.

Because of the wide range of information available, this chapter on financial statement analysis covers only the most common methods used by financial analysts. Nevertheless, the techniques presented in this chapter constitute an important step in gaining a thorough understanding of a company's position and prospects.

■ OBJECTIVES OF FINANCIAL STATEMENT ANALYSIS

Objective 2

Explain the different objectives of debt and equity investors in analyzing information.

Investors purchase capital stock expecting to receive dividends and an increase in the value of the stock. Creditors make loans with the expectation of receiving interest and eventual repayment. However, both investors and creditors bear the risk that they will not receive their expected returns. They use financial statement analysis to (1) predict the amount of expected returns and (2) assess the risks associated with those returns.

Because creditors generally have specific fixed amounts to be received and have the first claim on assets, they are most concerned with assessing short-term liquidity and long-term solvency. **Short-term liquidity** is an organization's ability to meet current payments as they become due. **Long-term solvency** is the ability to generate enough cash to repay long-term debts as they mature.

In contrast, equity investors are more concerned with profitability, dividends, and future security prices. Why? Because dividend payments depend on profitable operations, and stock price appreciation depends on the market's assessment of the company's prospects. However, creditors also assess profitability. Why? Because profitable operations are the prime source of cash to repay loans.

How can financial statement analysis help creditors and investors? After all, financial statements report on past results and current position, but creditors and investors want to predict future returns and their risks. Financial statement analysis is useful because past performance is often a good indicator of future performance, and current position is the base on which future performance must be built. For example, trends in past sales, operating expenses, and net income may continue. Furthermore, evaluation of management's past performance gives clues to its ability to generate future returns. Finally, the assets a company owns, the liabilities it must pay, its levels of receivables and inventories, its cash balance, and other indicators of current position all provide clues to its future prospects.

short-term liquidity
An organization's ability to meet current payments as they become due.

long-term solvency
An organization's ability to generate enough cash to repay long-term debts as they mature.

■ EVALUATING TRENDS AND COMPONENTS OF THE BUSINESS

Objective 3

Describe trend analysis and approaches to analyzing the components of a business.

This section discusses methods used to analyze financial statement data. These methods focus on trend analysis and assessing the components of the business. Trend analysis examines changes over time. Component analysis can mean several things. One application concentrates on the components of the financial statements themselves, the relative size of current assets, the level of investment in fixed assets, the gross margin percentage, and so on. At another level, component analysis means sorting out the parts of the company's business. The company can be separated into different business units or kinds of businesses, different geographic areas of production or marketing, or different customer groups such as private versus government.

Trend Analysis

Financial statements contain both the current year's and the previous year's amounts. In addition, annual reports must include the amounts of key financial items for at least the last five years. Many companies include ten years of data. Using these data, financial analysts can examine in detail the changes in the past year and can examine longer-term trends in several important items.

Consider the balance sheets and income statements of Oxley Company in Exhibits 15-1 and 15-2. The amounts are identical to the financial statements introduced in Chapter 5 in the Oxley Company illustration. (Recall that Oxley is a retailer of lawn and garden products.) However, two columns have been added to aid the comparison of 19X2 results with those of 19X1. The first new column shows the amount of the change in each item from 19X1 to 19X2. The second shows the percentage change, computed as follows:

$$\text{Percentage change 19X1 to 19X2} = \frac{\text{Amount of change}}{\text{19X1 amount}} \times 100$$

The percentage change shows the percentage by which the current-year amount exceeds or falls short of the base-year amount, 19X1 in this case. For example, Oxley's accounts receivables increased from $70,000 at the end of 19X1 to $95,000 at the end of 19X2, an increase of 35.7%:

$$\text{Percentage change} = \frac{\$95,000 - \$70,000}{\$70,000} \times 100 = 35.7\%$$

Exhibit 15-1	Oxley Company	Statement of Income (in thousands except earnings per share)		

	For the Year Ended December 31, 19X2	For the Year Ended December 31, 19X1	Increase (Decrease) Amount	Percentage
Sales	$999	$800	$199	24.9%
Cost of goods sold	399	336	63	18.8
Gross profit (or gross margin)	$ 600	$ 464	$136	29.3
Operating expenses:				
Wages	$214	$150	$ 64	42.7
Rent	120	120	0	0.0
Miscellaneous	100	50	50	100.0
Depreciation	40	40	0	0.0
Total operating expenses	$474	$ 360	$ 114	31.7
Operating income (or operating profit)	$126	$104	$ 22	21.2
Other revenue and expense:				
Interest revenue	36	36	0	0.0
Deduct: Interest expense	(12)	(12)	0	0.0
Income before income taxes	$150	$128	$ 22	17.2
Income tax expense	60	48	12	25.0
Net income	$ 90	$ 80	$ 10	12.5
Earnings per common share*	$ .45	$ .40	$ .05	12.5%

* Dividends per share, $.40 and $.20, respectively. For publicly held companies, there is a requirement to show earnings per share on the face of the income statement, but it is not necessary to show dividends per share. Calculation of earnings per share: $90,000 ÷ 200,000 = $.45, and $80,000 ÷ 200,000 = $.40.

(Place a clip on this page for easy reference.)

Exhibit 15-2   Oxley Company   Balance Sheet (in thousands)

	December 31		Increase (Decrease)	
	19X2	**19X1**	**Amount**	**Percentage**
ASSETS				
Current assets:				
Cash	$150	$ 57	$ 93	163.2%
Accounts receivable	95	70	25	35.7
Accrued interest receivable	15	15	0	0.0
Inventory of merchandise	20	60	(40)	(66.7)
Prepaid rent	10	—	10	*
Total current assets	$290	$202	$ 88	43.6
Long-term assets:				
Long-term note receivable	288	288	0	0.0
Equipment, less accumulated depreciation				
of $120 and $80	80	120	(40)	(33.3)
Total assets	$658	$610	$ 48	7.9%
LIABILITIES AND STOCKHOLDERS' EQUITY				
Current liabilities:				
Accounts payable	$ 90	$ 65	$ 25	38.5%
Accrued wages payable	24	10	14	140.0
Accrued income taxes payable	16	12	4	33.3
Accrued interest payable	9	9	0	0.0
Unearned sales revenue	—	5	(5)	(100.0)
Note payable—current portion	80	—	80	*
Total current liabilities	$219	$101	$118	116.8
Long-term note payable	40	120	(80)	(66.7)
Total liabilities	$259	$221	$ 38	17.2
Stockholders' equity:				
Paid-in capital[†]	$102	$102	$ 0	0.0
Retained income	297	287	10	3.5
Total stockholders' equity	$399	$389	$ 10	2.6
Total liabilities and stockholders' equity	$658	$610	$ 48	7.9%

* When the base-year amount is zero, no percentage change can be computed.
† Details are often shown in a supplementary statement or in footnotes. In this case, there are 200,000 common shares outstanding, $.25 par per share, or 200,000 × $.25 = $50,000. Additional paid-in capital is $52,000.

Notice that each percentage change is independent of the others. Unlike the amounts of change, the percentage changes cannot be added or subtracted to obtain subtotals.

Changes must be interpreted carefully. Both the amount and the percentage changes should be examined. For example, the amount of the sales increase, $199,000, seems much larger than the increase in operating income, $22,000. But the base for sales is much larger, so the percentage increase is only slightly larger, 24.9% to 21.2%. Examination of percentage changes alone can also be misleading. For instance, the 140% increase in accrued wages payable seems to dominate the percentage increases. But the increase is only $14,000, a relatively small amount in the overall picture.

What would an analyst conclude from Oxley Company's changes from 19X1 to 19X2? Consider Exhibit 15-1, the income statement. The sales increase, 24.9%, is larger than the increase in cost of goods sold, 18.8%, causing a 29.3% increase in gross profit. That is the good news. The bad news is that operating expenses increased by 31.7%. This would be of special concern because huge increases in only two items, wages and miscellaneous expenses, caused the entire increase. In addition, income tax expense increased by a larger percentage than pretax income (25.0% to 17.2%), meaning that the effective tax rate must have increased. In total, the nearly 25% increase in sales led to only a 12.5% increase in net income.

Changes in dollar amount and percentage terms are used to identify patterns. This procedure focuses the analysts' attention and encourges questions that probe for underlying causes. Examination of the balance sheet changes in Exhibit 15-2 might lead the analysts to question why the composition of the assets changed so considerably, with current assets increasing by 43.6% while equipment decreased by 33.3%. Within the current assets, cash and accounts receivable had substantial increases, and inventories plummeted. Total liabilities increased by 17.2%, but most significant is the 116.8% increase in current liabilities and 66.7% decrease in long-term liabilities. This change is attributable primarily to $80,000 of the note payable becoming due within the next year, thereby qualifying as a current liability.

The large percentage fluctuations can now be understood. Cash is being accumulated to pay an imminent debt obligation and the equipment is depreciating quickly. A plan for replacement of the equipment should be considered.

Financial analysts often examine changes over a series of years, not just the current year's changes. Exhibit 15-3 shows a five-year summary of key items for Oxley Company. Percentage changes could be computed for each year, using the earlier year as the base year. For example, percentage changes in sales are:

$$19X2$$
$$\left(\frac{\$999 - \$800}{\$800}\right) \times 100 = 24.9\%$$

$$19X1$$
$$\left(\frac{\$800 - \$765}{\$765}\right) \times 100 = 4.6\%$$

$$19X0$$
$$\left(\frac{\$765 - \$790}{\$790}\right) \times 100 = (3.2\%)$$

$$19Y9$$
$$\left(\frac{\$790 - \$694}{\$694}\right) \times 100 = 13.8\%$$

Sales growth rates are highly variable. In this business, weather might be one factor. Rates of new home construction might also play a role. Awareness of this variability may aid the analyst in determining the core economic factors that drive the business. We might learn that Oxley's sales decline in 19X0 was associated with a recession, or that the significant increase in 19X2 involved a new product.

EXHIBIT 15-3		For the Year Ended December 31				
		19X2	19X1	19X0	19Y9	19Y8
Oxley Company	Income Statement Data:					
Five-Year Financial	Sales	$999	$800	$765	$790	$694
Summary (in thou-	Gross profit	600	464	448	460	410
sands, except per	Operating income	126	104	85	91	78
share amounts)	Net income	90	80	62	66	56
	Earnings per share.	.45	.40	.31	.33	.28
	Dividends per share	.40	.20	.20	.20	.15
	Balance Sheet Data (as of December 31):					
	Total assets	$658	$610	$590	$585	$566
	Total liabilities	259	221	241	258	265
	Stockholders' equity	399	389	349	327	301

Common-Size Statements

component percentages Analysis and presentation of financial statements in percentage form to aid comparability.

common-size statement Financial statement expressed in component percentages.

To aid comparisons with a company's previous years and especially to aid the comparison of several companies that differ in size, income statements and balance sheets are often analyzed by percentage relationships, called **component percentages.** The resulting statements, in which the components are assigned a relative percentage, are called **common-size statements.** Consider Oxley Company's common-size statements in Exhibit 15-4. It is difficult to compare Oxley's $290,000 of current assets with a larger company's $480,000. But suppose the other company has total assets of $1 million. Oxley's 44% current asset *percentage* (shown in Exhibit 15-4) can be directly compared with the other company's $480,000 ÷ $1,000,000 = 48%.

The income statement percentages are usually based on sales = 100%. Oxley seems very profitable, but such percentages have more meaning when comparing the budgeted performance with another competitor's values, or with the industry average. Our concern that high margins attract price competition might be reduced if we learned that high margins were characteristic of the industry.

The behavior of each expense in relation to changes in total revenue is often revealing. That is, which expenses go up or down as sales fluctuate? For example, during these two years, rent, depreciation, and interest have been fixed in total but have decreased in relation to sales. In contrast, the wages have increased in total and as a percentage of sales. The latter is not a welcome sign. Exhibit 15-4 indicates that wages in 19X1 were $150 ÷ $800 = 19% of sales, whereas wages in 19X2 were $214 ÷ $999 = 21% of sales.

The balance sheet percentages are usually based on total assets = 100%. See Exhibit 15-4. The most notable feature of the balance sheet percentages is that both current assets and current liabilities are more prominent at the end of 19X2. This arises from the $80,000 debt coming due, which was also highlighted in our review of percentage changes.

Exhibit 15-4

Oxley Company
Common-Size
Statements
(in thousands except
percentages)

	For the Year Ended December 31			
	19X2		19X1	
Statement of Income				
Sales	$999*	100%	$800	100%
Cost of goods sold	399	40	336	42
Gross profit (or gross margin)	$600*	60%	$464	58%
Wages	$214	21%	$150	19%
Rent	120	12	120	15
Miscellaneous	100	10	50	6
Depreciation	40	4	40	5
Operating expenses	$474	47%	$360	45%
Operating income	$126	13%	$104	13%
Other revenue and expense	24	2	24	3
Pretax income	$150	15%	$128	16%
Income tax expense	60	6	48	6
Net income	$ 90	9%	$ 80	10%

	December 31			
	19X2		19X1	
Balance Sheet				
Current assets	$290	44%	$202	33%
Long-term note receivable	288	44	288	47
Equipment, net	80	12	120	20
Total assets	$658	100%	$610	100%
Current liabilities	$219	33%	$101	16%
Long-term note	40	6	120	20
Total liabilities	$259	39%	$221	36%
Stockholders' equity	399	61	389	64
Total liab. and stk. eq.	$658	100%	$610	100%
Working capital	$ 71		$101	

* Note the use of dollar signs in columns of numbers. Frequently, they are used at the top and bottom only and not for every subtotal. Their use by companies depends on the preference of management.

Management's Discussion and Analysis

management's
discussion and
analysis (MD&A)
A required section of
annual reports that
concentrates on
explaining the major
changes in the income
statement and the
major changes in liq-
uidity and capital
resources.

Both trends and component percentages are generally discussed in a required section of annual reports called **management's discussion and analysis** (often called **MD&A**). The MD&A section explains the major changes in the income statement and the major changes in liquidity and capital resources. The space most companies devote to the section in annual reports has increased dramatically in recent years. For example, a recent McDonald's Corporation annual report has a twelve-page MD&A section.

Exhibit 15-5 contains excerpts from the chairman's letter and management's discussion and analysis in the annual report of Pepsico. The annual report is fifty-two pages long. About half is discussion and analysis and half is

The Truth, the Whole Truth,...

The Securities Exchange Commission is serious about full disclosure. You might characterize the SEC approach as a *no surprises* concept. Management should share *material* information with investors as it becomes known. "Management's Discussion and Analysis" is one place where information is shared. A recent enforcement action against Caterpillar, Inc., manufacturer of heavy equipment, illustrates both the concept of timely disclosure and the concept of material facts. A few months after the 1989 annual report and the first quarter 1990 report were issued, Caterpillar announced that 1990 earnings were expected to be *well below* earlier projections. The majority of the decrease was associated with an earnings decline in its Brazilian subsidiary. The stock price fell sharply on this news. The SEC believed that Caterpillar's disclosure about the negative Brazilian events constituted a case of too little information too late.

Ultimately, the problem was that Caterpillar's segment reporting did not identify the fact that 23% of its 1989 profit of $497 million was generated in Brazil. In December 1989 Brazil elected a new president, whose administration adopted severe programs to curb Brazil's hyperinflation. The subsequent decline in economic activity in Brazil substantially affected 1990 earnings of many multinationals, including Ford and GM. Yet, Caterpillar's *1989 Annual Report* observed only a potential decline in sales due to "post election politics" in Brazil. Worse yet, the first quarter 1990 report indicated increased demand worldwide while barely mentioning uncertain economic conditions in Brazil, in spite of disclosures by management to Caterpillar's board of directors in February 1990 that the economic conditions in Brazil would have major negative effects on 1990 results.

The action against Caterpillar stresses the SEC's commitment to increase disclosure. As James Lyons noted in a 1992 *Forbes* article, "... if management is worried about something, it should say so."

Segment reporting is the area of greatest concern to analysts. In order to assess the entity's performance to date and to predict future earnings, analysts want to know how the parts of the company are doing. In the Caterpillar case, the issue was geographic: How is the Brazilian business doing? In the chapter, the Pepsico information includes reference to future uncertainty regarding the consequences of the devaluation of the Mexican peso during 1994 to 1995. It is also important to know how different lines of business are performing. An analyst following Ford might want to separate the automobile business from the truck business and the financing business in order to refine his or her forecasts. An analyst following Pepsico might want to separate restaurants like Kentucky Fried Chicken (KFC) and Taco Bell from the soft drink business. As this text is being written, FASB is developing new rules to guide the nature and extent of segment data to be required. ■

Source: Forbes *(May 25, 1992).* Pepsico 1994 Annual Report

financial statements and the related notes. The cover shows a picture of Cindy Crawford reading the annual report, and the report begins "To humanize the facts, figures, and financial data of our annual report, we decided to aim it at a real live person—a typical investor next door. We chose Cindy Crawford. So sit back, pop open a Pepsi, and, along with Cindy read about your company." The discussions compare 1992, 1993, and 1994. The edited version in Exhibit 15-5 captures the essence. Percentage comparisons are a common part of the discussion. Management then augments observed changes with examples of underlying causes.

Exhibit 15-5	**Chairman's Letter**
Pepsico 1994 Excerpts from Chairman's Letter and Management Discussion and Analyisis	As I was telling Cindy, Pepsico had a strong year in 1994—for the most part. Sales, earnings and dividends hit all-time highs. Particularly strong were domestic soft drinks and domestic snack foods, our two most profitable businesses. Our international beverage and snack businesses also had a big year. And across all of our international businesses, sales grew to more that $8 billion. That's bigger than all of Pepsico was just nine years ago.

continued

Exhibit 15-5

Pepsico
1994 Excerpts from
Chairman's Letter
and Management
Discusssion and
Analyisis
(*Continued*)

On the other hand, our restaurant segment slowed down in 1994. While sales grew a respectable 12% and earnings were nearly three-quarters of a billion dollars, that was still a good bit shy of the remarkable 17% average annual growth our restaurants had posted for well over a decade. In response, we've already realigned and strengthened management and created some promising new programs...

Measuring the Business

I'd like to share with you—and with Cindy—a little about the basic health of Pepsico. How we measure the business. How we gauge our progress. What we look at to determine if we're on the right track...

Four of Our Yardsticks

There are different ways to look at different businesses. Because Pepsico is a very large, multi-line, growth-oriented consumer products company, we look primarily at four measurements:

- Volume growth
- Operating profit growth
- Cash growth
- Investment returns

Here's how I think about them.

Volume Growth

Other than acquisitions, the only unassailable, completely healthy way for consumer business to grow year in and year out is to sell more products. In our case this means selling lots more bottles of Pepsi, bags of chips, buckets of chicken. Volume growth is probably the single best gauge of a consumer products company because it tells us whether we're satisfying consumers and how we're doing against our competitors. In 1994, volume was up at nearly all our businesses, especially in beverages and snack foods... So in terms of volume growth, most of our businesses are doing just fine.

Operating Profit Growth

Now obviously volume has to grow in a way that's profitable. And when you combine our strong volume growth with good profit margins, you're headed for the kind of operating profits that would make any investor smile. Over the last five years, our operating profit margin has been fairly steady, averaging 11%. As a result, our operating profits have grown at a compounded annual rate of 13%.
So based on operating profit growth, Pepsico is also in excellent shape.

Cash Growth

One of my favorite measures of financial strength, and one that says an awful lot about Pepsico, is cash. I'm talking about what's left after we pay for things like labor and raw materials.

All three of our business segments generate operating cash and plenty of it—totaling nearly $5 billion in 1994. And that's been growing steadily. Our segment operating cash grew at 9% in 1994 and at a compounded annual rate of 13% over the past five years.

Over the last five years with our strong cash flow we've been able to invest over $8 billion in existing businesses, invest nearly $4 billion in new ones, pay $2 billion in dividends, and repurchase more that $1 billion worth of Pepsico stock.

Investment Returns

Of course when you're investing $3 billion a year, as we did in 1994, it's important to be smart about it. That's where our fourth measurement comes in. We look for our individual investments to produce returns well over our 11% cost of capital. And the higher those returns are, the more value we create for our shareholders.

continued

Exhibit 15-5

Pepsico
1994 Excerpts from
Chairman's Letter
and Management
Discusssion and
Analyisis
(*Continued*)

If you look at our investment in Pepsico overall, measured by our return on equity, the results are excellent. In 1994 our return on equity was 27%, nearly our best in a decade. And over the last five years it's averaged about 25%.

Putting It All Together

So, as I pointed out to Cindy, these four ways we measure and manage our business-volume growth, operating profit growth, cash growth, and investment returns—tell me Pepsico is thriving. I hope you get the same feeling.

Wayne Calloway
Chairman of the Board and Chief Executive Officer.

MANAGEMENT DISCUSSION AND ANALYSIS

Marketplace Actions

Pepsico's domestic and international businesses operate in markets that are highly competitive and subject to global and local economic conditions including inflation, commodity price, and currency fluctuations, and governmental actions. In Mexico, for example, our businesses have benefited in past years from improving conditions. Conversely, the significant devaluation of the Mexican peso at the end of 1994 and continuing into 1995 will not only negatively impact reported earnings from Mexico due to translation, but is expected to create a much less favorable economic climate in the country. Pepsico's operating and investing strategies are designed, where possible, to mitigate these factors through aggressive actions on several fronts including: (a) enhancing the appeal and value of its products through brand promotion, product innovation, quality improvement and prudent pricing actions; (b) providing better service to customers; (c) increasing world-wide availability of its products; (d) acquiring businesses and forming alliances to increase market presence and utilize resources more efficiently; and (e) containing costs through efficient and effective purchasing, manufacturing, distribution and administrative processes.

Restructurings

Restructuring actions realign resources for more efficient and effective execution of operating strategies. As a result, Pepsico continually considers and executes restructuring actions that vary in size and impact, for example from a minor sales force reorganization at a local facility to a significant organizational and process redesign affecting an entire operating division. The resulting cost savings or profits from increased sales are reinvested in the business to increase Pepsico's shareholder value.

Currency Exchange Effects

In 1994, 1993 and 1992, international businesses represented 18.6%, 18.0% and 17.7%, respectively, of Pepsico's total segment operating profits. The following paragraphs describe the effects of currency exchange rate movements on Pepsico's reported results. See Other Factors Expected to Impact 1995 Results on page 26.

Translation of the income statements of international businesses into U.S. dollars affects year-over-year comparability of operating results. In 1994 and 1993, sales and operating profit growth rates for our consolidated international businsses were not materially impacted.

Changes in currency exchange rates also result in reported foreign exchange gains and losses. Pepsico reported a net foreign exchange gain of $4.5 million and $17.4 million in 1993 and 1992, respectively.

continued

Management's Analysis—Results of Operations

Net Sales rose $3.5 billion or 14% in 1994 of which $215 million or 1 point was contributed by net acquisitions. The balance of the increase reflected volume gains of $2.2 billion and $934 million due to additional restaurant units.

Cost of sales as a percentage of Net Sales was 48.2%, 47.7% and 48.3% in 1994, 1993 and 1992, respectively. The decline in the 1994 gross margin reflected a mix shift to lower-margin businesses in international beverages and worldwide restaurants, and lower net pricing in domestic beverages, partially offset by a mix shift to higher-margin packages and products in international snack foods and manufacturing efficiencies in domestic snack foods.

Selling, general and administrative expenses rose 14% in 1994 and 13% in 1993, reflecting base business growth.

Operating Profit increased 10% in 1994 and 23% in 1993. Excluding the Unusual Items, operating profit increased $262 million or 9% in 1994 and $342 million or 13% in 1993, driven by combined segment operating profit growth of 7% in 1994 and 14% in 1993. The 1994 increase reflected $850 million from higher volumes and $73 million from additional restaurant units, partially offset by higher operating expenses.

Interest expense, net of Interest income, increased 15% in 1994 and 2% in 1993. The 1994 increase reflected higher average borrowings partially offset by higher interest rates on investment balances.

Provision for Income Taxes as a percentage of pretax income was 33.0%, 34.5% and 31.4% in 1994, 1993 and 1992, respectively.

Income and Income Per Share before Cumulative Effect of Accounting Changes "income" and "income per share" in 1994 increased 12% to $1.8 billion and 13% to $2.22, respectively, and in 1993 increased 22% to $1.6 billion and 22% to $1.96, respectively. Excluding the Unusual Items, income and income per share rose 8% and 9%, respectively, in 1994 and 13% and 12%, respectively, in 1993. Growth in income per share was depressed by estimated dilution from acquisitions of $0.03 or 1 point in 1994 and $0.05 or 3 points in 1993, primarily due to international beverage acquisitions in both years.

The Mexican peso devaluation may unfavorably impact Net Sales and Net Income in 1995: however, due to many uncertainties in Mexico, we are unable to quantify the impacts.

Segment Reporting

The Pepsico management discussion in Exhibit 15-5 includes a comparison of domestic and international performance. Such detailed disclosure is part of the gradual evolution toward fuller disclosure during the 1980s and 1990s. The financial statements become thicker and more complex and are impressively adorned with detailed footnotes and supplementary information. Among the more controversial requirements was the issuance by the FASB in 1976 of *Statement No. 14*, "Financial Reporting for Segments of a Business Enterprise." Corporations must now disclose data about their operations in different industries and in foreign countries, their export sales, and their major customers. Almost twenty years later, the FASB is considering changes to these rules to help investors better understand the parts of the enterprise.

The purpose of consolidated financial statements is to provide an overall view of an economic entity. However, consolidated data can hide some of the details that might be useful in predicting profitability, risk, and growth. The purpose of segment disclosures is to facilitate such prediction.

Exhibit 15-6 lists the four types of disclosures required by *Statement No. 14.* An *industry segment* is a product or service or a group of related products or services. Management has much discretion in defining industry segments. The nature of the product, the nature of the production process, and the markets or marketing methods should be considered in identifying a company's segments. Examples of industry segments include the following:

- American Express Company: travel-related services; international banking services; investment services; IDS financial services; insurance services
- Alcoa: aluminum processing; finished products

If an industry segment meets any one of the three criteria for disclosure in Exhibit 15-6, the segment's revenue, profit, assets, depreciation, and capital expenditures must be reported.

Companies with significant operations in foreign countries must separately disclose the results of operations by geographic area. For example, American Express Company reports revenue, profits, and assets for the United States, Europe, and Asia/Pacific. Even companies without foreign operations must disclose foreign *sales* by geographic area if such export sales are 10% or more of total revenues.

Finally, companies must report aggregate sales to any customer accounting for more than 10% of revenues. For example, Ball Corporation, maker of packaging materials, including metal beverage containers for brewers and soft drink companies, reports that 23% of its sales were to Anheuser-Busch and 20% were to various agencies of the United States government. Exhibit 15-7 shows the industry and geographic segment information from Pepsico's 1994 annual report.

| Exhibit 15-6 | Main Provisions of FASB Statement No. 14 |

Type of Disclosure	Criteria Disclosure	Items to Be Disclosed
1. Industry segment	a. Revenue at least 10% of company revenue, b. Profit at least 10% of company profit, or c. Assets at least 10% of company assets.	a. Segment revenue b. Segment profit c. Segment assets d. Other (e.g., segment depreciation and capital expenditures)
2. Geographic segment	a. Foreign operations contribute at least 10% of company's revenue, or b. Foreign operations use more than 10% of the company's assets	a. Segment revenue b. Segment profit c. Segment assets
3. Export disclosures	At least 10% of revenues from export sales	Export sales by geographic area
4. Major customers	Any customer providing more than 10% of company's revenue	Customer identity and amount of revenue

■ FINANCIAL RATIOS

Objective 4

Review the basic financial ratios.

The cornerstone of financial statement analysis is the computation and interpretation of ratios. Exhibit 15-8 groups some of the most popular ratios into four categories. Most of these ratios have been introduced in earlier chapters, as indicated in the second column. (A dash in the column means that the ratio is being introduced in this chapter for the first time.)

Exhibit 15-7   Pepsico 1994 Segment and Geographic Disclosures

Net Sales	Growth Rate 1989-1994	1994	Operating Profits	Growth Rate 1989-1994	1994
Beverages:					
Domestic	7.2%	$ 6,541.2	Domestic	12.1%	$1,022.3
International	22.2%	3,146.3	International	20.0%	194.7
	10.9%	9,687.5		13.2%	1,217.0
Snack Foods:					
Domestic	9.3%	5,011.3	Domestic	8.9%	1,025.1
International	32.0%	3,253.1	International	27.1%	351.8
	15.5%	8,264.4		12.2%	1,376.9
Restaurants:					
Domestic	13.2%	8,693.9	Domestic	12.2%	658.8
International	26.4%	1,826.6	International	4.3%	71.5
	14.9%	10,520.5		11.3%	730.3
Combined Segments					
Domestic	10.1%	20,246.4	Domestic	11.1%	2,706.2
International	26.6%	8,226.0	International	20.6%	618.0
	13.6%	$28,472.4		12.3%	3,324.2

Geographic Areas	Net Sales 1994	Segment Operating Profits 1994	Identifiable Assets 1994
United States	$20,246.4	$2,706.2	$14,218.4
Europe	2,177.1	16.7	3,062.0
Mexico	2,022.8	261.4	994.7
Canada	1,244.3	81.6	1,342.1
Other	2,781.8	258.3	2,195.6
Combined Segments	$28,472.4	$3,324.2	21,812.8
Corporate			2,979.2
			$24,792.0

continued

Exhibit 15-7	Pepsico 1994 Segment and Geographic Disclosures (*Continued*)

	Depreciation Expense		Amortization of Intangible Assets	
	Growth Rate 1989-1994	*1994*	*Growth Rate 1989-1994*	*1994*
Beverages	14.9%	$ 385.4	7.6%	$164.8
Snack Foods	11.7%	297.0	17.8%	42.0
Restaurants	17.5%	538.8	28.9%	105.4
Corporate		7.0		
	15.0%	$1,228.2	14.0%	$312.2

	Identifiable Assets		Capital Spending	
	Growth Rate 1989-1994	*1994*	*Growth Rate 1989-1994*	*1994*
Beverages	9.1%	$ 9,566.0	20.4%	$ 677.1
Snack Foods	8.8%	5,043.9	15.6%	532.1
Restaurants	18.6%	7,202.9	20.3%	1,072.0
Corporate		2,979.2		7.2
	10.4%	$24,792.0	19.0%	$2,288.4

Evaluating Financial Ratios

time-series comparisons Comparisons of a company's financial ratios with its own historical ratios.

bench marks General rules of thumb specifying appropriate levels for financial ratios.

cross-sectional comparisons Comparisons of a company's financial ratios with the ratios of other companies or with industry averages.

Evaluation of a financial ratio requires a comparison. There are three main types of comparisons: (1) with a company's own historical ratios (called **time-series comparisons**), (2) with general *rules of thumb* or **bench marks,** and (3) with ratios of other companies or with industry averages (called **cross-sectional comparisons**).

Much can be learned by examining the *time-series trend* of a company's ratios. That is why annual reports typically contain a table of comparative statistics for five or ten years. For example, some of the items listed in the 1994 annual report of Pepsico are:

	1994	1993	1992	1991	1990
Income per share	$ (2.18)	$1.96	$ .46	$1.35	$1.35
Debt as a percentage of total capitalization	49%	50%	49%	51%	51%
Return on common stockholders' equity	(27.0)%	27.2%	23.9%	20.7%	24.8%

Exhibit 15-8   Some Typical Financial Ratios

Typical Name of Ratio	Introduced in Chapter	Numerator	Denominator	Using Appropriate Oxley Numbers Applied to December 31 of Year	
				19X2	**19X1**
Short-term liquidity ratios:					
Current ratio	4	Current assets	Current liabilities	290 ÷ 219 = 1.3	202 ÷ 101 = 2.0
Quick ratio	4	Cash + marketable securities + receivables	Current liabilities	(150 + 0 + 95) ÷ 219 = 1.1	(57 + 0 + 70) ÷ 101 = 1.3
Average collection period in days	6	Average accounts receivable x 365	Sales	[1/2(95 + 70) x 365] ÷ 999 = 30†	Unknown*
Inventory turnover	7	Cost of goods sold	Average inventory at cost	399 ÷ 1/2(20 + 60) = 10	Unknown*
Long-term solvency ratios:					
Total debt to total assets	10	Total liabilities	Total assets	259 ÷ 658 = 39.4%	221 ÷ 610 = 36.2%
Total debt to equity	10	Total liabilities	Stockholders' equity	259 ÷ 399 = 64.9%	221 ÷ 389 = 56.8%
Interest coverage	10	Income before interest and taxes	Interest expense	(150 + 12) ÷ 12 = 13.5	(128 + 12) ÷ 12 = 11.7
Profitability ratios:					
Return on stockholders' equity	4,12	Net income	Average stock- holders' equity	90 ÷ 1/2(399 + 389) = 22.8%	Unknown*
Gross profit rate or percentage	4	Gross profit or gross margin	Sales	600 ÷ 999 = 60%	464 ÷ 800 = 58%
Return on sales	4	Net income	Sales	90 ÷ 999 = 9%	80 ÷ 800 = 10%
Asset turnover	—	Sales	Average total assets available	999 ÷ 1/2(658 + 610) = 1.6	Unknown*
Pretax return on operating assets	—	Operating income	Average total assets available	126 ÷ 1/2(658 + 610) = 19.9%	Unknown*
Earnings per share	2	Net income less dividends on preferred stock, if any	Average common shares outstanding	90 ÷ 200 = $.45	80 ÷ 200 = $.40
Market price and dividend ratios:					
Price-earnings	2	Market price of common share (assume $4 and $3)	Earnings per share	4 ÷ .45 = 8.9	3 ÷ .40 = 7.5
Dividend-yield	2	Dividends per common share	Market price of common share (assume $4 and $3)	.40 ÷ 4 = 10.0%	.20 ÷ 3 = 6.7%
Dividend-payout	2	Dividends per common share	Earnings per share	.40 ÷ .45 = 89%	.20 ÷ .40 = 50%

* Insufficient data available because the *beginning* balance sheet balances for 19X1 are not provided. Without them, the *average* investment in receivables, inventory, total assets, or stockholders' equity during 19X1 cannot be computed.

† This may be easier to see as follows: Average receivables = 1/2(95 + 70) = 82.5. Average receivables as a percentage of annual sales = 82.5 ÷ 999 = 8.25%. Average collection period = 8.25% × 365 days = 30 days.

Ratios

Ratios are useful for financial analysis by investors because ratios capture critical dimensions of the economic performance of the entity. Where else might economic performance need to be measured? Where else might ratios pay off for managers? It turns out that ratios are increasingly a tool that managers use to guide, measure, and reward workers. If you compensate workers for actions that make the company more profitable, for actions that increase the value of the company's common stock, you are motivating the employees effectively.

Hewitt Associates, a compensation consulting firm, reports that 60% of the 1,941 large companies they surveyed in 1994 had profit-sharing programs. Such programs are based on the solid view that when profits rise, the company is doing the right thing. And when workers do the right thing, they should share in the benefits. The higher the profit, the more the workers should earn as their share.

Duke Power Co. in Charlotte, N.C., has decided that profit may not be the right measure. Suppose profit increases because you raise more capital and expand the company? Should the workers necessarily earn more? Duke Power decided to reward workers based on two factors: success in meeting goals and the return on equity (ROE). For one worker the goal might be defined as reduced injuries and for another as improved customer service. But everyone earns more for meeting ROE targets. ROE is a good measure of

efficiency because it can be improved by increasing profitability (the return on sales) and also by increasing the efficiency with which assets are employed (asset turnover).

In 1991, many workers had never heard of ROE, but by 1995 workers were watching the monthly financial results as carefully as their chidren look both ways before crossing the street. Now workers participate, and bonuses can exceed the base pay. As a result a $9.00 per hour worker can earn $20.00 per hour by achieving targets. And management is delighted to pay these bonuses because they are only paid when worker productivity is exceptional. The surprise is that workers can and do turn in exceptional performances when they know it will be recognized—not just by kind words, but by a management that puts its money where its mouth is.

Tawn Nhan, in a Washington Post article, gave the example of Neely Ashe, an engineer responsible for the coal division who has begun to cooperate more actively with the nuclear division. As Ashe said about the nuclear group, "I want to see them do well; it has an effect on my pay." Other companies are following this pattern. Glenayre Technologies and Nucor are also centered in Charlotte, N.C., and have similar bonus plans. ∎

Source: The Washington Post, *Sunday March 26, 1995, p. H5*

Broad *rules of thumb* often serve as bench marks for comparison. Historically, the most quoted bench mark is a current ratio of 2 to 1. Recently, changes in management practices have reduced cash and inventory levels, and average current ratios are moving toward 1 to 1. Other bench marks are described in *Industry Norms and Key Business Ratios* by Dun & Bradstreet, the financial services firm.

Bench marks are general guides. More specific comparisons come from cross-sectional comparisons; that is, by examining ratios of similar companies or from industry averages. Dun & Bradstreet informs its subscribers of the credit-worthiness of thousands of individual companies. In addition, the firm regularly compiles many ratios of the companies it monitors. Compare the ratios for Oxley Company in Exhibit 15-8 to some of the Dun & Bradstreet ratios for 1,712 retail nurseries and garden stores:

Dun & Bradstreet Ratios			Average Collection Period	Total Debt to Stockholders' Equity	Net Income on Sales	Net Income on Stockholders' Equity
	Current Ratio	Quick Ratio	(Days)	(Percent)	(Percent)	(Percent)
1,712 companies:						
Upper quartile	4.2	1.5	5.5	32.3	6.1	30.2
Median	2.0	0.5	11.3	92.8	2.5	12.6
Lower quartile	1.3	0.2	23.0	230.7	0.5	2.6
Oxley*	1.3	1.1	30.0	64.9	9.0	22.8

* Ratios are from Exhibit 15-8. Please consult that exhibit for an explanation of the components of each ratio.

The individual ratios are ranked from best to worst. The ratio ranked in the middle is the *median*. The upper quartile is the ratio ranked halfway between the median and the best value. The lower quartile is the ratio ranked halfway between the median and the worst value. The concept of best and worst must be considered carefully. Different constituencies may adopt different points of view. For example, a short-term creditor would think that a very high current ratio was good, because it means the assets are there to repay the debt. From management's perspective, however, it is possible that current assets are excessive.

Short-Term Liquidity Ratios

Questions concerning liquidity focus on whether there are sufficient current assets to satisfy current liabilities as they become due. The most commonly used liquidity ratio is the current ratio. The higher the current ratio, the more assurance the short-term creditor usually has about being paid in full and on time. As Exhibit 15-8 shows, Oxley's current ratio of 1.3 has declined from 2.0 and is unimpressive in relation to the industry median of 2.0, which is shown in the previous section.

The quick ratio measures shorter-term liquidity. The numerator includes only those current assets that can quickly be turned into cash: cash, marketable securities, and accounts receivable. Oxley's quick ratio has also declined in 19X2, from 1.3 to 1.1, but is still greater than the industry median of 0.5.

Liquidity is also affected by how soon accounts receivable will be collected and how soon inventory will be sold. The average collection period and inventory turnover are closely watched signals. Deteriorations through time in these ratios can help alert investors and creditors to problem areas. For example, a decrease in inventory turnover may suggest slower-moving (or even unsalable) merchandise or a worsening coordination of the buying and selling functions. An increase in the average collection period of receivables may indicate increasing acceptance of poor credit risks or less-energetic collection efforts. Whether the inventory turnover of 10 and the average collection period of 30 days are "fast" or "slow" depends on past performance and the performance of similar companies. Inventory turnover is not available from Dun & Bradstreet on an industry-comparable basis. The average collection period for Oxley is nearly three times as long as the industry median of 11.3 days.

Many analysts use sales *on account* in the denominator of the average collection period. This ratio focuses attention on how long it takes to collect credit accounts, in contrast to how long it takes to receive payment on sales in general. A company with many cash sales may have a short average collection period for total sales, even though there may be long delays in receiving payments for items sold on credit. Suppose half of Oxley's sales were for cash (including bank cards) and only half on open credit. The average collection period for *credit sales* would be

$$\frac{(1/2)(95 + 70) \times 365}{(1/2)(999)} = 60 \text{ days}$$

To be compared with industry averages, the averages must also be adjusted for credit sales. Suppose only one-fourth of the sales in retail nurseries are on credit. The industry median collection period for credit accounts would be $10.2 \div (1/4) = 40.8$ days.

Long-Term Solvency Ratios

Ratios of debt to assets and debt to equity are used for solvency evaluation. Although the focus is on the ability to repay long-term creditors, both creditors and shareholders watch these ratios to judge the degree of risk of insolvency and the stability of profits. Typically, companies with heavy debt in relation to ownership capital are in greater danger of suffering net losses or even insolvency when business conditions sour. Why? Because revenues and many expenses decline, but interest expenses and maturity dates do not change. Oxley's debt-to-equity ratio of 64.9% is below the industry median of 92.8%, reflecting less-than-average uncertainty concerning the company's ability to pay its debts on time.

Another solvency measure is the interest coverage ratio. It shows how much danger there is that operations will not generate operating income (before interest expense) at least as large as the company's interest expense. A common rule of thumb is that the interest coverage ratio should be at least five. Oxley's ratio of 13.5 comfortably exceeds this bench mark. The interest coverage ratio was discussed in more detail in Chapter 10.

Profitability Ratios

Earnings per share (EPS) is the best known of all financial ratios. It measures the "bottom line," earnings available to the holder of a share of common stock. It was introduced in Chapter 2, and extended discussion appears later in this chapter, where we examine some issues that arise for more complex companies than Oxley.

The primary profitability measure is return on stockholders' equity. Abbreviated ROE, this ratio relates an accounting measure of income to the level of ownership capital used to generate the income. As defined in Chapter 4 and discussed more extensively in Chapter 12, the ratio is:

ROE = Net income / Average shareholders' equity

Oxley's return of 22.8% is above the 1994 industry median of 12.6% shown on page 689. What explains Oxley's superior performance? Two additional profitability ratios help explain it. The return on sales was introduced in Chapter 4. Exhibit 15-8 shows that the return on sales has fallen from 10% to 9%. But the 9% level, which indicates that 9 cents of every dollar of sales is profit, places Oxley well above the 75th percentile of nurseries and garden stores according to Dun & Bradstreet. The second key to assessing Oxley's superior ROE is the efficiency with which Oxley uses its asset structure to generate sales. To accomplish this, we now examine some distinctions between operating performance and financial performance.

◼ OPERATING PERFORMANCE AND FINANCIAL PERFORMANCE

ROE, discussed above, is affected by financing choices. *Financial management* is concerned with where to get cash and how to use that cash to benefit the entity. Borrowed funds create interest costs and affect net income, the numerator of the ratio. *Operating management* is concerned with the day-to-day activities that generate revenues and expenses. Ratios to assess operating efficiency should not be affected by financial considerations.

Market Price and Dividend Ratios

Investors are particularly concerned with the market price of common shares. Both earnings and dividends are related to share price. The price-earnings (P/E) ratio shows how market participants value $1 of a company's earnings. Generally, high P/E means that investors expect earnings to grow faster than average, and a low P/E indicates small expected earnings growth. In 1995, the average economy-wide P/E ratio was 16, but some companies such as Microsoft, the computer software company, had P/E ratios over 35. In contrast, IBM had a P/E of 15 and McDonald's 21. Oxley's P/E of 8.9 is above last year's 7.5, but it is below the economy-wide average. Apparently, investors think Oxley has below-average growth potential.

Oxley doubled its dividend per share in 19X2, increasing the dividend yield to 10.0%. Therefore an investor who buys $1,000 of Oxley common stock will receive annual cash dividends of 10% × $1,000 = $100 if dividend rates do not change. Oxley is paying out 89% of earnings, as shown by the dividend-payout ratio. The high payout ratio may be one reason for the low projected growth; Oxley is not reinvesting much of its earnings.

Operating Performance

In general, we evaluate the overall success of an investment by comparing what the investment returns to us with the investment we initially made. In general, the rate of return on investment can be defined as:

$$\text{Rate of return on investment} = \frac{\text{Income}}{\text{Invested capital}} \tag{1}$$

EBIT Earnings before interest and taxes.

In various settings, we find it useful to define *income* differently, sometimes as net earnings and sometimes as either pretax income from operations or earnings before interest and taxes (**EBIT**). We also define *invested capital* differently, sometimes as the stockholders' equity and other times as the total capital provided by both debt and equity sources. These choices are determined by the purpose of the analysis.

    The measurement of *operating* performance (that is, how profitably assets are employed) should not be influenced by the management's *financial* decisions (that is, how assets are financed). Operating performance is best measured by **pretax operating rate of return on total assets:**

pretax operating rate of return on total assets
Operating income divided by average total assets available.

$$\begin{array}{c}\text{Pretax operating rate} \\ \text{of return on total assets}\end{array} = \frac{\text{Operating income}}{\text{Average total assets available}} \tag{2}$$

The right side of Equation 2 consists, in turn, of two important ratios:

$$\frac{\text{Operating income}}{\text{Average total assets available}} = \frac{\text{Operating income}}{\text{Sales}} \times \frac{\text{Sales}}{\begin{array}{c}\text{Average total} \\ \text{assets available}\end{array}} \tag{3}$$

Using Exhibits 15-1 and 15-2, pages 677-78, we can compute the following 19X2 results for Oxley Company:

operating income percentage on sales
Operating income divided by sales.

$$\frac{\$126}{\frac{1}{2}(\$658+\$610)} = \frac{\$126}{\$999} \times \frac{\$999}{\$634} = 19.9\%$$

These relationships are displayed in a boxed format in Exhibit 15-9.

    The right-side terms in Equation 3 are often called the **operating income percentage on sales** and the **total asset turnover (asset turnover),** respectively. Equation 3 may be reexpressed:

total asset turnover (asset turnover)
Sales divided by average total assets available.

$$\begin{array}{c}\text{Pretax operating rate} \\ \text{of return on total assets}\end{array} = \text{Operating income percentage on sales} \times \text{Total asset turnover}$$
$$19.9\% = 12.6\% \times 1.576 \text{ times} \tag{4}$$

Exhibit 15-9

Major Ingredients of Return on Total Assets

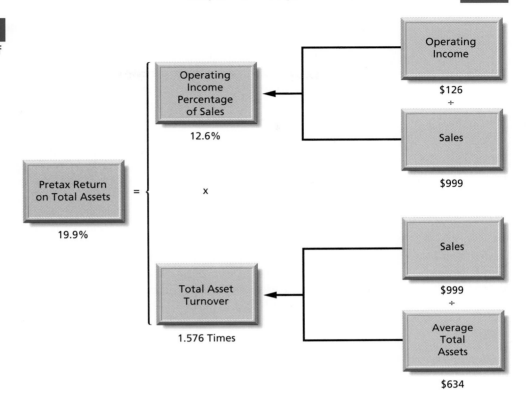

If ratios are used to evaluate operating performance, they should exclude extraordinary items that are regarded as nonrecurring items that do not reflect normal performance.

Equation 4 highlights two basic factors in profit making: operating margin percentage and turnover. An improvement in either will, by itself, increase the rate of return on total assets.

The ratios could be computed on the basis of figures after taxes, and often are. However, the peculiarities of the income tax laws may sometimes distort results—for example, the tax rate may change, or losses carried back or forward might eliminate the tax in certain years.

Financial Performance

A major aspect of financial performance is achieving an appropriate balance of debt and equity financing. Debt surrounds us. Governments issue debt securities of all kinds for many purposes. Businesses do likewise. Individuals have small loans (on refrigerators) and big loans (on homes).

In addition to a decision about how much debt is appropriate, a firm must choose how much to borrow short-term (e.g., accounts payable and some bank debt) and how much to borrow by issuing bonds or other longer-term debt. Short-term financing should ordinarily be for investments in current assets. Some entities have edged into deep financial water by using short-term debt for long-term investments (for example, plant and equipment). A notable example is the city of New York, which was unable to pay its debt during the 1970s.

The problem with short-term debt is that it must be quickly repaid or replaced with new financing. When the borrower encounters trouble and cannot repay, it will also be difficult to refinance. Lenders prefer healthy, profitable borrowers, not troubled ones. Such problems are especially severe during periods when interest rates are rising, since each new refinancing occurs at a higher interest rate and the cash flow required to cover interest requirements rises steadily.

Long-term investments should be financed by long-term capital: debt or stock. Debt is often a more attractive vehicle than common stock because (1) interest payments are deductible for income tax purposes but dividends are not, and (2) the ownership rights to voting and profits are kept by the present shareholders.

Trading on the Equity

capitalization (capitalization structure, capital structure) Owners' equity plus long-term debt.

Most companies have two basic types of long-term financing: long-term debt and stockholders' equity. The total of long-term financing is often called the **capitalization, capitalization structure,** or simply **capital structure** of a corporation. Suppose a company has long-term debt (in the form of bonds payable) and common stock as its capital structure. This means that common shareholders enjoy the benefits of all income in excess of interest on the bonds.

trading on the equity (financial leverage, leveraging, gearing) Using borrowed money at fixed interest rates with the objective of enhancing the rate of return on common equity.

Trading on the equity, (also referred to as using **financial leverage, leveraging,** or in the U.K., **gearing)** means using borrowed money at fixed interest rates with the objective of enhancing the rate of return on common shareholders' equity. There are costs and benefits to shareholders from trading on the equity. The costs are interest payments and increased risk, and the benefits are the larger returns to the common shareholders—as long as overall income is sufficiently large.

Consider three companies, A, B, and C, each in the same industry with $80,000 of average assets and with the same rate of return on total assets (ROA) in any year. However, the ROA varies: In Year 1 it is 20%, in Year 2 it is 10%, and in Year 3 it is 5%. The three companies have chosen very different capital structures. Company A has no debt, company B has $30,000 in debt, and Company C has $60,000 in debt. Company B pays 10% interest, while the more heavily indebted Company C must pay 12%. How do the shareholders fare in these three companies in different years? The results are summarized in Exhibit 15-10.

The first column of Exhibit 15-10 gives the income before interest expense. To clearly focus on leverage, this example ignores taxes. Recall that the return on assets is calculated as

return on total assets (ROA) Income before interest expense divided by average total assets.

$$\frac{\text{Rate of return}}{\text{on total assets}} = \frac{\text{Income before interest expense}}{\text{Average total assets}}$$

Therefore, income before interest expense equals rate of **return on total assets (ROA)** times average total assets. In this instance we assume a given ROA for each year and therefore can calculate income by multiplying ROA times the constant asset level of $80,000. The values are the same for all three companies within a year but vary from year to year. The interest expense is different for each company because each has a different level of debt. Our primary interest is the effect of leverage on the level of the **rate of return on common stockholders' equity (ROE)** defined as:

rate of return on stockholders' equity (ROE) Net income divided by average stockholders' equity.

$$\frac{\text{Rate of return}}{\text{on stockholders' equity}} = \frac{\text{Net income}}{\text{Average stockholders' equity}}$$

| Exhibit 15-10 | Trading on the Equity-Effects of Debt on Rates of Return |

	(1) Income before Interest	(2) Interest Expense	(3) Net Income	(4) Stockholders' Equity	(5) Return on Equity
	(ROA x Assets)*	(Debt x Interest Rate)†	(1) – (2)		(3) ÷ (4)
Year 1: 20% ROA					
Company A	$16,000	$ 0	$16,000	$80,000	20%
Company B	16,000	3,000	13,000	50,000	26%
Company C	16,000	7,200	8,800	20,000	44%
Year 2: 10% ROA					
Company A	$ 8,000	$ 0	$ 8,000	$80,000	10%
Company B	8,000	3,000	5,000	50,000	10%
Company C	8,000	7,200	800	20,000	4%
Year 3: 5% ROA					
Company A	$ 4,000	$ 0	$ 4,000	$80,000	5%
Company B	4,000	3,000	1,000	50,000	2%
Company C	4,000	7,200	(3,200)	20,000	(16%)

* All three companies have $80,000 in assets.
† Company A, no debt; Company B, $30,000 in debt at 10%; Company C, $60,000 in debt at 12%.

What do we learn from Exhibit 15-10? First, a debt-free, or *unlevered*, company has identical ROA and ROE. Note that Company A's ROE and ROA are identical in each year: 20%, 10%, and 5%. Second, when a company has an ROA greater than its interest rate, ROE exceeds ROA. This is called favorable financial leverage and describes both companies B and C in Year 1. They earn 20% on their assets and pay either 10% or 12% on their debt. The earnings in excess of the interest cost increase earnings available to shareholders. Year 2 is interesting because Company B has an ROA of 10%, which equals its interest rate. Thus, like Company A, Company B has an ROE of 10%. In contrast Company C experiences *unfavorable* financial leverage. Since its 10% ROA is less than the 12% interest cost, its ROE falls sharply to 4%.

Year 3 further stresses the effects of leverage in poor years. When ROA falls noticeably below the firm's interest cost, ROE falls sharply as well. Company B falls to an ROE of 2%, while the more highly leveraged Company C faces a loss year and negative ROE.

When a company is unable to earn at least the interest rate on the money borrowed, the return on equity will be lower than for the debt-free company. If earnings are low enough that the interest and principal payments on debt cannot be made, a company may be forced into bankruptcy. The possibility of bankruptcy increases the risk to the common stockholders even more than to debtholders.

Obviously, the more stable the income, the less dangerous it is to trade on the equity (or, as it is often called, to use *leveraging* or, in the United Kingdom, *gearing*). Therefore regulated utilities such as electric, gas, and telephone companies tend to have a much heavier proportion of debt than manufacturers of computers or steel. The *prudent* use of debt is part of intelligent financial management.

Income Tax Effects

Because interest payments are deductible as an expense for income tax purposes but dividends are not, if all other things are equal, the use of debt is less costly to the corporation than equity. Suppose additional capital of $10 million is going to be raised by a company either through long-term debt or through preferred stock. The latter is discussed in Chapter 12, page 543. The typical preferred stock is a part of shareholders' equity, and the dividend thereon is not deductible for income tax purposes. Moreover, the rate of preferred dividends is usually higher than the rate of interest because the preferred stockholders have a greater risk due to their lower-priority claim on the total assets of a company. Assume that an interest rate of 10% for debt and a preferred dividend rate of 11% are applicable. The income tax rate is 40%. Compare the effects of obtaining additional capital by these two methods shown in the accompanying table.

	$10 Million Long-Term Debt	$10 Million Preferred Stock
Income before interest expense (assumed)	$ 5,000,000	$5,000,000
Interest expense at 10% of long-term debt	1,000,000	—
Income before income taxes	$ 4,000,000	$5,000,000
Income tax expense at 40%	1,600,000	2,000,000
Net income	$ 2,400,000	$3,000,000
Dividends to preferred shareholders at 11%	—	1,100,000
Net income less dividends	$ 2,400,000	$ 1,900,000
Pretax cost of capital raised	10%	11%
After-tax cost of capital raised:		
$600,000* ÷ $10,000,000	6%	
$1,100,000 ÷ $10,000,000		11%

* Interest expense	$ 1,000,000
Income tax savings because of interest deduction:	
.40 x $1,000,000	400,000
Interest expense after tax savings	$ 600,000

Three points deserve emphasis:

1. Interest is tax deductible, so its after-tax cost can be considerably less than dividends on preferred stock. In other words, *net income attributable to common shareholders* can be substantially higher if debt is used.

2. Interest is an expense, whereas preferred dividends are not. Therefore *net income* is higher if preferred shares are used. Note that trading on the equity can benefit the common stockholders by the issuance of either long-term debt securities or preferred stock, provided that there are sufficient earnings on the additional assets acquired.

3. Failure to pay interest is an act of bankruptcy, which gives creditors rights to control or liquidate the company. Failure to pay dividends is not.

Measuring Safety

Investors in debt securities want assurance that future operations will easily provide cash sufficient to make the scheduled payments of interest and principal. Corporate borrowers have a natural concern for the degree of risk they assume by borrowing. Thus lenders and borrowers have a mutual aversion to excessive risks from debt, although lenders understandably have the stronger aversion.

Debt securities often have protective provisions, such as mortgage liens on real estate or restrictions on dividend payments to holders of common stock. However, these provisions are of minor importance compared with prospective earnings. Bondholders would like to avoid the trouble, costs, and inconvenience of foreclosure or bankruptcy litigation; they would rather receive a steady stream of interest and repayments of principal.

Debt-to-equity ratios are popular measures of risk. But they do not focus on the major concern of the holders of long-term debt: the ability to meet debt obligations on schedule. A ratio that focuses on interest-paying ability is **interest coverage** (sometimes called **times interest earned**). For example, in the table on page 696, interest coverage is:

interest coverage (times interest earned) Income before interest expense and income taxes divided by interest expense.

$$\text{Interest coverage} = \frac{\text{Income before interest expense and income taxes}}{\text{Interest expense}}$$
$$= \frac{\$5,000,000}{\$1,000,000} = 5.0 \text{ times}$$

The equation is self-explanatory. A rule of thumb for adequate safety of an industrial bond is that all interest charges should be earned at least five times in the poorest year in a span of seven to ten years that might be under review. The numerator does not deduct income taxes because interest expense is deductible for income tax purposes. In effect, income taxes, as a periodic "claim" on earnings, have a lower priority than interest. For instance, if the numerator were only $1 million, interest would be paid, leaving a net taxable income of zero. This tax-deductibility feature is a major reason why bonds are used much more widely than preferred stock.

■ PROMINENCE OF EARNINGS PER SHARE

Objective 6

Calculate EPS when preferred stock exists, shares outstanding change during the year, and dilution is a possibility.

Throughout this text we have viewed earnings per share (EPS) as a basic reporting element in the financial statements. However, we have generally expressed it in the context of a simple owners' equity structure consisting solely of common stock. Three issues that might complicate matters are discussed below: preferred stock, stock issues and redemptions, and the possibility of exercise of options or various convertible securities. If common stock is issued during the year, the weighted average number of shares must be calculated. If preferred stocks exist, the priority claims of those shareholders must be considered. Finally, if there are exchange privileges outstanding such as stock options or convertible securities, their potential effect must be considered.

Weighted Average Shares and Preferred Stock

When the capital structure is relatively simple, computations of EPS are straightforward. For example, consider the following calculation (figures assumed):

$$\text{Earnings per share of common stock} = \frac{\text{Net income}}{\text{Weighted- average number of shares outstanding during the period}}$$

$$= \frac{\$1,000,000}{800.000} = \$1.25$$

Computations of EPS are based on the weighted-average number of shares outstanding during a period. For example, suppose 750,000 shares were outstanding at the beginning of a calendar year, and 200,000 of additional shares were issued on October 1 (three months before the end of the year). The weighted average is based on the number of months that the shares were outstanding during the year. The basic computation can be accomplished in two different ways:

750,000 × weighting of 12/12= 750,000	750,000 × 9/12 = 562,500
200,000 × weighting of 3/12 = 50,000 *or*	950,000 × 3/12 = 237,500
Weighted average shares = 800,000	= 800,000

In addition, if the capital structure includes preferred stock that is nonconvertible, the dividends on preferred stock applicable to the current period, whether or not paid, should be deducted in calculating earnings applicable to common stock (figures assumed):

$$\text{Earnings per share of common stock} = \frac{\text{Net income} - \text{Preferred dividends}}{\text{Weighted} - \text{average number of shares outstanding during the period}}$$

$$= \frac{\$1,000,000 - \$200,000}{800,000} = \$1.00$$

Historical summaries of EPS must be made comparable by adjusting for changes in capitalization structure (for example, stock splits and stock dividends).

Primary and Fully Diluted EPS

Accounting Principles Board *Opinion No. 15*, "Earnings per Share," stresses that the foregoing simple computations are inadequate when companies have convertible securities, stock options, or other financial instruments that can be exchanged for or converted to common shares. For example, suppose a firm has some convertible preferred stock in its capital structure:

5% convertible preferred stock, $100 par, each share convertible into 2 common shares	100,000 shares
Common stock	1,000,000 shares

The simple EPS computation follows:

Computation of earnings per share:	
Net income	$10,500,000
Preferred dividends	500,000
Net income to common stock	$10,000,000
Earnings per share of common stock:	
$10,000,000 ÷ 1,000,000 shares	$ 10.00

However, note how EPS would be affected if the preferred stock were converted, that is, exchanged for common stock. *Dilution*, a reduction in EPS, will occur. EPS can be calculated *as if* conversion had occurred at the beginning of the fiscal year:

Net income	$10,500,000
Preferred dividends	0
Net income to common stock	$10,500,000
Earnings per share of common stock—assuming conversion:	
$10,500,000 ÷ 1,200,000 shares	$ 8.75

The potential earnings dilution of common stock is $10.00 – $8.75 = $1.25 per share.

APB *Opinion No. 15* requires companies to divide securities that could cause dilution into two categories: (1) common stock equivalents and (2) other sources of dilution. Common stock equivalents are securities whose major value is attributable to their being exchangeable for or convertible to common stock. There are complex rules, beyond the scope of this text, for identifying common stock equivalents. **Primary EPS** is the EPS calculated as if *common stock equivalents* that dilute EPS were converted. **Fully diluted EPS** is an EPS that includes assumed conversion of *all* potentially dilutive securities. Primary EPS is reported on the income statement. If primary and fully diluted EPS differ by more than 3%, both must be reported.

Assume that the convertible preferred stock in our example is not a common stock equivalent. EPS would be presented as follows:

primary EPS EPS calculated as if all common stock equivalents that dilute EPS were converted to common stock.

fully diluted EPS An earnings-per-share figure on common stock that assumes that all potentially dilutive convertible securities and stock options are exchanged for common stock.

Primary earnings per common share	
(Note A)	$10.00
Fully diluted earnings per common	
share (Note B)	$ 8.75

Note A: Per share data are based on the average number of common shares outstanding during each year, after recognition of the dividend requirements on the 5% preferred stock.

Note B: Per share data based on the assumption that the outstanding preferred stock is converted into common shares at the beginning of the year, reflecting the 200,000 shares issuable on conversion and eliminating the preferred dividend requirements.

■ DISCLOSURE OF NONRECURRING ITEMS

Security analysts evaluate the prospects of the firm relative to the future. Therefore it is very important to distinguish the elements of the current financial statements that reflect recurring aspects of the firm from those that represent one-time events or items that will not continue. These items fall into three major categories: special items, extraordinary items, and discontinued operations. Each category is explained briefly.

Special Items

special items
Expenses that are
large enough and
unusual enough to
warrant separate
disclosure.

Special items, which are large and somewhat unusual, represent a category of event that may recur with some frequency. During the 1980s and into the 1990s, the most common special item has been restructuring charges. A restructuring occurs when a firm decides to substantially change the size or scope or location of a part of the business. It often involves relocation, plant closings, and reductions in personnel. The costs will typically be incurred over an extended period of time, often several years, but GAAP requires that the total costs be estimated and recorded when the plan is made. In 1994 the FASB and the SEC acted to assure that restructuring changes did not include costs that will benefit future periods. Specifically they cannot include relocation and training costs for people who will continue to work for the firm. These are properly matched to future revenues. Disclosure occurs by reporting the cost as a separate line item among operating expenses, with discussion of the plan in the footnotes. The following example is condensed from the AT&T 1991 annual report:

AT&T and
Subsidiaries
Consolidated
Statements of
Income
Year Ended
December 31
(dollars in millions)

	1991
Sales and revenues	$63,089
Costs	38,825
Gross margin	24,264
Operating expenses	
Selling, general, and administrative expenses	16,220
Research and development expenses	3,114
Provision for business restructuring (D)	**3,572**
Total operating expenses	22,906
Operating income	1,358
Other income—net	977
Income before income taxes	883
Provision for income taxes	361
Net income	$ 522

(D) Business Restructuring and Other Charges
The 1991 charges were recorded as a $3,572 provision for business restructuring, $501 of selling, general and administrative expenses, $123 as cost of products and systems, and the remainder as other costs and expenses, including other income—net. The provision for business restructuring includes the estimated costs associated with force reductions and relocations, facility consolidations, contractual obligations, including lease buyouts, and other restructuring activities.

How would an analyst use this information to project future earnings? Since a restructuring of such magnitude is rare, the analyst might argue that the expense of $3,572 is nonrecurring. We should, then, adjust net earnings for the special item to make predictions and to better evaluate trends. However, the special item decreased the income tax provision. If we assume a 40% tax rate, the special item reduced taxable income by $3,572 and therefore reduced the tax provision by 40% of $3,572, or $1,429. The special item's after-tax effect would be $3,572 − (.40 × 3,572) = $2,143 million. In estimating future net income the analyst would add back $2,143 million to reported net income of $522 million and estimate the sustainable level at approximately $2,665 million. This proposed adjustment proved reasonable, even conservative. AT&T did not record additional special items in the next three years and net income reached $4,710 million in 1994.

Notice that because special items are reported with other expenses, they are reported before tax. Taxable income is thus reduced and income tax expense is affected. The next two segregated items discussed in this chapter, extraordinary items and discontinued operations, are more explicitly segregated in the financial statements. They are reported below income from continuing operations, and their income tax effects are calculated separately and reported separately, either parenthetically or in the footnotes. Exhibit 15-11 provides an example.

Extraordinary Items

The FASB and SEC insist that, with three exceptions, all items of revenue, expense, gain, and loss recognized during the period be shown in the current income statement. The three exceptions are: (1) correction of errors, such as the failure to recognize depreciation in a previous period, (2) tax effects of preacquisition loss carryforwards of purchased subsidiaries, and (3) specified foreign currency translation adjustments. In contrast, in earlier years, many special or *extraordinary items* were shown in the Statement of Retained Income and never appeared as a part of the computation of net income or EPS for any year. Today they are listed in a special section of the income statement and are included in net income.

Exhibit 15-11	Income from continuing operations before income taxes		$ 50
	Deduct applicable income taxes		20
Illustrated Partial Income Statement (in millions, data assumed)	Income from continuing operations		$ 30
	Discontinued operations (Note _____):		
	Income from operations of discontinued Division X (less applicable income taxes of $4)	$ 6	
	Loss on disposal of Division X, including provision of $3 for operating losses during phase-out period (less applicable income taxes of $6)	(9)	(3)
	Income before extraordinary items		$ 27
	Add extraordinary items:		
	Loss from earthquake (less applicable income taxes of $2)	(3)	
	Gain from early extinguishment of debt (less applicable income taxes of $8)	12	9
	Net income		$ 36
	Per share amounts (in dollars), assuming 4 million shares of common stock outstanding:		
	Income from continuing operations		$7.50
	Loss on discontinued operations		(.75)
	Income before extraordinary items		$6.75
	Extraordinary items		2.25
	Net income		$9.00

Only the following items are *excluded* from the determination of net income:

a. Charges or credits resulting from transactions in the company's own capital stock.
b. Transfers to and from accounts properly designated as appropriated retained earnings (such as general purpose contingency reserves or provisions for replacement costs of fixed assets).

Extraordinary items that affect net income are segregated and reported net of tax, as in Exhibit 15-11.

Through the years, the definition of extraordinary items has been narrowed considerably. Accounting Principles Board *Opinion No. 30* concluded that an event or transaction should be presumed to be an ordinary and usual activity of the reporting entity, and hence includable in income before extraordinary items, unless the evidence clearly supports its classification as an extraordinary item as defined in *Opinion No. 30*. **Extraordinary items** result from events that must have both an *unusual nature* and an *infrequency of occurrence*. Therefore writedowns of receivables and inventories are ordinary items, as are gains or losses on the sale or abandonment of fixed assets. The effects of a strike and many foreign currency revaluations are also ordinary items. *Opinion No. 30* specifically states that casualties such as an earthquake or government expropriation or prohibition are examples of events that are likely to qualify as extraordinary items.

extraordinary items
Items that are unusual in nature and infrequent in occurrence that are shown separately, net of tax, in the income statement.

In an average year, fewer than 10% of major U.S. companies report an extraordinary item; fewer than 5% have an extraordinary item greater than 10% of their net income. Most of the extraordinary items arise from extinguishment of debt as shown in the following extract from the 1994 income statement of Spectrum Control, Inc. (in thousands).

Income before extraordinary item	$ 982
Gain on extinguishment of debt, net of applicable income taxes	4,012
Net income	$4,994

A tragic illustration of an extraordinary charge was caused by criminal tampering with Tylenol capsules. The manufacturer, Johnson & Johnson, reported the following on its income statement (in millions):

Earnings before extraordinary charge	$146.5
Extraordinary charge—costs associated with the withdrawal	
of TYLENOL capsules (less applicable tax relief of $50.0)	50.0
Net earnings	$ 96.5

Discontinued Operations

discontinued operations The termination of a business segment reported separately, net of tax, in the income statement.

Discontinued operations involve the termination of a segment of the business, not just a single plant or location. *Opinion No. 30* states that the results of continuing operations should be reported separately from *discontinued operations*, although both must be reported on the income statement. Moreover, any gain or loss from the disposal of a segment of a business should be reported in conjunction with the related results of discontinued operations and not as an extraordinary item, as Exhibit 15-11 illustrates.

Amounts of applicable income taxes should be disclosed on the face of the income statement or in related notes. Revenues applicable to the discontinued operations should be disclosed separately in the related notes.

In a comparative income statement, the income or loss of the discontinued segment's operations should be condensed and reclassified from continuing operations to discontinued operations for both years. In this way, the income from continuing operations is placed on a comparable basis.

The CSX income statement for 1990, 1992, and 1994 on page 706 combines segment disclosures and a restructuring charge. Discontinued operations are shown separately, net of tax.

Financial presentations such as those in Exhibit 15-11 and the CSX Corporation example are often criticized as being unnecessarily complex. However, the financial results of an entity are often produced by a variety of complicated forces. Consequently, the simplifying of innately complex data is not easy. Indeed, too much condensation and summarization may be undesirable.

■ EFFICIENT MARKETS AND INVESTOR DECISIONS

efficient capital market One in which market prices "fully reflect" all information available to the public.

Much recent research in accounting and finance has concentrated on whether the stock markets are "efficient." An **efficient capital market** is one in which market prices "fully reflect" all information available to the public. Therefore searching for "underpriced" securities in such a market would be fruitless unless an investor has information that is not generally available. If the real-world markets are indeed efficient, a relatively inactive approach would be an appropriate investment strategy for most investors. The hallmarks of this approach are risk control, high diversification, and low turnover of securities. The role of accounting information would mainly be in identifying the different degrees of risk among various stocks so that investors can maintain desired levels of risk and diversification.

Objective 8

Explain the importance of efficient markets to accounting disclosures.

Research in finance and accounting during the past twenty years has reinforced the idea that financial ratios and other data such as reported earnings provide inputs to predictions of such economic phenomena as financial failure or earnings growth. Furthermore, many ratios are used simultaneously rather than one at a time for such predictions. Above all, the research has shown that accounting reports are only one source of information and that in the aggregate the market is not fooled by companies that choose the least-conservative accounting policies. In sum, the market as a whole sees through attempts by companies to gain favor through the choice of accounting policies that tend to boost immediate income. Thus there is evidence that the stock markets may indeed be relatively "efficient," at least in their reflection of most accounting data. However, the stock market crash of October 1987 and other reported "anomalies" prevent unqualified endorsement of stock market efficiency.

Suppose you are the chief executive officer of Company A. Reported earnings are $4 per share and the stock price is $40. You are contemplating changing your method of depreciation for investor-reporting purposes from accelerated to straight-line. Your competitors use straight-line. You think the Company A stock price unjustifiably suffers in comparison with other companies in the same industry.

CSX Corporation
and Subsidiaries
Consolidated
Statement of
Earnings (millions of
dollars, except per
share amounts)

	Years Ended December 31,		
	1994	**1992**	**1990**
Operating Revenue			
Transportation	$ 9,410	$ 8,550	$ 7,947
Non-Transportation	198	184	258
Total	9,608	8,734	8,205
Operating Expense			
Transportation	8,232	7,644	7,195
Non-Transportation	144	125	142
Productivity/Restructuring Charge	—	699	53
Total	8,376	8,468	7,390
Earnings (Loss)			
Operating Income	1,232	266	815
Other Income	55	3	41
Interest Expense	281	276	319
Earnings (Loss) from Continuing Operations before Income Taxes	1,006	(7)	537
Income Tax Expense	354	(27)	172
Earnings from Continuing Operations	652	20	365
Discontinued Operations, Net of Income Taxes:			
Earnings (Loss) from Energy Segment			(1)
Gain on Disposition of Energy Segment Assets			52
Net Earnings	$ 652	$ 20	$ 416
Per Common Share			
Earnings Per Share:			
From Continuing Operations	$ 6.23	$ .19	$ 3.63
From Discontinued Operations:			
Earnings (Loss) from Energy Segment			(.01)
Gain on Disposition of Energy Segment Assets			.53
Earnings Per Share	$ 6.23	$ .19	$ 4.15
Average Common Shares Outstanding (thousands)	104,652	102,907	98,252
Cash Dividends Paid Per Common Share	$ 1.76	$ 1.52	$ 1.40

If straight-line depreciation is adopted by Company A, reported earnings will be $5 instead of $4 per share. Would the stock price rise accordingly from $40 to $50? No, the empirical research on these issues indicates that the stock price would remain at $40 (all other things equal).

Remember that the market is efficient only with respect to *publicly available* information. Therefore accounting issues that deal with the disclosure of new information are important, but concerns about the format for reporting already available data are less important. William Beaver has commented on the implications of market efficiency for accounting regulators:

> Many reporting issues are trivial and do not warrant an expenditure of FASB resources. The properties of such issues are twofold: (1) There is essentially no difference in cost to the firm of reporting either method. (2) There is essentially no cost to statement users in adjusting from one method to the other. In such cases, there is a simple solution. Report one method, with sufficient footnote disclosure to permit adjustment to the other, and let the market interpret implications of the data for security prices.
>
> The FASB should shift its resources to those controversies where there is non-trivial additional cost to the firms or to investors in order to obtain certain types of information (for example, replacement cost accounting for depreciable assets). Whether such information should be a required part of reporting standards is a substantive issue.[1]

Be aware also that accounting statements are not the only source of financial information about companies. Some alternative sources were listed earlier in the chapter on page 674. However, financial statement information may be more directly related to the item of interest, and it may be more reliable, lower-cost, or more timely than information from alternative sources.

The research described above concentrates on the effects of accounting on investors in the aggregate. Individual investors must either incur the costs of conducting careful analyses or delegate that chore to professional analysts. In any event, intelligent analysis cannot be accomplished without an understanding of the assumptions and limitations of financial statements, including the presence of various alternative accounting methods.

■ FOREIGN-CURRENCY ISSUES

Objective 9

Explain some effects on financial statements from translating foreign currencies.

foreign-currency exchange rates The number of units of one currency that can be exchanged for one unit of another currency.

Today, companies conduct business in various countries and so must learn to do business using different currencies. Two problems arise. One problem is accounting for day-to-day transactions that occur in foreign currencies. Another problem is consolidating a subsidiary that exists in another country and does its own accounting in the currency of that country.

These issues are important because of fluctuating **foreign-currency exchange rates.** The foreign-currency exchange rate specifies how many units of one currency are required to obtain one unit of another currency. Recently, the conversion rate of Japanese yen into U.S. dollars has been approximately $.0111. This means that one yen buys 1.11 cents. The relation could be expressed as the conversion rate of U.S. dollars into Japanese yen, which would be ¥90. If conversion rates were constant, no accounting problems would arise, but the rates often change significantly. Forty years ago, the conversion rate of dollars into yen was ¥360. In the spring of 1991 it was around ¥138, and in the spring of 1995 around ¥90. During this time the value of the yen increased relative to the value of the dollar.

---

[1] William H. Beaver, "What Should Be the FASB's Objectives?" *Journal of Accountancy*, Vol. 136, p. 52.

Accounting for Transactions in Foreign Currencies

If a U.S. firm exports an automobile to Japan for $10,000, the sale will often be on credit and *denominated* in yen. The customer owes ¥900,000 (because the conversion rate at the time of the sale was ¥90). The U.S. firm will record the sale in dollars, and the receivable would be $10,000 on its books. After one month, the buyer remits ¥900,000 to the seller. Suppose the yen has fallen (or weakened) against the dollar, and the new exchange rate is ¥92. When the yen is converted to dollars the seller ends up with only $9,782.61 (¥900,000 / ¥92). The transaction has given rise to a loss of $217.39, which would be recorded as follows:

Cash	$9,782.61	
Loss on currency fluctuation	217.39	
Accounts receivable		$10,000.00

Not surprisingly, the currency exchange rate could move in the other direction and give rise to a gain. Many companies use sophisticated financial transactions to eliminate the effect of currency fluctuations, but these hedging transactions and their accounting are covered in more advanced courses.

Consolidating International Subsidiaries

The previous section dealt with a company in one country doing business with a company in another country. A more complex problem arises in an international parent-subsidiary relationship. Suppose a U.S. company (parent) owns a Japanese company (subsidiary, or sub) doing business in Japan in yen. At the end of the year the parent must consolidate the sub's financial data with its own and create a single set of statements. What exchange rate should be used?

GAAP requires that different exchange rates be used for different elements of the financial statements. Assets and liabilities of the sub are translated at the year-end exchange rate. The common stock account is translated at the historic rate existing when the sub was created. The average exchange rate during the year is used to account for the transactions in the income statement. These translated net income figures annually increase the retained earnings of the parent. Over time, the parent's retained earnings reflect yen translations at different exchange rates. The problem is apparent. If the assets of the sub equal its liabilities plus its owners' equity in yen, and different rates are used to translate assets, liabilities, and equity, then the consolidated balance sheet is forced out of balance. To bring it back in balance a **translation adjustment** is created, which is reported as part of shareholders' equity. Details of computing this translation adjustment are beyond the scope of this text.

The stockholders' equity sections of most multinational firms include foreign-currency translation adjustments. The title and amount of the translation adjustment and total stockholders' equity for some international companies follow:

translation adjustment A contra-account in stockholders' equity that arises when a foreign subsidiary is consolidated.

Company	Account Name	Amount	Total SE
Quaker Oats	Cumulative translation adjustment	(75.4)	446
Kellogg	Currency translation adjustment	(159)	1,808
McDonald's	Foreign currency translation adjustment	(115)	6,885

Summary Problem for Your Review

Problem

Exhibit 15-12 contains a condensed income statement and balance sheet for Gannett Company, Inc., the nation's largest newspaper group with eighty dailies, including *USA Today*.

Required

1. Compute the following ratios: (a) current ratio, (b) quick ratio, (c) average collection period, (d) total debt to stockholders' equity, (e) return on sales, and (f) return on stockholders' equity.
2. Using the 1994 Gannett values provided below and the following Dun & Bradstreet 1994-95 ratios for 503 newspaper companies, assess Gannett's liquidity, solvency, and profitability.

	Current Ratio	Quick Ratio	Average Collection Period	Total Debt to Stockholders' Equity	Net Income on Sales	Net Income on Stockholders' Equity
Upper quartile	5.5	4.0	28.1	18.0	9.0	27.4
Median	2.2	1.7	37.6	47.0	4.2	11.8
Lower quartile	1.3	0.9	46.5	151.4	1.0	3.4

Using only the ratios in requirement 1, assess Gannett Company's liquidity, solvency, and profitability.

Solution

Gannett's 1994 ratios are also provided for comparison, although data for their calculation are not provided in the problem.

				1991	1994
1. a.	Current ratio =	$\dfrac{636,101}{443,835}$		= 1.4	1.2
b.	Quick ratio =	$\dfrac{70,673+444,568}{443,835}$		= 1.2	1.1
c.	Average collection period =	$\dfrac{(1/2)(444,568+469,701)\times365}{3,382,035}$		= 49.3	44.7
d.	Total debt to stockholders' equity =	$\dfrac{2,144,593}{1,539,487}$	=	139.3%	103.0%
e.	Return on sales =	$\dfrac{301,649}{3,382,035}$	=	8.9%	12.2%

1991   1994

f. Return on stockholders' equity $= \dfrac{301,649}{(1/2)(1,539,487 + 2,063,077)}$

$= 16.8\%$ 25.0%

Exhibit 15-12	Income Statement	For the Year Ended *December 29, 1991*
Gannett	Revenues	$ 3,382,035
Company, Inc.	Operating expenses	(2,823,088)
(in thousands)	Operating income	558,947
	Interest expense	(71,057)
	Interest and other income	14,859
	Income before income taxes	502,749
	Provision for income taxes	(201,100)
	Net income	$ 301,649

		For the Year Ended	
		December 29,	December 30,
Balance Sheets		1991	1990
Assets			
Current assets:			
Cash and marketable securities		$ 70,673	$ 56,238
Receivables		444,568	469,071
Inventories		51,380	66,525
Prepaid expenses		69,480	76,856
Total current assets		636,101	668,690
Property, plant, and equipment, net		1,484,910	1,472,123
Intangible and other assets		1,563,069	1,685,332
Total assets		$ 3,684,080	$3,826,145
Liabilities and Shareholders' Equity			
Total current liabilities		$ 443,835	$ 500,203
Long-term liabilities		1,700,758	1,262,865
Total liabilities		2,144,593	1,763,068
Total shareholders' equity		1,539,487	2,063,077
Total liabilities and shareholders' equity		$ 3,684,080	$3,826,145

2. The measures of profitability improved significantly from 1991 to 1994. In 1994 Gannett continued to manage current assets aggressively while reducing the level of debt in the capital structure. The increased profitability in 1994 was caused by a number of factors including the increased popularity of *USA Today*, "the nation's newspaper." In 1994, Gannett was below the median on liquidity measures and more leveraged than the median. However, profitability was very high.

Highlights to Remember

Financial and operating information is available from many sources, including daily newspapers. Various regulations in the United States require the issuance of annual reports and govern their content. In addition, publicly traded companies must disclose particular information by filing 10-K, 8-K, and other forms with the SEC on a periodic basis.

Financial information is provided to aid investors in assessing the risk and return of a potential investment. Investors in debt are particularly concerned about the solvency and liquidity of the issuer, while equity investors are more interested in profitability.

Trend analysis is a form of financial statement analysis that concentrates on changes in the financial statements through time. It involves comparing relationships for a period of years or quarters. Common-size financial statements are constructed by expressing the elements of the balance sheet as a percentage of total assets and the elements of the income statement as a percentage of total revenue. They enhance the ability to compare one company with another or to conduct a trend analysis over time.

The basic financial ratios allow us to put numbers in perspective. By relating one part of the financial statements to another they facilitate questions such as "Given the change in revenues, was the change in accounts receivable reasonable?" and "Is the company's inventory level, given its size, comparable to industry norms?" The chapter reviews the ratios presented throughout the text.

Liquidity ratios deal with the immediate ability to make payments. Solvency ratios deal with the longer-term ability to meet obligations. Both are often incorporated into debt covenants to ensure lenders' rights. Profitability ratios are used to assess operating efficiency and performance.

Return on equity (ROE) is the most fundamental profitability ratio because it relates income to the shareholder's investment. Return on assets is one of several related elements that focuses on the profitable use of all assets. It can be further divided into the return on sales and the total asset turnover.

Earnings per share (EPS) is a fundamental measure of performance. In this chapter three complexities in calculating this measure were identified and incorporated into the calculation. Since preferred shares receive preference to dividends, their dividends are deducted from earnings in the numerator. Since shares outstanding may change during the year, the denominator is calculated as a weighted average over the year. The presence of options and convertible securities creates a potential to issue new shares as a result of the actions of others. Therefore, EPS is calculated on both a primary and a fully diluted basis.

Special items, extraordinary items, and discontinued operations are three categories of unusual and possibly nonrecurring items. Separately disclosing these allows analysts to refine forecasts of future performance based on current operations. Special items are included with other expenses but identified separately. Extraordinary items and discontinued items are shown separately below earnings from operations and net of their individual tax effects.

Efficient markets refer to the probability that the actions of analysts to carefully evaluate disclosures lead to their incorporating all available information into the market price for securities. Evidence suggests this is substantially, but not totally, true. This fact means that complete disclosure is more important than the form of the disclosure. For example, investors are unlikely to be confused in their efforts to price securities by differences in the methods of depreciation or inventory accounting in use.

Multinational companies do business in more than one country. Sometimes they export products produced in the home country to other markets. In this case, transactions with foreign customers are often in the customer's currency, although they are accounted for in the home currency. Exchange-rate fluctuations between the sale date and the collection date give rise to gains or losses, which appear in the seller's earnings statement and affect net earnings. In other cases, foreign subsidiaries manufacture and sell outside the home country. Foreign subsidiaries hold assets, conduct business, and account for it in their own currency. Translation problems arise when the subsidiary's financial statements are translated into the parent's currency for consolidation. In the United States such translations for consolidation give rise to translation adjustments recorded in stockholders' equity with no effect on consolidated net earnings.

Accounting Vocabulary

asset turnover, *p. 694*
bench marks, *p. 688*
capital structure, *p. 696*
capitalization, *p. 696*
capitalization structure, *p. 696*
common-size statement, *p. 680*
component percentages, *p. 680*
cross-sectional comparisons, *p. 688*
discontinued operations, *p. 704*
EBIT, *p. 694*
efficient capital market, *p. 705*
extraordinary items, *p. 704*
financial leverage, *p. 696*

financial statement analysis, *p. 674*
foreign-currency exchange rates, *p. 707*
fully diluted EPS, *p. 701*
gearing, *p. 696*
interest coverage, *p. 699*
leveraging, *p. 696*
long-term solvency, *p. 676*
management's discussion and analysis (MD&A), *p. 681*
operating income percentage on sales, *p. 694*
pretax operating rate of return on total assets, *p. 694*

primary EPS, *p. 701*
pro forma statement, *p. 675*
rate of return on stockholders' equity (ROE), *p. 696*
return on total assets (ROA), *p. 696*
short-term liquidity, *p. 676*
special items, *p. 702*
time-series comparisons, *p. 688*
times interest earned, *p. 699*
total asset turnover, *p. 694*
trading on the equity, *p. 696*
translation adjustment, *p. 708*

Assignment Material

Questions

15-1. Why do decision makers use financial statement analysis?

15-2. In addition to the basic financial statements, what information is usually presented in a

company's annual report?

15-3. Give three sources of information for investors besides accounting information.

15-4. "Financial statements report on *history*. Therefore they are not useful to creditors and investors who want to predict *future* returns and risk." Do you agree? Explain?

15-5. How do common-size statements aid comparisons with other companies?

15-6. What information is presented in the "management's discussion and analysis" (MD&A) section of annual reports?

15-7. Name three types of comparisons that are useful in evaluating financial ratios.

15-8. "Ratios are mechanical and incomplete." Explain.

15-9. Ratios are often grouped into four categories. What are the categories?

15-10. What two measures of operating performance are combined to give the pretax operating return on total assets?

15-11. "Trading on the equity means exchanging bonds for stock." Do you agree? Explain.

15-12. "Borrowing is a two-edged sword." Do you agree? Explain.

15-13. Why are companies with heavy debt in relation to ownership capital in greater danger when business conditions sour?

15-14. "The tax law discriminates against preferred stock and in favor of debt." Explain.

15-15. "An efficient capital market is one where securities are traded through stockbrokers." Do you agree? Explain.

15-16. Suppose the president of your company wanted to switch depreciation methods to increase reported net income: "Our stock is 10% below what I think it should be; changing the depreciation method will increase income by 10%, thus getting our share price up to its proper level." How would you respond?

15-17. Evaluate the following quotation from *Forbes*: "If IBM had been forced to expense [the software development cost of] $785 million, its earnings would have been cut by 72 cents a share. With IBM selling at 14 times earnings, expensing the costs might have knocked over $10 off IBM's share price."

15-18. Suppose you wanted to compare the financial statements of Colgate-Palmolive and Procter and Gamble. What concerns might you have in comparing their various ratios?

15-19. Suppose you wanted to evaluate the financial performance of IBM over the last ten years. What factors might affect the comparability of a firm's financial ratios over such a long period of time?

15-20. Suppose you worked for a small manufacturing company and the president said that you must improve your current ratio. Would you interpret this to mean that you should increase it or decrease it? How might you do so?

15-21. Suppose you work for a small local department store that manages its own accounts receivable with a private charge card. Your boss has told you to improve the accounts receivable turnover from 4 to 5 times. How would you go about this? What are the risks in your proposal that might affect the company negatively?

15-22. Would you expect the return on equity to be greater than or less than the return on assets? Explain.

15-23. Suppose the current ratio for your company changed from 2 to 1 to become 1.8 to 1. Would you expect the level of working capital to increase or to decrease? Why?

15-24. Suppose you compared the financial statements of an airline and a grocery store. Which would you expect to have the higher values for the following ratios: debt-to-equity ratio, current ratio, inventory turnover ratio, accounts receivable turnover ratio, and return on equity? Explain.

15-25. As the chief financial officer you have just been presented with a set of comparative ratios for your firm. Which of the following facts would you be likely to view as good news? Why? Consider each one as an independent case. Assume all else is unchanged.
  1. Increase in current ratio.
  2. Decrease in inventory turnover.
  3. Decrease in interest-coverage.
  4. Increase in return on sales.
  5. Increase in the price/earnings ratio.

15-26. Describe a circumstance under which each of the following independent events would be viewed as good news. Explain why. You may take the approach of management or of an investor.
  1. Interest rates have risen.
  2. The company reduced its accounts receivable turnover.
  3. The company created a stock option plan.
  4. The company increased its dividend.
  5. The company increased its inventory turnover.

When might the view of management and of an investor be different?

Exercises

15-27   Rate-of-Return Computations

1. Yokahama Company reported a 4% operating margin on sales, an 8% pretax operating return on total assets, and ¥2 billion of total assets. Compute (a) operating income, (b) total sales, and (c) total asset turnover.

2. Wales Corporation reported £600 million of sales, £32 million of operating income, and a total asset turnover of 4 times. Compute (a) total assets, (b) operating margin percentage on sales, and (c) pretax operating return on total assets.

3. Compare the two companies.

15-28   Common Stock Ratios and Book Value

You may wish to review Chapter 12. The Somar Corporation has outstanding 500,000 shares of 8% preferred stock with a $100 par value and 10.5 million shares of common stock of $1 par value. The current market price of the common is $24, and the latest annual dividend rate is $2 per share. Common treasury stock consists of 500,000 shares costing $7.5 million. The company has $150 million of additional paid-in capital, $15 million of retained income, and a $12 million bond sinking fund. Net income for the current year is $20 million.

Required   Compute the following:

1. Total stockholders' equity.
2. Common price/earnings ratio.
3. Common dividend-yield percentage.
4. Common dividend-payout percentage.
5. Book value per share of common.

15-29   Trading on the Equity

Baker Company has assets of $500 million, bonds payable of $200 million, and stockholders' equity of $300 million. The bonds bear interest at 10% per annum. Charlie Company, which is in the same industry, has assets of $500 million and stockholders' equity of $500 million. Prepare a comparative tabulation of Charlie Company and Baker Company for each of three years. Show income before interest, interest, net income, return on assets, and return on stockholders' equity. The income before interest for both companies was: Year 1, $50 million; Year 2, $25 million; and Year 3, $75 million. Ignore income taxes. Show all monetary amounts in millions of dollars. Comment on the results.

15-30   Using Debt or Equity

The Logan Corporation is trying to decide whether to raise additional capital of $30 million through a new issue of 12% long-term debt or of 10% preferred stock. The income tax rate is 40%. Compute net income less dividends for these alternatives, assuming that income before interest expense and taxes is $12 million. Show all dollar amounts in thousands. What is the after-tax cost of capital for debt and for preferred stock expressed in percentages? Comment on the comparison. Compute times interest earned for the first year.

15-31   EPS and Times Interest Earned Computations

Eastern Shipping Co. has outstanding 500,000 shares of common stock, $4 million of 8% preferred stock, and $8 million of 10% bonds payable. Its income tax rate is 40%.

1. Assume the company has $6 million of income before interest and taxes. Compute (a) EPS and (b) number of times bond interest has been earned.

2. Assume $4 million of income before interest and taxes, and make the same computations.

15-32 Debt Versus Preferred Stock

Southwestern Bell Corporation provides telephone services to Arkansas, Kansas, Missouri, Oklahoma, and Texas. In 1994, the company had operating income before taxes and interest of $2,790.3 million. Interest expense was $480.2 million on long-term debt of $5,848.3 million. The company has no preferred stock outstanding, although 10 million shares are authorized.

Suppose $4,000 million of preferred stock with a dividend rate of 12% had been issued instead of $4,000 million of the long-term debt. The debt had an effective interest rate of 8.21%. Assume that the income tax rate is 40%.

Required Compute net income and net income attributable to common shareholders under (a) the current situation with $5,848.3 million of long-term debt and no preferred stock, and (b) the assumed situation with $4,000 million of preferred stock and $1,848.3 million of long-term debt.

Problems

15-33 Common-Size Statements

(Alternate is 15-40.) SkyMart and Bullseye are both discount store chains. Condensed income statements and balance sheets for the two companies are shown in Exhibit 15-13. Amounts are in thousands.

Required
1. Prepare common-sized statements for SkyMart and Bullseye for 19X9.
2. Compare the financial performance for 19X9 and financial position at the end of 19X9 for SkyMart with the performance and position of Bullseye. Use only the statements prepared in requirement 1.

15-34 Financial Ratios

(Alternate is 15-36.) This problem uses the same data as 15-33, but it can be solved independently. SkyMart and Bullseye are both discount store chains. Condensed income statements and balance sheets for the two companies are shown in Exhibit 15-13. Amounts are in thousands.

Additional information:

* Cash dividends per share: SkyMart, $2.00; Bullseye, $1.50
* Market price per share: SkyMart, $30; Bullseye, $40
* Average shares outstanding for 19X9: SkyMart, 15 million; Bullseye, 7 million

Required
1. Compute the following ratios for both companies for 19X9: (a) current, (b) quick, (c) average collection period, (d) inventory turnover, (e) total debt to total assets, (f) total debt to total equity, (g) return on stockholders' equity, (h) gross profit rate, (i) return on sales, (j) asset turnover, (k) pretax return on assets, (l) earnings per share, (m) price/earnings, (n) dividend yield, and (o) dividend payout.
2. Compare the liquidity, solvency, profitability, and market price and dividend ratios of SkyMart with those of Bullseye.

15-35 Trend Analysis

Merck & Co., the pharmaceutical company, has frequently been ranked America's most admired company by *Fortune* magazine. The 1993 and 1994 income statements and balance sheets are in Exhibit 15-14. A few categories are slightly condensed.

Required
1. Prepare an income statement and balance sheet for Merck & Co. that has two columns, one showing the amount of change between 1993 and 1994 and the other showing the percentage of change.
2. Identify and discuss the most significant changes between 1993 and 1994.

Exhibit 15-13	Financial Statements for SkyMart and Bullseye

Income statements for the Year
Ended December 31, 19X9

	Skymart	Bullseye
Sales	$875,600	$491,750
Cost of sales	582,360	301,910
Gross profit	293,240	189,840
Operating expenses	174,130	147,160
Operating income	119,110	42,680
Other revenue (expense)	(21,930)	6,270
Pretax income	97,180	48,950
Income tax expense	38,870	19,580
Net income	$ 58,310	$ 29,370

Balance Sheets

	Skymart		Bullseye	
	December 31		December 31	
	19X9	*19X8*	*19X9*	*19X8*
Assets				
Current assets				
Cash	$ 12,100	$ 10,700	$ 8,200	$ 6,900
Marketable securities	5,300	5,300	4,100	3,800
Accounts receivable	36,700	40,100	21,300	20,500
Inventories	155,600	149,400	105,100	106,600
Prepaid expenses	17,100	16,900	8,800	8,400
Total current assets	226,800	222,400	147,500	146,200
Property and equipment, net	461,800	452,300	287,600	273,500
Other assets	14,700	13,900	28,600	27,100
Total assets	$703,300	$688,600	$463,700	$446,800
Liabilities and Stockholders' Equity				
Liabilities				
Current liabilities (summarized)	$ 91,600	$ 93,700	$ 61,300	$ 58,800
Long-term debt	156,700	156,700	21,000	21,000
Total liabilities	248,300	250,400	82,300	79,800
Stockholders' equity	455,000	438,200	381,400	367,000
Total liabilities and stockholders' equity	$703,300	$688,600	$463,700	$446,800

15-36   Financial Ratios
(Alternate is 15-34.) Merck & Co. is the largest company in the health-care industry in the United States. Two recent income statements and balance sheets are in Exhibit 15-14. Additional 1994 data are:

- Cash dividends, $1.20 per share
- Market price per share, $38
- Average common shares outstanding, 1,259,250,000

Required

Compute the following ratios for Merck & Co. for 1994: (a) current, (b) quick, (c) average collection period, (d) total debt to total assets, (e) total debt to total equity, (f) return on stockholders' equity, (g) return on sales, (h) asset turnover, (i) pretax return on assets, (j) earnings per share, (k) price/earnings, (l) dividend yield, and (m) dividend payout. Total debt includes current liabilities, long-term debt, and deferred income taxes and noncurrent liabilities.

Exhibit 15-14

Merck & Co., Inc. and Subsidiaries Consolidated Statement of Income (in millions)

Years Ended December 31	1994	1993
SALES	$14,969.8	$10,498.2
Costs, Expenses, and Other		
Materials and production	5,962.7	2,497.6
Marketing and administrative	3,177.5	2,913.9
Research and development	1,230.6	1,172.8
Other (income) expense, net	183.8	811.2
	10,554.6	7,395.5
Income before taxes	4,415.2	3,102.7
Taxes on income	1,418.2	936.5
Net income	$2,997.0	$2,166.2
Earnings Per Share of Common Stock	$2.38	$1.87

Consolidated Balance Sheet

December 31	1994	1993
ASSETS		
Current Assets		
Cash and cash equivalents	$1,604.0	$829.4
Short-term investments	665.7	712.9
Accounts receivable	2,351.5	2,094.3
Inventories	1,660.9	1,641.7
Prepaid expenses and taxes	639.6	456.3
Total current assets	6,921.7	5,734.6
Investments	1,416.9	1,779.9
Property, Plant, and Equipment, at cost		
Land	212.6	212.5
Buildings	2,604.5	2,386.1
Machinery, equipment, and office furnishings	4,029.4	3,769.0
Construction in progress	826.4	805.2
	7,672.9	7,172.8
Less allowance for depreciation	2,376.6	2,278.2
	5296.3	4,894.6
Investments	7,212.3	6,645.5
Other Assets	1,009.4	872.9
	$21,856.6	$19,927.5
LIABILITIES AND STOCKHOLDERS' EQUITY		
Current Liabilities		
Accounts payable and accrued liabilities	$2,715.4	$2,378.3
Loans payable	146.7	1,736.0
Income taxes payable	2,206.5	1,430.4
Dividends payable	380.0	351.0
Total current liabilities	5,448.6	5,895.7

continued

Exhibit 15-14			
Consolidated Balance Sheet (*Continued*)			

Long-term debt		1,145.9	1,120.8
Deferred income taxes and noncurrent liabilities		2,914.3	1,744.9
Minority Interests		1,208.8	1,144.4
Stockholders' Equity			
Common Stock			
Authorized—2,700,000,000 shares			
Issued — 1,483,167,594 shares — 1994		4,667.8	4,576.5
— 1,480,611,247 shares — 1993			
Retained earnings		10,942.0	9,393.2
		15,609.8	13,969.7
Less treasury stock, at cost			
235,341,571 shares—1994			
226,676,597 shares—1993		4,470.8	3,948.0
Total stockholders' equity		11,139.0	10,021.7
		$21,856.6	$19,927.5

15-37   Trend Analysis and Common-Size Statements

Jason Company furnished the following condensed data (in thousands):

	December 31		
	19X3	**19X2**	**19X1**
Cash	$ 25	$ 20	$ 15
Accounts receivable	90	70	50
Merchandise inventory	85	75	65
Prepaid expenses	10	10	10
Land	30	30	30
Building	70	75	80
Equipment	60	50	40
Total assets	$370	$330	$290
Accounts payable	$ 50	$ 40	$ 30
Taxes payable	20	15	10
Accrued expenses payable	15	10	5
Long-term debt	45	45	45
Paid-in capital	150	150	150
Retained income	90	70	50
Total liab. and stk. eq.	$370	$330	$290

	Year Ended December 31	
	19X3	**19X2**
Sales (all on credit)	$800	$750
Cost of goods sold	(440)	(420)
Operating expenses	(300)	(285)
Pretax income	60	45
Income taxes	(20)	(15)
Net income	$ 40	$ 30

Required

1. Prepare a trend analysis for Jason's income statement and balance sheet that compares 19X3 with 19X2.
2. Prepare common-size income statements for 19X3 and 19X2 and balance sheets for December 31, 19X3 and December 31, 19X2 for Jason Company.
3. Comment on Jason Company's performance and position for 19X3 compared with 19X2.

15-38   Financial Ratios

Consider the data for Jason Company in the preceding problem.

Required

1. Compute the following ratios for each of the last two years, 19X2 and 19X3:
   a. Current ratio
   b. Gross profit rate
   c. Percentage of net income to sales
   d. Ratio of total debt to stockholders' equity
   e. Inventory turnover
   f. Percentage of net income to stockholders' equity
   g. Average collection period for accounts receivable
2. For each of the following items, indicate whether the change from 19X2 to 19X3 for Jason Company seems to be favorable or unfavorable, and identify the ratios you computed above that most directly support your answer. The first item below is given as an example.
   a. Gross margin: favorable, b
   b. Return to owners
   c. Ability to pay current debts on time
   d. Collectibility of receivables
   e. Risks of insolvency
   f. Salability of merchandise
   g. Return on sales
   h. Operating success
   i. Overall accomplishment
   j. Future stability of profits
   k. Coordination of buying and selling functions
   l. Screening of risks in granting credit to customers

15-39   Computation of Financial Ratios

The financial statements of the Maxim Co are shown below.

The Maxim Co.
Balance Sheets
(in thousands of dollars)

	December 31	
	19X2	**19X1**
Assets		
Current assets:		
Cash	$ 1,000	$ 1,000
Short-term investments		1,000
Receivables, net	5,000	4,000
Inventories at cost	12,000	9,000
Prepayments	1,000	1,000
Total current assets	$ 19,000	$ 16,000
Plant and equipment, net	22,000	23,000
Total assets	$ 41,000	$ 39,000
Liabilities and Stockholders' Equity		
Current liabilities:		
Accounts payable	$ 10,000	$ 6,000
Accrued expenses payable	500	500

continued

The Maxim Co.
Balance Sheets
(in thousands of
dollars)

(*Continued*)

	December 31	
	19X2	**19X1**
Income taxes payable	1,500	1,500
Total current liabilities	$12,000	$ 8,000
8% bonds payable	$10,000	$10,000
Stockholders' equity:		
Preferred stock, 12%, par value $100 per share	$ 5,000	$ 5,000
Common stock, $10 par value	8,000	8,000
Premium on common stock	4,000	4,000
Unappropriated retained earnings	1,000	3,000
Reserve for plant expansion	1,000	1,000
Total stockholders' equity	$19,000	$21,000
Total liab. and stk. eq.	$41,000	$39,000

The Maxim Co.
Statement of Income
and Reconciliation of
Retained Earnings
for the Year Ended
December 31, 19X2
(in thousands of
dollars)

Sales (all on credit)		$44,000
Cost of goods sold		32,000
Gross profit on sales		$12,000
Other operating expenses:		
Selling expenses	$5,000	
Administrative expenses	2,000	
Depreciation	1,000	8,000
Operating income		$ 4,000
Interest expense		800
Income before income taxes		$ 3,200
Income taxes at 40%		$ 1,280
Net income		$ 1,920
Dividends on preferred stock		600
Net income for common stockholders		$ 1,320
Dividends on common stock		3,320
Net income retained		$ (2,000)
Unappropriated retained earnings, December 31, 19X1		3,000
Unappropriated retained earnings, December 31, 19X2		$ 1,000

Required

Compute the following for the 19X2 financial statements.

1. Pretax return on total assets.
2. Divide your answer to requirement 1 into two components: operating income percentage of sales and total asset turnover.
3. After-tax rate of return on total assets. Be sure to add the *after-tax* interest expense to net income.
4. Rate of return on total stockholders' equity. Did the preferred and common stockholders benefit from the existence of debt? Explain fully.
5. Rate of return on *common* stockholders' equity. This ratio is the amount of net income available for the common stockholders, divided by total stockholders' equity less the par value of preferred stock. Did the common stockholders benefit from the existence of preferred stock? Explain fully.

15-40 Common-Size Statements

(Alternate is 15-33). Exhibit 15-15 contains the slightly condensed income statement and balance sheets of 3M (formerly Minnesota Mining and Manufacturing Company), a multinational company with sales over $7.5 billion in the United States and over $7.5 billion abroad.

Required

1. Prepare common-size statements for 3M for 1993 and 1994.
2. Comment on the changes in component percentages from 1993 to 1994.

15-41 Liquidity Ratios

Exhibit 15-15 contains the slightly condensed income statement and balance sheets of Minnesota Mining and Manufacturing Company (3M), maker of Scotch brand tapes.

Required

1. Compute the following ratios for 1994: (a) current, (b) quick, (c) average collection period, and (d) inventory turnover.
2. Assess 3M's liquidity compared with the following industry averages:

Current ratio	1.8 times
Quick ratio	1.0 times
Average collection period	41.6 days
Inventory turnover	4.5 times

Exhibit 15-15

Minnesota Mining and Manufacturing Company (3M) and Subsidiaries Consolidated Statement of Income for the Years Ended December 31, 1994 and 1993 (amounts in millions, except per-share data)

	1994	1993
Net Sales	$15,079	$ 14,020
Operating Expenses		
Cost of goods sold	8,995	8,529
Selling, general, and administrative expenses	3,833	3,535
Total	12,828	12,064
Operating Income	2,251	1,956
Other Income and Expense		
Interest expense	87	50
Investment and other income—net	10	(96)
Total	97	(46)
Income before Income Taxes	2,154	2,002
Provision for Income Taxes	832	739
Net income	$ 1,322	$ 1,263
Average Shares Outstanding	423	434

Consolidated Balance Sheet as of December 31, 1994 and 1993 (dollars in millions)

	1994	1993
Assets		
Current Assets		
Cash and cash equivalents	$ 297	$ 274
Other securities	194	382
Accounts receivable—net	2,948	2,610
Inventories	2,763	2,401
Other current assets	726	696
Total current assets	6,928	6,363
Investments	536	455
Property, Plant, and Equipment—net	5,054	4,830
Other Assets	978	549
Total	$13,496	$12,197

continued

Consolidated Balance
Sheet as of
December 31, 1994
and 1993
(dollars in millions)

(*Continued*)

	1994	1993
Liabilities and Stockholders' Equity		
Current Liabilities		
Accounts payable	$ 996	$ 878
Payroll	328	331
Income taxes	110	290
Short-term debt	917	697
Other current liabilities	1,254	1,086
Total current liabilities	3,605	3,282
Other Liabilities	2,126	1,607
Long-Term Debt	1,031	796
Stockholders' Equity—net	6,734	6,512
Shares outstanding—1994: 419,793,702; 1993: 429,478,638		
Total	$13,496	$12,197

15-42   Solvency Ratios

Exhibit 15-15 contains the income statement and balance sheets of Minnesota Mining and Manufacturing Company (3M), a diversified manufacturing company with operations in the United States and fifty-one other countries.

Required

1. Compute the following ratios for 1994: (a) total debt to total assets and (b) total debt to total equity.
2. Assess 3M's solvency compared with the following industry averages:

Total debt to total assets	57.4%
Total debt to total shareholders' equity	115.3%

15-43   Profitability Ratios

Exhibit 15-15 contains the income statement and balance sheets of Minnesota Mining and Manufacturing Company (3M), a technology company with over one hundred technologies. A corporate objective is for significant sales to be generated by new products introduced in the last five years.

Required

1. Compute the following ratios for 1994: (a) return on stockholders' equity, (b) gross profit rate, (c) return on sales, (d) asset turnover, (e) pretax return on assets, and (f) earnings per share.
2. Assess 3M's profitability in 1994 compared with the following industry averages:

Return on stockholders' equity	12%
Gross profit rate	32%
Return on sales	3.2%
Asset turnover	2.66 times
Pretax return on assets	7.7%
Earnings per share	$1.94

15-44   Market Price and Dividend Ratios

Exhibit 15-15 contains the income statement and balance sheets of Minnesota Mining and Manufacturing Company (3M), a leader in bringing new technology-based products to the market. In 1994, 3M paid cash dividends of $1.76 per share and the market price was $50 per share.

Required

1. Compute the following ratios for 1994: (a) price/earnings, (b) dividend yield, and (c) dividend payout.
2. Assess 3M's market price and dividend ratios compared with the following industry averages:

Price earnings	16.0
Dividend yield	2.8%
Dividend payout	46%

15-45   Income Ratios and Asset Turnover

The following data are from the 1994 and 1990 annual reports of McDonald's Corporation, operator of over ten thousand McDonald's restaurants in fifty countries:

	1994	1990
Rate of return on stockholders' equity	19.40%	20.50%
Operating income percentage on sales	26.93%	24.04%
Total asset turnover	.65	.67
Average total assets	$12,814 million	$9,921 million
Interest expense (net)	$ 355 million	$ 413 million
Income tax expense	$ 662 million	$ 444 million

Required

1. Complete the following condensed income statement for 1994. Round to the nearest million.

	1994
Sales	$?
Operating expenses	?
Operating income	$?
Interest expense (net)	?
Pretax income	$?
Income tax expense	?
Net income	$?

2. Compute the following:
   a.   Pretax operating rate of return on total assets
   b.   Rate of return on sales
   c.   Average stockholders' equity
3. Compare the values for 1994 to 1990.

15-46   Income Ratios and Asset Turnover

Tribune Company, publisher of the *Chicago Tribune* and owner of the Chicago Cubs baseball team, included the following data in its 1991 annual report to stockholders (in millions of dollars expect percentages):

Net income	$ 242
Total assets:	
Beginning of year	2,536
End of year	2,785
Net income as a percent of:	
Total revenue	11.2%
Average stockholders' equity	19.9%

Required   Using only the above data, compute

1. Net income as a percentage of average assets
2. Total revenues
3. Average stockholders' equity
4. Asset turnover, using two different approaches
5. Compare the 1994 net income percentages of 11.2 and 19.9 to their 1991 values of 7.0% and 17.6%

15-47   Foreign-Currency Translation

British Petroleum (BP) prepares its accounts in British pounds. Since BP has U.S. shareholders, it provides supplemental data for U.S. shareholders by translating its financial statements into U.S. dollars. One of your classmates said that BP's U.S. dollar financial statements would be easy to use because there would be no foreign-currency translation adjustments included in owners' equity. The reason given was that all of the income statement and balance sheet amounts would be translated at year-end values, and foreign-currency translation adjustments arise when various income statement and balance sheet amounts are translated at different exchange rates. Comment on your classmate's assertion.

15-48   Industry Identification

(Cristi Gleason adapted.) Common size financial statements and selected ratio values are provided in Exhibit 15-16 for nine companies from the following industries:

1. Airplane manufacturer
2. Department store
3. Real Estate Investment Trust (REIT)
4. Telecommunications
5. Pharmaceutical
6. Newspaper
7. Grocery
8. Consumer Products
9. Athletic Franchise

Required   Use your knowledge of general business practices to match the industries to the company data.

15-49

(Cristi Gleason adapted.) Common size financial statements and selected ratio values are provided in Exhibit 15-17 for nine companies from the following industries:

1. Department Store
2. Telecommunications
3. Pharmaceutical
4. Petroleum
5. Newspaper
6. Grocery

7. Consumer Products
8. Utility
9. Home Building

Required   Use your knowledge of general business practices to match the industries to the company data.

15-50   Special Items: Litigation

In 1991 Polaroid's financial statements included the effect of patent infringement litigation against Eastman Kodak that began in 1976. Exhibit 15-17 includes an excerpt from Polaroid's footnote 14, which explains the litigation, and an excerpt from Polaroid's Financial Summary.

Required   Use the information in Exhibit 15-17 to respond to the following questions, assuming a 40% tax rate.

1. How would the litigation settlement have been shown in the 1991 Consolidated Statement of Earnings?
2. What disclosure would you argue was appropriate during the years 1976 through 1990 regarding this litigation?
3. The majority of the proceeds of the litigation settlement went to retire preferred stock, to repay debt, and to acquire treasury shares. Estimate the return on average common stockholders' equity for 1992 assuming that earnings from ongoing operations after tax, exclusive of the special item, are very similar to 1991.

Exhibit 15-16   (for Problem 15-48) (*Columns may not add due to rounding.*)

	A	B	C	D	E	F	G	H	I
	%	%	%	%	%	%	%	%	%
Balance Sheet									
Cash & Marketable Securities	1.52	5.15	12.31	58.58	0.58	8.36	0.44	1.39	10.40
Current Receivables	36.11	12.65	7.75	11.49	25.72	10.34	0.23	3.02	12.20
Inventories	4.58	6.68	23.20	0.00	23.30	1.20	0.00	26.19	11.27
Other Current Assets	5.23	2.64	5.26	7.16	2.24	2.25	0.90	2.25	5.25
Total Current Assets	47.45	27.31	48.52	77.23	51.84	22.15	1.57	32.85	39.11
Net Property, Plant, & Equip.	27.80	30.41	31.69	2.47	40.82	24.24	94.16	63.76	39.26
Other Non-current Assets	24.75	42.28	19.79	20.30	7.35	53.60	4.27	3.39	21.63
Total Assets	100.00	100.00	100.00	100.00	100.00	100.00	100.00	100.00	100.00
Current Liabilities	39.02	39.08	31.81	22.63	20.01	16.09	6.38	30.25	31.49
Long Term Liabilities	38.37	24.00	23.00	89.84	36.34	17.49	40.80	23.15	33.93
Owners' Equity	22.61	36.92	45.19	-12.46	43.65	66.41	52.82	46.60	34.59
Total Liabilities & Owners' Eq	100.00	100.00	100.00	100.00	100.00	100.00	100.00	100.00	100.00
Income Statement									
Revenues	100.00	100.00	100.00	100.00	100.00	100.00	100.00	100.00	100.00
Cost of Sales	59.02	29.41	76.63	30.44	68.51	53.38	29.23	74.68	57.28
Gross Profit	40.98	70.59	23.37	69.56	31.49	46.62	70.77	25.32	42.72
Interest expense	1.00	1.82	0.59	6.60	1.91	0.35	16.66	0.52	1.59
Research & Development	4.14	15.71	7.77	0.00	0.00	0.00	0.00	0.00	0.00
Selling, General, & Admin.	20.77	16.91	5.14	30.87	15.91	24.18	3.65	17.24	27.16
Other Expenses (Income)	–0.31	–2.92	–0.56	–16.84	0.00	–1.09	–0.93	0.09	0.82

Exhibit 15-16   (for Problem 15-48) (*Continued*)

	A	B	C	D	E	F	G	H	I
	%	%	%	%	%	%	%	%	%
Depreciation & Amortization	5.38	7.57	5.21	16.63	3.06	5.41	14.52	1.90	3.74
Income taxes	3.74	8.99	1.31	3.62	4.21	7.26	0.00	2.20	3.75
Net Income	6.27	22.52	3.90	28.68	6.40	10.51	36.88	3.37	7.30

Ratios

	A	B	C	D	E	F	G	H	I
Current Ratio	1.22	0.70	1.53	3.41	2.59	1.38	0.25	1.09	1.24
Long-Term Debt as % of Equity	63.38	39.69	26.84	−467.67	69.53	4.46	31.16	30.35	56.39
Return on Sales	6.27	22.52	3.90	28.68	6.58	10.51	36.88	3.37	7.30
Return on Assets	6.34	10.66	4.08	26.96	8.56	10.22	6.28	11.58	8.76
Return on Equity	30.10	25.92	9.16	−116.06	20.12	15.32	10.18	26.02	27.17
Inventory Turnover	12.93	1.62	3.99	INF	3.96	46.82	INF	9.76	5.98
Times Interest Earned	11.05	17.36	9.79	5.89	6.54	52.33	3.21	11.92	7.94

Exhibit 15-17   (for Problem 15-49) (*Columns may not add due to rounding.*)

	A	B	C	D	E	F	G	H	I
	%	%	%	%	%	%	%	%	%
Balance Sheet									
Cash & Marketable Securities	13.86	3.71	1.28	1.67	1.32	0.00	1.21	1.57	3.54
Current Receivables	13.85	14.52	15.73	18.30	7.90	3.87	2.94	0.00	17.09
Inventories	0.00	10.78	7.95	19.23	0.97	2.48	22.62	34.90	11.62
Other Current Assets	2.16	11.20	1.96	2.73	2.93	0.69	1.85	0.67	3.20
Total Current Assets	29.87	40.20	26.91	41.93	13.12	7.04	28.63	37.15	35.46
Net Property, Plant, & Equip.	55.35	48.14	61.39	43.22	36.93	84.64	49.91	1.41	32.37
Other Non-current Assets	14.78	11.66	11.69	14.86	49.95	8.31	21.47	61.45	32.18
Total Assets	100.00	100.00	100.00	100.00	100.00	100.00	100.00	100.00	100.00
Current Liabilities	19.17	46.90	32.30	21.91	14.38	9.35	36.31	29.84	24.90
Long-Term Liabilities	25.82	16.70	26.43	48.69	36.37	50.64	50.87	51.85	45.43
Owners' Equity	55.02	36.40	41.27	29.40	49.25	40.02	12.82	18.31	29.68
Total Liabilities & Owners' Eq	100.00	100.00	100.00	100.00	100.00	100.00	100.00	100.00	100.00
Income Statement									
Revenues	100.00	100.00	100.00	100.00	100.00	100.00	100.00	100.00	100.00
Cost of Sales	51.85	20.58	54.41	61.71	53.56	32.11	72.80	76.81	51.57
Gross Profit	48.15	79.42	45.59	38.29	46.44	67.89	27.20	23.19	46.43
Interest expense	1.15	1.21	0.68	3.15	1.19	5.28	1.42	6.39	1.14
Research & Development	0.00	13.21	0.77	0.00	0.00	0.00	0.00	0.00	0.00
Selling, General, & Admin.	28.42	35.89	8.09	27.25	37.48	23.03	21.19	11.79	31.50
Other Expenses (Income)	0.17	−0.43	27.00	0.50	−8.66	9.57	−0.15	1.05	1.09
Depreciation & Amortization	8.82	3.38	4.60	3.40	0.00	13.35	2.09	1.56	3.10
Income taxes	3.64	6.25	2.85	1.73	7.37	6.04	1.11	0.91	3.95
Net Income	5.96	19.80	1.60	2.26	9.05	10.63	1.53	1.49	7.65

Exhibit 15-17   (for Problem 15-49) *(Continued)*

	A	B	C	D	E	F	G	H	I
	%	%	%	%	%	%	%	%	%
Ratios									
Current Ratio	1.56	0.86	0.83	1.91	0.91	0.75	0.79	1.24	1.42
Long Term Debt as % of Equity	33.29	11.80	27.49	124.44	30.64	75.70	314.43	274.09	96.08
Return on Sales	5.96	19.80	1.62	2.26	9.05	10.63	1.53	1.49	7.65
Return on Assets	5.75	21.34	2.62	1.90	6.72	4.79	4.75	1.22	9.75
Return on Equity	11.59	58.42	6.28	6.34	13.56	12.27	46.69	8.08	31.37
Inventory Turnover	INF	2.20	9.83	2.88	32.45	5.66	10.05	2.33	5.62
Times Interest Earned	9.37	22.59	8.98	2.26	14.63	4.16	2.91	1.36	11.15

15-51   MD&A and Ethics

If certain conditions are met, the SEC requires companies to disclose information about future events that are reasonably likely to materially affect the firm's operations. Many companies are understandably reluctant to disclose such information. After all, positive predictions may not materialize and negative predictions may unduly alarm the investors. What ethical considerations should a company's managers consider when deciding what prospective information to disclose in the MD&A section of the annual report?

15-52   Wal-Mart Annual Report

Use the Wal-Mart financial statements and notes in Appendix A to respond to the following questions.

Required

1. Calculate return on common shareholders' equity for 1995. Compare it to the values for 1988 and 1984 (both were 32%).
2. Calculate inventory turnover for 1995 and compare it to the value for 1988 of 5.25 and for 1984 of 5.30.
3. Calculate debt-to-total-assets for 1995. Compare it to the values for 1988 of .560 and for 1984 of .554.

15-53   Compact D from Disclosure

Use the Compact D software to respond to the following. Choose two companies in each of two industries.

Required

Calculate the return on assets, return on equity, and return on sales for each of the companies. Compare and contrast the two companies in each industry and the averages for each industry.

16

Financial Statements: Conceptual Framework and Income Measurement

Learning Objectives

After studying this chapter, you should be able to

1   Describe the FASB's conceptual framework.

2   Identify the qualities that make information valuable.

3   Present examples of accounting standards in other countries that differ from those in the United States.

4   Explain how identical companies can report different net incomes because of their choice of accounting methods.

5   Describe the major differences between financial capital and physical capital.

6   Explain and illustrate four different ways of measuring income: (1) historical cost/nominal dollars, (2) current cost/nominal dollars, (3) historical cost/constant dollars, and (4) current cost/constant dollars.

Part One of this chapter provides an overview of the conceptual framework of accounting. It gives some insight into the development of policy making by the FASB as well as the political, social, and business forces that influence the FASB's decisions. The chapter gathers some of the concepts introduced in earlier chapters and adds others to provide a more complete picture of the concepts that underlie accounting. It also provides a synopsis and integration of the international diversity that characterizes accounting practice. We have stressed throughout the text that U.S. practices represent only one of a number of possible choices. Here we revisit and extend examples from throughout the text.

Part Two of this chapter focuses on concepts of income measurement. First, variations of methods of measuring income with GAAP are explored. Then alternatives to the traditional income measurement methods are discussed.

■ PART ONE: CONCEPTUAL FRAMEWORK OF ACCOUNTING

For years, accountants have sought a consistent set of concepts underlying accounting practice. But they still have a patchwork of generally accepted accounting principles (GAAP) that has slowly evolved over many years of accounting practice and regulatory effort. As a result, various accounting rules seem inconsistent within any single framework. For example, the lower-of-cost-or-market basis is applied differently to inventories, to short-term investments, and to long-term investments.

■ FASB'S CONCEPTUAL FRAMEWORK

Objective 1

Describe the FASB's conceptual framework.

accounting policy making Choosing the accounting measurement and disclosure methods required for financial reporting.

Between 1978 and 1984, the Financial Accounting Standards Board (FASB) issued four *Statements of Financial Accounting Concepts* (SFACs) relating to business enterprises.[1] Exhibit 16-1 summarizes the highlights of these SFACs. The statements provide the conceptual framework used by the FASB.

The principal task of the FASB is **accounting policy making**, which is choosing the accounting measurement and disclosure methods required for financial reporting. People refer to the board's function as rule making, standard setting, or regulation of financial reporting. Whatever its role is called, the board is a policy-making body that exercises judgment to choose among alternatives. There are no objective criteria to guide the FASB in making its decisions. The conceptual framework summarized in Exhibit 16-1 aids the exercise of judgment; it does not provide solutions to all the reporting issues faced by the FASB.

---

[1] The FASB has also issued two statements on a conceptual framework for nonbusiness organizations. These statements apply to "most human service organizations, churches, foundations, and some other organizations, such as those private nonprofit hospitals and nonprofit schools that receive a significant portion of their financial resources from sources other than the sale of goods and services." See Concepts Statement No. 4, "Objectives of Financial Reporting by Nonbusiness Organizations" (Stamford, CT: FASB, 1980); and Concepts Statement No. 6, "Elements of Financial Statements" (Stamford, CT: FASB, 1985).

Exhibit 16-1	Statement*	Highlights
Statements of Financial Accounting Concepts for Business Enterprises	SFAC No. 1, Objectives of Financial Reporting by Business Enterprises	• Accounting should provide information useful for making economic decisions • Statements should focus on external users, e.g., creditors and investors • Information should aid the prediction of cash flows • Earnings based on accrual accounting provide a better measure of performance than do cash receipts and disbursements
	SFAC No. 2, Qualitative Characteristics of Accounting Information	• Usefulness is evaluated in relation to the purposes to be served • Different information is useful for different decisions • Decision usefulness is the primary characteristic in the hierarchy of desirable characteristics • Both relevance and reliability are necessary for information to be useful • Relevance requires timeliness and either predictive or feedback value • Reliable information must faithfully represent the item being measured and be verifiable and neutral • Comparability and consistency aid usefulness • To be useful, information must be material, that is, reported amounts must be large enough to make a difference in decisions • Benefits from using information should exceed its cost
	SFAC No. 3, Elements of Financial Statements of Business Enterprises	• Defines the ten building blocks that comprise financial statements: (1) assets, (2) liabilities, (3) equity, (4) investments by owners, (5) distributions to owners, (6) comprehensive income, (7) revenues, (8) expenses, (9) gains, and (10) losses.
	SFAC No. 5, Recognition and Measurement in Financial Statements of Business Enterprises	• Specifies what information should be included in financial statements and when • All components of financial statements are important, not just a single "bottom-line" number • A statement of financial position provides information about assets, liabilities, and equity; it does not show the market value of the entity • Earnings measure periodic performance; comprehensive income recognizes all effects on equity except investments by or distributions to owners • Financial statements are based on the concept of financial capital maintenance • Measurement is and will continue to be based on nominal units of money • Revenue is recognized when it is earned and realized (or realizable) • Information based on current prices, if reliable and more relevant than alternative information, should be reported if costs involved are not too high

* SFAC Nos. 4 and 6 relate to nonbusiness entities and are not summarized here.

Accounting policy making is complex. Progress will continue to come in fits and starts. It will always be considered as too fast by some critics and too slow by others. Most people favor "improvements" in accounting—the quicker the better. But one person's improvement is often another person's impairment. Resolving these trade-offs is the essence of policy making.

Above all, students, accountants, managers, and others should recognize that the process of setting accounting standards is not confined to the development of a conceptual framework and its application to specific issues via exercises in impeccable logic and fact gathering. The process also includes the gaining of general acceptance and support. A major role of the conceptual framework is ultimately to enhance the likelihood that proposed statements will be generally accepted. The more plausible the logic and the more compelling the facts, the greater the chance of winning the support of diverse interests.

Lessons from History

Until the early 1930s, when the Securities and Exchange Commission was created by Congress, accounting practices in the United States evolved in accordance with the best professional judgment of CPAs and managers. Then private and public regulators entered the picture. To refresh your memory, see pages 65–67 for a description of the relationships among the Securities and Exchange Commission, the private regulatory bodies, and other interested groups such as managers, auditors, and investors. The Accounting Principles Board was the senior private regulatory body from 1959 to 1973, when it was succeeded by the FASB.

All of the regulatory bodies have been criticized for using piecemeal approaches, solving one accounting issue at a time. Again and again, critics have cited a need for a conceptual framework. As we saw earlier, the FASB has worked hard on constructing a conceptual framework. Meanwhile, the board also had to contend with an unending stream of specific accounting controversies that demanded immediate attention. Is there a lesson here? Why has the piecemeal approach persisted? The answer lies in a careful look at the policy-making process.

The term *generally accepted* is a key part of the familiar term *generally accepted accounting principles*. The policy-making process is much more complicated than having intelligent, experienced regulators apply logic and evidence to an issue and then promulgate rules that are subsequently followed by the affected parties. The use of logic and evidence is absolutely necessary, but it is insufficient. When the FASB considers a financial accounting standard, assorted interested parties present arguments to support their favored choices. The standards issued are often compromises among the contending interests; therefore the standards are not necessarily products of airtight logic.

The FASB's task is not only technical, but also political and educational. When the term *political* is used in this context, it means the ways of convincing interested persons about the wisdom of the board's decisions. In short, the FASB must tackle the task of obtaining general acceptance, particularly acceptance by the SEC and Congress.

Future Role of Government

In many countries accounting standards are set by a government agency. However, in the United States, most accounting reporting requirements are determined by the FASB, a private-sector institution, with the backing of the SEC, an agency of the federal government. The SEC was created by the Securities Acts of 1933 and 1934 and is empowered to ensure "full and fair" disclosures by corporations. The SEC has the ultimate legal authority over most financial reporting to investors. On several occasions, the SEC has taken an active role in the setting of accounting standards. For instance, it put pressure on the FASB toward wider use of "current-cost" accounting.

The FASB is very conscious that its pronouncements need the support of the SEC. Therefore, the board and the SEC are in constant touch. In turn, Congress maintains oversight of the SEC. If Congress becomes sufficiently unhappy with progress in the setting of financial accounting standards, it could specifically require that the role of the FASB be dampened or eliminated.

What looms ahead? Probably more government exercise of authority through the SEC. Despite the increasing activist role of congressional committees and other government entities, it remains highly likely that during the next ten years the FASB will continue to be the major single influence on changes in financial accounting standards.

■ CHOOSING AMONG REPORTING ALTERNATIVES

The FASB must make difficult decisions about reporting requirements. For example, should reporting of income tax expense include deferred taxes? How should the expense for pensions and the associated pension liability be measured? Should liabilities be shown at historical cost or current market value? The list could go on and on. The FASB has issued over one hundred twenty standards in just over twenty years and has shown no sign of slowing down. How does the FASB decide that one level of disclosure or one measurement method is acceptable and another is not?

The overriding criterion for choosing reporting alternatives is *cost/benefit*. Accounting should improve decision making. This is a benefit. But accounting information is an economic good that is costly to produce. A policy-making body such as the FASB must do its best to issue pronouncements whose perceived benefits exceed their perceived costs for the whole of society. The costs and benefits are hard to measure. They are widely diffused and fall unevenly throughout the economy. Nevertheless, the board should never lose sight of the fundamental cost-benefit test.

The costs of providing information include costs to both providers and users. Providers incur costs of data collecting and processing, of auditing, and of educating preparers. In addition, disclosure of sensitive information can lead to lost competitive advantages or increased labor union pressures. The costs to users of information include those passed on by the providers plus the costs of education, analysis, and interpretation.

The benefits of accounting information surely exist, but they are harder to pinpoint than the costs. A highly developed economy depends on accounting to inform investors and creditors whose collective decisions provide resources to sound and promising enterprises while withdrawing support from faltering entities.

An important concept in judging costs and benefits is materiality. Information is *material* when its inclusion or correct presentation would probably change the judgment of a reasonable person. Determining whether an item is material is a pervasive problem that is usually resolved by professional judgment on a case-by-case basis. The FASB should not get bogged down in issues whose effect is likely to be immaterial.

The FASB has identified a hierarchy of characteristics of information that lead to increased benefits. These are shown in Exhibit 16-2. Foremost is decision usefulness. Without usefulness there would be no benefits. The rest of the items specify what characteristics make information useful.

Exhibit 16-2

Qualities that Increase the Value of Information

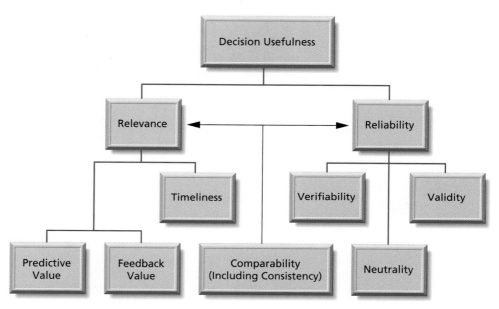

Source: Adapted from *Qualitative Characteristics of Accounting Information* (Stamford, CT: FASB, 1980), p. 15.

Relevance and Reliability

relevance The capability of information to make a difference to the decision maker.

Relevance and *reliability* are qualities that make accounting useful for decision making. **Relevance** is defined as the capability of information to make a difference to the decision maker. *Reliability* is defined in Chapter 1 (p. 0) as the quality of information that assures decision makers that the information captures the conditions or events that it purports to represent. The accounting literature is filled with arguments about the trade-offs between relevance and reliability. Consider the balance sheet value of Weyerhaeuser Company's timberlands, which are recorded at original cost. Most of the land was purchased more than fifty years ago. The historical cost is reliable, but not very relevant. In contrast, the current value of the land is more relevant, but estimates of this current value are subjective. The prevailing view in the United States is that many current market value estimates are not sufficiently reliable to be included in the accounting records, even though they are more relevant. However, in

Objective 2

Identify the qualities that make information valuable.

some countries current market values are routinely used. For example, British Petroleum subtracted the "replacement cost of sales" in obtaining "replacement cost operating profit" of £2,501 million in 1993.

For information to be relevant, it must help decision makers either predict the outcomes of future events (*predictive value*) or confirm or update past predictions (*feedback value*). Relevant information must also be available on a timely basis, that is, before a decision maker has to act. Information that does not help predict or confirm predictions, or is not available when it is needed, is not relevant.

Reliability is enhanced by *verifiability* (or *objectivity*), *neutrality*, and *validity*. **Verifiability** means that there would be a high extent of consensus among independent measurers of an item. For example, the amount paid for assets is highly verifiable, but the predicted cost to replace the assets usually is not.

Validity (also called **representational faithfulness**) means a correspondence between the accounting numbers and the resources or events those numbers purport to represent. Consider goodwill, which represents excess earning power when a group of assets is acquired (i.e., excess of cost over the fair market value of the net assets acquired). Suppose such earning power disappears before the goodwill is completely amortized. The amount of goodwill on the balance sheet would no longer be a valid measure of excess earning power.

Neutrality, or *freedom from bias*, means choosing accounting policies without attempting to achieve purposes other than measuring economic impact. In other words, financial reporting rules should not be used to achieve social policy objectives, nor should they be used to give an advantage to certain types of companies. For example, depreciation methods for reporting to shareholders should not be chosen to encourage or discourage investment.

Tampering with accounting policies (standards or principles) to promote national goals is a dangerous path. First, research has demonstrated that accounting measurements per se are unlikely to affect investors' decisions if the timing and amounts of the underlying cash flows are unaffected. Therefore such tampering is not likely to achieve its objectives. Second, tampering with policies would quickly erode the credibility of financial reporting to the detriment of the public interest.

The quality of neutrality underscores a fundamental approach taken by the FASB. Arguments about accounting issues should concentrate on how measurements and disclosure can improve the communication of economic phenomena. These issues should be resolved, however imperfectly, by determining how economic information is best disseminated in light of the costs and benefits for society as a whole.

The final items affecting usefulness are *comparability* and *consistency*. Information is more useful if it can be compared with similar information about other companies or with similar information for other reporting periods. For example, financial results for two companies are hard to compare if one uses FIFO and the other uses LIFO. Because identifying trends for a single company is difficult if accounting methods are continually changed, consistency in applying accounting methods over time is desirable. Moreover, firms must disclose their accounting methods so that users can determine the extent to which the financial statements of two firms are comparable.

---

verifiability A quality of information such that there would be a high extent of consensus among independent measurers of an item.

validity (representational faithfulness) A correspondence between the accounting numbers and the resources or events those numbers purport to represent.

neutrality Choosing accounting policies without attempting to achieve purposes other than measuring economic impact; freedom from bias.

Overview of Key Concepts

Exhibit 16-3 presents an overview of key concepts covered in this chapter and elsewhere in the text. A concrete example of each is provided, as is a listing of the chapters in the text that contain the main discussions or examples of the individual concepts. This entire tabulation should be a convenient guide for recalling and comparing some major ingredients of accounting's conceptual framework.

■ ACCOUNTING STANDARDS THROUGHOUT THE WORLD

This text has focused on the principles of accounting that are generally accepted in the United States. Nevertheless, practices of other countries have been mentioned throughout. This section elaborates on some of the basic differences among accounting reports in various countries.[2]

Although differences exist among countries, the most basic aspects of accounting are consistent throughout the world. Double-entry systems, accrual accounting, and the income statement and balance sheet are used worldwide. Therefore similarities in financial reporting exceed the differences.

Differences in Tax and Inflation Accounting

Objective 3

Present examples of accounting standards in other countries that differ from those in the U.S.

One major area of differences in financial reporting is the influence of the income tax law on reporting to shareholders. In Chapter 14, we emphasized that methods in the United States for reporting to tax authorities differ from those used for reporting to shareholders. In contrast, tax reporting and shareholder reporting are identical in many countries. For example, France has a "Plan Compatible" that specifies a National Uniform Chart of Accounts that is used for both tax returns and reporting to shareholders. German financial reporting is also determined primarily by tax laws. If accounting records are not kept according to strict tax laws, the German tax authorities can reject the records as a basis for taxation.

In some countries, tax laws have a major influence on shareholder reporting even if tax and shareholder reports are not required to be identical. In Japan, for example, certain principles are allowed for tax purposes only if they are also used for shareholder reporting. When such principles provide tax advantages, there is a tendency for companies to use them for reporting to shareholders.

In addition to the influence of the tax law, financial reporting of income taxes differs among countries. For example, in Argentina income tax expenses are recognized in financial statements only when payments are made to the government; in contrast, most countries accrue taxes when the related income is recognized. Sweden and Switzerland are two other countries that do not recognize deferred taxes. However, Britain, the Netherlands, and Canada recognize deferred taxes in a manner similar to the United States.

Another significant difference among countries is the extent to which financial statements account for inflation. In the 1980s, the FASB experimented with

---

[2] For elaboration of the material in this section see F. Choi and G. Mueller, *International Accounting* (Upper Saddle River, NJ: Prentice Hall, 1992), especially Chap. 3, pp. 77–136.

requiring supplementary disclosure of inflation-adjusted numbers. After years of accounting research on the value of these disclosures, the FASB concluded that the costs exceeded the benefits. Now no requirements for such supplementary disclosure exist in the United States. In contrast, many countries require full or partial adjustments for inflation for reporting to both shareholders and tax authorities. For example, Brazil has experienced persistent double- and triple-digit inflation rates and requires all statements to be adjusted for changes in the general price level in the manner described later in this chapter. Such inflation-adjusted statements are used for both tax and shareholder reporting. Argentina requires dual reporting. Companies must include two columns in financial statements, one for traditional historical-cost numbers and one for general price-level-adjusted numbers.

The Netherlands has been a leader in the application of current replacement-cost measurements to financial accounts, although it has no formal requirement mandating either historical cost or replacement cost. French financial statements include a partial inflation adjustment, using replacement cost for fixed assets. Similarly, Sweden allows (but does not require) the revaluation of certain property, plant, and equipment. Mexico requires inflation adjustments, but allows either price-level adjustments or current-cost statements.

Not surprisingly, countries that have experienced the lowest inflation rates have been the slowest to recognize inflation in their accounting statements. Japan has no recognition of inflation, and Germany has recommended supplementary disclosures, but few companies have responded.

Accounting Principles in Selected Countries

Accounting practices differ among countries for a variety of reasons, such as differences in government, economic systems, culture, and traditions. We will briefly discuss how accounting in the United Kingdom, France, Germany, and Japan differs from that in the United States.

The Companies' Laws in the *United Kingdom* provide general guidance for accounting standards, and details are specified by the Accounting Standards Board, a private-sector body sponsored by the accountancy profession. U.K. companies can use either historical-cost or current-cost accounting, or a mixture of the two. For example, British Petroleum reports both "Historical cost operating profit" and "Replacement cost operating profit" on its income statement. LIFO is not allowed for either tax or shareholder reporting; research expenditures are charged to expense, but development expenses can be capitalized; purchased goodwill is usually written off immediately.

France leads the way in national uniform accounting. Companies must use a National Uniform Chart of Accounts, and financial reporting requirements are extensive. Accounting records are considered legal control devices more than sources of information for decision makers. Accounting methods such as pooling-of-interests, LIFO, and capitalization of leases are not allowed. Research and development costs can be capitalized but must be amortized over no more than five years, and goodwill is amortized over five to twenty-five years. Future pension obligations are not recognized as liabilities. Two reporting requirements are unique to France: (1) companies must publish an annual social balance sheet relating to environmental matters and employee conditions and benefits, and (2) companies must publish comprehensive financial forecasts.

Exhibit 16-3

Frequently Encountered Terminology in Conceptual Frameworks of Accounting

Term	Short Description	Example	Chapters in this Text*
Cost and benefits	Accounting information is an economic good. It should be gathered as long as its benefits exceed its costs.	Decisions must be improved sufficiently to justify recording current values in addition to historical costs.	Mainly in 3, 8, 9
Relevance	Capability of information to make a difference to the decision maker.	Report of cash in bank is essential to determine how much money to borrow.	3, 16
Reliability	Dependability of information as representing what it purports to represent	The cost of the land was $1 million 1986 dollars.	1, 16
Verifiability (objectivity)	Characteristic of information that results in its reproducibility by a consensus of independent measurers.	Cash has high verifiability, accounts receivable less, inventories less yet, depreciable assets even less, and so on.	1, 3, 16
Validity (representational faithfulness)	Correspondence between numbers and effects portrayed.	The historical cost/constant dollar cost of the land described above may be $1.2 million 1996 dollars, but the $1.2 million does not represent the current cost or market value of the land.	16
Consistency	Applying the same accounting methods over a series of reporting periods.	Use of FIFO inventory over a series of years, not FIFO for two years, LIFO for three, and so on.	7
Neutrality (evenhandedness)	Choosing accounting policies on the basis of quantifying without bias, that is, without purposes other than measuring economic impact.	An example of lack of neutrality may clarify: choosing the flow-through method in accounting for the investment tax credit for purposes of achieving national goals of encouraging capital expenditures.†	14
Materiality	An item is material if the judgment of a reasonable person would have been changed or influenced by its omission or misstatement.	An error of $100 of revenue would be immaterial for a firm with $100,000 of revenue but material for a firm with $1,000.	3
Conservatism	Way of dealing with uncertainties. Avoids recognition of income on the basis of inadequate evidence but requires recognition of losses when assets have been impaired or liabilities incurred. In short, when in doubt, write it off.	Charging all research and development costs to expenses as incurred. Applying lower-of-cost-or-market methods to asset valuation.	6, 9, 13

Exhibit 16-3

Frequently Encountered Terminology in Conceptual Frameworks of Accounting (continued)

Term	Short Description	Example	Chapters in this Text*
Continuity (going concern)	Assumption that an entity will continue indefinitely or at least will not be liquidated in the near future.	Letterhead stationery on hand is classified as supplies or rubbish, depending on the going concern assumption.	3
Entity	The unit of accountability.	A parent corporation, a subsidiary, a retail store.	1, 13
Accrual accounting	Record financial effects in the periods affected regardless of when cash is received or paid.	Recognize receivables and payables and match expenses with revenues.	2, 3, 4
Recognition	Formally recording or incorporating an item in accounts and financial statements. An element may be recognized (recorded) or unrecognized (unrecorded).	Recognition requires revenues to be earned and realized. Increases or decreases in the value of land may be earned but unrealized. Advance payments on subscriptions may be realized but not earned.	1, 2, 4, 6
Matching and cost recovery	Matching is relating revenues and expenses to each other in a particular period.	Sales commission expenses are "matched" directly against related sales. Sales salaries, costs of heating, and depreciation on equipment are "matched" indirectly against current revenues because their benefits are considered to be exhausted in the current period.	2, 4, 6, 16

* Many of these criteria or basic ideas underlie this entire textbook.
† See Appendix 14 for discussion of the investment tax credit. Suppose flow-through is chosen because it is deemed to be the best possible measure of the economic impact of the enterprise. Then neutrality exists if flow-through is chosen.

U.S. GAAP versus Swedish GAAP

Three thousand miles of ocean is not all that separates Sweden and the United States. Cultural, legal, and economic factors have contributed to considerable differences in the accounting rules that are used in the financial statements of each country's business enterprises. How significant are these differences?

Consider AB Volvo, a major Swedish manufacturer of cars, trucks, and buses. Volvo's shares are traded on the over-the-counter (OTC) market in the United States. To trade in U.S. stock markets, the SEC requires Volvo to provide investors with details of the differences in net income and stockholders' equity computed using U.S. GAAP and using Swedish GAAP, as found in the table below.

What are the differences between U.S. and Swedish GAAP that affected Volvo? The adjustment for income taxes arose because deferred taxes are computed differently in Sweden than in the United States. In Sweden, tooling costs are expensed as incurred, but they are capitalized in the United States and amortized over a period not exceeding five years. Business combinations, especially amounts paid in excess of book values, are reported differently in Sweden than in the U.S. In the United States, interest costs incurred in the construction of property and equipment are capitalized, but they are expensed in Sweden. Sale-leaseback transactions are recorded differently in Sweden than in the U.S. Finally, when certain accounting policies change in the U.S. there is a one-time effect on income that does not appear on Swedish statements.

Were the differences significant? These adjustments caused net income in 1993 to be higher under U.S. GAAP then under Swedish GAAP by 6,404 million SEK and actually turned a loss into a gain. In 1992 the adjustments had the opposite effect, increasing the loss by $1,299 million SEK, a 39% increase. In 1993 shareholders' equity was higher under U.S. GAAP by 1,748 million SEK, a 6% difference, while in 1992 it was higher under Swedish GAAP by 3,791 million SEK, a 13% difference.

Volvo is not an isolated case. For example, Norsk Hydro, the largest company in Norway, had 1993 net income of 3,406 million NOK (Norwegian Kroner) under Norwegian GAAP and 2,996 NOK, or 12% less, under U.S. GAAP. Nokia, an international telecommunications and electronics company headquartered in Helsinki, compares its net income using Finnish Accounting Standards (FAS) to that computed using International Accounting Standards (IAS); FAS generated a net loss of 246 million FM (Finnish Mark) in 1993, compared with a loss of 1,150 million FM under IAS.

Overall, U.S. investor interest in foreign companies has increased. Why? Many stocks for companies outside the U.S. have posted returns far in excess of the U.S. stock market. For example, a price index covering 215 foreign stocks from 26 countries showed returns 25% greater than the Standard & Poor's 500-stock index between 1992 and 1994. To take advantage of these opportunities, many U.S. investors want to be able to understand the financial statements of non-U.S. companies in Sweden, Norway, Finland, and throughout the world. ■

Sources: "The Global Investor," Business Week *(September 19, 1994), pp. 96-104; AB Volvo,* Annual Report, *1993; Norsk Hydro,* Annual Report, *1993; Nokia,* Annual Report, *1993.*

| | In Millions of Swedish Kroner (SEK) | | | |
	Net Income (Loss)		Shareholders' Equity	
	1993	*1992*	*1993*	*1992*
Amounts in accordance with Swedish GAAP	(3,466)	(3,320)	27,088	29,721
Adjustments to confirm to U.S. GAAP:				
Foreign currency translation	(842)	(1,829)	(2,671)	(1,829)
Income taxes	(593)	1,118	2,101	(4,038)
Tooling costs	(629)	112	996	1,525
Business combinations	950	(111)	950	—
Interest costs	(39)	39	257	249
Leasing	41	41	(228)	(269)
Cumulative effect of change in accounting policies	7,012	(405)		
Other	504	(264)	343	571
Net increase (decrease) in net income (loss)	6,404	(1,299)		
Net increase (decrease) in shareholders' equity			1,748	(3,791)
Amounts in accordance with U.S. GAAP	2,938	(4,619)	28,836	25,930

Tax law dominates financial reporting in *Germany*; whatever is reported to shareholders must also be reported to tax authorities. Therefore, accounting standards are based on statutes and court decisions, and they are not necessarily directed at producing statements useful for decision making. Both FIFO and LIFO are allowed, but they must correspond to the physical flow of inventory. Goodwill must be written off over fifteen years. Depreciation is based on specific tax-depreciation schedules. Cash flow statements are not required, but many companies provide them anyway. Consolidated statements are required, but exceptions are granted for many companies. Although German accounting standards have grown closer to U.S standards since World War II, they remain significantly different.

Accounting and finance play a smaller role in *Japanese* companies and in the Japanese economy than in other industrialized countries. Accounting is dominated by the central government, especially the Ministry of Finance. There is extensive cross-ownership among Japanese firms, and banks are often heavily involved with companies to whom they lend money. Debt capital is used much more than equity capital. Because large creditors can obtain extensive information easily, there is less need for public financial disclosure to capital market participants such as individual investors. Japan almost reveres historical cost accounting; current cost data cannot even be given as supplementary information. Consolidated statements are required, though many significant subsidiaries are still excluded from the consolidated statements. Goodwill is based on the difference between purchase price and book value (not fair market value) of net assets acquired. Goodwill, research and development expenditures, and many other intangible assets must be written off over five years or less. Few leases are capitalized, and pension obligations are not recognized as liabilities. In general, Japanese accounting standards are very conservative. One study showed that the average net income for a Japanese firm is 58% below the amount that would be reported using U.S. accounting standards. This is one of the reasons that price-earnings ratios of Japanese firms average more than double those of U.S. firms.

This section has presented only a sample of the international differences in accounting standards. Until recently few people were very concerned about the differences. But the growing globalization of business enterprises and capital markets is creating much current interest in common, worldwide standards. There are too many cultural, social, and political differences among countries to expect complete worldwide standardization of financial reporting in the near future. In fact, complete harmonization of standards may not be desirable, because it could mask true cultural and economic differences among countries. However, the trend is clear. The International Federation of Accountants (IFAC), which was described in Chapter 1, is leading the way toward more standardization of accounting measurement and reporting practices throughout the world.

■ PART TWO: VARIATIONS IN INCOME MEASUREMENT

The measurement of income is easily the most controversial subject in accounting. The remainder of this chapter focuses on different methods of measuring income. First, we examine the impact of different allowable methods of measuring traditional, historical-cost income. Then we present alternative measures that are designed to account for inflation.

■ HISTORICAL COST INCOME MEASUREMENT

Objective 4

Explain how identical companies can report different net incomes because of their choice of accounting methods.

The most popular approach to income measurement is commonly labeled the historical-cost method, which is based on actual costs of acquiring assets. It has been described at length in this book. However, the label "historical cost" does not completely define the way income is measured. Disputes often occur in applying the historical-cost method. The majority of these disputes center on timing. For example, when are revenues recognized? When do the costs of assets become expenses?

Revenue Recognition

The timing of income is influenced most by the *recognition* principle. This book discusses revenue recognition in Chapters 2 and 6. It is a major feature of accrual accounting because it determines when revenues and the associated (matched) costs will be recorded. Thus it specifies when income will be reported.

Generally, revenue is recorded when goods or services are *delivered* to customers. However, there are some exceptions to the notion that delivery triggers the recording of revenue. For example, companies undertaking long-run construction projects often recognize revenue using a *percentage-of-completion method*. Consider the builder of an ocean liner. Such a company may portray performance better by spreading prospective revenues, related costs, and resulting net income over the life of the contract in proportion to the work accomplished. Otherwise all the net income would appear in one chunk upon completion of the project, as if it had been earned on a single day.

Second, in exceptionally rare cases, revenue is recorded in proportion to cash collections under long-run installment contracts. An illustration is the retail sales of undeveloped lots. These receivables are collectible over an extended period of time, and there is no reliable basis for estimating the degree of collectibility.

Uncertainty about the collectibility of receivables does not always delay the recording of revenue. Many accountants regard the revenue as realized but provide an ample allowance for uncollectible accounts. For example, a hospital can recognize revenue on the accrual basis as its services are delivered. However, its bad debts expense (which is conceptually an offset of gross revenue because it represents revenue never to be received) is a much higher percentage of revenue than in, for example, retail food stores.

Impact of Alternative Timing of Expenses

In addition to timing differences caused by revenue recognition, generally accepted accounting principles allow accountants to choose when to recognize certain expenses. Comparing two companies can be difficult if each chooses a different method for recognizing major expenses. To achieve comparability, analysts often reconstruct a company's financial statements to place them on a basis consistent with other companies in the same industry.

Suppose two companies, Miami Marine (MM) and Sarasota Sailboats (SS), began business in the same industry in 19X1. Each company would have had the following for 19X1, depending on the accounting method chosen:

	Amount	Difference
Beginning inventory	$ 0	
Purchases	270,000	
Ending inventory, if FIFO is used	110,000	$40,000
Ending inventory, if LIFO is used	70,000	
Depreciation, if accelerated is used	20,000	10,000
Depreciation, if straight-line is used	10,000	
Product introduction costs, original total amount	30,000	20,000
Product introduction costs, amortized amount	10,000	
Revenue	400,000	
Other expenses	100,000	
Common shares outstanding	10,000	
Income tax rate	40%	

For income-tax reporting purposes, the top management of MM and SS have both used accelerated (MACRS) depreciation and the immediate write-off of all product introduction costs. For all other items, assume that the same method would be used for tax purposes and stockholder reporting purposes.

For stockholder reporting purposes, the choice of accounting policies can have a dramatic effect on net income and earnings per share. Assume that MM takes one extreme stance; SS takes the other extreme. As Exhibit 16-4 shows, the choices of LIFO, accelerated depreciation (assumed equal to MACRS depreciation), and immediate write-off of product introduction costs will result in MM's earnings per share of $3.00. In contrast, SS's earnings per share would be $7.20.

Many managers regard the maximizing of immediate reported earnings per share as a worthy objective. They tend to choose the accounting policies favored by SS. Others tend to be more conservative and choose the MM policies. The point here is that similar operations may be portrayed differently in income statements. Note that all the data are the same as far as the underlying cash flows are concerned, with one exception: A company that used FIFO for stockholder reporting cannot use LIFO for tax purposes. Therefore SS's current payments for income taxes are $16,000 larger than MM's.

Perhaps accounting measurements will eventually become better standardized, and identical operations will be reported in more nearly identical figures. In the meantime, accountants and corporate executives should view increased disclosure and amplified description as the most pressing requirements in financial reporting. These requirements must be met if investors are to have sufficient data for making their own comparisons between companies.

Statement of Accounting Policies

As Exhibit 16-4 shows, the choice among generally accepted accounting practices can significantly affect the level of reported earnings. Information about the accounting principles, practices, procedures, or policies (words like these are used loosely) is essential for the intelligent analysis of financial statements. Companies must include a description of all significant accounting policies as an integral part of the financial report. The disclosure usually appears as a separate Summary of Significant Accounting Policies preceding the footnotes of financial statements.

Exhibit 16-5 displays some of the items in a typical summary, that of Procter & Gamble Company. The summary mentions many items covered in earlier chapters: consolidated statements, LIFO, goodwill, depreciation methods, and income taxes.

Exhibit 16-4

Stockholder Reporting
Possible Income Statements
for the Year Ended December 31, 19X1
(in thousands of dollars, except earnings per share)

	(1) Miami Marine (LIFO, MACRS, Immediate Write-off)	(2) Change from LIFO to FIFO	(3) Change from MACRS to Straight-line	(4) Change from Immediate Write-off to Amortization	(5) Sarasota Sailboat (FIFO, Straight-line, Amortization)
			Individual Effects		
Revenue	400				400
Expenses:					
Cost of goods sold	200	40			160
Depreciation	20		10		10
Product introduction costs	30			20	10
Other expenses	100				100
Total expenses	350				280
Income before income taxes	50				120
Income taxes:					
Currently payable	20*	16			36†
Deferred	—		4	8	12‡
Total income tax expense	20				48
Net income reported	30	24	6	12	72
Earnings per share on 10,000 shares	3.00	2.40	.60	1.20	7.20

* Income tax per the tax return would be .40 × $50 = $20.
† Same as for MM Company except that FIFO would boost the current income tax per the tax return by .4 × $40 = $16. Therefore the total would be $20 + $16 = $36.
‡ Additional income tax expense equal to the deferred tax liability must be reported as the result of showing $10 less depreciation expense and $20 less amortization expense, a total of $30 multiplied by the tax rate of 40% = $12.

Exhibit 16-5

The Procter &
Gamble Company
Summary of
Significant
Accounting Policies

PRINCIPLES OF CONSOLIDATION: The financial statements include the accounts of The Procter & Gamble Company and its majority-owned subsidiaries. Investments in 20% to 50% owned affiliates in which significant management control is exercised are included at original cost adjusted for the change in equity since acquisition. Other investments in affiliates are carried at cost.

INVENTORY VALUATION: Inventories are valued at the lower of cost or market. Cost for inventories in the United States is primarily determined by the last-in, first-out method. Cost is determined by the average cost method for substantially all of the remaining inventories.

GOODWILL AND OTHER INTANGIBLE ASSETS: Intangible assets are amortized on a straight-line basis over periods not exceeding forty years.

DEPRECIATION: For financial accounting purposes, depreciation is calculated on a straight-line basis over the estimated useful lives of the properties.

INCOME TAXES: Provision is made for the income tax effects of all transactions in the consolidated statement of earnings, including those for which actual tax payment or tax relief is deferred to future years. These deferrals result primarily from the use of shorter equipment lives and accelerated methods of depreciation for tax purposes.

OTHER EXPENSES: Advertising and research and development costs are charged against earnings in the year incurred.

■ INCOME MEASUREMENT AND PRICE CHANGES

Accountants traditionally have maintained that net income is a return *on* the capital invested by shareholders. Suppose an amount equal to the net income of a period is returned to the shareholders as dividends. In the absence of price changes, such a payment leaves the shareholders' invested capital at the end of the period equal to the beginning capital. However, when prices change, this relationship between income and capital is altered. In times of generally rising prices, paying dividends equal to net income, as conventionally measured, usually amounts to paying out some capital itself as well as the return on capital.

Complaints about Historical Cost

A pet theme of politicians and other critics of business is the "unconscionable" or "obscene" profits reported by American companies. In turn, many business executives insist that our traditional historical-cost basis for measuring income produces misleading results during a time of rising prices. Some managers have complained that the reported profits for most years in the past two decades have been so badly overstated that income taxes have been unfairly levied. In many cases, invested capital, rather than earned income, has been taxed.

The industries with huge investments in plant and equipment claim that their profits are badly misstated by generally accepted accounting principles. For instance, consider NYNEX, a company that emerged from the breakup of the Bell System. In a recent period of high inflation NYNEX reported net income of $1,095 million, which would have been a net loss of $82 million if depreciation had been adjusted for inflation.

The soaring inflation of the late 1970s in the United States raised many questions about the usefulness of traditional historical-cost financial statements. The FASB responded by issuing *Statement No. 33,* "Financial Reporting and Changing Prices." The statement required no changes in the primary financial statements. However, it required large companies to include supplementary inflation-adjusted schedules in their annual reports.

Statement No. 33 was experimental, and its requirements were in place for eight years. By 1987 inflation had subsided, and the FASB decided that inflation-adjusted disclosures would no longer be required. Although U.S. companies do not need to report inflation-adjusted numbers, a basic knowledge about reporting the effects of changing prices is useful for at least four reasons: (1) high inflation is still present in many countries, and most accounting reports in those countries report the effects of inflation; (2) if history is any indication, higher inflation rates will return to the United States sooner or later, and when they do, readers of financial statements will again become concerned with inflation-adjusted statements; (3) the cumulative effect of even a 2% or 3% rate is substantial; and (4) understanding the limitations of traditional financial statements is enhanced by knowing how inflation affects (or does not affect) such financial statements.

Income or Capital

Objective 5

Describe the major differences between financial capital and physical capital.

Before presenting alternatives to historical-cost accounting, we first concentrate on various concepts of income and capital. At first glance, the concept of income seems straightforward. Income is an entity's increase in wealth during a period, that is, the amount that could be paid out to shareholders at the end of the period and still leave the entity as well off as it was at the beginning of the period. In essence, shareholders invest capital and expect a return on the capital and an eventual return of the capital. To measure the shareholders' *return on capital*, the entity must measure the resources required to maintain invested capital at its original level, that is, the amount needed to preserve capital for the eventual *return of capital*. Excess resources resulting from the period's operations are income:

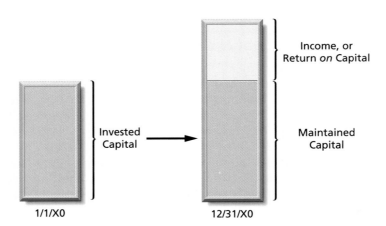

To measure income, accountants must define invested capital and identify how much of an entity's resources at the end of a period are required to maintain invested capital. The time-honored interpretation is that invested capital is a *financial concept*, based on the amount of money invested. That is, shareholders invest money with the expectation of an eventual return of an equal *amount of*

money (return *of* capital) together with additional amounts representing a return *on* capital. Maintaining capital requires keeping resources equal to the dollar value of the original investment. Any excess is income, the return *on* capital.

In contrast, some accountants and managers define capital as a *physical concept*, based on the company's real productive capacity. They identify the physical resources that make up capital at the beginning of the period. To maintain capital, the entity must set aside enough end-of-period resources to replace the beginning-of-period physical capacity. Only resources in excess of those required to replicate the initial productive capacity are considered income.

Consider an example where a company begins with owners' investment (capital) of $1,000, which is used immediately to purchase inventory. The inventory is sold a year later for $1,500. The cost of replacing the inventory has risen to $1,200.

The year began with *financial capital* of $1,000 and *physical capital* consisting of the inventory. At the end of the year there is $1,500 and no inventory. Suppose management wanted to pay investors a return on their investment but keep the original investment to begin a new year. How much can the company pay out?

Most accountants and managers would agree that income should measure the amount that can be paid out after retaining an amount that would leave the company as well off at the end of the year as at the beginning. But what do we mean by "as well off"?

If the beginning-of-the-year financial value is to be maintained, $500 of the $1,500 can be paid out and $1,000 kept. The $1,000 is equivalent to the financial investment in the business at the beginning of the year. This $500 measure of income is based on **financial capital maintenance**—that is, income emerges after financial resources are recovered.

But suppose income emerges only after recovering an amount that allows physical operating capability to be maintained, called **physical capital maintenance**. The physical resources consist of inventory, which costs $1,200 to replace. Therefore, of the $1,500 available at the end of the year, $1,200 must be spent to maintain inventory at its beginning-of-the-year level, and income is only $300.

financial capital maintenance A concept of income measurement whereby income emerges only after financial resources are recovered.

physical capital maintenance A concept of income measurement whereby income emerges only after recovering an amount that allows physical operating capability to be maintained.

	Financial Capital Maintenance	Physical Capital Maintenance
Sales	$1,500	$1,500
Cost of goods sold	1,000	1,200
Income	$ 500	$ 300

■ MEASUREMENT ALTERNATIVES UNDER CHANGING PRICES

inflation A general decline in the purchasing power of the monetary unit.

When prices of resources do not change, financial and physical capital maintenance give identical measures of income. But price changes are a fact of life. Some price changes are a result of **inflation**, a general decline in the purchasing power of the monetary unit or a general increase in the average cost of goods and services. In addition, price changes that result in a particular item becoming more or less expensive relative to other items can occur even in the absence of inflation.

Changing prices, and particularly inflation, have caused accountants to consider two types of changes in financial reporting: (1) Switch from measuring transactions in **nominal dollars**, which are dollar measurements that are not restated for fluctuations in the general purchasing power of the monetary unit, to **constant dollars,** which are restated in terms of current purchasing power. (2) Instead of reporting the **historical cost** of an asset, which is the amount originally paid to acquire it, use the **current cost**, which is generally the cost to replace it. Traditional accounting uses *nominal* (rather than constant) dollars and *historical* (rather than current) costs. Such accounting has almost exclusively dominated financial reporting in the United States throughout this century. Using historical costs implies maintenance of financial capital; current costs imply *physical* capital maintenance.

The two approaches, which can be applied separately or in combination, address separate but related problems caused by changing prices: (1) constant-dollar disclosures account for *general* changes in the purchasing power of the dollar, and (2) current-cost disclosures account for changes in *specific* prices. The two approaches create the following four alternatives for measuring income:

nominal dollars
Those dollars that are not restated for fluctuations in the general purchasing power of the monetary unit.

constant dollars
Dollar measurements that are restated in terms of current purchasing power.

historical cost The amount originally paid to acquire an asset.

current cost
Generally, the cost to replace an asset.

Objective 6

Explain and illustrate four different ways of measuring income: (1) historical cost/nominal dollars, (2) current cost/nominal dollars, (3) historical cost/constant dollars, (4) current cost/constant dollars.

	Historical Cost	Current Cost
Nominal Dollars	1 Historical cost/ nominal dollars	2 Current cost/ nominal dollars
Constant Dollars	3 Historical cost/ constant dollars	4 Current cost/ constant dollars

We will use the Greystone Company situation to compare the four basic methods of income measurement. Greystone has the following comparative balance sheets at December 31 (based on historical costs in nominal dollars):

	19X1	19X2
Cash	$ 0	$10,500
Inventory, 400 and 100 units, respectively	8,000	2,000
Total assets	$8,000	$12,500
Original paid-in capital	$8,000	$ 8,000
Retained income	—	4,500
Stockholders' equity	$8,000	$12,500

The company acquired all 400 units of inventory at $20 per unit (total of $8,000) on December 31, 19X1, and held the units until December 31, 19X2. Three hundred units were sold for $35 per unit (total of $10,500 cash) on December 31, 19X2. The replacement cost of the inventory at that date was $30 per unit. The general-price-level index was 100 on December 31, 19X1, and 110 on December 31, 19X2. (This means that a bundle of goods that cost $100 on December 31, 19X1 will cost $110 on December 31, 19X2.) We assume that these are the company's only transactions, and for simplicity, we ignore income taxes. Exhibit 16-6 shows Greystone's balance sheets and income statements prepared according to each of the four methods for measuring income.

Historical Cost/Nominal Dollars

The first two columns of Exhibit 16-6 show financial statements prepared using the time-honored historical cost/nominal dollars approach (Method 1). Basically, this method measures invested capital in nominal dollars. It is the most popular approach to income measurement and is commonly called the historical-cost method. Operating income (which equals net income in this case) is the excess of realized revenue ($10,500 in 19X2) over the "not restated" $6,000 historical costs of assets used in obtaining that revenue. As we have already seen, when the conventional accrual basis of accounting is used, an exchange transaction is ordinarily necessary before revenues (and resulting incomes) are recognized. Thus no income generally appears until the asset is sold; intervening price fluctuations are ignored.

Current Cost/Nominal Dollars

current-cost method
A measurement method using current costs and nominal dollars.

The second set of financial statements in Exhibit 16-6 illustrates a **current-cost method** that has especially strong advocates in the United Kingdom and Australia (Method 2). This method uses current cost/nominal dollars. The focus is on income from continuing operations. This model emphasizes that operating income should be "distributable" income. That is, Greystone could pay dividends in an amount of only $1,500, leaving enough assets to allow for replacement of the inventory that has just been sold.

Critics of traditional accounting claim that the $4,500 historical-cost measure of income from continuing operations is misleading because it overstates the net increment in distributable assets. If a $4,500 dividend were paid, the company would not be able to continue operations at the same level as before. The current cost statement reports only the $1,500 profit available after replacing the inventory. The $3,000 difference between the two operating incomes ($4,500 − $1,500 = $3,000) is frequently referred to as an "inventory profit" or an "inflated profit." Why? Because $9,000 instead of $6,000 is now necessary to replace the 300 units sold (300 × the increase in price from $20 to $30 equals the $3,000 difference).

Holding Gains and Physical Capital

The current-cost method stresses a separation between *income from continuing operations*, which is defined as the excess of revenue over the current costs of the assets consumed in obtaining that revenue, and *holding gains* (or *losses*), which are increases (or decreases) in the replacement costs of the assets held during the current period. Holding gains do not arise in historical cost/nominal dollar income statements. Why? Because with conventional accrual accounting, an exchange transaction is ordinarily necessary before revenues (and resulting incomes) are recognized. Intervening price fluctuations are ignored. In contrast, the current-cost method recognizes the impact on a company when the values of its assets change.

Exhibit 16-6

Greystone Company
Four Major Methods to Measure Income and Capital (in dollars)
Assumptions: Inventory, historical cost—$20/unit; Inventory,
current cost—$30/unit; Beginning index—100; Ending index—110

| | Nominal Dollars* | | | | Constant Dollars* | | | |
| | (Method 1) | | (Method 2) | | (Method 3) | | (Method 4) | |
	Historical Cost		Current Cost		Historical Cost		Current Cost	
Balance sheets as of								
December 31	19X1	19X2	19X1	19X2	19X1	19X2	19X1	19X2
Cash	—	10,500	—	10,500	—	10,500	—	10,500
Inventory, 400 and 100 units, respectively	8,000	2,000 [b]	8,000	3,000 [c]	8,800 [e]	2,200 [e]	8,800 [e]	3,000 [c]
Total assets	8,000	12,500	8,000	13,500	8,800	12,700	8,800	13,500
Original paid-in capital	8,000	8,000	8,000	8,000	8,800 [f]	8,800 [f]	8,800 [f]	8,800 [f]
Retained income (confined to income from continuing operations)		4,500		1,500		3,900		1,500
Revaluation equity (accumulated holding gains)				4,000				3,200
Total liab. & stk. eq.	8,000	12,500	8,000	13,500	8,800	12,700	8,800 [e]	13,500
Income statements for 19X2								
Sales, 300 units @ $35		10,500		10,500		10,500		10,500
Cost of goods sold, 300 units		6,000 [b]		9,000 [c]		6,600 [e]		9,000 [c]
Income from continuing operations (to retained income)		4,500		1,500		3,900		1,500
Holding gains:[a]								
On 300 units sold				3,000 [d]				2,400 [g]
On 100 units unsold				1,000 [d]				800 [g]
Total holding gains[a] (to revaluation equity)				4,000				3,200

* Nominal dollars are not restated for a general price index, whereas constant dollars are restated.
[a] Many advocates of the current-cost method favor showing these gains in a completely separate statement of holding gains rather than as a part of the income statement. Others favor including some or all of these gains as a part of income for the year.
[b] 100 × $20, [c] 100 × $30, [d] 300 × ($30 – $20), [e] 110/100 × $8,000, [f] 110/100 × $8,000.
   300 × $20.   300 × $30.   100 × ($30 – $20).   110/100 × $2,000,
   110/100 × $6,000.

[g] $9,000 – [(110/100) × $6,000] = $2,400 $3,000 – [(110/100) × $2,000] = $800
   or   or
   300 × [30 – (110/100) × $20] = $2,400.   100 × [$30 – (110/100) × $20] = $800.

Accountants differ sharply on how to account for holding gains. The "correct" accounting depends on distinctions between capital and income. That is, income cannot occur until invested capital is "recovered" or "maintained." The issue of capital versus income is concretely illustrated in Exhibit 16-6. The advocates of a physical concept of capital maintenance claim that *all* holding gains (both those gains related to the units sold and the gains related to the units unsold) should be excluded from income and become a part of stock-

revaluation equity
A part of stockholders' equity that includes all holding gains that are excluded from income.

holders' equity called **revaluation equity**. Why? Because holding gains represent the amount that must be reinvested to maintain physical capital at its beginning-of-the-year level. Holding gains become part *of* capital, not a return *on* capital.

For simplicity, income taxes are ignored in Exhibit 16-6. The historical cost-nominal dollar method (Method 1) is the only acceptable method for reporting on income tax returns in English-speaking countries. Many managers of heavy industries such as steel and aluminum claim that their capital is being taxed under the historical-cost/nominal-dollar method. These managers maintain that taxes should be levied only on *income from continuing operations*, as computed under the current-cost/nominal-dollar method (Method 2). To date, most governments have not responded to these logical protests.

Some U.S. companies, especially real estate companies, present current cost/nominal dollar financial statements as a supplement to their historical cost statements. An example is Catellus Development Co. of San Francisco, one of the country's largest publicly-held real estate companies. The company's reasoning is explained in a footnote to its financial statements:

> Current value basis consolidated balance sheets...provide supplemental information.... Because of the low historical cost basis of the Company's real estate assets, management believes that the historical cost basis presentation used in customary financial statements does not reflect the true economic value of the Company's holdings...Management believes that current value information provides meaningful information regarding the Company's economic condition and the value of its holdings in today's real estate market.

The company's current cost balance sheet and statement of changes in revaluation equity are in Exhibit 16-7. Notice that the current value of the company's properties exceeds the historical book value by $1,712,217,000 − $1,091,832,000 = $620,385,000. Further, revaluation equity which represents the difference between current cost and historical cost values for *all* assets and liabilities, not just properties, adds $476,171,000 to the stockholders' equity. Finally, from the statement of changes in revaluation equity you can see the revaluation equity includes holding gains on both properties sold and those still held.

Historical Cost/Constant Dollars

Method 3 of Exhibit 16-6 shows the results of applying general index numbers to historical costs. Essentially, the income measurements in each year are restated in terms of *constant dollars* (which possess the same general purchasing power of the current year) instead of the *nominal dollars* (which possess different general purchasing powers of various years).

Because of inflation, dollars spent or received in 19X2 have a different value than dollars spent or received in 19X1. Adding 19X1 dollars to 19X2 dollars is like adding apples and oranges. Constant-dollar accounting measures all items on the 19X2 financial statements in 19X2 dollars.

Consider the objections to Method 1. Deducting 6,000 19X1 dollars from 10,500 19X2 dollars to obtain $4,500 is akin to deducting 60 *centimeters* from 105 *meters* and calling the result 45. Grade-school tests are marked wrong when such nonsensical arithmetic is discovered, but accountants have been paid well for years for performing similar arithmetic.

Exhibit 16-7

Current Cost
Financial Statements
Catellus
Development
Corporation

Balance Sheet
December 31, 1993
(in thousands)

	Supplemental Current Value Basis	Historical Cost Basis
ASSETS		
Developable properties	$ 766,980	$ 592,497
Income producing properties	708,936	552,387
Surplus developable properties	103,104	75,078
Agricultural and other properties	177,100	12,198
Less accumulated depreciation		(140,328)
Less estimated disposition costs	(43,903)	
	1,712,217	1,091,832
Other assets and deferred charges	8,989	51,207
Notes receivable	10,098	9,579
Accounts receivable	7,195	7,195
Cash, cash equivalents, and investments	214,014	214,014
	$1,952,513	$1,373,827
LIABILITIES AND STOCKHOLDERS' EQUITY		
Mortgage and other debt	$ 645,083	$ 663,764
Accounts payable and accrued expenses	47,585	47,585
Deferred credits and other liabilities	13,109	22,200
Deferred income taxes	244,616	144,329
Total liabilities	950,393	847,878
Stockholders' equity:		
Preferred stock	322,500	322,500
Common stock	730	730
Paid-in capital	244,151	244,151
Retained earnings (accumulated deficit)	(41,432)	(41,432)
Revaluation equity	476,171	
Total stockholders' equity	1,002,120	525,949
Total	$1,952,513	$1,373,827

Statement of Changes in Revaluation Equity
for the Year Ended December 31, 1993
(in thousands)

Revaluation equity at beginning of year	$817,227
Revaluation equity attributable to properties sold	(43,227)
Reduction in value of properties held at beginning and end of year	(344,883)
Decrease in estimated disposition costs	10,554
Other changes *	36,500
Revaluation equity at end of year	$476,171

* Primarily a tax effect that is beyond the scope of this text.

Method 3, historical cost/constant dollars, shows how to remedy the foregoing objections. General indexes may be used to restate the amounts of historical-cost/nominal-dollar Method 1. Examples of such indexes are the Gross National

Product Implicit Price Deflator and the Consumer Price Index for All Urban Consumers (CPI). Anyone who has lived long enough to be able to read this book is aware that the purchasing power of the dollar is unstable. Index numbers are used to gauge the relationship between current conditions and some norm or base condition (which is assigned the index number of 100). For our purpose, a **general price index** compares the average price of a group of goods and services at one date with the average price of a similar group at another date.

A price index is an average. It does not measure the behavior of the individual component prices. Some individual prices may move in one direction and some in another. The general consumer price level may soar while the prices of eggs and chickens decline.

Do not confuse *general* indexes, which are used in constant-dollar accounting, with *specific* indexes. The two have entirely different purposes. Sometimes **specific price indexes** are used as a means of approximating the current costs of particular assets or types of assets. That is, companies use specialized indexes to get low cost approximations of current costs without hiring professional appraisers. For example, Inland Steel has used the Engineering News Record Construction Cost Index to value most of its property, plant, and equipment for purposes of using the current-cost method.

general price index
An index that compares the average price of a group of goods and services at one date with the average price of a similar group at another date.

specific price index
An index used to approximate the current costs of particular assets or types of assets.

Maintaining Invested Capital

The historical-cost/constant-dollar approach (Method 3) is *not* a fundamental departure from historical costs. Instead it maintains that all historical costs to be matched against revenue should be restated on some constant-dollar basis so that all revenues and all expenses can be expressed in dollars of the same (usually current) purchasing power. The restated figures are *historical costs* expressed in constant dollars via the use of a general price index.

The *current* dollar is typically employed because readers of financial statements tend to think in such terms instead of in terms of old dollars with significantly different purchasing power. The original units in inventory would be updated on each year's balance sheet along with their effect on stockholders' equity. For example, the December 31, 19X1 balance sheet would be restated for comparative purposes on December 31, 19X2:

	Not Restated Cost	Multiplier	Restated Cost
Inventory	$8,000	110/100	$8,800
Original paid-in capital	8,000	110/100	8,800

To extend the illustration, suppose all the inventory was held for two full years. The general price index rose from 110 to 132 during 19X3. The December 31, 19X2 balance sheet items would be restated for comparative purposes on December 31, 19X3, using 19X3 dollars:

	Restated Cost 12/31/X2	Multiplier	Restated Cost 12/31/X3
Inventory	$8,800	132/110	$10,560*
Original paid-in capital	8,800	132/110	10,560*

* The same restated 19X3 result could be tied to 19X1, the year of acquisition:
Inventory $8,000 × 132/100 = $10,560
Original paid-in capital $8,000 × 132/100 = $10,560

The restated amount is just that—a restatement of original *cost* in terms of current (19X3) dollars. It is not a gain in any sense. Therefore this approach should not be labeled as an adoption of "current-cost" accounting. Using this approach, if the specific current cost of the inventory goes up or down but the average price level remains unchanged, the restated cost is unaffected.

The restated historical-cost approach harmonizes with the concept of *maintaining the general purchasing power* of the invested capital (a *financial* concept of capital maintenance) in total rather than maintaining "specific invested capital," item by item.

The historical cost/constant dollar (i.e., inflation-adjusted) method is popular in countries that have experienced high inflation rates. It is required in several South American countries. Venezuela, which had accumulated inflation of 523% between 1989 and 1994, just recently switched to inflation-adjusted accounting methods. Venezuelan accounting authorities required supplemental inflation-adjusted statements beginning in 1992 and now require such adjustments in the primary financial statements. For example, consider Corimon, S.A.C.A., a Caracas-based producer of paints, coatings, and related products. The heading and first line of the company's income statement were:

Statement of Income Corimon, S.A.C.A. (expressed in values adjusted for the effects of inflation)		
	Years ended March 31,	
	1994	1993
	(millions of constant bolivars)	
Net sales	26,910	26,015

A footnote to the company's financial statements included the following:

> Traditional financial statements, prepared with historical numbers, are based on the premise that the value of money doesn't change with time, and therefore ignore fluctuations. The reality is that in inflationary economies, money is not stable and its value changes, deteriorating purchasing power with no reflection of the deterioration in the financial statements. As these changes are important, they are now reflected in our financial statements.

The general price index in Venezuela for March 31, 1993 was 211.6 and for March 31, 1994 was 311.7. Both the 26,910 and 26,015 million bolivars are expressed in March 31, 1994 bolivars, showing a sales increase of 3.4% in constant dollars. Suppose the 1993 sales had been expressed in March 31, 1993 bolivars: 26,015 × (211.6 ÷ 311.7) = 17,660 million bolivars. An increase in sales from 17,660 to 26,910 million bolivars makes it appear that sales increased by 52.4%. The inflation-adjusted increase of 3.4% is surely more meaningful to financial statement users than is the 52.4% nominal increase.

Current Cost/Constant Dollars

Method 4 of Exhibit 16-6 shows the results of applying general index numbers together with current costs. As the footnotes of the exhibit explain in more detail, the nominal gains reported under Method 2 are adjusted so that only gains in constant dollars are reported. For example, suppose you buy 100 units on December 31, 19X1 for $2,000 cash. If the current replacement cost of your inventory at December 31, 19X2 is $3,000 but the general price index has risen from 100 to 110, your nominal gain is $1,000, but your "real" gain in constant dollars in 19X2 is only $800: the $3,000 current cost minus the restated historical cost of $2,000 × 1.10 = $2,200.

Suppose the 100 units are held throughout 19X3 while the general price index rises from 110 to 132. The replacement cost rises from $30 to $34, a nominal holding gain for 19X3 of $4 × 100 = $400. However, the current-cost/ constant-dollar approach (Method 4) would report a real holding loss in 19X3:

		December 31	
	19X1	19X2	19X3
Original cost restated for changes in the price level	$2,000	$2,200	$2,640
Current cost	2,000	3,000	3,400
Increase in current cost		1,000*	400*
Increase due to price level		200†	440†
Holding gain (loss)		$ 800	$ (40)

*3,000 – 2,000 = 1,000, and 3,400 – 3,000 = 400
†2,200 – 2,000 = 200, and 2,640 – 2,200 = 440

Many theorists disagree on the relative merits of historical-cost approaches versus miscellaneous versions of current-cost approaches to income measurement. But there is general agreement among the theorists that, ignoring practical barriers, restatements in constant dollars would be an improvement because otherwise income includes illusory gains caused by using an unstable measuring unit.

Summary Problems for Your Review

Problem One

In 1970, a parcel of land, call it parcel 1, was purchased for $1,200. An identical parcel, 2, was purchased today for $3,600. The general-price-level index has risen from 100 in 1970 to 300 now. Fill in the blanks in the table below.

Parcel	(1) Historical Cost Measured in 1970 Purchasing Power	(2) Historical Cost Measured in Current Purchasing Power	(3) Historical Cost as Originally Measured
1	_____	_____	_____
2	_____	_____	_____
Total	======	======	======

1. Compare the figures in the three columns. Which total presents a nonsense result. Why?
2. Does the write-up of parcel 1 in column 2 result in a gain? Why?
3. Assume that these parcels are the only assets of the business. There are no liabilities. Prepare a balance sheet for each of the three columns.

Solution to Problem One

Parcel	(1) Historical Cost Measured in 1970 Purchasing Power	(2) Historical Cost Measured in Current Purchasing Power	(3) Historical Cost as Originally Measured
1	$1,200	$3,600	$1,200
2	1,200	3,600	3,600
Total	$2,400	$7,200	$4,800

1. The addition in column 3 produces a nonsense result. In contrast, the other sums are the results of applying a standard unit of measure. The computations in columns 1 and 2 are illustrations of a restatement of historical cost in terms of a common dollar, a standard unit of measure. Such computations have frequently been called adjustments for changes in the general price level. Whether the restatement is made using the 1970 dollar or the current dollar is a matter of personal preference; columns 1 and 2 yield equivalent results. Restatement in terms of the current dollar (column 2) is most popular because the current dollar has more meaning than the old dollar to the reader of the financial statements.

2. The mere restatement of identical assets in terms of different but equivalent measuring units cannot be regarded as a gain. Expressing parcel 1 as $1,200 in column 1 and $3,600 in column 2 is like expressing parcel 1 in terms of, say, either 1,200 square yards or $9 \times 1,200 = 10,800$ square feet. Surely, the "write-up" from 1,200 square yards to 10,800 square feet is not a gain; it is merely another way of measuring the same asset. The 1,200 square yards and the 10,800 square feet are equivalent; they are different ways of describing the same asset. That is basically what general-price-level accounting is all about. It says you cannot measure one plot of land in square yards and another in square feet and add them together before converting to some common measure. Unfortunately, column 3 fails to perform such a conversion before adding the two parcels together; hence the total is internally inconsistent.

3. The only items on the balance sheets would be:

	(1)	(2)	(3)
Land	$2,400	$7,200	$4,800
Paid-in capital	$2,400	$7,200	$4,800

Note that (1) is expressed in 1970 dollars, (2) is in current dollars, and (3) is a mixture of 1970 and current dollars.

Problem Two

Reexamine Exhibit 16-6, page 750. Suppose the replacement cost at December 31, 19X2 had been $25 instead of $30. Suppose also that the general price index had been 120 instead of 110. All other facts are unchanged. Use four columns to prepare balance sheets as of December 31, 19X2 (only) and income statements for 19X2 under the four concepts shown in Exhibit 16-6.

Solution to Problem Two

The solution is in Exhibit 16-8. In particular, compare Methods 2 and 4. The current cost of inventory items has risen 25% during a period when the general level has risen 20%.

Note too that the historical cost/constant dollar concept restates the old historical-cost amounts in 19X2 dollars rather than 19X1 dollars by multiplying the old dollars by 120/100.

| Exhibit 16-8 | Solution Exhibit for Summary Problem Two |

	Nominal Dollars		**Constant Dollars**	
	(Method 1) Historical Cost[a]	*(Method 2)* Current Cost	*(Method 3)* Historical Cost	*(Method 4)* Current Cost
Balance sheets, December 31, 19X2				
Cash	10,500	10,500	10,500	10,500
Inventory, 100 units	2,000	2,500 [b]	2,400 [d]	2,500 [b]
Total assets	12,500	13,000	12,900	13,000
Original paid-in capital	8,000	8,000 [d]	9,600 [e]	9,600 [e]
Retained income (confined to income from continuing operations)	4,500	3,000	3,300	3,000
Revaluation equity (accumulated holding gains)	—	2,000	—	400
Total stockholders' equity	12,500	13,000	12,900	13,000
Income statements for 19X2				
Sales, 300 units @ $35	10,500	10,500	10,500	10,500
Cost of goods sold, 300 units	6,000	7,500 [b]	7,200 [d]	7,500 [b]
Income from continuing operations	4,500	3,000	3,300	3,000
Holding gains (losses):				
On 300 units sold		1,500 [c]		300 [f]
On 100 units unsold		500 [c]		100 [f]
Total holding gains		2,000		400

[a] All numbers are the same as in Exhibit 16-6, page 750.
[b] 100 × $25   [c] 300 × ($25 – $20)   [d] 120/100 × $2,000   [e] 120/100 × $8,000
   300 × $25   100 × ($25 – $20)   120/100 × $6,000
[f] $7,500 – [(120/100) × 6,000] = $300
   $2,500 – [(120/100) × 2,000] = $100

Highlights to Remember

Accountants have sought a conceptual framework for years, but financial accounting standards are still largely set on a piecemeal basis. The entire standard-setting process is complex. It involves far more than technical aspects because the gaining of general acceptance is a political task.

Accounting standards vary from country to country. Attempts at international standards are progressing, but significant differences are likely to persist.

The assortment of alternatives among generally accepted accounting principles means that managers and accountants have some latitude in selecting the accounting policies of a specific entity. Publicly held companies must publish a statement of their accounting policies as a part of their annual financial reports.

The matching of historical costs with revenue is the generally accepted means of measuring net income. However, this method is often criticized in times of changing prices. Some critics suggest using general price indexes to adjust historical costs so that all expenses are measured in current dollars of the same purchasing power. Such adjustments do not represent a departure from historical cost. A more fundamental change is to base net income computations on some version of current costs. Proponents claim that such a measure is a better gauge of the distinctions between income (the return *on* capital) and capital maintenance (the return *of* capital).

Accounting Vocabulary

accounting policy making, *p. 730*
constant dollars, *p. 748*
current cost, *p. 748*
current-cost method, *p. 749*
financial capital maintenance,
  p. 747
general price index, *p. 753*

historical cost, *p. 748*
inflation, *p. 747*
neutrality, *p. 735*
nominal dollars, *p. 748*
physical capital maintenance,
  p. 747
relevance, *p. 734*

representational faithfulness,
  p. 735
revaluation equity, *p. 751*
specific price index, *p. 753*
validity, *p. 735*
verifiability, *p. 735*

Assignment Material

Questions

16-1. What are the major objectives of financial reporting as chosen by the FASB?

16-2. "Now that the FASB has a conceptual framework, accounting policy making is simply a matter of mechanically applying the framework to issues that arise." Do you agree? Explain.

16-3. What is the fundamental cost-benefit test in accounting policy making?

16-4. Name three types of costs of producing accounting information.

16-5. "It is better to be roughly right than precisely wrong." Interpret this statement in light of the qualitative characteristics of accounting.

16-6. "The ability of a dozen independent accountants to apply the same measurement methods and obtain the same result is an example of validity." Do you agree? Explain.

16-7. "Neutrality underscores a fundamental

approach that should be taken by the FASB." Describe the approach.

16-8. "Accounting theory is unimportant because it is impractical." Do you agree? Explain.

16-9. "Accounting policy making is a political endeavor." Do you agree? Explain.

16-10. "Accounting policies differ so much from country to country that accountants trained in one country have difficulty practicing in another, even if there is no language barrier." Do you agree? Explain.

16-11. How have high inflation rates influenced accounting policies in many countries?

16-12. Do you expect common, worldwide accounting standards within the next decade? Explain.

16-13. "Timing of expense recognition is not important. The important thing is that all expenses eventually be recognized on the income statement." Do you agree? Explain.

16-14. What is a statement of accounting policies?

16-15. "The FASB no longer requires reporting of inflation-adjusted data in annual reports. Therefore there is no reason to study inflation-adjusted financial statements." Do you agree? Explain.

16-16. Distinguish between the physical and the financial concepts of maintenance of invested capital.

16-17. "The choice among accounting measures of income is often expressed as either historical-cost accounting or general-price-level accounting or current-cost accounting." Do you agree? Explain.

16-18. Explain how net income is measured under the current-cost approach.

16-19. What is the common meaning of current cost?

16-20. Explain what a general price index represents.

16-21. Distinguish between general indexes and specific indexes.

16-22. "Specific indexes are used in nominal-dollar accounting but not in constant-dollar accounting." Do you agree? Explain.

16-23. "All holding gains should be excluded from income." What is the major logic behind this statement?

Exercises

16-24   Statements of Financial Accounting Concepts
Using your own words, describe the basic contents of *Statements of Financial Accounting Concepts* Numbers 1, 2, 3, and 5. Use only *one sentence* for each statement. Make each sentence as informative as possible.

16-25   Costs and Benefits of Information
The FASB recently required companies to include a liability for postretirement benefits on their balance sheets. Postretirement benefits are items such as health insurance that are provided to retired employees. Many companies argued against such a requirement. They maintained that the costs would exceed the benefits.

Required
1. Discuss the potential costs and benefits of mandatory reporting of a liability for postretirement benefits on companies' balance sheets.
2. Assess the relevance and reliability of measuring and reporting such a liability.

16-26   Characteristics of Information
International Paper Company shows the following under long-term assets in its balance sheet (in millions):

Forestlands	$786

A footnote described the forestlands as 6.2 million acres that are "stated at cost, less accumulated depletion." The average cost of the timberlands is $127 per acre. Suppose the current market price is estimated to be between $300 and $600 per acre, providing a best estimate of total market value of $450 × 6.2 million = $2,790 million.

Required
1. Which measure, the $786 million or $2,790 million, is more relevant? What characteristics make it relevant?
2. Which measure is more reliable? What characteristics make it reliable?
3. If you were an investor considering the purchase of common stock in International Paper, which measure would be most valuable to you? Explain.

16-27   Effect of Inventory and Depreciation Methods on Income
Chippewa Materials began business on January 2, 19X1, with a cash investment by shareholders of $50,000. Management immediately purchased inventory for $30,000 and a machine for $20,000. The machine has a useful life of four years and no salvage value.

The inventory was sold during 19X1 for $60,000, and it was replaced at a cost of $40,000. Ignore taxes.

Required
1. Compute operating income assuming Chippewa uses FIFO and straight-line depreciation.

2. Compute operating income assuming Chippewa uses LIFO and double-declining-balance depreciation.

3. Compare the answers in requirements 1 and 2. Does the choice of accounting method make a difference? Explain.

16-28   Effects of Transactions on Financial Statements

For each of the following numbered items, select the lettered transaction that indicates its effect on the corporation's financial statements. If a transaction has more than one effect, list all applicable letters. Assume that the total current assets exceed the total current liabilities both before and after every transaction described.

NUMBERED TRANSACTIONS

1. Sale on account at a gross profit.

2. Collection of account receivable.

3. Purchase of inventory on open account.

4. Payment of trade account payable.

5. Issuance of additional common shares as a stock dividend.

6. Sale for cash of a factory building at a selling price that substantially exceeds the book value.

7. The destruction of a building by fire. Insurance proceeds, collected immediately, slightly exceed book value.

8. The appropriation of retained earnings as a reserve for contingencies.

9. Issue of new shares in a three-for-one split of common stock.

LETTERED EFFECTS

a. Increases working capital.

b. Decreases working capital.

c. Increases current ratio.

d. Decreases current ratio.

e. Increases the book value per share of common stock.

f. Decreases the book value per share of common stock.

g. Increases total retained earnings.

h. Decreases total retained earnings.

i. Increases total stockholders' equity.

j. Decreases total stockholders' equity.

k. None of the above.

16-29   Financial and Physical Capital Maintenance

Hollywood Convenience Grocery began business on January 2, 19X3, with a cash investment of $70,000, which was used to immediately purchase inventory. One-half of the inventory was sold for $55,000 during January and was not replaced before the end of the month. The cost to replace the inventory would have been $40,000 on January 31.

Required

1. Using the financial capital maintenance concept, compute operating income for January.

2. Using the physical capital maintenance concept, compute operating income for January.

16-30   Holding Gains

Trajan Cedar Mill had cedar logs that were purchased for $20,000 on March 1, 19X2. During March Congress passed a law severely restricting the cutting of cedar trees, so the replacement cost of the logs jumped to $34,000. On March 31, half of the logs were sold for $17,000.

Required

Compute the holding gain on the logs for the month of March under (a) the historical cost/nominal dollar method and (b) the current cost/nominal dollar method.

16-31 Inventory in Constant Dollars

On December 31, 19X1, Lenhoff Company bought inventory for $9,000. During 19X2 half of the inventory was sold, and on December 31, 19X2, the inventory that was sold was replaced at a cost of $5,000. The price index was 110 on 12/31/X1 and 121 on 12/31/X2.

Required

Compute the inventory reported on the balance sheets of 12/31/X1 and 12/31/X2 assuming that Lenhoff uses (a) the historical cost/nominal dollar method of accounting and FIFO and (b) the historical cost/constant dollar method of accounting.

16-32 Meaning of General Index Applications and Choice of Base Year

Alamo County Hospital acquired land in mid-1976 for $3 million. In mid-1996 it acquired a substantially identical parcel of land for $6 million. The general-price-level index annual averages were:

1996—210.0   1986—100.0   1976—60.0

Required

1. In four columns, show the computations of the total cost of the two parcels of land expressed in (a) costs as traditionally recorded, (b) dollars of 1996 purchasing power, (c) 1986 purchasing power, and (d) 1976 purchasing power.
2. Explain the meaning of the figures that you computed in requirement 1.

Problems

16-33 Revenue Recognition and Percentage-of-Completion

Van den Boom Company contracted to build a large river bridge for the city of Amsterdam. The board of directors is about to meet to decide whether to adopt the completed-contract or the percentage-of-completion method of accounting. The percentage-of-completion method recognizes income based on incurred costs to date, divided by these known costs plus the estimated future costs to complete the contract. It computes an applicable percentage as follows:

$$\frac{\text{Percentage}}{\text{of completion}} = \frac{\text{Costs incurred to date}}{\left(\begin{array}{c}\text{Costs incurred} \\ \text{to date}\end{array}\right) + \left(\begin{array}{c}\text{Estimated additional} \\ \text{costs to compute}\end{array}\right)}$$

The percentage is applied to the total contract price to determine the recognized revenue for the period.

Van den Boom began business on January 1, 19X4. Construction activity for the year ended December 31, 19X4, revealed (in millions of Netherlands guilders, NG):

Total contract price	NG 88
Billings through December 31, 19X4	35
Cash collections	28
Contract costs incurred	42
Estimated additional costs to complete the contract	14

Any work remaining to be done is expected to be completed in 19X5. Ignore selling and other expenses as well as income taxes.

Required

Prepare a schedule computing the amount of revenue and income that would be reported for 19X4 under
    a. The completed-contract method
    b. The percentage-of-completion method (based on estimated costs)

16-34   Recognition Criteria

Fortune reported on a recent Supreme Court decision related to accrual accounting. The Internal Revenue Service (IRS) and several casinos disagreed on when to recognize revenue and expenses for progressive slot machines. These slot machines have no limit to the payoff. They pay a lucky winner the money others have put into the machine since the last payoff (less the house takeout, of course). The longer since the last win, the larger the jackpot. Progressive slots pay off on average every four and one-half months.

Suppose that on December 31, 1995, Harrah's Casino had a progressive slot machine that had not paid off recently. In fact, $1.2 million had been placed in the machine since its last payoff on February 13, 1995. Assume that the house's take out is 5%.

The IRS regarded the $1.2 million as revenue but allowed no expense until a payoff occurred. The casinos argued that an expense equal to 95% of the revenue will eventually be incurred, and accrual accounting would require recognition of the expense at the same time as the revenue is recorded.

Required

1. How much revenue should Harrah's recognize in 1995 from the machine? Explain fully.
2. How much expense should Harrah's recognize in 1995 from the machine? Explain fully.
3. The IRS argued that no expense should be recognized until a payoff to the winner had been made. What do you suppose was the basis for their argument?
4. Suppose you are a gambler who uses accrual accounting. How would you account for $100 placed into the progressive slot machine described above? Is this consistent with your answers to requirements 1 and 2? Why or why not?

16-35   Nature of Capital, Income, Revenue

(M. Wolfson, adapted) Here is a letter written by the financial vice-president of Acurex Corporation, a manufacturer of energy, environmental, and agricultural equipment:

Dear Professor:

We are engaged in a somewhat unusual government contract with the Department of Energy as a demonstration, or "showcase," program. We are designing and constructing a fuel delivery system for industrial boilers in which we will cost-share 35% of the total cost with the government. In return, we are awarded immediate title to all the equipment involved, including the government's 65% portion.

It seems to me that there is some real logic in reflecting the government's gift of 65% of total cost in current earnings, subject only to a test of net realizable value. I'd appreciate your thoughts.

Sincerely,

The company's net income the previous year was $1,007,000.

Required

Suppose the cost of the fuel delivery system is $1.2 million. This consists of about $600,000 in "hard assets" (equipment, etc.) and about $600,000 in designing costs. Via journal entries, show at least two ways in which the government contract could be reflected in Acurex's books, assuming the costs are all incurred prior to the end of the year. What is the effect of your two ways on the year's pretax income?

16-36   Japanese Annual Reports

Kobe Steel, Ltd., is one of the world's top twenty producers of iron and steel products and is also one of the most diversified corporations in Japan. The company's annual sales are about $8 billion at current exchange rates.

Kobe Steel maintains its records and prepares its financial statements in accordance with generally accepted accounting principles and practices in Japan. Selected parts of Kobe Steel's "Summary of Significant Accounting Policies" are reproduced below:

2. Summary of Significant Accounting Policies

Consolidation

The consolidated financial statements include the accounts of the Company and its significant majority-owned subsidiaries (the "Group"). Intercompany transactions and accounts have been eliminated. The difference, if considered significant, between the cost of investments and the equity in their net assets at their dates of acquisition is amortized over five years (forty years for acquisitions made by certain foreign consolidated subsidiaries).

Allowance for Doubtful Receivables

The allowance for doubtful receivables is provided in amounts sufficient to cover possible losses on collection. It is determined by adding the uncollectible amounts individually estimated for doubtful receivables to a maximum amount permitted for tax purposes which is calculated collectively.

Marketable Securities and Investment Securities

Listed equity securities, both in marketable securities and investment securities, except for certain equity securities of subsidiaries and affiliates in which the Company's ownership equals or exceeds 25 percent, are stated at the lower of moving average cost or market value. Other securities, excluding investments accounted for by the equity method, are stated at moving average cost. If significant impairment of value is deemed permanent, cost has been appropriately reduced.

Inventories

Inventories are valued at cost, as determined by the following methods:

Two main works of the Iron & Steel and Welding sector and three main plants of the Aluminum & Copper Division....... Last-in, first-out

Finished goods and work in process in the Machinery Division and one plant of the Iron & Steel and Welding sector....... Specific Identification

Others.. Weighted average

Depreciation

Depreciation of property, plant, and equipment is principally provided using the straight-line method over estimated useful lives.

Long-term Construction Contracts

Sales and related costs of certain long-term (over one year) construction contracts are recognized by the percentage of completion method.

Research and Development Expenses

Expenses for development of new products and research and application for new technologies, which are expected to contribute to future sales, are deferred and amortized over a five-year period.

Income Taxes

Income taxes are based on taxable income and charged to income on the taxes payable method. Deferred income taxes relating to timing differences between financial accounting and tax reporting purposes are not recognized by certain foreign consolidated subsidiaries.

Allowance for Special Repairs

Blast furnaces and hot blast stoves, including related machinery and equipment, periodically require substantial component replacement and repair. The estimated future costs of such work are provided for and charged to income on a straight-line basis over the period to the date of the anticipated replacement and repair. The difference between such estimated costs and actual costs is charged or credited to income at the time the work takes place.

Required   Identify the accounting policies used by Kobe Steel that would not be generally accepted in the United States.

16-37   Effects of Various Accounting Methods on Net Income

You are the manager of Hiramatsu Company, a profitable new company that has high potential growth. It is nearing the end of your first year in business and you must make some decisions regarding accounting policies for financial reporting to stockholders. Your controller and your certified public accountant have gathered the following information (all figures in thousands except tax rate):

Revenue	$40,000
Beginning inventory	0
Purchases	21,000
Ending inventory—if LIFO is used	6,000
Ending inventory—if FIFO is used	8,000
Depreciation—if straight-line is used	1,500
Depreciation—if double-declining-balance is used	3,000
Store-opening costs	4,000
Store-opening costs (amortized amount)	800
Other expenses	5,000
Income tax rate	40%
Common shares outstanding	2,000

Double-declining-balance depreciation will be used for tax purposes regardless of the method chosen for reporting to stockholders. For all other items, assume that the same method is used for tax purposes and for financial reporting purposes.

Required   1. Prepare a columnar income statement such as in Exhibit 16-4 on page 744. In column 1 show the results using LIFO, double-declining-balance depreciation, and direct write-off of store-opening costs. Show earnings per share as well as net income. In successive columns, show the separate effects on net income and earnings per share of substituting the alternative methods: column 2, FIFO inventory; column 3, straight-line depreciation; column 4, amortization of store-opening costs. In column 5, show the total results of choosing all the alternative methods (columns 2 through 4). Note that in columns 2 through 4 only single changes from column 1 should be shown; that is, column 3 does not show the effects of columns 2 and 3 together, nor does column 4 show the effects of columns 2, 3, and 4 together.
2. As the manager, which accounting policies would you adopt? Why?

16-38   Effects of Various Accounting Methods on Income

General Electric had the following data in its 1993 annual report (in millions of dollars except for earnings per share):

Total revenues	$60,562
Cost of goods and services sold	28,914
Depreciation, depletion, and amortization	3,261
Other expenses (summarized here)	21,812
Total expenses	53,987
Earnings before income taxes	6,575
Provision for income taxes	2,151
Net earnings	$ 4,424
Net earnings per share (in dollars)	$ 5.18

Inventories on December 31, 1993, were $3,824 million and on December 31, 1992, were $4,574 million. If FIFO had been used instead of LIFO, the FIFO inventories would have been higher by $1,629 million at December 31, 1993, and $1,808 million at December 31, 1992.

The company stated that most depreciation is computed by accelerated methods, primarily sum-of-the-years'-digits.

General Electric's marginal 1993 income tax rate was 35%.

Required Suppose General Electric had used straight-line depreciation for reporting to shareholders, resulting in depreciation, depletion, and amortization expense of $2,261 million rather than $3,261 million in 1993. Also suppose the company had used FIFO instead of LIFO. Recast all the above data for 1993, including the amount earned per common share. Show supporting computations.

16-39   Four Versions of Income and Capital
Baldridge Instruments Company has the following comparative balance sheets as of December 31 (based on historical costs in nominal dollars):

	19X4	19X5
Cash	$ —	$4,500
Inventory, 50 and 20 units, respectively	5,000	2,000
Total assets	$5,000	$6,500
Paid-in capital	$5,000	$5,000
Retained income	—	1,500
Stockholders' equity	$5,000	$6,500

The general-price-level index was 120 on December 31, 19X4, and 138 on December 31, 19X5. The company had acquired fifty units of inventory on December 31, 19X4, for $100 each and had held them throughout 19X5. Thirty units were sold on December 31, 19X5, for $150 cash each. The replacement cost of the inventory at that date was $120 per unit. Assume that these are the only transactions. Ignore income taxes.

Required Use four sets of columns to prepare comparative balance sheets as of December 31, 19X4 and 19X5, and income statements for 19X5 using (1) historical cost/nominal dollars, (2) current cost/nominal dollars, (3) historical cost/constant dollars, and (4) current cost/constant dollars.

16-40   Concepts of Income

Suppose you are in the business of investing in land and holding it for resale. On December 31, 19X2, a parcel of land had a historical cost of $100,000 and a current value (measured via use of a specific price index) of $300,000; the general price level had doubled since the land has acquired. Suppose also that the land was sold a year later on December 31, 19X3, for $360,000. The general price level rose by 5% during 19X3.

Required

1. Prepare a tabulation of income from continuing operations and holding gains for 19X3, using the four methods illustrated in Exhibit 16-6.
2. In your own words, explain the meaning of the results, giving special attention to what income represents.

16-41   LIFO and Current Costs

Blackstone Company began business on December 31, 19X1, when it acquired 200 units of inventory for $20 per unit. It held the inventory until December 31, 19X2, when it acquired 200 more units for $30 per unit and sold 300 units for $35 each. Assume that these are the company's only transactions, and ignore income taxes.

Required

1. Compute operating income using the historical-cost/nominal dollars method and a FIFO inventory method.
2. Compute operating income using the historical-cost/nominal dollars method and a LIFO inventory method.
3. Compute operating income using the current cost/nominal dollar method.
4. Explain the differences in operating income in requirements 1, 2, and 3.
5. Does historical cost/nominal dollar operating income using LIFO give results that approximate current cost operating income? Why or why not?

16-42   Reporting on Changing Prices

Transamerica Corporation, a large diversified company, reported operating income of $151 million on sales of $5,399 million. After adjusting for changes in specific prices (current costs), operating income was $107 million. Three other amounts reported were related to holding gains (in millions):

Effect of increase in general price level	$64
Excess of increase in specific prices over increase in general price level	$23
Increase in specific prices of inventories and property and equipment held during the year	$87

Required

1. Identify the holding gain under the current-cost/nominal-dollars method.
2. Identify the holding gain under the current-cost/constant-dollars method.
3. Explain why the holding gain in requirement 1 differs from that in requirement 2.

16-43   Depreciation and Price-Level Adjustments

Shapiro Legal Services purchased a computer with networking services for $400,000. This computer has an expected life of four years and an expected residual value of zero. Straight-line depreciation is used. The general price index is 150 at the date of acquisition; it increases 30 points annually during the next three years. The results follow:

Year	Price-Level Index	Historical-Cost/ Nominal-Dollar Depreciation	Multiplier	Historical-Cost/ Constant-Dollar Depreciation as Recorded
1	150	$100,000	$\frac{150}{150}$	$100,000
2	180	100,000	$\frac{180}{150}$	120,000
3	210	100,000	$\frac{210}{150}$	140,000
4	240	100,000	$\frac{240}{150}$	160,000
		$400,000		

Required

1. Convert the figures in the last column so that they are expressed in terms of fourth-year dollars. For example, the $120,000 second-year dollars would have to be restated by multiplying by 240/180.
2. Suppose in requirement 1 that revenue easily exceeds expenses for each year and that cash equal to the annual depreciation charge was invested in a noninterest-bearing cash account. If amounts equal to the unadjusted depreciation charge were invested each year, would sufficient cash have accumulated to equal the general purchasing power of $400,000 invested in the asset four years ago? If not, what is the extent of the total financial deficiency measured in terms of fourth-year dollars?
3. Suppose in requirement 2 that amounts equal to the constant-dollar depreciation for each year were used. What is the extent of the total financial deficiency?
4. Suppose in requirement 3 that the amounts were invested each year in assets that increased in value at the same rate as the increase in the general price level. What is the extent of the total financial deficiency?

16-44 Revenues in Constant Dollars
Alcoa, the aluminum company, reported the following total revenues (in millions):

	1993	1992	1991	1990	1989
Historical basis	$9,056	$9,492	$ 9,884	$10,710	$10,910
In average 1993 dollars	9,056	9,776	10,486	11,841	?

The average Consumer Price Index was 144.5 in 1993 and 124.0 in 1989.

Required Compute the following:

1. Total revenues for 1989 in average 1993 dollars. Round to the nearest million.
2. Percentage decrease in revenues between 1989 and 1993 on a historical cost basis.
3. Percentage decrease in revenues between 1989 and 1993 in average 1993 dollars.
4. Average Consumer Price Index for 1991.

16-45 Effects of General Versus Specific Price Changes
The following data are from the annual reports of Gannett Co., owner of 120 newspapers; Zayre Corporation, operator of 290 discount stores; and Goodyear Tire and Rubber Company:

(in millions)	Gannett	Zayre	Goodyear
Increase in specific prices of assets held during the year[*]	$45.8	$ 24.9	$ (4.7)
Less effect of increase in general price level	37.5	55.5	252.0
Excess of increase in specific prices over increase in the general price level[†]	$ 8.3	$(30.6)	$(256.7)

[*] Holding gain using current-cost/nominal-dollars method.
[†] Holding gain using current-cost/constant-dollars method.

Required

Compare and contrast the relationship between changes in the general price level and changes in the prices of the specific assets of each of the three companies.

16-46   Ethics and Business Practices

Ethical considerations affect business decisions of many companies. Consider the brief descriptions of how ethics affects each of the following three companies:

A. Baxter International, Inc. – This health-care company adopted an aggressive environmental and ethical policy in 1990. The company met its goal of having all its facilities in the United States achieve "state of the art" environmental status by 1993. Between 1990 and 1993 it reduced emissions of 17 toxic substances by 94%. In three years it reduced hazardous waste by 49%. In 1993 the company increased the percentage of women in its work force from 46% to 52% and the percentage of minorities from 28% to 29%. The company has a Corporate Responsibility Office that benchmarks Baxter's policies against companies known to have exemplary business practices. Baxter's commitment is to "assure that the company follows, at all times, the highest standards of corporate responsibility." (Note: All this information is contained in Baxter's annual report.)

B. SC Johnson Wax–Since its founding in 1896, Johnson Wax has been committed to putting something back into the community. As described in the August 1994 issue of *Management Accounting*, the company contributes a minimum of 5% of pretax profits to charities. It also promotes employee involvement in community service activities. Two areas where Johnson Wax has been especially supportive are education and the environment. From elementary schools through colleges and universities, a variety of programs improve the quality of education and thereby the quality of Johnson Wax's work force. For the environment, Johnson Wax first makes its operations as environmentally friendly as possible. In addition, the company supports numerous outside environmental activities that improve the communities in which it operates. Underlying the philanthropic vision is the belief that Johnson Wax will eventually benefit from contributing to worthy social causes.

C. Calvert Social Managed Fund–Calvert is the largest of approximately 33 U.S. mutual funds devoted to "ethical investing." Calvert directs more than $500 million into companies whose business practices meet certain ethical standards. According to *The Economist*, total assets in "ethical" mutual funds exceed $2.5 billion. These funds avoid companies for a variety of reasons, among them companies that damage the environment, make weapons, sell tobacco or alcohol, discriminate in employment, or use animals in testing products. Each fund has its own standards.

Required

Describe how ethical issues might affect the decisions of each company. Do you believe these firms view ethical behavior as primarily a cost or a benefit? List some specific costs for each company and some potential benefits.

16-47   Comprehensive Review: Reconstruct Transactions

Childrobics, Inc. was incorporated in New York State on May 7, 1993. The company owns and operates indoor recreation facilities for children and their families in the New York metropolitan area. The company prepared financial statements on February 28, 1994, for the period since incorporation. Slightly revised versions of the company's balance sheet and statement of cash flows are on page 771. Footnotes pointed out that, in exchange for a note payable of $250,000, the creditors supplied $146,000 in cash and $104,000 in property and equipment.

Required   Compute amounts to replace each of the question marks in Childrobics' balance sheet.

Childrobics, Inc.
Balance Sheet
February 28, 1994

ASSETS		
Current assets:		
Cash		$?
Property and equipment:		
At cost	$?	
Accumulated depreciation	?	
Net		?
Other assets		25,300
Total assets		$?
LIABILITIES AND STOCKHOLDERS' EQUITY		
Current liabilities:		
Accounts payable and accrued expenses	$?	
Deferred revenue	?	
Note payable	?	
Total current liabilities		$?
Stockholders' equity:		
Common stock–$.01 par value, 25,000,000 shares authorized, 975,000 shares issued and outstanding	?	
Additional paid-in capital	?	
Retained Earnings	?	
Total stockholders' equity		?
Total liabilities and stockholders' equity		$?

Childrobics, Inc.
Statement of Cash
Flows
for the Period Ended
February 28, 1994

OPERATING ACTIVITIES:		
Net income	$ 2,516	
Adjustment to reconcile net income to net cash provided by operating activities:		
Depreciation	10,947	
Change in assets and liabilities:		
Accounts payable and accrued expenses	59,871	
Deferred revenue – customer deposits	13,450	
Net cash – operating activities		$ 86,784
INVESTING ACTIVITIES:		
Purchases of property and equipment	$(192,583)	
Expenditures for other assets	(25,300)	
Net cash – investing activities		(217,883)
FINANCING ACTIVITIES:		
Loans	$ 146,000	
Common stock	25,000	
Net cash – financing activities		171,000
Net increase in cash		39,901
Cash – beginning of period		0
Cash – end of period		$ 39,901

16-48   Comprehensive Review: Reconstruct Transactions

Interlinq Software Corporation develops, sells, and supports PC-based systems for residential mortgage loan management. Its products are used by approximately 1,400 companies in all fifty states. Its main product is called MortgageWare.

Interlinq's balance sheets for 1992 and 1993 and statement of cash flows for 1993 are on pages 770–72w. In addition to the information in the two statements, you should know that Interlinq had two non-cash transactions that affected their statements. First, all of the preferred stock outstanding at the end of 1992 was converted to common stock during 1993. The balance sheet amount of $14,306 was transferred to the common stock accounts, split between common stock at par and additional paid-in capital. Second, a tax benefit was received from the exercise of stock options. This resulted in a decrease in taxes payable and an increase in paid in capital, both in the amount of $57,370.

Required

1. Compute the amount to replace each of the question marks in Interlinq's balance sheet and statement of cash flows. You might find it helpful to begin with the Statement of Cash Flows.
2. Assess the performance of Interlinq during 1993.

Interlinq Software Corporation
Balance Sheets
as of June 30, 1992 and 1993

Assets	1993	1992
Current assets:		
Cash and cash equivalents	$?	$1,829,264
Short-term investments, at cost	?	—
Certificates of deposit	?	32,754
Accounts receivable, less allowance for doubtful accounts of $128,592 in 1993 and $48,530 in 1992	1,787,572	1,159,186
Current portion of contracts receivable, less allowance for doubtful contracts of $92,725 in 1993 and $66,500 in 1992	463,926	194,607
Software license fee rights, less accumulated amortization of $217,838 in 1993 and $121,340 in 1992	?	104,010
Inventory	68,984	21,580
Prepaid expenses	?	14,943
Deferred income taxes	149,104	17,674
Total current assets	?	3,374,018
Furniture and equipment, at cost	?	2,188,595
Less accumulated depreciation and amortization	1,480,538	1,106,496
Net furniture and equipment	?	1,082,099
Contracts receivable, excluding current portion	332,360	171,401
Deposits	7,500	25,937
Capitalized software costs, less accumulated amortization of $1,986,427 in 1993 and $1,418,558 in 1992	?	1,001,492
Total Assets	$?	$5,654,947
Liabilities and Shareholders' Equity		
Current liabilities		
Bank notes payable	$?	$ 228,360
Current installments of obligations under capital leases	0	10,860
Accounts payable	?	294,759
Accrued profit sharing	?	185,325
Accrued commissions	205,013	132,797

continued

Other accrued liabilities	342,587	263,573
Customer deposits	435,834	266,623
Income taxes payable	?	100,693
Deferred software support fees	?	1,166,475
Total current liabilities	?	2,649,465
Noncurrent liabilities, excluding current installments:		
Deferred rent	?	45,291
Deferred software support fees	113,490	58,511
Total noncurrent liabilities	?	103,802
Shareholders' equity		
Series A redeemable convertible preferred stock, $.01 par value. Authorized 5,000,000 shares; issued and outstanding 1,430,575 shares in 1992	—	14,306
Common stock, $.01 par value. Authorized 30,000,000 shares; issued and outstanding 5,501,558 shares in 1993 and 1,083,962 shares in 1992	?	10,840
Additional paid-in capital	?	3,044,876
Retained earnings (deficit)	?	(168,342)
Total shareholders' equity	?	2,901,680
Total Liabilities and Shareholders' Equity	$?	$5,654,947

Interlinq Software Corporation
Statement of Cash Flows for the Year Ended June 30, 1993

Cash flows from operating activities:	
Net income	$ 2,598,603
Adjustments to reconcile net income to net cash provided by operating activities:	
Depreciation and amortization of furniture and equipment	609,935
Amortization of capitalized software costs	567,869
Amortization of software license fee rights	96,498
Loss on disposition of equipment	79,860
Change in certain assets and liabilities:	
Increase in accounts receivable	?
Increase in contracts receivable	(430,278)
Increase in inventory and prepaid expenses	(136,534)
Increase in deferred income taxes	?
Decrease in deposits	?
Increase in accounts payable	208,729
Increase in accrued profit sharing	34,285
Increase in accrued commissions, other accrued liabilities, and deferred rent	395,781
Increase in customer deposits	?
Increase in income taxes payable	152,024
Increase in deferred software support fees	768,554
Net cash provided by operating activities	?
Cash flows from investing activities:	
Purchases of furniture and equipment	(1,321,546)
Capitalized software costs	(980,514)
Proceeds from sale of certificates of deposit	32,754
Purchase of short-term investments	(1,500,000)
Proceeds from sale of furniture and equipment	176,245
Net cash used in investing activities	(3,593,061)

continued

continued

Interlinq Software Corporation Statement of Cash Flows for the Year Ended June 30, 1993 Continued

Cash flows from financing activities:	
Principal payments on bank note payable	(228,360)
Principal payments on long-term debt	—
Principal payments on capital leases	(10,860)
Proceeds from issuance of bank note payable	
Proceeds from issuance of long-term debt	—
Proceeds from issuance of common stock	10,635,055
Repurchase of common stock	—
Dividends paid	(71,529)
Net cash provided by financing activities	10,324,306
Net increase in cash and cash equivalents	$?

16-49 Wal-Mart Annual Report

Examine the income statement of Wal-Mart (p. 779). The cost of sales is based on the LIFO inventory method. The operating, selling, and general and administrative expenses include $1,070,000,000 of depreciation and amortization, which is computed using the straight-line method.

Suppose Wal-Mart had switched to replacement cost and accelerated depreciation at the beginning of fiscal 1995. Prior-year results were not restated. Therefore balance sheet amounts for January 31, 1994, were unaffected by the changes. As a result of the change, the ending inventory amount at January 31, 1995, was $14,415,000,000 instead of $14,064,000,000 and depreciation and amortization charged during fiscal 1995 was $1,170,000,000 instead of $1,070,000,000. For requirements 1 and 2, assume that the changes were made for shareholder reporting only; no change was made in tax statements.

Required

1. Compute the revised fiscal 1995 income before income taxes.
2. The effective tax rate is 37%. Compute the revised fiscal 1995 provision for income taxes and net income for Wal-Mart.

16-50 Compact D from Disclosure

Select any company from the ones available on Compact D. Be sure that amounts are available for both beginning and ending inventory and depreciation and amortization for the most recent fiscal year.

Suppose your company changed its inventory and depreciation methods beginning with the start of the most recent fiscal year. Prior-year results were not restated. Therefore balance sheet amounts at the beginning of the year were unaffected by the changes.

The changes caused the ending inventory value to be 10% lower than the amount shown in the statements and the annual depreciation and amortization to be 20% greater. (Such changes might result from a switch from FIFO to LIFO and from straight-line to accelerated depreciation. However, assume the given changes regardless of the inventory and depreciation methods currently being used.)

1. Compute the revised income before income taxes for the most recent fiscal year.
2. Compute the company's effective tax rate. Then compute the revised provision for income taxes, net income, and net income per share for your company in the most recent fiscal year.
3. Assume that your company reports the same cost of sales on its tax and shareholder income statements. However, the tax statement includes the new depreciation and amortization (that is, it is 20% higher on the tax statement than on shareholder reports). Now assume that the inventory method is changed as specified in the problem for both tax and shareholder reports, while the depreciation and amortization is changed in the shareholder report only. This makes tax and shareholder reports identical. What would be the effect of the change in tax reporting on the income taxes shown on the income statement for shareholder reporting? What would be the effect on the taxes currently payable and the deferred taxes on the reports to shareholders?
4. Assume that the changes in requirement 3 are allowed for both tax and shareholder reporting. What factors would affect your company's decision about whether or not to make the changes?

Wal-Mart Annual Report

Wal-Mart is a rapidly growing, very successful, innovative retailer. Its growth has been founded on a strategy of good service, low prices, and sophisticated relations with suppliers. Wal-Mart has innovated just-in-time inventory concepts at the retail level and has developed information-sharing computer networks that allow suppliers to anticipate Wal-Mart's delivery needs.

The 1995 letter to Wal-Mart's "Friends," its shareholders and employee Associates, communicated the details of another successful year. Material from that letter is summarized below, followed by numerous pages from the annual report. We appreciate Wal-Mart's permission to reproduce this information for use and analysis throughout your introduction to financial accounting.

The letter to shareholders reported another record year due to the contributions of the 622,000 Associates in the Wal-Mart family. Wal-Mart has been named the number-one American corporation in responsiveness to Shareholders by the United Shareholders Association and was ranked by *Fortune* magazine as one of the three most admired American corporations.

In 1995, total sales increased 22%, including sales growth from new stores. Sales increased 7% in "comparable stores," those open for two full years by the end of 1995. Return on beginning-of-the-year shareholders' equity was 24.9%. Wal-Mart stores increased to 2,176 in 1995, up 37 from 1994. Supporting the growth was a new investment of $4,500,000,000, and additional capital expenditures were planned for 1996. The financial results in the following pages include the standard financial statements and notes, management's discussion and analysis, the audit opinion, and the mandatory statement regarding responsibility for the financial statements.

■ MANAGEMENT'S DISCUSSION AND ANALYSIS

Results of Operations

Revenues

Sales for the three fiscal years ended January 31 and the respective total and comparable store percentage increases over the prior year were:

Fiscal Year	Sales (in millions)	Total Company Increases	Comparable Store Increase
1995	$82,494	22%	7%
1994	67,344	21%	6%
1993	55,484	26%	11%

The sales increase of 22% in fiscal 1995 compared with fiscal 1994 was attributed to 111 new stores, 6 new Supercenters, and 22 new Sam's Clubs; sales from the relocation or expansion of 69 existing Wal-Mart stores into Supercenters; comparative store sales increase of 7%; and the entry into the Canadian market through the purchase of 122 stores from Woolworth Canada, Inc., a subsidiary of Woolworth Corporation. Sam's Clubs sales as a percentage of total sales increased by 1.1%, part of which is attributable to the PACE units acquired in the fourth quarter of fiscal 1994. Supercenter sales as a percentage of total sales increased by .5% and Canada stores sales accounted for 1.5% of total sales.

The sales increase of 21% in fiscal 1994 compared with fiscal 1993 was attributable to 142 new stores, 1 new Supercenter, and 65 new Sam's Clubs; sales from the relocation or expansion of 37 existing Wal-Mart stores into Supercenters; comparative store sales increases of 6%; a 37% growth in the sales of the McLane Company, and the acquisition of 99 PACE Clubs in the fourth quarter. Sam's Clubs sales as a percentage of total sales decreased by .3% while the McLane Company sales as a percentage of total sales increased by .7%.

New Wal-Mart Stores and Sam's Clubs	1995	1994	1993
New Wal-Mart stores	111	142	161
New Supercenters	6	1	
Wal-Mart stores relocated or expanded to Supercenters	69	37	24
New Sam's Clubs	22	65	48
Acquired PACE clubs		99	
Acquired Canada Woolco stores	122		
New Canada stores	1		

Costs and Expenses

Cost of sales as a percentage of sales increased .1% in fiscal 1995 as compared with fiscal 1994 and decreased .3% in fiscal 1994 as compared with fiscal 1993. The increase in fiscal 1993 is primarily due to a larger percentage of consolidated sales attributable to Sam's Clubs resulting in part from the addition of the PACE Clubs. The cost of sales on Sam's Clubs is significantly higher as a percentage of sales than in Wal-Mart stores due to a lower markup on purchases. The decrease in fiscal 1994 as compared with fiscal 1993 was due to a larger percentage of consolidated sales attributed to departments within Wal-Mart stores which have higher markon percents and increases in markon percents in Sam's Clubs and McLane Company.

Operating, selling, and general and administrative expenses as a percentage of sales increased .2% and .3%, respectively, in each of the last two fiscal years when compared with the previous year. The increase in fiscal 1995 was primarily attributable to the acquisition of the Canada stores and higher payroll and payroll related benefit costs. The increase in fiscal 1994 was due principally to higher payroll and payroll-related benefit cost, depreciation costs and certain occupancy costs in part attributable to the Company's expansion program.

Interest Cost

Interest cost increased in fiscal 1995 and 1994 due primarily to increased indebtedness in each of the years, which is attributable to the expansion program. The cost of short-term borrowing increased as average short-term borrowing rates increased approximately 1.4% on fiscal 1995 compared with fiscal 1994. Interest cost will increase in fiscal 1996 with the additional borrowing required to finance the expansion program. The Company may use short-term borrowing arrangements to take advantage of the most favorable financing rates. See Note 2 of Notes to Consolidated Financial Statements for additional information on interest and debt.

Income Taxes

The effective income tax rate was 37.1% and 36.8% in fiscal 1995 and 1994 respectively. See Note 4 of Notes to Consolidated Financial Statements for additional information on income taxes.

■ LIQUIDITY AND CAPITAL RESOURCES

Cash Flow Information

Cash flow provided from operations was $2.9 billion in fiscal 1995. These funds, combined with long-term borrowings of $1.3 billion and proceeds from sale/leaseback transactions of $.5 billion, were used to finance capital expenditures of $3.7 billion, acquire the assets of 122 Canada Woolco stores, invest in international operations, pay dividends, provide working capital, and fund the operations of subsidiaries.

Borrowing Information

The Company had committed lines of credit of $1,175 million with 11 banks and informal lines with various banks totaling an additional $1,050 million which were used to support short-term borrowing and commercial paper. These lines of credit and their anticipated cyclical increases will be sufficient to finance the seasonal buildups in merchandise inventories and interim financing requirements for stores developed with sale/leaseback or other long-term financing objectives.

The Company has aggressively expanded during the past three years. Even though interest rates increased throughout fiscal 1995, the Company has taken advantage of interest rates in the past three years which have been substantially lower than those available in recent history. These favorable debt market conditions, combined with the Company's ability to generate significant cash flows from operations, have allowed it to continue this expansion and position itself to continue as the world's largest retailer. These increased borrowings to support the expansion programs have caused the Company's debt (including obligations under capital leases) to equity ratios to increase to .77:1 at the end of fiscal 1995, as compared with .75:1 and .56:1 at the end of fiscal 1994 and 1993, respectively. In view of the Company's significant working capital, its consistent ability to generate working capital from operations and the availability of external financing, the Company foresees no difficulty in providing funds necessary to fulfill its working capital needs and to finance its expansion plans.

Foreign Currency Translation

The Company has operations in Mexico through a joint venture with CIFRA, Mexico's largest retailer. In fiscal 1995 the value of the peso dropped significantly in relation to the dollar, and accordingly the Company's investment and shareholders' equity were reduced due to foreign currency translation adjustment of approximately $235 million related to the joint venture in Mexico. The Company also had a foreign currency translation reduction of approximately $21 million related to its Canadian operation.

The Company is evaluating strategies to reduce the risk of currency devaluation. Although the Company is currently exposed to this risk, any further devaluation of the peso or other currencies should not significantly impact the Company's consolidated operations or financial position.

Expansion

The Company plans to continue to enhance its position as the world's largest retailer through expansion in fiscal 1996. Expansion plans include 90 to 100 new Wal-Mart stores, 12 new Supercenters and 9 new Sam's Clubs along with the expansion or relocation of approximately 70 Wal-Mrt stores and 4 Sam's Clubs, and the conversion of approximately 80 Wal-Mart stores into Supercenters.

The Company will continue to develop its interests in Hong Kong, China, Argentina, Brazil and Canada with the planned addition of 20 to 25 new units. With the recent devaluation of the peso, the Company has slowed its planned expansion program in Mexico and will continue to evaluate future opportunities.

Also included in expansion plans for fiscal 1996 are three distribution centers. Total planned capital expenditures for 1996 approximate $4 billion. The Company may sell $1,051 million of public debt utilizing shelf registration statements previously filed with the Securities and Exchange Commission. Long-term and short-term borrowings along with cash provided from operations should provide adequate funding for the Company's fiscal 1996 expansion program.

■ CONSOLIDATED STATEMENTS OF INCOME

(Amounts in millions except per share data.) Fiscal years ended January 31,	1995	1994	1993
Revenues:			
Net Sales	$82,494	$67,344	$ 55,484
Other income-net	918	641	501
	83,412	67,985	55,985
Costs and Expenses:			
Cost of Sales	65,586	53,444	44,175
Operating, selling, and general and administrative expenses	12,858	10,333	8,321
Interest Costs:			
Debt	520	331	143
Capital leases	186	186	180
	79,150	64,294	52,819
Income Before Income Taxes	4,262	3,691	3,166
Provision for Income Taxes:			
Current	1,572	1,325	1,137
Deferred	9	33	34
	1,581	1,358	1,171
Net Income	$ 2,681	$ 2,333	$ 1,995
Net Income Per Share	$ 1.17	$ 1.02	$ .87

See accompanying notes.

Net Income Chart (millions of dollars)

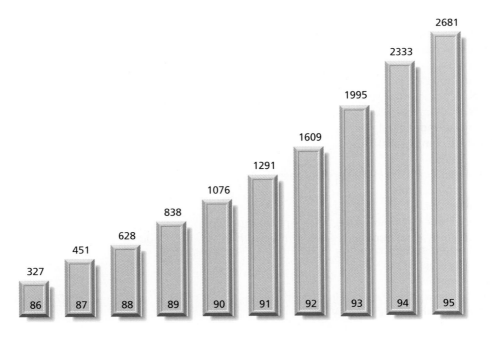

86	87	88	89	90	91	92	93	94	95
327	451	628	838	1076	1291	1609	1995	2333	2681

■ CONSOLIDATED BALANCE SHEETS

(Amounts in millions.) January 31,	1995	1994
Assets		
Current Assets:		
Cash and cash equivalents	$ 45	$ 20
Receivables	700	690
Recoverable costs from sale/leaseback	200	208
Inventories:		
At replacement cost	14,415	11,483
Less LIFO reserve	351	469
Inventories at LIFO cost	14,064	11,014
Prepaid expenses and other	329	182
Total Current Assets	15,338	12,114
Property, Plant, and Equipment, at Cost:		
Land	3,036	2,741
Buildings and improvements	8,973	6,818
Fixtures and equipment	4,768	3,981
Transportation equipment	313	260
	17,090	13,800
Less accumulated depreciation	2,782	2,173
Net property, plant, and equipment	14,308	11,627
Property under capital leases	2,147	2,059
Less accumulated amortization	581	510
Net property under capital leases	1,566	1,549
Other Assets and Deferred Charges	1,607	1,151
Total Assets	$32,819	$26,441
Liabilities and Shareholders' Equity		
Current Liabilities:		
Commercial paper	$ 1,795	$ 1,575
Accounts payable	5,907	4,104
Accrued liabilities	1,819	1,473
Accrued federal and state income taxes	365	183
Long-term debt due within one year	23	20
Obligations under capital leases due within one year	64	51
Total Current Liabilities	9,973	7,406
Long-Term Debt	7,871	6,156
Long-Term Obligations Under Capital Leases	1,838	1,804
Deferred Income Taxes	411	322
Shareholders' Equity:		
Preferred stock ($.10 par value; 100 shares authorized, none issued)		
Common stock ($.10 par value; 5,500 shares authorized, 2,297 and 2,299 issued and outstanding in 1995 and 1994, respectively)	230	230
Capital in excess of par value	539	536
Retained earnings	12,213	9,987
Foreign currency translation adjustment	(256)	—
Total Shareholders' Equity	12,726	10,753
Total Liabilities and Shareholders' Equity	$32,819	$26,441

■ CONSOLIDATED STATEMENTS OF SHAREHOLDERS' EQUITY

(Amounts in millions except per share data.)	Number of shares	Common stock	Capital in excess of par value	Retained earnings	Foreign currency translation adjustment	Total
Balance—January 31, 1992	$1,149	$115	$626	$ 6,249	$ —	$ 6,990
Net Income				1,995		1,995
Cash dividends ($.11 per share)				(241)		(241)
Two-for-one stock split	1,150	115	(115)			—
Other	1		16			16
Balance—January 31, 1993	2,300	230	527	8,003	—	8,760
Net Income				2,333		2,333
Cash dividends ($.13 per share)				(299)		(299)
Other	(1)		9	(50)		(41)
Balance—January 31, 1994	2,299	230	536	9,987	—	10,753
Net Income				2,681		2,681
Cash dividends ($.17 per share)				(391)		(391)
Foreign currency translation adjustment					(256)	(256)
Other	(2)		3	(64)		(61)
Balance—January 31, 1995	2,297	$230	$539	$12,213	$(256)	$12,726

See accompanying notes.

■ CONSOLIDATED STATEMENTS OF CASH FLOWS

(Amounts in millions.) Fiscal years ended January 31,	1995	1994	1993
Cash flows from operating activities:			
Net income	$2,681	$2,333	$1,995
Adjustments to reconcile net income to net cash provided by operating activities:			
Depreciation and amortization	1,070	849	649
Increase in accounts receivable	(84)	(165)	(106)
Increase in inventories	(3,053)	(1,324)	(1,884)
Increase in accounts payable	1,914	230	420
Increase in accrued liabilities	496	327	176
Other	(118)	(55)	28
Net cash provided by operating activities	2,906	2,195	1,278
Cash flow from investing activities:			
Payments for property, plant, and equipment	(3,734)	(3,644)	(3,756)
Acquisition of assets from PACE Membership Warehouses, Inc.	—	(830)	—
Acquisition of assets from Woolworth Canada, Inc.	(352)	—	—
Sale/leaseback arrangements and other property sales	502	272	416
Investment in international operations	(434)	(198)	(106)
Other investing activities	226	(86)	(60)
Net cash used in investing activities	(3,792)	(4,486)	(3,506)
Cash flows from financing activities:			
Increase (decrease) in commercial paper	220	(14)	1,135
Proceeds from issuance of long-term debt	1,250	3,108	1,367
Dividends paid	(391)	(299)	(241)
Payment of long-term debt	(37)	(19)	(8)
Payment of capital lease obligations	(70)	(437)	(60)
Other financing activities	(61)	(40)	6
Net cash provided by financing activities	911	2,299	2,209
Net increase (decrease) in cash and cash equivalents	25	8	(19)
Cash and cash equivalents at beginning of year	20	12	31
Cash and cash equivalents at end of year	$ 45	$ 20	$ 12
Supplemental disclosure of cash flow information:			
Income tax paid	$1,390	$1,366	$1,173
Interest paid	658	450	317
Capital lease obligations incurred	193	162	286

See accompanying notes.

■ NOTES TO CONSOLIDATED FINANCIAL STATEMENTS

1 Summary of Significant Accounting Policies

Segment information

The Company and its subsidiaries are principally engaged in the operation of mass merchandising stores.

Consolidation

The consolidated financial statements include the accounts of subsidiaries. Significant intercompany transactions have been eliminated in consolidation.

Cash and cash equivalents

The Company considers investments with a maturity of three months or less when purchased to be "cash equivalents."

Inventories

Inventories are stated principally at cost (last-in, first-out), which is not in excess of market, using the retail method for inventories in stores.

Pre-opening costs

Costs associated with the opening of stores are expensed during the first full month of operations. The costs are carried as prepaid expenses prior to the store opening.

Recoverable costs from sale/leaseback

All costs of acquisition and construction of properties for which the Company plans to sell and leaseback within one year are accumulated in current assets until properties are sold.

Interest during construction

In order that interest costs properly reflect only that portion relating to current operations, interest on borrowed funds during the construction of property, plant, and equipment is capitalized. Interest costs capitalized were $70 million, $65 million and $80 million in 1995, 1994, and 1993, respectively.

Depreciation and Amortization

Depreciation and amortization for financial statement purposes is provided on the straight-line method over the estimated useful lives of the various assets. For income tax purposes, accelerated methods are used with recognition of deferred income taxes for the resulting temporary differences.

Operating, selling, and general and administrative expenses

Buying, warehousing, and occupancy costs are included in operating, selling, and general and administrative expenses.

Income taxes

In fiscal 1994, the Company adopted Statement of Financial Accounting Standards No. 109, "Accounting for Income Taxes" (SFAS 109) prospectively as a change in accounting principle effective February 1, 1993. Under SFAS 109, the deferred tax provision is determined under the liability method, whereby deferred tax assets and liabilities are recognized based on differences between financial statement and tax bases of assets and liabilities using presently enacted tax rates. In fiscal year 1993, deferred income taxes were provided on timing differences between financial statement and taxable income.

Net income per share

Net income per share is based on the weighted average outstanding common-shares. The dilutive effect of stock options is insignificant and consequently has been excluded from the earnings per share computations.

Stock options

Proceeds from the sale of common stock issued under the stock option plans and related tax benefits which accrue to the Company are accounted for as capital transactions, and no charges or credits are made to income in connection with the plans.

2 Commercial Paper and Long-term Debt

Information on short-term borrowings and interest rates is as follows (dollar amounts in millions):

Fiscal year ended January 31,	1995	1994	1993
Maximum amount outstanding at month-end	$2,729	$2,395	$2,315
Average daily short-term borrowings	1,693	1,247	1,184
Weighted average interest rate	4.4%	3.0%	3.5%

At January 31, 1995, the Company had committed lines of credit of $1,175 million with 11 banks and informal lines of credit with various banks totaling an additional $1,050 million, which were used to support short-term borrowings and commercial paper. Short-term borrowings under these lines of credit bear interest at or below the prime rate.

Long-term debt at January 31 consists of (amounts in millions):

		1995	1994
8 5/8%	Notes due April 2001	$ 750	$ 750
5 7/8%	Notes due October 2005	750	750
9 1/10%	Notes due July 2000	500	500
5 1/2%	Notes due September 1997	500	500
6 1/8%	Notes due October 1999	500	500
5 1/2%	Notes due March 1998	500	500
6 1/2%	Notes due June 2003	500	500
7 1/4%	Notes due June 2013	500	500
7 1/2%	Notes due May 2004	500	—
7 8/10%-8 1/4%	Obligations from sale/leaseback transactions due 2014	484	—
7%-8%	Obligations from sale/leaseback transactions due 2013	322	335
8%	Notes due May 1996	250	250
6 3/8%	Notes due March 2003	250	250
6 3/4%	Notes due October 2023	250	250
8%	Notes due September 2006	250	—
8 1/2%	Notes due September 2024	250	—
6 7/8%	Eurobond due June 1999	250	—
5 1/8%	Eurobond due October 1998	250	250
10 7/8%	Debentures due August 2000	100	100
	Other	215	221
		$7,871	$6,156

Long-term debt is unsecured except for $220 million which is collateralized by property with an aggregate carrying value of approximately $358 million. Annual maturities on long-term debt during the next five years are (in millions):

Fiscal years ending January 31,	Annual maturity
1996	$ 23
1997	268
1998	523
1999	774
2000	806
Thereafter	5,500

The Company observes certain covenants under the terms of its note and debentures agreements, the most restrictive of which relates to amounts of additional secured debt and long-term leases.

The Company has entered into sale/leaseback transactions involving buildings while retaining title to the underlying land. These transactions were accounted for as financings and are included in long-term debt and the annual maturities schedules above. The resulting obligations are amortized over the lease terms. Future minimum lease payments for each of the five succeeding years as of January 31, 1995 are (in millions):

Fiscal years ending January 31,	Minimum Rentals
1996	$ 81
1997	72
1998	76
1999	76
2000	104
Thereafter	1,109

The fair value of the Company's long-term debt approximates $7,530 million based on the Company's current incremental borrowing rate for similar types of borrowing arrangements. The carrying amount of the short-term borrowings approximates fair value.

At January 31, 1995 and 1994, the Company had letters of credit outstanding totaling $580 and $808 million, respectively. These letters of credit were issued primarily for the purchase of inventory.

The Company has guaranteed the indebtedness of a joint venture for the development of real estate in Puerto Rico. At January 31, 1995, the amount guaranteed was approximately $54 million. The Company does not anticipate any joint venture defaults.

Under shelf registration statements previously filed with the Securities and Exchange Commission, the Company may issue debt securities aggregating $1,051 million.

3 Defined Contribution Plan

The Company maintains a profit sharing plan under which most full and many part-time Associates become participants following one year of employment. Annual contributions, based on the profitability of the Company, are made at the sole discretion of the Company. Contributions were $175 million, $166 million, and $166 million in 1995, 1994, and 1993, respectively.

4 Income Taxes

The Company prospectively adopted SFAS 109 as a change in accounting principle effective February 1, 1993; consequently, prior years' financial statements have not been restated. Due to the nature of the predominant cumulative differences in the Company's book tax bases of assets and liabilities, which relate to items that were both timing differences under Principles Board Opinion 11, "Accounting for Income Taxes" (APB 11), and temporary differences under SFAS 109, the cumulative impact of adoption was insignificant. The income tax provision consists of the following (in millions):

	1995	1994	1993
Current:			
Federal	$1,394	$1,193	$1,002
State and Local	178	132	135
Total current tax provision	1,572	1,325	1,137
Deferred:			
Federal	7	30	31
State and Local	2	3	3
Total deferred tax provision	9	33	34
Total provision for income taxes	$1,581	$1,358	$1,171

Deferred income taxes under SFAS 109 reflect the net tax effects of temporary differences between the carrying amounts of assets and liabilities for financial reporting purposes and the amounts used for income tax purposes. Items that give rise to significant portions of the deferred tax accounts at January 31 are as follows (in millions):

	1995	1994
Deferred tax liabilities:		
Property, plant, and equipment	$518	$408
Inventory	88	38
Other	8	9
Total deferred tax liabilities	614	455
Deferred tax assets:		
Amounts accrued for financial reporting purposes not yet deductible for tax purposes	230	114
Capital leases	114	95
Other	33	18
Total deferred tax assets	377	227
Net deferred tax liabilities	$237	$228

The components of the provision for deferred income taxes under APB 11 for the years ended January 31, 1993 are (in millions):

	1993
Depreciation	$68
Capital leases	(21)
Other	(12)
	$35

A reconciliation of the significant differences between the effective income tax rate and the federal statutory rate on pretax income follows:

	1995	1994	1993
Statutory tax rate	35.0%	35.0%	34.0%
State income taxes, net of federal income tax benefit	2.7%	2.4%	2.9%
Other	(0.6%)	(0.6%)	0.1%
Effective tax rate	37.1%	36.8%	37.0%

5 Acquisitions

In two unrelated cash transactions during fiscal 1994, the Company acquired selected assets of PACE Membership Warehouses, Inc., including the right to operate 107 of PACE's former locations, for $830 million, recording $336 million goodwill which is being amortized over 25 years.

   In fiscal 1995, the Company acquired selected assets related to 122 Woolco stores in Canada from Woolworth Canada, Inc., a subsidiary of Woolworth Corporation, for approximately $352 million, recording $221 million of leasehold and location value which is being amortized over 20 years. These transactions have been accounted for as purchases, and the results of operations for the acquired units since the dates of their acquisitions have been included on the Company's results. Pro forma results of operations are not presented due to insignificant differences from the historical results.

6 Stock Option Plans

At January 31, 1995, 76 million shares of common stock were reserved for insurance under stock option plans. The options granted under the stock option plans expire 10 years from date of grant and may be exercised in nine annual installments. Further information concerning the options is as follows:

	Shares	Option price per share	Total
Shares under option			
January 31, 1992	13,618,000	$ .67-27.25	$142,763,000
Options Granted	4,072,000	$25.75-30.82	118,430,000
Options Canceled	(1,134,000)	$ .67-30.82	(13,560,000)
Options Exercised	(2,092,000)	$ .67-27.25	(12,773,000)
January 31, 1993	14,464,000	$ 1.43-30.82	234,860,000
Options Granted	3,550,000	$25.00-27.25	90,377,000
Options Canceled	(803,000)	$ 1.43-30.82	(17,325,000)
Options Exercised	(1,335,000)	$ 1.43-30.82	(9,664,000)
January 31, 1994	15,867,000	$ 1.43-30.82	298,248,000
Options Granted	4,125,000	$21.63-26.75	95,689,000
Options Canceled	(1,013,000)	$ 1.43-30.82	(23,127,000)
Options Exercised	(1,019,000)	$ 2.08-27.25	(7,829,000)
January 31, 1995	17,969,000	$ 2.78-30.82	$362,981,000
(4,223,000 shares exercisable)			
Shares available for option:			
January 31, 1994	11,502,000		
January 31, 1995	58,107,000		

7 Long-term Lease Obligations

The Company and certain of its subsidiaries have long-term leases for stores and equipment. Rentals (including, for certain leases, amounts applicable to taxes, insurance, maintenance, other operating expenses, and contingent rentals) under all operating leases were $479 million in 1995, $361 million in 1994, and $313 million in 1993. Aggregate minimum annual rentals at January 31, 1995, under non-cancelable leases are as follows (in millions):

Fiscal years	Operating leases	Capital leases
1996	$ 386	$ 252
1997	403	251
1998	386	251
1999	334	249
2000	318	247
Thereafter	3,155	2,785
Total minimum rentals	$4,982	4,035
Less estimated executory costs		80
Net minimum lease payments		3,955
Less imputed interest at rates ranging from 6.1% to 14.0%		2,053
Present value of net minimum lease payments		$1,902

Certain of the leases provide for contingent additional rentals based on percentage of sales. Such additional rentals amounted to $42 million, $27 million, and $30 million in 1995, 1994, and 1993, respectively. Substantially all of the store leases have renewal options for additional terms from five to 25 years at the same or lower minimum rentals.

The Company has entered into lease commitments for land and buildings for 62 future locations. These lease commitments with real estate developers or through sale/leaseback arrangements provide for minimum rentals for 20 to 25 years, excluding renewal options, which, if consummated based on current cost estimates, will approximate $58 million annually over the lease terms.

8 Quarterly Financial Data (Unaudited)

| Amounts in millions (except per share information) | Quarter ended | | | |
	April 30,	July 31,	October 31,	January 31,
1995				
Net sales	$17,686	$19,942	$20,418	$24,448
Cost of sales	14,063	15,960	16,201	19,362
Net income	498	565	588	1,030
Net income per share	$ .22	$ .25	$ .26	$ .45
1994				
Net sales	$13,920	$16,237	$16,827	$20,360
Cost of sales	11,017	12,963	13,308	16,156
Net income	451	496	519	867
Net income per share	$ .20	$ .22	$ .23	$ .38

■ REPORT OF INDEPENDENT AUDITORS

The Board of Directors and Shareholders
Wal-Mart Stores, Inc.

We have audited the accompanying consolidated-balance sheets of Wal-Mart Stores, Inc., and Subsidiaries as of January 31, 1995 and 1994, and the related consolidated statements of income, shareholders' equity, and cash flows for each of the three years in the period ended January 31, 1995. These financial statements are the responsibility of the Company's management. Our responsibility is to express an opinion on these financial statements based on our audits.

We conducted our audits in accordance with generally accepted auditing standards. Those standards require that we plan and perform the audit to obtain reasonable assurance about whether the financial statements are free of material misstatement. An audit includes examining, on a test basis, evidence supporting the amounts and disclosures in the financial statements. An audit also includes assessing the accounting principles used and significant estimates made by management, as well as evaluating the overall financial statement presentation. We believe that our audits provide a reasonable basis for our opinion.

In our opinion, the financial statements referred to above present fairly, in all material respects, the consolidated financial position of Wal-Mart Stores, Inc. and Subsidiaries at January 31, 1995 and 1994, and the consolidated results of their operations and cash flows for each of the three years in the period ended January 31, 1995, in conformity with generally accepted accounting principles.

Ernst and Young LLP

Tulsa, Oklahoma
March 24, 1995

■ RESPONSIBILITY FOR FINANCIAL STATEMENTS

The financial statements and information of Wal-Mart Stores, Inc., and Subsidiaries presented in this Report have been prepared by management which has responsibility for their integrity and objectivity. These financial statements have been prepared in conformity with generally accepted accounting principles, applying certain estimates and judgments based upon currently available information and management's view of current conditions and circumstances.

Management has developed and maintains a system of accounting and controls, including an extensive internal audit program, designed to provide reasonable assurance that the Company's assets are protected from improper use and that accounting records provide a reliable basis for the preparation of financial statements. This system is continually reviewed, improved, and modified in response to changing business conditions and operations and to recommendations made by the independent auditors and the internal auditors. Management believes that the accounting and control systems provide reasonable assurance that assets are safeguarded and financial information is reliable.

The Company has adopted a Statement of Ethics to guide our management in the continued observance of high ethical standards of honesty, integrity, and fairness in the conduct of the business and in accordance with the law. Compliance with the guidelines and standards is periodically reviewed and is acknowledged in writing by all management associates.

The Board of Directors, through the activities of its Audit Committee consisting solely of outside Directors, participates in the process of reporting financial information. The duties of the Committee include keeping informed of the financial condition of the Company and reviewing its financial policies and procedures, its internal accounting controls, and the objectivity of its financial reporting. Both the Company's independent auditors and the internal auditors have free access to the Audit Committee and meet with the Committee periodically, with and without management present.

Paul R. Carter
Executive Vice President and Chief Financial Officer

■ CORPORATE INFORMATION

Registrar and Transfer Agent
Boatmen's Trust Company
510 Locust Street
Post Office Box 14768
St. Louis, Missouri 63178
800/456-9852

Independent Auditors
Ernst & Young LLP
3900 One Williams Center
Tulsa, Oklahoma 74172

Listings
New York Stock Exchange
Stock Symbol: WMT
Pacific Stock Exchange
Stock Symbol: WMT
Toronto Stock Exchange
Stock Symbol: WMT

Corporate Address
Wal-Mart Stores, Inc.
Bentonville, Arkansas
72716-8611
Telephone:
501/273-4000

Form 10-K and Other Reports
A copy of the Company's Annual Report on Form 10-K for the fiscal year ended January 31, 1995, as filed with the Securities and Exchange Commission, may be obtained without charge by writing to:
10-K Report
Wal-Mart Stores, Inc.
Bentonville, Arkansas
72716-8611

or by calling:
501/273-8446

Quarterly Reports

Beginning May 1, 1995, you may obtain the most recent quarterly financial data and current press release via fax (or mail) by calling 800/WAL-MART.

Diversity Report

A report on diversity programs may be obtained by writing the Company.

Annual Meeting

Our Annual Meeting of Shareholders will be held on Friday, June 2, 1995 at 10:00 a.m. in Bud Walton Arena on the University of Arkansas campus, Fayetteville, Arkansas. You are cordially invited to attend. A proxy statement, including a request for proxies, will be mailed to shareholders in early May 1995.

Market Price Of Common Stock	Fiscal years ended January 31,			
	1995		1994	
Quarter	High	Low	High	Low
April 30	$29.13	$24.00	$34.00	$26.38
July 31	25.88	22.75	28.50	24.88
October 31	26.00	22.75	27.25	23.50
January 31	24.13	20.88	29.88	24.38

Dividends Paid Per Share Fiscal years ended January 31, Quarterly			
1995		1994	
April 14	$0.0425	April 9	$0.0325
July 8	0.0425	July 9	0.0325
October 3	0.0425	October 4	0.0325
January 5	0.0425	January 5	0.0325

Recommended Readings

The following readings are suggested as an aid to those readers who want to pursue some topics in more depth than is possible in this book. There is a hazard in compiling a group of recommended readings. Inevitably, some worthwhile books or periodicals are overlooked. Moreover, such a list cannot include books published subsequent to the compilation here.

A systematic commitment to reading about current issues in business and accounting will benefit any student. On a daily basis, the *Wall Street Journal* is the primary source, although many daily papers in major cities provide good financial coverage. The Sunday business section of *The New York Times* is a valuable resource. *Forbes* and *Business Week* provide weekly business news and often address accounting topics.

Professional journals are typically available in university libraries. The *Journal of Accountancy* emphasizes financial accounting and is directed at the practicing CPA. *Accounting Horizons* stresses current, practice-oriented articles in all areas of accounting. *Management Accounting* focuses on management accounting. The *Harvard Business Review* and *Fortune*, which are aimed at general managers, contain many articles on planning and control.

The Accounting Review and the *Journal of Accounting Research* cover all phases of accounting at a more theoretical level than the preceding publications.

The *Opinions* of the Accounting Principles Board are available from the American Institute of CPAs, 1211 Avenue of the Americas, New York, NY 10036. The institute also has a series of research studies on a variety of topics. The pronouncements of the Financial Accounting Standards Board are available from the board's office, 401 Merritt 7, P.O. Box 5116, Norwalk, CT 06865-5116.

The Financial Executives Institute, 10 Madison Avenue, P.O. Box 1938, Morristown, NJ 07960, and the National Association of Accountants, 10 Paragon Drive, P.O. Box 433, Montvale, NJ 07645-0433, have long lists of accounting research publications.

Books on elementary financial accounting are available from almost all major publishers. The next steps in the study of financial accounting are in books entitled *Intermediate Accounting* and then *Advanced Accounting*, which are available from Harcourt Brace Jovanovich, Richard D. Irwin, Inc., McGraw-Hill Book Co., Prentice Hall, Inc., South-Western Publishing Co., Wiley-Hamilton, and other publishers.

For the analysis and interpretation of financial statements, especially in relationship to the market prices of stocks and bonds, see W.H. Beaver, *Financial Reporting: An Accounting Revolution*, second edition, and G. Foster, *Financial Statement Analysis*, second edition, both published by Prentice Hall, Inc.

There are many books on elementary management accounting. Also, many books entitled *Cost Accounting* stress a management approach. For examples, see C.T. Horngren, G.L. Sundem, and W.O. Stratton, *Introduction to Management Accounting*, the companion to this book, and *Cost Accounting: A Managerial Emphasis*, by C.T. Horngren, G. Foster, and S. Datar. Both are published by Prentice Hall, Inc.

Glossary

accelerated depreciation (p. 383) Any depreciation method that writes off depreciable costs more quickly than the ordinary straight-line method based on expected useful life.

account (p. 12) A summary record of the changes in a particular asset, liability, or owners' equity.

account format (p. 154) A classified balance sheet with the assets at the left.

account payable (p. 13) A liability that results from a purchase of goods or services on open account.

Accounting Principles Board (APB) (p. 66) The predecessor to the Financial Accounting Standards Board.

accounting cycle (p. 180) The multistage process by which accountants produce an entity's financial statements.

accounting policy making (p. 730) Choosing the accounting measurement and disclosure methods required for financial reporting.

accounts receivable (p. 246) Amounts owed to a company by customers as a result of delivering goods or services and extending credit in the ordinary course of business.

accounts receivable turnover (p. 254) Credit sales divided by average accounts receivable.

accrual basis (p. 44) Recognizes the impact of transactions on the financial statements in the time periods when revenues and expenses occur.

accrue (p. 137) Accumulation of a receivable or payable during a given period even though no explicit transaction occurs.

accumulated depreciation (p. 102) The cumulative sum of all depreciation recognized since the date of acquisition of the particular assets described.

adjustments (p. 136) The key final process (before the computation of ending account balances) of assigning the financial effects of transactions to the appropriate time - periods.

adjusting entries *See* adjustments

affiliated company (p. 593) A company that has 20% to 50% of its voting shares owned by another company.

aging of accounts receivable (p. 253) An analysis of the elements of individual accounts receivable according to the time elapsed after the dates of billing.

AICPA (p. 66) American Institute of Certified Public Accountants, the leading organization of the auditors of corporate financial reports.

allowance for bad debts *See* allowance for uncollectible accounts

allowance for depreciation *See* accumulated depreciation.

allowance for doubtful accounts *See* allowance for uncollectible accounts

allowance for uncollectible accounts (p. 249) A contra asset account that offsets total receivables by an estimated amount that will probably not be collected.

allowance method (p. 249) Method of accounting for bad debt losses using estimates of the amount of sales that will ultimately be uncollectible and a contra asset account, allowance for doubtful accounts.

amortization (p. 379) The systematic reduction of a lump-sum amount. When referring to long-lived assets, it usually means the allocation of the costs of intangible assets to the periods that benefit from these assets.

annual report (p. 5) A combination of financial statements, management discussion and analysis, and graphs and charts that is provided annually to investors.

annuity (p. 461) Equal cash flows to take place during successive periods of equal length.

APB Opinions (p. 66) A series of thirty-one opinions of the Accounting Principles Board, many of which are still the "accounting law of the land."

appropriated retained income *See* restricted retained income.

assets (p. 8) Economic resources that are expected to benefit future cash inflows or help reduce future cash outflows.

asset turnover *See* total asset turnover.

audit (p. 23) An examination of transactions and financial statements made in accordance with generally accepted auditing standards.

audit committee (p. 333) A committee of the board of directors that oversees the internal accounting controls, financial statements, and financial affairs of the corporation.

auditor (p. 201) An accountant who provides an independent examination of the financial statements.

auditor's opinion (p. 23) A report describing the auditor's examination of transactions and financial statements. It is included with the financial statements in an annual report issued by the corporation.

authorized shares (p. 542) The total number of shares that may legally be issued under the articles of incorporation.

available-for-sale securities (p. 589) Investments in equity or debt securities that are not held for active trading but may be sold before maturity.

average collection period *See* days to collect accounts receivable.

bad debts *See* uncollectible accounts.

bad debt recoveries (p. 254) Accounts receivable that were written off as uncollectible but then collected at a later date.

bad debts expense (p. 246) The cost of granting credit that arises from uncollectible accounts.

balance (p. 90) The difference between the total left-side and right-side amounts in an account at any particular time.

balance sheet ((p. 7) A financial statement that shows the financial status of a business entity at a particular instant in time.

balance sheet equation (p. 8) Assets = Liabilities + Owners' equity.

bank reconciliation (p. 341) An analysis that explains any difference between the cash balance shown by the depositor and that shown by the bank.

basket purchase (p. 380) The acquisition of two or more types of assets for a lump-sum cost.

bearer instrument *See* unregistered instrument.

bench marks (p. 688) General rules of thumb specifying appropriate levels for financial ratios.

betterment *See* improvement.

bonds (p. 436) Formal certificates of indebtedness that are typically accompanied by (1) a promise to pay interest in cash at a specified annual rate plus (2) a promise to pay the principal at a specific maturity date.

book of original entry (p. 93) A formal chronological record of how the entity's transactions affect the balances in pertinent accounts.

book value (p. 102) The balance of an account shown on the books, net of any contra accounts. For example, the book value of equipment is its acquisition cost minus accumulated depreciation.

book value per share of common stock (p. 565) Stockholders' equity attributable to common stock divided by the number of shares outstanding.

call premium (p. 439) The amount by which the redemption price exceeds par.

callable (p. 546) A characteristic of bonds or preferred stock that gives the issuer the right to redeem the security at a fixed price.

callable bonds (p. 438) Bonds subject to redemption before maturity at the option of the issuer.

capital (p. 19) A term used to identify owners' equities for proprietorships and partnerships.

capital improvement *See* improvement.

capital lease (p. 463) A lease that transfers substantially all the risks and benefits of ownership to the lessee.

capital stock certificate (p. 18) Formal evidence of ownership shares in a corporation.

capital structure *See* capitalization.

capitalization (p. 696) Owners' equity plus long-term debt.

capitalization structure *See* capitalization.

capitalized (p. 380) A cost that is added to an asset account, as distinguished from being expensed immediately.

carrying amount *See* book value.

carrying value *See* book value.

cash basis (p. 44) Accounting method that recognizes the impact of transactions on the financial statements only when cash is received or disbursed.

cash discounts (p. 241) Reductions of invoice prices awarded for prompt payment.

cash dividends (p. 57) Distributions of cash to stockholders that reduce retained income.

cash equivalents (p. 244) Highly liquid short-term investments that can easily be converted into cash.

cash flow (p. 494) Usually refers to net cash provided by operating activities.

cash flows from financing activities (p. 502) The third major section of the statement of cash flows describing flows to and from providers of capital.

cash flows from investing activities (p. 502) The second major section of the statement of cash flows describing purchase or sale of plant, property, equipment, and other long-lived assets.

cash flows from operating activities (p. 492) The first major section of the statement of cash flows. It shows the cash effects of transactions that affect the income statement.

cash flow statement *See* statement of cash flows.

certificates of deposit (p. 588) Short-term obligations of banks.

certified public accountant (CPA) (p. 22) In the United States, a person earns this designation by a combination of education, qualifying experience, and the passing of a two-day written national examination.

charge (p. 91) A word often used instead of debit.

chart of accounts (p. 94) A numbered or coded list of all account titles.

classified balance sheet (p. 149) A balance sheet that groups the accounts into subcategories to help readers quickly gain a perspective on the company's financial position.

closing entries (p. 196) Entries that transfer the revenues, expenses, and dividends declared balances from their respective accounts to the retained income account.

closing the books (p. 196) The final step taken in the accounting cycle to update retained earnings and facilitate the recording of the next year's transactions.

commercial paper (p. 588) Short-term notes payable issued by large corporations with top credit ratings.

common stock (p. 20) Stock representing the class of owners having a "residual" ownership of a corporation.

common-size statement (p. 680) Financial statement expressed in component percentages.

comparative financial statements (p. 182) Statements that present data for two or more reporting periods.

compensating balances (p. 245) Required minimum cash balances on deposit when money is borrowed from banks.

component percentages (p. 680) Analysis and presentation of financial statements in percentage form to aid comparability.

compound entry (p. 14, 97) An entry for a transaction that affects more than two accounts.

compound interest (p. 458) For any period, interest rate multiplied by a changing principal amount. The unpaid interest is added to the principal to become the principal for the new period.

compound interest method *See* effective-interest amortization.

conservatism (p. 288) Selecting the methods of measurement that yield lower net income, lower assets, and lower stockholders' equity in the early years.

consignment (p. 358) Goods shipped for future sales, title remaining with the shipper (consignor), for which the receiver (consignee), upon his or her acceptance, is accountable. The goods are part of the consignor's inventory until sold.

consistency (p. 281) Conformity from period to period with unchanging policies and procedures.

consolidated statements (p. 596) Combinations of the financial positions and earnings reports of the parent company with those of various subsidiaries into an overall report as a single entity.

constant dollars (p. 748) Dollar measurements that are restated in terms of current purchasing power.

contingent liability (p. 451) A potential liability that depends on a future event arising out of a past transaction.

continuity convention *See* going concern convention.

contra account (p. 102) A separate but related account that offsets or is a deduction from a companion account. An example is accumulated depreciation.

contra asset (p. 102) A contra account that offsets an asset.

contractual rate *See* nominal interest rate.

coupon rate *See* nominal interest rate.

convertible (p. 546) A characteristic of bonds or preferred stock that gives the holder the right to exchange the security for common stock.

convertible bonds (p. 439) Bonds that may, at the holder's option, be exchanged for other securities.

copyrights (p. 398) Exclusive rights to reproduce and sell a book, musical composition, film, and similar items.

corporate proxy (p. 542) A written authority granted by individual shareholders to others to cast the shareholders' votes.

corporation (p. 17) An organization that is an "artificial being" created by individual state laws.

cost of goods available for sale (p. 272) Sum of beginning inventory plus current year purchases.

cost of goods sold (p. 64) The original acquisition cost of the inventory that was sold to customers during the reporting period.

cost recovery (p. 45) The concept by which some purchases of goods or services are recorded as assets because their costs are expected to be recovered in the form of cash inflows (or reduced cash outflows) in future periods.

cost of sales *See* cost of goods sold.

cost valuation (p. 270) Process of assigning specific historical costs to items counted in the physical inventory.

cost-benefit criterion (p. 113) As a system is changed, its expected additional benefits should exceed its expected additional costs.

coupon rate *See* nominal interest rate.

covenant *See* protective covenant.

credit (p. 91) An entry or balance on the right side of an account.

creditor (p. 15) One to whom money is owed.

cross-referencing *See* keying of entries.

cross-sectional comparisons (p. 688) Comparisons of a company's financial ratios with the ratios of other companies or with industry averages.

cumulative (p. 543) A characteristic of preferred stock that requires that undeclared dividends accumulate and must be paid in the future before common dividends.

current assets (p. 149) Cash plus assets that are expected to be converted to cash or sold or consumed during the next twelve months or within the normal operating cycle if longer than a year.

current cost (p. 748) Generally, the cost to replace an asset.

current liabilities (p. 149) Liabilities that fall due within the coming year or within the normal operating cycle if longer than a year.

current ratio (p. 152) Current assets divided by current liabilities.

current yield (p. 438) Annual interest payments divided by the current price of a bond.

current-cost method (**p.** 749) A measurement method using current costs and nominal dollars.

cutoff error (p. 358) Failure to record transactions in the correct time period.

data processing (p. 110) The totality of the procedures used to record, analyze, store, and report on chosen activities.

date of record (p. 547) The date when ownership is fixed for determining the right to receive a dividend.

days to collect accounts receivable (p. 255) 365 divided by accounts receivable turnover.

debenture (p. 437) A debt security with a general claim against all assets rather than a specific claim against particular assets.

debit (p. 91) An entry or balance on the left side of an account.

debtor (p. 15) One who owes money.

declaration date (p. 547) The date the board of directors declares a dividend.

deferral method (p. 658) A method of accounting for tax credits associated with business investments whereby the tax savings reduce tax expense in each year of an asset's useful life.

deferred charges (p. 401) Similar to prepaid expenses, but they have longer-term benefits.

deferred credit *See* unearned revenue.

deferred revenue *See* unearned revenue.

deferred tax liability (p. 641) A tax liability that is predictable now because of timing differences but will only be payable when a future tax return is filed.

depletion (p. 379) The process of allocating the cost of natural resources to the period in which the resources are used.

depreciable value (p. 381) The amount of the acquisition cost to be allocated as depreciation over the total useful life of an asset. It is the difference between the total acquisition cost and the predicted residual value.

depreciation (p. 48) The systematic allocation of the acquisition cost of long-lived or fixed assets to the expense accounts of particular periods that benefit from the use of the assets.

depreciation schedule (p. 382) The listing of depreciation amounts for each year of an asset's useful life.

dilution (p. 556) Reduction in stockholders' equity per share or earnings per share that arises from some changes among shareholders' proportional interests.

direct method (p. 492) In a statement of cash flows, the method that calculates net cash provided by operating activities as collections minus operating disbursements.

discontinued operations (p. 704) The termination of a business segment reported separately, net of tax, in the income statement.

discount amortization (p. 443) The spreading of bond discount over the life of the bonds as expense.

discount on bonds (p. 439) The excess of face amount over the proceeds upon issuance of a bond.

discount rates (p. 460) The interest rates used in determining present values.

disposal value *See* residual value.

dividend arrearages (p. 544) Accumulated unpaid dividends on preferred stock.

double-declining-balance depreciation (DDB) (p. 383) The most popular form of accelerated depreciation. It is computed by doubling the straight-line rate and multiplying the resulting DDB rate by the beginning book value.

double-entry system (p. 88) The method usually followed for recording transactions, whereby at least two accounts are always affected by each transaction.

earnings *See* income.

EBIT (p. 694) Earnings before interest and taxes.

economic life *See* useful life.

effective-interest amortization (p. 443) An amortization method that uses a constant interest rate.

effective interest rate *See* yield to maturity.

efficient capital market (p. 705) One in which market prices "fully reflect" all information available to the public.

entity (p. 9) An organization or a section of an - organization that stands apart from other organizations and individuals as a separate economic unit.

equity method (p. 593) Accounting for an investment at acquisition cost adjusted for the investor's share of dividends and earnings or losses of the investee subsequent to the date of investment.

expenditures (p. 392) The purchases of goods or services, whether for cash or on credit.

expenses (p. 42) Decreases in owners' equity that arise because goods or services are delivered to customers.

explicit transactions (p. 136) Events such as cash receipts and disbursements, credit purchases, and credit sales that trigger nearly all day-to-day routine entries.

extraordinary items (p. 704) Items that are unusual in nature and infrequent in occurrence that are shown separately, net of tax, in the income statement.

F.O.B. destination (p. 275) Seller pays freight costs from the shipping point of the seller to the receiving point of the buyer.

F.O.B. shipping point (p. 275) Buyer pays freight costs from the shipping point of the seller to the receiving point of the buyer.

face amount (p. 437) The principal as indicated on the certificates of bonds or other debt instruments.

FASB Statements (p. 66) The FASB's rulings on generally accepted accounting principles.

financial accounting (p. 7) The field of accounting that serves external decision makers, such as stockholders, suppliers, banks, and government agencies.

Financial Accounting Standards Board (FASB) (p. 66) A private-sector body that determines generally accepted accounting standards in the United States.

financial capital maintenance (p. 747) A concept of income measurement whereby income emerges only after financial resources are recovered.

financial leverage *See* trading on the equity.

financial management (p. 490) Is mainly concerned with where to get cash and how to use cash for the benefit of the entity.

financial statement analysis (p. 674) Using financial statements to assess a company's performance.

financing activities (p. 491) In the statement of cash flows, obtaining resources as a borrower or issuer of securities and repaying creditors and owners.

financing lease *See* capital lease

finished goods inventory (p. 303) The accumulated costs of manufacture for goods that are complete and ready for sale.

first-in, first-out (FIFO) (p. 279) This method of accounting for inventory assumes that the units acquired earliest are used or sold first.

fiscal year (p. 41) The year established for accounting purposes.

fixed assets *See* tangible assets.

flow-through (p. 653) A method of accounting for tax credits whereby the entire tax savings reduces tax expense in the year the credit is earned.

Foreign Corrupt Practices Act (p. 331) A U.S. law that makes it an explicit responsibility of management to report on the adequacy of internal control.

foreign-currency exchange rates (p. 707) The number of units of one currency that can be exchanged for one unit of another currency.

franchises (p. 399) Privileges granted by a government, manufacturer, or distributor to sell a product or service in accordance with specified conditions.

freight in (p. 275) An additional cost of the goods acquired during the period, which is often shown in the purchases section of an income statement.

freight out (p. 275) The transportation costs borne by the seller of merchandise and often shown as a "shipping expense."

fully diluted EPS (p. 701) An earnings-per-share figure on common stock that assumes that all potentially dilutive convertible securities and stock options are exchanged for common stock.

future value (p. 459) The amount accumulated, including principal and interest.

gearing *See* trading on the equity.

general controls (p. 341) Internal accounting controls that focus on the organization and operation of the data-processing activity.

general journal (p. 93) The most common example of a book of original entry; a complete chronological record of transactions.

general ledger (p. 89) The collection of accounts that accumulates the amounts reported in the major financial statements.

general price index (p. 753) An index that compares the average price of a group of goods and services at one date with the average price of a similar group at another date.

generally accepted accounting principles (GAAP) (p. 9) A term that applies to the broad concepts or guidelines and detailed practices in accounting, including all the conventions, rules, and procedures that together make up accepted accounting practice at a given time.

going concern convention (p. 112) The assumption that in all ordinary situations an entity persists indefinitely.

goodwill (p. 399) The excess of the cost of an acquired company over the sum of the fair market value of its identifiable individual assets less the liabilities.

gross margin *See* gross profit.

gross margin percentage *See* gross profit percentage.

gross profit (p. 155) The excess of sales revenue over the cost of the inventory that was sold.

gross profit percentage (p. 159) Gross profit divided by sales.

gross profit test (p. 297) The comparing of gross profit percentages to detect any phenomenon worth investigating.

gross sales (p. 240) Total sales revenue before deducting sales returns and allowances.

held-to-maturity securities (p. 589) Debt securities that the investor expects to hold until maturity.

historical cost (p. 748) The amount originally paid to acquire an asset.

holding gain (p. 285) Increase in the replacement cost or other measure of current value of the inventory held during the current period.

implicit interest (p. 449) An interest expense that is not explicitly recognized in a loan agreement.

implicit transactions (p. 136) Events (such as the passage of time) that are temporarily ignored in day-to-day recording procedures and are recognized via end-of-period adjustments.

imprest basis (p. 353) A method of accounting for petty cash.

improvement (p. 394) An expenditure that is intended to add to the future benefits from an existing fixed asset.

imputed interest *See* implicit interest.

imputed interest rate (p. 449) The market interest rate that equates the proceeds from a loan with the present value of the loan payments.

income (p. 42) The excess of revenues over expenses.

income statement (p. 50) A report of all revenues and expenses pertaining to a specific time period.

independent opinion *See* auditor's opinion.

indirect method (p. 492) In a statement of cash flows, the method that adjusts the accrual net income to reflect only cash receipts and outlays.

inflation (p. 747) A general decline in the purchasing power of the monetary unit.

input controls (p. 340) Internal accounting controls that help guard against the entry of false or erroneous data.

intangible assets (p. 378) Rights or economic benefits, such as franchises, patents, trademarks, copyrights, and goodwill, that are not physical in nature.

interest coverage (p. 452, 699) Income before interest expense and income taxes divided by interest expense.

interest period (p. 458) The time period over which the interest rate applies.

interest rate (p. 458) The percentage applied to a principal amount to calculate the interest charged.

interim periods (p. 42) The time span established for accounting purposes that are less than a year.

internal control (p. 329) A system of both internal administrative control and internal accounting control.

interperiod tax allocation *See* tax deferral

International Accounting Standards Committee (IASC) (p. 67) An organization representing over one hundred accountancy boards from over seventy-five countries that is developing a common set of accounting standards to be used throughout the world.

inventory (p. 12) Goods held by a company for the purpose of sale to customers.

inventory profit *See* holding gain.

inventory shrinkage (p. 273) Difference between (a) the value of inventory that would occur if there were no theft, breakage, or losses of inventory and (b) the value of inventory when it is physically counted.

interperiod tax allocation *See* tax deferral.

inventory turnover (p. 294) The cost of goods sold divided by the average inventory held during the period.

investing activities (p. 491) Activities that involve (1) providing and collecting cash as a lender or as an owner of securities and (2) acquiring and disposing of plant, property, equipment, and other long-term productive assets.

inward transportation *See* freight in.

issued shares (p. 542) The aggregate number of shares potentially in the hands of shareholders.

journal entry (p. 93) An analysis of the effects of a transaction on the accounts, usually accompanied by an explanation.

journalizing (p. 93) The process of entering transactions into the journal.

keying of entries (p. 95) The process of numbering or otherwise specifically identifying each journal entry and each posting.

last-in, first-out (LIFO) (p. 279) This inventory method assumes that the units acquired most recently are used or sold first.

lease (p. 462) A contract whereby an owner (lessor) grants the use of property to a second party (lessee) for rental payments.

leasehold improvement (p. 401) Investments by a lessee in items that are not permitted to be removed from the premises when a lease expires, such as installation of new fixtures, panels, walls, and air-conditioning equipment.

leasehold (p. 400) The right to use a fixed asset for a specified period of time, typically beyond one year.

ledger (p. 89) A group of related accounts kept current in a systematic manner.

leveraging *See* trading on the equity.

liabilities (p. 8) Economic obligations of the organization to outsiders or claims against its assets by outsiders.

licenses *See* franchises.

LIFO increment *See* LIFO layer.

LIFO layer (p. 286) A separately identifiable additional segment of LIFO inventory.

LIFO reserve (p. 287) The difference between a company's inventory valued at LIFO and what it would be under FIFO.

limited liability (p. 18) A feature of the corporate form of organization whereby corporate creditors ordinarily have claims against the corporate assets only. The owners' personal assets are not subject to the creditors' grasp.

line of credit (p. 430) An agreement with a bank to provide automatically short-term loans up to some preestablished maximum.

liquidating value (p. 545) A measure of the preference to receive assets in the event of corporate liquidation.

long-lived assets (p. 378) Resources that are held for an extended time, such as land, buildings, equipment, natural resources, and patents.

long-term liabilities (p. 429) Obligations that fall due beyond one year from the balance sheet date.

long-term solvency (p. 676) An organization's ability to generate enough cash to repay long-term debts as they mature.

lower-of-cost-or-market method (LCM) (p. 288) The superimposition of a market-price test on an inventory cost method.

management accounting (p. 7) The field of accounting that serves internal decision makers, such as top executives, department heads, college deans, hospital administrators, and people at other management levels within an organization.

management reports (p. 331) Explicit statements in annual reports of publicly held companies that state management is responsible for all audited and unaudited information in the annual report.

management's discussion and analysis (MD&A) (p. 681) A required section of annual reports that concentrates on explaining the major changes in the income statement and the major changes in liquidity and capital resources.

market rate *See* yield to maturity.

marketable securities (p. 587) Any notes, bonds, or stocks that can readily be sold via public markets. The term is often used as a synonym for short-term investments.

matching (p. 45) The recording of expenses in the same time period as the related revenues are recognized.

materiality convention (p. 112) The concept that states that a financial statement item is material if its omission or misstatement would tend to mislead the reader of the financial statements under consideration.

minority interests (p. 602) The outside shareholders' interests, as opposed to the parent's interests, in a subsidiary corporation.

Modified Accelerated Cost Recovery System (MACRS) (p. 642) The basis for computing depreciation for tax purposes in the United States. It is based on arbitrary "recovery" periods instead of useful lives.

mortgage bond (p. 437) A form of long-term debt that is secured by the pledge of specific property.

multiple-step income statement (p. 155) An income statement that contains one or more subtotals that highlight significant relationships.

municipal bond interest (p. 637) Interest paid by states and local governments that is not treated as taxable income by the United States government.

net book value *See* book value.

net income (p. 50) The remainder after all expenses have been deducted from revenues.

net operating loss (NOL) (p. 654) An operating loss for tax purposes that can be carried back three years or forward fifteen years to offset taxable income in other years.

net sales (p. 240) Total sales revenue reduced by sales returns and allowances.

neutrality (p. 735) Choosing accounting policies without attempting to achieve purposes other than measuring economic impact; freedom from bias.

nominal dollars (p. 748) Those dollars that are not restated for fluctuations in the general purchasing power of the monetary unit.

nominal interest rate (p. 436) A contractual rate of interest paid on bonds.

notes payable (p. 8) Promissory notes that are evidence of a debt and state the terms of payment.

open account (p. 13) Buying or selling on credit, usually by just an "authorized signature" of the buyer.

operating activities (p. 491) Transactions that affect the income statement.

operating cycle (p. 41) The time span during which cash is used to acquire goods and serv-ices, which in turn are sold to customers, who in turn pay for their purchases with cash.

operating income (p. 155) Gross profit less all operating expenses.

operating income percentage on sales (p. 694) Operating income divided by sales.

operating lease (p. 463) A lease that should be accounted for by the lessee as ordinary rent expenses.

operating management (p. 490) Is mainly concerned with the major day-to-day activities that generate revenues and expenses.

operating profit *See* operating income.

operating statement *See* statement of income.

other postretirement benefits (p. 450) Benefits provided to retired workers in addition to a pension, such as life and health insurance.

output controls (p. 341) Internal accounting controls that check output against input and ensure that only authorized persons receive reports.

outstanding shares (p. 542) Shares in the hands of shareholders equal to issued shares less treasury shares.

owners' equity (p. 8) The residual interest in, or - remaining claim against, the organization's assets after deducting liabilities.

P&L statement *See* statement of income.

paid-in capital (p. 20) The total capital investment in a corporation by its owners at the inception of business and subsequently.

paid-in capital in excess of par value (p. 20) When issuing stock, the difference between the total amount received and the par value.

par value (p. 20, 437) The nominal dollar amount printed on stock certificates. *See* face amount

parent company (p. 596) A company owning more than 50% of the voting shares of another company, called the subsidiary company.

participating (p. 545) A characteristic of preferred stock that provides increasing dividends when common dividends increase.

partnership (p. 17) A special form of organization that joins two or more individuals together as co-owners.

patents (p. 398) Grants by the federal government to an inventor, bestowing (in the United States) the exclusive right for 17 years to produce and sell the invention.

payment date (p. 547) The date dividends are paid.

pensions (p. 450) Payments to former employees after they retire.

percentage of accounts receivable method (p. 252) An approach to estimating bad debts expense and uncollectible accounts at year end using the historical relations of uncollectibles to accounts receivable.

percentage of sales method (p. 251) An approach to estimating bad debts expense and uncollectible accounts based on the historical relations between credit sales and uncollectibles.

period costs (p. 45) Items identified directly as expenses of the time period in which they are incured.

periodic inventory system (p. 272) The system in which the cost of goods sold is computed periodically by relying solely on physical counts without keeping day-to-day records of units sold or on hand.

permanent accounts (p. 201) Balance sheet accounts.

permanent differences (p. 637) Differences between pretax income as reported to shareholders and taxable income as reported to the government because a revenue or expense item is recognized for one purpose but not the other.

perpetual inventory system (p. 271) A system that keeps a running, continuous record that tracks inventories and the cost of goods sold on a day-to-day basis.

physical capital maintenance (p. 747) A concept of income measurement whereby income emerges only after recovering an amount that allows physical operating capability to be maintained.

physical count (p. 273) The process of counting all the items in inventory at a moment in time.

plant assets *See* tangible assets.

pooling-of-interests method (p. 617) A way of accounting for the combination of two corporations based on the book values of the acquired company's net assets, as distinguished from the purchase method.

posting (p. 95) The transferring of amounts from the journal to the appropriate accounts in the ledger.

preemptive rights (p. 542) The rights to acquire a pro-rata amount of any new issues of capital stock.

preferred stock (p. 543) Stock that has some priority over other shares regarding dividends or the distribution of assets upon liquidation.

premium on bonds (p. 439) The excess of the proceeds over the face amount of a bond.

present value (p. 460) The value today of a future cash inflow or outflow.

pretax income (p. 144) Income before income taxes.

pretax operating rate of return on total assets (p. 694) Operating income divided by average total assets available.

primary EPS (p. 701) EPS calculated as if all common stock equivalents that dilute EPS were converted to common stock.

private accounting (p. 24) Accountants who work for businesses, government agencies, and other nonprofit organizations.

private placement (p. 436) A process whereby notes are issued by corporations when money is borrowed from a few sources, not from the general public.

privately owned (p. 17) A corporation owned by a family, a small group of shareholders, or a single individual, in which shares of ownership are not publicly sold.

pro forma statement (p. 675) A carefully formulated expression of predicted results.

processing controls (p. 340) Internal accounting controls relating to the design, programming, and operation of the system.

product costs (p. 45) Costs that are linked with revenues and are charged as expenses when the related revenue is recognized.

professional corporation (p. 542) A form of corporation providing professional people some corporate benefits without limited liability.

profit *See* income.

profitability evaluation (p. 158) The assessment of the likelihood that a company will provide investors with a particular rate of return on their investment.

promissory note (p. 430) A written promise to repay principal plus interest at specific future dates.

protective covenant (p. 438) A provision stated in a bond, usually to protect the bondholders' interests.

public accounting (p. 24) The field of accounting where services are offered to the general public on a fee basis.

publicly owned (p. 17) A corporation in which shares in the ownership are sold to the public.

purchase allowance *See* sales allowance.

purchase method (p. 616) A way of accounting for the acquisition of one company by another; based on the market prices paid for the acquired company's assets.

purchase returns *See* sales returns.

rate of return on common equity (ROE) (p. 564) Net income less preferred dividends divided by average common equity.

rate of return on stockholders' equity (ROE) (p. 696) Net income divided by average stockholders' equity.

raw material inventory (p. 303) Includes the cost of materials held for use in the manufacturing of a product.

receivables *See* accounts receivable.

recognition (p. 45) A test for determining whether revenues should be recorded in the financial statements of a given period. To be recognized, revenues must be earned and realized.

reconcile a bank statement (p. 245) To verify that the bank balance for cash is consistent with the accounting records.

redemption price (p. 546) The call price, which is typically 5% to 10% above the par value of the bond or stock.

registered instrument (p. 438) Bonds that require the interest and maturity payments to be made to specific owners.

reinvested earnings *See* retained earnings.

relevance (p. 734) The capability of information to make a difference to the decision maker.

reliability (p. 10) The quality of information that assures decision makers that the information captures the conditions or events it purports to represent.

replacement cost (p. 285) The cost at which an inventory item could be acquired today.

report format (p. 154) A classified balance sheet with the assets at the top.

representational faithfulness *See* validity.

reserve (p. 563) Has one of three meanings: (1) a restriction of dividend-declaring power as denoted by a specific subdivision of retained income, (2) an offset to an asset, or (3) an estimate of a definite liability of indefinite or uncertain amount.

reserve for doubtful accounts *See* allowance for uncollectible accounts.

residual value (p. 381) The amount received from disposal of a long-lived asset at the end of its useful life.

restricted retained income (p. 563) Any part of retained income that may not be reduced by dividend declarations.

results of operations *See* statement of income.

retail method *See* retail inventory method.

retail inventory method (p. 355) A popular inventory costing method based on sales prices, often used as a control device and for obtaining an inventory valuation for financial statement purposes.

retailer (p. 293) A company that sells items directly to the final users, individuals.

retained earnings (p. 64) A synonym for retained income.

retained income (p. 42) Additional owners' equity generated by income or profits.

return on sales ratio (p. 159) Net income divided by sales.

return on stockholders' equity ratio (p. 159) Net income divided by invested capital (measured by average stockholders' equity).

return on total assets (ROA) (p. 696) Income before interest expense divided by average total assets.

revaluation equity (p. 751) A part of stockholders' equity that includes all holding gains that are excluded from income.

revenues (p. 42) Gross increases in owners' equity arising from increases in assets received in exchange for the delivery of goods or services to customers.

reversing entries (p. 211) Entries that switch back all debits and credits made in a related preceding adjusting entry.

sales (p. 64) A synonym for revenues.

sales allowance (p. 240) Reduction of the selling price (the original price previously agreed upon).

sales returns (p. 240) Products returned by the customer.

sales revenues *See* sales.

salvage value *See* residual value.

scrap value *See* residual value.

Securities and Exchange Commission (SEC) (p. 66) The agency designated by the U.S. Congress to hold the ultimate responsibility for authorizing the generally accepted accounting principles for companies whose stock is held by the general investing public.

series (p. 546) Different groups of preferred shares issued at different times with different features.

shareholders' equity *See* stockholders' equity.

short-term debt securities (p. 588) Largely notes and bonds with maturities of one year or less.

short-term equity securities (p. 588) Capital stock in other corporations held with the intention to liquidate within one year as needed.

short-term investment (p. 587) A temporary investment in marketable securities of otherwise idle cash.

short-term liquidity (p. 676) An organization's ability to meet current payments as they become due.

simple entry (p. 96) An entry for a transaction that affects only two accounts.

simple interest (p. 458) For any period, interest rate multiplied by an unchanging principal amount.

single-step income statement (p. 155) An income statement that groups all revenues together and then lists and deducts all expenses together without drawing any intermediate subtotals.

sinking fund (p. 439) Cash or securities segregated for meeting obligations on bonded debt.

sinking fund bonds (p. 439) Bonds with indentures that require the issuer to make annual payments to a sinking fund.

sole proprietorship (p. 17) A separate organization with a single owner.

solvency (p. 152) An entity's ability to meet its financial obligations as they become due.

source documents (p. 91) The supporting original records of any transaction; they are memorandums of what happened.

special items (p. 702) Expenses that are large enough and unusual enough to warrant separate disclosure.

special journals (p. 211) Journals used to record particular types of voluminous transactions; examples are the sales journal and the cash receipts journal.

specific identification method (p. 279) This inventory method concentrates on the physical tracing of the particular items sold.

specific price index (p. 753) An index used to approximate the current costs of particular assets or types of assets.

specific write-off method (p. 248) This method of accounting for bad debt losses assumes all sales are fully collectible until proved otherwise.

stated rate *See* nominal interest rate.

stated value *See* par value.

statement of cash flows (p. 53) A required statement that reports the cash receipts and cash payments of an entity during a particular period.

statement of earnings *See* statement of income.

statement of financial condition *See* balance sheet.

statement of financial position *See* balance sheet.

statement of income (p. 64) A synonym for income statement.

statement of income and retained income (p. 61) A statement that includes a statement of retained income at the bottom of an income statement.

statement of operations *See* statement of income

statement of retained income (p. 60) A statement that lists the beginning balance in retained income, followed by a description of any changes that occurred during the period, and the ending balance.

statement of revenues and expenses *See* statement of income.

stock certificate *See* capital stock certificate.

stock dividends (p. 549) Distribution to stockholders of additional shares of any class of the distributing company's stock, without any payment to the company by the stockholders.

stock options (p. 564) Special rights usually granted to executives to purchase a corporation's capital stock.

stock split (p. 548) Issuance of additional shares to existing stockholders for no payments by the stockholders.

stockholders' equity (shareholders' equity) (p. 19) Owners' equity of a corporation. The excess of assets over liabilities of a corporation.

straight-line depreciation (p. 382) A method that spreads the depreciable value evenly over the useful life of an asset.

subordinated debentures (p. 437) Debt securities whose holders have claims against only the assets that remain after the claims of general creditors are satisfied.

subsidiary A (p. 596) corporation owned or controlled by a parent company through the ownership of more than 50% of the voting stock.

T-account (p. 89) Simplified version of ledger accounts that takes the form of the capital letter T.

tangible assets (p. 378) Physical items that can be seen and touched, such as land, natural resources, buildings, and equipment.

tax allocation *See* tax deferral.

tax credits (p. 653) Direct reductions in a company's income tax obligations.

tax deduction (p. 636) An item that may be deducted on the tax return to calculate taxable income.

tax deferral (p. 647) A method that measures reported income as if it were subject to the full current tax rate even though a more advantageous accounting method was used for tax purposes.

temporary accounts (p. 201) Accounts that are subjected to periodic closing, i.e., revenue, expense, and dividends declared accounts.

temporary difference *See* timing difference.

terminal value *See* residual value.

time-series comparisons (p. 688) Comparisons of a company's financial ratios with its own historical ratios.

times interest earned *See* interest coverage.

timing difference (p. 639) A situation that arises whenever revenue or expense items are recognized in one period for tax purposes and in another period for shareholder reporting.

total asset turnover (p. 694) Sales divided by average total assets available.

trade discounts (p. 241) Reductions to the gross selling price for a particular class of customers to arrive at the actual selling price (invoice price).

trade receivables *See* accounts receivable.

trademarks (p. 398) Distinctive identifications of a manufactured product or of a service taking the form of a name, a sign, a slogan, a logo, or an emblem.

trading on the equity (p. 696) Using borrowed money at fixed interest rates with the objective of enhancing the rate of return on common equity.

trading securities (p. 589) Current investments in equity or debt securities held for short-term profit.

transaction (p. 10) Any event that both affects the financial position of an entity and can be reliably recorded in money terms.

translation adjustment (p. 708) A contra-account in stockholders' equity that arises when a foreign subsidiary is consolidated.

treasury stock (p. 542) A corporation's issued stock that has subsequently been repurchased by the company and not retired.

trial balance (p. 104) A list of all accounts with their balances.

trust indenture (p. 438) A contract whereby the issuing corporation of a bond promises a trustee that it will abide by stated provisions.

turnover (p. 243) Often a synonym for sales or revenues outside the United States.

U.S. Treasury obligations (p. 588) Interest-bearing notes, bonds, and bills issued by the U.S. government.

uncollectible accounts (p. 246) Receivables determined to be uncollectible because debtors are unable or unwilling to pay their debts.

underwriters (p. 439) A group of investment bankers that buys an entire bond or stock issue from a corporation and then sells the bonds to the general investing public.

unearned revenue (p. 137) Revenue received and recorded before it is earned.

unit depreciation (p. 382) A method based on units of service when physical wear and tear is the dominating influence on the useful life of the asset.

unlimited liability (p. 542) Legal responsibility not limited by law or contract; personal assets can be seized to satisfy corporate debts.

unregistered instrument (p. 438) Bonds requiring interest to be paid to the individual who presents the interest coupons attached to the bond.

unsubordinated debenture (p. 437) A bond that is unsecured by specific pledged assets, giving its owner a general claim with a priority like an account payable.

useful life (p. 381) The time period over which an asset is depreciated.

validity (p. 735) A correspondence between the accounting numbers and the resources or events those numbers purport to represent.

verifiability (p. 735) A quality of information such that there would be a high extent of consensus among independent measurers of an item.

weighted-average cost (p. 279) This inventory method computes a unit cost by dividing the total acquisition cost of all items available for sale by the number of units available for sale.

wholesaler (p. 293) An intermediary that sells inventory items to retailers.

work in process inventory (p. 303) Includes the cost incurred for partially completed items, including raw materials, labor, and other costs.

work sheet (p. 204) A columnar approach to moving from a trial balance to the finished financial statements.

working capital (p. 151) The excess of current assets over current liabilities.

working capital ratio *See* current ratio.

write-down (p. 289) A reduction in carrying value to below cost in response to a decline in value.

working paper *See* work sheet.

yield to maturity (p. 439) The interest rate that equates market price at issue to the present value of principal and interest.

Index